*Ninth Edition*

# Annotated Model Rules of Professional Conduct

*Ellen J. Bennett*
*Helen W. Gunnarsson*

*Center for Professional Responsibility
American Bar Association*

www.americanbar.org

Cover and interior design by Zaccarine Design, Inc.

The ABA Model Rules of Professional Conduct, including Preamble, Scope, and Comment, were adopted by the ABA House of Delegates on August 2, 1983, and amended in 1987, 1989, 1990, 1991, 1992, 1993, 1994, 1995, 1997, 1998, 2000, 2002, 2003, 2007, 2008, 2009, 2012, 2013, 2016, and 2018. The analyses, conclusions, and views expressed in these annotations are those of the American Bar Association Center for Professional Responsibility's research lawyers.

Printed in the United States of America.

23 22 21 20 19     5 4 3 2 1

### Library of Congress Cataloging-in-Publication Data

Names: Bennett, Ellen J., editor. | Gunnarsson, Helen W., editor. | Center for Professional
   Responsibility (American Bar Association) | American Bar Association. House of
   Delegates. Model rules of professional conduct.
Title: Annotated model rules of professional conduct / Ellen J. Bennett, Helen W. Gunnarsson.
Description: Ninth edition. | Chicago, Illinois : Center for Professional Responsibiltiy,
   American Bar Association, [2019] | Includes bibliographical references and index.
Identifiers: LCCN 2019014489 (print) | LCCN 2019015418 (ebook) |
   ISBN 9781641054041 (ebook) | ISBN 9781641054034 (softcover : alk. paper)
Subjects: LCSH: American Bar Association. House of Delegates. Model rules of professional
   conduct | Legal ethics--United States. | LCGFT: Model acts.
Classification: LCC KF305 (ebook) | LCC KF305 .A2 2019 (print) | DDC 174/.30973--dc23
LC record available at https://lccn.loc.gov/2019014489

Discounts are available for books ordered in bulk. Special consideration is given to state bars, CLE programs, and other bar-related organizations. Inquire at Book Publishing, ABA Publishing, American Bar Association, 321 North Clark Street, Chicago, Illinois 60654-7598.

www.ShopABA.org

# Acknowledgments

The ninth edition of the *Annotated Model Rules of Professional Conduct* presents an authoritative and practical analysis of the lawyer ethics rules and the cases, ethics opinions, and other legal authorities essential to understanding them. The Model Rules of Professional Conduct were adopted by the ABA in 1983 and have been amended numerous times since.

This new edition of the Annotated Model Rules of Professional Conduct represents a major refinement of previous editions. It takes into account all amendments through August 2018, as well as the American Law Institute's *Restatement (Third) of the Law Governing Lawyers* (2000).

Special appreciation is in order to the many lawyers of the Center for Professional Responsibility who made this publication possible. Ellen J. Bennett, editor of the ninth edition, and Helen W. Gunnarsson, assistant editor, served as the principal authors, preparing the book and bringing it to completion with excellence and professionalism.

Special mention should also be made of Elizabeth J. Cohen, Robert A. Creamer, William Freivogel, Nancy G. Kisicki, and Keith Swisher, whose insightful writing is evidenced in several areas.

Finally, I would like to express my gratitude to Catherine Zaccarine, designer and typesetter, and Kirk A. Swanson, proofreader and copyeditor, for their professionalism, speed, and accuracy.

The Center for Professional Responsibility thanks the West Publishing Corporation for its generous gift of the West Professional Responsibility Law Library, the resource for much of the research reflected in this work.

This volume is dedicated to the memory of Jeanne P. Gray, Director of the Center for Professional Responsibility from 1983–2013, whose leadership and vision made this work possible.

*Tracy L. Kepler, Director*
*Center for Professional Responsibility*

# CONTENTS

# PREFACE

For more than one hundred years, the American Bar Association has provided leadership in legal ethics and professional responsibility through the adoption of professional standards that serve as models of the regulatory law governing the legal profession.

On August 27, 1908, the Association adopted the original Canons of Professional Ethics. These were based principally on the Code of Ethics adopted by the Alabama Bar Association in 1887, which in turn had been borrowed largely from the lectures of Judge George Sharswood, published in 1854 as Professional Ethics, and from the fifty resolutions included in David Hoffman's A Course of Legal Study (2d ed. 1836). Piecemeal amendments to the Canons occasionally followed.

In 1913, the Standing Committee on Professional Ethics of the American Bar Association was established to keep the Association informed about state and local bar activities concerning professional ethics. In 1919 the name of the Committee was changed to the Committee on Professional Ethics and Grievances; its role was expanded in 1922 to include issuing opinions "concerning professional conduct, and particularly concerning the application of the tenets of ethics thereto." In 1958 the Committee on Professional Ethics and Grievances was separated into two committees: a Committee on Professional Grievances, with authority to review issues of professional misconduct, and a Committee on Professional Ethics with responsibility to express its opinion concerning proper professional and judicial conduct. The Committee on Professional Grievances was discontinued in 1971. The name of the Committee on Professional Ethics was changed to the Committee on Ethics and Professional Responsibility in 1971 and remains so.

In 1964, at the request of President Lewis F. Powell Jr., the House of Delegates of the American Bar Association created a Special Committee on Evaluation of Ethical Standards (the "Wright Committee") to assess whether changes should be made in the then-current Canons of Professional Ethics. In response, the Committee produced the Model Code of Professional Responsibility. The Model Code was adopted by the House of Delegates on August 12, 1969, and subsequently by the vast majority of state and federal jurisdictions.

In 1977, the American Bar Association created the Commission on Evaluation of Professional Standards to undertake a comprehensive rethinking of the ethical premises and problems of the legal profession. Upon evaluating the Model Code and determining that amendment of the Code would not achieve a comprehensive statement of the law governing the legal profession, the Commission commenced a six-year study and drafting process that produced the Model Rules of Professional Conduct. The Model Rules were adopted by the House of Delegates of the American Bar Association on August 2, 1983.

Between 1983 and 2002, the House amended the Rules and Comments on fourteen different occasions. In 1997, the American Bar Association created the Commission on Evaluation of the Rules of Professional Conduct ("Ethics 2000 Commission") to comprehensively review the Model Rules and propose amendments as deemed appropriate. On February 5, 2002, the House of Delegates adopted a series of amendments that arose from this process.

In 2000, the American Bar Association created the Commission on Multijurisdictional Practice to research, study and report on the application of current ethics and bar admission rules to the multijurisdictional practice of law. On August 12, 2002, the House of Delegates adopted amendments to Rules 5.5 and 8.5 as a result of the Commission's work and recommendations.

In 2002, the American Bar Association created the Task Force on Corporate Responsibility to examine systemic issues relating to corporate responsibility arising out of the unexpected and traumatic bankruptcy of Enron and other Enron-like situations that had shaken confidence in the effectiveness of the governance and disclosure systems applicable to public companies in the United States. In August 11-12, 2003, the House of Delegates adopted amendments to Rules 1.6 and 1.13 as a result of the Task Force's work and recommendations.

In 2009, the American Bar Association created the Commission on Ethics 20/20 to perform a thorough review of the ABA Model Rules of Professional Conduct and the U.S. system of lawyer regulation in the context of advances in technology and global legal practice developments. On August 6, 2012, and February 11, 2013, the House of Delegates adopted a series of amendments to the Rules and Comments as a result of the Commission's work and recommendations.

In February 2016, the Section on International Law recommended amending Model Rule of Professional Conduct 5.5 and the ABA Model Rule for Registration of In-House Counsel to include language specifying that the court of highest appellate jurisdiction may, in its discretion, allow foreign in-house lawyers who do not meet the ABA definition of foreign lawyer because they cannot be "members of the bar" to be able to practice as in-house counsel in the U.S. and to be so registered. On February 8, 2016, the House of Delegates adopted the suggested amendments with further revisions.

In August 2016, the Standing Committee on Ethics and Professional Responsibility brought to the House of Delegates amendments to Model Rule 8.4, Misconduct. Proposed new paragraph (g) prohibited lawyers from discrimination and harassment in conduct related to the practice of law. On August 8, 2016, the House of Delegates adopted the recommended amendments.

In 2018, the Standing Committee on Ethics and Professional Responsibility suggested amendments to the Model Rules regulating lawyer advertising with the goal of simplifying those rules and making them more uniform. On August 6, 2018, the House of Delegates adopted the suggested amendments.

The American Bar Association continues to pursue its goal of assuring the highest standards of professional competence and ethical conduct. The Standing Committee on Ethics and Professional Responsibility, charged with interpreting the professional standards of the Association and recommending appropriate amendments and clarifications, issues opinions interpreting the Model Rules of Professional Conduct and the Model Code of Judicial Conduct. The opinions of the Committee are published by the American Bar Association in a series of bound volumes containing opinions from 1924 through 2013 and as individual PDFs starting with the 1984 opinions.

Requests that the Committee issue opinions on particular questions of professional and judicial conduct should be directed to the American Bar Association, Center for Professional Responsibility, 321 N. Clark Street, Chicago, Illinois 60654.

# ABA STANDING COMMITTEE ON ETHICS AND PROFESSIONAL RESPONSIBILITY (2018–2019)

BARBARA S. GILLERS, *Chair*
New York, New York

MICHAEL H. RUBIN
Baton Rouge, Louisiana

JOHN M. BARKETT
Miami, Florida

LYNDA C. SHELY
Scottsdale, Arizona

ROBERT HIRSHON
Ann Arbor, Michigan

ELIZABETH C. TARBERT
Tallahassee, Florida

THOMAS O. MASON
Washington, D.C.

NORMAN W. SPAULDING
Stanford, California

DOUGLAS RICHMOND
Chicago, Illinois

LISA DEITCH TAYLOR
Parsippany, New Jersey

---

## AMERICAN BAR ASSOCIATION CENTER FOR PROFESSIONAL RESPONSIBILITY

*Director*
TRACY L. KEPLER

*Ethics Counsel*
DENNIS A. RENDLEMAN

# ABA COMMISSION ON EVALUATION OF PROFESSIONAL STANDARDS (1977–1983)

# COMMISSION ON EVALUATION OF PROFESSIONAL STANDARDS
# CHAIR'S INTRODUCTION

The Commission on Evaluation of Professional Standards was appointed in the summer of 1977 by former ABA President William B. Spann, Jr. Chaired by Robert J. Kutak until his death in early 1983, the Commission was charged with evaluating whether existing standards of professional conduct provided comprehensive and consistent guidance for resolving the increasingly complex ethical problems in the practice of law. For the most part, the Commission looked to the former ABA Model Code of Professional Responsibility, which served as a model for the majority of state ethics codes. The Commission also referred to opinions of the ABA Standing Committee on Ethics and Professional Responsibility, as well as to decisions of the United States Supreme Court and of state supreme courts. After thoughtful study, the Commission concluded that piecemeal amendment of the Model Code would not sufficiently clarify the profession's ethical responsibilities in light of changed conditions. The Commission therefore commenced a drafting process that produced numerous drafts, elicited voluminous comment, and launched an unprecedented debate on the ethics of the legal profession.

On January 30, 1980, the Commission presented its initial suggestions to the bar in the form of a Discussion Draft of the proposed Model Rules of Professional Conduct. The Discussion Draft was subject to the widest possible dissemination and interested parties were urged to offer comments and suggestions. Public hearings were held around the country to provide forums for expression of views on the draft.

In the year following the last of these public hearings, the Commission conducted a painstaking analysis of the submitted comments and attempted to integrate into the draft those which seemed consistent with its underlying philosophy. The product of this analysis and integration was presented on May 31, 1981, as the proposed Final Draft of the Model Rules of Professional Conduct. This proposed Final Draft was submitted in two formats. The first format, consisting of blackletter Rules and accompanying Comments in the so-called restatement format, was submitted with the Commission's recommendation that it be adopted. The alternative format was patterned after the Model Code and consisted of Canons, Ethical Considerations, and Disciplinary Rules. In February 1982, the House of Delegates by substantial majority approved the restatement format of the Model Rules.

The proposed Final Draft was submitted to the House of Delegates for debate and approval at the 1982 Annual Meeting of the Association in San Francisco. Many organizations and interested parties offered their comments in the form of proposed amendments to the Final Draft. In the time allotted on its agenda, however, the House debated only proposed amendments to Rule 1.5. Consideration of the remainder of the document was deferred until the 1983 Midyear Meeting in New Orleans. The proposed Final Draft, as amended by the House in San Francisco, was reprinted in the November 1982 issue of the *ABA Journal*.

At the 1983 Midyear Meeting the House resumed consideration of the Final Draft. After two days of often vigorous debate, the House completed its review of the proposed amendments to the blackletter Rules. Many amendments, particularly in the area of confidentiality, were adopted. Debate on a Preamble, Scope, Terminology, and Comments, rewritten to reflect the New Orleans amendments, was deferred until the 1983 Annual Meeting in Atlanta, Georgia.

On March 11, 1983, the text of the blackletter Rules as approved by the House in February, together with the proposed Preamble, Scope, Terminology, and Comments, was circulated to members of the House, Section and Committee chairs, and all other interested parties. The text of the Rules reflected the joint efforts of the Commission and the House Drafting Committee to incorporate the changes approved by the House and to ensure stylistic continuity and uniformity. Recipients of the draft were again urged to submit comments in the form of proposed amendments. The House Committees on Drafting and Rules and Calendar met on May 23, 1983, to consider all of the proposed amendments that had been submitted in response to this draft. In addition, discussions were held among concerned parties in an effort to reach accommodation of the various positions. On July 11, 1983, the final version of the Model Rules was again circulated.

The House of Delegates commenced debate on the proposed Preamble, Scope, Terminology, and Comments on August 2, 1983. After four hours of debate, the House completed its consideration of all the proposed amendments and, upon motion of the Commission, the House voted to adopt the Model Rules of Professional Conduct, together with the ancillary material as amended. The task of the Commission had ended and it was discharged with thanks.

Throughout the drafting process, active participants included not only the members of the Commission but also the Sections and Committees of the American Bar Association and national, state, and local bar organizations. The work of the Commission was subject to virtually continuous scrutiny by academicians, practicing lawyers, members of the press, and the judiciary. Consequently, every provision of the Model Rules reflects the thoughtful consideration and hard work of many dedicated professionals. Because of their input, the Model Rules are truly national in derivation. The Association can take immense pride in its continued demonstration of leadership in the area of professional responsibility.

The Model Rules of Professional Conduct are intended to serve as a national framework for implementation of standards of professional conduct. Although the Commission endeavored to harmonize and accommodate the views of all the participants, no set of national standards that speaks to such a diverse constituency as the legal profession can resolve each issue to the complete satisfaction of every affected party. Undoubtedly there will be those who take issue with one or another of the Rules' provisions. Indeed, such dissent from individual provisions is expected. And the Model Rules, like all model legislation, will be subject to modification at the level of local implementation. Viewed as a whole, however, the Model Rules represent a responsible approach to the ethical practice of law and are consistent with professional obligations imposed by other law, such as constitutional, corporate, tort, fiduciary, and agency law.

I should not end this report without speaking of the Commission's debt to many people who have aided us in our deliberations, and have devoted time, energy, and goodwill to the advancement of our work over the last six years. It would probably be impossible to name each of the particular persons whose help was significant to us, and it surely would be unfortunate if the name of anyone were omitted from the list. We are, and shall remain, deeply grateful to the literally hundreds of people who aided us with welcome and productive suggestions. We think the bar should be grateful to each of them, and to our deceased members, Alan Barth of the District of Columbia, who we hardly had time to know, Bill Spann, who became a member after the conclusion of his presidential term, and our original chair, Bob Kutak.

The long work of the Commission and its resulting new codification of the ethical rules of practice demonstrate, it is submitted, the commitment of the American lawyer to his or her profession and to achievement of the highest standards.

*Robert W. Meserve*
*September 1983*

# ABA COMMISSION ON EVALUATION OF THE RULES OF PROFESSIONAL CONDUCT (1997–2002)

HON. E. NORMAN VEASEY, *Chair*
Wilmington, Delaware

SUSAN R. MARTYN
Toledo, Ohio

LAWRENCE J. FOX
Philadelphia, Pennsylvania

DAVID T. MCLAUGHLIN
New London, New Hampshire

ALBERT C. HARVEY
Memphis, Tennessee

RICHARD E. MULROY
Ridgewood, New Jersey

GEOFFREY C. HAZARD, JR.
Swarthmore, Pennsylvania

LUCIAN T. PERA
Memphis, Tennessee

HON. PATRICK E. HIGGINBOTHAM
Dallas, Texas

HON. HENRY RAMSEY, JR. (Ret.)
Berkeley, California

W. LOEBER LANDAU
New York, New York

HON. LAURIE D. ZELON
Los Angeles, California

MARGARET C. LOVE
Washington, D.C.

## LIAISONS

JAMES B. LEE
Salt Lake City, Utah
*Board of Governors*

SETH ROSNER
Greenfield Center, New York
*Board of Governors*

## REPORTERS

NANCY J. MOORE
Boston, Massachusetts
*Chief Reporter*

THOMAS D. MORGAN (1998–1999)
Washington, D.C.

CARL A. PIERCE
Knoxville, Tennessee

## CENTER FOR PROFESSIONAL RESPONSIBILITY

JEANNE P. GRAY
Chicago, Illinois
*Director*

CHARLOTTE K. STRETCH
Chicago, Illinois
*Counsel*

SUSAN M. CAMPBELL
Chicago, Illinois
*Paralegal*

# Commission on Evaluation of the Rules of Professional Conduct (Ethics 2000)
# Chair's Introduction

In mid-1997, ABA President Jerome J. Shestack, his immediate predecessor, N. Lee Cooper, and his successor, Philip S. Anderson, had the vision to establish the "Ethics 2000" Commission. These three leaders persuaded the ABA Board of Governors that the Model Rules adopted by the ABA House of Delegates in 1983 needed comprehensive review and some revision, and this project was launched. Though some might have thought it premature to reopen the Model Rules to such a rigorous general reassessment after only fourteen years, the evaluation process has proven that the ABA leadership was correct.

One of the primary reasons behind the decision to revisit the Model Rules was the growing disparity in state ethics codes. While a large majority of states and the District of Columbia had adopted some version of the Model Rules (then thirty-nine, now forty-two), there were many significant differences among the state versions that resulted in an undesirable lack of uniformity—a problem that had been exacerbated by the approximately thirty amendments to the Model Rules between 1983 and 1997. A few states had elected to retain some version of the 1969 Model Code of Professional Responsibility, and California remained committed to an entirely separate system of lawyer regulation.

But it was not only the patchwork pattern of state regulation that motivated the ABA leaders of 1997 to take this action. There were also new issues and questions raised by the influence that technological developments were having on the delivery of legal services. The explosive dynamics of modern law practice and the anticipated developments in the future of the legal profession lent a sense of urgency as well as a substantive dimension to the project. These developments were underscored by the work then underway on the American Law Institute's *Restatement of the Law Governing Lawyers*.

There was also a strong countervailing sense that there was much to be valued in the existing concepts and articulation of the Model Rules. The Commission concluded early on that these valuable aspects of the Rules should not be lost or put at risk in our revision effort. As a result, the Commission set about to be comprehensive, but at the same time conservative, and to recommend change only where necessary. In balancing the need to preserve the good with the need for improvement, we were mindful of Thomas Jefferson's words of nearly 185 years ago, in a letter concerning the Virginia Constitution, that "moderate imperfections had better be borne with; because, when once known, we accommodate ourselves to them, and find practical means of correcting their ill effects."

Thus, we retained the basic architecture of the Model Rules. We also retained the primary disciplinary function of the Rules, resisting the temptation to preach aspirationally about "best practices" or professionalism concepts. Valuable as the profession might find such guidance, it would not have—and should not be misperceived as having—a regulatory dimension. We were, however, always conscious of the educational role of the Model Rules. Finally, we tried to keep our changes to a minimum: when a particular provision was found not to be "broken" we did not try to "fix" it. Even so, as the reader will note, the Commission ended up making a large number of changes: some are relatively innocuous and nonsubstantive, in the nature of editorial or stylistic changes; others are substantive but not particularly controversial; and a few are both substantive and controversial.

The deliberations of the Commission did not take place in a vacuum and our determinations are not being pronounced *ex cathedra*. Rather, they are products of thorough research, scholarly analysis, and thoughtful consideration. Of equal importance, they have been influenced by the views of practitioners, scholars, other members of the legal profession, and the public. All these constituencies have had continual access to and considerable—and proper—influence upon the deliberations of the Commission throughout this process.

I must pause to underscore the openness of our process. We held over fifty days of meetings, all of which were open, and ten public hearings at regular intervals over a four-and-a-half-year period. There were a large number of interested observers at our meetings, many of whom were members of our Advisory Council of 250-plus persons, to offer comments and suggestions. Those observations were very helpful and influential in shaping the Report. Our public discussion drafts, minutes, and Report were available on our website for the world to see and comment upon. As a consequence, we received an enormous number of excellent comments and suggestions, many of which were adopted in the formulation of our Report.

Moreover, we encouraged state and local bar associations, ABA sections and divisions, other professional organizations, and the judiciary to appoint specially designated committees to work with and counsel the Commission. This effort was successful, and the Commission benefitted significantly from the considered views of these groups.

In heeding the counsel of these advisors, we were constantly mindful of substantial and high-velocity changes in the legal profession, particularly over the past decade. These changes have been highlighted by increased public scrutiny of lawyers and an awareness of their influential role in the formation and implementation of public policy; persistent concerns about lawyer honesty, candor, and civility; external competitive and technological pressures on the legal profession; internal pressures on law firm organization and management raised by sheer size, as well as specialization and lawyer mobility; jurisdictional and governance issues, such as multidisciplinary and multijurisdictional practice; special concerns of lawyers in nontraditional practice settings, such as government lawyers and in-house counsel; and the need to enhance public trust and confidence in the legal profession.

At the end of the day, our goal was to develop Rules that are comprehensible to the public and provide clear guidance to the practitioner. Our desire was to preserve all that is valuable and enduring about the existing Model Rules, while at the same time adapting them to the realities of modern law practice and the limits of professional discipline. We believe our product is a balanced blend of traditional precepts and forward-looking provisions that are responsive to modern developments. Our process has been thorough, painstaking, open, scholarly, objective, and collegial.

It is impossible here to go into detail about the changes proposed by the Commission. The changes recommended by the Commission clarified and strengthened a lawyer's duty to communicate with the client; clarified and strengthened a lawyer's duty to clients in certain specific problem areas; responded to the changing organization and structure of modern law practice; responded to new issues and questions raised by the influence that technological developments are having on the delivery of legal services; clarified existing Rules to provide better guidance and explanation to lawyers; clarified and strengthened a lawyer's obligations to the tribunal and to the justice system; responded to the need for changes in the delivery of legal services to low- and middle-income persons; and increased protection of third parties.

The ABA House of Delegates began consideration of the Commission's Report at the August 2001 Annual Meeting in Chicago and completed its review at the February 2002 Midyear Meeting in Philadelphia. At the August 2002 Annual Meeting in Washington, D.C., the ABA House of Delegates considered and adopted additional amendments to the Model Rules sponsored by the ABA Commission on Multijurisdictional Practice and the ABA Standing Committee on Ethics and Professional Responsibility. As state supreme courts consider implementation of these newly revised Rules, it is our fervent hope that the goal of uniformity will be the guiding beacon.

In closing, the Commission expresses its gratitude to the law firm of Drinker Biddle & Reath, whose generous contribution helped make possible the continued, invaluable support of the Commission's Chief Reporter. I also want to express personally my gratitude to and admiration for my colleagues. The chemistry, goodwill, good humor, serious purpose, collegiality, and hard work of the Commission members, Reporters, and ABA staff have been extraordinary. The profession and the public have been enriched beyond measure by their efforts. It has been a pleasure and a privilege for me to work with all of them.

*E. Norman Veasey*
*August 2002*

# PREAMBLE AND SCOPE

## PREAMBLE: A LAWYER'S RESPONSIBILITIES

[1] A lawyer, as a member of the legal profession, is a representative of clients, an officer of the legal system and a public citizen having special responsibility for the quality of justice.

[2] As a representative of clients, a lawyer performs various functions. As advisor, a lawyer provides a client with an informed understanding of the client's legal rights and obligations and explains their practical implications. As advocate, a lawyer zealously asserts the client's position under the rules of the adversary system. As negotiator, a lawyer seeks a result advantageous to the client but consistent with requirements of honest dealings with others. As an evaluator, a lawyer acts by examining a client's legal affairs and reporting about them to the client or to others.

[3] In addition to these representational functions, a lawyer may serve as a third-party neutral, a nonrepresentational role helping the parties to resolve a dispute or other matter. Some of these Rules apply directly to lawyers who are or have served as third-party neutrals. See, e.g., Rules 1.12 and 2.4. In addition, there are Rules that apply to lawyers who are not active in the practice of law or to practicing lawyers even when they are acting in a nonprofessional capacity. For example, a lawyer who commits fraud in the conduct of a business is subject to discipline for engaging in conduct involving dishonesty, fraud, deceit or misrepresentation. See Rule 8.4.

[4] In all professional functions a lawyer should be competent, prompt and diligent. A lawyer should maintain communication with a client concerning the representation. A lawyer should keep in confidence information relating to representation of a client except so far as disclosure is required or permitted by the Rules of Professional Conduct or other law.

[5] A lawyer's conduct should conform to the requirements of the law, both in professional service to clients and in the lawyer's business and personal affairs. A lawyer should use the law's procedures only for legitimate purposes and not to harass or intimidate others. A lawyer should demonstrate respect for the legal system and for those who serve it, including judges, other lawyers and public officials. While it is a lawyer's duty, when necessary, to challenge the rectitude of official action, it is also a lawyer's duty to uphold legal process.

[6] As a public citizen, a lawyer should seek improvement of the law, access to the legal system, the administration of justice and the quality of service rendered by the legal profession. As a member of a learned profession, a lawyer should cultivate knowledge of the law beyond its use for clients, employ that knowledge in reform of the law and work to strengthen legal education. In addition, a lawyer should further the public's understanding of and confidence in the rule of law and the justice system because legal institutions in a constitutional democracy depend on popular participation and support to maintain their authority. A lawyer should be mindful of deficiencies in the administration of justice and of the fact that the poor, and some-

times persons who are not poor, cannot afford adequate legal assistance. Therefore, all lawyers should devote professional time and resources and use civic influence to ensure equal access to our system of justice for all those who because of economic or social barriers cannot afford or secure adequate legal counsel. A lawyer should aid the legal profession in pursuing these objectives and should help the bar regulate itself in the public interest.

[7] Many of a lawyer's professional responsibilities are prescribed in the Rules of Professional Conduct, as well as substantive and procedural law. However, a lawyer is also guided by personal conscience and the approbation of professional peers. A lawyer should strive to attain the highest level of skill, to improve the law and the legal profession and to exemplify the legal profession's ideals of public service.

[8] A lawyer's responsibilities as a representative of clients, an officer of the legal system and a public citizen are usually harmonious. Thus, when an opposing party is well represented, a lawyer can be a zealous advocate on behalf of a client and at the same time assume that justice is being done. So also, a lawyer can be sure that preserving client confidences ordinarily serves the public interest because people are more likely to seek legal advice, and thereby heed their legal obligations, when they know their communications will be private.

[9] In the nature of law practice, however, conflicting responsibilities are encountered. Virtually all difficult ethical problems arise from conflict between a lawyer's responsibilities to clients, to the legal system and to the lawyer's own interest in remaining an ethical person while earning a satisfactory living. The Rules of Professional Conduct often prescribe terms for resolving such conflicts. Within the framework of these Rules, however, many difficult issues of professional discretion can arise. Such issues must be resolved through the exercise of sensitive professional and moral judgment guided by the basic principles underlying the Rules. These principles include the lawyer's obligation zealously to protect and pursue a client's legitimate interests, within the bounds of the law, while maintaining a professional, courteous and civil attitude toward all persons involved in the legal system.

[10] The legal profession is largely self-governing. Although other professions also have been granted powers of self-government, the legal profession is unique in this respect because of the close relationship between the profession and the processes of government and law enforcement. This connection is manifested in the fact that ultimate authority over the legal profession is vested largely in the courts.

[11] To the extent that lawyers meet the obligations of their professional calling, the occasion for government regulation is obviated. Self-regulation also helps maintain the legal profession's independence from government domination. An independent legal profession is an important force in preserving government under law, for abuse of legal authority is more readily challenged by a profession whose members are not dependent on government for the right to practice.

[12] The legal profession's relative autonomy carries with it special responsibilities of self-government. The profession has a responsibility to assure that its regulations are conceived in the public interest and not in furtherance of parochial or self-interested concerns of the bar. Every lawyer is responsible for observance of the Rules of Professional Conduct. A lawyer should also aid in securing their observance

by other lawyers. Neglect of these responsibilities compromises the independence of the profession and the public interest which it serves.

[13] Lawyers play a vital role in the preservation of society. The fulfillment of this role requires an understanding by lawyers of their relationship to our legal system. The Rules of Professional Conduct, when properly applied, serve to define that relationship.

## SCOPE

[14] The Rules of Professional Conduct are rules of reason. They should be interpreted with reference to the purposes of legal representation and of the law itself. Some of the Rules are imperatives, cast in the terms "shall" or "shall not." These define proper conduct for purposes of professional discipline. Others, generally cast in the term "may," are permissive and define areas under the Rules in which the lawyer has discretion to exercise professional judgment. No disciplinary action should be taken when the lawyer chooses not to act or acts within the bounds of such discretion. Other Rules define the nature of relationships between the lawyer and others. The Rules are thus partly obligatory and disciplinary and partly constitutive and descriptive in that they define a lawyer's professional role. Many of the Comments use the term "should." Comments do not add obligations to the Rules but provide guidance for practicing in compliance with the Rules.

[15] The Rules presuppose a larger legal context shaping the lawyer's role. That context includes court rules and statutes relating to matters of licensure, laws defining specific obligations of lawyers and substantive and procedural law in general. The Comments are sometimes used to alert lawyers to their responsibilities under such other law.

[16] Compliance with the Rules, as with all law in an open society, depends primarily upon understanding and voluntary compliance, secondarily upon reinforcement by peer and public opinion and finally, when necessary, upon enforcement through disciplinary proceedings. The Rules do not, however, exhaust the moral and ethical considerations that should inform a lawyer, for no worthwhile human activity can be completely defined by legal rules. The Rules simply provide a framework for the ethical practice of law.

[17] Furthermore, for purposes of determining the lawyer's authority and responsibility, principles of substantive law external to these Rules determine whether a client-lawyer relationship exists. Most of the duties flowing from the client-lawyer relationship attach only after the client has requested the lawyer to render legal services and the lawyer has agreed to do so. But there are some duties, such as that of confidentiality under Rule 1.6, that attach when the lawyer agrees to consider whether a client-lawyer relationship shall be established. See Rule 1.18. Whether a client-lawyer relationship exists for any specific purpose can depend on the circumstances and may be a question of fact.

[18] Under various legal provisions, including constitutional, statutory and common law, the responsibilities of government lawyers may include authority concerning legal matters that ordinarily reposes in the client in private client-lawyer relation-

ships. For example, a lawyer for a government agency may have authority on behalf of the government to decide upon settlement or whether to appeal from an adverse judgment. Such authority in various respects is generally vested in the attorney general and the state's attorney in state government, and their federal counterparts, and the same may be true of other government law officers. Also, lawyers under the supervision of these officers may be authorized to represent several government agencies in intragovernmental legal controversies in circumstances where a private lawyer could not represent multiple private clients. These Rules do not abrogate any such authority.

[19] Failure to comply with an obligation or prohibition imposed by a Rule is a basis for invoking the disciplinary process. The Rules presuppose that disciplinary assessment of a lawyer's conduct will be made on the basis of the facts and circumstances as they existed at the time of the conduct in question and in recognition of the fact that a lawyer often has to act upon uncertain or incomplete evidence of the situation. Moreover, the Rules presuppose that whether or not discipline should be imposed for a violation, and the severity of a sanction, depend on all the circumstances, such as the willfulness and seriousness of the violation, extenuating factors and whether there have been previous violations.

[20] Violation of a Rule should not itself give rise to a cause of action against a lawyer nor should it create any presumption in such a case that a legal duty has been breached. In addition, violation of a Rule does not necessarily warrant any other nondisciplinary remedy, such as disqualification of a lawyer in pending litigation. The Rules are designed to provide guidance to lawyers and to provide a structure for regulating conduct through disciplinary agencies. They are not designed to be a basis for civil liability. Furthermore, the purpose of the Rules can be subverted when they are invoked by opposing parties as procedural weapons. The fact that a Rule is a just basis for a lawyer's self-assessment, or for sanctioning a lawyer under the administration of a disciplinary authority, does not imply that an antagonist in a collateral proceeding or transaction has standing to seek enforcement of the Rule. Nevertheless, since the Rules do establish standards of conduct by lawyers, a lawyer's violation of a Rule may be evidence of breach of the applicable standard of conduct.

[21] The Comment accompanying each Rule explains and illustrates the meaning and purpose of the Rule. The Preamble and this note on Scope provide general orientation. The Comments are intended as guides to interpretation, but the text of each Rule is authoritative.

**State Rules Comparison**
http://ambar.org/MRPCStateCharts

# ANNOTATION
## EXTRADISCIPLINARY APPLICATION OF ETHICS RULES

The Scope section of the Model Rules emphatically disclaims any intent to regulate lawyer conduct outside the disciplinary context: the rules are "not designed to be a basis for civil liability," violation of a rule "should [not] create any presumption . . . that a legal duty has been breached," and an "antagonist in a collateral proceeding or transaction" does not implicitly have standing to enforce a rule. Scope [20]. (The predecessor Model Code of Professional Responsibility (1969) provided simply that it "[did] not undertake to define standards for civil liability.")

Nevertheless, courts have long looked to the ethics rules in nondisciplinary contexts, including malpractice, breach of fiduciary duty, disqualification, motions to suppress or preclude evidence, motions for sanctions, and disputes over fees. "[T]he reality is that lawyers can be disciplined, disbarred, disqualified or sued on the basis of these rules." Lawrence K. Hellman, *When "Ethics Rules" Don't Mean What They Say: The Implications of Strained ABA Ethics Opinions*, 10 Geo. J. Legal Ethics 317 (Winter 1997). *See* Gary A. Munneke & Anthony E. Davis, *The Standard of Care in Legal Malpractice: Do the Model Rules of Professional Conduct Define It?*, 22 J. Legal Prof. 33 (1998) (language admonishing against using rules as basis for civil liability "has been criticized as self-serving economic protectionism, drafted by the organized bar and ratified by the courts [that] consistently cite ethical rules to support decisions that modify the standards of civil liability"); Ted Schneyer, *The ALI's Restatement and the ABA's Model Rules: Rivals or Complements?*, 46 Okla. L. Rev. 25 (Spring 1993) (ABA's "jurisdictional modesty" was "purely defensive"; when "Model Rules could be used to shape lawyers' duties for nondisciplinary purposes without creating substantial new legal risks for lawyers, the drafters were not shy about trying to do so").

A 2002 amendment made an important concession to the rules' extradisciplinary functions: "[S]ince the Rules do establish standards of conduct by lawyers, a lawyer's violation of a Rule may be evidence of breach of the applicable standard of conduct." Scope [20]. Balancing this was a contemporaneous amendment noting that "violation of a Rule does not necessarily warrant any other nondisciplinary remedy, such as disqualification of a lawyer in pending litigation." *Id. Accord Restatement (Third) of the Law Governing Lawyers* § 52(2) & cmt. f (2000) (rule violation "may be considered by a trier of fact as an aid in understanding and applying" duties of competence and diligence required to meet standard of care).

According to the legislative history, these changes "reflect the decisions of courts on the relationship between these Rules and causes of action against a lawyer, including the admissibility of evidence of violation of a Rule in appropriate cases." American Bar Association, *A Legislative History: The Development of the ABA Model Rules of Professional Conduct, 1982–2013*, at 19 (2013). *See* Donald E. Campbell, *The Paragraph 20 Paradox: An Evaluation of the Enforcement of Ethical Rules as Substantive Law*, 8 St. Mary's J. Legal Mal. & Ethics 252 (2018) (discussing how courts determine when ethics rules should be considered as evidence of a substantive violation and when they should be excluded from consideration); *see also* Mark A. Armitage, *Professional Responsibility*, 53 Wayne L. Rev. 541 (Spring 2007) ("Indeed, it may not even be possible in an area like conflicts or fees to disentangle MRPC-based analyses from existing law."); John S. Dzienkowski, *Ethical Decisionmaking and the Design of Rules of Ethics*, 42 Hofstra L. Rev. 55 (Fall 2013) (ABA's fear that any new ethics rule addressing a cutting-edge issue—such as alternative litigation funding—will have collateral extradisciplinary effects "has proven to be a major obstacle to fundamental reform of the Model Rules"). *Compare Levine v. Haralson, Miller, Pitt, Feldman & McAnally, P.L.C.*, 418 P.3d 1007 (Ariz. 2018) ("The rules promulgated by our supreme court to regulate the practice of law establish a portion of the public policy of the state, 'have the same force and effect as state statutes,' and are 'equally binding.'" (cite omitted); without written fee agreement as required by ethics rules, lawyer not entitled to be paid under oral agreement or quantum meruit), *with In re Mardigian Estate*, 917 N.W.2d 325 (Mich. 2018) ("The rules of professional conduct promulgated by this Court should neither overrule nor give rise to substantive law."; fact that lawyer drafted will for friend leaving substantial bequest to lawyer and his family, in violation of Rule 1.8(c), does not itself create basis for voiding will).

## NO PRIVATE CAUSE OF ACTION FOR VIOLATING ETHICS RULE

Violation of an ethics rule does not give rise to a private cause of action. *See Karas v. Katten Muchin Rosenman LLP*, No. 07-1545-CV, 2009 WL 38898, 2009 BL 3320 (2d Cir. Jan. 8, 2009) (even if restrictive covenant violated New York's disciplinary rule, lawyer did not have cause of action against law firm for restraint of trade); *Schatz v. Rosenberg*, 943 F.2d 485 (4th Cir. 1991) ("plaintiffs cannot base a securities fraud or other misrepresentation claim on a violation of an ethical rule"); *Stahl v. Twp. of Montclair*, Civ. No. 12-3244 (SRC), 2013 WL 1867036, 2013 BL 117152 (D.N.J. May 2, 2013) (lawyers defending municipal employees from arrestee's harassment suit allegedly offered to drop criminal charges if he would drop civil suit; alleged violation of New Jersey's Rule 3.4(g) not actionable constitutional violation); *Laws v. Priority Trustee Servs. of N.C.*, 610 F. Supp. 2d 528 (W.D.N.C. 2009) (law firm's service as substitute trustee in foreclosure proceedings and also as counsel for lender did not give rise to causes of action for breach of contract, breach of fiduciary duty, constructive fraud, or unfair and deceptive trade practices; sole basis for all claims was ethics rules and ethics opinions); *B & O Mfg., Inc. v. Home Depot U.S.A., Inc.*, No. C 07-02864 JSW, 2007 WL 3232276, 2007 BL 192276 (N.D. Cal. Nov. 1, 2007) (alleged violation of rule on business transactions with client does not give rise to action to rescind contract); *Stratagene v. Parsons Behle & Latimer*, 315 F. Supp. 2d 765 (D. Md. 2004) (rejecting malpractice claim based upon violation of Rule 1.9; rules as "expression of public policy having the force of law" do not provide basis for court, in applying state law, to create cause of action); *Astarte, Inc. v. Pac. Indus. Sys., Inc.*, 865 F. Supp. 693 (D. Colo. 1994) (under Colorado law, lawyer ethics codes neither prescribe civil liability standards nor create private causes of action); *Terry Cove N., Inc. v. Marr & Friedlander, P.C.*, 521 So. 2d 22 (Ala. 1988) (sole remedy for rule violation is imposition of discipline); *Allen v. Allison*, 155 S.W.3d 682 (Ark. 2004) (alleged violations of antisolicitation rules could not be basis for civil conspiracy claim by former client dissatisfied with settlement offer firm obtained for him); *Biller Assocs. v. Peterken*, 849 A.2d 847 (Conn. 2004) (ethics rules do not give rise to cause of action); *Judy v. Preferred Commc'n Sys.*, 29 A.3d 248 (Del. Ch. 2011) (lawyers' substantive legal duties "may be congruent with the requirement and objectives of the Rules," but "provide no additional bases for the enforcement of such duties outside of the framework of disciplinary proceedings") (quoting *In re Infotechnology*, 582 A.2d 215 (Del. 1990)); *Smith v. Bateman Graham, P.A.*, 680 So. 2d 497 (Fla. Dist. Ct. App. 1996) (lawyer's alleged unethical conduct in soliciting clients of firm from which he was resigning could not be basis for injunction against further solicitation); *Coleman v. Hicks*, 433 S.E.2d 621 (Ga. Ct. App. 1993) (cannot base legal malpractice claim upon allegation that lawyers' excessive fees violated ethics code); *Nagy v. Beckley*, 578 N.E.2d 1134 (Ill. App. Ct. 1991) (no cause of action for "ethical malpractice" separate from legal malpractice claim; ethics rules not "independent font of tort liability"); *Liggett v. Young*, 877 N.E.2d 178 (Ind. 2007) (home builder had no cause of action against his lawyer for violating Rule 1.8(a) in contract to build custom home for lawyer); *McCabe v. Hoch*, 216 P.3d 720 (Kan. 2009) (cannot assert claim based upon opposing counsel's alleged violation "of his duty as an attorney and his ethical responsibilities to the Kansas Supreme Court"); *Teague v. St. Paul Fire & Marine Ins. Co.*, 10 So. 3d 806 (La. Ct. App. 2009) (failure of plastic surgeon's insurance defense counsel in medical malpractice case to keep him informed of settlement efforts did not constitute legal malpractice for purposes of surgeon's suit against them for settling without his approval); *Trierweiler v. Varnum, Riddering, Schmidt & Howlett, L.L.P.*, Nos. 256511, 261865, 2006 WL 1161546, 2006 BL 173699 (Mich. May 2, 2006) ("violation of the rules cannot 'give rise' to a cause of action for enforcement or for damages caused by a failure to comply"); *Baxt v. Liloia*, 714 A.2d 271 (N.J. 1998) (declining to hold that rules "in themselves create a duty or that a violation of the [rules], standing alone, can form the basis for a cause of action"); *Maritrans GP Inc. v. Pepper, Hamilton & Scheetz*, 602 A.2d 1277 (Pa. 1992) ("simply because a lawyer's conduct may violate the rules of ethics does not mean that the conduct is actionable, in damages or for injunctive relief"); *Joyner v. DeFriend*, 255 S.W.3d 281 (Tex. App. 2008) (plaintiffs could not sue prosecutor for conspiracy and fraud based upon allegations he violated ethics rules in handling evidence relating to death of their son); *see also Horn v. Wooster*, 165 P.3d 69 (Wyo. 2007) (no cause of action against co-counsel for legal malpractice) (discussed in Douglas R. Richmond, *Professional Responsibilities of Co-Counsel: Joint Venturers or Scorpions in a Bottle?*, 98 Ky. L.J. 461 (2009–2010)); *cf. B.W.T. v. Haynes & Haynes, P.C.*, 20 So. 3d 815 (Ala. Civ. App. 2009) (trial court lacked subject-matter jurisdiction to issue declaratory judgment that fee agreement did not violate Rule 1.5; any opinion would be merely advisory because state bar had not been joined).

## ETHICS RULES AS EVIDENCE OF STANDARDS OF CONDUCT AND CARE

Violation of an ethics rule does not itself create a presumption that a legal duty has been breached, according to Scope [20]. The modifier "itself" was added by amendment in 2002; it had appeared in early drafts of the Model Rules but was dropped by the time the rules were adopted in 1983. American Bar Association, *A Legislative History: The Development of the ABA Model Rules of Professional Conduct, 1982–2013*, at 12, 16–21 (2013). *Compare Elkind v. Bennett*, 958 So. 2d 1088 (Fla. Dist. Ct. App. 2007) (confidentiality as legal duty long predates ethics codes, and is enforceable as such in legal malpractice action), *with Lear Corp. v. Butzel Long, PC*, No. 258669, 2006 WL 1360286, 2006 BL 174731 (Mich. Ct. App. May 18, 2006) (although complaint properly alleged breach of fiduciary duty, it did not state cause of action because it relied entirely upon Rules 1.7 and 1.16).

However, most courts do look to the ethics rules as evidence of standards of conduct and care, particularly in actions for legal malpractice or breach of fiduciary duty. *See, e.g., CenTra, Inc. v. Estrin*, 538 F.3d 402 (6th Cir. 2008) (ethics rules are "probative and instructive . . . , particularly as they relate to CenTra's malpractice and fiduciary-duty claims") (applying Michigan law); *Avianca, Inc. v. Harrison*, 70 F.3d 637 (D.C. Cir. 1995) (evidence of rule violation creates rebuttable presumption of violation of lawyer's fiduciary duty to client) (applying District of Columbia law); *Jacobsen v. Oliver*, 555 F. Supp. 2d 72 (D.D.C. 2008) ("certain kinds of violations of certain ethical rules may demonstrate that an attorney has breached his fiduciary duty of loyalty"); *Sealed Party v. Sealed Party*, Civ. No. H-04-2229, 2006 WL 1207732, 2006 BL 139529 (S.D. Tex. May 4, 2006) (Texas and federal courts "regularly" refer to Texas rules to help define standards of lawyer conduct in tort cases; citing cases involving fees, withdrawal, aggregate settlements, and delivery of client funds); *RTC Mortg. Trust 1994 N-1 v. Fid. Nat'l Title Ins. Co.*, 58 F. Supp. 2d 503 (D.N.J. 1999) (violation of Rule 1.7 was evidence of lawyer's malpractice in action by third-party lender for whom lawyer, who represented both buyer and seller, had provided opinion letter); *Griffith v. Taylor*, 937 P.2d 297 (Alaska 1997) (rules are evidence of scope of lawyer's duties to client); *Allen v. Lefkoff, Duncan, Grimes & Dermer, P.C.*, 453 S.E.2d 719 (Ga. 1995) (bar rule admissible on standard of care if rule intended to protect person in plaintiff's position or addresses particular harm plaintiff suffered); *Owens v. McDermott, Will & Emery*, 736 N.E.2d 145 (Ill. App. Ct. 2000) (rules may be relevant to standard of care in malpractice case); *Stender v. Blessum*, 897 N.W.2d 491 (Iowa 2017) (adopting "majority approach" that violation of ethics rules does not establish per se claim for legal malpractice, but may be used as evidence of standard of care; discussing other approaches); *Leonard v. Reeves*, 82 So. 3d 1250 (La. Ct. App. 2012) (although rule violation does not constitute actionable legal malpractice, court would look to Rules 1.2, 1.3, and 1.4 in evaluating malpractice action arising out of allegedly incorrect legal advice); *Sargent v. Buckley*, 697 A.2d 1272 (Me. 1997) (former clients' allegation that lawyer violated Rule 1.9 stated cause of action for common-law breach of fiduciary duty, with bar rules providing "some evidence" of standard of care); *Fishman v. Brooks*, 487 N.E.2d 1377 (Mass. 1986) (rules are admissible evidence of negligence, on par with "liquor laws, workers' compensation, and building codes"); *Welsh v. Case*, 43 P.3d 445 (Or. Ct. App. 2002) ("Disciplinary rules, together with statutes and common-law principles relating to fiduciary relationships, all help define the duty component of the fiduciary duty owed by a lawyer to his or her client."); *McNair v. Rainsford*, 499 S.E.2d 488 (S.C. Ct. App. 1998) (failure to comply with ethics rules relevant to lawyer's alleged breach of duty of reasonable care); *Sands v. Menard*, 904 N.W.2d 789 (Wis. 2017) (while ethics rules "may guide courts in determining required standards of care generally, they may not be employed as an absolute defense in a civil action involving an attorney"). *But see Judy v. Preferred Commc'n Sys.*, 29 A.3d 248 (Del. Ch. 2011) (declining to look to Rule 1.16 to determine enforceability of retaining lien). *See generally* Nicola A. Boothe-Perry, *No Laughing Matter: The Intersection of Legal Malpractice and Professionalism*, 21 Am. U. J. Gender Soc. Pol'y & L. 1 (2012); Stephen E. Kalish, *How to Encourage Lawyers to Be Ethical: Do Not Use the Ethics Codes as a Basis for Regular Law Decisions*, 13 Geo. J. Legal Ethics 649 (Summer 2000); Gary A. Munneke & Anthony E. Davis, *The Standard of Care in Legal Malpractice: Do the Model Rules of Professional Conduct Define It?*, 22 J. Legal Prof. 233 (1998) (concluding certain ethics rules do articulate relevant standards of conduct and care that should be admissible as evidence in malpractice actions); Douglas R. Richmond, *Why Legal Ethics Rules Are Relevant to Lawyer Liability*, 38 St. Mary's L.J. 929 (2007); Charles W. Wolfram, *A Cautionary Tale: Fiduciary Breach as Legal Malpractice*, 34 Hofstra L. Rev. 689 (Spring 2006); Note, *The Evidentiary Use of the Ethics Codes in Legal Malpractice: Erasing a Double Standard*, 109 Harv. L. Rev. 1102 (Spring 1996) ("At the very least, the provisions of a jurisdiction's ethics code that relate to the facts of a malpractice suit should be admissible in helping to establish the proper standard of care.").

## • *Expert Testimony/Jury Instructions*

Consistent with the premise that ethics rules are evidence of standards of care and conduct, most courts permit expert witnesses in malpractice and fiduciary duty cases to use the ethics rules in reaching their conclusions; many courts also permit the rules to be used in jury instructions. *See, e.g., Mirabito v. Liccardo*, 5 Cal. Rptr. 2d 571 (Ct. App. 1992) (California disciplinary rules may be used as evidence and incorporated into jury instructions in legal malpractice action; expert witnesses may use rules to establish lawyer's breach of fiduciary duty to client); *Waldman v. Levine*, 544 A.2d 683 (D.C. 1988) (expert's use of Model Code in determining standard of care in legal malpractice case is appropriate and not unlike use of practice codes in other negligence contexts); *Mayol v. Summers, Watson & Kimpel*, 585 N.E.2d 1176 (Ill. App. Ct. 1992) (jury instructions in legal malpractice case may quote lawyer discipline rules to same extent as statutes and ordinances in instructions in other types of negligence actions); *Abramson v. Wildman*, 964 A.2d 703 (Md. Ct. Spec. App. 2009) (jury instruction on competence based upon Rule 1.1 warranted in client's breach-of-contract claim against lawyer; contract specified client "may expect our firm to be both sensitive and professionally responsible to your situation"); *Mainor v. Nault*, 101 P.3d 308 (Nev. 2004) (expert witnesses in legal malpractice action entitled to base their opinions upon ethics rules); *cf. Pierce v. Cook*, 992 So. 2d 612 (Miss. 2008) (even if former client's suit based upon lawyer's affair with wife sounded in legal malpractice rather than breach of contract, jury instruction on lawyer's duties was not impermissible use of ethics rules without requisite expert testimony: "Ordinary jurors [can] determine if an adulterous affair between an attorney and his client's wife is breach of a duty owed by an attorney to his client."). *Compare Lazy Seven Coal Sales Inc. v. Stone & Hinds, P.C.*, 813 S.W.2d 400 (Tenn. 1991) (expert may not testify that lawyer violated ethics rule, but may consider ethics rule violation in evaluating standard of care), *with Roy v. Diamond*, 16 S.W.3d 783 (Tenn. 1999) (trial court did not abuse discretion by admitting findings and judgment from disciplinary proceeding in subsequent legal malpractice action, in light of expert testimony in malpractice case that lawyer violated standard of care (as opposed to disciplinary rule)). *See generally* Pamela A. Bresnahan & Timothy H. Goodman, *Breach of Fiduciary Duty and Expert Testimony Regarding Attorney Ethics Rules*, 2003 Prof. Law. 53 (Symposium 2003); David S. Caudill, *The Roles of Attorneys as Courtroom Experts: Revisiting the Conventional Limitations and Their Exceptions*, 2 St. Mary's J. Legal Mal. & Ethics 136 (2012) (even though expert testimony on ethics rules does not establish standard of care and should not give impression that breach of ethics rules is actionable, "there should be no blanket prohibition on expert legal testimony concerning the Model Rules").

The minority view is that ethics rules are not admissible. *See Ex parte Toler*, 710 So. 2d 415 (Ala. 1998) (violation of ethics rules may not be used as evidence in legal malpractice action); *Orsini v. Larry Moyer Trucking, Inc.*, 833 S.W.2d 366 (Ark. 1992) (upholding trial court's refusal to allow introduction of Model Rules) (discussed in Mark A. Hagemeier, Note, Orsini v. Larry Moyer Trucking, Inc.: *Approaching a Definitive Use of the Model Rules of Professional Conduct in the Legal Malpractice Context in Arkansas*, 46 Ark. L. Rev. 607 (1993)); *Byers v. Cummings*, 87 P.3d 465 (Mont. 2004) (plaintiff in legal malpractice action must prove breach of duty established through expert testimony, not breach of disciplinary rules; plaintiff not entitled to instruction based upon Rule 1.4(b) duty to explain matter to extent necessary to permit client to make informed decisions about representation); *Harrington v. Pailthorp*, 841 P.2d 1258 (Wash. Ct. App. 1992) (violation of rules may not be used as evidence of malpractice); *see also Smith v. Morrison*, 47 A.3d 131 (Pa. Super. Ct. 2012) (in malpractice action for breach of fiduciary duty, jury instructions reciting ethics rules verbatim were properly rejected).

There is also authority for an approach that permits the ethics rules to be used but not identified or admitted. In *Hizey v. Carpenter*, 830 P.2d 646 (Wash. 1992), the court cited the disclaimer language in the Model Code's Preliminary Statement and barred testimony and jury instructions explicitly referring to the Code of Professional Responsibility or Rules of Professional Conduct. An expert witness would, however, be allowed to quote from the rules—without identifying the source of the language—if relevant to the expert's opinion on the applicable standard of care and the lawyer's conformity to it. *See Tilton v. Trezza*, 819 N.Y.S.2d 213 (Sup. Ct. 2006) (endorsing *Hizey*; expert may testify about ethical conduct under circumstances of case and may use language from Model Code but may not refer specifically to it); *Behnke v. Ahrens*, 294 P.3d 729 (Wash. Ct. App. 2012) (*Hizey* "preserved the propriety of using the ethical rules for reasons other than to impose malpractice liability"; court may consider ethics rules in client's action to recover attorneys' fees based upon breach of fiduciary duty); *cf. LK Operating, LLC v. Collection Grp., LLC*, 331 P.3d 1147 (Wash. 2014) (contract that violates Rule 1.8(a) "may not be enforced unless it can be shown that notwithstanding the violation the resulting contract does not violate the underlying public policy of the rule"; dissent believes *Hizey* requires greater separation between discipline and civil actions). *See generally* Marc R. Greenough, Note, *The Inadmissibility of Professional Ethical Standards in Legal Malpractice Actions After* Hizey v. Carpenter, 68 Wash. L. Rev. 395 (Apr. 1993) (criticizing *Hizey* for overreading disclaimer to give it more preclusive effect than drafters intended); Stephen E. Kalish, *How to Encourage Lawyers to Be Ethical: Do Not Use the Ethics Code as a Basis for Regular Law Decisions*, 13 Geo J. Legal Ethics 649 (Summer 2000) (endorsing *Hizey* for restricting ethics codes to "domain" separate from "regular law"; "[j]urors should be shielded from any explicit reference to an ethics code violation" lest they give it undue weight).

## DISQUALIFICATION

Violation of an ethics rule is not itself a sufficient basis for disqualification. *See, e.g., Dixon v. Golden-Masano-Bradley Law Firm*, Civ. No. 2:06-0392, 2006 WL 1737767, 2006 BL 71854 (E.D. Pa. June 23, 2006) ("disqualification depends upon the requirements and purpose of the rule and how it is applied in particular factual circumstances"); *Ridge-*

*way Nursing & Rehabilitation Facility, LLC v. Lane*, 415 S.W.3d 635 (Ky. 2013) (refusing to issue mandamus disqualifying lawyer for obtaining evidence in violation of Rule 4.2 when other remedies, such as excluding improperly obtained evidence, were available; lawyer may still be subject to discipline); *Schuff v. A.T. Klemens & Son*, 16 P.3d 1002 (Mont. 2000) (although ethics rule violation not prima facie grounds for disqualification, it is additional evidence that may "tip the scales"; lawyer who is not disqualified because court finds no prejudice may still be subject to discipline); *Musa v. Gillette Commc'ns*, 641 N.E.2d 233 (Ohio Ct. App. 1994) (violation of ethics code should not result in disqualification unless "absolutely necessary"; trial court's order of disqualification "in order to prevent the possibility of an ethical violation" was abuse of discretion).

Courts do, however, routinely look to the jurisdiction's ethics rules (and even the Model Rules themselves) in deciding disqualification motions. *In re EPIC Holdings, Inc.*, 985 S.W.2d 41 (Tex. 1998) (ethics rules "do not determine whether counsel is disqualified in litigation, but they do provide guidelines and suggest the relevant considerations"; citing cases); *see, e.g., In re Congoleum Corp.*, 426 F.3d 675 (3d Cir. 2005) (citing Rule 1.7 in disqualifying firm from serving as debtor's "special insurance counsel" in reorganization); *Cole v. Ruidoso Mun. Sch.*, 43 F.3d 1373 (10th Cir. 1994) (ABA Model Rules reflect "national standard" to be used in ruling on disqualification motions); *In re Dresser Indus., Inc.*, 972 F.2d 540 (5th Cir. 1992) (in federal courts, motions to disqualify are "governed by the ethical rules announced by the national profession"; court looks to ABA standards as well as ethics rules of forum state); *Kashi v. McGraw-Hill Global Educ. Holdings, LLC*, No. 17-1818, 2018 WL 4094958, 2018 BL 307566 (E.D. Pa. Aug. 27, 2018) (courts have power to disqualify lawyers for violating ethics rules, but only if disqualification is appropriate under particular facts; firm's disqualification not warranted despite ethics rule violations); *Paul v. Judicial Watch, Inc.*, 571 F. Supp. 2d 17 (D.D.C. 2008) (surveying jurisdictions and disqualifying lawyer for violation of Rule 1.9); *Harrison v. Fisons Corp.*, 819 F. Supp. 1039 (M.D. Fla. 1993) (courts ruling on claims of conflict of interest have consistently relied upon ethics codes); *Seeco, Inc. v. Hales*, 969 S.W.2d 193 (Ark. 1998) (whether lawyer violated ethics rules by participating in series of events contrived to force judge's recusal was relevant to motion seeking his disqualification); *People v. Donaldson*, 113 Cal. Rptr. 2d 548 (Ct. App. 2001) (looking to lawyer-witness rule in evaluating effect of prosecutor testifying in criminal case; Model Rules serve as "collateral source for guidance on proper professional conduct in California"); *State ex rel. Wallace v. Munton*, 989 S.W.2d 641 (Mo. Ct. App. 1999) (trial court has power to enforce Rule 3.7 by disqualifying lawyer who will be witness); *see also Grosser-Samuels v. Jacquelin Designs Enters., Inc.*, 448 F. Supp. 2d 772 (N.D. Tex. 2006) (lawyer disqualified for violating conflicts rule; motion for sanctions held in abeyance pending possible disciplinary action). *See generally* Mark J. Fucile, *Disqualification Motions and the RPC's: Recent Decisions Using Ethics Rules as the Basis for Disqualification*, 1999 Prof. Law. 9 (Symposium 1999) (Model Rules "now provide the key component in the substantive law of disqualification").

## LITIGATION MISCONDUCT

Litigation misconduct is dealt with in the first instance by the trial judge—via contempt, sanctions, and remedies involving fees and suppression or preclusion of evidence. These decisions may also look to the rules of professional conduct. *See, e.g.,* *Constand v. Cosby*, 229 F.R.D. 472 (E.D. Pa. 2005) (court would adopt and enforce Rule 3.6 (Trial Publicity) as procedural rule in high-profile paternity case; although court normally would refer offending counsel to disciplinary authorities, "an after-the-fact rebuke by the Disciplinary Board would not address the need for prompt action by the trial court"); *In re Marriage of Redmond*, 131 P.3d 1167 (Colo. App. 2005) (if trial court finds that court-appointed special advocate's alteration of dates on documents violated Rule 8.4(c), court may order full or partial fee refund); *Speicher v. Columbia Twp. Bd. of Election Comm'rs*, 832 N.W.2d 392 (Mich. 2012) (because legislature has given judiciary power to determine public policy as it relates to bar, judge has authority to apply rule against illegal or clearly excessive fees to lawyer's request for "actual attorney fees" under Open Meetings Act); *In re Estate of McCool*, 553 A.2d 761 (N.H. 1988) (estate lawyer who clearly violates conflicts rules forfeits legal fees as well as executor's fees); *see also In re Sledge*, 352 B.R. 742 (Bankr. E.D.N.C. 2006) (citing lawyer's failure to maintain "professional standard of care" and "adhere to the standards of conduct set forth in the Rules of Professional Responsibility," court ordered lawyer to reimburse clients for his fees); *cf. Portland Gen. Elec. Co. v. Duncan, Weinberg, Miller & Pembroke, P.C.*, 986 P.2d 35 (Or. Ct. App. 1999) (fee reduction is not available sanction for violating disciplinary rules on former-client conflicts, but is appropriate sanction for breach of fiduciary duty arising out of representing conflicting interests, and ethics rules are evidence of scope of that fiduciary duty); *In re Adoption of M.M.H.*, 981 A.2d 261 (Pa. Super. Ct. 2009) (ethics rule did not give adoption court authority to halve uncontested fee request it considered unreasonable). *See generally* Richard G. Johnson, *Integrating Legal Ethics & Professional Responsibility with Federal Rule of Civil Procedure 11*, 37 Loy. L.A. L. Rev. 819 (Winter 2004) (Rule 11 should be interpreted in light of ethics rules relevant to litigation; federal judges should be allowed to require compliance); Peter A. Joy, *The Relationship Between Civil Rule 11 and Lawyer Discipline: An Empirical Analysis Suggesting Institutional Choices in the Regulation of Lawyers*, 37 Loy. L.A. L. Rev. 765 (Winter 2004) (lack of correlation between Rule 11 sanctions and reported disciplinary cases involving litigation misconduct betokens wise institutional choice not to require discipline for every Rule 11 sanction); Jeffrey A. Webb & Blake W. Stribling, *Ten Years After* Burrow v. Arce: *The Current State of Attorney Fee Forfeiture*, 40 St. Mary's L.J. 967 (2009); Fred C. Zacharias, *Are Evidence-Related Ethics Provisions "Law"?*, 76 Fordham L. Rev. 1315 (Dec. 2007).

Note that a trial court's ruling regarding litigation misconduct is not conclusive in a disciplinary proceeding arising out of the same conduct. *See Ala. State Bar v. Caffey*, 938 So. 2d 942 (Ala. 2006) (trial court's judgment of criminal contempt for lawyer's disrespectful conduct did not conclusively establish violation of Rules 3.1(a), 3.2, 3.5(c), or 8.4; in disciplinary context, evidentiary hearing regarding state of mind and justification was required); *In re Boone*, 7 P.3d 270 (Kan. 2000) (failure to comply with court's orders violated Rule 8.4(d) even though magistrate in underlying litigation decided, based upon lawyer's corrective actions, that report to disciplinary administrator not required); *In re Panel Case No. 17289*, 669 N.W.2d 898 (Minn. 2003) (trial judge's decision not to impose Rule 11 sanctions did not preclude disciplinary authority from proceeding against lawyer for making frivolous claims); *In re Marra*,

87 P.3d 384 (Mont. 2004) (lawyer's "reliance" upon trial court's denial of other side's motion to disqualify him was not defense to charge that he violated Rule 1.10); *In re Eadie*, 36 P.3d 468 (Or. 2001) (rejecting argument that trial court's denial of opponent's motion to set aside default judgment for "fraud, misrepresentation, or other misconduct" precluded disciplinary panel from finding misrepresentation); *State ex rel. Clifford v. Office of Disciplinary Counsel*, 745 S.E.2d 225 (W. Va. 2013) (trial court's denial of disqualification motion alleging conflict of interest does not foreclose disciplinary action, but it "merits consideration" in determining whether to impose discipline); *cf. Goldstein v. Comm'n for Lawyer Discipline*, 109 S.W.3d 810 (Tex. App. 2003) (when divorce court considered comment to ethics rule in finding lawyer's fee unconscionable, no error to give finding preclusive effect in disciplinary proceeding).

## AGREEMENTS THAT VIOLATE ETHICS RULES

### • Agreements with Nonlawyers

Caselaw varies on the enforceability of a contract between a lawyer and nonlawyer that violates the lawyer ethics rules. Some courts have refused to permit lawyers to avoid contractual obligations by claiming the contracts violated the ethics rules. *See, e.g., Patterson v. Law Office of Lauri J. Goldstein, P.A.*, 980 So. 2d 1234 (Fla. Dist. Ct. App. 2008) (reversing summary judgment for defendant law firm in paralegal's action to enforce agreement giving her fee-based bonus; "public interest is not advanced if an attorney is permitted to promise a bonus arrangement that violates the fee-sharing rule, and then invoke the Rules as a shield from liability under that arrangement"); *Shimrak v. Garcia-Mendoza*, 912 P.2d 822 (Nev. 1996) (rejecting law firm's attempt to evade paying private investigator by claiming contract constituted unethical fee-splitting; "it would not be fair . . . to allow attorneys to receive free investigative services simply because of their claim that the other party to the contract was 'in pari delicto' with them"; furthermore, lawyer ethics rule did not apply to investigator); *see also Murdock v. Nalbandian*, Nos. 218-2008-CV-1062, 218-2009-EQ-0031, 2010 WL 8484210 (N.H. Super. Ct. Oct. 26, 2010) (if lawyer lending money to client does not comply with Rule 1.8(a), loan contracts voidable at client's election); *cf. Santiago v. Evans*, 547 F. App'x 923 (11th Cir. 2013) (client sold property to lawyer to repay loan from lawyer; lawyer's failure to comply with Rule 1.8(a) meant contract void as against public policy and lawyer could not enforce it).

Other courts, however, have refused to allow nonlawyers to enforce such contracts. *See, e.g., Fisher v. Carron*, No. 289687, 2010 WL 935742, 2010 BL 350844 (Mich. Ct. App. Mar. 16, 2010) (nonlawyer could not enforce lawyer's promise of share in legal fees earned from cases she referred; "to the extent that plaintiff elected to do business with a lawyer, plaintiff thereby exposed herself to the machinations of the rules that govern that profession"); *Bonilla v. Rotter*, 829 N.Y.S.2d 52 (App. Div. 2007) (private investigator's agreement to solicit personal injury clients in exchange for $2,500 out of any resulting settlement was illegal and he was "foreclosed from seeking the assistance of the courts" in enforcing it). *See generally* Mark A. Armitage, *Professional Responsibility*, 53 Wayne L. Rev. 541 (Spring 2007) (comparing case in which client successfully asserted rule violation as defense to lawyer's suit for fees with case in which client unsuccessfully tried to sue lawyer for rule violation, author suggests "[f]orm is elevated over substance when a duty on the part of a lawyer, and a correlative right of another, is enforceable [or not] depending upon whether the person is asserting 'a cause of action for enforcement of a rule or for damages' or a defense"; citing Michigan's Rule 1.0(b), which tracks Scope [20]); Benjamin P. Cooper, *Taking Rules Seriously: The Rise of Lawyer Rules as Substantive Law and the Public Policy Exception in Contract Law*, 35 Cardozo L. Rev. 267 (Oct. 2013) (examining how courts have split on enforcing rule-violative agreements, and calling for greater reliance on rules as source of law).

### • *Agreements among Lawyers*

Courts are similarly divided on the enforceability of rule-violative agreements among lawyers. Many courts refuse to enforce them. *See, e.g., Margolin v. Shemaria*, 102 Cal. Rptr. 2d 502 (Ct. App. 2000) (denial of referring lawyers' share in fees was appropriate remedy for failing to obtain client's written consent to fee-sharing, even though receiving lawyers breached their promise to referring lawyers to obtain consent); *Gagne v. Vaccaro*, 766 A.2d 416 (Conn. 2001) (court "should not allow itself to be made the instrument of enforcing obligations arising out of an agreement that is against public policy, either in law or in equity"; but lawyer who cannot enforce rule-violative agreement against successor counsel may still recover in quantum meruit or unjust enrichment); *Chandris, S.A. v. Yanakakis*, 668 So. 2d 180 (Fla. 1995) (contingent-fee agreement that does not comply with ethics rules is void; because fee-division agreement between out-of-state lawyer and Florida lawyer was born of void contingent-fee agreement between out-of-state lawyer and Florida client, it was unenforceable); *Christensen v. Eggen*, 577 N.W.2d 221 (Minn. 1998) (fee-splitting agreement between lawyers in different firms violated Rule 1.5(e) and was unenforceable as against public policy); *Londoff v. Vuylsteke*, 996 S.W.2d 553 (Mo. Ct. App. 1999) (promise to share fees unenforceable because it did not satisfy Rule 1.5(e)); *Kalled v. Albee*, 712 A.2d 616 (N.H. 1998) (because clients did not give informed consent to fee-sharing agreement between counsel as required by Rule 1.5(f)(1), agreement void as against public policy and unenforceable). *But see Poole v. Prince*, 61 So. 3d 258 (Ala. 2010) (surveying caselaw from other jurisdictions and concluding trial court lacked authority to invalidate agreement that violated Rule 1.5(e)).

But courts are also willing to give precedence to the equities. *See Daynard v. Ness, Motley, Loadholt, Richardson & Poole, P.A.*, 188 F. Supp. 2d 115 (D. Mass. 2002) (enforcing oral fee-sharing agreement between law professor and law firm that used his expertise to win "massive" settlements in tobacco suits would not offend public policy; allegedly illegal behavior was incidental and insubstantial); *Post v. Bregman*, 707 A.2d 806 (Md. 1998) (court can hold rule-violative fee agreement unenforceable to avoid anomalous result of helping lawyer enforce same agreement that subjects him to discipline, but must first analyze violation, public policies, and equities); *Robert L. Crill, Inc. v. Bond*, 76 S.W.3d 411 (Tex. App. 2001) (undisclosed fee-sharing agreement had no financial impact upon client, and thus was not void as against public policy); *see also* Nathan M. Crystal, *Enforcing Fee Splitting Rules: Equity Rather Than Strict Compliance*, 25 S.C. Law. 12 (May 2014) (strict compliance, though apparently the majority rule, is inconsistent with principles of fairness, contract law, and fee forfeiture).

# TERMINOLOGY

## Rule 1.0

*Terminology*

(a) "Belief" or "believes" denotes that the person involved actually supposed the fact in question to be true. A person's belief may be inferred from circumstances.

(b) "Confirmed in writing," when used in reference to the informed consent of a person, denotes informed consent that is given in writing by the person or a writing that a lawyer promptly transmits to the person confirming an oral informed consent. See paragraph (e) for the definition of "informed consent." If it is not feasible to obtain or transmit the writing at the time the person gives informed consent, then the lawyer must obtain or transmit it within a reasonable time thereafter.

(c) "Firm" or "law firm" denotes a lawyer or lawyers in a law partnership, professional corporation, sole proprietorship or other association authorized to practice law; or lawyers employed in a legal services organization or the legal department of a corporation or other organization.

(d) "Fraud" or "fraudulent" denotes conduct that is fraudulent under the substantive or procedural law of the applicable jurisdiction and has a purpose to deceive.

(e) "Informed consent" denotes the agreement by a person to a proposed course of conduct after the lawyer has communicated adequate information and explanation about the material risks of and reasonably available alternatives to the proposed course of conduct.

(f) "Knowingly," "known," or "knows" denotes actual knowledge of the fact in question. A person's knowledge may be inferred from circumstances.

(g) "Partner" denotes a member of a partnership, a shareholder in a law firm organized as a professional corporation, or a member of an association authorized to practice law.

(h) "Reasonable" or "reasonably" when used in relation to conduct by a lawyer denotes the conduct of a reasonably prudent and competent lawyer.

(i) "Reasonable belief" or "reasonably believes" when used in reference to a lawyer denotes that the lawyer believes the matter in question and that the circumstances are such that the belief is reasonable.

(j) "Reasonably should know" when used in reference to a lawyer denotes that a lawyer of reasonable prudence and competence would ascertain the matter in question.

(k) "Screened" denotes the isolation of a lawyer from any participation in a matter through the timely imposition of procedures within a firm that are reasonably adequate under the circumstances to protect information that the isolated lawyer is obligated to protect under these Rules or other law.

(l) "Substantial" when used in reference to degree or extent denotes a material matter of clear and weighty importance.

(m) "Tribunal" denotes a court, an arbitrator in a binding arbitration proceeding or a legislative body, administrative agency or other body acting in an adjudicative capacity. A legislative body, administrative agency or other body acts in an adjudicative capacity when a neutral official, after the presentation of evidence or legal argument by a party or parties, will render a binding legal judgment directly affecting a party's interests in a particular matter.

(n) "Writing" or "written" denotes a tangible or electronic record of a communication or representation, including handwriting, typewriting, printing, photostating, photography, audio or videorecording, and electronic communications. A "signed" writing includes an electronic sound, symbol or process attached to or logically associated with a writing and executed or adopted by a person with the intent to sign the writing.

## COMMENT

### Confirmed in Writing

[1] If it is not feasible to obtain or transmit a written confirmation at the time the client gives informed consent, then the lawyer must obtain or transmit it within a reasonable time thereafter. If a lawyer has obtained a client's informed consent, the lawyer may act in reliance on that consent so long as it is confirmed in writing within a reasonable time thereafter.

### Firm

[2] Whether two or more lawyers constitute a firm within paragraph (c) can depend on the specific facts. For example, two practitioners who share office space and occasionally consult or assist each other ordinarily would not be regarded as constituting a firm. However, if they present themselves to the public in a way that suggests that they are a firm or conduct themselves as a firm, they should be regarded as a firm for purposes of the Rules. The terms of any formal agreement between associated lawyers are relevant in determining whether they are a firm, as is the fact that they have mutual access to information concerning the clients they serve. Fur-

thermore, it is relevant in doubtful cases to consider the underlying purpose of the Rule that is involved. A group of lawyers could be regarded as a firm for purposes of the Rule that the same lawyer should not represent opposing parties in litigation, while it might not be so regarded for purposes of the Rule that information acquired by one lawyer is attributed to another.

[3] With respect to the law department of an organization, including the government, there is ordinarily no question that the members of the department constitute a firm within the meaning of the Rules of Professional Conduct. There can be uncertainty, however, as to the identity of the client. For example, it may not be clear whether the law department of a corporation represents a subsidiary or an affiliated corporation, as well as the corporation by which the members of the department are directly employed. A similar question can arise concerning an unincorporated association and its local affiliates.

[4] Similar questions can also arise with respect to lawyers in legal aid and legal services organizations. Depending upon the structure of the organization, the entire organization or different components of it may constitute a firm or firms for purposes of these Rules.

## Fraud

[5] When used in these Rules, the terms "fraud" or "fraudulent" refer to conduct that is characterized as such under the substantive or procedural law of the applicable jurisdiction and has a purpose to deceive. This does not include merely negligent misrepresentation or negligent failure to apprise another of relevant information. For purposes of these Rules, it is not necessary that anyone has suffered damages or relied on the misrepresentation or failure to inform.

## Informed Consent

[6] Many of the Rules of Professional Conduct require the lawyer to obtain the informed consent of a client or other person (e.g., a former client or, under certain circumstances, a prospective client) before accepting or continuing representation or pursuing a course of conduct. See, e.g., Rules 1.2(c), 1.6(a) and 1.7(b). The communication necessary to obtain such consent will vary according to the Rule involved and the circumstances giving rise to the need to obtain informed consent. The lawyer must make reasonable efforts to ensure that the client or other person possesses information reasonably adequate to make an informed decision. Ordinarily, this will require communication that includes a disclosure of the facts and circumstances giving rise to the situation, any explanation reasonably necessary to inform the client or other person of the material advantages and disadvantages of the proposed course of conduct and a discussion of the client's or other person's options and alternatives. In some circumstances it may be appropriate for a lawyer to advise a client or other person to seek the advice of other counsel. A lawyer need not inform a client or other person of facts or implications already known to the client or other person; nevertheless, a lawyer who does not personally inform the client or other person assumes the risk that the client or other person is inadequately informed and the consent is invalid. In determining whether the information and explanation provided are reasonably

adequate, relevant factors include whether the client or other person is experienced in legal matters generally and in making decisions of the type involved, and whether the client or other person is independently represented by other counsel in giving the consent. Normally, such persons need less information and explanation than others, and generally a client or other person who is independently represented by other counsel in giving the consent should be assumed to have given informed consent.

[7] Obtaining informed consent will usually require an affirmative response by the client or other person. In general, a lawyer may not assume consent from a client's or other person's silence. Consent may be inferred, however, from the conduct of a client or other person who has reasonably adequate information about the matter. A number of Rules require that a person's consent be confirmed in writing. See Rules 1.7(b) and 1.9(a). For a definition of "writing" and "confirmed in writing," see paragraphs (n) and (b). Other Rules require that a client's consent be obtained in a writing signed by the client. See, e.g., Rules 1.8(a) and (g). For a definition of "signed," see paragraph (n).

### Screened

[8] This definition applies to situations where screening of a personally disqualified lawyer is permitted to remove imputation of a conflict of interest under Rules 1.10, 1.11, 1.12 or 1.18.

[9] The purpose of screening is to assure the affected parties that confidential information known by the personally disqualified lawyer remains protected. The personally disqualified lawyer should acknowledge the obligation not to communicate with any of the other lawyers in the firm with respect to the matter. Similarly, other lawyers in the firm who are working on the matter should be informed that the screening is in place and that they may not communicate with the personally disqualified lawyer with respect to the matter. Additional screening measures that are appropriate for the particular matter will depend on the circumstances. To implement, reinforce and remind all affected lawyers of the presence of the screening, it may be appropriate for the firm to undertake such procedures as a written undertaking by the screened lawyer to avoid any communication with other firm personnel and any contact with any firm files or other information, including information in electronic form, relating to the matter, written notice and instructions to all other firm personnel forbidding any communication with the screened lawyer relating to the matter, denial of access by the screened lawyer to firm files or other information, including information in electronic form, relating to the matter and periodic reminders of the screen to the screened lawyer and all other firm personnel.

[10] In order to be effective, screening measures must be implemented as soon as practical after a lawyer or law firm knows or reasonably should know that there is a need for screening.

### State Rules Comparison

http://ambar.org/MRPCStateCharts

# CLIENT-LAWYER RELATIONSHIP

## Rule 1.1

### *Competence*

A lawyer shall provide competent representation to a client. Competent representation requires the legal knowledge, skill, thoroughness and preparation reasonably necessary for the representation.

## COMMENT

### *Legal Knowledge and Skill*

[1] In determining whether a lawyer employs the requisite knowledge and skill in a particular matter, relevant factors include the relative complexity and specialized nature of the matter, the lawyer's general experience, the lawyer's training and experience in the field in question, the preparation and study the lawyer is able to give the matter and whether it is feasible to refer the matter to, or associate or consult with, a lawyer of established competence in the field in question. In many instances, the required proficiency is that of a general practitioner. Expertise in a particular field of law may be required in some circumstances.

[2] A lawyer need not necessarily have special training or prior experience to handle legal problems of a type with which the lawyer is unfamiliar. A newly admitted lawyer can be as competent as a practitioner with long experience. Some important legal skills, such as the analysis of precedent, the evaluation of evidence and legal drafting, are required in all legal problems. Perhaps the most fundamental legal skill consists of determining what kind of legal problems a situation may involve, a skill that necessarily transcends any particular specialized knowledge. A lawyer can provide adequate representation in a wholly novel field through necessary study. Competent representation can also be provided through the association of a lawyer of established competence in the field in question.

[3] In an emergency a lawyer may give advice or assistance in a matter in which the lawyer does not have the skill ordinarily required where referral to or consultation or association with another lawyer would be impractical. Even in an emergency, however, assistance should be limited to that reasonably necessary in the circumstances, for ill-considered action under emergency conditions can jeopardize the client's interest.

[4] A lawyer may accept representation where the requisite level of competence can be achieved by reasonable preparation. This applies as well to a lawyer who is appointed as counsel for an unrepresented person. See also Rule 6.2.

## Thoroughness and Preparation

[5] Competent handling of a particular matter includes inquiry into and analysis of the factual and legal elements of the problem, and use of methods and procedures meeting the standards of competent practitioners. It also includes adequate preparation. The required attention and preparation are determined in part by what is at stake; major litigation and complex transactions ordinarily require more extensive treatment than matters of lesser complexity and consequence. An agreement between the lawyer and the client regarding the scope of the representation may limit the matters for which the lawyer is responsible. See Rule 1.2(c).

## Retaining or Contracting With Other Lawyers

[6] Before a lawyer retains or contracts with other lawyers outside the lawyer's own firm to provide or assist in the provision of legal services to a client, the lawyer should ordinarily obtain informed consent from the client and must reasonably believe that the other lawyers' services will contribute to the competent and ethical representation of the client. See also Rules 1.2 (allocation of authority), 1.4 (communication with client), 1.5(e) (fee sharing), 1.6 (confidentiality), and 5.5(a) (unauthorized practice of law). The reasonableness of the decision to retain or contract with other lawyers outside the lawyer's own firm will depend upon the circumstances, including the education, experience and reputation of the nonfirm lawyers; the nature of the services assigned to the nonfirm lawyers; and the legal protections, professional conduct rules, and ethical environments of the jurisdictions in which the services will be performed, particularly relating to confidential information.

[7] When lawyers from more than one law firm are providing legal services to the client on a particular matter, the lawyers ordinarily should consult with each other and the client about the scope of their respective representations and the allocation of responsibility among them. See Rule 1.2. When making allocations of responsibility in a matter pending before a tribunal, lawyers and parties may have additional obligations that are a matter of law beyond the scope of these Rules.

## Maintaining Competence

[8] To maintain the requisite knowledge and skill, a lawyer should keep abreast of changes in the law and its practice, including the benefits and risks associated with relevant technology, engage in continuing study and education and comply with all continuing legal education requirements to which the lawyer is subject.

### Definitional Cross-References

"Reasonably" See Rule 1.0(h)

### State Rules Comparison

http://ambar.org/MRPCStateCharts

## ANNOTATION

### INTRODUCTION

Competence was not an explicit ethical requirement until after 1970, when jurisdictions began adopting versions of the ABA Model Code of Professional Responsibility. Model Code DR 6-101(A) (Failing to Act Competently) (1969). Although the Model Code required competence, it did not define it, and so disciplinary agencies assessing adequacy of representation relied principally upon DR 6-101(A)(3) (forbidding neglect) and DR 6-101(A)(2) (requiring adequate preparation). *See In re Cohn*, 600 N.Y.S.2d 501 (App. Div. 1993) (neglect may be considered a species of failure to act competently; applying state's Code). Rule 1.1, in contrast, now defines competence by breaking it into four ingredients—knowledge, skill, thoroughness, and preparation.

#### • *2012 Amendments*

The comment was amended in 2012 to add paragraphs [6] and [7] under a new header, Retaining or Contracting With Other Lawyers. Former paragraph [6] was renumbered to paragraph [8], and language was added to make explicit that a lawyer's duty of competence includes keeping abreast of the benefits and risks associated with relevant technology. *See* American Bar Association, *A Legislative History: The Development of the ABA Model Rules of Professional Conduct, 1982–2013*, at 43 (2013).

### KNOWLEDGE

#### • *Legal Principles*

A lawyer is expected to be familiar with well-settled principles of law applicable to a client's needs. *See People ex rel. Goldberg v. Gordon*, 607 P.2d 995 (Colo. 1980) (treating corporation as tenancy in common among shareholders, then using probate proceeding to transfer joint-tenancy assets, demonstrated "total lack of understanding of fundamental principles essential to the practice of law"); *Fla. Bar v. Lecznar*, 690 So. 2d 1284 (Fla. 1997) (failure to name insurance company as defendant in personal injury suit within statutory time limit indicated failure to understand relevant legal doctrines or procedures); *In re Hagedorn*, 725 N.E.2d 397 (Ind. 2000) (failure to carry out essential adoption procedures); *In re Hult*, 410 P.3d 879 (Kan. 2018) (lawyer representing immigration client lacked sufficient knowledge of relevant law or procedure); *Att'y Grievance Comm'n v. Zhang*, 100 A.3d 1112 (Md. 2014) (lack of knowledge and failure to do research in annulment/divorce matter); *Commonwealth v. McDaniels*, 785 A.2d 120 (Pa. Super. Ct. 2001) (brief grossly misstated client's crimes and relevant standard for withdrawal from representation); *In re Moore*, 494 S.E.2d 804 (S.C. 1997) (erroneously believing statute of limitations in medical malpractice case would not run until after obtaining opinion by client's treating physician that malpractice occurred); *Office of Disciplinary Counsel v. Henry*, 664 S.W.2d 62 (Tenn. 1983) (filing "answers" to one client's murder indictment, and civil rights suit for another client alleging libel by receipt of pornography in mail); *Martin v. Nw. Wash. Legal Servs.*, 717 P.2d 779 (Wash. Ct. App. 1986) (failing to inquire about, discuss, or seek division of client's husband's military pension in course of marriage dissolution). *But see In re Yelverton*, 105 A.3d 413 (D.C. 2014) (lawyer for witness in criminal trial pursued "legally unfounded strategy," including filing motion for mistrial without standing and with no chance of success, but court declined to find violation of Rule 1.1 because actions were "sincerely undertaken for the purpose of protecting his client" and caused no harm). *See generally* American Bar Association, *Essential Qualities of the Professional Lawyer* 105 *et seq.* (2013); Christopher Sabis & Daniel Webert, *Understanding the "Knowledge" Element of Attorney Competence: A Roadmap for Novice Attorneys*, 15 Geo. J. Legal Ethics 915 (Summer 2002).

### • *Basic Research*

A lawyer must be able to ascertain applicable rules of law, whether or not commonly known or settled, using standard research sources. *See Baldayaque v. United States*, 338 F.3d 145 (2d Cir. 2003) (criminal defense lawyer "did no legal research" on client's case); *Att'y Grievance Comm'n v. Sperling*, 69 A.3d 478 (Md. 2013) ("decision to do nothing promptly" on learning of case's dismissal violated duty of competence); *Att'y Grievance Comm'n v. James*, 870 A.2d 229 (Md. 2005) (failure to do "even cursory research" regarding viability of claim); *State ex rel. Okla. Bar Ass'n v. Hensley*, 661 P.2d 527 (Okla. 1983) (intestacy laws not "peculiar to probate law" but "basic" and "readily ascertainable upon minimal research"); *In re Young*, 639 S.E.2d 674 (S.C. 2007) (filing RICO counterclaim in answer to adversaries' suit without researching state predicate offenses upon which claim was based); *In re Taylor*, 60 V.I. 356 (V.I. 2014) (failure to do any research before advising immigration client). *See generally* Lawrence Duncan MacLachlan, *Gandy Dancers on the Web: How the Internet Has Raised the Bar on Lawyers' Professional Responsibility to Research and Know the Law*, 13 Geo. J. Legal Ethics 607 (Summer 2000); Ellie Margolis, *Surfin' Safari—Why Competent Lawyers Should Research on the Web*, 10 Yale J.L. & Tech. 82 (Fall 2007).

### • *Procedure*

A lawyer is required to know and follow all applicable rules of procedure. *See In re Gluck*, 114 F. Supp. 3d 57 (E.D.N.Y. 2015) (repeated failure to comply with deadlines or appear at pretrial conferences); *People v. Beecher*, 350 P.3d 310 (Colo. O.P.D.J. 2014) (telling client not to appear at pretrial conference); *Burton v. Mottolese*, 835 A.2d 998 (Conn. 2003) (failure to stop speaking when objection was made); *Ky. Bar Ass'n v. Trumbo*, 17 S.W.3d 856 (Ky. 2000) (filing defective separation agreement without proper notarization of husband's signature; decree of dissolution later set aside); *In re Martin*, 982 So. 2d 765 (La. 2008) (criminal defense lawyer failed to provide statement of admission to federal probation office, precluding significant reduction in sentencing); *Att'y Grievance Comm'n v. Nichols*, 950 A.2d 778 (Md. 2008) (failure to list personal injury case on schedule of assets in bankruptcy); *Ryan v. Ryan*, 677 N.W.2d 899 (Mich. Ct. App. 2004) (filing of complaint without required verification or supporting affidavits); *In re Fru*, 829 N.W.2d 379 (Minn. 2013) (persistent failure to comply with immigration court orders and procedures over eight-year period was pattern of incompetence); *In re Gallegos*, 723 P.2d 967 (N.M. 1986) (lawyer did not apply for supersedeas bond to protect property during appeal, telling judge he "really had no idea how to proceed"); *In re Howe*, 843 N.W.2d 325 (N.D. 2014) (failing to comply with immigration court filing requirements); *In re Obert*, 282 P.3d 825 (Or. 2012) (filing untimely motions and notices and failing to follow explicit instructions from court was "pattern of ignorance of the most basic of applicable rules"); *In re Laprath*, 670 N.W.2d 41 (S.D. 2003) (demonstrating lack of understanding of basic legal procedure in multiple client matters and pro se defense to disciplinary complaint); *In re Winkel*, 577 N.W.2d 9 (Wis. 1998) (failing to have client execute disclaimer required under father's trust, resulting in greater tax liability for estate); *cf. In re Phillips*, 766 A.2d 47 (D.C. 2001) (lawyer serving as executor of estate did not follow required trust accounting procedures and court orders).

### • *Court Rules*

Violation of court rules may also constitute lack of competence under Rule 1.1. *See, e.g., Mendez v. Draham*, 182 F. Supp. 2d 430 (D.N.J. 2002) (repeated admonitions under Federal Rule of Civil Procedure 11 cast doubt on lawyer's continuing compliance with Rule 1.1, warranting referral to district chief judge for discipline); *In re McCord*, 722 N.E.2d 820 (Ind. 2000) (representing client before U.S. circuit court without being admitted to that court, misapplying rules governing federal appellate practice, and repeatedly failing to comply with procedural requirements); *In re Harris*, 180 P.3d 558 (Kan. 2008) (promising client to file bankruptcy matter immediately but failing to obtain electronic filing account, thereby violating court's mandatory electronic filing rule); *In re Krause*, 737 A.2d 874 (R.I. 1999) (failure to effectuate timely service of process demonstrated incompetence); *In re Moore*, 494 S.E.2d 804 (S.C. 1997) (failing to serve defendant within thirty days of filing lawsuit, thereby risking dismissal of case). *But see Ky. Bar Ass'n v. Fernandez*, 397 S.W.3d 383 (Ky. 2013) (experienced lawyer's numerous ethics and court rule violations did not show lack of knowledge or competence so as to violate Rule 1.1).

### • *Technology*

Rule 1.1 requires a lawyer to have a basic understanding of the benefits and risks associated with relevant technology. Cmt. [8]; ABA Formal Ethics Op. 477R (2017). *See, e.g.,* ABA Formal Ethics Op. 483 (2018) (duty to monitor for and respond to data breach); ABA Formal Ethics Op. 11-459 (2011) (protecting confidentiality of client's electronic communications); Ala. Ethics Op. 2010-02 (n.d.) (cloud computing); Alaska Ethics Op. 2014-3 (2014) (cloud computing); Ariz. Ethics Op. 09-04 (2009) (computer security); Cal. Ethics Op. 2010-179 (2010) (requiring basic awareness of available security for electronic technology used in lawyer's practice or associating with someone who does); D.C. Ethics Op. 371 (2016) (social media); Fla. Ethics Op. 12-3 (2013) (cloud computing); Ill. Ethics Op. 16-06 (2016) (cloud computing); N.H. Ethics Op. 2012-13/4 (2013) (lawyer must have basic understanding of technology and keep abreast of changes); N.Y. State Ethics Op. 842 (2010) (must keep up with advances in technology used in law practice); N.Y. Cnty. Ethics Op. 749 (2017) (electronically stored information [ESI] and e-discovery); N.Y. City Ethics Op. 2017-5 (2017) (international travel with electronic devices storing or with ability to access client data); N.Y. City Ethics Op. 2015-3 (2015) (must be able to recognize common e-mail trust account scams); N.C. Ethics Op. 2014-5 (2015) (advising client on effect of social media posts in litigation, on removal and preservation of posts, and on adjustment of social media privacy and security settings); Ohio Sup. Ct. Ethics Op. 2017-5 (2017) (virtual law office); Pa. Formal Ethics Op. 2014-300 (2014) (social media); Pa. Formal Ethics Op. 2009-100 (2009) (document metadata); Tenn. Formal Ethics Op. 2015-F-159 (2015) (cloud computing); W. Va. Ethics Op. 2015-02 (2015) (social media); Tex. Ethics Op. 665 (2016) (metadata); *cf.* Cal. Ethics Op. 2015-193 (2015) (electronically stored information [ESI] and e-discovery). *See generally* American Bar Association, *Essential Qualities of the Professional Lawyer* 189 *et seq.* (2013); Jan L. Jacobowitz & John G. Browning, *Legal Ethics and Social Media: A Practitioner's Handbook* (2017); Margaret M. DiBianca, *Ethical Risks Arising from Lawyers' Use of (and Refusal to Use) Social Media*, 12 Del. L. Rev. 179 (2011); Jon M. Garon, *Technology Requires Reboot of Professionalism and Ethics for Practitioners*, 16 J. Internet L., no. 4, at 3 (Oct. 2012); Louise Lark Hill, *Technology—A Motivation Behind Recent Model Rule Revisions*, 40 N. Ky. L. Rev. 315 (2013); Katy (Yin Yee) Ho, *Defining the Contours of an Ethical Duty of Technological Competence*, 30 Geo. J. Legal Ethics 853 (Fall 2017); Monica McCarroll, *Discovery and the Duty of Competence*, 26 Regent U. L. Rev. 81 (2013–2014); Michael McNerney & Emilian Papadopoulos, *Hacker's Delight: Law Firm Risk and Liability in the Cyber Age*, 62 Am. U. L. Rev. 1243 (June 2013); Amanda Moghaddam, "EZ ESI: Hands-on Advice for Handling and Using ESI in a Legal Malpractice Claim," *ABA/BNA Lawyers' Manual on Professional Conduct*, 33 Law. Man. Prof. Conduct 561 (Current Reports, Oct. 4, 2017).

## SKILL
### • *Drafting*

The skills required of a lawyer include the ability to draft pleadings and documents. *See, e.g., Philbrick v. Univ. of Conn.*, 51 F. Supp. 2d 164 (D. Conn. 1999) (admonishing lawyer for sloppy pleading that omitted crucial arguments); *In re Willis*, 505 A.2d 50 (D.C. 1985) (pleadings were sloppy, incoherent, incomplete, and misleading); *In re Hogan*, 490 N.E.2d 1280 (Ill. 1986) (nineteen pleadings or briefs contained incomprehensible arguments and writing); *In re Stern*, 11 N.E.3d 917 (Ind. 2014) (lawyer's pleadings were incomplete, difficult to understand, replete with spelling and grammatical errors, and included frivolous affirmative defenses); *Ky. Bar Ass'n v. Brown*, 14 S.W.3d 916 (Ky. 2000) (pleading was "little more than fifteen unclear and ungrammatical sentences slapped together as two pages of unedited text with an unintelligible message"); *Att'y Grievance Comm'n v. Costanzo*, 68 A.3d 808 (Md. 2013) (failure to do anything after retention but draft complaint having nothing to do with representation); *In re Hawkins*, 502 N.W.2d 770 (Minn. 1993) (repeated disregard of local bankruptcy rules coupled with incomprehensible written work containing numerous spelling, grammar, and typing errors); *In re Sheridan*, 813 A.2d 449 (N.H. 2002) (repeated failure to draft acceptable articles of incorporation); *In re Wallace*, 518 A.2d 740 (N.J. 1986) ("seriously deficient" drafting of promissory note); *In re Addison*, 611 S.E.2d 914 (S.C. 2005) (drafting conveyance documents with incorrect descriptions of realty); *In re Kagele*, 72 P.3d 1067 (Wash. 2003) (filing quiet title complaint with incorrect legal description of realty and failing to invoke prescriptive easement).

### • *Legal Analysis*

Competence includes the ability to analyze relevant rules and principles and apply them to clients' circumstances. *See, e.g., People v. Woodford*, 97 P.3d 968 (Colo.

O.P.D.J. 2004) (incorrectly advising that federal tax liens were dischargeable in bankruptcy); *In re Katz*, 981 A.2d 1133 (Del. 2009) (failing to realize or inform borrower clients that mortgage notes tendered by lender violated federal lending law and that lender failed to give three-day rescission rights); *Office of Disciplinary Counsel v. Au*, 113 P.3d 203 (Haw. 2005) (misrepresenting holding of published opinion); *In re Black*, 941 P.2d 1380 (Kan. 1997) ("failure to properly learn, observe and apply the rules for calculating child support demonstrates a lack of competency"); *Lieber v. Hartford Ins. Ctr. Inc.*, 15 P.3d 1030 (Utah 2000) (brief relied upon overruled case and misrepresented distinguishable caselaw as general rule; lawyer also maintained that case has no value as precedent if not recently cited); *Lawyer Disciplinary Bd. v. Turgeon*, 557 S.E.2d 235 (W. Va. 2000) (failure to understand how federal sentencing guidelines applied to client's case); *see also* Cal. Ethics Op. 2003-162 (2003) (lawyer who personally advocated nonpayment of income tax is still competent to advise if those beliefs do not prevent her "from performing an objective evaluation of her client's legal position"); *cf. Att'y Grievance Comm'n v. Dyer*, 162 A.3d 970 (Md. 2017) ("motion or pleading that ultimately proves to be unsuccessful or even lack merit is not per se a violation" of Rule 1.1).

## THOROUGHNESS AND PREPARATION
### • *Investigation and Research*

The interrelated obligations of thoroughness and preparation require a lawyer to investigate all relevant facts and research applicable law. *See, e.g., In re Dean*, 401 B.R. 917 (Bankr. D. Idaho 2008) (failing to investigate whether security interest in clients' motor home was perfected before filing bankruptcy petition); *People v. Boyle*, 942 P.2d 1199 (Colo. 1997) (failing to prepare adequately for hearing or to discover readily available evidence supporting asylum petition); *People v. Felker*, 770 P.2d 402 (Colo. 1989) (preparing for divorce hearing only on way to courthouse, then failing to consult with client about agreement to limit child support or to seek maintenance or support arrearages, equitable property division, attorneys' fees, or expenses); *In re Guy*, 756 A.2d 875 (Del. 2000) (failing to contact any of four potential criminal defense witnesses named by client); *Iowa Supreme Court Att'y Disciplinary Bd. v. Wright*, 840 N.W.2d 295 (Iowa 2013) (failure to conduct even cursory internet search or otherwise competently investigate and analyze Nigerian internet scam); *In re Rathbun*, 169 P.3d 329 (Kan. 2007) (failing to contact witnesses before bench criminal trial or call any witnesses at trial); *Att'y Grievance Comm'n v. Chasnoff*, 783 A.2d 224 (Md. 2001) (personal injury plaintiff's lawyer failed to visit scene of accident until two years afterward, did not attempt to locate witness who tried to help client on night of accident or attempt to preserve testimony of witnesses, and failed to have client monitor his medical condition to document lack of improvement); *In re Rios*, 965 N.Y.S.2d 418 (App. Div. 2013) (failing to ask client about exact location of accident in nonsuggestive manner); *In re Kovitz*, 504 N.Y.S.2d 400 (App. Div. 1986) (failing to investigate personal injury case for fourteen years, claiming it was trial tactic to outwait witnesses); *In re Summers*, 842 N.W.2d 842 (N.D. 2014) (failure to prepare for trial); *Toledo Bar Ass'n v. Wroblewski*, 512 N.E.2d 978 (Ohio 1987) (estate lawyer did not properly complete inventory and made no attempt to determine if any next of kin survived); *In re Greene*, 557 P.2d 644 (Or. 1976) (lawyer who was personal representative of estate failed to discover large savings account or ascertain true value of realty); *Beard v. Bd. of Prof'l Responsibility*, 288 S.W.3d 838 (Tenn. 2009) (recommending client settle matter by paying $10,000 even though court order, which lawyer neglected to read, found client was owed $6,700); *In re Winkel*, 577 N.W.2d 9 (Wis. 1998) (failing to obtain information concerning trust funds held by clients' business, including amounts of deposits and disbursements made and claims of contractors on funds, before clients surrendered assets to bank); *In re Fischer*, 499 N.W.2d 677 (Wis. 1993) (signing, as attorney of record, complex pleadings forwarded by "American Constitutional Coalition Foundation," which processed complaints from inmates challenging their incarceration, without meeting with inmates or otherwise attempting to ascertain basis for claims); *see also* Fla. Ethics Op. 00-4 (2000) (lawyer providing legal services over internet must inform client when matter's complexity requires meeting in person and, if client refuses, must decline representation or withdraw).

### • *Application to Client Matters*

After learning the relevant law and facts, a lawyer must then apply them to the clients' matters. *See Erpenbeck v. Ky. Bar Ass'n*, 295 S.W.3d 435 (Ky. 2009) (learning, but failing to inform lender client, of existing mortgages on two properties); *Att'y Grievance Comm'n v. Framm*, 144 A.3d 827 (Md. 2016) (lawyer hired to explain marital settlement agreement by client with diminished capacity abused discovery, failed to recognize inherent conflict of interest or conduct adequate research on guardianship petitions, and failed to explain to client that cost of continuing litigation might negate any possible benefit); *In re Fett*, 790 N.W.2d 840 (Minn. 2010) (advising client agent under power of attorney to transfer principal's assets to himself without explaining possible consequences); *In re Fayssoux*, 675 S.E.2d 428 (S.C. 2009) (failing to heed "red flags" of fraud and proceeding with twenty-eight fraudulent real estate closings); *In re Welcome*, 58 V.I. 236 (V.I. 2013) (failing to respond to dispositive motion); D.C. Ethics Op. 373 (2017) (criminal defense lawyer appointed in domestic violence case to represent defendant with parallel civil protection order matter should consider advising client on reciprocal effects of developments in each case on the other); Wash. Ethics Op. 201501 (2015) (lawyer advising client with marijuana-related business permitted under state law must also advise on risks under federal law).

### FAILURE TO COMPLY WITH ETHICS RULES

A lawyer's failure to comply with a duty imposed by another ethics rule may also constitute lack of competence under Rule 1.1. *See, e.g., In re Muhammad*, 3 So. 3d 458 (La. 2009) (accepting criminal defense matter though lawyer was related to both victim and defendant violated Rules 1.1 and 1.7); *Att'y Grievance Comm'n v. Zuckerman*, 944 A.2d 525 (Md. 2008) (failing to ensure settlement and judgment monies were promptly accounted for and disbursed facilitated office manager's embezzlement and so violated Rules 1.1 and 1.15); *Cincinnati Bar Ass'n v. Lawson*, 891 N.E.2d 749 (Ohio 2008) (failing to arrange service on defendant for several months even after being ordered to do so by presiding judge violated Rules 1.1 and 1.3); *State ex rel. Okla. Bar Ass'n v. Clausing*, 224 P.3d 1268 (Okla. 2009) (taking loan from trust he created for settlor and for which lawyer was trustee violated Rules 1.1, 1.7, and 1.8);

*In re Sturkey*, 657 S.E.2d 465 (S.C. 2008) (conversing with criminal defendant client within earshot of police officers violated Rules 1.1 and 1.6); *cf.* Rule 1.6, cmt. [18] (lawyer must "act competently to safeguard information relating to the representation of a client against unauthorized access by third parties and against inadvertent or unauthorized disclosure"). *But see In re Ward*, 881 N.W.2d 206 (N.D. 2016) (failure to respond to communications or otherwise maintain "cooperative relationship" with bankruptcy trustee violated Rule 1.3 but not Rule 1.1; court noted policy of discouraging "'stacking' or 'piling on'" charges of rule violations for same conduct).

## DELEGATION AND SUPERVISION

Because a lawyer is required to supervise subordinate lawyers and nonlawyer staff, the ethical obligation of competence cannot be avoided by referring a matter to another. *E.g., In re Herbst*, 931 A.2d 1016 (D.C. 2007) (allowing nonlawyer staff member to negotiate settlement of client's case); *Att'y Grievance Comm'n v. Zuckerman*, 944 A.2d 525 (Md. 2008) (failing to supervise nonlawyer office manager in charge of client trusts, thus allowing her to embezzle client funds); *In re Saab*, 547 N.E.2d 919 (Mass. 1989) (lawyer who had never handled domestic relations appeal turned it over to inexperienced junior associate whom he then failed to supervise); *In re Martin*, 699 S.E.2d 695 (S.C. 2010) (failure to timely file documents warranted discipline notwithstanding lawyer's assertions that he delegated tasks to nonlawyer staff); ABA Formal Ethics Op. 08-451 (2008) ("lawyer may outsource legal or nonlegal support services provided the lawyer remains ultimately responsible for rendering competent legal services to the client under Model Rule 1.1"); *accord* San Diego Cnty. Ethics Op. 2007-1 (2007); Colo. Ethics Op. 121 (2009); N.C. Ethics Op. 2007-12 (2008). *But see In re Wilkinson*, 805 So. 2d 142 (La. 2002) (failure to supervise work of law clerk warranted discipline under Rule 5.1 but not Rule 1.1). *See generally* Rule 5.1 (Responsibilities of Partners, Managers, and Supervisory Lawyers); Rule 5.3 (Responsibilities Regarding Nonlawyer Assistance).

## INEXPERIENCE

### • *New Lawyers*

Lack of competence may be a particular problem for the new or inexperienced lawyer. *E.g., Wise v. Washington County*, No. 10–1677, 2015 WL 1757730, 2015 BL 110240 (W.D. Pa. Apr. 17, 2015) (failure to adequately investigate or properly counsel client on risks and other substandard practice in civil rights case); *In re Landrith*, 124 P.3d 467 (Kan. 2005) (lawyer practicing for only four months engaged in egregious and protracted misbehavior); *In re Martin*, 982 So. 2d 765 (La. 2008) (lawyer mishandled first federal criminal defense case; inexperience cited as mitigating factor); *In re Yacavino*, 494 A.2d 801 (N.J. 1985) (new lawyer left alone and unsupervised in firm's outlying office failed to complete adoption; court condemned firm's attitude of leaving new lawyers to "sink or swim"); *Columbus Bar Ass'n v. Kizer*, 915 N.E.2d 314 (Ohio 2009) (lawyer neglected four separate matters within first four years of beginning practice); *see also* Rule 5.1 (Responsibilities of Partners, Managers, and Supervisory Lawyers). *See generally* Christopher Sabis & Daniel Webert, *Understanding the "Knowledge" Requirement of Attorney Competence: A Roadmap for Novice Attorneys*, 15 Geo. J. Legal Ethics 915 (Summer 2002).

### • *Unfamiliarity with Areas of Law*

Competence includes the ability to discern when an undertaking requires specialized knowledge or experience that a lawyer does not have and requires that the lawyer either acquire the expertise, associate with a specialist, or decline the undertaking and refer it to a competent specialist. *See In re Fisher*, 202 P.3d 1186 (Colo. 2009) (lawyer who had never handled case involving federal pension failed to investigate requirements for securing divorce client's rights to ex-husband's federal pension); *In re Deardorff*, 426 N.E.2d 689 (Ind. 1981) (new lawyer who told judge he had "no idea how to proceed" in joint will litigation should have asked for help instead of lying to clients for three years about case's status); *In re Terry*, 265 P.3d 537 (Kan. 2011) (lawyer with no experience in employment discrimination "failed to represent [plaintiff] with the legal knowledge, skill, thoroughness, and preparation reasonably necessary"); *Att'y Grievance Comm'n v. Kendrick*, 943 A.2d 1173 (Md. 2008) (lawyer refused for over eight years to admit ignorance of probate procedures or seek and accept help necessary to close estate); *In re Kaszynski*, 620 N.W.2d 708 (Minn. 2001) (ignorance of immigration law and procedures and failure to supply documentation required to support clients' claims for relief put clients in danger of deportation); *Miss. Bar v. Pegram*, 167 So. 3d 230 (Miss. 2014) (lawyer acknowledging lack of competence to handle criminal trial should not have agreed to act as sole counsel and should have limited role to negotiating pretrial diversion); *State ex rel. Counsel for Discipline v. Orr*, 759 N.W.2d 702 (Neb. 2009) (lawyer should have recognized specialized nature of franchising law and performed research necessary to become competent); *Richmond's Case*, 872 A.2d 1023 (N.H. 2005) ("Rule 1.1 mandates that a general practitioner must identify areas in which the lawyer is not competent"); *In re Yetman*, 552 A.2d 121 (N.J. 1989) (failure to refer complex matter beyond lawyer's competence is itself violation of duty of competence); *In re Peper*, 763 S.E.2d 205 (S.C. 2015) (lawyer recognized his lack of competence but failed to limit scope of representation and missed statute of limitations); *In re Dumke*, 635 N.W.2d 594 (Wis. 2001) (lawyer unfamiliar with sexual predator proceedings failed to hire or seek appointment of expert to evaluate testing methods and risk analysis upon which state based its opinion that client was sexually violent person); *see also* ABA Formal Ethics Op. 465 (2013) (must limit Groupon or deal-of-the-day offer to services and areas in which lawyer is competent); *cf.* N.C. Ethics Op. 2010-6 (2011) (advertising for matters in legal areas in which lawyer is inexperienced is permissible only if advertisement includes statement that lawyer will associate with experienced lawyer). *See generally* Christine M. Macey, *Referral Is Not Required: How Inexperienced Supreme Court Advocates Can Fulfill Their Ethical Obligations*, 22 Geo. J. Legal Ethics 979 (Summer 2009) ("if the first-time advocate is willing to prepare adequately and the well-informed client wants her to remain on the case, the lawyer has no ethical obligation to refer the case to a specialist"); Brad S. McLelland, *Attorney Competence or Lack Thereof—Under What Circumstances May an Attorney Ethically Handle a Matter in Which the Attorney Is Not Competent? Is an Ethical Rule Necessary to Restrain Such an Attorney?*, 22 J. Legal Prof. 297 (Spring 1998) (comparing provisions of Model Code and Rules permitting lawyer to provide services on emergency basis in legal field in which lawyer is unfamiliar).

## *Self-Education in Unfamiliar Area*

Although, as Comment [2] notes, it is possible for a lawyer to provide competent representation in a wholly novel field through "necessary study," the lawyer should not expect the client to pay for excessive amounts of time preparing for tasks that with experience become routine, *In re Estate of Larson*, 694 P.2d 1051 (Wash. 1985), or for "every minute of the lawyer's preparation." *Robert L. Wheeler, Inc. v. Scott*, 777 P.2d 394 (Okla. 1989) (fee award reduced when first-year associate assigned to case). *See generally* Rule 1.5 (Fees).

## SIXTH AMENDMENT CONSIDERATIONS

Incompetent representation by criminal defense counsel can violate the Sixth Amendment right to effective assistance of counsel. *See Strickland v. Washington*, 466 U.S. 668 (1984). However, the evaluation of competence for Sixth Amendment purposes may differ from the evaluation of competence for Rule 1.1 purposes. *See, e.g., In re Wolfram*, 847 P.2d 94 (Ariz. 1993) (ineffective assistance may serve as predicate for disciplinary action, but post-conviction relief does not necessarily equate to violation of ethics rules); *Fla. Bar v. Sandstrom*, 609 So. 2d 583 (Fla. 1992) (representation of murder defendant whose conviction was vacated on ground of ineffective assistance included "such a flagrant lack of preparation and such deficient performance" as to warrant suspension); *Att'y Grievance Comm'n v. Middleton*, 756 A.2d 565 (Md. 2000) (failure to move to suppress evidence, present favorable evidence, or prepare for cross-examination of prosecution witnesses resulted in post-conviction relief for defendant and discipline for lawyer); *In re Agrillo*, 604 N.Y.S.2d 171 (App. Div. 1993) (although reversal of client's conviction on ground of ineffective assistance will not always result in determination of professional misconduct, respondent's specific admissions—that he went to trial unprepared, failed to place his level of unpreparedness on record, and made no record of his alleged inability to hear trial testimony—clearly established ethics violations); *In re Longacre*, 122 P.3d 710 (Wash. 2005) (that lawyer's representation was previously held ineffective was not dispositive of later Rule 1.1 inquiry).

## PUBLIC DEFENDERS AND APPOINTED COUNSEL

The obligation to be adequately prepared may justify a refusal to proceed with the defense of a criminal case if a court-appointed lawyer or public defender has not had an adequate opportunity to prepare. *See In re Sherlock*, 525 N.E.2d 512 (Ohio Ct. App. 1987) (public defender's contempt vacated when order to proceed with trial required her to violate her professional responsibility under DR 6-101(A)(2), requiring adequate preparation); *see also Easley v. State*, 334 So. 2d 630 (Fla. Dist. Ct. App. 1976) (lawyer who usually handled civil cases but was appointed to represent criminal defendant properly advised client he felt incompetent to handle case; finding of criminal contempt for securing client's affidavit in support of motion to reconsider after denial of motion to withdraw as counsel reversed). *But see In re Roose*, 69 P.3d 43 (Colo. 2003) (affirming discipline of appointed lawyer who walked out of jury trial after being ordered to proceed despite her inexperience). The potential violation of Rule 1.1 may also be "good cause" for a lawyer to seek to avoid appointment by a court. *See* annotation to Rule 6.2.

## HEAVY CASELOADS

The duty to provide competent representation requires a lawyer to keep her case-load manageable to allow adequate time and effort for each client matter. *See Davis v. Ala. State Bar*, 676 So. 2d 306 (Ala. 1996) (disciplining lawyers who, "in an effort to turn over a huge volume of cases, neglected their clients and . . . prevented [associates] from providing quality and competent legal services"); *Att'y Grievance Comm'n v. Ficker*, 924 A.2d 1105 (Md. 2007) (running "high-volume operation" of criminal defense cases resulted in neglect of several clients' matters).

Excessive caseloads can be a significant problem for public defenders, prosecutors, other government lawyers, and lawyers appointed to represent indigent defendants. When heavy caseloads due to circumstances beyond such lawyers' control jeopardize their ability to render competent representation, the lawyers may be obligated to seek to withdraw. Rule 1.16(a)(1) (requiring withdrawal if continued representation would violate an ethics rule or other law); ABA Formal Ethics Op. 06-441 (2006) (public defender or lawyer appointed to defend indigent defendant "must move to withdraw from representation if she cannot provide competent and diligent representation"); *accord* Mich. Informal Ethics Op. RI-252 (1996); N.Y. State Ethics Op. 751 (2002); Or. Ethics Op. 2007-178 (2007); Utah Ethics Op. 96-07 (1996); *see also* American Bar Association, *ABA Guidelines for the Appointment and Performance of Defense Counsel in Death Penalty Cases*, 31 Hofstra L. Rev. 913 (Summer 2003) (see Guidelines 6.1 (Workload) and 10.3 (Obligations of Appointed Counsel Respecting Workload)); *cf. In re Edward S.*, 92 Cal. Rptr. 3d 725 (Ct. App. 2009) (public defender's heavy caseload and inadequate resources rendered competent representation impossible, warranting new trial); *Pub. Defender v. State*, 115 So. 3d 261 (Fla. 2013) (aggregate motion to withdraw granted when public defender's office had grossly excessive caseload precluding systemic competent representation); *State ex rel. Mo. Pub. Defender Comm'n v. Waters*, 370 S.W.3d 592 (Mo. 2012) (trial court erred in appointing public defender's office to represent defendant given office's certification of limited availability due to excessive caseload); *State ex rel. Okla. Bar Ass'n v. Ward*, 353 P.3d 509 (Okla. 2015) (declining to find prosecutor's inadequate trial preparation due to heavy caseload violated duty of competence); American Bar Association, *Eight Guidelines of Public Defense Related to Excessive Workloads* (Aug. 2009), available at https://www.amer icanbar.org/content/dam/aba/administrative/legal_aid_indigent_defendants/ ls_sclaid_def_eight_guidelines_of_public_defense.authcheckdam.pdf (see comment to Guideline 1: "if workloads are excessive, neither competent nor quality representation is possible"). *See generally* Peter A. Joy, *Rationing Justice by Rationing Lawyers*, 37 Wash. U. J.L. & Pol'y 205 (2011).

If withdrawal is not permitted, a lawyer must continue the representation to the best of her ability. Rule 1.16(c); S.C. Ethics Op. 04-12 (2004) (if court "denies the motion to withdraw, the attorney must continue the representation even if the attorney believes that the attorney's caseload prevents the attorney from providing competent representation").

## Rule 1.2

### *Scope of Representation and Allocation of Authority between Client and Lawyer*

(a) Subject to paragraphs (c) and (d), a lawyer shall abide by a client's decisions concerning the objectives of representation and, as required by Rule 1.4, shall consult with the client as to the means by which they are to be pursued. A lawyer may take such action on behalf of the client as is impliedly authorized to carry out the representation. A lawyer shall abide by a client's decision whether to settle a matter. In a criminal case, the lawyer shall abide by the client's decision, after consultation with the lawyer, as to a plea to be entered, whether to waive jury trial and whether the client will testify.

(b) A lawyer's representation of a client, including representation by appointment, does not constitute an endorsement of the client's political, economic, social or moral views or activities.

(c) A lawyer may limit the scope of the representation if the limitation is reasonable under the circumstances and the client gives informed consent.

(d) A lawyer shall not counsel a client to engage, or assist a client, in conduct that the lawyer knows is criminal or fraudulent, but a lawyer may discuss the legal consequences of any proposed course of conduct with a client and may counsel or assist a client to make a good faith effort to determine the validity, scope, meaning or application of the law.

## COMMENT

### *Allocation of Authority between Client and Lawyer*

[1] Paragraph (a) confers upon the client the ultimate authority to determine the purposes to be served by legal representation, within the limits imposed by law and the lawyer's professional obligations. The decisions specified in paragraph (a), such as whether to settle a civil matter, must also be made by the client. See Rule 1.4(a)(1) for the lawyer's duty to communicate with the client about such decisions. With respect to the means by which the client's objectives are to be pursued, the lawyer shall consult with the client as required by Rule 1.4(a)(2) and may take such action as is impliedly authorized to carry out the representation.

[2] On occasion, however, a lawyer and a client may disagree about the means to be used to accomplish the client's objectives. Clients normally defer to the spe-

cial knowledge and skill of their lawyer with respect to the means to be used to accomplish their objectives, particularly with respect to technical, legal and tactical matters. Conversely, lawyers usually defer to the client regarding such questions as the expense to be incurred and concern for third persons who might be adversely affected. Because of the varied nature of the matters about which a lawyer and client might disagree and because the actions in question may implicate the interests of a tribunal or other persons, this Rule does not prescribe how such disagreements are to be resolved. Other law, however, may be applicable and should be consulted by the lawyer. The lawyer should also consult with the client and seek a mutually accept-able resolution of the disagreement. If such efforts are unavailing and the lawyer has a fundamental disagreement with the client, the lawyer may withdraw from the rep-resentation. See Rule 1.16(b)(4). Conversely, the client may resolve the disagreement by discharging the lawyer. See Rule 1.16(a)(3).

[3] At the outset of a representation, the client may authorize the lawyer to take specific action on the client's behalf without further consultation. Absent a materi-al change in circumstances and subject to Rule 1.4, a lawyer may rely on such an advance authorization. The client may, however, revoke such authority at any time.

[4] In a case in which the client appears to be suffering diminished capacity, the lawyer's duty to abide by the client's decisions is to be guided by reference to Rule 1.14.

## Independence from Client's Views or Activities

[5] Legal representation should not be denied to people who are unable to afford legal services, or whose cause is controversial or the subject of popular disapproval. By the same token, representing a client does not constitute approval of the client's views or activities.

## Agreements Limiting Scope of Representation

[6] The scope of services to be provided by a lawyer may be limited by agreement with the client or by the terms under which the lawyer's services are made available to the client. When a lawyer has been retained by an insurer to represent an insured, for example, the representation may be limited to matters related to the insurance coverage. A limited representation may be appropriate because the client has limited objectives for the representation. In addition, the terms upon which representation is undertaken may exclude specific means that might otherwise be used to accomplish the client's objectives. Such limitations may exclude actions that the client thinks are too costly or that the lawyer regards as repugnant or imprudent.

[7] Although this Rule affords the lawyer and client substantial latitude to limit the representation, the limitation must be reasonable under the circumstances. If, for example, a client's objective is limited to securing general information about the law the client needs in order to handle a common and typically uncomplicated legal problem, the lawyer and client may agree that the lawyer's services will be limited to a brief telephone consultation. Such a limitation, however, would not be reasonable if the time allotted was not sufficient to yield advice upon which the client could rely. Although an agreement for a limited representation does not exempt a lawyer from

the duty to provide competent representation, the limitation is a factor to be considered when determining the legal knowledge, skill, thoroughness and preparation reasonably necessary for the representation. See Rule 1.1.

[8] All agreements concerning a lawyer's representation of a client must accord with the Rules of Professional Conduct and other law. See, e.g., Rules 1.1, 1.8 and 5.6.

## Criminal, Fraudulent and Prohibited Transactions

[9] Paragraph (d) prohibits a lawyer from knowingly counseling or assisting a client to commit a crime or fraud. This prohibition, however, does not preclude the lawyer from giving an honest opinion about the actual consequences that appear likely to result from a client's conduct. Nor does the fact that a client uses advice in a course of action that is criminal or fraudulent of itself make a lawyer a party to the course of action. There is a critical distinction between presenting an analysis of legal aspects of questionable conduct and recommending the means by which a crime or fraud might be committed with impunity.

[10] When the client's course of action has already begun and is continuing, the lawyer's responsibility is especially delicate. The lawyer is required to avoid assisting the client, for example, by drafting or delivering documents that the lawyer knows are fraudulent or by suggesting how the wrongdoing might be concealed. A lawyer may not continue assisting a client in conduct that the lawyer originally supposed was legally proper but then discovers is criminal or fraudulent. The lawyer must, therefore, withdraw from the representation of the client in the matter. See Rule 1.16(a). In some cases, withdrawal alone might be insufficient. It may be necessary for the lawyer to give notice of the fact of withdrawal and to disaffirm any opinion, document, affirmation or the like. See Rule 4.1.

[11] Where the client is a fiduciary, the lawyer may be charged with special obligations in dealings with a beneficiary.

[12] Paragraph (d) applies whether or not the defrauded party is a party to the transaction. Hence, a lawyer must not participate in a transaction to effectuate criminal or fraudulent avoidance of tax liability. Paragraph (d) does not preclude undertaking a criminal defense incident to a general retainer for legal services to a lawful enterprise. The last clause of paragraph (d) recognizes that determining the validity or interpretation of a statute or regulation may require a course of action involving disobedience of the statute or regulation or of the interpretation placed upon it by governmental authorities.

[13] If a lawyer comes to know or reasonably should know that a client expects assistance not permitted by the Rules of Professional Conduct or other law or if the lawyer intends to act contrary to the client's instructions, the lawyer must consult with the client regarding the limitations on the lawyer's conduct. See Rule 1.4(a)(5).

## Definitional Cross-References

"Fraudulent" See Rule 1.0(d)
"Informed consent" See Rule 1.0(e)
"Knows" See Rule 1.0(f)
"Reasonable" See Rule 1.0(h)

**State Rules Comparison**
http://ambar.org/MRPCStateCharts

## ANNOTATION

### Paragraph (a): Client Decides Objectives of Representation and Must Be Consulted about Means Employed

#### LAWYER MUST DEFER TO CLIENT ON OBJECTIVES AND CONSULT ABOUT MEANS

The general division of authority between lawyer and client is along the lines of "objectives" versus "means," but these realms of authority actually overlap. Rule 1.2(a) provides that a lawyer must "abide by" the client's instructions regarding the objectives of the representation and that the lawyer, "as required by Rule 1.4," must "consult with the client" about the means by which such objectives are to be pursued. Hence, the rule gives the client ultimate authority over the objectives, but somewhat less authority over the means employed. Just how much authority a client has regarding "means" is not entirely clear, nor is it always possible to distinguish between whether a particular decision relates to the "objectives" or to the "means."

The distinction between "objectives" and "means" is often expressed as the difference between decisions that directly affect the ultimate resolution of the case or the substantive rights of the client and decisions that are procedural or tactical in nature. The client generally has control over the former, and the lawyer over the latter. *See, e.g., Blanton v. Womancare, Inc.*, 696 P.2d 645 (Cal. 1985) (decisions affecting substantive rights differ from tactical decisions in extent to which they affect client's interest and involve "matters of judgment which extend beyond technical competence"); Conn. Informal Ethics Op. 97-37 (1997) (decision about whether to join third party in civil action is issue relating to objectives of representation and is therefore matter for client to decide). *See generally* Jonathan Barker & Matthew Cosentino, *Who's in Charge Here? The Ethics 2000 Approach to Resolving Lawyer-Client Conflicts*, 16 Geo. J. Legal Ethics 505 (Summer 2003).

#### • Lawyer Must Pursue Specific Objectives for Which Lawyer Was Retained

A lawyer who fails to carry out the objectives of a representation chosen by the client violates Rule 1.2. *See, e.g., In re Hagedorn*, 725 N.E.2d 397 (Ind. 2000) (failed to take steps to effectuate adoption though hired to do so); *In re Watson*, 121 P.3d 982 (Kan. 2005) (failed to diligently prosecute change of custody motion that client instructed him to pursue); *Att'y Grievance Comm'n v. Framm*, 144 A.3d 827 (Md. 2016) (lawyer hired by client with diminished capacity to explain marital settlement agreement then opposed client's answer in guardianship case); *In re Diviacchi*, 62 N.E.3d 38 (Mass. 2016) (failed to pursue client's goal of avoiding foreclosure); *Olson v. Fraase*, 421 N.W.2d 820 (N.D. 1988) (lawyer had duty to follow client's reasonable instructions to prepare documents to create joint tenancy, despite honest belief that instructions not in client's best interest); *In re Eugster*, 209 P.3d 435 (Wash. 2009) (lawyer for elderly client failed to diminish son's control of client's affairs as client requested and instead sought to have son appointed legal guardian); *In re Spangler*, 881 N.W.2d 35 (Wis. 2016) (lawyer never filed suit against client's former business associate as hired to do and misled client for years); D.C. Ethics Op. 353 (2010) (absent indications of risk of harm to incapacitated client, lawyer hired by agent under power of attorney must defer to agent on whether agent should step down due to potential conflicts because decision goes to objectives of representation); Phila. Ethics Op. 2008-11 (2008) (lawyer hired by insurer to defend driver/wife in husband's suit against her for accident injuring family must comply with wife's instruction to give only minimal defense and not hire expert); *cf.* N.H. Ethics Op. 2015-16/9 (2016) (court-appointed standby counsel for self-represented criminal defendant should ask court to define responsibilities).

In addition, a lawyer must adhere to a client's decision to cease pursuing previously sought objectives. *See, e.g., Burton v. Mottolese*, 835 A.2d 998 (Conn. 2003) (lawyer continued to litigate claim after clients instructed her to stop); *In re Friesen*, 991 P.2d 400 (Kan. 1999) (lawyer negotiated and accepted settlement without client's authorization after client directed lawyer to dismiss action); *In re Humphrey*, 15 So. 3d 960 (La. 2009) (after client discharged lawyer and filed consent to judgment through successor counsel, first lawyer filed notice of appeal); *see also Red Dog v. State*, 625 A.2d 245 (Del. 1993) (lawyer must respect defendant's decision to forgo further appeals and accept death penalty). On the lawyer's duty to withdraw from the representation upon being discharged, see the annotation to Rule 1.16.

### • *Lawyer's Implied Authorization regarding Means*

The command in Rule 1.2(a) that a lawyer "shall" consult about means was tempered in 2002 with the addition of the provision that a "lawyer may take such action on behalf of the client as is impliedly authorized to carry out the representation." This provision, paralleling that contained in Rule 1.6(a) (permitting disclosure of client information when "impliedly authorized in order to carry out the representation"), was added to avoid any implication that a lawyer must always consult to obtain authority to act. American Bar Association, *A Legislative History: The Development of the ABA Model Rules of Professional Conduct, 1982–2013*, at 58–59 (2013); *see, e.g., Puppolo v. Donovan & O'Connor, LLC*, 35 A.3d 166 (Vt. 2011) (decision to employ counsel necessitates accepting counsel's professional judgment regarding strategic decisions such as which expert to retain, and mere disagreement on strategy does not constitute "good cause" that would support motion to withdraw immediately before trial). For criticism of this provision, see Steven Lubet & Robert P. Burns, *Division of Authority Between Attorney and Client: The Case of the Benevolent Otolaryngologist*, 2003 U. Ill. L. Rev. 1275 (2003) ("[It] essentially eviscerates the notion of client control, or even meaningful input, concerning the means of representation. Moneyed clients will enjoy exceptional influence over their lawyers, as always. Marginal clients will be told where to draw the line.").

## LAWYER MUST ABIDE BY CLIENT'S DECISION REGARDING SETTLEMENT OF CLAIMS

A lawyer has no inherent power, merely because he or she represents a client, to settle the client's claim. *See Fennell v. TLB Kent Co.*, 865 F.2d 498 (2d Cir. 1989); *Koval v. Simon Telelect, Inc.*, 693 N.E.2d 1299 (Ind. 1998) ("a client's retention of an attorney does not in itself confer implied or apparent authority on that attorney to settle or compromise the client's claim"). Rule 1.2(a) specifically provides that it is the client who decides whether to accept a settlement offer and that the "lawyer shall abide by a client's decision" in such matters.

Accordingly, this rule requires a lawyer to get the client's specific authorization to enter a settlement agreement on the client's behalf. *Fitlife Brands, Inc. v. Supreme Sports Enhancement, LLC*, No. 8:14-CV-241, 2015 WL 12803646, 2015 BL 92945 (D. Neb. Apr. 1, 2015) (under Nebraska law, lawyer must have express authority to accept settlement; ordinary employment as lawyer will not suffice); *In re Friesen*, 991 P.2d 400 (Kan. 1999) (negotiating and accepting settlement without client's authorization after client directed lawyer to dismiss action); *In re O'Meara*, 54 A.3d 762 (N.H. 2012) (sending settlement demand to insurer's lawyer without clients' authorization); *State ex rel. Okla. Bar Ass'n v. Hummel*, 89 P.3d 1105 (Okla. 2004) (agreeing to modification of divorce decree without prior consultation with client); *In re Indeglia*, 765 A.2d 444 (R.I. 2001) (accepting settlement offer in direct contravention of client's instructions; whether lawyer believed client's position was unreasonable was "irrelevant"); *In re White*, 663 S.E.2d 21 (S.C. 2008) (accepting insurer's settlement offer without client's authorization); *In re Wysolmerski*, 702 A.2d 73 (Vt. 1997) (binding clients to unauthorized settlements); ABA Formal Ethics Op. 96-403 (1996) (lawyer hired by insurer to represent insured may not settle matter if lawyer knows that insured objects to settlement, without first giving insured opportunity to reject defense and assume responsibility for own defense); *see also In re Hawk*, 496 S.E.2d 261 (Ga. 1998) (lawyer settled case without telling insurance company client had fired him); *In re Harshey*, 740 N.E.2d 851 (Ind. 2001) (setting in motion chain of events resulting in court requiring client to accept settlement offer despite client's clearly expressed desire that offer be refused); *cf. In re Panel File No. 99-5*, 607 N.W.2d 429 (Minn. 2000) (failing to inform opposing counsel or magistrate of client's settlement offer despite client's explicit request that he do so).

Regarding the authorization required when there are multiple clients represented in a single undertaking, see the annotation to Rule 1.8 (Rule 1.8(g) requires that "each client" consent to any aggregate settlement).

### • Lawyer's Authority to Settle Claim

Whether a lawyer has authority to settle a claim is a matter of state substantive law. The issue generally arises in the context of client challenges to the enforceability of the resulting agreement. *See, e.g., Covington v. Cont'l Gen. Tire, Inc.*, 381 F.3d 216 (3d Cir. 2004) (refusing to enforce settlement to which lawyer agreed without client's express authority); *Santos v. Ruiz*, No. CV166063140, 2017 WL 6763525, 2017 BL 467723 (Conn. Super. Ct. Dec. 6, 2017) (discussing agency law and law governing lawyers with regard to apparent authority); *Gravens v. Auto-Owners Ins. Co.*, 666 N.E.2d 964

(Ind. Ct. App. 1996) ("the requirement that an attorney must obtain his client's authority or consent to settle a case is implicit in the client's right to exercise ultimate authority over the settlement"); *Barrow v. Penn*, 669 N.Y.S.2d 452 (App. Div. 1998) (reversing dismissal after ostensible settlement because lawyer had no authority to settle).

## LAWYER MAY NOT COERCE CLIENT TO APPROVE SETTLEMENT

### • *Fee Agreement May Not Be Used to Deprive Client of Right to Approve Settlement*

Although a client may grant the lawyer express authority to settle, a retainer agreement that forbids the client from settling a case without the lawyer's consent or that creates a financial disincentive to do so may be found to be against public policy and impermissible under Rule 1.2(a). *See, e.g., In re Grievance Proceeding*, 171 F. Supp. 2d 81 (D. Conn. 2001) (in federal grievance proceeding, written fee agreement delegating all settlement authority to lawyer found to violate Rule 1.2(a), but no discipline imposed because lawyer did not invoke those terms); *Compton v. Kittleson*, 171 P.3d 172 (Alaska 2007) (fee agreement guaranteeing lawyer greater of $175 per hour or one-third of recovery violated Rule 1.2 "because of its potential to restrict a client's exclusive right to accept or reject an offer of judgment"); *In re Lansky*, 678 N.E.2d 1114 (Ind. 1997) (provision in fee agreement by which client gave up right to determine whether to accept settlement offer violates Rule 1.2(a)); *In re Coleman*, 295 S.W.2d 857 (Mo. 2009) (provision that lawyer "shall have the exclusive right to determine when and for how much to settle this case" violates Rule 1.2(a)); Ariz. Ethics Op. 06-07 (2006) (lawyer may not provide in retainer agreement that lawyer may settle matter without client's consent if client's whereabouts unknown); Colo. Ethics Op. 134 (2018) (lawyer representing joint clients may not compel any client to join majority in accepting or rejecting aggregate settlement); Conn. Informal Ethics Op. 99-18 (1999) (contingent-fee agreement may not include clause requiring client to pay lawyer at hourly rate if client rejects settlement offer recommended by lawyer and defendant prevails; client has right to decide whether to accept settlement and economic pressure limiting that right violates rule); Nev. Ethics Op. 35 (2006) (retainer agreement may not give lawyer authority to settle matter without client consent); Wash. Ethics Op. 191 (1994) (fee agreement providing if client rejects settlement offer lawyer believes is reasonable, fee will be based upon larger of offer or amount recovered at trial is improper); *see also* David Hricik, *Dear Lawyer: If You Decide It's Not Economical to Represent Me, You Can Fire Me as Your Contingent Fee Client, but I Agree I Will Still Owe You a Fee*, 64 Mercer L. Rev. 363 (Winter 2013).

### • *Withdrawal from Case if Client Fails to Settle*

Similarly, a lawyer who withdraws from a case due to a client's unwillingness to settle may forfeit his or her entitlement to a fee. *See, e.g., Kay v. Home Depot, Inc.*, 623 So. 2d 764 (Fla. Dist. Ct. App. 1993) (denying fee recovery to lawyer whose only reason for withdrawing was that client refused settlement he advised); *May v. Seibert*, 264 S.E.2d 643 (W. Va. 1980) (acceptance of settlement terms solely within client's province, and refusal is not adequate grounds for lawyer's withdrawal). *But see Kannewurf v. Johns*, 632 N.E.2d 711 (Ill. App. Ct. 1994) (trial court did not abuse discretion in awarding quantum meruit fees to contingent-fee lawyer who withdrew when clients insisted he negotiate for settlement amount he believed unreasonable; lawyer found to have good cause to withdraw).

## RIGHTS OF CRIMINAL DEFENDANTS TO CONTROL CERTAIN ASPECTS OF LITIGATION

In both the civil and criminal realms, the objectives-versus-means criterion is used to analyze the division of authority between lawyer and client. However, a lawyer representing a criminal defendant must meet obligations imposed by the Constitution, as well as those imposed by the ethics rules. The decision-making authority of a criminal defendant is therefore broader than that of a client in a civil matter.

### • *Control over Substantive Decisions*

In addition to the general provision relating to control over the objectives and means of the representation, Rule 1.2(a) adds a more specific provision that in a criminal case, the lawyer must "abide by the client's decision, after consultation with the lawyer, as to a plea to be entered, whether to waive jury trial and whether the client will testify." *See McCoy v. Louisiana*, 584 U.S. __, 138 S. Ct. 1500 (2018) (defense lawyer in capital trial may not concede guilt against defendant's wishes, even if lawyer believes concession offers best opportunity to avoid death penalty); *In re Garnett*, 603 S.E.2d 281 (Ga. 2004) (ordering disbarment for, inter alia, refusing client's instruction to enter guilty plea); *State v. Jones*, 923 P.2d 560 (Mont. 1996) (client's decision to exercise right to jury trial rather than accept plea agreement cannot constitute good cause for lawyer withdrawal, as this would run directly afoul of Rule 1.2(a)); *McConnell v. State*, 212 P.3d 307 (Nev. 2009) ("[C]ounsel does not have the authority to override a defendant's decision to plead guilty. That decision is reserved to the client."); *cf. State v. A.N.J.*, 225 P.3d 956 (Wash. 2010) (lawyer's role is to evaluate evidence and likelihood of conviction so client may make informed decision whether to accept plea bargain); Wash. Ethics Op. 2194 (2009) (lawyer offered early, revocable plea bargain before discovery is given by prosecutor must explain pros and cons of arrangement and must abide by client's decision). *See generally* annotation to Rule 1.4 (Communication).

A lawyer's duty under Rule 1.2(a) to defer to certain client decisions in a criminal matter is a necessary corollary of a criminal defendant's constitutional right to make decisions regarding matters that are "fundamental" or "substantive" because they derive from constitutional guarantees. *United States v. Teague*, 953 F.2d 1525 (11th Cir. 1992) ("while defense counsel serves as an advocate for the client, it is the client who is the master of his or her own defense"). *E.g., Jones v. Barnes*, 463 U.S. 745 (1983) (decisions about fundamental matters, including whether to plead guilty, waive jury, testify, take appeal, and, with some limitations, act as own advocate, are for defendant); *United States v. Boyd*, 86 F.3d 719 (7th Cir. 1996) (fundamental choices for accused to make include whether to be represented by counsel, plead guilty, waive jury, or testify); *State v. Hausner*, 280 P.3d 604 (Ariz. 2012) (lawyer required to abide by client's decision to waive presentation of mitigation evidence and instruction to forgo argument for leniency after multiple murder convictions); *Helmedach v. Comm'r of Corr.*,

148 A.3d 1105 (Conn. App. Ct. 2016) (criminal defense counsel violated Rule 1.2(a) by waiting until after client testified to apprise her of plea offer); *Taylor v. State*, 28 A.3d 399 (Del. 2011) (defendant's not guilty plea was fundamental decision reserved to defendant, and defense counsel was prohibited from undermining client's decision by arguing for guilty-but-mentally-ill verdict); *Pruitt v. State*, 514 S.E.2d 639 (Ga. 1999) (after being informed of right to testify and present evidence, "a competent defendant, and not his counsel, makes the ultimate decision about whether to testify or present mitigation evidence"); *People v. Eyen*, 683 N.E.2d 193 (Ill. App. Ct. 1997) (defendant did not knowingly waive right to jury trial and was not bound by counsel's actions in requesting bench trial when defendant not present for pretrial hearing where type of trial decided); *State v. Debler*, 856 S.W.2d 641 (Mo. 1993) (defendant has right to make basic decisions regarding whether to plead guilty or go to trial, types of defenses to present at trial, and whether to testify; defense counsel advises defendant on effect of choices and then implements them); *People v. Clark*, 9 N.Y.S.3d 277 (App. Div. 2015) (client decides fundamental points such as how to plead, waiver of jury trial, nature of defense, and whether to testify or appeal; counsel makes strategic decisions such as jury selection and what evidence to present), *aff'd*, 69 N.E.3d 604 (N.Y. 2016); *accord* ABA Standards for Criminal Justice: Defense Function, Standard 4-5.2(b) (4th ed. 2015). *See generally* Erica J. Hashimoto, *Resurrecting Autonomy: The Criminal Defendant's Right to Control the Case*, 90 B.U. L. Rev. 1147 (June 2010); Christopher Pape, *Ineffective Assistance of Rule 1.2: Seeking an On the Record Waiver to Protect Defendant's Right to Testify*, 35 J. Legal Prof. 437 (2011).

## • *Tactics*

On the other hand, decisions that involve tactics and trial strategy may constitutionally be made by the lawyer after consultation with the client. *See generally* ABA Standards for Criminal Justice: Defense Function, Standard 4-5.2(d) (4th ed. 2015). Courts have thus deferred to the lawyer's judgment in a wide variety of matters. *See, e.g., Darden v. Wainwright*, 477 U.S. 168 (1986) (not ineffective assistance for defense lawyers in capital murder case not to introduce mitigating evidence at sentencing, for fear of opening door to evidence in rebuttal); *United States v. Washington*, 198 F.3d 721 (8th Cir. 1999) (decision to request mistrial is strategic one for counsel to make); *Poole v. United States*, 832 F.2d 561 (11th Cir. 1987) (defense lawyer's decision to stipulate to easily provable matter—that institutions defendant allegedly robbed were federally insured—was tactical, so client consent not needed); *People v. Williams*, 72 Cal. Rptr. 2d 58 (Ct. App. 1998) (defense lawyer authorized to waive formal recitation of reasons for enhanced sentence); *People v. Arko*, 183 P.3d 555 (Colo. 2008) ("decision to request a lesser offense instruction is strategic and tactical in nature, and is therefore reserved for defense counsel," not defendant).

Several opinions suggest it is not merely permissible, but preferable, for lawyers to make such tactical decisions. *See, e.g., United States v. Boyd*, 86 F.3d 719 (7th Cir. 1996) ("the more technical the legal rule, the less appropriate it is for the accused to make the choice personally"; decisions about when to challenge jurors are tactical and thus for lawyer to make); *McLaughlin v. State*, 173 P.3d 1014 (Alaska Ct. App. 2007) (having lawyer decide whether to pursue interlocutory review after conviction but before sentencing "is based on sound policy. Whether to petition for review is generally a complicated strategic and tactical decision that is best left to the attorney"); *State v. Davis*, 506 A.2d 86 (Conn. 1986) (general rule is still that witness selection is tactical decision for lawyer, notwithstanding state constitutional provision that gives defendant right "to be heard by himself and by counsel . . . and to have compulsory process to obtain witnesses in his behalf"); *State v. Mecham*, 9 P.3d 777 (Utah Ct. App. 2000) (lawyer retains responsibility for making tactical decisions, including whether to pursue motion to suppress evidence). *See generally* Alberto Bernabe, *Waiving Good-Bye to a Fundamental Right: Allocation of Authority Between Attorneys and Clients and the Right to a Public Trial*, 38 J. Legal Prof. 1 (Fall 2013).

## REPRESENTING CLIENTS WITH DIMINISHED CAPACITY

When a client's ability to make decisions about the representation is diminished, the division of decision-making authority between the lawyer and client may be affected by the lawyer's ability to take protective action in limited circumstances. For a discussion of this issue, see the annotation to Rule 1.14.

## Paragraph (b): Representation Not Endorsement of Client's Views or Conduct

Rule 1.2(b) says that representing a client does not in itself constitute an endorsement of the client's political, economic, social, or moral views or activities. There was no counterpart to this provision in the Model Code. The provision is intended to facilitate the representation of unpopular clients. *See* Andre A. Borgeas, *Necessary Adherence to Model Rule 1.2(b): Attorneys Do Not Endorse the Acts or Views of Their Clients by Virtue of Representation*, 13 Geo. J. Legal Ethics 761 (Summer 2000); *cf. LaBrake v. State*, 152 P.3d 474 (Alaska Ct. App. 2007) (lawyers "expected to represent people whose conduct may be questionable, and whose views on social and moral matters may differ significantly from the lawyer's"); Tenn. Formal Ethics Op. 96-F-140 (1996) (lawyer who believes his religious and moral beliefs will impair representation must allow court to determine propriety of withdrawal). *See generally* R.I. Ethics Op. 88-30 (1989) (lawyer who has no personal knowledge of client's dishonesty may continue to represent client after third person alleges client is "a fraud"; ethics rules do not require that lawyers represent only innocent clients).

## Paragraph (c): Limiting Scope of Representation

Rule 1.2(c), as amended in 2002, permits a lawyer to "limit the scope of the representation if the limitation is reasonable under the circumstances and the client gives informed consent." Previously, paragraph (c) allowed a lawyer to "limit the objectives of the representation if the client consents after consultation." Rule 1.2(c) (1998) [superseded]. The new version replaced the term "objectives" with "scope" because only the client can limit the objectives, and added the requirement that such limitations be "reasonable under the circumstances." The amendment was intended to give express permission for limited-representation agreements and "provide a framework within which lawyers may expand access to legal services by providing limited but nonetheless valuable legal services to low or moderate-income persons who otherwise would be unable to obtain counsel." American Bar Association, *A Legislative History: The Development of the ABA Model Rules of Professional Conduct, 1982–2013*, at 59 (2013). *See Disciplinary Counsel v. Lee*, 49 N.E.3d 1255 (Ohio 2016) (lawyer did not sustain burden of defining limited scope of representation to client, and client reasonably assumed lawyer was representing her); ABA Formal Ethics Op. 472 (2015) (lawyer should provide client with written confirmation of limitation of scope of representation); N.Y. City Ethics Op. 2016-2 (2016) (discussing disclosure and other requirements for limiting scope of representation of deposition witness); *see also* Pa. Formal Ethics Op. 2016-200 (2016) (discussing difficulty in assessing reasonability of limiting scope of representation and obtaining client's informed consent under Avvo Legal Services' "Flat Fee Limited Scope" program). *See generally* Kristen M. Blankley, *Adding by Subtracting: How Limited Scope Agreements for Dispute Resolution Representation Can Increase Access to Attorney Services*, 28 Ohio St. J. on Disp. Resol. 659 (2013).

Examples of limited-scope representation (also known as "unbundled" legal services) include limiting the representation to certain types of claims or transactions, specific tasks, or discrete stages of litigation or transactions. *See, e.g., Lerner v. Laufer*, 819 A.2d 471 (N.J. Super. Ct. App. Div. 2003) (lawyer retained specifically to review sufficiency, but not fairness, of marital property settlement agreement arrived at after mediation had no duty to investigate so as to advise on agreement's reasonableness); *see also Indianapolis Podiatry, P.C. v. Efroymson*, 720 N.E.2d 376 (Ind. Ct. App. 1999) (by disclosing to one client potential conflict with other client and limiting representation to exclude claims between the two, firm avoided breaching duty of loyalty); *Persels & Assocs., LLC v. Capital One Bank, (USA), N.A.*, 481 S.W.3d 501 (Ky. 2016) (permitting and providing guidance on limited representation; requiring adequate investigation of facts and disclosure of active assistance to tribunal); D.C. Ethics Op. 343 (2008) (limiting representation to "discrete legal issue or with respect to a discrete stage in the litigation" may allow lawyer to avoid conflict under Rule 1.9). *See generally* Kaitlyn Aitken, *Unbundled Legal Services: Disclosure Is Not the Answer*, 25 Geo. J. Legal Ethics 365 (Summer 2012); Jessica K. Steinberg, *In Pursuit of Justice? Case Outcomes and the Delivery of Unbundled Legal Services*, 18 Geo. J. on Poverty L. & Pol'y 453 (2011); Michele N. Struffolino, *Taking Limited Representation to the Limits: The Efficacy of Using Unbundled Legal Services in Domestic-Relations Matters Involving Litigation*, 2 St. Mary's J. Legal Mal. & Ethics 166 (2012). For a discussion of lawyers' participation in programs sponsored by courts or nonprofit organizations offering short-term limited legal services, see the annotation to Rule 6.5 (limiting a lawyer's risk of disqualification for conflicts of interest resulting from participation in such programs).

## GHOSTWRITING COURT DOCUMENTS FOR PRO SE LITIGANTS

Lawyers sometimes provide only limited, behind-the-scenes advice or document preparation for clients who wish to appear pro se or who cannot afford to hire a lawyer to litigate the matter. Some authorities have disapproved such surreptitious representation, especially when it involves a lawyer ghostwriting a document filed in court by a pro se litigant, because it misrepresents that the litigant is acting without the assistance of counsel and permits a lawyer to evade the responsibilities imposed by Rule 11 of the Federal Rules of Civil Procedure (requiring lawyers to certify there are grounds to support allegations made in court filings). *See, e.g., In re Dreamplay, Inc.*, 534 B.R. 106 (Bankr. D. Md. 2015) (permitting ghostwriting "would allow any attorney anywhere to dive into a case, no matter the jurisdiction, with free rein and no attendant responsibility"); *Chung v. El Paso Sch. Dist. #11*, No. 14-cv-01520-KLM, 2015 WL 225430, 2015 BL 9948 (D. Colo. Jan. 15, 2015) (lawyer for pro se litigant may not ghostwrite documents to submit to court or opposing counsel); *Sejas v. MortgageIT, Inc.*, No. 1:11cv469 (JCC), 2011 WL 2471205, 2011 BL 161287 (E.D. Va. June 20, 2011) (ghostwriting documents filed with court by pro se litigants "inconsistent with procedural, ethical, and substantive rules of court"); *Ricotta v. California*, 4 F. Supp. 2d 961 (S.D. Cal. 1998) (involvement in drafting pro se plaintiff's court documents was unprofessional conduct); *Johnson v. Bd. of Cnty. Comm'rs*, 868 F. Supp. 1226 (D. Colo. 1994) (practice of ghostwriting pleadings may subject lawyer to contempt of court "irrespective of the degree to which it is considered unprofessional by the governing bodies of the bar"); Ill. Ethics Op. 04-03 (2005) (lawyer acting as mediator in domestic relations matter between unrepresented spouses may not ghostwrite proposed judgment for spouses to file pro se); *cf.* Mass. Ethics Op. 98-1 (1998) (lawyer may provide limited background advice to pro se litigant, but not extensive services such as drafting litigation documents, which would mislead court and other parties).

To address such concerns, some authorities have explicitly required that any document filed by a litigant proceeding pro se also be signed by any lawyer who helped prepare it. *E.g., Duran v. Carris*, 238 F.3d 1268 (10th Cir. 2001) (participation in drafting pro se appellate brief must be acknowledged by signature); *Ellis v. Maine*, 448 F.2d 1325 (1st Cir. 1971) ("[i]f a brief is prepared in any substantial part by a member of the bar, it must be signed by him"); Conn. Informal Ethics Op. 98-5 (1998) (lawyer who prepares document for purportedly pro se litigant to file with court must inform court); Nev. Ethics Op. 34 (2009) (lawyer who gives substantial drafting assistance to pro se litigant in paperwork filed with court must reveal role by signing); *see also* Colo. R. Civ. P. 11(b) ("An attorney may . . . provide limited representation in accordance with Colo. RPC 1.2 to a pro se party involved in a court proceeding. Pleadings or papers filed by the pro se party that were prepared with the drafting assistance of the attorney shall include the attorney's name, address, telephone number and registration number"); Kan. Ethics Op. 09-01 (2009) (preparing document for pro se litigant to file in court is permissible if it includes legend "Prepared with Assistance of Counsel").

An increasing number of authorities, however, have found that lawyer ghostwriting is ethically permissible as long as the client provides informed consent and the ghostwriting would not result in misrepresentation—such as the client telling the court or allowing the court to believe he received no assistance from a lawyer—or violation of any other court order or ethics rule. *E.g., In re Hood*, 727 F.3d 1360 (11th Cir. 2013) (helping petitioner complete standard bankruptcy petition designed for pro se filing that resulted in no unfair advantage); ABA Formal Ethics Op. 07-446 (2007); Ala. Ethics Op. 2010-01 (2010); Mich. Informal Ethics Op. RI-347 (2010); N.J. Ethics Op. 713 (2007); N.Y. Cnty. Ethics Op. 742 (2010); N.C. Ethics Op. 2008-3 (2009); Pa.-Phila. Joint Formal Ethics Op. 2011-100 (2011); Utah Ethics Op. 08-01 (2008); *see also In re Liu*, 664 F.3d 367 (2d Cir. 2011) (helping pro se litigants draft petitions without disclosing assistance to court was not sanctionable misconduct); *cf. Green v. Champs-Elysees*, No. M2012-01352-COA-R3-CV, 2013 WL 1458890, 2013 BL 103687 (Tenn. Ct. App. Apr. 9, 2013) (assistance to pro se litigant, including drafting pleadings, may have violated ethics rules but did not amount to contempt of court); Ariz. Ethics Op. 05-06 (2005) ("the practice is not inherently misleading [because] a court or tribunal can generally determine whether [a] document was written with a lawyer's help"); Tenn. Formal Ethics Op. 2007-F-153 (2007) (lawyer may prepare pleading to assist pro se litigant in protecting right from dismissal under statute of limitations or other similar rule without disclosing assistance but may not provide further assistance without disclosure). *See generally* Salman Bhojani, *Attorney Ghostwriting for Pro Se Litigants—A Practical and Bright-Line Solution to Resolve the Split of Authority Among Federal Circuits and State Bar Associations*, 65 SMU L. Rev. 653 (Summer 2012); Kristen M. Blankley, *Adding by Subtracting: How Limited Scope Agreements for Dispute Resolution Representation Can Increase Access to Attorney Services*, 28 Ohio St. J. on Disp. Resol. 659 (2013); Jona Goldschmidt, *An Analysis of Ghostwriting Decisions: Still Searching for the Elusive Harm*, 95 Judicature 78 (Sept.–Oct. 2011); Molly M. Jennings & D. James Greiner, *The Evolution of Unbundling in Litigation Matters: Three Case Studies and a Literature Review*, 89 Denv. U. L. Rev. 825 (2012); Ira P. Robbins, *Ghostwriting: Filling in the Gaps of Pro Se Prisoners' Access to the Courts*, 23 Geo. J. Legal Ethics 271 (Spring 2010). Also see Rule 3.3 (Candor Toward the Tribunal) and Rule 8.4 (Misconduct).

## LIMITATION MUST BE REASONABLE

Rule 1.2(c) requires that any limitation placed upon the representation be "reasonable under the circumstances." *See, e.g., Hartford Accident & Indem. Co. v. Foster*, 528 So. 2d 255 (Miss. 1988) (insurance policy may not contain provisions limiting ethical obligations owed by insurance company lawyers to insured clients); Ala. Ethics Op. 2015-01 (2015) (personal injury lawyer may not unreasonably limit scope of engagement by refusing to negotiate liens on settlement proceeds without payment of additional fee); Del. Ethics Op. 2006-1 (2006) (approving retainer agreement that limits representation to uncontested divorce, as long as lawyer continues undertaking outside that limitation if instructed to do so by relevant court); N.Y. City Ethics Op. 2015-4 (2015) (discussing limiting scope of representation as local counsel); Utah Ethics Op. 2017-04 (2017) (pro hac vice lawyer, local counsel, and client may agree if reasonable that only pro hac vice lawyer will communicate directly with client); *see also Greenwich v. Markhoff*, 650 N.Y.S.2d 704 (App. Div. 1996) (law firm may be liable for malpractice for failure to file personal injury action on behalf of client even though retainer agreement purported to limit scope of representation to workers' compensation claim; retainer agreement did not obviate firm's duty to apprise client that personal injury action might lie); *cf. Nw. Immigrant Rights Project v. Sessions*, No. C17-716 RAJ, 2017 WL 3189032, 2017 BL 261597 (W.D. Wash. July 27, 2017) (granting preliminary injunction on First Amendment grounds against enforcement of regulation requiring notice of full appearance by lawyers participating in preparation of immigration matters); Rule 1.5, cmt. [5] (lawyer may not enter fee agreement "whose terms might induce the lawyer improperly to curtail services for the client or perform them in a way contrary to the client's interest").

Limiting representation of a divorcing spouse to mediation, and requiring withdrawal if the divorce becomes contested, is one of the defining features of the collaborative law process. Several ethics committees have held that limitation reasonable under Rule 1.2. *E.g.,* ABA Formal Ethics Op. 07-447 (2007); Ark. Ethics Op. 2011-3 (2011); Orange Cnty. Formal Ethics Op. 2011-01 (2011); Conn. Informal Ethics Op. 09-01 (2009); Ky. Ethics Op. E-425 (2005); Mo. Formal Ethics Op. 124 (2008); N.J. Ethics Op. 699 (2005); N.C. Ethics Op. 2002-1 (2002); N.D. Ethics Op. 12-01 (2012); Pa. Ethics Op. 2004-24 (2004); S.C. Ethics Op. 10-01 (2010); Wash. Ethics Op. 2170 (2007). *But see* Colo. Ethics Op. 115 (2007) (limitation impermissible because "course of action that 'reasonably should be pursued on behalf of the client,' [that is, representation in litigation] is foreclosed to the lawyer"); Me. Ethics Op. 208 (2014) (collaborative participation agreement should state whether lawyers may continue to represent participants if proceedings become contested); *cf. In re Mabray,* 355 S.W.2d 16 (Tex. App. 2010) (state collaborative law statute did not invalidate "cooperative law" agreement permitting lawyers for divorcing spouses to continue representing them if proceedings became contested). *See generally* John Lande & Forrest S. Mosten, *Collaborative Lawyers' Duties to Screen the Appropriateness of Collaborative Law and Obtain Clients' Informed Consent to Use Collaborative Law,* 25 Ohio St. J. on Disp. Resol. 347 (2010).

A series of federal bankruptcy decisions has disapproved as unreasonable contractual limitations on certain core consumer bankruptcy legal services, including representation concerning reaffirmation agreements. *See, e.g., In re Minardi,* 399 B.R. 841 (Bankr. N.D. Okla. 2009). *See generally* Gregory M. Duhl, *Divided Loyalties: The Attorney's Role in Bankruptcy Reaffirmations,* 84 Am. Bankr. L.J. 361, 379–84 (Fall 2010).

The ABA Standing Committee on the Delivery of Legal Services has resources on limited scope representation at https://www.americanbar.org/groups/delivery_ legal_services/resources.html.

## INFORMED CONSENT OF CLIENT: DISCLOSURE

Limited-scope representation is permissible under Rule 1.2 only if the lawyer first clearly explains the limitations to the client and their likely effect on the undertaking and the client then consents. *See, e.g., Johnson v. Bd. of Cnty. Comm'rs,* 85 F.3d 489 (10th Cir. 1996) (although separate representation permissible for government official sued in both official and individual capacity, lawyer may limit representation to official capacity only if he consults with client about his exposure in his individual capacity and client consents to limitation); *Johnson v. Office of Prof'l Conduct,* 342 P.3d 280 (Utah 2014) (reversing finding of violation of Rule 1.2 because lawyer disclosed limitation on scope of representation in retainer agreement); Colo. Ethics Op. 101 (1998) ("lawyer engaged in unbundled legal services must clearly explain the limitations of the representation, including the types of services which are not being provided and the probable effect of limited representation"); D.C. Ethics Op. 330 (2005) ("Because the tasks excluded from a limited services agreement will typically fall to the client to perform or not get done at all, it is essential that clients clearly understand the division of responsibilities under a limited representation agreement"); Phila. Ethics Op. 2010-4 (2010) (contract lawyer must verify that retaining firm disclosed limited scope of participation to client and obtained client's informed consent); *see also* ABA Formal

Ethics Op. 96-403 (1996) (lawyer hired by insurer to represent insured must advise insured that lawyer intends to proceed at direction of insurer in accordance with insurance contract); Mich. Informal Ethics Op. RI-358 (2013) (lawyer may, as condition of representation of one client, agree to limit scope of representation of other existing and potential future clients if lawyer determines she may provide competent representation to other clients and obtains their informed consent); N.Y. City Ethics Op. 2001-3 (2001) (lawyer may limit scope of representation to avoid conflict with current or former client, provided client whose representation is limited consents after full disclosure and limitation does not so restrict representation as to render it inadequate); *cf. In re Samad*, 51 A.3d 486 (D.C. 2012) (even though written retainer agreement limited representation to advice and did not include filing motions, lawyer had duty to ensure client understood "division of responsibilities"; that is, what lawyer would and would not do); *Indianapolis Podiatry, P.C. v. Efroymson*, 720 N.E.2d 376 (Ind. Ct. App. 1999) (when limiting scope of representation, extent of required disclosure to client is "similar, if not identical, to that required in the context of a conflict of interest"). *See generally* Rule 1.5(b) (requiring that scope of representation, as well as basis for fees, be communicated to client before representation begins or shortly thereafter).

## Paragraph (d): Counseling or Assisting in Unlawful or Fraudulent Conduct

### LAWYER MAY NOT ASSIST CLIENT IN CRIMINAL OR FRAUDULENT CONDUCT

A lawyer may not assist a client in conduct that the lawyer knows is criminal or fraudulent. *See People v. Chappell*, 927 P.2d 829 (Colo. 1996) (helping client violate child custody order, resulting in felony charges against client); *People v. Theodore*, 926 P.2d 1237 (Colo. 1996) (driving client to family home in violation of restraining order); *Att'y Grievance Comm'n v. Protokowicz*, 619 A.2d 100 (Md. 1993) (helping former client in breaking into client's wife's home, killing pet cat in microwave oven, and searching for evidentiary documents to steal for use in proceedings); *In re Houge*, 764 N.W.2d 328 (Minn. 2009) (hiring client and supervising activity that client was barred from performing under client's criminal probation terms); *In re LaDuca*, 299 A.2d 405 (N.J. 1973) (aiding client in extorting ransom for return of stolen property); *In re Siegel*, 471 N.Y.S.2d 591 (App. Div. 1984) (corporate counsel engaging in fraudulent scheme involving unrecorded cash sales of corporate merchandise with corporation president and chair of board); *In re Feeley*, 581 S.E.2d 487 (S.C. 2003) (helping client forge checks for payment of client's bond and lawyer's fees); Mich. Informal Ethics Op. RI-298 (1997) (lawyer may not assist title company in illegal or fraudulent conduct by agreeing to be named as drafter of deed, prepared by nonlawyer title company employee whom lawyer does not supervise, which lawyer does not review before delivery and execution); N.J. Ethics Op. 710 (2006) (lawyer may not participate in scheme whereby realty buyer and seller inflate sale price of property and credit inflated increment back to buyer at closing to enhance financing fees earned by mortgage service provider); N.Y. State Ethics Op. 2082 (2016) (in-house lawyer for finance company may not provide legal services to company's customers; doing so would constitute assisting in the unauthorized practice of law, a crime). *See generally* Landon C. Davis III, Isaac A. McBeth & Elizabeth Southall, *A Distinction Without a Difference? An Examination of the Legal and Ethical Difference Between Asset Protection and Fraudulent Transfers Under Virginia Law*, 47 U. Rich. L. Rev. 381 (2012).

Even passive assistance, such as withholding information from a court or the government, may violate Rule 1.2. *See, e.g., People v. Casey*, 948 P.2d 1014 (Colo. 1997) (lawyer failed to inform court that client charged with trespassing was using someone else's identity); *In re Price*, 429 N.E.2d 961 (Ind. 1982) (withholding information from government to assist client in obtaining Medicaid benefits illegally); *State ex rel. Okla. Bar Ass'n v. Golden*, 201 P.3d 862 (Okla. 2008) (lawyer convicted under federal misprision of felony statute was disbarred for same conduct); *cf. Chapman Lumber, Inc. v. Tager*, 952 A.2d 1 (Conn. 2008) (lawyer helped client defraud creditor by failing to reveal that client did not own building deeded to creditor to settle debt). *But see* Utah Ethics Op. 97-02 (1997) (lawyer's failure to give law enforcement authorities telephone number of client accused of crime does not amount to assisting client in committing crime).

## LAWYER MAY NOT ADVISE CLIENT TO ENGAGE IN CRIMINAL OR FRAUDULENT CONDUCT

Regardless of whether actual assistance is rendered, a lawyer may never advise a client to engage in criminal or fraudulent conduct. *See, e.g., People v. Gifford*, 76 P.3d 519 (Colo. O.P.D.J. 2003) (advising client to offer ex-wife real estate in exchange for favorable testimony in pending criminal case); *In re Temple*, 786 S.E.2d 684 (Ga. 2016) (advising payday lending company clients to knowingly violate usury laws); *In re Scionti*, 630 N.E.2d 1358 (Ind. 1994) (counseling father not to return child to mother, notwithstanding court order to do so); *In re Johnson*, 597 P.2d 740 (Mont. 1979) (advising client to disregard ruling of court); *Werme's Case*, 839 A.2d 1 (N.H. 2003) (advising client to disclose confidential court records to newspaper); *In re Edson*, 530 A.2d 1246 (N.J. 1987) (advising clients to invent evidence in defense of drunk-driving case); Vt. Ethics Op. 97-6 (1997) (lawyer may not advise client to refuse to submit to evidentiary test for alcohol when such refusal would constitute a crime, but may advise client of legal consequences of taking or refusing to take such test and of any good-faith argument for contesting validity of law); *cf.* Va. Ethics Op. 1802 (2010) (lawyer may advise client to surreptitiously record conversation to obtain relevant information if permissible under state and federal law).

This issue has come into relief in jurisdictions that expressly permit the limited use of marijuana—a crime under federal law. *See, e.g.*, Ariz. Ethics Op. 11-01 (2011) (permissible under Rule 1.2(d) for lawyer to assist clients wishing to start businesses or engage in other actions permitted under Arizona Medical Marijuana Act); Conn. Informal Ethics Op. 2013-02 (2013) (lawyer may advise and represent client concerning state requirements for licensing and regulation of businesses that grow or dispense marijuana for medical purposes but must inform client that such businesses violate federal criminal statutes, and lawyer may not assist client in criminal conduct); Me. Ethics Op. 199 (2010) (Rule 1.2 makes no "distinction between crimes which are enforced and those which are not," so lawyer must "determine whether the particular legal service being requested rises to the level of assistance in violating federal law"), Wash. Ethics Op. 201501 (2015) (Washington state lawyers may advise clients operating marijuana-related businesses on effect of relevant laws but not on how to violate them or conceal violations); Colo. R. 1.2, cmt. [14] ("A lawyer may counsel a client regarding the validity, scope, and meaning of Colorado constitution article XVIII, secs. 14 & 16, and may assist a client in conduct that the lawyer reasonably believes is permitted by these constitutional provisions and the statutes, regulations, orders, and other state or local provisions implementing them. In these circumstances, the lawyer shall also advise the client regarding related federal law and policy."). *See generally* A. Claire Frezza, *Counseling Clients on Medical Marijuana: Ethics Caught in Smoke*, 25 Geo. J. Legal Ethics 537 (Summer 2012); Sam Kamin & Eli Wald, *Marijuana Lawyers: Outlaws or Crusaders?* 91 Or. L. Rev. 869 (2013); Alec Rothrock, *Is Assisting Medical Marijuana Dispensaries Hazardous to a Lawyer's Professional Health?* 89 Denv. U. L. Rev. 1047 (2012); Anna El-Zein, Note, *Caught in a Haze: Ethical Issues for Attorneys Advising on Marijuana*, 82 Mo. L. Rev. 1171 (2017).

## WHEN LAWYER SHOULD INQUIRE INTO CLIENT'S AFFAIRS

A lawyer's assistance in unlawful conduct is not excused by a failure to inquire into the client's objectives. *See, e.g., In re Bloom*, 745 P.2d 61 (Cal. 1987) (aiding client in transporting plastic explosives to Libya; court dismissed argument that lawyer believed in good faith that transport was authorized by National Security Council); *Fla. Bar v. Brown*, 790 So. 2d 1081 (Fla. 2001) (by failing to consider legality of request of company president's request concerning campaign contribution reimbursement scheme, lawyer assisted in conduct he should have known was criminal or fraudulent); *Harrell v. Crystal*, 611 N.E.2d 908 (Ohio Ct. App. 1992) (advising clients on tax shelter investments without properly investigating or requesting IRS letter ruling); *see also* ABA Informal Ethics Op. 1470 (1981) (lawyer should not undertake representation without making further inquiry if facts suggest representation might aid client in fraud or crime); *cf. In re Tocco*, 984 P.2d 539 (Ariz. 1999) (violation of Rule 1.2(d) requires knowing misconduct; mere showing that lawyer reasonably should have known conduct violated rule, without more, was insufficient).

## TAKING GOOD-FAITH POSITION

Rule 1.2(d) permits a lawyer to assist a client in making a good-faith determination of the validity, scope, meaning, or application of the law. Applying this principle, ABA Formal Opinion 85-352 (1985) explained that a lawyer may advise a client to take a position on a tax return if the lawyer believes in good faith the position is warranted or supportable. A good-faith belief simply requires some realistic possibility of success, according to the opinion; the lawyer need not believe the position will actually prevail. *See* Ariz. Ethics Op. 88-02 (1988) (lawyer with good-faith doubt that health-care provider's proposed lien form is enforceable should explain possible consequences to client but need not advise against signing); Vt. Ethics Op. 97-6 (1997) (lawyer may not advise client to refuse to submit to evidentiary test for alcohol when such refusal would constitute a crime, but may advise client of legal consequences of taking or refusing to take such test and of any good-faith argument for contesting validity of law).

## Former Paragraph (e): Consultation with Client regarding Ethical and Legal Limitations on Lawyer's Conduct

Formerly, Rule 1.2 contained a paragraph (e), which stated that "[w]hen a lawyer knows that a client expects assistance not permitted by the rules of professional conduct or other law, the lawyer shall consult with the client regarding the relevant limitations on the lawyer's conduct." Rule 1.2(e) (1983) [superseded]. This provision was deleted from Rule 1.2 by amendment in 2002. The substance of the provision is now contained in Rule 1.4(a)(5).

## Rule 1.3

*Diligence*

**A lawyer shall act with reasonable diligence and promptness in representing a client.**

## COMMENT

[1] A lawyer should pursue a matter on behalf of a client despite opposition, obstruction or personal inconvenience to the lawyer, and take whatever lawful and ethical measures are required to vindicate a client's cause or endeavor. A lawyer must also act with commitment and dedication to the interests of the client and with zeal in advocacy upon the client's behalf. A lawyer is not bound, however, to press for every advantage that might be realized for a client. For example, a lawyer may have authority to exercise professional discretion in determining the means by which a matter should be pursued. See Rule 1.2. The lawyer's duty to act with reasonable diligence does not require the use of offensive tactics or preclude the treating of all persons involved in the legal process with courtesy and respect.

[2] A lawyer's work load must be controlled so that each matter can be handled competently.

[3] Perhaps no professional shortcoming is more widely resented than procrastination. A client's interests often can be adversely affected by the passage of time or the change of conditions; in extreme instances, as when a lawyer overlooks a statute of limitations, the client's legal position may be destroyed. Even when the client's interests are not affected in substance, however, unreasonable delay can cause a client needless anxiety and undermine confidence in the lawyer's trustworthiness. A lawyer's duty to act with reasonable promptness, however, does not preclude the lawyer from agreeing to a reasonable request for a postponement that will not prejudice the lawyer's client.

[4] Unless the relationship is terminated as provided in Rule 1.16, a lawyer should carry through to conclusion all matters undertaken for a client. If a lawyer's employment is limited to a specific matter, the relationship terminates when the matter has been resolved. If a lawyer has served a client over a substantial period in a variety of matters, the client sometimes may assume that the lawyer will continue to serve on a continuing basis unless the lawyer gives notice of withdrawal. Doubt about whether a client-lawyer relationship still exists should be clarified by the lawyer, preferably in writing, so that the client will not mistakenly suppose the lawyer is looking after the client's affairs when the lawyer has ceased to do so. For example, if a lawyer has handled a judicial or administrative proceeding that produced a result adverse to the client and the lawyer and the client have not agreed that the lawyer

will handle the matter on appeal, the lawyer must consult with the client about the possibility of appeal before relinquishing responsibility for the matter. See Rule 1.4(a) (2). Whether the lawyer is obligated to prosecute the appeal for the client depends on the scope of the representation the lawyer has agreed to provide to the client. See Rule 1.2.

[5] To prevent neglect of client matters in the event of a sole practitioner's death or disability, the duty of diligence may require that each sole practitioner prepare a plan, in conformity with applicable rules, that designates another competent lawyer to review client files, notify each client of the lawyer's death or disability, and determine whether there is a need for immediate protective action. Cf. Rule 28 of the American Bar Association Model Rules for Lawyer Disciplinary Enforcement (providing for court appointment of a lawyer to inventory files and take other protective action in absence of a plan providing for another lawyer to protect the interests of the clients of a deceased or disabled lawyer).

**Definitional Cross-References**
"Reasonable" *See* Rule 1.0(h)

**State Rules Comparison**
http://ambar.org/MRPCStateCharts

# ANNOTATION
## NATURE OF DUTY

Rule 1.3 states the lawyer's basic duty to perform the work for which the lawyer was engaged, within a reasonable time, and, as noted in Comment [1], "with commitment and dedication to the interests of the client." How diligently a lawyer performs his or her job not only affects the rights of the client, it also reflects upon the integrity of the lawyer: "Even when the client's interests are not affected in substance, . . . unreasonable delay can cause a client needless anxiety and undermine confidence in the lawyer's trustworthiness." Cmt. [3].

As a practical matter, violations of Rule 1.3's duty of diligence typically accompany violations of other ethics rules, most frequently Rule 1.1 (Competence), Rule 1.4 (Communication), Rule 1.15 (Safekeeping Property), Rule 3.2 (Expediting Litigation), Rule 5.1 (Responsibilities of Partners, Managers, and Supervisory Lawyers), and Rule 5.3 (Responsibilities Regarding Nonlawyer Assistance). In most cases, a lawyer's lack of diligence results from violation of another ethics rule (for example, missing a statute of limitations due to a lack of competence) or leads to another ethics violation (for example, missing a statute of limitations leading to failure to communicate this to the client). Nevertheless, a lawyer's ethical obligations under Rule 1.3 are separate and distinct from those of other ethics rules. *See generally* American Bar Association, *Essential Qualities of the Professional Lawyer* 117 *et seq.* (2013).

## PREJUDICE TO CLIENT

Lack of diligence often results in obvious prejudice to the client's interests. *See, e.g., People v. Mendus*, 360 P.3d 1049 (Colo. O.P.D.J. 2015) (inaction resulted in divorce clients losing custody and maintenance); *In re Francis*, 137 A.3d 187 (D.C. 2016) (failure to move for extension of time resulted in dismissal of client's complaint); *Fla. Bar v. Barcus*, 697 So. 2d 71 (Fla. 1997) (failure to move for rehearing or to set aside judgment of foreclosure); *In re Shearouse*, 472 S.E.2d 294 (Ga. 1996) (allowing statute of limitations to expire; failure to set aside foreclosure of property); *Office of Disciplinary Counsel v. Collins*, No. SCAD–15–0000709, 2016 WL 281995, 2016 BL 14935 (Haw. Jan. 20, 2016) (failure to appear or file motion to set aside order resulted in client's temporary loss of child custody); *In re Roswold*, 249 P.3d 1199 (Kan. 2011) (inaction ultimately resulted in case's dismissal); *In re Whitehead*, 28 So. 3d 249 (La. 2010) (failure to tell criminal defendant to appear at several hearings resulted in issuance of bench warrants and jailing of client); *Att'y Grievance Comm'n v. Chanthunya*, 133 A.3d 1034 (Md. 2016) (failure to appeal denial of one client's green card application and failure to prepare second client for asylum hearing impeded clients' naturalization); *In re Igbanugo*, 863 N.W.2d 751 (Minn. 2015) (delay of nearly two years in submitting documents to immigration court resulted in dismissal of asylum petition); *Parrish v. Miss. Bar*, 691 So. 2d 904 (Miss. 1996) (failure to tell workers' compensation client of scheduled physical examination resulted in client missing exam and claim being dismissed); *In re Bogard*, 49 N.Y.S.3d 684 (App. Div. 2017) (inaction resulted in clients' losing home in sheriff's foreclosure sale); *In re Widdel*, 899 N.W.2d 278 (N.D. 2017) (failure to file tax return diminished trust and estate assets); *In re Purvis*, 557 S.E.2d 651 (S.C. 2001) (real estate lawyer's failure to pay client's property taxes resulted in sale of client's property); *Lawyer Disciplinary Bd. v. Martin*, 693 S.E.2d 461 (W. Va. 2010) (failure to file tax returns resulted in penalties and interest charged to estate); *Bd. of Prof'l Responsibility v. Powers*, 322 P.3d 1287 (Wyo. 2014) (failure to timely complete disposition of estate-owned house, resulting in heir's bearing two years of carrying costs; failure to timely file notice of appeal, resulting in dismissal).

Actual prejudice to the client's matter, however, is not a necessary element of the disciplinary offense. *See, e.g., In re Douglass*, 859 A.2d 1069 (D.C. 2004) (failure to file suit within shorter of two arguably applicable statutes of limitations "not excused by the possibility that an action . . . still might have been timely"); *Iowa Supreme Court Bd. of Prof'l Ethics & Conduct v. Sather*, 534 N.W.2d 428 (Iowa 1995) (failure to manage estate proceedings properly or to respond to notices and complaint of court clerk and disciplinary board; discipline imposed even though matter was lawyer's own family estate, lawyer not compensated, and no apparent prejudice); *In re Dixon*, 996 So. 2d 1029 (La. 2008) (failure to serve adversary for several months, although "actions appear to have caused no significant harm to his client"); *Att'y Grievance Comm'n v. Davis*, 825 A.2d 430 (Md. 2003) ("no harm, no foul" not a viable defense to discipline inquiry under this rule); *In re Kurzman*, 871 N.W.2d 753 (Minn. 2015) (delay in filing properly prepared documents in child custody and visitation matter had no apparent effect on judge's decision but protracted time-sensitive proceedings and negatively affected client's relationship with legal profession); *In re Seaworth*, 603 N.W.2d 176

(N.D. 1999) (Rule 1.3 "does not require a client to be prejudiced by his or her lawyer's failure to act with reasonable diligence and promptness for a violation of the rule to occur"); *In re PRB Docket No. 2007-003*, 987 A.2d 273 (Vt. 2009) (lawyer disciplined for delay in responding to discovery even though "conduct did not result in actual substantial harm to his client, the public, the legal system, or the profession").

## PROMPTNESS
### • *Meeting Deadlines*

Rule 1.3 requires a lawyer to meet deadlines and appear at scheduled legal proceedings. *See, e.g., In re Brady*, 387 P.3d 1 (Alaska 2016) (failure to comply with pretrial deadlines in personal injury case); *In re Muhr*, 370 P.3d 677 (Colo. O.P.D.J. 2016) (failing to file suit within statute of limitations); *In re Shearouse*, 472 S.E.2d 294 (Ga. 1996) (dismissing case without client's knowledge or permission and letting statute of limitations expire); *Tiller v. Semonis*, 635 N.E.2d 572 (Ill. App. Ct. 1994) (duty under Rule 1.3 includes "tracking . . . cases and learning the date upon which a hearing is to occur . . . . [Failure to be notified] does not constitute an excuse"); *In re Davidson*, 761 N.E.2d 854 (Ind. 2002) (failure to appear for client's sentencing hearing); *In re Fickler*, 362 P.3d 1102 (Kan. 2015) (failure to timely file appellate brief); *Ky. Bar Ass'n v. Niehaus*, 539 S.W.3d 35 (Ky. 2018) (failure to respond to discovery by deadline); *State ex rel. Okla. Bar Ass'n v. Giger*, 37 P.3d 856 (Okla. 2001) (filing lawsuit after claim already time-barred and failing to respond to motion to dismiss); *In re Walwyn*, 531 S.W.3d 131 (Tenn. 2017) (missing appeal deadline, then waiting three and one-half years to file motion for leave to file late appeal); *In re Juarez*, 24 P.3d 1040 (Wash. 2001) (failing to file timely appellate brief or motion to extend time); *In re Urban*, 574 N.W.2d 651 (Wis. 1998) (failure to timely file estate inventories, respond to requests from department of revenue, distribute estate assets, or close estates).

### • *Unreasonable Delay*

Even without missing a formal deadline, a lawyer may be subject to discipline under Rule 1.3 for unreasonable delay. *See, e.g., People v. C de Baca*, 948 P.2d 1 (Colo. 1997) (waiting until shortly before statute of limitations was to run before informing client of suspension from practice and consequent inability to file complaint); *In re Benge*, 783 A.2d 1279 (Del. 2001) (trust provision required client to secure lawyer's consent to amend trust; lawyer took more than a year to consent, complying only in response to petition to compel); *In re Anderson*, 979 A.2d 1206 (D.C. 2009) (failure to pay client's medical providers for years after receiving settlement funds); *Fla. Bar v. Walton*, 952 So. 2d 510 (Fla. 2006) (withholding for seven months reimbursable costs ordered to be paid to client by opponent because opponent's payment was $0.23 short); *In re Hartin*, 764 S.E.2d 542 (Ga. 2014) (delay in filing uncontested divorce and qualified domestic relations order and recording quitclaim deed); *In re Cherry*, 715 N.E.2d 382 (Ind. 1999) (delay in filing petition for post-conviction relief for five and one-half years after conclusion of appeals process while client was incarcerated); *In re James*, 409 P.3d 848 (Kan. 2017) (unreasonable delay in multiple cases); *Ky. Bar Ass'n v. Burgin*, 412 S.W.3d 872 (Ky. 2013) (failing to deposit personal injury settlement check in trust account or take steps to have it replaced until several years later, after client filed bar complaint); *In re Brown*, 967 So. 2d 482 (La. 2007) (five-year delay in serving opponents with summons and not responding to their motion to dismiss suit); *In re Horton*, 979 N.Y.S.2d 918 (App. Div. 2014) (taking more than three years to complete work on qualified domestic relations order); *N.C. State Bar v. Scott*, 773 S.E.2d 520 (N.C. Ct. App. 2015) (failure to timely obtain title insurance policy and disburse real estate closing funds for title premium and property taxes); *Dayton Bar Ass'n v. Brown*, 921 N.E.2d 220 (Ohio 2009) (delay of more than a year in transferring elderly clients' assets into trust, thus postponing their anticipated move into nursing home and eligibility for Medicaid); *State ex rel. Okla. Bar Ass'n v. Minter*, 37 P.3d 763 (Okla. 2001) (failing to provide land purchaser with marketable title for more than three years, testifying it was "one of those things that got stuck on the back burner"); *In re Ricci*, 735 A.2d 203 (R.I. 1999) (retaining personal injury plaintiff client's settlement funds for a year before paying client's medical providers); *In re Longtin*, 713 S.E.2d 297 (S.C. 2011) (failure to file motions for default and proposed orders as directed by court, resulting in dismissal of multiple cases for want of prosecution); *In re Artery*, 709 N.W.2d 54 (Wis. 2006) (five-month delay in filing promised habeas petition).

The problem of undue delay can be particularly egregious in estate matters. *See, e.g., In re Edmonds*, 21 N.E.3d 447 (Ill. 2014) (nine-year delay in resolving estate's tax liability); *In re Bonnette*, 791 So. 2d 68 (La. 2001) (estate succession still not closed nine years after lawyer retained to handle it); *In re MacGibbon*, 535 N.W.2d 809 (Minn. 1995) (lawyer served first as counsel for personal representative and then as successor personal representative for more than thirty years; neglect in attempting to establish heirs "exacerbated the delays that are inherent in the process of probate administration"); *In re O'Brien*, 29 P.3d 1044 (N.M. 2001) (telling client delay in closing decedent's estate was result of waiting for final tax clearances from state taxation and revenue department, although estate was several thousands of dollars below threshold level for seeking tax clearance, and no evidence suggested lawyer ever took steps to obtain clearance); *In re Swanson*, 638 N.W.2d 240 (N.D. 2002) (lawyer appointed as executor failed to probate estate for more than thirteen years); *In re Biddle*, 773 S.E.2d 590 (S.C. 2015) (failure to file documents necessary to close one estate and failure to file petition to remove personal representative for breach of fiduciary duty in another).

## CARRYING OUT REPRESENTATION

In addition to requiring that a lawyer meet deadlines and appear at legal proceedings, Rule 1.3 mandates that a lawyer actively carry a matter forward. *See, e.g., Comm. on Prof'l Ethics v. Freed*, 341 N.W.2d 757 (Iowa 1983) ("We view respondent's retreat from the obligation he assumed as a serious matter, to be equated with the conduct of a surgeon who, without transferring responsibility, drops his scalpel and abandons his patient in the course of an operation.").

### • *Taking No Action*

It is the duty of diligence that requires a lawyer actually to perform the work for which he or she was retained. Thus, a lawyer who takes no action on a case is subject to discipline under Rule 1.3. *See, e.g., People v. Carrigan*, 358 P.3d 650 (Colo. O.P.D.J. 2015) (multiple instances of failing to perform any services for clients); *In re*

*Asher*, 772 A.2d 1161 (D.C. 2001) (failing to draft or file any documents to vacate judgment entered against client in connection with retail installment contract and security agreement, resulting in garnishment action against client); *In re Radford*, 746 N.E.2d 977 (Ind. 2001) (failure to take any meaningful action in several client matters); *In re Weaver*, 281 P.3d 502 (Kan. 2012) (lawyer formed loan modification business and solicited and collected retainer fees from clients but did nothing to provide them with legal services); *Ky. Bar Ass'n v. Gallaher*, 539 S.W.3d 29 (Ky. 2018) (taking no action or stopping work after minimal services in multiple matters); *In re Judice*, 26 So. 3d 747 (La. 2010) (failing to file workers' compensation case before period of prescription had elapsed); *Att'y Grievance Comm'n v. Thomas*, 127 A.3d 562 (Md. 2015) (failure to attend hearing in criminal matter or file petitions in divorce and guardianship matters); *In re Diviacchi*, 62 N.E.3d 38 (Mass. 2016) (persistent refusal to take action to prevent foreclosure, participate in settlement negotiations, or meet with client); *In re Howe*, 626 N.W.2d 650 (N.D. 2001) (did nothing to secure judgment for client's post-divorce award, resulting in client losing opportunity to lock in low interest rate on home refinance); *Disciplinary Counsel v. Hoff*, 921 N.E.2d 636 (Ohio 2010) (accepting $5,000 retainer to resolve federal tax deficiencies for client but failing even to communicate with IRS); *In re Veiga*, 783 A.2d 911 (R.I. 2001) (failure to file defamation suit before statute of limitations elapsed); *In re Atwater*, 725 S.E.2d 686 (S.C. 2012) (failure to diligently investigate or otherwise advance uncomplicated case for nearly a decade); *Lawyer Disciplinary Bd. v. Munoz*, 807 S.E.2d 290 (W. Va. 2017) (failure to take any action after court appointments in two habeas cases).

• *Failure to Complete Work*

Rule 1.3 imposes a duty to carry through to conclusion all matters related to the representation, unless the lawyer withdraws. *See, e.g., People v. Sandoval*, 334 P.3d 252 (Colo. O.P.D.J. 2014) (multiple instances of entering appearance and/or filing initial pleadings with no further action, or taking no action at all after being retained); *Statewide Grievance Comm. v. Gifford*, 820 A.2d 309 (Conn. App. Ct. 2003) (ceasing work on case after attending client's deposition and deciding her testimony was untrue); *In re Shaw*, 472 S.E.2d 307 (Ga. 1996) (failure to complete adoption proceedings or disburse money held in trust for medical expenses); *In re Putsey*, 675 N.E.2d 703 (Ind. 1997) (ceasing work after filing bankruptcy petition and motion to dismiss civil suit); *Ky. Bar Ass'n v. Sparks*, 538 S.W.3d 284 (Ky. 2018) (failure to take any action after filing suit); *In re Swafford*, 238 So. 3d 957 (La. 2018) (failure to complete succession work); *Att'y Grievance Comm'n v. Smith*, 109 A.3d 1184 (Md. 2015) (prosecutor in child sex abuse case failed to notify victim or foster mother of proceeding, resulting in their losing ability to participate in trial or sentencing hearing and being unaware of conditions of defendant's release); *In re Bartley*, 53 N.Y.S.3d 643 (App. Div. 2017) (successfully overturned denial of unemployment benefits, but decision reversed after failure to oppose employer's appeal); *In re Howe*, 843 N.W.2d 325 (N.D. 2014) (failure to timely file application for cancellation of removal or obtain and submit supporting documents to immigration court); *State ex rel. Okla. Bar Ass'n v. Wilcox*, 318 P.3d 1114 (Okla. 2014) (failure to seek reimbursement for client's travel expenses from workers' compensation insurer); *In re Hedesh*, 776 S.E.2d 260 (S.C. 2015) (failure to ensure closing documents were timely recorded); *Lawyer Disciplinary Bd. v. Thorn*, 783 S.E.2d 321 (W. Va. 2016) (multiple failures to carry out representations).

Similarly, a lawyer may not simply abandon a case or client. *See, e g , People v. Weatherford*, 357 P.3d 1251 (Colo. O.P.D.J. 2015) (failing to file any documents in divorce case or return client's calls after client completed financial disclosures as instructed); *In re Lyles*, 494 S.E.2d 338 (Ga. 1998) (abandoning client's case without notifying client or returning unearned fees or client's documents); *In re Vaughan*, 801 So. 2d 1058 (La. 2001) (accepting child support matter and then closing his office without notifying client); *In re Lazroe*, 29 N.Y.S.3d 843 (App. Div. 2016) (failing to act on one personal injury matter and ceasing work on another without notifying clients); *In re Jones-Burgess*, 753 S.E.2d 532 (S.C. 2014) (multiple instances of taking no action after being retained and then closing law office without notifying clients); *In re Wickersham*, 310 P.3d 1237 (Wash. 2013) (lawyer failed to appear at hearings or withdraw from cases and abandoned practice without notice to clients); Ariz. Ethics Op. 2010-02 (2010) (lawyer and law firm must cooperate to inform clients of lawyer's departure from firm and to ensure client matters handled competently and diligently); *cf.* Phila. Ethics Op. 2014-100 (2015) (law firm succession plan is best practice, though not required by ethics rules, to prevent potential violations of Rule 1.3's duty of diligence and other rules as result of lawyer's sudden death or disability).

### • *Inadequate Investigation and Preparation*

Rule 1.3 requires an adequate level of preparation and investigation for each particular representation. *See, e.g., Fla. Bar v. Kinney*, 606 So. 2d 367 (Fla. 1992) (failure to file suit on time against insolvent insurer, not realizing insolvent insurers subject to reduced statutes of limitations); *Tiller v. Semonis*, 635 N.E.2d 572 (Ill. App. Ct. 1994) (duty of diligence includes tracking clients' cases and ascertaining hearing dates); *In re Miller*, 759 N.E.2d 209 (Ind. 2001) (criminal defense lawyer did not respond to client's letters, never visited client during his ninety-day hospital stay, and met defendant for first time at second court appearance); *In re Harris*, 180 P.3d 558 (Kan. 2008) (lawyer handling bankruptcy case failed to get username and password for bankruptcy court's mandatory electronic filing system); *In re Ungar*, 25 So. 3d 101 (La. 2009) (failing to investigate all terms of aggregate settlement negotiated by co-counsel so clients could make informed decision whether to accept); *Att'y Grievance Comm'n v. Williams*, 132 A.3d 232 (Md. 2016) (failure to propound any discovery on behalf of medical malpractice client or take other action to advance her claim); *In re Kovitz*, 504 N.Y.S.2d 400 (App. Div. 1986) (failing to investigate personal injury case for fourteen years, claiming it was trial tactic to outwait witnesses); *Cleveland Metro. Bar Ass'n v. Kaplan*, 921 N.E.2d 645 (Ohio 2010) (failing to ensure bankruptcy client's payroll service took bankruptcy plan deductions from client's paycheck, resulting in dismissal of case for failure to fund plan); *In re Konnor*, 694 N.W.2d 376 (Wis. 2005) (lawyer for estate failed to investigate suspicion that rent owed estate was being misappropriated by decedent's brothers); Phila. Ethics Op. 2014-2 (2014) (duty of diligence necessitates locating pertinent witnesses and preparing them to testify); Va. Ethics Op. 1865 (2012) (lawyer holding settlement funds must exercise reasonable diligence to ascertain validity of third-party claim).

#### • Heavy Caseloads

Comment [2] to Rule 1.3 explains that a "lawyer's work load must be controlled so that each matter can be handled competently." *See, e.g., In re Mance*, 869 A.2d 339 (D.C. 2005) (neglect of client's criminal appeal caused in part by "overwhelming case load"); *Pub. Defender v. State*, 115 So. 3d 261 (Fla. 2013) (aggregate motion to withdraw granted when public defender's office had grossly excessive caseload precluding systemic competent representation); *State ex rel. Mo. Pub. Defender Comm'n v. Waters*, 370 S.W.3d 592 (Mo. 2012) (trial court erred in appointing public defender's office to represent defendant given office's certification of limited availability due to excessive caseload); ABA Formal Ethics Op. 465 (2013) (lawyer considering offering Groupon or "daily deal" coupons must limit number of deals offered, to preserve lawyer's ability to handle caseload promptly, competently, and diligently); Ala. Ethics Op. 2012-01 (2012) (participation in "daily deal" marketing arrangement risks creation of unmanageable caseload); *see also* annotation to Rule 1.1, "Heavy Caseloads." *But see State ex rel. Okla. Bar Ass'n v. Ward*, 353 P.3d 509 (Okla. 2015) (declining to find violation of Rule 1.3 where prosecutor "spent just about every waking moment" preparing for trial while continuing to manage rest of heavy caseload). *See generally* Heather Baxter, *Too Many Clients, Too Little Time: How States Are Forcing Public Defenders to Violate Their Ethical Obligations*, 25 Fed. Sent'g Rep. 91 (Dec. 2012).

### LAWYER NOT RELIEVED OF ETHICAL OBLIGATION BY DELEGATING WORK

A lawyer who agrees to represent a client is not relieved of ethical obligations by delegating the work to others. *See, e.g., In re Dickens*, 174 A.3d 283 (D.C. 2017) (ignoring "clear warning signs" that firm partner was mismanaging trust and estate client's assets); *In re Robinson*, 495 S.E.2d 28 (Ga. 1998) (lawyer undertook representation and then, without formally withdrawing, assigned cases to legal assistants or other lawyers who did not pursue claims); *Att'y Grievance Comm'n v. Narasimhan*, 92 A.3d 512 (Md. 2014) (immigration lawyer forwarded clients' requests for information to associate but never followed up after associate responded inadequately); *Sheridan's Case*, 781 A.2d 7 (N.H. 2001) (lawyer who delegated oversight of estate to associate but remained counsel and commissioner of record was responsible for untimely filings of accounts for estate); *State ex rel. Okla. Bar Ass'n v. Sheridan*, 84 P.3d 710 (Okla. 2003) (although office manager's behavior exacerbated violations, lawyer himself "was the one who failed to fulfill his responsibilities to his clients"); *In re Johnson*, 689 S.E.2d 623 (S.C. 2010) (failing to attend real estate closing and allowing his nonlawyer office assistant to conduct it instead); *cf. In re Bailey*, 115 So. 3d 458 (La. 2013) (lawyer's failure to have his wife, who served as his office manager and trustee of client's settlement funds, file timely accountings and tax returns resulted from conflict of interest and failure to supervise, not lack of diligence). *See generally* Rule 5.1 (Responsibilities of Partners, Managers, and Supervisory Lawyers); Rule 5.3 (Responsibilities Regarding Nonlawyer Assistance).

## Rule 1.4

### Communication

(a) A lawyer shall:

(1) promptly inform the client of any decision or circumstance with respect to which the client's informed consent, as defined in Rule 1.0(e), is required by these Rules;

(2) reasonably consult with the client about the means by which the client's objectives are to be accomplished;

(3) keep the client reasonably informed about the status of the matter;

(4) promptly comply with reasonable requests for information; and

(5) consult with the client about any relevant limitation on the lawyer's conduct when the lawyer knows that the client expects assistance not permitted by the Rules of Professional Conduct or other law.

(b) A lawyer shall explain a matter to the extent reasonably necessary to permit the client to make informed decisions regarding the representation.

## COMMENT

[1] Reasonable communication between the lawyer and the client is necessary for the client effectively to participate in the representation.

### Communicating with Client

[2] If these Rules require that a particular decision about the representation be made by the client, paragraph (a)(1) requires that the lawyer promptly consult with and secure the client's consent prior to taking action unless prior discussions with the client have resolved what action the client wants the lawyer to take. For example, a lawyer who receives from opposing counsel an offer of settlement in a civil controversy or a proffered plea bargain in a criminal case must promptly inform the client of its substance unless the client has previously indicated that the proposal will be acceptable or unacceptable or has authorized the lawyer to accept or to reject the offer. See Rule 1.2(a).

[3] Paragraph (a)(2) requires the lawyer to reasonably consult with the client about the means to be used to accomplish the client's objectives. In some situations—depending on both the importance of the action under consideration and the feasibil-

ity of consulting with the client—this duty will require consultation prior to taking action. In other circumstances, such as during a trial when an immediate decision must be made, the exigency of the situation may require the lawyer to act without prior consultation. In such cases the lawyer must nonetheless act reasonably to inform the client of actions the lawyer has taken on the client's behalf. Additionally, paragraph (a)(3) requires that the lawyer keep the client reasonably informed about the status of the matter, such as significant developments affecting the timing or the substance of the representation.

[4] A lawyer's regular communication with clients will minimize the occasions on which a client will need to request information concerning the representation. When a client makes a reasonable request for information, however, paragraph (a)(4) requires prompt compliance with the request, or if a prompt response is not feasible, that the lawyer, or a member of the lawyer's staff, acknowledge receipt of the request and advise the client when a response may be expected. A lawyer should promptly respond to or acknowledge client communications.

## Explaining Matters

[5] The client should have sufficient information to participate intelligently in decisions concerning the objectives of the representation and the means by which they are to be pursued, to the extent the client is willing and able to do so. Adequacy of communication depends in part on the kind of advice or assistance that is involved. For example, when there is time to explain a proposal made in a negotiation, the lawyer should review all important provisions with the client before proceeding to an agreement. In litigation a lawyer should explain the general strategy and prospects of success and ordinarily should consult the client on tactics that are likely to result in significant expense or to injure or coerce others. On the other hand, a lawyer ordinarily will not be expected to describe trial or negotiation strategy in detail. The guiding principle is that the lawyer should fulfill reasonable client expectations for information consistent with the duty to act in the client's best interests, and the client's overall requirements as to the character of representation. In certain circumstances, such as when a lawyer asks a client to consent to a representation affected by a conflict of interest, the client must give informed consent, as defined in Rule 1.0(e).

[6] Ordinarily, the information to be provided is that appropriate for a client who is a comprehending and responsible adult. However, fully informing the client according to this standard may be impracticable, for example, where the client is a child or suffers from diminished capacity. See Rule 1.14. When the client is an organization or group, it is often impossible or inappropriate to inform every one of its members about its legal affairs; ordinarily, the lawyer should address communications to the appropriate officials of the organization. See Rule 1.13. Where many routine matters are involved, a system of limited or occasional reporting may be arranged with the client.

## Withholding Information

[7] In some circumstances, a lawyer may be justified in delaying transmission of information when the client would be likely to react imprudently to an imme-

diate communication. Thus, a lawyer might withhold a psychiatric diagnosis of a client when the examining psychiatrist indicates that disclosure would harm the client. A lawyer may not withhold information to serve the lawyer's own interest or convenience or the interests or convenience of another person. Rules or court orders governing litigation may provide that information supplied to a lawyer may not be disclosed to the client. Rule 3.4(c) directs compliance with such rules or orders.

### Definitional Cross-References
"Informed consent" *See* Rule 1.0(e)
"Knows" *See* Rule 1.0(f)
"Reasonably" *See* Rule 1.0(h)

### State Rules Comparison
http://ambar.org/MRPCStateCharts

# ANNOTATION
## *Paragraph (a): Duty to Keep Client Informed*
### OVERVIEW

As originally promulgated, Rule 1.4(a) simply stated that "[a] lawyer shall keep a client reasonably informed about the status of a matter and promptly comply with reasonable requests for information." Model Rule 1.4(a) (1983) [superseded]. In 2002, the rule was amended to identify five specific requirements. *See* American Bar Association, *A Legislative History: The Development of the ABA Model Rules of Professional Conduct, 1982–2013*, at 76–78 (2013).

The comment was amended in 2012 to make explicit that a lawyer should promptly acknowledge or respond to client communications through any medium, not just telephone calls as previously worded. *See* American Bar Association, *A Legislative History: The Development of the ABA Model Rules of Professional Conduct, 1982–2013*, at 79 (2013).

## *Paragraph (a)(1): Duty to Inform Client of Matters Requiring Client's Informed Consent*

Paragraph (a)(1) requires a lawyer to "promptly inform the client of any decision or circumstance with respect to which the client's informed consent, as defined in Rule 1.0(e), is required by these Rules." The rules specifically require a lawyer to obtain a client's informed consent in a variety of situations. For example, Rule 1.2(c) requires informed consent if a lawyer wants to limit the scope of representation. Most often, however, a client's informed consent is required when a lawyer seeks a waiver of duties relating to confidentiality and/or conflicts of interest. *E.g., Iowa Supreme Court Att'y Disciplinary Bd. v. Qualley*, 828 N.W.2d 282 (Iowa 2013) (collection lawyers failed to inform client of their conflict of interest); ABA Formal Ethics Op. 477R (2017) (informed consent regarding security precautions may be required for certain electronic communications). For a discussion of these situations, see the annotations to Rules 1.6, 1.7, 1.8, 1.9, 1.11, 1.12, 1.18, and 2.3.

## Paragraph (a)(2): Duty to Consult with Client about Means

Rule 1.4(a)(2) requires a lawyer to "reasonably consult with the client about the means by which the client's objectives are to be accomplished." This language is almost identical to that contained in Rule 1.2(a), which states that "as required by Rule 1.4, [a lawyer] shall consult with the client as to the means by which [the client's objectives] are to be pursued." Rule 1.4(a)(2), however, adds the word "reasonably," to preclude an interpretation that the lawyer would always be required to consult, even when a particular act is impliedly authorized. American Bar Association, *A Legislative History: The Development of the ABA Model Rules of Professional Conduct, 1982–2013*, at 77 (2013).

Some ethics opinions have concluded that under these rules, the "means" by which a representation is to be accomplished encompasses the personnel by whom it is to be accomplished if they include lawyers hired outside the firm, and that clients should be informed of such outsourcing. *See* ABA Formal Ethics Op. 08-451 (2008); N.C. Ethics Op. 2007-12 (2008); Ohio Ethics Op. 2009-6 (2009); Va. Ethics Op. 1850 (2010).

For discussion of a lawyer's duty to consult with a client regarding the means for pursuing the client's objectives, see the annotation to Rule 1.2.

## Paragraph (a)(3): Duty to Inform Clients of Status

Rule 1.4(a)(3) requires lawyers to keep clients informed about the status of their legal matters. *See People v. Carter*, 364 P.3d 1164 (Colo. O.P.D.J. 2015) (failing to notify client of withdrawal); *In re Kerr*, 805 S.E.2d 15 (Ga. 2017) (providing misleading information and failing to respond to client's inquiries); *In re Clothier*, 344 P.3d 370 (Kan. 2015) (failure to apprise client that estranged wife had moved to modify temporary orders in pending divorce); *In re Sarama*, 26 So. 3d 770 (La. 2010) (lawyer representing client in unpaid tax matter took $17,000 from client without informing him whether money was for payment of tax debt or fees); *Att'y Grievance Comm'n v. London*, 47 A.3d 986 (Md. 2012) (alleged difficulty in reaching client did not excuse failure to inform client of case's status); *In re Harris*, 868 A.2d 1011 (N.J. 2005) (failing to return client phone calls and otherwise ceasing communication for months at a time); *In re Howe*, 843 N.W.2d 325 (N.D. 2014) (failing to inform clients of deadlines, hearing dates, or costs and expenses); *Threadgill v. Bd. of Prof'l Responsibility*, 299 S.W.3d 792 (Tenn. 2009) (failing to keep client informed of status of negotiations with, and payments to, subrogees entitled to share of settlement proceeds); *In re Taylor*, 60 V.I. 356 (V.I. 2014) (ceasing to update clients on cases or respond to communications); *In re Gorokhovsky*, 824 N.W.2d 804 (Wis. 2012) (lawyer neither consulted with client before filing motion to modify sentence nor sought to withdraw motion after client objected); *Bd. of Prof'l Responsibility v. Allred*, 378 P.3d 594 (Wyo. 2016) (failed to answer client's telephone calls or respond to client's e-mails); ABA Formal Ethics Op. 483 (2018) (duty to inform client of data breach); Ga. Ethics Op. 16-1 (2016) (honoring one joint client's request to withhold certain information from other client is inconsistent with duty to keep clients informed); N.Y. City Ethics Op. 2017-5 (2017) (international border search or seizure of lawyer's electronic device containing confidential information requires notification to clients); N.Y. City Ethics Op. 2015-6 (2015) (accidental destruction of client files requires notification to clients); Ohio Ethics Op. 2010-6 (2010) (lawyer may not use comprehensive power of attorney in contingent-fee agreement to make decisions concerning all aspects of case, including settlement, and thereby avoid duty to communicate with client).

The lawyer must inform the client if the client's case has been dismissed. *See, e.g., People v. Nelson*, 40 P.3d 840 (Colo. O.P.D.J. 2002) (failing to inform clients that cases dismissed due to lawyer's failure to prosecute); *In re Ballew*, 695 S.E.2d 573 (Ga. 2010) (failing to inform client of settlement and dismissal of cases); *Idaho State Bar v. Souza*, 129 P.3d 1251 (Idaho 2006) (failure to tell client of filing personal injury suit three days after limitation period had run and consequent dismissal); *In re Ehrlich*, 351 P.3d 1268 (Kan. 2015) (failure to inform client that personal injury suit was dismissed for failure to serve defendant); *Ky. Bar Ass'n v. Bader*, 531 S.W.3d 20 (Ky. 2017) (failure to tell client case was dismissed after two years of inaction); *In re Elbert*, 698 So. 2d 949 (La. 1997) (failing to inform clients of dismissal resulting from failure to file case in proper venue and effect service within proper time limits); *Att'y Grievance Comm'n v. Williams*, 132 A.3d 232 (Md. 2016) (near complete failure to communicate with client, including informing her of case's dismissal with prejudice) *In re Zeitler*, 866 A.2d 171 (N.J. 2005) (repeatedly neglecting matters to point of dismissal and failing to inform clients); *see also In re Rosenthal*, 446 A.2d 1198 (N.J. 1982) (lawyer should inform client of imminent dismissal even if client has announced intention to no longer prosecute claim, as it is always possible for client to change mind).

## NOTIFICATION OF MATERIAL ERRORS REQUIRED

If a lawyer materially errs or fails to follow client instructions on a material matter, the rule requires the lawyer to inform the client. ABA Formal Ethics Op. 481 (2018). An error is "material," the opinion states, if it is "(a) reasonably likely to harm or prejudice a client; or (b) of such a nature that it would reasonably cause a client to consider terminating the representation even in the absence of harm or prejudice." The opinion goes on to explain that Rule 1.4 requires prompt notification of the client in case of a material error but imposes no such duty for former clients. *See* Colo. Ethics Op. 113 (2005) (must notify client of "material adverse developments, including those resulting from the lawyer's own errors"); Minn. Ethics Op. 21 (2009) (must inform client if lawyer's conduct in representation creates nonfrivolous potential malpractice claim); Mo. Informal Ethics Op. 2017-02 (n.d.) (must notify client of nonlawyer assistant's confidentiality breach); N.C. Ethics Op. 2015-4 (2015) (must disclose material errors).

Attempts to cover up the mistake compound the ethics violation. *See, e.g., People v. Belair*, 413 P.3d 357 (Colo. O.P.D.J. 2018) (sending client invoices and reports over fifteen-year period falsely stating that patent filings were "in good order" when lawyer never prepared some patent applications and abandoned others); *In re Schoeneman*, 891 A.2d 279 (D.C. 2006) (telling client that discrimination case was "fine" when in fact it had been dismissed); *In re Thomas*, 740 A.2d 538 (D.C. 1999) (misleading client into thinking her money was in escrow account and then ceasing to provide her with any information); *Fla. Bar v. Fredericks*, 731 So. 2d 1249 (Fla. 1999) (falsely telling client that lawsuit was filed and resolved in client's favor, when in fact no suit was filed); *In re Hagedorn*, 725 N.E.2d 397 (Ind. 2000) (failing to take steps to effectuate adoption and misleading clients about status of proceedings); *In re Hasty*, 227 P.3d 967 (Kan. 2010) (failing to tell client that file misplaced, discovery deadlines missed, and client's pleadings ordered stricken); *Att'y Grievance Comm'n v. Faber*, 817 A.2d 205 (Md. 2003) (falsely telling client her bankruptcy petition was filed); *In re Hyde*, 950 P.2d 806 (N.M. 1997) (neglecting client matters, misleading clients about status of case and work performed, failing to follow clients' instructions, and billing for work not done); *In re Brousseau*, 697 A.2d 1079 (R.I. 1997) (lawyer who disagreed with client's instructions to file partition suit ignored client's instructions and falsely stated that suit filed); *In re Stockholm*, 785 S.E.2d 361 (S.C. 2016) (misleading clients whose cases lawyer failed to have served within statute of limitations by telling them matters had settled).

For cases involving a lawyer's attempt to undo the damage resulting from the lawyer's own error through additional acts of misconduct, see *People v. Muhr*, 370 P.3d 677 (Colo. O.P.D.J. 2016) (failing to tell client of missed statute of limitations for filing suit, then misleading client into thinking case was settled by preparing false settlement statement and sending check from firm's operating account); *In re Thyden*, 877 A.2d 129 (D.C. 2005) (failing to tell client of sanction entered against client by bankruptcy court and appeal of sanction to district court); *Fla. Bar v. Bazley*, 597 So. 2d 796 (Fla. 1992) (failing to tell client claim barred by workers' compensation statute; falsely telling client lawyer filed and won civil action and was collecting judgment, advancing payments to client out of his own funds); *In re Mays*, 495 S.E.2d 30 (Ga. 1998) (falsely telling client that suit settled, when lawyer actually let statute of limitations run and used his own funds to pay purported settlement); and *In re Fontenot*, 230 So. 3d 185 (La. 2017) (settling case without telling clients, then lying about terms and paying out funds in excess of settlement from trust account).

### • Consultation with Ethics Counsel

A few authorities have addressed whether the ethical duty to keep a client reasonably informed extends to disclosing that the lawyer has consulted with his law firm's in-house ethics counsel on an issue of professional responsibility having to do with the client. *See, e.g., Garvy v. Seyfarth Shaw LLP*, 966 N.E.2d 523 (Ill. App. Ct. 2012) (Rule 1.4's disclosure requirements did not override law firm's expectation of confidentiality in communications with in-house ethics counsel); ABA Formal Ethics Op. 08-453 (2008) ("[c]ompliance with Rule 1.4 would not require the firm to reveal that its opinions and advice are the result of an ethics consultation"); N.Y. State Ethics Op. 789 (2005) (law firm need not disclose consultations with in-house ethics counsel on professional responsibility issue having to do with client).

### LAWYER MUST COMMUNICATE PROMPTLY

A lawyer must promptly convey important information about the client's matter. *See In re Banks*, No. 17-10456, 2018 WL 735351, 2018 BL 40262 (Bankr. W.D. La. Feb. 2, 2018) (waiting almost forty-five days after being retained to contact bankruptcy client, then failing to timely respond to calls or e-mails or inform client of dismissal of petition); *People v. Primavera*, 942 P.2d 496 (Colo. 1997) (waiting six months, until only nine days before scheduled hearing, before notifying incarcerated client of court appointment to represent him in dependency and neglect matter, then waiting three days before informing client of court order allowing children to return to home of client's former wife, whose boyfriend had allegedly molested them); *In re Baxter*, 940 P.2d 37 (Kan. 1997) (delaying informing client of agreement with adverse party to forgo part of attorneys' fee demand, for which lawyer sought reimbursement from client, and of settlement check having been received by firm and deposited into wrong account); *Att'y Grievance Comm'n v. Bellamy*, 162 A.3d 848 (Md. 2017) (delaying informing client of important proceedings until day before); *Cleveland Metro. Bar Ass'n v. Thomas*, 925 N.E.2d 959 (Ohio 2010) (delaying informing personal injury client of dismissal and denial of motions to vacate and reinstate); *State ex rel. Okla. Bar Ass'n v. Wilcox*, 227 P.3d 642 (Okla. 2009) (delaying notifying client of receipt of workers' compensation payments until after deadline to negotiate checks passed); ABA Formal Ethics Op. 481 (2018) (prompt notification of material error required); N.Y. City Ethics Op. 2017-2 (2017) (must inform client promptly on discovering another lawyer has fraudulently billed client so client may decide whether to provide informed consent to reporting misconduct); N.Y. City Ethics Op. 2015-3 (2015) (lawyer victimized by trust account e-mail scam must promptly notify affected clients); N.C. Ethics Op. 2015-4 (2015) (must promptly notify client of error that may have materially prejudiced client's interests); Or. Ethics Op. 2005-162 (2005) (union-member lawyer on strike must continue to keep employer-client promptly informed about developments in legal matters).

## SETTLEMENT OFFERS

Under Rule 1.2, whether to settle a matter is the client's decision. Thus, under both Rules 1.2 and 1.4, a lawyer must communicate a settlement offer unless the lawyer is aware from prior discussions that the client would reject the offer. *See Burton v. Mottolese*, 835 A.2d 998 (Conn. 2003) (failing to convey defendants' offers to waive claims for fees and costs and waive fees awarded defendants as sanctions in exchange for withdrawal of suit); *In re Steele*, 868 A.2d 146 (D.C. 2005) (failing to inform client of scheduled settlement conference and defendant's initial settlement offer); *In re Ballew*, 695 S.E.2d 573 (Ga. 2010) (failing to inform client of settlement offers lawyer accepted and consequent dismissal of cases); *Comm. on Prof'l Ethics v. Behnke*, 486 N.W.2d 275 (Iowa 1992) (handling client's personal injury claim by telephone, with only one subsequent meeting, and settling it without consulting client); *In re Elbert*, 698 So. 2d 949 (La. 1997) (failing to communicate settlement offer to clients); *Green v. Va. State Bar*, 677 S.E.2d 227 (Va. 2009) (making settlement offer without informing or getting authorization from clients); *In re Pfefer*, 344 P.3d 1200 (Wash. 2015) (failing to communicate settlement offer before statute of limitations lapsed); *cf. First Nat'l Bank of LaGrange v. Lowrey*, 872 N.E.2d 447 (Ill. App. Ct. 2007) (in legal malpractice case, lawyer breached standard of care by "failing to advise" of settlement offer; citing Rule 1.4).

In addition, a lawyer must tell the client enough about the circumstances of the offer so that the client may consider alternatives, including retaining other counsel or deciding not to go forward at all. *See, e.g., Rice v. Perl*, 320 N.W.2d 407 (Minn. 1982) (failing to disclose law firm's professional relationship with insurance claim adjuster responsible for settling client's claim); *Hartford Accident & Indem. Co. v. Foster*, 528 So. 2d 255 (Miss. 1988) (must fully explain all ramifications of any offer of settlement).

## CRIMINAL REPRESENTATION

A lawyer representing a criminal defendant has a duty under Rule 1.4 to promptly inform and consult with the client about issues over which a client has decision-making authority. The obligation is also a function of the defendant's constitutional rights. *See, e.g., Canaan v. McBride*, 395 F.3d 376 (7th Cir. 2005) (failing to inform defendant of right to testify at penalty phase of trial and so breaching constitutional "duties to consult with the defendant on important decisions and to keep the defendant informed of important developments"); *In re Wolfram*, 847 P.2d 94 (Ariz. 1993) (failing to consult with client about possibility of jury instruction on lesser-included offenses violated duty of communication as well as duty of diligence); *Helmedach v. Comm'r of Corr.*, 148 A.3d 1105 (Conn. App. Ct. 2016) (failing to inform defendant of favorable plea offer until after she took stand and spent two and one-half days testifying); *People v. Mena*, 792 N.E.2d 790 (Ill. App. Ct. 2003) (failing to perfect appeal, respond to client's letters, or apprise client of steps necessary to complete appeal); *Dew v. State*, 843 N.E.2d 556 (Ind. Ct. App. 2006) (failure to convey prosecution's plea agreement proposal amounts to ineffective assistance of counsel; citing Rule 1.4); *In re Longacre*, 122 P.3d 710 (Wash. 2005) (failing to discuss plea offers with client); *Lawyer Disciplinary Bd. v. Munoz*, 807 S.E.2d 290 (W. Va. 2017) (failure to communicate after court appointments to file habeas petitions); *Bd. of Prof'l Responsibility v. Powers*, 322 P.3d 1287 (Wyo. 2014) (failure to communicate with imprisoned client about post-conviction sentence modification motion); Va. Ethics Op. 1880 (2015) (must advise criminal defendant of appeal option even if lawyer believes frivolous); *cf. In re LaFont*, 898 So. 2d 339 (La. 2005) (Rule 1.4 required lawyer to communicate clearly that making plea agreement would not guarantee commutation of sentence). Also see the annotation to Rule 1.2.

## MISSING CLIENTS

Even when a lawyer loses track of a client, the duty to communicate important information persists and requires at least a reasonable effort to find the client to deliver the information. *See* Ariz. Ethics Op. 06-07 (2006) (duty to consult with client before settling matter persists even if client's whereabouts unknown); La. Ethics Op. 05-RPCC-001 (2005) (when closing practice, lawyer should send form letter to last known addresses of clients whose whereabouts unknown, notifying them of lawyer's termination of representation and of opportunity to obtain their files and property); Ohio Sup. Ct. Ethics Op. 2005-10 (2005) (before reporting client property to state as unclaimed, lawyer must make reasonable effort to contact client at last known address); S.C. Ethics Op. 98-07 (n.d.) (lawyer retained to pursue personal injury suit for missing client may not treat matter as terminated until he makes reasonable effort to locate client). Whether more is required after reasonable effort has failed to locate a client depends upon the information to be conveyed and the circumstances of the representation. *See, e.g., Burke v. Lewis*, 122 P.3d 533 (Utah 2005) (trial judge properly appointed lawyer to represent litigant whose whereabouts unknown, even though lawyer could not communicate with client); Alaska Ethics Op. 2004-3 (2004) (lawyer facing impending limitation deadline for client who cannot be located may file suit without express authorization if lawyer believes prior communications with client conferred implied authorization and failure to file would have material, adverse effect); N.Y. State Ethics Op. 787 (2005) (lawyer who jointly represents wife in personal injury claim and missing husband in loss of consortium claim may not settle wife's claim and thereby lose husband's claim without his consent; if husband cannot be found, lawyer must withdraw from both representations).

## DELAYING OR AVOIDING TELLING CLIENT

Comment [7] to Rule 1.4 suggests that "[i]n some circumstances, a lawyer may be justified in delaying transmission of information when the client would be likely to react imprudently to an immediate communication." The comment gives as an example the case of a lawyer withholding a client's psychiatric diagnosis if the examining psychiatrist indicates disclosure would be harmful to the client, but also states the lawyer may not withhold information merely to serve the interests or convenience of the lawyer or a third person. *See, e.g.*, D.C. Ethics Op. 327 (2005) (lawyer representing multiple defendants who all waived client-lawyer confidentiality vis-à-vis co-defendants may not withhold material information because one client later changes his mind); Ill. Ethics Op. 13-10 (2013) (although court rule forbids lawyer from giving incarcerated client copies of discovery obtained from prosecution, lawyer must discuss contents with client); N.D. Ethics Op. 97-12 (1997) (avoiding disclosing client's psychological records to client permissible if lawyer reasonably believes disclosure would result in substantial harm to client or others, but lawyer should urge client to discuss records directly with psychologist, with or without lawyer present); Va. Ethics Op. 1864 (2014) (criminal defense lawyer may agree with prosecutor that he may share but will not provide copies of discretionary discovery materials obtained from prosecution to client); *cf. Ill. State Bar Ass'n Mut. Ins. Co. v. Frank M. Greenfield & Assocs., P.C.*, 980 N.E.2d 1120 (Ill. App. Ct. 2012) (lawyer's malpractice insurance policy's clause requiring lawyer to obtain insurer's written consent before admitting liability to client was void as against public policy by interfering with lawyer's ethical obligation of disclosure).

Comment [7] also explains that a lawyer must comply with court rules or orders prohibiting disclosure, such as protective orders containing "attorneys' eyes only" restrictions, to a client. *E.g., Aging Backwards, LLC v. Esmonde-White*, No. 1:16-CV-20758, 2016 BL 318832 (S.D. Fla. Sept. 26, 2016); *Powell Mountain Energy, LLC v. Manalapan Land Co.*, Civ. No. 09-305-JBC, 2011 WL 3880512, 2011 BL 223860 (E.D. Ky. Aug. 31, 2011).

## COMMUNICATING THROUGH OTHERS

A lawyer may not delegate the ethical duty to communicate with a client, although subordinates may assist in client communication with proper supervision. Rule 5.3 (Responsibilities Regarding Nonlawyer Assistance). *E.g., In re Reger*, 421 P.3d 25 (Alaska 2018) (inadequate supervision of nonlawyer assistant, who failed to communicate with clients); *In re Galbasini*, 786 P.2d 971 (Ariz. 1990) (failure to supervise nonlawyer employees and consequently "had no idea who his clients were"); *Mays v. Neal*, 938 S.W.2d 830 (Ark. 1997) (lawyer delegated all contact with client to nonlawyer assistant, never met or spoke with client despite client's requests, settled case without seeking client's approval, and never informed client of receipt of settlement check); *In re Francis*, 137 A.3d 187 (D.C. 2016) (local counsel who was sole counsel of record had duty to keep client informed of litigation status, either personally or by informing lead counsel); *Fla. Bar v. Glueck*, 985 So. 2d 1052 (Fla. 2008) (allowing nonlawyer employees of immigration consulting firm with which his firm shared office to conduct most client communications); *In re Hamer*, 808 S.E.2d 647 (Ga. 2017) (delegating communication with clients to nonlawyer assistant without proper supervision); *In re Farmer*, 950 P.2d 713 (Kan. 1997) (failing to return calls or inform clients of court orders and instructing nonlawyer staff to "handle" client phone calls); *Att'y Grievance Comm'n v. Kimmel*, 955 A.2d 269 (Md. 2008) (law firm partners failed to respond to inquiries of client whose case assigned to out-of-state associate); Iowa Ethics Op. 13-02 (2013) (lawyer sponsoring out-of-state lawyer for pro hac vice admission may not delegate responsibilities to communicate with and educate client to out-of-state lawyer); Mich. Informal Ethics Op. RI-349 (2010) (lawyer may direct nonlawyer assistant to communicate with client if lawyer properly trains and supervises assistant); N.H. Ethics Op. 2009-10/2 (2010) (lawyer may communicate with client through qualified, impartial interpreter); Utah Ethics Op. 17-04 (2017) (lawyer acting as local counsel must ensure communication requirements of Rule 1.4 are met).

Similarly, a lawyer risks violating Rule 1.4 by communicating with a third party instead of directly with the client. *See, e.g., People v. Rivers*, 933 P.2d 6 (Colo. 1997) (lawyer hired by client's girlfriend to represent client, then subsequently fired by girlfriend, had duty to notify client to determine whether he still wanted lawyer to represent him); *Machado v. Statewide Grievance Comm.*, 890 A.2d 622 (Conn. App. Ct. 2006) (lawyer who communicated with incarcerated client through client's business partner failed to inform client after business partner terminated representation); *In re Dreier*, 671 A.2d 455 (D.C. 1996) (relying on intermediary to communicate with client); *Fla. Bar v. Jasperson*, 625 So. 2d 459 (Fla. 1993) (lawyer retained by wife to handle joint bankruptcy never met with husband yet prepared and filed joint petition, depriving husband of right to make informed decision); *In re Howe*, 843 N.W.2d 325 (N.D. 2014) (blaming failure to inform immigration clients of rescheduled hearing date on unavailability of their daughter, who acted as translator); *cf. Att'y Grievance Comm'n v. Lee*, 890 A.2d 273 (Md. 2006) (lawyer who had difficulty communicating directly with imprisoned client, and who previously communicated with client's mother, disciplined for failing to continue communication through mother).

## WHEN LAWYER LEAVES FIRM OR PRACTICE OF LAW

Lawyers who cease practicing law must notify their clients. *See, e.g., People v. Martin*, 223 P.3d 728 (Colo. O.P.D.J. 2009) (ceasing to respond to client communications and abandoning practice); *In re Cohen*, 612 S.E.2d 294 (Ga. 2005) (lawyer living in Florida failed to tell Georgia client he adopted inactive status in Georgia and then failed to appear at arraignment); *In re Ragland*, 697 N.E.2d 44 (Ind. 1998) (failing to inform client he was suspended from practice); *In re Hughes*, 874 So. 2d 746 (La. 2004) (continuing to accept new clients and demand retainers just days before assuming office as judge); *In re Orren*, 590 N.W.2d 127 (Minn. 1999) (abandoning law practice without notifying clients); *Disciplinary Counsel v. Bellew*, 97 N.E.3d 438 (Ohio 2017) (failing to tell client of suspension from law practice); *In re Wickersham*, 310 P.3d 1237 (Wash. 2013) (leaving state and abandoning practice without notifying clients); *Lawyer Disciplinary Bd. v. Sirk*, 810 S.E.2d 276 (W. Va. 2018) (failing to tell bankruptcy client lawyer had closed office and no longer had bankruptcy software access or electronic filing capability); La. Ethics Op. 05-RPCC-001 (2005) (lawyer closing practice must inform all clients in time to allow them to hire new counsel).

Similarly, lawyers have a duty to inform their clients if they will be leaving their firms or their practices, so that clients have the opportunity to choose between following the lawyer or remaining with the firm. *See, e.g.,* ABA Formal Ethics Op. 99-414 (1999) (lawyer responsible for client's matter and remaining members of law firm must ensure client is timely informed of lawyer's impending departure); Ariz. Ethics Op. 10-02 (2010) (lawyer with significant substantive involvement in matter must notify client of impending firm departure so client may choose who will continue representation); Colo. Ethics Op. 116 (2007) (both departing lawyer and firm must notify clients of lawyer's departure, preferably jointly); Ky. Ethics Op. E-424 (2005) (lawyer departing firm must inform clients in whose representation lawyer played significant role); Mo. Informal Ethics Op. 970197 (n.d.) (lawyer must give notice of departure to clients with whom lawyer had significant contact); Neb. Ethics Op. 13-03 (2013) (lawyer selling practice to other firm lawyers should notify clients); Pa.-Phila. Joint Formal Ethics Op. 2007-300 (2007) (both departing lawyer and firm must notify clients of lawyer's departure; joint notice preferable); R.I. Ethics Op. 2003-07 (2003); S.C. Ethics Op. 97-30 (1997); *see also* D.C. Ethics Op. 221 (1991) (law firm may not restrict departing lawyer's right to send departure announcements to clients and may not restrict lawyer's responses to client inquiries about departure); *cf. Feldman & Pinto, P.C. v. Seithel*, Civ. No. 11-5400, 2011 WL 6758460, 2011 BL 324804 (E.D. Pa. Dec. 22, 2011) (lawyer's letter stating she "left" firm and inviting clients to sign forms indicating choice of law firm was misleading, as she was fired); Phila. Ethics Op. 2013-4 (2013) (law firm's bounce-back message responding to e-mails sent to former partner must include former partner's new contact information). *But see* Conn. Informal Ethics Op. 00-25 (2000) (lawyer may—but is not required to—notify clients of pending departure from firm); Ill. Ethics Op. 12-14 (2012) (associate lawyer has no duty to notify clients before leaving firm unless associate's involvement in matters substantial enough that his departure might reasonably affect clients' decisions); Ohio Sup. Ct. Ethics Op. 98-5 (1998) (lawyer may notify clients he is leaving firm and indicate willingness to provide legal services). For discussion of a lawyer's duty to notify clients when withdrawing from representation, see the annotation to Rule 1.16. For discussion of a lawyer's duties when departing a law firm, see *ABA/BNA Lawyers' Manual on Professional Conduct*, "Types of Practice: Private Firm: Withdrawal and Termination," pp. 91:701 *et seq.*

## Paragraph (a)(4): Duty to Comply Promptly with Reasonable Requests for Information

A lawyer must promptly comply with a client's reasonable requests for information. *See People v. Carter*, 364 P.3d 1164 (Colo. O.P.D.J. 2015) (failing to respond to client's letters requesting information); *In re Benge*, 783 A.2d 1279 (Del. 2001) (lawyer who drafted trust document that required lawyer's consent to amendments to document failed to respond to client's phone calls and letters seeking lawyer's consent); *In re Bernstein*, 707 A.2d 371 (D.C. 1998) (failing to inform clients lawsuit filed on their behalf until lawyer discharged, eighteen months after filing); *Fla. Bar v. Flowers*, 672 So. 2d 526 (Fla. 1996) (failing to respond to client's questions about orders to show cause in guardianship case); *In re Wenger*, 112 P.3d 199 (Kan. 2005) (repeated failure to return phone calls from clients seeking information); *Ky. Bar Ass'n v. Hines*, 399 S.W.3d 750 (Ky. 2013) (failing to respond to letters from corporate client's representatives); *In re Swafford*, 238 So. 3d 957 (La. 2018) (failure to respond to client's requests for information); *Att'y Grievance Comm'n v. Narasimhan*, 92 A.3d 512 (Md. 2014) (failing to respond to immigration clients' requests for information, then forwarding them to associate, who responded inadequately); *In re Saltzstein*, 896 N.W.2d 864 (Minn. 2018) (failure to respond to clients' inquiries or provide copy of retainer agreement, accounting for funds delivered or services rendered, or client's file); *Cleveland Metro. Bar Ass'n v. Fonda*, 7 N.E.3d 1164 (Ohio 2014) (failure to correct client's clear belief that he was proceeding on matter outside scope of engagement letter); *State ex rel. Okla. Bar Ass'n v. Bradley*, 338 P.3d 629 (Okla. 2014) (failure to provide statements for services performed, refunds, and case files); *Garland v. Bd. of Prof'l Responsibility*, 536 S.W.3d 811 (Tenn. 2017) (failing to respond to client's reasonable requests for information as result of delegating client communication to staff); *Robinson v. Va. State Bar*, No. 151501, 2016 WL 3208972, 2016 BL 155283 (Va. Apr. 14, 2016) (failure to provide client with billing statements); *cf.* ABA Formal Ethics Op. 471 (2015) (discussing duty to provide former client with documents on request even if already provided to client during representation).

However, a lawyer's failure to respond to every request does not necessarily violate the rule. *See, e.g., In re Schoeneman*, 777 A.2d 259 (D.C. 2001) (failure to return client's phone calls for three weeks did not violate Rule 1.4 because client and lawyer spoke monthly and lawyer regularly informed client of his activities); *cf. Lawyer Disciplinary Bd. v. Chittum*, 689 S.E.2d 811 (W. Va. 2010) (no violation for failure to return client's calls placed after representation had ended).

## Paragraph (a)(5): Duty to Consult with Client about Ethical and Legal Limitations on Lawyer's Conduct

Paragraph (a)(5) of Rule 1.4 was formerly Rule 1.2(e). It was moved in 2002 in accordance with the decision to consolidate rules imposing duties of communication with a client in Rule 1.4. American Bar Association, *A Legislative History: The Development of the ABA Model Rules of Professional Conduct, 1982–2013*, at 77 (2013). If a lawyer perceives the client expects assistance that would be unethical or illegal for the lawyer to provide, the rule requires the lawyer to inform the client of the limitations on the lawyer's conduct. *See In re Marshall*, 680 N.E.2d 1098 (Ind. 1997) (agreeing to represent client in out-of-state matter, but failing to inform client he was not licensed to practice law in that state); *In re Breslin*, 793 A.2d 645 (N.J. 2002) (failing to explain to former client lawyer would not participate in illegal scheme when former client presented him with envelope containing son's résumé and bundles of money for delivery to police commissioner); ABA Formal Ethics Op. 08-453 (2008) (if firm's ethics counsel concludes lawyer's proposed conduct in representation would violate ethics rules, then that "requires an explanation to the client of the possible consequences of the proposed action"); Conn. Informal Op. 2013-02 (2013) (when providing advice regarding marijuana business activities permissible under state law, lawyer should advise client of restrictions on lawyer's ability to assist client in conduct that violates federal law); Mo. Informal Ethics Op. 2014-04 (n.d.) (must advise client setting up business to produce and distribute federally controlled substance of limitations on lawyer's actions); *cf. People v. Doherty*, 945 P.2d 1380 (Colo. 1997) (lawyer should have responded to client's creation of false evidence by informing him of ethical problem it caused instead of neglecting case and ceasing communication).

### Paragraph (b): Duty to Explain Matters to Client

Rule 1.4(b) requires a lawyer to explain a matter to a client to the extent reasonably necessary for the client to make informed decisions concerning the representation. *See Iowa Supreme Court Att'y Disciplinary Bd. v. Qualley*, 828 N.W.2d 282 (Iowa 2013) (collection lawyers failed to provide homeowners association client with material information concerning association's interest in bidding at sheriff's sale); *Ky. Bar Ass'n v. Helmers*, 353 S.W.3d 599 (Ky. 2011) (failing to inform mass tort clients of aggregate settlement terms before obtaining signed releases); *Att'y Grievance Comm'n v. Aita*, 181 A.3d 774 (Md. 2018) (sending letter in English, which client could not read or write, stating "[i]f you do not understand this document . . . it is your responsibility to have it translated" did not permit client to make informed decision); *Att'y Grievance Comm'n v. Framm*, 144 A.3d 827 (Md. 2016) (failing to provide mentally impaired client with written explanation of advice); *In re Marshall*, 157 P.3d 859 (Wash. 2007) (filing appeal of dismissal of several clients' claims without first consulting or explaining action to clients; Rule 1.4(b) requires "more than mailing the notice of appeal to the client after the fact"); D.C. Ethics Op. 373 (2017) (appointed criminal defense lawyer must explain scope of representation to defendant, including matters excluded); N.Y. City Ethics Op. 2017-7 (2017) (lawyer may take into consideration joint clients' sophistication and experience in deciding whether particular disclosure or explanation is required); Pa. Ethics Op. 2011-010 (2011) (lawyer who received inadvertently sent e-mail from opposing party or counsel must "advise the client of the nature of the information, if not the specific content"); Va. Ethics Op. 1872 (2013) (lawyer conducting virtual law practice may not fulfill communication duties by merely uploading information to client but must obtain confirmation that client understands advice given). *But see Att'y Grievance Comm'n v. Rand*, 57 A.3d 976 (Md. 2012) (lawyer who advised client at initial meeting of consequences of failing to file employment grievance did not violate Rule 1.4 by not reiterating advice over three-year period).

Accordingly, a lawyer must explain the legal effect of entering an agreement or executing a legal document, including the risks, benefits, and alternatives. *See, e.g.,* *In re Morse*, 470 S.E.2d 232 (Ga. 1996) (asking client to sign settlement agreement without explaining its legal effect); *In re Ragland*, 697 N.E.2d 44 (Ind. 1998) (failing to explain impact of settlement and indemnity agreement); *In re Flack*, 33 P.3d 1281 (Kan. 2001) (failing to meet individually with clients to explain estate plans and relying upon nonlawyer staff to explain plans to clients); *Hodges v. Reasonover*, 103 So. 3d 1069 (La. 2012) (failing to disclose effects of mandatory arbitration clause in engagement agreement); *In re Fett*, 790 N.W.2d 840 (Minn. 2010) (advising agent under power of attorney to transfer principal's assets to himself without discussing prohibition on self-dealing); *In re Hall*, 329 P.3d 870 (Wash. 2014) (failing to explain conflict of interest and potential adverse consequences of lawyer's being made client's trustee); *In re Winkel*, 577 N.W.2d 9 (Wis. 1998) (failing to inform clients about risk of criminal prosecution if clients surrendered business assets to bank and law firm without arranging to pay subcontractor bills); ABA Formal Ethics Op. 02-425 (2002) (must explain advantages and disadvantages of arbitration clause in proposed fee agreement to client, including that arbitration normally results in client's waiver of significant rights, such as right to jury trial, broad discovery, and appeal); Me. Ethics Op. 202 (2011) (must discuss with client potential effects of jury waiver clause in engagement agreement); Mo. Informal Ethics Op. 2014-04 (n.d.) (must advise client setting up business to produce and distribute federally controlled substance of inconsistencies between state and federal law); N.H. Ethics Op. 2008-09/1 (2009) (lawyer who drafts will or trust naming lawyer as fiduciary must "frankly discuss all available options pertaining to the selection of fiduciaries"); Ohio Sup. Ct. Ethics Op. 2012-3 (2012) (lawyer who mentions or whose client asks about alternative litigation financing must explain risks and benefits of such arrangements); Phila. Ethics Op. 2013-8 (2014) (lawyer should discuss impact of litigation funding arrangement and alternatives with client before making referral); Tex. Ethics Op. 586 (2008) (lawyer must explain significant risks and benefits of binding arbitration clause in retainer agreement). For discussion of a lawyer's duty to explain fee agreements to clients, see the annotation to Rule 1.5.

When a lawyer is aware of facts suggesting a client's objectives in a transaction are at risk, the lawyer must apprise the client of those facts and their legal implications so the client can make an informed decision about alternative courses of action. *See In re Sullivan*, 727 A.2d 832 (Del. 1999) (lawyer whose failure to file brief resulted in dismissal of appeal sent letter to client more than a year later, informing her there were "no claims pending" in her case); *Stephen v. Sallaz & Gatewood, Chtd.*, 248 P.3d 1256 (Idaho 2011) (failing to inform client of her husband's significantly higher property valuation before finalizing property settlement); *In re Cable*, 715 N.E.2d 396 (Ind. 1999) (failing to tell client he was too busy to handle appeal); *Att'y Grievance Comm'n v. Cassidy*, 766 A.2d 632 (Md. 2001) (lawyer hired to draft and record deed failed to tell client he was suspended, which was vital information because law requires certification by lawyer to record deed); *In re Howe*, 626 N.W.2d 650 (N.D. 2001) (failing to tell client lawyer was not following through on reducing award to judgment, so client, who was seeking loan with favorable interest rate, could not make informed decision to secure replacement counsel before interest rate increased); Ariz. Ethics Op. 97-6 (1997) (criminal defense lawyer whose client enters cooperation agreement with law enforcement agencies must fully advise client of real-world consequences of such cooperation, including fact that agencies did not have resources to protect client or his family); Mass. Ethics Op. 09-03 (2009) (lawyer jointly representing employer and employee in immigration matter must inform both if employment authorization revoked); *cf. State ex rel. Okla. Bar Ass'n v. Helton*, 394 P.3d 227 (Okla. 2017) (lawyer "technically" violated Rule 1.4 in failing to reduce terms of business transaction with client to writing, advise client to seek advice of independent counsel, or obtain client's written informed consent, even though evidence showed client was fully informed and agreed to terms); ABA Formal Ethics Op. 465 (2013) (lawyer offering coupon deal must explain whether additional services beyond those included in deal will be necessary to achieve client's objective).

## Rule 1.5

*Fees*

(a) A lawyer shall not make an agreement for, charge, or collect an unreasonable fee or an unreasonable amount for expenses. The factors to be considered in determining the reasonableness of a fee include the following:

(1) the time and labor required, the novelty and difficulty of the questions involved, and the skill requisite to perform the legal service properly;

(2) the likelihood, if apparent to the client, that the acceptance of the particular employment will preclude other employment by the lawyer;

(3) the fee customarily charged in the locality for similar legal services;

(4) the amount involved and the results obtained;

(5) the time limitations imposed by the client or by the circumstances;

(6) the nature and length of the professional relationship with the client;

(7) the experience, reputation, and ability of the lawyer or lawyers performing the services; and

(8) whether the fee is fixed or contingent.

(b) The scope of the representation and the basis or rate of the fee and expenses for which the client will be responsible shall be communicated to the client, preferably in writing, before or within a reasonable time after commencing the representation, except when the lawyer will charge a regularly represented client on the same basis or rate. Any changes in the basis or rate of the fee or expenses shall also be communicated to the client.

(c) A fee may be contingent on the outcome of the matter for which the service is rendered, except in a matter in which a contingent fee is prohibited by paragraph (d) or other law. A contingent fee agreement shall be in a writing signed by the client and shall state the method by which the fee is to be determined, including the percentage or percentages that shall accrue to the lawyer in the event of settlement, trial or appeal; litigation and other expenses to be deducted from the recovery; and whether such expenses are to be deducted before or after the contingent fee is calculated. The agreement must clearly notify the client of any expenses for which the client will be liable whether or not the client is the prevailing party. Upon conclusion of a contingent fee matter, the lawyer shall provide the client with a written statement stating the outcome of the matter and, if there is a recovery, showing the remittance to the client and the method of its determination.

(d) A lawyer shall not enter into an arrangement for, charge, or collect:

(1) any fee in a domestic relations matter, the payment or amount of which is contingent upon the securing of a divorce or upon the amount of alimony or support, or property settlement in lieu thereof; or

(2) a contingent fee for representing a defendant in a criminal case.

(e) A division of a fee between lawyers who are not in the same firm may be made only if:

(1) the division is in proportion to the services performed by each lawyer or each lawyer assumes joint responsibility for the representation;

(2) the client agrees to the arrangement, including the share each lawyer will receive, and the agreement is confirmed in writing; and

(3) the total fee is reasonable.

## COMMENT

### Reasonableness of Fee and Expenses

[1] Paragraph (a) requires that lawyers charge fees that are reasonable under the circumstances. The factors specified in (1) through (8) are not exclusive. Nor will each factor be relevant in each instance. Paragraph (a) also requires that expenses for which the client will be charged must be reasonable. A lawyer may seek reimbursement for the cost of services performed in-house, such as copying, or for other expenses incurred in-house, such as telephone charges, either by charging a reasonable amount to which the client has agreed in advance or by charging an amount that reasonably reflects the cost incurred by the lawyer.

### Basis or Rate of Fee

[2] When the lawyer has regularly represented a client, they ordinarily will have evolved an understanding concerning the basis or rate of the fee and the expenses for which the client will be responsible. In a new client-lawyer relationship, however, an understanding as to fees and expenses must be promptly established. Generally, it is desirable to furnish the client with at least a simple memorandum or copy of the lawyer's customary fee arrangements that states the general nature of the legal

services to be provided, the basis, rate or total amount of the fee and whether and to what extent the client will be responsible for any costs, expenses or disbursements in the course of the representation. A written statement concerning the terms of the engagement reduces the possibility of misunderstanding.

[3] Contingent fees, like any other fees, are subject to the reasonableness standard of paragraph (a) of this Rule. In determining whether a particular contingent fee is reasonable, or whether it is reasonable to charge any form of contingent fee, a lawyer must consider the factors that are relevant under the circumstances. Applicable law may impose limitations on contingent fees, such as a ceiling on the percentage allowable, or may require a lawyer to offer clients an alternative basis for the fee. Applicable law also may apply to situations other than a contingent fee, for example, government regulations regarding fees in certain tax matters.

## Terms of Payment

[4] A lawyer may require advance payment of a fee, but is obliged to return any unearned portion. See Rule 1.16(d). A lawyer may accept property in payment for services, such as an ownership interest in an enterprise, providing this does not involve acquisition of a proprietary interest in the cause of action or subject matter of the litigation contrary to Rule 1.8(i). However, a fee paid in property instead of money may be subject to the requirements of Rule 1.8(a) because such fees often have the essential qualities of a business transaction with the client.

[5] An agreement may not be made whose terms might induce the lawyer improperly to curtail services for the client or perform them in a way contrary to the client's interest. For example, a lawyer should not enter into an agreement whereby services are to be provided only up to a stated amount when it is foreseeable that more extensive services probably will be required, unless the situation is adequately explained to the client. Otherwise, the client might have to bargain for further assistance in the midst of a proceeding or transaction. However, it is proper to define the extent of services in light of the client's ability to pay. A lawyer should not exploit a fee arrangement based primarily on hourly charges by using wasteful procedures.

## Prohibited Contingent Fees

[6] Paragraph (d) prohibits a lawyer from charging a contingent fee in a domestic relations matter when payment is contingent upon the securing of a divorce or upon the amount of alimony or support or property settlement to be obtained. This provision does not preclude a contract for a contingent fee for legal representation in connection with the recovery of post-judgment balances due under support, alimony or other financial orders because such contracts do not implicate the same policy concerns.

## Division of Fee

[7] A division of fee is a single billing to a client covering the fee of two or more lawyers who are not in the same firm. A division of fee facilitates association of more than one lawyer in a matter in which neither alone could serve the client as well, and

most often is used when the fee is contingent and the division is between a referring lawyer and a trial specialist. Paragraph (e) permits the lawyers to divide a fee either on the basis of the proportion of services they render or if each lawyer assumes responsibility for the representation as a whole. In addition, the client must agree to the arrangement, including the share that each lawyer is to receive, and the agreement must be confirmed in writing. Contingent fee agreements must be in a writing signed by the client and must otherwise comply with paragraph (c) of this Rule. Joint responsibility for the representation entails financial and ethical responsibility for the representation as if the lawyers were associated in a partnership. A lawyer should only refer a matter to a lawyer whom the referring lawyer reasonably believes is competent to handle the matter. See Rule 1.1.

[8] Paragraph (e) does not prohibit or regulate division of fees to be received in the future for work done when lawyers were previously associated in a law firm.

## Disputes over Fees

[9] If a procedure has been established for resolution of fee disputes, such as an arbitration or mediation procedure established by the bar, the lawyer must comply with the procedure when it is mandatory, and, even when it is voluntary, the lawyer should conscientiously consider submitting to it. Law may prescribe a procedure for determining a lawyer's fee, for example, in representation of an executor or administrator, a class or a person entitled to a reasonable fee as part of the measure of damages. The lawyer entitled to such a fee and a lawyer representing another party concerned with the fee should comply with the prescribed procedure.

### Definitional Cross-References
"Confirmed in writing" *See* Rule 1.0(b)
"Firm" *See* Rule 1.0(c)
"Writing" and "Written" and "Signed" *See* Rule 1.0(n)

### State Rules Comparison
http://ambar.org/MRPCStateCharts

## ANNOTATION

### Paragraph (a): Reasonable Fees and Expenses

Rule 1.5(a) as first promulgated in 1983 affirmatively required a lawyer's fee to be "reasonable." The current phrasing prohibiting "unreasonable" fees harks back to the predecessor Model Code and was restored in 2002 on the theory that the new wording had been making it "harder than necessary to impose discipline for excessive fees." American Bar Association, *A Legislative History: The Development of the ABA Model Rules of Professional Conduct, 1982–2013,* at 97 (2013) (rephrasing not intended as substantive change). *See Restatement (Third) of the Law Governing Lawyers* § 34 (2000) (prohibiting lawyer from charging fee "larger than is reasonable under the circumstances"). *See generally* Gabriel J. Chin & Scott C. Wells, *Can a Reasonable Doubt Have an Unreasonable Price? Limitations on Attorneys' Fees in Criminal Cases,* 41 B.C. L. Rev.

1 (Dec. 1999) (finding only two cases imposing discipline based solely upon size of fee, authors conclude that "virtually all" applications of Rule 1.5(a) also involve dishonesty or misconduct; authors propose disclosure standard instead); Alex B. Long, *Attorney-Client Fee Agreements That Offend Public Policy*, 61 S.C. L. Rev. 287 (Winter 2009); Ankur Parekh & Jay R. Pelkofer, *Lawyers, Ethics, and Fees: Getting Paid Under Model Rule 1.5*, 16 Geo. J. Legal Ethics 767 (Summer 2003); *ABA/BNA Lawyers' Manual on Professional Conduct*, "Fees: Amount of Fee," pp. 41:301 *et seq.*

The 2002 amendment also prohibits unreasonable expenses. *See* American Bar Association, *A Legislative History: The Development of the ABA Model Rules of Professional Conduct, 1982–2013*, at 97 (2013).

## FACTORS TO CONSIDER

Paragraph (a) lists eight factors to be considered, if relevant, in assessing a fee's reasonableness. Comment [1] emphasizes that these factors "are not exclusive. Nor will each factor be relevant in each instance." For additional factors that courts have considered in the context of either a disciplinary proceeding or a prevailing party's recovery of fees pursuant to contract (as opposed to recovery of fees pursuant to statute, which is discussed below), see *In re Estate of Johnson*, 119 P.3d 425 (Alaska 2005) (in estate context, trial court may also consider size of estate insofar as it affects lawyer's exposure to liability); *Corbello v. Iowa Prod.*, 850 So. 2d 686 (La. 2003) (lists ten factors "derived from" Rule 1.5: result obtained, responsibility incurred, importance of litigation, amount of money involved, extent and character of work performed, number of appearances made, intricacies of facts involved, counsel's diligence and skill, court's own knowledge, and counsel's legal knowledge, attainment, and skill); *Mani v. Mani*, 869 A.2d 904 (N.J. 2005) (in addition to requiring affidavit of reasonableness under Rule 1.5(a), court awarding fees in divorce will consider parties' relative financial status and good or bad faith in conduct of action, but may not consider underlying issue of marital fault); and *In re Egger*, 98 P.3d 477 (Wash. 2004) (additional factor is "[w]hether the fee agreement or confirming writing demonstrates that the client had received a reasonable and fair disclosure of material elements of the fee agreement and of the lawyer's billing practices"). *Cf. Shaffer v. Superior Court*, 39 Cal. Rptr. 2d 506 (Ct. App. 1995) (size of lawyer's profit margin not appropriate factor in evaluating fee); *In re Hoffman*, 834 N.W.2d 636 (N.D. 2013) (criminal defense lawyer's nonrefundable minimum fee of $30,000 was reasonable in light of red flags, including lawyer's concern that client, who just fired first lawyer, would be switching lawyers again to get another continuance). Comm. on Lawyer Bus. Ethics, ABA Section of Bus. Law, Report, *Business and Ethics Implications of Alternative Billing Practices*, 54 Bus. Law. 175 (Nov. 1998) (recommending two additional factors: size and complexity of matter, and client's experience and sophistication in business matters).

The court determining a fee's reasonableness may not ignore particular factors if they are relevant. *See, e.g., Schumacher v. AK Steel Corp. Ret. Accumulation Pension Plan*, 995 F. Supp. 2d 835 (S.D. Ohio 2014) (contingency risk alone will not justify enhancement); *Rodriguez v. Ancona*, 868 A.2d 807 (Conn. App. Ct. 2005) (by looking solely to amount involved and results obtained in fixing fees as percentage of damage award, court abused discretion by "seizing from the full panoply of relevant factors merely one factor, to the exclusion and disregard of the others"); *Heng v. Rotech Med. Corp.*, 720 N.W.2d 54 (N.D. 2006) (all reasonableness factors must be considered; no single factor controls; *see also Microtek Med., Inc. v. 3M Co.*, 942 So. 2d 122 (Miss. 2006) (upholding fee award of more than $223,000; trial court painstakingly addressed factors listed in Rule 1.5(a) before finding fee reasonable in light of case's difficulty and lawyer's skill and lost opportunity costs).

## STATUTORY FEE AWARDS

Decisions in statutory fee award cases must be considered separately from fee decisions in other contexts; they are distinguished by the much greater emphasis on degree of success, and by the much greater judicial discretion involved. *See Perdue v. Kenny A.*, 559 U.S. 542 (2010) (superior performance can be basis for enhancing attorneys' fees award under federal fee-shifting statute in civil rights case in extraordinary circumstances); *Noel v. Ribbits*, No. WWMCV084007022S, 2012 WL 1511377 (Conn. Super. Ct. Apr. 4, 2012) (public policy favors court's exercise of discretion to award substantial fees when cases involve "small sums and large principles" (quoting *Rodriguez v. Ancona*, 868 A.2d 807 (Conn. App. Ct. 2005))).

When awarding statutory fees "the primary concern . . . is that the fee awarded be reasonable, that is, one that is adequately compensatory to attract competent counsel yet which avoids producing a windfall for lawyers." *Huizinga v. Genzink Steel Supply & Welding Co.*, 984 F. Supp. 2d 741 (W.D. Mich. 2013).

In the vast majority of fee-award cases the court uses the "lodestar" approach, which multiplies the number of hours the prevailing party's lawyer reasonably expended by a reasonable hourly billing rate set with reference to the prevailing market rate. *Kalloo v. Unlimited Mech. Co. of NY, Inc.*, 977 F. Supp. 2d 209 (E.D.N.Y. 2013) ("reasonable hourly rate" is what paying client would be willing to pay; court should approximate market rates prevailing in community for similar services by lawyers of reasonably comparable skill, experience, and reputation).

The court then considers the Rule 1.5(a) "reasonableness" factors to the extent they have not already been subsumed in the lodestar calculation. *Blum v. Stenson*, 465 U.S. 886 (1984); *see Speicher v. Columbia Twp. Bd. of Election Comm'rs*, 832 N.W.2d 392 (Mich. Ct. App. 2012) (public policy expressed in Rule 1.5(a) extends to all situations in which fees sought, including plaintiff's counsel's Open Meetings Act claim against defendants for plaintiff's "actual" attorneys' fees). In statutory fee cases the most important of these is the degree of success. *See Dajbabic v. Rick's Café*, 995 F. Supp. 2d 210 (E.D.N.Y. 2014). The court may then consider factors not enumerated in Rule 1.5(a); these usually include the case's "undesirability" and the size of awards in similar cases. *See Carter v. Caleb Brett LLC*, 757 F.3d 866 (9th Cir. 2014); *Johnson v. Ga. Highway Express, Inc.*, 488 F.2d 714 (5th Cir. 1974). The court may then make a percentage reduction, although it is preferable to adjust the hours or rate at the first step rather than to adjust the lodestar. *Fischer v. SJB-P.D. Inc.*, 214 F.3d 1115 (9th Cir. 2000). When a court makes only a small adjustment to a fee request it need give only a brief explanation; the court may reduce the figure by up to 10 percent (a "haircut") purely as an exercise of its discretion. *Gonzales v. City of Maywood*, 729 F.3d 1196 (9th Cir. 2013).

## ILLEGALITY

Illegal conduct in setting or seeking a fee violates Rule 1.5(a). *See, e.g., In re Bach*, 966 A.2d 350 (D.C. 2009) (accepting fees from estate without filing required petition); *Iowa Supreme Court Bd. of Prof'l Ethics & Conduct v. McKittrick*, 683 N.W.2d 554 (Iowa 2004) (compounding interest and imposing it before charges billed); *Att'y Grievance Comm'n v. Somerville*, 842 A.2d 811 (Md. 2004) (taking $1,000 from estate checking account amounted to collection of unreasonable fee, as well as crime); *In re Zak*, 73 N.E.3d 262 (Mass. 2017) (charging advance fees for mortgage assistance relief services when doing so is prohibited by federal and state law); *State ex rel. Okla. Bar Ass'n v. Gassaway*, 196 P.3d 495 (Okla. 2008) (attempt to trade legal services for sexual favors violated, among other rules, Rule 1.5); *see also In re Igbanugo*, 863 N.W.2d 751 (Minn. 2015) (failure to credit payments client made and continuing to bill client $17,451 after court determined outstanding legal fees were $2,944); *cf. Iowa Supreme Court Bd. of Prof'l Ethics & Conduct v. Tofflemire*, 689 N.W.2d 83 (Iowa 2004) (full-time employee of state's labor division abused sick leave policy so she could also work as contract lawyer for state public defender, submitting false bills and altering checks in support of reimbursement claims).

### • Fees Exceeding Legislative Cap

A contract calling for fees in excess of a legislative cap violates Rule 1.5(a). *See, e.g., In re Wimmershoff*, 3 P.3d 417 (Colo. 2000) (fee in workers' compensation case exceeded statutory maximum of 20 percent); *In re Stephens*, 851 N.E.2d 1256 (Ind. 2006) (fee agreement designed to circumvent statutory cap in medical malpractice case); *Comm. on Legal Ethics v. Burdette*, 445 S.E.2d 733 (W. Va. 1994) (workers' compensation claimant cannot waive statutory limit on attorneys' fees, nor may lawyer request waiver); *In re Konopka*, 498 N.W.2d 853 (Wis. Ct. App. 1993) (contract granting probate lawyer 4 percent of gross value of estate's inventory contravened fee statute declaring that estate's value shall not be controlling factor); *cf. In re Amendment to Rules Regulating Fla. Bar*, 939 So. 2d 1032 (Fla. 2006) (approving amendment permitting lawyer to condition medical malpractice representation upon client's waiver of fee caps set by state constitution).

## UNREASONABLE FEES

### • Bill-Padding; Double-Billing

Padding bills or billing the same work to more than one client violates Rule 1.5(a), as well as other rules. *See, e.g., In re Burghoff*, 374 B.R. 681 (Bankr. N.D. Iowa 2007) (charging $5,373 for 25.5 hours preparing briefs largely plagiarized from article written by others); *People v. Espinoza*, 35 P.3d 552 (Colo. O.P.D.J. 2001) (inflating billing entries and charging for phantom time expenditures); *In re Dyer*, 750 So. 2d 942 (La. 1999) (padding some expenses and inventing others; "it defies belief that so many 'mistakes' could occur in favor of respondent, and none in favor of his client"); *Att'y Grievance Comm'n v. Hess*, 722 A.2d 905 (Md. 1999) (giving client 15 percent discount but then inflating bills to make up for it); *In re Kellington*, 852 N.W.2d 395 (N.D. 2014) (double-billing, billing for overhead and billing at wrong hourly rate); *State ex rel. Okla. Bar Ass'n v. Kinsey*, 212 P.3d 1186 (Okla. 2009) (scheduling false appointments, and billing clients for work not done and travel expenses not incurred); *In re Vanderbeek*, 101 P.3d 88 (Wash. 2004) (disbarment for habitually inflating client bills, charging excessive fees for simple form pleadings, withdrawal notices, and short letters demanding payment of fees); Or. Ethics Op. 2005-170 (2005) (lawyer who spends one hour in court at docket call for four different clients may not charge each client for a full hour; time savings must be passed on to clients); *see also In re Wall*, 73 N.E.3d 170 (Ind. 2017) (lawyer worked with corporation that charged recurring monthly fees not tied to work on client matters and nonrefundable retainers not charged to reserve lawyer's time).

Billing in quarter-hour increments is likely to result in unreasonable fees. *See Yellowbook, Inc. v. Brandeberry*, 708 F.3d 837 (6th Cir. 2013) (quarter-hour billing tends to generate bills 15 percent higher than one-tenth-hour billing); *Welch v. Metro. Life Ins. Co.*, 480 F.3d 942 (9th Cir. 2007) (frequency of quarter-hour and half-hour charges for letters, telephone calls, and intraoffice conferences necessitated 20 percent across-the-board reduction); *Hawkins v. Astrue*, Civ. No. 09-7460, 2010 WL 5375948, 2010 BL 406989 (E.D. La. Nov. 24, 2010) (billing in quarter-hour increments to review one-page documents is unreasonable; entries reduced to one-tenth hour); *Bd. of Prof'l Responsibility v. Casper*, 318 P.3d 790 (Wyo. 2014) (practice of billing minimum of fifteen-minute increments for tasks such as signing subpoenas, stipulated orders, and one-page letters resulted in charging unreasonable fee); *see also Kelmendi v. Detroit Bd. of Educ.*, No. 12-14949, 2017 WL 1502626, 2017 BL 139115 (E.D. Mich. Apr. 27, 2017) (because lawyers billed only in quarter-hour increments and most time entries were rounded up to a half or full hour, court imposed across-the-board 5 percent reduction "to counter the likelihood that some hours involved rounding that led to slight overbilling"). *See generally* Sonia S. Chan, *ABA Formal Opinion 93-379: Double-Billing, Padding, and Other Forms of Overbilling*, 9 Geo. J. Legal Ethics 611 (Winter 1996); Kevin Hopkins, *Law Firms, Technology, and the Double-Billing Dilemma*, 12 Geo. J. Legal Ethics 95 (Fall 1998) ("modified hourly billing," as alternative to traditional hourly billing arrangement, itself often results in double-billing); Lisa G. Lerman, *A Double Standard for Lawyer Dishonesty: Billing Fraud Versus Misappropriation*, 34 Hofstra L. Rev. 847 (Spring 2006); "Risk Managers Always Say Avoid Fee Disputes but What Should Firms Do to Achieve This?," *ABA/BNA Lawyers' Manual on Professional Conduct*, 29 Law. Man. Prof. Conduct 688 (Current Reports, Oct. 23, 2013); Susan Saab Fortney, *The Billable Hours Derby: Empirical Data on the Problems and Pressure Points*, 33 Fordham Urb. L.J. 171 (Nov. 2005); Lisa G. Lerman, *Blue-Chip Bilking: Regulation of Billing and Expense Fraud by Lawyers*, 12 Geo. J. Legal Ethics 205 (Winter 1999); Christine Parker & David Ruschena, *The Pressures of Billable Hours: Lessons from a Survey of Billing Practices Inside Law Firms*, 9 U. St. Thomas L.J. 619 (Fall 2011); Douglas R. Richmond, *For a Few Dollars More: The Perplexing Problems of Unethical Billing Practices by Lawyers*, 60 S.C. L. Rev. 63 (Autumn 2008); Douglas R. Richmond, *The New Law Firm Economy, Billable Hours, and Professional Responsibility*, 29 Hofstra L. Rev. 207 (Fall 2000).

• *Fees for Doing Nothing*

It is by definition unreasonable to charge for work not done. *In re Cleaver-Bascombe*, 892 A.2d 396 (D.C. 2006) (submission of false Criminal Justice Act voucher for work not actually done by counsel appointed for indigent criminal defendant violates Rule 1.5(a) regardless of whether lawyer actually collects on voucher); *In re O'Farrell*, 942 N.E.2d 799 (Ind. 2011) (charging and collecting flat fees that were nonrefundable even if client-lawyer relationship terminated before completion of representation); *In re Moser*, 56 So. 3d 239 (La. 2011) ("pre-billing" clients for work before doing it); *Att'y Grievance Comm'n v. Gage-Cohen*, 101 A.3d 1043 (Md. 2014) (per se unreasonable to charge for work not done); *Att'y Grievance Comm'n v. Brady*, 30 A.3d 902 (Md. 2011) (though hourly rate of $220 to represent home purchaser in civil action against vendors not unreasonable, $10,000 in fees unreasonable in light of lawyer's neglect and abandonment of case); *In re O'Brien*, 29 P.3d 1044 (N.M. 2001) (lawyer charged $5,000 without work product to justify it; "any fee is excessive when absolutely no services are provided"); *In re McKechnie*, 708 N.W.2d 310 (N.D. 2006) (failure to commence federal civil rights action or refund unearned portion of $2,500 up-front payment); *Flowers v. Bd. of Prof'l Responsibility*, 314 S.W.3d 882 (Tenn. 2010) (charging fees and costs for services not performed and then not reimbursing); *see also In re Placide*, 414 P.3d 1124 (Wash. 2018) (keeping fee for work not performed; lawyer's offer to return fee, which client declined, did not satisfy duty not to charge or collect unreasonable fee).

• *Fees for Doing Very Little*

Charging a lot for doing very little is just as likely to violate Rule 1.5(a) as charging for doing nothing. *See, e.g., Budget Rent-A-Car Sys., Inc. v. Consol. Equity LLC*, 428 F.3d 717 (7th Cir. 2005) (appellee's lawyer filed petition seeking $4,626 to produce short jurisdictional memo citing five cases, and $4,354 to prepare sanctions motions and statement of fees and costs: "[i]t is inconceivable that this is the going market price for such exiguous submissions"; request "so exorbitant as to constitute an abuse of the process of the court asked to make the award"); *Fla. Bar v. Petersen*, 248 So. 3d 1069 (Fla. 2018) ($6,500 fee excessive when lawyer filed complaint and conducted preliminary discovery but took no significant action thereafter); *In re Calahan*, 930 So. 2d 916 (La. 2006) (unreasonable to charge $12,500, or 40 percent of recovery, to write one-page demand letter to client's previous lawyer to complain of alleged excessive fee); *Att'y Grievance Comm'n v. Monfried*, 794 A.2d 92 (Md. 2002) (hearing judge's failure to find violation of Rule 1.5 was clear error; lawyer received flat fee of $1,000 to represent client in parole revocation but did nothing beyond making a few phone calls to get hearing date scheduled); *Commonwealth v. Ennis*, 808 N.E.2d 783 (Mass. 2004) (unreasonable for defense counsel to claim sixty-four hours for short response to interlocutory appeal of suppression order in which he repeated his arguments from motion to suppress); *In re McCray*, 755 N.W.2d 835 (N.D. 2008) (lawyer charged $590 over ten-month period for less than twelve minutes, which lawyer spent mailing dispute letter to credit reporting agencies in client's own name); *In re Wyllie*, 19 P.3d 338 (Or. 2001) (lawyer charged $1,850 and collected $750 after agreeing to work for hourly fee of $150; worked for two and a half hours, and charged additional $50 for missed appointment); *In re Van Camp*, 257 P.3d 599 (Wash. 2011) (keeping entire

$25,000 retainer for doing little work in matter that should have resulted in routine settlement); *cf. In re Brothers*, 70 P.3d 940 (Wash. 2003) (lawyer who normally charged $50 to prepare quitclaim deeds instead charged one-third of value of property transferred, or $36,663).

### • Doing Very Little, and Doing It Badly

In assessing a fee's reasonableness, what is ultimately at issue is "the reasonable value of the services rendered and value received by the client." *Regions Bank v. Automax USA, LLC*, 858 So. 2d 593 (La. Ct. App. 2003); *see People v. Woodford*, 81 P.3d 370 (Colo. O.P.D.J. 2003) ($2,500 may be reasonable fee for preparation of trust, but not if documents incompetently prepared, do not address client's objectives, and completely lack value to client); *In re McCann*, 894 A.2d 1087 (Del. 2005) (charging $25,249 and taking more than fifteen years to complete work on estate unreasonable, as was charging $25,000 for work on estate in which lawyer did not file inventory or accounting and was removed as personal representative by court); *Fla. Bar v. Carlon*, 820 So. 2d 891 (Fla. 2002) (lawyer charged $500 to open file and $3,000 for looking in *Martindale-Hubbell* and writing identical letters to twelve lawyers in unsuccessful effort to find Arizona lawyer to handle case); *Idaho State Bar v. Frazier*, 28 P.3d 363 (Idaho 2001) (after saying he could resolve estate matter for $5,500, lawyer charged more than $100,000 and mismanaged it such that another lawyer had to close it); *Att'y Grievance Comm'n v. Framm*, 144 A.3d 827 (Md. 2016) (unreasonable to charge for filing defective pleadings, representing adverse party, and violating court rules and orders); *In re Pearlman*, 955 A.2d 995 (R.I. 2010) (charging $3,500 for two one-page wills poorly drafted "to an extreme extent" and fee of 5 percent of decedent's gross estate plus retainer of $9,500); *In re Sinnott*, 845 A.2d 373 (Vt. 2004) (lawyer charged client for negotiating debt with credit card company even though client ended up doing negotiations himself).

### • Work That Benefits Lawyer, Not Client

Work done for the lawyer's own benefit may not be billed to the client. *See, e.g., Att'y Grievance Comm'n v. Kreamer*, 946 A.2d 500 (Md. 2008) (time spent completing time sheets is overhead expense); *Att'y Grievance Comm'n v. Culver*, 849 A.2d 423 (Md. 2004) (may not charge client for vacating discovery sanction imposed as result of counsel's incompetence); *In re Lawyers Responsibility Bd. Panel No. 94-17*, 546 N.W.2d 744 (Minn. 1996) (charging client for time spent responding to client's ethics complaint violates Rule 1.5(a) as well as Rule 8.4(d)); *In re Napolitano*, 662 N.Y.S.2d 56 (App. Div. 1997) (charging for time spent responding to client's complaint was attempt to collect illegal fee); *In re Gorokhovsky*, 824 N.W.2d 804 (Wis. 2012) (charging client $400 for pursuing fees from him); *In re Kitchen*, 682 N.W.2d 780 (Wis. 2004) (when clients filed grievance against him, lawyer charged them $175 to retrieve their file to answer inquiries); Me. Ethics Op. 139 (1994) ("We are struck at the outset by the novelty of the suggestion that the [a]ttorney's personal defense against a complaint of professional misconduct could be construed, under any circumstances, as the rendition of legal services to a client."); *see also* Conn. Informal Ethics Op. 03-05 (2003) (may not bill client for defending grievance brought by opposing party unless original agreement so provides, or lawyer and client reach new agreement); N.C. Ethics Op. 2000-7 (2000) (may not charge client for time participating in state bar's fee dispute resolution program).

Note, however, that this rule may not apply in statutory fee cases. *See Wolff v. Royal Am. Mgmt., Inc.*, 545 F. App'x 791 (11th Cir. 2013) (if federal law allows attorneys' fees to prevailing party, time litigating both entitlement to and amount of fees is compensable).

### • *Doing Way Too Much*

Fees for excessive lawyering violate Rule 1.5(a). *See Coffey's Case*, 880 A.2d 403 (N.H. 2005) (estimated fee of $30,000 and actual fee of $64,242.89, for 225 hours writing brief and eighty-five hours preparing for oral argument in probate appeal clearly excessive; lawyer already familiar with case, no transcript to review, and typical appeal would require thirty to seventy-five hours); *In re Dorothy*, 605 N.W.2d 493 (S.D. 2000) (lawyer tried to charge almost $60,000 and did charge more than $47,000 for uncomplicated child custody and support representation; overly extensive briefing was of little or no value); *see also In re Estate of Langland*, Nos. 255287, 256134, 258476, 2006 WL 1752261 (Mich. Ct. App. June 27, 2006) (probate court did not err in awarding attorneys' fees as sanction against lawyer who failed to distinguish "preserving a record for appellate review from merely beating a dead horse" with repeated objections and demands for evidentiary hearings).

### • *Doing Remedial Work*

Lawyers are expected to provide competent representation (see Rule 1.1); they may not charge clients for time necessitated by their own inexperience. *See, e.g., Heavener v. Meyers*, 158 F. Supp. 2d 1278 (E.D. Okla. 2001) (500 hours for straightforward Fourth Amendment excessive-force claim and nineteen hours for research on Eleventh Amendment defense indicated excessive billing due to counsel's inexperience); *In re Poseidon Pools of Am., Inc.*, 180 B.R. 718 (Bankr. E.D.N.Y. 1995) (denying compensation for various document revisions; "we note that given the numerous times throughout the Final Application that Applicant requests fees for revising various documents, Applicant fails to negate the obvious possibility that such a plethora of revisions was necessitated by a level of competency less than that reflected by the Applicant's billing rates"); *Att'y Grievance Comm'n v. Manger*, 913 A.2d 1 (Md. 2006) ("While it may be appropriate to charge a client for case-specific research or familiarization with a unique issue involved in a case, general education or background research should not be charged to the client."); *In re Hellerud*, 714 N.W.2d 38 (N.D. 2006) (reduction in hours, fee refund of $5,651.24, and reprimand for lawyer unfamiliar with North Dakota probate work who charged too many hours at too high a rate for simple administration of cash estate; "it is counterintuitive to charge a higher hourly rate for knowing less about North Dakota law").

### • *Too Many Lawyers*

Participation by too many lawyers is another kind of overlawyering that can result in an unreasonable fee. *See Heavener v. Meyers*, 158 F. Supp. 2d 1278 (E.D. Okla. 2001) (forty-nine invoice entries for "discussion" with co-counsel constituted "prime example of fee-padding"); *Carr v. Fort Morgan Sch. Dist.*, 4 F. Supp. 2d 998 (D. Colo. 1998) (reducing fee request; "[i]f the attorneys possess the skill required to charge the rates they are charging for their legal services, which this Court has determined they do, such constant collaboration, review, preparation and consultation is not necessary"); *Richmont Capital Partners I, L.P. v. J.R. Invs. Corp.*, Civ. No. 20281, 2004 WL 1152295, 2004 BL 3043 (Del. Ch. May 20, 2004) (rejecting amount requested; three lawyers worked fifty-nine hours total to answer complaints and prepare motions for admissions pro hac vice, and four lawyers worked 223 hours total drafting responses to motions to dismiss raising no novel issues).

### • *Charging Lawyer Rates for Nonlawyer Work*

A lawyer may not bill nonlawyer services at lawyer rates, no matter who performs them. *See Hermida v. Archstone*, 950 F. Supp. 2d 298 (D. Mass. 2013) (tasks considered administrative or clerical, which may not be billed at lawyer's rates even if lawyer performs them, include organizing, distributing, and copying documents; drafting correspondence; researching facts and collecting data; checking legal cites; scheduling and logistical planning; filing court documents and managing docket); *In re Green*, 11 P.3d 1078 (Colo. 2000) (charging lawyer's hourly rate for faxing documents, calling court clerk's office, and delivering documents to opposing counsel unreasonable as matter of law); *Comm. on Prof'l Ethics & Conduct v. Zimmerman*, 465 N.W.2d 288 (Iowa 1991) (charging full hourly rate for attending ward's birthday party and discussing ward's toiletry needs); *In re Charges of Unprof'l Conduct in Panel Case No. 23236*, 728 N.W.2d 254 (Minn. 2007) (supervising lawyer billed at contractual lawyer rate of $205 per hour for work done by lawyer on restricted status and unable to practice law; should have used paralegals' rate); *Goeldner v. Miss. Bar*, 891 So. 2d 130 (Miss. 2004) (unreasonable to bill law clerk's services at $175 per hour upon law school graduation; "[u]ntil admittance to the bar, a person with a J.D. is no more than a 'law clerk'"); *Cincinnati Bar Ass'n v. Alsfelder*, 816 N.E.2d 218 (Ohio 2004) (lawyer charged "attorney's time" to unsophisticated client whom he befriended with advice about "anything and everything," including boyfriends, vehicles, and restaurants; "[the lawyer] attempted to charge for his counsel in the manner that a therapist might, overlooking that an attorney, unless a qualified therapist, may no more engage in that profession than a therapist may practice law without a license"); *In re Dorothy*, 605 N.W.2d 493 (S.D. 2000) (when client ran out of gas en route to meet with lawyer, lawyer offered to bring him gas but then charged him $100 per hour for it); *In re Compton*, 744 N.W.2d 78 (Wis. 2008) (lawyer billed state public defender's office for 120 hours of legal services for work actually performed by paralegal).

### CLIENT'S AGREEMENT

A lawyer violates Rule 1.5 "by charging fees that exceed an agreed-upon fee even if those fees might have been deemed reasonable absent the agreement." *In re Isler*, 315 P.3d 711 (Ariz. 2014). *See also Att'y Grievance Comm'n v. Olszewski*, 107 A.3d 1159 (Md. 2015) (when retainer specified a fee of 33.3 percent on amount collected, lawyer's attempt to collect additional 15 percent on uncollected funds was unreasonable). However, the fact that a client agrees to a fee does not itself make a fee reasonable;

a lawyer may still be disciplined for charging an unreasonable fee notwithstanding the client's agreement. *See In re Guste*, 118 So. 3d 1023 (La. 2012) (after representation completed, lawyer and client entered agreement for lawyer to provide personal services to client at her usual lawyer rate); *Att'y Grievance Comm'n v. Braskey*, 836 A.2d 605 (Md. 2003) (by disbursing $9,000 of remaining settlement to himself after taking one-fourth of gross settlement proceeds pursuant to contingent-fee agreement, lawyer "went beyond collecting an unreasonable fee" and was "fee gouging," even if client consented); *In re Sinnott*, 845 A.2d 373 (Vt. 2004) (cannot charge unreasonable fees even if clients will pay them); *cf. Wright ex rel. Wright v. Wright*, 337 S.W.3d 166 (Tenn. 2011) (court determining reasonableness of lawyer's fee for representing minor may not look to fee agreement with minor's representative as presumptive benchmark). *See generally* Kathryn Thompson, *Let's Be Reasonable: Client Consent to a Fee Agreement Doesn't Mean It's Ethical*, 94 A.B.A. J. 26 (Mar. 2008).

Outside the disciplinary context see *Paul, Weiss, Rifkind, Wharton & Garrison v. Koons*, 780 N.Y.S.2d 710 (Sup. Ct. 2004) (summary judgment for law firm seeking $3.9 million in hotly contested custody fight between wealthy artist who instructed firm to "leave no stone unturned" and his politically prominent wife; court would not "police the conduct of wealthy litigants who choose to share their wealth with counsel through extravagant litigation"), and *In re Adoption of M.M.H.*, 981 A.2d 261 (Pa. Super. Ct. 2009) (trial court lacked authority to cut lawyer's fees in adoption proceeding down to amount it deemed reasonable for locale; violation of Rule 1.5 is basis for discipline, not fee reduction).

## INVESTMENT IN CLIENT AS FEE

Comment [4], added in 2002, notes that fees paid in property instead of money "often have the essential qualities of a business transaction with the client," and therefore "may" be subject to the requirements of Rule 1.8(a), which governs lawyer/client business transactions. American Bar Association, *A Legislative History: The Development of the ABA Model Rules of Professional Conduct, 1982–2013*, at 95–96 (2013). Caselaw and ethics opinions are more emphatic. *See Iowa Supreme Court Att'y Disciplinary Bd. v. Kaiser*, 736 N.W.2d 544 (Iowa 2007) (lawyer acquiring stock in client must comply with Rule 1.8(a)); ABA Formal Ethics Op. 00-418 (2000) (lawyer who acquires ownership interest in client in exchange for legal services, either in lieu of cash fee or as investment opportunity, must comply with Rule 1.8(a)); N.Y. State Ethics Op. 913 (2012) (same); *see also Richmond's Case*, 904 A.2d 684 (N.H. 2006) (no inherent conflict between Rule 1.5 and Rule 1.8(a); though Rule 1.5 permits lawyer to accept property as fee, lawyer must still comply with requirements of Rule 1.8(a)). *See generally* Poonam Puri, *Taking Stock of Taking Stock*, 87 Cornell L. Rev. 99 (Nov. 2001).

Although fee agreements are subject to continued review for reasonableness as circumstances change, the reasonableness of a fee that takes the form of an investment or an interest in the client is looked at prospectively, not retrospectively. *See Bauermeister v. McReynolds*, 571 N.W.2d 79 (Neb. 1997) ($4 million potential fee based upon 5 to 10 percent likelihood of success of private landfill business venture not excessive under "lean forward" fee agreement wherein "if successful, everyone profits; if not, then they all lose together"), *modified on denial of reh'g*, 575 N.W.2d 354 (Neb.

1998); N.Y. State Ethics Op. 913 (2012) (evaluating reasonableness of modification and fairness of transaction in hindsight would overlook lawyer's assumption of risk that venture would fail); N.Y. City Ethics Op. 2000-3 (2000) (determination of whether fee taken in client securities is excessive depends upon value when agreement reached; though this may create "spectacular windfalls in relation to the compensation that would normally be received on a cash basis," reward stems from acceptance of investment risk); Pa. Formal Ethics Op. 2001-100 (2001) (determination "should be made based on the information available at the time of the transaction and not with the benefit of hindsight"). *But see Holmes v. Loveless*, 94 P.3d 338 (Wash. Ct. App. 2004) (error to continue to enforce thirty-year-old contingent-fee agreement under which law firm was to continue to receive 5 percent of cash distributions from joint venture—a successful shopping center—in exchange for initial two and a half years of discounted legal services; discount, valued at $8,000, had already generated income of $380,000; "we agree with the joint venture's contention that the time has been reached when making additional distributions under the agreement would result in an excessive fee").

## EXPENSES CHARGEABLE TO CLIENT

Lawyers may not bill clients for general office overhead—that is, routine costs such as "maintaining a library, securing malpractice insurance, renting of office space, purchasing utilities and the like." ABA Formal Ethics Op. 93-379 (1993). Clients reasonably expect these expenses to be "subsumed within the charges the lawyer is making for professional services." *Id. See Precision Seed Cleaners v. Country Mut. Ins. Co.*, 976 F. Supp. 2d 1228 (D. Or. 2013) (clerical tasks are overhead expenses to be absorbed by counsel); *Spicer v. Chi. Bd. Options Exch., Inc.*, 844 F. Supp. 1226 (N.D. Ill. 1993) (cost of special ventilation of office in days after major flood was part of firm's general overhead, as was expense of keeping track of filings, deadlines, and dockets); *N.C. State Bar v. Gilbert*, 566 S.E.2d 685 (N.C. 2002) (lawyer who had never handled personal injury case charged clients full cost of medical encyclopedias for his library); San Diego Cnty. Ethics Op. 2013-3 (2013) (may not bill for secretarial overtime unless attributable to "some emergency or time exigency").

Although some costs and expenses may be billed separately, they may not be used as a profit center. Comment [1] explains that "[a] lawyer may seek reimbursement for the cost of services performed in-house, such as copying, or for other expenses incurred in-house, such as telephone charges, either by charging a reasonable amount to which the client has agreed in advance or by charging an amount that reasonably reflects the cost incurred by the lawyer." *See* ABA Formal Ethics Op. 93-379 (1993) ("The lawyer's stock in trade is the sale of legal services, not photocopy paper, tuna fish sandwiches, computer time or messenger services."); *cf.* N.C. Ethics Op. 2005-11 (2006) (when lender requires real estate buyer's lawyer to submit estimate of anticipated recording and courier costs before lender will issue loan package, lawyer may, with full disclosure, inflate estimate and keep any excess, provided charges not clearly excessive).

Access charges for electronic legal research are normally treated as overhead, but may be passed along to the client if the client has given informed consent. *See*

*Guerrant v. Roth*, 777 N.E.2d 499 (Ill. App. Ct. 2002) (contingent-fee lawyer cannot recover computer-aided research expenses from client unless agreement expressly so provides); *cf. Heng v. Rotech Med. Corp.*, 720 N.W.2d 54 (N.D. 2006) (reversing portion of fee award attributable to electronic research and adopting prevailing view that fees for electronic legal research are not recoverable as costs but are part of "reasonable attorney's fees" already included in statutory fee award).

Whatever the firm's payment to the database provider is based upon—for example, a discounted rate or a flat fee for unlimited access—the firm must try to track the amount actually attributable to the particular client. Pa. Ethics Op. 2006-30 (2006) (law firm may recoup cost of computerized legal research by billing clients pro rata percentage of monthly access fee, provided clients give informed consent).

If a lawyer is required by ethics rules or laws to retain certain client information, the lawyer may not add a storage charge at the end of the representation. Nassau Cnty. (N.Y.) Ethics Op. 06-02 (2006) (lawyer may, however, charge reasonable amount or actual cost for storing documents lawyer is not required to keep).

Note that a court may find a particular expense reasonable in one context but may disallow it in another context: "[A] court that would decline to question a law firm's right to bill a client for particular expenses may well hold that those same types of expenses are unreasonable in a bankruptcy matter or a fee-shifting case when someone other than the client will have to bear them." Douglas R. Richmond, "Pinch Points When Charging Expenses to Clients," *ABA/BNA Lawyers' Manual on Professional Conduct*, 29 Law. Man. Prof. Conduct 787 (Current Reports, Dec. 4, 2013) (alerting lawyers to distinction though finding judicial perspective "dubious").

### • *Outsourcing Legal Work/Contract Lawyers*

According to an ABA ethics opinion, if a contract lawyer's services are billed as costs and expenses, the billing lawyer may not charge more than the actual cost plus a reasonable allocation of overhead directly associated with that contract lawyer. ABA Formal Ethics Op. 00-420 (2000) (collecting authorities); *see also* ABA Formal Ethics Op. 08-451 (2008) (for outsourced work performed off-site and without need for infrastructural support, only permissible markup would be reasonable allocation of cost of supervising the work).

If the contract lawyer's services are billed as legal services rather than costs, a markup may be permitted subject to the overarching reasonableness requirement of Rule 1.5(a). ABA Formal Ethics Op. 00-420 (2000); *see Carlson v. Xerox Corp.*, 596 F. Supp. 2d 400 (D. Conn. 2009) (appropriate to bill contract lawyers' time as legal services in light of evidence of how billing lawyers trained, supervised, and monitored them, in some instances removing them for inadequate performance).

Disclosure, however, is required. *See* L.A. Cnty. Ethics Op. 518 (2006) (whether or not markup added, billing lawyer must disclose basis of costs passed on to client for contract lawyer); Haw. Ethics Op. 47 (2004) (firm must disclose, preferably in writing, rate at which contract lawyer will be billed to client); Md. Ethics Op. 2001-31 (2001) (surcharge permissible if contract lawyer's services billed as legal services and revealed in retainer agreement).

## • *Outsourcing Nonlawyer Work*

Regarding work outsourced to nonlawyers, see Conn. Informal Ethics Op. 03-08 (2003) (cost of paying outside firm to collect medical records is considered overhead built into lawyer's fee and cannot be passed on to client); Fla. Ethics Op. 07-2 (2007) (firm may charge client actual cost of its overseas provider of paralegal services unless charge would normally be covered as overhead; in contingent-fee case, however, cannot charge separately for outsourced paralegal work normally performed by client's own lawyer and incorporated into fee); and N.Y. City Ethics Op. 2006-3 (2006) (absent contrary agreement, charges for legal support services performed by nonlawyer overseas should include no more than direct costs plus reasonable allocation of overhead expenses directly associated with those services). *See generally* Ohio Ethics Op. 2009-6 (2009) (lawyer may outsource legal or support services domestically or abroad, directly to lawyers or nonlawyers or indirectly through independent service provider; any amount over actual cost must be reasonable, such as a reasonable amount to cover lawyer's supervision).

## CONTINGENT-FEE CASES AND FEE AWARDS

Whether a contingent-fee lawyer may include a fee award in the amount on which the percentage is calculated, or may even retain both, turns on the precise wording of both the statute involved and the fee agreement. *See Gobert v. Williams*, 323 F.3d 1099 (5th Cir. 2003) (Title VII case permitting lawyer to retain statutory and contingent fee; fee agreement specified court-awarded fees would belong to lawyer); *Quint v. A.E. Staley Mfg. Co.*, 245 F. Supp. 2d 162 (D. Me.) (awarding statutory as well as contingent fees when fee agreement assigned to counsel the right to request fee award), *aff'd*, 84 F. App'x 101 (1st Cir. 2003); *Burrell v. Yale Univ.*, No. X02 CV 00-0159421-S, 2005 WL 1670613 (Conn. Super. Ct. May 26, 2005) (condemning civil rights plaintiffs' lawyers for seeking to calculate statutory fee award as one-third of jury award, which already included fees: "[W]hen fully exposed for what it is, [this formula] represents the type of matter that makes the public cynical about the legal profession. The court has examined the factors governing the reasonableness of an attorney's fee in Rule 1.5(a) of the Rules of Professional Conduct and finds nothing there to justify such exorbitant rates."); *Dowles v. ConAgra, Inc.*, 25 So. 3d 889 (La. Ct. App. 2009) (lawyer in Family and Medical Leave Act case could keep both; fee agreement specified that fee award would be lawyer's property); *Albunio v. City of New York*, 11 N.E.3d 1104 (N.Y. 2014) (absent explicit agreement to the contrary, lawyer is entitled to greater of either contingent fee or statutory award; collecting cases); *Finnell v. Seismic*, 67 P.3d 339 (Okla. 2003) (Oklahoma law prohibits lawyer from retaining contingent fee and statutory fee award); *Heldreth v. Rahimian*, 637 S.E.2d 359 (W. Va. 2006) (keeping both would be either double recovery or windfall); N.C. Ethics Op. 2002-4 (2003) (although lawyer not per se barred from collecting contingent fee in addition to portion of court-awarded fee if consistent with fee agreement and not clearly excessive, collecting full amount of both "ordinarily" violates Rule 1.5(a)); Okla. Ethics Op. 325 (2009) (although lawyer and client may not agree that lawyer will retain any attorneys' fee awarded by statute or settlement in addition to contingent fee, they may agree that percentage will be based upon aggregate of the two amounts); *Restatement*

*(Third) of the Law Governing Lawyers* § 38 cmt. f (2000) (agreement permitting lawyer to receive both contractual fee and fee award, without crediting award against contract fee, is presumptively unreasonable); *cf. Pickett v. Sheridan Health Care Ctr.*, 664 F.3d 632 (7th Cir. 2011) (court calculating lodestar erred in reducing hourly rate to offset contingent-fee recovery; statutory and contingent fees represent distinct entitlements; analyzed in Don Zupanec, *Attorneys' Fees—Lodestar—Consideration of Contingent Fee*, 27 Fed. Litigator 15 (Feb. 2012)).

A lawyer who takes a case on a contingent-fee basis must reveal the agreement to the court if the court is considering awarding fees. *See Warnell v. Ford Motor Co.*, 205 F. Supp. 2d 956 (N.D. Ill. 2002) (class counsel in sex discrimination class action "double-dipped" by taking $2.75 million fee award on $12 million settlement in addition to contingent fee, yielding total award of more than $3.4 million; ordered to disgorge contingent fee); *Jenkins v. McCoy*, 882 F. Supp. 549 (S.D. W. Va. 1995) (a year after awarding statutory fees, court learned that plaintiff's lawyer had also taken percentage pursuant to contingent-fee agreement; court ordered it repaid to plaintiff and criticized lawyer for violating court's trust); *In re Struthers*, 877 P.2d 789 (Ariz. 1994) (agreement in collection cases granting lawyer contingent fee and any court-awarded fee is facially invalid and misleads court; court would not award fees if it knew award would provide double recovery for lawyer and no benefit to client).

The Supreme Court has held that in civil rights cases in which fees are awarded pursuant to 42 U.S.C. § 1988, the statute controls what the losing defendant must pay rather than what the prevailing plaintiff must pay his or her lawyer. Therefore, if the court awards less than the amount in the contingent-fee agreement, the plaintiff remains obligated for the difference. *Venegas v. Mitchell*, 495 U.S. 82 (1990).

## SIMULTANEOUS NEGOTIATION OF SETTLEMENT AND ATTORNEYS' FEES

Whenever a lawyer negotiates attorneys' fees as part of a settlement there is a potential conflict of interest. A plaintiff's lawyer has an interest in securing the best possible fee award, but is duty-bound to negotiate the best possible settlement for the client.

In *Evans v. Jeff D.*, 475 U.S. 717 (1986), the Supreme Court unanimously declined to prohibit the simultaneous negotiation of fees and settlement and, by a six-to-three vote, also declined to ban settlements conditioned upon the waiver of fees. A statutory fee award, at least under 42 U.S.C. § 1988, belongs to the client and may be waived or compromised by the client, the Court said. *Cf. Ramirez v. Sturdevant*, 26 Cal. Rptr. 2d 554 (Ct. App. 1994) (any settlement resulting from simultaneous negotiation of fees and merits is presumed tainted by conflict between lawyer and client and will not be approved unless lawyer establishes that in protecting own interests he or she did not slight those of client). For analysis see *ABA/BNA Lawyers' Manual on Professional Conduct*, "Fees: Simultaneous Negotiation of Fees and Merits," pp. 41:1601 *et seq. See generally* Daniel Nazer, Note, *Conflict and Solidarity: The Legacy of* Evans v. Jeff D., 17 Geo. J. Legal Ethics 499 (Spring 2004).

Lawyers have attempted to avoid the conflict by using retainer provisions that either transfer the right to a fee award from the client to the lawyer or prohibit the client from waiving the right. *See Pony v. Cnty. of Los Angeles*, 433 F.3d 1138 (9th Cir. 2006) (provision in retainer agreement assigning right to apply for attorneys' fees void as matter of law; right to seek statutory attorneys' fees in civil rights action under 42 U.S.C. § 1983 is substantive cause of action and thus cannot be contractually transferred); *Babcock v. Rezak*, No. 96-CV-0394E(SC), 2004 WL 1574623 (W.D.N.Y. June 23, 2004) (construing ambiguous assignment in fee agreement against firm and refusing to let firm seek fees in face of client's desire to waive them to facilitate settlement: "[The law firm's] interest in section 1988 fees is diametrically opposed to that of [the client]. This Court finds that preservation of an attorney's undivided loyalty is a special circumstance justifying denial of section 1988 fees."). *See generally* L.A. Cnty. Ethics Op. 515 (2006) (discussing lawyer-client agreement to split statutory fee award).

## Paragraph (b): Communicating Basis for Legal Fees

### EXPLAINING FEE AGREEMENT

Rule 1.5(b) requires a lawyer to "communicate" to a client who is not a regular client (and to a regular client, if the terms are changing) the basis upon which the lawyer will charge for fees and expenses. According to the rule, this must be done before or within a reasonable time after commencing the representation, and "preferably" in writing. *See, e.g., In re Freeman*, 835 N.E.2d 494 (Ind. 2005) (fee agreements that did not establish how hourly rate would apply against retainers violated Rule 1.5(b)); *In re Salwowski*, 819 N.E.2d 823 (Ind. 2004) (lawyer failed to explain clearly how fee would be calculated; billed at $125 per hour after agreeing to represent client in bankruptcy for $1,500, and partner then improperly ordered outstanding bills transferred to client's bankruptcy billing statement even though pre-petition debt to firm protected); *Att'y Grievance Comm'n v. Davy*, 80 A.3d 322 (Md. 2013) (two written retainer agreements, each accompanied by "nonrefundable engagement fees," did not clarify whether lawyer handling client's bankruptcy, client's company's bankruptcy, or both); *Balducci v. Cige*, 192 A.3d 1064 (N.J. Super. Ct. App. Div. 2018) (fee agreement unenforceable because lawyer failed to adequately explain effect of complicated provisions to client); *In re Hellerud*, 714 N.W.2d 38 (N.D. 2006) (requiring lawyer to refund $820 charged for legal assistant's work; lawyer had not made clear he would charge assistant's time at $275 per hour); *In re Fink*, 22 A.3d 461 (Vt. 2011) (disciplining lawyer for violating Rule 1.5(b) even though he did not attempt to collect on agreement: "The purpose of the rule was not fulfilled because the parties were unclear about the exact terms of the agreement."); *In re Van Camp*, 257 P.3d 599 (Wash. 2011) (failure to explain the confusing phrase "earned retainer" violated Rule 1.5(b)); ABA Formal Ethics Op. 94-389 (1994) (lawyers should discuss different fee arrangements with prospective clients); *see also In re Ifill*, 878 A.2d 465 (D.C. 2005) (violation of Rule 1.5(b); lawyer failed to honor client's request for retainer agreement or written confirmation of amounts paid); *cf.* Neb. Ethics Op. 17-03 (2017) (lawyer may accept payment in form of digital currencies such as bitcoin, but should disclose to client that funds will be converted into U.S. dollars immediately upon receipt).

### • Writing "Preferred"

Rule 1.5(b) requires that the lawyer communicate to the client the scope of the representation and the basis of the fee and expenses "preferably in writing." As discussed below, a written agreement is required only in the case of a contingent fee agreement (Rule 1.5(c)) or a fee-sharing agreement between lawyers not in the same firm (Rule 1.5(e)).

## MODIFICATION OF AGREEMENTS

Modification of a fee agreement during a representation is permitted if the lawyer can show the modification was reasonable under the circumstances at the time it was made (Rule 1.5(a)), and was explained to and accepted by the client (Rules 1.4, 1.5(b)). ABA Formal Ethics Op. 11-458 (2011). But "[e]xcept . . . for periodic rate increases, and absent an unanticipated change in circumstances, attempts by a lawyer to change a fee arrangement to increase the lawyer's compensation are likely to be found unreasonable and unenforceable." *Id.; see In re Thayer*, 745 N.E.2d 207 (Ind. 2001) (lawyer negotiated 40 percent contingent-fee agreement but after settlement presented client with new written agreement raising percentage to 50 percent, claiming additional 10 percent was "to prevent the medical provider or others from attaching the proceeds"); *Ky. Bar Ass'n v. Basinger*, 53 S.W.3d 92 (Ky. 2001) (lawyer attempted to charge contingent fee after indicating he would charge hourly fee); *Att'y Grievance Comm'n v. Olszewski*, 107 A.3d 1159 (Md. 2015) (failure to communicate unilateral modification of fee agreement); *In re Light*, 615 N.W.2d 164 (S.D. 2000) (lawyer presented client with agreement increasing contingent fee from 30 to 33⅓ percent without explanation); *In re Marshall*, 217 P.3d 291 (Wash. 2009) (lawyer who agreed to represent client for flat fee of $5,000, then tried to "squeeze" her for $21,787.50, violated Rule 1.5(a)); *see also In re Hefron*, 771 N.E.2d 1157 (Ind. 2002) (lawyer agreed to represent client on hourly basis to recover estate assets but when he learned substantial assets were easily recoverable, he insisted client sign new agreement giving him percentage); *Forbes v. Am. Bldg. Maint. Co.*, 198 P.3d 1042 (Wash. Ct. App. 2005) (enforcing renegotiated contingent-fee agreement providing for higher potential recovery to lawyer in client's employment discrimination suit; fact that client would no longer be in arrears under prior hybrid fee agreement constituted adequate consideration). *Compare In re Hammerle*, 952 N.E.2d 751 (Ind. 2011) (criminal defense lawyer and client, believing trial would take longer than anticipated, changed from hourly rate to flat capped sum; fact that modification ended up benefiting lawyer after client unexpectedly pleaded guilty made new fee unreasonable), *with Pezold, Richey, Caruso & Barker v. Cherokee Nation Indus., Inc.*, 46 P.3d 161 (Okla. Civ. App. 2001) (client having trouble paying hourly rate bills negotiated switch to contingent-fee agreement; after case settled at conference that evening, court properly awarded almost $800,000 in fees pursuant to new agreement). *See generally* Douglas R. Richmond, *Changing Fee Agreements During Representations: What Are the Rules?*, 15 Prof. Law., no. 3, at 2 (2004).

## ADVANCES VERSUS RETAINERS

Although a lawyer may require a client to advance money for legal fees (see Comment [4]), the advance remains the property of the client until earned. Pursuant to Rule 1.15, the advance must be placed in the lawyer's trust account and may be withdrawn only as the lawyer has earned it. Any unearned portion must be returned to the client at the end of the representation in accordance with Rule 1.16(d). *See, e.g., Ala. State Bar v. Hallett*, 26 So. 3d 1127 (Ala. 2009) (lawyer violated Rule 1.5(a) by charging divorce client flat fee that he treated as nonrefundable retainer); *In re Sather*, 3 P.3d 403 (Colo. 2000) (designating advance fee as "nonrefundable retainer" is misleading and interferes with lawyer-client relationship); *In re Mance*, 980 A.2d 1195 (D.C. 2009) (flat fee must be treated as client funds until earned); *In re O'Farrell*, 942 N.E.2d 799 (Ind. 2011) (nonrefundable "engagement fee" in family law matters unreasonable because lawyer claimed entitlement to entire fee whether earned or not); *In re Kendall*, 804 N.E.2d 1152 (Ind. 2004) (advance payments for future services are by definition refundable; therefore, agreement characterizing advance payment as nonrefundable violated reasonableness requirement of Rule 1.5(a)); *In re Dawson*, 8 P.3d 856 (N.M. 2000) (unearned nonrefundable fees are unreasonable); *Columbus Bar Ass'n v. Halliburton-Cohen*, 832 N.E.2d 42 (Ohio 2005) (lawyer violated correlative Model Code provision by charging divorce client spurious "lost opportunity" fee amounting to impermissible nonrefundable retainer); Alaska Ethics Op. 2009-01 (2009) (misleading to describe fee or retainer in any way as "non-refundable"); Conn. Informal Ethics Op. 00-02 (2000) (concept of retainer's nonrefundability is "slippery as a watermelon seed"); N.C. Ethics Op. 2005-13 (2006) (minimum fee billed against lawyer's hourly rate is client's money, unearned portion of which must be returned to client to avoid collecting excessive fee); Okla. Ethics Op. 317 (2002) (any advance payment should be held in trust account until earned, with unearned portion refunded to client at end of representation). *See generally* Tyler Moore, Current Development, *Flat Fee Fundamentals: An Introduction to the Ethical Issues Surrounding the Flat Fee After* In re Mance, 23 Geo. J. Legal Ethics 701 (Summer 2010); Douglas R. Richmond, *Understanding Retainers and Flat Fees*, 34 J. Legal Prof. 113 (2009) (explaining retainers and flat-fee agreements and analyzing controversy over "nonrefundable" retainers); Alec Rothrock, *The Forgotten Flat Fee: Whose Money Is It and Where Should It Be Deposited?*, 1 Fla. Coastal L.J. 293 (Spring–Summer 1999) (flat fees are like fee advances; they should be held in trust account until earned).

At the other extreme is a general retainer. Because it buys the lawyer's availability for a particular representation or a particular time period, it may be considered earned when paid. *See, e.g., Ryan v. Butera*, 193 F.3d 210 (3d Cir. 1999) (general nonrefundable retainer of $1 million for only ten weeks of work enforceable when client offered initial, one-time payment as "carrot" to attract counsel with "specific capability" despite client's history of nonpayment of legal fees); *Iowa Supreme Court Disciplinary Bd. v. Piazza*, 756 N.W.2d 690 (Iowa 2008) (distinguishing between "general retainer," where fee is earned when paid whether or not lawyer actually performs services for client, and "special retainer," which pays for specific service and remains client's property until earned); *In re Lochow*, 469 N.W.2d 91 (Minn. 1991) (nonrefundable retainer may be appropriate if lawyer must forgo representation of other clients and lose business as result of engagement; if retainer reasonable, it may be immediately earned, but agreement must be in writing and approved by client); N.C. Ethics Op. 2008-10 (2008) (distinguishing between nonrefundable retainers, which are prohibited, and general retainers, which are paid solely to ensure lawyer's availability for specific time period). *See generally* Lester Brickman & Lawrence A. Cunningham, *Nonrefundable Retainers: A Response to Critics of the Absolute Ban*, 64 U. Cin. L. Rev. 11 (Fall 1995); Steven

Lubet, *The Rush to Remedies: Some Conceptual Questions About Nonrefundable Retainers*, 73 N.C. L. Rev. 271 (Nov. 1994) (questioning whether blanket ban justified).

In some jurisdictions, nonrefundable fees are permitted for reasons other than to secure a lawyer's availability if certain conditions are met. *See, e.g.*, Me. Ethics Op. 211 (2014) (Maine Rule 1.5(h) permits lawyers to charge nonrefundable fees, not limited to availability retainers, if certain conditions are met); N.Y. City Ethics Op. 2015-2 (2015) (fee agreement requiring client to pay flat, nonrefundable monthly fee may be permissible in some circumstances if fee is not excessive, fully earned, and does not impede client's right to terminate representation and agreement clearly discloses how fee is calculated, what services are covered and under what circumstances fee becomes fully earned; state's rule explicitly prohibits nonrefundable fees, but permits "reasonable minimum fee" if agreement clearly states circumstances under which fee is incurred and how it will be calculated ); Tenn. Rule 1.5(f) (prescribing circumstances under which lawyer may charge "nonrefundable fee that is earned before any legal services are rendered").

## *Paragraph (c): Contingent Fees*

### TYPES OF CONTINGENT-FEE ARRANGEMENTS

The most common form of contingent-fee agreement gives the lawyer a specified percentage of any recovery, whether obtained by settlement or judgment after trial. Other forms include a "reverse" contingent fee that is based upon the amount of money the lawyer's services save the client, and an agreement giving the lawyer a percentage of expected profits. *See* ABA Formal Ethics Op. 94-389 (1994) (fee agreement may provide for "higher percentage fee as the amount of the recovery goes up or the amount of savings increases," such as 15 percent of first $100,000 recovered or saved, 20 percent on next $25,000, and 25 percent on anything thereafter); L.A. Cnty. Ethics Op. 507 (2001) (as fee for preparing and prosecuting patent application, lawyer may accept 5 percent of any proceeds); Ky. Ethics Op. E-359 (1993) (lawyer using reverse contingent fee should expect to bear burden of proving that amount and method of computing it are reasonable under circumstances); Pa. Ethics Op. 92-76 (1992) (approving contingent fee based upon amount client saves in tax appeal); *see also In re Powell*, 953 N.E.2d 1060 (Ind. 2011) (terms of contingent-fee agreement may have been reasonable at outset, but matter so quickly resolved that lawyer should have realized his fee had become unreasonable); *Brown & Sturm v. Frederick Rd. Ltd. P'ship*, 768 A.2d 62 (Md. Ct. Spec. App. 2001) (reverse contingent-fee agreement by which lawyers claimed almost $5 million for reduction of IRS tax liability was unreasonable at inception; it was based upon inflated property valuation and bore little relation to time, labor, novelty, and risk involved). *See generally* Lester Brickman, *Effective Hourly Rates of Contingency Fee Lawyers: Competing Data and Non-Competitive Fees*, 81 Wash. U. L.Q. 653 (Fall 2003); Lester Brickman, *Contingent Fee Abuses, Ethical Mandates, and the Disciplinary System: The Case Against Case-by-Case Enforcement*, 53 Wash. & Lee L. Rev. 1339 (1996); Herbert M. Kritzer, *Advocacy and Rhetoric vs. Scholarship and Evidence in the Debate over Contingency Fees: A Reply to Professor Brickman*, 82 Wash. U. L.Q. 477 (Summer 2004); Paul Lansing, Michael Fricke & Suzanne Davis, *The Ethics of Contin-*

*gent Fees in Legal Service Businesses,* 33 J. Legal Prof. 301 (2009); Douglas R. Richmond, *Turns of the Contingent Fee Key to the Courthouse Door,* 65 Buff. L. Rev. 915 (Dec. 2017) (noting expanding use of contingent-fee arrangements and surveying ethical issues involved); Adam Shainfeld, *A Critical Survey of the Law, Ethics, and Economics of Attorney Contingent Fee Arrangements,* 54 N.Y.L. Sch. L. Rev. 773 (2009/2010); Jim O. Stuckey, II, *"Reverse Contingency Fees": A Potentially Profitable and Professional Solution to the Billable Hour Trap,* 17 Prof. Law., no. 3, at 25 (2005).

The 2002 amendments to Comment [3] deleted the requirement that a lawyer offer a client alternative arrangements if there is doubt about whether a contingent fee is in the client's best interest. For criticism of this deletion, and argument that the 2002 amendments to Rule 1.5 facilitate abuse of contingent fees, see Lester Brickman, *The Continuing Assault on the Citadel of Fiduciary Protection: Ethics 2000's Revision of Model Rule 1.5,* 2003 U. Ill. L. Rev. 1181 (2003) (symposium issue).

## INTERFERING WITH CLIENT'S CONTROL OF CASE

Rule 1.2(a) requires the lawyer to abide by the client's decision regarding settlement. Therefore, a contingent-fee agreement must not impinge upon the client's settlement authority. *See, e.g.,* Neb. Ethics Op. 95-1 (1995) (may not include provision in contingent-fee agreement preventing client from settling case without lawyer's approval; may not include provision giving lawyer either percentage fee or customary hourly fee, whichever greater, if client settles without lawyer's approval); N.Y. Cnty. Ethics Op. 736 (2006) (contingent-fee agreement may not give lawyer authority to convert to hourly fee if client refuses "reasonable" settlement offer); Or. Ethics Op. 2005-54 (2005) (fee agreement may not provide that if client rejects "reasonable" settlement offer, lawyer entitled to agreed-upon percentage of rejected amount plus hourly fee from point of rejection forward); Phila. Ethics Op. 2001-1 (2002) (contingent-fee agreement may not authorize payment on hourly or quantum meruit basis if client rejects lawyer's settlement advice; however, fee-conversion clause triggered by client's decision to depart from agreement's clearly articulated objectives—for example, equitable versus monetary relief—may be permissible); *cf.* L.A. Cnty. Ethics Op. 505 (2001) (lawyer may offer fee waiver or very advantageous fee structure in return for client's promise not to agree to any settlement that includes confidentiality clause, with client to pay reasonable value of lawyer's services otherwise). *Compare Weiner v. Burr, Pease & Kurtz, P.C.,* 221 P.3d 1 (Alaska 2009) (when client already made settlement offer, contingent-fee agreement triggering higher fee if firm engaged in "substantial litigation" did not impermissibly burden client's right to settle; higher fee contingent upon insurer's rejection of offer), *and Little v. Amber Hotel Co.,* 136 Cal. Rptr. 3d 97 (Ct. App. 2011) (enforcing fee agreement that simply preserved lawyer's right to any fee award court would make, without regard to terms on which clients might choose to settle), *with Compton v. Kittleson,* 171 P.3d 172 (Alaska 2007) (agreement that if clients decided to settle for any amount that would yield less than $175 per hour for lawyer, contingent fee would be retroactively converted into hourly fee was impermissible burden upon clients' right to settle case). *See generally* Alex B. Long, *Attorney-Client Fee Agreements That Offend Public Policy,* 61 S.C. L. Rev. 287 (Winter 2009).

A contingent-fee agreement that penalizes the client for discharging the lawyer also violates the rules. *See, e.g., Guy Bennett Rubin PA v. Guettler*, 73 So. 3d 809 (Fla. Dist. Ct. App. 2011) (termination clause in contingent-fee contract requiring client to pay hourly rate for work done before discharge chills client's right to switch lawyers or to abandon case); *In re Lansky*, 678 N.E.2d 1114 (Ind. 1997) (agreement guaranteeing lawyer 40 percent of gross recovery if client discharges him before resolution of case unreasonable); *Hoover Slovacek LLP v. Walton*, 206 S.W.3d 557 (Tex. 2006) (retainer provision entitling firm to present value of its contingent fee if discharged before contingency occurs violates public policy and is unenforceable); Va. Ethics Op. 1812 (2005) (impermissible to include provision that if client terminates agreement, "reasonable value of Attorney's services shall be valued at $200 per hour," or alternative provision that lawyer may, "where permitted by law, elect compensation based on the agreed contingent fee for any settlement offer made to Client prior to termination"). *See generally* Tiffanie S. Clausewitz, *On the Trail to Increased Client Protection: Attorney Contingent Fee Contract Termination in Light of* Hoover v. Walton, 39 St. Mary's L.J. 539 (2009).

## RISK OF NONRECOVERY

A contingent fee may not be permissible if there is no real risk of total nonrecovery. *See, e.g., In re Sulzer Hip Prosthesis & Knee Prosthesis Liab. Litig.*, 290 F. Supp. 2d 840 (N.D. Ohio 2003) (unethical to enter contingent-fee agreements with plaintiff class members after both sides already signed memorandum outlining full settlement; no significant risk of nonrecovery); *In re Newman*, 958 N.E.2d 792 (Ind. 2011) (declaring it unreasonable to charge hourly fee payable upon client's receipt of estate distribution plus 25 percent of that distribution, but declining to find contingent-fee agreements per se unethical whenever no risk of total nonrecovery); *In re Hogan Trust*, No. 242530, 2004 WL 1178192, 2004 BL 21736 (Mich. Ct. App. May 27, 2004) (affirming probate court's fee reduction of nearly $400,000 under contingent-fee agreement to $75,000 plus costs and requiring lawyer to return rest to trust; fees unreasonable in light of $45,000 "engagement fee" that "altered the risk-shifting effect" of contingent-fee agreement); Or. Ethics Op. 2005-124 (2005) (although personal injury lawyer may use fee agreement based upon recovery of personal injury protection benefits as well as disputed portion of any award, if sole claim is uncontested personal injury protection claim without separate personal injury case, anything other than de minimis contingent fee is clearly excessive); *cf. Att'y Grievance Comm'n v. Ashworth*, 851 A.2d 527 (Md. 2004) (25 percent contingent-fee agreement for representing plaintiff in dispute with former employer not unreasonable even though matter settled within days and without litigation; "attorneys with excellent skills and reputations often can obtain satisfactory settlements with the expenditure of less effort than those lawyers without such reputation and skill"); *State ex rel. Okla. Bar Ass'n v. Flaniken*, 85 P.3d 824 (Okla. 2004) (rejecting "upon reflection" test by which reasonableness of fee determined in hindsight, court declined to find violation when lawyer lawfully contracted for one-third of client's recovery in probate matter that turned out not to involve anticipated will contest).

ABA Formal Opinion 94-389 holds that it is not per se unethical to charge a contingent fee even though liability is clear and recovery certain, and the amount is the only real issue. ABA Formal Ethics Op. 94-389 (1994). For a scathing critique of this opinion, see Lester Brickman, *ABA Regulation of Contingency Fees: Money Talks, Ethics Walks*, 65 Fordham L. Rev. 247 (Oct. 1996).

## CONTINGENT-FEE AGREEMENTS MUST BE IN WRITING

Rule 1.5(c) requires a written contingent-fee agreement, signed by the client, specifying the lawyer's percentage and explaining which costs and expenses the client is expected to bear. *See, e.g., Statewide Grievance Comm. v. Timbers*, 796 A.2d 565 (Conn. App. Ct. 2002) (failure to secure written contingent-fee agreement or communicate with client about fee); *In re Anonymous*, 657 N.E.2d 394 (Ind. 1995) (workers' compensation board's fee schedule did not obviate need for compliance with ethics requirement of written contingent-fee agreement); *Rasner v. Ky. Bar Ass'n*, 57 S.W.3d 826 (Ky. 2001) (failure to memorialize agreement with client for one-third contingent fee to recover insurance proceeds); *In re Fink*, 22 A.3d 461 (Vt. 2011) (failure to put contingent fee in writing); Ill. Ethics Op. 98-03 (1999) (law firm functioning as business broker between intellectual property clients who are inventors and promoters must reduce fee agreement to writing if fee contingent upon success of contemplated venture).

Although failure to reduce the contingent-fee agreement to writing violates Rule 1.5(c), it does not necessarily deprive the lawyer of all fees. *See, e.g., Mullens v. Hansel-Henderson*, 65 P.3d 992 (Colo. 2002) (quantum meruit recovery permitted in face of noncomplying contingent-fee agreement; lawyer performed all contracted services); *In re Williams*, 693 A.2d 327 (D.C. 1997) (lawyer sued client in small-claims court for his contingent fee, and client then filed complaint against lawyer for never reducing fee agreement to writing; small-claims suit settled, but lawyer admonished in disciplinary proceeding for violating Rules 1.5(b) and 1.5(c)); *Partee v. Compton*, 653 N.E.2d 454 (Ill. App. Ct. 1995) (even though lawyer had not signed contingent-fee agreement, clients not permitted to avoid paying on contract after they "reap[ed] the benefits of its execution"; summary judgment granted for lawyer without prejudice to clients' "other remedies available to them under the Code of Professional Responsibility"); *Starkey, Kelly, Blaney & White v. Estate of Nicolaysen*, 796 A.2d 238 (N.J. 2002) (though oral contingent-fee agreement unenforceable, lawyer entitled to recover reasonable value of legal services under quantum meruit theory). *But see Levine v. Haralson, Miller, Pitt, Feldman & McAnally, P.L.C.*, 418 P.3d 1007 (Ariz. Ct. App. 2018) (lawyer wishing to be compensated on contingent-fee basis "must have a written fee agreement signed by the client"; quantum meruit recovery is unavailable if no written agreement).

## PREMATURE TERMINATION OF CONTINGENT-FEE ENGAGEMENT

A contingent-fee lawyer who is discharged without cause may seek recovery on a quantum meruit basis. *See Baker v. Shapero*, 203 S.W.3d 697 (Ky. 2006) (abandoning Kentucky's unusual policy of permitting recovery on contract when contingent-fee lawyer discharged without cause and announcing that state would join majority of jurisdictions limiting lawyer to quantum meruit recovery); *see also In re Harris*, 934 P.2d 965 (Kan. 1997) (even if client discharged lawyer without cause, $4,000 for ten hours of work would be reduced to quantum meruit recovery of $900; without hiring second lawyer or filing suit, client successfully negotiated settlement of claim for $10,000 more than lawyer had thought it worth); *Bank of Am., N.A. v. Prestige Imports, Inc.* 54 N.E.3d 589 (Mass. App. Ct. 2016) (lawyer who withdraws from contingent-fee matter due to conduct of client is entitled to fees on quantum meruit basis; client "degraded and humiliated" lawyer over course of several years); *cf. Keck & Assocs., P.C. v. Vasey*, 834 N.E.2d 486 (Ill. App. Ct. 2005) (dismissing quantum meruit claim when contingent-fee client discharged lawyer with cause after final adverse judgment and rejected lawyer's advice to appeal); *In re Stowman Law Firm, P.A.*, 870 N.W.2d 755 (Minn. 2015) (lawyer who withdrew from contingent-fee case due to client's refusal to settle is not entitled to recover in quantum meruit). *See generally* Jonathan J. Fox, Comment, *Fixing Compensation Pursuant to a Contingent Fee Contract Following a Premature Termination of the Attorney-Client Relationship*, 57 Loy. L. Rev. 861 (Winter 2011); David Hricik, *Dear Lawyer: If You Decide It's Not Economical to Represent Me, You Can Fire Me as Your Contingent Fee Client, but I Agree I Will Still Owe You a Fee*, 64 Mercer L. Rev. 363 (Winter 2013).

## Paragraph (d): Contingent Fees in Domestic Relations Matters and Criminal Cases

### DOMESTIC RELATIONS MATTERS

In domestic relations matters, Rule 1.5(d) prohibits fee agreements that are contingent upon "the securing of a divorce or upon the amount of alimony or support, or property settlement in lieu thereof." The prohibition protects against overreaching in highly emotional situations and reflects a policy of promoting reconciliation.

This provision, however, does not prohibit contingent-fee arrangements involving post-judgment domestic relations matters; these do not raise the same policy concerns as contingent fees for securing a divorce or for obtaining a certain amount of alimony, support, or property. Cmt. [6]; *see Gil v. Gil*, 956 A.2d 593 (Conn. App. Ct. 2008) (rule not applicable to agreement permitting husband's counsel to collect as additional compensation any attorneys' fees awarded after dissolution due to wife's contempt); *Doe v. Doe*, 34 P.3d 1059 (Haw. Ct. App. 2001) (vacating order excluding post-judgment interest on child support arrearage and limiting fees to lodestar amount with no consideration of contingent-fee contract between lawyer and ex-wife; comment expressly authorizes contingent fees in agreements to enforce judgments for past-due child support); R.I. Ethics Op. 2006-03 (2006) (lawyer may represent wife on contingent-fee basis in dispute with husband about value of stock to which she is entitled under marital settlement agreement); *cf. Chief Disciplinary Counsel v. Cohen*, No. FSTCV084014502S, 2010 WL 5158379 (Conn. Super. Ct. Dec. 2, 2010) (bonus clause triggering higher fees in matters of "extraordinary difficulty" or requiring "special expertise" did not turn domestic relations retainer into prohibited contingent fee). *But see Marquis & Aurbach v. Eighth Judicial Dist. Court*, 146 P.3d 1130 (Nev. 2006) (fee contingent upon modification of property settlement agreement that disposed of both alimony and community property violated state's version of Rule 1.5(d)); *Medina v. Draslow*, 53 N.Y.S.3d 116 (App. Div. 2017) (charging contingent fee in post-judgment divorce matter violated N.Y. Rule 1.5(d)(5)(i), but lawyer could recover under quantum meruit). *See generally* Denise Fields, Comment, *Risky Business or Clever Thinking? An Examination of the Ethical Considerations of Disguised Contingent Fee Agreements in Domestic Relations Matters,* 75 UMKC L. Rev. 1065 (Summer 2007).

## CRIMINAL CASES

Rule 1.5(d) forbids contingent-fee arrangements in criminal cases. *See* N.Y. Cnty. Ethics Op. 714 (1996) (because state's ban, like Model Rule, explicitly refers to representing "a defendant in a criminal case," it must be applied to corporate criminal defendants as well as individuals even though fines, rather than incarceration, at stake). A fee based upon acquittal creates a conflict of interest because it may tempt a defense lawyer to push for trial rather than a plea bargain, or to forgo mitigating evidence if it could lead to conviction of a lesser-included offense. *See generally* Lindsey N. Godfrey, Note, *Rethinking the Ethical Ban on Criminal Contingent Fees: A Common Sense Approach to Asset Forfeiture,* 79 Tex. L. Rev. 1699 (May 2001); Adam Silberlight, *Gambling with Ethics and Constitutional Rights: A Look at Issues Involved with Contingent Fee Arrangements in Criminal Defense Practice,* 27 Seattle U. L. Rev. 805 (Winter 2004).

Use of a contingent-fee agreement in representing a criminal defendant does not in itself constitute ineffective assistance of counsel. *See Downs v. Fla. Dep't of Corr.,* 738 F.3d 240 (11th Cir. 2013) ($10,000 bonus fee in murder case if defendant acquitted of all felony charges did not create conflict or deprive defendant of effective assistance); *Commonwealth v. Facella,* 679 N.E.2d 221 (Mass. App. Ct. 1996) (unethical agreement with criminal defendant to negotiate change of plea to guilty, charging $10,000 initially and additional $15,000 if lawyer could negotiate sentence of under ten years, did not entitle defendant to evidentiary hearing on his claim of ineffective assistance of counsel).

The ABA Guidelines for the Appointment and Performance of Defense Counsel in Death Penalty Cases (2003) unequivocally disapprove of flat fees in death penalty cases because the client's interests are pitted against the lawyer's interest in doing no "more than what is minimally necessary to qualify for the flat payment." (See the "History of Guideline" following Guideline 9.1(B)(1), quoting from the ABA Standards for Criminal Justice: Providing Defense Services, Commentary to Standard 5-2.4 (3d ed. 1993)). *See State v. Cheatham,* 292 P.3d 318 (Kan. 2013) (overworked, inexperienced defense lawyer's flat-fee arrangement in capital murder case so fundamentally undermined representation that defendant did not need to prove actual prejudice).

### • Related Civil Action

The prohibition does not automatically apply to fee agreements for defending a client who plans a civil action arising out of the arrest. *See Landsman v. Moss,* 579 N.Y.S.2d 450 (App. Div. 1992) (contingent-fee arrangement that gave lawyer first $12,000 recovered in client's malicious prosecution action as compensation for lawyer's work defending client in criminal action did not violate prohibition against contingent fees in criminal cases, but did violate rule against acquiring proprietary interest in client's cause of action); Ind. Ethics Op. 1991-4 (1991) (lawyer may agree that criminal defense fee will be paid from recovery in client's planned civil action for false arrest or by client if no recovery in civil action; fee not contingent upon successful criminal defense but upon success in civil case); N.Y. State Ethics Op. 1146 (2018) (where lawyer represents client in personal injury case and criminal matter, arrangement in which fee in criminal case is contingent on outcome of personal injury matter does not violate rule); Pa. Ethics Op. 2004-17 (2004) (prohibition of Rule 1.5(d)(2) does not preclude contingent-fee arrangement with bank fraud defendant whereby lawyer's fee in federal criminal case will be paid out of defendant's recovery in related civil qui tam action).

### Paragraph (e): Fee Division across Firms

Rule 1.5(e) provides that if lawyers not in the same firm share fees, then (1) the division must be proportionate to the work performed or each lawyer must assume joint responsibility, (2) the client must agree in writing, and (3) the total fee must be reasonable. Paragraph (e) applies when one lawyer refers a case to another lawyer, when a client's initial lawyer is replaced by successor counsel, or when lawyers affiliate as co-counsel or local counsel. *See, e.g., Statewide Grievance Comm. v. Dixon*, 772 A.2d 160 (Conn. App. Ct. 2001) (Rule 1.5(e) violated when client did not know of or consent to division of fees between current and former counsel); *Corcoran v. Ne. Ill. Reg'l Commuter R.R. Corp.*, 803 N.E.2d 87 (Ill. App. Ct. 2003) (even though receiving firm waived its own fee when wrongful-death case settled for no more than what client had already been offered, referring lawyer could still recover referral fee of $140,000 from client based upon his compliance with written disclosure requirement and assumption of same responsibility as receiving firm); *Cleveland Bar Ass'n v. Mishler*, 886 N.E.2d 818 (Ohio 2008) (paying another lawyer on hourly basis for appearing in lawyer's place at client's deposition and at mediation conference, without charging client for other lawyer's work and without sharing contingent fee, did not violate fee-sharing rule); *see also In re Wall*, 73 N.E.3d 170 (Ind. 2017) (lawyer treated as independent contractor was not in "same firm" with Florida corporation offering clients bankruptcy, mortgage modification, and foreclosure defense services); ABA Formal Ethics Op. 464 (2013) (lawyers do not violate ban on sharing fees with non-lawyers by sharing fees with lawyers who practice in firm that includes nonlawyer owners, as is permitted in D.C. and some foreign countries); *cf.* ABA Formal Ethics Op. 475 (2016) (when one lawyer receives earned fee subject to fee sharing arrangement with another lawyer, the other lawyer is considered "third person" under Rule 1.15 and receiving lawyer must handle funds accordingly). *See generally* Kellie E. Billings, *What Attorneys Should Know: A Comprehensive Analysis of Proposed Rule 8A*, 35 St. Mary's L.J. 1015 (2004) (reviewing history of referral-fee regulation in different jurisdictions).

### DEPARTING LAWYERS

Comment [8] was added in 2002 to explain that Rule 1.5(e) does not apply if the fee is being divided between lawyers who used to be associated in a firm but have gone their separate ways. *See Norton Frickey, P.C. v. James B. Turner, P.C.*, 94 P.3d 1266 (Colo. App. 2004) (rule "does not prohibit or regulate division of fees to be received

in the future for work done when lawyers were previously associated in a law firm");
*Walker v. Gribble*, 689 N.W.2d 104 (Iowa 2004) (agreement between lawyer and former partner about division of lucrative contingent fee permissible as part of overall
separation from firm); *Frasier, Frasier & Hickman, L.L.P. v. Flynn*, 114 P.3d 1095 (Okla.
Civ. App. 2005) (Rule 1.5(e) does not prohibit law firm from sharing fees with former
partner under separation agreement covering matters entrusted to firm before partner's departure); *Piaskoski & Assocs. v. Ricciardi*, 686 N.W.2d 675 (Wis. Ct. App. 2004)
(Rule 1.5(e) not applicable if lawyers were in same firm when representation began);
Ill. Ethics Op. 03-06 (2004) (rule does not prohibit separation agreement under which
partner who is leaving firm to become state's attorney will share fees for cases he
brought to firm; he need not retain responsibility for cases, take fee in proportion to
services rendered, or obtain client consent).

## JOINT RESPONSIBILITY

Rule 1.5(e) accords with what one ethics opinion called "the modern trend [that]
permits a lawyer to receive a portion of the fees generated by a matter solely in consideration for a referral if the lawyer assumes joint responsibility." N.Y. Cnty. Ethics
Op. 715 (1996). Comment [7] explains that joint responsibility "entails financial and
ethical responsibility for the representation as if the lawyers were associated in a
partnership." *See* Tex. Ethics Op. 590 (2009) (agreement that requires departing lawyer to pay firm percentage of fees he receives for representing firm clients after he
departs, without requiring firm to perform services or assume joint responsibility,
is impermissible); Wis. Formal Ethics Op. EF-10-02 (2010) (referring lawyer's duties
include obligations to monitor progress of case and remain available to client, and
to maintain financial responsibility for representation). *But see* Ariz. Ethics Op. 04-02
(2004) (requirement of joint responsibility satisfied if referring lawyer assumes financial responsibility for any malpractice during representation; referring lawyer not
necessarily required to have "substantive involvement"); Ill. Rule 1.5(e) (requires
only "joint financial responsibility").

"Implicit in the terms of the fee division allowed by Rule 1.5(e) is . . . that the
referring lawyer who divides a legal fee has undertaken the representation of the client." ABA Formal Ethics Op. 474 (2016). Accordingly, a lawyer who is prohibited by
the ethics rules from undertaking a representation may not share in the legal fee generated by that matter. *See In re Babies*, 315 B.R. 785 (Bankr. N.D. Ga. 2004) (fee-sharing
arrangement between Georgia lawyer and Illinois lawyers did not satisfy Georgia
Rule 1.5(e)'s requirement of joint responsibility if fee not apportioned according to
work performed; joint responsibility requires more than financial responsibility and
therefore could not be assumed by Illinois lawyers without pro hac vice admission
to Georgia bar); *Evans & Luptak, PLC v. Lizza*, 650 N.W.2d 364 (Mich. Ct. App. 2002)
(agreement that allows firm to receive payment for referring client with which it had
conflict is unenforceable); *Cruse v. O'Quinn*, 273 S.W.3d 766 (Tex. App. 2008) (because
fee-sharer must maintain joint responsibility, suspended and disbarred lawyer may
not recover fees in cases not concluded before disbarment); ABA Formal Ethics Op.
474 (2018) (referring lawyer with conflict of interest cannot share legal fee); N.Y. State
Ethics Op. 745 (2001) (lawyer disqualified due to conflict of interest cannot assume

joint responsibility and thus may not be paid referral fee); N.Y. City Ethics Op. 2016-1 (2016) (lawyer with unwaivable or unwaived conflict of interest who refers client to other lawyer may not share fees generated by that matter); Pa. Ethics Op. 2018-010 (2018) (conflicted referring lawyer cannot receive fee).

## WRITTEN CONSENT TO FEE DIVISION REQUIRED

The 2002 amendments to Rule 1.5 add a requirement that the client agree in writing to the participation of each lawyer, including the share each will receive. *See In re Storment*, 786 N.E.2d 963 (Ill. 2002) (failure to obtain written client consent to fee division not "mere technical violation"; lawyer suspended); *In re Stochel*, 792 N.E.2d 874 (Ind. 2003) (without client consent, lawyer paid $16,000 to referring lawyer whose only contact with client had been initial consultation for which he had already been paid $250); *In re Hart*, 605 S.E.2d 532 (S.C. 2004) (lawyer disciplined for, inter alia, not putting his standard 50/50 fee split with referring lawyers in writing in seventy cases; no client complained, all clients consented, and lawyer self-reported); Pa. Ethics Op. 2018-010 (2018) (fee-sharing agreement cannot be enforced if clients were not advised of it); *see also Naughton v. Pfaff*, 57 N.E.3d 503 (Ill. App. Ct. 2016) (failure of referring lawyer to ensure client signed fee-sharing agreement precluded him from recovering under oral agreement).

"[T]he division of fees must be agreed to either before or within a reasonable time after commencing the representation." ABA Formal Ethics Op. 474 (2016). *See Wagner & Wagner, LLP v. Atkinson, Haskins, Nellis, Brittingham, Gladd & Carwile, P.C.*, 596 F.3d 84 (2d Cir. 2010) (cannot cure lack of informed consent by charade of giving client "joint responsibility" letter after settlement reached); *Saggese v. Kelley*, 837 N.E.2d 699 (Mass. 2005) (written consent must be obtained before lawyer makes referral); *see also* Cal. Rule 1.5.1 (client must consent "either at the time the lawyers enter into the agreement to divide the fee or as soon thereafter as reasonably practicable"). *See generally* Constance L. Rudnick & Elizabeth N. Mulvey, *Splitting Hairs in Fee Splitting*, 50 Boston B.J., Mar./Apr. 2006, at 14 (criticizing *Saggese*).

## ENFORCEABILITY OF FEE-SHARING
## AGREEMENT THAT VIOLATES RULE 1.5(e)

Enforceability of fee-division agreements that do not comply with Rule 1.5 varies among jurisdictions. For a thorough analysis see "Special Report: Rule 1.5(e) Looms Large in Lawyers' Disputes over Fee-Sharing Agreements," *ABA/BNA Lawyers' Manual on Professional Conduct*, 30 Law. Man. Prof. Conduct 18 (Current Reports, Mar. 26, 2014). *See generally* Benjamin P. Cooper, *Taking Rules Seriously: The Rise of Lawyer Rules as Substantive Law and the Public Policy Exception in Contract Law*, 35 Cardozo L. Rev. 267 (Oct. 2013) (examines split among courts about substantive impact of agreements that violate lawyer ethics rules and urges courts to take rules more seriously as source of law); Douglas R. Richmond, *Professional Responsibilities of Co-Counsel: Joint Venturers or Scorpions in a Bottle?*, 98 Ky. L.J. 461 (2009–2010).

Courts disfavor lawyers' attempts to assert their own lack of compliance with Rule 1.5(e) to avoid honoring an obligation to share a fee with another lawyer. *See, e.g., Grasso v. Galanter*, No. 2:12-cv-00738-GMN-NJK, 2013 WL 5537289 (D. Nev. Oct.

4, 2013); *Barnes, Crosby, Fitzgerald & Zeman, LLP v. Ringler*, 151 Cal. Rptr. 3d 134 (Ct. App. 2012) (lawyer was himself responsible for preventing other lawyer from complying with consent and disclosure requirements); *cf. Thompson v. Hiter*, 826 N.E.2d 503 (Ill. App. Ct. 2005) (law firm discharged by client before settlement not entitled to portion of fee earned by lawyer who brought case to firm and then handled it after firm's discharge; firm failed to obtain written agreement as required by rule).

## RESOLUTION OF FEE DISPUTES

Comment [9] notes that a lawyer should "conscientiously consider" voluntarily submitting to any established arbitration or mediation procedure to resolve a fee dispute. An ABA ethics opinion goes further and permits a retainer agreement that requires binding arbitration of fee disputes and malpractice claims if the client is fully apprised of the advantages and disadvantages of arbitration and has given informed consent. ABA Formal Ethics Op. 02-425 (2002); *see Slater-Moore v. Goeldner*, 113 So. 3d 521 (Miss. 2013) (rejecting client's challenge to inclusion of fee-arbitration provisions in retainer contracts and enforcing law firm's motion to compel arbitration of her fee dispute). *See generally* Lester Brickman, *Attorney-Client Fee Arbitration: A Dissenting View*, 1990 Utah L. Rev. 227 (1990) (resort to arbitration may amount to functional equivalent of client waiving the "correlative rights that devolve upon him as a consequence of the attorney's fiduciary obligation").

The ABA's Model Fee Arbitration Rules are available at https://www.american bar.org/groups/professional_responsibility/resources/client_protection/fee/.

The ethical implications of arbitrating client-lawyer disputes are also discussed in the annotation to Rule 1.8(h).

## Rule 1.6

### *Confidentiality of Information*

(a) A lawyer shall not reveal information relating to the representation of a client unless the client gives informed consent, the disclosure is impliedly authorized in order to carry out the representation or the disclosure is permitted by paragraph (b).

(b) A lawyer may reveal information relating to the representation of a client to the extent the lawyer reasonably believes necessary:

(1) to prevent reasonably certain death or substantial bodily harm;

(2) to prevent the client from committing a crime or fraud that is reasonably certain to result in substantial injury to the financial interests or property of another and in furtherance of which the client has used or is using the lawyer's services;

(3) to prevent, mitigate or rectify substantial injury to the financial interests or property of another that is reasonably certain to result or has resulted from the client's commission of a crime or fraud in furtherance of which the client has used the lawyer's services;

(4) to secure legal advice about the lawyer's compliance with these Rules;

(5) to establish a claim or defense on behalf of the lawyer in a controversy between the lawyer and the client, to establish a defense to a criminal charge or civil claim against the lawyer based upon conduct in which the client was involved, or to respond to allegations in any proceeding concerning the lawyer's representation of the client;

(6) to comply with other law or a court order; or

(7) to detect and resolve conflicts of interest arising from the lawyer's change of employment or from changes in the composition or ownership of a firm, but only if the revealed information would not compromise the attorney-client privilege or otherwise prejudice the client.

(c) A lawyer shall make reasonable efforts to prevent the inadvertent or unauthorized disclosure of, or unauthorized access to, information relating to the representation of a client.

# COMMENT

[1] This Rule governs the disclosure by a lawyer of information relating to the representation of a client during the lawyer's representation of the client. See Rule 1.18 for the lawyer's duties with respect to information provided to the lawyer by a prospective client, Rule 1.9(c)(2) for the lawyer's duty not to reveal information relating to the lawyer's prior representation of a former client and Rules 1.8(b) and 1.9(c)(1) for the lawyer's duties with respect to the use of such information to the disadvantage of clients and former clients.

[2] A fundamental principle in the client-lawyer relationship is that, in the absence of the client's informed consent, the lawyer must not reveal information relating to the representation. See Rule 1.0(e) for the definition of informed consent. This contributes to the trust that is the hallmark of the client-lawyer relationship. The client is thereby encouraged to seek legal assistance and to communicate fully and frankly with the lawyer even as to embarrassing or legally damaging subject matter. The lawyer needs this information to represent the client effectively and, if necessary, to advise the client to refrain from wrongful conduct. Almost without exception, clients come to lawyers in order to determine their rights and what is, in the complex of laws and regulations, deemed to be legal and correct. Based upon experience, lawyers know that almost all clients follow the advice given, and the law is upheld.

[3] The principle of client-lawyer confidentiality is given effect by related bodies of law: the attorney-client privilege, the work product doctrine and the rule of confidentiality established in professional ethics. The attorney-client privilege and work product doctrine apply in judicial and other proceedings in which a lawyer may be called as a witness or otherwise required to produce evidence concerning a client. The rule of client-lawyer confidentiality applies in situations other than those where evidence is sought from the lawyer through compulsion of law. The confidentiality rule, for example, applies not only to matters communicated in confidence by the client but also to all information relating to the representation, whatever its source. A lawyer may not disclose such information except as authorized or required by the Rules of Professional Conduct or other law. See also Scope.

[4] Paragraph (a) prohibits a lawyer from revealing information relating to the representation of a client. This prohibition also applies to disclosures by a lawyer that do not in themselves reveal protected information but could reasonably lead to the discovery of such information by a third person. A lawyer's use of a hypothetical to discuss issues relating to the representation is permissible so long as there is no reasonable likelihood that the listener will be able to ascertain the identity of the client or the situation involved.

## *Authorized Disclosure*

[5] Except to the extent that the client's instructions or special circumstances limit that authority, a lawyer is impliedly authorized to make disclosures about a client when appropriate in carrying out the representation. In some situations, for example, a lawyer may be impliedly authorized to admit a fact that cannot properly be disputed or to make a disclosure that facilitates a satisfactory conclusion to a

matter. Lawyers in a firm may, in the course of the firm's practice, disclose to each other information relating to a client of the firm, unless the client has instructed that particular information be confined to specified lawyers.

## *Disclosure Adverse to Client*

[6] Although the public interest is usually best served by a strict rule requiring lawyers to preserve the confidentiality of information relating to the representation of their clients, the confidentiality rule is subject to limited exceptions. Paragraph (b)(1) recognizes the overriding value of life and physical integrity and permits disclosure reasonably necessary to prevent reasonably certain death or substantial bodily harm. Such harm is reasonably certain to occur if it will be suffered imminently or if there is a present and substantial threat that a person will suffer such harm at a later date if the lawyer fails to take action necessary to eliminate the threat. Thus, a lawyer who knows that a client has accidentally discharged toxic waste into a town's water supply may reveal this information to the authorities if there is a present and substantial risk that a person who drinks the water will contract a life-threatening or debilitating disease and the lawyer's disclosure is necessary to eliminate the threat or reduce the number of victims.

[7] Paragraph (b)(2) is a limited exception to the rule of confidentiality that permits the lawyer to reveal information to the extent necessary to enable affected persons or appropriate authorities to prevent the client from committing a crime or fraud, as defined in Rule 1.0(d), that is reasonably certain to result in substantial injury to the financial or property interests of another and in furtherance of which the client has used or is using the lawyer's services. Such a serious abuse of the client-lawyer relationship by the client forfeits the protection of this Rule. The client can, of course, prevent such disclosure by refraining from the wrongful conduct. Although paragraph (b)(2) does not require the lawyer to reveal the client's misconduct, the lawyer may not counsel or assist the client in conduct the lawyer knows is criminal or fraudulent. See Rule 1.2(d). See also Rule 1.16 with respect to the lawyer's obligation or right to withdraw from the representation of the client in such circumstances, and Rule 1.13(c), which permits the lawyer, where the client is an organization, to reveal information relating to the representation in limited circumstances.

[8] Paragraph (b)(3) addresses the situation in which the lawyer does not learn of the client's crime or fraud until after it has been consummated. Although the client no longer has the option of preventing disclosure by refraining from the wrongful conduct, there will be situations in which the loss suffered by the affected person can be prevented, rectified or mitigated. In such situations, the lawyer may disclose information relating to the representation to the extent necessary to enable the affected persons to prevent or mitigate reasonably certain losses or to attempt to recoup their losses. Paragraph (b)(3) does not apply when a person who has committed a crime or fraud thereafter employs a lawyer for representation concerning that offense.

[9] A lawyer's confidentiality obligations do not preclude a lawyer from securing confidential legal advice about the lawyer's personal responsibility to comply with these Rules. In most situations, disclosing information to secure such advice will be impliedly authorized for the lawyer to carry out the representation. Even when

the disclosure is not impliedly authorized, paragraph (b)(4) permits such disclosure because of the importance of a lawyer's compliance with the Rules of Professional Conduct.

[10] Where a legal claim or disciplinary charge alleges complicity of the lawyer in a client's conduct or other misconduct of the lawyer involving representation of the client, the lawyer may respond to the extent the lawyer reasonably believes necessary to establish a defense. The same is true with respect to a claim involving the conduct or representation of a former client. Such a charge can arise in a civil, criminal, disciplinary or other proceeding and can be based on a wrong allegedly committed by the lawyer against the client or on a wrong alleged by a third person, for example, a person claiming to have been defrauded by the lawyer and client acting together. The lawyer's right to respond arises when an assertion of such complicity has been made. Paragraph (b)(5) does not require the lawyer to await the commencement of an action or proceeding that charges such complicity, so that the defense may be established by responding directly to a third party who has made such an assertion. The right to defend also applies, of course, where a proceeding has been commenced.

[11] A lawyer entitled to a fee is permitted by paragraph (b)(5) to prove the services rendered in an action to collect it. This aspect of the rule expresses the principle that the beneficiary of a fiduciary relationship may not exploit it to the detriment of the fiduciary.

[12] Other law may require that a lawyer disclose information about a client. Whether such a law supersedes Rule 1.6 is a question of law beyond the scope of these Rules. When disclosure of information relating to the representation appears to be required by other law, the lawyer must discuss the matter with the client to the extent required by Rule 1.4. If, however, the other law supersedes this Rule and requires disclosure, paragraph (b)(6) permits the lawyer to make such disclosures as are necessary to comply with the law.

## Detection of Conflicts of Interest

[13] Paragraph (b)(7) recognizes that lawyers in different firms may need to disclose limited information to each other to detect and resolve conflicts of interest, such as when a lawyer is considering an association with another firm, two or more firms are considering a merger, or a lawyer is considering the purchase of a law practice. See Rule 1.17, Comment [7]. Under these circumstances, lawyers and law firms are permitted to disclose limited information, but only once substantive discussions regarding the new relationship have occurred. Any such disclosure should ordinarily include no more than the identity of the persons and entities involved in a matter, a brief summary of the general issues involved, and information about whether the matter has terminated. Even this limited information, however, should be disclosed only to the extent reasonably necessary to detect and resolve conflicts of interest that might arise from the possible new relationship. Moreover, the disclosure of any information is prohibited if it would compromise the attorney-client privilege or otherwise prejudice the client (e.g., the fact that a corporate client is seeking advice on a corporate takeover that has not been publicly announced; that a person has consulted

a lawyer about the possibility of divorce before the person's intentions are known to the person's spouse; or that a person has consulted a lawyer about a criminal investigation that has not led to a public charge). Under those circumstances, paragraph (a) prohibits disclosure unless the client or former client gives informed consent. A lawyer's fiduciary duty to the lawyer's firm may also govern a lawyer's conduct when exploring an association with another firm and is beyond the scope of these Rules.

[14] Any information disclosed pursuant to paragraph (b)(7) may be used or further disclosed only to the extent necessary to detect and resolve conflicts of interest. Paragraph (b)(7) does not restrict the use of information acquired by means independent of any disclosure pursuant to paragraph (b)(7). Paragraph (b)(7) also does not affect the disclosure of information within a law firm when the disclosure is otherwise authorized, see Comment [5], such as when a lawyer in a firm discloses information to another lawyer in the same firm to detect and resolve conflicts of interest that could arise in connection with undertaking a new representation.

[15] A lawyer may be ordered to reveal information relating to the representation of a client by a court or by another tribunal or governmental entity claiming authority pursuant to other law to compel the disclosure. Absent informed consent of the client to do otherwise, the lawyer should assert on behalf of the client all nonfrivolous claims that the order is not authorized by other law or that the information sought is protected against disclosure by the attorney-client privilege or other applicable law. In the event of an adverse ruling, the lawyer must consult with the client about the possibility of appeal to the extent required by Rule 1.4. Unless review is sought, however, paragraph (b)(6) permits the lawyer to comply with the court's order.

[16] Paragraph (b) permits disclosure only to the extent the lawyer reasonably believes the disclosure is necessary to accomplish one of the purposes specified. Where practicable, the lawyer should first seek to persuade the client to take suitable action to obviate the need for disclosure. In any case, a disclosure adverse to the client's interest should be no greater than the lawyer reasonably believes necessary to accomplish the purpose. If the disclosure will be made in connection with a judicial proceeding, the disclosure should be made in a manner that limits access to the information to the tribunal or other persons having a need to know it and appropriate protective orders or other arrangements should be sought by the lawyer to the fullest extent practicable.

[17] Paragraph (b) permits but does not require the disclosure of information relating to a client's representation to accomplish the purposes specified in paragraphs (b)(1) through (b)(6). In exercising the discretion conferred by this Rule, the lawyer may consider such factors as the nature of the lawyer's relationship with the client and with those who might be injured by the client, the lawyer's own involvement in the transaction and factors that may extenuate the conduct in question. A lawyer's decision not to disclose as permitted by paragraph (b) does not violate this Rule. Disclosure may be required, however, by other Rules. Some Rules require disclosure only if such disclosure would be permitted by paragraph (b). See Rules 1.2(d), 4.1(b), 8.1 and 8.3. Rule 3.3, on the other hand, requires disclosure in some circumstances regardless of whether such disclosure is permitted by this Rule. See Rule 3.3(c).

### Acting Competently to Preserve Confidentiality

[18] Paragraph (c) requires a lawyer to act competently to safeguard information relating to the representation of a client against unauthorized access by third parties and against inadvertent or unauthorized disclosure by the lawyer or other persons who are participating in the representation of the client or who are subject to the lawyer's supervision. See Rules 1.1, 5.1 and 5.3. The unauthorized access to, or the inadvertent or unauthorized disclosure of, information relating to the representation of a client does not constitute a violation of paragraph (c) if the lawyer has made reasonable efforts to prevent the access or disclosure. Factors to be considered in determining the reasonableness of the lawyer's efforts include, but are not limited to, the sensitivity of the information, the likelihood of disclosure if additional safeguards are not employed, the cost of employing additional safeguards, the difficulty of implementing the safeguards, and the extent to which the safeguards adversely affect the lawyer's ability to represent clients (e.g., by making a device or important piece of software excessively difficult to use). A client may require the lawyer to implement special security measures not required by this Rule or may give informed consent to forgo security measures that would otherwise be required by this Rule. Whether a lawyer may be required to take additional steps to safeguard a client's information in order to comply with other law, such as state and federal laws that govern data privacy or that impose notification requirements upon the loss of, or unauthorized access to, electronic information, is beyond the scope of these Rules. For a lawyer's duties when sharing information with nonlawyers outside the lawyer's own firm, see Rule 5.3, Comments [3]-[4].

[19] When transmitting a communication that includes information relating to the representation of a client, the lawyer must take reasonable precautions to prevent the information from coming into the hands of unintended recipients. This duty, however, does not require that the lawyer use special security measures if the method of communication affords a reasonable expectation of privacy. Special circumstances, however, may warrant special precautions. Factors to be considered in determining the reasonableness of the lawyer's expectation of confidentiality include the sensitivity of the information and the extent to which the privacy of the communication is protected by law or by a confidentiality agreement. A client may require the lawyer to implement special security measures not required by this Rule or may give informed consent to the use of a means of communication that would otherwise be prohibited by this Rule. Whether a lawyer may be required to take additional steps in order to comply with other law, such as state and federal laws that govern data privacy, is beyond the scope of these Rules.

### Former Client

[20] The duty of confidentiality continues after the client-lawyer relationship has terminated. See Rule 1.9(c)(2). See Rule 1.9(c)(1) for the prohibition against using such information to the disadvantage of the former client.

**Definitional Cross-References**
"Firm" *See* Rule 1.0(c)
"Fraud" *See* Rule 1.0(d)
"Informed consent" *See* Rule 1.0(e)
"Reasonably" *See* Rule 1.0(h)
"Reasonably believes" *See* Rule 1.0(i)
"Substantial" *See* Rule 1.0(l)

**State Rules Comparison**
http://ambar.org/MRPCStateCharts

# ANNOTATION

## OVERVIEW

Rule 1.6 sets out the lawyer's professional duty to protect the confidentiality of client information. This ethical duty derives from both the law of agency and the law of evidence. *See Restatement (Third) of Agency* § 8.05 (2006) (agent may not disclose or use "confidential information" of principal for agent's own purposes or those of third party); *Restatement (Third) of the Law Governing Lawyers* §§ 59–67, 68–86 (2000) (confidentiality rules derived from agency law and professional regulations; evidentiary attorney privilege protects confidential client-lawyer communications from coerced disclosure in course of legal proceedings).

Compliance with the duty of confidentiality under this rule requires not only that lawyers avoid improperly disclosing protected information, but also that they act reasonably and competently to preserve confidentiality. *See* Rule 1.6(c), cmts. [18], [19]. In addition, under Rule 1.8(b), lawyers may not use protected information to the client's disadvantage without the client's consent. *See also* Rule 1.9(c) (Duties to Former Clients); Rule 1.13 (Organization as Client); Rule 1.18(b) (Duties to Prospective Client); Rule 3.3 (Candor Toward the Tribunal); Rule 4.1(b) (Truthfulness in Statements to Others).

### • *2012 Amendments*

Rule 1.6 was amended in 2012 to address issues relating to conflicts and technology. Paragraph (b)(7) and Comments [13] and [14] were added to permit limited disclosure of information "to detect and resolve conflicts of interest arising from the lawyer's change of employment or from changes in the composition or ownership of a firm." Former Comments [13] through [18] were consequently renumbered [15] through [20], paragraph (c)—requiring a lawyer to make reasonable efforts to prevent inadvertent or unauthorized disclosure of client information, or unauthorized access to the information—was added, and Comments [18] and [19] were amended accordingly. *See* American Bar Association, *A Legislative History: The Development of the ABA Model Rules of Professional Conduct, 1982–2013*, at 143–46 (2013).

### • *Relationship of Rule 1.6 to Attorney-Client Privilege*

The attorney-client evidentiary privilege is so closely related to the ethical duty of confidentiality that the terms "privileged" and "confidential" are often used interchangeably. But the two are entirely separate concepts, applicable under different sets of circumstances and using different standards. The ethical duty is extremely broad: it protects from disclosure all "information relating to the representation," and applies at all times. The attorney-client privilege, however, is more limited: it protects from compelled disclosure the substance of a lawyer-client communication made for the purpose of obtaining or imparting legal advice or assistance, and applies only in the context of a legal proceeding governed by the rules of evidence. *See* Rule 1.6, cmt. [3]; *Restatement (Third) of the Law Governing Lawyers* §§ 68–86 (2000).

Accordingly, a court's determination that particular information is not privileged is not the same as a determination that the lawyer has no ethical obligation to protect the information from disclosure in other contexts. *See, e.g., Hays v. Page Perry, LLC*, 92 F. Supp. 3d 1315 (N.D. Ga. Mar. 17, 2015) ("that certain confidential information may be discoverable [under crime-fraud exception to attorney-client privilege] does not mean that attorneys may volunteer such information outside of a judicial proceeding"); *Newman v. State*, 863 A.2d 321 (Md. 2004) (confidentiality rule "not limited to matters communicated in confidence by the client but also to all information relating to the representation . . . whereas the attorney-client privilege only protects communications between the client and the attorney"); *Spratley v. State Farm Mut. Ins. Co.*, 78 P.3d 603, 608 n.2 (Utah 2003) (ethical duty of confidentiality not coextensive with attorney-client privilege: "privilege might be waived allowing compelled disclosure by an attorney while the duty of confidentiality is still in full force"). Conversely, a lawyer's voluntary and permissible disclosure under one of the confidentiality exceptions does not itself waive or otherwise disrupt the privileged nature of a communication for purposes of a subsequent attempt to compel disclosure. *See In re Grand Jury Investigation*, 902 N.E.2d 929 (Mass. 2009) (disclosure of client's threat to harm judge was permitted by Rule 1.6, but communication remained privileged and lawyer could not be compelled to testify about it at subsequent criminal proceeding). *See generally* Michael W. Glenn, *Principles, Politics and Privilege: How the Crime-Fraud Exception Can Preserve the Strength of the Attorney-Client Privilege for Government Lawyers and Their Clients*, 40 Fordham Urb. L.J. 1447 (May 2013); Mitchell M. Simon, *Discreet Disclosures: Should Lawyers Who Disclose Confidential Information to Protect Third Parties Be Compelled to Testify Against Their Clients?* 49 S. Tex. L. Rev. 307 (Winter 2007).

Although a determination of whether a lawyer must reveal client information in an adversarial proceeding will turn on rules of evidence rather than rules of ethics, the lawyer's ethical duty of confidentiality governs important aspects of the lawyer's response to a demand for information. When a demand is first made upon a lawyer, through legal process, to disclose client information, Rule 1.6 requires the lawyer to assert "all nonfrivolous claims" that the information is protected from disclosure by the attorney-client privilege or other applicable law. Cmt. [15]; *see, e.g.,* R.I. Ethics Op. 2000-8 (2000) (lawyer questioned at deposition about matters related to representation of deceased client is required by Rule 1.6 to invoke lawyer-client privilege and ethical duty of confidentiality and, if applicable, work-product doctrine; lawyer must comply with final order of court seeking disclosure).

For further analysis of the relationship between the ethical duty of confidentiality and the attorney-client privilege, see *ABA/BNA Lawyers' Manual on Professional Conduct*, "Confidentiality: Protected Information," pp. 55:301 *et seq.*

## *Paragraph (a): Protected Information*

### LAWYER MAY NOT DISCLOSE INFORMATION
### RELATING TO REPRESENTATION OF CLIENT

Rule 1.6(a) prohibits a lawyer from disclosing any "information relating to the representation of a client," in the absence of implied or express consent or an applicable exception specified in the rule. *See, e.g., People v. Albani*, 276 P.3d 64 (Colo. O.P.D.J. 2011) (criminal defense lawyer disclosed prosecution's plea offers and related discussions with client to court without client's consent); *In re Steele*, 45 N.E.3d 777 (Ind. 2015) (recording conversations with clients and replaying them to staff and relatives for "personal amusement"); *Disciplinary Counsel v. Holmes*, No. 2018-0818, 2018 WL 5292330 (Ohio Oct. 25, 2018) (two lawyers shared client information); *In re Peshek*, 798 N.W.2d 879 (Wis. 2011) (assistant public defender published confidential information in blog posts from which clients' identities could be deduced); ABA Formal Ethics Op. 463 (2013) ("mandatory reporting of suspicion [of money laundering or terrorist financing related to] a client is in conflict with Rules 1.6 and 1.8"); Phila. Ethics Op. 2018-1 (2018) (lawyer must conduct reasonably diligent search for missing client but may not disclose confidential information); Utah Ethics Op. 05-02 (2005) (criminal defense lawyer may not reveal client's prior convictions when requested by court at sentencing hearing without client's informed consent). The range of protected information is extremely broad, covering information received from the client or any other source, even public sources, and, according to Comment [4], even information that is not itself protected but may lead to the discovery of protected information by a third party. *See, e.g., In re Goebel*, 703 N.E.2d 1045 (Ind. 1998) (in effort to convince criminal client who threatened to murder guardianship client that lawyer did not know latter's whereabouts, lawyer showed criminal client returned envelope containing incorrect address for her; however, criminal client was able to guess mistake in address, go to her home, and murder her husband).

### • *Previously Disclosed or Publicly Available Information*

In contrast to both the attorney-client privilege (applicable only to communications made "in confidence," and waived upon disclosure) and Rule 1.9(c)(1) (permitting lawyers to "use" information relating to the representation of a former client to the disadvantage of that client when the "information has become generally known"), Rule 1.6 contains no exception permitting disclosure of information previously disclosed or publicly available. *See, e.g., In re Anonymous*, 932 N.E.2d 671 (Ind. 2010) (neither client's prior disclosure of information relating to her divorce representation to friends nor availability of information in police reports and other public records absolved lawyer of violation of Rule 1.6); *Iowa Supreme Court Att'y Disciplinary Bd. v. Marzen*, 779 N.W.2d 757 (Iowa 2010) (all lawyer-client communications, even those including publicly available information, are confidential); *In re Bryan*,

61 P.3d 641 (Kan. 2003) (disclosing, in court documents, existence of defamation suit against former client); *State ex rel. Okla. Bar Ass'n v. Chappell*, 93 P.3d 25 (Okla. 2004) (lawyer in fee dispute with former employer violated Rule 1.6 by filing motion referring to criminal charges that were filed and later dismissed against former client); *Lawyer Disciplinary Bd. v. McGraw*, 461 S.E.2d 850 (W. Va. 1995) ("[t]he ethical duty of confidentiality is not nullified by the fact that the information is part of a public record or by the fact that someone else is privy to it"); *In re Harman*, 628 N.W.2d 351 (Wis. 2001) (lawyer violated Rule 1.6(a) by disclosing to prosecutor former client's medical records he obtained during prior representation; irrelevant whether those records "lost their 'confidentiality'" by being made part of former client's medical malpractice action); ABA Formal Ethics Op. 480 (2018) (rule protects from disclosure information relating to a representation, "including information contained in a public record"); Ariz. Ethics Op. 2000-11 (2000) (lawyer must "maintain the confidentiality of information relating to representation even if the information is a matter of public record"); Nev. Ethics Op. 41 (2009) (contrasting broad language of Rule 1.6 with narrower language of *Restatement (Third) of the Law Governing Lawyers*); Pa. Ethics Op. 2009-10 (2009) (absent client consent, lawyer may not report opponent's misconduct to disciplinary board even though it is recited in court's opinion); *cf.* Cal. Formal Ethics Op. 2016-195 (n.d.) (must protect confidential client information even if publicly available); David Hricik, *The Same Thing Twice: Copying Text from One Client's Patent into Another's Application*, 5 Landslide, no. 5, at 22 (May/June 2013) (discussing whether copying text from one client's patent application into another's may breach duty of confidentiality). *But see In re Sellers*, 669 So. 2d 1204 (La. 1996) (lawyer violated Rule 4.1 by failing to disclose existence of collateral mortgage to third party; because "mortgage was filed in the public record, disclosure of its existence could not be a confidential communication, and was not prohibited by Rule 1.6"); *In re Lim*, 210 S.W.3d 199 (Mo. 2007) (no violation of duty of confidentiality when lawyer sent letter to INS opining that former clients "lack the good moral character needed to obtain immigration benefits" because they "lied and deceived our office" and owed lawyer money, because lawyer's opinion was not confidential information and debt was matter of public record); *Hunter v. Va. State Bar*, 744 S.E.2d 611 (Va. 2013) (state bar's interpretation of Rule 1.6 as prohibiting posting publicly available client information about completed cases on lawyer's blog violated First Amendment); *cf.* N.Y. State Ethics Op. 1057 (2015) (documents filed by client in other court do not fall within "generally known" exception in Comment [4A] to N.Y. Rule 1.6 unless reported in public media or widely publicized by client and therefore are confidential information that lawyer may not disclose in support of motion to withdraw).

### • *Disclosure of Client Identity*

Rule 1.6 prohibits the disclosure of a client's identity unless the client consents or the disclosure is impliedly authorized. *See, e.g.*, Conn. Informal Ethics Op. 17-01 (2017) (lawyer for real estate seller is impliedly authorized to complete state tax form requiring disclosure of seller's Social Security number); Ill. Ethics Op. 12-03 (2012) (may not provide business networking group members with client names without clients' consent); N.Y. State Ethics Op. 1088 (2016) (lawyer may not disclose client name in advertising if client has requested representation remain confidential or disclosure would be detrimental or embarrassing to client, but may do so under New York rule's exception if fact of representation is generally known); Phila. Ethics Op. 2014-6 (2014) (law firm representing union members through union legal services plan contract may not disclose names of members with pending cases to union after contract terminated); Wash. Ethics Op. 201802 (2018) (informed consent required before disclosing client's name to outside entity such as insurer, risk or human resources manager, or third-party litigation administrator); Wis. Formal Ethics Op. EF-17-02 (2017) (informed consent required before including client names in advertising materials).

A lawyer may use hypotheticals to discuss issues relating to the representation as long as "there is no reasonable likelihood that the listener will be able to ascertain the identity of the client or the situation involved." Cmt. [4]. *See* ABA Formal Ethics Op. 480 (2018) (use of hypotheticals in lawyer blogs and public commentary); ABA Formal Ethics Op. 98-411 (1998) (lawyer may consult another lawyer who is not associated with him for advice on client matter by framing request for consultation as hypothetical without revealing client's identity); Ill. Ethics Op. 12-15 (2012) (may post to online bar association discussion group seeking guidance on client matter if no information relating to representation is disclosed without client's informed consent and inquiry would not risk identifying client); N.Y. State Ethics Op. 1026 (2014) (lawyer may not publish work of fiction based on real client if reasonable chance exists that reader might thereby ascertain client's identity); Or. Ethics Op. 2011-184 (2011) (seeking guidance on client matter by consulting lawyer outside firm or in post to online bar association discussion group permissible if no information relating to representation is disclosed without client's informed consent and inquiry carries no risk of identifying client).

In the context of litigation, however, the general rule is that a client's identity is not protected by the attorney-client privilege unless "the net effect of the disclosure would be to reveal the nature of a client communication." 1 Kenneth S. Broun et al., *McCormick on Evidence* § 90 (7th ed. 2013). *See, e.g., United States v. BDO Seidman*, 337 F.3d 802 (7th Cir. 2003) (court likened tax practitioner-client privilege to attorney-client privilege in requiring disclosure of information regarding identity of accounting firm's clients who consulted with firm regarding their participation in potentially abusive tax shelters); *In re Subpoena to Testify Before Grand Jury (Alexiou v. United States)*, 39 F.3d 973 (9th Cir. 1994) (requiring testimony about identity of client who paid with counterfeit $100 bill; client's name not considered confidential unless "intertwined" with confidential information or last link tying client to crime); *Brett v. Berkowitz*, 706 A.2d 509 (Del. 1998) (client identity privileged in exceptional cases when disclosure would provide "last link" in chain of evidence implicating client in crime and would reveal confidential communication between lawyer and client); *State v. Gonzalez*, 234 P.3d 1 (Kan. 2010) (public defender could not be compelled to disclose identity of client when defender already disclosed nature of client's statement). *See generally* Steven Goode, *Identity, Fees and the Attorney-Client Privilege*, 59 Geo. Wash. L. Rev. 307 (Jan. 1991).

## • *Financial and Billing Information*

The rule also prohibits a lawyer from revealing a client's financial or billing information without the client's consent. *See, e.g., Bd. of Prof'l Responsibility v. Casper*, 318 P.3d 790 (Wyo. 2014) (complete billing records of former client filed with lien for fees to which lawyer was not entitled contained confidential information); ABA Formal Ethics Op. 484 (2018) (may refer client to finance company but may not reveal client information except as permitted by Rule 1.6(a) or (b)); N.Y. State Ethics Op. 1061 (2015) (must obtain client's informed consent before reporting client's payment history to subscription-based data clearinghouse); N.Y. City Ethics Op. 2017-2 (2017) (must obtain client's informed consent before reporting partner's fraudulent billing to disciplinary agency); R.I. Ethics Op. 2002-02 (2002) (lawyer for municipal council may not comply with individual council member's request for unredacted itemized billing statement unless council consents). The issue arises often in the context of insurance representation, when a lawyer hired by an insurance company to represent an insured is asked to submit information supporting the lawyer's bills to the insurer or a third-party auditor hired by the insurer, or real estate transactions, when a title insurance company asks to audit the lawyer's trust account containing deposits relating to transactions the company is insuring. Ethics committees commonly find that a lawyer is impliedly authorized to give billing information to an insurer if it will not adversely affect the interests of the insured, but not to submit this information to a third-party auditor without the informed consent of the insured. *E.g.*, ABA Formal Ethics Op. 01-421 (2001); Alaska Ethics Op. 2006-3 (2006) (insurance defense counsel may not give confidential bills to noninsurer contractors for electronic or computerized screening); Conn. Informal Ethics Op. 2011-7 (2011); Fla. Ethics Op. 12-04 (2013); Mass. Ethics Op. 2000-4 (2000); Neb. Ethics Op. 2000-1 (2000); N.H. Ethics Op. 2000-01/05 (2000); N.Y. State Ethics Op. 987 (2013); Pa. Formal Ethics Op. 2001-200 (2001); S.C. Ethics Op. 12-08 (2012); *accord In re Rules of Prof'l Conduct*, 2 P.3d 806 (Mont. 2000) (insurance defense counsel may not give detailed description of legal services to third-party auditors absent fully informed consent of insureds). *But see* D.C. Ethics Op. 290 (1999) (may not provide client billing information to insurer or insurer's auditing agency without client's informed consent).

On the other hand, generally neither confidentiality nor the evidentiary attorney-client privilege will protect billing information or fee agreements if disclosure would not reveal the substance of confidential communications between a lawyer and a client. *See, e.g., DiBella v. Hopkins*, 403 F.3d 102 (2d Cir. 2005) (time records and billing statements not privileged when they do not contain detailed accounts of legal services rendered); *United States v. Naegele*, 468 F. Supp. 2d 165 (D.D.C. 2007) (lawyer's billing statements that were general and did not reveal any litigation strategy or other specifics of representation not protected by attorney-client privilege); *L.A. Cnty. Bd. of Supervisors v. Superior Court*, 386 P.3d 773 (Cal. 2016) ("the contents of an invoice are privileged only if they either communicate information for the purpose of legal consultation or risk exposing information that was communicated for such a purpose. This latter category includes any invoice that reflects work in active and ongoing litigation."); *Att'y Grievance Comm'n v. Zdravkovich*, 852 A.2d 82 (Md. 2004) (lawyer's bank statements not attorney-client communications and neither confidential nor privileged); *Hewes v. Langston*, 853 So. 2d 1237 (Miss. 2003) (simple invoice normally not protected by attorney-client privilege, but "itemized legal bills necessarily reveal confidential information and thus fall within the privilege"); *In re Dyer*, 817 N.W.2d 351 (N.D. 2012) (monthly bank trust account statements contained no information about specific clients and were not confidential).

## DISCLOSURES EXPRESSLY OR IMPLIEDLY AUTHORIZED

Lawyers must obviously disclose a great deal of "information relating to the representation of a client" simply to do their jobs. These disclosures are permissible when the client has expressly or impliedly authorized them.

### • Implied Authorization

Like Rule 1.2(a), which allows a lawyer to "take such action on behalf of the client as is impliedly authorized to carry out the representation," Rule 1.6(a) specifically permits disclosure of client information when "impliedly authorized . . . to carry out the representation." The permission is generally limited to disclosures that are clearly necessary to advance the representation of a client, such as facts "that cannot properly be disputed" or "a disclosure that facilitates a satisfactory conclusion to a matter." Rule 1.6, cmt. [5]. *See* ABA Formal Ethics Op. 08-450 (2008) (without informed consent of client, lawyer may not reveal information to another, jointly represented client when disclosure would be harmful to first client, such as denial of insurance protection; "[i]mplied authority applies only when the lawyer reasonably perceives that disclosure is necessary to the representation of the client whose information is protected by Rule 1.6 . . . and no client may be presumed impliedly to have authorized such [harmful] disclosures"); Ga. Ethics Op. 16-1 (2016) (jointly represented clients do not impliedly consent to disclosure of confidences).

In general, what is "impliedly authorized" depends upon the particular circumstances of the representation. *See, e.g.*, ABA Formal Ethics Op. 483 (2018) (lawyer experiencing data breach may reveal information relating to representation to law enforcement if lawyer reasonably believes disclosure is impliedly authorized, will advance client's interests, and will not adversely affect client's material interests); ABA Formal Ethics Op. 01-421 (2001) (lawyer hired by insurance company to defend insured normally has implied authorization to share with insurer information that will advance insured's interests); ABA Informal Ethics Op. 86-1518 (1986) (may disclose to opposing counsel, without client consultation, inadvertent omission of contract provision); Ark. Ethics Op. 96-1 (1996) (in real estate transaction, many disclosures are impliedly authorized; many documents become public records, and other parties to transaction receive information such as purchase price, amount of offer, amount accepted, and condition of property; disclosures to obtain title insurance are also impliedly authorized); *see also Lawyer Disciplinary Bd. v. McGraw*, 461 S.E.2d 850 (W. Va. 1995) (state attorney general not impliedly authorized to disclose to third party that state agency changing its position on environmental issue, notwithstanding that position change would be matter of public record); Mont. Ethics Op. 050621 (2005) (criminal defense lawyer may not, without client's prior consent, tell judge or prosecutor whether client contacted him, even though client's bond conditioned upon regularly phoning defense counsel); *cf.* ABA Formal Ethics Op. 93-370 (1993) (unless client consents, lawyer should not reveal to judge—and judge should not require lawyer to disclose—client's instructions on settlement authority limits or lawyer's advice about settlement).

### Disclosures within Firm

Comment [5] states that lawyers in a firm are impliedly authorized to discuss with each other information regarding a firm client "unless the client has instructed that the particular information be confined to specified lawyers." This is because clients who choose to be represented by law firms typically do so because of the expertise within law firms "and such a client expects that the firm will utilize all its available resources for the client's benefit." ABA Formal Ethics Op. 08-453 (2008) (impliedly authorized exception includes consulting "ethics counsel" within law firm regarding ethics implications of consulting lawyer's conduct).

### Disclosures When Working with Outside Lawyers and Nonlawyers

Lawyers and law firms sometimes outsource legal and nonlegal support services, which necessarily involves the disclosure of client information outside the firm. Limited disclosures to a lawyer outside a law firm have been found to be impliedly authorized "when the consulting lawyer reasonably believes the disclosure will further the representation by obtaining the consulted lawyer's experience or expertise for the benefit of the consulting lawyer's client." ABA Formal Ethics Op. 98-411 (1998) (consulting lawyer may not disclose information protected by attorney-client privilege or information that would harm client; "[h]ypothetical or anonymous consultations thus are favored where possible"); *see also* Me. Ethics Op. 171 (1999) (client consent not required when consultation is for client's benefit, consulted lawyer does not have conflicting interests, and no privileged information disclosed). *But see In re Mandelman,* 514 N.W.2d 11 (Wis. 1994) (asking other lawyers for help on several client matters and transferring client files without seeking clients' consent).

Similarly, limited disclosure to a nonlawyer independent contractor may be impliedly authorized when necessary to carry out the representation. *See, e.g.,* Vt. Ethics Op. 2003-03 (n.d.) (permissible to use outside computer consultant to manage case files when necessary to carry out representation); *see also* ABA Formal Ethics Op. 95-398 (1995) (lawyer who gives computer maintenance company access to client files must make reasonable efforts to ensure use of adequate procedures to protect confidential client information).

In determining whether a particular disclosure is impliedly authorized, the relationship between the law firm and the outside service provider must also be considered. If the relationship involves a high degree of supervision and control, such that the provider is "tantamount to an employee," client consent is not typically required. ABA Formal Ethics Op. 08-451 (2008) (acknowledging that other rules, such as Rule 1.2(a) or Rule 1.4, might require lawyers to consult with clients before engaging temporary legal or nonlegal services). However, if the relationship between the firm and the provider is "attenuated, as in a typical outsourcing relationship," the firm may not disclose client information without the client's consent. *Id. See* Colo. Ethics Op. 121 (2008) (disclosure of confidential information to outsourced lawyers not admitted in Colorado usually requires client's informed consent; factors to consider include degree of attenuation of relationship of lawyer and outsourced worker); Fla. Ethics Op. 07-2 (2008) (in determining whether client should be informed of participation of overseas providers, lawyer should consider "whether a client would reasonably expect the lawyer or law firm to personally handle the matter and whether the non-lawyers will have more than a limited role in the provision of the services"; disclosure of information should be limited to "information necessary to complete the work for the particular client"); N.C. Ethics Op. 2007-12 (2008) (disclosure of confidential information to overseas outsourced workers requires written informed consent from client); Ohio Ethics Op. 2009-6 (2009) (disclosure of confidential information to outsourced workers requires informed consent of client); Va. Ethics Op. 1850 (2010) (lawyer must obtain client's informed consent before revealing client confidences to outsourced workers).

### Representing Clients with Diminished Capacity

A lawyer who takes action under Rule 1.14 to protect the interests of a client with diminished capacity is, according to Rule 1.14(c), "impliedly authorized under Rule 1.6(a) to reveal information about the client, but only to the extent reasonably necessary to protect the client's interests." For discussion of a lawyer's obligations when representing a client with diminished capacity, see the annotation to Rule 1.14.

### • Informed Consent

When disclosure of particular information is not "impliedly authorized" or otherwise covered by the rule's exceptions, client consent is required. Previously, the rules required client consent "after consultation." The 2002 amendment to the rule changed the language throughout the rules to require "informed consent." This was not intended as a substantive change. See American Bar Association, A Legislative History: The Development of the ABA Model Rules of Professional Conduct, 1982–2013, at 130 (2013).

Informed consent requires an understanding of the risks and benefits attendant upon disclosure. See Rule 1.0(e) (defining "informed consent" throughout rules to denote "the agreement by a person to a proposed course of conduct after the lawyer has communicated adequate information and explanation about the material risks of and reasonably available alternatives to the proposed course of conduct"); see also Rule 1.0, cmts. [6], [7] (providing additional explanation of what informed consent generally requires). It usually requires an affirmative response by the client; the lawyer may not assume consent from a client's silence. Rule 1.0, cmt. [7]; see ABA Formal Ethics Op. 01-421 (2001) ("disclosure to the client . . . in order to obtain informed consent within the meaning of Rule 1.6 must adequately and fairly identify the effects of disclosure and non-disclosure on the client's interests," including risk that information may then be disclosed to others, that lawyer-client privilege may be waived, and that information could be used to client's disadvantage); see also McClure v. Thompson, 323 F.3d 1233 (9th Cir. 2003) (even if criminal defense lawyer had client's consent to disclose to authorities locations of two murder victims' bodies, consent not "informed" as lawyer had not advised client about potential harmful consequences of disclosure); *Banner v. City of Flint*, 136 F. Supp. 2d 678 (E.D. Mich. 2000) (lawyer who obtained confidences from initial consultation with prospective client violated rule when he deposed her in another matter without explaining availability of attorney-client privilege), *aff'd in part, rev'd in part*, 99 F. App'x 29 (6th Cir. 2004) (affirming district court's finding of Rule 1.6 violation, court held rule requires lawyer to advise client "about the advantages *and disadvantages* of revelation in language the client can understand"); *In re Smith*, 991 N.E.2d 106 (Ind. 2013) (client's exclamation of approval in response to lawyer's suggestion that he might write a book about her did not constitute informed consent); *Commonwealth v. Downey*, 842 N.E.2d 955 (Mass. App. Ct. 2006) (murder defendants did not give informed consent for lawyers to wear body microphones during trial at request of television production company; neither lawyer explained arrangement's potential pitfalls); *In re Vogel*, 482 S.W.3d 520 (Tenn. 2016) (former client's request for explanation of lawyer's reasons for withdrawing, cc'd to judge, did not constitute informed consent to lawyer's sending copy of response with explanation casting client in negative light to judge); *cf.* N.J. Ethics Op. 719 (2010) (lawyer may not require estate administrator client as condition of representation to consent to disclosure of confidential information to surety company for surety company's benefit).

Unlike a conflicts waiver, informed consent to the disclosure of confidential information under Rule 1.6 need not be confirmed in writing.

## DUTY OF CONFIDENTIALITY TOWARD PROSPECTIVE CLIENTS, FORMER OR DECEASED CLIENTS, AND ORGANIZATIONAL CLIENTS

A lawyer's duty of confidentiality extends to a prospective client who consults a lawyer in good faith for the purpose of obtaining legal representation or advice, even though the lawyer performs no legal services for the would-be client and declines the representation. Rule 1.18(b) provides that "a lawyer who has learned information from a prospective client shall not use or reveal that information, except as Rule 1.9 would permit with respect to information of a former client." For a discussion of the ethical duties owed to prospective clients, see the annotation to Rule 1.18.

The lawyer's duty to preserve client confidences continues after the lawyer-client relationship has concluded (Comment [20]), and even after the client dies. *See Restatement (Third) of the Law Governing Lawyers* § 60 cmt. e (2000); *State ex rel. Counsel for Discipline v. Tonderum*, 840 N.W.3d 487 (Neb. 2013) (revealing confidential information after being fired by client); *In re Parrinello*, 67 N.Y.S.3d 355 (App. Div. 2017) (revealing confidential information about deceased client); Me. Ethics Op. 213 (2016) (law firm may not donate ancient, inactive client files with possible historical value to library or educational institution or allow files to be reviewed by outside party unless exception to Rule 1.6 applies or firm reasonably ascertains that original client consented; waiver from family or personal representative of deceased client's estate is insufficient); N.Y. State Ethics Op. 1084 (2016) (criminal defense lawyer may not reveal deceased convicted client's statements potentially exonerating co-defendant absent direct or implied authorization by client); *cf.* Haw. Ethics Op. 38 (1999) (may disclose information relating to representation of deceased client if doing so would effectuate client's estate plan); Kan. Ethics Op. 01-01 (2001) (lawyer whose client inherited property from former client is impliedly authorized to disclose information from deceased client's file to effectuate inheritance). This duty is specifically addressed in Rule 1.9(c)(2) (lawyer may not "reveal information relating to the representation [of a former client] except as these Rules would permit or require with respect to a client"). See the annotation to Rule 1.9 for discussion. *Cf. SEC v. Carrillo Huettel LLP*, No. 13 Civ. 1735, 2015 WL 1610282, 2015 BL 99612 (S.D.N.Y. Apr. 8, 2015) (weight of authority is that attorney-client privilege terminates with dissolution of corporation).

For a discussion of the duty of confidentiality in the corporate context, see the annotation to Rule 1.13 (Organization as Client).

### Paragraph (b): Exceptions to Duty of Confidentiality— Permissive Disclosure

Rule 1.6 sets out seven circumstances in which a lawyer is permitted—but not required—to disclose information relating to a client's representation. Although non-disclosure in these circumstances would not violate this rule, it could violate other rules or law. Cmts. [12], [17]; *see* Utah Ethics Op. 97-12 (1998) (lawyer who suspects client of committing child abuse may, but need not, report suspected behavior under Rule 1.6, but state statute may require lawyer to report). As discussed below, any disclosures made pursuant to one of these exceptions must be narrowly tailored to avoid any unnecessary disclosure.

### Paragraph (b)(1): Disclosure to "Prevent Reasonably Certain Death or Substantial Bodily Harm"

In 2002, Rule 1.6(b)(1) was amended to permit disclosure "to prevent reasonably certain death or substantial bodily harm." (Former Rule 1.6(b)(1) permitted disclosure "to prevent the *client* from committing a *criminal act* that the lawyer believes is likely to result in *imminent* death or substantial bodily harm" (emphases added).) The exception was broadened to authorize disclosure to prevent accidental, but serious, physical harm that is reasonably certain to occur, either because "it will be suffered imminently or . . . there is a present and substantial threat that a person will suffer such harm at a later date if the lawyer fails to take action necessary to eliminate the threat," such as sometimes happens in the case of toxic torts. Cmt. [6]; *see Restatement (Third) of the Law Governing Lawyers* § 66 (2000) (disclosure permitted if necessary to prevent reasonably certain death or serious bodily harm); *see also* American Bar Association, *Essential Qualities of the Professional Lawyer* 130–31 (2013); *cf.* Ken Strutin, *Preserving Attorney-Client Confidentiality at the Cost of Another's Innocence: A Systemic Approach*, 17 Tex. Wesleyan L. Rev. 499 (2011) ("Rule 1.6(b)(1) has not gone far enough to guide lawyers confronted with private confessions exonerating third parties.").

Most jurisdictions have adopted some form of this exception to Rule 1.6, and permit disclosure to prevent death or serious bodily harm. *See, e.g., In re Grand Jury Investigation*, 902 N.E.2d 929 (Mass. 2009) (lawyer properly disclosed client's threat to harm judge); *State v. Hansen*, 862 P.2d 117 (Wash. 1993) (no violation of confidentiality by telling judge that individual who called lawyer to retain him threatened to kill judge and two lawyers in case); N.H. Ethics Op. 2014-15/5 (2015) (disclosure of confidential information permissible even over elder client's objection if lawyer reasonably believes there is actual or threatened physical or psychological abuse, but lawyer must first seek client's consent); N.Y. City Ethics Op. 2018-1 (2018) (disclosure of confidential information about prospective client with diminished capacity permissible to prevent substantial harm); R.I. Ethics Op. 98-12 (1998) (lawyer threatened by imprisoned client may report action to parole board or attorney general, or apply for restraining order); *see also McClure v. Thompson*, 323 F.3d 1233 (9th Cir. 2003) (criminal defense lawyer who disclosed to authorities locations of bodies of two murder victims did not violate duty of confidentiality, as lawyer reasonably believed victims still alive and disclosure necessary to prevent their imminent death or substantial bodily harm). Some jurisdictions *require* such disclosure. *See, e.g.,* Conn. Informal Ethics Op. 08-06 (n.d.) (lawyer who reasonably believes client intends to kill others associated with case when he gets out of prison must make necessary disclosure to prevent harm); Ill. Ethics Op. 2017-01 (2017) (criminal defense lawyer's knowledge of client's addiction and use of heroin, without more, does not require disclosure under death or serious bodily harm provision); Ill. Ethics Op. 12-08 (2012) (must report information from divorce client regarding spouse's history of and interest in soliciting minors for sex to law enforcement authorities if lawyer believes disclosure is reasonably necessary to prevent child sexual abuse, which constitutes "substantial bodily harm" within meaning of Rule 1.6); Ind. Ethics Op. 2015-2 (2015) (requiring lawyer to report child abuse or neglect if lawyer believes it necessary to prevent "reasonably certain death or substantial bodily harm"; otherwise, lawyer may not report absent client's informed consent); Iowa Ethics Op. 10-02 (2010) (lawyer must disclose information relating to representation if lawyer believes disclosure reasonably necessary to prevent death or substantial bodily harm); *cf. In re R.L.R.*, 116 So. 3d 570 (Fla. Dist. Ct. App. 2013) (lawyer for juvenile runaway in foster care proceeding may not disclose juvenile's location without juvenile's consent because disclosure not necessary to prevent death, substantial bodily harm, or commission of crime); *In re Christina W.*, 639 S.E.2d 770 (W. Va. 2006) (lawyer appointed as guardian ad litem for minor in abuse and neglect proceeding owes child "general" duty of confidentiality under Rule 1.6 but must disclose to court information from child regarding abuse even if child directs lawyer to keep information confidential).

## *Paragraphs (b)(2) and (b)(3): Economic Crimes and Frauds*

### • *2003 Amendments*

In 2003, the ABA adopted paragraphs (b)(2) and (b)(3) of Rule 1.6. *See ABA/BNA Lawyers' Manual on Professional Conduct*, 19 Law. Man. Prof. Conduct 467 (Current Reports, Aug. 13, 2003). This marked the first time the rules permitted disclosure of client information when the client uses or has used the lawyer's services to commit a crime or fraud resulting in substantial injury to the property or financial interests of another. (The predecessor Model Code did, however, have a limited exception permitting a lawyer to reveal the "intention of [a] client to commit a crime and the information necessary to prevent the crime." DR 4-101(A).) *See generally* American Bar Association, *A Legislative History: The Development of the ABA Model Rules of Professional Conduct, 1982–2013*, at 139–44 (2013).

Even before these amendments were adopted by the ABA in 2003, most state rules already contained provisions permitting limited disclosure to prevent or rectify the consequences of a client's fraudulent or criminal behavior.

## Paragraph (b)(2): Disclosure to Prevent Crime or Fraud Resulting in Financial Injury or Property Damage

Rule 1.6(b)(2) permits a lawyer to disclose information relating to the representation of a client "to prevent the client from committing a crime or fraud that is reasonably certain to result in substantial injury to the financial interests or property of another and in furtherance of which the client has used or is using the lawyer's services." Only a few jurisdictions have adopted the ABA version of Rule 1.6(b)(2) verbatim. Some jurisdictions permit disclosure to prevent a crime or a fraud regardless of the type of consequences likely to result, some permit disclosure whether or not the lawyer's services are involved, some permit disclosure to prevent a criminal but not a fraudulent act, some permit disclosure to prevent anyone from committing a crime or fraud, and some require disclosure. *See, e.g., Lane's Case*, 889 A.2d 3 (N.H. 2005) (lawyer properly disclosed former client's confidences in effort to prevent former client from stealing money from mother or deceased father's estate); Alaska Ethics Op. 2003-2 (2003) (lawyer for personal representative of estate may, but is not required to, reveal personal representative's criminal or fraudulent conduct to court or beneficiaries); Nassau Cnty. (N.Y.) Ethics Op. 01-07 (2001) (law firm that withdrew from representing legatees of decedent's estate because they planned to conceal existence of additional legatee may, but is not required to, reveal information about additional legatee); *cf. Fla. Bar v. Knowles*, 99 So. 3d 918 (Fla. 2012) (because immigration client's alleged remark that she would do anything, including lie in court, to avoid deportation was not sufficient to create reasonable belief that she would commit crime, lawyer should not have disclosed comment to prosecutor).

Absent authority to disclose a client's past crimes or frauds under Rule 1.6(b)(3) or an analogous provision, a lawyer may not disclose a client's wrongful past actions to prevent their continuing consequences and may not even disclose a client's continuing crime or fraud if to do so would also reveal past wrongdoing. *See, e.g., United States v. Quest Diagnostics Inc.*, 734 F.3d 154 (2d Cir. 2013) (company's former general counsel's disclosures of company information and participation in qui tam suit under False Claims Act went beyond what might have been reasonably necessary to prevent client's alleged wrongdoing); *Danon v. Vanguard Grp., Inc.*, No. 100711/13, 2015 WL 7594570, 2015 BL 388118 (N.Y. Sup. Ct. Nov. 16, 2015) (neither bringing qui tam action nor disclosure of client's tax information and strategies in complaint were reasonably necessary to prevent client from committing tax fraud); *In re Botimer*, 214 P.3d 133 (Wash. 2009) (lawyer sent letter to IRS stating that client incorrectly reported her income on tax returns and failed to pay gift taxes); Ariz. Ethics Op. 2001-14 (2001) (lawyer for defendant in criminal appeal may not reveal client's use of false name in trial court); Conn. Informal Ethics Op. 01-13 (2001) (lawyer may not disclose client's continuing failure to file tax form); N.Y. City Ethics Op. 2002-1 (2002) (lawyer consulted for advice concerning client's theft of car may not disclose client's continuing crime of possessing stolen property); N.Y. Cnty. Ethics Op. 746 (2013) (former corporate counsel may not disclose client information or collect reward under whistleblower statute unless disclosure permitted by Rule 1.6 or necessary to correct fraud, crime, or false evidence presented to tribunal). For criticism of this line of authorities, see Dennis J. Ventry, Jr., *Stitches for Snitches: Lawyers as Whistleblowers*, 50 U.C. Davis L. Rev. 1455 (Apr. 2017). *See generally* Kathleen M. Boozang, Note and Comment, *The New Relators: In-House Counsel and Compliance Officers*, 6 J. Health & Life Sci. L. 16 (Oct. 2012).

### Paragraph (b)(3): Disclosure to Prevent, Mitigate, or Rectify Financial Injury or Property Damage from Client's Crime or Fraud

Rule 1.6(b)(3) permits a lawyer to disclose information relating to the representation of a client "to prevent, mitigate or rectify substantial injury to the financial interests or property of another that is reasonably certain to result or has resulted from the client's commission of a crime or fraud in furtherance of which the client has used the lawyer's services." Many jurisdictions have similar provisions. *See, e.g., A. v. B.*, 726 A.2d 924 (N.J. 1999) (law firm drafting wills for husband and wife may reveal existence of husband's illegitimate child to wife upon learning of child's existence from another client; husband's deliberate failure to inform wife of child's existence constituted fraud on wife); Md. Ethics Op. 2001-18 (2002) (lawyer for personal representative of estate who discovers evidence that client misappropriated estate's funds may not disclose this unless lawyer's services used to further misappropriation); Nev. Ethics Op. 25 (2001) (lawyer who was consulted but not retained by person who used lawyer's advice to perpetrate fraud on bankruptcy court may reveal information to court); *see also In re Lackey*, 37 P.3d 172 (Or. 2002) (National Guard judge-advocate suspended for disclosing client confidences and secrets; disclosures intended to embarrass or injure officers with whom he had work-related conflicts, not to remedy government fraud); *cf. In re Smith*, 991 N.E.2d 106 (Ind. 2013) (lawyer's disclosure of client's alleged false statements in job application to federal government years after client left federal employment could not mitigate or rectify alleged fraud); *In re Schafer*, 66 P.3d 1036 (Wash. 2003) (lawyer impermissibly disclosed client confidences and secrets to IRS, FBI, and press in course of exposing judge's misconduct).

### OTHER RULES GOVERNING DISCLOSURE OF CRIMINAL OR FRAUDULENT CONDUCT

#### • Disclosure Required by Crime-Fraud Exception to Attorney-Client Privilege

Under a generally recognized crime-fraud exception to the attorney-client privilege, a lawyer is not barred from disclosing otherwise privileged information about a client who consults the lawyer to further the commission of a crime or a fraud. *See, e.g., Restatement (Third) of the Law Governing Lawyers* § 82 (2000) (privilege does not apply when client "(a) consults a lawyer for the purpose, later accomplished, of obtaining assistance to engage in a crime or fraud or aiding a third person to do so, or (b) regardless of the client's purpose at the time of consultation uses the lawyer's advice or other services to engage in or assist a crime or fraud"); *In re Grand Jury Investigation*, Misc. No. 17-2336 (BAH), 2017 WL 4898143, 2017 BL 404277 (D.D.C. Oct. 2, 2017) (collecting cases).

Because of the differences between the ethical duty of confidentiality and the attorney-client privilege and their respective exceptions, a determination that disclosure of client information is permitted by the crime-fraud exception to the ethics rule does not necessarily lead to the same result under the crime-fraud exception to the attorney-client privilege. *See, e.g., State v. Boatwright*, 401 P.3d 657 (Kan. Ct. App. 2017) (reversing trial court's admission of lawyer's testimony about client's statement of intent to kill ex-fiancee based on crime exception found in Kansas Rule 1.6 (b) (1); Rule 1.6 is not rule of evidence governing admissibility of testimony, and crime-fraud exception to attorney client privilege did not apply); *Newman v. State*, 863 A.2d 321 (Md. 2004) (although lawyer had, pursuant to Rule 1.6, properly informed court presiding over custody matter of client's threat to murder her husband and child, lawyer's testimony about those statements at subsequent criminal proceeding was barred by attorney-client privilege); *In re Grand Jury Investigation*, 902 N.E.2d 929 (Mass. 2009) (ethical permissibility of informing judge of client's threat to kill judge not inconsistent with finding that client's statements were privileged; subpoena quashed); *Danon v. Vanguard Grp., Inc.*, No. 100711/13, 2015 WL 7594570, 2015 BL 388118 (N.Y. Sup. Ct. Nov. 16, 2015) (distinguishing crime-fraud exception to attorney-client privilege from exception to duty of confidentiality).

### • *Disclosure Required by Rule 3.3*

When a matter is before a tribunal, a lawyer may be required by Rule 3.3 to reveal to the court information otherwise protected under Rule 1.6 to avoid assisting a client in perpetrating a crime or fraud. For discussion of a lawyer's duty of candor to a tribunal, see the annotation to Rule 3.3.

### • *Disclosure of Unlawful Conduct by Corporate Constituents*

For discussion of a lawyer's obligations with respect to disclosure of unlawful conduct by someone "associated" with a corporate or other organizational client, see the annotation to Rule 1.13.

## *Paragraph (b)(4): Disclosure to Secure Legal Ethics Advice*

In 2002, a new exception—Rule 1.6(b)(4)—was added, permitting disclosure "to secure legal advice about the lawyer's compliance with these Rules." (This provision was originally numbered 1.6(b)(2), but renumbered when other paragraphs of Rule 1.6 were added in 2003.)

Although disclosure to secure ethics advice will "[i]n most situations" be impliedly authorized, Rule 1.6(b)(4) permits disclosure even without implicit authorization "because of the importance of a lawyer's compliance with the Rules of Professional Conduct." Cmt. [9]. *See* ABA Formal Ethics Op. 08-453 (2008) (disclosure to in-house law firm ethics counsel is typically impliedly authorized and is also expressly authorized by Rule 1.6(b)(4)); Pa. Ethics Op. 2017-016 (2017) (law firm faced with in camera hearing by special master into its "professional considerations" for moving to withdraw may disclose confidential information to its counsel because of need for advice to ensure compliance with ethics rules). For cases holding that the attorney-client privilege protects a lawyer's communications with in-house ethics counsel from disclosure to the lawyer's client, see *St. Simons Waterfront, LLC v. Hunter, Maclean, Exley & Dunn, P.C.*, 746 S.E.2d 98 (Ga. 2013); *Garvy v. Seyfarth Shaw LLP*, 966 N.E.2d 523 (Ill. App. Ct. 2012); and *RFF Family P'ship v. Burns & Levinson, LLP*, 991 N.E.2d 1066 (Mass. 2013).

## Paragraph (b)(5): Disclosure to Support Claim or Defense

Rule 1.6(b)(5) permits disclosure (1) "to establish a claim or defense . . . in a controversy between the lawyer and the client," (2) "to establish a defense to a criminal charge or civil claim against the lawyer based upon conduct in which the client was involved," and (3) "to respond to allegations in any proceeding concerning the lawyer's representation of the client." (Rule 1.6(b)(5) was originally enacted as Rule 1.6(b)(2), renumbered in 2002 as 1.6(b)(3), and renumbered in 2003 as 1.6(b)(5).)

### DISCLOSURE TO COLLECT FEE

A lawyer "entitled" to a fee is permitted by paragraph (b)(5) to disclose information relating to the representation, including proof of the services rendered, when reasonably necessary to collect the lawyer's fee. This accords with the principle that the beneficiary of a fiduciary relationship may not exploit it to the detriment of the fiduciary. Cmt. [11]. The disclosure must be limited to that necessary to establish or collect the fee, whether through litigation, obtaining an attorneys' lien, attaching client property, or other means. *See, e.g., Pedersen & Houpt v. Summit Real Estate Grp.*, 877 N.E.2d 4 (Ill. App. Ct. 2007) (exception extended beyond lawyer's assertion of breach-of-contract claim to include claim for fraudulent misrepresentation when necessary to recover total outstanding fee); D.C. Ethics Op. 236 (1993) (when client has filed bankruptcy petition to discharge debt owed to lawyer's firm, lawyer may reveal limited information about client's assets if lawyer has good-faith expectation of recovering more than minimal amount); N.C. Ethics Op. 2004-6 (2004) (lawyer in fee dispute with former corporate client permitted to reveal information necessary to pierce corporate veil if lawyer has good-faith belief claim warranted); Or. Ethics Op. 2005-104 (2005) (may disclose information relating to representation of client who justified nonpayment of bill by claiming lawyer committed malpractice); *see also Att'y Grievance Comm'n v. Powers*, 164 A.3d 138 (Md. 2017) (disclosing confidential information by suing former client in federal court that lawyer knew or should have known lacked jurisdiction); Ariz. Ethics Op. 93-11 (1993) (may not initiate criminal proceedings against client who paid with check drawn on insufficient funds; criminal complaints rarely necessary to collect fee). *See generally Restatement (Third) of the Law Governing Lawyers* § 65 (2000) (disclosure of client confidences permitted in self-defense and in compensation disputes when reasonably necessary); *ABA/BNA Lawyers' Manual on Professional Conduct*, "Confidentiality: Disclosure: Attorneys' Claims and Defenses," pp. 55:701 *et seq.*

## DISCLOSURE TO COLLECTION AGENCIES AND CREDIT BUREAUS

Although lawyers generally may refer delinquent client accounts to collection agencies if disclosure of client information is minimized, reporting clients to credit bureaus that maintain records and provide reports is disfavored. *See, e.g.,* Alaska Ethics Op. 2000-3 (2000) (lawyer may not report delinquent client's status to credit bureau); Mont. Ethics Op. 001027 (2000) (may use collection agency to collect legal fees if all other reasonable methods of collection are exhausted and disclosure is minimized, but referral to credit bureau is not necessary for debt collection, is punitive, and risks unauthorized disclosures of client information); N.Y. State Ethics Op. 684 (1996) (may not report to credit bureau that client failed to pay past-due fee); Ohio Sup. Ct. Ethics Op. 91-16 (1991) (firm may use collection agency but should reveal confidences only to degree necessary to collect fee); Phila. Ethics Op. 90-23 (1991) (firm may disclose names of client to collection agency; confidentiality must be otherwise preserved); S.C. Ethics Op. 94-11 (1994) (may use collection agency, but not credit bureau); Tex. Ethics Op. 652 (2016) (may refer delinquent client to collection agency but not to credit bureau). *But see* Conn. Informal Ethics Op. 2010-06 (2010) (may notify credit bureaus of judgment obtained against former client); Fla. Ethics Op. 90-2 (1991) (firm may subscribe to credit-reporting service and provide information regarding undisputed debts owed only by former—not current—clients); Kan. Ethics Op. 94-5 (1994) (may refer client account to credit bureau but may not reveal information unrelated to collecting debt).

## SUITS BY FORMER IN-HOUSE COUNSEL
## AGAINST FORMER EMPLOYER

Whether, and to what extent, former in-house counsel may sue their former employers for employment-related matters varies among jurisdictions, and has changed over time.

The Model Code version of the exception, DR 4-101(C)(4), applied only to fee disputes and self-defense. This meant that wrongful discharge suits were not permitted unless they could be maintained without violating client confidences. *See, e.g., GTE Prods. Corp. v. Stewart,* 653 N.E.2d 161 (Mass. 1995); *Wise v. Consol. Edison Co. of N.Y.,* 723 N.Y.S.2d 462 (App. Div. 2001); *Willy v. Coastal States Mgmt. Co.,* 939 S.W.2d 193 (Tex. App. 1997); *cf. Gen. Dynamics Corp. v. Superior Court,* 876 P.2d 487 (Cal. 1994) (in-house counsel may maintain suit for retaliatory discharge that does not require revealing privileged client confidences and secrets; client communications regarding committing crimes or fraud are not privileged).

Model Rule 1.6(b)(5), however, expanded the exception to permit disclosure to establish a claim against a client. ABA Formal Ethics Op. 01-424 (2001) (rules permit in-house lawyer to bring wrongful discharge suit against former employer and disclose information necessary to establish claim); *e.g., Heckman v. Zurich Holding Co. of Am.,* 242 F.R.D. 606 (D. Kan. 2007) (plaintiff entitled to maintain retaliatory discharge action under Kansas law and to reveal confidential information necessary to establish claim); *Alexander v. Tandem Staffing Solutions, Inc.,* 881 So. 2d 607 (Fla. Dist. Ct. App. 2004) (whistleblower claim by former in-house counsel against employer constituted controversy between lawyer and client within meaning of Florida's version of Rule 1.6(b)(5)); *accord Burkhart v. Semitool, Inc.*, 5 P.3d 1031 (Mont. 2000) (former in-house counsel may reveal client confidences to extent reasonably necessary to prove wrongful discharge claim); *Crews v. Buckman Labs Int'l*, 78 S.W.3d 852 (Tenn. 2002) (same); *Spratley v. State Farm Mut. Auto. Ins. Co.*, 78 P.3d 603 (Utah 2003) (same). *But see Balla v. Gambro, Inc.*, 584 N.E.2d 104 (Ill. 1991) (refusing to extend tort of retaliatory discharge to in-house counsel). *See generally* Brenda Marshall, Note, *In Search of Clarity: When Should In-House Counsel Have the Right to Sue for Retaliatory Discharge?*, 14 Geo. J. Legal Ethics 871 (Spring 2001); *ABA/BNA Lawyers' Manual on Professional Conduct*, "Confidentiality: Disclosure: Attorneys' Claims and Defenses," pp. 55:701 *et seq.*

Several courts have addressed in-house lawyers' suits under federal law. *See, e.g., Van Asdale v. Int'l Game Tech.*, 577 F.3d 989 (9th Cir. 2009) (distinguishing *Balla v. Gambro, Inc.*, 584 N.E.2d 104 (Ill. 1991), and holding that former in-house counsel may bring action under Sarbanes-Oxley Act); *Stinneford v. Spiegel Inc.*, 845 F. Supp. 1243 (N.D. Ill. 1994) (in-house counsel may bring suit under Age Discrimination in Employment Act).

## DISCLOSURE TO DEFEND CLAIMS BROUGHT BY CLIENTS AND THIRD PARTIES AGAINST LAWYER

Rule 1.6(b)(5) permits disclosure to defend claims or charges brought against the lawyer by third parties as well as clients. As noted in Comment [10], such charges may arise in civil, criminal, disciplinary, or other proceedings, and may be based upon wrongs allegedly committed by the lawyer against the client, or by the lawyer and client against a third person. *See, e.g., Hamilton v. Rubin*, LC No. 04-40221-CZ, 2006 WL 1751901 (Mich. Ct. App. June 27, 2006) (disclosures regarding representation of plaintiff, a former client, were permissible under self-defense exception in out-of-state action by plaintiff's associate, another former client, accusing lawyer of fraud, conspiracy, and malpractice relating to sale of business interest in which plaintiff was involved); *Hélie v. McDermott, Will & Emery*, 869 N.Y.S.2d 27 (App. Div. 2008) (self-defense exception may be invoked against allegations of malpractice by nonclient); *In re Dyer*, 817 N.W.2d 351 (N.D. 2012) (lawyers permitted to disclose trust account records and client bills in bar disciplinary proceeding); Or. Ethics Op. 2005-104 (2005) (may disclose information relating to representation of former client to defend against disciplinary complaint filed by opposing party in matter); *cf. Qualcomm Inc. v. Broadcom Corp.*, No. 05CV1958-RMB (BLM), 2008 WL 638108, 2008 BL 308505 (S.D. Cal. Mar. 5, 2008) (client's criticism and blaming of its own lawyers for discovery violations constituted sufficient "accusatory adversity" to invoke exception to attorney-client privilege and justify disclosure of confidential information in connection with motion for sanctions); N.Y. State Ethics Op. 1094 (2016) (may not provide client's former lawyer with client file to facilitate defense against client's ethics complaint without client's consent). It is not necessary that the lawyer be named as a party to a proceeding in which the client or third party makes claims of wrongdoing on the part of the lawyer. *See, e.g., Hartman v. Cunningham*, 217 S.W.3d 408 (Tenn. Ct. App. 2006) (self-defense exception applied to lawyer's affidavit submitted to refute claim in former client's malpractice case against successor counsel for failing to advise him of potential claim against affiant-lawyer).

## FORMAL COMPLAINT NOT NECESSARY

A lawyer accused of wrongful conduct in connection with the representation of a client, or with complicity in a client's wrongful conduct, need not wait until formal charges are filed. "The lawyer's right to respond arises when an assertion of such complicity has been made. . . . [T]he defense may be established by responding directly to a third party who has made such an assertion." Cmt. [10]. *See, e.g., In re Bryan*, 61 P.3d 641 (Kan. 2003) (formal proceedings not required before disclosure in self-defense could be made under Rule 1.6(b)); Pa. Ethics Op. 96-48 (1996) (lawyer whose former clients defended against SEC fraud complaint by alleging lawyer's lack of due diligence may discuss matter with SEC even though lawyer not named in complaint); S.C. Ethics Op. 94-23 (1994) (lawyer under investigation by Social Security Administration regarding handling of client's disability claim may disclose client information to defend himself even though no formal grievance proceeding pending). Mere criticism of the lawyer, however, may be insufficient to warrant disclosures in self-defense, even when the criticisms appear in the press. *See, e.g., Louima v. City of New York*, No. 98 CV 5083(SJ), 2004 WL 2359943 (E.D.N.Y. Oct. 5, 2004) ("mere press reports" about lawyer's conduct do not justify disclosure of client information even if reports false and accusations unfounded); *People v. Isaac*, No. 15PDJ099, 2016 WL 6124510, 2016 BL 349912 (Colo. O.P.D.J. Sept. 22, 2016) (including client confidences and information related to representations in public internet posts responding to negative online client reviews); *In re Skinner*, 758 S.E.2d 788 (Ga. 2014) (posting former client's confidential information in response to negative online reviews); *In re Steele*, 45 N.E.3d 777 (Ind. 2015) (punishing clients who posted negative online reviews by posting responses that included confidential information); N.Y. State Ethics Op. 1032 (2014) (may not disclose confidential information in response to former client's negative online review); Nassau Cnty. (N.Y.) Ethics Op. 2016-1 (2016) (same); N.Y. Cnty. Ethics Op. 711 (1997) (client's criticism of lawyer to neighbor was mere gossip and did not trigger exception to confidentiality rule); Tex. Ethics Op. 662 (2016) (may not disclose confidential information in response to former client's negative online review); Utah Ethics Op. 05-01 (2005) (criminal defense lawyer may not voluntarily disclose client confidences to prosecutor or to court in response to claim that lawyer's prior advice was confusing; no "controversy" between lawyer and client). *But see* Ariz. Ethics Op. 93-02 (1993) (interpreting "controversy" to include disagreement in public media). *See generally* Jenna C. Newmark, Note, *The Lawyer's "Prisoner's Dilemma": Duty and Self-Defense in Postconviction Ineffectiveness Claims*, 79 Fordham L. Rev. 699 (Nov. 2010).

## THREATENING TO DISCLOSE CONFIDENTIAL INFORMATION

A lawyer is not permitted to threaten disclosure to intimidate or retaliate against a client. *See, e.g., Fla. Bar v. Carricarte*, 733 So. 2d 975 (Fla. 1999) (former corporate counsel whose employment was terminated threatened to reveal client's trade secrets unless company gave him "severance pay"); *State ex rel. Counsel for Discipline v. Wilson*, 634 N.W.2d 467 (Neb. 2001) (lawyer threatened to disclose client information to INS and to court unless client paid for services lawyer previously provided at no charge); *In re Boelter*, 985 P.2d 328 (Wash. 1999) (threatening to disclose confidential information if client did not pay bill). *But see In re Lim*, 210 S.W.3d 199 (Mo. 2007) (no violation when lawyer threatened to report client to collection agency and then to report client's debt to INS if bill not paid).

## Paragraph (b)(6): Disclosure to Comply with Law or Court Order

Paragraph (b)(6), added to Rule 1.6 in 2002, permits disclosure "to comply with other law or a court order." Previously the comment addressed this issue; the amendment specifically allowing disclosure was not intended as a substantive change. American Bar Association, *A Legislative History: The Development of the ABA Model Rules of Professional Conduct, 1982–2013*, at 132 (2013). Typically, a lawyer is requested to provide information as a result of a discovery request or subpoena; the lawyer must make all nonfrivolous arguments that the information is protected from disclosure and, unless the client has otherwise directed, must resist disclosure until a court or other tribunal orders it. Cmt. [15]; *see, e.g.*, ABA Formal Ethics Op. 473 (2016) (lawyer receiving court order or subpoena—whether from governmental agency or anyone else—for records relating to representation of current or former client must, if so instructed by client or if client is unavailable, seek to limit order or subpoena on any legitimate grounds available to protect confidentiality, but is not required to appeal order absent appropriate arrangements with available client; disclosure must be limited to extent reasonably necessary for compliance, and lawyer should seek protective orders to limit access to tribunal and those with need to know); D.C. Ethics Op. 288 (1999) (lawyer subpoenaed by congressional subcommittee to produce client files must seek to quash or limit subpoena on all available grounds; if subcommittee overrides objections and threatens lawyer with contempt, then lawyer may—but is not required to—produce documents; threat of fines and imprisonment under federal law meets "required by law" exception); Neb. Ethics Op. 11-05 (2011) (lawyer who served as guardian ad litem for minor may disclose information about representation to state legislative committee only if subpoenaed and ordered to do so after having made all meritorious arguments against disclosure); N.D. Ethics Op. 15-04 (2015) (court's mere question to public defender regarding client's whereabouts, without ordering lawyer to answer, does not trigger exception); Pa. Ethics Op. 2002-106 (2003) (lawyer may comply with arbitration panel's order to disclose client information after raising issue of confidentiality). *See generally* Rebecca Aviel, *The Boundary Claim's Caveat: Lawyers and Confidentiality Exceptionalism*, 86 Tul. L. Rev. 1055 (May 2012).

The required-by-law exception may be triggered by statutes, administrative agency regulations, or court rules. *See, e.g., United States v. Legal Servs. for N.Y.C.*, 249 F.3d 1077 (D.C. Cir. 2001) (appropriations act requiring federally funded legal aid organizations to give client names to auditors triggered required-by-law exception to state's confidentiality rule); *FTC v. Trudeau*, No. 03 C 3904, 2013 WL 842599 (N.D. Ill. Mar. 6, 2013) (Fed. R. Civ. P. 45 constitutes "law" requiring lawyers to reveal confidential information, and lawyers must comply with court order requiring compliance with subpoena even if confidential information must thereby be revealed); *Hope for Families & Cmty. Serv., Inc. v. Warren*, No. 3:06-CV-1113-WKW (WO), 2009 WL 174970, 2009 BL 20317 (M.D. Ala. Jan. 26, 2009) (Rule 1.6 "cannot be used as a shield to producing discovery when it is sought from opposing counsel through compulsion of law in a judicial proceeding"); ABA Formal Ethics Op. 11-460 (2011) (employer's lawyer in employee dispute may disclose that employer accessed employee's e-mails on company server if lawyer reasonably believes disclosure may be necessary to comply with applicable law); N.C. Ethics Op. 2005-9 (2006) (lawyer for public company may reveal confidential information about corporate misconduct to SEC under permissive-disclosure regulations authorized by Sarbanes-Oxley Act, even if disclosure would otherwise be prohibited by state's ethics rules); Vt. Ethics Op. 2015-1 (n.d.) (lawyer does not violate confidentiality rule by complying with federal rule requiring disclosure of all evidence relating to client's disability claim because it constitutes "other law" within meaning of Rule 1.6). However, the exception is not triggered by contracts or other agreements between private parties. *See* Va. Ethics Op. 1811 (2005) (contractual obligation to reveal information did not trigger exception).

A much-litigated example of a law requiring disclosure of client information is the Internal Revenue Code, which, in 26 U.S.C. § 6050, compels lawyers to disclose, through IRS Form 8300, the identities of clients and the amounts and payment dates of all cash fees in excess of $10,000. This provision has consistently been upheld against attacks based upon confidentiality and privilege. *See, e.g., United States v. Goldberger & Dubin, P.C.,* 935 F.2d 501 (2d Cir. 1991) (rejecting challenges to disclosures based upon Fourth, Fifth, and Sixth Amendments and holding that lawyer-client privilege must bow to federal statute that "implicitly precludes its application"). *See generally ABA/ BNA Lawyers' Manual on Professional Conduct,* "Confidentiality: Required by Law or Court Order," pp. 55:1201 *et seq.* Similar issues also arise in connection with the IRS's "John Doe" summonses of law firms in connection with investigations of abusive tax shelters, *see, e.g., In re Tax Liabs. of John Does,* No. 03C 4190, 2003 WL 21791551 (N.D. Ill. June 19, 2003) (approving first such summons and ordering firm to reveal names of clients investing in tax shelter transactions organized or sold by law firm), and with its efforts to collect unpaid taxes from lawyers, *see, e.g., United States v. Servin,* 721 F. App'x 156 (3d Cir. 2018) (ordering compliance with summonses from IRS requiring disclosure of lawyer's current client list and list of cases that settled or will settle within specific time period, including parties' names and addresses). Additional reporting requirements are found in the USA Patriot Act, including a requirement that anyone who must file a Form 8300 must also file a suspicious activity report (SAR) with the Treasury Department's Financial Crimes Enforcement Network. *But see* N.Y. City Ethics Op. 2004-02 (2004) (unclear whether required-by-law exception would permit lawyer representing both corporation and corporate employee to file SAR without advance consent of employee). *See generally* Kevin Shepherd, *USA Patriot Act and the Gatekeeper Initiative: Surprising Implications for Transactional Lawyers,* 16 Prob. & Prop. 26 (Sept./Oct. 2002).

The issue also arises in connection with statutes requiring that child abuse be reported. *See, e.g.,* N.Y. City Ethics Op. 1997-2 (1997) (lawyer employed by social service agency may disclose information relating to abuse of minor client to social service agency if required by law). *See generally* Rebecca Aviel, *When the State Demands Disclosure,* 33 Cardozo L. Rev. 675 (Dec. 2011); Robert P. Mosteller, *Child Abuse Reporting Laws and Attorney-Client Confidences: The Reality and the Specter of Lawyer as Infor-*

*mant*, 42 Duke L.J. 203 (Nov. 1992); Robin A. Rosencrantz, Note, *Rejecting "Hear No Evil, Speak No Evil": Expanding the Attorney's Role in Child Abuse Reporting*, 8 Geo. J. Legal Ethics 327 (Winter 1995).

## Paragraph (b)(7): Disclosure to Detect and Resolve Conflicts of Interest

Paragraph (b)(7) was added in 2012 to explicitly allow a lawyer to disclose information relating to the representation of a client to detect and resolve conflicts of interest that may arise from the lawyer's changing employment or a law firm's merger or sale, even without the client's consent, as long as the disclosure does not compromise the attorney-client privilege or otherwise harm the client. The addition of paragraph (b)(7) was intended to "codify what has long been common practice and acknowledged as essential in ethics opinions: Lawyers must have the ability to disclose limited information to lawyers in other firms in order to detect and prevent conflicts of interest." ABA Resolution and Report to House of Delegates, No. 105F (May 7, 2012), *available at* https://www.americanbar.org/content/dam/aba/administrative/ethics_2020/2012_hod_annual_meeting_105f.authcheckdam.pdf. *See, e.g.*, ABA Formal Ethics Op. 09-455 (2009) (lawyers may disclose basic client information necessary for conflicts analysis because rules require detection and resolution of conflicts, which is impossible without disclosure); D.C. Ethics Op. 312 (2002) (finding, under rule protecting only "confidences" and "secrets," that client's identity and basic information regarding nature of representation are not generally protected); Kan. Ethics Op. 07-01 (2007) (suggesting lawyer's current firm limit access to "middle counsel" such as retired partner or paralegal employed in separate conflicts-checking unit of new firm); Ky. Ethics Op. E-443 (2017) (lawyers or law firms considering merging practices may disclose basic information sufficient to determine whether conflicts of interest exist unless client would object, disclosure would adversely affect client interests, or information is privileged); Boston Ethics Op. 04-01 (2005) (limited disclosures for conflicts checking permissible under implied-authorization exception because any other reading leaves lawyers in untenable position); Pa.-Phila. Joint Formal Ethics Op. 2007-300 (2007) (lawyer negotiating to join new firm should disclose no more information regarding clients' identity and matters than necessary without client consent); *cf.* N.C. Ethics Op. 2010-12 (2011) (law firm may reveal basic information about identity of clients and matters worked on by former clerk who is candidate for lawyer position at another firm that wishes to perform conflicts check as part of hiring process); Phila. Ethics Op. 2014-1 (2014) (ethics committee encourages use of Rule 1.6 disclosure provision to run conflicts check as soon as possible upon lawyer's joining law firm). *See generally* James M. Fischer, *Large Law Firm Lateral Hire Conflicts Checking: Professional Duty Meets Actual Practice*, 36 J. Legal Prof. 167 (Fall 2011).

## Paragraph (c): Acting Competently to Preserve Confidentiality

Paragraph (c) was added in 2012 to make explicit that lawyers must act reasonably to prevent inadvertent or unauthorized disclosure of, or unauthorized access to, information relating to a representation. At the same time, the comment was amended to provide that a third party's unauthorized access to, or the inadvertent or unauthorized disclosure of, information relating to a client's representation will not constitute a violation of Rule 1.6 if the lawyer has made reasonable efforts to prevent the access or disclosure. Cmt. [18]. The rule extends not only to the lawyer but also to "other persons who are participating in the representation of the client or who are subject to the lawyer's supervision." *Id. See, e.g., Statewide Grievance Comm. v. Paige*, No. CV030198335S, 2004 WL 1833462 (Conn. Super. Ct. July 14, 2004) (lawyer's custom of reusing paper containing client information as scrap impermissibly gave others access to protected information); *In re Toigo*, 385 P.3d 585 (Nev. 2016) (abandoning client files in home office after being evicted so that others could access client information); ABA Formal Ethics Op. 08-451 (2008) (lawyer must act competently to minimize risk of disclosure of protected information by outside service providers); N.J. Ethics Op. 692 (2002) (lawyer must act reasonably to protect client information when destroying client files); Ohio State Bar Ethics Op. 2011-02 (2011) (law firm that outsources human resources functions must ensure client information remains confidential); *see also State ex rel. Okla. Bar Ass'n v. McGee*, 48 P.3d 787 (Okla. 2002) (despite lawyer's claim that he was unaware of secretary's preparation of letter impermissibly disclosing confidential information, lawyer "stands ultimately responsible for work done by all non-lawyer staff"). This duty is particularly important when considering outsourcing to foreign jurisdictions whose confidentiality rules may be different from those at home. *See, e.g.,* Colo. Ethics Op. 121 (2008); Va. Ethics Op. 1850 (2010). *See generally ABA/BNA Lawyers' Manual on Professional Conduct*, "Confidentiality: Overview," pp. 55:101 *et seq.*; Mary C. Daly & Carole Silver, *Flattening the World of Legal Services? The Ethical and Liability Minefields of Offshore Legal and Law-Related Services*, 38 Geo. J. Int'l L. 401 (Spring 2007); Madelyn Tarr, *Law Firm Cybersecurity: The State of Preventative and Remedial Regulation Governing Data Breaches in the Legal Profession*, 15 Duke L. & Tech. Rev. 234 (May 20, 2017); Mark L. Tuft, *Supervising Offshore Outsourcing of Legal Services in a Global Environment: Re-Examining Current Ethical Standards*, 43 Akron L. Rev. 825 (2010). For a discussion of the lawyer's responsibilities regarding support staff, see the annotation to Rule 5.3 (Responsibilities Regarding Nonlawyer Assistance).

## ELECTRONIC COMMUNICATIONS AND DATA STORAGE

Transmitting and storing electronic communications, whether by phone (landline or cell phone), by fax, in the cloud, or over the internet pose unique problems related to maintaining client confidences because of the ease with which communications and data may be accessed by unauthorized and unknown persons. Electronic documents also raise the issue of "metadata"—that is, information "hidden" in a document that may reveal details about the document's preparation, prior drafts, and authorship. Even online legal research may result in a lawyer's inadvertently revealing client information to unknown entities.

ABA Formal Opinion 477R states "A lawyer generally may transmit information relating to the representation of a client over the internet without violating the Model Rules of Professional Conduct where the lawyer has undertaken reasonable efforts to prevent inadvertent or unauthorized access. However, a lawyer may be required to take special security precautions to protect against the inadvertent or unauthorized disclosure of client information when required by an agreement with the client or by law, or when the nature of the information requires a higher degree of security." ABA Formal Ethics Op. 477R (2017). Such precautions may include obtaining a client's informed consent to use a particular means of communication, using encrypted e-mail, refraining from using the "cc" or "bcc" functions in e-mails, "scrubbing" a document of its metadata, limiting online tracking, or using a more secure means of communication. *See* cmts. [18], [19]; Alaska Ethics Op. 2018-1 (2018) (lawyers should avoid using "cc" or "bcc" options to send clients copies of e-mails because of risk of inadvertent disclosure of confidential information if client then selects "reply all"); Fla. Ethics Op. 10-2 (2010) (providing guidance on measures to protect confidentiality in using or disposing of devices containing "storage media," such as printers, copiers, facsimile machines, and scanners); Ky. Ethics Op. E-442 (2017) (recommending forwarding e-mail to client instead of using "cc" function so as not to disclose client's identity or other information related to representation); N.Y. State Ethics Op. 1076 (2015) (lawyer should consider forwarding e-mails to client instead of using "cc" or "bcc"). A lawyer must also take reasonable steps to ensure the technology and procedures involved in storing and transmitting electronic client information—whether the lawyer's own or that of outside service providers—are adequate to protect confidentiality. *See, e.g.*, Ala. Ethics Op. 2010-02 (2010); Ariz. Ethics Op. 09-04 (2009); Iowa Ethics Op. 11-01 (2011); Mass. Ethics Op. 12-03 (2012); Mo. Informal Ethics Op. 2014-02 (2014); Nev. Ethics Op. 33 (2006); N.J. Ethics Op. 701 (2006); N.Y. State Ethics Op. 1019 (2014); N.C. Ethics Op. 2011-6 (2012); Ohio State Bar Ethics Op. 2013-03 (2013); Pa. Formal Ethics Op. 2011-200 (2011); Tex. Ethics Op. 665 (2016); Vt. Ethics Op. 2010-6 (2012); *see also* ABA Formal Ethics Op. 483 (2018) ("Rule 1.6 is not violated even if data is lost or accessed if the lawyer has made reasonable efforts to prevent the loss or access."; suggesting measures to prevent unauthorized or inadvertent disclosure once data breach has occurred); Alaska Ethics Op. 2016-1 (2016) (impractical for lawyer to implement technology to detect surreptitiously placed incoming e-mail tracking software); Ill. Ethics Op. 18-01 (2018) (duty to use reasonable precautions does not require lawyer to protect incoming e-mails from tracking software or "web bugs"); Pa. Formal Ethics Op. 2017-300 (n.d.) (same). *See generally ABA/BNA Lawyers' Manual on Professional Conduct*, "Confidentiality: Electronic Communications," pp. 55:401 *et seq.*; Shea Boyd, *The Attorney's Ethical Obligations with Regard to the Technologies Employed in the Practice of Law*, 29 Geo. J. Legal Ethics 849 (Fall 2016); Kristin J. Hazelwood, *Technology and Client Communications: Preparing Law Students and New Lawyers to Make Choices That Comply with the Ethical Duties of Confidentiality, Competence, and Communication*, 83 Miss. L.J. 245 (2014); Sarah Jane Hughes, *Did the National Security Agency Destroy the Prospects for Confidentiality and Privilege When Lawyers Store Clients' Files in the Cloud—And What, if Anything, Can Lawyers and Law Firms Realistically Do in Response?*, 41 N. Ky. L. Rev. 405 (2014); Anne Klinefelter, *When to Research Is to Reveal: The Growing Threat to Attorney and Client Confidentiality from Online Tracking*, 16 Va. J.L. & Tech. 1 (Spring 2011); Whitney Morgan, *Baring All: Legal Ethics and Confidentiality of Electronically Stored Information in the Cloud*, 24 Cath. U. J. L. & Tech. 469 (Spring 2016); Nathan Powell, *Electronic Ethics: Lawyers' Ethical Obligations in a Cyber Practice*, 29 Geo. J. Legal Ethics 1237 (Fall 2016); Cheryl B. Preston, *Lawyers' Abuse of*

*Technology*, 103 Cornell L. Rev. 879 (May 2018); Eli Wald, *Legal Ethics' Next Frontier: Lawyers and Cybersecurity*, 19 Chap. L. Rev. 501 (Spring 2016).

### • *Portable Devices and Border Searches*

When common usage of cell phones began, many ethics opinions advised lawyers to be cautious and to warn clients of the risk that calls on cellular phones may be intercepted. *See, e.g.,* Ill. Ethics Op. 90-7 (1990); Iowa Ethics Op. 90-44 (1990); N.Y. City Ethics Op. 94-11 (1994); N.C. Ethics Op. RPC 215 (1995); Wash. Ethics Op. 91-1 (1991); *see also* Mass. Ethics Op. 94-5 (1994) (lawyer may not use cellular phone to discuss confidential matters with client without informed consent, if risk that conversations may be overheard); N.H. Ethics Op. 1991-92/6 (1991) (lawyer may not discuss client information via cellular phone without client consent unless scrambler or similar device used); *cf.* Minn. Ethics Op. 19 (1999) (distinguishing between digital cordless and cellular phones when used within digital service area and analog cordless and cellular telephones, which are less secure and require consultation with client regarding risks).

As mobile phone usage has become ubiquitous, ethics opinions have evolved to state that communications by cell phone generally pose no special problem unless there is a realistic threat of interception. *See, e.g.,* Ariz. Ethics Op. 95-11 (1995) (lawyer may use cellular phone to contact client but should exercise caution if genuine risk of interception); Del. Ethics Op. 2001-2 (2001) (absent extraordinary circumstances suggesting communication may be intercepted, communication of client information via cell phone does not violate Rule 1.6).

More recently, concerns have arisen regarding the potential for search and seizure of smartphones and other portable electronic devices when crossing international borders. *See* N.Y. City Ethics Op. 2017-5 (2018) (lawyer crossing U.S. border must take reasonable precautions to avoid disclosure of client information in case government border agent requests access to lawyer's electronic devices); ABA Executive Summary, Electronic Device Advisory for Mid-Year Meeting Attendees (2018), *available at* https://www.americanbar.org/content/dam/aba/administrative/professional_responsibility/scepr_electronic_device_advisory_exec_summary.pdf (discussing January 2018 directive of U.S. Customs and Border Protection regarding border searches of electronic devices, lawyers' ethical obligations under Model Rules, and suggested protective measures).

### • *E-mail*

ABA Formal Opinion 477R states that for most matters unencrypted e-mail will be acceptable for lawyer-client communication but under some circumstances, such as where highly sensitive information is involved, "reasonable efforts" may require additional security safeguards, such as encryption, or even avoiding electronic communication altogether. The opinion also provides suggestions for how to determine what security measures will be reasonable. ABA Formal Ethics Op. 477R (2017); *see also* ABA Formal Ethics Op. 2011-459 (2011) ("lawyer sending or receiving substantive communications with a client via e-mail or other electronic means ordinarily must warn the client about the risk of sending or receiving electronic communications using a computer or other device, or e-mail account, where there is a significant risk that a third party may gain access"); Iowa Ethics Op. 15-01 (2015) (same); Tex. Ethics Op. 648 (2015) (confidential information may be sent via e-mail but lawyer may need to warn client of risks and/or consider additional precautions such as encryption or using other means of communication). *See generally* Rebecca Bolin, *Risky Mail: Concerns in Confidential Attorney-Client Email*, 81 U. Cin. L. Rev. 601 (Winter 2012); Adam C. Losey, *Clicking Away Confidentiality: Workplace Waiver of Attorney-Client Privilege*, 60 Fla. L. Rev. 1179 (Dec. 2008).

As for information received from nonclients through unsolicited e-mails or other electronic communications, authorities generally conclude the lawyer has no duty to protect the confidentiality of unsolicited information if the lawyer had no opportunity to avoid its receipt or warn that it would not be kept confidential. *See* Ariz. Ethics Op. 2002-04 (2002); Nev. Ethics Op. 32 (2005); Va. Ethics Op. 1842 (2008); Wash. Ethics Op. 2080 (2006). For an in-depth discussion of this issue, see *ABA/BNA Lawyers' Manual on Professional Conduct*, "Confidentiality: Electronic Communications," pp. 55:401 *et seq.* Also see the annotation to Rule 1.18 (Duties to Prospective Client).

### • *Metadata*

ABA Formal Opinion 06-552 suggests that a lawyer who is concerned about inadvertently disclosing client information via metadata contained in electronic documents may be able to limit the likelihood of its transmission by "scrubbing" the metadata from the document or sending the document in a paper, facsimile, or scanned format that does not contain metadata. ABA Formal Ethics Op. 06-552 (2006). Indeed, all state ethics opinions that have addressed the issue impose a duty upon the sending lawyer to use reasonable care to prevent unauthorized disclosure of confidential information through metadata. *See, e.g.,* Me. Ethics Op. 196 (2008); Minn. Ethics Op. 22 (2010); Miss. Ethics Op. 259 (2012); N.C. Ethics Op. 2009-1 (2010); Or. Ethics Op. 2011-187 (2011; rev. 2015); Vt. Ethics Op. 2009-1 (2009); Wash. Ethics Op. 2216 (2012); W. Va. Ethics Op. 2009-01 (2009); Wis. Formal Ethics Op. EF-12-01 (2012). However, authorities do not always agree about what constitutes reasonable care. *Compare* D.C. Ethics Op. 341 (2007) (lawyers have duty to employ reasonably available technical means to remove metadata before sending document), *with* N.Y. State Ethics Op. 782 (2004) (no absolute duty to scrub metadata unless lawyer knows document contains confidential information or that receiving lawyer likely to mine for metadata). *Cf.* Fed. R. Civ. P. 34(b)(2)(E) (party must generally produce documents with electronically stored information "as they are kept in the usual course of business"; that is, with metadata intact). *See generally* Elizabeth W. King, *The Ethics of Mining for Metadata Outside of Formal Discovery*, 113 Penn St. L. Rev. 801 (Winter 2009).

### • *Virtual Law Offices, Social Networking Websites, Blogs, and Similar Communication Modes*

Communicating directly with clients through postings to websites—including law firm portals, social networking sites, lawyer blogs, bulletin boards, chat rooms, and listservs—poses obvious risks, as does providing lists of contacts on networking sites or providing links to other websites. In general, a lawyer's duty with respect to these modes of communication is to be competent and exercise reasonable care, as with more traditional communications. *See, e.g.,* Pa. Formal Ethics Op. 2010-200 (2010) (lawyer practicing in virtual law office must take reasonable measures to protect confidentiality of client information); *see also* ABA Formal Ethics Op. 480 (2018) (discussing confidentiality obligations for lawyers commenting publicly via blogs and other media); Cal. Formal Ethics Op. 2012-184 (2012) (lawyer wishing to conduct virtual law practice must take reasonable steps to ensure provider's technology adequate to protect confidentiality of client information).

Users may be unaware of the extent to which others may have access to their uploaded information or to which it may be used by third parties to discover client information. Some commentators suggest lawyers and law firms develop policies and procedures for the use of social networking. *See generally* Jan L. Jacobowitz & John G. Browning, *Legal Ethics and Social Media: A Practitioner's Handbook* 127-38 (2017); Vanessa S. Browne-Barbour, *"Why Can't We Be 'Friends'?": Ethical Concerns in the Use of Social Media,* 57 S. Tex. L. Rev. 551 (Summer 2016); Steven C. Bennett, *Ethics of Lawyer Social Networking,* 73 Alb. L. Rev. 113 (2009); Pamela A. Bresnahan & Lucian T. Pera, *The Impact of Technological Developments on the Rules of Attorney Ethics Regarding Attorney-Client Privilege, Confidentiality, and Social Media,* 7 St. Mary's J. Legal Mal. & Ethics 2 (2016); John G. Browning, *Keep Your "Friends" Close and Your Enemies Closer: Walking the Ethical Tightrope in the Use of Social Media,* 3 St. Mary's J. Legal Mal. & Ethics 204 (2013); Margaret M. DiBianca, *Ethical Risks Arising from Lawyers' Use of (and Refusal to Use) Social Media,* 12 Del. L. Rev. 179 (2011).

## • *Cloud Storage*

Methods of storing and synchronizing client files and information in the cloud—that is, on remote servers owned by third parties, sometimes referred to as software as a service (SaaS), platform as a service (PaaS), or infrastructure as a service (IaaS)—pose risks similar to other electronic media and require a similar standard of care: A lawyer must exercise reasonable care to protect the information's confidentiality by, for example, acquiring a basic understanding of the technology involved and using due diligence to ascertain whether cloud providers' security is adequate. *See, e.g.,* Conn. Informal Ethics Op. 2013-07 (2013); Iowa Ethics Op. 11-01 (2011); Mass. Ethics Op. 12-03 (2012); N.H. Ethics Op. 2012-13/4 (2013); N.Y. State Ethics Op. 940 (2012); N.C. Ethics Op. 2011-6 (2011); Ohio State Bar Ethics Op. 2013-03 (2013); Pa. Formal Ethics Op. 2011-200 (2011); Vt. Ethics Op. 2010-6 (2012); Wash. Ethics Op. 2215 (2012). *See generally* Christopher W. Folk, *The Internet of Things and Cybersecurity: What Does a Lawyer Need to Know,* 33 Syracuse J. Sci. & Tech. L. 48 (2016-17); Jack Lerner, Michael Frank, Michelle Lee & Diana Wade, *The Duty of Confidentiality in the Surveillance Age,* 17 J. Internet L., no. 10, at 1 (Apr. 2014); Roland L. Trope & Sarah Jane Hughes, *Red Skies in the Morning—Professional Ethics at the Dawn of Cloud Computing,* 38 Wm. Mitchell L. Rev. 111 (2011).

## DISCLOSURE UNDER OTHER ETHICS RULES

Rule 1.6 permits, but does not require, disclosure under certain circumstances. Other ethics rules, however, affirmatively require disclosure. Most do so only when the disclosure would not violate Rule 1.6 (for example, see Rules 4.1, 8.1, and 8.3), but some, such as Rule 3.3 (Candor Toward the Tribunal), require disclosure of information even if it is otherwise protected by Rule 1.6. Finally, other rules, such as Rule 1.13 (Organization as Client), may permit the disclosure of information whether or not Rule 1.6 would permit it. *See generally* Peter R. Jarvis & Trisha M. Rich, *The Law of Unintended Consequences: Whether and When Mandatory Disclosure Under Model Rule 4.1(b) Trumps Discretionary Disclosure Under Model Rule 1.6(b)*, 44 Hofstra L. Rev. 421 (Winter 2015).

## DISCLOSURE STRICTLY LIMITED TO ESSENTIAL INFORMATION

Any disclosure permitted under Rule 1.6 must be strictly limited to that which "the lawyer reasonably believes . . . is necessary to accomplish one of the purposes specified" in paragraph (b). Cmt. [16]. *See, e.g., Cross v. United States*, Nos. 5:16-cv-06097, 5:15-cr-00079, 2016 WL 4766490, 2016 BL 296385 (S.D. W. Va. Sept. 12, 2016) (criminal defense lawyer may disclose information regarding client communications to extent reasonably necessary to comply with court order and to fully respond to allegations of ineffective assistance of counsel); *In re Bryan*, 61 P.3d 641 (Kan. 2003) (lawyer's many disclosures of adverse information about former client, including informing store manager where client worked that client had history of making false claims, were not reasonably necessary to defend against client's accusations that lawyer was stalking her); *Cleveland Metro. Bar Ass'n v. Heben*, 81 N.E.3d 469 (Ohio 2017) (disclosures of communications with client about representation's scope, legal advice to client, and other protected information in affidavit supporting motion to withdraw were inappropriate and unnecessary); *Lawyer Disciplinary Bd. v. Farber*, 488 S.E.2d 460 (W. Va. 1997) (affidavit reporting on lawyer's plea discussions with defendant filed in support of motion to withdraw); ABA Formal Ethics Op. 476 (2016) (disclosure in support of motion to withdraw for nonpayment of fees must be limited to what is sufficient for court to decide motion); D.C. Ethics Op. 364 (2013) (disclosure of confidences and secrets to respond to former client's claim of ineffective assistance of counsel must be reasonably limited to only what is necessary); Neb. Ethics Op. 12-11 (2012) (lawyer sued by federal agency for civil fraud with two co-defendant former clients may disclose confidential client information only to extent necessary for lawyer's own defense); Nev. Ethics Op. 55 (2018) (criminal defense lawyer may disclose information to extent reasonably necessary to defend against former client's allegations of ineffective assistance of counsel); N.Y. State Ethics Op. 1057 (2015) (lawyer should ordinarily confine reasons in support of withdrawal to "professional considerations"; if court requests or orders disclosure of confidential information, lawyer should disclose no more than necessary without client's informed consent and should take protective measures such as requesting in camera examination); Or. Ethics Op. 2005-136 (2005; rev. 2014) (disclosures made by former in-house counsel to support wrongful termination action against former employer must be made in least public manner possible); *see also In re Boyce*, 613 S.E.2d 538 (S.C. 2005) (lawyer sent letter to client and client's employer threatening to sue both in effort to collect fee); N.Y. City Ethics Op. 1986-8 (1986) (suggesting lawyer disclosing confidential information to collect fee should do so only to court in camera, with request that information be kept under seal); *cf.* ABA Formal Ethics Op. 10-456 (2010) (lawyer's concern about protecting reputation in response to claims of ineffective assistance almost always can be addressed by disclosures in setting subject to judicial supervision); Cal. Formal Ethics Op. 2015-192 (n.d.) (lawyer ordered to disclose confidential information when moving to withdraw must exhaust reasonable efforts at compromise short of disclosure or refusing to comply with court order, including requesting relief from order and, if grounds for withdrawing are permissive, considering withdrawing motion to withdraw).

## DUTIES OF RECIPIENT OF UNINTENDED DISCLOSURES

Rule 4.4(b) was amended in 2002 to address the ethical obligations of a lawyer who is the unintended recipient of documents that appear to be confidential; the lawyer in this position is directed only to "promptly notify the sender." For discussion of this issue, see the annotation to Rule 4.4.

# CLIENT-LAWYER RELATIONSHIP

## Rule 1.7

*Conflict of Interest: Current Clients*

(a) Except as provided in paragraph (b), a lawyer shall not represent a client if the representation involves a concurrent conflict of interest. A concurrent conflict of interest exists if:

(1) the representation of one client will be directly adverse to another client; or

(2) there is a significant risk that the representation of one or more clients will be materially limited by the lawyer's responsibilities to another client, a former client or a third person or by a personal interest of the lawyer.

(b) Notwithstanding the existence of a concurrent conflict of interest under paragraph (a), a lawyer may represent a client if:

(1) the lawyer reasonably believes that the lawyer will be able to provide competent and diligent representation to each affected client;

(2) the representation is not prohibited by law;

(3) the representation does not involve the assertion of a claim by one client against another client represented by the lawyer in the same litigation or other proceeding before a tribunal; and

(4) each affected client gives informed consent, confirmed in writing.

## COMMENT

### General Principles

[1] Loyalty and independent judgment are essential elements in the lawyer's relationship to a client. Concurrent conflicts of interest can arise from the lawyer's responsibilities to another client, a former client or a third person or from the lawyer's own interests. For specific Rules regarding certain concurrent conflicts of interest, see Rule 1.8. For former client conflicts of interest, see Rule 1.9. For conflicts of interest involving prospective clients, see Rule 1.18. For definitions of "informed consent" and "confirmed in writing," see Rule 1.0(e) and (b).

[2] Resolution of a conflict of interest problem under this Rule requires the lawyer to: 1) clearly identify the client or clients; 2) determine whether a conflict of interest exists; 3) decide whether the representation may be undertaken despite the existence of a conflict, i.e., whether the conflict is consentable; and 4) if so, consult with the clients affected under paragraph (a) and obtain their informed consent, confirmed in

writing. The clients affected under paragraph (a) include both of the clients referred to in paragraph (a)(1) and the one or more clients whose representation might be materially limited under paragraph (a)(2).

[3] A conflict of interest may exist before representation is undertaken, in which event the representation must be declined, unless the lawyer obtains the informed consent of each client under the conditions of paragraph (b). To determine whether a conflict of interest exists, a lawyer should adopt reasonable procedures, appropriate for the size and type of firm and practice, to determine in both litigation and non-litigation matters the persons and issues involved. See also Comment to Rule 5.1. Ignorance caused by a failure to institute such procedures will not excuse a lawyer's violation of this Rule. As to whether a client-lawyer relationship exists or, having once been established, is continuing, see Comment to Rule 1.3 and Scope.

[4] If a conflict arises after representation has been undertaken, the lawyer ordinarily must withdraw from the representation, unless the lawyer has obtained the informed consent of the client under the conditions of paragraph (b). See Rule 1.16. Where more than one client is involved, whether the lawyer may continue to represent any of the clients is determined both by the lawyer's ability to comply with duties owed to the former client and by the lawyer's ability to represent adequately the remaining client or clients, given the lawyer's duties to the former client. See Rule 1.9. See also Comments [5] and [29].

[5] Unforeseeable developments, such as changes in corporate and other organizational affiliations or the addition or realignment of parties in litigation, might create conflicts in the midst of a representation, as when a company sued by the lawyer on behalf of one client is bought by another client represented by the lawyer in an unrelated matter. Depending on the circumstances, the lawyer may have the option to withdraw from one of the representations in order to avoid the conflict. The lawyer must seek court approval where necessary and take steps to minimize harm to the clients. See Rule 1.16. The lawyer must continue to protect the confidences of the client from whose representation the lawyer has withdrawn. See Rule 1.9(c).

## Identifying Conflicts of Interest: Directly Adverse

[6] Loyalty to a current client prohibits undertaking representation directly adverse to that client without that client's informed consent. Thus, absent consent, a lawyer may not act as an advocate in one matter against a person the lawyer represents in some other matter, even when the matters are wholly unrelated. The client as to whom the representation is directly adverse is likely to feel betrayed, and the resulting damage to the client-lawyer relationship is likely to impair the lawyer's ability to represent the client effectively. In addition, the client on whose behalf the adverse representation is undertaken reasonably may fear that the lawyer will pursue that client's case less effectively out of deference to the other client, i.e., that the representation may be materially limited by the lawyer's interest in retaining the current client. Similarly, a directly adverse conflict may arise when a lawyer is required to cross-examine a client who appears as a witness in a lawsuit involving another client, as when the testimony will be damaging to the client who is represented in the lawsuit. On the other hand, simultaneous representation in unrelated matters of

clients whose interests are only economically adverse, such as representation of competing economic enterprises in unrelated litigation, does not ordinarily constitute a conflict of interest and thus may not require consent of the respective clients.

[7] Directly adverse conflicts can also arise in transactional matters. For example, if a lawyer is asked to represent the seller of a business in negotiations with a buyer represented by the lawyer, not in the same transaction but in another, unrelated matter, the lawyer could not undertake the representation without the informed consent of each client.

### Identifying Conflicts of Interest: Material Limitation

[8] Even where there is no direct adverseness, a conflict of interest exists if there is a significant risk that a lawyer's ability to consider, recommend or carry out an appropriate course of action for the client will be materially limited as a result of the lawyer's other responsibilities or interests. For example, a lawyer asked to represent several individuals seeking to form a joint venture is likely to be materially limited in the lawyer's ability to recommend or advocate all possible positions that each might take because of the lawyer's duty of loyalty to the others. The conflict in effect forecloses alternatives that would otherwise be available to the client. The mere possibility of subsequent harm does not itself require disclosure and consent. The critical questions are the likelihood that a difference in interests will eventuate and, if it does, whether it will materially interfere with the lawyer's independent professional judgment in considering alternatives or foreclose courses of action that reasonably should be pursued on behalf of the client.

### Lawyer's Responsibilities to Former Clients and Other Third Persons

[9] In addition to conflicts with other current clients, a lawyer's duties of loyalty and independence may be materially limited by responsibilities to former clients under Rule 1.9 or by the lawyer's responsibilities to other persons, such as fiduciary duties arising from a lawyer's service as a trustee, executor or corporate director.

### Personal Interest Conflicts

[10] The lawyer's own interests should not be permitted to have an adverse effect on representation of a client. For example, if the probity of a lawyer's own conduct in a transaction is in serious question, it may be difficult or impossible for the lawyer to give a client detached advice. Similarly, when a lawyer has discussions concerning possible employment with an opponent of the lawyer's client, or with a law firm representing the opponent, such discussions could materially limit the lawyer's representation of the client. In addition, a lawyer may not allow related business interests to affect representation, for example, by referring clients to an enterprise in which the lawyer has an undisclosed financial interest. See Rule 1.8 for specific Rules pertaining to a number of personal interest conflicts, including business transactions with clients. See also Rule 1.10 (personal interest conflicts under Rule 1.7 ordinarily are not imputed to other lawyers in a law firm).

[11] When lawyers representing different clients in the same matter or in substantially related matters are closely related by blood or marriage, there may be a significant risk that client confidences will be revealed and that the lawyer's family relationship will interfere with both loyalty and independent professional judgment. As a result, each client is entitled to know of the existence and implications of the relationship between the lawyers before the lawyer agrees to undertake the representation. Thus, a lawyer related to another lawyer, e.g., as parent, child, sibling or spouse, ordinarily may not represent a client in a matter where that lawyer is representing another party, unless each client gives informed consent. The disqualification arising from a close family relationship is personal and ordinarily is not imputed to members of firms with whom the lawyers are associated. See Rule 1.10.

[12] A lawyer is prohibited from engaging in sexual relationships with a client unless the sexual relationship predates the formation of the client-lawyer relationship. See Rule 1.8(j).

## *Interest of Person Paying for a Lawyer's Service*

[13] A lawyer may be paid from a source other than the client, including a co-client, if the client is informed of that fact and consents and the arrangement does not compromise the lawyer's duty of loyalty or independent judgment to the client. See Rule 1.8(f). If acceptance of the payment from any other source presents a significant risk that the lawyer's representation of the client will be materially limited by the lawyer's own interest in accommodating the person paying the lawyer's fee or by the lawyer's responsibilities to a payer who is also a co-client, then the lawyer must comply with the requirements of paragraph (b) before accepting the representation, including determining whether the conflict is consentable and, if so, that the client has adequate information about the material risks of the representation.

## *Prohibited Representations*

[14] Ordinarily, clients may consent to representation notwithstanding a conflict. However, as indicated in paragraph (b), some conflicts are nonconsentable, meaning that the lawyer involved cannot properly ask for such agreement or provide representation on the basis of the client's consent. When the lawyer is representing more than one client, the question of consentability must be resolved as to each client.

[15] Consentability is typically determined by considering whether the interests of the clients will be adequately protected if the clients are permitted to give their informed consent to representation burdened by a conflict of interest. Thus, under paragraph (b)(1), representation is prohibited if in the circumstances the lawyer cannot reasonably conclude that the lawyer will be able to provide competent and diligent representation. See Rule 1.1 (competence) and Rule 1.3 (diligence).

[16] Paragraph (b)(2) describes conflicts that are nonconsentable because the representation is prohibited by applicable law. For example, in some states substantive law provides that the same lawyer may not represent more than one defendant in a capital case, even with the consent of the clients, and under federal criminal statutes certain representations by a former government lawyer are prohibited, despite the informed consent of the former client. In addition, decisional law in some

states limits the ability of a governmental client, such as a municipality, to consent to a conflict of interest.

[17] Paragraph (b)(3) describes conflicts that are nonconsentable because of the institutional interest in vigorous development of each client's position when the clients are aligned directly against each other in the same litigation or other proceeding before a tribunal. Whether clients are aligned directly against each other within the meaning of this paragraph requires examination of the context of the proceeding. Although this paragraph does not preclude a lawyer's multiple representation of adverse parties to a mediation (because mediation is not a proceeding before a "tribunal" under Rule 1.0(m)), such representation may be precluded by paragraph (b)(1).

## Informed Consent

[18] Informed consent requires that each affected client be aware of the relevant circumstances and of the material and reasonably foreseeable ways that the conflict could have adverse effects on the interests of that client. See Rule 1.0(e) (informed consent). The information required depends on the nature of the conflict and the nature of the risks involved. When representation of multiple clients in a single matter is undertaken, the information must include the implications of the common representation, including possible effects on loyalty, confidentiality and the attorney-client privilege and the advantages and risks involved. See Comments [30] and [31] (effect of common representation on confidentiality).

[19] Under some circumstances it may be impossible to make the disclosure necessary to obtain consent. For example, when the lawyer represents different clients in related matters and one of the clients refuses to consent to the disclosure necessary to permit the other client to make an informed decision, the lawyer cannot properly ask the latter to consent. In some cases the alternative to common representation can be that each party may have to obtain separate representation with the possibility of incurring additional costs. These costs, along with the benefits of securing separate representation, are factors that may be considered by the affected client in determining whether common representation is in the client's interests.

## Consent Confirmed in Writing

[20] Paragraph (b) requires the lawyer to obtain the informed consent of the client, confirmed in writing. Such a writing may consist of a document executed by the client or one that the lawyer promptly records and transmits to the client following an oral consent. See Rule 1.0(b). See also Rule 1.0(n) (writing includes electronic transmission). If it is not feasible to obtain or transmit the writing at the time the client gives informed consent, then the lawyer must obtain or transmit it within a reasonable time thereafter. See Rule 1.0(b). The requirement of a writing does not supplant the need in most cases for the lawyer to talk with the client, to explain the risks and advantages, if any, of representation burdened with a conflict of interest, as well as reasonably available alternatives, and to afford the client a reasonable opportunity to consider the risks and alternatives and to raise questions and concerns. Rather, the writing is required in order to impress upon clients the seriousness of the decision the

client is being asked to make and to avoid disputes or ambiguities that might later occur in the absence of a writing.

## Revoking Consent

[21] A client who has given consent to a conflict may revoke the consent and, like any other client, may terminate the lawyer's representation at any time. Whether revoking consent to the client's own representation precludes the lawyer from continuing to represent other clients depends on the circumstances, including the nature of the conflict, whether the client revoked consent because of a material change in circumstances, the reasonable expectations of the other clients and whether material detriment to the other clients or the lawyer would result.

## Consent to Future Conflict

[22] Whether a lawyer may properly request a client to waive conflicts that might arise in the future is subject to the test of paragraph (b). The effectiveness of such waivers is generally determined by the extent to which the client reasonably understands the material risks that the waiver entails. The more comprehensive the explanation of the types of future representations that might arise and the actual and reasonably foreseeable adverse consequences of those representations, the greater the likelihood that the client will have the requisite understanding. Thus, if the client agrees to consent to a particular type of conflict with which the client is already familiar, then the consent ordinarily will be effective with regard to that type of conflict. If the consent is general and open-ended, then the consent ordinarily will be ineffective, because it is not reasonably likely that the client will have understood the material risks involved. On the other hand, if the client is an experienced user of the legal services involved and is reasonably informed regarding the risk that a conflict may arise, such consent is more likely to be effective, particularly if, e.g., the client is independently represented by other counsel in giving consent and the consent is limited to future conflicts unrelated to the subject of the representation. In any case, advance consent cannot be effective if the circumstances that materialize in the future are such as would make the conflict nonconsentable under paragraph (b).

## Conflicts in Litigation

[23] Paragraph (b)(3) prohibits representation of opposing parties in the same litigation, regardless of the clients' consent. On the other hand, simultaneous representation of parties whose interests in litigation may conflict, such as coplaintiffs or codefendants, is governed by paragraph (a)(2). A conflict may exist by reason of substantial discrepancy in the parties' testimony, incompatibility in positions in relation to an opposing party or the fact that there are substantially different possibilities of settlement of the claims or liabilities in question. Such conflicts can arise in criminal cases as well as civil. The potential for conflict of interest in representing multiple defendants in a criminal case is so grave that ordinarily a lawyer should decline to represent more than one codefendant. On the other hand, common representation of persons having similar interests in civil litigation is proper if the requirements of paragraph (b) are met.

[24] Ordinarily a lawyer may take inconsistent legal positions in different tribunals at different times on behalf of different clients. The mere fact that advocating a legal position on behalf of one client might create precedent adverse to the interests of a client represented by the lawyer in an unrelated matter does not create a conflict of interest. A conflict of interest exists, however, if there is a significant risk that a lawyer's action on behalf of one client will materially limit the lawyer's effectiveness in representing another client in a different case; for example, when a decision favoring one client will create a precedent likely to seriously weaken the position taken on behalf of the other client. Factors relevant in determining whether the clients need to be advised of the risk include: where the cases are pending, whether the issue is substantive or procedural, the temporal relationship between the matters, the significance of the issue to the immediate and long-term interests of the clients involved and the clients' reasonable expectations in retaining the lawyer. If there is significant risk of material limitation, then absent informed consent of the affected clients, the lawyer must refuse one of the representations or withdraw from one or both matters.

[25] When a lawyer represents or seeks to represent a class of plaintiffs or defendants in a class-action lawsuit, unnamed members of the class are ordinarily not considered to be clients of the lawyer for purposes of applying paragraph (a)(1) of this Rule. Thus, the lawyer does not typically need to get the consent of such a person before representing a client suing the person in an unrelated matter. Similarly, a lawyer seeking to represent an opponent in a class action does not typically need the consent of an unnamed member of the class whom the lawyer represents in an unrelated matter.

## Nonlitigation Conflicts

[26] Conflicts of interest under paragraphs (a)(1) and (a)(2) arise in contexts other than litigation. For a discussion of directly adverse conflicts in transactional matters, see Comment [7]. Relevant factors in determining whether there is significant potential for material limitation include the duration and intimacy of the lawyer's relationship with the client or clients involved, the functions being performed by the lawyer, the likelihood that disagreements will arise and the likely prejudice to the client from the conflict. The question is often one of proximity and degree. See Comment [8].

[27] For example, conflict questions may arise in estate planning and estate administration. A lawyer may be called upon to prepare wills for several family members, such as husband and wife, and, depending upon the circumstances, a conflict of interest may be present. In estate administration the identity of the client may be unclear under the law of a particular jurisdiction. Under one view, the client is the fiduciary; under another view the client is the estate or trust, including its beneficiaries. In order to comply with conflict of interest rules, the lawyer should make clear the lawyer's relationship to the parties involved.

[28] Whether a conflict is consentable depends on the circumstances. For example, a lawyer may not represent multiple parties to a negotiation whose interests are fundamentally antagonistic to each other, but common representation is permissible where the clients are generally aligned in interest even though there is some

difference in interest among them. Thus, a lawyer may seek to establish or adjust a relationship between clients on an amicable and mutually advantageous basis; for example, in helping to organize a business in which two or more clients are entrepreneurs, working out the financial reorganization of an enterprise in which two or more clients have an interest or arranging a property distribution in settlement of an estate. The lawyer seeks to resolve potentially adverse interests by developing the parties' mutual interests. Otherwise, each party might have to obtain separate representation, with the possibility of incurring additional cost, complication or even litigation. Given these and other relevant factors, the clients may prefer that the lawyer act for all of them.

## Special Considerations in Common Representation

[29] In considering whether to represent multiple clients in the same matter, a lawyer should be mindful that if the common representation fails because the potentially adverse interests cannot be reconciled, the result can be additional cost, embarrassment and recrimination. Ordinarily, the lawyer will be forced to withdraw from representing all of the clients if the common representation fails. In some situations, the risk of failure is so great that multiple representation is plainly impossible. For example, a lawyer cannot undertake common representation of clients where contentious litigation or negotiations between them are imminent or contemplated. Moreover, because the lawyer is required to be impartial between commonly represented clients, representation of multiple clients is improper when it is unlikely that impartiality can be maintained. Generally, if the relationship between the parties has already assumed antagonism, the possibility that the clients' interests can be adequately served by common representation is not very good. Other relevant factors are whether the lawyer subsequently will represent both parties on a continuing basis and whether the situation involves creating or terminating a relationship between the parties.

[30] A particularly important factor in determining the appropriateness of common representation is the effect on client-lawyer confidentiality and the attorney-client privilege. With regard to the attorney-client privilege, the prevailing rule is that, as between commonly represented clients, the privilege does not attach. Hence, it must be assumed that if litigation eventuates between the clients, the privilege will not protect any such communications, and the clients should be so advised.

[31] As to the duty of confidentiality, continued common representation will almost certainly be inadequate if one client asks the lawyer not to disclose to the other client information relevant to the common representation. This is so because the lawyer has an equal duty of loyalty to each client, and each client has the right to be informed of anything bearing on the representation that might affect that client's interests and the right to expect that the lawyer will use that information to that client's benefit. See Rule 1.4. The lawyer should, at the outset of the common representation and as part of the process of obtaining each client's informed consent, advise each client that information will be shared and that the lawyer will have to withdraw if one client decides that some matter material to the representation should be kept from the other. In limited circumstances, it may be appropriate for

the lawyer to proceed with the representation when the clients have agreed, after being properly informed, that the lawyer will keep certain information confidential. For example, the lawyer may reasonably conclude that failure to disclose one client's trade secrets to another client will not adversely affect representation involving a joint venture between the clients and agree to keep that information confidential with the informed consent of both clients.

[32] When seeking to establish or adjust a relationship between clients, the lawyer should make clear that the lawyer's role is not that of partisanship normally expected in other circumstances and, thus, that the clients may be required to assume greater responsibility for decisions than when each client is separately represented. Any limitations on the scope of the representation made necessary as a result of the common representation should be fully explained to the clients at the outset of the representation. See Rule 1.2(c).

[33] Subject to the above limitations, each client in the common representation has the right to loyal and diligent representation and the protection of Rule 1.9 concerning the obligations to a former client. The client also has the right to discharge the lawyer as stated in Rule 1.16.

## Organizational Clients

[34] A lawyer who represents a corporation or other organization does not, by virtue of that representation, necessarily represent any constituent or affiliated organization, such as a parent or subsidiary. See Rule 1.13(a). Thus, the lawyer for an organization is not barred from accepting representation adverse to an affiliate in an unrelated matter, unless the circumstances are such that the affiliate should also be considered a client of the lawyer, there is an understanding between the lawyer and the organizational client that the lawyer will avoid representation adverse to the client's affiliates, or the lawyer's obligations to either the organizational client or the new client are likely to limit materially the lawyer's representation of the other client.

[35] A lawyer for a corporation or other organization who is also a member of its board of directors should determine whether the responsibilities of the two roles may conflict. The lawyer may be called on to advise the corporation in matters involving actions of the directors. Consideration should be given to the frequency with which such situations may arise, the potential intensity of the conflict, the effect of the lawyer's resignation from the board and the possibility of the corporation's obtaining legal advice from another lawyer in such situations. If there is material risk that the dual role will compromise the lawyer's independence of professional judgment, the lawyer should not serve as a director or should cease to act as the corporation's lawyer when conflicts of interest arise. The lawyer should advise the other members of the board that in some circumstances matters discussed at board meetings while the lawyer is present in the capacity of director might not be protected by the attorney-client privilege and that conflict of interest considerations might require the lawyer's recusal as a director or might require the lawyer and the lawyer's firm to decline representation of the corporation in a matter.

**Definitional Cross-References**
"Confirmed in writing" *See* Rule 1.0(b)
"Informed consent" *See* Rule 1.0(e)
"Reasonably believes" *See* Rule 1.0(i)
"Tribunal" *See* Rule 1.0(m)

**State Rules Comparison**
http://ambar.org/MRPCStateCharts

## ANNOTATION

### GENERAL PROHIBITION

Rule 1.7(a) sets forth the basic prohibition against representation involving conflicting interests ("concurrent conflicts"). The rule identifies two types of concurrent conflicts: direct-adversity conflicts (Rule 1.7(a)(1)) and material-limitation conflicts (Rule 1.7(a)(2)).

#### • *2002 Amendments*

Until the 2002 amendments, the rule used different formulas for each type of conflict: a representation directly adverse to another client was permissible with both clients' consent if the lawyer reasonably believed the relationship with the existing client would not be adversely affected, and a representation that may have been materially limited by the lawyer's interests or responsibilities to others was permissible with client consent if the lawyer reasonably believed the representation would not be adversely affected. The reporter to the Ethics 2000 Commission noted that "[l]awyers frequently [became] confused" when applying this distinction. *See* American Bar Association, *A Legislative History: The Development of the ABA Model Rules of Professional Conduct, 1982–2013*, at 175 (2013).

The reworded test in amended Rule 1.7(a)(2) ("significant risk that the representation . . . will be materially limited") does not represent a substantive change; the drafters' intent was to reflect how the rule was already being interpreted by courts and ethics committees. American Bar Association, *A Legislative History: The Development of the ABA Model Rules of Professional Conduct, 1982–2013*, at 175 (2013).

Rule 1.7(b) then sets forth a single standard of consentability and informed consent governing direct-adversity and material-limitation conflicts alike. Paragraph (b) adds a requirement that informed consent always be confirmed in writing.

The comment was amended in 2002 to address some recurring fact settings and to encompass concerns formerly addressed by Model Rule 2.2 (Intermediary). (Rule 2.2 was deleted in 2002 because it incorrectly suggested that intermediation was something other than an instance of common representation. American Bar Association, *A Legislative History: The Development of the ABA Model Rules of Professional Conduct, 1982–2013*, at 181 (2013).) Much of the former Rule 2.2 survives in Rule 1.7's Comments [26] through [28] (nonlitigation conflicts) and Comments [29] through [33] (special considerations in common representation). *See generally* William Freivogel, *A Short History of Conflicts of Interest. The Future?*, 20 Prof. Law., no. 2, at 3 (2010); Charles W. Wolfram, *Ethics 2000 and Conflicts of Interest: The More Things Change . . .*, 70 Tenn. L. Rev. 27 (Fall 2002).

## STANDING TO SEEK DISQUALIFICATION

The general rule is that only a former or current client has standing to bring a motion to disqualify counsel on the basis of a conflict of interest. *In re Yarn Processing Patent Validity Litig.*, 530 F.2d 83 (5th Cir. 1976) (often cited in standing cases); *O'Hanlon v. AccessU2 Mobile Solutions, LLC*, No. 18-cv-00185-RBJ-NYW, 2018 WL 3586395, 2018 BL 266269 (D. Colo. July 26, 2018); *Ellison v. Chartis Claims, Inc.*, 35 N.Y.S.3d 922 (App. Div. 2016); *In re Technicool Sys., Inc.*, 896 F.3d 382 (5th Cir. 2018) (standing rule especially strict in bankruptcy cases).

In exceptional circumstances courts will forgive lack of standing. *See, e.g., Smith v. TFI Family Servs., Inc.*, No. 17-02235-JTM-GEB, 2018 WL 2926474, 2018 BL 203503 (D. Kan. June 8, 2018) ("public interest" warranted exception in case involving allegations of child abuse in foster care); *Steel Workers Pension Trust v. The Renco Grp., Inc.*, Civ. No. 16-190, 2016 WL 3633079, 2016 BL 218766 (W.D. Pa. July 7, 2016) (court's duty to ensure compliance with ethics rules); *In re CellCyte Genetic Corp. Sec. Litig.*, No. C08–47RS, 2008 WL 5000156 (W.D. Wash. Nov. 20, 2008) (to "protect the integrity of the process and to protect the litigants"); *DeBlasio v. Stone*, Nos. 11–1152, 11–1153, 2012 WL 6097653, 2012 BL 321586 (W. Va. Dec. 7, 2012) (standing not a requirement if the conflict calls "in question the fair and efficient administration of justice"). *See generally* Ivy Johnson, *Standing to Raise a Conflict of Interest*, 23 N. Ill. U. L. Rev. 1 (Fall 2002); Douglas R. Richmond, *The Rude Question of Standing in Attorney Disqualification Disputes*, 25 Am. J. Trial Advoc. 17 (Summer 2001).

## *Paragraph (a): Conflict Identification*

### RULE 1.7(a)(1): DIRECTLY ADVERSE INTERESTS

#### • *Representing Opposing Parties in Same Lawsuit*

Representation of opposing persons in the same lawsuit is prohibited by Rule 1.7(a)(1); this conflict is not waivable. Rule 1.7(b)(3); *see, e.g., Ex parte Osbon*, 888 So. 2d 1236 (Ala. 2004) (in divorce proceeding, husband's lawyer subpoenaed wife's records from mental health agency; lawyer's partner responded on behalf of agency); *Vinson v. Vinson*, 588 S.E.2d 392 (Va. Ct. App. 2003) (representing both husband and wife in divorce proceeding was "gross conflict of interest"); *cf. Fremont Indem. Co. v. Fremont Gen. Corp.*, 49 Cal. Rptr. 3d 82 (Ct. App. 2006) (when lawyer's two clients adverse in proceeding in which lawyer not involved, lawyer's duty of loyalty not implicated and disqualification not justified); D.C. Ethics Op. 326 (2004) (lawyer may refer prospective client to another lawyer even though prospective client adverse to current client of lawyer in same matter).

#### • *Representing Someone in Unrelated Suit against Existing Client*

Rule 1.7(a)(1) prohibits a lawyer from representing anyone directly adverse to a current client, even if the matters are unrelated. *See Harrison v. Fisons Corp.*, 819 F.

Supp. 1039 (M.D. Fla. 1993) (even though law firm represented bank only as guardian of estate, firm could not be adverse to bank on unrelated matters; no distinction between fiduciary and individual capacity); *Fla. Bar v. Adorno*, 60 So. 3d 1016 (Fla. 2011) (settling class action for small group without informing remaining class members was direct adversity and violated Florida's version of Model Rule 1.7(a)(1)); *State ex rel. Neb. State Bar Ass'n v. Frank*, 631 N.W.2d 485 (Neb. 2001) (lawyer may not represent client in workers' compensation claim against employer's insurer whom lawyer already represents in unrelated litigation); Ill. Ethics Op. 04-01 (2004) (lawyer cannot represent real estate buyer if one of lawyer's clients is trying to collect debt owed by seller); Pa. Ethics Op. 00-67 (2000) (solicitor for political subdivision may not represent discharged subordinates of separately elected official whom they are suing for wrongful discharge; political subdivision is nominal defendant in employment suit); S.C. Ethics Op. 05-14 (2005) (without consent, lawyer may not represent mortgagor in foreclosure proceeding if mortgagee is client in other foreclosure proceedings); *see also* ABA Formal Ethics Op. 92-367 (1992) (generally, lawyer may not undertake representation that will require cross-examination of another client as adverse witness). *See generally* Daniel J. Bussel, *No Conflict*, 25 Geo. J. Legal Ethics 207 (Spring 2012) (frontal attack on Rule 1.7(a)(1); author argues "American Rule" should be changed to "substantial relationship" standard); Edwin S. Gault, Jr., Note, *Simultaneous Representation of Adverse Interests: Suing One Client on Behalf of Another*, 15 Miss. C. L. Rev. 189 (Fall 1994); Thomas D. Morgan, *Suing a Current Client*, 9 Geo. J. Legal Ethics 1157 (Summer 1996) (proposition that "a lawyer may never take a position directly adverse to a current client" is not the rule, nor should it be); Brian J. Redding, *Suing a Current Client: A Response to Professor Morgan*, 10 Geo. J. Legal Ethics 487 (Spring 1997); Norman W. Spaulding, *Reinterpreting Professional Identity*, 74 U. Colo. L. Rev. 1 (Winter 2003); Gregory Zimmer, *Suing a Current Client: Responsibility and Respectability in the Conduct of the Legal Profession*, 11 Geo. J. Legal Ethics 371 (Winter 1998).

When a lawyer is employed by a government entity, analysis of conflicts depends upon identifying precisely which government entity is the client. *See, e.g., Brown & Williamson Tobacco Corp. v. Pataki*, 152 F. Supp. 2d 276 (S.D.N.Y. 2001) (law firm that represented state agencies not disqualified from representing tobacco company in its suit challenging state statute); ABA Formal Ethics Op. 97-405 (1997) (lawyer not barred by Rule 1.7 from simultaneously performing legal services for government entity and private clients against another government entity in same jurisdiction, as long as two entities not considered same client); Ill. Ethics Op. 01-07 (2002) (two lawyers in same firm may continue to represent two different governmental units that function under separate boards and are not currently adverse on any issues).

## • *Intellectual Property Opinions*

The following authorities provide that a law firm is being directly adverse to a client when it opines on that client's intellectual property, on behalf of another client: *Andrew Corp. v. Beverly Mfg. Co.*, 415 F. Supp. 2d 919 (N.D. Ill. 2006); Phila. Ethics Op. 2012-11 (2013); Va. Ethics Op. 1774 (2003). *See* Samuel C. Miller, *Ethical Considerations in Rendering Patent Opinions and the Impact of* Knorr, Echostar *and* Andrew, 88 J. Pat. & Trademark Off. Soc'y 1091 (Dec. 2006).

## • *Multiple Representation in Nonlitigation Context*

Comment [7] points out that direct adversity "can also arise in transactional matters." *See, e.g., Iowa Supreme Court Bd. of Prof'l Ethics & Conduct v. Wagner*, 599 N.W.2d 721 (Iowa 1999) (may not represent both buyer and seller in residential real estate transaction); *In re Herriott*, 42 Misc. 3d 1214(A), 986 N.Y.S.2d 868 (N.Y. Sur. Ct. 2014) (sale of real estate by decedent's estate to co-executor voided, in part because same lawyer represented buyer and seller); *N.C. State Bar v. Merrell*, 777 S.E.2d 103 (N.C. Ct. App. 2015) (lawyer suspended for representing lenders and borrower in commercial real estate closing); R.I. Ethics Op. 2017-02 (2017) (same law firm may not represent buyer and seller in sale of business; neither screen nor consent will cure); *cf.* ABA Formal Ethics Op. 05-434 (2004) (ordinarily, no direct adversity when lawyer is engaged to draft estate plan for father disinheriting son, whom lawyer represents on unrelated matters).

## • *Competing for Limited Funds or Resources*

Parties competing for limited funds or resources can create a current client conflict. *See In re Sea Star Line, LLC*, No. 3:15-cv-1297-J-20MCR, 2017 WL 485700, 2017 BL 35388 (M.D. Fla. Feb. 6, 2017), and *In re Seastreak, LLC*, No. 2:13-00315 (WJM), 2014 WL 1272125, 2014 BL 84732 (D.N.J. Mar. 27, 2014) (same ferry accident; limited funds; law firm representing multiple claimants must deal with the conflict); *Smith v. Ga. Energy USA, LLC*, No. CV 208-020, 2014 U.S. Dist. LEXIS 133899 (S.D. Ga. Sept. 23, 2014) (class action regarding miscalibrated gas pumps; lawyer representing class and individual claimants directed to produce plan to deal with limited funds); *Bridgepoint Constr. Servs. Inc. v. Newton*, 237 Cal. Rptr. 3d 598 (Ct. App. 2018) (lawyer disqualified primarily for representing two claimants seeking same funds); Fla. Ethics Op. 02-3 (2002) (lawyer may not represent driver and passenger as plaintiffs if defendant's insurance not adequate to satisfy both unless clients agree among themselves on ultimate distribution of proceeds); N.C. Ethics Op. 2001-6 (2001) (lawyer may not represent multiple claimants in workers' compensation case where one could win at expense of others); *see also Celgard, LLC v. LG Chem, LTD*, 594 F. App'x 669 (Fed. Cir. 2014) (when lawyer represents party seeking to enjoin seller from selling products to buyers, and nonparty buyers are clients of lawyer on other matters, lawyer's representation is directly adverse to clients/nonparties/buyers).

## • *Competing for One License*

Parties seeking licenses, permits, and the like can create a current client conflict. *E.g.,* D.C. Ethics Op. 356 (2010) (bidding contest; lawyer represents one bidder while another bidder is a client on other matters; conflict).

## • *Insurance Defense Representation*

Client-identity issues often underlie the conflicts that arise in insurance defense representation. Jurisdictions are divided over whether a lawyer hired by an insurance company to represent one of its insureds also represents the insurance company. *Compare Nev. Yellow Cab Corp. v. Eighth Judicial Dist. Court*, 152 P.3d 737 (Nev. 2007) (lawyer represents both carrier and insured), *with Weitz Co. v. Ohio Cas. Ins.*

*Co.*, No. 11-cv-00694 –REB-BNB, 2011 WL 2535040, 2011 BL 168996 (D. Colo. June 27, 2011) (only insured is client, relying on Colo. Ethics Op. 91 (1993)). *See generally* Aviva Abramovsky, *The Enterprise Model of Managing Conflicts of Interest in the Tripartite Insurance Defense Relationship*, 27 Cardozo L. Rev. 193 (Oct. 2005); *Restatement (Third) of the Law Governing Lawyers* § 134 cmt. f (2000) (lawyer designated to represent insured does not automatically represent insurer).

ABA Formal Opinion 05-435 (2004) addresses the situation in which a lawyer simultaneously represents an insurance company in one matter and a plaintiff suing one of the company's insureds in an unrelated proceeding in which the company is not a party but is providing the defense. The opinion concludes that "such simultaneous representation does not, without more, result in 'direct adversity' under Rule 1.7(a)(1)" unless the insurer is a named party in the second proceeding. Although the insurer's economic interest in litigation is ordinarily aligned with that of the insured's, "economic adversity alone between the insurer and the plaintiff in the second action is not . . . the sort of direct adversity that constitutes a concurrent conflict of interest under the Model Rules." *Id.*; *accord Stonebridge Cas. Ins. Co. v. D.W. Van Dyke & Co.*, No. 10-CV-81157, 2015 WL 8330980, 2015 BL 409102 (S.D. Fla. Oct. 23, 2015) (following ABA Op. 05-435).

### • *Disqualification Not Inevitable*

Because the decision on disqualification is committed to the court's discretion, a violation of Rule 1.7(a) does not always result in disqualification—particularly if the complaining party cannot show it was harmed. *See, e.g., Hempstead Video, Inc. v. Inc. Vill. of Valley Stream*, 409 F.3d 127 (2d Cir. 2005); *Bayshore Ford Truck Sales, Inc. v. Ford Motor Co.*, 380 F.3d 1331 (11th Cir. 2004); *Lanard Toys Ltd. v. Dolgencorp LLC*, No. 3:15-cv-849-J-34PDB, 2016 WL 7326855, 2016 BL 419166 (M.D. Fla. Dec. 16, 2016) (overlap brief; no confidential information involved); *Blankenchip v. CitiMortgage, Inc.*, Civ. No. 2:14-02309 WBS AC, 2016 WL 6821867, 2016 BL 385382 (E.D. Cal. Nov. 18, 2016) (slight overlap "de minimis"); *HLP Props., LLC v. Consol. Edison Co. of N.Y., Inc.*, Civ. No. 01383 (LGS), 2014 WL 5285926, 2014 BL 289700 (S.D.N.Y. Oct. 16, 2014) (weighed harm, did not disqualify); *Garland v. Ford Motor Co.*, No. 2:12-0021, 2015 WL 1401030, 2015 BL 84904 (M.D. Tenn. Mar. 26, 2015) (Rule 1.7 violation, but no harm).

### • *"Hot-Potato" Rule*

This title concerns a lawyer dropping one client in order to take on a matter adverse to that client. It is discussed in the annotation to Rule 1.9.

## RULE 1.7(a)(2): MATERIAL-LIMITATION CONFLICTS

Rule 1.7(a)(2) focuses not on direct adversity of interests, but on the extent to which a representation is likely to be limited because of interests jeopardizing the lawyer's exercise of independent professional judgment.

### • *Responsibilities to Other Clients*

Multiple representation that does not involve direct adversity of interests under Rule 1.7(a)(1) can still pose a conflict under Rule 1.7(a)(2) if responsibilities to one client could materially limit the representation of another. *See, e.g., In re Shay*, 756 A.2d 465 (D.C. 2000) (conflict materially limited lawyer's representation of couple in estate planning when lawyer knew at time wills drafted that husband, unbeknownst to wife, was actually married to another person); *Idaho State Bar v. Frazier*, 28 P.3d 363 (Idaho 2001) (no violation of Rule 1.7 when lawyer representing both trust and beneficiary's estate bills trust fees and costs to beneficiary's estate, because no evidence that interests of estates not aligned or representation of estates affected); *In re Twohey*, 727 N.E.2d 1028 (Ill. 2000) (lawyer advised client to invest money in another client's company); *In re Toups*, 773 So. 2d 709 (La. 2000) (assistant district attorney representing husband in divorce case should have withdrawn after client's wife filed criminal complaint against husband); *In re Bullis*, 723 N.W.2d 667 (N.D. 2006) (lawyer for computer software company also represented company's landlord, its chief financial officer, an investor, a creditor, and corporation that bought company; construing "adversely affect" test rather than "materially limit" test); *In re Marshall*, 157 P.3d 859 (Wash. 2007) (lawyer represented multiple plaintiffs in discrimination case without adequately explaining possible conflicts or obtaining waivers); N.Y. City Ethics Op. 2001-2 (2001) (detailed analysis of multiple representation in transactional matters); S.C. Ethics Op. 00-17 (2000) (lawyer may represent multiple parties at real estate closings if lawyer complies with requirements of Rule 1.7); *see also* D.C. Ethics Op. 301 (2000) (law firm representing 3,000 special education students seeking benefits from government may also represent class member in personal injury action against same defendant; possibility of conflict "remote").

In litigation, multiple representation of co-parties in civil matters is permitted if there is no "substantial discrepancy" among positions, testimony, or settlement prospects. Cmt. [23]; *see, e.g., Patterson v. Balsamico*, 440 F.3d 104 (2d Cir. 2006) (although defense of any 42 U.S.C. § 1983 action against municipality and its officers/employees presents potential joint-representation conflict, employee's motion for new trial properly denied; his defense consistent with that of municipality, and counsel never argued that employee acted outside scope of his employment); *Miller v. Alagna*, 138 F. Supp. 2d 1252 (C.D. Cal. 2000) (city's lawyers defending city and police officers in civil rights suit knew of potential conflicting defenses at outset but did not obtain informed consent; officers fired them after city fired officers; officers then moved successfully to disqualify them from continuing to represent city); *J & J Snack Foods Corp. v. Kaffrissen*, Civ. No. 98-5743, 2000 WL 562736, 2000 BL 1391 (E.D. Pa. May 9, 2000) (during settlement of wrongful death case, corporation first intervened to recoup what it spent on decedent's medical care and then sued beneficiaries and their counsel for it; when counsel represented himself and continued to represent beneficiaries as his co-defendants, court—concerned that one beneficiary did not understand she had potential malpractice action against him—disqualified him from representing any beneficiaries); *In re Adoption of Baby Girl T*, 21 P.3d 581 (Kan. Ct. App. 2001) (lawyer may represent both adoptive and birth parents with fully informed consent of all); Pa. Ethics Op. 00-78B (2000) (lawyer may represent child as well as child's onlooker sibling in personal injury case arising out of dog bite; child and sibling not making competing claims against limited settlement fund). *See generally* Debra Lyn Bassett, *Three's a Crowd: A Proposal to Abolish Joint Representation*, 32 Rutgers L.J. 387 (Winter

2001); R. David Donoghue, *Conflicts of Interest: Concurrent Representation*, 11 Geo. J. Legal Ethics 319 (Winter 1998); Ze'ev Eiger & Brandy Rutan, Note, *Conflicts of Interest: Attorneys Representing Parties with Adverse Interests in the Same Commercial Transaction*, 14 Geo. J. Legal Ethics 945 (Summer 2001); Carrie Menkel-Meadow, *Ethics and the Settlement of Mass Torts: When the Rules Meet the Road*, 80 Cornell L. Rev. 1159 (May 1995); Geoffrey P. Miller, *Conflicts of Interest in Class Action Litigation: An Inquiry into the Appropriate Standard*, 2003 U. Chi. Legal F. 581 (2003); Dina Mishra, Note, *When the Interests of Municipalities and Their Officials Diverge: Municipal Dual Representation and Conflicts of Interest in § 1983 Litigation*, 119 Yale L.J. 86 (Oct. 2009); Jack B. Weinstein, *Ethical Dilemmas in Mass Tort Litigation*, 88 Nw. U. L. Rev. 469 (Winter 1994); William E. Wright, Jr., *Ethical Considerations in Representing Multiple Parties in Litigation*, 79 Tul. L. Rev. 1523 (June 2005).

## • Duties to Prospective Clients

Conflicts arising out of the duty to protect information received from a prospective client are discussed in the annotation to Rule 1.18.

## • Positional Conflicts

Positional or issue conflicts arise when a lawyer's successful advocacy of a client's legal position in one case could be detrimental to the interests of a different client in another case. *See Williams v. State*, 805 A.2d 880 (Del. 2002) (lawyer who argued in one pending capital appeal that trial court was required to give great weight to jury's recommendation against death penalty permitted under Rule 1.7(b) to withdraw from second capital appeal in which he would be arguing that trial court gave too much weight to jury's recommendation favoring death penalty); ABA Formal Ethics Op. 93-377 (1993) (law firm may not concurrently represent clients whose matters would require firm to argue directly contrary positions in same jurisdiction unless neither case likely to lead to precedent harmful to other and each client gives informed consent). *See generally* Helen A. Anderson, *Legal Doubletalk and the Concern with Positional Conflicts: A "Foolish Consistency"?*, 111 Penn St. L. Rev. 1 (Summer 2006); John S. Dzienkowski, *Positional Conflicts of Interest*, 71 Tex. L. Rev. 457 (Feb. 1993); Douglas R. Richmond, *Choosing Sides: Issue or Positional Conflicts of Interest*, 51 Fla. L. Rev. 383 (July 1999).

## • Corporate-Family Conflicts

See the annotation to Rule 1.13(g) for discussion of conflicts presented by simultaneous representation of an organization and one or more of its constituents.

## • Simultaneous Representation of Co-Parties in Criminal Cases

In criminal cases, most of the caselaw on conflicts of interest involves interpreting the Sixth Amendment right to effective assistance of counsel. Key decisions from the Supreme Court include *Mickens v. Taylor*, 535 U.S. 162 (2002) (when trial court fails to address potential conflict of interest about which it reasonably should have known, defendant must establish that conflict adversely affected his lawyer's performance); *Wheat v. United States*, 486 U.S. 153 (1988) (district court has discretion to disqualify defense counsel even if defendant waives conflict); and *Glasser v. United States*, 315 U.S. 60 (1942) (federal courts may not force defendant to accept appointment of counsel who is representing another defendant in same proceeding). (*Glasser* was extended to state court proceedings in *Holloway v. Arkansas*, 435 U.S. 475 (1978).) *See generally* Jeffrey Scott Glassman, Note, Mickens v. Taylor: *The Court's New Don't-Ask, Don't-Tell Policy for Attorneys Faced with a Conflict of Interest*, 18 St. John's J. Legal Comment. 919 (Summer 2004); Mark W. Shiner, *Conflicts of Interest Challenges Post* Mickens v. Taylor: *Redefining the Defendant's Burden in Concurrent, Successive, and Personal Interest Conflicts*, 60 Wash. & Lee L. Rev. 965 (Summer 2003).

### • *Lawyer's Own Financial and Professional Interests*

A lawyer's financial interests may conflict with a client's interests. *See Doe v. Nielsen*, 883 F.3d 716 (7th Cir. 2018) (law firm disqualified in immigration case where law firm manager was being sued by SEC for defrauding immigration clients; court cited Ill. Rule 1.7(a)(2)); *In re Evans*, 902 A.2d 56 (D.C. 2006) (when lawyer whose title company was insuring real estate in loan transaction learned that actual owner was unprobated estate of borrower's deceased mother-in-law, lawyer initiated probate proceeding on borrower's behalf to transfer title to her but did not explain his own financial interest in facilitating closing); *In re Bruzga*, 27 A.3d 804 (N.H. 2011) (lawyer continued to represent client after state opened Medicaid fraud investigation into how lawyer and client were administering trust and estate); *In re Simon*, 20 A.3d 421 (N.J. 2011) (after motion to withdraw for nonpayment of fees denied, lawyer defending client in murder prosecution created conflict forcing his withdrawal by suing client for fees); *Wixom v. Wixom*, 332 P.3d 1063 (Wash. Ct. App. 2014) (sanctions entered jointly against lawyer and client, and on appeal lawyer tried to assign all sanctions to client; lawyer disqualified); ABA Formal Ethics Op. 484 (2018) (discussing ethical duties when lawyers refer clients to fee financing companies); ABA Formal Ethics Op. 04-432 (2004) (advancing bail on behalf of accused client may pose conflict if amount of bail is "material" to lawyer); ABA Formal Ethics Op. 02-427 (2002) (discussing propriety of lawyer taking security interest in client's property to guarantee payment of fees); D.C. Ethics Op. 367 (2014) (discussing extent to which lawyer can negotiate employment with party or law firm adverse to client).

For discussion of the propriety of acquiring an ownership interest in a client, see the annotation to Rule 1.8(a). For discussion of the conflict presented by simultaneous negotiation of settlement and attorneys' fees, see the annotation to Rule 1.5.

Professional interests that are not purely financial can also materially limit a representation. *See Gerber v. Riordan*, No. 3:06-CV-1525, 2012 WL 366543, 2012 BL 22154 (N.D. Ohio Jan. 31, 2012) (permitting withdrawal in face of client criticisms and accusations); ABA Formal Ethics Op. 08-453 (2008) (discussing law firm ethics counsel's duties to clients versus duties to law firm); ABA Formal Ethics Op. 97-406 (1997) (not necessarily improper for two lawyers to represent adverse interests at same time that one lawyer represents the other; each lawyer must evaluate whether relationship could materially limit representation of third-party client, but disclosure of their relationship is "prudent"); ABA Formal Ethics Op. 94-384 (1994) (lawyer usually need not withdraw from representation when opponent files grievance against him or her, but if lawyer's interest in avoiding discipline could materially limit representation, lawyer first must reasonably conclude representation will not be adversely affected and then must seek client's consent); Conn. Informal Ethics Op. 00-8 (2000) (no material-limitation conflict when lawyer drafts will and serves as both executor of and lawyer for estate, or when lawyer drafts will and subsequent trust agreement under which lawyer serves as co-trustee); Pa. Ethics Op. 02-1 (2002) (lawyer who represents asylum applicant in case pending with immigration court and employs applicant as translator may have conflict of interest if representation of applicant is materially limited by lawyer's own interests as applicant's employer; material limitation may result if applicant's employment terminated); *cf. Sands v. Menard, Inc.*, 787 N.W.2d 384 (Wis. 2010) (order of reinstatement in general counsel's wrongful-termination suit violated public policy; parties' "mutual animosity and distrust" created personal-interest conflict under Rule 1.7(a)(2)).

The issue can arise when criminal defense counsel is asked to advise a client about a plea deal that would require waiving the right to file an ineffective assistance claim. *See Cooper v. State*, 356 S.W.3d 148 (Mo. 2011) (defense lawyer's conflict non-waivable under Rule 1.7, but plea agreement may still be enforceable); Kan. Ethics Op. 17-02 (2017) (violation of Rule 1.7(a) for defense lawyer to ask defendant to waive ineffective assistance claim or for prosecutor to seek waiver of prosecutorial misconduct claim; collecting authorities). It can also occur when a lawyer for a personal-injury plaintiff is asked to execute a release in favor of defendants as a condition of settlement. *See* Phila. Ethics Op. 2011-7 (2012) (agreeing with other jurisdictions; plaintiff's lawyer may not agree to indemnify settling defendants).

When a lawyer for a corporation serves on the corporation's board of directors, the two sets of duties may come into conflict. *See generally* ABA Formal Ethics Op. 98-410 (1998) (suggesting ways to minimize risk of violating ethics rules); Susanna M. Kim, *Dual Identities and Dueling Obligations: Preserving Independence in Corporate Representation*, 68 Tenn. L. Rev. 179 (Winter 2001); Bethany Smith, Note, *Sitting on vs. Not Sitting on Your Client's Board of Directors*, 15 Geo. J. Legal Ethics 597 (Spring 2002); Patrick W. Straub, Note, *ABA Task Force Misses the Mark: Attorneys Should Not Be Discouraged from Serving on Their Corporate Clients' Board of Directors*, 25 Del. J. Corp. L. 261 (2000); Stephen M. Zaloom, *Status of the Lawyer-Director: Avoiding Ethical Misconduct*, 8 U. Miami Bus. L. Rev. 229 (Spring 2000).

## • Lawyer's Family Ties and Personal Relationships

Family ties and personal relationships can create a material-limitation conflict. *See, e.g., Petrovic v. Amoco Oil Co.*, 200 F.3d 1140 (8th Cir. 1999) (law firm representing plaintiff class disqualified because two class representatives were close relatives—husband and sister-in-law—of partner in firm; clear danger their interests would conflict with class's interests when making decisions that could affect law firm's fees); *In re Driscoll*, 856 N.E.2d 840 (Mass. 2006) (lawyer for bank lending money to his secretary notarized secretary's husband's signature on loan documents without witnessing signature; had she been a stranger, lawyer would have sought verification from husband); *Haley v. Boles*, 824 S.W.2d 796 (Tex. App. 1992) (lawyer excused from handling indigent criminal-defense case because one firm partner was spouse of prosecutor assigned to case); Ariz. Ethics Op. 2001-12 (2001) (when assistant public defender is in romantic relationship with law enforcement officer who regularly investigates and arrests office's clientele, informed client consent required to defend any client in whose case officer is involved; if officer is expected to testify, conflict ordinarily nonconsentable); N.Y. State Ethics Op. 738 (2001) (improper for lawyer to refer real estate client to title abstract company in which lawyer's spouse has ownership interest for other than purely ministerial work; intimate relationship and economic interests of husband and wife inseparable). *See generally* Stephen W. Simpson, *From Lawyer-Spouse to Lawyer-Partner: Conflicts of Interest in the 21st Century*, 19 Geo. J. Legal Ethics 405 (Spring 2006).

### • *Sex with Clients*

A sexual relationship with a client that arises during the course of the representation can interfere with the lawyer's ability to exercise independent professional judgment on the client's behalf. The 2002 amendments to the Model Rules identify sex with clients as a specific instance of a material-limitation conflict. *See* Rule 1.8(j); *see also* Rule 1.7, cmt. [12].

Even in the absence of the specific prohibition, however, courts have had no trouble applying Rule 1.7 or its Model Code predecessor to lawyer-client sexual relationships. *See, e.g., Horaist v. Doctor's Hosp. of Opelousas*, 255 F.3d 261 (5th Cir. 2001); *In re Ryland*, 985 So. 2d 71 (La. 2008); *In re O'Leary*, 69 A.3d 1121 (Md. Ct. Spec. App. 2013); *In re Mayer*, 722 S.E.2d 800 (S.C. 2012); *cf. In re Anonymous*, 699 S.E.2d 693 (S.C. 2010) (sex with client's wife is "per se violation of Rule 1.7"). *See generally* Phillip R. Bower & Tanya E. Stern, *Conflict of Interest? The Absolute Ban on Lawyer-Client Sexual Relationships Is Not Absolutely Necessary*, 16 Geo. J. Legal Ethics 535 (Summer 2003); Linda Fitts Mischler, *Personal Morals Masquerading as Professional Ethics: Regulations Banning Sex Between Domestic Relations Attorneys and Their Clients*, 23 Harv. Women's L.J. 1 (Spring 2000).

This topic is also addressed in the annotation to Rule 1.8(j).

### • *Responsibilities to Others*

Responsibilities attendant upon other kinds of relationships, in addition to personal relationships and lawyer-client relationships, can also create material-limitation conflicts under Rule 1.7(a)(2). *See Berry v. Saline Mem'l Hosp.*, 907 S.W.2d 736 (Ark. 1995) (lawyer who had served on hospital's board of governors may not represent patient seeking hospital records under state's freedom of information act for use in patient's action against hospital's insurer; as former board member, lawyer had fiduciary duty not to act to hospital's detriment); Conn. Informal Ethics Op. 00-17 (2000) (lawyer who is town councilman may not represent plaintiff in personal injury action against employee of town and town itself; representation would be materially limited by lawyer's duties to town); D.C. Ethics Op. 337 (2007) (lawyer's responsibilities to person employing her as expert witness may materially limit her ability to represent someone adverse to him in related matter); Ill. Ethics Op. 00-01 (2000) (conflict of interest exists between lawyer's representation of one client and other similar clients if lawyer complies with client's accountant's request to sign confidentiality agreement prohibiting lawyer from revealing accountant's strategies for reducing client's tax obligations). *Compare United States v. Daniels*, 163 F. Supp. 2d 1288 (D. Kan. 2001) (motion to disqualify denied; even though lawyer defending physician in fraud case was being paid by physician's malpractice insurer and was representing physician and insurer in malpractice actions brought by fraud victims, physician was also being defended by two independent criminal defense lawyers and had knowingly waived conflict), *with State v. Culbreath*, 30 S.W.3d 309 (Tenn. 2000) (district attorney and his staff disqualified from prosecuting indecency case because of district attorney's use of private lawyer who received substantial compensation from special interest group opposed to sexually oriented businesses). *See generally* Nancy J. Moore, *Ethical Issues in Third-Party Payment: Beyond the Insurance Defense Paradigm*, 16 Rev. Litig. 585 (Summer 1997).

Payment of a client's fees by a third person, including an insurance company, is discussed in the annotations to Rules 1.8(f) and 5.4(c).

## *Paragraph (b): Client Consent*

### INFORMED CONSENT

If a lawyer reasonably believes that no client will be adversely affected, and if the representation is not prohibited by law and does not involve one client asserting a claim against another, the lawyer may represent conflicting interests if each affected client gives informed consent, confirmed in writing. Rule 1.0(e) defines "informed consent" to mean that the lawyer has "communicated adequate information and explanation about the material risks of and reasonably available alternatives to the proposed course of conduct." *See, e.g., Centra, Inc. v. Estrin*, 538 F.3d 402 (6th Cir. 2008) (client's "vague and general" knowledge of firm's prior work "not an adequate foundation for informed consent"); *Anderson v. Nassau Cnty. Dep't of Corr.*, 376 F. Supp. 2d 294 (E.D.N.Y. 2005) (granting employer-defendants' motion to disqualify plaintiff's counsel, whose firm concurrently represented different employee in similar Title VII action in which plaintiff was fellow defendant; irrelevant that firm already disqualified in that action; employee's offer to withdraw her claims against plaintiff to cure conflict "can only be viewed to support the . . . possible diminution in the vigor of representation that the Second Circuit has sought to prevent in granting motions to disqualify counsel"); *Discotrade Ltd. v. Wyeth-Ayerst Int'l, Inc.*, 200 F. Supp. 2d 355 (S.D.N.Y. 2002) (disqualification granted; "it is clear from the documentary record that [counsel] knew it had not secured an effective waiver before filing this lawsuit"); *Image Technical Servs., Inc. v. Eastman Kodak Co.*, 820 F. Supp. 1212 (N.D. Cal. 1993) (no exception for international law firms with multinational clients; duty to obtain fully informed consent applies "no matter how difficult the communication hurdles"); *In re Evans*, 902 A.2d 56 (D.C. 2006) (rejecting lawyer's argument that pursuant to "company policy" of his title company it was lawyer's associate's responsibility to inform client of lawyer's interest in company; lawyer's admission that he had not personally ensured client gave informed consent established violation of Rule 1.7); *Iowa Supreme Court Att'y Disciplinary Bd. v. Clauss*, 711 N.W.2d 1 (Iowa 2006) (lawyer for creditor also undertook to represent debtor in seeking to lift injunction against her business operations; warning client that lawyer represents both sides is not enough to validate waiver); *In re Wyllie*, 19 P.3d 338 (Or. 2001) (lawyer for three co-defendants hired by father of one to give second opinion about feasibility of pleas to lesser charges not excused from disclosing likely conflict of interest among co-defendants simply because co-defendants were already represented by appointed trial lawyer); *Fullmer v. State Farm Ins. Co.*, 514 N.W.2d 861 (S.D. 1994) (defendant must be advised by independent counsel and informed that her proposed new counsel served as witness for co-defendant in earlier trial before her consent to representation can be deemed valid); *In re Guardianship of Lillian P.*, 617 N.W.2d 849 (Wis. Ct. App. 2000) (waiver requires lawyer to disclose nature of all conflicts or potential conflicts relating to lawyer's representation of client's interests, and how they could affect lawyer's exercise of independent professional judgment for client; client must understand risks involved in not choosing other representation). *See generally* Peter R. Jarvis & Bradley F. Tellam, *When Waiver Should Not Be Good Enough: An Analysis of Current Client Conflicts Law*, 33 Willamette L. Rev. 145 (Winter 1997); Fred C. Zacharias, *Waiving Conflicts of Interest*, 108 Yale L.J. 407 (Nov. 1998).

### • *Written Confirmation*

Rule 1.7(b)(4) requires that a client's informed consent to a lawyer's conflict of interest be "confirmed in writing." This writing may be made by the client, or by the lawyer confirming an oral consent from the client. This approach was adopted by the 2002 amendments to the Model Rules. *See* Cmt. [20]; *see also* Rule 1.0(b).

### • *Government-Entity Consent*

Jurisdictions differ about whether a government entity may waive its counsel's conflict of interest. Some jurisdictions adhere to a per se government-cannot-consent rule, relying upon the public interest and reasoning that a government lawyer may use—or suggest an ability to use—his or her position to secure consent improperly or to gain an improper advantage for a private client. *See, e.g., State ex rel. Morgan Stanley & Co. v. MacQueen*, 416 S.E.2d 55 (W. Va. 1992) (government inherently incapable of consenting to its law firm's concurrent representation of government employees who, though not named as parties, are indirectly accused of acting contrary to government's interest); N.J. Ethics Op. 697 (2005) (noting that in adopting Model Rules, court had specifically chosen to retain per se rule, "essentially a protective remnant of the appearance-of-impropriety rule"); Ohio Sup. Ct. Ethics Op. 2014-2 (2014).

Other jurisdictions, however, have come to reject this rationale. *See, e.g., Pfizer, Inc. v. Farr*, No. M2011-0139-COA-R10-CV, 2012 WL 2370619, 2012 BL 159661 (Tenn. Ct. App. June 22, 2012); Ill. Ethics Op. 95-5 (1995); Iowa Ethics Op. 06-03 (2006); Md. Ethics Op. 99-28 (1999) (modifying prior opinions); N.Y. State Ethics Op. 629 (1992) (modifying prior opinions); Pa. Ethics Op. 2006-24 (2006).

### • *Prospective Waivers*

The effectiveness of a client's prospective waiver of a conflict depends upon whether the conflict is consentable in the first place, and how clearly the waiver identifies the anticipated conflict. *Compare Celgene Corp. v. KV Pharm. Co.*, Civ. No. 07-4819

(SDW), 2008 WL 2937415, 2008 BL 158060 (D.N.J. July 29, 2008), *Worldspan, L.P. v. Sabre Grp. Holdings, Inc.*, 5 F. Supp. 2d 1356 (N.D. Ga. 1998) (disqualification despite advance waivers), *and Sheppard, Mullin, Richter & Hampton, LLP v. J-M Mfg., Inc.*, 425 P.3d 1 (Cal. 2018) (not enforced where law firm did not disclose existing relationship), *with In re Fisker Auto. Holdings, Inc. S'holder Litig.*, Civ. No. 13-2100-DBS-SRF, 2018 WL 3991470, 2018 BL 322151 (D. Del. Aug. 9, 2018) (views prospective waiver favorably), *Galderma Labs., L.P. v. Actavis Mid Atl. LLC*, 927 F. Supp. 2d 390 (N.D. Tex. 2013) (specifically rejecting *Celgene* and approving general, open-ended waiver), *Visa U.S.A., Inc. v. First Data Corp.*, 241 F. Supp. 2d 1100 (N.D. Cal. 2003) (disqualification avoided by advance waiver), *and Grovick Props., LLC v. 83-10 Astoria Blvd., LLC*, 990 N.Y.S.2d 601 (App. Div. 2014) (conflict specifically identified in waiver; disqualification reversed). *See also* ABA Formal Ethics Op. 05-436 (2005) (lawyer may obtain advance waiver from client allowing lawyer to represent unidentified future clients with interests potentially adverse to existing client's interests; waiver more apt to be enforceable if client is "experienced user of legal services" or independently represented in connection with waiver); D.C. Ethics Op. 309 (2001) (lawyer may seek prospective waiver in connection with firm's current or future clients in matters not substantially related to matter firm is undertaking for client; unless client independently represented, waiver must specify types of potential adverse representations and types of adverse clients); N.Y. State Ethics Op. 829 (2009) (approving advance waivers); N.Y. City Ethics Op. 2006-1 (2006) (law firm may ask sophisticated clients to execute prospective waivers permitting it to represent multiple clients in same transactional matter, if clients' interests not starkly antagonistic and certain other requirements met; opinion includes three sample waivers). *See generally* Comment [22] to Rule 1.7; Michael J. DiLernia, *Advance Waivers of Conflicts of Interest in Large Law Firm Practice*, 22 Geo. J. Legal Ethics 97 (Winter 2009); Angela R. Elbert & Sarah G. Malia, *Playing Both Sides? Navigating the Murky Waters of Advance Conflict Waivers*, 19 Prof. Law., no. 1, at 14 (2008); Lauren Nicole Morgan, Note, *Finding Their Niche: Advance Conflicts Waivers Facilitate Industry-Based Lawyering*, 21 Geo. J. Legal Ethics 963 (Summer 2008); Peter Jarvis, Allison Martin Rhodes & Calon Russel, "Clearly Enforceable Future Conflicts Waivers," *ABA/BNA Lawyers' Manual on Professional Conduct*, 30 Law. Man. Prof. Conduct 692 (Current Reports, Oct. 22, 2014).

## Rule 1.8

### *Conflict of Interest: Current Clients: Specific Rules*

(a) A lawyer shall not enter into a business transaction with a client or knowingly acquire an ownership, possessory, security or other pecuniary interest adverse to a client unless:

(1) the transaction and terms on which the lawyer acquires the interest are fair and reasonable to the client and are fully disclosed and transmitted in writing in a manner that can be reasonably understood by the client;

(2) the client is advised in writing of the desirability of seeking and is given a reasonable opportunity to seek the advice of independent legal counsel on the transaction; and

(3) the client gives informed consent, in a writing signed by the client, to the essential terms of the transaction and the lawyer's role in the transaction, including whether the lawyer is representing the client in the transaction.

(b) A lawyer shall not use information relating to representation of a client to the disadvantage of the client unless the client gives informed consent, except as permitted or required by these Rules.

(c) A lawyer shall not solicit any substantial gift from a client, including a testamentary gift, or prepare on behalf of a client an instrument giving the lawyer or a person related to the lawyer any substantial gift unless the lawyer or other recipient of the gift is related to the client. For purposes of this paragraph, related persons include a spouse, child, grandchild, parent, grandparent or other relative or individual with whom the lawyer or the client maintains a close, familial relationship.

(d) Prior to the conclusion of representation of a client, a lawyer shall not make or negotiate an agreement giving the lawyer literary or media rights to a portrayal or account based in substantial part on information relating to the representation.

(e) A lawyer shall not provide financial assistance to a client in connection with pending or contemplated litigation, except that:

(1) a lawyer may advance court costs and expenses of litigation, the repayment of which may be contingent on the outcome of the matter; and

(2) a lawyer representing an indigent client may pay court costs and expenses of litigation on behalf of the client.

(f) A lawyer shall not accept compensation for representing a client from one other than the client unless:

(1) the client gives informed consent;

(2) there is no interference with the lawyer's independence of professional judgment or with the client-lawyer relationship; and

(3) information relating to representation of a client is protected as required by Rule 1.6.

(g) A lawyer who represents two or more clients shall not participate in making an aggregate settlement of the claims of or against the clients, or in a criminal case an aggregated agreement as to guilty or nolo contendere pleas, unless each client gives informed consent, in a writing signed by the client. The lawyer's disclosure shall include the existence and nature of all the claims or pleas involved and of the participation of each person in the settlement.

(h) A lawyer shall not:

(1) make an agreement prospectively limiting the lawyer's liability to a client for malpractice unless the client is independently represented in making the agreement; or

(2) settle a claim or potential claim for such liability with an unrepresented client or former client unless that person is advised in writing of the desirability of seeking and is given a reasonable opportunity to seek the advice of independent legal counsel in connection therewith.

(i) A lawyer shall not acquire a proprietary interest in the cause of action or subject matter of litigation the lawyer is conducting for a client, except that the lawyer may:

(1) acquire a lien authorized by law to secure the lawyer's fee or expenses; and

(2) contract with a client for a reasonable contingent fee in a civil case.

(j) A lawyer shall not have sexual relations with a client unless a consensual sexual relationship existed between them when the client-lawyer relationship commenced.

(k) While lawyers are associated in a firm, a prohibition in the foregoing paragraphs (a) through (i) that applies to any one of them shall apply to all of them.

## COMMENT

### Business Transactions between Client and Lawyer

[1] A lawyer's legal skill and training, together with the relationship of trust and confidence between lawyer and client, create the possibility of overreaching when the lawyer participates in a business, property or financial transaction with a client, for

example, a loan or sales transaction or a lawyer investment on behalf of a client. The requirements of paragraph (a) must be met even when the transaction is not closely related to the subject matter of the representation, as when a lawyer drafting a will for a client learns that the client needs money for unrelated expenses and offers to make a loan to the client. The Rule applies to lawyers engaged in the sale of goods or services related to the practice of law, for example, the sale of title insurance or investment services to existing clients of the lawyer's legal practice. See Rule 5.7. It also applies to lawyers purchasing property from estates they represent. It does not apply to ordinary fee arrangements between client and lawyer, which are governed by Rule 1.5, although its requirements must be met when the lawyer accepts an interest in the client's business or other nonmonetary property as payment of all or part of a fee. In addition, the Rule does not apply to standard commercial transactions between the lawyer and the client for products or services that the client generally markets to others, for example, banking or brokerage services, medical services, products manufactured or distributed by the client, and utilities' services. In such transactions, the lawyer has no advantage in dealing with the client, and the restrictions in paragraph (a) are unnecessary and impracticable.

[2] Paragraph (a)(1) requires that the transaction itself be fair to the client and that its essential terms be communicated to the client, in writing, in a manner that can be reasonably understood. Paragraph (a)(2) requires that the client also be advised, in writing, of the desirability of seeking the advice of independent legal counsel. It also requires that the client be given a reasonable opportunity to obtain such advice. Paragraph (a)(3) requires that the lawyer obtain the client's informed consent, in a writing signed by the client, both to the essential terms of the transaction and to the lawyer's role. When necessary, the lawyer should discuss both the material risks of the proposed transaction, including any risk presented by the lawyer's involvement, and the existence of reasonably available alternatives and should explain why the advice of independent legal counsel is desirable. See Rule 1.0(e) (definition of informed consent).

[3] The risk to a client is greatest when the client expects the lawyer to represent the client in the transaction itself or when the lawyer's financial interest otherwise poses a significant risk that the lawyer's representation of the client will be materially limited by the lawyer's financial interest in the transaction. Here the lawyer's role requires that the lawyer must comply, not only with the requirements of paragraph (a), but also with the requirements of Rule 1.7. Under that Rule, the lawyer must disclose the risks associated with the lawyer's dual role as both legal adviser and participant in the transaction, such as the risk that the lawyer will structure the transaction or give legal advice in a way that favors the lawyer's interests at the expense of the client. Moreover, the lawyer must obtain the client's informed consent. In some cases, the lawyer's interest may be such that Rule 1.7 will preclude the lawyer from seeking the client's consent to the transaction.

[4] If the client is independently represented in the transaction, paragraph (a)(2) of this Rule is inapplicable, and the paragraph (a)(1) requirement for full disclosure is satisfied either by a written disclosure by the lawyer involved in the transaction or by the client's independent counsel. The fact that the client was independently repre-

sented in the transaction is relevant in determining whether the agreement was fair and reasonable to the client as paragraph (a)(1) further requires.

## Use of Information Related to Representation

[5] Use of information relating to the representation to the disadvantage of the client violates the lawyer's duty of loyalty. Paragraph (b) applies when the information is used to benefit either the lawyer or a third person, such as another client or business associate of the lawyer. For example, if a lawyer learns that a client intends to purchase and develop several parcels of land, the lawyer may not use that information to purchase one of the parcels in competition with the client or to recommend that another client make such a purchase. The Rule does not prohibit uses that do not disadvantage the client. For example, a lawyer who learns a government agency's interpretation of trade legislation during the representation of one client may properly use that information to benefit other clients. Paragraph (b) prohibits disadvantageous use of client information unless the client gives informed consent, except as permitted or required by these Rules. See Rules 1.2(d), 1.6, 1.9(c), 3.3, 4.1(b), 8.1 and 8.3.

## Gifts to Lawyers

[6] A lawyer may accept a gift from a client, if the transaction meets general standards of fairness. For example, a simple gift such as a present given at a holiday or as a token of appreciation is permitted. If a client offers the lawyer a more substantial gift, paragraph (c) does not prohibit the lawyer from accepting it, although such a gift may be voidable by the client under the doctrine of undue influence, which treats client gifts as presumptively fraudulent. In any event, due to concerns about overreaching and imposition on clients, a lawyer may not suggest that a substantial gift be made to the lawyer or for the lawyer's benefit, except where the lawyer is related to the client as set forth in paragraph (c).

[7] If effectuation of a substantial gift requires preparing a legal instrument such as a will or conveyance, the client should have the detached advice that another lawyer can provide. The sole exception to this Rule is where the client is a relative of the donee.

[8] This Rule does not prohibit a lawyer from seeking to have the lawyer or a partner or associate of the lawyer named as executor of the client's estate or to another potentially lucrative fiduciary position. Nevertheless, such appointments will be subject to the general conflict of interest provision in Rule 1.7 when there is a significant risk that the lawyer's interest in obtaining the appointment will materially limit the lawyer's independent professional judgment in advising the client concerning the choice of an executor or other fiduciary. In obtaining the client's informed consent to the conflict, the lawyer should advise the client concerning the nature and extent of the lawyer's financial interest in the appointment, as well as the availability of alternative candidates for the position.

## Literary Rights

[9] An agreement by which a lawyer acquires literary or media rights concerning the conduct of the representation creates a conflict between the interests of the client

and the personal interests of the lawyer. Measures suitable in the representation of the client may detract from the publication value of an account of the representation. Paragraph (d) does not prohibit a lawyer representing a client in a transaction concerning literary property from agreeing that the lawyer's fee shall consist of a share in ownership in the property, if the arrangement conforms to Rule 1.5 and paragraphs (a) and (i).

### Financial Assistance

[10] Lawyers may not subsidize lawsuits or administrative proceedings brought on behalf of their clients, including making or guaranteeing loans to their clients for living expenses, because to do so would encourage clients to pursue lawsuits that might not otherwise be brought and because such assistance gives lawyers too great a financial stake in the litigation. These dangers do not warrant a prohibition on a lawyer lending a client court costs and litigation expenses, including the expenses of medical examination and the costs of obtaining and presenting evidence, because these advances are virtually indistinguishable from contingent fees and help ensure access to the courts. Similarly, an exception allowing lawyers representing indigent clients to pay court costs and litigation expenses regardless of whether these funds will be repaid is warranted.

### Person Paying for a Lawyer's Services

[11] Lawyers are frequently asked to represent a client under circumstances in which a third person will compensate the lawyer, in whole or in part. The third person might be a relative or friend, an indemnitor (such as a liability insurance company) or a co-client (such as a corporation sued along with one or more of its employees). Because third-party payers frequently have interests that differ from those of the client, including interests in minimizing the amount spent on the representation and in learning how the representation is progressing, lawyers are prohibited from accepting or continuing such representations unless the lawyer determines that there will be no interference with the lawyer's independent professional judgment and there is informed consent from the client. See also Rule 5.4(c) (prohibiting interference with a lawyer's professional judgment by one who recommends, employs or pays the lawyer to render legal services for another).

[12] Sometimes, it will be sufficient for the lawyer to obtain the client's informed consent regarding the fact of the payment and the identity of the third-party payer. If, however, the fee arrangement creates a conflict of interest for the lawyer, then the lawyer must comply with Rule 1.7. The lawyer must also conform to the requirements of Rule 1.6 concerning confidentiality. Under Rule 1.7(a), a conflict of interest exists if there is significant risk that the lawyer's representation of the client will be materially limited by the lawyer's own interest in the fee arrangement or by the lawyer's responsibilities to the third-party payer (for example, when the third-party payer is a co-client). Under Rule 1.7(b), the lawyer may accept or continue the representation with the informed consent of each affected client, unless the conflict is nonconsentable under that paragraph. Under Rule 1.7(b), the informed consent must be confirmed in writing.

## Aggregate Settlements

[13] Differences in willingness to make or accept an offer of settlement are among the risks of common representation of multiple clients by a single lawyer. Under Rule 1.7, this is one of the risks that should be discussed before undertaking the representation, as part of the process of obtaining the clients' informed consent. In addition, Rule 1.2(a) protects each client's right to have the final say in deciding whether to accept or reject an offer of settlement and in deciding whether to enter a guilty or nolo contendere plea in a criminal case. The rule stated in this paragraph is a corollary of both these Rules and provides that, before any settlement offer or plea bargain is made or accepted on behalf of multiple clients, the lawyer must inform each of them about all the material terms of the settlement, including what the other clients will receive or pay if the settlement or plea offer is accepted. See also Rule 1.0(e) (definition of informed consent). Lawyers representing a class of plaintiffs or defendants, or those proceeding derivatively, may not have a full client-lawyer relationship with each member of the class; nevertheless, such lawyers must comply with applicable rules regulating notification of class members and other procedural requirements designed to ensure adequate protection of the entire class.

## Limiting Liability and Settling Malpractice Claims

[14] Agreements prospectively limiting a lawyer's liability for malpractice are prohibited unless the client is independently represented in making the agreement because they are likely to undermine competent and diligent representation. Also, many clients are unable to evaluate the desirability of making such an agreement before a dispute has arisen, particularly if they are then represented by the lawyer seeking the agreement. This paragraph does not, however, prohibit a lawyer from entering into an agreement with the client to arbitrate legal malpractice claims, provided such agreements are enforceable and the client is fully informed of the scope and effect of the agreement. Nor does this paragraph limit the ability of lawyers to practice in the form of a limited-liability entity, where permitted by law, provided that each lawyer remains personally liable to the client for his or her own conduct and the firm complies with any conditions required by law, such as provisions requiring client notification or maintenance of adequate liability insurance. Nor does it prohibit an agreement in accordance with Rule 1.2 that defines the scope of the representation, although a definition of scope that makes the obligations of representation illusory will amount to an attempt to limit liability.

[15] Agreements settling a claim or a potential claim for malpractice are not prohibited by this Rule. Nevertheless, in view of the danger that a lawyer will take unfair advantage of an unrepresented client or former client, the lawyer must first advise such a person in writing of the appropriateness of independent representation in connection with such a settlement. In addition, the lawyer must give the client or former client a reasonable opportunity to find and consult independent counsel.

## Acquiring Proprietary Interest in Litigation

[16] Paragraph (i) states the traditional general rule that lawyers are prohibited from acquiring a proprietary interest in litigation. Like paragraph (e), the general rule

has its basis in common law champerty and maintenance and is designed to avoid giving the lawyer too great an interest in the representation. In addition, when the lawyer acquires an ownership interest in the subject of the representation, it will be more difficult for a client to discharge the lawyer if the client so desires. The Rule is subject to specific exceptions developed in decisional law and continued in these Rules. The exception for certain advances of the costs of litigation is set forth in paragraph (e). In addition, paragraph (i) sets forth exceptions for liens authorized by law to secure the lawyer's fees or expenses and contracts for reasonable contingent fees. The law of each jurisdiction determines which liens are authorized by law. These may include liens granted by statute, liens originating in common law and liens acquired by contract with the client. When a lawyer acquires by contract a security interest in property other than that recovered through the lawyer's efforts in the litigation, such an acquisition is a business or financial transaction with a client and is governed by the requirements of paragraph (a). Contracts for contingent fees in civil cases are governed by Rule 1.5.

### Client-Lawyer Sexual Relationships

[17] The relationship between lawyer and client is a fiduciary one in which the lawyer occupies the highest position of trust and confidence. The relationship is almost always unequal; thus, a sexual relationship between lawyer and client can involve unfair exploitation of the lawyer's fiduciary role, in violation of the lawyer's basic ethical obligation not to use the trust of the client to the client's disadvantage. In addition, such a relationship presents a significant danger that, because of the lawyer's emotional involvement, the lawyer will be unable to represent the client without impairment of the exercise of independent professional judgment. Moreover, a blurred line between the professional and personal relationships may make it difficult to predict to what extent client confidences will be protected by the attorney-client evidentiary privilege, since client confidences are protected by privilege only when they are imparted in the context of the client-lawyer relationship. Because of the significant danger of harm to client interests and because the client's own emotional involvement renders it unlikely that the client could give adequate informed consent, this Rule prohibits the lawyer from having sexual relations with a client regardless of whether the relationship is consensual and regardless of the absence of prejudice to the client.

[18] Sexual relationships that predate the client-lawyer relationship are not prohibited. Issues relating to the exploitation of the fiduciary relationship and client dependency are diminished when the sexual relationship existed prior to the commencement of the client-lawyer relationship. However, before proceeding with the representation in these circumstances, the lawyer should consider whether the lawyer's ability to represent the client will be materially limited by the relationship. See Rule 1.7(a)(2).

[19] When the client is an organization, paragraph (j) of this Rule prohibits a lawyer for the organization (whether inside counsel or outside counsel) from having a sexual relationship with a constituent of the organization who supervises, directs or regularly consults with that lawyer concerning the organization's legal matters.

## Imputation of Prohibitions

[20] Under paragraph (k), a prohibition on conduct by an individual lawyer in paragraphs (a) through (i) also applies to all lawyers associated in a firm with the personally prohibited lawyer. For example, one lawyer in a firm may not enter into a business transaction with a client of another member of the firm without complying with paragraph (a), even if the first lawyer is not personally involved in the representation of the client. The prohibition set forth in paragraph (j) is personal and is not applied to associated lawyers.

## Definitional Cross-References

"Firm" *See* Rule 1.0(c)
"Informed consent" *See* Rule 1.0(e)
"Knowingly" *See* Rule 1.0(f)
"Substantial" *See* Rule 1.0(l)
"Writing" and "Signed" *See* Rule 1.0(n)

## State Rules Comparison

http://ambar.org/MRPCStateCharts

# ANNOTATION

Rule 1.8 addresses ten specific situations in which a lawyer's personal interests may compromise a client's representation or otherwise harm a client. In most of these situations, the conflict cannot be cured by informed client consent. The lawyer must either avoid the situation or comply with conditions designed to protect the client.

## • *2002 Amendments*

Several paragraphs and related comments were amended in 2002. Treatment of family relationships among lawyers was moved from former paragraph (i) to Rule 1.7, Comment [11]. Former paragraph (j) (acquiring a proprietary interest in litigation) was renumbered as paragraph (i). Two new paragraphs were added: paragraph (j), prohibiting most client-lawyer sexual relationships, and paragraph (k), imputing all prohibitions of Rule 1.8, except paragraph (j), to associated lawyers. Previously, only the prohibition of paragraph (c) on substantial gifts to lawyers was imputed. American Bar Association, *A Legislative History: The Development of the ABA Model Rules of Professional Conduct, 1982–2013*, at 207–21 (2013).

## *Paragraph (a): Business Transactions between Client and Lawyer*

Rule 1.8(a) prohibits business transactions between a lawyer and a client unless the lawyer complies with specific conditions designed to protect the client. These protections are consistent with the common law governing the client-lawyer relationship as well as the law of agency. *See Restatement (Third) of the Law Governing Lawyers* § 126 (2000); *Restatement (Third) of Agency* § 8.03 (2006) (agent has duty not to deal with principal as or on behalf of adverse party in transaction connected with agency relationship).

As explained in Comment [1], Rule 1.8(a) does not apply to ordinary client-lawyer fee arrangements, which are governed by Rule 1.5, or to standard commercial transactions between a lawyer and client "for products or services that the client generally markets to others." It does apply, however, to lawyers who sell their clients goods or services related to the practice of law, such as title insurance or investment services, even if the transaction is not closely related to the subject matter of the representation. *See In re Spencer*, 330 P.3d 538 (Or. 2014) (lawyer acted as real estate broker for bankruptcy client).

If Rule 1.8(a) applies, paragraph (a)(1) requires that the transaction be objectively fair and reasonable to the client. *See In re Miller*, 66 P.3d 1069 (Wash. 2003) (rejecting "sophisticated client" defense); ABA Formal Ethics Op. 00-416 (2000) (lawyer may purchase accounts receivable from client and pursue collection for lawyer's benefit as long as transaction fair and reasonable to client and Rule 1.8 conditions met). Paragraph (a)(1) also requires that the terms of the transaction be fully disclosed in a manner reasonably understandable to the client. *See Fla. Bar v. Ticktin*, 14 So. 3d 928 (Fla. 2009) (press release stating lawyer would assume management of indicted client's business not sufficient disclosure). Paragraph (a)(2) requires that the client be advised in writing of the desirability of seeking the advice of independent counsel and be given a reasonable opportunity to do so; the fact that a client is independently represented in a transaction will be relevant in determining whether the transaction was fair and reasonable. Paragraph (a)(3) requires informed consent, in a writing signed by the client, to the essential terms of the transaction and the lawyer's role in the transaction, including whether the lawyer is representing the client in the transaction. *See In re Trewin*, 684 N.W.2d 121 (Wis. 2004) (clients' signatures on loan documents not sufficient consent).

## COMMON SITUATIONS

Loans involving lawyers and clients are among the most common situations in which Rule 1.8(a) applies. *See, e.g., Calvert v. Mayberry*, No. 16SC413, 2019 WL 1510451 (Colo. Apr. 8, 2019) (rebuttable presumption that Rule 1.8(a) violation renders contract void as against public policy); *In re Torre*, 127 A.3d 690 (N.J. 2015) (lawyer solicited unsecured loan from long-time client); *In re Crary*, 638 N.W.2d 23 (N.D. 2002) (lawyer took loans from elderly client and sold her annuities with undisclosed commissions). Also typical are sales and investment transactions that unfairly favor the lawyer or in which the lawyer fails to provide adequate disclosure. *See, e.g., In re Davis*, 740 N.E.2d 855 (Ind. 2001) (lawyer persuaded client to invest settlement funds in lawyer's business); *In re Lupo*, 851 N.E.2d 404 (Mass. 2006) (lawyer bought real estate from elderly aunt for substantially less than fair market value).

Rule 1.8(a) also applies to the use of client funds for a lawyer's own purposes. *See, e.g., In re Viehe*, 762 A.2d 542 (D.C. 2000) (lawyer entrusted with blank checks for real estate purchase wrote checks for personal use); *In re Letellier*, 742 So. 2d 544 (La. 1999) (lawyer with power of attorney for elderly client loaned client funds to lawyer's corporation); *In re Severson*, 860 N.W.2d 658 (Minn. 2015) (lawyer used client funds for business investments). However, a lawyer's agreement to serve as a fiduciary under a client's will or trust drafted by the lawyer is not a business transaction under Rule 1.8(a), although the lawyer must comply with Rules 1.4(b) and 1.7(a)(2). *See* ABA Formal Ethics Op. 02-426 (2002).

Other common situations are nonmonetary fee arrangements. Comment [1] explains that Rule 1.8(a) applies when a lawyer accepts an interest in a client's business or other nonmonetary property as payment of all or part of a fee. *See In re Snyder*, 35 S.W.3d 380 (Mo. 2000) (accepting quitclaim real estate interest in lieu of cash fee); *Disciplinary Counsel v. Bucio*, 93 N.E.3d 951 (Ohio 2017) (suspension for taking land worth far more than hourly fee); *see also* N.H. Ethics Op. 2017-18/01 (2017) (rule applies to any agreement, including barter transaction, to exchange goods or services for legal services).

When a lawyer acquires stock of a client in lieu of or in addition to a cash fee, a determination that the fee is reasonable under the factors enumerated in Rule 1.5(a) does not resolve whether the transaction is also "fair and reasonable to the client" within the meaning of Rule 1.8(a). ABA Formal Ethics Op. 00-418 (2000) (must consider additional factors, including risk of enterprise failing and stock's marketability); *accord* D.C. Ethics Op. 300 (2000); N.Y. City Ethics Op. 2000-3 (2000); *see also In re Richmond*, 904 A.2d 684 (N.H. 2006) (rejecting argument that Rules 1.5 and 1.8(a) are inconsistent); *cf. Buechel v. Bain*, 766 N.E.2d 914 (N.Y. 2001) (although federal law permits fee agreement granting lawyer interest in client's patent, lawyer must nevertheless comply with state ethics rules). *See generally* John S. Dzienkowski & Robert J. Peroni, *The Decline in Lawyer Independence: Lawyer Equity Investments in Clients*, 81 Tex. L. Rev. 405 (Dec. 2002).

Rule 1.8(i), discussed below, specifically excepts contingent-fee agreements and liens authorized by law (statute, common law, or contract) to secure legal fees from Rule 1.8(a). Comment [16] explains, however, that when a lawyer acquires a security interest in property other than that recovered through the litigation, such an acquisition is subject to the rule. *E.g., Petit-Clair v. Nelson*, 782 A.2d 960 (N.J. Super. Ct. App. Div. 2001) (mortgages on residences of corporate officers securing fees for continued representation of corporation void for failure to comply with rule); ABA Formal Ethics Op. 02-427 (2002) (lawyer acquiring contractual security interest in client property to secure fees must comply with rule); *accord* N.Y. State Ethics Op. 1104 (2016).

## CHANGING FEE AGREEMENTS

Although Rule 1.8(a) does not apply to ordinary client-lawyer fee agreements, it may be relevant to modifications during the course of a representation. *See, e.g., In re Corcella*, 994 N.E.2d 1127 (Ind. 2013) (lawyer switched from hourly to contingent fee without complying with rule); *In re Curry*, 16 So. 3d 1139 (La. 2009) (inserting more favorable terms into original agreement violated rule); *see also* ABA Formal Ethics Op. 11-458 (2011) (changing existing fee agreement permissible if reasonable and accepted by client; modification that involves lawyer acquiring interest in client's business or property subject to Rule 1.8(a)); *cf. Restatement (Third) of the Law Governing Lawyers* § 18(1)(a) (2000) (client may avoid modification unless lawyer shows modification fair and reasonable to client).

## REFERRAL ARRANGEMENTS

Most jurisdictions consider Rule 1.8(a) applicable when a lawyer receives compensation for referrals to nonlawyer professionals such as investment advisors. *See* Ariz. Ethics Op. 05-01 (2005); D.C. Ethics Op. 361 (2011); N.J. Ethics Op. 696 (2005); *see In re Phillips*, 107 P.3d 615 (Or. 2005) (lawyer advised clients to consult insurance agents without disclosing shared commissions); *cf.* Rule 7.2(b)(4) (lawyer may refer clients to another lawyer or nonlawyer professional if reciprocal referral agreement not exclusive and clients informed of its existence and nature). Rule 1.8(a) also applies when the referral is made to an entity in which the lawyer has a financial interest. *See* ABA Formal Ethics Op. 484 (2018) (lawyer may refer clients to lender to finance legal fees, but must comply with Rule 1.8(a) if lawyer has financial interest in lender); *see also* Rule 5.7, cmt. [5] (lawyer must comply with Rule 1.8(a) when referring clients to law-related service entity in which lawyer has interest); *cf.* Rule 7.2(b)(5) (lawyer may give "nominal" gifts as expression of appreciation not intended or expected as compensation for referral). Some jurisdictions have concluded that compensated referrals are improper even with full disclosure and consent. *See, e.g.,* Me. Ethics Op. 184 (2004); Tex. Ethics Op. 536 (2001).

## *Paragraph (b): Use of Information Related to Representation*

Rule 1.8(b) governs the use (in contrast to disclosure, which is governed by Rule 1.6) of information relating to the representation of a current client. Once the client-lawyer relationship has ended, Rule 1.9 governs both the disclosure and use of protected information.

Rule 1.8(b) prohibits a lawyer from using information relating to the representation of a client to the client's disadvantage without the client's informed consent, unless permitted or required by other rules. Comment [5] explains, for example, that if a lawyer knows a client intends to develop several parcels of land, the lawyer may not use that information to buy one of the parcels in competition with the client or to recommend that another client make such a purchase. *See In re Guidone*, 653 A.2d 1127 (N.J. 1994) (lawyer used client information to acquire interest in partnership buying property from client); *Disciplinary Counsel v. Ward*, 34 N.E.3d 74 (Ohio 2015) (lawyer used knowledge of client's business affairs to formulate litigation strategy adverse to client); ABA Formal Ethics Op. 05-435 (2005) (lawyer who simultaneously represents liability insurer and claimant against one of its insureds in unrelated matter may not use information relating to representation of insurer for claimant's benefit); ABA Formal Ethics Op. 02-426 (2002) (lawyer acting as fiduciary may have conflict using information gained in representation of beneficiary in unrelated matter); ABA Formal Ethics Op. 92-367 (1992) (seeking third-party discovery of client may involve information within contemplation of Rule 1.8(b)).

Comment [5] notes that Rule 1.8(b) does not prohibit a lawyer from using client information in a way that does not disadvantage the client. In this respect, Rule 1.8(b) differs from general fiduciary and agency law. *See Restatement (Third) of the Law Governing Lawyers* § 60(2) (2000) (lawyer who uses client's confidential information for pecuniary gain must account to client for any profit); *Restatement (Third) of Agency* § 8.05 (2006) (agent may not use principal's confidential information for own purposes).

## *Paragraph (c): Gifts to Lawyers*

Rule 1.8(c) prohibits a lawyer from soliciting a substantial gift from a client or preparing an instrument by which a client gives a substantial gift to the lawyer or the lawyer's relative, unless the lawyer or other recipient is related to the client. The rule defines "related persons" to include relatives or others with whom the lawyer or client maintains a "close, familial relationship." *See In re Devaney*, 870 A.2d 53 (D.C. 2005) (lawyer prepared instrument conveying property to himself and his family); *In re Boulger*, 637 N.W.2d 710 (N.D. 2001) (lawyer drafted codicil giving himself large contingent gift); *see also In re Colman*, 885 N.E.2d 1238 (Ind. 2008) (lawyer who "actively participated" in drafting will naming lawyer and son beneficiaries violated rule even though will prepared by another lawyer).

Comment [6] notes that a lawyer may accept a substantial gift that was not solicited, but cautions that the gift must meet "general standards of fairness" and may be voidable under the doctrine of undue influence, which treats client gifts as presumptively fraudulent. *See, e.g., Olson v. Estate of Watson*, 52 S.W.3d 865 (Tex. App. 2001) (will leaving testator's entire estate to lawyer's family unenforceable); *cf. Restatement (Third) of the Law Governing Lawyers* § 127(2) (2000) (lawyer may not accept substantial gift from client unless lawyer related to client or client has received or been encouraged to seek independent advice). *But see In re Mardigian Estate*, 917 N.W.2d 325 (Mich. 2018) (presumption of undue influence rebuttable; violation of rule "merely constitutes grounds for invoking attorney disciplinary process").

Rule 1.8(c) permits small gifts, as well as gifts from clients who are related to the lawyer. Comment [8] further notes that the rule permits a lawyer to seek appointment to a fiduciary position, including that of a client's executor, but cautions that the arrangement may create a conflict of interest within the meaning of Rule 1.7. *See also* ABA Formal Ethics Op. 02-426 (2002) (lawyer may act as fiduciary under will or trust prepared by lawyer; absent special circumstances, lawyer acting as fiduciary may appoint himself or other firm lawyers to represent him in that capacity if compensation reasonable).

## *Paragraph (d): Literary Rights*

Rule 1.8(d) prohibits a lawyer, while representing a client, from acquiring the client's literary or media rights to a portrayal or account based in substantial part upon information relating to the representation. *See Restatement (Third) of the Law Governing Lawyers* § 36(3) (2000) (similar to Rule 1.8(d)). Comment [9] explains that a lawyer's acquisition of such rights creates a conflict between the interests of the client and the personal interests of the lawyer. *See In re Henderson*, 78 N.E.3d 1092 (Ind. 2017) (prosecutor disciplined for book deal about scandalous murder case); *Commonwealth v. Downey*, 842 N.E.2d 955 (Mass. App. Ct. 2006) (defense counsel's agreement to wear concealed microphone during murder trial required new trial); *Harrison v. Miss. Bar*, 637 So. 2d 204 (Miss. 1994) (agreement with film producer for rights to lawyer's life story, including representation of current client, violated rule); *cf.* D.C. Ethics Op. 334 (2006) (rule not applicable to lawyer's agreement to sell own story about pending case). Comment [9] also notes that a lawyer's fee may consist of an interest in literary property that is the subject of a representation if the fee arrangement conforms to Rules 1.5, 1.8(a), and 1.8(i).

### *Paragraph (e): Financial Assistance*

With two exceptions discussed below, Rule 1.8(e) prohibits a lawyer from providing financial assistance, including loans or guarantees of third-party loans, to a client in connection with pending or contemplated litigation. The prohibition is designed to avoid encouraging clients to pursue litigation that might not otherwise be brought, as well as avoid giving lawyers too great a financial stake in the litigation. *See Restatement (Third) of the Law Governing Lawyers* § 36(2) (2000) (prohibitions similar to Rule 1.8(e)); *see also* N.M. Ethics Op. 2017-01 (2017) (plaintiff's lawyer may not agree to indemnify opposing party from third-party claims to settlement funds); *cf.* ABA Formal Ethics Op. 04-432 (2004) (no per se prohibition on posting bail for client, but must be no significant risk that representation will be materially limited by lawyer's personal interest in recovering advance).

The first exception, stated in paragraph (e)(1), permits a lawyer to advance court costs and litigation expenses and to condition repayment upon recovery, which Comment [10] analogizes to a contingent fee. The second, expressed in paragraph (e)(2), permits a lawyer for an indigent client to pay court costs and litigation expenses outright. *See* Conn. Informal Ethics Op. 00-21 (2000) (lawyer may pay indigent client's deposition travel expenses); Pa. Ethics Op. 2000-14 (2000) (lawyer may post appeal bond for indigent client); *cf.* Wash. Ethics Op. 2149 (2007) (lawyer for nonprofit group providing guardianship services to indigents may not pay costs of proceedings because client is organization rather than indigent person).

### ASSISTING INDIGENT CLIENTS

Most jurisdictions do not allow an exception for assisting indigent clients. *See, e.g., In re Kratina,* 746 N.W.2d 378 (Neb. 2008) (improper to pay travel expenses for client medical treatment); *Lawyer Disciplinary Bd. v. Nessel,* 769 S.E.2d 484 (W. Va. 2015) (prohibition absolute; no exception for "altruistic intent"). *But see Fla. Bar v. Taylor,* 648 So. 2d 1190 (Fla. 1994) (no violation to give indigent client used clothing for child and $200 for necessities as "act of humanitarianism"); *cf.* Va. Ethics Op. 1830 (2006) (public defender may give indigent client nominal amount to buy personal items at jail commissary; gift not "in connection with" client's case). A few jurisdictions have amended the rule to permit various forms of financial assistance to indigent clients. *See, e.g.,* Minn. Rule 1.8(e)(3) (lawyer may guarantee loan to enable indigent client to withstand litigation delay). *See generally* Philip G. Schrag, *The Unethical Ethics Rule: Nine Ways to Fix Model Rule of Professional Conduct 1.8(e),* 28 Geo. J. Legal Ethics 39 (Winter 2015).

### LOANS FOR LITIGATION EXPENSES

Some jurisdictions have concluded that although there are risks, a lawyer in a contingent-fee matter may borrow funds from a lending institution to defray litigation expenses. *See, e.g., Chittenden v. State Farm Mut. Auto. Ins. Co.,* 788 So. 2d 1140 (La. 2001) (with adequate disclosure and consent, lawyer may make agreement obligating client to repay interest on loan obtained by lawyer for litigation and living expenses); Ky. Ethics Op. E-420 (2002) (lawyer may borrow to finance litigation expenses in contingent-fee case and deduct interest from proceeds of action, but may not grant lender security interest in contingent fee; collecting opinions). A lawyer may also assist a client seeking nonrecourse funding from an alternative litigation finance provider in exchange for an interest in the proceeds from the litigation, but the lawyer must advise the client of the risks, including waiver of the attorney-client privilege. *See, e.g.,* N.Y. City Ethics Op. 2011-2 (2011); Ohio Sup. Ct. Ethics Op. 2012-3 (2012). *See generally* Douglas R. Richmond, *Other People's Money: The Ethics of Litigation Funding,* 56 Mercer L. Rev. 649 (Winter 2005).

## Paragraph (f): Person Paying for a Lawyer's Services

Rule 1.8(f) imposes conditions on a lawyer's acceptance of compensation from someone other than the client. Comment [11] notes that third-party payors frequently have interests that differ from those of the client, including interests in minimizing the lawyer's fee and learning how a representation is progressing. For these reasons, Rule 1.8(f) requires: (1) informed client consent; (2) no interference with the lawyer's independence of professional judgment or with the client-lawyer relationship; and (3) protection of information relating to the representation. The second condition is similar to Rule 5.4(c), which provides that a lawyer shall not permit a person who recommends, employs, or pays the lawyer to render legal services to another to direct or regulate the lawyer's professional judgment in rendering such services; both rules may apply in some situations. *See, e.g.,* ABA Formal Ethics Op. 02-428 (2002) (lawyer may draft will for testator at request of existing client who pays lawyer and is potential beneficiary, provided testator gives informed consent and Rules 1.8(f) and 5.4(c) followed); *see also* ABA Formal Ethics Op. 07-448 (2007) (defendant who refuses representation by appointed lawyer has no basis to contend lawyer obligated to avoid conflicts); *Restatement (Third) of the Law Governing Lawyers* § 134 (2000) (imposing conditions similar to Rule 1.8(f)). *See generally* Nancy J. Moore, *Ethical Issues in Third-Party Payment: Beyond the Insurance Defense Paradigm,* 16 Rev. Litig. 585 (Summer 1997).

Comment [12] notes that Rule 1.7 also applies if the fee arrangement creates a conflict of interest for the lawyer. Although the two rules express the criteria differently ("materially limited" in Rule 1.7 and "interference with the lawyer's independence of professional judgment or with the client-lawyer relationship" in Rule 1.8(f)), no different substantive standard was apparently intended. *See* Geoffrey C. Hazard, Jr., W. William Hodes & Peter R. Jarvis, *The Law of Lawyering* § 13.21 (4th ed. 2015); *see also* Neb. Ethics Op. 17-03 (2017) (lawyer may accept digital currencies from third-party payors if no interference with lawyer's independent relationship with client).

## INSURANCE DEFENSE

Under a typical liability insurance policy, an insurer appoints and pays a lawyer to defend a claim made against an insured. This tripartite relationship among insurer, insured, and defense counsel is often characterized by commentators as the "eternal triangle." *See* Douglas R. Richmond, *Lost in the Eternal Triangle of Insurance Defense Ethics*, 9 Geo. J. Legal Ethics 475 (Winter 1996) (conflicts inevitable in eternal triangle; defense counsel should embrace principle that insured is sole client).

Jurisdictions differ on whether defense counsel represents the insured, the insurer, or both. Some hold that the insured is the defense lawyer's only client. *See, e.g., Essex Ins. Co. v. Tyler*, 309 F. Supp. 2d 1270 (D. Colo. 2004); *In re Rules of Prof'l Conduct*, 2 P.3d 806 (Mont. 2000); *cf. Hornberger v. Wendel*, 764 N.W.2d 371 (Minn. Ct. App. 2009) (attorney-client relationship between lawyer and insured created as matter of law when insurer retained defense counsel). Others suggest a "dual client" relationship with both the insured and the insurer absent a conflict of interest, although the insured is usually considered the "primary" client. *See, e.g., Nev. Yellow Cab Corp. v. Eighth Judicial Dist. Court*, 152 P.3d 737 (Nev. 2007) (adopting "majority view" that defense lawyer represents insurer and insured, but insured is primary client); *see also* ABA Formal Ethics Op. 08-450 (2008) (lawyer representing multiple clients, as in insurance defense, must protect confidential information of each and may need to withdraw from representing one or both clients if conflict arises); ABA Formal Ethics Op. 96-403 (1996) (Model Rules offer no guidance on whether lawyer retained by insurer represents insured, insurer, or both; if insured objects to settlement insurer is authorized to make, lawyer must give insured opportunity to reject insurer's defense and assume defense at insured's expense). Some states require insurance defense lawyers to provide insureds with written statements of the terms and scope of the representation. *See* Fla. Rule 4-1.8(j); Ohio Rule 1.8(f)(4); Wis. Rule 1.2(e). *See generally* Thomas D. Morgan, *What Insurance Scholars Should Know About Professional Responsibility*, 4 Conn. Ins. L.J. 1 (1997–1998).

Many insurers in the 1990s sought to control defense costs by imposing billing guidelines on defense counsel and requiring submission of fee and expense statements to third-party auditors. Numerous state opinions concluded this practice violated Rule 1.8(f) and other ethics rules. *See* ABA Formal Ethics Op. 01-421 (2001) (collecting opinions and concluding lawyers must obtain informed consent to disclose bills to outside auditors). *See generally* Susan Randall, *Managed Litigation and the Professional Obligations of Insurance Defense Lawyers*, 51 Syracuse L. Rev. 1 (2001).

Some insurers have sought to control costs by establishing "captive" firms, lawyers employed directly by insurers, to represent insureds in claims defense. Such arrangements have been permitted in most states, but found to violate Rule 1.8(f) as well as Rules 1.7 and 5.5 in others. *See, e.g., Brown v. Kelton*, 380 S.W.3d 361 (Ark. 2011) (defense by employee lawyers presents conflicts of interest and constitutes unauthorized practice of law); *Unauthorized Practice of Law Comm'n v. Am. Home Ins. Co.*, 261 S.W.3d 24 (Tex. 2008) (staff lawyer may defend insured if insurer's and insured's interests congruent and affiliation fully disclosed). An ABA ethics opinion concluded that insurance staff counsel may ethically represent insureds as long as the lawyers (1) exercise independent professional judgment in the representations, and (2) inform all insureds at the earliest opportunity practicable that the lawyers are employed by the insurer. ABA Formal Ethics Op. 03-430 (2003); *cf. Golden v. State Farm Mut. Auto. Ins. Co.*, 745 F.3d 252 (7th Cir. 2014) (insurer need not disclose staff defense counsel to insured when policy issued).

## CRIMINAL DEFENSE

In criminal cases, third-party payment of a defendant's legal fees may raise due process and Sixth Amendment concerns. *See, e.g., Wood v. Georgia*, 450 U.S. 261 (1981) ("inherent dangers" when defense counsel paid by third party; trial court on notice must inquire further to protect defendant's rights); *United States v. Schwarz*, 283 F.3d 76 (2d Cir. 2002) (conviction reversed because large retainer paid by union to defend two officers created nonconsentable conflict); Ariz. Ethics Op. 2001-06 (2001) (lawyer may not contract with county to represent indigent defendants if authorizations required from nonlawyer third parties that could induce lawyer to act contrary to clients' interests); *cf. Devaney v. United States*, 47 F. Supp. 2d 130 (D. Mass. 1999) (rejecting claim that lawyer pursued plea bargain to minimize fees paid by defendant's brother-in-law; no violation by mere third-party fee payment).

## Paragraph (g): Aggregate Settlements or Plea Agreements

Rule 1.8(g) prohibits a lawyer who represents two or more clients from participating in making an aggregate settlement of the claims of or against the clients, or in a criminal case an aggregated agreement as to guilty or nolo contendere pleas, unless each client gives informed consent in a writing signed by the client. The required disclosure must include the existence and nature of all claims or pleas involved and the participation of each person in the settlement. *See Restatement (Third) of the Law Governing Lawyers* § 128 cmt. d(i) (2000) (lawyer must inform each client of all settlement terms, including what other claimants will receive); *In re Gatti*, 333 P.3d 994 (Or. 2014) (lawyer failed to obtain each client's informed written consent to allocation of lump-sum settlement); ABA Formal Ethics Op. 06-438 (2006) (lawyer must advise each client of total settlement amount, nature and amount of each client's participation, fees and costs to be paid to lawyer, and how costs will be apportioned to each client). *See generally* American Law Institute, *Principles of the Law of Aggregate Litigation* (2010).

The informed-consent requirement cannot be met by obtaining advance consent to a decision that will be made by the lawyer or a majority of the claimant group. *See, e.g., Abbott v. Kidder Peabody & Co.*, 42 F. Supp. 2d 1046 (D. Colo. 1999) (engagement agreement permitting steering committee to control settlement created nonconsentable conflict); *Tax Auth., Inc. v. Jackson Hewitt, Inc.*, 898 A.2d 512 (N.J. 2006) (lawyer may not obtain advance consent to accept majority vote on settlement); *cf.* Colo. Ethics Op. 134 (2018) (lawyer may prepare advance agreement providing majority rule, but agreement not binding when settlement proposal considered; lawyer may need to withdraw if dispute arises among clients). *See generally* Carol A. Needham, *Advance Consent to Aggregate Settlements: Reflections on Attorneys' Fiduciary Obligations and Professional Responsibility Duties*, 44 Loy. U. Chi. L.J. 511 (Winter 2012).

## Paragraph (h): Limiting Liability and Settling Malpractice Claims

Rule 1.8(h) was split into two paragraphs in 2002 to clarify that it addresses two separate situations. Paragraph (h)(1) prohibits agreements prospectively limiting a lawyer's liability to a client for malpractice unless the client is independently represented in making the agreement. The 2002 amendment also deleted the former additional condition "unless permitted by law" because, as the drafters explained, they were unaware of any such law. American Bar Association, *A Legislative History: The Development of the ABA Model Rules of Professional Conduct, 1982–2013*, at 217 (2013); *cf. Restatement (Third) of the Law Governing Lawyers* § 54(2) (2000) (agreements prospectively limiting lawyer's malpractice liability unenforceable).

Comment [14] resolves three significant issues concerning the application of paragraph (h)(1). First, it does not prohibit pre-dispute agreements to arbitrate legal malpractice claims. *See* ABA Formal Ethics Op. 02-425 (2002) (retainer agreement may require binding arbitration of fee disputes and malpractice claims provided client fully apprised of advantages and disadvantages of arbitration and gives informed consent; agreement must not limit liability to which lawyer would otherwise be exposed). A few courts have enforced generic pre-dispute arbitration clauses, but others have refused. *See, e.g., Bezio v. Draeger*, 737 F.3d 819 (1st Cir. 2013) (arbitration enforced despite failure to specify malpractice claims or advise of consequences); *Hodges v. Reasonover*, 103 So. 3d 1069 (La. 2012) (no per se rule against arbitrating malpractice claims; lawyer did not make necessary disclosures); *Castillo v. Arrieta*, 368 P.3d 1249 (N.M. Ct. App. 2016) (arbitration denied because lawyer did not explain implications); *Royston, Rayzor, Vickery, & Williams, LLP v. Lopez*, 467 S.W.3d 494 (Tex. 2015) (generic arbitration clause enforced). Second, it does not prohibit lawyers from practicing in limited-liability entities. *See* ABA Formal Ethics Op. 96-401 (1996) (law firm may practice as limited-liability entity if lawyers remain personally liable for own acts or omissions). Third, it does not prohibit agreements limiting the scope of the representation in accordance with Rule 1.2. *See* N.Y. City Ethics Op. 2001-3 (2001) (lawyer may limit scope of representation to avoid conflicts of interest if client consents and limitation does not render lawyer's advice inadequate).

Paragraph (h)(2) prohibits a lawyer from settling an existing or potential claim with an unrepresented client or former client unless that person is advised in writing of the desirability of seeking independent counsel and is given a reasonable opportunity to do so. *See In re Braun*, 734 N.E.2d 535 (Ind. 2000) (lawyer did not advise client to consult independent counsel before client agreed to release lawyer from liability and withdraw disciplinary complaint in exchange for fee refund); *see also* N.J. Ethics Op. 721 (2011) (request that client withdraw or not file disciplinary charge as part of settlement violates Rule 8.4(d)). The phrase "or potential claim" was added in 2002 to make clear that the prohibition applies to unasserted possible claims as well as actual claims. American Bar Association, *A Legislative History: The Development of the ABA Model Rules of Professional Conduct, 1982–2013*, at 218 (2013); *see also In re Greenlee*, 143 P.3d 807 (Wash. 2006) (interpreting prior version of rule to cover potential claims).

### Paragraph (i): Acquiring Proprietary Interest in Litigation

Rule 1.8(i) restricts a lawyer's ability to acquire a proprietary interest in a client's cause of action or the subject matter of litigation. Paragraph (i) was renumbered in 2002; it was formerly paragraph (j). This rule, like Rule 1.8(e), is derived from common-law doctrines of champerty and maintenance, and it is designed to avoid giving the lawyer too great a stake in the representation. Comment [16] notes the additional concern that a client may find it more difficult to discharge a lawyer who has an ownership interest in the litigation. *See* ABA Formal Ethics Op. 00-416 (2000) (lawyer may purchase accounts receivable from client if transaction complies with Rule 1.8(a), but if accounts are subject of litigation conducted by lawyer, lawyer must either acquire entire claim or withdraw from representation).

The general prohibition is subject to three significant exceptions. First, paragraph (e) permits certain advances for litigation costs. Second, paragraph (i)(1) exempts liens "authorized by law." A 2002 amendment substituted "authorized" for "granted" to clarify that the exemption included contractual liens. American Bar Association, *A Legislative History: The Development of the ABA Model Rules of Professional Conduct, 1982–2013*, at 219 (2013). Third, paragraph (i)(2) recognizes contingent fees in civil matters. *See also Restatement (Third) of the Law Governing Lawyers* § 43 (2000) (general discussion of lawyer liens).

### Paragraph (j): Client-Lawyer Sexual Relationships

Rule 1.8(j) prohibits all client-lawyer sexual relationships, including consensual relationships, except those predating the formation of the client-lawyer relationship. The per se prohibition was adopted in 2002, after several jurisdictions had enacted similar rules, because a specific rule has "the advantage not only of alerting lawyers more effectively to the dangers of sexual relationships with clients but also of alerting clients that the lawyer may have violated ethical obligations in engaging in such conduct." American Bar Association, *A Legislative History: The Development of the ABA Model Rules of Professional Conduct, 1982–2013*, at 219 (2013). Jurisdictions without specific rules had typically addressed client-lawyer sex under rules dealing with misconduct or conflicts of interest. *See, e.g., In re Bash*, 880 N.E.2d 1182 (Ind. 2008) (attempted sexual relations with client violated Rule 8.4(a)); *In re Berg*, 955 P.2d 1240 (Kan. 1998) (sexual relations with vulnerable divorce clients warranted disbarment despite lack of express prohibition); *see also Restatement (Third) of the Law Governing Lawyers* § 16 cmt. e (2000) (lawyer may not enter sexual relationship with client that would abuse client's dependence or create risk to lawyer's independent judgment); ABA Formal Ethics Op. 92-364 (1992) (lawyer's fiduciary obligation to client implies lawyer should not abuse client's trust by taking sexual or emotional advantage).

Comment [17] cites the fiduciary nature of the client-lawyer relationship and explains that the client's own emotional involvement renders it unlikely that the client could give adequate informed consent. *See, e.g., In re Paschal*, 772 S.E.2d 271 (S.C. 2015) (lawyer suspended for sex with married client); *Lawyer Disciplinary Bd. v. White*, 811 S.E.2d 893 (W. Va. 2018) (lawyer disbarred for sex with vulnerable client). Comment [18] observes that sexual relationships that predate the client-lawyer relationship are exempt from the rule because concerns for exploitation and client dependency may be diminished in such situations, but nevertheless cautions that the lawyer must consider whether the relationship will pose a material limitation on the representation within the meaning of Rule 1.7(a)(2). When the client is an organization, Comment [19] explains that the prohibition is limited to relationships with constituents of the organization who supervise, direct, or regularly consult with the lawyer about the organization's legal matters. *See, e.g., In re Bergman,* 382 P.3d 455 (Kan. 2016) (suspension for secret affair with company president).

### Paragraph (k): Imputation of Prohibitions

Rule 1.8(k) was added in 2002. Previously, imputation of a conflict under Rule 1.8 was determined by the general imputation rule, Rule 1.10(a), and only the prohibition on gifts to lawyers (Rule 1.8(c)) was imputed to other lawyers associated in a firm. American Bar Association, *A Legislative History: The Development of the ABA Model Rules of Professional Conduct, 1982–2013,* at 220 (2013). Rule 1.8(k) now imputes almost all the Rule 1.8 prohibitions to every lawyer associated in a firm. Only the prohibition of Rule 1.8(j) (client-lawyer sexual relationships) is deemed personal and exempt from imputation.

## Rule 1.9

### *Duties to Former Clients*

(a) A lawyer who has formerly represented a client in a matter shall not thereafter represent another person in the same or a substantially related matter in which that person's interests are materially adverse to the interests of the former client unless the former client gives informed consent, confirmed in writing.

(b) A lawyer shall not knowingly represent a person in the same or a substantially related matter in which a firm with which the lawyer formerly was associated had previously represented a client

(1) whose interests are materially adverse to that person; and

(2) about whom the lawyer had acquired information protected by Rules 1.6 and 1.9(c) that is material to the matter; unless the former client gives informed consent, confirmed in writing.

(c) A lawyer who has formerly represented a client in a matter or whose present or former firm has formerly represented a client in a matter shall not thereafter:

(1) use information relating to the representation to the disadvantage of the former client except as these Rules would permit or require with respect to a client, or when the information has become generally known; or

(2) reveal information relating to the representation except as these Rules would permit or require with respect to a client.

## COMMENT

[1] After termination of a client-lawyer relationship, a lawyer has certain continuing duties with respect to confidentiality and conflicts of interest and thus may not represent another client except in conformity with this Rule. Under this Rule, for example, a lawyer could not properly seek to rescind on behalf of a new client a contract drafted on behalf of the former client. So also a lawyer who has prosecuted an accused person could not properly represent the accused in a subsequent civil action against the government concerning the same transaction. Nor could a lawyer who has represented multiple clients in a matter represent one of the clients against the others in the same or a substantially related matter after a dispute arose among

the clients in that matter, unless all affected clients give informed consent. See Comment [9]. Current and former government lawyers must comply with this Rule to the extent required by Rule 1.11.

[2] The scope of a "matter" for purposes of this Rule depends on the facts of a particular situation or transaction. The lawyer's involvement in a matter can also be a question of degree. When a lawyer has been directly involved in a specific transaction, subsequent representation of other clients with materially adverse interests in that transaction clearly is prohibited. On the other hand, a lawyer who recurrently handled a type of problem for a former client is not precluded from later representing another client in a factually distinct problem of that type even though the subsequent representation involves a position adverse to the prior client. Similar considerations can apply to the reassignment of military lawyers between defense and prosecution functions within the same military jurisdictions. The underlying question is whether the lawyer was so involved in the matter that the subsequent representation can be justly regarded as a changing of sides in the matter in question.

[3] Matters are "substantially related" for purposes of this Rule if they involve the same transaction or legal dispute or if there otherwise is a substantial risk that confidential factual information as would normally have been obtained in the prior representation would materially advance the client's position in the subsequent matter. For example, a lawyer who has represented a businessperson and learned extensive private financial information about that person may not then represent that person's spouse in seeking a divorce. Similarly, a lawyer who has previously represented a client in securing environmental permits to build a shopping center would be precluded from representing neighbors seeking to oppose rezoning of the property on the basis of environmental considerations; however, the lawyer would not be precluded, on the grounds of substantial relationship, from defending a tenant of the completed shopping center in resisting eviction for nonpayment of rent. Information that has been disclosed to the public or to other parties adverse to the former client ordinarily will not be disqualifying. Information acquired in a prior representation may have been rendered obsolete by the passage of time, a circumstance that may be relevant in determining whether two representations are substantially related. In the case of an organizational client, general knowledge of the client's policies and practices ordinarily will not preclude a subsequent representation; on the other hand, knowledge of specific facts gained in a prior representation that are relevant to the matter in question ordinarily will preclude such a representation. A former client is not required to reveal the confidential information learned by the lawyer in order to establish a substantial risk that the lawyer has confidential information to use in the subsequent matter. A conclusion about the possession of such information may be based on the nature of the services the lawyer provided the former client and information that would in ordinary practice be learned by a lawyer providing such services.

## Lawyers Moving Between Firms

[4] When lawyers have been associated within a firm but then end their association, the question of whether a lawyer should undertake representation is more

complicated. There are several competing considerations. First, the client previously represented by the former firm must be reasonably assured that the principle of loyalty to the client is not compromised. Second, the rule should not be so broadly cast as to preclude other persons from having reasonable choice of legal counsel. Third, the rule should not unreasonably hamper lawyers from forming new associations and taking on new clients after having left a previous association. In this connection, it should be recognized that today many lawyers practice in firms, that many lawyers to some degree limit their practice to one field or another, and that many move from one association to another several times in their careers. If the concept of imputation were applied with unqualified rigor, the result would be radical curtailment of the opportunity of lawyers to move from one practice setting to another and of the opportunity of clients to change counsel.

[5] Paragraph (b) operates to disqualify the lawyer only when the lawyer involved has actual knowledge of information protected by Rules 1.6 and 1.9(c). Thus, if a lawyer while with one firm acquired no knowledge or information relating to a particular client of the firm, and that lawyer later joined another firm, neither the lawyer individually nor the second firm is disqualified from representing another client in the same or a related matter even though the interests of the two clients conflict. See Rule 1.10(b) for the restrictions on a firm once a lawyer has terminated association with the firm.

[6] Application of paragraph (b) depends on a situation's particular facts, aided by inferences, deductions or working presumptions that reasonably may be made about the way in which lawyers work together. A lawyer may have general access to files of all clients of a law firm and may regularly participate in discussions of their affairs; it should be inferred that such a lawyer in fact is privy to all information about all the firm's clients. In contrast, another lawyer may have access to the files of only a limited number of clients and participate in discussions of the affairs of no other clients; in the absence of information to the contrary, it should be inferred that such a lawyer in fact is privy to information about the clients actually served but not those of other clients. In such an inquiry, the burden of proof should rest upon the firm whose disqualification is sought.

[7] Independent of the question of disqualification of a firm, a lawyer changing professional association has a continuing duty to preserve confidentiality of information about a client formerly represented. See Rules 1.6 and 1.9(c).

[8] Paragraph (c) provides that information acquired by the lawyer in the course of representing a client may not subsequently be used or revealed by the lawyer to the disadvantage of the client. However, the fact that a lawyer has once served a client does not preclude the lawyer from using generally known information about that client when later representing another client.

[9] The provisions of this Rule are for the protection of former clients and can be waived if the client gives informed consent, which consent must be confirmed in writing under paragraphs (a) and (b). See Rule 1.0(e). With regard to the effectiveness of an advance waiver, see Comment [22] to Rule 1.7. With regard to disqualification of a firm with which a lawyer is or was formerly associated, see Rule 1.10.

**Definitional Cross-References**

"Confirmed in writing" *See* Rule 1.0(b)
"Firm" *See* Rule 1.0(c)
"Informed consent" *See* Rule 1.0(e)
"Knowingly" and "Known" *See* Rule 1.0(f)
"Writing" *See* Rule 1.0(n)

**State Rules Comparison**
http://ambar.org/MRPCStateCharts

## ANNOTATION

### OVERVIEW OF RULE 1.9

Rule 1.9(a) is the core rule on conflicts with former clients. Two key issues are (1) whether the client is "current" or "former," and (2) whether the proposed representation is "substantially related" to the former representation. A third important issue is whether the new representation is "materially adverse" to the former client. *See generally* N.Y. State Ethics Op. 1008 (2014) (discussion of current versus former client).

Rule 1.9(b) applies when a representation in a substantially related matter would be materially adverse to the interests of a client of the lawyer's former firm, rather than to the interests of the lawyer's own former client. In this scenario a conflict arises only if the lawyer acquired protected information that would be material.

Both Rule 1.9(a) and Rule 1.9(b) permit the representation with the former client's informed consent, confirmed in writing.

Rule 1.9(c)(1) governs the use of a former client's protected information, and Rule 1.9(c)(2) separately governs the disclosure of that information.

### *Paragraph (a): The Former-Client Rule*

### WAS THERE EVER A LAWYER-CLIENT RELATIONSHIP?

Application of Rule 1.9 begins with a determination of whether the lawyer and the putative former client ever actually formed a lawyer-client relationship. *See, e.g., City of Waukegan v. Martinovich*, No. 03 C 3984, 2005 WL 3465567, 2005 BL 62452 (N.D. Ill. Dec. 16, 2005) (disqualifying defendant's lawyer in environmental cleanup action because plaintiff employed her in remediation project; nature of her work belied argument she had been nonlegal "consultant"); *Stratagene v. Invitrogen Corp.*, 225 F. Supp. 2d 608 (D. Md. 2002) (former associate's "discrete and limited" administrative work on plaintiff's patent application sufficed to create lawyer-client relationship disqualifying her from representing defendant plaintiff was suing for infringement of related patent); *In re Estate of Klehm*, 842 N.E.2d 1177 (Ill. App. Ct. 2006) (law firm that represented sons solely in their roles as beneficiaries of father's estate not disqualified from representing executor of mother's estate in citation proceeding against sons); *In re James*, 679 S.E.2d 702 (W. Va. 2009) (lawyer who agreed to represent defendant in drunk-driving accident after meeting with both defendant's and victim's parents did not form attorney-client relationship with victim's parents). *See generally* Susan R. Martyn, *Accidental Clients*, 33 Hofstra L. Rev. 913 (Spring 2005); Ingrid A. Minott, Note, *The Attorney-Client Relationship: Exploring the Unintended Consequences of Inadvertent Formation*, 86 U. Det. Mercy L. Rev. 269 (Winter 2009).

## • *Organizational Clients*

When the lawyer has represented an organization, rather than an individual, it is not always clear who enjoys former-client status for purposes of Rule 1.9. Most of the confusion arises in three situations: (1) corporate affiliates, (2) organizations and their individual constituents, and (3) mergers and asset sales. For a discussion of these relationships, see the annotation to Rule 1.13.

## • *Insurance Defense Representation*

Issues relating to insurance defense representation are discussed in the annotations to Rules 1.7(a) and 1.8(f).

## • *Common-Interest Agreements*

When parties in a litigated matter have common interests their lawyers sometimes enter a common-interest or joint-defense agreement to share information and strategy, with each lawyer agreeing to keep the information of the other lawyers' clients confidential. This obligation may result in disqualifying one of the lawyers from later representing someone adverse to a nonclient member of the group in a substantially related matter. Rationales, however, vary. *See, e.g., In re Gabapentin Patent Litig.*, 407 F. Supp. 2d 607 (D.N.J. 2005) (joint-defense agreement created implied lawyer-client relationship between counsel for one defendant and other signatories; counsel's new firm therefore needed each signatory's consent before it could represent plaintiff in same matter); *City of Kalamazoo v. Mich. Disposal Serv.*, 151 F. Supp. 2d 913 (W.D. Mich. 2001) (lawyer-client relationship between one co-defendant and counsel for another co-defendant in environmental litigation was created by joint-defense agreement; counsel disqualified from representing plaintiffs in subsequent environmental suit against first co-defendant); *Meza v. H. Muehlstein & Co.*, 98 Cal. Rptr. 3d 422 (Ct. App. 2009) (disqualifying law firm representing plaintiff in toxic tort action in which new associate had represented one of multiple defendants; although that defendant had been dismissed, remaining defendants had shared confidential information with associate pursuant to common-interest doctrine); *Nat'l Med. Enters. v. Godbey*, 924 S.W.2d 123 (Tex. 1996) (lawyer who promised in joint-defense agreement to maintain confidentiality of information received from corporation while representing company's ex-employees disqualified, along with lawyer's entire firm, from subsequently representing parties adverse to corporation); ABA Formal Ethics Op. 95-395 (1995) (disqualifying fiduciary obligation "almost surely" exists in joint-defense consortium that entailed sharing of confidential information); D.C. Ethics Op. 349 (2009) (although not prohibited by Rule 1.9 from undertaking representation adverse to member of former client's joint-defense group, lawyer "may have acquired contractual and fiduciary obligations to nonclient group member that will preclude him from representing an adverse party in a substantially related matter"). *See generally* Bradley C. Nahrstadt & W. Brandon Rogers, *In Unity There Is Strength: The Advantages (and Disadvantages) of Joint Defense Groups*, 80 Def. Couns. J. 29 (Jan. 2013).

### • *Accommodation Clients*

Rule 1.9 accords with the majority of courts in refusing to recognize the concept of an accommodation client—someone the lawyer briefly represents as a favor to another client or another lawyer, but who will not thereafter "count" as a former client. *See, e.g., Exterior Sys., Inc. v. Noble Composites, Inc.*, 175 F. Supp. 2d 1112 (N.D. Ind. 2001) (rejecting accommodation-client doctrine and collecting cases); *Universal City Studios, Inc. v. Reimerdes*, 98 F. Supp. 2d 449 (S.D.N.Y. 2000) (rejecting law firm's argument that it was representing particular company only as accommodation to parent corporation, its long-standing client, and denying firm permission to withdraw in order to sue company in unrelated matter); *cf. Streit v. Covington & Crowe*, 98 Cal. Rptr. 2d 193 (Ct. App. 2000) (firm whose only connection to plaintiff's case was that it covered hearing on motion "as a professional courtesy" to her counsel could nevertheless be sued for legal malpractice; no such thing as "limited-liability representation" no matter how perfunctory the involvement). *See generally* Susan R. Martyn, *Accidental Clients*, 33 Hofstra L. Rev. 913 (Spring 2005); Douglas R. Richmond, *Accommodation Clients*, 35 Akron L. Rev. 59 (2001).

### • *Former Prospective Clients*

For a discussion of representing a client whose interests are materially adverse to an individual who previously consulted with but did not hire the lawyer, see the annotation to Rule 1.18.

### • *Short-Term Limited Legal Services under Rule 6.5*

When a lawyer participating in a qualified legal services program renders short-term assistance to program beneficiaries, Rule 6.5(a)(1) specifies that although a lawyer-client relationship is indeed established, the lawyer will be subject to Rule 1.9(a) only if the lawyer actually knows that the representation involves a conflict of interest. For further discussion, see the annotation to Rule 6.5.

### • *Lawyer Serving as Expert Witness*

According to ABA Formal Opinion 97-407, a lawyer testifying as an expert witness does not establish a lawyer-client relationship with the party for Rule 1.9 purposes. ABA Formal Ethics Op. 97-407 (1997); *see Commonwealth Ins. Co. v. Stone Container Corp.*, 178 F. Supp. 2d 938 (N.D. Ill. 2001) (adopting reasoning of ABA opinion); *see also* D.C. Ethics Op. 337 (2007) (serving as expert witness does not create lawyer-client relationship with party; firm hiring lawyer-expert should explain lawyer's role to client at outset of engagement).

## IS THE CLIENT A "FORMER" CLIENT?

Once a lawyer-client relationship has been found to exist, the next issue is to determine whether the relationship has ended or is ongoing. Rule 1.9 applies only to former clients; conflicts of interest involving current clients are governed by Rules 1.7 and 1.8, both of which are more restrictive than Rule 1.9.

When a lawyer is retained for a specific matter, the representation terminates when the matter has been resolved. Rule 1.3, cmt. [4]; *see Revise Clothing, Inc. v. Joe's Jeans Subsidiary, Inc.*, 687 F. Supp. 2d 381 (S.D.N.Y. 2010) (no explicit termination required; retainer agreement specified that law firm's representation limited to particular dispute). When the lawyer's representation is not limited to a particular matter, however, a question of fact can arise about whether the representation has terminated. *See Jones v. Rabanco, Ltd.*, No. CO3-3195P, 2006 WL 2237708, 2006 BL 101731 (W.D. Wash. Aug. 3, 2006) (when settlement agreement evinced intent that lawyer represent client if contract issues arose, three years of noncommunication between them did not terminate lawyer-client relationship); *Shearing v. Allergan Inc.*, No. CV-S-93-866-DWH(LRL), 1994 WL 382450 (D. Nev. Apr. 5, 1994) (current-client rule applied and required disqualification even though client had not engaged firm for more than a year; firm had regularly acted as client's outside counsel for thirteen years and never formally ended relationship); *Hatfield v. Seville Centrifugal Bronze*, 732 N.E.2d 1077 (Ohio C.P. 2000) (when lawyer provides annual advice and services to client and does not tell client representation has ceased, relationship continues for following year for conflicts purposes); *see also Credit Index, LLC v. RiskWise Int'l, LLC*, 746 N.Y.S.2d 885 (Sup. Ct.) ("as-needed" nature of legal advice rendered over firm's four-year relationship with client did not permit firm to represent client's opponent), *aff'd*, 744 N.Y.S.2d 326 (App. Div. 2002); Pa. Ethics Op. 2008-48 (2008) (company for which law firm annually performs legal services regarding stock transfers and maintains decade's worth of board minutes and company by-laws is current client even though firm has not performed new services for two years); *cf. Artromick Int'l, Inc. v. Drustar, Inc.*, 134 F.R.D. 226 (S.D. Ohio 1991) (no disqualification; although client was disputing lawyer's last bill, lawyer had done no legal work for it for more than a year, and it had been using new lawyer); *Gray v. Gray*, No. E2001-COA-R3-CV, 2002 WL 31093931, 2002 BL 15886 (Tenn. Ct. App. Sept. 19, 2002) (no ongoing lawyer-client relationship between husband in divorce action and wife's lawyer, who had prepared couple's wills ten years earlier); Pa. Ethics Op. 2001-08 (2001) (law firm that performed corporate work for company for two years and then no further work for two years may represent company's opponent in unrelated matter unless company establishes reasonable belief it remains current client).

### • *"Hot-Potato" Gambit*

To facilitate application of Rule 1.9 rather than the more stringent criteria of Rules 1.7 and 1.8 applicable to current clients, lawyers have been known to seek to withdraw from representing less "desirable" clients in an effort to convert them into former clients. The attempt to drop one client to take on another—called the "hot-potato" gambit—has been roundly condemned. *See, e.g., Altova GmbH v. Syncro Soft SRL*, 320 F. Supp. 3d 314 (D. Mass. 2018); *McLain v. Allstate Prop. & Cas. Ins. Co.*, Civ. No. 3:16CV843-TSL-RHW, 2017 WL 1513090, 2017 BL 136582 (S.D. Miss. Apr. 25, 2017); *Markham Concepts, Inc. v. Hasbro, Inc.*, 196 F. Supp. 3d 345 (D.R.I. 2016); *W. Sugar Coop. v. Archer-Daniels-Midland Co.*, 98 F. Supp. 3d 1074 (C.D. Cal. 2015) (firm dropped client when conflict raised). *See generally* John Leubsdorf, *Conflicts of Interest: Slicing the Hot Potato Doctrine*, 48 San Diego L. Rev. 251 (Feb.–Mar. 2011).

## Thrust-Upon Conflicts

Courts have, however, allowed firms to withdraw from representing one client to continue (rather than begin) representing another client when an unforeseeable conflict arises through no fault of the lawyer. *See, e.g., Microsoft Corp. v. Commonwealth Scientific & Indus. Research Org.*, Nos. 6:06 CV 549, 6:06 CV 550, 2007 WL 4376104, 2007 BL 171431 (E.D. Tex. Dec. 13, 2007) (permitting lawyer to withdraw because client actively concealed facts creating conflict; "[t]he 'thrust upon' exception applies when unforeseeable developments cause two current clients to become directly adverse"); *see also* D.C. Ethics Op. 272 (1997) (if certain conditions can be met, law firm may continue to represent longtime regulatory client in adversary proceeding before administrative agency, even after different client whom it represents on unrelated matters hires separate counsel and unexpectedly initiates administrative proceeding against first client); N.Y. City Ethics Op. 2005-5 (2005) ("thrust-upon" conflicts do not implicate hot-potato rule; opinion recommends flexible approach in which "overriding factor should be the prejudice the withdrawal or continued representation will cause the parties"). *See generally* Jay M. Levin & Jennifer A. Ziznewski, *Law Firm and Client Mergers: How to Comply with Ethical Requirements During a Transition*, 40 Brief 24 (Winter 2011).

## ARE THE MATTERS SUBSTANTIALLY RELATED?

Once it is established there was a lawyer-client relationship and it has terminated, the next issue in determining whether a lawyer may undertake a representation adverse to the former client is the relationship between the two matters: If the two matters are the same or substantially related, the subsequent adverse representation is prohibited without the former client's consent.

The substantial-relationship test grew out of caselaw on disqualification. *See T.C. Theatre Corp. v. Warner Bros. Pictures*, 113 F. Supp. 265 (S.D.N.Y. 1953) ("the former client need show no more than that the matters embraced within the pending suit wherein his former attorney appears on behalf of his adversary are substantially related to the matters or cause of action wherein the attorney previously represented him"). Rule 1.9(a) specifically adopts the "substantial relationship" rubric. Comments [1], [2], and [11] contain some language suggesting a definition.

Comment [3], adopted in 2002, explains that matters are "substantially related" for purposes of Rule 1.9 "if they involve the same transaction or legal dispute" or, alternatively, "if there otherwise is a substantial risk that confidential factual information as would normally have been obtained in the prior representation would materially advance the client's position in the subsequent matter."

Put another way, might the lawyer have learned things in the prior matter that would give the lawyer's client an advantage in the current matter? Hundreds of reported decisions have considered application of the "substantial relationship" test, almost always in a disqualification context, and the variety of results is wide. *See, e.g., Holmes v. Credit Protection Ass'n*, No. 1:17-cv-3995-WTL-MPB, 2018 WL 5777324, 2018

BL 406262 (S.D. Ind. Nov. 2, 2018) (disqualification ordered; representations involved overlapping issues and lawyer worked on prior matter for sixty hours, had access to file for several years and consulted with company on strategy); *TWiT, LLC v. Twitter, Inc.*, No. 18-cv-00341-JSC, 2018 WL 2470942, 2018 BL 194996 (N.D. Cal. June 1, 2018) (firm may represent defendant in suit for trademark infringement and breach of contract although it previously represented plaintiff in matter involving third party's threatened patent suit against it; no substantial relationship between matters); *Acad. of Allergy & Asthma in Primary Care v. La. Health Serv. & Indem. Co.*, Civ. No. 18-399, 2018 WL 4739690, 2018 BL 361993 (E.D. La. Oct. 2, 2018) (earlier negotiations with state medical board substantially related to this suit for insurance coverage); *Moore v. Olson*, 351 P.3d 1066 (Alaska 2015) (earlier negotiation of airport hangar lease not substantially related to enforcement of business break-up settlement agreement); *Costello v. Buckley*, 199 Cal. Rptr. 3d 891 (Ct. App. 2016) (lawyer defending a collection case had previously represented the plaintiff in easement matter; there was substantial relationship between matters because lawyer would have learned about plaintiff's relationship with defendant); *McCleary v. City of Des Moines Zoning Bd.*, 900 N.W.2d 617 (Iowa Ct. App. 2017) (earlier preparation of letter of intent for city not substantially related to this zoning challenge); *In re Catherine A.*, 65 N.Y.S.3d 339 (App. Div. 2017) (custody case in which lawyer is adverse to mother not substantially related to earlier criminal drug case in which lawyer represented mother); *Adams Creek Assocs. v. Davis*, 652 S.E.2d 677 (N.C. Ct. App. 2007) (suit for trespass to property not substantially related to earlier suit to establish ownership of same property).

### • *Passage of Time*

The passage of time can render information obtained in a prior representation "obsolete," according to Comment [3]. In the following cases the passage of ten years or more between matters did not preclude a finding of substantial relationship: *Fallacaro v. Fallacaro*, No. FA 980719606S, 1999 WL 241743 (Conn. Super. Ct. Apr. 8, 1990); *Niemi v. Girl Scouts of Minn.*, 768 N.W.2d 385 (Minn. Ct. App. 2009); *Gjoni v. Swan Club*, 2 N.Y.S.3d 341 (App. Div. 2015); *In re Gadbois*, 786 A.2d 393 (Vt. 2001).

### • *Playbook*

When a lawyer has represented an organizational client, the client may feel that the lawyer's general familiarity with its procedures and policies would give a subsequent client an unfair edge over it in another matter. This kind of general knowledge is called "playbook" information. *See* Charles W. Wolfram, *Former Client Conflicts*, 10 Geo. J. Legal Ethics 677 (Summer 1997). It may be a factor in ruling on a motion to disqualify, but according to Comment [3] it ordinarily is not in itself cause for disqualification. Courts are split as to recognition of "playbook" information as disqualifying. *See, e.g., Watkins v. Trans Union*, 869 F.3d 514 (7th Cir. 2017) (not disqualifying; in 2-1 decision, majority and minority opinions provide good examples of different approaches to playbook); *Olajide v. Palisades Collection, LLC*, No. 15-CV-7673 (JMF), 2016 WL 1448859, 2016 BL 113505 (S.D.N.Y. Apr. 12, 2016) ("general knowledge" of former client not enough); *Sonos, Inc. v. D&M Holdings Inc.*, No. 14-1330-RGA, 2015 WL 5277194, 2015 BL 291446 (D. Del. Sept. 9, 2015) (knowledge of general litigation strategy not disqualifying); *Micrografx, LLC v. Samsung Telecomm'ns Am., LLC*, No. 3:13-CV-3599-N, 2014 WL 12586177, 2014 BL 331274 (N.D. Tex. Mar. 7, 2014) (similarity of technology disqualifying in patent infringement case; smartphone, tablets, and graphic libraries); *Cuevas v. Joint Benefit Trust*, No. 13–cv–00045–JST, 2013 WL 4647404, 2013 BL 231639 (N.D. Cal. Aug. 29, 2013) (disqualifying; lawyer representing union members in discrimination suit against union formerly represented union in discrimination cases); *Childress v. Trans Union, LLC*, No. 1:12-cv-00184-TWP-DML, 2013 WL 1828050, 2013 BL 403343 (S.D. Ind. Apr. 30, 2013) (disqualifying; different FCRA cases); *De La Cruz v. V.I. Water & Power Auth.*, No. 1:07-cv-9, 2012 WL 1648318, 2012 BL 112319 (D.V.I. May 8, 2012) (different cases involved exposed power lines, but disqualifying).

## ARE THE INTERESTS MATERIALLY ADVERSE?

Rule 1.9 prohibits the subsequent representation only if the interests of the new client would be materially adverse to those of the former client. *See, e.g., Plotts v. Chester Cycles LLC*, No. CV-14-00428-PHX-GMS, 2016 WL 614023, 2016 BL 43138 (D. Ariz. Feb. 16, 2016) (law firm cannot handle Title VII case against company after it had represented company's one-third owner in divorce and adverse holding in Title VII case could significantly harm the owner); *Colorpix Sys. of Am. v. Broan Mfg. Co.*, 131 F. Supp. 2d 331 (D. Conn. 2001) (disqualifying law firm from representing insurer suing company whose parent and sister corporations firm defended in prior subrogation action brought on same theory; any judgment against company would affect parent's bottom line); *In re Jones & McClain, LLP*, 271 B.R. 473 (Bankr. W.D. Pa. 2001) (interests of law firm partner filing involuntary bankruptcy petition against firm were adverse to interests of former client, a firm partner who might have to pay law firm's debts); *Sec. Investor Prot. Corp. v. R.D. Kushnir & Co.*, 246 B.R. 582 (Bankr. N.D. Ill. 2000) (interests of bankrupt securities brokerage firm and its principal were adverse because trustee had potential causes of action against principal for failure to supervise broker-employee); *Simpson Performance Prods., Inc. v. Horn, PC*, 92 P.3d 283 (Wyo. 2004) (lawyer represented manufacturer of safety equipment in investigating possible suit against National Association of Stock Car Auto Racing, and then represented manufacturer's former CEO in suing NASCAR over same incident; no adversity of interests within meaning of Rule 1.9); ABA Formal Ethics Op. 99-415 (1999) (only direct adversity qualifies as "material adversity").

## CONSENT

Under both paragraph (a) and paragraph (b) of Rule 1.9, a lawyer who would otherwise be disqualified may nevertheless undertake the representation if the "former client gives informed consent, confirmed in writing." For a definition and explanation of "informed consent," see Rule 1.0(e) and Comments [6] and [7] to Rule 1.0. *See generally* Richard W. Painter, *Advance Waiver of Conflicts*, 13 Geo. J. Legal Ethics 289 (Winter 2000).

Neither the rule nor the comments explain how to obtain the former client's consent to the proposed new representation without violating the duty of confidentiality to the prospective client. See the annotation to Rule 1.18.

• *Standing to Disqualify*

The question of who has standing to move for disqualification is discussed in the annotation to Rule 1.7.

## Paragraph (b): Client of Lawyer's Former Firm

When the lawyer's former firm, rather than the lawyer personally, represented someone whose interests are materially adverse to those of the prospective client, the lawyer will be disqualified only if he or she personally acquired protected information that would be material to the new matter. *See Victorinox AG v. B&F Sys., Inc.*, 709 F. App'x 44 (2d Cir. 2017) (no exchange of information at prior firm); *Loop AI Labs Inc. v. Gatti*, No. 15-cv-00798-HSG, 2016 WL 344874, 2016 BL 23546 (N.D. Cal. Jan. 28, 2016) (following *Adams v. Aerojet-Gen. Corp.*, 104 Cal. Rptr. 2d 116 (Ct. App. 2001), holding that firm-switching lawyer not automatically disqualified on basis of imputed knowledge from case involving client of former firm; focus upon whether lawyer's responsibilities and interactions with colleagues at prior firm made it likely he obtained confidential information relating to current case); *In re ProEducation Int'l, Inc.*, 587 F.3d 296 (5th Cir. 2009) (former firm's representation of creditor in case did not warrant lawyer's disqualification from representing different creditor in same case; lawyer had not personally represented or gained information about creditor represented by former firm); *Hermann v. GutterGuard Inc.*, 199 F. App'x 745 (11th Cir. 2006) (disqualifying partner who monitored team meetings of firm lawyers representing clients in employment matters and attended meeting in which confidential information of former client discussed); *Edward v. 360° Commc'ns*, 189 F.R.D. 433 (D. Nev. 1999) (no disqualification of plaintiff's lawyer despite prior employment by opponent's law firm; lawyer not directly involved in case while working with firm, and affidavits by lawyer and firm members rebutted presumption that lawyer privy to confidential information about case); *Dieter v. Regents of Univ. of Cal.*, 963 F. Supp. 908 (E.D. Cal. 1997) (lawyers who previously worked for law firm that represented adverse party not disqualified; they worked out of different office and had no involvement in or knowledge of matter); *The Park Apartments at Fayetteville, LP v. Plants*, 545 S.W.3d 755 (Ark. 2018) (lawyer for defendant formerly worked at legal aid office, but not in department bringing this case; defendants' legal staff not disqualified); *Green v. Toledo Hosp.*, 764 N.E.2d 979 (Ohio 2002) (refusing to disqualify lawyer even though nonlawyer employee had worked for opponent's lawyer; presumption that employee disclosed confidential information adequately rebutted); *see also Hempstead Video, Inc. v. Inc. Vill. of Valley Stream*, 409 F.3d 127 (2d Cir. 2005) (noting and joining "strong trend" toward allowing presumption of confidence-sharing within firm to be rebutted); Or. Ethics Op. 2005-120 (2005; rev. 2015) (acquisition of material confidential information can arise from informal exchanges within firm even if lawyer did no work on client's matters); Pa. Ethics Op. 2006-052 (2006) (lawyer may represent prospective plaintiff in civil lawsuit despite his former law firm's prior representation of prospective defendant; even if matters substantially related, lawyer will not be disqualified unless he acquired information about defendant that is material to current lawsuit). *See generally* Eli Wald, *Lawyer Mobility and Legal Ethics:*

*Resolving the Tension Between Confidentiality Requirements and Contemporary Lawyers' Career Paths*, 31 J. Legal Prof. 199 (2007).

On the issue of imputed disqualification, see the annotation to Rule 1.10.

## Paragraph (c): Using or Disclosing Information Related to Representation of Former Client

Rule 1.9(c) separately regulates use and disclosure of confidential information. Paragraph (c) applies whether or not a subsequent representation is involved, and it applies even if the lawyer's former firm—rather than the individual lawyer—represented the former client.

### USING INFORMATION

Rule 1.9(c)(1) prohibits a lawyer from *using* information about a former client except in ways that would be permitted were the relationship still in effect. *See United States v. Quest Diagnostics Inc.*, 734 F.3d 154 (2d Cir. 2013) (New York's version of Model Rule 1.9(c)(1) prevented former general counsel from being relator in qui tam action against his former employer; federal False Claims Act does not trump ethics rules); *Hulzebos v. City of Sioux Falls*, Civ. No. 13-4024, 2013 WL 5297152, 2013 BL 252124 (D.S.D. Sept. 19, 2013) (former lawyer for city handling employment matters could not, under Rule 1.9(c), represent city employee against city in employment matter); *In re Wilder*, 764 N.E.2d 617 (Ind. 2002) (suspending lawyer for representing unmarried couple in organizing business and subsequently representing one of them in unwinding business when their personal relationship deteriorated; lawyer used documents acquired while representing couple); *Lane's Case*, 889 A.2d 3 (N.H. 2005) (discipline unwarranted; lawyer's use of accounting prepared by former client-executor was to former client's advantage, not disadvantage); *In re Gadbois*, 786 A.2d 393 (Vt. 2001) (wife's lawyer's remark that his presence as "known" character, having represented husband in divorce thirteen years ago, would help settle subsequent divorce did not support board's conclusion he used former client secrets for personal advantage).

The sole exception is that the lawyer may use information that has become generally known. According to ABA Formal Opinion 479, information is generally known "if it is widely recognized by members of the public in the relevant geographic area or it is widely recognized in the former client's industry, profession, or trade." The opinion explains that "the fact that the information may have been discussed in open court, or may be available in court records, in public libraries, or in other public repositories does not, standing alone, mean that the information is generally known." ABA Formal Ethics Op. 479 (2017); *see Pallon v. Roggio*, Nos. 04-3625 (JAP), 06-1068 (FLW), 2006 WL 2466854, 2006 BL 91075 (D.N.J. Aug. 24, 2006) (information must be within basic understanding and knowledge of public; discovery materials widely available to public through internet or other source not "generally known" within meaning of rule); *Steel v. Gen. Motors Corp.*, 912 F. Supp. 724 (D.N.J. 1995) (defendant company's litigation techniques and trial strategies and content of its form pleadings, while widely known to lawyers involved in similar cases against company, are not generally known); *In re Anonymous*, 932 N.E.2d 671 (Ind. 2010) (no evidence that information relating to husband's accusations against former client, or even divorce filing, was generally known); *In re Tennant*, 392 P.3d 143 (Mont. 2017) (lawyer used knowledge derived from representation to bid on former clients' property; lawyer not permitted to take advantage of former clients "by retroactively relying on public records of their information for self-dealing"); *see also* N.Y. State Ethics Op. 1128 (2017) ("information is not 'generally known' simply because it is in the public domain or available in a public file"). *But see State v. Mancilla*, No. A06-581, 2007 WL 2034241, 2007 BL 59053 (Minn. Ct. App. July 17, 2007) (lawyer's cross-examination of former client regarding prior convictions would not have violated Rule 1.9(c) because "prior convictions were matters of public record and, therefore, fall within the generally-known-information exception"). *See generally Turner v. Commonwealth*, 726 S.E.2d 325 (Va. 2012) (Lemons, J., concurring) (analyzing "generally known" for purposes of Rule 1.9(c)).

## DISCLOSING INFORMATION

Rule 1.9(c)(2) prohibits any *disclosure* (as opposed to use) of former-client information that would not be permitted in connection with a current client, regardless of whether the information has become generally known. *See In re Harman*, 628 N.W.2d 351 (Wis. 2001) (lawyer disciplined for disclosing former client's medical records to prosecutor; irrelevant that records made public when filed in former client's medical malpractice action). For a discussion of the duty of confidentiality, see the annotation to Rule 1.6.

## Rule 1.10

### *Imputation of Conflicts of Interest: General Rule*

(a) While lawyers are associated in a firm, none of them shall knowingly represent a client when any one of them practicing alone would be prohibited from doing so by Rules 1.7 or 1.9, unless

(1) the prohibition is based on a personal interest of the disqualified lawyer and does not present a significant risk of materially limiting the representation of the client by the remaining lawyers in the firm; or

(2) the prohibition is based upon Rule 1.9(a) or (b), and arises out of the disqualified lawyer's association with a prior firm, and

(i) the disqualified lawyer is timely screened from any participation in the matter and is apportioned no part of the fee therefrom;

(ii) written notice is promptly given to any affected former client to enable the former client to ascertain compliance with the provisions of this Rule, which shall include a description of the screening procedures employed; a statement of the firm's and of the screened lawyer's compliance with these Rules; a statement that review may be available before a tribunal; and an agreement by the firm to respond promptly to any written inquiries or objections by the former client about the screening procedures; and

(iii) certifications of compliance with these Rules and with the screening procedures are provided to the former client by the screened lawyer and by a partner of the firm, at reasonable intervals upon the former client's written request and upon termination of the screening procedures.

(b) When a lawyer has terminated an association with a firm, the firm is not prohibited from thereafter representing a person with interests materially adverse to those of a client represented by the formerly associated lawyer and not currently represented by the firm, unless:

(1) the matter is the same or substantially related to that in which the formerly associated lawyer represented the client; and

(2) any lawyer remaining in the firm has information protected by Rules 1.6 and 1.9(c) that is material to the matter.

(c) A disqualification prescribed by this Rule may be waived by the affected client under the conditions stated in Rule 1.7.

(d) The disqualification of lawyers associated in a firm with former or current government lawyers is governed by Rule 1.11.

## COMMENT

### Definition of "Firm"

[1] For purposes of the Rules of Professional Conduct, the term "firm" denotes lawyers in a law partnership, professional corporation, sole proprietorship or other association authorized to practice law; or lawyers employed in a legal services organization or the legal department of a corporation or other organization. See Rule 1.0(c). Whether two or more lawyers constitute a firm within this definition can depend on the specific facts. See Rule 1.0, Comments [2]–[4].

### Principles of Imputed Disqualification

[2] The rule of imputed disqualification stated in paragraph (a) gives effect to the principle of loyalty to the client as it applies to lawyers who practice in a law firm. Such situations can be considered from the premise that a firm of lawyers is essentially one lawyer for purposes of the rules governing loyalty to the client, or from the premise that each lawyer is vicariously bound by the obligation of loyalty owed by each lawyer with whom the lawyer is associated. Paragraph (a)(1) operates only among the lawyers currently associated in a firm. When a lawyer moves from one firm to another, the situation is governed by Rules 1.9(b) and 1.10(a)(2) and 1.10(b).

[3] The rule in paragraph (a) does not prohibit representation where neither questions of client loyalty nor protection of confidential information are presented. Where one lawyer in a firm could not effectively represent a given client because of strong political beliefs, for example, but that lawyer will do no work on the case and the personal beliefs of the lawyer will not materially limit the representation by others in the firm, the firm should not be disqualified. On the other hand, if an opposing party in a case were owned by a lawyer in the law firm, and others in the firm would be materially limited in pursuing the matter because of loyalty to that lawyer, the personal disqualification of the lawyer would be imputed to all others in the firm.

[4] The rule in paragraph (a) also does not prohibit representation by others in the law firm where the person prohibited from involvement in a matter is a nonlawyer, such as a paralegal or legal secretary. Nor does paragraph (a) prohibit representation if the lawyer is prohibited from acting because of events before the person became a lawyer, for example, work that the person did while a law student. Such persons, however, ordinarily must be screened from any personal participation in the matter to avoid communication to others in the firm of confidential information that both the nonlawyers and the firm have a legal duty to protect. See Rules 1.0(k) and 5.3.

[5] Rule 1.10(b) operates to permit a law firm, under certain circumstances, to represent a person with interests directly adverse to those of a client represented by

a lawyer who formerly was associated with the firm. The Rule applies regardless of when the formerly associated lawyer represented the client. However, the law firm may not represent a person with interests adverse to those of a present client of the firm, which would violate Rule 1.7. Moreover, the firm may not represent the person where the matter is the same or substantially related to that in which the formerly associated lawyer represented the client and any other lawyer currently in the firm has material information protected by Rules 1.6 and 1.9(c).

[6] Rule 1.10(c) removes imputation with the informed consent of the affected client or former client under the conditions stated in Rule 1.7. The conditions stated in Rule 1.7 require the lawyer to determine that the representation is not prohibited by Rule 1.7(b) and that each affected client or former client has given informed consent to the representation, confirmed in writing. In some cases, the risk may be so severe that the conflict may not be cured by client consent. For a discussion of the effectiveness of client waivers of conflicts that might arise in the future, see Rule 1.7, Comment [22]. For a definition of informed consent, see Rule 1.0(e).

[7] Rule 1.10(a)(2) similarly removes the imputation otherwise required by Rule 1.10(a), but unlike section (c), it does so without requiring that there be informed consent by the former client. Instead, it requires that the procedures laid out in sections (a)(2)(i)–(iii) be followed. A description of effective screening mechanisms appears in Rule 1.0(k). Lawyers should be aware, however, that, even where screening mechanisms have been adopted, tribunals may consider additional factors in ruling upon motions to disqualify a lawyer from pending litigation.

[8] Paragraph (a)(2)(i) does not prohibit the screened lawyer from receiving a salary or partnership share established by prior independent agreement, but that lawyer may not receive compensation directly related to the matter in which the lawyer is disqualified.

[9] The notice required by paragraph (a)(2)(ii) generally should include a description of the screened lawyer's prior representation and be given as soon as practicable after the need for screening becomes apparent. It also should include a statement by the screened lawyer and the firm that the client's material confidential information has not been disclosed or used in violation of the Rules. The notice is intended to enable the former client to evaluate and comment upon the effectiveness of the screening procedures.

[10] The certifications required by paragraph (a)(2)(iii) give the former client assurance that the client's material confidential information has not been disclosed or used inappropriately, either prior to timely implementation of a screen or thereafter. If compliance cannot be certified, the certificate must describe the failure to comply.

[11] Where a lawyer has joined a private firm after having represented the government, imputation is governed by Rule 1.11(b) and (c), not this Rule. Under Rule 1.11(d), where a lawyer represents the government after having served clients in private practice, nongovernmental employment or in another government agency, former-client conflicts are not imputed to government lawyers associated with the individually disqualified lawyer.

[12] Where a lawyer is prohibited from engaging in certain transactions under Rule 1.8, paragraph (k) of that Rule, and not this Rule, determines whether that

prohibition also applies to other lawyers associated in a firm with the personally prohibited lawyer.

**Definitional Cross-References**

"Firm" *See* Rule 1.0(c)
"Knowingly" *See* Rule 1.0(f)
"Partner" *See* Rule 1.0(g)
"Screened" *See* Rule 1.0(k)
"Tribunal" *See* Rule 1.0(m)
"Written" *See* Rule 1.0(n)

**State Rules Comparison**

http://ambar.org/MRPCStateCharts

# ANNOTATION

## INTRODUCTION

Rule 1.10 is the general rule of imputation of conflicts of interest. Except under limited circumstances, while lawyers are associated in a firm none of them may knowingly represent a client if any one of them would be prohibited from doing so by Rule 1.7 (Conflict of Interest: Current Clients) or Rule 1.9 (Duties to Former Clients). Rule 1.10 does not apply to the prohibitions of Rule 1.8; those situations are subject to Rule 1.8(k). Imputation involving former or current government officers and employees is regulated by Rule 1.11 (Special Conflicts of Interest for Former and Current Government Officers and Employees). Imputation and screening under Rule 1.18 (Duties to Prospective Client) are governed by Rule 1.18(c). If a lawyer is disqualified under Rule 3.7 (Lawyer as Witness) as a necessary trial witness, imputation is determined by Rule 3.7(c).

### • *2002 Amendments*

There were three significant amendments to Rule 1.10 in 2002. The first eliminated most "personal-interest" conflicts (those arising from a lawyer's own personal interest rather than interests of current clients, third parties, or former clients) from imputation. Second, new paragraph (d) clarified that Rule 1.11, and not Rule 1.10, governs imputation of conflicts of interest of current or former government lawyers. Third, new Comment [4] explained that when nonlawyers such as paralegals, secretaries, and law students are personally disqualified, imputation of their conflicts may be avoided if they are screened to protect any confidential information from their prior employment. *See* American Bar Association, *A Legislative History: The Development of the ABA Model Rules of Professional Conduct, 1982–2013*, at 260–67 (2013).

### • *2009 Amendments*

Rule 1.10(a) was amended in February and August 2009 to permit nonconsensual screening to remove imputation when lawyers in private practice change employment. *See* American Bar Association, *A Legislative History: The Development of the ABA*

*Model Rules of Professional Conduct, 1982–2013*, at 268–74 (2013). Before these amendments, nonconsensual screening of a personally disqualified lawyer was not recognized in many states as a way to avoid imputation of conflicts in the private-firm context unless the conflict arose from the lateral hire's activities before becoming a lawyer.

### *Paragraph (a): Lawyers Associated in a Firm*

Comment [2] explains that imputation gives effect to the principle that every lawyer in a firm owes a duty of loyalty to the firm's clients. *See also Restatement (Third) of the Law Governing Lawyers* § 123 cmt. b (2000) (rationale for imputation reflects three concerns: lawyers in firms ordinarily share each other's interests; affiliated lawyers ordinarily share confidential client information; and clients would have difficulty proving complete isolation of adverse representation by affiliated lawyer).

Imputation under Rule 1.10(a) applies while lawyers are associated in a firm. Rule 1.0(c) defines a "firm" or "law firm" to denote "a lawyer or lawyers in a law partnership, professional corporation, sole proprietorship or other association authorized to practice law; or lawyers employed in a legal services organization or the legal department of a corporation or other organization." Comment [3] to Rule 1.0 notes that a government law department is ordinarily considered a "firm" for purposes of the ethics rules, but imputation involving former or current government officers and employees is regulated by Rule 1.11.

Commentators have noted considerable variety among the relationships to which Rule 1.10 has been applied. *See, e.g.,* Donald R. Lundberg, *A Firm by Any Other Name Is Just as Conflicted: Quasi-Law Firms and Imputed Conflicts of Interest*, 53 Res Gestae 36 (Sept. 2009) (whether lawyers constitute a firm should depend upon reasonable public perception rather than internal financial arrangements); Thomas D. Morgan, *Conflicts of Interest and the New Forms of Professional Associations*, 39 S. Tex. L. Rev. 215 (Mar. 1998) (trying to define "firm" not as useful as analyzing expectations of confidentiality and loyalty arising in particular arrangements). *See also United States ex rel. Bahsen v. Boston Scientific Neuromodulation Corp.*, 147 F. Supp. 3d 239 (D.N.J. 2015) (lawyer "seconded" to firm client considered associated with firm for purposes of imputation); *Mustang Enters., Inc. v. Plug-In Storage Sys., Inc.*, 874 F. Supp. 881 (N.D. Ill. 1995) (two firms using "affiliated firm" designation treated as two offices of one firm); Conn. Informal Ethics Op. 15-06 (2015) (conflicts of lawyer practicing with more than one firm at same time imputed to each firm); N.Y. State Ethics Op. 876 (2011) (if lawyers of two firms practice together in third firm, conflicts imputed to all three firms).

Rule 1.10(a)(1) exempts conflicts that arise out of a lawyer's personal interests from imputation unless the conflict would materially limit the firm's other lawyers in carrying out the representation in question. *See* ABA Formal Ethics Op. 08-453 (2008) (misconduct of lawyer consulting in-firm ethics counsel may limit ability of other firm lawyers to represent relevant client).

### "OF COUNSEL" RELATIONSHIPS

The practical meaning of "of counsel" can vary widely among law firms and even within a firm. ABA Formal Opinion 90-357 (1990) superseded several prior opinions and concluded that the term should be limited to lawyers with whom a firm has a close, regular, and personal relationship; the opinion offered four examples of relationships appropriate for the "of counsel" designation: a part-time practitioner, an inactive retired partner, a probationary partner-to-be, and a permanent firm lawyer with a status between partner and associate. As a general matter, "of counsel" lawyers are treated like firm partners or associates for conflicts purposes. *See Restatement (Third) of the Law Governing Lawyers* §123 cmt. c(ii) (2000) (imputation ordinarily applies to "of counsel" lawyers).

When lawyers are "of counsel" to more than one firm, the consequence is "to make them all effectively a single firm, for purposes of attribution of disqualifications." ABA Formal Ethics Op. 90-357 (1990); *accord* Mass. Ethics Op. 01-1 (2001) (firms treated as one for conflicts purposes); N.Y. State Ethics Op. 793 (2006) (if two firms share "of counsel" lawyer, conflicts of each imputed to other). However, the "of counsel" title alone may not be dispositive. A relationship appropriately described as "of counsel" for purposes of, for example, Rule 7.1, Comment [7] (Communications Concerning a Lawyer's Services), may not necessarily require imputation under Rule 1.10. *See Hempstead Video, Inc. v. Inc. Vill. of Valley Stream*, 409 F.3d 127 (2d Cir. 2005) (relationship with "of counsel" lawyer who had limited contact with firm too attenuated to impute conflicts; per se approach rejected); *Gray v. Mem'l Med. Ctr., Inc.*, 855 F. Supp. 377 (S.D. Ga. 1994) (declining to impute firm's disqualification to "of counsel" lawyer with whom it sporadically consulted).

## TEMPORARY AND CONTRACT LAWYERS

The primary guidance in applying the conflicts rules to temporary lawyers continues to be ABA Formal Opinion 88-356 (1988), which defines a temporary lawyer as "a lawyer engaged by a firm for a limited period, either directly or through a lawyer placement agency." *See also* ABA Formal Ethics Op. 00-420 (2000) (contract lawyer is "any lawyer retained by a lawyer or law firm who is not employed permanently for general assignment by the lawyer or law firm engaged by the client"). ABA Formal Opinion 88-356 also explains that whether a temporary lawyer is treated as "associated" with a firm depends upon the lawyer's access to information relating to the representation of other firm clients and the consequent risk of improper disclosure or misuse of information. A temporary lawyer who works on a number of matters and has access to information relating to the representation of other firm clients may be held to be associated with the firm under Rule 1.10. *See, e.g.,* Ala. Ethics Op. 2007-3 (2007); Ga. Ethics Op. 05-09 (2006). But if the relationship is limited and the lawyer is screened from confidential information of firm clients, the result may be different. *See* N.Y. City Ethics Op. 2007-2 (2007). *See generally* Kathleen Maher, *The Permanent Legacy of the ABA Opinion on Temporary Lawyers*, 13 Prof. Law., no. 1, at 18 (2001).

## SHARING OFFICE SPACE

Lawyers sharing office space may be deemed "associated in a firm" if they share information and staff or if they hold themselves out as a firm. *See Monroe v. City of Topeka*, 988 P.2d 228 (Kan. 1999) (indicia of lawyers presenting themselves to public as a firm for purposes of imputed disqualification include sharing office space, telephone, and mailing address); D.C. Ethics Op. 303 (2001) (whether sharing office space leads to imputed disqualification depends upon specific arrangements); Or. Ethics Op. 2005-50 (2005) (imputation if lawyers share common employee with access to protected information).

## LEGAL SERVICES ORGANIZATIONS

Whether a legal services organization, or individual components of it, will be considered a "firm" for purposes of imputation usually depends on the specific circumstances. *See, e.g.,* Colo. Ethics Op. 117 (2007) (under procedures of state legal services program, organization and its affiliated panels not considered one firm); N.Y. State Ethics Op. 794 (2006) (volunteer lawyers who supervise students in law school clinic considered associated if students work in common space and share access to physical files; conflicts of each volunteer imputed to firms of all participating lawyers). *See generally* Peter A. Joy & Robert R. Kuehn, *Conflict of Interest and Competency Issues in Law Clinic Practice,* 9 Clinical L. Rev. 493 (Fall 2002).

## CO-COUNSEL

When lawyers or law firms serve as co-counsel in a matter, the conflicts of one are not generally imputed to the other. *See Restatement (Third) of the Law Governing Lawyers* § 123 cmt. c(iii) (2000) (conflict imputed within firm not extended to lawyers in another firm working on another matter); *see also Ex parte Wheeler,* 978 So. 2d 1 (Ala. 2007) (no imputation to co-counsel without showing of actual disclosure; would otherwise result in "double imputation"); *Kelly v. Paulsen,* 44 N.Y.S.3d 263 (App. Div. 2016) (imputation to co-counsel requires "close, regular, and personal" relationship); N.Y. State Ethics Op. 1141 (2017) (law school clinic and legal aid organization that act as co-counsel in discrete matters not associated for purposes of imputation); *cf. Pound v. Cameron,* 36 Cal. Rptr. 3d 922 (Ct. App. 2005) (no relevant distinction between hiring or associating as co-counsel lawyer with other side's confidential information).

## COUNSEL FOR CO-PARTIES

Imputation issues may arise from agreements to cooperate in representing co-parties. *See, e.g., In re Gabapentin Patent Litig.,* 407 F. Supp. 2d 607 (D.N.J. 2005) (although lawyers' former client, a co-defendant in multidistrict litigation, waived imputation of their disqualification when lawyers joined plaintiff's firm, lawyers had "imputed" attorney-client relationship with other participants in joint-defense agreement who did not waive); *cf. Essex Chem. Corp. v. Hartford Accident & Indem. Co.,* 993 F. Supp. 241 (D.N.J. 1998) (although counsel for one defendant withdrew due to conflict, court did not impute disqualification to other defense counsel absent showing that confidential information actually shared). *See generally* Claudia T. Salomon & Jeremy D. Andersen, *Imputing Conflicts Across Firms,* 27 J. Legal Prof. 81 (2002–2003).

## SCREENING NONLAWYERS

Comment [4] reflects the clear majority view that conflicts of nonlawyers, as well as conflicts arising from work done before a person became a lawyer, will not ordinarily be imputed if the nonlawyers are screened to protect confidential information.

("Screened" is defined in Rule 1.0(k) and Comments [8], [9], and [10] to Rule 1.0.) *See also Restatement (Third) of the Law Governing Lawyers* § 123 cmt. f (2000) (duty of confidentiality of nonlawyers not imputed; may be screened); ABA Informal Ethics Op. 88-1526 (1988) (paralegals and independent contractors such as investigators may be screened); *In re Johnston*, 872 N.W.2d 300 (N.D. 2015) (adopting majority rule for paralegals; reviewing cases); Tex. Ethics Op. 650 (2015) (law firm marketing assistant may be screened).

## LATERAL LAWYER CONFLICTS

Lawyers moving between firms (lateral lawyers) have duties to former clients under Rule 1.9(b), which prohibits a lawyer from knowingly representing a person, in the same or a substantially related matter, adverse to a client of the lawyer's former firm about whom the lawyer had acquired material confidential information. This duty is imputed to lawyers in the new firm by Rule 1.10(a). As noted in Comment [5] to Rule 1.9, however, lateral lawyers carry only those conflicts based on actual knowledge. Comment [6] to Rule 1.9 further explains that in the absence of information to the contrary, it can be inferred that lawyers are privy only to information of those clients actually served. Thus, lateral lawyers are ordinarily permitted to rebut the presumption that they acquired protected information at their former firm. *See, e.g., In re ProEducation Int'l, Inc.*, 587 F.3d 296 (5th Cir. 2009) (lateral could rebut presumption of acquisition of confidential information of former firm's client); *Luce v. Alcox*, 848 N.E.2d 552 (Ohio Ct. App. 2006) (presumption of shared confidences rebuttable).

### • *Removing Imputation for Lateral Lawyers*

Until the 2009 amendments to Rule 1.10(a), the Model Rules did not authorize screening to remove the imputation of a lateral lawyer's conflicts in the private-employment context. *See, e.g., U.S. Filter Corp. v. Ionics, Inc.*, 189 F.R.D. 26 (D. Mass. 1999) (screen disapproved although lateral billed only 1.6 hours on matter). Before 2009, however, several states adopted rules authorizing screening in the private-firm context, and some courts in other jurisdictions recognized screens absent a rule. *See, e.g.,* Ill. Rule 1.10(b) (1990); *Cummin v. Cummin*, 695 N.Y.S.2d 346 (App. Div. 1999) (screen prevented disqualification); *see also Papyrus Tech. Corp. v. N.Y. Stock Exch.*, 325 F. Supp. 2d 270 (S.D.N.Y. 2004) (minor participation in former firm's representation sufficient to disqualify lateral, but not enough to impute disqualification to new firm that instituted effective screen; collecting cases); *Kirk v. First Am. Title Ins. Co.*, 108 Cal. Rptr. 3d 620 (Ct. App. 2010) (disqualification not warranted when tainted lawyer screened; court expressed concern for clients who lose lawyer of choice); *Restatement (Third) of the Law Governing Lawyers* § 124(2) (2000) (screening permitted if lateral's knowledge "unlikely to be significant" to subsequent matter).

The 2009 amendments to Rule 1.10(a) permit a firm to remove imputation of a lawyer's disqualification if it is based upon Rule 1.9(a) or (b) and arises out of the lawyer's association with a prior firm, provided the disqualified lawyer is timely screened and apportioned no part of the fee in the matter. Comment [8] explains that the fee restriction does not prohibit the screened lawyer from receiving a salary or partnership share established by prior independent agreement. Subparagraphs (a)(2)

(ii) and (a)(2)(iii) list the procedural steps required in addition to those contained in the general definition of "screened" in Rule 1.0(k).

At least eighteen jurisdictions have adopted a screening rule substantially similar to Rule 1.10(a)(2). *See, e.g.,* D.C. Rule 1.10(b); Or. Rule 1.10(c). Those rules permit screening of a lateral lawyer regardless of the lawyer's level of involvement with the former firm's client or matter. Another fourteen states have adopted rules under which the availability of screening depends on the lateral lawyer's knowledge or involvement regarding the relevant matter or former client. *See, e.g.,* Ariz. Rule 1.10(d)(1) (screening permitted if lateral did not have "primary responsibility" for matter that causes disqualification); Cal. Rule 1.10(a)(2) (screening permitted if lateral did not "substantially participate" in same or substantially related matter); Mass. Rule 1.10(d)(2) (screening permitted if lateral had neither involvement nor information "sufficient to provide a substantial benefit" to new firm's client). Some states, however, continue to disallow screening in the private-firm context. *See, e.g., Audio MPEG, Inc. v. Dell, Inc.,* 219 F. Supp. 3d 563 (E.D. Va. 2016) (lateral screened, no evidence of shared information; but screening "would not cure the impropriety").

### Paragraph (b): Imputation after a Lawyer Leaves Firm

After a lawyer leaves a firm, Rule 1.10(b) permits the firm to represent a person with interests adverse to a client or former client of the departed lawyer as long as the new matter is not substantially related to the matter in which the departed lawyer represented the client and no remaining lawyer has (either in memory or in accessible files) any information protected by Rules 1.6 or 1.9(c) that is material to the new matter. *See, e.g., Reilly v. Computer Assocs. Long-Term Disability Plan,* 423 F. Supp. 2d 5 (E.D.N.Y. 2006) (no disqualification where departed lawyer adequately screened during five-month affiliation).

### Paragraph (c): Consent and Waiver

If all affected clients give informed consent under the conditions stated in Rule 1.7, paragraph (c) permits them to waive the imputation of disqualification otherwise prescribed by Rule 1.10(a). See the annotation to Rule 1.7.

### Paragraph (d): Former or Current Government Lawyer Associations

Under the 2002 amendments to Rules 1.10 and 1.11, the disqualification of lawyers associated with former or current government lawyers is governed by Rule 1.11 rather than Rule 1.10. As a result, Comment [11] to Rule 1.10 notes that when a lawyer undertakes representation of the government, any former-client conflicts resulting from previous employment are not imputed to associated government lawyers. Comment [2] to Rule 1.11 nevertheless suggests "ordinarily it will be prudent to screen such lawyers."

## Rule 1.11

### *Special Conflicts of Interest for Former and Current Government Officers and Employees*

(a) Except as law may otherwise expressly permit, a lawyer who has formerly served as a public officer or employee of the government:

(1) is subject to Rule 1.9(c); and

(2) shall not otherwise represent a client in connection with a matter in which the lawyer participated personally and substantially as a public officer or employee, unless the appropriate government agency gives its informed consent, confirmed in writing, to the representation.

(b) When a lawyer is disqualified from representation under paragraph (a), no lawyer in a firm with which that lawyer is associated may knowingly undertake or continue representation in such a matter unless:

(1) the disqualified lawyer is timely screened from any participation in the matter and is apportioned no part of the fee therefrom; and

(2) written notice is promptly given to the appropriate government agency to enable it to ascertain compliance with the provisions of this Rule.

(c) Except as law may otherwise expressly permit, a lawyer having information that the lawyer knows is confidential government information about a person acquired when the lawyer was a public officer or employee, may not represent a private client whose interests are adverse to that person in a matter in which the information could be used to the material disadvantage of that person. As used in this Rule, the term "confidential government information" means information that has been obtained under governmental authority and which, at the time this Rule is applied, the government is prohibited by law from disclosing to the public or has a legal privilege not to disclose and which is not otherwise available to the public. A firm with which that lawyer is associated may undertake or continue representation in the matter only if the disqualified lawyer is timely screened from any participation in the matter and is apportioned no part of the fee therefrom.

(d) Except as law may otherwise expressly permit, a lawyer currently serving as a public officer or employee:

(1) is subject to Rules 1.7 and 1.9; and

(2) shall not:

(i) participate in a matter in which the lawyer participated personally and substantially while in private practice or nongovernmental employment, unless the appropriate government agency gives its informed consent, confirmed in writing; or

(ii) negotiate for private employment with any person who is involved as a party or as lawyer for a party in a matter in which the lawyer is participating personally and substantially, except that a lawyer serving as a law clerk to a judge, other adjudicative officer or arbitrator may negotiate for private employment as permitted by Rule 1.12(b) and subject to the conditions stated in Rule 1.12(b).

(e) As used in this Rule, the term "matter" includes:

(1) any judicial or other proceeding, application, request for a ruling or other determination, contract, claim, controversy, investigation, charge, accusation, arrest or other particular matter involving a specific party or parties, and

(2) any other matter covered by the conflict of interest rules of the appropriate government agency.

## COMMENT

[1] A lawyer who has served or is currently serving as a public officer or employee is personally subject to the Rules of Professional Conduct, including the prohibition against concurrent conflicts of interest stated in Rule 1.7. In addition, such a lawyer may be subject to statutes and government regulations regarding conflict of interest. Such statutes and regulations may circumscribe the extent to which the government agency may give consent under this Rule. See Rule 1.0(e) for the definition of informed consent.

[2] Paragraphs (a)(1), (a)(2) and (d)(1) restate the obligations of an individual lawyer who has served or is currently serving as an officer or employee of the government toward a former government or private client. Rule 1.10 is not applicable to the conflicts of interest addressed by this Rule. Rather, paragraph (b) sets forth a special imputation rule for former government lawyers that provides for screening and notice. Because of the special problems raised by imputation within a government agency, paragraph (d) does not impute the conflicts of a lawyer currently serving as an officer or employee of the government to other associated government officers or employees, although ordinarily it will be prudent to screen such lawyers.

[3] Paragraphs (a)(2) and (d)(2) apply regardless of whether a lawyer is adverse to a former client and are thus designed not only to protect the former client, but also to prevent a lawyer from exploiting public office for the advantage of another client.

For example, a lawyer who has pursued a claim on behalf of the government may not pursue the same claim on behalf of a later private client after the lawyer has left government service, except when authorized to do so by the government agency under paragraph (a). Similarly, a lawyer who has pursued a claim on behalf of a private client may not pursue the claim on behalf of the government, except when authorized to do so by paragraph (d). As with paragraphs (a)(1) and (d)(1), Rule 1.10 is not applicable to the conflicts of interest addressed by these paragraphs.

[4] This Rule represents a balancing of interests. On the one hand, where the successive clients are a government agency and another client, public or private, the risk exists that power or discretion vested in that agency might be used for the special benefit of the other client. A lawyer should not be in a position where benefit to the other client might affect performance of the lawyer's professional functions on behalf of the government. Also, unfair advantage could accrue to the other client by reason of access to confidential government information about the client's adversary obtainable only through the lawyer's government service. On the other hand, the rules governing lawyers presently or formerly employed by a government agency should not be so restrictive as to inhibit transfer of employment to and from the government. The government has a legitimate need to attract qualified lawyers as well as to maintain high ethical standards. Thus a former government lawyer is disqualified only from particular matters in which the lawyer participated personally and substantially. The provisions for screening and waiver in paragraph (b) are necessary to prevent the disqualification rule from imposing too severe a deterrent against entering public service. The limitation of disqualification in paragraphs (a)(2) and (d)(2) to matters involving a specific party or parties, rather than extending disqualification to all substantive issues on which the lawyer worked, serves a similar function.

[5] When a lawyer has been employed by one government agency and then moves to a second government agency, it may be appropriate to treat that second agency as another client for purposes of this Rule, as when a lawyer is employed by a city and subsequently is employed by a federal agency. However, because the conflict of interest is governed by paragraph (d), the latter agency is not required to screen the lawyer as paragraph (b) requires a law firm to do. The question of whether two government agencies should be regarded as the same or different clients for conflict of interest purposes is beyond the scope of these Rules. See Rule 1.13 Comment [9].

[6] Paragraphs (b) and (c) contemplate a screening arrangement. See Rule 1.0(k) (requirements for screening procedures). These paragraphs do not prohibit a lawyer from receiving a salary or partnership share established by prior independent agreement, but that lawyer may not receive compensation directly relating the lawyer's compensation to the fee in the matter in which the lawyer is disqualified.

[7] Notice, including a description of the screened lawyer's prior representation and of the screening procedures employed, generally should be given as soon as practicable after the need for screening becomes apparent.

[8] Paragraph (c) operates only when the lawyer in question has knowledge of the information, which means actual knowledge; it does not operate with respect to information that merely could be imputed to the lawyer.

[9] Paragraphs (a) and (d) do not prohibit a lawyer from jointly representing a private party and a government agency when doing so is permitted by Rule 1.7 and is not otherwise prohibited by law.

[10] For purposes of paragraph (e) of this Rule, a "matter" may continue in another form. In determining whether two particular matters are the same, the lawyer should consider the extent to which the matters involve the same basic facts, the same or related parties, and the time elapsed.

### Definitional Cross-References

"Confirmed in writing" *See* Rule 1.0(b)

"Firm" *See* Rule 1.0(c)

"Informed consent" *See* Rule 1.0(e)

"Knowingly" and "Knows" *See* Rule 1.0(f)

"Screened" *See* Rule 1.0(k)

"Written" *See* Rule 1.0(n)

### State Rules Comparison

http://ambar.org/MRPCStateCharts

## ANNOTATION

### OVERVIEW

Lawyers formerly employed by the government—whether or not in a "lawyer" capacity—are not subject to the general rule on former-client conflicts. Under Rule 1.11(a) the trigger for disqualifying a lawyer formerly employed by the government is *personal and substantial participation* in the *same* matter, as opposed to actual *representation* in the same *or a substantially related* matter. And if a former government lawyer is disqualified based upon personal and substantial participation in the same matter, his new colleagues can use screening and notice to avoid imputation. In the private sector, nonconsensual screening would not prevent imputation.

Lawyers currently employed by the government—whether or not in a "lawyer" capacity—must comply with the general rules on conflicts; Rule 1.11(d) expressly incorporates Rules 1.7 and 1.9. However, their conflicts are not imputed to their governmental colleagues.

In addition, Rule 1.11(c) prohibits a lawyer currently or formerly employed by the government from representing a private client if the lawyer possesses "confidential government information"—narrowly defined in paragraph (c)—that is damaging to someone with adverse interests. This prohibition supplements the lawyer's duties of confidentiality under Rules 1.6 and 1.9(c), which are fully applicable to government lawyers.

#### • *Moving from One Government Agency to Another*

Rule 1.11 applies "not only to lawyers moving from government service to private practice (and vice versa) but also to lawyers moving from one government agency to another." American Bar Association, *A Legislative History: The Development of the ABA*

*Model Rules of Professional Conduct, 1982–2013*, at 291 (2013) (explaining why rule was retitled in 2002 from "Successive Government and Private Employment" to "Special Conflicts of Interest for Former and Current Government Officers and Employees"). When a lawyer moves from one governmental agency to another, it "may be appropriate," according to Comment [5], "to treat that second agency as another client for purposes of this Rule, as when a lawyer is employed by a city and subsequently is employed by a federal agency." Comment [4] similarly notes that "successive clients [may be] a government agency and another client, public or private." *See* American Bar Association, *A Legislative History: The Development of the ABA Model Rules of Professional Conduct, 1982–2013*, at 294 (2013) (noting rule's applicability to "successive representation between distinct government agencies").

However, paragraph (c), on the disqualifying effect of confidential government information, addresses subsequent (or concurrent) representation of "private" clients only. Similarly, paragraph (d), on lawyers currently serving as public officers or employees, is phrased in terms of matters in which they participated while in "private practice or nongovernmental employment."

On the distinction between representing the government and being paid by the government, see *Humphrey ex rel. State v. McLaren*, 402 N.W.2d 535 (Minn. 1987). *See also* Ronald D. Rotunda & John S. Dzienkowski, *Lawyer's Deskbook on Professional Responsibility* § 1.11-3(a) & n.3 (2018–2019) (private practitioner who represents government agency "is accepting private employment from the government agency"; "mere fact that the government is paying a lawyer does not mean that the lawyer works on behalf of the government"); Martin Cole, *Government Lawyer Conflicts*, 70 Bench & B. Minn. 12 (Sept. 2013) (Rule 1.11 does not apply to lawyers in private practice who also represent governmental clients).

Whether two government agencies should be regarded as the same or different clients is "beyond the scope of these Rules," according to Comment [5]. Rule 1.13 does, however, touch upon the related problem of identifying the government client in the first place; see the annotation to Rule 1.13 for discussion.

### Paragraph (a): Participation versus Representation

Rule 1.11(a) provides that unless the appropriate government agency consents, a lawyer who has been a public officer or employee—whether or not in a "lawyer" capacity—is disqualified from representing any client, whether private or governmental, if the lawyer participated personally and substantially in the same matter as a public officer or employee.

Rule 1.11 as amended in 2002 displaces Rule 1.9(a) and (b), which overlapped with it confusingly. Codifying the holding of ABA Formal Opinion 97-409 (1997), the amended rule makes *personal and substantial participation* in the *same* matter (as opposed to *representation* in the same *or a substantially related* matter) the touchstone of disqualification from any subsequent representation, adverse or not. Comment [4] explains the rationale:

> [T]he rules governing lawyers presently or formerly employed by a government agency should not be so restrictive as to inhibit transfer of employ-

ment to and from the government. . . . Thus a former government lawyer is
disqualified only from particular matters in which the lawyer participated
personally and substantially.

*Compare Violet v. Brown*, 9 Vet. App. 530 (Vet. App. 1996) (superseded) (even though
Board of Veterans Appeals former counsel's involvement in decision being appealed
was "minimal," court found a "representation" within meaning of Rule 1.9 and
therefore disqualified him from representing appellant), *with Sperry v. Shinseki*, 24
Vet. App. 1 (Vet. App. 2010) (*Violet* no longer controls; under Rule 1.11, veteran's lawyer who, as counsel for secretary of Veterans Affairs, signed unopposed motion for
remand in veteran's case was not disqualified from representing veteran on appeal).
*See In re White*, 11 A.3d 1226 (D.C. 2011) (lawyer who supervised investigation of
age-discrimination complaint as head of D.C. human rights office became co-counsel
for complainant and seriously interfered with administration of justice by sharing
inside knowledge of human rights proceeding with co-counsel); *In re Coleman*, 895
N.Y.S.2d 122 (App. Div. 2010) (disqualification of petitioner's counsel in probate proceeding reversed; responsibility as former chief court attorney of surrogate's court
law department to review and assign every incoming case was administrative rather
than substantive); Pa. Ethics Op. 2008-11 (2008) (lawyer may accept court appointment to represent convicted defendant at sentencing phase even though lawyer was
assistant district attorney during trial; lawyer had no role in and no information about
case); R.I. Ethics Op. 2009-01 (2009) (former part-time assistant municipal solicitor
who prosecuted misdemeanors in district court and housing matters in municipal
court may represent clients in misdemeanor and housing matters in which she did
not personally and substantially participate).

Rule 1.11 applies regardless of alignment of interests, and applies whenever
the lawyer has served as a public officer or employee of any kind—even if not in
a "lawyer" capacity. In this regard it is broader than Rule 1.9, the general rule on
former-client conflicts, which is limited to subsequent adverse representation. *See
Filippi v. Elmont Union Free Sch. Dist. Bd. of Educ.*, 722 F. Supp. 2d 295 (E.D.N.Y. 2010)
(associate's service as vice president of school board required disqualification of her
firm from representing employee suing board and its officials for discrimination);
*Park-N-Shop, Ltd. v. City of Highwood*, 864 F. Supp. 82 (N.D. Ill. 1994) (lawyer on city
council when mayor granted liquor license to plaintiff not prohibited from representing plaintiff in suit about license renewal; participation "tangential"); Ill. Ethics Op.
96-07 (1997) (Rule 1.11 applies to lawyer who worked as nonlawyer child welfare
supervisor in state's Department of Children and Family Services and later wanted
to represent parents and children in juvenile court); *cf.* Pa. Ethics Op. 2008-08 (2008)
(part-time township solicitor not public officer or employee within meaning of Rule
1.11; receipt of township manager's e-mail about pending employee grievance therefore disqualifies lawyer and firm from later representing employee unless township
and employee consent).

For analysis of the differences between Rules 1.9 and 1.11, see *Babineaux v. Foster*,
Civ. No. 04-1679, 2005 WL 711604, 2005 BL 88697 (E.D. La. Mar. 21, 2005) (rejecting
application of Rule 1.9). *See generally* John M. Burman, *Ethics for Lawyers Who Repre-*

*sent Governmental Entities as Part of Their Private Practices*, 10 Wyo. L. Rev. 357 (2010); Martha Harrell Chumbler, *Conflicts of Interests Relating to Former and Current Government Clients*, 35 Urb. Law. 671 (Fall 2003); Patrick J. Johnston, *Amended Model Rule of Professional Conduct 1.11: Long-Standing Controversy, Imperfect Remedy, and New Questions*, 11 Widener J. Pub. L. 83 (2002).

## PUBLIC DEFENDERS

Public defenders are usually government employees appointed by a judge to represent private individuals who are being prosecuted by fellow government employees. This makes for an awkward fit with Rule 1.11; as a result, successive-employment conflicts in this context are frequently analyzed under Rule 1.9 instead. *See Richard B. v. State Dep't of Health & Soc. Servs.*, 71 P.3d 811 (Alaska 2003) (because public defender represents private individuals, his move to private firm governed by Rule 1.9 rather than Rule 1.11; firm therefore may not use screening to avoid imputation of his conflicts); *State v. Wilson*, 195 S.W.3d 23 (Mo. Ct. App. 2006) (Rule 1.9 governs prosecutor who was former public defender); D.C. Ethics Op. 313 (2002) (military lawyer assigned to represent court-martial defendant may continue to represent him after entering private practice; lawyer not "accepting other employment" within District of Columbia's Rule 1.11 because client remains the individual rather than the government; same rationale applies to "former public defenders and former federal officers and employees who were authorized, while working for the government, to represent particular individuals or groups of individuals"). *But see People v. Shari*, 204 P.3d 453 (Colo. 2009) (court would share parties' "assumption that public defenders are 'government attorneys' under Rule 1.11"). *See generally* Randy Lee, *Related Representations in Civil and Criminal Matters: The Night the D.A. Ditched His Date for the Prom*, 29 N. Ky. L. Rev. 281 (2002).

## "PERSONAL AND SUBSTANTIAL"

Rule 1.11(a) uses the same "personal and substantial participation" threshold as Rule 1.12, which deals with disqualification of former judges and third-party neutrals. The phrase comes from the Ethics in Government Act of 1978, 18 U.S.C. § 207 (2018), where it is defined as participation "through decision, approval, disapproval, recommendation, the rendering of advice, investigation or other such action." *See, e.g., Arroyo v. City of Buffalo*, No. 15-CV-753A(F), 2017 WL 3085835, 2017 BL 251611 (W.D.N.Y. July 20, 2017) (no disqualification for former prosecutor representing plaintiff suing police who shot plaintiff's dog while executing search warrant; although as prosecutor he had spoken to officer about incident, no evidence he had participated substantially in official investigation, deliberations about whether charges should be filed, or prosecution); *United States v. Dancy*, No. 3:08CR189, 2008 WL 4329414, 2008 BL 207850 (E.D. Va. Sept. 16, 2008) (disqualification of defense counsel vacated; even though during her previous employment as prosecutor with multijurisdictional grand jury she was "obviously involved personally" in investigation by allowing subpoenas to be issued under her authority, her participation was not substantial); *Richards v. Lewis*, Civ. No. 05-0069, 2005 WL 2645001, 2005 BL 42302 (D.V.I. Oct. 14, 2005) (employment discrimination plaintiff's counsel's involvement, while assistant

attorney general, in plaintiff's related unfair labor practice charge against police commissioner was "limited, pro forma and ultimately nominal" notwithstanding that she
signed routine general denial on commissioner's behalf); *United States v. Philip Morris
Inc.*, 312 F. Supp. 2d 27 (D.D.C. 2004) (under Rule 1.11(a), former Department of Justice special litigation counsel's work preparing for and then responding to tobacco
company suits challenging FDA's Youth Tobacco Rulemaking initiative prohibited
him from representing tobacco company seeking to intervene to defend its privilege
logs in government's suit against affiliated tobacco company); *Sperry v. Shinseki*, 24
Vet. App. 1 (Vet. App. 2010) (veteran's lawyer had not, in his former job as counsel for
secretary of Veterans Affairs, participated personally and substantially in veteran's
case by signing unopposed motion for remand); *In re White*, 11 A.3d 1226 (D.C. 2011)
(rejecting lawyer's argument that although she was supposed to be personally and
substantially involved in matter she "did not do what she was supposed to do, and
therefore she cannot be held responsible for a Rule 1.11(a) violation"; lawyer's claim
that she did not "feel responsible" was irrelevant); *In re Sofaer*, 728 A.2d 625 (D.C.
1999) ("[A] single act of approving or participating in a critical step may be substantial if the act is of significance to the matter. This requires more than official responsibility, knowledge, perfunctory involvement, or involvement in only administrative
or peripheral issues."); *Registe v. State*, 697 S.E.2d 804 (Ga. 2010) (former prosecutor
who applied for search warrants in attempt to locate fugitive suspect thereby participated personally and substantially in investigation even though he did not appear in
court; disqualified from serving as defense counsel); *Sorci v. Iowa Dist. Court for Polk
Cnty.*, 671 N.W.2d 482 (Iowa 2003) (former assistant county attorney had substantial
responsibility, applying predecessor Model Code standard, in any juvenile protective
proceedings in which she (1) advised state social workers, prosecutors, or agents,
(2) wrote letters or reports about case, (3) signed pleadings filed on state's behalf, or
(4) appeared for state in court; subsequent disciplinary proceedings at *Iowa Supreme
Court Att'y Disciplinary Bd. v. Johnson*, 728 N.W.2d 199 (Iowa 2007)); *State v. Rivadeneira*, No. A-1033-09T4, 2010 WL 3075573, 2010 BL 366990 (N.J. Super. Ct. App. Div. Aug.
3, 2010) (former prosecutor's management of sex crimes unit trial team and detectives precluded him from representing criminal defendant even though he went into
private practice before defendant identified as target of unit's investigation); *Royer v.
Dillow*, No. 13 CA 71, 2014 WL 98601 (Ohio Ct. App. Jan. 9, 2014) (disqualification of
plaintiff's counsel in wrongful-death lawsuit reversed; on remand, trial court must
conduct hearing on counsel's level of involvement, as city's part-time law director, in
criminal case against same defendant arising out of same accident); D.C. Ethics Op.
315 (2002) (former EPA lawyer may represent private client challenging agency's final
rules even though he drafted status reports and participated in discussions about
timing of rulemaking proceedings; participation did not go beyond "official responsibility . . . or involvement on an administrative or peripheral issue" within meaning
of federal regulations); Md. Ethics Op. 2001-29 (2001) (lawyer formerly employed by
municipal police department's legal affairs office to prosecute officers in administrative hearings and defend department—but not individual officers—against civil
lawsuits not per se prohibited from representing private clients suing municipality
or individual officers); N.J. Ethics Op. 614 (1988) (substantial responsibility does not

include "bare 'overall' or 'ultimate' responsibility"); N.Y. State Ethics Op. 966 (2013) (part-time town clerk with solely ministerial duties may represent client in matter pending in another town court even though client also has matter pending before clerk's court); N.Y. State Ethics Op. 748 (2001) ("fact that a former government lawyer was counsel for the government in unrelated matters [when] defendant's case was investigated or prosecuted is not enough to demonstrate personal and substantial participation"); Tex. Ethics Op. 574 (2006) (former employee of state regulatory agency may represent client in matter that originated while he worked there but in which he did not participate personally and substantially). *Compare Sec. Investor Prot. Corp. v. Vigman*, 587 F. Supp. 1358 (C.D. Cal. 1984) (when SEC regional administrator signed complaint and trial brief he assumed, as matter of law, "personal and substantial responsibility of ensuring that there existed good ground to support the SEC's case"; citing Fed. R. Civ. P. 11), *with Sec. Gen. Life Ins. Co. v. Superior Court*, 718 P.2d 985 (Ariz. 1986) (no "personal and substantial responsibility"; although matters involving insurance company were before lawyer's department while he was director of insurance, he was not aware of details and merely signed orders his staff gave him).

## CONSENT BY GOVERNMENT AGENCY

A former public officer's or employee's conflict of interest may be waived by the "appropriate government agency" if the relevant regulations permit the agency to consent. *Cf.* Neb. Ethics Op. 08-01 (2008) (although Rule 1.11 authorizes public entities to waive conflicts, prosecution cannot give consent when state law does not provide mechanism for county attorney, who is statutory counsel for "state, county, and public," to obtain it).

The ability of public entities to waive a conflict of interest is discussed in the annotation to Rule 1.7.

## *Paragraph (b): Screening*

A conflict that results from an individually disqualified lawyer's service as a public officer or employee will not be imputed to his or her firm colleagues if the lawyer is timely screened and the appropriate government agency is notified in writing. American Bar Association, *A Legislative History: The Development of the ABA Model Rules of Professional Conduct, 1982–2013*, at 292 (2013) (screening for former government employees "encourage[s] lawyers to work in the public sector without fear that their service will unduly burden their future careers in the private sector"); *see, e.g., Calhoun v. Commonwealth*, 492 S.W.3d 132 (Ky. 2016) (fact that public defender withdrew and took job as assistant prosecutor did not require disqualification of entire prosecutor's office when lawyer adequately screened); *State v. Clausen*, 104 So. 3d 410 (La. 2012) (disqualifying criminal defense firm that employed former prosecutor who had been involved in defendant's case; affidavit that he had not discussed or been involved with case since leaving prosecutor's office did not satisfy Rule 1.11's screening requirements); *People v. Davenport*, 779 N.W.2d 257 (Mich. 2009) (two-prosecutor office effectively implemented "measures to prevent improper communications" and screen incoming lawyer who had been representing criminal defendant); *In re Essex Equity Holdings USA v. Lehman Bros., Inc.*, 909 N.Y.S.2d 285 (Sup. Ct. 2010) (firm's practice of "creating silos of isolation" was not functional equivalent of screening, nor were former prosecutor's conversations with his former supervisors about "what [he] could and could not handle" if he joined firm functional equivalent of written notice to appropriate government agency); *see also In re Charlisse C.*, 194 P.3d 330 (Cal. 2008) (on mother's motion to disqualify publicly funded law center that represented her in past from now representing her child in dependency proceeding, lower court should have determined whether center adequately protected mother's confidences "through timely, appropriate, and effective screening measures and structural safeguards"); Pa. Ethics Op. 2004-08 (2004) (criminal defense lawyer who takes part-time position as domestic violence prosecutor may not handle any criminal defense work in same county; disqualification not imputed to firm colleagues if district attorney for county of prosecution consents and screening and notice requirements met; "better practice would be to obtain the written consent and approval of the prospective criminal defendant"); *cf.* Ariz. Ethics Op. 16-01 (2016) (of counsel relationship can result in imputation under Rule 1.11). *See generally* Brad Andrews, *A New Analysis of When Public Defender Conflicts of Interest Are Imputed*, 53 Advoc. (Idaho) 13 (May 2010); Shira Mizrahi, Note, *Up Against the Wall: A Guide to the Effective Screening of Former Government Attorneys in New York*, 10 Cardozo Pub. L. Pol'y & Ethics J. 131 (Fall 2011).

Screening as a way of avoiding imputing the conflicts of a former public officer or employee to his new colleagues was first approved by an ABA ethics opinion construing the predecessor Model Code. The Code itself made no mention of screening; the opinion was prompted by the "concern of many government agencies as well as . . . many former government lawyers now in practice" over the harsh consequences of what was then an inflexible rule. ABA Formal Ethics Op. 342 (1975). The opinion is criticized in Lawrence K. Hellman, *When "Ethics Rules" Don't Mean What They Say: The Implications of Strained ABA Ethics Opinions*, 10 Geo. J. Legal Ethics 317 (Winter 1997). *See generally* Robert A. Creamer, *Three Myths About Lateral Screening*, 13 Prof. Law., no. 2, at 20 (Winter 2002) (distinguishing between private lawyers and former government lawyers for screening purposes is illogical and discriminatory).

Rule 1.0(k) defines screening as "the isolation of a lawyer from any participation in a matter through the timely imposition of procedures within a firm that are reasonably adequate under the circumstances to protect information that the isolated lawyer is obligated to protect under these Rules or other law." Comments [9] and [10] to Rule 1.0 explain the available "isolation" procedures.

For discussion of screening outside the context of former governmental employment, see the annotation to Rule 1.10.

## *Paragraph (c): "Confidential Government Information"*

Rule 1.11(c) provides that a lawyer who acquired "confidential government information about a person" while a public officer or employee may not thereafter represent a private client whose interests are adverse to that person "in a matter in which the information could be used to the material disadvantage of that person." Confidential government information is specially defined in paragraph (c) as information "obtained under governmental authority and which . . . the government is prohibited by law from disclosing to the public or has a legal privilege not to disclose and which is not otherwise available to the public." *See United States v. Villaspring Health Care Ctr. Inc.*, Civ. No. 3:11-43-DCR, 2011 WL 5330790, 2011 BL 285930 (E.D. Ky. Nov. 7, 2011) (disqualifying lawyer from defending facility in federal False Claims Act case and rejecting argument that in course of investigating health care facility as assistant attorney general he gained no confidential information not already known to facility; lawyer also interviewed facility's former employees and gained "strategic insights, such as his knowledge of the strengths and weaknesses of the evidence"); *Kronberg v. LaRouche*, No. 1:09cv947(AJT/TRJ), 2010 WL 1443934, 2010 BL 79579 (E.D. Va. Apr. 9, 2010) (plaintiff who testified in federal criminal prosecution of defendant twenty years ago and was now suing him for libel could not be represented by former assistant U.S. attorney who participated in the prosecution; Rule 1.11(c) required disqualification notwithstanding that he had not used, would not use, and did not remember any confidential government information); *Baltimore County v. Barnhart*, 30 A.3d 291 (Md. Ct. Spec. App. 2011) (although former county attorney dealt with legal issues involving county's pension obligations, she had not acquired confidential information she could use to county's detriment in representing county retiree in pension dispute); *see also Tina X v. John X*, 32 N.Y.S.3d 332 (App. Div. 2016) (violation of Rule 1.11(c) for court to appoint lawyer to represent children in custody matter when he had previously been involved in prosecuting mother on child endangerment charges, but rule violation alone did not warrant vacatur of stipulated order).

Note that "confidential government information" protected under Rule 1.11(c) is different from the information protected under Rule 1.6, which covers only information relating to the *representation* of a client. *See* Or. Ethics Op. 2005-120 (rev. 2015) (confidential government information under Rule 1.11(c) "may encompass information that would not otherwise constitute confidential client information under [Rule] 1.6"). For example, under Rule 1.11(c) it is not necessary that the former public officer or employee was working as a lawyer when she acquired the information; administrative, policy, and advisory positions also trigger the prohibition. In addition, information that has become publicly available is not considered confidential government information for purposes of Rule 1.11's ban on subsequent adverse representation, but it is enough to trigger Rule 1.9(b)'s prohibition on subsequent adverse representation and it is still protected from disclosure (by the lawyer) under Rule 1.9(c)(2).

## KNOWLEDGE NOT IMPUTED

Rule 1.11(c) operates only when the lawyer has "actual knowledge" of the information; the rule "does not operate with respect to information that merely could be imputed to the lawyer." Cmt. [8]. *See Babineaux v. Foster*, Civ. No. 04-1679, 2005 WL 711604, 2005 BL 88697 (E.D. La. Mar. 21, 2005) (rejecting city's argument, in moving to disqualify former assistant city attorney from representing plaintiff in employment discrimination suit against city, that because mayor copied attorney on "confidential" response letter "it can be presumed that other confidential communications transpired"); *Walker v. State Dep't of Transp. & Dev.*, 817 So. 2d 57 (La. 2002) (former assistant attorney general's assertion in solicitation letter to other lawyers that he knew inner operations of Department of Transportation and knew location of documents essential to proving case against department did not require his disqualification from representing personal injury plaintiffs; no evidence he actually obtained confidential information related to particular cases in which he was representing plaintiffs); *NAACP v. State*, 711 A.2d 1355 (N.J. Super. Ct. App. Div. 1998) (reversing denial of pro hac vice admission, court looked to Rule 1.11 to decide that former government lawyer's work in developing entry-level exam for law enforcement candidates would not have warranted his disqualification from later representing employment discrimination plaintiffs attacking exam's validity; "nine-year hiatus between [his] employment with the U.S. Department of Justice and the filing of the pro hac vice application certainly suffices to mitigate any concern that this former officeholder might be seen to be taking advantage of information acquired in fresh governmental service"); *cf.* Ark. Ethics Op. 2002-1 (2002) (former counsel to federal administrative agency may give expert testimony for defendants being sued by same agency fifteen years later; statements about enforcement policies followed during his tenure, general comments on enforcement strategy, and discussions of particular enforcement actions did not involve "confidential government information"). *But see* Neb. Ethics Op. 08-01 (2008) (because county attorneys have access to information concerning all nonsupport defendants in state, part-time county attorney may not represent any party in child support matter).

## No Waiver

Unlike a conflict resulting from participation in a matter, a conflict resulting from possession of "confidential government information" cannot be waived. *See* Pa. Ethics Op. 94-132 (1994) (former government lawyer who obtains confidential information while employed by Department of Justice may not represent client in matter in which she was involved as government lawyer, even with government consent); S.C. Ethics Op. 97-41 (1998) (former special prosecutor for solicitor's office may represent victims in civil suit against criminal defendant being prosecuted by solicitor's office if solicitor's office consents, unless she had access to confidential information that could lead to unfair advantage).

## *Paragraph (d): Lawyers Currently Employed by Government*

Lawyers currently serving as public officers or employees are expressly made subject to the general-purpose rules on former-client and current-client conflicts, Rules 1.9 and 1.7, respectively.

## Prior Nongovernmental Participation

According to paragraph (d)(2)(i), a lawyer serving as a public officer or employee may not participate in a matter in which he or she participated personally and substantially while in "private practice or nongovernmental employment," unless the appropriate government agency consents. *See* R.I. Ethics Op. 2007-04 (2007) (lawyer who becomes town council member may not participate in matter about which he was consulted while in private practice; preliminary investigation constituted personal and substantial participation even though lawyer declined representation). The prohibition is designed "to prevent a lawyer from exploiting public office for the advantage of another client," according to Comment [3]; it is symmetrical with that of

Rule 1.11(a)(2), which applies when the move is in the other direction. *Cf.* Mass. Ethics Op. 07-02 (2007) (prohibition not applicable to new commissioner of state agency who, in private practice, represented agency itself rather than individuals dealing with it).

Note that it is the current governmental employer, rather than the former private client, whose consent Rule 1.11(d)(2)(i) requires. The former client's interests, however, are protected by Rule 1.11(d)(1)'s incorporation of Rule 1.9, which already requires the former client's consent if the interests were materially adverse.

## CONCURRENTLY REPRESENTING PRIVATE PARTY

According to Comment [9], a lawyer representing a government agency may "jointly" represent a private party if permitted by Rule 1.7 and not otherwise prohibited by law. *See* Utah Ethics Op. 06-01 (2006) (proposed pro bono work of one government lawyer will not create conflict imputable to others in same government office if she does not participate in their conflicting work, and if all comply strictly with Rule 1.7); Vt. Ethics Op. 2003-4 (2003) (applying Rule 1.11 "by analogy" as well as Rule 1.7 to private lawyer's part-time work for attorney general's office). *See generally* John M. Burman, *Ethics for Lawyers Who Represent Governmental Entities as Part of Their Private Practices*, 10 Wyo. L. Rev. 357 (2010); David Halperin, *Ethics Breakthrough or Ethics Breakdown? Kenneth Starr's Dual Roles as Private Practitioner and Public Prosecutor*, 15 Geo. J. Legal Ethics 231 (Winter 2002).

## NO IMPUTATION, BUT SCREENING "PRUDENT"

Comment [2] notes that even though there is no imputation of a government lawyer's disqualification to his or her colleagues, "ordinarily it will be prudent to screen such lawyers." *See United States v. Goot*, 894 F.2d 231 (7th Cir. 1990) (criminal defendant's lawyer's appointment as new U.S. attorney for district of prosecution did not disqualify other assistants; screening in effect before lawyer took office, and presumption of shared confidences rebutted by appointment of acting U.S. attorney and by affidavits that no secrets disclosed); *In re Grand Jury Investigation*, 918 F. Supp. 1374 (S.D. Cal. 1996) (U.S. attorney's office not disqualified from investigating specific incidents of state court corruption even though one assistant U.S. attorney, not assigned to investigation, represented one subject during state's investigation of same allegations); *Brown v. City of Hartford*, 127 A.3d 278 (Conn. App. Ct. 2015) (conflict of city's corporation counsel, based on prior representation of plaintiff, not imputed to entire office; current action commenced after counsel joined office, and counsel had neither participated in current action nor divulged plaintiff's confidences); *McMillen v. State*, No. A08-1917, 2010 WL 10367, 2010 BL 1648 (Minn. Ct. App. Jan. 5, 2010) (disqualification of lawyer who represented criminal defendant as public defender before joining county attorney's office would not be imputed; no claim that lawyer shared confidential information with prosecutors); *State v. Eighth Judicial Dist. Court (Zogheib)*, 321 P.3d 882 (Nev. 2014) (conflict of former criminal defense counsel who became head of prosecutor's office not imputed to entire office when prosecutor was not personally handling matter and screening procedures were adequate); *State ex rel. Tyler v. MacQueen*, 447 S.E.2d 289 (W. Va. 1994) (prosecutor's office not disqualified as long as personally disqualified prosecutor effectively screened from case); *see also* N.C. Ethics Op. 2003-14 (2004) (former defense lawyer, now prosecutor, may not handle habitual-felon trial of defendant whom he represented on underlying felony conviction; other lawyers in office may, with proper screening and notice); *cf. State v. Stenger*, 760 P.2d 357 (Wash. 1988) (disqualifying prosecutor's office in death case when prosecutor's prior representation of defendant on unrelated charge involved information interwoven with decision to seek death penalty; screening would be unavailing because prosecutor assisted in preparation of press release and attended press conference and post-arrest briefing at sheriff's office).

## NEGOTIATING FOR PRIVATE EMPLOYMENT

Rule 1.11(d)(2)(ii) prohibits a lawyer working for the government from negotiating for private employment with anyone "involved as a party or as lawyer for a party in a matter in which the lawyer is participating personally and substantially." It represents a compromise protecting the government lawyer's marketability without sacrificing the government's interest in conflict-free service. *See Airline Pilots Ass'n v. U.S. Dep't of Transp.*, 899 F.2d 1230 (D.C. Cir. 1990) (not improper for secretary of Department of Transportation to negotiate for employment with law firm representing major airline in matter not then pending before DOT; more stringent requirement "would mean, effectively, that high government officials could not, before leaving their posts, negotiate with many, if any, of the District's large law firms"; construing federal conflict-of-interest statute, 18 U.S.C. § 208); *In re Relphorde*, 596 N.E.2d 903 (Ind. 1992) (lawyer who entered fee agreement with criminal defendant he was appointed to represent as indigent found to have negotiated for private employment in matter in which he was participating as public employee); *Commonwealth v. Maricle*, 10 S.W.3d 117 (Ky. 1999) (mandamus requiring disqualification of defense lawyers at firm joined by former prosecutor who continued to participate in prosecution of their client while negotiating for job); *Rissler v. Jefferson Cnty. Bd. of Zoning Appeals*, 693 S.E.2d 321 (W. Va. 2010) (given that zoning board's lawyer "most likely" negotiating terms of forthcoming employment with developer's counsel shortly before leaving board, he should have been disqualified as board's counsel in connection with developer's application). *See generally* Anne Bowen Poulin, *Conflicts of Interest in Criminal Cases: Should the Prosecution Have a Duty to Disclose?*, 47 Am. Crim. L. Rev. 1135 (Summer 2010).

Rule 1.11(d)(2)(ii) does not apply to judicial law clerks, who are understood to be "in the market"; special provision is made for them in Rule 1.12.

## *Paragraph (e): "Matter"*

A "matter," as specifically defined by Rule 1.11(e), does not include legislation, rulemaking, and other policy determinations. This definition codifies an ABA ethics opinion that construed the analogous provision of the predecessor Model Code:

[W]ork as a government employee in drafting, enforcing or interpreting government or agency procedures, regulations, or laws, or in briefing abstract principles of law does not disqualify the lawyer [under Model Code DR

9-101(b)] from subsequent private employment involving the same regulations, procedures or points of law; the same "matter" is not involved because there is lacking the discrete, identifiable transactions or conduct involving a particular situation and specific parties.

ABA Formal Ethics Op. 342 (1975). *See, e.g., United States v. Villaspring Health Care Ctr. Inc.*, Civ. No. 3:11-43-DCR, 2011 WL 5330790, 2011 BL 285930 (E.D. Ky. Nov. 7, 2011) (federal government's False Claims Act suit against health care facility involved same matter as state's criminal probe of health care facility; former assistant state attorney general's participation in investigation precluded him from continuing to defend facility in civil case); *Green v. City of New York*, No. 10 Civ. 8214(PKC), 2011 WL 2419864 (S.D.N.Y. June 7, 2011) (subsequent suit involving different parties may be considered same as first matter depending upon scope of lawyer's work on first matter; "It is relevant whether the lawyer merely gathered and produced documents, responded to pleadings and attended court conferences or, rather, served as counselor and advisor on the broad subject at hand."); *Hitchens v. State*, 931 A.2d 437 (Del. 2007) (probation revocation proceeding in which prosecutor on original charge now representing defendant as assistant public defender did not involve same matter as original prosecution); *In re Sofaer*, 728 A.2d 625 (D.C. 1999) (lawyer violated Rule 1.11(a) by undertaking to represent Libyan government in connection with civil and criminal disputes and litigation arising from bombing of airplane over Scotland after serving as legal advisor in State Department and personally and substantially participating in government's investigation of bombing and in related diplomatic and legal activities); D.C. Ethics Op. 297 (2001) (former U.S. Department of Interior lawyer who was actively involved in proposed regulations may represent Indian tribe in negotiated rulemaking regarding regulations; rulemaking of general application not "matter" within meaning of Rule 1.11(a)); Pa. Ethics Op. 2012-14 (2012) (lawyer who, as probation officer, supervised defendant's probation may represent defendant on new probation violation charges filed after lawyer left probation department); Utah Ethics Op. 15-01 (2015) (any proceeding before board of pardons involving same offender is same "matter" for purposes of Rules 1.11(a)(2) and 1.12(a)).

Comment [10] notes that a matter "may continue in another form," and that "[i]n determining whether two particular matters are the same, the lawyer should consider the extent to which the matters involve the same basic facts, the same or related parties, and the time elapsed." *See, e.g., Reed v. Astrue*, Civ. No. 09-824-SLR, 2011 WL 2112009, 2011 BL 139346 (D. Del. May 26, 2011) (lawyer may represent plaintiff seeking disability benefits even though he defended Social Security Administration's denial of her earlier claim; "Given that claimants are permitted to come back to the well multiple times, and . . . administrative records related to each attempt can (and usually do) include substantially all medical records ever presented to defendant," contrary ruling would "essentially [preclude] attorneys of long standing . . . from representing repeat filers"); *In re Sec. Investor Prot. Corp. v. Vigman*, 587 F. Supp. 1358 (C.D. Cal. 1984) ("discrete series" of transactions involving specific situation and specific parties in ten-year-old civil action was "part and parcel" of subsequent, broader suit alleging widespread securities fraud; former SEC regional administrator disqualified from representing plaintiff in later suit); *State ex rel. Jefferson Cnty. Bd. of Zoning Appeals v. Wilkes*, 655 S.E.2d 178 (W. Va. 2007) (disqualifying former county lawyer and his firm from representing private developer before zoning board in permit application on which lawyer worked as counsel for zoning board; rejecting trial court's conclusion that each stage in consideration of conditional-use permit application is separate "matter"); S.C. Ethics Op. 05-01 (2005) (former deputy solicitor who prosecuted child molester for sexual abuse at boys' residential home may not work on civil case involving abuse at same home even though new case involves different boy and different perpetrator). *See generally* Patricia E. Salkin, *Crime Doesn't Pay and Neither Do Conflicts of Interest in Land Use Decisionmaking*, 40 Urb. Law. 561 (Summer 2008).

Rule 1.11(e)(2)'s definition also incorporates "any other matter covered by the conflict of interest rules of the appropriate government agency." *See EEOC v. Exxon Corp.*, 202 F.3d 755 (5th Cir. 2000) (settlement of oil company's criminal liability for oil spill was same "particular matter" within meaning of Ethics in Government Act as EEOC's discrimination suit over oil company's policy disqualifying employees who have undergone substance-abuse treatment from certain safety-sensitive positions, because policy was required by government as condition of oil-spill settlement; court declined, however, to apply Rule 1.11 to former government lawyers' expert testimony for defense); *Royer v. Dillow*, No. 13 CA 71, 2014 WL 98601 (Ohio Ct. App. Jan. 9, 2014) (under state conflict-of-interest statute, matter "includes any case, proceeding, application, determination, issue, or question, but does not include the proposal, consideration, or enactment of statutes, rules, ordinances, resolutions, or charter or constitutional amendments"). A particular government agency's conflict-of-interest rules may be stricter in some respects than Rule 1.11. *See* "Speakers Detail Dilemmas, Restrictions Facing Present, Former Government Lawyers," *ABA/BNA Lawyers' Manual on Professional Conduct*, 29 Law. Man. Prof. Conduct 559 (Current Reports, Aug. 28, 2013). Comment [1] further notes that statutes and government regulations regarding conflicts of interest may limit the ability of a particular government agency to give consent.

## Rule 1.12

### *Former Judge, Arbitrator, Mediator or Other Third-Party Neutral*

(a) Except as stated in paragraph (d), a lawyer shall not represent anyone in connection with a matter in which the lawyer participated personally and substantially as a judge or other adjudicative officer or law clerk to such a person or as an arbitrator, mediator or other third-party neutral, unless all parties to the proceeding give informed consent, confirmed in writing.

(b) A lawyer shall not negotiate for employment with any person who is involved as a party or as lawyer for a party in a matter in which the lawyer is participating personally and substantially as a judge or other adjudicative officer or as an arbitrator, mediator or other third-party neutral. A lawyer serving as a law clerk to a judge or other adjudicative officer may negotiate for employment with a party or lawyer involved in a matter in which the clerk is participating personally and substantially, but only after the lawyer has notified the judge or other adjudicative officer.

(c) If a lawyer is disqualified by paragraph (a), no lawyer in a firm with which that lawyer is associated may knowingly undertake or continue representation in the matter unless:

(1) the disqualified lawyer is timely screened from any participation in the matter and is apportioned no part of the fee therefrom; and

(2) written notice is promptly given to the parties and any appropriate tribunal to enable them to ascertain compliance with the provisions of this rule.

(d) An arbitrator selected as a partisan of a party in a multimember arbitration panel is not prohibited from subsequently representing that party.

## COMMENT

[1] This Rule generally parallels Rule 1.11. The term "personally and substantially" signifies that a judge who was a member of a multimember court, and thereafter left judicial office to practice law, is not prohibited from representing a client in a matter pending in the court, but in which the former judge did not participate. So also the fact that a former judge exercised administrative responsibility in a court does

not prevent the former judge from acting as a lawyer in a matter where the judge had previously exercised remote or incidental administrative responsibility that did not affect the merits. Compare the Comment to Rule 1.11. The term "adjudicative officer" includes such officials as judges pro tempore, referees, special masters, hearing officers and other parajudicial officers, and also lawyers who serve as part-time judges. Paragraphs C(2), D(2) and E(2) of the Application Section of the Model Code of Judicial Conduct provide that a part-time judge, judge pro tempore or retired judge recalled to active service, shall not "act as a lawyer in a proceeding in which the judge has served as a judge or in any other proceeding related thereto." Although phrased differently from this Rule, those Rules correspond in meaning.

[2] Like former judges, lawyers who have served as arbitrators, mediators or other third-party neutrals may be asked to represent a client in a matter in which the lawyer participated personally and substantially. This Rule forbids such representation unless all of the parties to the proceedings give their informed consent, confirmed in writing. See Rule 1.0(e) and (b). Other law or codes of ethics governing third-party neutrals may impose more stringent standards of personal or imputed disqualification. See Rule 2.4.

[3] Although lawyers who serve as third-party neutrals do not have information concerning the parties that is protected under Rule 1.6, they typically owe the parties an obligation of confidentiality under law or codes of ethics governing third-party neutrals. Thus, paragraph (c) provides that conflicts of the personally disqualified lawyer will be imputed to other lawyers in a law firm unless the conditions of this paragraph are met.

[4] Requirements for screening procedures are stated in Rule 1.0(k). Paragraph (c)(1) does not prohibit the screened lawyer from receiving a salary or partnership share established by prior independent agreement, but that lawyer may not receive compensation directly related to the matter in which the lawyer is disqualified.

[5] Notice, including a description of the screened lawyer's prior representation and of the screening procedures employed, generally should be given as soon as practicable after the need for screening becomes apparent.

### Definitional Cross-References
"Confirmed in writing" *See* Rule 1.0(b)
"Firm" *See* Rule 1.0(c)
"Informed consent" *See* Rule 1.0(e)
"Knowingly" *See* Rule 1.0(f)
"Screened" *See* Rule 1.0(k)
"Tribunal" *See* Rule 1.0(m)
"Writing" and "Written" *See* Rule 1.0(n)

### State Rules Comparison
http://ambar.org/MRPCStateCharts

## ANNOTATION

### INTRODUCTION: REACH OF RULE

Rule 1.12 sets out the conflicts-of-interest rules for lawyers who have served as or clerked for judges or other adjudicative officers, or who have served as third-party neutrals. The rule thus extends far beyond former judges.

### • *Judges, Adjudicators, Law Clerks*

As first formulated in the predecessor Model Code (DR 9-101(A)), the rule prohibited subsequent representation in a matter in which the lawyer had acted on the merits "in a judicial capacity."

With the adoption of the Model Rules in 1983, the rule was broadened to include personal and substantial participation "as a judge or other adjudicative officer, arbitrator or law clerk to such a person." *See, e.g., Ill. Wood Energy Partners, L.P. v. County of Cook*, 667 N.E.2d 477 (Ill. App. Ct. 1995) (member of zoning board of appeals); *Pappas v. Waggoner's Heating & Air, Inc.*, 108 P.3d 9 (Okla. Civ. App. 2004) (in case of first impression, court construed "judge or other adjudicative officer"—within meaning of state's 1983 version of rule—to include mediators); *State ex rel. Ten S. Mgmt. Co. v. Wilson*, 745 S.E.2d 263 (W. Va. 2013) (hearing officer at administrative review of state human rights commission's "no probable cause" determination acts as adjudicative officer even though complaint's merits not adjudicated; assistant attorney general who served as hearing officer may not then represent complainant before commission); Ariz. Ethics Op. 89-1 (1989) (hearing officer for state agency); Conn. Informal Ethics Op. 99-32 (1999) (part-time judicially appointed state court trial referee must comply with Rule 1.12 as well as applicable canons of Code of Judicial Conduct); Ohio Sup. Ct. Ethics Op. 2017-4 (2017) (former magistrate must comply with Rule 1.12); Utah Ethics Op. 15-01 (2015) (former member or hearing officer of board of pardons); *see also Radford v. Radford*, 371 P.3d 1158 (Okla. Civ. App. 2016) (rule applied to paralegal formerly employed by guardian ad litem who acted as third-party neutral).

### • *Mediators and Other Third-Party Neutrals*

In 2002, in an effort to take into account "a more expansive category of neutrals that participate in court-based and private dispute resolution," the ABA extended Model Rule 1.12 to include mediators and "other third-party neutrals." American Bar Association, *A Legislative History: The Development of the ABA Model Rules of Professional Conduct, 1982–2013*, at 305 (2013). At the same time, the drafters eliminated any references to arbitrators' law clerks, explaining that "arbitrators, like mediators and other third-party neutrals, typically do not have law clerks." *Id.* "Third-party neutral" is defined in paragraph [3] of the Preamble as a nonrepresentational role helping parties resolve a dispute; according to Comment [1] to Rule 2.4, it includes facilitators, evaluators, and decision makers. *See In re Dhillon*, Bankr. No. 10-41700, Adv. No. 11-4015, 2011 WL 3651308, 2011 BL 214489 (Bankr. S.D. Ill. Aug. 18, 2011) (lawyer acted as third-party neutral in facilitating lease of restaurant and therefore disqualified from representing lessors in lessees' bankruptcy).

Under Rule 1.12, a lawyer who has served as a third-party neutral is analogized to a former judge for conflicts purposes. This means that the former third-party neutral's disqualification from a subsequent representation can be cured by the parties' consent. It also means that when a third-party neutral's work in a matter disqualifies him or her from a subsequent representation, the firm is not automatically disqualified. Screening, along with notice, can protect against imputed disqualification. The drafters chose this approach after hearing testimony that third-party neutrals "do not share confidential information with other lawyers in the firm in the same way that lawyers representing clients do." American Bar Association, *A Legislative History: The Development of the ABA Model Rules of Professional Conduct, 1982–2013*, at 306 (2013). *Cf.* Carrie Menkel-Meadow, *The Evolving Complexity of Dispute Resolution Ethics*, 30 Geo. J. Legal Ethics 389 (Summer 2017) (arguing that Rule 1.12 fails to deal with many forms of conflicts of interest that can arise with the use of mediation and arbitration).

Jurisdictions disagree on whether a lawyer-mediator who conducts a domestic relations mediation may then prepare documents for the parties. *See* Ohio Ethics Op. 2009-4 (2009) (surveying authority from other jurisdictions and concluding that lawyer-mediator may prepare documents for one of the parties as long as lawyer did not negotiate to do this at outset of mediation); Tex. Ethics Op. 583 (2008) (lawyer may not agree to mediate divorce settlement and also prepare documents effectuating agreement). This issue is also addressed in the annotation to Rule 2.4 (Lawyer Serving as Third-Party Neutral).

Controversy exists over the decision to group mediators with other kinds of third-party neutrals. *See Moore v. Altra Energy Techs., Inc.*, 295 S.W.3d 404, 407 n.14 (Tex. 2009) (mediation party might not be willing to disclose sensitive information if aware that mediator's law firm could later represent opponent in same dispute; "may be appropriate to reconsider" treating mediators as adjudicatory officials). *See generally* Aron H. Schnur, Note, *I Never Agreed to This! Reconsidering the Inclusion of Attorney-Mediators Under Model Rule 1.12*, 23 Geo. J. Legal Ethics 813 (Summer 2010) (availability of screening under 2009 amendment to Model Rule 1.10 warrants reexamination of decision to evaluate mediators' downstream conflicts under Rule 1.12 rather than more rigorous Rule 1.9).

## • *Judicial Clerks*

Note that court rules governing former judicial clerks may be more restrictive than Rule 1.12. U.S. Supreme Court Rule 7, for example, bars former clerks from participating in any Supreme Court cases for two years and bars them forever from participating in any cases that were pending before the court during clerkship; rules in most courts include similar provisions. *See In re Violation of Rule 50*, 502 F. App'x 981 (Fed. Cir. 2013) (strongly admonishing law firm at which former court clerk provided advice in matter he did not realize was pending during his clerkship; although firm's conflicts committee inadvertently missed it, "the appeal number alone should have raised a red flag"); *cf. Bradley v. State*, 16 P.3d 187 (Alaska Ct. App. 2001) (court's own rule absolutely barred all former law clerks from any participation in cases pending during their clerkships; looking to Rule 1.12, however, court carved out similar exceptions for consent and for lack of personal involvement).

## Paragraph (a): Representation in Same Matter
### WHAT IS A "MATTER"?

Rule 1.12 applies only to representation in connection with the *same* matter in which the lawyer participated as judge, law clerk, or third-party neutral. This is more permissive than the rule on former-client conflicts; under Rule 1.9 (Duties to Former Clients), a lawyer may not represent interests adverse to a former client if the matter is the same *or substantially related. See Durham County v. Richards & Assocs., Inc.*, 742 F.2d 811 (4th Cir. 1984) (dispute about motion to compel arbitration of contractor's claims against owner did not involve same "matter" as prior arbitration of another contractor's damage claims against general contractor on same project; no disqualification of contractor's lawyer even though he arbitrated other contractor's damage claims); *Hossaini v. Vaelizadeh*, No. 4:11CV3502, 2011 WL 3422782, 2011 BL 202753 (D. Neb. Aug. 4, 2011) (lawyer who mediated child custody dispute may represent mother in tort litigation with father arising out of their failed romance; matters had "little in common except for the fact that [the same parties] are involved in both"); *In re Marrone*, Civ. No. 02-9364, 2003 WL 22416375 (E.D. Pa. Oct. 22, 2003) (affirming disqualification of debtor's counsel in bankruptcy proceedings; when serving as bankruptcy judge, counsel assigned two of debtor's "numerous" previous bankruptcies); *Meyer v. Foti*, 720 F. Supp. 1234 (E.D. La. 1989) (no disqualification of firm representing sheriff and his lawyers in suit by federal magistrate; correctness of decisions district court made while two firm members serving as judicial clerks had no bearing upon issues in current suit); *Schultz v. Schultz*, 783 So. 2d 329 (Fla. Dist. Ct. App. 2001) (trial court abused its discretion by disqualifying wife's counsel in divorce solely because retired partner in counsel's firm was appointed arbitrator in shareholder suit against husband and his company; matters were different); *In re Moncus*, 733 S.E.2d 330 (Ga. 2012) (lawyer violated rule by filing motions to terminate probation of three criminal defendants whose probationary sentences he had himself imposed while serving as municipal court judge); *In re W.R.*, 966 N.E.2d 1139 (Ill. App. Ct. 2012) (new trial ordered; per se violation when father's lawyer in juvenile neglect case had three years earlier mediated family court case between parents involving same custody and visitation issues); *James v. Miss. Bar*, 962 So. 2d 528 (Miss. 2007) (lawyer violated Rule 1.12 by representing woman seeking to modify post-divorce child custody order; as chancellor, lawyer signed temporary order regarding husband's visitation rights); *In re Onorevole*, 511 A.2d 1171 (N.J. 1986) (no violation of Rule 1.12(a) when retired administrative law judge who heard budget appeal involving township board of education was later retained as private lawyer by same board to investigate and bring tenure charges against its superintendent); *In re de Brittingham*, 319 S.W.3d 95 (Tex. 2010) (lawyer who as justice had served on appeals court panel affirming two trial court orders in ancillary probate proceeding disqualified from representing relators in mandamus arising from same ancillary proceeding; "matter" not limited to discrete appeal or proceeding); Ala. Ethics Op. 93-04 (1993) (former judge may not represent party in motion related to divorce decree he signed, even if decree based upon waiver and agreement and required minimal judicial participation); N.Y. State Ethics Op. 1064 (2015) (lawyer who served as "emergency judge" in neglect action and issued consent order to put child in foster care may not later represent parent in permanent neglect proceeding, nor may lawyer represent client in child support modification action if her judicial orders relating to custody and visitation will be revisited in current action); S.C. Ethics Op. 93-26 (1993) (former family court judge may not represent party alleging violation of order he entered as judge unless all parties to proceeding consent after disclosure, even though order routine and entered on consent); Utah Ethics Op. 15-01 (2015) (any proceeding before board of pardons involving same offender is same "matter" for purposes of Rules 1.11(a) (2) and 1.12(a)); *cf. Archuleta v. Turley*, 904 F. Supp. 2d 1185 (D. Utah 2012) (prisoner's habeas action in federal court was same matter as his state habeas action on which state's attorney participated as court clerk, notwithstanding state's argument that it was different proceeding before different judge of different sovereign; court denied reconsideration by order dated Jan. 15, 2013).

"Matter" in the more general context of former government employment is discussed in the annotation to Rule 1.11.

## What Is "Personal and Substantial" Participation?

Like Rule 1.11, which regulates conflicts of interest for former and current government officers and employees, Rule 1.12 does not come into play unless participation in the prior matter was "personal and substantial." *See, e.g., Ill. Wood Energy Partners, L.P. v. County of Cook*, 667 N.E.2d 477 (Ill. App. Ct. 1995) (law firm representing plaintiff seeking zoning certificate not disqualified by its "of counsel" lawyer's prior service on zoning board of appeals; lawyer did not participate in any way in plaintiff's application while on board); R.I. Ethics Op. 2007-01 (2007) (former probate judge may represent clients in probate court, but if he participated personally and substantially as judge in matter, he must secure all parties' consent).

Participation on the merits or in settlement discussions is considered personal and substantial. *See, e.g., Monument Builders of Pa., Inc. v. Catholic Cemeteries Ass'n, Inc.*, 190 F.R.D. 164 (E.D. Pa. 1999) (lawyer who, as judicial clerk, "had a hand in construing settlement agreements" in antitrust class action may not, fifteen years later, represent plaintiff in action alleging breach of agreements); *Floyd v. State*, 495 S.W.3d 82 (Ark. 2016) (former judge disqualified from representing criminal defendant; signing affidavit of probable cause for arrest warrant and presiding over plea-and-arraignment hearing constituted substantial participation in case); *In re Hoffman*, 670 N.W.2d 500 (N.D. 2003) ("considering and granting a default divorce constitutes personal and substantial involvement"); Md. Ethics Op. 85-23 (1985) (former judicial clerk who becomes firm member may not participate in matter in which, as clerk, he reviewed motion for default judgment and exceptions to answers to interrogatories and made recommendations to judge); S.C. Ethics Op. 99-06 (1999) (if judge acted on merits, irrelevant that he was incorporating rulings of other judges or approving consent orders); *see also* Ill. Ethics Op. 94-9 (1994) (former judge who advises another lawyer about matter over which he presided while on bench violates Rule 1.12(a) even though judge not compensated and not part of lawyer's firm); N.C. Ethics Op. 2010-8 (2010) (lawyer who consulted with couple about mediating their contemplated separation may not subsequently represent husband in wife's equitable distribution action; even though mediation did not occur, consultation constituted substantial participation); *cf.* Phila. Ethics Op. 2005-4 (2005) (passage of time between service as referee and proposed employment as lawyer is irrelevant to Rule 1.12).

Nominal or ministerial responsibility does not trigger Rule 1.12. *See, e.g., Sec. Gen. Life Ins. Co. v. Superior Court*, 718 P.2d 985 (Ariz. 1986) (former director of Department of Insurance not disqualified by Rule 1.12 from representing insurance company in litigation; no evidence he either acted in adjudicative capacity or participated personally and substantially); *Duncan v. Cropsey*, 437 S.E.2d 787 (Ga. Ct. App. 1993) (refusing to disqualify former supreme court justice from defending lawyer in action for attorneys' fees related to litigation that was appealed to supreme court during former justice's tenure there; supreme court's only action was to transfer case to appellate court); Or. Ethics Op. 2005-120 (rev. 2007) (lawyer "must have done something more than review the status of a matter in court or at docket call or permit the entry of a stipulated order"); Pa. Ethics Op. 2012-23 (2012) (lawyer serving as magisterial district judge may continue to represent grandparents in custody proceeding against parents even though mother appeared before him in eviction court; upon recognizing her he recused himself, and different judge signed order incorporating parties' stipulation); *cf. Comparato v. Schait*, 848 A.2d 770 (N.J. 2004) (former judicial law clerk who calendared motions and performed related ministerial tasks had not participated personally and substantially in matrimonial matter before joining firm representing wife, but court directed her to continue to screen herself anyway). *But see Hamed v. Yusuf*, Civ. Nos. SX–12–CV–370, SX–14–CV–287, SX–14–CV–278, 2018 WL 1320364 (V.I. Super. Ct. Mar. 14, 2018) (although former law clerk's involvement in case consisted of cataloguing motions and general research, her nearly two-year-long participation and exposure to broad range of facts and legal issues "was sufficiently 'personal and substantial'" to warrant disqualification).

## *Paragraph (b): When Judges and Judicial Clerks Negotiate for Employment*

A lawyer participating personally and substantially in a matter as an adjudicator or third-party neutral may not negotiate for employment with the parties or their counsel. *See* Or. Ethics Op. 2009-181 (2009) (hearing officer for state agency does not violate Rule 1.12(b) by "mere submission" of employment application to state's department of justice, which represents state in hearings, or by negotiating for employment with department of justice while it represents state in appealing from his decision).

Rule 1.12(b) makes special provision for judicial clerks, who are expected to be thinking about their employment prospects. Judicial clerks may negotiate for employment even with those involved in a matter in which they are participating personally and substantially, as long as they notify their judges. They are not required to notify others involved in the matter. *See generally* Linda H. Green, *The Spotless Reputation and Federal Law Clerk Employment Negotiations*, 25 U. Mem. L. Rev. 127 (Fall 1994).

## Paragraph (c): Disqualification Imputed
## Unless Lawyer Screened

Rule 1.12(c) imputes any disqualification under Rule 1.12(a) to the lawyer's entire firm, even if the relationship is merely of counsel. ABA Formal Ethics Op. 357 (1990); *see* Ariz. Ethics Op. 16-01 (2016) (lawyer who is "of counsel" to firm is "associated" with firm for purposes of Rule 1.12(c)).

Imputation can be avoided if the disqualified lawyer is screened and receives no part of the fee from the matter, and written notice is given to the parties and to "any appropriate tribunal." (Consent is not required.) *See Parallel Networks, LLC v. Abercrombie & Fitch Co.*, No. 6:10-CV-111, 2016 WL 3883392, 2016 BL 109705 (E.D. Tex. Apr. 1, 2016) (informing plaintiff three weeks after the fact that former judge in matter had joined defendants' team constituted adequate notice); *Am. Tax Funding, LLC v. City of Schenectady*, No. 1:12-CV-1026 (MAD/RFT), 2014 WL 6804297, 2014 BL 338978 (N.D.N.Y. Dec. 2, 2014) (disqualification of lawyer who as law clerk had attended settlement conference not imputed to twenty-lawyer firm that implemented timely and effective screen; opinion discusses how to evaluate screening in small firms); *Monument Builders of Pa., Inc. v. Catholic Cemeteries Ass'n, Inc.*, 190 F.R.D. 164 (E.D. Pa. 1999) (former judicial clerk's disqualification would not be imputed to her firm; she worked primarily from home and promptly notified court of conflict, and firm ready to establish screens); *Foster v. Traul*, 175 P.3d 186 (Idaho 2007) (although former judicial clerk whom defense firm hired worked on court's grant of firm's motion for summary judgment, screening prevented firm's disqualification); *In re Marriage of Thornton*, 486 N.E.2d 1288 (Ill. App. Ct. 1985) (approving procedures used by firm representing husband in divorce action to screen out participation of firm member who, as judge, ruled on wife's discovery requests; firm denied him access to file and refused to allow anyone to talk with him about it); *Ryan's Express Transp. Servs., Inc. v. Amador Stage Lines, Inc.*, 279 P.3d 166 (Nev. 2012) (remanded for hearing into whether law firm adequately screened shareholder who as settlement judge learned confidential information about client's opponent); *Burkhardt v. Kastell*, No. A-2724-17T3, 2018 WL 2921911, 2018 BL 202806 (N.J. Super. Ct. App. Div. June 8, 2018) (reversing disqualification of firm with which parties' former mediator had become affiliated when rule's screening and notice requirements complied with; rejecting lower court's analysis basing disqualification on "appearance of impropriety" and adversary's "discomfort"); *Manditch v. Manditch*, 937 N.Y.S.2d 883 (App. Div. 2012) (abuse of discretion to deny plaintiff's motion to disqualify defense firm in matrimonial action once justice who presided over case became firm partner; opinion notes firm's failure to comply with notice requirements of state's Rule 1.12(d), analogous to Model Rule 1.12(c)); *Pappas v. Waggoner's Heating & Air, Inc.*, 108 P.3d 9 (Okla. Civ. App. 2004) (former mediator's disqualification not imputed to his firm: mediation contract unrelated to firm, mediator maintained separate filing system not available to firm members, firm's litigation file in matter not available to former mediator, and no information would be exchanged); *Hamed v. Yusuf*, Civ. Nos. SX–12–CV–370, SX–14–CV–287, SX–14–CV–278, 2018 WL 1320364 (V.I. Super. Ct. Mar. 14, 2018) (screening procedures in two-member firm were "sufficient to safeguard the public perception of and public trust in the judicial system"); *see also* Rule 1.0(k) (definition of "screened"); *cf.* Cal. Rule 1.12(c)(1) (screening and notice cannot prevent disqualification of entire firm if conflict arose from lawyer's service as mediator or settlement judge).

### Paragraph (d): Partisan Arbitrators on Multimember Arbitration Panels

Service as a party's designee on an arbitration panel does not implicate Rule 1.12. *See Feinberg v. Katz*, No. 01 Civ. 2739(CSH), 2003 WL 260571 (S.D.N.Y. Feb. 5, 2003) (looking to Rule 1.12(d) to deny motion to disqualify defense counsel who served as defendant's appointee on arbitration panel in related matter; "if a partisan arbitrator is not expected to be neutral, he cannot then be acting in a 'judicial capacity'"); *Dobuzinsky v. Middlesex Mut. Assurance Co.*, No. 376243, 1995 WL 574769 (Conn. Super. Ct. Sept. 22, 1995) (in case of first impression, court concluded that plain language of Rule 1.12(d) militated against disqualifying plaintiffs' counsel in action against insurance company; court rejected defense argument that counsel "may have gained an unfair advantage" by having arbitrated plaintiffs' uninsured motorist claim). *See generally* Seth H. Lieberman, *Something's Rotten in the State of Party-Appointed Arbitration: Healing ADR's Black Eye That Is "Nonneutral Neutrals,"* 5 Cardozo J. Conflict Resol. 215 (Spring 2004) ("party-appointed arbitrators" are really "party-appointed advocates").

## Rule 1.13

### *Organization as Client*

(a) A lawyer employed or retained by an organization represents the organization acting through its duly authorized constituents.

(b) If a lawyer for an organization knows that an officer, employee or other person associated with the organization is engaged in action, intends to act or refuses to act in a matter related to the representation that is a violation of a legal obligation to the organization, or a violation of law that reasonably might be imputed to the organization, and that is likely to result in substantial injury to the organization, then the lawyer shall proceed as is reasonably necessary in the best interest of the organization. Unless the lawyer reasonably believes that it is not necessary in the best interest of the organization to do so, the lawyer shall refer the matter to higher authority in the organization, including, if warranted by the circumstances, to the highest authority that can act on behalf of the organization as determined by applicable law.

(c) Except as provided in paragraph (d), if

(1) despite the lawyer's efforts in accordance with paragraph (b) the highest authority that can act on behalf of the organization insists upon or fails to address in a timely and appropriate manner an action or a refusal to act, that is clearly a violation of law; and

(2) the lawyer reasonably believes that the violation is reasonably certain to result in substantial injury to the organization,

then the lawyer may reveal information relating to the representation whether or not Rule 1.6 permits such disclosure, but only if and to the extent the lawyer reasonably believes necessary to prevent substantial injury to the organization.

(d) Paragraph (c) shall not apply with respect to information relating to a lawyer's representation of an organization to investigate an alleged violation of law, or to defend the organization or an officer, employee or other constituent associated with the organization against a claim arising out of an alleged violation of law.

(e) A lawyer who reasonably believes that he or she has been discharged because of the lawyer's actions taken pursuant to paragraphs (b) or (c), or who withdraws under circumstances that require or permit the lawyer to take action under either of those paragraphs, shall proceed as the lawyer reasonably believes necessary to assure that the organization's highest authority is informed of the lawyer's discharge or withdrawal.

(f) In dealing with an organization's directors, officers, employees, members, shareholders or other constituents, a lawyer shall explain the identity of the client when the lawyer knows or reasonably should know that the organization's interests are adverse to those of the constituents with whom the lawyer is dealing.

(g) A lawyer representing an organization may also represent any of its directors, officers, employees, members, shareholders or other constituents, subject to the provisions of Rule 1.7. If the organization's consent to the dual representation is required by Rule 1.7, the consent shall be given by an appropriate official of the organization other than the individual who is to be represented, or by the shareholders.

# COMMENT

## The Entity as the Client

[1] An organizational client is a legal entity, but it cannot act except through its officers, directors, employees, shareholders and other constituents. Officers, directors, employees and shareholders are the constituents of the corporate organizational client. The duties defined in this Comment apply equally to unincorporated associations. "Other constituents" as used in this Comment means the positions equivalent to officers, directors, employees and shareholders held by persons acting for organizational clients that are not corporations.

[2] When one of the constituents of an organizational client communicates with the organization's lawyer in that person's organizational capacity, the communication is protected by Rule 1.6. Thus, by way of example, if an organizational client requests its lawyer to investigate allegations of wrongdoing, interviews made in the course of that investigation between the lawyer and the client's employees or other constituents are covered by Rule 1.6. This does not mean, however, that constituents of an organizational client are the clients of the lawyer. The lawyer may not disclose to such constituents information relating to the representation except for disclosures explicitly or impliedly authorized by the organizational client in order to carry out the representation or as otherwise permitted by Rule 1.6.

[3] When constituents of the organization make decisions for it, the decisions ordinarily must be accepted by the lawyer even if their utility or prudence is doubtful. Decisions concerning policy and operations, including ones entailing serious risk, are not as such in the lawyer's province. Paragraph (b) makes clear, however, that when the lawyer knows that the organization is likely to be substantially injured by action of an officer or other constituent that violates a legal obligation to the organization or is in violation of law that might be imputed to the organization, the lawyer must

proceed as is reasonably necessary in the best interest of the organization. As defined in Rule 1.0(f), knowledge can be inferred from circumstances, and a lawyer cannot ignore the obvious.

[4] In determining how to proceed under paragraph (b), the lawyer should give due consideration to the seriousness of the violation and its consequences, the responsibility in the organization and the apparent motivation of the person involved, the policies of the organization concerning such matters, and any other relevant considerations. Ordinarily, referral to a higher authority would be necessary. In some circumstances, however, it may be appropriate for the lawyer to ask the constituent to reconsider the matter; for example, if the circumstances involve a constituent's innocent misunderstanding of law and subsequent acceptance of the lawyer's advice, the lawyer may reasonably conclude that the best interest of the organization does not require that the matter be referred to higher authority. If a constituent persists in conduct contrary to the lawyer's advice, it will be necessary for the lawyer to take steps to have the matter reviewed by a higher authority in the organization. If the matter is of sufficient seriousness and importance or urgency to the organization, referral to higher authority in the organization may be necessary even if the lawyer has not communicated with the constituent. Any measures taken should, to the extent practicable, minimize the risk of revealing information relating to the representation to persons outside the organization. Even in circumstances where a lawyer is not obligated by Rule 1.13 to proceed, a lawyer may bring to the attention of an organizational client, including its highest authority, matters that the lawyer reasonably believes to be of sufficient importance to warrant doing so in the best interest of the organization.

[5] Paragraph (b) also makes clear that when it is reasonably necessary to enable the organization to address the matter in a timely and appropriate manner, the lawyer must refer the matter to higher authority, including, if warranted by the circumstances, the highest authority that can act on behalf of the organization under applicable law. The organization's highest authority to whom a matter may be referred ordinarily will be the board of directors or similar governing body. However, applicable law may prescribe that under certain conditions the highest authority reposes elsewhere, for example, in the independent directors of a corporation.

## Relation to Other Rules

[6] The authority and responsibility provided in this Rule are concurrent with the authority and responsibility provided in other Rules. In particular, this Rule does not limit or expand the lawyer's responsibility under Rules 1.8, 1.16, 3.3 or 4.1. Paragraph (c) of this Rule supplements Rule 1.6(b) by providing an additional basis upon which the lawyer may reveal information relating to the representation, but does not modify, restrict, or limit the provisions of Rule 1.6(b)(1)–(6). Under paragraph (c) the lawyer may reveal such information only when the organization's highest authority insists upon or fails to address threatened or ongoing action that is clearly a violation of law, and then only to the extent the lawyer reasonably believes necessary to prevent reasonably certain substantial injury to the organization. It is not necessary that the lawyer's services be used in furtherance of the violation, but

it is required that the matter be related to the lawyer's representation of the organization. If the lawyer's services are being used by an organization to further a crime or fraud by the organization, Rules 1.6(b)(2) and 1.6(b)(3) may permit the lawyer to disclose confidential information. In such circumstances Rule 1.2(d) may also be applicable, in which event, withdrawal from the representation under Rule 1.16(a)(1) may be required.

[7] Paragraph (d) makes clear that the authority of a lawyer to disclose information relating to a representation in circumstances described in paragraph (c) does not apply with respect to information relating to a lawyer's engagement by an organization to investigate an alleged violation of law or to defend the organization or an officer, employee or other person associated with the organization against a claim arising out of an alleged violation of law. This is necessary in order to enable organizational clients to enjoy the full benefits of legal counsel in conducting an investigation or defending against a claim.

[8] A lawyer who reasonably believes that he or she has been discharged because of the lawyer's actions taken pursuant to paragraph (b) or (c), or who withdraws in circumstances that require or permit the lawyer to take action under either of these paragraphs, must proceed as the lawyer reasonably believes necessary to assure that the organization's highest authority is informed of the lawyer's discharge or withdrawal.

### Government Agency

[9] The duty defined in this Rule applies to governmental organizations. Defining precisely the identity of the client and prescribing the resulting obligations of such lawyers may be more difficult in the government context and is a matter beyond the scope of these Rules. See Scope [18]. Although in some circumstances the client may be a specific agency, it may also be a branch of government, such as the executive branch, or the government as a whole. For example, if the action or failure to act involves the head of a bureau, either the department of which the bureau is a part or the relevant branch of government may be the client for purposes of this Rule. Moreover, in a matter involving the conduct of government officials, a government lawyer may have authority under applicable law to question such conduct more extensively than that of a lawyer for a private organization in similar circumstances. Thus, when the client is a governmental organization, a different balance may be appropriate between maintaining confidentiality and assuring that the wrongful act is prevented or rectified, for public business is involved. In addition, duties of lawyers employed by the government or lawyers in military service may be defined by statutes and regulation. This Rule does not limit that authority. See Scope.

### Clarifying the Lawyer's Role

[10] There are times when the organization's interest may be or become adverse to those of one or more of its constituents. In such circumstances the lawyer should advise any constituent, whose interest the lawyer finds adverse to that of the organization of the conflict or potential conflict of interest, that the lawyer cannot represent such constituent, and that such person may wish to obtain independent representa-

tion. Care must be taken to assure that the individual understands that, when there is such adversity of interest, the lawyer for the organization cannot provide legal representation for that constituent individual, and that discussions between the lawyer for the organization and the individual may not be privileged.

[11] Whether such a warning should be given by the lawyer for the organization to any constituent individual may turn on the facts of each case.

## Dual Representation

[12] Paragraph (g) recognizes that a lawyer for an organization may also represent a principal officer or major shareholder.

## Derivative Actions

[13] Under generally prevailing law, the shareholders or members of a corporation may bring suit to compel the directors to perform their legal obligations in the supervision of the organization. Members of unincorporated associations have essentially the same right. Such an action may be brought nominally by the organization, but usually is, in fact, a legal controversy over management of the organization.

[14] The question can arise whether counsel for the organization may defend such an action. The proposition that the organization is the lawyer's client does not alone resolve the issue. Most derivative actions are a normal incident of an organization's affairs, to be defended by the organization's lawyer like any other suit. However, if the claim involves serious charges of wrongdoing by those in control of the organization, a conflict may arise between the lawyer's duty to the organization and the lawyer's relationship with the board. In those circumstances, Rule 1.7 governs who should represent the directors and the organization.

### Definitional Cross-References
"Knows" *See* Rule 1.0(f)
"Reasonably" *See* Rule 1.0(h)
"Reasonably believes" *See* Rule 1.0(i)
"Reasonably should know" *See* Rule 1.0(j)
"Substantial" *See* Rule 1.0(l)

### State Rules Comparison
http://ambar.org/MRPCStateCharts

# ANNOTATION

In many ways, representing an entity can be the most conceptually complex area of professional responsibility. It is fitting, then, that the corresponding Model Rule—Rule 1.13—is both complex and detailed. In terms of sheer length, for example, it is the third-longest rule (trailing narrowly behind Rule 1.8 and Rule 3.8), and it covers a diverse range of issues, including the lawyer's role, internal fraud and investigations, "noisy" withdrawal, and dual representation.

## *Paragraph (a): Organization Is Client*
### LAWYER REPRESENTS ORGANIZATION

Unless a lawyer has also formed a lawyer-client relationship with a constituent, Rule 1.13 clarifies that a lawyer employed or retained by an organization represents the organization itself, not the individual constituents who act for it. Thus, the Model Rules embrace the "entity theory" of organizational representation. Rule 1.13(a); *accord Restatement (Third) of the Law Governing Lawyers* § 96(1) cmt. b (2000) ("The so-called 'entity' theory of organizational representation . . . is now universally recognized in American law, for purposes of determining the identity of the direct beneficiary of legal representation of corporations and other forms of organizations."); *see also Murray v. Metro. Life Ins. Co.,* 583 F.3d 173 (2d Cir. 2009) (lawyer for mutual insurance company represents entity, not policyholders); ABA Formal Ethics Op. 08-453 (2008) (law firm's ethics counsel typically represents firm itself, not individual lawyers within firm); Alaska Ethics Op. 2012-3 (2012) (lawyer for corporation not lawyer for constituents without more); Colo. Ethics Op. 120 (2008) (organization's lawyer does not automatically represent its constituents); N.J. Ethics Op. 664 (1992) (lawyer who represents corporation in collections matters has lawyer-client relationship with corporation, not with corporation's credit manager). *See generally* 3 Ronald E. Mallen & Jeffrey M. Smith, *Legal Malpractice* § 26:5 (2009) (discussing potential conflicts of entity lawyer in numerous contexts, including corporate formation, closely held corporations, and shareholder derivative actions); D. Ryan Nayar, *Almost Clients: A Closer Look at Attorney Responsibility in the Context of Entity Representation,* 41 Tex. J. Bus. L. 313 (Winter 2006); Ellen A. Pansky, *Between an Ethical Rock and Hard Place: Balancing Duties to the Organizational Client and Its Constituents,* 37 S. Tex. L. Rev. 1167 (Oct. 1996); George Rutherglen, *Lawyer for the Organization: An Essay on Legal Ethics,* 1 Va. L. & Bus. Rev. 141 (Fall 2006); Joan C. Rogers, "Corporate Lawyers Must Take Steps to Minimize Client Identity Problems," *ABA/BNA Lawyers' Manual on Professional Conduct,* 29 Law. Man. Prof. Conduct 624 (Current Reports, Sept. 25, 2013); William H. Simon, *Whom (or What) Does the Organization's Lawyer Represent? An Anatomy of Intraclient Conflict,* 91 Cal. L. Rev. 57 (Jan. 2003).

Even if an organization's lawyer does not represent a particular constituent, the lawyer may have authority under Rule 4.2 to prevent another lawyer from communicating with the constituent about specific matters. This is discussed in the annotation to Model Rule 4.2 (Communication with Person Represented by Counsel).

### • *Closely Held Corporations*

Although closely held corporations often look and feel quite distinct from widely held corporations, the entity-representation rule usually applies to closely held corporations just as it does to widely held corporations. *See Kirsch v. Dean,* No. 3:16-CV-00299-CRS, 2016 WL 7177765 (W.D. Ky. Dec. 7, 2016) (two 50 percent owners; only corporation was client); *Concordia Partners, LLC v. Ward,* No. 2:12-cv-138-GZS, 2012 WL 3229300, 2012 BL 438471 (D. Me. Aug. 6, 2012) (lawyer for corporation not lawyer for controlling officer, who was member of family who owned it); *Clemente v. Martinelli,* 102 N.E.3d 1030 (Mass. App. Ct. 2018) (lawyer for corporation not lawyer for an owner and director); *Oram v. 6 B's, Inc.*, No. 332925, 2018 WL 442213, 2018 BL 14335 (Mich. Ct. App. Jan. 16, 2018) (lawyer for one member of LLC not necessarily lawyer for LLC); Ariz. Ethics Op. 2002-06 (2002) (lawyer retained to form new corporation may limit representation to corporation and not represent its incorporating constituents, provided constituents consent after lawyer makes appropriate disclosures); D.C. Ethics Op. 216 (1991) (corporation's lawyer may represent corporation against one of two 50 percent shareholders, as long as lawyer acts consistently with corporation's interests); R.I. Ethics Op. 2005-10 (2005) (lawyers who represented corporation in obtaining permits for real estate development may later represent company to which real estate was sold in connection with same permits, even though two principals/shareholders of first corporation objected to selling real estate; former client was corporation, not constituents, and new representation not adverse to corporation's interests); *see also Ky. Bar Ass'n v. Hines*, 399 S.W.3d 750 (Ky. 2013) (corporation's lawyer violated Rule 1.13(a) by assisting minority shareholders in filing suit on behalf of corporation, against wishes of majority of board); Or. Ethics Op. 2005-85 (2005) (lawyer for corporation with two stockholders who are not in same family does not automatically represent stockholders as individuals as well, nor does lawyer who represents two unrelated stockholders automatically represent their corporation); *cf. Razin v. A Milestone, LLC*, 67 So. 3d 391 (Fla. Dist. Ct. App. 2011) (lawyer not disqualified from representing LLC in lawsuit even though managing member of LLC who retained him was the one suing organization; operating documents authorized managing member to retain counsel for LLC).

That said, it is not uncommon in closely held corporations for (1) a constituent's interests to be essentially identical to the corporation's interests or (2) the constituent to rely upon the corporation's lawyer for personal legal services. In such situations, the entity's lawyer can—even unwittingly—become the individual's lawyer as well. *See Quatama Park Townhomes Owners Ass'n, v. RBC Real Estate Fin., Inc.*, No. 3:18-cv-00023-SB, 2018 WL 3689902, 2018 BL 277939 (D. Or. Aug. 3, 2018) (totality of circumstances rendered directors' belief that they were clients not unreasonable); *Philin Corp. v. Westhood, Inc.*, No. CV-04-1228-HU, 2005 WL 582695 (D. Or. Mar. 11, 2005) (interests of closely held family corporation and shareholder sufficiently identical to warrant disqualification of law firm representing party adverse to corporation, given that firm lawyer consulted with shareholder in same matter); *United States v. Edwards*, 39 F. Supp. 2d 716 (M.D. La. 1999) (lawyer for close corporation established to obtain riverboat gambling license had lawyer-client relationship with corporation's sole shareholder because their interests identical and shareholder reasonably expected lawyer-client relationship existed; factors include whether lawyer ever represented shareholder in individual matters, whether lawyer's services billed to and paid by corporation, whether shareholders treat corporation as corporation or partnership, and whether shareholder reasonably believes lawyer acts as shareholder's individual lawyer); *Luce v. Alcox*, 848 N.E.2d 552 (Ohio Ct. App. 2006) (minority shareholder in closely held corporation who brought suit on behalf of corporation against majority shareholder deemed to have been in lawyer-client relationship with corporation's lawyers, who were now representing majority shareholder); *First Republic Bank v. Brand*, 51 Pa. D. & C.4th 167 (Pa. C.P. 2001) (creating ten-factor test to determine whether close corporation's lawyer and corporate shareholder in implied attorney-client relationship). *See generally* Darian M. Ibrahim, *Solving the Everyday Problem of Client Identity in the Context of Closely Held Businesses*, 56 Ala. L. Rev. 181 (Fall 2004); Lawrence E. Mitchell, *Professional Responsibility and the Close Corporation: Toward a Realistic Ethic*, 74 Cornell L. Rev. 466 (Mar. 1989); Bryan J. Pechersky, Note, *Representing General Partnerships and Close Corporations: A Situational Analysis of Professional Responsibility*, 73 Tex. L. Rev. 919 (Mar. 1995).

## • Corporate Families

By representing one entity the lawyer does not thereby become the lawyer for affiliated entities. Rule 1.7, cmt. [34] ("A lawyer who represents a corporation or other organization does not, by virtue of that representation, necessarily represent any constituent or affiliated organization, such as a parent or subsidiary."); *see also* ABA Formal Ethics Op. 95-390 (1995) ("A lawyer who represents a corporate client is not by that fact alone necessarily barred from a representation that is adverse to a corporate affiliate of that client in an unrelated matter."). This general rule, however, will give way whenever there is (1) an agreement to the contrary, (2) substantial organizational overlap, or (3) shared confidential information. Rule 1.7, cmt. [34] (lawyer may need client consent for, or be barred from, representation adverse to affiliate when "the circumstances are such that the affiliate should also be considered a client of the lawyer, there is an understanding between the lawyer and the organizational client that the lawyer will avoid representation adverse to the client's affiliates, or the lawyer's obligations to either the organizational client or the new client are likely to limit materially the lawyer's representation of the other client"); *see also GSI Commerce Solutions, Inc. v. BabyCenter, LLC*, 618 F.3d 204 (2d Cir. 2010) (lawyers for parent company disqualified from representation adverse to subsidiary in light of financial interdependence and "substantial operational commonality" between parent and subsidiary, including wholly owned status of subsidiary, shared in-house legal department and other services, such as accounting and human resources, and management overlap); *Boynton Beach Firefighters' Pension Fund v. HCP, Inc.*, No. 3:16-cv-1106, 2017 WL 5759361, 2017 BL 425053 (N.D. Ohio Nov. 28, 2017) (no disqualification); *Atlantic Specialty Ins. Co. v. Premera Blue Cross*, No. C15-1927-TSZ, 2016 WL 1615430, 2016 BL 129407 (W.D. Wash. Apr. 22, 2016) (because of shared insurance claims handling, firm disqualified); *Lennar Mare, LLC v. Steadfast Ins. Co.*, 105 F. Supp. 3d 1100 (E.D. Cal. 2015) (entities too close, firm disqualified); *HLP Props., LLC v. Consol. Edison Co. of N.Y., Inc.*, No. 14 Civ. 01383 (LGS), 2014 WL 5285926, 2014 BL 289700 (S.D.N.Y. Oct. 16, 2014) (law firm represented parent while suing subsidiary; although parent and subsidiary were one for conflicts purposes, court denied disqualification because prejudice to client outweighed harm to parent); *Standard Ret. Servs., Inc. v. Ky. Bancshares, Inc.*, No. 5:14-026-DCR, 2014 WL 4783016, 2014 BL 267266 (E.D. Ky. Sept. 24, 2014) (lawyer representing one subsidiary of parent not disqualified from opposing another subsidiary of that same parent by virtue of that relationship alone); N.Y. City Ethics Op. 2007-3 (2007) (explaining relevant factors to discern "whether the affiliate is de facto a current client"); Pa. Ethics Op. 01-62 (2001) (representation of multiple franchisees of franchisor in connection with advice on leases poses no apparent Rule 1.7 conflict). *See generally*

3 Ronald E. Mallen & Jeffrey M. Smith, *Legal Malpractice* § 26:5 (2009) (discussing cases and ethics opinions in parent-subsidiary context); Darian Ibrahim, *Solving the Everyday Problem of Client Identity in the Context of Closely Held Businesses*, 56 Ala. L. Rev. 181 (Fall 2004); Michael Sacksteder, *Formal Opinion 95-390 of the ABA's Ethics Committee: Corporate Clients, Conflicts of Interest, and Keeping the Lid on Pandora's Box*, 91 Nw. U. L. Rev. 741 (Winter 1997); John Steele, *Corporate Affiliate Conflicts: A Reasonable Expectations Test*, 29 W. St. U. L. Rev. 283 (Spring 2002); Charles W. Wolfram, *Corporate-Family Conflicts*, 2 J. Inst. for Study Legal Ethics 295 (1999).

## • *Corporate Restructuring*

In corporate mergers, asset transfers, and other changes in corporate structure, whether the lawyer-client relationship transfers along with the ownership of the corporation depends upon the nature of the transaction. *See generally* Henry Sill Bryans, *Business Successors and the Transpositional Attorney-Client Relationship*, 64 Bus. Law. 1039 (Aug. 2009).

## ORGANIZATIONS OTHER THAN CORPORATIONS

### • *Partnerships*

A lawyer for a partnership does not automatically represent the partners individually. *See Hopper v. Frank*, 16 F.3d 92 (5th Cir. 1994) (lawyer hired by individual partners to assist in sale of limited partnership assets had lawyer-client relationship with partnership alone rather than with partners; "there is no logical reason to distinguish partnerships from corporations or other legal entities in determining the client the lawyer represents"); *Eurycleia Partners, LP v. Seward & Kissel, LLP*, 910 N.E.2d 976 (N.Y. 2009) (lawyer for limited partnership does not owe fiduciary duty to individual limited partners); *Minor v. Combo Stores Co.*, 937 N.Y.S.2d 272 (App. Div. 2012) (lawyer who had represented individual not disqualified from later representing party against partnerships that individual managed); *Vanderschaaf v. Bishara*, No. M2017-00412-COA-R3-CV, 2018 WL 4677455, 2018 BL 354162 (Tenn. Ct. App. Sept. 28, 2018) (lawyer for two-person partnership not lawyer for one of the partners); ABA Formal Ethics Op. 91-361 (1991) (lawyer for partnership represents entity, not individual partners, unless specific circumstances indicate otherwise); Ill. Ethics Op. 13-02 (2013) (lawyer for partnership not, without more, lawyer for partners; when lawyer represents partnership and partners, lawyer may not take a side in dispute among them); Md. Ethics Op. 95-54 (1995) (lawyer for limited partnership, hired by general partner who is removed and contests removal, may continue representation when requested by new, disputed general partner; lawyer represents partnership, not individual constituent); Or. Ethics Op. 2005-85 (2005) (lawyer who represents partnership with two owners who are not related does not automatically also represent owners as individuals, nor does lawyer who represents two unrelated owners automatically represent their partnership).

But as with counsel for a closely held corporation, counsel for the partnership can easily become an individual partner's lawyer as well, whether intentionally or not. *See, e.g., Responsible Citizens v. Superior Court*, 20 Cal. Rptr. 2d 756 (Ct. App. 1993) (factors to consider include type and size of partnership, nature and scope of lawyer's engagement by partnership, kind and extent of contacts between lawyer and individual partner, and lawyer's access to information relating to partner's interests); *Rice v. Strunk*, 670 N.E.2d 1280 (Ind. 1996) (if partnership structured so its business is managed by "an aggregation of the general partners," lawyer-client relationship exists between partnership's lawyer and each general partner, but if management placed in hands of fewer than all partners, lawyer represents only partnership; other circumstances may also create lawyer-client relationship with individual partners). *See generally* James M. Fischer, *Representing Partnerships: Who Is/Are the Client(s)?*, 26 Pac. L.J. 961 (July 1995).

• *Governmental Organizations*

Precisely defining the identity of a governmental client can be difficult; as Comment [9] notes, depending upon the circumstances, the client may be a specific agency, a branch of government, or "the government as a whole." Ultimately, the question is one of law. N.Y. City Ethics Op. 2004-03 (2004) (who is governmental client, and whether government lawyer may represent more than one agency, is more dependent on facts and law than on ethics rules); *see, e.g., Brown & Williamson Tobacco Corp. v. Pataki*, 152 F. Supp. 2d 276 (S.D.N.Y. 2001) (law firm that represented limited number of state agencies on limited number of issues under contract with state budget department did not represent state government as a whole); *Salt Lake Cnty. Comm'n v. Salt Lake Cnty. Att'y*, 985 P.2d 899 (Utah 1999) (county lawyer had lawyer-client relationship with county as entity and not with commission or individual commissioners); ABA Formal Ethics Op. 97-405 (1997) (discussing how to identify government client for conflicts purposes); Cal. Formal Ethics Op. 2001-156 (2001) (city lawyer generally represents municipal corporate entity acting through its constituent subentities and officials; if city charter does not give constituent parts of city government any authority to act independently of city, city lawyer does not represent constituent subentities and officials separately); Conn. Informal Ethics Op. 03-01 (2003) (city corporation counsel may represent city in civil lawsuit filed by city employee concerning employee's transfer to another department, even though employee sometimes appears as witness for city in property code enforcement proceedings); Mass. Ethics Op. 03-01 (2003) (lawyer for municipality who advised department head in his official capacity at deposition in suit between two private parties may represent municipality in unrelated lawsuit brought by department head after his departure from municipal employment, and may introduce deposition testimony to impeach him; department head could not have reasonably assumed lawyer had been representing him personally); R.I. Ethics Op. 2002-02 (2002) (municipal lawyer must comply with municipal council's request for redacted itemized statement of prior bills; lawyer may not comply with individual council member's request for unredacted bills unless council, which is client, consents); *see also Restatement (Third) of the Law Governing Lawyers* § 97 cmt. c (2000) (relevant factors include terms of retention or other manifestations of reasonable understanding, anticipated scope and nature of lawyer's services, particular regulatory arrangements relevant to lawyer's work, and history and traditions of office); *cf.* D.C. Rule 1.6(k) ("The client of the government lawyer is the agency that employs the lawyer unless expressly provided to the contrary by appropriate law, regulation, or order."). *See generally* Elisa E. Ugarte, *The Government Lawyer and the Common Good*, 40 S. Tex. L. Rev. 269 (Spring 1999); Note, *Government Counsel and Their Obligations*, 121 Harv. L. Rev. 1409 (Mar. 2008); Note, *Rethinking the Professional Responsibility of Federal Agency Lawyers*, 115 Harv. L. Rev. 1170 (Feb. 2002).

- *Other Types of Associations*

Similarly, lawyers for other types of entities do not necessarily represent the constituents. *See, e.g., United States v. Int'l Bhd. of Teamsters*, 119 F.3d 210 (2d Cir. 1997) (lawyer for campaign organization of candidate for union president did not represent campaign manager who consulted him about alleged campaign contribution violations); *Integrity Nat'l Corp. v. DSS Servs., Inc.*, No. PWG-17-160, 2017 WL 2812807, 2017 BL 225148 (D. Md. June 29, 2017) (lawyer represented joint venture, not constituent firms); *Killion v. Coffey*, No. 13-1808-RMB-KMW, 2014 WL 2931327, 2014 BL 181351 (D.N.J. June 30, 2014) (lawyer who had legal services agreement with police officers' union did not represent union members for whom he provided no legal services); *Frey v. City of Hoboken*, No. A-2918-15T4, 2018 WL 3468165, 2018 BL 256096 (N.J. Super. Ct. App. Div. July 19, 2018) (law firm for union not law firm for members); ABA Formal Ethics Op. 92-365 (1992) (trade association's lawyer does not automatically represent individual members, although circumstances in particular instance may support finding that lawyer-client relationship with individual member has arisen; identifying factors for consideration); D.C. Ethics Op. 305 (2001) (lawyer for trade association generally not prohibited from representing association or another client in matter adverse to member of association, unless circumstances support member's expectation of lawyer-client relationship); Or. Ethics Op. 2005-27 (2005) (lawyer for trade association may also represent one association member against another member, who is not present or former client, in matter unrelated to lawyer's representation of association). *See generally* Robert R. Keatinge, *The Implications of Fiduciary Relationships in Representing Limited Liability Companies and Other Unincorporated Associations and Their Partners or Members*, 25 Stetson L. Rev. 389 (Winter 1995); Susan P. Koniak & George M. Cohen, *In Hell There Will Be Lawyers Without Clients or Law*, 30 Hofstra L. Rev. 129 (Fall 2001) (discussing indeterminate obligations of class counsel).

The nature of some unincorporated associations, however, may be such that the interests of the entity cannot be distinguished from the interests of the individual constituents. In that circumstance, courts are likely to find that the entity's lawyer represents the individual constituents as well. *See, e.g., City of Kalamazoo v. Mich. Disposal Serv.*, 151 F. Supp. 2d 913 (W.D. Mich. 2001) (lawyer-client relationship existed between individual defendant in environmental litigation and lawyer who also served as common counsel for all defendants under joint-defense agreement; defense group existed solely to represent individual members' interests in litigation); *Al-Yusr Townsend & Bottum Co. v. United Mid-East Co.*, Civ. No. 95-1168, 1995 WL 592548 (E.D. Pa. Oct. 4, 1995) (interests of individual members of joint venture "so intertwined" with those of joint venture that court compelled to conclude venture's lawyer had lawyer-client relationship with each co-venturer); *Franklin v. Callum*, 804 A.2d 444 (N.H. 2002) (lawyer who performs legal work for unincorporated waste disposal project that has no independent legal status separate from its member districts represents each district as well as project).

## Confidentiality Issues between Organization and Constituents

The ethical duty of confidentiality typically runs to the organization itself rather than to any of its constituents. *See, e.g.,* N.J. Ethics Op. 664 (1992) (when corporation's credit manager told corporation's lawyer about corporation's criminal and fraudulent activities, lawyer's duty was to disclose allegations to president and directors and keep allegations confidential from disclosure to others; client was corporation, not employee); R.I. Ethics Op. 2003-04 (2003) (lawyer representing unincorporated condominium association and seeking to withdraw from representation—because board breached its contract with him and consistently failed to accept his legal advice—may not tell individual unit owners why he is seeking to withdraw). *But see Restatement (Third) of the Law Governing Lawyers* § 131 cmt. e (2000) (lawyer may be prohibited from sharing confidential information with entity-employer if that information obtained from constituent who "reasonably appeared to be consulting the lawyer as present or prospective client with respect to the person's individual interests, and the lawyer failed to warn the associated person that the lawyer represents only the organization and could act against the person's interests as a result").

As a general matter, the corporate attorney-client privilege similarly belongs to the corporation, not its constituents. Because the privilege is beyond the scope of this annotation, however, see the following sources for discussion: *ABA/BNA Lawyers' Manual on Professional Conduct,* "Types of Practice: Corporate: Privilege/Confidentiality," pp. 91:2201 *et seq.;* Gary H. Collins & David Z. Seide, *Warning the Witness: A Guide to Internal Investigations and the Attorney-Client Privilege* (2010); Edna Selan Epstein, *The Attorney-Client Privilege and the Work-Product Doctrine* (5th ed. 2007).

## In-House Lawyers: Lawyers Who Are Also Employees or Shareholders

In-house counsel are not only an entity's lawyers but also its employees, and possibly its shareholders as well. When an in-house lawyer asserts a claim against the entity, the ethical constraints attending the lawyer's role as counsel—particularly the duty of confidentiality—can make the claim difficult to pursue. Courts have taken both supportive and unsupportive views of such claims. *See, e.g., Van Asdale v. Int'l Game Tech.,* 577 F.3d 989 (9th Cir. 2009) (in-house counsel may pursue whistleblower action under Sarbanes-Oxley Act; any resulting risks to attorney-client confidentiality or privilege can be adequately addressed by court's equitable powers, such as protective orders or in camera proceedings); *Heckman v. Zurich Holding Co. of Am.,* 242 F.R.D. 606 (D. Kan. 2007) (in-house counsel may pursue whistleblower claim under Kansas law; court granted motion for protective order for corporation's confidential information, but denied request for selective waiver protection of corporation's attorney-client privilege); *Gen. Dynamics Corp. v. Superior Court,* 876 P.2d 487 (Cal. 1994) (in-house counsel may pursue retaliatory discharge claim if possible to do so without breaching attorney-client privilege); *Balla v. Gambro, Inc.,* 584 N.E.2d 104 (Ill. 1991) (disallowing in-house "whistleblower" lawyer's claim for retaliatory discharge; permitting such claims would have chilling effect on communications between lawyer and employer/client); *Burkhart v. Semitool, Inc.*, 5 P.3d 1031 (Mont. 2000) (in-house counsel may reveal confidential information when necessary to establish wrongful discharge claim); *Tartaglia v. UBS PaineWebber Inc.*, 961 A.2d 1167 (N.J. 2008) (former in-house counsel has common-law cause of action for wrongful discharge because she was allegedly fired for complaining about company policy that forced her to violate ethics rule concerning conflicts of interest, which is expression of state public policy); *Mancheski v. Gabelli Grp. Capital Partners, Inc.*, 802 N.Y.S.2d 473 (App. Div. 2005) (although former corporate counsel and his law firm were disqualified from representing shareholders against corporation, former corporate counsel is not himself precluded from suing corporation in his capacity as shareholder, notwithstanding his duty to preserve corporation's confidences and secrets); *Crews v. Buckman Labs. Int'l, Inc.*, 78 S.W.3d 852 (Tenn. 2002) (in-house counsel may bring retaliatory discharge action against former employer and may disclose employer-client's confidences to extent necessary to establish claim); ABA Formal Ethics Op. 01-424 (2001) ("The Model Rules do not prevent an in-house lawyer from pursuing a suit for retaliatory discharge when a lawyer was discharged for complying with her ethical obligations. . . . The lawyer must take reasonable affirmative steps, however, to avoid unnecessary disclosure and limit the information revealed."). *See generally* S.C. Ethics Op. 06-12 (2006) (in-house counsel whose professional independence is unethically infringed by nonlawyer supervisor may need to raise issue with higher authority pursuant to Rule 1.13(b)); Susanna M. Kim, *Dual Identities and Dueling Obligations: Preserving Independence in Corporate Representation*, 68 Tenn. L. Rev. 179 (Winter 2001); Rachel S. Richman, *A Cause Worth Quitting For? The Conflict Between Professional Ethics and Individual Rights in Discriminatory Treatment of Corporate Counsel*, 75 Ind. L.J. 963 (Summer 2000); Sally R. Weaver, *Ethical Dilemmas of Corporate Counsel: A Structural and Contextual Analysis*, 46 Emory L.J. 1023 (Summer 1997).

## Paragraph (b): Actions Inconsistent with Organization's Interests

### 2003 AMENDMENTS

Rule 1.13(b) was amended in 2003, following the release of a report by the ABA Task Force on Corporate Responsibility (available at 59 Bus. Law. 145 (Nov. 2003)) and the promulgation of new regulations by the Securities and Exchange Commission (SEC). *See generally* Lawrence A. Hamermesh, *The ABA Task Force on Corporate Responsibility and the 2003 Changes to the Model Rules of Professional Conduct*, 17 Geo. J. Legal Ethics 35 (Fall 2003). These changes respond to the challenges highlighted by—but by no means limited to—the corporate scandals of the Enron era. *See generally In re Enron Corp.*, 235 F. Supp. 2d 549 (S.D. Tex. 2002) (lawyers for Enron who co-authored misleading financial reports could be responsible for securities violations as principal violators); Thomas D. Morgan, *Lawyer Law: Comparing the ABA Model Rules of Professional Conduct with the ALI Restatement (Third) of the Law Governing Lawyers* 168 (2005) ("Few issues have been more challenging for lawyers over the years, and few

have involved potentially greater liability for the lawyer who sees serious misconduct by a constituent official and fails to act in the best interests of the organizational
client."); Milton C. Regan, Jr., *Teaching Enron*, 74 Fordham L. Rev. 1139 (Dec. 2005).

The most significant change to Rule 1.13 is the creation of a new exception to
the lawyer's duty of confidentiality. In limited circumstances, the amended rule
permits—though does not require—a lawyer to go outside the organization with
information relating to misconduct by a constituent that is likely to cause substantial harm to the organization. *See* American Bar Association, *A Legislative History:
The Development of the ABA Model Rules of Professional Conduct, 1982–2013*, at 326–31
(2013). Also in 2003, the ABA made analogous amendments to the confidentiality
obligation of Rule 1.6, which are discussed in the annotation to Rule 1.6 (paragraphs
(b)(2)–(3)).

## WHEN CONSTITUENT'S CONDUCT
## LIKELY TO HARM ORGANIZATION

Under Rule 1.13(b), when a lawyer for an organization "knows" a constituent of
the organization is engaged in improper conduct likely to result in substantial harm
to the organization, the lawyer must proceed "as is reasonably necessary in the best
interest of the organization." *See* Rule 1.0(f) (defining "knows" as denoting "actual
knowledge of the fact in question" that may be "inferred from circumstances"); Rule
1.13, cmt. [3] ("knowledge can be inferred from circumstances, and a lawyer cannot
ignore the obvious"). Rule 1.13(b) is, in a sense, a specific application of the lawyer's
duties of competence, diligence, and communication to the organizational context.
*See, e.g., Restatement (Third) of the Law Governing Lawyers* § 96 cmt. e (2000) ("A lawyer
is . . . required to act diligently and to exercise care by taking steps to prevent reasonably foreseeable harm to a client. Thus, [the *Restatement*, like Rule 1.13(b),] requires a
lawyer to take action to protect the interests of the client organization with respect to
certain breaches of legal duty to the organization by a constituent.").

Rule 1.13(b) identifies two kinds of constituent misconduct that can trigger this
duty to act: a violation of a legal obligation to the organization, or a violation of law
that reasonably might be imputed to the organization. *See In re Harding*, 223 P.3d 303
(Kan. 2010) (city attorney violated Rule 1.13 by failing to act in best interests of city
when faced with misconduct, failing to refer matter to city's highest authority, and
failing to advise high-level city officials that attorney's representation of city might
be adverse to their interests); *In re DeMers*, 901 N.Y.S.2d 858 (App. Div. 2010) (disciplining zoning board's lawyer for violating Rule 1.13(b) by failing to take action in
response to board's continuing violations of state law); *see also* Rule 1.13, cmt. [4] (in
determining how to proceed when learning of violation, lawyer should consider seriousness of violation and its consequences, responsibility in organization and apparent motivation of person involved, and organizational policies); *Restatement (Third)
of the Law Governing Lawyers* § 96 cmt. f (2000) (lawyer should assess "the degree and
imminence of threatened financial, reputational, and other harms to the organization; the probable results of litigation that might ensue against the organization or
for which it would be financially responsible; the costs of taking measures within the
organization to prevent or correct the harm; the likely efficaciousness of measures

that might be taken; and similar considerations"); *Restatement (Third) of the Law Governing Lawyers* § 97 cmt. j (2000) (with respect to governmental client, lawyer may need to consider potential public and private injury, including injury to public interest in integrity of government and to nonproprietary rights, such as deprivations of right to vote or to be free from invidious discrimination); Mich. Informal Ethics Op. RI-345 (2008) (explaining compliance with Rule 1.13 in situation in which high-level corporate officer intends to destroy discovery documents); *cf. FDIC v. Clark*, 978 F.2d 1541 (10th Cir. 1992) (lawyer may have duty to take action and not simply take at face value constituent's false or misleading assurances). *See generally* William H. Simon, *Introduction: The Post-Enron Identity Crisis of the Business Lawyer*, 74 Fordham L. Rev. 947 (Dec. 2005).

## • *Climbing Corporate Ladder*

Unless the lawyer reasonably believes the organization's best interests do not so require, the lawyer must report misconduct "up the ladder" to higher authorities in the organization, including, if necessary, "the highest authority that can act on behalf of the organization [under] applicable law." Rule 1.13(b). In a private organization, the highest authority will ordinarily be the corporation's board of directors or similar governing body. Cmt. [5]; *see also Restatement (Third) of the Law Governing Lawyers* § 97 cmt. j (2000) (lawyer representing governmental clients may need to consider whether to refer matter "to allied governmental agencies, such as the government's general legal office, such as a state's office of attorney general").

If the company is public, the lawyer may be independently required by law to inform the company's highest authority of certain misconduct. The Sarbanes-Oxley Act of 2002 (15 U.S.C. § 7201) and the SEC regulations promulgated pursuant to it (17 C.F.R. §§ 205.1–205.7) require a lawyer to report evidence of a material violation of securities laws or a breach of fiduciary duty by the company or its agent to the company's general counsel or CEO and, if no adequate response is received, to the company's audit committee, independent directors, or board of directors. The lawyer can also fulfill the SEC obligation by reporting to the company's "qualified legal compliance committee," if the company has created one. *See generally* Thomas G. Bost, *Corporate Lawyers After the Big Quake: The Conceptual Fault Line in the Professional Duty of Confidentiality*, 19 Geo. J. Legal Ethics 1089 (Fall 2006); John M. Burman, *Non-SEC Whistle-Blowing Obligations of Lawyers Who Represent Organizations*, 46 Washburn L.J. 127 (Fall 2006); Roger C. Cramton et al., *Legal and Ethical Duties of Lawyers After Sarbanes-Oxley*, 49 Vill. L. Rev. 725 (2004); Beverley Earle & Gerald A. Madek, *The New World of Risk for Corporate Attorneys and Their Boards Post-Sarbanes-Oxley: An Assessment of Impact and a Prescription for Action*, 2 Berkeley Bus. L.J. 185 (Spring 2005); Caroline Harrington, Note, *Attorney Gatekeeper Duties in an Increasingly Complex World: Revisiting the "Noisy Withdrawal" Proposal of SEC Rule 205*, 22 Geo. J. Legal Ethics 893 (Summer 2009); Sung Hui Kim, *Gatekeepers Inside Out*, 21 Geo. J. Legal Ethics 411 (Spring 2008); Fred C. Zacharias, *Coercing Clients: Can Lawyer Gatekeeper Rules Work?*, 47 B.C. L. Rev. 455 (May 2006).

While the revised duties in Rule 1.13 are similar to the SEC's rules of practice, there are important differences between the two. For example, Rule 1.13(b) requires a lawyer to climb the corporate ladder when the lawyer "knows" of a violation of a legal duty "likely" to result in substantial corporate injury. SEC Rule 205, in contrast, is triggered by "credible evidence, based upon which it would be unreasonable . . . for a prudent attorney not to conclude that it is reasonably likely that a material violation has occurred, is ongoing, or is about to occur." 17 C.F.R. § 205.2(e).

## Paragraph (c): "Reporting Out"

Pursuant to paragraph (c), the lawyer is permitted to "report out"—that is, to "reveal information relating to the representation" outside the organization—if the lawyer (1) goes up the organizational ladder and informs the organization's highest authority of misconduct "that is clearly a violation of law" reasonably certain to result in substantial injury to the organization, and (2) the highest authority nevertheless fails to address the problem "in a timely and appropriate manner." *See* ABA Formal Ethics Op. 08-453 (2008) (law firm's ethics counsel may have duty to "disclose misconduct of a consulting lawyer to law firm management," and if that is ineffective, may have discretion to disclose misconduct "to external regulatory authorities"); *see also Hays v. Page Perry, LLC*, 627 F. App'x 892 (11th Cir. 2015) (rule permits but does not require lawyer to report client/entity's regulatory noncompliance to government agency).

Before the 2003 amendment to the rule, however, a lawyer in this position could only resign; there was no provision in the Model Rules allowing the lawyer to go outside the organization. *See* American Bar Association, *A Legislative History: The Development of the ABA Model Rules of Professional Conduct, 1982–2013*, at 309–25 (2013) (proposed reporting-out provision similar to Rule 1.13(c) was defeated in 1983); *cf.* 17 C.F.R. §§ 205.3(d)(2)(i)–(iii) (lawyer may report to SEC to extent necessary to (1) prevent company from committing material securities law violation likely to cause substantial financial injury to company or investors, (2) prevent company from committing or suborning perjury, or making false statements in SEC investigation, or (3) rectify consequences of material securities violation by company).

Note that the 2003 amendments to the confidentiality rule (Rule 1.6) do not permit disclosure—whether to prevent, rectify, or mitigate injury—unless the lawyer's services are being used to further the particular crime or fraud. *See* Rule 1.6(b)(2)–(3). Rule 1.13(c) contains no such limitation. *But see* Monroe H. Freedman & Abbe Smith, *Understanding Lawyers' Ethics* § 5.07 (4th ed. 2010) (containing critical discussion of paragraphs (b) and (c) of Rule 1.13 and arguing that Rule 1.13—even as amended—is still more protective of corporate fraud, as opposed to fraud by individuals addressed under Rule 1.6, because Rule 1.13 instructs corporate lawyer to act only to prevent "substantial injury to the organization" and to consider "best interest" of organization, as opposed to interests of others).

## Paragraph (d): Lawyer Investigating or Defending Claim Arising out of Corporate Wrongdoing

Rule 1.13(d) limits the "reporting out" authority contained in Rule 1.13(c). If the lawyer has been retained to investigate an alleged violation of law by the organization, or to defend the organization or a constituent against claims arising out of an alleged violation of law, the lawyer does not have the option of reporting out under Rule 1.13(c). In these circumstances, it is thought, there is a compelling need to promote full and frank disclosure by organizational constituents without fear of disclosure by the lawyer to third parties. *See* Rule 1.13, cmt. [7]. The SEC rules make a similar exception. *See* 17 C.F.R. §§ 205.3(b)(6), 205.3(b)(7).

### *Paragraph (e): Lawyer's Continuing Obligations upon Discharge or Withdrawal under Circumstances Governed by Paragraphs (b) and (c)*

If a lawyer takes corrective action pursuant to paragraphs (b) or (c) and as a result is discharged or withdraws, Rule 1.13(e) requires the lawyer to take reasonably necessary steps to notify the organization's highest authority. *Cf.* 17 C.F.R. § 205.3(b)(10) (lawyer who reasonably believes he was discharged for reporting evidence of material violation of law may so notify corporation's board of directors or any committee thereof). Note that Rule 1.13(e) requires only reasonable steps to ensure that the entity's highest authority is "informed of the lawyer's discharge or withdrawal," and is silent about whether the lawyer is also permitted to disclose the circumstances under which the withdrawal or termination occurred. *See* Rule 1.13, cmt. [8]. The ABA Task Force on Corporate Responsibility, whose report inspired Rule 1.13(e), clarifies that a broad reading was intended. *See Report of the ABA Task Force on Corporate Responsibility*, 59 Bus. Law. 145 (Nov. 2003) ("[T]he lawyer's professional obligations to act in the best interest of the organization should require the lawyer to take reasonable steps to assure that the organization's highest authority is aware of the withdrawal or discharge, *and the lawyer's understanding of the circumstances that brought it about.*" (emphasis added)).

Before the 2003 amendments, Rule 1.13(c) simply permitted the lawyer faced with certain corporate misconduct to withdraw pursuant to Rule 1.16. It neither required nor authorized any disclosure or other remedial action.

### *Paragraph (f): Lawyer Must Clarify Role If Constituent's Interests Adverse to Those of Organization*

To protect constituents and the organization from problems that could result from confusion about the lawyer's role, Rule 1.13(f) requires the lawyer to clarify the identity of the client when *the lawyer knows or reasonably should know* the organization's interests are adverse to those of a constituent. The italicized language was added in 2002, replacing the phrase, "it is apparent." *See State ex rel. Thomas v. Schneider*, 130 P.3d 991 (Ariz. Ct. App. 2006) (when interests of city and its officials may conflict, then pursuant to Rule 1.13(f), city attorney should inform city officials of "the scope of the attorney's representation so that those who might otherwise believe a confidential relationship exists do not compromise their legal interests"); D.C. Ethics Op. 269 (1997) (lawyer conducting investigation of possible wrongdoing by corporation and its employees must make clear that lawyer represents corporation and will divulge information to it). *See generally* Ariana R. Levinson, *Legal Ethics in the Employment Law Context: Who Is the Client?*, 37 N. Ky. L. Rev. 1 (2010).

Rule 1.13(f) ordinarily should be read together with Rule 4.3 for a fuller understanding of potential "Upjohn warnings" in this context. *See United States v. Ruehle*, 583 F.3d 600 (9th Cir. 2009) (lawyers conducting internal corporate investigations may provide a "so-called Upjohn or corporate Miranda warning," which advises constituent "that the corporate lawyers do not represent the individual employee; that anything said by the employee to the lawyers will be protected by the company's attorney-client privilege subject to waiver of the privilege in the sole discretion of the company; and that the individual may wish to consult with his own attorney if he has any concerns about his own potential legal exposure" (citing *Upjohn Co. v. United States*, 449 U.S. 383 (1981))); Rule 1.13, cmt. [10] (providing standard warnings in situations in which lawyer should reasonably know constituent's interests are adverse to organization's interests). *See generally* Gary H. Collins & David Z. Seide, *Warning the Witness: A Guide to Internal Investigations and the Attorney-Client Privilege* (2010); Edward C. Brewer, *Ethics of Internal Investigations in Kentucky and Ohio*, 27 N. Ky. L. Rev. 721 (2000).

See the annotation to Rule 4.3 (Dealing with Unrepresented Person) for further discussion.

## FAILURE TO CLARIFY ROLE MAY RESULT IN LAWYER-CLIENT RELATIONSHIP WITH CONSTITUENT

When the lawyer does not clarify the nature of his or her role in representing the organization, a constituent may conclude that the lawyer represents the constituent as well as the organization. If this belief is reasonable, it may give rise to a lawyer-client relationship between the lawyer and the constituent. *See Manion v. Nagin*, 394 F.3d 1062 (8th Cir. 2005) (by giving corporation's executive director legal advice about his employment agreement, corporation's lawyer established lawyer-client relationship with director: "If Nagin was truly working exclusively as [the corporation's] lawyer, he should have responded to Manion's questions by clarifying that he worked only for [the corporation] and suggested Manion seek outside counsel."); *Home Care Indus., Inc. v. Murray*, 154 F. Supp. 2d 861 (D.N.J. 2001) (corporation's law firm disqualified from representing it in suit over enforceability of CEO's severance agreement: "Given that the rapport between the Skadden Firm and [the CEO] . . . was a delicate one, the Skadden Firm should have taken precautions to clarify any ambiguity concerning its duty to represent [the corporation] as separate and distinct from its officers."); N.Y. State Ethics Op. 743 (2001) (lawyer for labor union who fails to inform employee that lawyer does not represent employee risks possibility of inadvertently creating lawyer-client relationship with employee in connection with disclosure of information that employee considers secret and does not want publicized); *cf.* D.C. Ethics Op. 328 (2005) (lawyer who represents constituent of organization should make clear to organization's nonclient constituents that his client's interests may differ from those of organization). *See generally* Mary C. Daly, *Avoiding the Ethical Pitfall of Misidentifying the Organizational Client*, 574 PLI/Lit 399 (1997); Jeffrey Willis & Jamie Heisler Ibrahim, *Avoiding Disqualification: 10 Tips When Representing Corporate Clients*, Ariz. Att'y, June 2009, at 34; Note, *An Expectations Approach to Client Identity*, 106 Harv. L. Rev. 687 (Jan. 1993).

## *Paragraph (g): Multiple Representation*

Rule 1.13(g) permits a lawyer to represent both an organization and one or more of its constituents, subject to the Rule 1.7 provisions governing conflicts of interest. *See Guillen v. City of Chicago*, 956 F. Supp. 1416 (N.D. Ill. 1997) (city lawyer representing city and police officers in civil rights action not disqualified from also representing city paramedics at deposition); *Ontiveros v. Constable*, 199 Cal. Rptr. 3d 836 (Ct. App. 2016) (lawyer cannot represent corporation and CEO in derivative action if CEO accused of fraud); *Campellone v. Cragan*, 910 So. 2d 363 (Fla. Dist. Ct. App. 2005) (lawyer disqualified from representing both entity and majority shareholder in derivative suit alleging serious misconduct by majority shareholder); *Frank Settelmeyer & Sons, Inc. v. Smith & Harmer, Ltd.*, 197 P.3d 1051 (Nev. 2008) (lawyers did not have conflict of interest in representing corporation and majority shareholder in dissolution action); *Campbell v. McKeon*, 905 N.Y.S.2d 589 (App. Div. 2010) (holding similar to *Campellone*); *see also* Cal. Formal Ethics Op. 2003-163 (2003) (lawyer for corporation who represents constituent in unrelated matter may not advise corporation in matter adverse to client); Conn. Informal Ethics Op. 99-19 (1999) (law firm may represent corporation in employment matters and one of its employees in unrelated matter, but may not represent either of them if corporation undertakes adverse action, such as firing employee); Conn. Informal Ethics Op. 99-13 (1999) (lawyer employed by financial institution's trade association may represent individual member financial institutions, subject to conflict-of-interest provisions of Rule 1.7); N.Y. City Ethics Op. 2004-03 (2004) (advising government lawyers on possible conflicts of interest "(a) among government agency clients; (b) between a government agency and its constituents represented by the government lawyer; and (c) between an agency and unrepresented constituents"); N.Y. City Ethics Op. 2004-02 (2004) (discussing factors lawyer should consider in determining whether and how to represent organization and its constituents when organization faced with government investigation); R.I. Ethics Op. 2003-02 (2003) (lawyer for corporation may not represent one of its shareholders in action for involuntary dissolution; representation would be adverse to corporation's interests and would be materially limited by lawyer's responsibilities to corporation). *See generally Restatement (Third) of the Law Governing Lawyers* § 131 cmt. g (2000) (in derivative actions against organizational client, lawyer ordinarily may not represent individual defendants unless "the disinterested directors conclude that no basis exists for the claim that the defending officers and directors have acted against the interests of the organization" and lawyer obtains "the effective consent of all clients"). Importantly, the organization's consent to a potentially conflicting dual representation must be given by a constituent other than one who will be represented by the organization's lawyer. *See, e.g., Fanning v. John A. Sheppard Mem'l Ecological Reservation, Inc.*, No. 2:18-cv-01183, 2018 WL 5316009, 2018 BL 395765 (S.D. W. Va. Oct. 26, 2018) (informed consent requirement not satisfied by engagement letter that failed to mention conflict, and was signed by the represented board member; dual representation prohibited).

## Rule 1.14

### *Client with Diminished Capacity*

(a) When a client's capacity to make adequately considered decisions in connection with a representation is diminished, whether because of minority, mental impairment or for some other reason, the lawyer shall, as far as reasonably possible, maintain a normal client-lawyer relationship with the client.

(b) When the lawyer reasonably believes that the client has diminished capacity, is at risk of substantial physical, financial or other harm unless action is taken and cannot adequately act in the client's own interest, the lawyer may take reasonably necessary protective action, including consulting with individuals or entities that have the ability to take action to protect the client and, in appropriate cases, seeking the appointment of a guardian ad litem, conservator or guardian.

(c) Information relating to the representation of a client with diminished capacity is protected by Rule 1.6. When taking protective action pursuant to paragraph (b), the lawyer is impliedly authorized under Rule 1.6(a) to reveal information about the client, but only to the extent reasonably necessary to protect the client's interests.

## COMMENT

[1] The normal client-lawyer relationship is based on the assumption that the client, when properly advised and assisted, is capable of making decisions about important matters. When the client is a minor or suffers from a diminished mental capacity, however, maintaining the ordinary client-lawyer relationship may not be possible in all respects. In particular, a severely incapacitated person may have no power to make legally binding decisions. Nevertheless, a client with diminished capacity often has the ability to understand, deliberate upon, and reach conclusions about matters affecting the client's own well-being. For example, children as young as five or six years of age, and certainly those of ten or twelve, are regarded as having opinions that are entitled to weight in legal proceedings concerning their custody. So also, it is recognized that some persons of advanced age can be quite capable of handling routine financial matters while needing special legal protection concerning major transactions.

[2] The fact that a client suffers a disability does not diminish the lawyer's obligation to treat the client with attention and respect. Even if the person has a legal

representative, the lawyer should as far as possible accord the represented person the status of client, particularly in maintaining communication.

[3] The client may wish to have family members or other persons participate in discussions with the lawyer. When necessary to assist in the representation, the presence of such persons generally does not affect the applicability of the attorney-client evidentiary privilege. Nevertheless, the lawyer must keep the client's interests foremost and, except for protective action authorized under paragraph (b), must to look to the client, and not family members, to make decisions on the client's behalf.

[4] If a legal representative has already been appointed for the client, the lawyer should ordinarily look to the representative for decisions on behalf of the client. In matters involving a minor, whether the lawyer should look to the parents as natural guardians may depend on the type of proceeding or matter in which the lawyer is representing the minor. If the lawyer represents the guardian as distinct from the ward, and is aware that the guardian is acting adversely to the ward's interest, the lawyer may have an obligation to prevent or rectify the guardian's misconduct. See Rule 1.2(d).

## *Taking Protective Action*

[5] If a lawyer reasonably believes that a client is at risk of substantial physical, financial or other harm unless action is taken, and that a normal client-lawyer relationship cannot be maintained as provided in paragraph (a) because the client lacks sufficient capacity to communicate or to make adequately considered decisions in connection with the representation, then paragraph (b) permits the lawyer to take protective measures deemed necessary. Such measures could include: consulting with family members, using a reconsideration period to permit clarification or improvement of circumstances, using voluntary surrogate decisionmaking tools such as durable powers of attorney or consulting with support groups, professional services, adult-protective agencies or other individuals or entities that have the ability to protect the client. In taking any protective action, the lawyer should be guided by such factors as the wishes and values of the client to the extent known, the client's best interests and the goals of intruding into the client's decisionmaking autonomy to the least extent feasible, maximizing client capacities and respecting the client's family and social connections.

[6] In determining the extent of the client's diminished capacity, the lawyer should consider and balance such factors as: the client's ability to articulate reasoning leading to a decision, variability of state of mind and ability to appreciate consequences of a decision; the substantive fairness of a decision; and the consistency of a decision with the known long-term commitments and values of the client. In appropriate circumstances, the lawyer may seek guidance from an appropriate diagnostician.

[7] If a legal representative has not been appointed, the lawyer should consider whether appointment of a guardian ad litem, conservator or guardian is necessary to protect the client's interests. Thus, if a client with diminished capacity has substantial property that should be sold for the client's benefit, effective completion of the transaction may require appointment of a legal representative. In addition, rules of

procedure in litigation sometimes provide that minors or persons with diminished capacity must be represented by a guardian or next friend if they do not have a general guardian. In many circumstances, however, appointment of a legal representative may be more expensive or traumatic for the client than circumstances in fact require. Evaluation of such circumstances is a matter entrusted to the professional judgment of the lawyer. In considering alternatives, however, the lawyer should be aware of any law that requires the lawyer to advocate the least restrictive action on behalf of the client.

### *Disclosure of the Client's Condition*

[8] Disclosure of the client's diminished capacity could adversely affect the client's interests. For example, raising the question of diminished capacity could, in some circumstances, lead to proceedings for involuntary commitment. Information relating to the representation is protected by Rule 1.6. Therefore, unless authorized to do so, the lawyer may not disclose such information. When taking protective action pursuant to paragraph (b), the lawyer is impliedly authorized to make the necessary disclosures, even when the client directs the lawyer to the contrary. Nevertheless, given the risks of disclosure, paragraph (c) limits what the lawyer may disclose in consulting with other individuals or entities or seeking the appointment of a legal representative. At the very least, the lawyer should determine whether it is likely that the person or entity consulted with will act adversely to the client's interests before discussing matters related to the client. The lawyer's position in such cases is an unavoidably difficult one.

### *Emergency Legal Assistance*

[9] In an emergency where the health, safety or a financial interest of a person with seriously diminished capacity is threatened with imminent and irreparable harm, a lawyer may take legal action on behalf of such a person even though the person is unable to establish a client-lawyer relationship or to make or express considered judgments about the matter, when the person or another acting in good faith on that person's behalf has consulted with the lawyer. Even in such an emergency, however, the lawyer should not act unless the lawyer reasonably believes that the person has no other lawyer, agent or other representative available. The lawyer should take legal action on behalf of the person only to the extent reasonably necessary to maintain the status quo or otherwise avoid imminent and irreparable harm. A lawyer who undertakes to represent a person in such an exigent situation has the same duties under these Rules as the lawyer would with respect to a client.

[10] A lawyer who acts on behalf of a person with seriously diminished capacity in an emergency should keep the confidences of the person as if dealing with a client, disclosing them only to the extent necessary to accomplish the intended protective action. The lawyer should disclose to any tribunal involved and to any other counsel involved the nature of his or her relationship with the person. The lawyer should take steps to regularize the relationship or implement other protective solutions as soon as possible. Normally, a lawyer would not seek compensation for such emergency actions taken.

**Definitional Cross-References**

"Reasonably" *See* Rule 1.0(h)

"Reasonably believes" *See* Rule 1.0(i)

"Substantial" *See* Rule 1.0(l)

**State Rules Comparison**

http://ambar.org/MRPCStateCharts

## ANNOTATION

### OVERVIEW

Rule 1.14 addresses a lawyer's ethical obligations when a client's capacity to make adequately considered decisions in connection with a representation is diminished. Paragraph (a) directs the lawyer to maintain a "normal" client-lawyer relationship to the extent possible. If the lawyer believes the client is at risk of harm and cannot act in his or her own interest, paragraph (b) permits the lawyer to take "reasonably necessary protective action" under specified conditions. Paragraph (c) explicitly provides that disclosure of client information for the purpose of taking protective action under paragraph (b) is "impliedly authorized" by Rule 1.6 (Confidentiality of Information), "but only to the extent reasonably necessary to protect the client's interests."

#### • *2002 Amendments*

As originally promulgated in 1983, Model Rule 1.14 referred to the representation of a client "under a disability." In 2002 the wording was broadened to refer to a client "with diminished capacity" to reflect the continuum of a client's capacity. Paragraph (b) was expanded to include examples of protection that may be taken short of seeking the appointment of a guardian, and to require a risk of substantial harm before action may be taken. In addition, paragraph (c) was added to clarify the lawyer's confidentiality obligations under Rule 1.6. The comment was expanded to give guidance in evaluating a client's diminished capacity and in determining whether protective action should be taken. *See* American Bar Association, *A Legislative History: The Development of the ABA Model Rules of Professional Conduct, 1982–2013*, at 344–49 (2013).

### *Paragraph (a): Duty to Maintain Normal Client-Lawyer Relationship*

Rule 1.14(a) requires a lawyer to maintain, as far as reasonably possible, a "normal" client-lawyer relationship with a client with diminished capacity. *Accord Restatement (Third) of the Law Governing Lawyers* § 24(1) (2000). "This obligation implies that the lawyer should continue to treat the client with attention and respect, attempt to communicate and discuss relevant matters, and continue as far as reasonably possible to take action consistent with the client's directions and decisions." ABA Formal Ethics Op. 96-404 (1996); *see* Or. Ethics Op. 2005-159 (2005) (except in extreme cases, lawyer can usually explain decisions client faces in simple terms and elicit response sufficient to allow lawyer to proceed with representation).

Comment [1] explains that a "normal client-lawyer relationship is based on the assumption that the client, when properly advised and assisted, is capable of making decisions about important matters." The rule recognizes that although a severely incapacitated client "may have no power to make legally binding decisions," a client with diminished capacity will in many cases have "the ability to understand, deliberate upon, and reach conclusions about matters affecting the client's own well-being." Cmt. [1]. Accordingly, a lawyer representing a client with diminished capacity is required, to the extent "reasonably possible," to communicate with that client, work with him, and comply with his objectives concerning the representation. *See In re Flack*, 33 P.3d 1281 (Kan. 2001) (failure to abide by client's estate planning objectives, as far as reasonably possible, after being informed of client's medical and mental disability violated rule); *In re Lee*, 754 A.2d 426 (Md. Ct. Spec. App. 2000) (duty to maintain normal client-lawyer relationship precludes lawyer from using assessment of client's best interests to justify waiving client's rights without consultation, divulging client's confidences, disregarding client's wishes, and presenting evidence against client in guardianship proceeding); *In re Guardianship of Henderson*, 838 A.2d 1277 (N.H. 2003) (lawyer disregarded client's wishes and told court it would be "reasonable" to appoint client's mother as client's guardian; guardianship order reversed because client did not have full assistance of counsel to attack guardianship petition); Colo. Ethics Op. 126 (2015) (maintaining normal relationship means lawyer may not use own assessment of client's "best interests" to justify waiver of client's rights without consultation, revealing client's confidences, disregarding client's wishes, or presenting evidence against client); *see also In re Laprath*, 670 N.W.2d 41 (S.D. 2003) (lawyer prepared documents and had them signed by client whom lawyer considered incompetent, acted against client's wishes, and filed petition seeking to be appointed client's guardian when client complained). *See generally* David A. Green, *"I'm OK— You're OK": Educating Lawyers to "Maintain a Normal Client-Lawyer Relationship" with a Client with a Mental Disability*, 28 J. Legal Prof. 65 (2003–2004) (arguing that ethics rules should provide lawyers with more guidance and urging mandatory training on subject).

## REPRESENTATION OF MINOR

Rule 1.14 explicitly applies to the representation of those whose decision-making ability is diminished "because of minority." Although children may not have the power to make legally binding decisions, their opinions are generally entitled to some weight in legal proceedings. *See* Cmt. [1]; N.Y. City Ethics Op. 1997-2 (1997) (listing factors to be considered in assessing child's capacity).

A lawyer is not necessarily required to follow the instructions of a minor client if the lawyer believes they contravene the client's best interests. The lawyer's precise obligations will depend upon a variety of factors, including the client's level of maturity, the nature of the legal matter, the specific facts, and the particular jurisdiction involved. *See, e.g., Castro v. Hochuli*, 543 P.3d 705 (Ariz. Ct. App. 2015) (lawyer for child in dependency proceeding must seek appointment of guardian ad litem if child is unable to express preference or expresses preference harmful to child); *In re Marriage of Hartley*, 886 P.2d 665 (Colo. 1995) (lawyer appointed to represent child in custody matter acts as both guardian and advocate and need not represent child's views without question); *In re Christina W.*, 639 S.E.2d 770 (W. Va. 2006) ("while the child's opinions are to be given consideration where the child has demonstrated an adequate level of competency, there is no requirement that the child's wishes govern"); Conn. Informal Ethics Op. 94-29 (1994) (if lawyer thinks minor client's position is not in client's best interests, lawyer should seek appointment of guardian to protect client's interests and should then represent client's position before court; if lawyer finds this repugnant, he may seek to withdraw, but may not express opinion on merits or use client's confidences to advocate for position not favored by client); Ind. Ethics Op. 2015-2 (n.d.) (lawyer who learns minor client is victim of abuse or neglect must report it to authorities if child is at risk of reasonably certain death or substantial bodily harm; if no such risk, disclosure requires child's informed consent); Mass. Ethics Op. 93-6 (1993) (lawyer must comply with thirteen-year-old client's instructions even if lawyer believes doing so is not in client's best interests, unless lawyer determines client incapable of making reasoned decisions in matter; otherwise, lawyer may seek to withdraw); N.Y. City Ethics Op. 1997-2 (1997) (lawyer for minor lacking decision-making capacity may make decisions, including decisions to disclose confidential information, that client cannot make in reasoned way); S.D. Ethics Op. 2004-5 (2004) (lawyer need not comply with request of minor client in abuse and neglect case to advocate for placement that lawyer believes is not in client's best interests; may take protective action such as by advocating for different placement or seeking appointment of guardian ad litem); *see also In re Kristen B.*, 78 Cal. Rptr. 3d 495 (Ct. App. 2008) (lawyer for child in dependency case must advocate for minor's best interests, even if different from minor's wishes); L.A. Cnty. Ethics Op. 504 (2000) (if lawyer believes minor client is capable of making informed decision, lawyer must follow client's instructions not to disclose that client was sexually assaulted; if not, lawyer should take protective action, including seeking appointment of guardian ad litem, but may not disclose information unless appointment made).

The substantive law of the jurisdiction will also govern the obligations of a lawyer representing a minor. These obligations may vary depending upon whether the matter involves child custody, juvenile delinquency, abuse and neglect, or some other type of proceeding. In some jurisdictions, a lawyer may be required to serve as both counsel and guardian ad litem for a single client. For a discussion of the ethical issues arising when counsel is also the guardian ad litem, see *ABA/BNA Lawyers' Manual on Professional Conduct*, "Lawyer-Client Relationship: Client with Diminished Capacity," pp. 31:601 *et seq. See generally* Bruce A. Boyer, *Representing Child-Clients with "Diminished Capacity": Navigating an Ethical Minefield*, 24 Prof. Law., no. 1, at 36 (2016); Elizabeth J. Cohen, "Speakers Note Complexities of Representing Children," *ABA/BNA Lawyers' Manual on Professional Conduct*, 32 Law. Man. Prof. Conduct 367 (Current Reports, June 15, 2016); Conference, *Ethical Issues in the Legal Representation of Children*, 64 Fordham L. Rev. 1281 (Mar. 1996); Jan C. Costello, *Representing Children in Mental Disability Proceedings*, 1 J. Center for Child. & Cts. 101 (1999); Bruce A. Green, *Lawyers as Nonlawyers in Child Custody and Visitation Cases: Questions from the "Legal Ethics" Perspective*, 73 Ind. L.J. 665 (Spring 1998); David R. Katner, *Coming to Praise, Not to Bury, the New ABA Standards of Practice for Lawyers Who Represent Children in*

*Abuse and Neglect Cases*, 14 Geo. J. Legal Ethics 103 (Fall 2000); Ellen Marrus, *Please Keep My Secret: Child Abuse Reporting Statutes, Confidentiality, and Juvenile Delinquency*, 11 Geo. J. Legal Ethics 509 (Spring 1998); Martha Matthews, *Ten Thousand Tiny Clients: The Ethical Duty of Representation in Children's Class-Action Cases*, 64 Fordham L. Rev. 1435 (Mar. 1996); Symposium, *American Bar Association Model Act Governing Representation of Children in Abuse, Neglect, and Dependency Proceedings*, 36 Nova L. Rev. 309 (2012).

## WHEN CLIENT ALREADY HAS LEGAL REPRESENTATIVE

As noted in Comment [4], when a legal representative has already been appointed for the client the lawyer should ordinarily look to the representative to make decisions on the client's behalf. *See In re Guardianship of Hocker*, 791 N.E.2d 302 (Mass. 2003) ("permanent guardian stands in the place of the ward in making decisions about the ward's well-being, and the guardian is held to high standards of fidelity in exercising this authority for the ward's benefit"); *In re Kuhn*, 785 N.W.2d 195 (N.D. 2010) (lawyer violated rule by drafting new will for incompetent client without communicating with client's court-appointed guardian/conservator); *see also In re Jarvis*, 349 P.3d 445 (Kan. 2015) (lawyer who acted as client's legal representative without authorization of client's guardian violated multiple ethics rules). Nevertheless, the lawyer must still assess the client's interests independently and act in accordance with them—even if contrary to the representative's instructions. *See D.C. Ethics Op.* 353 (2010) (lawyer hired by person holding durable power of attorney to represent incapacitated client in litigation must follow that person's directives unless doing so would create risk of substantial harm warranting protective action); N.C. Ethics Op. 98-18 (1999) (lawyer may withhold information from minor client's guardian if lawyer believes guardian acting adversely to client's interests); Or. Ethics Op. 2005-159 (2005) (although lawyer normally takes direction from client's guardian ad litem, lawyer must still independently assess client's interests and guardian's assertion of them); *see also Schult v. Schult*, 699 A.2d 134 (Conn. 1997) (lawyer for minor child in custody dispute may advocate position contrary to position of child's guardian ad litem if court determines "such dual, conflicting advocacy" is in child's best interests); N.C. Ethics Op. 98-16 (1999) (even though client declared incompetent by state and guardian appointed, lawyer representing client in appeal of determination of incompetence not required to treat client as incompetent or defer to decisions of guardian relating to lawyer's representation of client). *See generally* Nina A. Kohn & Catheryn Koss, *Lawyers for Legal Ghosts: The Legality and Ethics of Representing Persons Subject to Guardianship*, 91 Wash. L. Rev. 581 (June 2016) (recommending changes to Model Rule 1.14 to address representation of persons subject to guardianship).

## *Paragraph (b): Protective Action*

Rule 1.14(b) permits a lawyer to take "reasonably necessary protective action" if the lawyer "reasonably believes that the client has diminished capacity, is at risk of substantial physical, financial or other harm unless action is taken and cannot adequately act in the client's own interest."

## ASSESSING CLIENT'S CAPACITY

To determine what, if any, protective action is appropriate, the lawyer must first assess the client's capacity. Comment [6] suggests that a lawyer consider and balance the following factors: "the client's ability to articulate reasoning leading to a decision, variability of state of mind and ability to appreciate consequences of a decision; the substantive fairness of a decision; and the consistency of a decision with the known long-term commitments and values of the client." *See In re Brantley*, 920 P.2d 433 (Kan. 1996) (lawyer disciplined for filing conservatorship proceedings without meeting personally with client to determine client's state of mind or client's understanding of financial affairs); Ind. Ethics Op. 2001-2 (2001) (failure to ascertain client's physical and mental condition and evaluate client's capacity violates Rule 1.14); Or. Ethics Op. 2005-159 (2005) (lawyer should "examine whether the client can give direction on the decisions that the lawyer must ethically defer to the client"); *see also In re Eugster*, 209 P.3d 435 (Wash. 2009) (lawyer fired by elderly client responded by filing petition to appoint guardian for her claiming she was "delusional," without making reasonable inquiry into her competency and despite fact that lawyer had considered her competent to sign estate planning documents months earlier).

If necessary, the lawyer may seek the aid of others to assess the client's capacity. *See, e.g.,* ABA Formal Ethics Op. 96-404 (1996) (suggesting that, in addition to appropriate diagnostician, lawyer consult with client's family or other interested persons who can help assess client's capacity); Mo. Informal Ethics Op. 990095 (1999) (lawyer who believes elderly client shows signs of Alzheimer's disease may seek assistance from social service agency to determine if guardian needed); N.Y. City Ethics Op. 1997-2 (1997) (in assessing client's capacity, lawyer must take into account information derived from communications with client and relevant information reasonably available from other sources; lawyer may also seek guidance from other professionals and concerned parties); N.D. Ethics Op. 00-06 (2000) (lawyer who believes divorce client will accept offer contrary to her best interests so she can avoid disclosing substance abuse problem must determine if client able to consider her decision adequately; lawyer may consult with professional to determine nature and extent of client's disability); Pa. Ethics Op. 87-214 (1988) (lawyer who reasonably believes client cannot handle her financial affairs and day-to-day health care needs may seek court appointment of physician to report to court on threshold issue of client's competence); *see also* Ky. Ethics Op. E-439 (2016) (lawyer who consults professional to assess client's capacity should consider how other professional's mandatory reporting requirements would affect client's best interest). *See generally* ABA Comm'n on Law and Aging & Am. Psychological Ass'n, *Assessment of Older Adults with Diminished Capacity: A Handbook for Lawyers* (2005); Charles P. Sabatino, *Representing a Client with Diminished Capacity: How Do You Know It and What Do You Do About It?*, 16 J. Am. Acad. Matrim. Law. 481 (2000).

### • *Client with Poor Judgment*

A client's poor judgment does not suffice to warrant protective action under Rule 1.14(b). ABA Formal Ethics Op. 96-404 (1996) ("Rule 1.14(b) does not authorize the lawyer to take protective action because the client is not acting in what the lawyer believes to be the client's best interest"); *accord* Colo. Ethics Op. 126 (2015); N.H.

Ethics Op. 2014-15/5 (n.d.); *Restatement (Third) of the Law Governing Lawyers* § 24 cmt. c (2000) (lawyer should not construe as proof of disability a client's insistence upon view of client's welfare that lawyer considers unwise or at variance with lawyer's views); *see* Conn. Informal Ethics Op. 05-12 (2005) (lawyer who believes elderly client is competent to make financial decisions may not take "protective action" by disclosing to third parties lawyer's concern that client's arrangements with personal care provider are ill-considered and will cause client to run out of funds); Me. Ethics Op. 84 (1988) ("It goes without saying that the attorney must have far stronger grounds for acting to seek the appointment of a guardian or to suggest that family members do so than mere disagreement with the client.").

## SPECTRUM OF PROTECTIVE MEASURES

Rule 1.14(b) envisions a spectrum of protective action, from consulting with individuals who can take protective action to seeking appointment of a legal representative or guardian. Comment [5] suggests several protective measures to consider, including consulting family members, using a reconsideration period to permit clarification or improvement of the circumstances surrounding the client's incapacity, using voluntary surrogate decision-making tools such as durable powers of attorney, or consulting support groups, professional services, adult-protective agencies, or other entities that can protect the client.

"Reasonably necessary" protective action is generally the "least restrictive action under the circumstances." ABA Formal Ethics Op. 96-404 (1996); Vt. Ethics Op. 2006-1 (2006) (same); *see also* Conn. Informal Ethics Op. 04-10 (2004) (lawyer may not ask law enforcement authorities to take suicidal client into custody under outstanding warrant as protective measure but may take less drastic measures, such as counseling against suicide, contacting client's family or medical professionals, or, as last resort, initiating steps for involuntary commitment).

### • *Seeking Appointment of Guardian*

Rule 1.14(b) permits the lawyer for a client with diminished capacity to seek appointment of a guardian to protect the client's interests if there is no less drastic alternative. ABA Formal Ethics Op. 96-404 (1996) (appointment of guardian is "serious deprivation of the client's rights and ought not be undertaken if other, less drastic, solutions are available"); *accord* Conn. Informal Ethics Op. 97-19 (1997); *see also In re S.H.*, 987 P.2d 735 (Alaska 1999) ("If the requirements of Rule 1.14 are met, a lawyer may seek a guardian to protect the client's interests despite the client's disapproval."); Ill. Ethics Op. 12-10 (2012) (lawyer who believes divorce client cannot make decisions in own best interest may seek guardianship based upon confidential information); Or. Ethics Op. 2005-159 (2005) (lawyer should seek appointment of guardian only when client "consistently demonstrates lack of capacity to act in his or her own interests and . . . is unlikely . . . to assist in the proceedings"). *See generally* American Bar Association, *A Practical Tool for Lawyers: Steps in Supporting Decision-Making* (identifying decision-making options less restrictive than guardianship), *available at* http://www.americanbar.org/groups/law_aging/resources/guardianship_law_practice/practical_tool.html.

However, a lawyer should not seek to be appointed as the client's guardian "except in the most exigent of circumstances, that is, where immediate and irreparable harm will result from the slightest delay," and even then, only on a temporary basis. ABA Formal Ethics Op. 96-404 (1996); *accord In re Laprath*, 670 N.W.2d 41 (S.D. 2003); Colo. Ethics Op. 126 (2015).

Similarly, a lawyer normally should not represent a third party petitioning for guardianship over the lawyer's client. ABA Formal Ethics Op. 96-404 (1996); *accord Att'y Grievance Comm'n v. Framm*, 144 A.3d 827 (Md. 2016); *In re Wyatt*, 982 A.2d 396 (N.H. 2009); *Dayton Bar Ass'n v. Parisi*, 965 N.E.2d 268 (Ohio 2012); *see* Mass. Ethics Op. 05-5 (2005) (lawyer may not represent longtime client's son seeking appointment as client's guardian); Va. Ethics Op. 1769 (2003) (legal aid lawyer may not represent daughter seeking appointment of guardian for elderly mother represented by same office in unrelated matter but may seek appointment of guardian if warranted under Rule 1.14); *see also* S.C. Ethics Op. 06-06 (2006) (law firm may petition court for appointment of conservator and/or guardian for impaired client, but may not represent client's daughter in proceeding to have herself named unless she is already acting as client's legal representative). *But see* R.I. Ethics Op. 2004-1 (2004) (lawyer may represent party seeking appointment as guardian over elderly client if lawyer "reasonably believes that a guardianship is in the elderly client's best interest").

## WITHDRAWAL FROM REPRESENTATION

A lawyer who concludes that representing a client with diminished capacity has become unreasonably difficult may seek to withdraw if the client will not be prejudiced, but withdrawal is not generally favored. *See* ABA Formal Ethics Op. 96-404 (1996) (withdrawal may leave disabled client vulnerable at very time client is in greatest need of assistance; better to continue representation and seek appropriate protective action); Me. Ethics Op. 84 (1988) (withdrawal leaves client without advice when it seems most needed); Mich. Informal Ethics Op. CI-882 (1983) (probability that client would have "same difficulties with any other lawyer retained . . . does not bind the attorney to remain in a relationship which the client may have rendered unreasonably difficult for the attorney to continue"); N.Y. State Ethics Op. 746 (2001) ("seeking to withdraw is generally seen as the least satisfactory response because doing so leaves the client without assistance when it is most needed"); *see also Hawkins v. Principi*, No. 03-2108 , 2004 WL 396064, 2004 BL 30951 (Vet. App. Feb. 20, 2004) (denying lawyer's motion to withdraw from representing long-time client who could neither recognize him nor remember prior representation; cannot end relationship due to client's diminished capacity, but should maintain as normal a relationship as possible); D.C. Ethics Op. 353 (2010) (if client's surrogate decision maker "were to engage in the conduct described in Rule 1.16(b) that would ordinarily cause a lawyer to withdraw, that is a circumstance under which the lawyer should take protective action," such as seeking substitute surrogate decision maker). *But see* Colo. Ethics Op. 131 (2017) (lawyer who represents client in adult protective proceeding should seek to withdraw and request appointment of guardian ad litem if client's incapacity is so severe that lawyer cannot continue lawyer-client relationship).

## *Paragraph (c): Disclosing Information about Client with Diminished Capacity*

### IMPLIED AUTHORIZATION TO REVEAL INFORMATION

Paragraph (c) of Rule 1.14, added in 2002, makes clear that although a lawyer must protect the confidences of a client with diminished decision-making capacity, when taking protective action pursuant to paragraph (b) the lawyer is "impliedly authorized" under Rule 1.6(a) to disclose information about the client "to the extent reasonably necessary to protect the client's interests." This provision is in accord with earlier interpretations of lawyers' confidentiality obligations. *See* ABA Formal Ethics Op. 96-404 (1996) (limited disclosure appropriate "to aid in the lawyer's assessment of the client's capacity as well as in the decision of how to proceed"); ABA Informal Ethics Op. 89-1530 (1989) (lawyer may consult client's physician concerning medical condition that interferes with client's ability to communicate or make decisions concerning representation, even though client has not consented and is currently incapable of doing so); Ill. Ethics Op. 00-02 (2000) (lawyer representing adult with psychiatric condition in disability benefit proceeding may not give psychiatric report to client's father unless lawyer believes client so disabled that guardian should be appointed); Me. Ethics Op. 84 (1988) (lawyer who believes elderly client incapable of making rational financial decisions may so inform client's son, as long as son has no adverse interest in client's affairs); Neb. Ethics Op. 91-4 (1991) (lawyer may disclose confidential communications to extent necessary to protect client's best interests if lawyer believes client incompetent); N.Y. City Ethics Op. 1987-7 (1987) (lawyer with alcoholic client may seek conservator and may disclose confidential information to court if necessary to safeguard client's interests; lawyer should seek judicial permission to make disclosures in camera and should request that file be kept under seal); *see also In re Christina W.*, 639 S.E.2d 770 (W. Va. 2006) (child's lawyer who also serves as guardian ad litem must disclose child's confidences to court against child's wishes if "honoring the duty of confidentiality would result in the [child's] exposure to a high risk of probable harm"); Colo. Ethics Op. 126 (2015) (lawyer must exercise care with respect to what information is disclosed, to whom, and how it will be used); N.Y. State Ethics Op. 1059 (2015) (lawyer representing unaccompanied minor in immigration removal proceedings must obtain informed consent of client, or in some cases child's parent or guardian, before disclosing confidential client information); *cf. In re Mullins*, 649 N.E.2d 1024 (Ind. 1995) (lawyer sought emergency guardianship over client in chronic vegetative state when client's parents authorized withdrawal of hydration and nutrition; lawyer faxed client's medical information to local news media in apparent effort to gain support for her position and oppose client's parents).

### • *Suicidal Client*

As to whether a lawyer may disclose a client's intent to commit suicide, compare Conn. Informal Ethics Op. 00-5 (2000) (lawyer may reveal client's intent to commit suicide only if lawyer reasonably believes client cannot adequately act in own interest; intent to commit suicide does not always evidence an inability to act in one's own interest), and Mass. Ethics Op. 01-2 (2001) (Rule 1.14 permits lawyer to disclose client's threat to commit suicide if lawyer has reasonable belief threat results from "mental disorder or disability that makes the client incapable of making a rational decision about the important matter of deciding to continue living"), with Alaska Ethics Op. 2005-1 (2005) (Rule 1.14 permits lawyer to tell "proper authorities," such as court, mental health professionals, or appropriate detention facility personnel, that client charged with felony plans to commit suicide rather than go to jail; any other interpretation "would defeat the purpose of Rule 1.14(b)—namely protecting the health and safety of a client who the lawyer reasonably believes is unable to act in his or her own interest"), and S.C. Ethics Op. 99-12 (1999) (lawyer may reveal client's threat to take own life; "'overriding social concern' for the preservation of human life dictates that a lawyer may, and even should, take reasonable steps to preserve the life and well-being of his client and others"). *See also* Model Rule 1.6(b)(1) (permitting disclosure "to prevent reasonably certain death or substantial bodily harm").

## CRIMINAL PROCEEDINGS

Criminal prosecution of a defendant who is not competent to stand trial is barred by the Due Process Clause of the Fourteenth Amendment. *Medina v. California*, 505 U.S. 437 (1992); *see Drope v. Missouri*, 420 U.S. 162 (1975); *Pate v. Robinson*, 383 U.S. 375 (1966); *see also Holmes v. Levenhagen*, 600 F.3d 756 (7th Cir. 2010) (suspending habeas corpus proceeding of seriously impaired death row inmate until mental illness abates or symptoms controlled). Accordingly, a lawyer with a good-faith doubt about the competency of a criminal defense client must raise the issue with the court. *See, e.g., Robidoux v. O'Brien*, 643 F.3d 334 (1st Cir. 2011) (if there are "substantial indications" that defendant not competent to stand trial, defense lawyer has "settled" duty to raise issue with court); *United States v. Boigegrain*, 155 F.3d 1181 (10th Cir. 1998) (defense counsel "is not only allowed to raise the competency issue, but, because of the importance of the prohibition on trying those who cannot understand proceedings against them, she has a professional duty to do so when appropriate"; not ineffective assistance of counsel to raise issue against client's wishes), *cert. denied*, 525 U.S. 1083 (1999); *Red Dog v. State*, 625 A.2d 245 (Del. 1993) (if criminal defense lawyer for capital murder defendant has reasonable and objective basis to doubt client's competency to decide to forgo further appeals, lawyer must inform court and ask for judicial determination of client's competency); *Blakeney v. United States*, 77 A.3d 328 (D.C. 2013) (criminal defense lawyer must raise competency issue if "objectively reasonable counsel would have reason to doubt" client's competency, even if client objects); *People v. Holt*, 21 N.E. 3d 695 (Ill. 2014) (when defendant contends she is fit to stand trial but evidence clearly indicates otherwise, defense lawyer not obligated to adopt client's position, since doing so would violate lawyer's duty to client and suborn violation of due process). *But see* ABA Criminal Justice Mental Health Standard 7-4.3(c) (2016 amendment provides that "Defense counsel *may* [replacing "should"] seek an ex parte evaluation of the defendant's competence to proceed whenever counsel has a good faith doubt about the defendant's competence," even over defendant's objection [emphasis added]; "should" wording retained, however, in parallel provisions relating to prosecutors and courts).

However, prior to raising the issue of a client's competency, lawyers are advised to consider the ramifications of doing so. *See* Ky. Ethics Op. E-440 (2016) (lawyer who has serious questions about client's competency to stand trial may have duty to raise issue, but should consider whether this would be detrimental to client's legal interests); Utah Ethics Op. 17-03 (2017) (lawyer should raise issue of client's competency only if after trying other approaches lawyer cannot otherwise protect client's interests and autonomy); Rodney J. Uphoff, *Ethical Problems Facing the Criminal Defense Lawyer: Practical Answers to Tough Questions* 34 (ABA Criminal Justice Section 1995) (criminal defense counsel should "weigh the client's choice on raising the issue along with the seriousness of the client's mental impairment, the nature of the defendant's case, counsel's ability to raise effective defenses, and the lawyer's assessment of the costs and benefits of various actions."); *see also United States v. Pfeifer*, 121 F. Supp. 3d 1255 (M.D. Ala. 2015) (when defense lawyer believed that wishes of client, who had been declared incompetent to stand trial, might conflict with client's best interests, court appointed guardian ad litem to advocate for client's best interests in subsequent competency and related proceedings). *See generally* Norma Schrock, *Defense Counsel's Role in Determining Competency to Stand Trial*, 9 Geo. J. Legal Ethics 639 (Winter 1996); Christopher Slobogin & Amy Mashburn, *The Criminal Defense Lawyer's Fiduciary Duty to Clients with Mental Disability*, 68 Fordham L. Rev. 1581 (Apr. 2000).

## • *Client's Refusal to Contest Death Penalty*

Whether a criminal defense lawyer may take "protective action" on behalf of a client who does not wish to contest a death penalty depends upon whether the lawyer reasonably believes the client is competent to make the decision. *See, e.g., Red Dog v. State*, 625 A.2d 245 (Del. 1993) (lawyer seeking competency determination for client wanting to forgo appeal of death sentence must, at minimum, demonstrate "objective and reasonable basis for believing that the client cannot act in his own interest"); *see also* Va. Ethics Op. 1816 (2005) (criminal defense lawyer whose suicidal client wants to be executed and directs lawyer not to present evidence in defense may take protective action if lawyer believes client unable to make rational, informed decision; depending upon degree of impairment, lawyer might seek mental evaluation, appointment of guardian, and/or go forward with defense anyway). *See generally* J.C. Oleson, *Swilling Hemlock: The Legal Ethics of Defending a Client Who Wishes to Volunteer for Execution*, 63 Wash. & Lee L. Rev. 147 (Winter 2006) (arguing that lawyers should not go along with death-row client's decision to forgo further appeals and volunteer for execution "because it is impossible to distinguish the will of the client from the situational effects of death-row syndrome").

## EMERGENCY LEGAL ASSISTANCE

Comments [9] and [10] were adopted in 1997 to clarify the lawyer's role when an individual with seriously diminished capacity needs immediate legal assistance but is not able to initiate a client-lawyer relationship. Comment [9] explains that a lawyer may take emergency protective legal action when the individual's health, safety, or financial interests are threatened with imminent and irreparable harm if the individual—or another acting in good faith—has consulted with the lawyer and the lawyer reasonably believes that the individual "has no other lawyer, agent or other representative available." In such emergency situations, the lawyer should act on behalf of the individual only to the extent reasonably necessary to maintain the status quo or otherwise avoid imminent and irreparable harm. Comment [10] advises the lawyer to "keep the confidences of the person *as if* dealing with a client," and to "take steps to regularize the relationship or implement other protective solutions as soon as possible" (emphasis added).

## Rule 1.15

### *Safekeeping Property*

(a) A lawyer shall hold property of clients or third persons that is in a lawyer's possession in connection with a representation separate from the lawyer's own property. Funds shall be kept in a separate account maintained in the state where the lawyer's office is situated, or elsewhere with the consent of the client or third person. Other property shall be identified as such and appropriately safeguarded. Complete records of such account funds and other property shall be kept by the lawyer and shall be preserved for a period of [five years] after termination of the representation.

(b) A lawyer may deposit the lawyer's own funds in a client trust account for the sole purpose of paying bank service charges on that account, but only in an amount necessary for that purpose.

(c) A lawyer shall deposit into a client trust account legal fees and expenses that have been paid in advance, to be withdrawn by the lawyer only as fees are earned or expenses incurred.

(d) Upon receiving funds or other property in which a client or third person has an interest, a lawyer shall promptly notify the client or third person. Except as stated in this Rule or otherwise permitted by law or by agreement with the client, a lawyer shall promptly deliver to the client or third person any funds or other property that the client or third person is entitled to receive and, upon request by the client or third person, shall promptly render a full accounting regarding such property.

(e) When in the course of representation a lawyer is in possession of property in which two or more persons (one of whom may be the lawyer) claim interests, the property shall be kept separate by the lawyer until the dispute is resolved. The lawyer shall promptly distribute all portions of the property as to which the interests are not in dispute.

## COMMENT

[1] A lawyer should hold property of others with the care required of a professional fiduciary. Securities should be kept in a safe deposit box, except when some other form of safekeeping is warranted by special circumstances. All property that is the property of clients or third persons, including prospective clients, must be kept

separate from the lawyer's business and personal property and, if monies, in one or more trust accounts. Separate trust accounts may be warranted when administering estate monies or acting in similar fiduciary capacities. A lawyer should maintain on a current basis books and records in accordance with generally accepted accounting practice and comply with any recordkeeping rules established by law or court order. See, e.g., ABA Model Rules for Client Trust Account Records.

[2] While normally it is impermissible to commingle the lawyer's own funds with client funds, paragraph (b) provides that it is permissible when necessary to pay bank service charges on that account. Accurate records must be kept regarding which part of the funds are the lawyer's.

[3] Lawyers often receive funds from which the lawyer's fee will be paid. The lawyer is not required to remit to the client funds that the lawyer reasonably believes represent fees owed. However, a lawyer may not hold funds to coerce a client into accepting the lawyer's contention. The disputed portion of the funds must be kept in a trust account and the lawyer should suggest means for prompt resolution of the dispute, such as arbitration. The undisputed portion of the funds shall be promptly distributed.

[4] Paragraph (e) also recognizes that third parties may have lawful claims against specific funds or other property in a lawyer's custody, such as a client's creditor who has a lien on funds recovered in a personal injury action. A lawyer may have a duty under applicable law to protect such third-party claims against wrongful interference by the client. In such cases, when the third-party claim is not frivolous under applicable law, the lawyer must refuse to surrender the property to the client until the claims are resolved. A lawyer should not unilaterally assume to arbitrate a dispute between the client and the third party, but, when there are substantial grounds for dispute as to the person entitled to the funds, the lawyer may file an action to have a court resolve the dispute.

[5] The obligations of a lawyer under this Rule are independent of those arising from activity other than rendering legal services. For example, a lawyer who serves only as an escrow agent is governed by the applicable law relating to fiduciaries even though the lawyer does not render legal services in the transaction and is not governed by this Rule.

[6] A lawyers' fund for client protection provides a means through the collective efforts of the bar to reimburse persons who have lost money or property as a result of dishonest conduct of a lawyer. Where such a fund has been established, a lawyer must participate where it is mandatory, and, even when it is voluntary, the lawyer should participate.

**State Rules Comparison**
http://ambar.org/MRPCStateCharts

# ANNOTATION
## GENERAL APPLICATION

Rule 1.15 imposes obligations of safekeeping, accounting, and delivery when a lawyer comes into possession of someone else's money or property. *See, e.g., Office of Disciplinary Counsel v. Adams*, No. SCAD-17-0000163, 2018 WL 1182888, 2018 BL 77729 (Haw. Mar. 7, 2018) ("grossly negligent recordkeeping" and overdrawing trust account with disbursements to self); *Att'y Grievance Comm'n v. Powell*, 192 A.3d 633 (Md. 2018) (disbursing estate funds for fees without court approval while representing personal representative for estate of decedent); *In re Dolgoff*, 18 N.Y.S.3d 922 (App. Div. 2015) (commingling personal funds with client funds, failing to keep appropriate records, withdrawing trust funds payable to cash and using them for personal purposes); *N.C. State Bar v. Merrell*, 777 S.E.2d 103 (N.C. 2015) (incorrectly identifying ownership of trust funds resulted in misappropriation); *Lawyer Disciplinary Bd. v. Haught*, 757 S.E.2d 609 (W. Va. 2014) (failing to safeguard or keep proper records of client funds after depositing them into IOLTA account); ABA Formal Ethics Op. 482 (2018) (discussing lawyer's obligations regarding property held in trust in event of disaster); D.C. Ethics Op. 374 (2018) (lawyer must safeguard prospective client's property, whether tangible or intangible, until decision on representation is made); *cf.* N.Y. City Ethics Op. 2015-3 (2015) (lawyer who has disbursed trust account funds as result of e-mail scam must promptly notify clients whose funds were in account).

Generally, Rule 1.15 is applied only when a lawyer obtains possession of another's property in connection with the representation of a client; all paragraphs save paragraph (d) expressly include such a limitation. *See* Cmt. [5] (rule inapplicable when lawyer holds funds in capacity other than as lawyer); American Bar Association, *A Legislative History: The Development of the ABA Model Rules of Professional Conduct, 1982–2013*, at 361 (2013). Some authorities, however, have applied Rule 1.15(d) to lawyers holding funds in scenarios other than the representation of a client. *See, e.g., People v. Rishel*, 50 P.3d 938 (Colo. O.P.D.J. 2002) (lawyer who belonged to group that pooled funds to purchase baseball tickets violated equivalent of Rule 1.15(d) by misusing funds); *In re McCann*, 894 A.2d 1087 (Del. 2005) (lawyer disciplined under equivalent of Rule 1.15(d) for failing to pay firm payroll taxes); *Att'y Grievance Comm'n v. Johnson*, 976 A.2d 245 (Md. 2009) (provisions of Rule 1.15(d) "ha[ve] been interpreted by this Court to apply 'generally' to the fiduciary duties connected with an attorney's holding of 'any property'[; so] the practice of law is not a prerequisite for an attorney to have violated" rule); *see also* Ariz. Ethics Op. 04-03 (2004) (lawyer who received funds from former client's sale of home cannot withdraw unpaid fees from those funds because he did not represent former client in home sale; Rule 1.15(d) nevertheless applies and requires former client's instructions for disbursement).

## *Paragraph (a): Identifying and Safeguarding Property of Others*

### ANTICOMMINGLING RULE

Rule 1.15(a) requires a lawyer to keep the property of others separate from the lawyer's own property. *See, e.g., In re Hagedorn*, 725 N.E.2d 397 (Ind. 2000) (lawyer appointed as guardian for individual and representative payee for individual's Social Security and Supplemental Security Income checks failed to keep guardianship funds separate from her own); *In re Baxter*, 940 P.2d 37 (Kan. 1997) (lawyer deposited settlement check in firm's business account and used funds for business expenses before mistake discovered); *Att'y Grievance Comm'n v. Weiers*, 102 A.3d 332 (Md. 2014) (failure to timely withdraw earned fees from trust account resulted in impermissible commingling); *In re Johnson*, 827 N.E.2d 206 (Mass. 2005) (lawyer deposited settlement checks in his firm's operating account); *In re Klotz*, 909 N.W.2d 327 (Minn. 2018) (having client deposit funds monthly into lawyer's business account for transfer to trust account to pay to client's creditor); *Disciplinary Counsel v. Corner*, 47 N.E.3d 847 (Ohio 2016) (commingling personal and client funds); *In re DiPippo*, 765 A.2d 1219 (R.I. 2001) (lawyer failed to deposit settlement proceeds in trust account); *Bd. of Prof'l Responsibility v. Sheppard*, 556 S.W.3d 139 (Tenn. 2018) (improperly transferring client funds from trust account to operating account to pay law firm expenses); *see also* Cal. Formal Ethics Op. 2005-169 (2005) (linking operating account to client trust account to cover inadvertent overdrafts in trust account permissible because accounts remain separate); Conn. Informal Ethics Op. 04-04 (2004) (lawyers who deposited personal funds in trust accounts to qualify for preferred-subscriber status for bank's stock violated rule).

The prohibition against commingling ensures that a lawyer's creditors will not be able to attach clients' property. *See In re Anonymous*, 698 N.E.2d 808 (Ind. 1998) (commingling of lawyer and client funds would subject clients to "unacceptable risks," such as attachment by creditors, or intended or unintended misappropriation by lawyer); *In re Glorioso*, 819 So. 2d 320 (La. 2002) (by commingling, lawyer put clients' funds at risk of being seized by IRS to satisfy lawyer's tax liability).

At the same time, the prohibition prevents lawyers from shielding personal assets from their own creditors by hiding funds in client trust accounts. *See In re Johnson*, 809 S.E.2d 797 (Ga. 2018) (lawyer deposited personal funds into client trust account to shield them from his creditors); *In re Lund*, 19 P.3d 110 (Kan. 2001) (lawyer claimed trust account held only client funds in effort to avoid garnishment by his ex-wife to satisfy outstanding judgment); *Att'y Grievance Comm'n v. Powell*, 192 A.3d 633 (Md. 2018) (depositing personal and family members' funds into client trust account to avoid scrutiny of IRS or divorce court); *In re Rebeau*, 787 N.W.2d 168 (Minn. 2010) (lawyer deposited earned fees in client trust account to shield funds from IRS); *Disciplinary Counsel v. Vogtsberger*, 895 N.E.2d 158 (Ohio 2008) (lawyer may not use client trust account as "'safe haven' for his money to avoid his personal financial responsibilities"); *In re Tidball*, 503 N.W.2d 850 (S.D. 1993) (lawyer commingled funds and used bank drafts to avoid garnishment by lawyer's personal creditors); *In re Trejo*, 185 P.3d 1160 (Wash. 2008) (lawyer used out-of-state client trust account to shield assets from garnishment by ex-wife).

## CONVERSION AND MISAPPROPRIATION

### • *Client Funds*

Misappropriation of client funds usually is an obvious violation of the rule and is dealt with by disbarment or other severe disciplinary sanction. *E.g., People v. Heaphy*, No. 14PDJ110, 2015 WL 11081955, 2015 BL 461238 (Colo. O.P.D.J. Sept. 9, 2015); *In re Malyszek*, 182 A.3d 1232 (D.C. 2018); *In re Cheatham*, 820 S.E.2d 668 (Ga. 2018); *In re Steele*, 45 N.E.3d 777 (Ind. 2015); *Att'y Disciplinary Bd. v. Stowe*, 830 N.W.2d 737 (Iowa 2013); *Ky. Bar Ass'n v. Mathews*, 308 S.W.3d 194 (Ky. 2010); *In re Dunn*, 241 So.

3d 984 (La. 2018); *Att'y Grievance Comm'n v. Cherry-Mahoi*, 879 A.2d 58 (Md. 2005); *In re Klotz*, 909 N.W.2d 327 (Minn. 2018) (intentional misappropriation); *In re Farris*, 472 S.W.3d 549 (Mo. 2015); *Disciplinary Counsel v. Riek*, 925 N.E.2d 980 (Ohio 2010); *In re Beck*, 773 S.E.2d 576 (S.C. 2015); *cf. Disciplinary Counsel v. Parnoff*, 152 A.3d 1222 (Conn. 2016) (rejecting mandatory disbarment for lawyer who erroneously believed former client's only interest in arbitration award proceeds was to pay another lawyer's fees and transferred disputed funds to personal account); *Att'y Disciplinary Bd. v. Powell*, 830 N.W.2d 355 (Iowa 2013) (court makes "distinction for purposes of sanctions between conduct involving trust fund violations and conduct in the nature of stealing").

### • *Stealing from Firm*

A court may apply Rule 1.15 in addition to Rule 8.4 (Misconduct) to a lawyer who misuses money that belongs to a law firm. *See, e.g., In re Morrell*, 684 A.2d 361 (D.C. 1996) (lawyer misappropriated hundreds of thousands of dollars from client, received compensation from both client and firm for same work, and also received kickback); *In re Christian*, 135 P.3d 1062 (Kan. 2006) (associate converted fees paid to himself on behalf of firm); *Hamilton v. Ky. Bar Ass'n*, 180 S.W.3d 470 (Ky. 2005) (associate who settled contingent-fee case at new firm failed to notify former firm that originally filed case and failed to tender former firm's share of fee); *Att'y Grievance Comm'n v. Kahl*, 84 A.3d 103 (Md. 2014) (accepting fees but not reporting them to firm and transferring funds without authorization from trust account to personal account); *State ex rel. Neb. State Bar Ass'n v. Frederiksen*, 635 N.W.2d 427 (Neb. 2001) (lawyer took $15,000 from his firm because he was dissatisfied with his compensation); *In re Sigman*, 104 A.3d 230 (N.J. 2014) (arranging for fees to be payable to lawyer instead of firm and failing to notify or pay firm its share); *In re Reynolds*, 39 P.3d 136 (N.M. 2002) (lawyer deposited more than $90,000 in firm and client estate funds in separate trust account he opened in his own name for his own use); *Disciplinary Counsel v. Jackson*, 56 N.E.3d 936 (Ohio 2016) (failing to share fees from court-appointed and other work with firm); *State ex rel. Okla. Bar Ass'n v. Biggers*, 981 P.2d 803 (Okla. 1999) (converting funds belonging to law firm and clients); *cf. In re Black*, 156 P.3d 641 (Kan. 2007) (county attorney failed to account for monies paid by traffic offenders to reimburse county's court costs). Also see the annotation to Rule 8.4.

### • *Administration of Estates and Trusts*

Rule 1.15 also applies to a lawyer's misuse of money when administering estates and trusts. *See, e.g., People v. Gallegos*, 229 P.3d 306 (Colo. O.P.D.J. 2010) (lawyer appointed as personal representative of deceased client's estate disbarred for misappropriating $500,000 of estate funds); *In re Merritt-Bagwell*, 122 A.3d 874 (D.C. 2015) (lawyer appointed guardian for minor's estate paid fees to herself without court approval); *In re Prince*, 494 S.E.2d 337 (Ga. 1998) (lawyer representing administratrix of estate took estate funds for personal use); *In re Stochel*, 34 N.E.3d 1207 (Ind. 2015) (lawyer serving as receiver converted receivership funds); *In re Arbour*, 915 So. 2d 345 (La. 2005) (withdrawing $40,000 in legal fees from probate estate without court approval); *Att'y Grievance Comm'n v. Kent*, 136 A.3d 394 (Md. 2016) (lawyer acting as trustee misappropriated funds); *In re O'Brien*, 894 N.W.2d 162 (Minn. 2017) (misappropriating over $300,000 from trust for which lawyer served as trustee); *In re Orsini*, 661 N.Y.S.2d 321 (App. Div. 1997) (converting funds from five estates, failing to reimburse more than $30,000 from three of those estates, and frequently commingling personal funds with client funds); *Cleveland Metro. Bar Ass'n v. Zoller and Mamone*, 73 N.E.3d 476 (Ohio 2016) (firm associates who were signatories on special client account failed to ensure account was separate, interest-bearing trust account or "to maintain even a modicum of oversight" that would have alerted them to "obvious improprieties," including overdrafts, resulting bank fees, and partner's overbilling); *State ex rel. Okla. Bar Ass'n v. Besly*, 136 P.3d 590 (Okla. 2006) (lawyer acting as executrix for estate paid herself legal fees from estate funds without court approval); *In re Brousseau*, 697 A.2d 1079 (R.I. 1997) (lawyer acting as administrator in probate estate withdrew funds for personal use); *In re Konnor*, 694 N.W.2d 376 (Wis. 2005) (lawyer acting as personal representative of estate allowed his brother to steal estate checkbook and forge three checks).

### • Safekeeping of Personal Property

The lawyer is responsible for safekeeping property, whether money or personal property, including documents and information held in electronic format and virtual currencies. *See, e.g., Fla. Bar v. Grosso*, 760 So. 2d 940 (Fla. 2000) (lawyer failed to safeguard and promptly return client's firearms); *Idaho State Bar v. Frazier*, 28 P.3d 363 (Idaho 2001) (theft of estate jewelry in lawyer's custody discovered after lawyer left items in briefcase at law office and at jeweler's for unreasonably long period); *In re Rathbun*, 124 P.3d 1 (Kan. 2005) (lawyer failed to deliver mail that client entrusted to him for forwarding to estranged husband); *In re Gold*, 693 So. 2d 148 (La. 1997) (after declining representation lawyer refused to return documents brought for his review by prospective client); *Att'y Grievance Comm'n v. Ghatt*, 192 A.3d 656 (Md. 2018) (lawyer acting as escrow agent facilitated fraudulent advanced fees scheme; lawyer had duty to investigate suspicious nature of transactions and safeguard funds until resolved); *In re Donohue*, No. 69228, 2016 WL 4079666, 2016 BL 253248 (Nev. July 22, 2016) (failure to limit paralegal's access to clients' sensitive financial information, resulting in paralegal's using one client's credit card for personal purchases and stealing another's identity); *Innes v. Marzano-Lesnevich*, 87 A.3d 775 (N.J. Super. Ct. App. Div. 2014), *aff'd as modified*, 136 A.3d 108 (N.J. 2016) (law firm representing wife in divorce turned over minor child's passport to client in spite of agreement prohibiting parents from traveling abroad with child); *In re Becker*, 504 N.W.2d 303 (N.D. 1993) (client's jewelry stolen from lawyer's car); *Columbus Bar Ass'n v. Kiesling*, 925 N.E.2d 970 (Ohio 2010) (lawyer failed to provide copies of several years' worth of tax returns required to administer estate of client's deceased husband); *In re Blackmon*, 629 S.E.2d 369 (S.C. 2006) (lawyer who retained original wills and deeds became incommunicado after testators' deaths); Conn. Informal Ethics Op. 92-21 (1992) (abstract of real estate title search prepared for client was client property and must be given to client upon request); Neb. Ethics Op. 17-3 (2017) (must safeguard digital currencies such as bitcoin separate from lawyer's property); N.Y. City Ethics Op. 2015-3 (2015) (lawyer following e-mail fraudster's instructions to transfer funds from trust account violates duty to preserve client funds); Ohio State Bar Ethics Op. 2013-03 (2013) (law firm must identify and safeguard electronic client information stored in cloud); *cf.* N.C. Ethics Op. 2015-6 (2015) (lawyer who has taken reasonable steps to maintain security of client trust funds as required by Rule 1.15 not required to replace client funds stolen by hacker).

Retaining liens—allowing for the retention of client papers and property until the lawyer is compensated for services rendered—are recognized in some jurisdictions. See the annotation to Rule 1.16.

## INTENT

No intent element is expressly included in Rule 1.15 and some authorities suggest that no intent need be proven to establish a violation. *See In re Mayeaux*, 762 So. 2d 1072 (La. 2000) (lawyer's "mistake, good faith, or lack of conscious wrongdoing does not negate an infraction of the rule"); *Att'y Grievance Comm'n v. Sperling*, 185 A.3d 76 (Md. 2018) ("an unintentional violation of 1.15(a) is still a violation"); *State ex rel. Okla. Bar Ass'n v. Helton*, 394 P.3d 227 (Okla. 2017) (lawyer who unintentionally overpaid himself out of funds that were to be held for client's benefit committed simple conversion); *Restatement (Third) of the Law Governing Lawyers* § 5 cmt. d (2000) ("Some few offenses, such as those requiring maintenance of office books and records . . . are absolute in form, thus warranting a finding of a violation . . . no matter what the lawyer's state of mind"). *But see* Nancy J. Moore, *Mens Rea Standards in Lawyer Disciplinary Codes*, 23 Geo. J. Legal Ethics 1 (Winter 2010) (arguing that some intent element should be implicit in Rule 1.15; "commingling lawyer and client funds and improper use of client funds . . . are almost always the product of either knowing or negligent conduct, and there is little reason to believe that bar counsel would have any difficulty in proving negligence when it occurs").

## LACK OF HARM NOT A DEFENSE

That a lawyer's commingling, temporary use, or improper accounting of client funds causes no actual harm to a client is not a defense to a charge under Rule 1.15. *See In re Anonymous*, 698 N.E.2d 808 (Ind. 1998) ("that client funds were never . . . at risk" is irrelevant to charge of commingling under rule); *In re Webre*, No. 2017-B-1861, 2018 WL 456373, 2018 BL 16753 (La. Jan. 12, 2018) (after depositing client funds into personal account instead of trust account, lawyer refunded unearned balance from trust account, causing no harm to client but "potential harm to other clients"); *Att'y Grievance Comm'n v. Whitehead*, 890 A.2d 751 (Md. 2006) (lawyer withdrew fees earned as conservator without court approval, though he promptly returned unapproved fees); *In re Klotz*, 909 N.W.2d 327 (Minn. 2018) (intentional misappropriation, commingling, and mismanagement of client's funds did not permanently injure any client but "harmed the public and the profession because it eroded the public's trust in lawyers and reflects poorly on the profession"); *Cleveland Metro. Bar Ass'n v. Walker*, 32 N.E.3d 437 (Ohio 2015) (commingling personal and client funds, failing to properly reconcile trust account or keep proper records); *In re PRB Docket No. 2013.160*, 118 A.3d 523 (Vt. 2015) (holding uncashed title insurance trust account checks payable to law firm for seven months); *In re Trejo*, 185 P.3d 1160 (Wash. 2008) (discipline warranted even if commingling causes no actual harm because it causes potential harm of having client funds attached by lawyer's creditors).

## INTEREST-BEARING ACCOUNTS
### • Generally

If a lawyer is holding a substantial sum of money for a client or will be holding funds for a considerable period of time, the lawyer may be required, absent client consent to do otherwise, to deposit such monies in an interest-bearing account and pay the interest to the client upon final disbursement. *See, e.g., Fla. Bar v. Dancu*, 490 So. 2d 40 (Fla. 1986) (court characterized lawyer's keeping interest earned on client's insurance benefits as "stealing a client's money").

### • IOLTA

For instances when a lawyer is holding funds in amounts too small or durations too short to earn interest, most states have established Interest on Lawyer Trust Account (IOLTA) plans. IOLTA plans allow such funds to be pooled and thus to earn interest. The interest is paid into a special fund that uses the income for public purposes, usually the provision of legal services to those with low incomes. All jurisdictions have created some sort of IOLTA program. See the "Status of IOLTA Programs" chart maintained by the ABA Commission on IOLTA, available at https://www. americanbar.org/groups/interest_lawyers_trust_accounts/resources/status_of_ iolta_programs/.

Although in *Phillips v. Wash. Legal Found.*, 524 U.S. 156 (1998), the Supreme Court held interest generated by funds in IOLTA accounts to be the private property of the client for Fifth Amendment purposes, it held in a later case that an IOLTA plan does not work a compensable "taking":

> It is neither unethical nor illegal for lawyers to deposit their clients' funds in a single bank account. A state law that requires client funds that could not otherwise generate net earnings for the client to be deposited in an IOLTA account is not a "regulatory taking." A law that requires that the interest on those funds be transferred to a different owner for a legitimate public use, however, could be a *per se* taking requiring the payment of "just compensation" to the client. Because that compensation is measured by the owner's pecuniary loss—which is zero whenever the Washington law is obeyed— there has been no violation of the Just Compensation Clause of the Fifth Amendment in this case.

*Brown v. Legal Found. of Wash.*, 538 U.S. 216, 240 (2003).

## RECORDKEEPING

Rule 1.15(a) requires lawyers to keep complete records of all funds held in connection with the representation of clients. *See, e.g., In re Fountain*, 878 A.2d 1167 (Del. 2005) ("multi-year failure to maintain proper books and records and safeguard client funds"); *Fla. Bar v. Smiley*, 622 So. 2d 465 (Fla. 1993) (failing to properly maintain required records for client trust account: ledger cards, monthly statements and reconciliations, and cash receipts and disbursements journal); *In re Coulter*, 816 S.E.2d 1 (Ga. 2018) (failing to maintain complete records or accurately account for client's funds); *In re Mossler*, 6 N.E.3d 387 (Ind. 2017) (failing to maintain proper trust account records); *In re Pearson*, 888 N.W.2d 319 (Minn. 2016) (failing to maintain trust account records); *In re Gonzalez*, 85 N.Y.S.3d 226 (App. Div. 2018) (failing to reconcile or keep records of special account and failing to keep records of property of clients and others); *In re Chinquist*, 714 N.W.2d 469 (N.D. 2006) (accepting advance cash fee payments from client without creating receipts or retaining records of time spent on case); *Disciplinary Counsel v. Joltin*, 67 N.E.3d 780 (Ohio 2016) (failing to keep trust account records for five years); *In re Jordan*, 809 S.E.2d 409 (S.C. 2017) (repeated commingling and overpayments from trust account covered up by poor recordkeeping); Mo. Informal Ethics Op. 20040052 (2004) (lawyer must keep records of all transactions involving client funds and property for five years after representation ends; construing prior version of rule). *Compare In re Murray*, 920 N.E.2d 862 (Mass. 2010) (failure to keep records of bundles of cash found in hospitalized client's home created rebuttable presumption that lawyer misused funds), *with In re Mulroe*, 956 N.E.2d 422 (Ill. 2011) ("careless bookkeeping" and failure to follow prescribed procedures for safekeeping client funds did not create presumption of dishonesty). *See generally* Irene M. Ricci, *Client Trust Funds: How to Avoid Ethical Problems*, 11 Geo. J. Legal Ethics 245 (Winter 1998).

Although a lawyer may delegate the work to another person, the lawyer remains ultimately responsible for compliance with recordkeeping requirements. *In re Bailey*, 821 A.2d 851 (Del. 2003) (managing partner of firm failed to prevent firm bookkeeper's improper withdrawal of client funds from trust); *In re Robinson*, 74 A.3d 688 (D.C. 2013) (lawyer should have carefully monitored subordinate tasked with trust account administration after first overdraft and should have removed subordinate after second overdraft); *In re Peloquin*, 338 P.3d 568 (Kan. 2014) (failure to supervise office manager); *Att'y Grievance Comm'n v. Sperling*, 185 A.3d 76 (Md. 2018) (sole signatory on firm client trust account failed to review account records or perform monthly reconciliations and therefore was unaware that his employer, a suspended lawyer, had misappropriated client funds); *In re Montpetit*, 528 N.W.2d 243 (Minn. 1995) (lawyer should have known secretary improperly maintained trust account books and records; lawyers charged with knowledge of requirements for handling client funds); *State ex rel. Okla. Bar Ass'n v. Mayes*, 977 P.2d 1073 (Okla. 1999) (lax supervision of nonlawyer office manager allowed commingling and conversion); *In re David*, 690 S.E.2d 579 (S.C. 2010) (delegating accounting of client trust account to single, untrained, nonlawyer employee); *In re Light*, 615 N.W.2d 164 (S.D. 2000) (leaving management of firm trust account to associate and clerical staff, allowing unearned fees to be taken out of trust); *In re PRB No. 2013-145*, 165 A.3d 130 (Vt. 2017) (firm's failure to reconcile IOLTA account or keep records discovered after bookkeeper suddenly left). See the annotation to Rule 5.3 for discussion of a lawyer's responsibilities when delegating the management of a client trust account to a nonlawyer.

For review of the ABA Model Rules for Client Trust Account Records, adopted in 2010, see https://www.americanbar.org/content/dam/aba/administrative/professional_responsibility/aba_model_rules_on_client_trust_account_records.pdf.

## Paragraph (b): Deposit of Personal Funds to Avoid Bank Charges

Paragraph (b), added in 2002, incorporates an accommodation that many jurisdictions had already been making, either by amendment or by interpretation, to permit lawyers to deposit personal funds in trust accounts to pay bank charges. The personal funds deposited may not be greater than necessary to pay the charges. *See, e.g., In re Yacobi,* 811 S.E.2d 791 (S.C. 2018) (depositing more personal funds than necessary to cover trust account shortages and fees and failing to remove overage); L.A. Cnty. Ethics Op. 485 (1995) (lawyer may keep personal funds in trust account to pay bank charges if amount bears reasonable relationship to amount of charges expected, but not as buffer against possible overdrafts in trust account, whether overdrafts caused by bank or lawyer error); Md. Ethics Op. 00-18 (1999) (law firm may deposit funds in trust account to cover bank charges for returned checks, or may arrange for charges to be deducted from firm's operating account); R.I. Ethics Op. 93-57 (1993) (lawyer may deposit own monies in trust account to avoid service charges, as long as amount is minimum necessary to avoid charges and lawyer does not use funds for any other purpose).

## Paragraph (c): Deposit of Legal Fees and Expenses

In 2002, paragraph (c) was added because of reports that "the single largest class of claims made to client protection funds is for the taking of unearned fees." American Bar Association, *A Legislative History: The Development of the ABA Model Rules of Professional Conduct, 1982–2013,* at 360 (2013). The rule is now explicit that a lawyer must deposit in a client trust account any legal fees and expenses that have been paid in advance, and may withdraw them only as earned or incurred. Rule 1.16(d) imposes a complementary obligation to refund any unearned or unused advances at the termination of a representation. See the annotation to Rule 1.16.

### CHARACTER OF ADVANCE PAYMENTS

Jurisdictions differ in determining the point at which legal fees paid to a lawyer become the lawyer's property. In general, fees paid in advance of the performance of legal services are client funds until earned and therefore must be placed in a client funds account. *See, e.g., In re Sather,* 3 P.3d 403 (Colo. 2000) (unless fee agreement "expressly states that a fee is an engagement retainer and explains how the fee is earned upon receipt, it will be presumed that any advance fee is a deposit from which [the] lawyer will be paid"); *In re Lochow,* 469 N.W.2d 91 (Minn. 1991) (advance payments of lawyers' fees are client funds, which must be placed in client trust account until earned); *In re Montclare,* 376 P.3d 811 (N.M. 2016) (real estate transferred to lawyer as flat fee payment must be safeguarded and returned promptly to client if any portion of fee is not earned); *State ex rel. Okla. Bar Ass'n v. Friesen,* 384 P.3d 1129 (Okla. 2016) (improper to treat as earned entire fee for reaching structured settlement in wrongful death matter, setting up annuities, trusts, and children's college accounts, and preparing wills, where lawyer knew some work could not be performed for years to come due to children's ages); Alaska Ethics Op. 2012-2 (2012) (flat or fixed fees must be deposited in lawyer's trust account until earned unless agreed otherwise in detailed writing); D.C. Ethics Op. 355 (2010) (advance fee payment must be placed in lawyer's trust account unless otherwise agreed; in absence of agreement about how lawyer is determined to have earned portions of fixed fee, lawyer has burden of establishing that he earned fees transferred out of trust account); Mo. Formal Ethics Op. 128 (2010) ("all flat fees must be deposited into a lawyer trust account and promptly removed when actually earned"); N.Y. State Ethics Op. 983 (2013) (lawyer may, at client's request, treat unearned portion of advance retainer for concluded matter as advance retainer for unspecified future legal services and must then maintain funds in trust account).

Some types of advance payment, however, have been held to be the lawyer's property upon receipt. A fee paid in exchange for the lawyer's future availability, some authorities reason, is earned upon receipt and so becomes the lawyer's funds, not to be deposited in a client trust account. *See, e.g., Dowling v. Chi. Options Assocs., Inc.*, 875 N.E.2d 1012 (Ill. 2007) (distinguishing "general retainers" and "advance payment retainers," which are considered earned upon receipt and placed in lawyer's general account, from "security retainer," which must be placed in client trust account and withdrawn only as services are performed). Several authorities have held that with the consent of the client, a fee paid in advance for a legal matter, the amount of which does not depend upon the amount of the lawyer's time spent on the matter, becomes the lawyer's property upon receipt. *See, e.g., id.* (calling such fee an "advance payment retainer," which is property of lawyer upon payment if client agrees to such treatment in written retainer agreement); *In re Kendall*, 804 N.E.2d 1152 (Ind. 2004) (flat fee paid in advance for work regardless of lawyer time becomes property of lawyer upon receipt and need not be held separately); Or. Ethics Op. 2005-151 (2005; rev. 2011) (when retaining agreement expressly states fixed fee is earned upon receipt, it may not be deposited in client trust account); *cf. Cluck v. Comm'n for Lawyer Discipline*, 214 S.W.3d 736 (Tex. App. 2007) (fee paid under written agreement that expressly said future hourly charges would be billed against it could not be characterized as "retainer"; it was advance to be deposited in client trust). Note that the lawyer may still be required by Rule 1.16(d) to refund, at the end of the representation, any portion of such fee that has not been "earned." See the annotation to Rule 1.16. *See generally* Tyler Moore, *Flat Fee Fundamentals: An Introduction to the Ethical Issues Surrounding the Flat Fee After* In re Mance, 23 Geo. J. Legal Ethics 701 (Summer 2010); Douglas R. Richmond, *Understanding Retainers and Flat Fees*, 34 J. Legal Prof. 113 (Fall 2009).

For discussion of whether and when fees belong to the lawyer or client, see the annotation to Rule 1.5.

## CREDIT CARD PAYMENTS

Numerous ethics opinions have approved advance payments of fees and expenses via credit cards, as long as the payments are credited to a client trust account. *See* Conn. Informal Ethics Op. 05-14 (2005); D.C. Ethics Op. 348 (2009); Kan. Ethics Op. 01-02 (2001); Ky. Ethics Op. E-426 (2007); Md. Ethics Op. 2003-06 (2003); Mich. Informal Ethics Op. RI-344 (2008); N.C. Ethics Op. 2009-4 (2009); Ohio Ethics Op. 2007-3 (2007); Utah Ethics Op. 97-06 (1997); *cf.* Haw. Ethics Op. 45 (2015) (credit card payments for unearned retainers or flat fees and earned fees may not be commingled). Because, however, most issuers of credit cards impose administrative costs and allow consumers a period to charge back the entire amount of a payment in case of a dispute—even if, for instance, a lawyer already deducted part of the payment as reimbursement of expenses—lawyers must ensure such costs or "chargebacks" do not come from other clients' funds in trust. *See In re White-Steiner*, 198 P.3d 1195 (Ariz. 2009) (lawyer unwittingly allowed credit card administrative fees to be deducted from client trust funds); La. Ethics Op. 12-RPCC-019 (2012) (lawyer must ensure credit card company takes "chargebacks" and transaction costs from operating account and not client trust account); Mich. Informal Ethics Op. RI-344 (2008) (lawyer must either arrange for "chargebacks" and issuer fees to be charged from lawyer's operating account or wait to withdraw earned fees and reimbursements until card issuer's dispute period elapses); Va. Ethics Op. 1848 (2009) (lawyer should arrange for "chargebacks" and administrative fees to be charged from lawyer's operating account); *cf.* Haw. Ethics Op. 45 (2015) (lawyer must deposit funds sufficient to pay credit card expenses into trust account unless client has given advance consent to pay charges); Pa. Ethics Op. 2011-028 (2011) (lawyer who accepts payments through PayPal or similar company must ensure transaction fees are paid by lawyer and not from client trust account funds, and that company will not freeze lawyer's trust account in event of payment dispute).

## MARKETING AND REFERRAL ARRANGEMENTS

Lawyers who participate in group coupon or "daily deal" marketing arrangements must determine whether to deposit the funds transmitted by the marketing organization into their general or client trust accounts. The key to this determination, as ABA Formal Opinion 465 observes, is whether a deal is structured as a coupon for a discount or as a fee for legal services to be rendered in the future. If the former, the funds forwarded to the lawyer by the marketing organization are not legal fees and may be deposited in the lawyer's general account. If the latter, the funds paid to the lawyer are advance legal fees, which must be deposited in the lawyer's trust account. ABA Formal Ethics Op. 465 (2013); *see, e.g.,* Md. Ethics Op. 2012-07 (2012); N.C. Ethics Op. 2011-10 (2011); S.C. Ethics Op. 11-05 (2011).

State authorities that have approved these arrangements generally opine that payments for legal services that are not rendered must be refunded in full, including the fee retained by the marketing company. *See, e.g.,* Md. Ethics Op. 2012-07 (2012); Neb. Ethics Op. 2012-03 (2012); N.H. Ethics Op. 2013/14-08 (2013); N.Y. State Ethics Op. 897 (2011); *cf.* N.C. Ethics Op. 2011-10 (2011) (payment deposited in lawyer's trust account must be refunded to purchaser who fails to claim services, but entire payment, including sum retained by marketing company, must be refunded to purchaser if lawyer determines conflict or other circumstances preclude lawyer from providing services).

Jurisdictions that have disapproved lawyers' use of group coupon and other third-party marketing and referral arrangements cite the difficulty of complying with Rule 1.15, among other considerations. *E.g.,* Ala. Ethics Op. 2012-01 (2012); Ariz. Ethics Op. 13-01 (2013); Ind. Ethics Op. 2012-1 (2012); Ohio Sup. Ct. Ethics Op. 2016-3

(2016); *see also* N.H. Ethics Op. 2013/14-08 (2013) (monies from sale of group discount coupon for legal services are not legal fees and do not implicate Rule 1.15, but structure of group prepaid legal fee deal, which requires compliance with Rule 1.15, is unlikely to be feasible); Pa. Formal Ethics Op. 2016-200 (2016) (lawyer risks violating Rule 1.15 by participating in arrangement with flat fee limited scope referral business that collects legal fee and remits it to lawyer after services are performed because lawyer may not delegate possession or distribution of legal fees paid in advance); Utah Ethics Op. 17-05 (2017) (questioning whether lawyer can protect client funds if third-party referral service is given access to lawyer's trust account).

## Paragraph (d): Notification and Delivery of Funds

### REQUIREMENT OF PROMPT NOTIFICATION AND DELIVERY

Paragraph (d) (renumbered from paragraph (b) in 2002) provides that when a lawyer receives funds or property in which a client or third party has an interest, the lawyer must promptly (1) notify the client or third party, (2) deliver the funds or property to the client or third party when due, and (3) render a full accounting upon request. *See, e.g., In re Hawk*, Misc. No. 115-006, 2016 WL 7157977, 2016 BL 405332 (S.D. Ga. Dec. 6, 2016) (failure to make timely restitution to clients after paralegal's embezzlement of trust account funds); *Ligon v. Tapp*, 519 S.W.3d 315 (Ark. 2017) (refusal to distribute proceeds from sale of marital home to divorce client after representation ended); *In re Att'y G*, 302 P.3d 248 (Colo. 2013) (lawyer not entitled to assert retaining lien over fee-guarantor's passport and therefore must return it); *In re Nave*, 280 A.3d 86 (D.C. 2018) (failure to promptly disburse settlement funds to client's medical providers); *Fla. Bar v. Silver*, 788 So. 2d 958 (Fla. 2001) (lawyer failed to notify medical clinic promptly about final settlement); *In re Johnson*, 53 N.E.3d 1177 (Ind. 2016) (failing to provide refunds or accountings for funds received, time spent, and disbursements made when requested by former clients); *In re Biscanin*, 390 P.3d 886 (Kan. 2017) (failure to return client's funds until at least six weeks after demand); *Ky. Bar Ass'n v. Burgin*, 412 S.W.3d 872 (Ky. 2013) (leaving endorsed settlement check in file for several years instead of promptly depositing check in trust account and properly disbursing proceeds); *In re Curry*, 16 So. 3d 1139 (La. 2009) (tardy and incomprehensible accounting); *Att'y Grievance Comm'n v. Hodes*, 105 A.3d 533 (Md. 2014) (lawyer serving as trustee transferred trust funds to himself instead of distributing them to beneficiary); *In re Hartke*, 529 N.W.2d 678 (Minn. 1995) (using client funds to cover day-to-day operating expenses without consent of client, and failing to disburse settlement monies promptly); *In re Moore*, 4 P.3d 664 (N.M. 2000) (failing to abide by promise to treating physician to pay for physician's services from proceeds of personal injury settlement); *Office of Disciplinary Counsel v. Sanborn*, 690 N.E.2d 1272 (Ohio 1998) (over ten-year period, lawyer misappropriated funds from estate for which he was fiduciary and failed to notify survivors of receipt of estate's funds); *In re Starr*, 952 P.2d 1017 (Or. 1998) (even if client "expects the lawyer to receive funds on the client's behalf, the lawyer has an affirmative duty to notify the client promptly and expressly when the lawyer in fact receives the funds"); *In re Hall*, 329 P.3d 870 (Wash. 2014) (refusal to return clients' original estate planning documents); ABA Formal Ethics Op. 475 (2016) (earned fee subject to division under agreement with other lawyer must be held and safeguarded separate from lawyer's own property, other lawyer must be promptly notified, and funds promptly delivered and accounted for); D.C. Ethics Op. 357 (2010) (absent agreement otherwise, lawyer must promptly provide paper copies of electronically maintained client records to client upon request if reasonable); La. Ethics Op. 05-RPCC-0004 (2005) (after notifying client and creditor of receipt of funds, lawyer must promptly distribute any portion of funds not in dispute; lawyer may retain only disputed portion); Tex. Ethics Op. 606 (2011) (lawyer must promptly return unearned fees at close of representation, even if lawyer suspects funds derived from criminal activity). *See generally* David R. Yates, *Accounting of Funds: What Do Lawyers Owe Their Clients?*, 25 J. Legal Prof. 255 (2001).

## MISSING CLIENTS

Several state ethics opinions have advised that when lawyers hold funds for clients whose whereabouts are unknown, the money may be disposed of under state laws governing unclaimed property. *E.g.*, Colo. Ethics Op. 95 (1993) (nominal sums may be kept indefinitely; larger sums may be disposed of under state unclaimed-property act if reasonable efforts to locate client fail); D.C. Ethics Op. 359 (2011) (lawyer should make reasonable efforts to locate missing client promptly after funds due and, if unsuccessful, should dispose of property under unclaimed-property statute); Kan. Ethics Op. 00-94 (2000) (lawyer must dispose of unclaimed funds under state unclaimed-property statute after appropriate efforts to contact client fail); Ohio Ethics Op. 2008-03 (2008) (following statutory procedures for unclaimed property for missing clients' monies in lawyer trust accounts does not violate Rule 1.15); Pa. Ethics Op. 2003-13 (2003) (lawyer may ethically obey state treasury department's demand that he report and turn over to it as escheated any unclaimed funds in his trust and escrow accounts). For discussion of a lawyer's duty to make reasonable efforts to locate missing clients, see the annotation to Rule 1.4.

## *Paragraph (e): Property Claimed by Both the Lawyer and Another Person*

Paragraph (e) (renumbered from paragraph (c)) was amended in 2002. The former version covered disputes between the lawyer and "another person." The revised language covers disputes between "two or more persons (one of whom may be the lawyer)." The current rule envisions at least three kinds of disputes: client-lawyer, client-creditor, and lawyer-client's creditor. The amended rule continues to require that the lawyer segregate disputed property until the dispute is resolved, and adds a sentence clarifying the lawyer's duty to distribute promptly any portion of the property not in dispute. *See* American Bar Association, *A Legislative History: The Development of the ABA Model Rules of Professional Conduct, 1982–2013*, at 360 (2013).

## WHEN LAWYER AND CLIENT BOTH HAVE CLAIMS

If the lawyer and client disagree about how to divide the funds, the lawyer must distribute any undisputed portion and hold the disputed funds in trust until the matter is resolved. *See, e.g., Att'y Disciplinary Bd. v. Rhinehart*, 827 N.W.2d 169 (Iowa

2013) (clients' refusal to discuss dispute over funds did not justify lawyer's disbursing funds to himself instead of keeping monies in trust account); *In re Harris*, 934 P.2d 965 (Kan. 1997) (using trust funds that were subject of ongoing fee dispute with client); *Att'y Grievance Comm'n v. Sacks*, 183 A.3d 86 (Md. 2018) (failure to deposit disputed retainer fees into trust account); *In re Hoffman*, 834 N.W.2d 636 (N.D. 2013) ($30,000 nonrefundable fee was reasonable and properly deposited in lawyer's operating account upon receipt, but once client discharged lawyer and requested partial refund, lawyer should have segregated disputed funds in trust account until resolution of dispute); *State ex rel. Okla. Bar Ass'n v. Wilcox*, 318 P.3d 1114 (Okla. 2014) (depositing workers' compensation client's temporary total disability checks into lawyer's mother's checking account, arguing that client gave permission because lawyer had advanced transportation expenses); *In re Starr*, 952 P.2d 1017 (Or. 1998) (lawyer required to leave disputed funds in trust account until dispute resolved, regardless of lawyer's lien on some or all of disputed funds); *Roberts v. Va. State Bar*, 818 S.E.2d 45 (Va. 2018) (withdrawing disputed funds from trust account as partial quantum meruit fee after client demanded refund); *In re Strand*, 505 N.W.2d 134 (Wis. 1993) (withdrawing client's funds from trust account as partial payment of fee while dispute pending); *see also In re Haar*, 698 A.2d 412 (D.C. 1997) (withdrawing legal fee from account belonging to both client and lawyer constituted negligent misappropriation of client funds when client disputed lawyer's right to those funds); *Richmond's Case*, 904 A.2d 684 (N.H. 2006) (selling securities from clients' accounts and using proceeds to pay legal fee arrearages); *In re Lee*, 835 N.W.2d 836 (N.D. 2013) (Crothers, J., concurring specially) (distinguishing paragraphs (a) and (e) and arguing that same conduct does not warrant finding of violation of both paragraphs); *cf.* Md. Ethics Op. 2009-03 (n.d.) (contingent-fee lawyer who receives settlement check that client refuses to endorse should hold check, withdraw from representation, and file suit for fees); Nev. Ethics Op. 51 (2014) (criminal defense lawyer who receives envelope of cash from unknown source for representation of three defendants, one of whom will be represented by different lawyer, must deposit cash into trust account until agreement is reached on apportionment of funds); Phila. Ethics Op. 2013-4 (2013) (law firm wishing to apply retainer balance to unbilled time on matter being handled by former partner who requested funds be transferred to him must hold funds in escrow account until dispute resolved).

## DUTY TO PROTECT CLAIMS OF CLIENT'S CREDITORS

Third parties, such as creditors of the client, may have valid claims against client funds or property held by a lawyer. The lawyer may have a duty under applicable law to protect these claims against wrongful interference by the client and to refuse to surrender the money or property to the client. Rule 1.15, cmt. [4]; *see, e.g., In re Lee*, 95 A.3d 66 (D.C. 2014) (misappropriating insurance payment in which client's mortgagee had interest); *Fla. Bar v. Bailey*, 803 So. 2d 683 (Fla. 2001) (client transferred stock into his lawyer's foreign investment account to facilitate turnover of funds to U.S. government in exchange for sentence reduction, but lawyer used it to pay himself instead); *In re Kirby*, 766 N.E.2d 351 (Ind. 2002) (lawyer who executed "doctor's lien" settled case without notifying doctor); *Ky. Bar Ass'n v. Burgin*, 412 S.W.3d 872 (Ky.

2013) (lawyer arranged for replacement settlement check to be payable to client alone and disbursed entire amount to client instead of reserving funds to satisfy Medicaid lien); *Thomas B. Olson & Assoc. v. Leffert Jay & Polglaze P.A.*, 756 N.W.2d 907 (Minn. Ct. App. 2008) (law firm holding portion of settlement funds subject to predecessor firm's pending lien petition "may have . . . a fiduciary duty" to predecessor firm; citing Rule 1.15); *Winship v. Gem City Bone & Joint, P.C.*, 185 P.3d 1252 (Wyo. 2008) (lawyer liable to client's treating physicians for failing to disburse settlement proceeds in compliance with client's assignment to physicians). *See generally* Charles M. Cork III, *A Lawyer's Ethical Obligations When the Client's Creditors Claim a Share of the Tort Settlement Proceeds*, 39 Tort Trial & Ins. Prac. L.J. 121 (Fall 2003). However, according to Comment [4], a "lawyer should not unilaterally assume to arbitrate a dispute between the client and the third party," and may therefore need to file an interpleader to resolve the dispute. *See, e.g., Hsu v. Parker*, 688 N.E.2d 1099 (Ohio Ct. App. 1996) (when dispute arose about proceeds claimed by client and physicians, lawyer should have filed complaint in interpleader).

Several state authorities have addressed a lawyer's duty to release funds to a third party. *See, e.g.,* Ala. Ethics Op. 2003-02 (2003) (lawyer who sends "protection letter" to client's creditor in anticipation of settlement must pay creditor from settlement funds, despite client's contrary instruction, if no dispute about debt); Conn. Informal Ethics Op. 01-08 (2001) (lawyer must not surrender to client property that lawyer comes to possess if lawyer knows of valid judgment or lien or assignment concerning property, or of letter of protection directly related to property); D.C. Ethics Op. 293 (2000) (discussing "just claims" of third parties and lawyer's obligations regarding disputed funds); Md. Ethics Op. 2004-06 (2003) (if lawyer determines limitation period has run on creditor's legal claim for disputed funds he has held in trust for several years, he may disburse funds to client); Mo. Informal Ethics Op. 970215 (1997) (lawyer who advised client to agree with creditor to pay outstanding debt out of proceeds of settlement of unrelated matter may not thereafter disburse settlement funds to client without consent of creditor); N.C. Ethics Op. 2001-11 (2002) (lawyer authorized by client to pay medical provider upon settlement may, when client changes mind, hold disputed funds in trust until impasse resolved by agreement or court order); Pa. Ethics Op. 2004-118 (2004) (lawyer who settled client's suit and escrowed money to satisfy workers' compensation lien must continue to hold funds in escrow notwithstanding client's demand to give client the money); S.C. Ethics Op. 05-08 (2005) (even in absence of letter of protection, lawyer who knows insurer has subrogation claim against settlement proceeds may not pay all proceeds to client but must retain sufficient funds to pay subrogation claim); *cf. Biller Assocs. v. Peterken*, 849 A.2d 847 (Conn. 2004) (rule did not create fiduciary duty for lawyer to protect creditor of client despite lawyer's acknowledgment of debt to creditor). *See generally* M. Collette Gibbons & Elin Brenner, *Divided Loyalties: A Lawyer's Duties to a Client's Creditors*, 10 Prob. & Prop. 24 (Dec. 1996); Sylvia Stevens, *The "Pushmi-Pullyu": Resolving Third-Party Claims to Client Funds*, 60 Or. St. B. Bull. 25 (Sept. 2000).

## Rule 1.16

*Declining or Terminating Representation*

(a) Except as stated in paragraph (c), a lawyer shall not represent a client or, where representation has commenced, shall withdraw from the representation of a client if:

(1) the representation will result in violation of the Rules of Professional Conduct or other law;

(2) the lawyer's physical or mental condition materially impairs the lawyer's ability to represent the client; or

(3) the lawyer is discharged.

(b) Except as stated in paragraph (c), a lawyer may withdraw from representing a client if:

(1) withdrawal can be accomplished without material adverse effect on the interests of the client;

(2) the client persists in a course of action involving the lawyer's services that the lawyer reasonably believes is criminal or fraudulent;

(3) the client has used the lawyer's services to perpetrate a crime or fraud;

(4) the client insists upon taking action that the lawyer considers repugnant or with which the lawyer has a fundamental disagreement;

(5) the client fails substantially to fulfill an obligation to the lawyer regarding the lawyer's services and has been given reasonable warning that the lawyer will withdraw unless the obligation is fulfilled;

(6) the representation will result in an unreasonable financial burden on the lawyer or has been rendered unreasonably difficult by the client; or

(7) other good cause for withdrawal exists.

(c) A lawyer must comply with applicable law requiring notice to or permission of a tribunal when terminating a representation. When ordered to do so by a tribunal, a lawyer shall continue representation notwithstanding good cause for terminating the representation.

(d) Upon termination of representation, a lawyer shall take steps to the extent reasonably practicable to protect a client's interests, such as giving reasonable notice to the client, allowing time for employment of other counsel, surrendering papers and property to which the client

**is entitled and refunding any advance payment of fee or expense that has not been earned or incurred. The lawyer may retain papers relating to the client to the extent permitted by other law.**

# COMMENT

[1] A lawyer should not accept representation in a matter unless it can be performed competently, promptly, without improper conflict of interest and to completion. Ordinarily, a representation in a matter is completed when the agreed-upon assistance has been concluded. See Rules 1.2(c) and 6.5. See also Rule 1.3, Comment [4].

## *Mandatory Withdrawal*

[2] A lawyer ordinarily must decline or withdraw from representation if the client demands that the lawyer engage in conduct that is illegal or violates the Rules of Professional Conduct or other law. The lawyer is not obliged to decline or withdraw simply because the client suggests such a course of conduct; a client may make such a suggestion in the hope that a lawyer will not be constrained by a professional obligation.

[3] When a lawyer has been appointed to represent a client, withdrawal ordinarily requires approval of the appointing authority. See also Rule 6.2. Similarly, court approval or notice to the court is often required by applicable law before a lawyer withdraws from pending litigation. Difficulty may be encountered if withdrawal is based on the client's demand that the lawyer engage in unprofessional conduct. The court may request an explanation for the withdrawal, while the lawyer may be bound to keep confidential the facts that would constitute such an explanation. The lawyer's statement that professional considerations require termination of the representation ordinarily should be accepted as sufficient. Lawyers should be mindful of their obligations to both clients and the court under Rules 1.6 and 3.3.

## *Discharge*

[4] A client has a right to discharge a lawyer at any time, with or without cause, subject to liability for payment for the lawyer's services. Where future dispute about the withdrawal may be anticipated, it may be advisable to prepare a written statement reciting the circumstances.

[5] Whether a client can discharge appointed counsel may depend on applicable law. A client seeking to do so should be given a full explanation of the consequences. These consequences may include a decision by the appointing authority that appointment of successor counsel is unjustified, thus requiring self-representation by the client.

[6] If the client has severely diminished capacity, the client may lack the legal capacity to discharge the lawyer, and in any event the discharge may be seriously adverse to the client's interests. The lawyer should make special effort to help the client consider the consequences and may take reasonably necessary protective action as provided in Rule 1.14.

## Optional Withdrawal

[7] A lawyer may withdraw from representation in some circumstances. The lawyer has the option to withdraw if it can be accomplished without material adverse effect on the client's interests. Withdrawal is also justified if the client persists in a course of action that the lawyer reasonably believes is criminal or fraudulent, for a lawyer is not required to be associated with such conduct even if the lawyer does not further it. Withdrawal is also permitted if the lawyer's services were misused in the past even if that would materially prejudice the client. The lawyer may also withdraw where the client insists on taking action that the lawyer considers repugnant or with which the lawyer has a fundamental disagreement.

[8] A lawyer may withdraw if the client refuses to abide by the terms of an agreement relating to the representation, such as an agreement concerning fees or court costs or an agreement limiting the objectives of the representation.

## Assisting the Client upon Withdrawal

[9] Even if the lawyer has been unfairly discharged by the client, a lawyer must take all reasonable steps to mitigate the consequences to the client. The lawyer may retain papers as security for a fee only to the extent permitted by law. See Rule 1.15.

### Definitional Cross-References

"Fraud" and "Fraudulent" *See* Rule 1.0(d)
"Reasonable" *See* Rule 1.0(h)
"Reasonably believes" *See* Rule 1.0(i)
"Tribunal" *See* Rule 1.0(m)

### State Rules Comparison

http://ambar.org/MRPCStateCharts

## ANNOTATION

### OVERVIEW

Rule 1.16 explains when a lawyer must or may decline or withdraw from a representation, and sets out the lawyer's obligations upon termination of the representation. A lawyer should not undertake representation unless it can be performed competently, promptly, and without conflict of interest. Cmt. [1]. Once a lawyer agrees to represent a client, the duties of competence (Rule 1.1) and diligence (Rule 1.3) imply an obligation to continue the representation through completion.

When withdrawing from the representation, the lawyer should take steps to protect the client's interests. If the matter is before a tribunal, the lawyer must comply with applicable legal procedures and must continue the representation if the tribunal so orders. Even after the representation ceases the lawyer retains certain obligations, including the duty to return documents and unearned fees, as well as the duties of confidentiality and loyalty. *See generally* Rule 1.9 (Duties to Former Clients).

## Paragraph (a): Mandatory Withdrawal and Prohibited Representation

Paragraph (a) requires a lawyer to decline or withdraw from certain representation, unless a tribunal orders otherwise.

## Paragraph (a)(1): Violation of Law or Ethics Rule

Paragraph (a)(1) provides that a lawyer must decline or withdraw from a representation that would result in violation of the Rules of Professional Conduct or other law. *See Cargile v. Viacom Int'l, Inc.*, 282 F. Supp. 2d 1316 (N.D. Fla. 2003) (failed to withdraw after realizing claim had no merit and client refused to dismiss it); *In re Humphrey*, 725 N.E.2d 70 (Ind. 2000) (failed to withdraw after case dismissed due to lawyer's lack of diligence); *In re Works*, 404 P.3d 681 (Kan. 2017) (after concluding appeal lacked merit, appointed appellate counsel took no action; should have withdrawn); *In re Polk*, 174 So. 3d 1131 (La. 2015) (failed to withdraw after becoming ineligible to practice law); *Att'y Grievance Comm'n v. Moore*, 152 A.3d 639 (Md. 2017) (failed to terminate representation until after closing practice and taking job that prohibited practicing law); ABA Formal Ethics Op. 07-449 (2007) (lawyer simultaneously representing judge in one matter and client appearing before judge in another must withdraw if judge refuses to disclose the representation; failure to withdraw would amount to assisting judge in unethical conduct, a violation of Rule 8.4(f)); ABA Formal Ethics Op. 06-441 (2006) (lawyer who believes her workload would render her unable to meet basic ethical duties required in representing client must decline or withdraw from that representation).

### CONFLICT OF INTEREST

A lawyer is prohibited from representing a client if doing so would result in a conflict of interest. *See People v. DeAtley*, 333 P.3d 61 (Colo. 2014) (abuse of discretion to deny motion to withdraw when court found conflict of interest due to client's malpractice suit); *People v. Riddle*, 35 P.3d 146 (Colo. O.P.D.J. 1999) (failed to withdraw after commencing sexual relationship with client); *In re Hull*, 767 A.2d 197 (Del. 2001) (failed to withdraw after conflict arose between spouses lawyer represented in bankruptcy matter); *In re Hunter*, 734 A.2d 654 (D.C. 1999) (should have withdrawn because of personal involvement with government witness against criminal client); *Att'y Grievance Comm'n v. Shapiro*, 108 A.3d 394 (Md. 2015) (should have withdrawn immediately after learning that client had potential malpractice action against him); *Bryan Corp. v. Abrano*, 52 N.E.3d 95 (Mass. 2016) (must decline representation if lawyer can "reasonably anticipate" conflict with existing client); *Grievance Adm'r v. Rostash*, 577 N.W.2d 452 (Mich. 1998) (lawyer assisted prosecutor in representing clients in civil matters and agreed to split fees with prosecutor, knowing prosecutor was handling underlying criminal case out of which civil claims arose); *In re Munden*, 559 S.E.2d 589 (S.C. 2002) (failed to withdraw when conflict arose from lawyer's adulterous relationship with client's spouse); Ga. Ethics Op. 16-1 (2016) (honoring client's request to keep information confidential from joint client will in most circumstances require lawyer to withdraw from the joint representation); S.D. Ethics Op. 96-3 (1996) (if client wants to appeal conviction and argue ineffective assistance of appointed counsel, counsel should inform client of conflict and move to withdraw); Tex. Ethics Op. 593 (2010) (lawyer who fails to file lawsuit for client within limitations period "must terminate the lawyer-client relationship and inform the client [of] the malpractice"). For analysis of situations in which a lawyer's taking on a new client or a new matter creates a conflict that may require withdrawal, see the annotations to Rules 1.7 and 1.9.

## ASSISTING CLIENT'S MISCONDUCT

A lawyer is required to withdraw if the lawyer knows continued representation will help the client commit a crime or fraud. *See, e.g., In re Am. Cont'l Corp. / Lincoln Sav. & Loan Litig.*, 794 F. Supp. 1424 (D. Ariz. 1992) (must withdraw if client refuses to stop violating law); *O'Brien v. Cleveland (In re O'Brien)*, 423 B.R. 477 (Bankr. D.N.J. 2010) (lawyer should have withdrawn from participating in mortgage rescue transaction as soon as he realized transaction was fraudulent); *Iowa Supreme Court Att'y Disciplinary Bd. v. Bieber*, 824 N.W.2d 514 (Iowa 2012) (failed to withdraw from representing buyer in real estate transaction knowing transaction would defraud lender); *In re Sharp*, 802 So. 2d 588 (La. 2001) (failed to withdraw once it became clear client intended to commit illegal act); *In re Edwardson*, 647 N.W.2d 126 (N.D. 2002) (lawyer who believed client had fraudulently withheld discoverable documents should have withdrawn); Fla. Ethics Op. 04-1 (2005) (lawyer who knows client will testify falsely at trial must move to withdraw); Utah Ethics Op. 00-06 (2000) (lawyer who knows client committed perjury must attempt to persuade client to rectify perjury and if unsuccessful must seek to withdraw); *see also* Rule 1.2(d) (prohibiting lawyer from assisting client in criminal or fraudulent act).

Withdrawal is permissive, rather than mandatory, if the lawyer only suspects (but does not know) the client is using the lawyer's services to commit a crime or fraud, or if the client only suggests doing so. *See* Cmt. [2]; *see also In re Hopkins*, 687 A.2d 938 (D.C. 1996) (lawyer for beneficiary in probate matter had no duty to withdraw when she only "suspected that her client might engage in wrongdoing"); *Calley v. Thomas M. Woodruff, P.A.*, 751 So. 2d 599 (Fla. Dist. Ct. App. 1998) (withdrawal not required absent well-founded belief client would commit perjury); Mich. Informal Ethics Op. RI-345 (2008) (in-house lawyer need not withdraw when corporate officer informs lawyer of intent to destroy discoverable documents); R.I. Ethics Op. 2008-02 (2008) (lawyer may withdraw if he concludes based on conflicting evidence that client is lying to further fraudulent claim, but withdrawal is mandatory if lawyer knows client is lying). Also see the discussion below regarding permissive withdrawal under paragraphs (b)(2) and (b)(3).

For discussion of a lawyer's obligations when faced with the possibility of client perjury, see the annotation to Rule 3.3.

## *Paragraph (a)(2): Physically or Mentally Unable to Provide Effective Representation*

Under paragraph (a)(2), a lawyer must decline or withdraw from a representation he or she is physically or mentally incapable of providing effectively. *See People v. Mendus*, 360 P.3d 1049 (Colo. O.P.D.J. 2015) (lawyer whose mental health problems impaired her ability to competently represent clients should have withdrawn even though clients wanted her to continue); *In re Barnes*, 691 N.E.2d 1225 (Ind. 1998) (lawyer should have withdrawn from bankruptcy case once it became apparent he was too depressed to complete it); *Iowa Supreme Court Att'y Disciplinary Bd. v. Kingery*, 871 N.W.2d 109 (Iowa 2015) (bipolar disorder and alcoholism coinciding with "extended period of professional dysfunction"); *In re Murrow*, 336 P.3d 859 (Kan. 2014) (severe depression impaired lawyer's ability to represent clients); *Att'y Grievance Comm'n v. Wallace*, 793 A.2d 535 (Md. 2002) (failure to withdraw upon realizing personal problems interfered with ability to represent client); *Disciplinary Counsel v. Wickerham*, 970 N.E.2d 932 (Ohio 2012) (lawyer's purported addiction to prescription drugs and difficulties dealing with own child custody matter materially impaired her ability to represent clients); *State ex rel. Okla. Bar Ass'n v. Southern*, 15 P.3d 1 (Okla. 2000) (failure to withdraw despite severe, untreated vitamin deficiency that essentially destroyed lawyer's short-term memory and exacerbated his depression); *In re Fitzharris*, 782 S.E.2d 596 (S.C. 2016) (lawyer's physical and mental health problems contributed to mishandling of client matter); *Lawyer Disciplinary Bd. v. Dues*, 624 S.E.2d 125 (W. Va. 2005) (persisted in representation even though worsening health prevented him from finalizing settlement); *see also Mulkey v. Meridian Oil, Inc.*, 143 F.R.D. 257 (W.D. Okla. 1992) (law firm should not actively seek new clients when one lawyer's emotional problems and another's accident rendered firm unable to handle existing caseload competently).

## *Paragraph (a)(3): Lawyer Is Discharged*

Paragraph (a)(3) requires a lawyer to withdraw if discharged by the client. *See People v. Doering*, 35 P.3d 719 (Colo. O.P.D.J. 2001); *Burton v. Mottolese*, 835 A.2d 998 (Conn. 2003); *In re Mance*, 869 A.2d 339 (D.C. 2005); *Fla. Bar v. Nunes*, 734 So. 2d 393 (Fla. 1999); *In re Williams*, 764 N.E.2d 613 (Ind. 2002); *Att'y Grievance Comm'n v. Lewis*, 85 A.3d 865 (Md. 2014); *In re Samborski*, 644 N.W.2d 402 (Minn. 2002); *State ex rel. Okla. Bar Ass'n v. Israel*, 25 P.3d 909 (Okla. 2001); *In re Schiller*, 808 S.E.2d 378 (S.C. 2017); *In re Eugster*, 209 P.3d 435 (Wash. 2009).

Comment [4] recognizes the general principle that a client has a right to discharge a lawyer "at any time, with or without cause." *See Olsen & Brown v. City of Englewood*, 889 P.2d 673 (Colo. 1995) (client may discharge lawyer at any time, for any reason); *Campbell v. Bozeman Investors of Duluth*, 964 P.2d 41 (Mont. 1998) (agreeing with "majority of jurisdictions" that client may discharge lawyer at any time, for any reason, or for no reason); Ill. Ethics Op. 99-08 (2000) (even though trust provision directs trustee to hire particular law firm, trustee always free as matter of public policy to fire firm and hire someone else, or to hire someone else in the first place); *accord Restatement (Third) of the Law Governing Lawyers* § 32(1) (2000).

However, this right is subject to limitations in certain circumstances. *See, e.g., Coyle v. Bd. of Chosen Freeholders of Warren Cnty.*, 787 A.2d 881 (N.J. 2002) (Rule 1.16(a)(3) not intended to apply to public counsel with statutory terms); *Crews v. Buckman Labs. Int'l, Inc.*, 78 S.W.3d 852 (Tenn. 2002) (in-house counsel claiming to have been fired for complying with ethical duty may bring retaliatory discharge suit against former employer); *see also Perlowski v. Elsam T. Killam & Assocs.*, 894 A.2d 1251 (N.J.

Super. Ct. Law Div. 2005) (independent contractor serving as corporate counsel may sue for damages if corporation fires him in violation of state's age discrimination law).

## Paragraph (b): Permissive Withdrawal

Paragraph (b) explains when a lawyer is permitted—but not required—to withdraw from representation. As with paragraph (a), paragraph (b) is subject to the power of a court to order continued representation. In 2002, the rule was amended by moving the provision now in paragraph (b)(1) out of the introductory paragraph in Rule 1.16(b), to clarify that the remaining paragraphs in Rule 1.16(b) permit the lawyer to withdraw even if there will be a material adverse effect on the client. Paragraphs (b)(2) through (b)(7) address those situations. American Bar Association, *A Legislative History: The Development of the ABA Model Rules of Professional Conduct, 1982–2013*, at 378 (2013).

## Paragraph (b)(1): No Material Adverse Impact

Paragraph (b)(1) permits a lawyer to withdraw from a representation at any time if the withdrawal will have no material adverse impact upon the interests of the client. *See Coleman-Adebayo v. Johnson*, 668 F. Supp. 2d 29 (D.D.C. 2009) ("a lawyer may withdraw . . . at any time so long as her doing so does not affect her client's interest in a materially adverse way"); *see also* D.C. Ethics Op. 353 (2010) (lawyer representing incapacitated client and dealing with relative who held power of attorney should not withdraw when relative accused of misusing client's money; withdrawal might cause substantial harm to client's interests); *cf.* John Lande, *Possibilities for Collaborative Law: Ethics and Practice of Lawyer Disqualification and Process Control in a New Model of Lawyering*, 64 Ohio St. L.J. 1315 (2003) (analyzing conflict between no-adverse-impact provision of rule and provision included in collaborative lawyers' retainer agreements requiring lawyer's withdrawal in event of litigation).

## Paragraphs (b)(2) and (b)(3): Client's Conduct Is Criminal or Fraudulent

Paragraphs (b)(2) and (b)(3) (renumbered in 2002 from paragraphs (b)(1) and (b)(2), respectively) permit a lawyer to withdraw when the client pursues an action that the lawyer reasonably believes is criminal or fraudulent, or when the client has used the lawyer's services to perpetrate a crime or fraud. *See, e.g., Matza v. Matza*, 627 A.2d 414 (Conn. 1993) (lawyer's allegations that client engaged in fraud in connection with dissolution of marriage proceedings justified lawyer's withdrawal, notwithstanding adverse effects on client's interests); *In re Young*, 849 So. 2d 25 (La. 2003) (because lawyer may seek withdrawal only if client "persists" in plan to commit perjury, lawyer must first seek to dissuade client); *State v. Berrysmith*, 944 P.2d 397 (Wash. Ct. App. 1997) (lawyer who reasonably believed client was about to perjure himself permitted to withdraw); ABA Formal Ethics Op. 92-366 (1992) (lawyer who knows client is using or will use lawyer's services or work product to perpetrate fraud must withdraw; lawyer whose client used lawyer's services in past to perpetrate fraud that is now completed may, but not required to, withdraw); R.I. Ethics Op. 95-38 (1995) (lawyer who discovered corporate client's principal committed fraud and perjury, which lawyer revealed to court and was permitted to withdraw, may decline representation of principal during appeal); *see also* Rule 1.2(d) (prohibiting lawyer from assisting client in criminal or fraudulent conduct).

### Paragraph (b)(4): Client Insists upon Taking Action That Lawyer Considers Repugnant or with Which Lawyer Has Fundamental Disagreement

In 2002, paragraph (b)(4) (renumbered from paragraph (b)(3)) was amended. Before amendment, the paragraph provided that a lawyer may withdraw if the client "insists upon pursuing an objective that the lawyer considers repugnant or imprudent." The paragraph now permits withdrawal when a client insists upon "taking action that the lawyer considers repugnant or with which the lawyer has a fundamental disagreement." The change from "pursuing an objective" to "taking action" permits the lawyer to withdraw regardless of whether the client's action concerns the objectives or the means of achieving those objectives. Substituting "with which the lawyer has a fundamental disagreement" for "imprudent" narrows the situations in which the lawyer may withdraw to those that seriously threaten the lawyer's autonomy due to a fundamental disagreement about objectives or means. American Bar Association, *A Legislative History: The Development of the ABA Model Rules of Professional Conduct, 1982–2013*, at 378 (2013).

### CONDUCT REPUGNANT

Paragraph (b)(4) permits a lawyer to withdraw when the client insists upon pursuing a course of action that although lawful is nevertheless repugnant to the lawyer. *See Red Dog v. State*, 625 A.2d 245 (Del. 1993) (client's decision to accept death penalty not, in itself, irrational; if lawyer unable to represent client intent upon accepting decision, or if death penalty repugnant to lawyer, lawyer may seek to withdraw if client not prejudiced); *State v. Jones*, 923 P.2d 560 (Mont. 1996) (disagreement with client's decision not to accept plea bargain and to exercise right to jury trial not cause for withdrawal); *see also* Tenn. Formal Ethics Op. 96-F-140 (1996) (lawyer who believes his religious and moral beliefs will impair representation must allow court to determine propriety of withdrawal).

### CLIENT REFUSES TO FOLLOW LAWYER'S ADVICE

A client's refusal to follow the lawyer's advice is not necessarily adequate grounds for withdrawal, particularly if the advice involves a decision that is properly left to the client. *See, e.g., Nichols v. Butler*, 953 F.2d 1550 (11th Cir. 1992) ("The decision by a defendant to exercise his fundamental right to testify at his own criminal trial, without more, is clearly not a sufficient reason for his attorney to seek to withdraw, even where that decision is against the advice of counsel."); *May v. Seibert*, 264 S.E.2d 643 (W. Va. 1980) (acceptance of settlement terms solely within client's province; refusal not adequate grounds for lawyer's withdrawal). For discussion of the allocation of authority between a lawyer and a client, see the annotation to Rule 1.2.

## *Paragraph (b)(5): Client Fails to Fulfill Obligations*

Paragraph (b)(5) (renumbered in 2002 from paragraph (b)(4)) permits withdrawal if the client fails substantially to fulfill an obligation regarding the representation. The client must first be given reasonable warning that the lawyer will withdraw if the obligation is not fulfilled. *See, e.g., Brandon v. Blech*, 560 F.3d 536 (6th Cir. 2009) (rule satisfied when firm gave client over three weeks' notice it would withdraw unless client paid past-due bills); *In re Franke*, 55 A.3d 713 (Md. Ct. Spec. App. 2012) (warning of intent to withdraw given two months before trial was reasonable when client made no attempt to pay more than $120,000 in fees).

Withdrawal may be permitted under this provision when a client fails to cooperate or communicate with the lawyer or to pay the lawyer's fees and expenses. *See, e.g., Sanford v. Maid-Rite Corp.*, 816 F.3d 546 (8th Cir. 2016) (failure to pay legal fees and provide lawyers with information critical to defense; clients warned several times); *Fid. Nat'l Title Ins. Co. of N.Y. v. Intercnty. Nat'l Title Ins. Co.*, 310 F.3d 537 (7th Cir. 2002) (client failed to pay substantial bill); *Koon Chun King Kee Soy Sauce Factory Ltd. v. Kun Fung USA Trading Co.*, No. 07-CV-2568, 2009 WL 605786, 2009 BL 47603 (E.D.N.Y. Mar. 9, 2009) (client failed to notify lawyer of whereabouts and failed to respond to lawyer's communications); *Hammond v. T.J. Litle & Co.*, 809 F. Supp. 156 (D. Mass. 1992) (lawyers allowed to withdraw based upon client's failure to pay pursuant to retainer agreement, even though failure not deliberate but resulted from financial inability); *Crane v. Crane*, 657 A.2d 312 (D.C. 1995) (lawyer permitted to withdraw when client refused to communicate with lawyer and made no arrangements to pay for past services); *see also King v. NAIAD Inflatables of Newport, Inc.*, 11 A.3d 64 (R.I. 2010) (abuse of discretion to deny motion to withdraw based upon client's failure to fulfill financial obligation; trial court failed to accord adequate weight to financial burden on law firm if forced to continue representing nonpaying client); *cf. In re Egwim*, 291 B.R. 559 (Bankr. N.D. Ga. 2003) (lawyer seeking to withdraw from Chapter 7 bankruptcy case for nonpayment must "demonstrate that a reasonable arrangement for the debtor's payment of fees is not possible and [that] counsel has consulted with the debtor to minimize the adverse effects of the withdrawal").

## *Paragraph (b)(6): Continued Representation Would Be Unreasonably Difficult*

Paragraph (b)(6) (renumbered in 2002 from paragraph (b)(5)) permits withdrawal when continued representation would place an unreasonable financial burden upon the lawyer or the representation has been rendered unreasonably difficult by the client.

### UNREASONABLE FINANCIAL BURDEN

A lawyer may be permitted to withdraw if the financial commitment required to continue the representation becomes unreasonably burdensome. *See, e.g., City of Joliet v. Mid-City Nat'l Bank of Chi.*, 998 F. Supp. 2d 689 (N.D. Ill. 2014) (law firm permitted to withdraw before completing trial when clients unable to pay outstanding fee of $5 million); *In re Franke*, 55 A.3d 713 (Md. Ct. Spec. App. 2012) (withdrawal permissible under paragraphs (b)(5) and (b)(6) of Rule 1.16 when client made no attempt to pay more than $120,000 in fees); *In re Withdrawal of Att'y*, 594 N.W.2d 514 (Mich. Ct. App. 1999) (withdrawal permitted when little or no likelihood of recovering attorneys' fees, more than 1,000 hours still required and more than 4,000 already expended, and other, more experienced counsel available). *Compare Smith v. R.J. Reynolds Tobacco Co.*, 630 A.2d 820 (N.J. Super. Ct. App. Div. 1993) (lawyers who spent ten years and $6 million pursuing high-profile tobacco liability case may withdraw if they submit "expert proofs" that recovery would be substantially less than value of work required), *with Haines v. Liggett Grp.*, 814 F. Supp. 414 (D.N.J. 1993) (tobacco liability lawyer not permitted to withdraw upon basis of cost; plaintiff would not find another lawyer due to high cost of tobacco litigation, and public had interest in continuation of case).

## CLIENT'S CONDUCT RENDERS
## REPRESENTATION UNREASONABLY DIFFICULT

Paragraph (b)(6) also provides that a lawyer need not continue representation when the client's conduct renders the representation unreasonably difficult. *See, e.g., Whiting v. Lacara*, 187 F.3d 317 (2d Cir. 1999) (client's desire to dictate legal strategies and to sue lawyer if those strategies not followed created "impossible" situation for lawyer; withdrawal permitted); *Kannewurf v. Johns*, 632 N.E.2d 711 (Ill. App. Ct. 1994) (client's unreasonable decision regarding objectives of representation and manner of settlement negotiations rendered lawyer's continued representation unreasonably difficult); *Ashker v. Int'l Bus. Machs. Corp.*, 607 N.Y.S.2d 488 (App. Div. 1994) (client's threats, accusations, and refusal to accept lawyer's advice rendered representation unreasonably difficult); *see also In re Kiley*, 947 N.E.2d 1 (Mass. 2011) (client did not render representation unreasonably difficult by sending documents to opposing counsel when lawyer was attempting to withdraw and had stopped advising client); N.M. Ethics Op. 1995-1 (1995) (lawyer whose client insists upon drafting documents and appearing in court without lawyer may seek to withdraw). As for clients who can no longer be located, compare Alaska Ethics Op. 2004-3 (2004) (lawyer who investigated claim for out-of-state client and concluded it was viable but could not locate client may file suit and then move to withdraw), with S.C. Ethics Op. 98-07 (1998) (lawyer hired on contingent-fee basis in personal injury matter who is unable to locate client after exercising reasonable diligence may assume representation terminated and is not obligated to file suit). *See generally* James P. Hemmer, *Resignation of Corporate Counsel: Fulfillment or Abdication of Duty*, 39 Hastings L.J. 641 (Mar. 1988) (when demands of corporate agents differ from corporation's expectations of representation and make representation unreasonably difficult, withdrawal from matter appropriate).

### Paragraph (b)(7): "Other Good Cause"

Paragraph (b)(7) (renumbered in 2002 from paragraph (b)(6)) permits withdrawal for "other good cause." *See City of Joliet v. Mid-City Nat'l Bank of Chi.*, 998 F. Supp. 2d 689 (N.D. Ill. 2014) (breakdown in lawyer-client relationship constitutes good cause to withdraw under Rule 1.16(b)(7); client threatened to sue for malpractice and individual with ownership interest in client filed suit against firm in unrelated matter); *WSF, Inc. v. Carter*, 803 So. 2d 445 (La. Ct. App. 2001) (withdrawal permitted when lawyer unable to continue after discovering certain criminal aspects of client's background); ABA Formal Ethics Op. 94-384 (1994) (opposing lawyer's filing disciplinary complaint during ongoing matter may be "other good cause" for withdrawal); *cf. Lasser v. Nassau Cmty. Coll.*, 457 N.Y.S.2d 343 (App. Div. 1983) (withdrawal justified when client required lawyer to seek approval from another lawyer for any actions undertaken on client's behalf).

## *Paragraph (c): Permission of Court*

Paragraph (c) provides that a lawyer must comply with applicable law requiring notice to or permission of the tribunal to withdraw, and stresses that the right to withdraw is subject to a court's authority to order the lawyer to continue the representation. Thus, regardless of the reason for seeking to withdraw as counsel, and regardless of whether the withdrawal is mandatory under paragraph (a) or permissive under paragraph (b), a lawyer is required to continue the representation if so ordered by a court. *See In re Fuller*, 621 N.W.2d 460 (Minn. 2001) (lawyer had duty to withdraw after discovering client's fraud but violated Rule 1.16(c) and (d) by ceasing representation without filing proper motion in accordance with court rules); *Columbus Bar Ass'n v. Nyce*, 98 N.E.3d 226 (Ohio 2018) (trial counsel failed to formally withdraw as required by local rule after clients retained new counsel to prosecute appeal); *Hawkins v. Comm'n for Lawyer Discipline*, 988 S.W.2d 927 (Tex. App. 1999) (though ordered to continue appointed representation, lawyer told client representation had ceased and refused to advise or act for client); *In re Pfefer*, 344 P.3d 1200 (Wash. 2015) (notice of withdrawal "effective immediately" did not comply with court rule's notice requirement); *see also Harris v. State*, 224 So. 3d 76 (Miss. 2017) (appointed counsel guilty of direct criminal contempt by refusing to continue representation after court denied motion to withdraw).

### DISCRETION OF COURT

Courts have wide discretion in ruling on a motion to withdraw; the court will consider not only the ethics rules, but also whether withdrawal would adversely affect the parties or impede the administration of justice. *See Sanford v. Maid-Rite Corp.*, 816 F.3d 546 (8th Cir. 2016) (reversing denial of motion to withdraw when lawyers had good cause to withdraw and no prejudice would result to client or third parties); *Brandon v. Blech*, 560 F.3d 536 (6th Cir. 2009) (same; case "inactive, with no impending deadlines"); *Fid. Nat'l Title Ins. Co. v. Intercnty. Nat'l Title Ins. Co.*, 310 F.3d 537 (7th Cir. 2002) (despite grounds to withdraw under Rule 1.16, leave to withdraw may be denied if lawyer engaged in "strategic conduct" or if "severe prejudice to third parties" would result); *Ohntrup v. Firearms Ctr.*, 802 F.2d 676 (3d Cir. 1986) (permission to withdraw denied when lawyer represented foreign clients with no agent in United States; withdrawal would foreclose possibility of efficient communication between litigants and court); *Bruce Lee Enters., LLC v A.V.E.L.A., Inc.*, No. 1:10 C 2333 (MEA), 2014 WL 1087934 (S.D.N.Y. Mar. 19, 2014) (lawyer waited until eve of trial to move to withdraw claiming client discharged him three months earlier; granting motion would have had "severe impact" on progress of five-year-old case whose trial date already postponed twice); *Rusinow v. Kamara*, 920 F. Supp. 69 (D.N.J. 1996) (plaintiff's counsel in car accident case not permitted to withdraw after learning of evidence that could impeach plaintiff's credibility and suggested insurance fraud or perjury; counsel did not demonstrate availability of substitute counsel, and trial two weeks away); *Gibbs v. Lappies*, 828 F. Supp. 6 (D.N.H. 1993) (lawyers retained by liability insurer to represent insured in personal injury case may not withdraw three months before trial on ground insurer unable to pay fees; client did not consent and withdrawal would necessitate continuance); *In re Cuddy*, 322 B.R. 12 (Bankr. D. Mass. 2005) (denying lawyer's motion to withdraw in part because "a pro se debtor presents often monumental problems of case administration"); *State v. Jones*, 923 P.2d 560 (Mont. 1996) (abuse of discretion to deny motion to withdraw in face of lawyer's disclosure of confidential information that created "obvious conflict of interest").

## CRIMINAL CASES

When a lawyer seeks to withdraw from representing a defendant in a criminal case, the defendant's constitutional right to counsel must be considered. *See United States v. Gonzalez-Lopez*, 548 U.S. 140 (2006) (trial court has "wide latitude in balancing the [Sixth Amendment] right to counsel of choice against the needs of fairness . . . and against the demands of its calendar"); *State v. Williams*, 300 P.3d 788 (Utah Ct. App. 2013) ("[a] trial court's ruling on a motion to withdraw is discretionary, but the court abuses its discretion if its denial of the motion violates the defendant's constitutional right to counsel"); *see also Ronquillo v. People*, 404 P.3d 264 (Colo. 2017) (joining majority concluding that Sixth Amendment right to counsel of choice includes right to fire counsel without good cause, even if defendant seeks to replace retained counsel with court-appointed one, but indigent defendant required to show good cause to fire court-appointed lawyer; court must ensure defendant understands and accepts consequences).

## APPOINTED COUNSEL'S RIGHT TO WITHDRAW

As recognized in Comment [3], when a lawyer has been appointed to represent a client, withdrawal ordinarily requires approval of the appointing authority. As for the ethical duties of appointed counsel seeking to withdraw, it is Rule 6.2, rather than Rule 1.16, that is primarily applicable. For a full discussion, see the annotation to Rule 6.2.

## *Paragraph (d): Duties upon Termination of Representation*

## DUTY TO PROTECT CLIENT'S INTEREST

Paragraph (d) provides that upon termination of representation a lawyer must take reasonable steps to protect the client's interest, such as giving reasonable notice, allowing time for employment of other counsel, surrendering papers and property to which the client is entitled, and refunding any advance payments of unearned fees or unincurred expenses. *See, e.g., In re Mitchell*, 727 A.2d 308 (D.C. 1999) (lawyer failed to advise client that firm had filed for bankruptcy and client's retainer—deposited in firm's general expense account—had become property of bankruptcy estate); *In re Works*, 404 P.3d 681 (Kan. 2017) (lawyer who disregarded client's instructions to appeal criminal matters failed to withdraw or to explain to client steps necessary to perfect appeal); *In re Soderberg*, 316 P.3d 762 (Kan. 2014) (lawyer withdrew without correcting deficiencies in qualified domestic relations order she prepared at end of divorce proceedings); *In re Greenman*, 860 N.W.2d 368 (Minn. 2015) (terminating representation days before hearing without filing notice with court and failing to appear at hearing resulted in dismissal of client's claims); *In re Quintana*, 29 P.3d 527 (N.M. 2001) (suspension from practice of law involuntarily terminates representation; it does not extinguish lawyer's responsibility to protect client interests); *In re Baehr*, 639 N.W.2d 708 (Wis. 2002) (while serving disciplinary suspension, lawyer failed to forward clients' court-issued notices or respond to calls); Va. Ethics Op. 1817 (2005) (criminal defense lawyer whose error caused dismissal of appeal must, before attempting to withdraw, inform client of error and conflict it creates and offer to help client pursue other relief); *cf.* N.C. Ethics Op. 2007-8 (2007) (usually "the act of withdrawal is a professional obligation of the lawyer, for the benefit of the lawyer" and so cost must be borne by lawyer). *See generally* Meegan B. Nelson, *When Clients Become "Ex-Clients": The Duties Owed After Discharge*, 26 J. Legal Prof. 233 (2001–2002).

## • *Reasonable Notice*

A lawyer must give a client reasonable notice before withdrawing from the representation. *See, e.g., In re Hamer*, 808 S.E.2d 647 (Ga. 2017) (client learned of lawyer's motion to withdraw after court granted it); *In re Trickey*, 46 P.3d 554 (Kan. 2002) (failure to notify client in time to secure other counsel); *Att'y Grievance Comm'n v. Pinno*, 85 A.3d 159 (Md. 2014) (abandonment of clients without notice); *Miss. Bar v. Pegram*, 167 So. 3d 230 (Miss. 2014) (withdrawing on day of trial without prior notice to client); *In re Coleman*, 295 S.W.3d 857 (Mo. 2009) (failure to notify client of motions to withdraw from three cases); *Cleveland Metro. Bar Ass'n v. Fonda*, 7 N.E.3d 1164 (Ohio 2014) (failure to advise client of intent to withdraw notwithstanding client's clear belief lawyer would continue representation); *State ex rel. Okla. Bar Ass'n v. Wagener*, 48 P.3d 771 (Okla. 2002) (failure to notify client of withdrawal from case or provide client with information enabling him to protect his interests); *In re Paulson*, 216 P.3d 859 (Or. 2009) (client found out from opposing counsel the day before trial that his lawyer had been suspended); *Eureste v. Comm'n for Lawyer Discipline*, 76 S.W.3d 184 (Tex. App. 2002) (failure to notify client of plan to withdraw or that office being closed); *In re Baratki*, 902 N.W.2d 250 (Wis. 2017) (lawyer abandoned divorce client without seeking court permission or giving client reasonable notice); Ariz. Ethics Op. 01-08 (2001) (lawyer who lost communication with client may withdraw, but must give client written notice of withdrawal and mail notice to "all known addresses as well as all addresses which may be discovered by the lawyer through the exercise of reasonable diligence"); *see also In re Burton*, 442 B.R. 421 (Bankr. W.D.N.C. 2009) (bankruptcy lawyer's retainer agreement included improper provision allowing lawyer to withdraw without notice if periodic fees not paid).

## • *Client's Papers and Property*

Upon termination of representation, the lawyer has a duty to surrender promptly papers and other property to which the client is entitled. *See, e.g., People v. Stillman*, 42 P.3d 88 (Colo. O.P.D.J. 2002) (failure to surrender client file); *In re Edwards*, 990 A.2d 501 (D.C. 2010) (failure to return unused portion of funds lawyer was holding to negotiate with client's creditors); *In re Moore*, 684 S.E.2d 71 (Ga. 2009) (failure to release escrowed money to client after realty transaction failed to close); *In re Brown*, 766 N.E.2d 363 (Ind. 2002) (failure to surrender client's file promptly); *In re Sechtem*, 49 P.3d 541 (Kan. 2002) (failure to forward clients' files to clients' new counsel); *Att'y Grievance Comm'n v. Powers*, 164 A.3d 138 (Md. 2017) (two-month delay in surrendering file in midst of ongoing litigation); *In re Greenman*, 860 N.W.2d 368 (Minn. 2015) (failure to return files for over sixteen months after initial request); *In re Harris*, 868 A.2d 1011 (N.J. 2005) (failure to return complete case file after termination); *In re Ward*, 881 N.W.2d 206 (N.D. 2016) (same); *Akron Bar Ass'n v. Holda*, 926 N.E.2d 626 (Ohio 2010) (three-month delay in turning over file to new lawyer after being discharged); *State ex rel. Okla. Bar Ass'n v. Vincent*, 48 P.3d 797 (Okla. 2002) (failure to return client's documents after termination); *Bd. of Prof'l Responsibility v. Sallee*, 469 S.W.3d 18 (Tenn. 2015) (failure to surrender key items from file after clients fired her).

A client is not necessarily entitled, however, to every document created in the course of a representation. *See, e.g., Sage Realty Corp. v. Proskauer Rose Goetz & Mendelsohn*, 689 N.E.2d 879 (N.Y. 1997) (law firm "should not be required to disclose documents which might violate a duty of nondisclosure owed to a third party, or otherwise imposed by law"); D.C. Ethics Op. 350 (2009) (lawyer who withdrew after discovering he drafted documents based upon client's misrepresentations had no duty to surrender those documents to client); *Restatement (Third) of the Law Governing Lawyers* § 46 cmt. c (2000) (lawyers may refuse to turn over certain internal law firm documents or documents whose disclosure would violate duty owed to another or would likely cause serious harm to client); *see also In re Anonymous*, 914 N.E.2d 265 (Ind. 2009) (reprimanding lawyer for failure to comply with former client's request for copies of discovery documents, but declaring request for "all other court documents" to be too vague; rule does not require lawyer "to honor all demands . . . for copies of everything in [client] files"). *Compare* Mont. Ethics Op. 100412 (2010) (lawyer may, under certain circumstances, withhold client's psychotherapy records from client if disclosure would not serve client's interests), *with* S.C. Ethics Op. 98-10 (1998) (lawyer who was sent client's mental health records by client's treating physician must release records to client when requested after representation ended, even though records marked "not to be shown to the patient").

The extent to which a lawyer is required to surrender work product depends on the jurisdiction. Under the majority view, a client is presumptively entitled to the entire file unless the lawyer can show good cause to withhold certain documents. *See Sage Realty Corp. v. Proskauer Rose Goetz & Mendelsohn*, 689 N.E.2d 879 (N.Y. 1997); *see also SEC v. McNaul*, 277 F.R.D. 439 (D. Kan. 2011) (adopting majority "entire file" approach; collecting cases). The minority view employs an "end product" approach, under which a client is entitled to the end product of the lawyer's services but must make a showing of need to obtain access to the lawyer's work product. *Id.* (collecting cases). *E.g., In re ANR Advance Transp. Co.*, 302 B.R. 607 (E.D. Wis. 2003) (Wisconsin follows minority rule). Under either approach, a lawyer is unlikely to be required to turn over documents containing the lawyer's personal impressions or relating to law firm administration. *See People v. Preston*, 276 P.3d 78 (Colo. O.P.D.J. 2011) (no duty to surrender personal work product if unnecessary to protect client's interests, including documents relating to firm administration, conflicts checks, personnel assignments, and lawyer's personal impressions); *see also* Ohio Ethics Op. 2010-2 (2010) (notes of lawyer's "passing thoughts" probably not "reasonably necessary" to representation and need not be surrendered). *See generally ABA/BNA Lawyers' Manual on Professional Conduct,* "Lawyer-Client Relationship: Duties Upon Withdrawal," pp. 31:1201 *et seq.*; Allison D. Rhodes & Robert W. Hillman, *Client Files and Digital Law Practices: Rethinking Old Concepts in an Era of Lawyer Mobility*, 43 Suffolk U. L. Rev. 897 (2010); Fred C. Zacharias, *Who Owns Work Product?*, 2006 U. Ill. L. Rev. 127 (2006).

For guidance on the types of documents that must be surrendered to a client upon termination of the representation see ABA Formal Ethics Op. 471 (2015).

## Costs of Surrendering File

In general, a lawyer who wishes to keep a copy of a client's file must assume the copying costs unless otherwise specified in the retainer agreement. *See Apa v. Qwest Corp.*, 402 F. Supp. 2d 1247 (D. Colo. 2005) (rule requires counsel to surrender papers to which client entitled, which court "understands to mean without additional cost to the client"); *In re Henry*, 684 S.E.2d 624 (Ga. 2009) (discharged lawyer's charging client for copying file "improper"); *In re Admonition Issued to X.Y.*, 529 N.W.2d 688 (Minn. 1995) (absent written agreement, unethical to charge client for copying file after discharge); Conn. Informal Ethics Op. 00-3 (2000) (absent express agreement before termination of representation, lawyer must pay cost of copying files); Kan. Ethics Op. 92-05 (1992) (lawyer may not charge client copying costs for court papers, documents generated by client, or discovery documents for which client paid, but may charge reasonable fee for copying other materials); Ohio Ethics Op. 2010-2 (2010) ("[a]ny expense . . . incurred by a lawyer in turning over a client's file . . . must be borne by the lawyer"); *see also In re Anseth*, 562 N.W.2d 385 (N.D. 1997) (discharged lawyer need not bear cost of returning documents, but should make them readily available to client); N.Y. State Ethics Op. 766 (2003) (lawyer may charge former client reasonable costs of assembly and delivery of files as reflected by retainer agreement or customary fee schedule).

## • Unearned Fees and Unincurred Expenses

The lawyer is also required to return to the client any unearned fees and unincurred expenses. *See, e.g., In re Green*, 622 S.E.2d 332 (Ga. 2005) (lawyer abandoned cases and then failed to refund advance fees); *In re Cosby*, 844 N.E.2d 478 (Ind. 2006) (failure to refund unearned fees and advanced costs in two cases); *In re Arnett*, 52 P.3d 892 (Kan. 2002) (failure to complete work or return unearned fee); *Ky. Bar Ass'n v. Glidewell*, 307 S.W.3d 625 (Ky. 2010) (failure to return unearned portion of fee after client's death); *Att'y Grievance Comm'n v. Lewis*, 85 A.3d 865 (Md. 2014) (failure to provide copy of file or return unearned fees); *In re Crissey*, 645 N.W.2d 141 (Minn.

2002) (failure to repay unearned fees); *In re Carlton*, 993 P.2d 736 (N.M. 2000) (failure to refund unearned fee); *In re Haley*, 622 S.E.2d 538 (S.C. 2005) (lawyer failed to refund $3,000 advance for case he failed to pursue); Conn. Informal Ethics Op. 04-11 (2004) (after divorce client's reconciliation with spouse, lawyer must refund advanced fees and may not continue to hold them as credit for cost of future legal services).

In most cases, unearned fees must be returned even if designated as "nonrefundable" or "flat" fees. *See State ex rel. Counsel for Discipline v. Wintroub*, 765 N.W.2d 482 (Neb. 2009) (most courts find nonrefundable fee agreements not invalid per se, but refuse to enforce them on case-by-case basis if fee not earned; collecting cases); *see also Ala. State Bar v. Hallett*, 26 So. 3d 1127 (Ala. 2009) (lawyer who collected $100,000 "flat fee" required to refund half after conceding in post-trial fee petition that $50,000 was "reasonable" fee); *In re Sather*, 3 P.3d 403 (Colo. 2000) (attempt to label fees as "nonrefundable" did not relieve lawyer of duty to return unearned fees upon discharge); *Dowling v. Chi. Options Assocs.*, 875 N.E.2d 1012 (Ill. 2007) (advanced fees already property of lawyer still "are subject to a lawyer's duty to refund any unearned fees, pursuant to Rule 1.16"); *In re Hoffman*, 834 N.W.2d 636 (N.D. 2013) (no Rule 1.5 or Rule 1.15 violation to charge "nonrefundable" "minimum fee" or deposit it in operating account, but lawyer must still refund any unearned portion if fired); *Bd. of Prof'l Responsibility v. Hiatt*, 382 P.3d 778 (Wyo. 2016) (failure to refund unearned portion of "non-refundable flat fee"); Mo. Formal Ethics Op. 128 (2010) (Rule 1.16 requires any fee, even flat fee or security retainer that has become property of lawyer, to be refunded if not earned); Douglas R. Richmond, *Understanding Retainers and Flat Fees*, 34 J. Legal Prof. 113 (2009) ("lawyers cannot escape their Rule 1.16(d) duty simply by labeling fees as earned upon receipt or declaring them non-refundable"). *But see Grievance Adm'r v. Cooper*, 757 N.W.2d 867 (Mich. 2008) (lawyer who retained "minimum fee" after being discharged did not violate Rule 1.16(d) when agreement was clear that fee nonrefundable).

## CONFIDENTIALITY

A lawyer must protect client confidences when moving to withdraw and thereafter. Rule 1.6 (Confidentiality of Information); Rule 1.9 (Duties to Former Clients). *See Lawyer Disciplinary Bd. v. Farber*, 488 S.E.2d 460 (W. Va. 1997) (lawyer attached affidavit to motion to withdraw revealing confidential information potentially damaging to client).

Nevertheless, the lawyer may be required to explain the reason for the withdrawal to the court. Comment [3] recognizes this potential conflict by declaring that if withdrawal is sought because the client demands unprofessional conduct on the lawyer's part, it "ordinarily should be accepted as sufficient" for the lawyer to explain to the court that professional considerations require termination of employment. If the court does not find it sufficient, the lawyer must take steps to limit disclosure. *See People v. Hagos*, 250 P.3d 596 (Colo. App. 2009) (lawyer seeking to withdraw due to client's insistence upon presenting perjured testimony need tell court only that "irreconcilable conflict" has developed; if court denies motion, lawyer should make record of disagreement outside presence of trial court for purposes of appellate review); *In re Gonzalez*, 773 A.2d 1026 (D.C. 2001) (motion to withdraw stated client failed to pay legal bills and made misrepresentations; could have submitted information in camera with appropriate redactions). *See generally* ABA Formal Ethics Op. 476 (2016) (providing guidance on protecting client confidences when moving to withdraw from representing client in civil proceeding based on client's failure to pay fees).

## RETAINING LIENS

Paragraph (d) provides that a "lawyer may retain papers relating to the client to the extent permitted by other law." As the rule suggests, jurisdictions differ on whether, and the extent to which, a lawyer may assert a retaining lien on a client's papers or property as security for the payment of legal fees. *E.g., In re Douglass*, 859 A.2d 1069 (D.C. 2004) (because District of Columbia's rules permit retaining liens only for work product for which lawyer has not received payment, lawyer violated rules by retaining client's entire file); *In re Brussow*, 286 P.3d 1246 (Utah 2012) (retaining liens impermissible under Utah rules); Haw. Formal Ethics Op. 28 (amended 2015) (until retaining liens explicitly approved under Hawaii law, they are implicitly forbidden by Rule 1.16); Ky. Ethics Op. E-395 (1997) (lawyer may not retain file due to fee dispute, but must surrender file except for work product); La. Ethics Op. 05-RPCC-003 (2005) (retaining liens not permitted under Louisiana rules). Several other state professional rules—such as Minn. Rule 1.16(g), N.C. Rule 1.16 cmt. [10], and N.D. Rules 1.16(e) and 1.19(a)—prohibit retaining liens.

Regardless of whether a jurisdiction permits retaining liens, lawyers must take appropriate steps to protect their client's interests. *See Defendant A v. Idaho State Bar*, 2 P.3d 147 (Idaho 2000) (no violation in retaining client's file to ensure payment of outstanding fees when lawyer made file available to new counsel to copy and no imminent prejudice to client); *Att'y Grievance Comm'n v. Rand*, 128 A.3d 107 (Md. 2015) (even if lawyer had valid retaining lien, he could not assert it because of his unethical billing and recordkeeping practices and fact that client matter was still pending); *Campbell v. Bozeman Investors of Duluth*, 964 P.2d 41 (Mont. 1998) (discharged lawyers claiming possessory lien failed to protect client's interests by retaining file while claim still pending); *In re Tillman*, 462 S.E.2d 283 (S.C. 1995) (assertion of lien inappropriate unless client deliberately fails to pay clearly agreed-upon fee); Iowa Ethics Op. 07-08 (2007) (lien for unpaid fees permissible only if it clearly will not prejudice client); Miss. Ethics Op. 144 (1988) (violation of rule if retention of file will prevent client from obtaining another lawyer or proceeding with case in timely manner); N.Y. State Ethics Op. 591 (1988) (may not assert retaining lien on client's papers to enhance ability to negotiate general release from liability); Or. Ethics Op. 2005-90 (2005) (if client does not have resources to pay in full, retaining lien must yield to fiduciary duty to protect client on client's payment of what client can afford); Pa. Ethics Op. 96-157 (1996) (rev.) (must give file to former client if failure to do so would substantially prejudice client's interests, even though lawyer has valid retaining lien on file for outstanding costs); S.C. Ethics Op. 02-11 (2002) (lawyer may not withhold file of former client until outstanding invoice paid, if doing so would prejudice client); Va. Ethics Op. 1690 (1997) (lawyer's assertion of retaining lien almost invariably results in prejudice to client's interests, in which case assertion of lien prohibited); *see also In re Att'y G.*, 302 P.3d 248 (Colo. 2013) (impermissible to assert retaining lien on client's passport); *In re Newman*, 958 N.E.2d 792 (Ind. 2011) (retaining client's file in estate matter improper when lawyer already filed charging lien); *In re Lim*, 210 S.W.3d 199 (Mo. 2007) (immigration lawyer reprimanded for withholding clients' labor certifications after termination of matter until fees paid). For discussion of a lawyer's ethical obligations regarding attorneys' liens, see *ABA/BNA Lawyers' Manual on Professional Conduct*, "Fees: Attorneys' Liens," pp. 41:2101 *et seq.*, and "Lawyer-Client Relationship: Duties Upon Withdrawal," pp. 31:1201 *et seq.*

## Rule 1.17

### *Sale of Law Practice*

A lawyer or a law firm may sell or purchase a law practice, or an area of law practice, including good will, if the following conditions are satisfied:

(a) The seller ceases to engage in the private practice of law, or in the area of practice that has been sold, [in the geographic area] [in the jurisdiction] (a jurisdiction may elect either version) in which the practice has been conducted;

(b) The entire practice, or the entire area of practice, is sold to one or more lawyers or law firms;

(c) The seller gives written notice to each of the seller's clients regarding:

(1) the proposed sale;

(2) the client's right to retain other counsel or to take possession of the file; and

(3) the fact that the client's consent to the transfer of the client's files will be presumed if the client does not take any action or does not otherwise object within ninety (90) days of receipt of the notice.

If a client cannot be given notice, the representation of that client may be transferred to the purchaser only upon entry of an order so authorizing by a court having jurisdiction. The seller may disclose to the court in camera information relating to the representation only to the extent necessary to obtain an order authorizing the transfer of a file.

(d) The fees charged clients shall not be increased by reason of the sale.

## COMMENT

[1] The practice of law is a profession, not merely a business. Clients are not commodities that can be purchased and sold at will. Pursuant to this Rule, when a lawyer or an entire firm ceases to practice, or ceases to practice in an area of law, and other lawyers or firms take over the representation, the selling lawyer or firm may obtain compensation for the reasonable value of the practice as may withdrawing partners of law firms. See Rules 5.4 and 5.6.

## Termination of Practice by the Seller

[2] The requirement that all of the private practice, or all of an area of practice, be sold is satisfied if the seller in good faith makes the entire practice, or the area of practice, available for sale to the purchasers. The fact that a number of the seller's clients decide not to be represented by the purchasers but take their matters elsewhere, therefore, does not result in a violation. Return to private practice as a result of an unanticipated change in circumstances does not necessarily result in a violation. For example, a lawyer who has sold the practice to accept an appointment to judicial office does not violate the requirement that the sale be attendant to cessation of practice if the lawyer later resumes private practice upon being defeated in a contested or a retention election for the office or resigns from a judiciary position.

[3] The requirement that the seller cease to engage in the private practice of law does not prohibit employment as a lawyer on the staff of a public agency or a legal services entity that provides legal services to the poor, or as in-house counsel to a business.

[4] The Rule permits a sale of an entire practice attendant upon retirement from the private practice of law within the jurisdiction. Its provisions, therefore, accommodate the lawyer who sells the practice on the occasion of moving to another state. Some states are so large that a move from one locale therein to another is tantamount to leaving the jurisdiction in which the lawyer has engaged in the practice of law. To also accommodate lawyers so situated, states may permit the sale of the practice when the lawyer leaves the geographical area rather than the jurisdiction. The alternative desired should be indicated by selecting one of the two provided for in Rule 1.17(a).

[5] This Rule also permits a lawyer or law firm to sell an area of practice. If an area of practice is sold and the lawyer remains in the active practice of law, the lawyer must cease accepting any matters in the area of practice that has been sold, either as counsel or co-counsel or by assuming joint responsibility for a matter in connection with the division of a fee with another lawyer as would otherwise be permitted by Rule 1.5(e). For example, a lawyer with a substantial number of estate planning matters and a substantial number of probate administration cases may sell the estate planning portion of the practice but remain in the practice of law by concentrating on probate administration; however, that practitioner may not thereafter accept any estate planning matters. Although a lawyer who leaves a jurisdiction or geographical area typically would sell the entire practice, this Rule permits the lawyer to limit the sale to one or more areas of the practice, thereby preserving the lawyer's right to continue practice in the areas of the practice that were not sold.

## Sale of Entire Practice or Entire Area of Practice

[6] The Rule requires that the seller's entire practice, or an entire area of practice, be sold. The prohibition against sale of less than an entire practice area protects those clients whose matters are less lucrative and who might find it difficult to secure other counsel if a sale could be limited to substantial fee-generating matters. The purchasers are required to undertake all client matters in the practice or practice area, subject to client consent. This requirement is satisfied, however, even if a purchaser is unable to undertake a particular client matter because of a conflict of interest.

### Client Confidences, Consent and Notice

[7] Negotiations between seller and prospective purchaser prior to disclosure of information relating to a specific representation of an identifiable client no more violate the confidentiality provisions of Model Rule 1.6 than do preliminary discussions concerning the possible association of another lawyer or mergers between firms, with respect to which client consent is not required. See Rule 1.6(b)(7). Providing the purchaser access to detailed information relating to the representation, such as the client's file, however, requires client consent. The Rule provides that before such information can be disclosed by the seller to the purchaser the client must be given actual written notice of the contemplated sale, including the identity of the purchaser, and must be told that the decision to consent or make other arrangements must be made within 90 days. If nothing is heard from the client within that time, consent to the sale is presumed.

[8] A lawyer or law firm ceasing to practice cannot be required to remain in practice because some clients cannot be given actual notice of the proposed purchase. Since these clients cannot themselves consent to the purchase or direct any other disposition of their files, the Rule requires an order from a court having jurisdiction authorizing their transfer or other disposition. The court can be expected to determine whether reasonable efforts to locate the client have been exhausted, and whether the absent client's legitimate interests will be served by authorizing the transfer of the file so that the purchaser may continue the representation. Preservation of client confidences requires that the petition for a court order be considered in camera. (A procedure by which such an order can be obtained needs to be established in jurisdictions in which it presently does not exist).

[9] All elements of client autonomy, including the client's absolute right to discharge a lawyer and transfer the representation to another, survive the sale of the practice or area of practice.

### Fee Arrangements Between Client and Purchaser

[10] The sale may not be financed by increases in fees charged the clients of the practice. Existing arrangements between the seller and the client as to fees and the scope of the work must be honored by the purchaser.

### Other Applicable Ethical Standards

[11] Lawyers participating in the sale of a law practice or a practice area are subject to the ethical standards applicable to involving another lawyer in the representation of a client. These include, for example, the seller's obligation to exercise competence in identifying a purchaser qualified to assume the practice and the purchaser's obligation to undertake the representation competently (see Rule 1.1); the obligation to avoid disqualifying conflicts, and to secure the client's informed consent for those conflicts that can be agreed to (see Rule 1.7 regarding conflicts and Rule 1.0(e) for the definition of informed consent); and the obligation to protect information relating to the representation (see Rules 1.6 and 1.9).

[12] If approval of the substitution of the purchasing lawyer for the selling lawyer is required by the rules of any tribunal in which a matter is pending, such approval must be obtained before the matter can be included in the sale (see Rule 1.16).

## Applicability of the Rule

[13] This Rule applies to the sale of a law practice of a deceased, disabled or disappeared lawyer. Thus, the seller may be represented by a non-lawyer representative not subject to these Rules. Since, however, no lawyer may participate in a sale of a law practice which does not conform to the requirements of this Rule, the representatives of the seller as well as the purchasing lawyer can be expected to see to it that they are met.

[14] Admission to or retirement from a law partnership or professional association, retirement plans and similar arrangements, and a sale of tangible assets of a law practice, do not constitute a sale or purchase governed by this Rule.

[15] This Rule does not apply to the transfers of legal representation between lawyers when such transfers are unrelated to the sale of a practice or an area of practice.

### Definitional Cross-References
"Law firm" *See* Rule 1.0(c)
"Written" *See* Rule 1.0(n)

### State Rules Comparison
http://ambar.org/MRPCStateCharts

## ANNOTATION

### WHY THE RULE WAS ADOPTED

Until the late twentieth century, it was considered unethical to sell a law practice. Even though it was not directly prohibited by either the Model Rules or the predecessor Model Code, it was said to violate rules against disclosing confidences, compensating someone for securing legal business, and sharing fees with nonlawyers. *See, e.g., O'Hara v. Ahlgren, Blumenfeld & Kempster*, 511 N.E.2d 879 (Ill. App. Ct.) (public policy considerations underlying prohibition against sharing fees with nonlawyers used as basis for striking down attempted sale of goodwill of deceased lawyer by widow), *aff'd*, 537 N.E.2d 730 (Ill. 1989); *Lake Cnty. Bar Ass'n v. Patterson*, 413 N.E.2d 840 (Ohio 1980) (purchase violated prohibition against compensating someone to secure legal business); *see also* Robert L. Ostertag, *Sale of a Law Practice*, 15 Experience, Winter 2005, at 18. *See generally* Geoffrey C. Hazard, Jr., W. William Hodes & Peter R. Jarvis, *The Law of Lawyering* § 22.03 (4th ed. 2015) (Supp. 2017-1) (identifying "rule of tradition" against sale of law practice on basis of public interest and status of law as profession that deals with people, not merchandise).

Inability to sell a law practice placed sole practitioners and their clients at a disadvantage when compared with law firm members and their clients. Firm lawyers could always use agreements by which the firm would either pay for the interest of a retiring partner, or agree to continue her salary and benefits for a given period without requiring performance of any services. Sole practitioners, however, could not. D.C. Ethics Op. 294 (1999); *see also* Kan. Ethics Op. 93-14 (1993) (prohibition on sale of goodwill by sole practitioners constitutes unequal protection of law); Barton T. Crawford, *The Sale of a Legal Practice in North Carolina: Goodwill and Discrimination Against the Sole Practitioner*, 32 Wake Forest L. Rev. 993 (Fall 1997).

The ban also left the clients of a sole practitioner to fend for themselves when their lawyer retired or died. *See* American Bar Association, *A Legislative History: The Development of the ABA Model Rules of Professional Conduct, 1982–2013*, at 383 (2013). *See generally* Demetrios Dimitriou, *What Should Be Your Concerns? Purchase or Sale of a Solo Practice*, 19 Law Prac. Mgmt., Nov./Dec. 1993, at 44.

In 1990 the ABA adopted Model Rule 1.17, and for the first time expressly permitted the sale of a law practice, "including good will."

### • *2002 and 2012 Amendments*

In 2002 the rule was amended to require the purchaser to honor the seller's fee agreements and to eliminate the requirement that a single purchaser buy the entire practice. In 2012, Comment [7] was amended to reflect changes made to Rule 1.6. *See generally* American Bar Association, *A Legislative History: The Development of the ABA Model Rules of Professional Conduct, 1982–2013*, at 387 *et seq.* (2013). These amendments are discussed in more detail below.

### RULE'S REQUIREMENTS

Under Rule 1.17, a lawyer or law firm is permitted to buy or sell a law practice or, pursuant to a 2002 amendment, an area of practice, including the associated goodwill. *See* N.Y. State Ethics Op. 961 (2013) (retiring lawyer may sell practice in exchange for percentage of fees collected by purchaser proportionate to services seller has already rendered or that fairly represents value of goodwill, but may not pay percentage of fees for new clients referred after sale); *see also* Mass. Ethics Op. 2014-4 (2014) (value of goodwill may include potential value of fees from future business of retiring lawyer's current clients, but not fees earned from new clients he refers after he retires).

The rule imposes conditions, set out in paragraphs (a) through (d), relating to the selling lawyer's ability to continue to engage in private practice, how much of the practice is sold and to whom, and notice to clients. These conditions are "intended to protect clients from breaches of confidentiality, conflicts of interests, and other abuses that may occur when a lawyer who is not a current member of a law firm purchases the good will of the law firm." N.C. Ethics Op. 98-6 (1998); *accord* Neb. Ethics Op. 13-03 (n.d.); *cf.* N.Y. State Ethics Op. 1133 (2017) (mere act of taking possession of retired lawyer's client files did not amount to a sale of law practice and did not implicate Rule 1.17).

Note that "[t]he Rule applies to the sale of a law practice of a deceased, disabled or disappeared lawyer." Cmt. [13]. The comment explains that although in such cases the seller may be represented by a nonlawyer, the purchaser must be a lawyer who must comply with the rule's requirements. *Id. See* Fla. Ethics Op. 03-1 (2004) (purchasing lawyer must comply with rule).

### *Paragraph (a): Limiting Seller's Ability to Engage in Private Practice*

Paragraph (a) requires the selling lawyer to cease private practice (or cease practicing in a specific area of law) in the jurisdiction or geographic area in which the practice was conducted. *See* Ill. Ethics Op. 07-02 (2007) (lawyer seeking to retire may not sell law practice, including goodwill, to associate and continue working for firm on "of counsel" basis; lawyer may, however, sell firm's tangible assets and continue working there); Me. Ethics Op. 210 (2014) (sole practitioner may not sell practice and continue to work as employee or independent contractor). *But see* Neb. Ethics Op. 13-03 (n.d.) (lawyer who sells practice may continue in private practice, including serving in "of counsel" capacity with same firm; Nebraska rule omits prohibition on continuing in private practice following sale of firm).

The rule does not prohibit the selling lawyer from assisting the purchaser or purchasers "in the orderly transition of active client matters for a reasonable period of time after the closing of the sale," according to ABA Formal Opinion 468; however, clients may not be charged for this work. ABA Formal Ethics Op. 468 (2014); *accord* Conn. Informal Ethics Op. 15-08 (2015) (selling lawyer may perform legal work necessary for transition of active matters and may be held out as "of counsel" during that time; if practice area sold, may not accept new matters, be co-counsel, or divide fee by taking joint responsibility for matter in that practice area).

## *Paragraph (b): Sale of Entire Practice or Practice Area to One or More Lawyers*

Paragraph (b) requires the entire practice, or an entire practice area, to be sold to one or more lawyers or firms. *See* N.D. Ethics Op. 15-08 (2015) (lawyer with two offices in state may not sell practice associated with one office and continue practicing in the same fields and same geographic area as practice to be sold).

The rule as originally adopted in 1990 required that the entire practice be sold to a single purchaser. The rationale was that purchasers could otherwise take only the most profitable cases in a practice, and leave some clients unrepresented. American Bar Association, *A Legislative History: The Development of the ABA Model Rules of Professional Conduct, 1982–2013*, at 390 (2013).

This requirement, however, was not tailored properly to accomplish its purpose, and was eliminated in 2002. The Ethics 2000 Commission gave this explanation for the change:

> The Commission believes that the present requirement is unduly restrictive and potentially disserves clients. While it remains important to ensure the disposition of the entire caseload, it is not necessary to require that all cases must be sold to a single buyer. For example, it may make better sense to allow the sale of family-law cases to a family lawyer and bankruptcy cases to a bankruptcy lawyer. Common sense would suggest the lawyer should sell the cases to the most competent practitioner and not be limited by such a "single buyer" rule, and paragraph (b) has been redrafted accordingly.

American Bar Association, *A Legislative History: The Development of the ABA Model Rules of Professional Conduct, 1982–2013*, at 390 (2013).

Note that the rule applies to the sale of the practice (or practice area) to someone not already part of the firm. As Comment [14] explains, "[a]dmission to or retirement from a law partnership or professional association, retirement plans and similar arrangements, and a sale of tangible assets of a law practice, do not constitute a sale or purchase governed by this Rule." *See* Neb. Ethics Op. 13-03 (n.d.) (rule inapplicable to sale of practice to current firm lawyer); N.C. Ethics Op. 98-6 (1998) (Rule 1.17 inapplicable if purchaser already member of firm; client interests not implicated by transfer of shares in professional corporation to existing employees in exchange for capital contributions); *see also Chance v. McCann*, 966 A.2d 29 (N.J. Super. Ct. App. Div. 2009) (Rule 1.17 did not apply to lawyer simply retiring from practice and not selling practice to third party; New Jersey's Rule 1.17(f) is substantially similar to Comment [14] of Model Rule 1.17).

## Paragraph (c): Notice to Clients

Paragraph (c) requires the seller to give written notice to each client about the proposed sale and the client's right to retain other counsel or to retrieve the file, and of the fact that the client's consent will be presumed if the client takes no action within ninety days. *See In re Pinck*, 94 A.3d 905 (N.J. 2014) (lawyer failed to provide advance written notice to client of sale of law practice); *In re McCray*, 825 N.W.2d 468 (N.D. 2012) (lawyer failed to notify clients of sale by certified mail as required by North Dakota rule); *In re Cutchin*, 771 S.E.2d 845 (S.C. 2015) (lawyer attempted to sell practice without satisfying rule's notice requirements; South Carolina's rule also requires lawyers to publish notice in newspaper).

If the lawyer is unable to notify the client, the rule prohibits transferring the representation of that client without a court order.

## Paragraph (d): Sale May Not Result in Increased Fees

Paragraph (d) prohibits requiring clients to pay higher fees as a result of the sale. Note that as originally adopted, this provision contained an exception permitting the purchaser to refuse to accept a client who does not agree to a higher fee, up to the rate the purchaser had been charging for similar services before initiating negotiations with the seller. In 2002, this exception was dropped and the rule now requires the purchaser to honor the seller's fee arrangements with all her clients; the purchaser is not permitted to charge the clients more than the seller had agreed to charge. Many jurisdictions had already imposed this requirement before the ABA acted. American Bar Association, *A Legislative History: The Development of the ABA Model Rules of Professional Conduct, 1982–2013*, at 390 (2013); *see In re Fitzgerald*, 59 N.Y.S.3d 364 (App. Div. 2017) (lawyer who purchased law practice improperly charged forty-four transferred clients additional fees); *see also* ABA Formal Ethics Op. 468 (2014) (clients may not be charged for "time spent only on the transition of matters"); Conn. Informal Ethics Op. 15-08 (2015) (may not charge for transitional work, which is "required only because of the sale and does not advance clients' causes"); *cf.* Ariz. Ethics Op. 09-01 (2009) (law firm requirement that departing associate pay firm $3,500 for each client she continues to represent violates Rule 1.17's policy of "disfavoring arrangements that create an incentive to charge clients greater fees").

According to Comment [10], the purchaser must also honor the arrangements between the seller and client about the scope of the work to be done.

## CONFIDENTIALITY

Comment [7] to Rule 1.17 explains that preliminary negotiations between the seller and a prospective purchaser "no more violate the confidentiality provisions of Model Rule 1.6 than do preliminary discussions concerning the possible association of another lawyer or mergers between firms, with respect to which client consent is not required." It cautions, however, that "detailed information relating to the representation, such as the client's file," cannot be disclosed without client consent. Note that Comment [7] was amended in 2012 to refer to Rule 1.6(b)(7), new in 2012, which permits limited disclosure of client information to detect and resolve conflicts of interest arising from "the lawyer's change of employment or from changes in the composition or ownership of a firm." Rule 1.6(b)(7); American Bar Association, *A Legislative History: The Development of the ABA Model Rules of Professional Conduct, 1982–2013*, at 393 (2013).

Interpreting the confidentiality obligations, an Arizona ethics opinion holds that a lawyer seeking to sell a law practice does not need client consent to disclose the identities of his clients and give "high-level, general descriptions of the work performed" unless disclosure would "adversely affect a client's material interest" or a client has instructed the lawyer not to disclose the information. Ariz. Ethics Op. 2006-01 (2006). The lawyer may not, however, disclose the amount of fees paid by specific clients without client consent, and the potential purchaser must maintain the confidentiality of the information disclosed by the seller, even if the sale falls through. *Id.*; *cf.* N.D. Ethics Op. 00-02 (2000) (purchasing firm that agrees to keep seller's closed files for at least ten years thereby assumes obligation to keep files confidential).

## SELLING PRACTICE WHEN LAWYER
## DISBARRED OR SUSPENDED

According to a South Carolina ethics opinion, Rule 1.17 does not permit a lawyer who has been disbarred or suspended to sell his practice. S.C. Ethics Op. 2003-06 (2003). The opinion reasons that because the ethics rule requires that the seller's "active" clients be given written notice of the proposed sale, it cannot apply to the practices of disbarred or suspended lawyers, who by definition no longer have "active" clients. (The ABA Model Rule, unlike the South Carolina rule, does not phrase the notification requirement in terms of "active" clients.) *Accord* Pa. Ethics Op. 2015-038 (2015) (suspended lawyer would not be able to meet rule's notice requirements; also, court might not permit lawyer to retire).

A Maine ethics opinion reaches the opposite conclusion: a suspended or disbarred lawyer has by definition "ceased to engage in the private practice of law in the State of Maine" and may therefore sell his practice if he complies with the bar rules and the disciplinary enforcement rules. Me. Ethics Op. 178 (2002); *cf. In re Lieber*, 834 N.W.2d 200 (Minn. 2013) (lawyer who sold practice one day after referee recommended his disbarment but before formal suspension and ultimate disbarment had no duty to notify clients of suspension as required by court rule, because he no longer had any clients).

## Rule 1.18

### Duties to Prospective Client

(a) A person who consults with a lawyer about the possibility of forming a client-lawyer relationship with respect to a matter is a prospective client.

(b) Even when no client-lawyer relationship ensues, a lawyer who has learned information from a prospective client shall not use or reveal that information, except as Rule 1.9 would permit with respect to information of a former client.

(c) A lawyer subject to paragraph (b) shall not represent a client with interests materially adverse to those of a prospective client in the same or a substantially related matter if the lawyer received information from the prospective client that could be significantly harmful to that person in the matter, except as provided in paragraph (d). If a lawyer is disqualified from representation under this paragraph, no lawyer in a firm with which that lawyer is associated may knowingly undertake or continue representation in such a matter, except as provided in paragraph (d).

(d) When the lawyer has received disqualifying information as defined in paragraph (c), representation is permissible if:

(1) both the affected client and the prospective client have given informed consent, confirmed in writing; or:

(2) the lawyer who received the information took reasonable measures to avoid exposure to more disqualifying information than was reasonably necessary to determine whether to represent the prospective client; and

(i) the disqualified lawyer is timely screened from any participation in the matter and is apportioned no part of the fee therefrom; and

(ii) written notice is promptly given to the prospective client.

## COMMENT

[1] Prospective clients, like clients, may disclose information to a lawyer, place documents or other property in the lawyer's custody, or rely on the lawyer's advice. A lawyer's consultations with a prospective client usually are limited in time and depth and leave both the prospective client and the lawyer free (and sometimes

required) to proceed no further. Hence, prospective clients should receive some but not all of the protection afforded clients.

[2] A person becomes a prospective client by consulting with a lawyer about the possibility of forming a client-lawyer relationship with respect to a matter. Whether communications, including written, oral, or electronic communications, constitute a consultation depends on the circumstances. For example, a consultation is likely to have occurred if a lawyer, either in person or through the lawyer's advertising in any medium, specifically requests or invites the submission of information about a potential representation without clear and reasonably understandable warnings and cautionary statements that limit the lawyer's obligations, and a person provides information in response. See also Comment [4]. In contrast, a consultation does not occur if a person provides information to a lawyer in response to advertising that merely describes the lawyer's education, experience, areas of practice, and contact information, or provides legal information of general interest. Such a person communicates information unilaterally to a lawyer, without any reasonable expectation that the lawyer is willing to discuss the possibility of forming a client-lawyer relationship, and is thus not a "prospective client." Moreover, a person who communicates with a lawyer for the purpose of disqualifying the lawyer is not a "prospective client."

[3] It is often necessary for a prospective client to reveal information to the lawyer during an initial consultation prior to the decision about formation of a client-lawyer relationship. The lawyer often must learn such information to determine whether there is a conflict of interest with an existing client and whether the matter is one that the lawyer is willing to undertake. Paragraph (b) prohibits the lawyer from using or revealing that information, except as permitted by Rule 1.9, even if the client or lawyer decides not to proceed with the representation. The duty exists regardless of how brief the initial conference may be.

[4] In order to avoid acquiring disqualifying information from a prospective client, a lawyer considering whether or not to undertake a new matter should limit the initial consultation to only such information as reasonably appears necessary for that purpose. Where the information indicates that a conflict of interest or other reason for non-representation exists, the lawyer should so inform the prospective client or decline the representation. If the prospective client wishes to retain the lawyer, and if consent is possible under Rule 1.7, then consent from all affected present or former clients must be obtained before accepting the representation.

[5] A lawyer may condition a consultation with a prospective client on the person's informed consent that no information disclosed during the consultation will prohibit the lawyer from representing a different client in the matter. See Rule 1.0(e) for the definition of informed consent. If the agreement expressly so provides, the prospective client may also consent to the lawyer's subsequent use of information received from the prospective client.

[6] Even in the absence of an agreement, under paragraph (c), the lawyer is not prohibited from representing a client with interests adverse to those of the prospective client in the same or a substantially related matter unless the lawyer has received from the prospective client information that could be significantly harmful if used in the matter.

[7] Under paragraph (c), the prohibition in this Rule is imputed to other lawyers as provided in Rule 1.10, but, under paragraph (d)(1), imputation may be avoided if the lawyer obtains the informed consent, confirmed in writing, of both the prospective and affected clients. In the alternative, imputation may be avoided if the conditions of paragraph (d)(2) are met and all disqualified lawyers are timely screened and written notice is promptly given to the prospective client. See Rule 1.0(k) (requirements for screening procedures). Paragraph (d)(2)(i) does not prohibit the screened lawyer from receiving a salary or partnership share established by prior independent agreement, but that lawyer may not receive compensation directly related to the matter in which the lawyer is disqualified.

[8] Notice, including a general description of the subject matter about which the lawyer was consulted, and of the screening procedures employed, generally should be given as soon as practicable after the need for screening becomes apparent.

[9] For the duty of competence of a lawyer who gives assistance on the merits of a matter to a prospective client, see Rule 1.1. For a lawyer's duties when a prospective client entrusts valuables or papers to the lawyer's care, see Rule 1.15.

## Definitional Cross-References

"Confirmed in writing" *See* Rule 1.0(b)
"Firm" *See* Rule 1.0(c)
"Informed consent" *See* Rule 1.0(e)
"Knowingly" *See* Rule 1.0(f)
"Reasonable" and "Reasonably" *See* Rule 1.0(h)
"Screened" *See* Rule 1.0(k)
"Written" *See* Rule 1.0(n)

## State Rules Comparison

http://ambar.org/MRPCStateCharts

## ANNOTATION

### 2012 AMENDMENTS

In 2012, Rule 1.18 was amended to define a prospective client as someone who "consults with" a lawyer about the possibility of forming a lawyer-client relationship with respect to a matter, rather than as someone who "discusses" the possibility. References in the comment to discussions, conversations, and interviews were all changed to conform to the new wording, and Comment [2] was expanded to explain how to tell if a communication—written, oral, or electronic—constitutes a consultation. The idea was to clarify the rule's application to electronic communications and give lawyers more guidance about how to avoid the inadvertent creation of a client-lawyer relationship. American Bar Association, *A Legislative History: The Development of the ABA Model Rules of Professional Conduct, 1982–2013*, at 404 (2013). The 2012 amendment also added the final sentence of Comment [2] declaring that a lawyer does not owe any duties under Rule 1.18 to a person who is trying to preemptively disqualify the lawyer from representing an opponent. *Id.*

## *Paragraph (a): Who Is a Prospective Client?*

### CONSULTATION

Under Rule 1.18(a), anyone who consults with a lawyer in good faith about the possibility of forming a lawyer-client relationship with respect to a matter is considered a prospective client. *See Disciplinary Counsel v. Cicero*, 982 N.E.2d 650 (Ohio 2012) (individual under federal investigation who met with lawyer and expressed dissatisfaction with current counsel was prospective client; lawyer advised him about recoverability of memorabilia seized during drug raid, told him he could "sit in . . . jail" or "start cooperating," and quoted him a fee); N.Y. City Ethics Op. 2018-1 (2018) (person becomes prospective client once she consults lawyer about representation, even if she lacks capacity to retain lawyer); *see also Jimenez v. Rivermark Cmty. Credit Union*, No. 3:15–CV–00128–BR, 2015 WL 2239669, 2015 BL 140013 (D. Or. May 12, 2015) (fact that lawyer was contacted by husband did not preclude wife, who did not speak English, from being prospective client).

Whether the lawyer is paid a fee is not dispositive. *See United States v. Carlisle*, No. 3:13-CR-012 JD, 2014 WL 958027, 2014 BL 67492 (N.D. Ind. Mar. 12, 2014) (prospective client did not become client by paying lawyer a dollar to ensure attorney-client privilege; disqualification would be analyzed under Rule 1.18 rather than Rule 1.9); *Kuntz v. Disciplinary Bd.*, 869 N.W.2d 117 (N.D. 2015) (payment of initial consultation fee does not itself create lawyer-client relationship; Rule 1.18 governed relationship). *See generally* Peter A. Joy & Kevin C. McMunigal, *Client or Prospective Client: What's the Difference?*, 27 Crim. Just. 51 (Fall 2012); Susan R. Martyn, *Accidental Clients*, 33 Hofstra L. Rev. 913 (Spring 2005) (discussing potential-client problem in scenarios involving beauty contests, public speeches, advertising, e-lawyering, social gatherings, consultations with other lawyers, referral fees, and unrepresented parties); Ingrid A. Minott, Note, *The Attorney-Client Relationship: Exploring the Unintended Consequences of Inadvertent Formation*, 86 U. Det. Mercy L. Rev. 269 (Winter 2009); Fred C. Zacharias, *The Pre-Employment Ethical Role of Lawyers: Are Lawyers Really Fiduciaries?*, 49 Wm. & Mary L. Rev. 569 (Nov. 2007).

Because the relationship is matter-specific, a person can be both a current and a prospective client. *See Bell v. Cumberland County*, Civ. No. 09-6485 (JHR/JS), 2012 WL 1900570, 2012 BL 127366 (D.N.J. May 23, 2012) (when firm's client in workers' compensation matter discussed husband's death, she became firm's prospective client with respect to wrongful death claim; "if a current client discusses a new matter with an attorney, he/she becomes a prospective client for the purpose of the new matter").

Note that the universe of prospective clients as specially defined by Rule 1.18(a) is much smaller than the infinite universe of prospective clients as the phrase is generally understood. *See, e.g.*, ABA Formal Ethics Op. 10-457 (2010) (not every visitor to lawyer's website is prospective client for purposes of Rule 1.18).

### REASONABLE EXPECTATION OF RELATIONSHIP

Comment [2] provides that someone who communicates information unilaterally, "without any reasonable expectation that the lawyer is willing to discuss the possibility of forming a client-lawyer relationship," is not a prospective client protected by Rule 1.18. Relying upon this language, the court in *Matthews v. United States*, No. 07-00030, 2010 WL 503038, 2010 BL 26046 (D. Guam Feb. 9, 2010), held that defense counsel owed no Rule 1.18 duties to a plaintiff who called him the previous year about a possible claim against the federal government. Given that the caller "insisted that he describe his circumstances" even after the lawyer explained he was a Navy JAG Corps reservist and could not represent or advise him, the caller did not become a prospective client simply because the lawyer let him keep talking "out of courtesy." *See also Conn v. U.S. Steel Corp.*, No. 2:07-CV-00213-JVB-PRC, 2009 WL 260955, 2009 BL 19880 (N.D. Ind. Feb. 2, 2009) (employment discrimination plaintiff's meeting with union lawyer did not make her his prospective client under Rule 1.18; her actions "prior to, during, and after the meeting at the Country Lounge Inn indicate that she kept [him] at arm's length"); San Diego Cnty. Ethics Op. 2006-1 (2006) (information in nonclient's unsolicited e-mail need not be treated as confidential if lawyer did not have chance to warn sender or stop flow of information); N.Y. City Ethics Op. 2013-1 (2013) ("[m]eetings and other communications that do not focus on a particular representation, such as introductory and general promotional calls or visits, as well as social meetings, by themselves generally should not give rise to prospective client duties"; construing "discusses with" version of Rule 1.18).

In an unusual fact situation, one court held that if an acquaintance shares sensitive information with a lawyer in a purely social context but later asks the lawyer for a referral about the matter involved, the subsequent consultation makes the person a prospective client and retroactively imbues the initial social exchange with confidentiality. *In re Anonymous*, 932 N.E.2d 671 (Ind. 2010) (discussed in Donald R. Lundberg, *"Listen, Do You Want to Know a Secret?" Keeping Client Confidences*, 54 Res Gestae 21 (Oct. 2010)). *See also Miness v. Ahuja*, 762 F. Supp. 2d 465 (E.D.N.Y. 2010) ("totality of the parties' relationship" warranted disqualification under Rule 1.18; lawyer and his longtime friend/golf partner had detailed discussions of underlying issues over many years, during course of which lawyer offered his legal services).

### • *Electronic Communications*

A 2010 ABA ethics opinion noted that website marketing can give rise to "unanticipated reliance or unexpected inquiries or information from website visitors seeking legal advice," and analyzed how a lawyer's response to a website-initiated inquiry can trigger duties under Rule 1.18. ABA Formal Ethics Op. 10-457 (2010). Two years later the ABA's Commission on Ethics 20/20 amended Rule 1.18 and its Comment [2] "to help lawyers understand how to avoid the inadvertent creation of such relationships in an increasingly technology-driven world, and to ensure that the public does not misunderstand the consequences of communicating electronically with a lawyer." ABA Report to the House of Delegates No. 105(b) (Aug. 2012), *available at* https://www.americanbar.org/content/dam/aba/administrative/ethics_2020/2012_hod_annual_meeting_105b_filed_may_2012.authcheckdam.pdf.

On the danger of electronic communications triggering responsibilities under Rule 1.18, see N.H. Ethics Op. 2009-10/1 (n.d.) (firm whose website invites e-mails from public, but uses click-through electronic disclaimer requiring waiver of confidentiality and/or conflicts before visitor discloses anything, must be able to prove waiver is sufficiently informed; should also consider effect of advance waiver on possible privilege claim later), and S.C. Ethics Op. 12-03 (2003) (may not participate in "Just Answer" website inviting specific questions about specific legal matters and offering specific legal advice, notwithstanding website's "buried" warning and disclaimer). *See generally* Jan L. Jacobowitz & Danielle Singer, *The Social Media Frontier: Exploring a New Mandate for Competence in the Practice of Law*, 68 U. Miami L. Rev. 445 (Winter 2014); Martin Whittaker, *Ethical Considerations Related to Blogs, Chat Rooms, and Listservs*, 21 Prof. Law., no. 2, at 3 (2012) (chat rooms and listservs more likely to implicate Rule 1.18 duties than websites and blogs).

## GOOD FAITH

To be considered a prospective client under Rule 1.18, an individual must have consulted the lawyer in good faith for the purpose of securing representation. *See Bernacki v. Bernacki*, 1 N.Y.S.3d 761 (Sup. Ct. 2015) (husband in divorce case who contacted twelve of the most experienced divorce lawyers in county in attempt to disqualify them from representing wife was not prospective client; wife's lawyer not disqualified as result of phone messages left by husband ostensibly seeking representation); Ill. Ethics Op. 12-18 (2012) (may not advise clients to taint-shop; if lawyer can prove he was consulted by someone who had no intention of hiring him, he is free to undertake subsequent adverse representation); N.Y. State Ethics Op. 923 (2012) (purported real estate buyer who turns out to be con artist trying to defraud lawyer does not qualify as prospective client; lawyer free to provide information to bank or law enforcement authorities); Va. Ethics Op. 1794 (2004) (no duty of confidentiality owed to person who posed as prospective client and shared confidences with lawyer to create conflict of interest); *see also* N.Y. City Ethics Op. 2015-3 (2015) (person attempting to defraud lawyer through internet-based trust account scam does not qualify as prospective client, but lawyer may not disclose person's confidential information prior to concluding person is attempting to commit fraud). *See generally* Kenneth D. Agran, Note, *The Treacherous Path to the Diamond-Studded Tiara: Ethical Dilemmas in Legal Beauty Contests*, 9 Geo. J. Legal Ethics 1307 (Summer 1996) (analyzing competitive interviewing process in which prospective client interviews several different law firms for same job).

## *Paragraph (b): Using or Revealing Information*

### CONFIDENTIALITY

Rule 1.18(b) codifies the well-settled proposition that information learned in a consultation is protected whether or not any lawyer-client relationship ensues. *See* American Bar Association, *A Legislative History: The Development of the ABA Model Rules of Professional Conduct, 1982–2013*, at 399 (2013) (obligation to treat all communications with prospective client as confidential "is a well-settled matter under the law of attorney-client privilege, and the fact that Model Rule 1.9 does not now technically cover these communications is an omission that [Rule 1.18(b)] corrects"); ABA Formal Ethics Op. 90-358 (1990) ("Information imparted to a lawyer by a would-be client seeking legal representation is protected from revelation or use under Model

Rule 1.6 even though the lawyer does not undertake representation of or perform legal work for the would-be client."); *see also In re Beguelin*, 417 P.3d 1118 (Nev. 2018) (after declining to represent divorce client upon learning she was friend's wife, lawyer called friend to tell him his wife wanted divorce); Ill. Ethics Op. 18-03 (2018) (lawyer who consults with represented person about legal representation may not inform that person's counsel); N.Y. State Ethics Op. 1126 (2017) (lawyer who drafted trust document for now-deceased couple may not disclose that one spouse misappropriated trust assets after learning about it from prospective client); R.I. Ethics Op. 2016-06 (2016) (lawyer may not tell current client that prospective client may have assets to which current client is entitled); Wis. Formal Ethics Op. EF-17-01 (2017) (lawyer may not list prospective client's name in marketing materials); *cf.* N.Y. City Ethics Op. 2018-1 (2018) (if prospective client has diminished capacity, Rule 1.14 permits lawyer to reveal otherwise protected information to extent necessary to protect his interests).

The proposition holds whether the lawyer is consulted by the prospective client personally or by someone acting on her behalf. *In re Modanlo*, 342 B.R. 230 (D. Md. 2006); *see* D.C. Ethics Op. 346 (2009) (when prospective client authorizes lawyer to approach another lawyer about taking his case, first lawyer is acting as prospective client's agent; second lawyer must therefore treat information as confidential under Rule 1.18); *see also Jimenez v. Rivermark Cmty. Credit Union*, No. 3:15–CV–00128–BR, 2015 WL 2239669, 2015 BL 140013 (D. Or. May 12, 2015) (fact that lawyer was contacted by husband, acting as wife's English-language facilitator, did not preclude wife from being prospective client); *De David v. Alaron Trading Corp.*, No. 10 CV 3502, 2012 WL 1429564 (N.D. Ill. Apr. 23, 2012) (corporation became prospective client when its representative discussed possibility of retaining lawyer to determine if it was subject to U.S. investment laws); *Richman v. Eighth Judicial Dist. Court*, No. 60676, 2013 WL 3357115, 2013 BL 36501 (Nev. May 31, 2013) (rejecting argument that Rule 1.18 "does not recognize a prospective client by agency"; all four founders of real estate firm and related entities became prospective clients when two of the founders consulted with lawyer about allegations against all founders, partners, real estate firm, and founders' law firm); N.C. Ethics Op. 2005-4 (2006) (duty of confidentiality under Rule 1.18 arises when someone consults lawyer about legal issue "on behalf of a friend or family member").

## USE OF INFORMATION: FORMER PROSPECTIVE CLIENTS TREATED AS FORMER CLIENTS

Rule 1.18 departs from ABA Formal Opinion 90-358 (1990) by putting prospective clients on par with former—rather than current—clients when it comes to protecting information. The difference is this: Although a lawyer may neither use nor reveal information relating to the representation of a current client, she may use information relating to the representation of a former client once it is generally known. (The prohibition against revelation does not change.) See the annotations to Rules 1.8 and 1.9 for discussion.

## Paragraph (c): Subsequent Adverse Representation in Substantially Related Matter

### INFORMATION THAT COULD BE SIGNIFICANTLY HARMFUL

Rule 1.18(c) separates the prohibition against using or revealing information learned in a consultation (the duty of confidentiality) from the prohibition against subsequent adverse representation in a substantially related matter (sometimes loosely characterized as a duty of loyalty).

Although a lawyer owes a former prospective client the same duty of confidentiality owed a former "full-fledged" client, the duty characterized as one of loyalty is different. Only if the erstwhile prospective client revealed information that could be significantly harmful to him will the lawyer be prohibited from representing someone with materially adverse interests in a substantially related matter. This is "less exacting than the corresponding restriction on representations that are materially adverse to a former client," as to whom the bar against acting adversely in a substantially related matter is "automatic." N.Y. City Ethics Op. 2013-1 (2013). *See Kidd v. Kidd,* 219 So. 3d 1021 (Fla. 2017) (when no confidential information was divulged during consultation with prospective client, lawyer may represent adversary); *State ex rel. Thompson v. Dueker,* 346 S.W.3d 390 (Mo. Ct. App. 2011) (error to disqualify wife's lawyer under Rule 1.9's irrefutable-presumption test when husband had been only a former prospective client; Rule 1.18 required husband to show he actually imparted disqualifying information); *Kuntz v. Disciplinary Bd.,* 869 N.W.2d 117 (N.D. 2015) (no disqualification where initial consultation did not involve receipt of information that was confidential or could be deemed prejudicial); N.Y. State Ethics Op. 960 (2013) (if lawyer did not receive significantly harmful information from home buyer who consulted him about suing seller over home's structural damage, lawyer may represent contractor seeking payment from buyer for whom he did repair work).

"[I]n order for information to be deemed 'significantly harmful' within the context of RPC 1.18, disclosure of that information cannot be simply detrimental in general to the former prospective client, but the harm suffered must be prejudicial in fact to the former prospective client within the confines of the specific matter in which disqualification is sought, a determination that is exquisitely fact-sensitive." *O Builders & Assocs., Inc. v. Yuna Corp.,* 19 A.3d 966 (N.J. 2011) (motion to disqualify denied; prospective client claimed only that she disclosed information "concerning pending litigation and business matters" and disclosed "business, financial and legal information . . . believe[d] to be related to the current [lawsuit]"). *See Xiao Hong Liu v. VMC E. Coast LLC,* No. 16 CV 5184 (AMD)(RML), 2017 WL 4564744, 2017 BL 363855 (E.D.N.Y. Oct. 11, 2017) ("Courts have held that information is not 'significantly harmful' if it is public information, if it merely regards the 'history of the dispute,' or if it is 'likely to be revealed at [the moving party's] deposition or in other discovery'"; collecting cases); *Benevida Foods, LLC v. Advance Magazine Publishers Inc.,* No. 15cv2729 (LTS)(DF), 2016 WL 3453342, 2016 BL 200831 (S.D.N.Y. June 15, 2016) (prospective client's assessment of own claims, financial situation and risk tolerance, and litigation and settlement strategies are types of information that, if shared, could be "significantly harmful" to it); *De David v. Alaron Trading Corp.,* No. 10 CV 3501, 2012 WL

1429564 (N.D. Ill. Apr. 23, 2012) (opinions and impressions of documents and facts, even if public, would establish privileged communications that, if revealed, would cause significant harm); *Factory Mut. Ins. Co. v. APComPower, Inc.*, 662 F. Supp. 2d 896 (W.D. Mich. 2009) (using Rule 1.18 approach, court disqualified plaintiff's lawyer in crane accident case; in earlier consultation with defendant's insurer, lawyer received engineering report significantly harmful to defendant); *Sturdivant v. Sturdivant*, 241 S.W.3d 740 (Ark. 2006) (disqualifying law firm that undertook representation of former wife in change-of-custody proceeding, unaware that former husband already consulted it and disclosed "everything he knew and his concerns about the children and his former wife"; although husband testified he had not disclosed information that would be harmful to his case, court reasoned this is not something prospective client would necessarily know); *Mayers v. Stone Castle Partners, LLC*, 1 N.Y.S.3d 58 (App. Div. 2015) (disclosure of confidential information to adversaries' lawyer did not warrant disqualification when information had been made generally known and adversaries were aware of it); *In re Carpenter*, 863 N.W.2d 223 (N.D. 2015) (information disclosed by prospective client who spent over 300 hours searching public records in attempt to locate heirs was "significantly harmful" within meaning of Rule 1.18(c)); John M. Burman, *Waiving a Conflict of Interest and Revoking That Waiver: Part III—Conflicts Involving Prospective and Former Prospective Clients*, 34 Wyo. Law. 46, n.53 (June 2011) (use of "significantly" in Rule 1.18 "suggests that the harm must be serious. Civil or criminal liability would seem to easily qualify. Embarrassment, or inconvenience, by contrast, does not seem to be 'significant.'"); *see also Keuffer v. O.F. Mossberg & Sons, Inc.*, 373 P.3d 14 (Mont. 2017) (rule violated when defendant's out-of-state counsel used fact that plaintiff consulted defendant's local counsel to intimidate plaintiff during deposition; both firms disqualified); *cf. Richman v. Eighth Judicial Dist. Court*, No. 60676, 2013 WL 3357115, 2013 BL 36501 (Nev. May 31, 2013) (disqualification did not require evidentiary hearing; court properly concluded that when company's founders consulted lawyer about allegations being made against them and others, they necessarily disclosed information about company's formation and operations that could be significantly harmful in different plaintiffs' later suit making substantially similar allegations).

## *Paragraph (d)(1): Consent*

Even if the lawyer receives disqualifying information under paragraph (c), Rule 1.18(d)(1) permits subsequent adverse representation if both the affected client and the former prospective client give informed consent, confirmed in writing. Comment [5] notes that a lawyer may condition a consultation upon the prospective client's informed consent that nothing "disclosed during the consultation will prohibit the lawyer from representing a different client in the matter," and that "[i]f the agreement expressly so provides, the prospective client may also consent to the lawyer's subsequent use of information received from the prospective client." *See* John M. Burman, *Waiving a Conflict of Interest and Revoking That Waiver: Part III—Conflicts Involving Prospective and Former Prospective Clients*, 34 Wyo. Law. 46 (June 2011).

Prospective waivers are discussed in the annotations to Rules 1.7 and 1.9.

## Paragraph (d)(2): Avoiding Imputation

Unlike a former client, a former prospective client cannot prevent other lawyers in the firm from undertaking a subsequent adverse representation over his objection. Rule 1.18(d)(2)'s express endorsement of nonconsensual screening is actually consistent with the caselaw predating the rule's adoption.

If the lawyer minimized the disclosures entailed in the initial consultation, the firm will be free to proceed with the subsequent representation as long as it screens the individual lawyer and notifies the former prospective client. *See* N.Y. City Ethics Op. 2013-1 (2013) ("[P]aragraph (d) requires the lawyer to take reasonable measures to limit the receipt of information as specified; it does not require that the information received in fact be so limited."); N.C. Ethics Op. 2003-8 (2003) (second representation may proceed if lawyer notifies former prospective client and promptly implements screening procedures; former prospective client's consent not necessary); *see also In re Modanlo*, 342 B.R. 230 (D. Md. 2006) (although creditor's firm would not be disqualified based upon debtor's initial consultation with one of its lawyers, court "[o]ut of an abundance of caution" ordered firm to formally screen lawyer from debtor's personal bankruptcy case); *Capital Prop. Assocs., LP v. Capital City Econ. Dev. Auth.*, No. X07CV044001923S, 2006 WL 1391382 (Conn. Super. Ct. May 5, 2006) (lawyers for real estate developer suing municipal entity for "jilting" him met with competitor seeking to replace him; looking to Rule 1.18, court ruled that complete failure to quarantine information prohibited firm from later deposing would-be replacement developer unless it used outside counsel and erected external screen); *cf. Benevida Foods, LLC v. Advance Magazine Publishers Inc.*, No. 15cv2729 (LTS)(DF), 2016 WL 3453342, 2016 BL 200831 (S.D.N.Y. June 15, 2016) (declining to impute conflict to co-counsel when no evidence confidences actually shared with it). *See generally* Caroline Buddensick, Current Development, *Risks Inherent in Online Peer Advice: Ethical Issues Posed by Requesting or Providing Advice Via Professional Electronic Mailing Lists*, 22 Geo. J. Legal Ethics 715 (Summer 2009); Jennifer Vaculik, Note, *Bidding by the Bar: Online Auction Sites for Legal Services*, 82 Tex. L. Rev. 445 (Dec. 2003) (if law firms participating in online auctions cannot limit exposure to information, they risk not only having to withdraw their bids but also having to tell current clients to find other counsel).

## Rule 2.1

### Advisor

In representing a client, a lawyer shall exercise independent professional judgment and render candid advice. In rendering advice, a lawyer may refer not only to law but to other considerations such as moral, economic, social and political factors, that may be relevant to the client's situation.

## COMMENT

### Scope of Advice

[1] A client is entitled to straightforward advice expressing the lawyer's honest assessment. Legal advice often involves unpleasant facts and alternatives that a client may be disinclined to confront. In presenting advice, a lawyer endeavors to sustain the client's morale and may put advice in as acceptable a form as honesty permits. However, a lawyer should not be deterred from giving candid advice by the prospect that the advice will be unpalatable to the client.

[2] Advice couched in narrow legal terms may be of little value to a client, especially where practical considerations, such as cost or effects on other people, are predominant. Purely technical legal advice, therefore, can sometimes be inadequate. It is proper for a lawyer to refer to relevant moral and ethical considerations in giving advice. Although a lawyer is not a moral advisor as such, moral and ethical considerations impinge upon most legal questions and may decisively influence how the law will be applied.

[3] A client may expressly or impliedly ask the lawyer for purely technical advice. When such a request is made by a client experienced in legal matters, the lawyer may accept it at face value. When such a request is made by a client inexperienced in legal matters, however, the lawyer's responsibility as advisor may include indicating that more may be involved than strictly legal considerations.

[4] Matters that go beyond strictly legal questions may also be in the domain of another profession. Family matters can involve problems within the professional competence of psychiatry, clinical psychology or social work; business matters can involve problems within the competence of the accounting profession or of financial specialists. Where consultation with a professional in another field is itself something a competent lawyer would recommend, the lawyer should make such a recommendation. At the same time, a lawyer's advice at its best often consists of recommending a course of action in the face of conflicting recommendations of experts.

## Offering Advice

[5] In general, a lawyer is not expected to give advice until asked by the client. However, when a lawyer knows that a client proposes a course of action that is likely to result in substantial adverse legal consequences to the client, the lawyer's duty to the client under Rule 1.4 may require that the lawyer offer advice if the client's course of action is related to the representation. Similarly, when a matter is likely to involve litigation, it may be necessary under Rule 1.4 to inform the client of forms of dispute resolution that might constitute reasonable alternatives to litigation. A lawyer ordinarily has no duty to initiate investigation of a client's affairs or to give advice that the client has indicated is unwanted, but a lawyer may initiate advice to a client when doing so appears to be in the client's interest.

## State Rules Comparison

http://ambar.org/MRPCStateCharts

## ANNOTATION

### INDEPENDENT PROFESSIONAL JUDGMENT— AVOIDING CONFLICTS OF INTEREST

Rule 2.1's mandate to "exercise independent professional judgment" is derived from Canon 5 of the Model Code (A Lawyer Should Exercise Independent Professional Judgment on Behalf of a Client). The duty to exercise independent professional judgment underlies the ethics rules relating to conflicts of interest and has a provenance in the common law. *See, e.g., Smoot v. Lund,* 369 P.2d 933 (Utah 1962) ("Where an attorney is hired solely to represent the interests of a client, his fiduciary duty is of the highest order and he must not represent interests adverse to those of the client. It is also true that because of his professional responsibility and the confidence and trust which his client may legitimately repose in him, he must adhere to a high standard of honesty, integrity and good faith in dealing with his client."). *See generally* American Bar Association, *Essential Qualities of the Professional Lawyer* 134–36 (2013); Kevin H. Michels, *Lawyer Independence: From Ideal to Viable Legal Standard,* 61 Case W. Res. L. Rev. 85 (Fall 2010).

Although Rule 2.1 is the ethics rule that clearly enunciates the lawyer's duty to exercise independent professional judgment in representing a client, it is not invoked nearly as frequently as the ethics rules that address specific threats to that independence. These issues are fully addressed in the annotations to Rule 1.7 (Conflict of Interest: Current Clients), Rule 1.8 (Conflict of Interest: Current Clients: Specific Rules), and Rule 5.4 (Professional Independence of a Lawyer); also see Rule 1.9 (Duties to Former Clients) and Rule 1.18 (Duties to Prospective Client).

#### • Insurance Defense

Independence is of particular concern for lawyers hired by insurance companies to defend insureds because insurance companies may seek to place restrictions upon the representation. In general, a lawyer may comply with these restrictions, but only to the extent they do not interfere with the lawyer's independent professional judgment in representing the insured. *See, e.g., In re Rules of Prof'l Conduct & Insurer-Imposed Billing Rules & Procedures,* 2 P.3d 806 (Mont. 2000) (insurance defense counsel who comply with insurer's requirements that lawyer obtain insurer's approval before scheduling depositions, conducting research, employing experts, or preparing motions would "violate their duties under the Rules of Professional Conduct to exercise their independent judgment and to give their undivided loyalty to insureds"); ABA Formal Ethics Op. 01-421 (2001) (lawyer hired by insurer to represent insureds may not comply with insurer's guidelines or directives relating to representation if these would "impair materially the lawyer's independent professional judgment"); Conn. Informal Ethics Op. 09-03 (2009) (lawyer may not represent both employer and its insurer in workers' compensation matter if employer desires, and insurer opposes, maximum recovery for employee); Okla. Ethics Op. 327 (2009) (in-house lawyer defending insurer's policyholders must ignore compensation incentive to take cases to trial and make settlement decisions in best interest of insureds); Utah Ethics Op. 02-03 (2002) (although insurance defense lawyer is not per se prohibited from agreeing to insurer's billing procedures or guidelines or agreeing to flat-fee arrangement, lawyer may not permit insurer's directives to materially impair lawyer's independent professional judgment in representing insured); *cf.* Conn. Informal Ethics Op. 00-9 (2000) (lawyer for government agency that adjudicates benefit claims may not accept directions from nonlawyer supervisor regarding proper disposition of cases if those directions conflict with lawyer's exercise of professional judgment); Ohio Sup. Ct. Ethics Op. 2012-3 (2012) (must ensure alternative litigation funding company providing nonrecourse loan to client "does not attempt to dictate the lawyer's representation of the client").

### • *Obligations to Others*

Outside of the insurance defense context, the possibility that a lawyer's independent professional judgment may be compromised by allegiances to others can arise in a variety of situations. Frequently they involve allegiances to people or entities who are sources of ongoing business for the lawyer. *See In re Haitbrink,* 375 P.3d 296 (Kan. 2016) (associating with nonlawyer for renegotiation and modification of residential real estate loans); Ariz. Ethics Op. 98-09 (1998) (accepting referral fee from investment advisor to whom lawyer referred client prohibited because fee may affect lawyer's independent professional judgment); Colo. Ethics Op. 106 (1999) (participating in referral agencies or bar-sponsored referral services permissible only if they do not require lawyer to accept referred clients, do not compensate lawyer on basis of fees paid by referred clients, and do not interfere with lawyer's independent professional judgment); Haw. Ethics Op. 46 (2003) (prohibiting accepting referral fee from nonlawyer service providers whom lawyer recommends to clients); Ill. Ethics Op. 10-02 (2009) (prohibiting accepting referrals from real estate agent if conditioned upon lawyer's using agent's affiliated title insurer exclusively); Ind. Ethics Op. 2012-1 (2012) (lawyer's professional independence might be undermined by participation in group coupon or "daily deal" arrangement); Mich. Informal Ethics Op. RI-325 (2001) (business arrangement with company that markets legal documents and kits might impede lawyer's exercise of independent professional judgment if lawyer's role would be to complete form documents already sold to clients); Neb. Ethics Op. 06-10 (2007) (prohibiting referrals of estate planning clients from company that sells form plans to clients before referrals because arrangement prevents lawyer's full exercise of independent professional judgment); Pa. Formal Ethics Op. 2016-200 (2016) (flat fee limited scope referral arrangement interferes with lawyer's independent professional judgment by impermissibly delegating to nonlawyer assessment of whether legal services were satisfactorily rendered).

Some authorities have invoked Rule 2.1 in situations involving lawyers' undertaking multiple representations. *See In re Key*, 582 S.E.2d 400 (S.C. 2003) (to hasten closing of real estate sale, lawyer agreed to represent both buyer and seller); Va. Ethics Op. 1836 (2008) (Rule 2.1 requires city lawyer who represents several municipal agents and bodies to give candid advice even if one client "might strongly disagree").

Rule 2.1 has also been invoked when obligations to adversaries or third parties might interfere with a lawyer's independent judgment on behalf of the client. *E.g.*, Ariz. Ethics Op. 03-05 (2003) (prohibiting indemnifying parties to personal injury settlement agreement against potential liens on settlement funds); N.J. Ethics Op. 719 (2010) (lawyer representing estate administrator may not comply with surety bond conditions that include protecting surety company's interests); S.C. Ethics Op. 08-07 (2008) (prohibiting indemnifying defendant, defendant's counsel, and defendant's insurer against Medicaid or Medicare liens on personal injury settlement proceeds); Tenn. Formal Ethics Op. 2010-F-154 (2010) (lawyer representing personal injury plaintiff may not agree to indemnify or hold harmless parties being released as part of settlement to ensure payment of medical expenses and liens); *see also Scheffler v. Adams & Reese LLP*, 950 So. 2d 641 (La. 2007) (lawyer not liable to former co-counsel for causing mutual client to fire both lawyers because Rule 2.1 requires undivided loyalty to client, which "should not be diluted by fiduciary duty owed to some other person, such as co-counsel").

### • *Personal Interests*

Rule 2.1 likewise proscribes a lawyer from letting personal interests affect his or her independence in representing a client. *See Richardson-Merrell, Inc. v. Koller*, 472 U.S. 424 (1985) (although lawyer "disqualified for misconduct may well have a personal interest in pursuing an immediate appeal, an interest which need not coincide with the interests of the client," personal desire for vindication does not amount to ground for appeal: "As a matter of professional ethics, . . . the decision to appeal should turn entirely on the client's interest"; citing Rules 1.7(b) and 2.1); *Lieberman v. Lieberman*, 160 So. 3d 73 n.4 (Fla. 2014) ("An attorney who is too personally involved with the issues in a litigation should consider withdrawing or risk violating ethical duties owed to the client.").

In many cases the personal interest is in receiving a financial benefit. *See, e.g., Chief Disciplinary Counsel v. Rozbicki*, 91 A.3d 932 (Conn. App. Ct. 2014) (lawyer serving as executor of estate of friend and former employer whose will directed repayment of loan to lawyer from life insurance policy proceeds failed to candidly advise beneficiaries of alternatives for administering estate); *Coffey's Case*, 880 A.2d 403

(N.H. 2005) (advising elderly client to deed lawyer his home for anticipated legal fees); *In re Spencer*, 330 P.3d 538 (Or. 2014) (lawyer serving bankruptcy client in dual role as real estate agent must exercise independent professional judgment in advising on home purchase); *In re Pfeiffer*, 796 S.E.2d 839 (S.C. 2017) (fraudulent lending scheme involving business co-owned by lawyer, who also acted as business's general counsel, violated Rule 2.1, among other rules); ABA Formal Ethics Op. 00-418 (2000) (lawyer who owns stock in client's business must avoid conflicts of interest and exercise independent professional judgment in rendering legal advice); Ariz. Ethics Op. 99-09 (1999) (lawyer practicing estate planning may offer securities and insurance brokerage services to clients only with informed consent and must not let his own financial interests compromise independent professional judgment in representing clients); Conn. Informal Ethics Op. 08-01 (n.d.) (lawyer representing several clients for injuries resulting from same product may not agree to proposed settlement requiring lawyer to forgo fees from clients who do not accept settlement); Ind. Ethics Op. 2008-3 (2008) (lawyer who refers client to financial advisor may not take percentage of advisor's fees); N.H. Ethics Op. 2008-09/1 (2009) (lawyer may not use form will naming himself as paid fiduciary; lawyer may name himself as fiduciary only at client's request after informing client of other available options); W. Va. Ethics Op. 05-02 (2005) (lawyer may advise client to get loan to cover living expenses, to be repaid from proceeds of client's suit, only if his interests in protecting contingent fee do not materially affect advice regarding loan); *see also* ABA Formal Ethics Op. 94-389 (1994) (lawyer not ethically obligated to solicit early offer of settlement in contingent-fee cases; such a rule would diminish discretion that is part of independent professional judgment).

Sometimes the conflicting personal interest involves family, friends, or institutions to which the lawyer has personal loyalty. *See* Md. Ethics Op. 2003-08 (2003) (lawyer who chairs his church's "legacy" committee may not prepare wills pro bono for parishioners who want to bequeath property to church); Neb. Ethics Op. 06-12 (2007) (lawyer whose father is municipality's prosecutor may represent criminal defendants in municipal courts only if he determines his "professional judgment will not be affected by the relationship"); Wash. Ethics Op. 2154 (2007) (lawyer may refer client to realty broker who employs lawyer's wife but "must also be mindful of RPC 2.1, which requires him to 'exercise independent professional judgment'").

## • *Sexual Relations with Clients*

In 2002, Rule 1.8 was amended to add paragraph (j), which provides that a "lawyer shall not have sexual relations with a client unless a consensual sexual relationship existed between them when the client-lawyer relationship commenced." In the absence of this explicit provision the issue has been analyzed under Rules 1.7 and 1.8 (conflict-of-interest rules), Rule 2.1, Rule 8.4(d) (prohibiting conduct "prejudicial to the administration of justice"), or some combination. *See, e.g., In re Berg*, 955 P.2d 1240 (Kan. 1998) (lawyer knew or should have known that engaging in sexual relationships with clients could prejudice clients' legal rights); *In re Fuerst*, 157 So. 3d 569 (La. 2014) (sexual encounter with divorce client during six-month waiting period to confirm divorce violated Rule 2.1); *State ex rel. Okla. Bar Ass'n v. Downes*, 121 P.3d 1058

(Okla. 2005) ("lawyer's sexual advances toward a client exploit the attorney-client relationship [and the] client's consent does not excuse the lawyer's actions"); *In re Halverson*, 998 P.2d 833 (Wash. 2000) (lawyer who engaged in sexual relationship with divorce client failed to exercise independent professional judgment by, inter alia, not advising client of potential ramifications relationship might have upon dissolution or representation); Va. Ethics Op. 1853 (2009) (although no rule "specifically prohibits sexual relationships between lawyer and client . . . the lawyer must consider that such conduct could . . . interfere with the lawyer's independent professional judgment (Rule 2.1) [and] create a conflict of interest between the lawyer and the client"). *See generally* Kathleen Maher, *Sex with Clients: The Progeny of ABA Opinion 92-364*, 12 Prof. Law., no. 2, at 20 (Winter 2001).

## CANDID ADVICE

Rule 2.1 requires that the lawyer's advice to a client be candid. As Comment [1] states, "[a] client is entitled to straightforward advice expressing the lawyer's honest assessment"; although legal advice may involve "unpleasant facts and alternatives that a client may be disinclined to confront[,] . . . a lawyer should not be deterred from giving candid advice by the prospect that the advice will be unpalatable to the client." *See In re O'Connor*, 553 N.E.2d 481 (Ind. 1990) (assuring client lawyer would secure client's son's release, even though lawyer knew son not yet eligible for work release); *Kidwell v. Sybaritic, Inc.*, 749 N.W.2d 855 (Minn. Ct. App. 2008) (in-house lawyer's advice to management regarding its possibly illegal activity was part of counsel's "most basic duties to his or her client—to be competent, to be diligent, to use good judgment, to render candid advice"); *Evans v. State*, 477 S.W.2d 94 (Mo. 1972) (in criminal case, lawyer duty-bound to advise defendant regarding advantages and disadvantages of choosing plea); *In re Harrison*, 587 S.E.2d 105 (S.C. 2003) (lawyer's investigation showed personal injury case had no merit but lawyer failed to so advise client until after limitation period expired); Ariz. Ethics Op. 15-01 (2015) (criminal defense counsel may not advise client to accept plea agreement containing waiver of ineffective assistance of counsel claim because it would compromise duty to exercise independent judgment and provide candid advice); Ariz. Ethics Op. 97-06 (1997) (criminal defense lawyer whose client enters cooperation agreement with law enforcement agency must fully advise client of risks, including agency's lack of resources to protect him); Ohio Sup. Ct. Ethics Op. 2012-3 (2012) (lawyer must provide candid advice regarding risks and benefits of nonrecourse civil litigation advance from alternative litigation finance company); *see also Wise v. Washington County*, Civ. No. 10-1677, 2015 WL 1757730, 2015 BL 110240 (W.D. Pa. Apr. 17, 2015) (failure to properly advise plaintiff client on risks of litigating claims); *In re Rokahr*, 681 N.W.2d 100 (S.D. 2004) (lawyer recognized existence of statutory easement and counseled client that creating and recording easement was therefore unnecessary but acceded to client's demand, thereby allowing client to override independent professional judgment). *See generally* Milan Markovic, *Advising Clients After Critical Legal Studies and the Torture Memos*, 114 W. Va. L. Rev. 109 (Fall 2011).

Lawyers must not allow their interest in collecting fees for resolving cases to diminish their candor to clients. *See Ky. Bar Ass'n v. Helmers*, 353 S.W.3d 599 (Ky. 2011) (failing to exercise independent professional judgment regarding firm scheme of misleading clients into accepting smaller portion of aggregate settlement in fen-phen litigation so that lawyers' fee portion would increase, and failing to advise clients candidly regarding settlement); *Stanley v. Bd. of Prof'l Responsibility*, 640 S.W.2d 210 (Tenn. 1982) (misleading parents of youthful offender into believing their child would be prosecuted to induce parents to pay lawyer large fee for his legal services); N.Y. City Ethics Op. 2011-2 (2011) (conflict may arise when advising client about financing if client cannot afford to litigate without third-party advance of legal fees).

For further discussion of a lawyer's duty of candor toward clients, see the annotation to Rule 8.4 (Rule 8.4(c) prohibits dishonesty, including dishonesty to clients). For discussion of a lawyer's duty to communicate with clients, see the annotation to Rule 1.4.

## ADVICE ABOUT NONLEGAL CONSIDERATIONS

Rule 2.1 specifically condones a lawyer's reference to nonlegal considerations—such as moral, economic, social, and political factors—when giving advice. As the comment explains, advice given in purely legal terms may be inadequate, particularly when other considerations, such as cost or the effect upon others, are important to the client. Thus, "[a]lthough a lawyer is not a moral advisor as such, moral and ethical considerations impinge upon most legal questions and may decisively influence how the law will be applied." Cmt. [2]; *see also Restatement (Third) of the Law Governing Lawyers* § 94(3) (2000) ("In counseling a client, a lawyer may address nonlegal aspects of a proposed course of conduct, including moral, reputational, economic, social, political, and business aspects."). *See generally* Kristen M. Blankley, *The Ethics and Practice of Drafting Pre-Dispute Resolution Clauses*, 49 Creighton L. Rev. 743 (Sept. 2016); Amanda Boote & Anne H. Dechter, *Slipped Up: Model Rule 2.1 and Counseling Clients on the "Grease Payments" Exception to the Foreign Corrupt Practices Act*, 23 Geo. J. Legal Ethics 471 (Summer 2010); Michael S. McGinniss, *Virtue and Advice: Socratic Perspectives on Lawyer Independence and Moral Counseling of Clients*, 1 Tex. A&M L. Rev. 1 (Fall 2013); Larry O. Natt Gantt II, *More Than Lawyers: The Legal and Ethical Implications of Counseling Clients on Nonlegal Considerations*, 18 Geo. J. Legal Ethics 365 (Spring 2005); Olumuyiwa Odeniyide, *Restoring Public Trust: Why In-House Counsel Should Encourage Companies to Disclose the Use of Corporate Funds for Political Spending*, 28 Geo. J. Legal Ethics 799 (Summer 2015); W. Bradley Wendel, *Government Lawyers in the Trump Administration*, 69 Hastings L.J. 275 (Dec. 2017); Fred C. Zacharias, *Integrity Ethics*, 22 Geo. J. Legal Ethics 541 (Spring 2009); Michael Zhou, *Giving Moral Advice in Sharia-Compliant Finance*, 27 Geo. J. Legal Ethics 1021 (Summer 2014).

This provision only rarely finds its way into court and ethics opinions. *See, e.g., Friedman v. Comm'r of Pub. Safety*, 473 N.W.2d 828 (Minn. 1991) (in declaring that person stopped for drunk driving has right to counsel before deciding whether to submit to blood alcohol test, court commented "[i]f the objective of DWI prosecution is to get drunk drivers off the highway, into treatment, and on the way to sobriety, an attorney can play a very important role [citing Rule 2.1's language permitting reference to moral and social factors]. The lawyer may be able to persuade a problem drinker to seek treatment."); *In re Marriage of Foran*, 834 P.2d 1081 (Wash. Ct. App.

1992) (in affirming decision invalidating prenuptial contract for being economically unfair, court warned that lawyers handling prenuptial contracts "should seriously consider the implications of RPC 2.1 [citing portion of rule permitting reference to moral, economic, social, and political factors]. Marital tranquility is not achieved by a contract which is economically unfair or achieved by unfair means."); N.Y. City Ethics Op. 2011-2 (2011) (lawyer's duty to provide candid advice to client who inquires about alternative litigation financing arrangements includes discussing client's economic resources, including possibility of more efficient use of those resources).

## Rule 2.2
### *Intermediary*

[Deleted 2002]

[Model Rule 2.2 was deleted in 2002. Issues relating to lawyers acting as intermediaries are dealt with in the comment to Rule 1.7. Intermediation and the conflict-of-interest issues it raises are no longer treated separately from any other multiple-representation conflicts. For further explanation of the deletion of Rule 2.2, see American Bar Association, *A Legislative History: The Development of the ABA Model Rules of Professional Conduct, 1982–2013*, at 419–22 (2013).]

## Rule 2.3

### Evaluation for Use by Third Persons

(a) A lawyer may provide an evaluation of a matter affecting a client for the use of someone other than the client if the lawyer reasonably believes that making the evaluation is compatible with other aspects of the lawyer's relationship with the client.

(b) When the lawyer knows or reasonably should know that the evaluation is likely to affect the client's interests materially and adversely, the lawyer shall not provide the evaluation unless the client gives informed consent.

(c) Except as disclosure is authorized in connection with a report of an evaluation, information relating to the evaluation is otherwise protected by Rule 1.6.

## COMMENT

### Definition

[1] An evaluation may be performed at the client's direction or when impliedly authorized in order to carry out the representation. See Rule 1.2. Such an evaluation may be for the primary purpose of establishing information for the benefit of third parties; for example, an opinion concerning the title of property rendered at the behest of a vendor for the information of a prospective purchaser, or at the behest of a borrower for the information of a prospective lender. In some situations, the evaluation may be required by a government agency; for example, an opinion concerning the legality of the securities registered for sale under the securities laws. In other instances, the evaluation may be required by a third person, such as a purchaser of a business.

[2] A legal evaluation should be distinguished from an investigation of a person with whom the lawyer does not have a client-lawyer relationship. For example, a lawyer retained by a purchaser to analyze a vendor's title to property does not have a client-lawyer relationship with the vendor. So also, an investigation into a person's affairs by a government lawyer, or by special counsel employed by the government, is not an evaluation as that term is used in this Rule. The question is whether the lawyer is retained by the person whose affairs are being examined. When the lawyer is retained by that person, the general rules concerning loyalty to client and preservation of confidences apply, which is not the case if the lawyer is retained by someone else. For this reason, it is essential to identify the person by whom the lawyer is retained. This should be made clear not only to the person under examination, but also to others to whom the results are to be made available.

## Duties Owed to Third Person and Client

[3] When the evaluation is intended for the information or use of a third person, a legal duty to that person may or may not arise. That legal question is beyond the scope of this Rule. However, since such an evaluation involves a departure from the normal client-lawyer relationship, careful analysis of the situation is required. The lawyer must be satisfied as a matter of professional judgment that making the evaluation is compatible with other functions undertaken in behalf of the client. For example, if the lawyer is acting as advocate in defending the client against charges of fraud, it would normally be incompatible with that responsibility for the lawyer to perform an evaluation for others concerning the same or a related transaction. Assuming no such impediment is apparent, however, the lawyer should advise the client of the implications of the evaluation, particularly the lawyer's responsibilities to third persons and the duty to disseminate the findings.

## Access to and Disclosure of Information

[4] The quality of an evaluation depends on the freedom and extent of the investigation upon which it is based. Ordinarily a lawyer should have whatever latitude of investigation seems necessary as a matter of professional judgment. Under some circumstances, however, the terms of the evaluation may be limited. For example, certain issues or sources may be categorically excluded, or the scope of search may be limited by time constraints or the noncooperation of persons having relevant information. Any such limitations that are material to the evaluation should be described in the report. If after a lawyer has commenced an evaluation, the client refuses to comply with the terms upon which it was understood the evaluation was to have been made, the lawyer's obligations are determined by law, having reference to the terms of the client's agreement and the surrounding circumstances. In no circumstances is the lawyer permitted to knowingly make a false statement of material fact or law in providing an evaluation under this Rule. See Rule 4.1.

## Obtaining Client's Informed Consent

[5] Information relating to an evaluation is protected by Rule 1.6. In many situations, providing an evaluation to a third party poses no significant risk to the client; thus, the lawyer may be impliedly authorized to disclose information to carry out the representation. See Rule 1.6(a). Where, however, it is reasonably likely that providing the evaluation will affect the client's interests materially and adversely, the lawyer must first obtain the client's consent after the client has been adequately informed concerning the important possible effects on the client's interests. See Rules 1.6(a) and 1.0(e).

## Financial Auditors' Requests for Information

[6] When a question concerning the legal situation of a client arises at the instance of the client's financial auditor and the question is referred to the lawyer, the lawyer's response may be made in accordance with procedures recognized in the legal profession. Such a procedure is set forth in the American Bar Association Statement of Policy Regarding Lawyers' Responses to Auditors' Requests for Information, adopted in 1975.

**Definitional Cross-References**
"Informed consent" *See* Rule 1.0(e)
"Knows" *See* Rule 1.0(f)
"Reasonably believes" *See* Rule 1.0(i)
"Reasonably should know" *See* Rule 1.0(j)

**State Rules Comparison**
http://ambar.org/MRPCStateCharts

## ANNOTATION

### GENERAL PROVISIONS

A client sometimes needs a lawyer to supply an evaluation of a matter for someone else's use. For example, a lawyer for a business might be asked to render an evaluation of the business for a prospective purchaser, or an opinion for a government agency about the legality of securities the client has registered for sale. *See* Cmt. [1]. Rule 2.3 addresses the lawyer's ethical obligations in providing such information to others.

Rule 2.3(a) states that as a general matter, it is permissible for a lawyer to provide an evaluation of a client matter to a third party "if the lawyer reasonably believes that [doing so] is compatible with other aspects of the lawyer's relationship with the client." This corresponds to Rule 1.2(a)'s provision that a "lawyer may take such action on behalf of the client as is impliedly authorized to carry out the representation."

Under paragraph (b), if "the lawyer knows or reasonably should know that the evaluation is likely to affect the client's interests materially and adversely," the lawyer is not permitted to provide the evaluation without the client's informed consent. *See* Ohio Sup. Ct. Ethics Op. 2012-3 (2012) (lawyer must obtain client's informed consent before preparing case evaluation for alternative litigation finance provider); *see also* Edward J. Levin, *Real Estate Finance Opinion Report of 2012 History and Summary*, 27-FEB Prob. & Prop. 52 (Jan./Feb. 2013).

Paragraph (c) makes clear that the information relating to the evaluation remains subject to the lawyer's confidentiality duties under Rule 1.6.

Rule 2.3 itself deals only with the lawyer's duty to the client, addressing the circumstances under which a lawyer may provide an evaluation to a third person and the extent to which information relating to the evaluation may be disclosed. The comment, however, goes further and provides guidance on information the evaluation may include, and how to deal with limitations on that information. The comment also points out that a lawyer may have a legal duty to the recipient of the evaluation, but that issues related to that legal duty are beyond the scope of the rule. In fact, it is those legal duties to third persons, as well as the lawyer's obligations under a variety of government regulations, that have created most of the caselaw and commentary on the subject. There is virtually no reported disciplinary authority construing and applying Rule 2.3.

## • Disclosure of Material Limitations

The comment advises that any material limitations on the scope of the opinion or the investigation upon which it is based should be described in the report. Cmt. [4]; *accord Restatement (Third) of the Law Governing Lawyers* § 95 cmt. c (2000) (lawyer's evaluation not guarantee that facts are accurate; "[a] lawyer normally may rely on facts provided by corporate officers and other agents of a client that the lawyer reasonably believes to be appropriate sources for such facts without further investigation or specific disclosure, unless the recipient of the opinion objects or the version of the facts provided or other circumstances indicate that further verification is required").

The extent to which a lawyer has relied upon the conclusions of others should also be noted in the opinion. *See* N.Y. City Bar Ass'n, *Report by Special Committee on Lawyer's Role in Securities Transactions*, 33 Bus. Law. 1343 (Mar. 1978) (if lawyer relies upon opinions of other lawyers, opinion letter should so state; by stating this reliance, lawyer represents that he or she considers reliance reasonable).

## • False Statements

A lawyer making an evaluation may not "knowingly make a false statement of material fact or law in providing an evaluation under this Rule." Cmt. [4]; *accord Restatement (Third) of the Law Governing Lawyers* § 95 (2000) (in providing information, evaluation, or opinion, lawyer must not make false statements); Comm. on Legal Opinions, ABA Section of Bus. Law, *Guidelines for the Preparation of Closing Opinions*, 57 Bus. Law. 875 (Feb. 2002) (opinion giver should not render opinion that will mislead recipient); *see also* Rule 4.1 (Truthfulness in Statements to Others).

## • Extent of Investigation: Customary Diligence

Rule 2.3 does not specify how much investigation the lawyer must perform for an evaluation. Comment [4] simply notes that "[o]rdinarily a lawyer should have whatever latitude of investigation seems necessary as a matter of professional judgment." Lawyers supplying evaluations for use by third persons have developed a consensus that a "customary practice" is recognized in the profession regarding the investigation and preparation of such evaluations. *See Statement on the Role of Customary Practice in the Preparation and Understanding of Third-Party Legal Opinions*, 63 Bus. Law. 1277 (Aug. 2008) (noting "[t]he *Restatement* identifies customary practice as a source of the criteria for determining whether the opinion giver has satisfied its obligations of competence and diligence"; citing *Restatement (Third) of the Law Governing Lawyers*, §§ 51, 52, 95 (2000)).

## CONFIDENTIALITY

Rule 2.3(c) explicitly provides that, except to the extent a lawyer is authorized to disclose client information "in connection with a report of an evaluation," information relating to the evaluation remains subject to the lawyer's duty of confidentiality under Rule 1.6. Thus, even though a lawyer has provided an evaluation of a matter affecting a client to a third party, the ethics rules prohibit the lawyer from disclosing additional client information to that party and from disclosing the same evaluation to someone else without the client's consent (unless an exception under Rule 1.6(b) applies). The rules, of course, do not prevent the third party from disclosing the information to others (although an agreement may accomplish this). In addition, disclosing otherwise confidential client information to a third party can result in waiver of the attorney-client privilege in connection with that information. *E.g., FDIC v. White Birch Ctr., Inc.*, No. CV 94-0312372 S, 1995 WL 127916 (Conn. Super. Ct. Mar. 14, 1995) (lawyer obliged to give testimony regarding opinion letter; he "should answer any questions regarding the validity of any acknowledgment he took, the scope of his power of attorney, and the basis for his opinion letter advising that the borrowers and guarantors had the requisite corporate authority"); *accord Restatement (Third) of the Law Governing Lawyers* § 79 (2000) ("The attorney-client privilege is waived if the client, the client's lawyer, or another authorized agent of the client voluntarily discloses the communication in a nonprivileged communication."). *But see Hewlett-Packard Co. v. Bausch & Lomb, Inc.*, 115 F.R.D. 308 (N.D. Cal. 1987) (attorney-client privilege not waived when party voluntarily disclosed lawyer's opinion letter to prospective purchaser but took substantial steps to assure purchaser maintained confidentiality); *cf. United States v. Sidley Austin Brown & Wood LLP*, No. 03 C 9355, 2004 WL 905930 (N.D. Ill. Apr. 28, 2004) (law firm that provided opinion letters concerning fraudulent tax shelters ordered to provide IRS with recipient names).

For discussion of a lawyer's duty to obtain a client's informed consent before disclosing information relating to the representation, see the annotation to Rule 1.6.

## ETHICAL VERSUS LEGAL DUTIES
## OWED THIRD PERSONS AND CLIENTS

When a lawyer makes an evaluation for the use of a third party—which typically takes the form of an opinion letter in support of a contemplated transaction—the lawyer's greatest risk is that of being sued by the third party if things go wrong. As Comment [3] notes, any legal obligation a lawyer may have to a third party is "beyond the scope of this Rule," but there are reported civil liability cases, rather than discipline cases, that cite Rule 2.3 and involve lawyers preparing evaluations for the use of third parties. *See, e.g., SEC v. Fehn*, 97 F.3d 1276 (9th Cir. 1996) (affirming finding that lawyer who helped prepare several deficient Form 10-Qs for filing with SEC aided and abetted violations of securities laws); *Mehaffy, Rider, Windholz & Wilson v. Cent. Bank Denver N.A.*, 892 P.2d 230 (Colo. 1995) (lawyers for town and its development authority who, to induce bank to purchase development bonds, issued opinion letters to bank stating town and authority complied with appropriate procedures before issuing bonds could be liable to bank for negligent misrepresentation, though not for malpractice); *see also* N.Y. State Ethics Op. 969 (2013) (lawyer may ask client for indemnification against third-party claims based upon lawyer's opinion letter). *See generally* Bruce C. Young & Charles E. McCallum, *Ethical Considerations in Third Party Opinion Practice: Withdrawal from an Opinion Engagement and Disaffirmance of a Previously Issued Opinion*, 69 Bus. Law. 979 (May 2014); *Report of the ABA Business Law Section Task Force on Delivery of Document Review Reports to Third Parties*, 67 Bus. Law. 99 (Nov. 2011).

## GUIDANCE FOR SPECIFIC TRANSACTIONS

The Model Rules do not give specific, technical guidance to lawyers preparing third-party evaluations. For many transactions, however, that type of guidance comes from a series of specialized bar reports, ethics opinions, and regulatory compilations. The bar reports were originally inspired by James J. Fuld, *Legal Opinions in Business Transactions: An Attempt to Bring Some Order Out of Chaos*, 28 Bus. Law. 915 (Apr. 1973). The reports have come principally from the TriBar Opinion Committee and the Committee on Legal Opinions of the ABA Section of Business Law. Combined, the two have drafted and published more than a dozen reports and model opinions on various topics in the ABA Section of Business Law's periodical, *The Business Lawyer*. The ABA Section of Business Law has collected and republished all of them, too, in *Collected ABA and TriBar Opinion Reports 2009* (2009). *See generally* Robert D. Pannell, *Legal Opinions in Business Transactions: The Modern Roots of a Professional Discipline*, 69 Bus. Law. 923 (May 2014).

### • *Financial Auditors' Requests for Information—Compliance with Recognized Procedures*

When a financial auditor's request for information concerning a client's legal status is referred to the client's lawyer, Comment [6] directs the lawyer to the procedures set forth in *ABA Statement of Policy Regarding Lawyers' Responses to Auditors' Requests for Information*, 31 Bus. Law. 1709 (Aug. 1976), *available at* http://apps.americanbar.org/buslaw/newsletter/0039/materials/pp3.pdf. This statement of policy—essentially a treaty between the ABA and the American Institute of Certified Public Accountants—reflects a compromise between lawyers' desires to protect client confidences fully and accountants' desires to render audit reports without excessive qualifications regarding the underlying information.

### • *Tax Opinions*

A lawyer or firm issuing an opinion about certain tax-sheltering transactions must abide by specific provisions of the U.S. Treasury Department's regulations for IRS practitioners, which are published as IRS Circular 230 and codified at 31 C.F.R. §§ 10.35–10.37 (2017). ABA Formal Opinion 346 (rev. 1982), issued by the ABA Standing Committee on Ethics and Professional Responsibility in 1982, also provides guidance. The two sets of standards were originally developed concurrently—although IRS Circular 230 has since been revised—and were designed to address the same practices.

### • *Securities Opinions*

Securities matters frequently call for legal opinions, and several authorities provide guidance concerning various transactions.

A federal law—15 U.S.C. § 78d-3, part of the Sarbanes-Oxley Act of 2002—imposes obligations upon lawyers doing work in connection with registered securities and empowers the SEC to discipline lawyers who violate those obligations. Under the rulemaking authority granted in 15 U.S.C. § 78w, the SEC has issued regulations that bear upon certain duties of lawyers preparing evaluations for use by third parties. *See*

17 C.F.R. §§ 205.1–205.7 (2018). For instance, the regulations permit a lawyer to disclose confidential information to the SEC without client consent to, inter alia, "rectify the consequences of a material violation [of federal securities law] by the issuer that caused, or may cause, substantial injury to the financial interest or property of the issuer or investors in the furtherance of which the attorney's services were used." 17 C.F.R. § 205.3(d)(2)(iii) (2018); *see also* Rule 1.6; Rule 1.13. *See generally ABA/BNA Lawyers' Manual on Professional Conduct*, "Types of Practice: Corporate: Misconduct," pp. 91:2401 *et seq.* The SEC's regulations expressly claim to preempt standards that are inconsistent. 17 C.F.R. §§ 205.1, 205.6(c) (2018); *see also* N.C. Ethics Op. 2005-9 (2006) (SEC regulations preempt state's professional conduct rules to extent SEC rules allow disclosure not otherwise permitted by state rules).

An ABA ethics opinion articulates guidelines for issuance of assumed-facts opinions concerning sales of unregistered securities. ABA Formal Ethics Op. 335 (1974). Regarding the ethical issues confronted by lawyers offering opinions in connection with the issuance of public bonds, see John R. Axe, *Conflicts of Interest Involving Bond Counsel*, 27 Urb. Law. 991 (Fall 1995).

### • *Real Estate Secured Transactions*

Principles from the reports of the TriBar Committee and the Committee on Legal Opinions have been applied to evaluations prepared by lawyers for real estate secured transactions. *See* Joint Drafting Comm., ABA Section of Real Prop., Trust & Estate Law, Comm. on Legal Opinions in Real Estate Transactions; American College of Real Estate Lawyers, Attorneys' Opinions Comm.; & American College of Mortgage Attorneys, Opinions Comm., *Real Estate Finance Opinion Report of 2012*, 47 Real Prop. Tr. & Est. L.J. 213 (Fall 2012); Robert J. Krapf & Edward J. Levin, *An Overview of the Real Estate Finance Opinion Report of 2012*, 14 Del. L. Rev. 153 (2014); *see also* Opinion Comm. of Real Prop. & Fin. Servs. Section, Haw. State Bar Ass'n, *Hawaii 2000 Report Regarding Lawyers' Opinion Letters in Mortgage Loan Transactions*, 22 U. Haw. L. Rev. 347 (Spring 2000).

## Rule 2.4

### *Lawyer Serving as Third-Party Neutral*

(a) A lawyer serves as a third-party neutral when the lawyer assists two or more persons who are not clients of the lawyer to reach a resolution of a dispute or other matter that has arisen between them. Service as a third-party neutral may include service as an arbitrator, a mediator or in such other capacity as will enable the lawyer to assist the parties to resolve the matter.

(b) A lawyer serving as a third-party neutral shall inform unrepresented parties that the lawyer is not representing them. When the lawyer knows or reasonably should know that a party does not understand the lawyer's role in the matter, the lawyer shall explain the difference between the lawyer's role as a third-party neutral and a lawyer's role as one who represents a client.

## COMMENT

[1] Alternative dispute resolution has become a substantial part of the civil justice system. Aside from representing clients in dispute-resolution processes, lawyers often serve as third-party neutrals. A third-party neutral is a person, such as a mediator, arbitrator, conciliator or evaluator, who assists the parties, represented or unrepresented, in the resolution of a dispute or in the arrangement of a transaction. Whether a third-party neutral serves primarily as a facilitator, evaluator or decisionmaker depends on the particular process that is either selected by the parties or mandated by a court.

[2] The role of a third-party neutral is not unique to lawyers, although, in some court-connected contexts, only lawyers are allowed to serve in this role or to handle certain types of cases. In performing this role, the lawyer may be subject to court rules or other law that apply either to third-party neutrals generally or to lawyers serving as third-party neutrals. Lawyer-neutrals may also be subject to various codes of ethics, such as the Code of Ethics for Arbitrators in Commercial Disputes prepared by a joint committee of the American Bar Association and the American Arbitration Association or the Model Standards of Conduct for Mediators jointly prepared by the American Bar Association, the American Arbitration Association and the Society of Professionals in Dispute Resolution.

[3] Unlike nonlawyers who serve as third-party neutrals, lawyers serving in this role may experience unique problems as a result of differences between the role of a third-party neutral and a lawyer's service as a client representative. The potential for

confusion is significant when the parties are unrepresented in the process. Thus, paragraph (b) requires a lawyer-neutral to inform unrepresented parties that the lawyer is not representing them. For some parties, particularly parties who frequently use dispute-resolution processes, this information will be sufficient. For others, particularly those who are using the process for the first time, more information will be required. Where appropriate, the lawyer should inform unrepresented parties of the important differences between the lawyer's role as third-party neutral and a lawyer's role as a client representative, including the inapplicability of the attorney-client evidentiary privilege. The extent of disclosure required under this paragraph will depend on the particular parties involved and the subject matter of the proceeding, as well as the particular features of the dispute-resolution process selected.

[4] A lawyer who serves as a third-party neutral subsequently may be asked to serve as a lawyer representing a client in the same matter. The conflicts of interest that arise for both the individual lawyer and the lawyer's law firm are addressed in Rule 1.12.

[5] Lawyers who represent clients in alternative dispute-resolution processes are governed by the Rules of Professional Conduct. When the dispute-resolution process takes place before a tribunal, as in binding arbitration (see Rule 1.0(m)), the lawyer's duty of candor is governed by Rule 3.3. Otherwise, the lawyer's duty of candor toward both the third-party neutral and other parties is governed by Rule 4.1.

### Definitional Cross-References
"Knows" *See* Rule 1.0(f)
"Reasonably should know" *See* Rule 1.0(j)

### State Rules Comparison
http://ambar.org/MRPCStateCharts

## ANNOTATION

Model Rule 2.4, adopted in 2002, addresses a lawyer's responsibilities when serving as a third-party neutral. Paragraph (a) explains what a third-party neutral is, and paragraph (b) requires a lawyer serving as a third-party neutral to explain her nonrepresentational role to any unrepresented parties. *See* American Bar Association, *A Legislative History: The Development of the ABA Model Rules of Professional Conduct, 1982–2013*, at 436 (2013) (rule adopted "to promote dispute-resolution parties' understanding of the lawyer-neutral's role"). *See generally* James J. Alfini, *Mediation as a Calling: Addressing the Disconnect Between Mediation Ethics and the Practice of Lawyer Mediators*, 49 S. Tex. L. Rev. 829 (Summer 2008); Carrie Menkel-Meadow, *Maintaining ADR Integrity*, 17 Alternatives to High Cost Litig. 1 (Jan. 2009); Carrie Menkel-Meadow, *The Lawyer as Consensus-Builder: Ethics for a New Practice*, 70 Tenn. L. Rev. 63 (Fall 2002) (conventional lawyer ethics rules have "scant relevance" when lawyer acts as facilitator).

Note that although paragraph (b) imposes the rule's only ethical obligation, many obligations and prohibitions are imposed by other standards and court rules that specifically regulate the conduct of mediators and arbitrators—lawyers and non-lawyers alike. *See generally* Susan Nauss Exon, *How Can a Mediator Be Both Impartial and Fair? Why Ethical Standards of Conduct Create Chaos for Mediators*, 2006 J. Disp. Resol. 387 (2006); Andrea C. Yang, Note, *Ethics Codes for Mediator Conduct: Necessary but Still Insufficient*, 22 Geo. J. Legal Ethics 1229 (Summer 2009); Paula M. Young, *Rejoice! Rejoice! Rejoice, Give Thanks, and Sing: ABA, ACR, and AAA Adopt Revised Model Standards of Conduct for Mediators*, 5 Appalachian J.L. 195 (Spring 2006).

The Model Standards of Conduct for Mediators, as adopted in 1994 and revised in 2005 by the ABA, the American Arbitration Association, and the Association for Conflict Resolution (successor to the group Comment [2] cites as the Society of Professionals in Dispute Resolution), and the Code of Ethics for Arbitrators in Commercial Disputes, approved by the ABA and the American Arbitration Association in 2004, are available at https://www.americanbar.org/groups/dispute_resolution/policy_standards/. For additional resources, see the ABA Section on Dispute Resolution's website at https://www.americanbar.org/groups/dispute_resolution/.

## Paragraph (a): What Is a Third-Party Neutral?

Rule 2.4 defines a third-party neutral as one who helps two or more nonclients "reach a resolution of a dispute or other matter that has arisen between them," and specifically cites arbitrators and mediators as examples. Comment [1] adds conciliators and evaluators as other examples, and further explains that third-party neutrals may also assist the parties "in the arrangement of a transaction." *See In re Dhillon*, No. 10-41700, Adv. No. 11-4015, 2011 WL 3651308, 2011 BL 214489 (Bankr. S.D. Ill. Aug. 18, 2011) (after lawyer connected restaurant seller with prospective buyers, who were his former clients, he facilitated inspection, agreed to draft lease according to parties' agreement, and asked questions to clarify terms to which parties were agreeing; "this fits in squarely with the definition of a third-party neutral as one who arranges a transaction"). *See generally* Cris Currie, *Mediating Off the Grid*, 59 Disp. Resol. J. 9 (May–July 2004) (critiquing distinction between evaluative ("traditional") and facilitative ("professional") approaches to mediation); Ellen E. Deason, *Combinations of Mediation and Arbitration with the Same Neutral: A Framework for Judicial Review*, 5 Y.B. on Arb. & Mediation 409 (2013) (analyzing hybrid "med-arbs," "arb-meds," and "mediation windows"); Byron G. Stier, *The Gulf Coast Claims Facility as Quasi-Public Fund: Transparency and Independence in Claim Administrator Compensation*, 30 Miss. C. L. Rev. 255 n.16 (2011) (summarizing experts' opinions rejecting applicability of Rule 2.4 to administrator of compensation fund making offers to one claimant at a time).

## NONREPRESENTATIONAL ROLES ONLY

Rule 2.4 addresses only nonrepresentational roles. *See* Preamble [3] ("lawyer may serve as a third-party neutral, a nonrepresentational role helping the parties to resolve a dispute or other matter"). *See generally* Robert Rubinson, *The Model Rules of Professional Conduct and Serving the Non-Legal Needs of Clients: Professional Regulation in a Time of Change*, 2008 J. Prof. Law. 119 (2008) (Preamble recognizes nonrepresentational role as "something that lawyers do, although the words seem to stop short of defining this role as the practice of law").

The extent to which a lawyer is subject to the lawyer ethics rules when serving in a nonrepresentational role may depend on whether the lawyer/mediator is providing legal advice, or whether, as set out in Rule 5.7, the lawyer's provision of mediation services is separate and distinct from the lawyer's provision of legal services. *See* N.J. Ethics Op. 711 (2007) (lawyers handling mediation who advise clients on their legal rights and obligations are practicing limited-representation law under Rule 1.2(c) "for the sole purpose of serving as a third-party neutral" under Rule 2.4; they are governed by lawyer ethics rules but must also explain they cannot and will not "act as the client's individual lawyer"); N.C. Dispute Resolution Comm'n Op. 25 (2013), *available at* https://www.nccourts.gov/assets/inline-files/25.2013.pdf?pXih vbVIAXoz0axmImqlm1G8uRteHHD9 (service as mediator is not practice of law; noting that the Standards of Professional Conduct for Mediators prohibit mediators from giving legal advice to parties); *see also* N.Y. State Ethics Op. 1026 (2014) (lawyer is subject to ethics rules when providing mediation services if those services are provided in manner not distinct from legal services). In any event, lawyers are subject to some ethics rules, such as Rule 8.4, whether or not they are representing clients. *Cf.* Or. Ethics Op. 2005-135 (2005) (lawyer serving as arbitrator, mediator, or court-appointed special master must deposit any fees paid in advance into separate trust account; Oregon's version of Rule 1.15 does not limit its application to funds held in connection with a representation).

## • *Representational Mediation Compared*

Although Model Rule 2.4's adoption coincided with the deletion of former Rule 2.2 (Lawyer as Intermediary), the rules address distinctly different roles. Former Rule 2.2 was about representational mediation—that is, serving as go-between among clients; it was deleted when the drafters decided representational mediation would be "better dealt with" in the comment to Rule 1.7 (Conflict of Interest: Current Clients). American Bar Association, *A Legislative History: The Development of the ABA Model Rules of Professional Conduct, 1982–2013,* at 421–22 (2013). Much of the old Rule 2.2 survives in Comments [26]–[35] to Rule 1.7.

A mediator within the meaning of Rule 2.4 is therefore not analogous to an intermediary within the meaning of former Rule 2.2. *See* Douglas H. Yarn, *Lawyer Ethics in ADR and the Recommendations of Ethics 2000 to Revise the Model Rules of Professional Conduct: Considerations for Adoption and State Application,* 54 Ark. L. Rev. 207 (2001) (symposium issue); *cf. Chang's Imps., Inc. v. Srader,* 216 F. Supp. 2d 325 (S.D.N.Y. 2001) (summary judgment for lawyer-mediator in malpractice action by mediation party seeking to hold him to lawyer's standard of care); *Furia v. Helm,* 4 Cal. Rptr. 3d 357 (Ct. App. 2003) (demurrer sustained; lawyer who agreed to serve as neutral mediator in clients' dispute with contractor could not be liable to contractor for legal malpractice); N.Y. State Ethics Op. 900 (2011) (Rule 1.7 not applicable to assistant county attorney serving as mediator in child permanency proceedings; mediator does not "represent a client" in the mediation). *See generally* Rebekah Ryan Clark, Comment, *The Writing on the Wall: The Potential Liability of Mediators as Fiduciaries,* 2006 BYU L. Rev. 1033 (2006).

## • *Different Kinds of ADR*

Rule 2.4 does not differentiate among mediators who help the parties reach their own agreements, evaluators who make preliminary settlement recommendations, and arbitrators who make the decisions themselves. Comment [1] simply notes that a third-party neutral may serve primarily as facilitator, evaluator, or decision maker, depending upon the process being used.

The caselaw, however, draws an important distinction between mediators and other kinds of third-party neutrals: Mediators are far likelier to acquire sensitive information from the parties or their counsel. This is likely to be determinative when courts decide whether a lawyer's prior service as a third-party neutral will require the lawyer's disqualification from a particular representation. See discussion under "Conflicts Downstream" below.

A proposed Model Rule 4.5 drafted in 2002 by the Commission on Ethics and Standards in ADR as an alternative to Model Rule 2.4 would have defined four different kinds of alternative dispute resolution: adjudicative, evaluative, facilitative, and hybrid. CPR-Geo. Comm'n on Ethics & Standards in ADR, *Model Rule for the Lawyer as Third-Party Neutral* (2002), *available at* https://www.cpradr.org/resource-center/protocols-guidelines/ethics-codes/model-rule-for-the-lawyer-as-third-party-neutral. *See generally* Carrie Menkel-Meadow, *Are There Systemic Ethics Issues in Dispute System Design? And What We Should [Not] Do About It: Lessons from International and Domestic Fronts*, 14 Harv. Negot. L. Rev. 195 (Winter 2009) (mediation models may be evaluative, facilitative, transformative, understanding, narrative, or eclectic; negotiation models range from "adversarial-competitive" to "collaborative and problem-solving").

## CONFIDENTIALITY

Rule 1.6 (Confidentiality of Information) limits a lawyer's ability to disclose "information relating to the representation of a client." The rule is not designed to apply to information acquired as a third-party neutral, a role that is by definition nonrepresentational.

However, as Comment [3] to Rule 1.12 (Former Judge, Arbitrator, Mediator or Other Third-Party Neutral) acknowledges, third-party neutrals "typically owe the parties an obligation of confidentiality under law or codes of ethics governing third-party neutrals." *See, e.g.*, 28 U.S.C. § 652(d) (2010) (requiring each federal district court to adopt alternative dispute resolution program that prohibits disclosure of "confidential dispute resolution communications"); Am. Bar Ass'n, Am. Arb. Ass'n & Ass'n for Conflict Resolution, Model Standards of Conduct for Mediators, Standard V(A) (2005) ("A mediator shall maintain the confidentiality of all information obtained by the mediator in mediation, unless otherwise agreed to by the parties or required by applicable law"); *see also* ABA Section of Dispute Resolution, Comm. on Mediator Ethical Guidance, Op. SODR 2009-2 (2009), *available at* https://www.americanbar.org/content/dam/aba/directories/dispute_resolution/0047_sodr_2009_2.pdf (lawyer-mediator may not tell one party that other party is considering criminal prosecution if mediation fails, but may use "general reality-testing questions to ensure that the party has considered risks associated with not reaching a mediated settlement"); ABA Section of Dispute Resolution, Comm. on Mediator Ethical Guidance, Op. SODR 2008-1 (2008), *available at* https://www.americanbar.org/content/dam/aba/directories/dispute_resolution/0042_sodr_2008_1.pdf (lawyer-mediator not required by Model Standards of Conduct for Mediators to warn parties of risk that at some point she may not be entitled to maintain confidentiality of what they have told her); Or. Ethics Op. 2005-167 (rev. 2014) (mediation confidentiality statute made no exception permitting mediator to disclose one party's attempted fraud on other; mediator's only option was to withdraw). *See generally* Michael E. Brown & Nicholas C. Duggan, *Mediation as Malpractice? The Effect of California Mediation Confidentiality Statutes*, 79 Def. Couns. J. 94 (Jan. 2012); James R. Coben & Peter M. Thompson, *Disputing Irony: A Systematic Look at Litigation About Mediation*, 11 Harv. Negot. L. Rev. 43 (Spring 2006) (authors' review of all 1,223 cases arising out of mediation that were reported 1993 through 2003 revealed surprisingly "cavalier" attitude toward mediation confidentiality once litigation ensues); Ellen E. Deason, *The Need for Trust as a Justification for Confidentiality in Mediation: A Cross-Disciplinary Approach*, 54 U. Kan. L. Rev. 1387 (June 2006); T. Noble Foster & Selden Prentice, *The Promise of Confidentiality in Mediation: Practitioners' Perceptions*, 2009 J. Disp. Resol. 163 (2009); Art Hinshaw, *Mediators as Mandatory Reporters of Child Abuse: Preserving Mediation's Core Values*, 34 Fla. St. U. L. Rev. 271 (Winter 2007); Maureen E. Laflin, *The Mediator as Fugu Chef: Preserving Protections Without Poisoning the Process*, 49 S. Tex. L. Rev. 943 (Summer 2008); Samara Zimmerman, Note, *Judges Gone Wild: Why Breaking the Mediation Confidentiality Privilege for Acting in "Bad Faith" Should Be Reevaluated in Court-Ordered Mandatory Mediation*, 11 Cardozo J. Conflict Resol. 353 (Fall 2009).

On a mediator's ability to comply with Rule 8.3's duty to report lawyer misconduct, see Ill. Ethics Op. 2011-01 (2011) (lawyer-mediator must report rule violation; obligation to report not restricted to information learned while representing client, nor is it abrogated by confidentiality provisions of mediation statutes). *See also* Uniform Mediation Act § 6(a)(6) (2003) (mediation privilege inapplicable to claims of professional misconduct). *See generally* Ellen E. Deason, *The Quest for Uniformity in Mediation Confidentiality: Foolish Consistency or Crucial Predictability?*, 85 Marq. L. Rev. 79 (Fall 2001); Rosemary J. Matthews, Comment, *Do I Have to Say More? When Mediation Confidentiality Clashes with the Duty to Report*, 34 Campbell L. Rev. 205 (Fall 2011).

## WRITING UP THE AGREEMENT

Jurisdictions differ regarding whether the lawyer may write up the mediated agreement. *See, e.g.*, Ky. Ethics Op. E-438 (2015) (lawyer-mediator may assist parties in preparing mediation agreement but not in preparing ancillary documents after mediation has concluded); Mo. Informal Ethics Op. 2010-0055 (n.d.) (lawyer may prepare documents effectuating marital dissolution agreement reached in mediation if both parties give informed consent, confirmed in writing, but may represent only one spouse and must clearly explain this to the other); N.Y. State Ethics Op. 736 (2001) (recognizing that divorce mediator does not have lawyer-client relationship with either party but nonetheless prohibiting him from writing up their agreement unless he can satisfy test for dual representation of clients with conflicting interests); N.C.

Ethics Op. 2012-2 (2013) (lawyer who has successfully mediated dispute between two pro se parties may help them prepare summary reflecting their understanding, but may not jointly represent them in preparing new business contract even if both consent); Ohio Ethics Op. 2009-4 (2009) (lawyer who mediated domestic relations matter but did not negotiate to subsequently represent either party may prepare legal documents—such as petitions and decrees—for one of them if both give informed written consent); Tex. Ethics Op. 583 (2008) (contracting to prepare mediated divorce agreement for unrepresented spouses constitutes impermissible representation of opposing parties; same conclusion whether lawyer or someone else was mediator); Wash. Ethics Op. 2223 (2012) (lawyer-mediator may not prepare documents memorializing unrepresented spouses' agreement; preparing "complex and customized provisions using original language and choices" is not mediation but representation, and would violate Rule 1.7). For a succinct analysis, see Robert L. Kehr, "When a Lawyer-Mediator Prepares the Settlement Agreement," *ABA/BNA Lawyers' Manual on Professional Conduct*, 27 Law. Man. Prof. Conduct 384 (Current Reports, June 8, 2011).

Note that some jurisdictions have modified the rule by spelling out the circumstances in which the lawyer would be permitted to write up the mediated agreement. *See, e.g.*, Or. Rule 2.4(b)(1); Tenn. Rule 2.4(e); Utah Rule 2.4(c)(1) (lawyer may prepare implementing documents and file them with court, "informing the court of the mediator's limited representation of the parties for the sole purpose of obtaining such legal approval as may be necessary").

## CONFLICTS DOWNSTREAM

Comment [4] explains that conflict-of-interest issues resulting from a lawyer's service as a third-party neutral—whether as evaluator, decision maker, facilitator, conciliator, or mediator—are to be resolved under Rule 1.12. Rule 1.12, which originally addressed conflicts stemming from service as a judge or arbitrator, was amended in 2002, when Rule 2.4 was adopted, to specifically embrace mediators and other third-party neutrals.

This is a departure from the preexisting caselaw, in which conflicts arising from service as a mediator among nonclients had typically been analyzed under the "substantially-related-matter" test of Rule 1.9 (former clients), rather than the more permissive "same-matter" test of Rule 1.12. In caselaw predating Rule 2.4, therefore, parties who had appeared before a mediator were analogized to former clients of the mediator—even when the mediator was an actual judicial officer: "[A] judge who has participated in mediation or settlement efforts . . . becomes a confidant of the parties, on a par with the parties' own lawyers." *In re County of Los Angeles*, 223 F.3d 990 (9th Cir. 2000). *E.g.*, *Poly Software Intern., Inc. v. Su*, 880 F. Supp. 1487 (D. Utah 1995) ("Where a mediator has received confidential information in the course of mediation, that mediator should not thereafter represent anyone in connection with the same or a substantially factually related matter unless all parties to the mediation proceeding consent after disclosure."); *Cho v. Superior Court*, 45 Cal. Rptr. 2d 863 (Ct. App. 1995) ("When a litigant has bared its soul in confidential settlement conferences with a judicial officer, that litigant could not help but be horrified to find that the judicial officer has resigned to join the opposing law firm—which is now pressing or defending the lawsuit against that litigant."); *accord Fields-D'Arpino v. Rest. Assocs., Inc.*, 39 F. Supp. 2d 412 (S.D.N.Y. 1999); *Bauerle v. Bauerle*, 616 N.Y.S.2d 275 (App. Div. 1994); *see also McKenzie Constr. v. St. Croix Storage Corp.*, 961 F. Supp. 857 (D.V.I. 1997) ("not unreasonable to assume that confidential information was disclosed" to mediator). *But see Clark v. Alfa Ins. Co.*, Civ. No. 00-AR-3296-S, 2001 WL 34394281 (N.D. Ala. Feb. 7, 2001) (if all mediation parties must be treated as former clients regardless of specific information mediator in fact obtained, "all lawyers in North Alabama who want to be mediators can (1) change their minds; (2) limit their law practices to mediation; or (3) expose themselves to ethical violation complaints"; court sua sponte looked to Rule 1.7(b) instead and found counsel's representation of plaintiff not materially limited by obligations flowing from his prior service as mediator in someone else's discrimination complaint against same defendant); *Moore v. Altra Energy Techs., Inc.*, 295 S.W.3d 404, 406 n.1 (Tex. 2009) (in state without Rule 2.4, court looked to state's version of Rule 1.12 in ruling on motion to disqualify lawyer who received confidential information during service as mediator; Texas rules, however, define tribunal to include mediator). *See generally* James R. Coben & Peter M. Thompson, *Disputing Irony: A Systematic Look at Litigation About Mediation*, 11 Harv. Negot. L. Rev. 43 (Spring 2006).

By turning to Rule 1.12, Rule 2.4 allows a former third-party neutral's disqualification from a subsequent representation to be cured by the written informed consent of all the parties. Even more important, Rule 1.12 lets firm colleagues use screening and notice to protect themselves from imputation. *Compare Matluck v. Matluck*, 825 So. 2d 1071 (Fla. Dist. Ct. App. 2002) (former husband's counsel formed law firm with lawyer who unsuccessfully mediated dissolution proceedings; entire firm must be disqualified regardless of screening), *and* Va. Ethics Op. 1826 (2006) (because state's unique Rule 2.10(e) made no exception for screening, imputation could not be avoided unless affected client gave informed written consent), *with In re County of Los Angeles*, 223 F.3d 990 (9th Cir. 2000) ("We hold that the vicarious disqualification of a firm does not automatically follow the personal disqualification of a former settlement judge [who upon retirement joined the firm], where the settlement negotiations are substantially related (but not identical) to the current representation. Screening mechanisms that are both timely and effective . . . will rebut the presumption that the former judge disclosed confidences to other members of the firm."). *See* Aron H. Schnur, Note, *I Never Agreed to This! Reconsidering the Inclusion of Attorney-Mediators Under Model Rule 1.12*, 23 Geo. J. Legal Ethics 813 (Summer 2010) (availability of screening under 2002 amendment to Rule 1.10 warrants reexamination of decision to evaluate mediators' downstream conflicts under Rule 1.12 rather than more rigorous Rule 1.9). *See generally* Paul M. Lurie, *Using Screening Walls and Advance Waivers to Manage Mediation Conflicts of Interest*, 24 Alternatives to High Cost Litig. 49 (Mar. 2006).

## Paragraph (b): Explaining Role

Rule 2.4(b) imposes obligations similar to those of Rule 4.3 (Dealing with Unrepresented Person), which is limited to lawyers representing clients, on the theory that an unrepresented participant in dispute resolution might have some misconceptions if the third-party neutral happens to be a lawyer. American Bar Association, *A Legisla-*

*tive History: The Development of the ABA Model Rules of Professional Conduct, 1982–2013,* at 437 (2013); *see In re Dhillon,* No. 10-41700, Adv. No. 11-4015, 2011 WL 3651308, 2011 BL 214489 (Bankr. S.D. Ill. Aug. 18, 2011) (before negotiations began, lawyer informed parties he would not be representing anybody; he "did everything he could have and should have done to properly make himself a third-party neutral at the negotiations"); N.Y. State Ethics Op. 878 (2011) (lawyer-mediator explaining her role as third-party neutral will "most often" have to disclose she is a lawyer). *See generally* Michael T. Colatrella, Jr., *Informed Consent in Mediation: Promoting Pro Se Parties' Informed Settlement Choice While Honoring the Mediator's Ethical Duties,* 15 Cardozo J. Conflict Resol. 705 (Spring 2014) (distinguishing between pro se party's informed consent to enter mediation ("participation consent"), which is mediator's responsibility, and pro se party's acceptance of settlement terms ("outcome consent"), which is not).

# ADVOCATE

## Rule 3.1
### *Meritorious Claims and Contentions*

A lawyer shall not bring or defend a proceeding, or assert or controvert an issue therein, unless there is a basis in law and fact for doing so that is not frivolous, which includes a good faith argument for an extension, modification or reversal of existing law. A lawyer for the defendant in a criminal proceeding, or the respondent in a proceeding that could result in incarceration, may nevertheless so defend the proceeding as to require that every element of the case be established.

## COMMENT

[1] The advocate has a duty to use legal procedure for the fullest benefit of the client's cause, but also a duty not to abuse legal procedure. The law, both procedural and substantive, establishes the limits within which an advocate may proceed. However, the law is not always clear and never is static. Accordingly, in determining the proper scope of advocacy, account must be taken of the law's ambiguities and potential for change.

[2] The filing of an action or defense or similar action taken for a client is not frivolous merely because the facts have not first been fully substantiated or because the lawyer expects to develop vital evidence only by discovery. What is required of lawyers, however, is that they inform themselves about the facts of their clients' cases and the applicable law and determine that they can make good faith arguments in support of their clients' positions. Such action is not frivolous even though the lawyer believes that the client's position ultimately will not prevail. The action is frivolous, however, if the lawyer is unable either to make a good faith argument on the merits of the action taken or to support the action taken by a good faith argument for an extension, modification or reversal of existing law.

[3] The lawyer's obligations under this Rule are subordinate to federal or state constitutional law that entitles a defendant in a criminal matter to the assistance of counsel in presenting a claim or contention that otherwise would be prohibited by this Rule.

**State Rules Comparison**
http://ambar.org/MRPCStateCharts

## ANNOTATION

### INTRODUCTION

A lawyer has a professional obligation to the client, the court, and the lawyer's adversaries not to advance meritless or frivolous arguments. *In re Girardi*, 611 F.3d 1027 (9th Cir. 2010) (pursuing suit to enforce foreign judgment against corporate entity not party to foreign suit "clearly constitutes 'conduct unbecoming a member of the court's bar,' because it violates the ABA's Model Rules [3.1 and 3.3]"); *In re Oladiran*, No. MC-10-0025-PHX-DGC, 2010 WL 3775074, 2010 BL 223466 (D. Ariz. Sept. 21, 2010) (filing bad-faith "motion for an honest and honorable court system" and frivolous lawsuits against federal judges that were clearly barred by judicial immunity); *In re Olsen*, 326 P.3d 1004 (Colo. 2014) (filing employment lawsuit without reasonable investigation and continuing to litigate in face of "credible evidence" that "completely contradicted" client's "implausible" allegations); *In re Yelverton*, 105 A.3d 413 (D.C. 2014) (filing numerous "repetitive," "unfounded," and "patently frivolous" motions, including motion for mistrial on behalf of victim in criminal matter); *In re Holste*, 358 P.3d 850 (Kan. 2015) (naming individual who was not party to contract as defendant in breach of contract suit); *In re O'Dwyer*, 221 So. 3d 1 (La. 2017) (filing "56-page, sometimes illegible, handwritten complaint full of inappropriate and 'irrelevant rhetoric,'" alleging without support that opposing counsel destroyed evidence, and asserting "baseless claims" against judges and disciplinary authorities); *Att'y Grievance Comm'n v. Worsham*, 105 A.3d 515 (Md. 2014) ("numerous frivolous arguments" attempting to justify lawyer's failure to file tax returns and pay taxes); *In re Caranchini*, 956 S.W.2d 910 (Mo. 1997) (pursuing claim even after clear no basis for claim existed); *N.C. State Bar v. Berman*, 761 S.E.2d 754 (N.C. 2014) (intentionally omitting required material allegations from complaint); *In re McAteer*, 183 A.3d 1133 (R.I. 2018) (obtaining default judgment after settling claim and receiving payment in full); *Barrett v. Va. State Bar*, 675 S.E.2d 827 (Va. 2009) (suspended lawyer filed frivolous claim in his pro se divorce); *In re Scannell*, 239 P.3d 332 (Wash. 2010) (defending disciplinary charges by dragging out proceedings with frivolous filings and objections, and unwarranted delays); *Bd. of Prof'l Responsibility v. Richard*, 335 P.3d 1036 (Wyo. 2014) ("consistent pattern of misbehavior" and "obstructionist tactics" before multiple courts, including repeated "intentional, willful refusal" to respond to discovery and "total lack of concern for honest communication with opposing counsel and the courts"); Ky. Ethics Op. E-441 (2017) (lawyer ghostwriting pleading for pro se litigant must conduct investigation sufficient to be satisfied that allegations have factual and legal foundation); Mo. Informal Ethics Op. 2015-01 (2015) (workers' compensation lawyer who does not know claimant's salary may not claim maximum amount allowed by law in pleadings and later submit corrected amount to agency); N.C. Ethics Op. 2008-3 (2009) (Rule 3.1 applies to lawyer ghostwriting papers for pro se litigant even though neither appearing in court nor signing pleadings); Va. Ethics Op. 1874 (2014) (prohibiting ghostwriting frivolous pleading for pro se litigant). *See generally* Geoffrey C. Hazard, W. William Hodes & Peter R. Jarvis, *The Law of Lawyering* § 30.02 (4th ed. 2015 & Supp. 2017-2) ("Part of the mythology of the adversary system is that litigating lawyers may do anything and everything to help advance a client's cause. The reality is that rules of professional conduct, rules of procedure, and the law of malicious prosecution and abuse of process have always prohibited or punished after the fact a lawyer's assertion of frivolous claims and defenses."); Nathan Crystal, *Limitations on Zealous Representation in an Adversarial System*, 32 Wake Forest L. Rev. 671 (Fall 1997); James B. Danford, Jr., *An Airliner and Perhaps a Lawyer's License Disappear*, 28 Geo. J. Legal Ethics 487 (Summer 2015); Margaret Raymond, *Professional Responsibility for the Pro Se Attorney*, 1 St. Mary's J. Legal Mal. & Ethics 2 (2011); Fred C. Zacharias, *Integrity Ethics*, 22 Geo. J. Legal Ethics 41 (Spring 2009).

## DETERMINING WHEN CLAIM IS FRIVOLOUS

Under the Model Code, DR 7-102(A)(1) provided that a lawyer may not take action on behalf of a client "when he knows or when it is obvious that such action would serve merely to harass or maliciously injure another."

In contrast, Rule 3.1 articulates a standard that eschews any reference to a lawyer's state of mind and instead requires that the lawyer's position have "a basis in law and fact . . . that is not frivolous." American Bar Association, *A Legislative History: The Development of the ABA Model Rules of Professional Conduct, 1982–2013*, at 442 (2013) ("A 'not frivolous' standard was recommended, rather than one based upon the concepts 'harass' or 'maliciously injure,' to track in litigation the prevailing standard in the law of procedure."). *See In re Graham*, 453 N.W.2d 313 (Minn. 1990) (applying "reasonable lawyer" standard, rather than "actual malice" standard, in disciplining lawyer charged with making false statements about judges and government lawyers in frivolous motions to recuse); *Lawyer Disciplinary Bd. v. Neely*, 528 S.E.2d 468 (W. Va. 1998) (Rule 3.1 uses objective standard for determining propriety of pleadings and other court documents); *Bd. of Prof'l Responsibility v. Stinson*, 337 P.3d 401 (Wyo. 2014) (expert testimony unnecessary for finding Rule 3.1 violation where evidence showed lawyer included assertions in answer and counterclaim with no good-faith basis and to publicly embarrass opponent); Va. Ethics Op. 1879 (2015) (government lawyer directed to file administrative charges must first exercise independent professional judgment to determine whether charges are nonfrivolous); *see also* Geoffrey C. Hazard, W. William Hodes & Peter R. Jarvis, *The Law of Lawyering* § 30.11 (4th ed. 2015 & Supp. 2017-2) (observing that even under objective standard "some element of subjectivity remains" but discipline "should be imposed only if the lawyer *persists* in the error after it is called to the lawyer's attention or if the error is the result of something more than a simple and isolated mistake of fact or law.").

### • *Motives of Lawyer or Client*

When first adopted, the comment stated that an action would be considered frivolous if the "client desires to have the action taken primarily for the purpose of harassing or maliciously injuring a person." Rule 3.1, cmt. [2] (1983) [superseded]. But in 2002 this language was deleted "because the client's purpose is not relevant to the objective merits of the client's claim." American Bar Association, *A Legislative History: The Development of the ABA Model Rules of Professional Conduct, 1982–2013*, at 444 (2013); *cf. In re McGraw*, 414 P.3d 841 (Or. 2018) (lawyer's personal motive for legal position is irrelevant to whether it is frivolous).

Nevertheless, objectively frivolous claims are often occasioned by intent to harass, embarrass, or otherwise injure or inconvenience a party, or by some other improper motive. *See, e.g., In re Wells*, 36 So. 3d 198 (La. 2010) (lawyer charged with extortion filed civil suit against prosecutor and judges); *Att'y Grievance Comm'n v. Phillips*, 155 A.3d 476 (Md. 2017) (filing frivolous motion for protective order and to quash subpoena to obstruct and delay bar counsel's investigation of misconduct); *In re Selmer*, 568 N.W.2d 702 (Minn. 1997) (lawyer repeatedly asserted baseless claims of racial discrimination to thwart creditor's collection efforts); *In re Hess*, 406 S.W.3d 37 (Mo. 2013) (deliberately filing frivolous claims against former clients to obtain fees to which lawyer not entitled); *In re Coaty*, 985 A.2d 1020 (R.I. 2010) (lawyer who was fired by client and instructed to deliver case file to new lawyer instead filed suit against client and new lawyer); *In re Samuels*, 666 S.E.2d 244 (S.C. 2008) (lawyer filed frivolous counter-suit against heating contractor who sued lawyer and his wife to collect $2,600 bill); *In re Voss*, 795 N.W.2d 415 (Wis. 2011) (lawyer maliciously disseminated highly personal information about former client, including voluminous psychiatric and other medical records, to court and in lawyer disciplinary proceeding); N.Y. City Ethics Op. 2015-5 (2015) (lawyer may not threaten to report opposing counsel's conduct to lawyer disciplinary agency to coerce more favorable settlement terms); *cf. Manistee Apartments, LLC v. City of Chicago*, 844 F.3d 630 (7th Cir. 2016) (suggesting test for "identifying and quickly disposing of frivolous claims" might be "where we suspect the lawyers, rather than the claimants, are the only potential beneficiaries"); *In re Foster*, 253 P.3d 1244 (Colo. 2011) (pro se lawyer's "lengthy post-dissolution litigation campaign" in which he initiated probate, civil, and criminal proceedings against ex-wife, including 630 trial court transactions, nine appeals, and several petitions for certiorari with state supreme court over twelve-year span, was nonsham litigation protected by First Amendment right to petition, save for appeal containing frivolous claim of trial judge bias). *See generally* American Bar Association, *Essential Qualities of the Professional Lawyer* 39 (2013). Note that Rule 4.4(a) prohibits a lawyer from using "means that have no substantial purpose other than to embarrass, delay, or burden a third person."

## • *Nonfrivolous Basis in Law and Fact*

Rule 3.1 requires that a position asserted by a lawyer have a nonfrivolous basis in law and fact. *See, e.g., In re Partington*, Civ. No. 11-00753 SOM, 2017 WL 4560070, 2017 BL 366267 (D. Haw. Oct. 12, 2017) (intentionally mischaracterized military judge's rulings in appellate brief to falsely argue that client was acquitted); *Iowa Supreme Court Bd. of Prof'l Ethics & Conduct v. Ronwin*, 557 N.W.2d 515 (Iowa 1996) (disciplinary proceedings against lawyer for filing frivolous lawsuits and making false accusations of criminal conduct against lawyers and judges did not infringe upon lawyer's constitutional right of free speech); *In re Zimmerman*, 19 P.3d 160 (Kan. 2001) (lawyer who stated he had no good-faith basis for responding to opposing party's motion for summary judgment could not have had good-faith basis for filing notice of appeal of order granting motion); *In re Mire*, 197 So. 3d 656 (La. 2016) (unsupported, repeated allegations of "incompetence and/or corruption" on part of trial judge); *Att'y Grievance Comm'n v. Mixter*, 109 A.3d 1 (Md. 2015) (filing and refusing to dismiss bad-faith lawsuit that included filing more than 100 meritless motions to compel compliance with over 120 unenforceable subpoenas); *In re Butler,* 868 N.W.2d 243 (Minn. 2015) (repeatedly filing frivolous lawsuits on behalf of foreclosure defendants in face of clear contrary precedent, even after being sanctioned); *In re Richards,* 986 P.2d 1117 (N.M. 1999) (lawyer's misplaced reliance upon U.S. Supreme Court case would have become apparent had lawyer researched and read cases distinguishing it); *In re Zappin,* 73 N.Y.S.3d 182 (App. Div. 2018) (frivolous and abusive pro se litigation against wife, her parents, and her lawyers); *N.C. State Bar v. Livingston,* 809 S.E.2d 183 (N.C. 2017) (filing frivolous complaint against other lawyers); *In re Ruffin,* 610 S.E.2d 803 (S.C. 2005) (no violation of Rule 3.1 when lawyer-litigant relied upon expertise of hired counsel regarding viability of RICO claim); *Lawyer Disciplinary Bd. v. Neely,* 528 S.E.2d 468 (W. Va. 1998) (mere fact that some allegations in complaint later prove false is insufficient to constitute violation of Rule 3.1). *But see In re S.C.,* 88 A.3d 1220 (Vt. 2014) ("even an arguably frivolous claim will not be deemed to violate Rule 3.1 where . . . a court categorically refuses to grant motions to withdraw [by appointed counsel in parental rights termination proceeding] in deference to overriding state interests"); N.C. Ethics Op. 2009-15 (2010) ("prosecutor who knows that she has no admissible evidence supporting a DWI charge to present at trial must dismiss the charge prior to calling the case for trial").

The availability of a clear affirmative defense does not necessarily render a claim frivolous. N.C. Ethics Op. 2003-13 (2004) (lawyer may file obviously time-barred claim because limitation period is "merely an affirmative defense"); Or. Ethics Op. 2005-21 (2005) (lawyer may file complaint for client even if lawyer knows defendant has valid affirmative defense); Pa. Ethics Op. 96-80 (1996) (lawyer may file claim known to be time-barred but must counsel client that this is an available affirmative defense). *But see Trainor v. Ky. Bar Ass'n,* 311 S.W.3d 719 (Ky. 2010) (disciplining lawyer for filing medical malpractice suit more than two years after expiration of limitation period).

## • *Good-Faith Argument for Extension, Modification, or Reversal of Existing Law*

Rule 3.1 characterizes as nonfrivolous a good-faith argument for an extension, a modification, or a reversal of existing law. *See, e.g., Att'y Grievance Comm'n v. Dyer,* 162 A.3d 970 (Md. 2017) (motions and series of appeals were not shown to be factually or legally unfounded); *In re Richards,* 986 P.2d 1117 (N.M. 1999) (lawyer failed to provide good-faith argument for extending, modifying, or reversing existing law: "[A] case upon which a lawyer relies to argue for the extension, modification, or reversal of existing law, must say what the lawyer says it says. Moreover, when relying upon an exception to a general rule of law, the position the lawyer asserts must either come within the exception, or provide a cogent argument for broadening the exception."); *Toledo Bar Ass'n v. Rust,* 921 N.E.2d 1056 (Ohio 2010) (dismissing Rule 3.1 charges for lawyer's filing suit that was ultimately dismissed by probate court because "the fact that he had [prior to filing suit] some arguably viable legal support for his actions is enough to avoid disciplinary sanction"); *see also In re Boone,* 7 P.3d 270 (Kan. 2000) (that lawyer failed to make good-faith argument for extension of existing law to trial court, resulting in dismissal, demonstrated that lawyer filed frivolous case despite lawyer's subsequently making such argument to disciplinary panel).

## DUTY TO INVESTIGATE

As Comment [2] states, a claim or defense "is not frivolous merely because the facts have not first been fully substantiated or because the lawyer expects to develop vital evidence only by discovery. What is required of lawyers, however, is that they inform themselves about the facts of their clients' cases and the applicable law and determine that they can make good faith arguments in support of their clients' positions." *See, e.g., In re Alexander,* 300 P.3d 536 (Ariz. 2013) (deputy county attorney maintained frivolous RICO complaint against judges, county board, and others without adequately investigating validity of allegations); *In re Bontrager,* 407 P.3d 1235 (Colo. O.P.D.J. 2017) (failure to investigate facts or become informed of law before filing suit and persisting in advancing nonmeritorious claims on appeal); *In re Zohdy,* 892 So. 2d 1277 (La. 2005) (lawyer who sought to intervene in chemical products liability class action failed to investigate whether his clients were exposed to chemical); *Att'y Grievance Comm'n v. Zhang,* 100 A.3d 1112 (Md. 2014) (lawyer pursued client's husband's impotence as annulment ground with no facts to support assertion); *Weatherbee v. Va. State Bar,* 689 S.E.2d 753 (Va. 2010) (lawyer named doctor as defendant in medical malpractice suit without adequately investigating whether named defendant was same person identified in client's medical records); *Lawyer Disciplinary Bd. v. Neely,* 528 S.E.2d 468 (W. Va. 1998) (lawyer who exhausted all avenues of presuit investigation may need discovery to complete development of case: "action or claim is not frivolous if after a reasonable investigation, all the facts have not been first substantiated"). *See generally* Jan L. Jacobowitz & John G. Browning, *Legal Ethics and Social Media: A Practitioner's Handbook* 29 (2017) (on reviewing client's social media postings before accepting the representation).

Authorities have recognized that a lawyer's duty to protect a client's interests in exigent situations—for example, when a limitation deadline is imminent—may necessitate a truncated investigation. *See* Neb. Ethics Op. 08-03 (2008) (if expiration of limitation period imminent, lawyer may file suit for client whom lawyer can no longer find as long as lawyer determines claim not frivolous); Or. Ethics Op. 2005-59 (2005) (when not possible for lawyer to conduct prefiling investigation regarding all potential defendants to be joined, lawyer may join additional defendants if lawyer cannot get extension of limitation period, lawyer acts with diligence following filing to determine whether viable action exists, and claims are promptly dismissed if not viable).

## CRIMINAL PROCEEDINGS

Rule 3.1 provides that in criminal proceedings, as well as in civil proceedings that could result in incarceration, a lawyer may defend a client in a way that requires every element of the case to be established. This provision reflects the constitutional principle that due process requires the state to prove every element of a crime charged and prohibits shifting the burden to the defendant by procedural rule or otherwise. *See Patterson v. New York,* 432 U.S. 197 (1977); *Mullaney v. Wilbur,* 421 U.S. 684 (1975). Accordingly, the criminal defense lawyer has an ethical obligation to force the government to prove its case. *See* D.C. Ethics Op. 320 (2003) (lawyer for criminal defendant must require government to bear burden of proof).

The tension between a criminal defendant's constitutional right to representation and a lawyer's ethical duty not to proffer frivolous claims has presented peculiar problems for lawyers appointed to defend indigent criminal defendants. In *Anders v. California*, 386 U.S. 738 (1967), the Supreme Court held that an appointed appellate lawyer may not simply present a "no-merits" letter to an appellate court if the client wants to appeal a criminal conviction, even if the lawyer reasonably believes there is no merit to an appeal. Instead, the lawyer must also prepare "a brief referring to anything in the record that might arguably support the appeal. . . . [T]he court—not counsel—then proceeds . . . to decide whether the case is wholly frivolous." But in *Smith v. Robbins*, 528 U.S. 259 (2000), the Court held that "the *Anders* procedure is merely one method of satisfying the requirements of the Constitution for indigent criminal appeals. States may—and, we are confident, will—craft procedures that, in terms of policy, are superior to, or at least as good as, that in *Anders*." The requirements for lawyers appointed to pursue meritless criminal appeals continue to evolve. *See Mosley v. State*, 908 N.E.2d 599 (Ind. 2009) (withdrawal with accompanying *Anders* brief not permitted; if client desires appeal, lawyer must brief appeal even if it raises frivolous issues, Rule 3.1 notwithstanding); *State v. Malcolm*, No. A-0744-08T4, 2010 WL 2868179, 2010 BL 353701 (N.J. Super. Ct. App. Div. July 19, 2010) (notwithstanding Rule 3.1, lawyer representing criminal defendant in post-conviction hearing must advance claims that client requests and may not "denigrate or dismiss the client's claims, . . . negatively evaluate them, or . . . render aid and support to the state's opposition"); *State v. Wilson*, 83 N.E.3d 942 (Ohio 2017) (if defendant insists, appointed counsel must file appeal even if counsel believes it to be frivolous and may not withdraw on that ground alone; Comment [3] to Rule 3.1 makes criminal defendant's rights superior to lawyer's duty to avoid frivolous filing); N.C. Ethics Op. 2016-2 (2016) (lawyer appointed to represent convicted criminal defendant who has filed post-conviction motion that lawyer believes to be frivolous need not so advise court nor file amended motion but must seek to withdraw if defendant insists that lawyer argue motion); Va. Ethics Op. 1880 (2015) (public defender or appointed counsel must file appeal if defendant insists, even if lawyer believes it to be frivolous, and will not violate Rule 3.1 in doing so); *see also* N.C. Ethics Op. 2008-17 (2009) (trial lawyer for indigent parent in juvenile neglect, abuse, or dependency case may sign notice of appeal although "lawyer may not believe that the appeal has merit"); *cf. State v. Schowengerdt*, 409 P.3d 38 (Mont. 2018) ("duty of loyalty and confidentiality is balanced with counsel's role as an officer of the court and is therefore limited by the duty to comply with law and the rules of professional conduct" and therefore "does not require counsel to 'assist the client in presenting false evidence'"). *But see United States v. Turner*, 677 F.3d 570 (3d Cir. 2012) (*Anders* does not permit court-appointed lawyers who do not seek to withdraw to file "hybrid" appellate brief containing frivolous as well as meritorious arguments). *See generally* Monroe H. Freedman, *The Professional Obligation to Raise Frivolous Issues in Death Penalty Cases*, 31 Hofstra L. Rev. 1167 (Summer 2003).

For a discussion of the special duties of prosecutors, see the annotation to Rule 3.8.

## RELATED OBLIGATIONS

Rule 3.1 is one of many prohibitions against frivolous or baseless conduct in the course of litigation. Rule 3.4(d) bars frivolous pretrial discovery requests, and Rule 3.2 requires reasonable efforts to expedite litigation. A federal statute, 28 U.S.C. § 1927, penalizes lawyers who "unreasonably and vexatiously" multiply litigation; 28 U.S.C. § 1912 and Rule 38 of the Federal Rules of Appellate Procedure address frivolous appeals. *See, e.g., Harris N.A. v. Hershey*, 711 F.3d 794 (7th Cir. 2013) (frivolity of appeal, pro se lawyer-appellant's sophistication, and financial interest in delay warranted Rule 38 sanctions); *Sawukaytis v. Comm'r of Internal Revenue*, 102 F. App'x 29 (6th Cir. 2004) (appellant's lawyer should have realized client's claim was frivolous and should have discouraged client from further vexatious litigation, warranting joint award of Rule 38 sanctions); *Wise v. Washington County*, Civ. No. 10-1677, 2015 WL 1757730, 2015 BL 110240 (W.D. Pa. Apr. 17, 2015) (citing Rule 3.1 in granting motion for sanctions under 28 U.S.C. § 1927 for bringing meritless equal protection and punitive damages claims).

Many states also have adopted so-called anti-SLAPP ("strategic lawsuit against public participation") statutes that penalize nonmeritorious claims against persons who publicly oppose a litigant's actions. *See generally LoBiondo v. Schwartz*, 970 A.2d 1007 (N.J. 2009) (canvassing existing anti-SLAPP statutes and analyzing interplay of anti-SLAPP law with Rule 3.1).

Lawyers' violations of these related obligations generally do not automatically constitute violations of Rule 3.1. *See, e.g., People v. Forsyth*, 292 P.3d 1248 (Colo. O.P.D.J. 2012) (disciplinary board not bound by appeals court's finding that lawyer filed frivolous appeal, and "disciplinary authorities have seldom seen fit to rebuke lawyers who already have been sanctioned under [Fed. R. Civ. P.] 11"); *Att'y Grievance Comm'n v. Brown*, 725 A.2d 1069 (Md. 1999) (mere fact that lawyer sanctioned by court for filing meritless case insufficient to prove Rule 3.1 violation; specific findings regarding underlying facts necessary); *State ex rel. Okla. Bar Ass'n v. Wilcox*, 227 P.3d 642 (Okla. 2009) (trial court's finding action frivolous, for purposes of award of attorneys' fees against nonprevailing party, does not require finding violation of Rule 3.1); *In re Osicka*, 765 N.W.2d 775 (Wis. 2009) (finding that lawyer violated civil procedure rule by filing frivolous claim does not itself establish Rule 3.1 violation). *See generally* Andrew Perlman, *The Parallel Law of Lawyering in Civil Litigation*, 79 Fordham L. Rev. 1965 (Apr. 2011).

## • *Rule 11*

Rule 3.1 parallels and can be analyzed in tandem with Rule 11 of the Federal Rules of Civil Procedure. *See, e.g., Obert v. Republic W. Ins. Co.*, 264 F. Supp. 2d 106 (D.R.I. 2003) (disciplining lawyers under Rule 3.1 by revoking pro hac vice admission and sanctioning under Rule 11 for same conduct); *In re Boone*, 66 P.3d 896 (Kan. 2003) (lawyer disciplined by state authorities under Rule 3.1 after being sanctioned under Rule 11 by federal district court); Richard G. Johnson, *Integrating Legal Ethics and Professional Responsibility with Federal Rule of Civil Procedure 11*, 37 Loy. L.A. L. Rev. 819 (Winter 2004). Rule 11 requires that every pleading, motion, or other paper of a party be signed by the lawyer representing the party or, if none, by the party. The signature constitutes a certification that, among other things, "the claims, defenses, and other legal contentions are warranted by existing law or by a nonfrivolous argument for extending, modifying, or reversing existing law or for establishing new law" and "the factual contentions have evidentiary support or, if specifically so identified, will likely have evidentiary support after a reasonable opportunity for further investigation or discovery." Fed. R. Civ. P. 11(b)(2), (b)(3). *See generally* Georgene M. Vairo, *Rule 11 Sanctions: Case Law, Perspectives and Preventive Measures* (Richard G. Johnson ed., 3d ed. 2004); Lonnie T. Brown, *Ending Illegitimate Advocacy: Reinvigorating Rule 11 Through Enhancement of the Ethical Duty to Report*, 62 Ohio St. L.J. 1555 (2001).

## Rule 3.2

### *Expediting Litigation*

**A lawyer shall make reasonable efforts to expedite litigation consistent with the interests of the client.**

## COMMENT

[1] Dilatory practices bring the administration of justice into disrepute. Although there will be occasions when a lawyer may properly seek a postponement for personal reasons, it is not proper for a lawyer to routinely fail to expedite litigation solely for the convenience of the advocates. Nor will a failure to expedite be reasonable if done for the purpose of frustrating an opposing party's attempt to obtain rightful redress or repose. It is not a justification that similar conduct is often tolerated by the bench and bar. The question is whether a competent lawyer acting in good faith would regard the course of action as having some substantial purpose other than delay. Realizing financial or other benefit from otherwise improper delay in litigation is not a legitimate interest of the client.

### Definitional Cross-References

"Reasonable" *See* Rule 1.0(h)

### State Rules Comparison

http://ambar.org/MRPCStateCharts

## ANNOTATION

### GENERAL PROBLEM OF DILATORY LAWYERING

Rule 3.2 recognizes that lawyers' dilatory tactics may impede the administration of justice, thus burdening opposing parties and wasting public resources. *See Roadway Express, Inc. v. Piper*, 447 U.S. 752 (1980) ("glacial pace of much litigation breeds frustration with the federal courts and, ultimately, disrespect for the law"); *Davis v. Coca-Cola Bottling Co.*, 516 F.3d 955 (11th Cir. 2008) ("shotgun pleadings"—that is, "nebulous," general allegations in complaints and affirmative defenses—undermine "the public's respect for the courts—the ability of the courts to process efficiently, economically, and fairly the business placed before them"); *Att'y Grievance Comm'n v. Williams*, 132 A.3d 232 (Md. 2016) (failing to timely serve medical malpractice complaints and creating discovery delays, ultimately resulting in dismissal with prejudice); *Collins v. CSX Transp., Inc.*, 441 S.E.2d 150 (N.C. 1994) ("'gamesmanship' and actions designed to minimize adequate notice to one's adversary have no place within the principles of professionalism governing the conduct of participants in litigation"); *Columbus Bar Ass'n v. Finneran*, 687 N.E.2d 405 (Ohio 1997) ("Dilatory practices bring the administration of justice into disrepute. . . . [A] procedure or tactic that had no substantial purpose other than delay constituted representation outside the bounds of the spirit and intent of our law.").

While Rule 1.3 sets forth the general requirement that lawyers "act with reasonable diligence and promptness in representing a client," Rule 3.2 specifically requires lawyers to attempt to "expedite litigation." Lawyers who fail to make reasonable efforts to do so are subject to discipline. *See People v. Maynard*, 238 P.3d 672 (Colo. O.P.D.J. 2009) ("establish[ing] a pattern and practice of filing matters at the last possible minute as a tactic to delay proceedings"); *In re Henry*, 684 S.E.2d 624 (Ga. 2009) (fired lawyer refused to give up file to successor, necessitating successor's obtaining court order and filing discipline complaint to get file); *In re Barnes*, 691 N.E.2d 1225 (Ind. 1998) (failing to make reasonable effort to expedite bankruptcy action, which led to dismissal of case); *In re James*, 409 P.3d 848 (Kan. 2015) (multiple instances of unreasonable delay); *Lawyer Disciplinary Bd. v. Blyler*, 787 S.E.2d 596 (W. Va. 2016) (estate lawyer failed to notify court or client for more than three years after state tax department's seizure of estate funds to satisfy lawyer's delinquent personal tax obligation).

But the rule qualifies the duty to expedite litigation by stating it must be "consistent with the interests of the client." *See* Ariz. Ethics Op. 90-16 (1990) (discussing under what circumstances lawyer may decline to approve prevailing opponent's draft agreed judgment order, to delay its entry and consequent deadline for appeal, where lawyer's real motive is that imminent resolution of another pending case might warrant reconsideration or reversal); Alan C. Eidsness & Lisa T. Spencer, *Confronting Ethical Issues in Practice: The Trial Lawyer's Dilemma*, 45 Fam. L.Q. 21 (Spring 2011) (acceding to divorce client's request to delay proceeding to explore possible reconciliation is likely not ethics violation); Ernest F. Lidge, III, *Client Interests and a Lawyer's Duty to Expedite Litigation: Does Model Rule 3.2 Impose Any Independent Obligations?*, 83 St. John's L. Rev. 307 (Winter 2009) (dilatory actions may be proper if not violations of other duties under rules and if consistent with interests of client). *But see In re Boone*, 7 P.3d 270 (Kan. 2000) (requesting extension to respond to summary judgment motion merely in hopes that caselaw would develop to support case found to violate Rule 3.2); *In re Howe*, 843 N.W.2d 325 (N.D. 2014) (rejecting, as inconsistent with Rule 3.2, argument that deliberately delaying immigration proceedings was tactic in clients' best interest); N.C. Ethics Op. 2003-1 (2003) (prohibiting asserting improper defenses to valid claim merely to accommodate client's desire to postpone payment of claim).

## FAILURE TO PROSECUTE/DEFEND CLAIM OR OVERZEALOUS ADVOCACY

Rule 3.2 requires that a lawyer prosecute or defend a client's claim without undue delay. This means all necessary filings and service must be made promptly. *See In re Shahab*, 809 S.E.2d 795 (Ga. 2018) (failing to file or advance immigration applications); *In re Smith*, 659 N.E.2d 896 (Ill. 1995) (failure to file dissolution petition until ten weeks after accepting retainer and delay in attempting proper service); *In re Romero*, 690 N.E.2d 707 (Ind. 1998) (six-year delay in drafting and filing order in domestic relations case); *In re Fahrenholtz*, 392 P.3d 125 (Kan. 2017) (abandoning practice without taking necessary action on pending matters); *In re Toaston*, 225 So. 3d 1066 (La. 2017) (failure to appear or file pleadings and repeatedly obtaining continuances); *Att'y Grievance Comm'n v. Mitchell*, 126 A.3d 72 (Md. 2015) (failing to obtain service on defendant, resulting in dismissal, then failing to move to reinstate); *In re Crandall*, 699 N.W.2d 769 (Minn. 2005) (lawyer failed to respond to motion to dismiss); *Carter v. Miss. Bar*, 654 So. 2d 505 (Miss. 1995) (inaction after accepting retainer fee); *State ex rel. Okla. Bar Ass'n v. Thomas*, 886 P.2d 477 (Okla. 1994) (failing to file proper forms to commence workers' compensation cases, resulting in expiration of limitation period); *In re Holt*, 103 A.3d 147 (R.I. 2014) (failing to obtain qualified domestic relations order for more than ten years after divorce judgment); *In re Davis*, 783 S.E.2d 304 (S.C. 2016) (failure to advance matters and failure to withdraw when lawyer's physical and/or mental condition impaired her ability to represent clients); *Lawyer Disciplinary Bd. v. Rossi*, 769 S.E.2d 464 (W. Va. 2015) (failure to file appearance or defend suit); *see also State ex rel. Okla. Bar Ass'n v. O'Laughlin*, 373 P.3d 1005 (Okla. 2016) (failing to file clients' tax returns).

Overzealous advocacy has also been held to violate Rule 3.2. *See, e.g., In re Mire*, 197 So. 3d 656 (La. 2016) (filing "numerous, unfounded motions to recuse" trial judge and repeated appeals); *In re Murrin*, 821 N.W.2d 195 (Minn. 2012) (lawyer attempting to recover monies from Ponzi scheme operators engaged in pattern of filing "seemingly endless pleadings that contained frivolous claims and were unnecessarily burdensome in length, violated court orders, wasted courts' resources, delayed litigation, and prejudiced the administration of justice"); *Rose v. Office of Prof'l Conduct*, 424 P.3d 134 (Utah 2017) ("fil[ing] a constant stream of motions, corrections to motions, amendments to motions, fil[ing] corrected or amended motions after the opposing parties had filed their response, fil[ing] lawsuits [i]n other courts, and fil[ing] appeals which had no basis").

## APPEARING AT HEARINGS AND OBEYING COURT ORDERS

Rule 3.2 also requires appearances at scheduled hearings and adherence to court orders. *See, e.g., Aka v. U.S. Tax Court*, 854 F.3d 30 (D.C. Cir. 2017) (entering appearance and then "vanishing"); *In re Staples*, 66 N.E.3d 939 (Ind. 2017) (failure to appear at scheduled hearings or file motion, even when ordered to do so, or timely respond to court's inquiries); *In re Herrington*, 222 P.3d 492 (Kan. 2010) (failure to appear at scheduled hearings for several clients); *In re McClanahan*, 26 So. 3d 756 (La. 2010) (failure to appear for trial in two cases); *Att'y Grievance Comm'n v. Storch*, 124 A.3d 204 (Md. 2015) (failure to turn over estate property as ordered); *In re O'Gara*, 746 N.W.2d 130 (Minn. 2008) (failure to appear at two court hearings in two different client matters); *In re Stricker*, 808 S.W.2d 356 (Mo. 1991) (failure to appear at scheduled conference on time); *In re Zeitler*, 866 A.2d 171 (N.J. 2005) (sending "uninformed per diem attorney" to several trial calls until case finally dismissed); *State ex rel. Okla. Bar Ass'n v. Perry*, 936 P.2d 897 (Okla. 1997) (failure to attend pretrial conference and hearing); *In re Longtin*, 713 S.E.2d 297 (S.C. 2011) (repeated failure to comply with court orders to file default motions and orders and other paperwork, resulting in dismissals); *In re DeRuiz*, 99 P.3d 881 (Wash. 2004) (lawyer for criminal defendant failed to appear at series of pretrial hearings); *Lawyer Disciplinary Bd. v. Munoz*, 807 S.E.2d 290 (W. Va. 2017) (failing to file habeas petitions as ordered).

## DILATORY DISCOVERY PRACTICES

Dilatory discovery tactics violate Rule 3.2. *See, e.g., In re Golding*, 700 N.E.2d 464 (Ind. 1998) (failure to answer discovery requests); *In re Boone*, 7 P.3d 270 (Kan. 2000) (filing requests to extend time for discovery without plans to conduct discovery, asserting requests were precautionary measures, in case lawyer later determined formal discovery needed); *Ky. Bar Ass'n v. McDaniel*, 170 S.W.3d 400 (Ky. 2005) (failure to answer discovery requests led to case being twice dismissed); *In re Schnyder*, 918 So. 2d 455 (La. 2006) (failure to respond to discovery); *Att'y Grievance Comm'n v. Williams*, 132 A.3d 232 (Md. 2016) (providing late, unexecuted, undated discovery responses and failing to appear or have client appear for deposition, resulting in dismissal of complaint); *In re Moe*, 851 N.W.2d 868 (Minn. 2014) (failing to respond to discovery, even after court order); *Terrell v. Miss. Bar*, 635 So. 2d 1377 (Miss. 1994) (failing to respond to correspondence regarding discovery requests and trial date or follow court's order to comply with discovery requests, and delaying sending release to finalize settlement agreement); *In re Caranchini*, 956 S.W.2d 910 (Mo. 1997) (pursuing baseless claims and engaging in voluminous needless discovery); *In re Carter*, 779 S.E.2d 194 (S.C. 2015) (failure to complete discovery); *In re PRB Docket No. 2007-003*, 987 A.2d 273 (Vt. 2009) (long delay in full production of requested documents); *cf. Alford v. Aaron Rents, Inc.*, No. 3:08-cv-683 MJR-DGW, 2010 WL 2765260, 2010 BL 404563 (S.D. Ill. May 17, 2010) (lawyers raised so many improper objections and arguments at so many depositions that presiding judge ordered they be conducted at courthouse under his supervision).

## DELAYING DISPOSITION

Action or inaction that delays a final disposition, even if it causes no harm to the client, can violate Rule 3.2. *See In re Shannon*, 876 P.2d 548 (Ariz. 1994) (lawyer for judgment creditor refused to file satisfaction of judgment until judgment debtor filed motion to compel); *People v. Maynard*, 238 P.3d 672 (Colo. O.P.D.J. 2009) (filing "repetitive motions that delayed the proceedings, many of which were frivolous" in federal suit designed to relitigate matters decided in prior state lawsuit); *In re Romero*, 690 N.E.2d 707 (Ind. 1998) (taking six years to file order in domestic relations case, though delay caused no "economic or legal harm to [lawyer's] client"); *In re Zohdy*, 892 So. 2d 1277 (La. 2005) (trying to impede final settlement of class case by filing improper motions, objections to settlement, and frivolous appeal); *In re Butler*, 868 N.W.2d 243 (Minn. 2015) (repeatedly dismissing and refiling same lawsuits under different names); *In re Reuwer*, 795 S.E.2d 17 (S.C. 2016) (failure to prepare proposed custody and parenting order for more than two years); *In re Lopez*, 106 P.3d 221 (Wash. 2005) (failing to file defense brief in sentencing appeal); *Lawyer Disciplinary Bd. v. Munoz*, 807 S.E.2d 290 (W. Va. 2017) (failing to file habeas petitions); *cf. NASCO, Inc. v. Calcasieu Television & Radio, Inc.*, 894 F.2d 696 (5th Cir. 1990) (bad-faith effort to delay inevitable judgment against clients); *Blowers v. Lerner*, No. 1:15-cv-889-GBL-MSN, 2016 WL

4575315, 2016 BL 286739 (E.D. Va. Aug. 31, 2016) (failing to notify client of settlement offer that would have ended litigation); N.Y. State Ethics Op. 991 (2013) (delaying foreclosure proceeding by, for example, requesting unnecessary loan documentation, so real estate LLC partly owned by lawyer would benefit, would violate Rule 3.2). *But see Att'y Grievance Comm'n v. Dyer*, 162 A.3d 970 (Md. 2017) (unsuccessful motions and appeals did not unreasonably delay proceedings); *Bd. of Prof'l Responsibility v. Stinson*, 370 P.3d 72 (Wyo. 2016) (finding no violation of Rule 3.2 because slow progress of litigation was attributable to both sides and benefited lawyer's client).

## APPELLATE PROCESS

The responsibility to expedite litigation applies at the appellate as well as trial level. *See In re Brady*, 387 P.3d 1 (Alaska 2016) (failure to file documents by court-ordered deadlines); *In re Mattson*, 924 N.E.2d 1248 (Ind. 2010) (lawyer appointed to represent criminal defendants on appeal failed to timely file rule-compliant brief in one case, and failed to file any brief in another); *In re Thomas*, 193 P.3d 907 (Kan. 2008) (failure to file appellate briefs on time, in one case filing five motions for extension); *Chauvin v. Ky. Bar Ass'n*, 294 S.W.3d 442 (Ky. 2009) (failure to file appellate brief on time); *In re White*, 699 So. 2d 375 (La. 1997) (failure to file appellate brief after being granted extension and being repeatedly reminded of deadline by clerk's office); *In re Pierce*, 706 N.W.2d 749 (Minn. 2005) (failure to file brief in client's appeal of conviction); *In re Locklair*, 795 S.E.2d 9 (S.C. 2016) (failing to timely correct deficient notice of appeal, order trial court transcript, or otherwise advance appeal); *Lawyer Disciplinary Bd. v. Hart*, 775 S.E.2d 75 (W. Va. 2015) (failure to file appeals); *see also State ex rel. Counsel for Discipline v. Herzog*, 762 N.W.2d 608 (Neb. 2009) ("filing an appeal on behalf of someone no longer legally one's client in and of itself violates [Rule 3.2]").

## Rule 3.3

*Candor Toward the Tribunal*

(a) A lawyer shall not knowingly:

(1) make a false statement of fact or law to a tribunal or fail to correct a false statement of material fact or law previously made to the tribunal by the lawyer;

(2) fail to disclose to the tribunal legal authority in the controlling jurisdiction known to the lawyer to be directly adverse to the position of the client and not disclosed by opposing counsel; or

(3) offer evidence that the lawyer knows to be false. If a lawyer, the lawyer's client, or a witness called by the lawyer, has offered material evidence and the lawyer comes to know of its falsity, the lawyer shall take reasonable remedial measures, including, if necessary, disclosure to the tribunal. A lawyer may refuse to offer evidence, other than the testimony of a defendant in a criminal matter, that the lawyer reasonably believes is false.

(b) A lawyer who represents a client in an adjudicative proceeding and who knows that a person intends to engage, is engaging or has engaged in criminal or fraudulent conduct related to the proceeding shall take reasonable remedial measures, including, if necessary, disclosure to the tribunal.

(c) The duties stated in paragraphs (a) and (b) continue to the conclusion of the proceeding, and apply even if compliance requires disclosure of information otherwise protected by Rule 1.6.

(d) In an ex parte proceeding, a lawyer shall inform the tribunal of all material facts known to the lawyer that will enable the tribunal to make an informed decision, whether or not the facts are adverse.

## Comment

[1] This Rule governs the conduct of a lawyer who is representing a client in the proceedings of a tribunal. See Rule 1.0(m) for the definition of "tribunal." It also applies when the lawyer is representing a client in an ancillary proceeding conducted pursuant to the tribunal's adjudicative authority, such as a deposition. Thus, for example, paragraph (a)(3) requires a lawyer to take reasonable remedial measures

if the lawyer comes to know that a client who is testifying in a deposition has offered evidence that is false.

[2] This Rule sets forth the special duties of lawyers as officers of the court to avoid conduct that undermines the integrity of the adjudicative process. A lawyer acting as an advocate in an adjudicative proceeding has an obligation to present the client's case with persuasive force. Performance of that duty while maintaining confidences of the client, however, is qualified by the advocate's duty of candor to the tribunal. Consequently, although a lawyer in an adversary proceeding is not required to present an impartial exposition of the law or to vouch for the evidence submitted in a cause, the lawyer must not allow the tribunal to be misled by false statements of law or fact or evidence that the lawyer knows to be false.

## Representations by a Lawyer

[3] An advocate is responsible for pleadings and other documents prepared for litigation, but is usually not required to have personal knowledge of matters asserted therein, for litigation documents ordinarily present assertions by the client, or by someone on the client's behalf, and not assertions by the lawyer. Compare Rule 3.1. However, an assertion purporting to be on the lawyer's own knowledge, as in an affidavit by the lawyer or in a statement in open court, may properly be made only when the lawyer knows the assertion is true or believes it to be true on the basis of a reasonably diligent inquiry. There are circumstances where failure to make a disclosure is the equivalent of an affirmative misrepresentation. The obligation prescribed in Rule 1.2(d) not to counsel a client to commit or assist the client in committing a fraud applies in litigation. Regarding compliance with Rule 1.2(d), see the Comment to that Rule. See also the Comment to Rule 8.4(b).

## Legal Argument

[4] Legal argument based on a knowingly false representation of law constitutes dishonesty toward the tribunal. A lawyer is not required to make a disinterested exposition of the law, but must recognize the existence of pertinent legal authorities. Furthermore, as stated in paragraph (a)(2), an advocate has a duty to disclose directly adverse authority in the controlling jurisdiction that has not been disclosed by the opposing party. The underlying concept is that legal argument is a discussion seeking to determine the legal premises properly applicable to the case.

## Offering Evidence

[5] Paragraph (a)(3) requires that the lawyer refuse to offer evidence that the lawyer knows to be false, regardless of the client's wishes. This duty is premised on the lawyer's obligation as an officer of the court to prevent the trier of fact from being misled by false evidence. A lawyer does not violate this Rule if the lawyer offers the evidence for the purpose of establishing its falsity.

[6] If a lawyer knows that the client intends to testify falsely or wants the lawyer to introduce false evidence, the lawyer should seek to persuade the client that the evidence should not be offered. If the persuasion is ineffective and the lawyer continues to represent the client, the lawyer must refuse to offer the false evidence. If

only a portion of a witness's testimony will be false, the lawyer may call the witness to testify but may not elicit or otherwise permit the witness to present the testimony that the lawyer knows is false.

[7] The duties stated in paragraphs (a) and (b) apply to all lawyers, including defense counsel in criminal cases. In some jurisdictions, however, courts have required counsel to present the accused as a witness or to give a narrative statement if the accused so desires, even if counsel knows that the testimony or statement will be false. The obligation of the advocate under the Rules of Professional Conduct is subordinate to such requirements. See also Comment [9].

[8] The prohibition against offering false evidence only applies if the lawyer knows that the evidence is false. A lawyer's reasonable belief that evidence is false does not preclude its presentation to the trier of fact. A lawyer's knowledge that evidence is false, however, can be inferred from the circumstances. See Rule 1.0(f). Thus, although a lawyer should resolve doubts about the veracity of testimony or other evidence in favor of the client, the lawyer cannot ignore an obvious falsehood.

[9] Although paragraph (a)(3) only prohibits a lawyer from offering evidence the lawyer knows to be false, it permits the lawyer to refuse to offer testimony or other proof that the lawyer reasonably believes is false. Offering such proof may reflect adversely on the lawyer's ability to discriminate in the quality of evidence and thus impair the lawyer's effectiveness as an advocate. Because of the special protections historically provided criminal defendants, however, this Rule does not permit a lawyer to refuse to offer the testimony of such a client where the lawyer reasonably believes but does not know that the testimony will be false. Unless the lawyer knows the testimony will be false, the lawyer must honor the client's decision to testify. See also Comment [7].

### Remedial Measures

[10] Having offered material evidence in the belief that it was true, a lawyer may subsequently come to know that the evidence is false. Or, a lawyer may be surprised when the lawyer's client, or another witness called by the lawyer, offers testimony the lawyer knows to be false, either during the lawyer's direct examination or in response to cross-examination by the opposing lawyer. In such situations or if the lawyer knows of the falsity of testimony elicited from the client during a deposition, the lawyer must take reasonable remedial measures. In such situations, the advocate's proper course is to remonstrate with the client confidentially, advise the client of the lawyer's duty of candor to the tribunal and seek the client's cooperation with respect to the withdrawal or correction of the false statements or evidence. If that fails, the advocate must take further remedial action. If withdrawal from the representation is not permitted or will not undo the effect of the false evidence, the advocate must make such disclosure to the tribunal as is reasonably necessary to remedy the situation, even if doing so requires the lawyer to reveal information that otherwise would be protected by Rule 1.6. It is for the tribunal then to determine what should be done—making a statement about the matter to the trier of fact, ordering a mistrial or perhaps nothing.

[11] The disclosure of a client's false testimony can result in grave consequences to the client, including not only a sense of betrayal but also loss of the case and

perhaps a prosecution for perjury. But the alternative is that the lawyer cooperate in deceiving the court, thereby subverting the truth-finding process which the adversary system is designed to implement. See Rule 1.2(d). Furthermore, unless it is clearly understood that the lawyer will act upon the duty to disclose the existence of false evidence, the client can simply reject the lawyer's advice to reveal the false evidence and insist that the lawyer keep silent. Thus the client could in effect coerce the lawyer into being a party to fraud on the court.

## Preserving Integrity of Adjudicative Process

[12] Lawyers have a special obligation to protect a tribunal against criminal or fraudulent conduct that undermines the integrity of the adjudicative process, such as bribing, intimidating or otherwise unlawfully communicating with a witness, juror, court official or other participant in the proceeding, unlawfully destroying or concealing documents or other evidence or failing to disclose information to the tribunal when required by law to do so. Thus, paragraph (b) requires a lawyer to take reasonable remedial measures, including disclosure if necessary, whenever the lawyer knows that a person, including the lawyer's client, intends to engage, is engaging or has engaged in criminal or fraudulent conduct related to the proceeding.

## Duration of Obligation

[13] A practical time limit on the obligation to rectify false evidence or false statements of law and fact has to be established. The conclusion of the proceeding is a reasonably definite point for the termination of the obligation. A proceeding has concluded within the meaning of this Rule when a final judgment in the proceeding has been affirmed on appeal or the time for review has passed.

## Ex Parte Proceedings

[14] Ordinarily, an advocate has the limited responsibility of presenting one side of the matters that a tribunal should consider in reaching a decision; the conflicting position is expected to be presented by the opposing party. However, in any ex parte proceeding, such as an application for a temporary restraining order, there is no balance of presentation by opposing advocates. The object of an ex parte proceeding is nevertheless to yield a substantially just result. The judge has an affirmative responsibility to accord the absent party just consideration. The lawyer for the represented party has the correlative duty to make disclosures of material facts known to the lawyer and that the lawyer reasonably believes are necessary to an informed decision.

## Withdrawal

[15] Normally, a lawyer's compliance with the duty of candor imposed by this Rule does not require that the lawyer withdraw from the representation of a client whose interests will be or have been adversely affected by the lawyer's disclosure. The lawyer may, however, be required by Rule 1.16(a) to seek permission of the tribunal to withdraw if the lawyer's compliance with this Rule's duty of candor results in such an extreme deterioration of the client-lawyer relationship that the lawyer can no longer competently represent the client. Also see Rule 1.16(b) for the circumstances

in which a lawyer will be permitted to seek a tribunal's permission to withdraw. In connection with a request for permission to withdraw that is premised on a client's misconduct, a lawyer may reveal information relating to the representation only to the extent reasonably necessary to comply with this Rule or as otherwise permitted by Rule 1.6.

**Definitional Cross-References**
"Fraudulent" *See* Rule 1.0(d)
"Knowingly" and "Known" and "Knows" *See* Rule 1.0(f)
"Reasonable" *See* Rule 1.0(h)
"Reasonably believes" *See* Rule 1.0(i)
"Tribunal" *See* Rule 1.0(m)

**State Rules Comparison**
http://ambar.org/MRPCStateCharts

# ANNOTATION

## *Paragraph (a)(1): Statements to a Tribunal*

### "TRIBUNAL"

Rule 3.3 requires candor to a tribunal. Rule 1.0(m), added in 2002, defines a tribunal as "a court, an arbitrator in a binding arbitration proceeding or a legislative body, administrative agency or other body acting in an adjudicative capacity." Rule 1.0(m) also explains that a body is deemed to act in an adjudicative capacity "when a neutral official, after the presentation of evidence or legal argument . . . will render a binding legal judgment directly affecting a party's interests in a particular matter." *See In re Cleaver-Bascombe*, 892 A.2d 396 (D.C. 2006) (committee erred in holding that neither superior court's accounting branch nor judge functioned as "tribunal" when processing lawyer's Criminal Justice Act voucher); *State ex rel. Okla. Bar Ass'n v. Dobbs*, 94 P.3d 31 (Okla. 2004) (state commission charged with supervising public service corporations was not exercising adjudicative powers by requiring change-of-ownership notification letter; lawyer's misrepresentations to it therefore did not violate Rule 3.3); *In re Bihlmeyer*, 515 N.W.2d 236 (S.D. 1994) (state industrial commission was tribunal). *Compare In re Vohra*, 68 A.3d 766 (D.C. 2013) (forging clients' signatures on visa applications to U.S. Citizenship and Immigration Services violated rule), *with* N.Y. State Ethics Op. 1011 (2014) (visa petitions to U.S. Departments of Labor and Homeland Security were not before a tribunal; rejecting conclusion of *Vohra* and other authorities).

The rule also applies to any "ancillary proceeding conducted pursuant to the tribunal's adjudicative authority, such as a deposition." Cmt. [1]. *See In re Michael*, 836 N.W.2d 753 (Minn. 2013) (lying at own contempt hearing); *In re Rodriguez*, 306 P.3d 893 (Wash. 2013) (lying at own deposition in own disciplinary investigation); *see also* ABA Formal Ethics Op. 06-439 (2006) (Rule 3.3 does not apply to mediation except with respect to "statements made to a tribunal when the tribunal itself is participating in settlement negotiations, including court-sponsored mediation in which a judge participates"). The ABA opinion was criticized as "debatable" in Douglas R. Richmond, *Lawyers' Professional Responsibilities and Liabilities in Negotiations*, 22 Geo. J. Legal Ethics 249 (Winter 2009) (suggesting some courts might hold Rule 3.3(a)(1) applicable to "mediations conducted pursuant to the court's adjudicatory authority").

If the tribunal's judgment will not be binding, Rule 3.3 does not apply. This means the lawyer need abide only by Rule 4.1's requirement of truthfulness, rather than by Rule 3.3's more rigorous requirement of candor. The major differences are that Rule 3.3 applies to all statements regardless of materiality, and can even require a lawyer to disclose information protected by Rule 1.6 (Confidentiality of Information).

However, if the lawyer is representing a client before a legislative body or administrative agency in a nonadjudicative proceeding, Rule 3.9 requires the lawyer to comply with Rule 3.3(a) through (c). See the annotation to Rule 3.9 for discussion.

## STATEMENTS MADE IN REPRESENTING CLIENT

Rule 3.3(a)(1) prohibits a lawyer from knowingly making a false statement of fact or law to a tribunal—whether material or not, whether oral or written, and whether in an affidavit, a pleading, or another document. *See, e.g., Ligon v. Price*, 200 S.W.3d 417 (Ark. 2004) (lawyer repeatedly offered judge's staff false excuses for delay, promising forthcoming pleadings that were never filed); *In re Owens*, 806 A.2d 1230 (D.C. 2002) (lawyer made false statements to administrative law judge to cover up her attempt to violate judge's sequestration order); *In re Dodge*, 108 P.3d 362 (Idaho 2005) (deputy prosecuting attorney told magistrate at probable cause hearing that defendant "pulled a shotgun"; report indicated only that he carried, not pulled, gun); *In re Hall*, 181 So. 3d 643 (La. 2015) (anticipating order for hair follicle drug test, lawyer bought detoxifying shampoo for client, then told court that client was not using illegal drugs); *In re Bailey*, 848 So. 2d 530 (La. 2003) (misrepresentation to court about scheduling conflict); *Att'y Grievance Comm'n v. Woolery*, 198 A.3d 835 (Md. 2018) (lawyer seeking trustee's removal falsely asserted that trustee had undertaken representation of a party); *In re Winter*, 770 N.W.2d 463 (Minn. 2009) (in moving to reopen client's immigration proceedings based upon predecessor's ineffectiveness, lawyer falsely claimed to have filed disciplinary complaint against predecessor; although actual filing not technically required before moving to reopen based upon ineffectiveness, claim's immateriality was not a defense); *Loigman v. Twp. Comm. of Middletown*, 889 A.2d 426 (N.J. 2006) (as pretext to exclude someone from courtroom, lawyer claimed he would be calling him as witness); *Hackos v. Smith*, 669 S.E.2d 761 (N.C. Ct. App. 2008) (filing record on appeal that differed materially from record proposed to opposing counsel); *In re Dixon*, No. S-1-SC-37204, 2019 WL 244456, 2019 BL 16132 (N.M. Jan. 17, 2019) (lawyer falsely claimed he had filed motion to bring client into lawsuit); *Disciplinary Counsel v. Rohrer*, 919 N.E.2d 180 (Ohio 2009) (at juvenile court hearing on violation of gag order, lawyer falsely claimed his staff "misconstrued" his directions in sending copy of motion to newspaper); *State ex rel. Okla. Bar Ass'n v. Brooking*, 411 P.3d 377 (Okla. 2018) (lawyer turned back date on clerk's filing stamp to show pleading as filed on earlier date); *Tri-Cities Holdings, LLC v. Tenn. Health Servs. & Dev. Agency*, No. 201500058COAR3CV, 2016 WL 721067, 2016 BL 50640 (Tenn. Ct.

App. Feb. 22, 2016) (permission to appear pro hac vice in administrative proceeding revoked after lawyer misrepresented status of related federal litigation); *In re Atta*, 882 N.W.2d 810 (Wis. 2016) (lawyer falsely denied romantic relationship with client); *In re Kalal*, 643 N.W.2d 466 (Wis. 2002) (lawyer gave false answers to court's questions about whether he or his firm had ever been penalized by another court for late filings; "Forgetfulness is okay. Spin is okay. False statements of facts, material or not, are not okay."); R.I. Ethics Op. 2014-04 (2014) (if estate administratrix tells her lawyer she diverted estate's funds, Rule 3.3(a) prohibits lawyer from filing accounting; lawyer should seek to withdraw); *cf. In re Larsen*, 379 P.3d 1209 (Utah 2016) (misstatement made recklessly did not violate rule barring only knowing misstatements; note that state later amended rule to bar both knowing and reckless false statements); *In re S.C.*, 88 A.3d 1220 (Vt. 2014) (although lawyer appointed for parent in termination of parental rights appeal believes appeal lacks merit, lawyer may make a good faith argument without claiming parent should prevail). *See generally* Bruce A. Green, *Candor in Criminal Advocacy*, 44 Hofstra L. Rev. 1105 (2016) (discussing and comparing candor responsibilities of prosecutors and defense lawyers); Peter J. Henning, *Lawyers, Truth, and Honesty in Representing Clients*, 20 Notre Dame J.L. Ethics & Pub. Pol'y 209 (2006) (observing that because of competing obligations, lawyer's behavior should be guided not by dedication to truth but by honesty with clients, opponents, and judicial system); W. William Hodes, *Seeking the Truth Versus Telling the Truth at the Boundaries of the Law: Misdirection, Lying, and "Lying with an Explanation,"* 44 S. Tex. L. Rev. 53 (Winter 2002) (analyzing distinction between arguments and evidence); Douglas R. Richmond, *Lawyers' Professional Responsibilities and Liabilities in Negotiations*, 22 Geo. J. Legal Ethics 249 (Winter 2009) ("lawyer who violates Rule 3.3(a) necessarily violates Rule 8.4(c) as well"); Keith W. Rizzardi, *Sea Level Lies: The Duty to Confront the Deniers*, 44 Stetson L. Rev. 75 (2014) (duty of candor bars lawyers from denying existence of sea level rise).

### • *Statements or Omissions that Mislead*

Failure to make a disclosure can be "the equivalent of an affirmative misrepresentation." Rule 3.3, cmt. [3]. "Any differences between 'false' and 'misleading' statements are irrelevant for Rule 3.3(a)(1) purposes . . . . Courts routinely employ Rule 3.3(a)(1) and equivalent rules to discipline lawyers who have misled through their silence." Douglas R. Richmond, *Appellate Ethics: Truth, Criticism, and Consequences*, 23 Rev. Litig. 301, 310-11 (Spring 2004). *See, e.g., Kim v. 511 E. 5th St., LLC*, No. 12 Civ. 8096 (JCF), 2016 WL 6833928, 2016 BL 391452 (S.D.N.Y. Nov. 7, 2016) (lawyers mischaracterized cited cases as having approved their hourly fees); *In re Decloutte*, No. 14-35557, 2018 WL 3078153, 2018 BL 219110 (Bankr. S.D. Tex. June 20, 2018) (lawyer failed to disclose that after she tried to secure fees by endorsing settlement check payable to client, she facilitated client's arrest for allegedly stealing from her); *In re Alcorn*, 41 P.3d 600 (Ariz. 2002) (lawyers for one defendant did not tell court they settled with plaintiffs and secretly agreed to conduct sham trial to create record for plaintiffs to use in seeking reconsideration of court's grant of summary judgment in favor of second defendant); *In re Cardwell*, 50 P.3d 897 (Colo. 2002) (defense lawyer had obligation to speak up when client pleading guilty to driving while alcohol-impaired falsely denied any prior convictions for alcohol-related offenses); *Daniels v. Alander*, 844 A.2d 182 (Conn. 2004) (associate sitting at counsel table remained silent when senior lawyer materially misrepresented out-of-state counsel's statements about client's parallel proceeding in another jurisdiction); *In re Singleton*, 111 P.3d 630 (Kan. 2005) (lawyer failed to inform judge of outstanding order for discovery in case, and instructed secretary to prepare dismissal order without signature blocks for opposing counsel and present it to judge as an agreed order); *In re Wells*, 36 So. 3d 198 (La. 2010) (lawyer presented lease agreement to court knowing parties bound by later lease agreement, and claimed to be acting as counsel for both client and corporation though he knew client transferred majority interest in corporation to third party); *In re Bruno*, 956 So. 2d 577 (La. 2007) (member of plaintiffs' litigation committee paid employee of corporate opponent for information but remained silent when co-counsel, in response to corporation's motion to disqualify, denied it); *Att'y Grievance Comm'n v. Hecht*, 184 A.3d 429 (Md. 2018) (suspended lawyer gave client false reason for substitute counsel's absence and client innocently conveyed it to court); *Brundage v. Estate of Carambio*, 951 A.2d 947 (N.J. 2008) ("if an attorney has an obligation to speak in order to comply with his or her duty of candor to the tribunal, then silence also may also be a violation of the RPC"); *In re Eicher*, 661 N.W.2d 354 (S.D. 2003) (lawyer moved to dismiss criminal charges against client based on state's failure to produce videotape he claimed was exculpatory, but failed to tell court he had copy of videotape); Ill. Ethics Op. 16-02 (2016) (criminal defense lawyer who moved for particular jury instruction and then discovered controlling authority making it reversible error to fail to give the instruction may not adopt strategy of remaining silent, hoping for error); *see also In re Budd*, No. 14-61192, 2015 WL 4522591, 2015 BL 237620 (Bankr. W.D. Va. July 24, 2015) (lawyer who submitted order with typed signature of opposing counsel was falsely representing that opposing counsel had reviewed and consented to it); *In re Seelig*, 850 A.2d 477 (N.J. 2004) (applying New Jersey's unique Rule 3.3(a)(5)—which required disclosure of material fact if omission may tend to mislead tribunal (amended in 2004 to "is reasonably certain to mislead" tribunal)—lawyer representing client on reckless-driving charges should have told municipal court client was also facing manslaughter charges arising out of same incident so judge would not be misled about double-jeopardy implications of accepting guilty plea) (discussed in Richard Silverman, Note, *Is New Jersey's Heightened Duty of Candor Too Much of a Good Thing?*, 19 Geo. J. Legal Ethics 951 (Summer 2006)). *See generally* Douglas R. Richmond, *Professional Responsibilities of Law Firm Associates*, 45 Brandeis L.J. 199 (Winter 2007).

## • *Duty to Correct Own Material False Statement*

Rule 3.3(a)(1) also requires a lawyer to "correct a false statement of material fact or law previously made to the tribunal by the lawyer." *See* N.Y. State Ethics Op. 797 (2006) (lawyer who certifies client's affidavit of eligibility to act as executor but then learns of client's disabling felony conviction must withdraw certification); *see also* Colo. Ethics Op. 123 (2011) (lawyer who must make remedial disclosure of protected information to correct false statement must still oppose admission of that information into evidence).

This requirement was added in 2002 at the same time the materiality threshold was deleted from the rule's prohibition on making false statements of fact or law to a tribunal. The lawyer's obligation to correct his own material false statements under Rule 3.3(a)(1) is thus symmetrical with the duty to remedy under Rule 3.3(a)(3) when a lawyer comes to learn that he has offered material evidence that is false. *See* American Bar Association, *A Legislative History: The Development of the ABA Model Rules of Professional Conduct, 1982–2013*, at 474 (2013).

Note that the materiality threshold remains a feature of Rule 4.1 (Truthfulness in Statements to Others); Rule 4.1(a) prohibits untruthful statements to third persons, as opposed to tribunals, only if they are material.

### • *Statements about Bar Status or Representational Capacity*

A lawyer who misstates his eligibility to serve as counsel violates Rule 3.3(a)(1). *See, e.g., In re Cohen*, 612 S.E.2d 294 (Ga. 2005) (Florida lawyer on inactive status in Georgia represented criminal defendant in Georgia, filing pleadings without disclosing his inactive status); *In re Hall*, 377 P.3d 1149 (Kan. 2016) (lawyer applying for admission pro hac vice failed to disclose administrative suspension of his Kansas license); *Disciplinary Counsel v. Mitchell*, 921 N.E.2d 634 (Ohio 2010) (suspended lawyer attempted to appear in juvenile court using false middle name); *State ex rel. Okla. Bar Ass'n v. Mothershed*, 66 P.3d 420 (Okla. 2003) (Oklahoma lawyer who had not passed Arizona bar exam filed pleadings with Arizona court using his Oklahoma registration number as though it were an Arizona number); *In re Paulson*, 216 P.3d 859 (Or. 2009) (suspended lawyer moved to postpone several matters, falsely claiming his disciplinary case was on appeal), *adhered to as modified on reconsideration*, 225 P.3d 41 (Or. 2010).

Nor may a lawyer falsely claim to be acting in a representational capacity. *See, e.g., In re Roose*, 69 P.3d 43 (Colo. 2003) (lawyer misidentified herself as appointed counsel after being removed by order of trial court); *In re Shearin*, 764 A.2d 774 (D.C. 2000) (lawyer told court at various times that she did, and did not, represent "conference" of Methodist churches and its bishop in contentious internecine church litigation); *In re Broome*, 815 So. 2d 1 (La. 2002) (lawyer filed pleading misrepresenting himself as counsel even though client had not authorized representation); *cf. Att'y Grievance Comm'n v. Goodman*, 850 A.2d 1157 (Md. 2004) (assistant public defender filed complaint under another lawyer's name).

### • *Notarizing Signature*

A lawyer who notarizes a signature on a document submitted to the court is making a statement within the meaning of Rule 3.3(a)(1). *See, e.g., In re Uchendu*, 812 A.2d 933 (D.C. 2002) (lawyer signed clients' names on verified probate filings in several cases, sometimes notarizing signatures as well; irrelevant that lawyer had clients' permission); *In re Porter*, 930 So. 2d 875 (La. 2006) (lawyer for couple bringing defamation action let husband, with wife's permission, sign wife's name on verification and then notarized signature); *Att'y Grievance Comm'n v. Geesing*, 80 A.3d 718 (Md. 2013) (lawyer directed staff to sign his name and to notarize his signature on affidavits); *State ex rel. Okla. Bar Ass'n v. Dobbs*, 94 P.3d 31 (Okla. 2004) (lawyer's false notarization of client's signature violated Rule 3.3(a)(1), whether or not lawyer had client's permission); *cf. People v. Peters*, 82 P.3d 389 (Colo. O.P.D.J. 2003) (lawyer's process server signed blank affidavits of service for lawyer to fill in and then get notarized; although lawyer violated Rule 8.4 because he knew jurats were false, he did not, by filing them, "adopt the statements made in those affidavits as [his] own" and therefore did not violate Rule 3.3(a)(1)). *See generally* Michael L. Closen & Charles N. Faeber, *The Case That There Is a Common Law Duty of Notaries Public to Create and Preserve Detailed Journal Records of Their Official Acts*, 42 J. Marshall L. Rev. 231, 319 n.349 (Winter 2009) (notary-related lawyer discipline cases frequently involve absent document-signers).

### • *Statements Relating to Discovery*

Misrepresenting the status of discovery or the availability of information sought in discovery violates Rule 3.3(a)(1). *See, e.g., People v. Poll*, 65 P.3d 483 (Colo. O.P.D.J. 2003) (lawyer falsely implied clients were to blame for lawyer's delay in discovery response and falsely said he could not locate client representative); *Henry v. Statewide Grievance Comm.*, 957 A.2d 547 (Conn. App. Ct. 2008) (lawyer convinced court to issue bench warrant for witness by falsely claiming he failed to appear at deposition); *In re Hermina*, 907 A.2d 790 (D.C. 2006) (lawyer justified failure to respond to discovery by falsely claiming another judge's order precluded him); *In re Carey*, 89 S.W.3d 477 (Mo. 2002) (lawyer intentionally withheld information from discovery); *In re Edwardson*, 647 N.W.2d 126 (N.D. 2002) (false excuses for failure to comply with discovery); *see also In re Kline*, 311 P.3d 321 (Kan. 2013) (after hearing on mandamus, state's attorney general tried to change his assistant's straightforward and truthful answer to court's question about scope of investigation by filing spurious "motion to clarify"). Generally, false statements made in discovery must be corrected. *See KCI USA, Inc. v. Healthcare Essentials, Inc.*, No. 1:14CV549, 2018 WL 3428711, 2018 BL 251903 (N.D. Ohio July 16, 2018) (once on notice of client's discovery violations and lawyers' resulting violations, lawyers were required to advise court of need to correct or supplement discovery).

### • *Statements about Judicial Officers*

False statements concerning judicial officers have been held to violate Rule 3.3 as well as the more specific prohibition in Rule 8.2. *See, e.g., In re Crenshaw*, 815 N.E.2d 1013 (Ind. 2004) (attempting to bring about judge's disqualification, lawyer falsely complained to state's civil rights commission and commission on judicial qualifications that judge discriminated against her); *Att'y Grievance Comm'n v. DeMaio*, 842 A.2d 802 (Md. 2004) (in motion to "modify" dismissal of his appeal, lawyer falsely accused chief judge and clerk of corruption and conspiracy); *Office of Disciplinary Counsel v. Wrona*, 908 A.2d 1281 (Pa. 2006) (lawyer's motions in child support matter falsely accused judge and court personnel of criminally altering audiotapes of proceedings); *cf. Welsh v. Mounger*, 912 So. 2d 823 (Miss. 2005) (on order to show cause, court sanctioned lawyer for violating Rule 3.3 by repeatedly claiming, in motions for recusal and reconsideration, that defendant was "the single largest individual major donor to [the justice's] election campaign," even after court corrected him). See the annotation to Rule 8.2 on false and reckless statements about judges.

## STATEMENTS MADE IN LAWYER'S "PERSONAL" CAPACITY

Comment [1], added in 2002, declares that Rule 3.3 governs the conduct of "a lawyer who is representing a client" in the proceedings of a tribunal. The blackletter rule has no such qualifier, and many cases apply Rule 3.3 to a lawyer's "personal" conduct. *See, e.g., People v. Ritland*, 327 P.3d 914 (Colo. O.P.D.J. 2014) (lawyer seeking to adopt her relative's baby circumvented procedures by falsely listing her own husband as father on baby's birth certificate and filing petition for stepparent adoption); *People v. Albright*, 91 P.3d 1063 (Colo. O.P.D.J. 2003) (misrepresentations about assets and income on personal bankruptcy filing); *In re Usher*, 987 N.E.2d 1080 (Ind. 2013) (false responses to requests for admission in civil suit against lawyer by social acquaintance whose employment prospects lawyer tried to ruin after she rejected his romantic advances); *In re Rumsey*, 71 P.3d 1150 (Kan. 2003) (after client stopped paying him, lawyer filed petition against client's mother as well as client, falsely claiming they both engaged him); *In re Richmond*, 996 So. 2d 282 (La. 2008) (false statement of domicile in notice of candidacy qualifying form); *In re Angwafo*, 899 N.E.2d 778 (Mass. 2009) (in her own family court proceedings, lawyer misrepresented her financial and marital status); *In re Scott*, 657 N.W.2d 567 (Minn. 2003) (false statements of fact to court in lawyer's own marital dissolution and custody case); *In re O'Meara*, 834 A.2d 235 (N.H. 2003) (in own divorce case, lawyer misstated date of subpoena and filed pleading with "gross embellishments on the truth"); *In re Barker*, 572 S.E.2d 460 (S.C. 2002) (false statements in lawyer's own divorce); *Diaz v. Comm'n for Lawyer Discipline*, 953 S.W.2d 435 (Tex. App. 1997) (Rule 3.3(a)(1) applies even if lawyer made his statements as party); *In re Simmerly*, 285 P.3d 838 (Wash. 2012) (after client fired him during pendency of motion for sanctions against both of them and declared bankruptcy, lawyer filed proof of claim seeking payment for post-termination work defending himself against sanctions motion); *see also In re Conteh*, 284 P.3d 724 (Wash. 2012) (lawyer violated Rule 3.3(a) by submitting false employment history on his application for asylum, to which employment history was material, but not by submitting same history on bar application, to which it was not material). *But see In re Ivy*, 350 P.3d 758 (Alaska 2015) (lawyer providing false testimony in litigation against her brother did not violate Rules 3.3 and 3.4; citing comment, Rule 3.3's inclusion under heading "Advocate" and ability to address dishonesty in lawyer's personal capacity under Rule 8.4); *Iowa Supreme Court Att'y Disciplinary Bd. v. Rhinehart*, 827 N.W.2d 169 (Iowa 2013) (citing comment as well as rule's inclusion under heading "Advocate" to hold that lawyer's fraudulent concealment of assets in his own marriage dissolution did not violate Rule 3.3 because he was not representing a client, although it did violate rules prohibiting fraud and conduct prejudicial to administration of justice).

The rule has also been applied to a lawyer's statements as a third-party witness. *See Andrews v. Ky. Bar Ass'n*, 169 S.W.3d 862 (Ky. 2005) (sending letter to bar counsel containing false statements about someone else's pending disciplinary case and enclosing falsified supporting evidence); *In re Finneran*, 919 N.E.2d 698 (Mass. 2010) (as speaker of commonwealth house of representatives, lawyer gave false testimony in federal voting rights lawsuit); *In re Dornay*, 161 P.3d 333 (Wash. 2007) (falsely testifying at her friend's divorce trial that she had never seen him in a rage). *But see State ex rel. Okla. Bar Ass'n v. Dobbs*, 94 P.3d 31 (Okla. 2004) (lawyer who testified falsely as witness in criminal proceeding against another did not violate Rule 3.3; rule "addresses professional misconduct *as an advocate* for making false statements to a tribunal, not false statements by a lawyer as a witness").

For fuller treatment of the application of Rule 3.3 to lawyers pro se, see Margaret Raymond, *Professional Responsibility for the Pro Se Attorney*, 1 St. Mary's J. Legal Mal. & Ethics 2, 28-30 & nn.104-116 (2011) (rule intended to protect court and process, as opposed to clients, and therefore should be fully applicable to pro se lawyers); *see also In re Yana*, No. 100284C, 2014 WL 309314 (N. Mar. I. Jan. 28, 2014) (Rule 3.3 applies when lawyer represents a client, including when lawyer is his own client).

### • Statements to Admission and Disciplinary Authorities

Although lying to lawyer admission or disciplinary authorities is specifically prohibited by Rule 8.1, Rule 3.3 has also been invoked in that context. *See, e.g., In re Shehane*, 575 S.E.2d 503 (Ga. 2003) (lawyer fabricated letters and postal receipts to buttress falsehood told to investigative panel); *Iowa Supreme Court Att'y Disciplinary Bd. v. Barnhill*, 885 N.W.2d 408 (Iowa 2016) (lawyer falsely claimed she had paid fee arbitration award); *In re Harris*, 847 So. 2d 1185 (La. 2003) (lawyer presented perjured testimony in his own disciplinary proceeding); *Att'y Grievance Comm'n v. Butler*, 172 A.3d 486 (Md. 2017) (lawyer falsely testified at disciplinary hearing that he had self-reported disciplinary investigation to Inspector General of USAID); *In re Sishodia*, 60 N.Y.S.3d 153 (App. Div. 2017) (lawyer who managed firm during principal attorney's suspension falsely told reinstatement committee that suspended lawyer had not participated in representing clients); *In re Diggs*, 544 S.E.2d 628 (S.C. 2001) (lawyer filed false compliance report with commission on continuing legal education); *In re Arendt*, 684 N.W.2d 79 (S.D. 2004) (lawyer fabricated document to show disciplinary board he complied with rule on business transactions with clients); *see also* Rule 8.1, cmt. [3] (lawyers representing bar applicants and disciplinary respondents are governed by, "in some cases, Rule 3.3"). *But see In re Albrecht*, 845 N.W.2d 184 (Minn. 2014) (lawyer who was not representing a client when he made misleading statements to disciplinary authorities did not violate Rule 3.3).

## Paragraph (a)(2): Failure to Disclose Legal Authority Known to Be Directly Adverse to Client's Position

Rule 3.3(a)(2) (renumbered from 3.3(a)(3) in 2002) requires a lawyer to disclose "legal authority in the controlling jurisdiction" that the lawyer knows is "directly adverse" to the client's position and that has not been presented by opposing counsel. *See Former Emps. of Chevron Prods. Co. v. U.S. Sec'y of Labor*, 245 F. Supp. 2d 1312 (Ct. Int'l Trade 2002) (duty covers "any legal authority in the controlling jurisdiction," including appellate courts, courts of coordinate jurisdiction, and even lower courts); *Massey v. Prince George's County*, 907 F. Supp. 138 (D. Md. 1995) (in excessive-force case involving use of police dog, defense counsel did not tell district judge of appellate decision against same defendants, represented by same office, on same issue) (discussed in Christopher W. Deering, *Candor Toward the Tribunal: Should an Attorney Sacrifice Truth and Integrity for the Sake of the Client?*, 31 Suffolk U. L. Rev. 59 (1997)); *Tyler v. State*, 47 P.3d 1095 (Alaska Ct. App. 2001) (endorsing, after extensive analysis, majority approach that lawyer must disclose authorities court "should, in fairness, consider when making its decision"); *Aquasol Condo. Ass'n, Inc. v. HSBC Bank USA*, No. 3D17-352, 2018 WL 4609002 (Fla. Dist. Ct. App. Sept. 26, 2018) (appellate lawyer failed to cite and acknowledge controlling adverse case in which lawyer himself was counsel of record); *Brundage v. Estate of Carambio*, 951 A.2d 947 (N.J. 2008) (unpublished decision of another trial court in same jurisdiction not "legal authority in the controlling jurisdiction"; palimony plaintiff's lawyer did not violate rule by failing to disclose he represented another plaintiff in separate palimony case whose dismissal he was currently appealing); *see also Thul v. Onewest Bank*, No. 12 C 6380, 2013 WL 212926 (N.D. Ill. Jan. 18, 2013) (rejecting lawyers' attempts to distinguish new and adverse Seventh Circuit case they had not cited, court noted they had cited older and nonbinding cases on same issue); *cf.* Ill. Ethics Op. 12-07 (2012) (Rule 3.3(a)(2) does not require lawyer to tell court of existence of agreement between client and unrepresented adversary that would be potential defense; lawyer believes agreement is unenforceable). *See generally* Elaine Bucklo, *The Temptation Not to Disclose Adverse Authority*, 40 Litig., no. 2, at 26 (Winter 2014); J. Lyn Entrikin Goering, *Legal Fiction of the "Unpublished" Kind: The Surreal Paradox of No-Citation Rules and the Ethical Duty of Candor*, 1 Seton Hall Cir. Rev. 27 (Spring 2005); Susan J. Irion, *How to Deal Like a Professional with Adverse Legal Authority*, 27 Litig., no. 2, at 49 (Winter 2011); Douglas R. Richmond, *Appellate Ethics: Truth, Criticism, and Consequences*, 23 Rev. Litig. 301 (Spring 2004); Douglas R. Richmond, *The Ethics of Zealous Advocacy: Civility, Candor and Parlor Tricks*, 34 Tex. Tech L. Rev. 3 (2002); Kathryn M. Stanchi, *Playing with Fire: The Science of Confronting Adverse Material in Legal Advocacy*, 60 Rutgers L. Rev. 381 (Winter 2008).

## *Paragraph (a)(3): False Evidence*

### OFFERING FALSE EVIDENCE

Rule 3.3(a)(3) prohibits a lawyer from knowingly offering false evidence. (The special exception for a criminal defense lawyer who knows his client intends to testify falsely is discussed below.) *See, e.g., In re Scahill*, 767 N.E.2d 976 (Ind. 2002) (in marital dissolution action, husband's lawyer continued to include couple's IRA on schedule of marital assets to be divided by court though he knew his client dissipated it); *In re Bailey*, 848 So. 2d 530 (La. 2003) (attempting to introduce altered medical report into evidence); *In re Krigel*, 480 S.W.3d 294 (Mo. 2016) (lawyer's questions were designed to mislead trial court about birth father's interest in raising child); *cf. Patsy's Brand, Inc. v. I.O.B. Realty, Inc.*, No. 98 CIV 10175(JSM), 2002 WL 59434 (S.D.N.Y. Jan. 16, 2002) (citing rule, court sua sponte sanctioned law firm for permitting its client to submit false affidavit; although client insisted affidavit was true, "no reasonable lawyer would believe it" in light of other evidence known to law firm); *Lucas v. State*, 572 S.E.2d 274 (S.C. 2002) (defense lawyer acted appropriately under Rule 3.3 by moving to withdraw because client intended to call witness who planned to give perjured testimony; denial of motion to withdraw did not deprive defendant of fair trial). *See generally* Monroe H. Freedman, *The Cooperating Witness Who Lies—A Challenge to Defense Lawyers, Prosecutors, and Judges*, 7 Ohio St. J. Crim. L. 739 (Spring 2010) (putting burden on defense counsel is "least appropriate way" to deal with cooperating witness who lies).

## REMEDIAL MEASURES

Although the prohibition against offering false evidence is not limited by materiality, the duty to remedy is not triggered unless the evidence is material. This duty arises whether the evidence was offered by the lawyer, the client, or a witness called by the lawyer. *See* Bruce A. Green, *Ethically Representing a Lying Cooperator: Disclosure as the Nuclear Deterrent*, 7 Ohio St. J. Crim. L. 639, 642 n.13 (Spring 2010) (Rule 3.3(a)(3) "appears to be directed solely at lawyers for parties in an adjudication, not at witnesses' lawyers"; author questions whether either Rule 3.3(a)(3) or 3.3(b) would apply to lawyer for criminal co-defendant who testifies untruthfully as cooperating witness).

Reasonable remedial measures include "remonstrating" with the client privately, withdrawing, and, whether or not the lawyer withdraws, making such disclosure to the tribunal "as is reasonably necessary to remedy the situation." Cmt. [10]. *See In re Grasso*, 586 B.R. 110 (Bankr. E.D. Pa. 2018) (lawyer knew client's testimony was false and misleading and failed to correct the record or disclose client's perjury); *People v. Miller*, No. 16PDJ067, 2017 WL 2634659, 2017 BL 208516 (Colo. O.P.D.J. 2017) (lawyer failed to correct misleading statements in client's affidavit); *Idaho State Bar v. Warrick*, 44 P.3d 1141 (Idaho 2002) (prosecutor who knew witness's testimony was false when presented should have taken prompt corrective action and not waited until following day, by which time court and defense counsel already knew); N.Y. State Ethics Op. 837 (2010) (when client tells lawyer that document about which he testified during arbitration proceeding was forged, lawyer's withdrawal would not be remedial measure; lawyer may, however, tell tribunal that specific item of evidence and related testimony are being withdrawn).

## CRIMINAL CASES: CLIENT PERJURY

Under paragraph (a)(3) (formerly paragraph (c)), a lawyer *may* refuse to offer evidence the lawyer reasonably believes—but does not know—is false. This does not apply to testimony by a client who is a defendant in a criminal proceeding; a criminal defense lawyer must honor the client's decision to testify unless she "knows" the testimony will be false, according to Comment [9]. *See generally* Nathan M. Crystal, *False Testimony by Criminal Defendants: Still Unanswered Ethical and Constitutional Questions*, 2003 U. Ill. L. Rev. 1529 (2003); Stephen Gillers, *Monroe Freedman's Solution to the Criminal Defense Lawyer's Trilemma Is Wrong as a Matter of Policy and Constitutional Law*, 34 Hofstra L. Rev. 821 (Spring 2006) (requiring criminal defense counsel to remedy completed client perjury does not implicate defendant's constitutional rights); Geoffrey C. Hazard, Jr., *The Client Fraud Problem as a Justinian Quartet: An Extended Analysis*, 25 Hofstra L. Rev. 1041 (Summer 1997) ("there is a good case that the balance between candor to the court and loyalty to the client should be struck differently for a criminal defense attorney than for other advocates"; author concludes that "requiring a criminal defense lawyer to 'blow the whistle' on client perjury is futile or counterproductive").

The blackletter rule makes no other special accommodations for Sixth Amendment rights, but the comment makes an accommodation for defense lawyers in jurisdictions still using the narrative approach to deal with client perjury. Comment [7] notes that courts in some jurisdictions have required defense counsel to present the client as a witness "or to give a narrative statement if the accused so desires, even if counsel knows that the testimony or statement will be false. The obligation of the advocate under the Rules of Professional Conduct is subordinate to such requirements." Under the narrative approach, defense counsel asks the client to testify but does not then participate by asking questions, and does not use the false testimony in closing argument. The Supreme Court disapproved of the narrative approach in dictum in *Nix v. Whiteside*, 475 U.S. 157 (1986), whereupon the ABA declared that lawyers could no longer use the narrative approach to insulate themselves from charges of assisting client perjury. ABA Formal Ethics Op. 87-353 (1987); *see* Ala. Ethics Op. 2009-1 (n.d.) (reaching same conclusion; narrative approach "inconsistent with the requirements of Rule 3.3 and inconsistent with the lawyer's obligations as an officer of the court"); Raymond J. McKoski, *Prospective Perjury by a Criminal Defendant: It's All About the Lawyer*, 44 Ariz. St. L. Rev. 1575 (Winter 2012) (criticizing current approaches—including withdrawing, presenting narrative testimony, or asking judge for guidance—for failing to recognize "the purpose of rules fashioning a lawyer's response to prospective client perjury is not to prevent false testimony but to protect the lawyer").

The addition of Comment [7] in 2002 acknowledges that the narrative approach still survives as one of the imperfect options available in the client perjury dilemma. American Bar Association, *A Legislative History: The Development of the ABA Model Rules of Professional Conduct, 1982–2013*, at 474 (2013) ("where a court insists that a criminal defendant be permitted to testify in the defendant's defense, the lawyer commits no ethical violation in allowing the client to do so even if the lawyer knows the client intends to lie"); *see Foster v. Smith*, No. 1:07-CV-854, 2014 WL 1230551 (W.D. Mich. Mar. 25, 2014) (collecting cases approving of narrative approach); *Miller v. State*, 764 S.E.2d 135 (Ga. 2014) (narrative approach did not result in ineffective assistance of counsel); *Commonwealth v. Mitchell*, 781 N.E.2d 1237 (Mass. 2003) (defendant may testify through open narrative); *see also State v. Chambers*, 994 A.2d 1248, 1258 n.12 (Conn. 2010) (collecting cases using narrative approach); D.C. Rule 3.3(b) (lawyer unable to dissuade client or to withdraw may use narrative approach); *cf. Brown v. Commonwealth*, 226 S.W.3d 74 (Ky. 2007) (reversing conviction based upon ineffective assistance; court's use of narrative approach was proper, but court should not have let trial counsel leave room while defendant gave his narrative). *See generally* Norman Lefstein, *Client Perjury in Criminal Cases: Still in Search of an Answer*, 1 Geo. J. Legal Ethics 521 (Winter 1988) (disclosure to court "leads to confusion and uncertainty in the courtroom"; narrative approach assures "the client will still be able to tell his or her story to the fact finder"); L. Timothy Perrin, *The Perplexing Problem of Client Perjury*, 76 Fordham L. Rev. 1707 (Dec. 2007).

### • *"Knowledge"*

The level of knowledge sufficient to trigger the prohibition against presenting a criminal defense client's false testimony is very high. For analysis see *State v. Chambers*, 994 A.2d 1248, 1260–64 & nn.13–16 (Conn. 2010) (standards have included "good cause to believe," "knowledge beyond a reasonable doubt," "a firm factual basis," and "a good faith determination"). *See also Commonwealth v. Mitchell*, 781 N.E.2d 1237 (Mass. 2003) (inconsistencies in evidence and strong physical and forensic evidence implicating defendant are insufficient to require counsel to investigate, or to disclose criminal defendant's intent to commit perjury; after analyzing various standards, court endorses "firm-basis-in-fact" threshold); *State v. McDowell*, 669 N.W.2d 204 (Wis. Ct. App. 2003) (as matter of law, except in most extraordinary circumstances defense counsel cannot "know" defendant will testify falsely); *cf. United States v. Midgett*, 342 F.3d 321 (4th Cir. 2003) (defense lawyer's "mere belief, albeit a strong one supported by other evidence," was insufficient basis to refuse assistance in presenting client's testimony). *See generally* Erin K. Jaskot & Christopher J. Mulligan, Current Development, *Witness Testimony and the Knowledge Requirement: An Atypical Approach to Defining Knowledge and Its Effect on the Lawyer as an Officer of the Court*, 17 Geo. J. Legal Ethics 845 (Summer 2004); Jay Sterling Silver, *Truth, Justice and the American Way: The Case Against the Client Perjury Rules*, 47 Vand. L. Rev. 339 (Mar. 1994); Brian Slipakoff & Roshini Thayaparan, Current Development, *The Criminal Defense Attorney Facing Prospective Client Perjury*, 15 Geo. J. Legal Ethics 935 (Summer 2002).

## Paragraph (b): When Lawyer Knows of Criminal or Fraudulent Conduct Relating to Proceeding

Until the rule was amended in 2002 this obligation (formerly found in Rule 3.3(a)(2)) was defined as a duty to take reasonable remedial measures necessary to avoid assisting the *client* in a criminal or fraudulent act. *See, e.g., In re Winthrop*, 848 N.E.2d 961 (Ill. 2006) (absent proof that lawyer represented client's agent as well as client, cannot discipline lawyer (under former Rule 3.3(a)(2)) for failing to tell court of agent's "suspicious" use of client's funds).

The rule, redesignated as Rule 3.3(b), now states that a lawyer "who knows that a *person* intends to engage, is engaging or has engaged in criminal or fraudulent conduct *related to the proceeding* shall take reasonable remedial measures, including, if necessary, disclosure to the tribunal" (emphases added). The new wording reflects a "special obligation" on the part of lawyers "to protect a tribunal against criminal or fraudulent conduct that undermines the integrity of the adjudicative process." Cmt. [12]. *See also* American Bar Association, *A Legislative History: The Development of the ABA Model Rules of Professional Conduct, 1982–2013*, at 474 (2013) (amendment means obligation to avoid assisting in client crime or fraud "is replaced by a broader obligation to ensure the integrity of the adjudicative process").

The obligation to take reasonable remedial measures is not triggered unless the lawyer is aware of the fraudulent or criminal quality of the act (whether the act is completed, ongoing, or intended). *See* ABA Formal Ethics Op. 466 (2014) (lawyer who reviews internet presence of juror or potential juror and finds evidence of conduct that is criminal or fraudulent, including conduct contemptuous of court instructions, must take remedial measures including, if necessary, reporting conduct to court); Md. Ethics Op. 2004-19 (2004) (lawyer may not tell court of former client's misrepresentation in bankruptcy petition unless lawyer knows misrepresentation intended to defraud); Phila. Ethics Op. 2011-4 (2011) (filing copy of estate tax return disclosing existence of client's siblings constituted notice to register of wills under Rule

3.3(b) that client misrepresented herself to be sole heir in her application for letters of administration); Va. Ethics Op. 1777 (2003) (lawyer who learns former client for whom he obtained discharge in bankruptcy did not notify court of subsequent inheritance may not notify court unless lawyer knows nondisclosure resulted from fraud rather than mistake).

## GHOSTWRITING

Authorities disagree on whether ghostwriting, where an attorney prepares documents for a pro se litigant without disclosing her role to the court, violates the duty of candor. *See In re Liu*, 664 F.3d 367 (2d Cir. 2011) (ghostwriting did not violate Rule 3.3); *Duran v. Carris*, 238 F.3d 1268 (10th Cir. 2001) (ghostwritten briefs are not allowed); *In re Smith*, No. 12-11603, 2013 WL 1092059, 2013 BL 24487 (Bankr. E.D. Tenn. Jan. 30, 2013) (collecting cases and finding disclosure of assistance is material and required in bankruptcy proceeding); ABA Formal Ethics Op. 07-446 (2007) (pro se litigant's receipt of lawyer's assistance is not material to merits of case and is not fraudulent or dishonest conduct requiring remedial measures); Va. Ethics Op. 1874 (2014) (ethics rules do not prohibit undisclosed assistance to pro se litigant). *See generally* Daniel J. O'Brien, *Ghostwriting and Its Constitutional Support*, 28 Geo. J. Legal Ethics 771 (Summer 2015); Debra Lyn Bassett, *Characterizing Ghostwriting*, 5 St. Mary's J. Legal Mal. & Ethics 286 (2015).

Ghostwriting is also discussed in the annotation to Rule 8.4(c).

## *Paragraph (c): Duration and Extent of Duty*

Rule 3.3(c) specifies that the obligations of paragraphs (a) and (b) continue to the conclusion of a proceeding and apply "even if compliance requires disclosure of information otherwise protected by Rule 1.6." Comment [13] was amended in 2002 to clarify that the "conclusion of the proceeding" means "when a final judgment in the proceeding has been affirmed on appeal or the time for review has passed." *See F.L.C. v. Ala. State Bar*, 38 So. 3d 698 (Ala. 2009) (omission of sole heir from probate petition was ongoing misrepresentation; limitation period for bringing disciplinary action under Rule 3.3(a)(1) as well as Rule 3.3(b) therefore did not begin to run until probate court notified of heir's existence); *Holden v. Blevins*, 837 A.2d 1053 (Md. Ct. Spec. App. 2003) (proceeding has not concluded until appeal rights of every party are exhausted, including right to petition for certiorari; Ariz. Ethics Op. 05-05 (2005) (client in unemployment compensation proceeding admitted perjury and then fired her lawyer; if client still receiving benefits subject to modification, lawyer must inform tribunal that "certain evidence is unreliable"); Ill. Ethics Op. 13-05 (2013) (obligation to tell administrative law judge that client appealing denial of benefits misrepresented her assets on her initial application arises only if lawyer has no other way to undo effect of client's false evidence); Md. Ethics Op. 2005-15 (2005) (if witness for client confesses during appeal that he lied at trial, lawyer must urge witness to rectify and must notify court if witness will not; witness's subsequent recantation of confession requires lawyer to investigate "sufficiently to either rule out the perjury or to reach a conclusion that a reasonable person would not believe the witness lied"); N.Y. State Ethics Op. 837 (2010) (rule does not authorize disclosure that jeopardizes client without serving any remedial purpose); N.Y. City Ethics Op. 2013-2 (2013) (if lawyer learns of evidence's falsity after close of proceeding, disclosure obligation depends upon whether it is still possible to amend, modify, or vacate judgment or to reopen proceeding); Phila. Ethics Op. 2008-9 (2008) (when estate receives additional assets but client, executrix, takes them and will not answer lawyer's messages, duty arises under Rule 3.3(b) if lawyer filed inventory or status report with register of wills, or any document with Orphans' Court, that sets forth estate's assets); R.I. Ethics Op. 2007-06 (2007) (for purposes of rule, Social Security disability proceeding not "concluded" until lawyer files fee petition; if client receives overpayment, lawyer who has not yet filed fee petition must notify judge if client will not); *cf.* N.D. Ethics Op. 05-03 (2005) (under state's unique Rule 3.3 requiring that lawyer seek to withdraw "without disclosure" upon learning of client's false evidence, divorce lawyer who learns parties entered secret side agreement that conflicts with their stipulation may not disclose arrangement to court); N.Y. Rule 3.3(c) (unique version of rule does not limit lawyer's duty to remedy to duration of the proceeding).

## *Paragraph (d): Ex Parte Proceedings*

Rule 3.3(d) requires a lawyer in an ex parte proceeding to inform the tribunal of "all material facts known to the lawyer that will enable the tribunal to make an informed decision, whether or not the facts are adverse." *See, e.g., Ndreko v. Ridge*, 351 F. Supp. 2d 904 (D. Minn. 2004) (at emergency hearing, counsel did not tell district court that client's petition for review of removal order was pending before circuit court of appeals, which already denied two motions to stay deportation); *People v. Ritland*, 327 P.3d 914 (Colo. O.P.D.J. 2014) (lawyer tried to adopt her relative's baby as "stepparent" to circumvent requirement of notice to baby's biological father; her failure to tell court her husband was not the father violated Rule 3.3(d)); *Daniels v. Alander*, 844 A.2d 182 (Conn. 2004) (in effort to persuade judge to assume jurisdiction, lawyer at emergency child custody application relating to out-of-state decree misrepresented client's out-of-state counsel's willingness to proceed on emergency basis); *In re Mullins*, 649 N.E.2d 1024 (Ind. 1995) (lawyer seeking emergency guardianship over client in persistent vegetative state did not tell court of parallel proceedings to withdraw client's nourishment and hydration); *In re Holste*, 358 P.3d 850 (Kan. 2015) (lawyer seeking default judgment failed to tell court that defendant was seeking extension of time to file answer); *cf.* N.Y. City Ethics Op. 2019-1 (2019) (rule does not apply to proceedings in which opposing party is absent by choice or appears pro se); Pa. Ethics Op. 2005-10 (2005) (if notice given to all parties and they do not show up, lawyer has no obligation to present adverse evidence unless failure to do so would mislead court). *See generally* Susan P. Koniak, *Feasting While the Widow Weeps:* Georgine v. Amchem Products, Inc., 80 Cornell L. Rev. 1046 (May 1995) (arguing that even when adversaries present and represented, ex parte rule should apply if alignment is such that there really is no "opposing party"—for example, when parties present an agreed settlement).

# ADVOCATE

## Rule 3.4

*Fairness to Opposing Party and Counsel*

A lawyer shall not:

(a) unlawfully obstruct another party's access to evidence or unlawfully alter, destroy or conceal a document or other material having potential evidentiary value. A lawyer shall not counsel or assist another person to do any such act;

(b) falsify evidence, counsel or assist a witness to testify falsely, or offer an inducement to a witness that is prohibited by law;

(c) knowingly disobey an obligation under the rules of a tribunal, except for an open refusal based on an assertion that no valid obligation exists;

(d) in pretrial procedure, make a frivolous discovery request or fail to make reasonably diligent effort to comply with a legally proper discovery request by an opposing party;

(e) in trial, allude to any matter that the lawyer does not reasonably believe is relevant or that will not be supported by admissible evidence, assert personal knowledge of facts in issue except when testifying as a witness, or state a personal opinion as to the justness of a cause, the credibility of a witness, the culpability of a civil litigant or the guilt or innocence of an accused; or

(f) request a person other than a client to refrain from voluntarily giving relevant information to another party unless:

(1) the person is a relative or an employee or other agent of a client; and

(2) the lawyer reasonably believes that the person's interests will not be adversely affected by refraining from giving such information.

## COMMENT

[1] The procedure of the adversary system contemplates that the evidence in a case is to be marshalled competitively by the contending parties. Fair competition in the adversary system is secured by prohibitions against destruction or concealment of evidence, improperly influencing witnesses, obstructive tactics in discovery procedure, and the like.

[2] Documents and other items of evidence are often essential to establish a claim or defense. Subject to evidentiary privileges, the right of an opposing party, including

the government, to obtain evidence through discovery or subpoena is an important procedural right. The exercise of that right can be frustrated if relevant material is altered, concealed or destroyed. Applicable law in many jurisdictions makes it an offense to destroy material for purpose of impairing its availability in a pending proceeding or one whose commencement can be foreseen. Falsifying evidence is also generally a criminal offense. Paragraph (a) applies to evidentiary material generally, including computerized information. Applicable law may permit a lawyer to take temporary possession of physical evidence of client crimes for the purpose of conducting a limited examination that will not alter or destroy material characteristics of the evidence. In such a case, applicable law may require the lawyer to turn the evidence over to the police or other prosecuting authority, depending on the circumstances.

[3] With regard to paragraph (b), it is not improper to pay a witness's expenses or to compensate an expert witness on terms permitted by law. The common law rule in most jurisdictions is that it is improper to pay an occurrence witness any fee for testifying and that it is improper to pay an expert witness a contingent fee.

[4] Paragraph (f) permits a lawyer to advise employees of a client to refrain from giving information to another party, for the employees may identify their interests with those of the client. See also Rule 4.2.

### Definitional Cross-References
"Knowingly" *See* Rule 1.0(f)
"Reasonably" *See* Rule 1.0(h)
"Reasonably believes" *See* Rule 1.0(i)
"Tribunal" *See* Rule 1.0(m)

### State Rules Comparison
http://ambar.org/MRPCStateCharts

## ANNOTATION

Rule 3.4 explains the lawyer's duties to adverse parties and counsel to ensure litigation is conducted fairly. As Comment [1] notes, "[t]he procedure of the adversary system contemplates that the evidence in a case is to be marshalled competitively by the contending parties. Fair competition in the adversary system is secured by prohibitions against destruction or concealment of evidence, improperly influencing witnesses, obstructive tactics in discovery procedure, and the like."

When a lawyer engages in abusive litigation tactics, it is normally the presiding judge who takes initial corrective action, including retrial, exclusion of evidence, disqualification, and monetary sanctions. In deciding what sanctions to impose, a court is likely to consider Rule 3.4 as well as other ethics rules. *See, e.g., Whittenburg v. Werner Enters. Inc.*, 561 F.3d 1122 (10th Cir. 2009) (ordering retrial because of improper closing argument); *Mezu v. Morgan State Univ.*, 269 F.R.D. 565 (D. Md. 2010) (threatening monetary sanctions against lawyers for all parties for abusive deposition behavior); *Briggs v. McWeeny*, 796 A.2d 516 (Conn. 2002) (affirming disqualification of lawyer who attempted to prevent dissemination and production of report adverse to client's interests).

## Paragraph (a): Alteration, Destruction, or Concealment of Evidence; Obstruction of Another's Access to Evidence

### DESTRUCTION OR ALTERATION OF EVIDENCE

Paragraph (a) prohibits a lawyer from altering or destroying "a document or other material having potential evidentiary value." *See In re Enna*, 971 A.2d 110 (Del. 2009) (lawyer subject to order of protection destroyed tape recording of argument with his wife); *In re Zeiger*, 692 A.2d 1351 (D.C. 1997) (altering client's medical records before submitting them to opposing party's insurance company); *Idaho State Bar v. Gantenbein*, 986 P.2d 339 (Idaho 1999) (intentionally altering medical report before submitting it to opposing counsel in personal injury case); *Ky. Bar Ass'n v. Maze*, 397 S.W.3d 891 (Ky. 2013) (county attorney on trial for vote fraud and under FBI investigation instructed office secretary to dispose of documents that would have shown jury tampering); *Att'y Grievance Comm'n v. White*, 731 A.2d 447 (Md. 1999) (lawyer who was plaintiff in employment discrimination case destroyed portions of autobiographical manuscript relevant to her claims); *In re Caranchini*, 956 S.W.2d 910 (Mo. 1997) (using forged document to support client's claim); *Cleveland Metro. Bar Ass'n v. Azman*, 66 N.E.3d 695 (Ohio 2016) (lawyer being sued by his former firm accessed other firm employees' accounts and deleted e-mails without authorization); *Sutch v. Roxborough Mem'l Hosp.*, 151 A.3d 241 (Pa. Super. Ct. 2016) (attempted tampering with witness's testimony); *In re Tornow*, 835 N.W.2d 912 (S.D. 2013) (destroying tape recording so it could not be produced in anticipated litigation); *In re Poole*, 125 P.3d 954 (Wash. 2006) (backdating accounting paperwork of former client who sued lawyer in dispute over fees); *Lawyer Disciplinary Bd. v. Smoot*, 716 S.E.2d 491 (W. Va. 2010) (defense lawyer disassembled and produced only portion of independent medical examination of pro se black-lung claimant); D.C. Ethics Op. 371 (2016) (must include social media postings in advising client on duty to preserve evidence and avoid spoliation); Mich. Informal Ethics Op. RI-345 (2008) (acceding to request of corporate client's CEO to return discoverable documents so he may destroy them would violate Rule 3.4(a)); Mo. Informal Ethics Op. 2014-02 (n.d.) (may not remove metadata with evidentiary value from documents before turning them over in discovery).

### • Duty to Safeguard Physical Evidence of Client Crimes

In 2002, language was added to Comment [2] calling attention to the law regarding a lawyer's possession of physical evidence of client crimes. The new language states that "[a]pplicable law may permit a lawyer to take temporary possession of physical evidence of client crimes for the purpose of conducting a limited examination that will not alter or destroy material characteristics of the evidence. In such a case, applicable law may require the lawyer to turn the evidence over to the police or other prosecuting authority, depending on the circumstances." *See In re Olson*, 222 P.3d 632 (Mont. 2009) (failure to turn over photographs removed from client's residence did not violate rule; lawyer "was not, at that point in the proceedings, obligated to turn the items over to the police or prosecutor by virtue of a statute or court order"); W. Va. Ethics Op. 2015-03 (2015) (lawyer holding evidence may be required to turn it over to law enforcement); *cf.* W. Va. Ethics Op. 98-02 (1998) (criminal defense lawyers holding fruits or instrumentalities of crime must resolve "two competing important public policies: the policy supporting the attorney-client privilege and the policy which prohibits an attorney from engaging in the obstruction of justice"); *Restatement (Third) of the Law Governing Lawyers* § 119 (2000) (when reasonably necessary, lawyer may take possession of physical evidence of client's crime and retain it for reasonable period; lawyer may conduct tests "that do not alter or destroy material characteristics of the evidence," but must notify prosecuting authorities and turn evidence over to them).

## OBSTRUCTING ANOTHER PARTY'S ACCESS TO EVIDENCE

Rule 3.4(a) also prohibits a lawyer from "unlawfully obstruct[ing] another party's access to evidence . . . ." *See In re Stover*, 104 P.3d 394 (Kan. 2005) (disobeying court order to give former client access to computer lawyer used for client's representation); *Att'y Grievance Comm'n v. Protokowicz*, 619 A.2d 100 (Md. 1993) (helping former client break into former client's wife's house to remove documents useful as evidence in client's pending divorce); *In re Eisenstein*, 485 S.W.3d 759 (Mo. 2016) (divorce lawyer's client surreptitiously obtained opposing counsel's direct examination questions and spouse's personal financial information and gave them to lawyer who did not notify opposing counsel until second day of trial); *In re Forrest*, 730 A.2d 340 (N.J. 1999) (failing to notify opposing counsel of client's death); *In re Dvorak*, 611 N.W.2d 147 (N.D. 2000) (denying access to witness or attempting to dissuade witness from providing information); *Lawyer Disciplinary Bd. v. Busch*, 754 S.E.2d 729 (W. Va. 2014) (prosecutor ignored, then refused one defense counsel's requests for information contained on computer hard drives and obstructed another defense counsel's access to recorded witness statements); Ky. Ethics Op. E-422 (2003) (improper to issue deposition subpoena duces tecum to nonparty and unilaterally cancel deposition after documents tendered without also disclosing documents to opponent); Md. Ethics Op. 2017-02 (2017) (blanket prohibition on contacting organization's current and former employees may be impermissible); Phila. Ethics Op. 2008-13 (2008) (plaintiffs' lawyer in case in which injured clients' common-law marriage is contested must inform opponent if clients file separate declaratory judgment action regarding marriage and such action is within scope of discovery requests); *see also State ex rel. Okla. Bar Ass'n v. Miller*, 309 P.3d 108 (Okla. 2013) (prosecutor failed to disclose assistance to key witness).

### • *Procuring Absence of Witness*

Procuring or attempting to procure the absence of witnesses also constitutes the obstruction of evidence in violation of Rule 3.4(a). *See, e.g., Harlan v. Lewis*, 982 F.2d 1255 (8th Cir. 1993) (defense lawyer for one physician in medical malpractice case suggested to other treating physician that he not testify for plaintiffs); *Sanderson v. Boddie-Noell Enters., Inc.*, 227 F.R.D. 448 (E.D. Va. 2005) (plaintiff's lawyer contacted employer of defendant's expert witness and suggested witness's testifying breached employment contract); *In re Geisler*, 614 N.E.2d 939 (Ind. 1993) (obstructing prosecutor's access to evidence by assisting witness's unavailability for service and trial); *In re Jensen*, 191 P.3d 1118 (Kan. 2008) (advising nonparty witness subpoenaed by adversary that witness "did not need to appear at the scheduled hearing unless he heard from" lawyer); *State ex rel. Okla. Bar Ass'n v. Cox*, 48 P.3d 780 (Okla. 2002) (telling physician friend that if he testified for lawyer's opponent, lawyer would have to "dig up dirt" about physician); Utah Ethics Op. 99-06 (1999) (as part of plea bargain in DUI case, neither prosecutor nor defense lawyer may seek agreement of police officer to ignore subpoena in defendant's parallel state administrative proceeding); *Restatement (Third) of the Law Governing Lawyers* § 116(3) (2000) ("lawyer may not unlawfully induce or assist a prospective witness to evade or ignore process obliging the witness to appear to testify"). *But see Att'y Grievance Comm'n v. Dyer*, 162 A.3d 970 (Md. 2017) (advising clients not to attend depositions on ground that subpoenas violated First Amendment rights did not unlawfully obstruct opponent's access to evidence).

## UNLAWFUL CONCEALMENT OF EVIDENCE VERSUS LEGITIMATE FAILURE TO DISCLOSE

Rule 3.4(a) prohibits a lawyer from "unlawfully" concealing material having potential evidentiary value. This does not impose a duty to volunteer all relevant information that a lawyer has, but prohibits concealing potential evidence a lawyer has a legal duty to disclose. *Sherman v. State*, 905 P.2d 355 (Wash. 1995) ("RPC 3.4 does not itself create a duty of disclosure"); *see also Miss. Bar v. Land*, 653 So. 2d 899 (Miss. 1994) (failing to reveal insurance investigator's report regarding accident in response to interrogatories and document requests); *In re Carey*, 89 S.W.3d 477 (Mo. 2002) (in response to discovery requests, lawyer denied existence of "conversations and documents which had in fact occurred and did exist"); *In re Olson*, 222 P.3d 632 (Mont. 2009) (failure to turn over certain items to prosecution did not violate rule because lawyer "was not, at that point in the proceedings, obligated to turn the items over . . . by virtue of a statute or court order"); *State ex rel. Okla. Bar Ass'n v. Upton*, 991 P.2d 544 (Okla. 1999) (withholding subpoenaed documents not a violation because civil procedure statute allowed withholding after proper objection).

## COUNSELING OR ASSISTING IN DESTRUCTION OR CONCEALMENT OF EVIDENCE

Rule 3.4(a) prohibits a lawyer from counseling another person to violate, or assisting another person in violating, the other provisions of the paragraph. This provision is similar to that of Rule 1.2(d) (prohibiting a lawyer from counseling a client to engage in—or assisting a client in—criminal or fraudulent conduct), and Rule 8.4(a) (prohibiting a lawyer from assisting or inducing person in violating the ethics rules).

A number of ethics committees have opined that lawyers may advise clients to restrict access to or delete potentially damaging information from their social media websites but also may have a duty to ensure the information is preserved in case it becomes subject to discovery. *See, e.g.,* D.C. Ethics Op. 371 (2016); Fla. Ethics Op. 14-1 (2015; rev. 2016); N.Y. Cnty. Ethics Op. 745 (2013); N.C. Ethics Op. 2014-5 (2014); Pa.

Formal Ethics Op. 2014-300 (2014); Phila. Ethics Op. 2014-5 (2014); W. Va. Ethics Op. 2015-02 (2015). *See generally* Jan L. Jacobowitz & John G. Browning, *Legal Ethics and Social Media: A Practitioner's Handbook* 56-57, 77-78 (2017).

## Paragraph (b): Falsifying Evidence, Assisting with False Testimony, or Offering Unlawful Inducement to Witness

Rule 3.4(b) prohibits a lawyer from falsifying evidence. *See, e.g., Fla. Bar v. Salnik,* 599 So. 2d 101 (Fla. 1992) (using judge's stamp to forge judgment, which lawyer then sent to opposing counsel to intimidate him); *Idaho State Bar v. Gantenbein,* 986 P.2d 339 (Idaho 1999) (lawyer in personal injury case intentionally altered medical report, submitted it to opposing counsel, and republished it in subsequent administrative and federal court proceedings); *In re Swarts,* 30 P.3d 1011 (Kan. 2001) (after learning evidence consisting of brown paper sack containing handkerchief was missing, county prosecutor brought his own to court and placed it on counsel table during plea change and sentencing hearing); *In re Watkins,* 656 So. 2d 984 (La. 1995) (making false statements to obtain Social Security benefits for clients); *In re Neitlich,* 597 N.E.2d 425 (Mass. 1992) (misrepresenting to court and to client's ex-wife's counsel purchase price of client's condominium); *In re Fuller,* 621 N.W.2d 460 (Minn. 2001) (submitting false evidence in disciplinary proceeding); Utah Ethics Op. 03-02 (2003) (knowingly submitting false billing statements to opposing counsel, insurer, or court violates rule); *cf. In re Ivy,* 350 P.3d 758 (Alaska 2015) (testifying falsely on own behalf did not violate Rule 3.4 because rule applies only in context of client representation).

This prohibition is a counterpart to Rule 3.3's prohibition against offering false evidence. Rule 3.4(b) casts this obligation as being owed to an opposing party and counsel, while Rule 3.3 casts the obligation as part of a lawyer's duty of candor toward a tribunal. A single act, of course, can violate both obligations. *See In re Dynan,* 98 P.3d 444 (Wash. 2004) (inflating hourly rate in fee petition filed with court and served on opponent).

### COUNSELING OR ASSISTING WITNESS TO GIVE FALSE TESTIMONY

A lawyer may not advise or assist a witness—whether a client or not—to give false testimony. *See, e.g., Goodsell v. Miss. Bar,* 667 So. 2d 7 (Miss. 1996) (allowing witness to testify about matter lawyer knew to be untrue); *In re Oberhellmann,* 873 S.W.2d 851 (Mo. 1994) (advising witness to testify falsely concerning residence); *Feld's Case,* 737 A.2d 656 (N.H. 1999) (allowing clients to testify inaccurately at deposition and failing to correct record); *In re Edson,* 530 A.2d 1246 (N.J. 1987) (counseling and assisting witness to testify falsely during trial); *In re Geoghan,* 686 N.Y.S.2d 839 (App. Div. 1999) (offering to have client testify falsely in criminal matter in exchange for defendant's settlement of civil matter); *Office of Disciplinary Counsel v. Valentino,* 730 A.2d 479 (Pa. 1999) (advising mother to testify falsely at arbitration hearing); *see also In re Moeller,* 582 N.W.2d 554 (Minn. 1998) (directing secretary to forge clients' signatures on retainer agreements and counseling client to stage workplace accident); N.Y. Cnty. Ethics Op. 741 (2010) (on learning client lied in deposition, lawyer must counsel him to correct testimony and if client will not, lawyer must take other remedial measures). *See generally* Roberta K. Flowers, *Witness Preparation: Regulating the Profession's "Dirty Little Secret,"* 38 Hastings Const. L.Q. 1007 (Summer 2011).

## OFFERING ILLEGAL INDUCEMENT TO WITNESS

Rule 3.4(b) also forbids a lawyer to offer a witness an inducement that is prohibited by law. *See, e.g., Fla. Bar v. Wohl,* 842 So. 2d 811 (Fla. 2003) (drafting agreement for witness to receive up to $1 million "bonus" if information she provided proved useful); *Iowa Supreme Court Att'y Disciplinary Bd. v. Gailey,* 790 N.W.2d 801 (Iowa 2010) (offering favorable divorce settlement to witness in exchange for testimony at witness's estranged husband's criminal trial); *In re Hingle,* 717 So. 2d 636 (La. 1998) (bribing witness); *In re Geoghan,* 686 N.Y.S.2d 839 (App. Div. 1999) (offering to have client testify falsely in criminal matter in exchange for defendant's settlement of civil matter); *In re Bonet,* 29 P.3d 1242 (Wash. 2001) (prosecutor offered to dismiss criminal charges against potential witness for defendant if witness would absent himself from defendant's trial by invoking witness's right against self-incrimination); *cf. Murray v. Just In Case Bus. Lighthouse, LLC,* 374 P.3d 443 (Colo. 2016) (trial court has discretion on whether to admit testimony of witness improperly paid by lawyer).

## WITNESS FEES

According to Comment [3], "it is not improper to pay a witness's expenses or to compensate an expert witness on terms permitted by law. The common law rule in most jurisdictions is that it is improper to pay an occurrence witness any fee for testifying and that it is improper to pay an expert witness a contingent fee."

### • *Occurrence Witnesses*

Most jurisdictions permit occurrence witnesses to be paid for time and expenses incurred as witnesses, provided such payments do not amount to inducements to testify in particular ways. *E.g.,* ABA Formal Ethics Op. 96-402 (1996) (nonexpert witness may be compensated for time spent attending trial or deposition or preparing for testimony if payment not conditioned upon content of testimony and does not violate any law); *accord* Ariz. Ethics Op. 97-7 (1998); Cal. Formal Ethics Op. 1997-149 (1997); Colo. Ethics Op. 103 (1998); Del. Ethics Op. 2003-3 (2003); Phila. Ethics Op. 2014-2 (2014); *see also* Ala. Ethics Op. 93-2 (1993) (witness may be repaid for expenses and lost time if compensation reasonable considering witness's occupation and normal wages); Conn. Informal Ethics Op. 92-30 (1992) (lawyer who drafted will for testator and testified as witness—without representing any party—in subsequent will contest may be compensated for time lost to testify); N.H. Ethics Op. 1992-93/10 (1993) (fact or opinion witness may be reimbursed for attorneys' fees that witness incurred defending contempt action arising out of litigation); S.C. Ethics Op. 2008-05 (2008) (defense lawyer may advise client to pay fees of prosecution witness's own lawyer if witness insists his own lawyer be present at interview, to extent such payment "may be legally permissible"); Vt. Ethics Op. 2009-06 (2009) (to secure attendance of out-of-state witness, lawyer may offer to reimburse lost wages and pay statutory attendance fees); W. Va. Ethics Op. 2017-01 (2017) (payment to fact witness for reasonable expenses and value of time spent in preparation and testifying should be accompanied by written fee agreement and may not be tied to outcome); *cf.* N.Y. State Ethics Op. 997 (2014) (lawyer may buy video surveillance tape footage to use as evidence in litigation, and purchase price may be contingent upon case outcome if tape has not been fraudulently altered and payment is not disguised witness payment). *See generally* George C. Harris, *Testimony for Sale: The Law and Ethics of Snitches and Experts*, 28 Pepp. L. Rev. 1 (2000); Douglas R. Richmond, *Compensating Fact Witnesses: The Price Is Sometimes Right*, 42 Hofstra L. Rev. 905 (Spring 2014).

Accordingly, a witness may not be paid for "telling the truth" or on a contingent-fee basis. *See, e.g., Commonwealth v. Miranda,* 934 N.E.2d 222 (Mass. 2010) (affirming verdict even though prosecutor certified cooperation of eyewitnesses who then received $2,000 reward for testimony, but stating "prosecutors in the future may not provide (or participate in providing) monetary awards to witnesses contingent on a defendant's conviction"); *Comm. on Legal Ethics v. Sheatsley,* 452 S.E.2d 75 (W. Va. 1994) (lawyer violated rule by acquiescing in payment of compensation to witness contingent upon content of testimony or outcome of case); *see also Golden Door Jewelry Creations, Inc. v. Lloyds Underwriters Non-Marine Ass'n,* 117 F.3d 1328 (11th Cir. 1997) (barring use of testimony from paid witnesses was adequate penalty for violating Rule 3.4(b)); *Wagner v. Lehman Bros. Kuhn Loeb Inc.,* 646 F. Supp. 643 (N.D. Ill. 1986) (disqualification for promising to remit percentage of potential recovery in case to induce witness to "tell the truth"); *cf. United States v. Cervantes-Pacheco,* 826 F.2d 310 (5th Cir. 1987) (overruling per se exclusion of testimony of informant paid contingent fee; concurring opinion noted practice violates Rule 3.4); Phila. Ethics Op. 2003-7 (2003) (treating physician who is also lawyer may accept noncontingent fee for his time in testifying as physician, but may not accept referral fee as lawyer); Tex. Ethics Op. 614 (2012) (lawyer may participate in settlement agreement conditioning payment upon party's execution of witness affidavit on subject matter of unrelated lawsuit as long as specific content of affidavit not subject to approval). *But see Addamax Corp. v. Open Software Found., Inc.,* 151 F.R.D. 504 (D. Mass. 1993) (lawyer who stated subpoena duces tecum might be withdrawn if affiant recanted affidavit did not violate Model Code's rule barring payment of "compensation" to witness contingent upon content of testimony).

## • Expert Witnesses

An expert, unlike a lay witness, may be compensated for his or her testimony, but fees must be reasonable and generally may not be contingent upon the outcome of a case. *See, e.g., Murray v. Just In Case Bus. Lighthouse, LLC,* 374 P.3d 443 (Colo. 2016) (agreement to pay expert witness 10 percent of any judgment or settlement violated rule); *New Eng. Tel. & Tel. Co. v. Bd. of Assessors,* 468 N.E.2d 263 (Mass. 1984) (majority rule "is that an expert witness may not collect compensation which by agreement was contingent on the outcome of a controversy"); *see also Swafford v. Harris,* 967 S.W.2d 319 (Tenn. 1998) (contingent-fee contract for services of physician acting as medical-legal expert is void against public policy); Ky. Ethics Op. E-394 (1996) (prohibiting compensating expert witness on contingent-fee basis, or paying "bonus" if recovery exceeds particular amount). *But see D.C.* Ethics Op. 233 (1993) (noting District of Columbia's version of Rule 3.4 permits payments of contingent fees to expert witnesses as long as not based upon percentage of recovery). *See generally* Steven Lubet, *Expert Witnesses: Ethics and Professionalism*, 12 Geo. J. Legal Ethics 465 (Spring 1999).

## *Paragraph (c): Obeying Obligation to Tribunal*

### COURT ORDERS

Paragraph (c) prohibits lawyers from disobeying, or advising their clients to disobey, court orders. *See, e.g., Ligon v. Stilley*, 371 S.W.3d 615 (Ark. 2010) (having subpoenas and deposition notices issued contrary to judge's order); *People v. Mason*, 212 P.3d 141 (Colo. O.P.D.J. 2009) (practicing law while suspended); *Fla. Bar v. Committe*, 136 So. 3d 1111 (Fla. 2014) (ignoring court order to pay sanctions); *In re Hagedorn*, 725 N.E.2d 397 (Ind. 2000) (lawyer appointed as guardian failed to file inventory and accounting as ordered by court and took fee from guardianship funds without court approval); *In re Mire*, 197 So. 3d 656 (La. 2016) (failing to disgorge bankruptcy fee as ordered); *Att'y Grievance Comm'n v. Storch*, 124 A.3d 204 (Md. 2015) (disobeying multiple orders to turn over estate property); *In re Butler*, 868 N.W.2d 243 (Minn. 2015) (failing to pay more than $300,000 in court-ordered sanctions and attorneys' fees); *Farley's Case*, 794 A.2d 116 (N.H. 2002) (converting client's funds after ordered by court not to dispose of or convey client's assets); *State ex rel. Okla. Bar Ass'n v. Braswell*, 975 P.2d 401 (Okla. 1998) (lawyer's being held in contempt for failing to pay sanctions established violation of Rule 3.4(c)); *In re Carter*, 779 S.E.2d 194 (S.C. 2015) (failure to comply with order to pay over funds that should have been held in trust account); *Bailey v. Bd. of Prof'l Responsibility*, 441 S.W.3d 223 (Tenn. 2014) (disobeying court order to refrain from making speaking objections); *Lawyer Disciplinary Bd. v. Martin*, 693 S.E.2d 461 (W. Va. 2010) (lawyer replaced as executor of decedent's estate failed to comply with court order to refund fees and turn over file to successor for months); *In re Ratzel*, 578 N.W.2d 194 (Wis. 1998) (disobeying court order to refrain from further representation in estate matter); *Bd. of Prof'l Responsibility v. Bustos*, 224 P.3d 873 (Wyo. 2010) (after federal appellate court issued order to show cause regarding lawyer's failure to file appellate brief, lawyer "did nothing"); *see also In re Dickstein*, No. 10–C–07932, 2015 WL 4527632 (Cal. Bar Ct. July 15, 2015) (lawyer guilty of criminal contempt for moving to withdraw for nonpayment of fees in violation of court order); *Iowa Supreme Court Att'y Disciplinary Bd. v. Stowers*, 823 N.W.2d 1 (Iowa 2012) (sending e-mails threatening to disclose confidential documents subject to protective order); Colo. Ethics Op. 130 (2017) (disseminating filings or information subject to protective order violates Rule 3.4(c)); Mo. Informal Ethics Op. 2017-04 (n.d.) (discussing procedures to follow on receipt of court order to turn over confidential information to law enforcement). *But see Ky. Bar Ass'n v. Blum*, 404 S.W.3d 841 (Ky. 2013) (persisting in "inappropriate" and "specious legal claims and filings" contrary to judge's repeated admonitions did not violate Rule 3.4(c), which "does not encompass violations of warnings, admonitions, or other statements made by a trial judge in an attempt to urge an attorney to conform his conduct to the recommended courtroom practice").

## COURT RULES

Rule 3.4 also prohibits lawyers from disobeying the rules of a tribunal. *See, e.g., In re Gabriel*, 837 P.2d 149 (Ariz. 1992) (failing to comply with discovery requests and orders in personal injury suit in which lawyer was defendant); *In re Howes*, 52 A.3d 1 (D.C. 2012) (assistant U.S. attorney improperly issued witness vouchers); *Ky. Bar Ass'n v. Schilling*, 361 S.W.3d 304 (Ky. 2012) (lawyer serving as examiner in bankruptcy case violated court rules and Bankruptcy Code in failing to disclose fee arrangements); *In re Smith*, 29 So. 3d 1232 (La. 2010) (continuing to represent criminal defendants after being sworn in as assistant district attorney); *In re Fuller*, 621 N.W.2d 460 (Minn. 2001) (failing to disclose or obtain court's approval for fees as required by bankruptcy rules); *Mathes v. Miss. Bar*, 637 So. 2d 840 (Miss. 1994) (accepting fees from two clients without first petitioning court for necessary approval); *In re Alcantara*, 676 A.2d 1030 (N.J. 1995) (violating Rule 4.2 by talking with another lawyer's client without permission, and Rule 3.4(f) by asking that person to refrain from giving testimony favorable to state, thereby also violating Rule 3.4(c)); *Disciplinary Bd. of Supreme Court v. Robb*, 618 N.W.2d 721 (N.D. 2000) (failing to follow court rule governing withdrawal from representation); *State ex rel. Okla. Bar Ass'n v. Kruger*, 421 P.3d 306 (Okla. 2018) ("Byzantine abuse" of court procedures in disciplinary proceedings, including "routinely" ignoring deadlines and failing to comply with statutes, court rules, and orders mandating production of records); *In re Nelson*, 750 S.E.2d 85 (S.C. 2013) (assistant prosecutor repeatedly communicated ex parte by phone and text message with cousin serving as juror in criminal trial prosecuted by other lawyers in assistant prosecutor's office); ABA Formal Ethics Op. 93-378 (1993) (lawyer representing client in civil matter is not prohibited by Model Rules from engaging in ex parte contacts with opponent's expert witness, but must conform to tribunal's discovery rules, which frequently include restrictions on lawyer-witness contacts); W. Va. Ethics Op. 2015-01 (2015) (lawyer appearing as stand-in counsel must comply with rules of court regarding appearance, withdrawal, and substitution); *see also* ABA Formal Ethics Op. 94-386 (rev. 1995) (Rule 3.4(c) does not prohibit lawyers from citing other jurisdiction's unpublished opinions in jurisdiction that does not have such ban, but lawyers must inform court to which opinion is cited of issuing court's limitation). *But see Iowa Supreme Court Att'y Disciplinary Bd. v. Rhinehart* (Iowa 2013) (Rule 3.4(c) did not apply to lawyer who deliberately failed to disclose material information in discovery in his own divorce case).

## *Paragraph (d): Abusing Pretrial Procedure*

### GENERAL PROHIBITION

A lawyer's duty of fairness to the opposing party and counsel prohibits the lawyer from abusing pretrial discovery procedures. Paragraph (d) states that a lawyer shall not make a frivolous discovery request or fail to make a reasonably diligent effort to comply with a legally proper discovery request by an opposing party. *See, e.g., Peters v. Comm. on Grievances for U.S. Dist. Court for S. Dist. of N.Y.*, 748 F.3d 456 (2d Cir. 2014) (violating confidentiality order by copying deposition transcripts for use in related action); *Meier v. Meier*, 835 So. 2d 379 (Fla. Dist. Ct. App. 2003) (lawyer must produce documents upon valid request by adverse party despite client's instruction to withhold them); *Idaho State Bar v. Gantenbein*, 986 P.2d 339 (Idaho 1999) (falsifying medical report and obstructing opposing counsel's efforts to determine who altered it); *In re Harris*, 186 P.3d 737 (Kan. 2008) (failing to provide responses to discovery); *Jones's Case*, 628 A.2d 254 (N.H. 1993) (falsely representing to opponent and court that neither he nor client had copy of certain letter); *Moseley v. Va. State Bar*, 694 S.E.2d 586 (Va. 2010) (after filing contract suit prohibited by arbitration clause, lawyer demanded voluminous discovery and denied existence of arbitration clause); *Bd. of Prof'l Responsibility v. Richard*, 335 P.3d 1036 (Wyo. 2014) ("consistent pattern of misbehavior" and "obstructionist tactics" before multiple courts, including repeated "intentional, willful refusal" to respond to discovery and "total lack of concern for honest communication with opposing counsel and the courts"); *see also* Rule 3.1 (Meritorious Claims and Contentions); Rule 3.2 (Expediting Litigation). *See generally* Babak Shamsi, *Some of Them Want to Abuse You: A Critique of Attorney Responses to Deposition Abuse*, 22 Geo. J. Legal Ethics 1135 (Summer 2009) (arguing policy of Rule 3.4 is served if lawyers suspend depositions when abusive questions asked or answers offered, and seek protective order instead of allowing deposition to proceed).

## Paragraph (e): Limiting Trial Tactics

### IMPROPER QUESTIONS OR STATEMENTS

Paragraph (e) prohibits lawyer misconduct at trial and limits certain trial tactics. It prohibits a lawyer from alluding to irrelevant matters or matters not supported by admissible evidence. *See, e.g., Gilster v. Primebank*, 747 F.3d 1007 (8th Cir. 2014) (Title VII plaintiff's lawyer improperly referred to her personal experience as sexual harassment victim in closing argument); *Whittenburg v. Werner Enters. Inc.*, 561 F.3d 1122 (10th Cir. 2009) ("violat[ing] the cardinal rule of closing argument: that counsel must confine comments to evidence in the record and to reasonable inferences from that evidence"); *Falkowski v. Johnson*, 148 F.R.D. 132 (D. Del. 1993) (plaintiff's lawyer's reference to insurance in automobile case requires retrial); *Grosjean v. Imperial Palace, Inc.*, 212 P.3d 1068 (Nev. 2009) ("attorneys violate the 'golden rule' by asking the jurors to place themselves in the plaintiff's position or nullify the jury's role by asking it to 'send a message' to the defendant instead of evaluating the evidence"); *Amelia's Auto., Inc. v. Rodriguez*, 921 S.W.2d 767 (Tex. App. 1996) (criticism of opposing counsel during cross-examination of opposing party violated ethics rules); *cf. Att'y Grievance Comm'n v. Alison*, 709 A.2d 1212 (Md. 1998) (though trial judge ordered mistrial for comments violating Rule 3.4(e)—including that one can "expect to get jerked around" when dealing with insurance company—comments did not "rise to the level requiring discipline"); *State v. Jones*, 558 S.E.2d 97 (N.C. 2002) (citing Rule 3.4(e) regarding prosecutor's improper remarks in closing argument, including describing defendant as "lower than the dirt on a snake's belly").

Paragraph (e) also prohibits a lawyer from asserting personal knowledge regarding facts at issue, except when testifying as a witness. *See, e.g., People v. Segal*, 40 P.3d 852 (Colo. O.P.D.J. 2002) (defense lawyer told jury that police officer's description of post-arrest events occurring in presence of lawyer was false and that "I was present"); *Holt v. Commonwealth*, 219 S.W.3d 731 (Ky. 2007) (prosecutor must not "make a statement of fact, the credence of which is always more or less strengthened by his official position"); *Smith v. Rudolph*, 51 N.Y.S.3d 507 (App. Div. 2017) (repeated assertions during trial of personal knowledge of facts in issue).

Paragraph (e) also prohibits a lawyer from stating a personal opinion regarding the justness of a cause, the credibility of a witness, the culpability of a civil litigant, or the guilt or innocence of an accused. *See, e.g., United States v. Brown*, 508 F.3d 1066 (D.C. Cir. 2007) (it is "for the jury, and not the prosecutor, to say which witnesses [are] telling the truth"); *Michael v. State*, 529 A.2d 752 (Del. 1987) ("Defense counsel, like the prosecutor, must refrain from interjecting personal beliefs and facts outside of the record into the argument to the jury"); *Lainhart v. State*, 916 N.E.2d 924 (Ind. Ct. App. 2009) (prosecutor vouched for honesty of police officer witnesses in voir dire and closing argument); *State v. Morris*, 196 P.3d 422 (Kan. Ct. App. 2008) (referring to defense witness in closing argument, prosecutor stated, "I think that her motives are a little suspect here, quite honestly"); *Harne v. Deadmond*, 954 P.2d 732 (Mont. 1998) (defense counsel personally vouched for credibility of client in closing argument); *State v. Bujnowski*, 532 A.2d 1385 (N.H. 1987) (prosecutor expressed personal opinions regarding credibility of witnesses' testimony and defendant's guilt to jury in closing argument); *cf. Cox v. State*, 696 N.E.2d 853 (Ind. 1998) (prosecutor's assertions in opening statement that defendant lied to police were not improper expressions of opinion of credibility of witness because defendant did not testify and record contained evidence that defendant did, in fact, lie). *See generally* Silas Crawford, *May an Attorney Assert His or Her Opinion as to the Credibility of Witnesses or the Guilt or Innocence of Defendants?*, 22 J. Legal Prof. 243 (Spring 1998) (discussing manner in which courts deal with improper statements of opinion by prosecutors).

### *Paragraph (f): Discouraging Voluntary Disclosure*

Paragraph (f) prohibits a lawyer from asking a person other than a client to refrain from voluntarily giving relevant information to "another party," unless that person is a relative, employee, or other agent of a client and the lawyer believes the person's interests will not be adversely affected by complying with the request. *See, e.g., Castaneda v. Burger King Corp.*, No. C 08-4262 WHA (JL), 2009 WL 2382688 (N.D. Cal. July 31, 2009) (if, as alleged, plaintiffs' counsel advised putative class members not to talk to defendants' counsel before class certification, this would violate rule); *Briggs v. McWeeny*, 796 A.2d 516 (Conn. 2002) (instructing witness and his counsel not to discuss damaging engineering report with anyone); *WellStar Health Sys., Inc. v. Kemp*, 751 S.E.2d 445 (Ga. Ct. App. 2013) (lawyers defending hospital corporation in wrongful death lawsuit sought to pressure plaintiff's expert physician to withdraw by telephoning general counsel of physician's employer); *Ky. Bar Ass'n v. Unnamed Att'y*, 414 S.W.3d 412 (Ky. 2013) (attorney who represented lawyer in disciplinary proceeding participated in improper settlement agreement requiring complainant to refuse to cooperate with bar disciplinary authorities); *In re Stanford*, 48 So. 3d 224 (La. 2010) (criminal defense lawyers procured affidavit from victim that included confidentiality provision discouraging testimony); *In re Kornreich*, 693 A.2d 877 (N.J. 1997) (attempting to dissuade witness from returning from another state to testify at trial); *see also In re Smith*, 848 P.2d 612 (Or. 1993) (lawyer for workers' compensation client sent letter to examining doctor threatening to sue him and insurer if doctor expressed particular medical opinion in course of compensation proceeding); Colo. Ethics Op. 120 (2008) (may not instruct corporate constituent not to provide information to corporation's opponent unless lawyer determines it will not be harmful to constituent); Ind. Ethics Op. 2014-1 (2014) (nondisparagement provision in settlement agreement may violate Rule 3.4(f) if it prohibits lawyer from "privately and voluntarily providing evidence to third parties for their use in litigation, upon request"); Pa. Formal Ethics Op. 2016-300 (2016) (prohibiting clause in settlement agreement precluding lawyer from subsequent use of information obtained during representation); Utah Ethics Op. 04-06 (2004) (corporation's lawyer may not direct opposing counsel not to contact corporate employees who are outside control group unless those employees have formed actual client-lawyer relationship with lawyer); Va. Ethics Op. 1854 (2010) (prosecutor may not condition plea offer upon defense lawyer's not telling defendant identity of certain prosecution witness). *See generally* Jon Bauer, *Buying Witness Silence: Evidence-Suppressing Settlements and Lawyers' Ethics*, 87 Or. L. Rev. 481 (2008).

# ADVOCATE

## Rule 3.5

### *Impartiality and*
### *Decorum of the Tribunal*

A lawyer shall not:

(a) seek to influence a judge, juror, prospective juror or other official by means prohibited by law;

(b) communicate ex parte with such a person during the proceeding unless authorized to do so by law or court order;

(c) communicate with a juror or prospective juror after discharge of the jury if:

(1) the communication is prohibited by law or court order;

(2) the juror has made known to the lawyer a desire not to communicate; or

(3) the communication involves misrepresentation, coercion, duress or harassment; or

(d) engage in conduct intended to disrupt a tribunal.

## COMMENT

[1] Many forms of improper influence upon a tribunal are proscribed by criminal law. Others are specified in the ABA Model Code of Judicial Conduct, with which an advocate should be familiar. A lawyer is required to avoid contributing to a violation of such provisions.

[2] During a proceeding a lawyer may not communicate ex parte with persons serving in an official capacity in the proceeding, such as judges, masters or jurors, unless authorized to do so by law or court order.

[3] A lawyer may on occasion want to communicate with a juror or prospective juror after the jury has been discharged. The lawyer may do so unless the communication is prohibited by law or a court order but must respect the desire of the juror not to talk with the lawyer. The lawyer may not engage in improper conduct during the communication.

[4] The advocate's function is to present evidence and argument so that the cause may be decided according to law. Refraining from abusive or obstreperous conduct is a corollary of the advocate's right to speak on behalf of litigants. A lawyer may stand firm against abuse by a judge but should avoid reciprocation; the judge's default is no justification for similar dereliction by an advocate. An advocate can present the cause, protect the record for subsequent review and preserve professional integrity by patient firmness no less effectively than by belligerence or theatrics.

[5] The duty to refrain from disruptive conduct applies to any proceeding of a tribunal, including a deposition. See Rule 1.0(m).

**Definitional Cross-References**

"Known" *See* Rule 1.0(f)

"Tribunal" *See* Rule 1.0(m)

**State Rules Comparison**

http://ambar.org/MRPCStateCharts

# ANNOTATION

## *Paragraph (a): Improper Influence*

### "PROHIBITED BY LAW"

Rule 3.5(a) prohibits a lawyer from seeking to "influence a judge, juror, prospective juror or other official by means prohibited by law." Comment [1] defines "law" to include the code of judicial conduct as well as the criminal law.

The prohibition is not limited to gifts and loans, as was its predecessor in the Model Code. Rule 3.5(a) targets any attempt to exert improper influence, including threats and other forms of pressure. *See, e.g., In re Zeno*, 517 F. Supp. 2d 591 (D.P.R. 2007) (when judge asked for more detail on Criminal Justice Act voucher she was reviewing, lawyer announced he would be filing a complaint against her; veiled threat and manipulative intent violated Rule 3.5(a)); *In re Wilder*, 764 N.E.2d 617 (Ind. 2002) (improperly obtaining ex parte temporary restraining order violates Rule 3.5 (as well as Rule 8.4(f)) by assisting judge in conduct that violates judicial code); *In re McCool*, 172 So. 3d 1038 (La. 2015) (online petitions, blogposts, and Twitter messages exhorting public to contact judges to express "horror" over proceedings in friend's custody case violated Rule 3.5(a) &(b)); *State ex rel. Counsel for Discipline v. Gast*, 896 N.W.2d 583 (Nev. 2017) (urging judge to consider judge's reputation and religious upbringing was attempt to influence judge to decide case on improper grounds, in violation of judicial code); *In re Garaas*, 652 N.W.2d 918 (N.D. 2002) (saying trial judge would be placing himself "at risk" if he continued with the proceedings was "clear threat to sue the judge personally" in violation of Rule 3.5(a)); *Lisi v. Several Att'ys*, 596 A.2d 313 (R.I. 1991) (judge coerced dozens of lawyers into lending him money; sanctions varied depending upon circumstances, including expectation of quid pro quo); Or. Ethics Op. 2005-56 (2005) (lawyers may contribute to vacation fund for semi-retired judge who still sits part-time if no intent to influence; citing state's bribery law, opinion warns that intent is fact-specific). *Compare* Me. Ethics Op. 161 (1998) (lawyers may not make or solicit contributions to support national center providing educational programs for judges even though benefit to any particular judge would be attenuated), *with* S.C. Ethics Op. 16-03 (2016) (gift from local bar association to judge permissible because likelihood of actual influence is minimal, but all contributions must be anonymous).

This is also discussed in the annotation to Rule 8.4(f).

Some authorities have also considered whether a lawyer's having influence over a judge's tenure and emoluments of office may itself count as improper influence over a judge before whom the lawyer appears. *Compare* N.M. Ethics Op. 2002-1 (2002) (lawyer should not represent clients before tribunals on which lawyer as public official has oversight or fiscal influence), *and* Okla. Ethics Op. 322 (n.d.) (lawyer serving on city council, which selects judges and approves court's budget, may not practice in city municipal courts; even though "simply being a member of the city council arguably is not an affirmative act committed with an intent to influence a judge," effect may be comparable), *with* S.C. Ethics Op. 09-06 (2009) (lawyer whose partner has been elected mayor may continue practicing in city court even though mayor sits on council; fact that council appoints city court judges does not, without more, prohibit "ordinary advocacy").

## JUDICIAL AWARDS AND HONORS

Judicial awards and honors may implicate Rule 3.5(a) as well as Rule 8.4(e) (misconduct to state or imply an ability to influence improperly a government agency or official). *See* ABA Informal Ethics Op. 86-1416 (1986) (lawyers' group with clearly defined litigation posture may not establish award program to honor particular judges before whom its members likely to appear); *cf.* N.Y. State Ethics Op. 953 (2013) (bar association members may help pay for portrait to be painted of retiring judge and presented to the courthouse, with their contributions to be publicly recognized: "We doubt that such an honor is a 'thing of value' within the meaning of Rule 3.5(a)(1).").

## HOSPITALITY AND SMALL GIFTS

Rule 3.5(a) is to be read in conjunction with Rule 3.13(B) of the Model Judicial Code, which permits judges to accept "ordinary social hospitality," and "items with little intrinsic value." *In re Corboy*, 528 N.E.2d 694 (Ill. 1988). *See* Ky. Ethics Op. E-351 (1992) (lawyer may not provide loans or gifts but may extend ordinary social hospitality to judge before whom lawyer practices); R.I. Ethics Op. 91-41 (1991) (lawyer may send flowers to judge who is hospitalized—act of ordinary social hospitality involving minimal monetary value); S.C. Ethics Op. 16-03 (2016) (application of rule requires honest assessment of lawyer's relationship with judge, occasion for, and nature of gift; "lawyer must decide whether, in light of such considerations, an outsider to the relationship would perceive the gift to arise out of the recipient's status as a judge, rather than the recipient's status as a friend"); *cf.* Va. Ethics Op. 1804 (2004) (lawyer may submit letter to judicial disciplinary body in support of judge before whom lawyer practices who is being investigated; letter is not gift but "represents participation as a citizen in a government process").

## *Paragraph (b): Unauthorized Ex Parte Communication*

### EX PARTE COMMUNICATION WITH JUDGES

Paragraph (b) prohibits ex parte communication with a judge during the course of a legal proceeding unless the communication is authorized by law or court order. *See Ex parte R.D.N.*, 918 So. 2d 100 (Ala. 2005) (reversing child custody order made on ex parte recommendation of guardian ad litem; "[i]f a guardian ad litem is to argue the case 'as any other attorney involved in [the] case,' . . . then it follows that rules of ethics [also] apply"); *In re Price*, 899 N.E.2d 645 (Ind. 2009) (lawyer procured emergency custody order without trying to serve mother); *Hancock v. Bd. of Prof'l Responsibility*, 447 S.W.3d 844 (Tenn. 2014) (after judge denied his fee petition but before lawyer filed appeal, lawyer e-mailed judge demanding explanation and apology); *In re McGrath*, 280 P.3d 1091 (Wash. 2012) (ex parte letters to judge disparaging opposing party because of her Canadian citizenship and asking judge to freeze her assets); Ky. Ethics Op. E-419 (2002) (improper for prosecutors to convene meeting with local judges to establish "shared understandings" on issues in pending and future criminal cases); N.C. Ethics Op. 97-3 (1997) (prosecutor may not initiate ex parte contact with judge to ask if judge will recuse himself from case); Pa. Ethics Op. 2007-29 (2008) (neither lawyer nor law students working at legal clinic may discuss legal research with judge who will be adjudicating cases they plan to file); *cf. State ex rel. Okla. Bar Ass'n v. Hine*, 937 P.2d 996 (Okla. 1997) (Rule 3.5 is limited to conduct as advocate and was therefore not violated when lawyer not representing any party in pending litigation sent letter to judge discussing facts of case with intent to influence outcome; letter did, however, violate Rule 8.4(d)). *See generally* George M. Cohen, *Beyond the No-Contact Rule: Ex Parte Contact by Lawyers with Nonclients*, 87 Tul. L. Rev. 1197 (June 2013) (discussing scope of Rule 3.5(b) and comparing it with Model Code and *Restatement*); Rachel C. Lee, *Ex Parte Blogging: The Legal Ethics of Supreme Court Advocacy in the Internet Era*, 61 Stan. L. Rev. 1535 (Apr. 2009) ("[B]logging directed at the Court by advocates endangers the impartiality of the Justices and the institutional legitimacy of the Court, and threatens to tilt the playing field in favor of certain interests. These risks appear substantial enough to potentially justify regulation.").

Under Rule 3.5(b), ex parte communication is barred regardless of the lawyer's motivation. *See, e.g., In re Bemis*, 938 P.2d 1120 (Ariz. 1997) (attempt to communicate ex parte with judge improper even though lawyer believed it was necessary to protect client's interests, and was not trying to gain unfair advantage); *In re Anonymous*, 729 N.E.2d 566 (Ind. 2000) (lawyer's good-faith belief he was acting in child's best interest did not justify ex parte contact with judge to obtain emergency child-custody transfer); *In re Marek*, 609 N.E.2d 419 (Ind. 1993) (motive irrelevant; lawyer sent note to trial judge discussing allegations of opposing party's sexual misconduct but did not serve copy on opposing party); *In re Lee*, 977 So. 2d 852 (La. 2008) (lawyer's disclosure of information to judge about opposing counsel's complicity in destroying evidence not justified by "good faith belief that he was disclosing another attorney's misconduct"); L.A. Cnty. Ethics Op. 514 (2005) (to avoid inadvertent ex parte communication, lawyers communicating on listserv to which judges subscribe should not discuss pending legal matters).

The prohibition applies even if the judge initiates the contact. *See* Ill. Ethics Op. 93-12 (1993) (lawyer who receives ex parte request from judge to prepare order in pending matter should suggest including opposing counsel, or should advise opposing counsel of judge's request); Mich. Informal Ethics Op. RI-195 (1994) (lawyer may not comply with judge's request to draft findings of fact and conclusions of law without notice to opposing counsel).

A lawyer who is representing a judge may, however, suggest the judge recuse himself from conducting a proceeding in which the lawyer represents a party. *See* ABA Formal Ethics Op. 07-449 (2007) (lawyer may remonstrate ex parte with client-judge to recuse himself from case lawyer involved in; "an attempt to dissuade a judge from conducting a proceeding [is not] an ex parte conversation . . . within the meaning of Rule 3.5"); Mich. Formal Ethics Op. R-20 (2008) ("communication with the judge by the judge's lawyer in this situation for the limited purpose of requesting the judge to raise the issue of disqualification is not within the meaning of 'communication about a pending matter'").

### • Communication regarding Administrative or Procedural Matters

Rule 3.5(b) presupposes that a proceeding is involved. The rule prohibits ex parte communication during "the" proceeding, but nowhere does the rule identify any proceedings. As originally adopted in 1983 the rule did not refer to proceedings at all; the quoted language was added in 2002 to be consistent with new paragraph (c), which was being added to permit certain "post-discharge" communications with jurors. See American Bar Association, *A Legislative History: The Development of the ABA Model Rules of Professional Conduct, 1982-2013*, at 495-96 (2013).

Rule 3.5(b) is more prohibitive than the Model Code of Judicial Conduct, which permits judges to engage in certain ex parte communications for "scheduling, administrative, or emergency purposes," Rule 2.9(A)(1). *See also Restatement (Third) of the Law Governing Lawyers* § 113 cmt. c (2000) ("routine and customary communications" for purposes such as scheduling hearings are permissible).

Rule 3.5(b) applies even if the communication is not on the merits. Its predecessor in the Model Code of Professional Responsibility was limited to communication on the merits; California and some other jurisdictions still use this wording, but the phrase is broadly construed. *See Matthew Zheri Corp. v. New Motor Vehicle Bd.*, 64 Cal. Rptr. 2d 705 (Ct. App. 1997) (communication is on the merits within California's Rule 5-300 if it is information in which opponents would be interested); San Diego Cnty. Formal Ethics Op. 2013-2 (2013) (communication that refers to a pending matter will "virtually always" be considered on the merits).

### • Communication Authorized by Law or Court Order

Rule 3.5(b) contains an exception for communication that is "authorized . . . by law or court order." Because there is no longer an exception for scheduling or administrative matters, whether any given communication is permissible must be determined by each jurisdiction's court rules, civil procedure rules, and caselaw. *See, e.g.*, Ill. Ethics Op. 93-12 (1994) (assistant state's attorney may not contact judge ex parte to obtain emergency stay of bail reduction order except as permitted by statute); N.C. Ethics Op. 2001-15 (2002) (statute allowing prosecutor to apply to judge "at any time" for bond modification does not permit application ex parte); Or. Ethics Op. 2005-134 (2005) (county counsel is authorized by state law to give ex parte advice to county hearing officer reviewing land use decisions of county planning board); *cf. In re Carmick*, 48 P.3d 311 (Wash. 2002) (though ex parte application otherwise permissible, lawyer who falsely said all parties had approved his proposed order could not invoke exception for communication authorized by law). *See generally* Leslie W. Abramson, *The Judicial Ethics of Ex Parte and Other Communications*, 37 Hous. L. Rev. 1343 (Winter 2000) (analyzing different treatment of ex parte communications in judicial and lawyer ethics rules); Roberta K. Flowers, *An Unholy Alliance: The Ex Parte Relationship Between the Judge and the Prosecutor*, 79 Neb. L. Rev. 251 (2000) (investigation, discovery, and safety are areas of permissible ex parte communication; author suggests safeguards to avoid impermissibly cooperative relationship between prosecutor and trial judge).

The acknowledgement that an ex parte communication during the proceeding may be authorized by court order (as well as by law) was added in 2002 to "alert lawyers to the availability of judicial relief in the rare situation in which an ex parte communication is needed." American Bar Association, *A Legislative History: The Development of the ABA Model Rules of Professional Conduct, 1982–2013*, at 496 (2013). *See Stevens v. State*, 770 N.E.2d 739 (Ind. 2002) (trial court may, upon showing of good cause, permit defendant's request for public funds to be made ex parte).

## • *Written Submissions to Judges*

As a rule, copies of all submissions to a judge must be furnished simultaneously to opposing counsel. *See In re Eadie*, 36 P.3d 468 (Or. 2001) (filing disqualification motion without notice to opposing counsel); *In re White*, 492 S.E.2d 82 (S.C. 1997) (after entry of default, lawyer wrote letter to judge commenting on merits of case and making disparaging comments about opposing counsel and parties without sending copy to opposing counsel); *Barrett v. Va. State Bar*, 611 S.E.2d 375 (Va. 2005) (lawyer acting pro se in own divorce sent letter to judge and guardian ad litem without copying wife's lawyer).

Last-minute delivery of papers to opposing counsel is not enough. *See, e.g., In re Wilder*, 764 N.E.2d 617 (Ind. 2002) (sending secretary to opposing counsel's office with copies of pleadings while lawyer met with judge to obtain temporary injunction did not amount to meaningful notice); N.C. Ethics Op. 97-5 (1998) (must simultaneously copy opposing counsel on any written communication to judge, and must tell judge opposing counsel has not yet had chance to respond); Phila. Ethics Op. 98-15 (1999) (communication with judge must be "contemporaneous" with communication to opposing party, "at a minimum by the same method of communication").

## EX PARTE COMMUNICATION WITH ADMINISTRATIVE LAW JUDGES AND OTHER OFFICIALS

The prohibition on ex parte communication with judges and other officials under Rule 3.5(b) has been held to apply to communication with administrative law judges and others serving in similar capacities. *See, e.g., Matthew Zaheri Corp. v. Mitsubishi Motor Sales of Am.*, 64 Cal. Rptr. 2d 705 (Ct. App. 1997) (no principled distinction between judge and administrative law judge for purposes of ethics rule); *In re Lacava*, 615 N.E.2d 93 (Ind. 1993) (members of medical malpractice review panel are "officials" for purposes of Rule 3.5); N.Y. State Ethics Op. 838 (2010) (unless agency has its own rule, Rule 3.5 applies to adversarial administrative agency matter in which decision is to be rendered by neutral official); Okla. Ethics Op. 313 (2000) (court-appointed commissioners in eminent domain proceeding are "officials" or "other decision makers" under state's version of Rule 3.5(b)); Phila. Ethics Op. 95-8 (1995) (lawyer may not communicate ex parte with arbitrator his client selected unless parties have otherwise agreed or arbitration rules allow it). *Compare* Kan. Ethics Op. 2000-06 (2002) (rule does not apply to city zoning officials because zoning matters not adversarial), *with* Tex. Ethics Op. 604 (2011) (lawyer may not communicate or cause client to communicate privately with state agency board members to influence them about planned permit application).

### • *When Hearing Officer Is Also Agency Head*

Many statutory schemes provide for hearings before administrative agency heads, department heads, or their appointees. When the agency head is simultaneously the "client" of the state or municipal lawyer handling the case, questions arise about whether communication between staff counsel and the agency head are permitted or perhaps required, in light of counsel's obligations to "keep [his or her] client reasonably informed about the status of the matter" (Rule 1.4(a)(3)), and to ascertain the client's "decisions concerning the objectives of representation" (Rule 1.2(a)). *See In re Op. No. 583 of Advisory Comm. on Prof'l Ethics*, 526 A.2d 692 (N.J. 1987) (ex parte communication permitted during prosecutorial phase, when agency head functions primarily as client, but not during review phase, when agency head reviews administrative officer's report and may reject or modify it).

### EX PARTE COMMUNICATION WITH JURORS DURING COURSE OF LEGAL PROCEEDINGS

Rule 3.5(b) bars ex parte communication with jurors during a legal proceeding "unless authorized . . . by law or court order." *See, e.g., Fla. Bar v. Peterson*, 418 So. 2d 246 (Fla. 1982) (misconduct to sit with two jurors at restaurant during trial recess, despite lack of ulterior motive); *In re Nelson*, 750 S.E.2d 85 (S.C. 2013) (assistant prosecutor repeatedly communicated with cousin on jury before and during criminal trial handled by lawyer's office colleagues).

Researching jurors or venire members through social-media websites that generate "friend" requests or notifications that the lawyer is "following" the juror is generally deemed a violation of the rule. *See, e.g., Sluss v. Commonwealth*, 381 S.W.3d 215 (Ky. 2012) (lawyer may research jurors using social-media websites if no communications or notifications to jurors result); N.Y. City Ethics Op. 2012-2 (2012) (same); N.Y. Cnty. Ethics Op. 743 (2011) (sending "friend" request to or "following" juror through social media constitutes communication prohibited by Rule 3.5); Or. Ethics Op. 2013-189 (2013) (may not e-mail juror asking for access to juror's social-media website). *But see* ABA Formal Ethics Op. 466 (2014) (may not send social-media connection request to juror, but notification to juror that lawyer accessed juror's internet profile page as result of juror's internet settings is not communication from lawyer).

## *Paragraph (c): Communication with Jurors after Discharge of Jury*

Paragraph (c) was added in 2002 in light of a decision finding the blanket prohibition against post-trial contact in the prior version of the Model Rules unconstitutionally overbroad as applied to post-verdict juror communication. *Rapp v. Disciplinary Bd. of Haw. Supreme Court*, 916 F. Supp. 1525 (D. Haw. 1996).

Paragraph (c) permits the communication unless it is already prohibited by law or court order, or the lawyer knows the juror does not want to be contacted, or it involves misrepresentation, coercion, duress, or harassment. This permits more post-verdict juror contact than the pre-amendment version of the rule but also affords jurors greater protection than the predecessor Model Code, which limited the prohibition to questions or comments "calculated merely to harass or embarrass the juror to influence his actions in future jury service." DR 7-108. American Bar Association, *A Legislative History: The Development of the ABA Model Rules of Professional Conduct, 1982–2013*, at 496 (2013). *See Adams v. Ford Motor Co.*, 653 F.3d 299 (3d Cir. 2011) (lawyer's post-verdict telephone call to juror inquiring about damage award and allocation of fault did not violate Rule 3.5(c)(2) or (3)); *State v. Cabrera*, 984 A.2d 149 (Del. Super. Ct. 2008) (upholding Rule 3.5(c) against convicted murderer's constitutional challenge); Wash. Ethics Op. 2204 (2010) (after verdict, prosecutors may discuss case with jurors and disclose evidence excluded from trial).

## COMMUNICATION PROHIBITED BY LAW OR COURT ORDER

Rule 3.5(b), on communication during the proceeding, is phrased as a prohibition with exceptions, but Rule 3.5(c)(1), on post-discharge communication, is phrased the other way around. Rule 3.5(c)(1) permits post-discharge communication unless the communication is already prohibited by law or court order. "Law" includes rules of evidence and civil procedure, and local rules of court. *See Williams v. Lawton*, 207 P.3d 1027 (Kan. 2009) (under Rule 3.5 and rules of civil procedure "attorneys may discuss a trial with willing jurors after their discharge . . . without seeking permission . . . unless contrary orders have been given"); *L.S. v. Miss. Bar*, 649 So. 2d 810 (Miss. 1994) (lawyer who contacted juror and alternate juror after lengthy medical malpractice case and falsely represented he had approval to do so violated Rule 3.5 by disobeying court's order not to talk to them); Or. Ethics Op. 2005-143 (2005) (if prohibited by state law and local rule of district court, Rule 3.5(c) prohibits lawyer from interviewing jurors after discharge); *see also Diettrich v. Nw. Airlines, Inc.*, 168 F.3d 961 (7th Cir. 1999) (lawyers' use of post-verdict dialogue with jury to support motion to overturn verdict was outside scope of district court's permission to interview jurors informally, and impermissibly "invite[d] the court to open the black box that is the jury room"); *Commonwealth v. Moore*, 52 N.E.3d 126 (Mass. 2016) (suggesting an instruction to discharged jurors that they are free to decline to talk to counsel and a protocol for notifying opposing counsel); *cf. Troy v. State*, 57 So. 3d 828 (Fla. 2011) (upholding state rule's prohibition on initiating communication with juror unless lawyer has reason to believe verdict is subject to challenge; no right to a fishing expedition).

## COMMUNICATION INVOLVING MISREPRESENTATION, COERCION, DURESS, OR HARASSMENT

Rule 3.5(c)(3) prohibits post-discharge communication with jurors that involves "misrepresentation, coercion, duress or harassment." *See, e.g.,* Mo. Informal Ethics Op. 970168 (1997) (criminal defense lawyer may contact discharged jurors while case on appeal, but must avoid conduct or questioning that may be viewed as harassment); Pa. Ethics Op. 91-52 (1991) (lawyer whose client was found liable in product-liability case may assign paralegal to telephone jurors for post-trial interviews, provided no intimidation or pressure); Phila. Ethics Op. 91-27 (1991) (after verdict in civil case, lawyer may distribute questionnaire about jurors' backgrounds, views on political issues, and reactions to specifics of trial, provided (1) no violation of local court rules and customs regarding prior judicial approval; (2) no harassment or embarrassment; (3) no attempt to influence juror's actions in future; and (4) questionnaire states juror has right to refuse to answer any question).

### *Paragraph (d): Conduct Intended to Disrupt Tribunal*

Paragraph (d) (renumbered in 2002 from paragraph (c)) prohibits a lawyer from engaging in "conduct intended to disrupt a tribunal." Its analog in the predecessor Model Code was limited to behavior when appearing before a tribunal as a lawyer, but was phrased in more general terms to prohibit engaging in "undignified or discourteous conduct which is degrading to a tribunal." The flavor survives in Comment [4]'s language about "[r]efraining from abusive or obstreperous conduct," which is frequently cited in opinions interpreting Rule 3.5(d). *See Fla. Bar v. Martocci,* 791 So. 2d 1074 (Fla. 2001) (lawyer crossed line from zealous advocacy to misconduct; profane, belittling insults to opposing litigant, her family, and her counsel included sticking out his tongue and calling litigant "nut case" and "stupid idiot"); *Lawyer Disciplinary Bd. v. Turgeon,* 557 S.E.2d 235 (W. Va. 2000) (lawyer for murder defendant violated Rule 3.5 by referring to prosecutor as "coke dealer" in front of jury and falsely telling jury both defendant and his wife had taken polygraph tests); *see also* Rule 8.4(d) (prohibiting conduct prejudicial to the administration of justice).

A judge's improper actions will not excuse a lawyer's violation of Rule 3.5(d); "the judge's default is no justification for similar dereliction by an advocate." Cmt. [4]. The advice to the lawyer is to "stand firm against abuse by a judge but . . . avoid reciprocation." *Id. See, e.g., Office of Disciplinary Counsel v. Breiner,* 969 P.2d 1285 (Haw. 1999) (lawyer's belief he was object of abusive trial judge could not justify disrespectful and argumentative courtroom conduct); *In re Turner,* 631 N.E.2d 918 (Ind. 1994) (court acknowledged that small-claims court judge had not remained in control of courtroom and had appeared to give preferential treatment to lawyer's opponent, but reprimanded lawyer for saying it was a "Mickey Mouse Court" and walking out); *see also Office of Disciplinary Counsel v. Mills,* 755 N.E.2d 336 (Ohio 2001) ("even if [the magistrate or opposing counsel] had acted improperly, the appropriate response is not to retaliate with a temper tantrum").

Normally, the disruptive conduct prohibited by Rule 3.5(d) is addressed by the judge hearing the matter, who may use any of a variety of sanctions including contempt. *See, e.g., United States v. Ortlieb*, 274 F.3d 871 (5th Cir. 2001) (affirming criminal contempt conviction of defense lawyer under 18 U.S.C. § 401(1) for vulgar and inappropriate comments to prosecutor and court at bench conferences during six-week trial); *United States v. Engstrom*, 16 F.3d 1006 (9th Cir. 1994) (affirming revocation of lawyer's pro hac vice status and suspension from practice within district but reversing criminal contempt, for lawyer's disrespectful and confrontational remarks to district judge in challenging his impartiality); *Boswell v. Gumbaytay*, No. 2:07-CV-135-WKW, 2009 WL 1515884, 2009 BL 350920 (M.D. Ala. June 1, 2009) (disqualification, reference to state bar, and report to chief judge of district court; lawyer kept filing "abusive and harassing documents replete with demeaning and derogatory name-calling and vituperous accusations" even after monetary sanctions were imposed); *GMAC Bank v. HTFC Corp.*, 248 F.R.D. 182 (E.D. Pa. 2008) (lawyer and client jointly and severally liable for fees and costs awarded under Fed. R. Civ. P. 30(d)(2) & 37(a)(5)(A) for abuse of opposing counsel during deposition; opinion warns of possible referral for discipline if behavior continues); *Miss. Bar v. Lumumba*, 912 So. 2d 871 (Miss. 2005) (lawyer held in contempt and later disciplined for, among other things, offering to advise judge how he "can, perhaps, get along better with lawyers in the future"); *see also Thomas v. Tenneco Packaging Co.*, 293 F.3d 1306 (11th Cir. 2002) (collecting cases sanctioning lawyers for unsubstantiated accusations and demeaning comments directed at opposing counsel). *See generally* Douglas R. Richmond, *Alternative Sanctions in Litigation*, 47 N.M. L. Rev. 209 (Summer 2017).

## INSIDE OR OUTSIDE COURTROOM

Rule 3.5(d) clearly applies to disruptive behavior inside the courtroom. *See, e.g., In re Moncier*, 550 F. Supp. 2d 768 (E.D. Tenn. 2008) (disrupted proceeding by interrupting and talking over judge); *Fla. Bar v. Norkin*, 132 So. 3d 77 (Fla. 2013) (rudeness, yelling, and antagonistic style towards bench "made it difficult for the judges to conduct proceedings"); *In re Romious*, 240 P.3d 945 (Kan. 2010) (calling municipal court a "kangaroo court" during public proceedings); *In re Larvadain*, 664 So. 2d 395 (La. 1995) (cursing, trying to intimidate judge, and accusing him of racism); *In re Coe*, 903 S.W.2d 916 (Mo. 1995) (lawyer openly argued with court's rulings, gestured, and accused trial court of unfair practices); *In re Vincenti*, 704 A.2d 927 (N.J. 1998) (disbarring lawyer who engaged in pattern of harassment, intimidation, and insulting behavior toward judges, witnesses, and opposing counsel); *Ciardi v. Office of Prof'l Conduct*, 379 P.3d 1287 (Utah 2016) (interrupted calendar call, ignored judge's instructions to sit down, caused disturbance as bailiff escorted him from courtroom); *cf. In re Kirschner*, 793 N.W.2d 196 (N.D. 2011) (failing to appear in court for scheduled trial).

The rule has also been applied to conduct not technically in the courtroom. *See, e.g., Fla. Bar v. Wasserman*, 675 So. 2d 103 (Fla. 1996) (profane out-of-court statements to judicial assistant and contemptuous behavior toward judge during hearing); *In re Moore*, 665 N.E.2d 40 (Ind. 1996) (in judge's chambers, lawyer struck opposing counsel). *But see In re Stuhff*, 837 P.2d 853 (Nev. 1992) (filing and serving disciplinary complaint on judge did not involve "in-court disruption"; more appropriate to treat it as conduct prejudicial to administration of justice).

In 2002, Comment [5] was added to clarify that the prohibition applies to any proceeding of a tribunal, including a deposition. American Bar Association, *A Legislative History: The Development of the ABA Model Rules of Professional Conduct, 1982–2013*, at 497 (2013). *See, e.g., Fla. Bar v. Ratiner*, 238 So. 3d 117 (Fla. 2018) (lawyer said "lie, lie, lie" during opposing counsel's examination of witness, and kept kicking leg of counsel table loudly and disruptively; disbarred in light of previous record); *Fla. Bar v. Ratiner*, 46 So. 3d 35 (Fla. 2013) (when opposing counsel placed evidence sticker on lawyer's laptop during eight-day deposition, lawyer "forcefully leaned" over table and harangued him, tearing sticker up and tossing it towards him; sanctions included mental health counseling, letters of apology, and either videotaping or bringing an approved co-counsel to any proceedings judge is not presiding over); *In re McClure*, 652 N.E.2d 863 (Ind. 1995) (lawyer threw contents of soft drink cup on plaintiff's counsel deposing lawyer's wife, who was also his co-defendant, and grabbed him "near or around his neck, restraining him in his chair").

## DOCUMENTS

The rule extends to pleadings and briefs. *See, e.g., In re Cordova-Gonzalez*, 996 F.2d 1334 (1st Cir. 1993) (pleadings with vitriolic slurs "degrading to the law, the bar and the court"); *In re Oladiran*, No. MC-10-0025-PHX-DGC, 2010 WL 3775074, 2010 BL 223466 (D. Ariz. Sept. 21, 2010) ("motion for an honest and honorable court system" referring to judge as "Dishonorable" and a "brainless coward" was "abusive, obstreperous, and disrupted the proceedings"); *People v. Maynard*, 238 P.3d 672 (Colo. O.P.D.J. 2009) (repeated motions to recuse assigned judge, filed up to eve of trial, as tactic to delay proceedings); *In re Shearin*, 721 A.2d 157 (Del. 1998) (appellate brief contained personal attacks on trial judge and suggested judge had been bribed by opponent); *In re McClellan*, 754 N.E.2d 500 (Ind. 2001) (petition for rehearing said court's prior decision "reads like a bad lawyer joke"); *Ky. Bar Ass'n v. Blum*, 404 S.W.3d 841 (Ky. 2013) (lawyer "filed repetitive pleadings, delayed the adjudicatory process, and sought extra-judicial resolution in order to receive a de novo tribunal hearing" contrary to court's order).

Letters and e-mails to the court have also been found to violate Rule 3.5(d). *See, e.g., In re Madison*, 282 S.W.3d 350 (Mo. 2009) (angry letters to judges who ruled against lawyer's clients); *Hancock v. Bd. of Prof'l Responsibility*, 447 S.W.3d 844 (Tenn. 2014) (e-mail to judge after denial of fee petition with "threatening tone" was "abusive" and "obstreperous" conduct). *See generally* W. Bradley Wendel, *Free Speech for Lawyers*, 28 Hastings Const. L.Q. 305 (Winter 2001) (suggesting synthesis of constitutional, ethical, and regulatory norms).

This topic is discussed in the annotation to Rule 8.2 (Judicial and Legal Officials) and Rule 8.4 (Misconduct).

## Rule 3.6
### *Trial Publicity*

(a) A lawyer who is participating or has participated in the investigation or litigation of a matter shall not make an extrajudicial statement that the lawyer knows or reasonably should know will be disseminated by means of public communication and will have a substantial likelihood of materially prejudicing an adjudicative proceeding in the matter.

(b) Notwithstanding paragraph (a), a lawyer may state:

(1) the claim, offense or defense involved and, except when prohibited by law, the identity of the persons involved;

(2) information contained in a public record;

(3) that an investigation of a matter is in progress;

(4) the scheduling or result of any step in litigation;

(5) a request for assistance in obtaining evidence and information necessary thereto;

(6) a warning of danger concerning the behavior of a person involved, when there is reason to believe that there exists the likelihood of substantial harm to an individual or to the public interest; and

(7) in a criminal case, in addition to subparagraphs (1) through (6):

(i) the identity, residence, occupation and family status of the accused;

(ii) if the accused has not been apprehended, information necessary to aid in apprehension of that person;

(iii) the fact, time and place of arrest; and

(iv) the identity of investigating and arresting officers or agencies and the length of the investigation.

(c) Notwithstanding paragraph (a), a lawyer may make a statement that a reasonable lawyer would believe is required to protect a client from the substantial undue prejudicial effect of recent publicity not initiated by the lawyer or the lawyer's client. A statement made pursuant to this paragraph shall be limited to such information as is necessary to mitigate the recent adverse publicity.

(d) No lawyer associated in a firm or government agency with a lawyer subject to paragraph (a) shall make a statement prohibited by paragraph (a).

## COMMENT

[1] It is difficult to strike a balance between protecting the right to a fair trial and safeguarding the right of free expression. Preserving the right to a fair trial necessarily entails some curtailment of the information that may be disseminated about a party prior to trial, particularly where trial by jury is involved. If there were no such limits, the result would be the practical nullification of the protective effect of the rules of forensic decorum and the exclusionary rules of evidence. On the other hand, there are vital social interests served by the free dissemination of information about events having legal consequences and about legal proceedings themselves. The public has a right to know about threats to its safety and measures aimed at assuring its security. It also has a legitimate interest in the conduct of judicial proceedings, particularly in matters of general public concern. Furthermore, the subject matter of legal proceedings is often of direct significance in debate and deliberation over questions of public policy.

[2] Special rules of confidentiality may validly govern proceedings in juvenile, domestic relations and mental disability proceedings, and perhaps other types of litigation. Rule 3.4(c) requires compliance with such rules.

[3] The Rule sets forth a basic general prohibition against a lawyer's making statements that the lawyer knows or should know will have a substantial likelihood of materially prejudicing an adjudicative proceeding. Recognizing that the public value of informed commentary is great and the likelihood of prejudice to a proceeding by the commentary of a lawyer who is not involved in the proceeding is small, the Rule applies only to lawyers who are, or who have been involved in the investigation or litigation of a case, and their associates.

[4] Paragraph (b) identifies specific matters about which a lawyer's statements would not ordinarily be considered to present a substantial likelihood of material prejudice, and should not in any event be considered prohibited by the general prohibition of paragraph (a). Paragraph (b) is not intended to be an exhaustive listing of the subjects upon which a lawyer may make a statement, but statements on other matters may be subject to paragraph (a).

[5] There are, on the other hand, certain subjects that are more likely than not to have a material prejudicial effect on a proceeding, particularly when they refer to a civil matter triable to a jury, a criminal matter, or any other proceeding that could result in incarceration. These subjects relate to:

(1) the character, credibility, reputation or criminal record of a party, suspect in a criminal investigation or witness, or the identity of a witness, or the expected testimony of a party or witness;

(2) in a criminal case or proceeding that could result in incarceration, the possibility of a plea of guilty to the offense or the existence or contents of any confession, admission, or statement given by a defendant or suspect or that person's refusal or failure to make a statement;

(3) the performance or results of any examination or test or the refusal or failure of a person to submit to an examination or test, or the identity or nature of physical evidence expected to be presented;

(4) any opinion as to the guilt or innocence of a defendant or suspect in a criminal case or proceeding that could result in incarceration;

(5) information that the lawyer knows or reasonably should know is likely to be inadmissible as evidence in a trial and that would, if disclosed, create a substantial risk of prejudicing an impartial trial; or

(6) the fact that a defendant has been charged with a crime, unless there is included therein a statement explaining that the charge is merely an accusation and that the defendant is presumed innocent until and unless proven guilty.

[6] Another relevant factor in determining prejudice is the nature of the proceeding involved. Criminal jury trials will be most sensitive to extrajudicial speech. Civil trials may be less sensitive. Non-jury hearings and arbitration proceedings may be even less affected. The Rule will still place limitations on prejudicial comments in these cases, but the likelihood of prejudice may be different depending on the type of proceeding.

[7] Finally, extrajudicial statements that might otherwise raise a question under this Rule may be permissible when they are made in response to statements made publicly by another party, another party's lawyer, or third persons, where a reasonable lawyer would believe a public response is required in order to avoid prejudice to the lawyer's client. When prejudicial statements have been publicly made by others, responsive statements may have the salutary effect of lessening any resulting adverse impact on the adjudicative proceeding. Such responsive statements should be limited to contain only such information as is necessary to mitigate undue prejudice created by the statements made by others.

[8] See Rule 3.8(f) for additional duties of prosecutors in connection with extrajudicial statements about criminal proceedings.

## Definitional Cross-References
"Firm" *See* Rule 1.0(c)
"Knows" *See* Rule 1.0(f)
"Reasonable" *See* Rule 1.0(h)
"Reasonably should know" *See* Rule 1.0(j)
"Substantial" *See* Rule 1.0(l)

## State Rules Comparison
http://ambar.org/MRPCStateCharts

## ANNOTATION
### LAWYER MAY NOT USE PUBLICITY TO PREJUDICE CASE
Rule 3.6 restricts a lawyer who is taking or has taken part in a matter from making out-of-court statements that the lawyer "knows or reasonably should know" will be publicly disseminated and "will have a substantial likelihood of materially prejudicing an adjudicative proceeding in the matter." Rule 3.6(a). *See, e.g., Kramer v. Tribe*, 156 F.R.D. 96 (D.N.J. 1994) (lawyers' use of media "to publicize their cases as a litigation tactic . . . must stop if the integrity of the judicial enterprise is to be preserved"); *In re Brizzi*, 962 N.E.2d 1240 (Ind. 2012) (prosecutor stated at press conference about mur-

der case that he "would not trade all the money and drugs in the world for the life of one person, let alone seven," that defendant "deserves the ultimate penalty," and that "[t]he evidence is overwhelming" and any other result "would be a travesty"); *State ex rel. Counsel for Discipline v. Island*, 894 N.W.2d 804 (Neb. 2017) (defense counsel issued press release during criminal trial suggesting prosecutor lacked integrity); Pa. Formal Ethics Op. 2014-300 (2014) (lawyer involved in pending matter may not post about matter on social media); W. Va. Ethics Op. 2015-02 (2015) (lawyer's statements on social media website are restricted by Rule 3.6, even if privacy settings limiting access are in place); *see also* ABA Formal Ethics Op. 480 (2018) (Rule 3.6 among rules that apply to participating lawyer's comments about matter in blogs, tweets, and other public communications). *See generally* Nicholas A. Battaglia, *The Casey Anthony Trial and Wrongful Exonerations: How "Trial by Media" Cases Diminish Public Confidence in the Criminal Justice System*, 75 Alb. L. Rev. 1579 (2012); Erwin Chemerinsky, *Silence Is Not Golden: Protecting Lawyer Speech Under the First Amendment*, 47 Emory L.J. 859 (Summer 1998); Leigh A. Krahenbuhl, *Advocacy in the Media: The Blagojevich Defense and a Reformulation of Rule 3.6*, 61 Duke L.J. 167 (Oct. 2011).

Not all public statements about a matter create a substantial likelihood of prejudice. *See United Servs. Auto. Ass'n v. Lisanby*, 47 So. 3d 1172 (Miss. 2010) (lawyer's assertion to reporter that his client "should win" would not have substantial likelihood of material prejudice "even if overheard by the jurors"); *see also EEOC v. McCormick & Schmick's Seafood Rests., Inc.*, No. WMN-08-CV-984, 2011 WL 1526967, 2011 BL 332301 (D. Md. Mar. 17, 2011) (EEOC radio announcement inviting "black individuals who applied for employment at or used to work for" restaurant to telephone agency "in connection with the class race discrimination lawsuit" fell within Rule 3.6(b)'s safe-harbor investigation exception); N.Y. State Ethics Op. 977 (2013) (lawyer may use social media to disseminate survey and link to online petition in support of client's administrative trademark proceeding if no substantial likelihood of prejudice exists). *See generally* Nicola A. Boothe-Perry, *The "Friend"ly Lawyer: Professionalism and Ethical Considerations of the Use of Social Networking During Litigation*, 24 U. Fla. J.L. & Pub. Pol'y 127 (Apr. 2013) (discussing desirability of additional ethical guidance for lawyers' communications via social media regarding matters in litigation); Jessica A. Hinkie, *Free Speech and Rule 3.6: How the Object of Attorney Speech Affects the Right to Make Public Criticism*, 20 Geo. J. Legal Ethics 695 (Summer 2007) (noting that "target of attorney speech is undoubtedly a part of a Rule 3.6 determination, with judges receiving more protection from attorney speech than either prosecutors or the court system as a whole").

By its terms, the rule applies not only to lawyers currently representing clients but also to those who "participated in the investigation or litigation of a matter." Rule 3.6(a). *See In re Duncan*, 533 S.E.2d 894 (S.C. 2000) (lawyer who had been replaced by public defender took recording of conversation with client provided by public defender to local television station "to influence the upcoming trial to the [former] client's advantage"); *In re Sommers*, 851 N.W.2d 458 (Wis. 2014) (lawyer posted to internet and sent to all state supreme court justices his letter to chief justice asserting prosecutorial misconduct in case in which lawyer served as defense counsel during pendency of disciplinary charges against both lawyers based on their conduct in same case).

## CONSTITUTIONALITY

The constitutionality of Rule 3.6's "substantial likelihood of material prejudice" standard was the subject of a landmark decision by the U.S. Supreme Court. In *Gentile v. State Bar*, 501 U.S. 1030 (1991), a divided Court approved the standard, holding that when lawyers are participating in a pending proceeding, the U.S. Constitution does not require a "clear and present danger of prejudice" standard. The Court reasoned that lawyers participating in pending cases have "special access to information through discovery and client communication." Their statements pose a heightened threat to the fair administration of justice, "since [they] are likely to be received as especially authoritative." In addition, statements made during the pendency of a case are "likely to influence the actual outcome of the trial" or "prejudice the jury venire, even if an untainted panel can ultimately be found." *Cf. United States v. Wecht*, 484 F.3d 194 (3d Cir. 2007) (amending district court rule that prohibited certain pretrial lawyer speech to comply with *Gentile*/Rule 3.6 standard: "we now exercise our supervisory authority to require that district courts apply Local Rule 83.1 to prohibit only speech that is substantially likely to materially prejudice ongoing criminal proceedings").

However, the *Gentile* Court ultimately ruled that the Nevada rule (virtually identical to the version of Model Rule 3.6 in effect at the time), as interpreted by the Nevada Supreme Court, was void for vagueness because of its safe-harbor provision. Allowing a lawyer to state the general nature of a claim or defense "without elaboration" conflicted with the provision (since relocated to the comment) admonishing that certain comments were likely to prejudice a jury. "The lawyer has no principle for determining when his remarks pass from the safe harbor of the general to the forbidden sea of the elaborated," the Court declared. *See* L. Cooper Campbell, Gentile v. State Bar *and Model Rule 3.6: Overly Broad Restrictions on Attorney Speech and Pretrial Publicity*, 6 Geo. J. Legal Ethics 583 (Winter 1993); *see also* Colo. Ethics Op. 130 (2017) (noting restrictions of Rule 3.6 and stating they must be balanced with lawyer's constitutional right to free expression).

### • *Amendments after* Gentile

Rule 3.6 was amended substantially in 1994 to cure the constitutional problems identified in *Gentile*. Current paragraph (c), for example, was added to allow lawyers to make extrajudicial statements to protect clients from "recent publicity not initiated by the lawyer or the lawyer's client," the justification offered by Gentile himself to the Nevada disciplinary authorities. Details of the 1994 amendments to the rule are set out in American Bar Association, *A Legislative History: The Development of the ABA Model Rules of Professional Conduct, 1982–2013*, at 508–11 (2013). *See generally* Christopher A. Brown, Note, *The Worsening Problem of Trial Publicity: Is "New" Model Rule 3.6 Solution or Surrender?*, 29 Ind. L. Rev. 379 (1995); Catherine Cupp Theisen, Comment, *The New Model Rule 3.6: An Old Pair of Shoes*, 44 U. Kan. L. Rev. 837 (July 1996).

In 2002, the "reasonable person" standard of Rule 3.6(a) was replaced by a "reasonable lawyer" standard: the likelihood that a statement will be publicized, as well as its potential for prejudice, are to be judged against what a lawyer reasonably should know. *See* American Bar Association, *A Legislative History: The Development of the ABA Model Rules of Professional Conduct, 1982–2013*, at 511–12 (2013); *cf. Bd. of Prof'l*

*Responsibility v. Murray*, 143 P.3d 353 (Wyo. 2006) (prosecutor's comments to local newspaper reporter about pending case violated rule modeled on pre-2002 version of Model Rule 3.6, as "reasonable person would expect" comments to be publicly disseminated).

## • *"Public Record"*

A lawyer's public recitation of facts contained in public records such as court pleadings is protected by the "safe harbor" provision of Rule 3.6(b)(2). *See Muex v. State*, 800 N.E.2d 249 (Ind. Ct. App. 2003) (affirming criminal conviction despite prosecutor's pretrial newspaper interview discussing affidavit of probable cause because defendant "does not provide cogent argument as to why the Affidavit of Probable Cause was not a public document"); *PCG Trading, LLC v. Seyfarth Shaw, LLP*, 951 N.E.2d 315 (Mass. 2011) (lawyer's remark, quoted in legal publication, that defendant law firm "misstated the facts," directly tracked allegations of complaint, which was public record); *see also Att'y Grievance Comm'n v. Gansler*, 835 A.2d 548 (Md. 2003) (because term "public record" in Rule 3.6(b)'s safe-harbor exception had no "settled definition," it would be construed as broadly as possible to include "anything in the public domain, including public court documents, media reports, and comments made by police officers"; in future, phrase "should refer only to public government records—the records and papers on file with a government entity to which an ordinary citizen would have lawful access"). *See generally* William Scott Croft, *Free Speech & Fair Trial—Striking the Balance: A Case Comment and Analysis of the Maryland Trial Publicity Rule as Applied in* Attorney Grievance Commission of Maryland v. Douglas F. Gansler, 19 Geo. J. Legal Ethics 345 (Winter 2006).

## GAG ORDERS

The U.S. Supreme Court in *Gentile* approved the "substantial likelihood of material prejudice" standard in the disciplinary context. However, when it comes to "gag orders"—injunctions that often apply to any public comment and that may apply not only to lawyers but also to parties and witnesses—the constitutional standard remains unsettled. *See, e.g., United States v. Scarfo*, 263 F.3d 80 (3d Cir. 2001) (applying *Gentile* standard to invalidate gag order imposed upon disqualified defense lawyer); *United States v. Brown*, 218 F.3d 415 (5th Cir. 2000) ("substantial likelihood" that comments by trial participants would prejudice court's ability to conduct fair trial); *In re Morrissey*, 168 F.3d 134 (4th Cir. 1999) (concluding "reasonable likelihood" standard constitutionally permissible under *Gentile*); *United States v. Cutler*, 58 F.3d 825 (2d Cir. 1995) (upholding order requiring defense lawyer to comply with local rule prohibiting certain categories of remarks if remarks "reasonably likely to interfere with fair trial or administration of justice"); *United States v. Schock*, No. 16-cr-30061, 2016 WL 7176578, 2016 BL 411302 (C.D. Ill. Dec. 9, 2016) (defendant's public statements, including assertions of innocence, did not meet standard for gag order, but court admonished parties to continue to comply with Rule 3.6); *Doe v. Rose*, No. CV-15-07503-MWF-JCx, 2016 WL 9107137 (C.D. Cal. Sept. 30, 2016) (gag order requires lawyers "to do what they already have an obligation to do" under California rule identical to Model Rule 3.6); *Graham v. Weber*, No. CIV 13-4100, 2015 WL 5797857, 2015 BL

327733 (D.S.D. Oct. 5, 2015) (affirming *Gentile*'s standard in denying request for gag order in post-conviction action; proceeding underway was unlikely to be affected by out-of-court statements, possibility of trial was too speculative to warrant gag order, and public had legitimate interest in publicity); *Laugier v. City of New York*, No. 13-CV-6171 (JMF), 2014 WL 6655283, 2014 BL 331148 (S.D.N.Y. Nov. 24, 2014) (adopting New York Rule 3.6 as order of court and warning counsel that violation may be punished as any other violation of court orders); *United States v. McGregor*, 838 F. Supp. 2d 1256 (M.D. Ala. 2012) (ordering prosecutor and defense counsel to comply with state ethics rule governing trial publicity is less restrictive than, and preferable to, gag order); *United States v. Corbin*, 620 F. Supp. 2d 400 (E.D.N.Y. 2009) (refusing to impose defendant's requested gag order on prosecution because "defendant's generalized assertions are insufficient to establish a reasonable likelihood of prejudice or of denying a fair trial"); *Constand v. Cosby*, 229 F.R.D. 472 (E.D. Pa. 2005) (adopting Rule 3.6 as case management order rather than outright gag order; "a gag order stilling counsel's voice outside the courtroom is not the answer"); *Ex parte Wright*, 166 So. 3d 618 (Ala. 2014) (proposed gag orders were impermissibly overbroad in that, among other things, they did not provide for exceptions for speech specifically permitted under Alabama Rule 3.6(c)(7)); *Atlanta Journal-Constitution v. State*, 596 S.E.2d 694 (Ga. Ct. App. 2004) (order requiring lawyers, parties, and witnesses to tell questioning media only "no comment" or "whatever we have to say will be [or has been] said in court" reversed; it was broader than prohibition in Rule 3.6, not based upon finding of substantial likelihood of prejudice, and applied to lawyers and nonlawyers alike); *Breiner v. Takao*, 835 P.2d 637 (Haw. 1992) ("serious and imminent threat" to defendant's right to fair trial); *Twohig v. Blackmer*, 918 P.2d 332 (N.M. 1996) (trial judge's order prohibiting all extrajudicial statements by lawyers to media during highly publicized trial invalid absent showing of "clear and present danger" to fair trial); *Nat'l Broad. Co. v. Cooperman*, 501 N.Y.S.2d 405 (App. Div. 1986) (invalidating gag order that restrained lawyer from communicating with news media on any matter related to criminal trial); *Commonwealth v. O'Brien*, No. 2706 EDA 2016, 2017 WL 5664772, 2017 BL 427381 (Pa. Super. Ct. Nov. 27, 2017) (discussing rationale for gag order prohibiting both prosecution and defense counsel from extrajudicial statements except as permitted by Rule 3.6); *Davenport v. Garcia*, 834 S.W.2d 4 (Tex. 1992) (gag order prohibiting all discussion of civil case outside courtroom violated free-speech protections of state constitution). *Compare United States v. Salameh*, 992 F.2d 445 (2d Cir. 1993) (gag order prohibiting defense counsel from publicly making any statements that "have anything to do with this case" overly broad), *with United States v. McVeigh*, 964 F. Supp. 313 (D. Colo. 1997) (complete ban on extrajudicial statements by lawyers and support personnel was best method of ensuring media references to case would have minimal impact upon nonsequestered jurors; order placed no restrictions upon protected activities of news media). *See generally* Erwin Chemerinsky, *Lawyers Have Free Speech Rights, Too: Why Gag Orders on Trial Participants Are Almost Always Unconstitutional*, 17 Loy. L.A. Ent. L. Rev. 311 (1997); Eileen A. Minnefor, *Looking for Fair Trials in the Information Age: The Need for More Stringent Gag Orders Against Trial Participants*, 30 U.S.F. L. Rev. 95 (Fall 1995); Gerald F. Uelmen, *Leaks, Gags and Shields: Taking Responsibility*, 37 Santa Clara L. Rev. 943 (1997).

## TIMING OF STATEMENT

Whether the lawyer's statement is the subject of a disciplinary proceeding or a motion in a pending proceeding, its timing has proved to be an important criterion in assessing its potential for prejudice. *See, e.g., United States v. Megale*, 235 F.R.D. 151 (D. Conn. 2006) (rule limiting criminal defense lawyers' ability to identify potential witnesses before trial "is constitutional, as long as there is a 'substantial likelihood of materially prejudicing' the judicial process by disseminating the information"); *United States v. Bingham*, 769 F. Supp. 1039 (N.D. Ill. 1991) (lawyers representing members of Chicago street gang violated local rule regarding public discussion of criminal litigation by making statements on eve of jury selection, criticizing judge's decision to impanel anonymous jury); *State v. Grossberg*, 705 A.2d 608 (Del. Super. Ct. 1997) (counsel for high-school students charged with murdering their newborn "timed his statements for maximum impact to coincide with his entry into the case [and] rekindle public interest and provide him with a significant audience within the venire"); *Iowa Supreme Court Bd. of Prof'l Ethics & Conduct v. Visser*, 629 N.W.2d 376 (Iowa 2001) (single newspaper article generated by lawyer's letter published almost two years before in city more than fifty miles from trial not reasonably likely to have affected proceedings; court assessed its potential both prospectively and retrospectively); *Maldonado v. Ford Motor Co.*, 719 N.W.2d 809 (Mich. 2006) (plaintiff's lawyer's public descriptions of excluded evidence coupled with plaintiff's "statement five days before trial that 'Metro Detroit' judges were biased . . . were substantially likely to materially prejudice the proceedings"); *Commonwealth v. McCullum*, 602 A.2d 313 (Pa. 1992) (nine-month period between publicity and trial sufficient "cooling-off" time to dissipate any prejudice); Or. Ethics Op. 2007-179 (2007) (lawyer may describe allegations of filed complaint at press conference early in litigation; because trial not imminent, statements not substantially likely to materially prejudice litigation).

## LAWYER AS COMMENTATOR

Journalists frequently turn to lawyers for perspectives on significant cases. Rule 3.6 does not apply to "outside" lawyers in this role. As Comment [3] notes, the "public value of informed commentary is great and the likelihood of prejudice to a proceeding by the commentary of a lawyer who is not involved in the proceeding is small."

Various sources discuss the "legal commentator" role. *See, e.g.*, Erwin Chemerinsky & Laurie Levenson, People v. Simpson: *Perspectives on the Implications for the Criminal Justice System: The Ethics of Being a Commentator*, 69 S. Cal. L. Rev. 1303 (May 1996); Rachel C. Lee, *Ex Parte Blogging: The Legal Ethics of Supreme Court Advocacy in the Internet Era*, 61 Stan. L. Rev. 1535 (Apr. 2009) ("[the] net effect of [the rule's exceptions] and the 'substantial likelihood of material prejudice' standard is that a good deal of publicity—particularly the sort likely to be contained in blog posts directed at the Supreme Court—is perfectly permissible").

ABA Formal Opinion 480 (2018) emphasizes that a lawyer who is involved in the investigation or adjudication of a matter and posts commentary on the matter on blogs, listservs, or other social media platforms may violate Rule 3.6(a) if it would create a substantial likelihood of material prejudice to the matter's adjudication.

## PROSECUTORS

Rule 3.8(f) also imposes obligations regarding extrajudicial remarks upon prose-cutors specifically, and expressly incorporates Rule 3.6. See the annotation to Rule 3.8 (Special Responsibilities of a Prosecutor). *See also* ABA Criminal Justice Standards on Fair Trial and Public Discourse, *available at* https://www.americanbar.org/groups/criminal_justice/standards.html. In matters involving discipline of prosecutors, both rules are sometimes invoked. *See, e.g., Lawyer Disciplinary Bd. v. Sims,* 574 S.E.2d 795 (W. Va. 2002); N.J. Ethics Op. 731 (2017) (prosecutors may not display seized contra-band while making out-of-court announcements). *Compare Att'y Grievance Comm'n v. Gansler,* 835 A.2d 548 (Md. 2003) (disciplining lawyer under Rule 3.6), *with In re Gansler,* 889 A.2d 285 (D.C. 2005) (reciprocally disciplining same lawyer for same conduct under Rule 3.8). *See generally* Jan L. Jacobowitz & John G. Browning, *Legal Ethics and Social Media: A Practitioner's Handbook* 56-57, 77-78 (2017); Laurie L. Leven-son, *Prosecutorial Sound Bites: When Do They Cross the Line?,* 44 Ga. L. Rev. 1021 (Spring 2010).

## Rule 3.7

### Lawyer as Witness

(a) A lawyer shall not act as advocate at a trial in which the lawyer is likely to be a necessary witness unless:

(1) the testimony relates to an uncontested issue;

(2) the testimony relates to the nature and value of legal services rendered in the case; or

(3) disqualification of the lawyer would work substantial hardship on the client.

(b) A lawyer may act as advocate in a trial in which another lawyer in the lawyer's firm is likely to be called as a witness unless precluded from doing so by Rule 1.7 or Rule 1.9.

## COMMENT

[1] Combining the roles of advocate and witness can prejudice the tribunal and the opposing party and can also involve a conflict of interest between the lawyer and client.

### Advocate-Witness Rule

[2] The tribunal has proper objection when the trier of fact may be confused or misled by a lawyer serving as both advocate and witness. The opposing party has proper objection where the combination of roles may prejudice that party's rights in the litigation. A witness is required to testify on the basis of personal knowledge, while an advocate is expected to explain and comment on evidence given by others. It may not be clear whether a statement by an advocate-witness should be taken as proof or as an analysis of the proof.

[3] To protect the tribunal, paragraph (a) prohibits a lawyer from simultaneously serving as advocate and necessary witness except in those circumstances specified in paragraphs (a)(1) through (a)(3). Paragraph (a)(1) recognizes that if the testimony will be uncontested, the ambiguities in the dual role are purely theoretical. Paragraph (a)(2) recognizes that where the testimony concerns the extent and value of legal services rendered in the action in which the testimony is offered, permitting the lawyers to testify avoids the need for a second trial with new counsel to resolve that issue. Moreover, in such a situation the judge has firsthand knowledge of the matter in issue; hence, there is less dependence on the adversary process to test the credibility of the testimony.

[4] Apart from these two exceptions, paragraph (a)(3) recognizes that a balancing is required between the interests of the client and those of the tribunal and the

opposing party. Whether the tribunal is likely to be misled or the opposing party is likely to suffer prejudice depends on the nature of the case, the importance and probable tenor of the lawyer's testimony, and the probability that the lawyer's testimony will conflict with that of other witnesses. Even if there is risk of such prejudice, in determining whether the lawyer should be disqualified, due regard must be given to the effect of disqualification on the lawyer's client. It is relevant that one or both parties could reasonably foresee that the lawyer would probably be a witness. The conflict of interest principles stated in Rules 1.7, 1.9 and 1.10 have no application to this aspect of the problem.

[5] Because the tribunal is not likely to be misled when a lawyer acts as advocate in a trial in which another lawyer in the lawyer's firm will testify as a necessary witness, paragraph (b) permits the lawyer to do so except in situations involving a conflict of interest.

## Conflict of Interest

[6] In determining if it is permissible to act as advocate in a trial in which the lawyer will be a necessary witness, the lawyer must also consider that the dual role may give rise to a conflict of interest that will require compliance with Rules 1.7 or 1.9. For example, if there is likely to be substantial conflict between the testimony of the client and that of the lawyer the representation involves a conflict of interest that requires compliance with Rule 1.7. This would be true even though the lawyer might not be prohibited by paragraph (a) from simultaneously serving as advocate and witness because the lawyer's disqualification would work a substantial hardship on the client. Similarly, a lawyer who might be permitted to simultaneously serve as an advocate and a witness by paragraph (a)(3) might be precluded from doing so by Rule 1.9. The problem can arise whether the lawyer is called as a witness on behalf of the client or is called by the opposing party. Determining whether or not such a conflict exists is primarily the responsibility of the lawyer involved. If there is a conflict of interest, the lawyer must secure the client's informed consent, confirmed in writing. In some cases, the lawyer will be precluded from seeking the client's consent. See Rule 1.7. See Rule 1.0(b) for the definition of "confirmed in writing" and Rule 1.0(e) for the definition of "informed consent."

[7] Paragraph (b) provides that a lawyer is not disqualified from serving as an advocate because a lawyer with whom the lawyer is associated in a firm is precluded from doing so by paragraph (a). If, however, the testifying lawyer would also be disqualified by Rule 1.7 or Rule 1.9 from representing the client in the matter, other lawyers in the firm will be precluded from representing the client by Rule 1.10 unless the client gives informed consent under the conditions stated in Rule 1.7.

## Definitional Cross-References
"Firm" *See* Rule 1.0(c)
"Substantial" *See* Rule 1.0(l)

## State Rules Comparison
http://ambar.org/MRPCStateCharts

# ANNOTATION

## POLICIES BEHIND ADVOCATE-WITNESS RULE

The prohibition against a lawyer serving as an advocate at trial and testifying as a witness in the same trial is aimed at eliminating confusion about the lawyer's role. As an advocate, the lawyer's task is to present the client's case and to test the evidence and arguments put forth by the opposing side. A witness, however, provides sworn testimony concerning facts about which he or she has personal knowledge or expertise. When a lawyer takes on both roles, jurors are likely to be confused about "whether a statement by an advocate-witness should be taken as proof or as an analysis of the proof." Rule 3.7, cmt. [2].

Confusion regarding the lawyer's role could prejudice a party or call into question the impartiality of the judicial process itself. *See People v. Rivera*, 986 N.E.2d 634 (Ill. 2013) (rule protects against possibility that "attorney-witness may not be a fully objective witness, causing harm to the client's cause, or the trier of fact may grant undue weight to the attorney's testimony, unfairly disadvantaging the opposing party"); *Jensen v. Poindexter*, 352 P.3d 1201 (Okla. 2015) (rule protects integrity of judicial process by eliminating possibility that lawyer will not be an objective witness, reducing risk that fact-finder may confuse roles of witness and advocate, and promoting public confidence in a fair judicial system); *see also Smith v. Wharton*, 78 S.W.3d 79 (Ark. 2002) (by sitting with trial counsel and actively participating in trial though he expected to testify, lawyer "reassumed his role as an advocate" and therefore should not have been allowed to testify; appellate court would disregard his testimony and would send copy of its opinion to disciplinary committee); *State ex rel. Neb. State Bar Ass'n v. Neumeister*, 449 N.W.2d 17 (Neb. 1989) (lawyer suspended for not withdrawing; trial court's failure to disqualify "will not exonerate him from discipline where it is found that his conduct is in violation of disciplinary rules"). *See generally* Douglas R. Richmond, *Lawyers as Witnesses*, 36 N.M. L. Rev. 47 (Winter 2006).

Because the advocate-witness rule protects opposing parties and the integrity of the judicial system as a whole, the client's consent to the representation or willingness to forgo the lawyer's testimony will not prevent disqualification if the lawyer's testimony is deemed "necessary." *See Premium Prods., Inc. v. Pro Performance Sports, LLC*, 997 F. Supp. 2d 433 (E.D. Va. 2014) (rule "not subject to client waiver because the interests served by the rule extend beyond those of a single client"); *MacArthur v. Bank of N.Y.*, 524 F. Supp. 1205 (S.D.N.Y. 1981) (disqualifying defendant bank's law firm despite bank's willingness to stay with firm and forgo its lawyer's necessary testimony; bank could obtain other counsel, but could not obtain substitute for his testimony); *Freeman v. Vicchiarelli*, 827 F. Supp. 300 (D.N.J. 1993) (disqualifying lawyer for malicious prosecution plaintiff who was sole witness to plaintiff's version of conversation with prosecutor and police officer in underlying case, notwithstanding plaintiff's willingness to forgo his testimony); *cf. Real Estate Training Int'l, LLC v. Nick Vertucci Cos.*, 124 F. Supp. 3d 1005 (C.D. Cal. 2015) (client consent defeated motion to disqualify in light of California rule permitting lawyer to serve as both trial counsel and witness with client's informed written consent).

In criminal matters, there is a heightened risk of prejudice to the defendant when a prosecutor or defense lawyer testifies. *See, e.g., United States v. Edwards,* 154 F.3d 915 (9th Cir. 1998) (advocate-witness rule protects jurors from being unduly influenced by "prestige and prominence" of prosecutor's office; improper vouching by prosecutor constituted error even though circumstances did "not fit neatly under either the advocate-witness rule or vouching rule"); *People v. Finley,* 141 P.3d 911 (Colo. App. 2006) (Sixth Amendment violated when court permitted defense lawyer to resume representing defendant at sentencing after testifying against him on his motion to withdraw plea).

Improper statements by a prosecutor at trial may violate Rule 3.7 even though the prosecutor does not actually take the stand. *See People v. Blue,* 724 N.E.2d 920 (Ill. 2000) (prosecutors' improper "objections" that were "thinly veiled" attempts to introduce evidence violated Rule 3.7); *Walker v. State,* 818 A.2d 1078 (Md. 2003) (invoking Rule 3.7 in reversal of conviction for prosecutor's "prejudicial assertions of personal knowledge of facts" during examination of witness); *State v. Lehrkamp,* 400 P.3d 697 (Mont. 2017) (prosecutor impermissibly stepped into role of crime victim and witness by advocating for sentence based on personal feelings). For discussion of the special ethical duties of prosecutors, see the annotation to Rule 3.8.

## MOTIONS TO DISQUALIFY OPPOSING COUNSEL AS TACTICAL ABUSE

Courts considering disqualification motions premised upon the advocate-witness rule have long recognized their potential for abuse as litigation tactics and have described disqualification as a "drastic measure," to be imposed only when "absolutely necessary." *Weeks v. Samsung Heavy Indus. Co.,* 909 F. Supp. 582 (N.D. Ill. 1996); *Zurich Ins. Co. v. Knotts,* 52 S.W.3d 555 (Ky. 2001); *City of Akron v. Carter,* 942 N.E.2d 409 (Ohio Ct. App. 2010); *see Murray v. Metro. Life Ins. Co.,* 583 F.3d 173 (2d Cir. 2009) (to guard against "opportunistic abuse," motions to disqualify under Rule 3.7 are "subject to fairly strict scrutiny"); *Klupt v. Krongard,* 728 A.2d 727 (Md. Ct. Spec. App. 1999) (courts closely scrutinize motions to disqualify opposing counsel due to concern that movant may be trying to "block, harass, or otherwise hinder the other party's case"); *S. & S. Hotel Ventures v. 777 S.H. Corp.,* 508 N.E.2d 647 (N.Y. 1987) (disqualification of lawyer denies party right to be represented by counsel of its choice, and can prolong and derail proceedings to strategic benefit of one party over another); *see also Lane v. State,* 80 So. 3d 280 (Ala. Crim. App. 2010) (improper disqualification of criminal defense lawyer who was not necessary witness under Rule 3.7 violated Sixth Amendment right to counsel of choice); *Utilimaster Corp. v. Dep't of State Revenue,* 967 N.E.2d 92 (Ind. T.C. 2012) (denying state revenue department's motion to disqualify opposing counsel as an "attempt to conceal its failure to timely pursue discovery"); *State v. Van Dyke,* 827 A.2d 192 (N.H. 2003) (admonishing trial courts "to review motions to disqualify defense counsel in criminal cases cautiously to minimize the potential for abuse of the advocate-witness rule and the risk that a criminal defendant will be deprived unnecessarily of his chosen counsel").

Thus, the mere fact that a party states an intention to call a lawyer as a witness is not grounds for disqualification under the rule. *See Devins v. Peitzer,* 622 So. 2d 558

(Fla. Dist. Ct. App. 1993) (refusing to disqualify lawyer for estate merely because contestants announced intention to call him as adverse witness on their behalf); *City of Akron v. Carter*, 942 N.E.2d 409 (Ohio Ct. App. 2010) (party's stated intention to call opponent's lawyer to testify is "insufficient basis for disqualification" under Rule 3.7); *State v. Sanders*, 534 S.E.2d 696 (S.C. 2000) (defendant's right to counsel violated by removal of lawyer under Rule 3.7 based upon state's assertion that it would call lawyer as witness; lawyer's subsequent testimony "added little to the State's case"; proper procedure is for trial court to conduct evidentiary hearing to assess necessity of counsel's anticipated testimony); Utah Ethics Op. 04-02 (2004) (no blanket requirement under Rule 3.7 that lawyer withdraw once opposing lawyer announces intention to call her as witness).

## Paragraph (a): Lawyer May Not Act as Advocate at Trial if Likely to Be Necessary Witness

### GENERAL TEST

Rule 3.7 requires disqualification when it is "likely" the lawyer will be a "necessary" witness. *In re Gibrick*, 562 B.R. 183 (Bankr. N.D. Ill. 2017) (courts have "variously described" circumstances under which lawyer is necessary witness, such as when it is "foreseeable"; when lawyer is aware of facts making it "obligatory" for him to testify; when lawyer has "crucial information [that] must be divulged"; and when lawyer's testimony is "essential to the case"; collecting cases); *see Venters v. Sellers*, 261 P.3d 538 (Kan. 2011) (rule requires specific showing of necessity and even then, "judge should apply a balancing test rather than automatically disqualify" lawyer); *Holbrook v. Benson*, 3 N.E.3d 788 (Ohio Ct. App. 2013) (abuse of discretion to disqualify lawyer without finding testimony admissible and necessary); *State v. Johnson*, 968 N.E.2d 541 (Ohio Ct. App. 2011) (abuse of discretion to disqualify defense counsel based upon finding he was "potential" witness, rather than "necessary" witness); *see also People v. Hagos*, 250 P.3d 596 (Colo. App. 2009) (rule requires determination of "who is 'likely' to be a 'necessary' witness" despite fact that "unpredictable nature of jury trials" and "ebb and flow of strategy and tactics" make it "impossible" to know in advance who will actually be one); *People v. Rivera*, 986 N.E.2d 634 (Ill. 2013) (no abuse of discretion in disqualifying defense counsel at time when he knew he would testify for client at suppression hearing; fact that he was not called as witness at trial "irrelevant").

This standard replaces that of the predecessor Model Code, which required disqualification when it was "obvious" the lawyer "ought to be called" as a witness, and gives greater weight to the client's choice of counsel. Model Code DR 5-101(B), DR 5-102(A).

### • Testimony Must Be Relevant and Material

For a lawyer to be disqualified under Rule 3.7, the anticipated testimony must be relevant and material. *Sec. Gen. Life Ins. Co. v. Superior Court*, 718 P.2d 985 (Ariz. 1986); *Helena Country Club v. Brocato*, 535 S.W.3d 272 (Ark. 2018); *Brooks v. S.C. Comm'n on Indigent Def.*, 797 S.E.2d 402 (S.C. Ct. App. 2017); *see United States v. Prantil*, 764

F.2d 548 (9th Cir. 1985) (defendant had compelling need to call prosecutor as material witness; prosecutor participated in events at issue); *Abrishamian v. Wash. Med. Grp., P.C.*, 86 A.3d 681 (Md. Ct. Spec. App. 2014) (lawyer's "substantive centrality to the issues in the case should have compelled him to back out at the beginning" of representation); *State ex rel. Karr v. McCarty*, 417 S.E.2d 120 (W. Va. 1992) (prosecutor whose testimony necessary to establish chain of custody of taped telephone conversations, integrity of which was contested, was properly disqualified); *see also Hamrick v. Union Twp.*, 81 F. Supp. 2d 876 (S.D. Ohio 2000) (lawyer who investigated allegations of sexual misconduct at police department disqualified from representing alleged victims in action against department); *Kennedy v. Eldridge*, 135 Cal. Rptr. 3d 545 (Ct. App. 2011) (lawyer disqualified from representing son in custody and support action involving grandson; applying Model Rule 3.7); Mass. Ethics Op. 05-05 (2005) (lawyer who believes elderly client needs guardian but knows client opposes guardianship may not represent client's son in seeking guardianship lest lawyer be called to testify). *Compare Caravousanos v. Kings Cnty. Hosp.*, 896 N.Y.S.2d 818 (Sup. Ct. 2010) (lawyer who negotiated and drafted agreement adjudged ambiguous will likely be necessary witness regarding parties' intent), *with Leonardo v. Leonardo II*, 746 N.Y.S.2d 90 (App. Div. 2002) (lawyer who drafted partnership agreements not disqualified from representing party in partition suit; dispute did not require court to go behind terms of agreement to determine parties' intent).

### • *Evidence Must Be Unobtainable Elsewhere*

A "necessary" witness under Rule 3.7 is one whose testimony is unobtainable elsewhere. *See Macheca Transp. Co. v. Phila. Indem. Ins. Co.*, 463 F.3d 827 (8th Cir. 2006) (abuse of discretion to disqualify lawyer without considering whether other witness available; "[t]estimony may be relevant and even highly useful, but still not strictly necessary"); *Waldrop v. Discover Bank*, No. 15-14689-JDL, 2016 WL 6090849, 2016 BL 346838 (Bankr. W.D. Okla. Oct. 18, 2016) (no disqualification where testimony would be "merely cumulative or collaborative of other witnesses"); *Hershewe v. Givens*, 89 F. Supp. 3d 1288 (M.D. Ala. 2015) (refusing to take "drastic measure" of disqualifying defendant's lawyers when plaintiff had not even taken "preliminary step of attempting to identify other witnesses"); *K.R. ex rel. Doe v. Clarity Child Guidance Ctr.*, 4 F. Supp. 3d 856 (W.D. Tex. 2014) (lawyer's pre-litigation advocacy did not make him necessary witness; information sought would be privileged or cumulative; disqualifying lawyer on this basis would have "chilling effect on pre-litigation negotiations"); *United States v. Melton*, 948 F. Supp. 2d 998 (N.D. Iowa 2013) (disqualification because counsel's testimony "was possibly relevant" as rebuttal witness was "contrary to law"; court must consider whether lawyer is only witness available); *Finkel v. Frattarelli Bros., Inc.*, 740 F. Supp. 2d 368 (E.D.N.Y. 2010) ("Where counsel's testimony would be merely cumulative of testimony provided by others, disqualification is not appropriate."); *Harter v. Univ. of Indianapolis*, 5 F. Supp. 2d 657 (S.D. Ind. 1998) ("A necessary witness is not the same thing as the 'best' witness. If the evidence that would be offered by having an opposing attorney testify can be elicited through other means, then the attorney is not a necessary witness."); *Martin v. State*, 779 S.E.2d

342 (Ga. 2015) (lawyers who were only witnesses other than judge to disputed conversation held in chambers were properly disqualified); *Smaland Beach Ass'n, Inc. v. Genova*, 959 N.E.2d 955 (Mass. 2012) (advice-of-counsel defense does not itself render lawyer necessary witness; court must determine if alternate sources of information exist, if lawyer's testimony would be cumulative or marginally relevant, or if disqualification foreseeable); *Chappell v. Cosgrove*, 916 P.2d 836 (N.M. 1996) (lawyer who accompanied client to meeting that became subject of litigation should not have been disqualified unless similar testimony could not have been obtained from others who attended meeting); *Fuller v. Collins*, 982 N.Y.S.2d 484 (App. Div. 2014) (plaintiff's lawyer should have been disqualified; he and defendant were sole source of knowledge about underlying contract discussions); *see also United States v. Watson*, 87 F.3d 927 (7th Cir. 1996) (lawyer-witness rule does not bar every assistant U.S. attorney who interviews suspect from representing government at trial when interview statement is at issue; assistant U.S. attorney should conduct interview in presence of third party who can later testify about it).

### EFFECT OF LAWYER AFFIDAVITS

The advocate-witness rule does not automatically apply whenever a lawyer submits an affidavit. *See, e.g., Zurich Ins. Co. v. Knotts*, 52 S.W.3d 555 (Ky. 2001) (lawyer representing plaintiffs in bad faith insurance claim is not disqualified "merely because he files a personal affidavit in opposition to a motion for summary judgment"); *Bank One Lima N.A. v. Altenburger*, 616 N.E.2d 954 (Ohio Ct. App. 1992) (lawyer did not become necessary witness by submitting affidavit stating only that documents attached to it were received by him from opposing counsel); Ariz. Ethics Op. 03-01 (2003) (lawyer's verification of pleading does not, by itself, make lawyer necessary witness); Mont. Ethics Op. 050317 (2005) (prosecutor does not become necessary witness merely by submitting affidavit in support of request for filing criminal information); *see also Tracy v. Dennie*, 411 S.W.3d 702 (Ark. 2012) (admission of attorney ad litem's written report in child custody matter did not violate Rule 3.7); *State ex rel. A.D. v. State*, 6 P.3d 1137 (Utah 2000) (court did not abuse discretion in quashing subpoena to compel guardian ad litem, as lawyer for children, to testify in proceeding to terminate parental rights; lawyer did not become witness simply by verifying termination petition or by fulfilling her statutory duty to make recommendations to court regarding best interests of children). *See generally* Douglas R. Richmond, *Lawyers as Witnesses*, 36 N.M. L. Rev. 47 (Winter 2006) (no reason to apply rule to lawyer affidavits in summary judgment proceedings; "no chance" judge will be confused or unfairly influenced by lawyer's dual roles).

However, the rule may be implicated if the lawyer's affidavit purports to include expert testimony. *See, e.g., Jarzyna v. Home Props., L.P.*, 201 F. Supp. 3d 650 (E.D. Pa. 2016) (striking affidavit through which plaintiff's lawyer attempted to provide expert testimony); *Mauze v. Curry*, 861 S.W.2d 869 (Tex. 1993) (plaintiffs' lawyer in legal malpractice case became necessary witness by submitting affidavit opining, as sole expert witness, that defendant was negligent).

## GENERALLY LIMITED TO ACTING AS TRIAL COUNSEL

Unlike disqualification based upon conflicting interests, disqualification under Rule 3.7 is generally limited to representation at trial. *See Droste v. Julien*, 477 F.3d 1030 (8th Cir. 2007) (in most jurisdictions, lawyer disqualified as necessary witness may still represent client in pretrial stage; collecting cases); *Ambush v. Engelberg*, 282 F. Supp. 3d 58 (D.D.C. 2017) (because lawyer who is likely to be necessary witness may represent client during pretrial proceedings, pretrial motion to disqualify is premature); *Merrill Lynch Bus. Fin. Servs., Inc. v. Nudell*, 239 F. Supp. 2d 1170 (D. Colo. 2003) (Rule 3.7 does not automatically require disqualification from pretrial activities such as "participating in strategy sessions, pretrial hearings, settlement conferences, or motions practice"); *Main Events Prods., LLC v. Lacy*, 220 F. Supp. 2d 353 (D.N.J. 2002) (lawyer likely to testify at trial need not be disqualified from pretrial matters); *Smaland Beach Ass'n, Inc. v. Genova*, 959 N.E.2d 955 (Mass. 2012) (lawyer considered necessary witness may participate in pretrial proceedings, but "prudent" to first obtain client consent after consultation); *Liapis v. Second Judicial Dist. Court*, 282 P.3d 733 (Nev. 2012) (abuse of discretion to disqualify lawyer at pretrial stage); *Cunningham v. Sams*, 588 S.E.2d 484 (N.C. Ct. App. 2003) (reversing portion of disqualification order prohibiting representation in pretrial activities); *Anderson Producing Inc. v. Koch Oil Co.*, 929 S.W.2d 416 (Tex. 1996) (lawyer did not violate advocate-witness rule by continuing to draft pleadings, engage in settlement negotiations, and assist with trial strategy after learning he would probably be called as witness at trial); ABA Informal Ethics Op. 89-1529 (1989) (lawyer who expects to testify on contested issue at trial may represent client in pretrial proceedings, if client consents after consultation and lawyer reasonably believes representation will not be adversely affected by client's interest in expected testimony); *see also Heard v. Foxshire Assocs., LLC*, 806 A.2d 348 (Md. Ct. Spec. App. 2002) (ethics rules distinguish between "trial" and "hearing" and do not prohibit lawyer from giving evidence on behalf of client before administrative agency). *But see Abrishamian v. Wash. Med. Grp., P.C.*, 86 A.3d 681 (Md. Ct. Spec. App. 2014) ("Disqualification of counsel at the trial level can extend to any aspect of the litigation the circuit court deems appropriate under the circumstances"; court properly prohibited lawyer from involvement in all stages of trial, including discovery); *Jensen v. Poindexter*, 352 P.3d 1201 (Okla. 2015) (lawyer's actions in making himself necessary witness and engaging in conduct that likely tainted fact-finding process warranted disqualification from all aspects of underlying paternity case).

However, some courts would disqualify a lawyer under Rule 3.7 from participating in pretrial activities involving evidence that, if admitted at trial, would reveal the lawyer's dual role. *See Williams v. Borden Chem. Inc.*, 501 F. Supp. 2d 1219 (S.D. Iowa 2007) (lawyer who was to be fact witness at trial could engage in pretrial activities other than taking and appearing at depositions; depositions may be offered into evidence at trial, revealing lawyer's dual role); *Lowe v. Experian*, 328 F. Supp. 2d 1122 (D. Kan. 2004) (disqualification not required for pretrial activities "such as participating in strategy sessions, pretrial hearings or conferences, settlement conferences, or motions practice," but may be required if activities involve "obtaining evidence which, if admitted at trial, would reveal the attorney's dual role"); *World Youth Day*

*Inc. v. Famous Artist Merch. Exch. Inc.*, 866 F. Supp. 1297 (D. Colo. 1994) (lawyer who was necessary trial witness not permitted to participate in depositions or other pretrial activity that would reveal lawyer's dual role if admitted at trial); *see also Waite, Schneider, Bayless & Chesley Co. v. Davis*, 253 F. Supp. 3d 997 (S.D. Ohio 2015) (lawyer who should have foreseen he would be a witness at trial violated rule by participating in pretrial discovery likely to generate evidence used at trial).

Rule 3.7 does not apply to appellate or post-trial representation. *See* ABA Informal Ethics Op. 83-1503 (1983) (neither Model Code nor Model Rules prohibit lawyer who withdrew as counsel of record in anticipation of testifying from assisting substitute counsel or arguing appeal, or from testifying at trial on remand if appeal succeeds; however, lawyer may do so only if testimony is not issue on appeal and no conflict of interest exists between lawyer and client); *see also United States v. Berger*, 251 F.3d 894 (10th Cir. 2001) (although lawyers who testified at hearing not disqualified from representation on appeal, court concerned about possible confusion at oral argument over whether lawyers were offering analysis of record "or were instead supplementing the record by expounding on facts within their personal knowledge"); *Willacy v. State*, 967 So. 2d 131 (Fla. 2007) ("rule does not mandate the withdrawal of counsel who must testify in a post-trial hearing").

There is a split of authority over the applicability of the lawyer-witness rule to administrative proceedings. *See generally* Arnold Rochvarg, *The Attorney as Advocate and Witness: Does the Prohibition of an Attorney Acting as Advocate and Witness at a Judicial Trial Also Apply in Administrative Adjudications?*, 26 J. Nat'l Ass'n Admin. L. Judges 1 (Spring 2006) (arguing for adoption of modified rule expressly for administrative adjudications).

## EXCEPTIONS

Rule 3.7 provides three exceptions to the general prohibition against lawyers testifying and serving as trial counsel in the same case.

### • *Testifying about Uncontested Issues, or about Nature and Value of Legal Services*

Paragraph (a)(1) permits a lawyer to testify regarding an uncontested issue. In this situation, "the ambiguities in the dual role are purely theoretical." Cmt. [3]. *See Branch v. State*, 882 So. 2d 36 (Miss. 2004) (defense lawyer whose testimony at trial merely authenticated physical evidence need not be disqualified); *see also People v. Pasillas-Sanchez*, 214 P.3d 520 (Colo. App. 2009) (exception does not apply to testimony about undisputed facts even though offered in support of disputed issue).

The second exception, contained in paragraph (a)(2), allows a lawyer to testify about the "nature and value of legal services rendered in the case." Cmt. [3]. *See, e.g., Bernier v. DuPont*, 715 N.E.2d 442 (Mass. App. Ct. 1999) (lawyer for executrix in probate matter should have been allowed to testify regarding amount of legal fees at issue in case); *In re Marriage of Perry*, 293 P.3d 170 (Mont. 2013) (lawyer's testimony concerning nature of legal services rendered was proper under Rule 3.7(a)(2)). In the circumstances that give rise to these two exceptions, the general concerns addressed by Rule 3.7 are absent or reduced.

## • *Substantial Hardship*

The third exception to the advocate-witness prohibition is contained in paragraph (a)(3), which permits a lawyer to testify if disqualification "would work substantial hardship on the client." This exception requires "a balancing . . . between the interests of the client and those of the tribunal and the opposing party." Cmt. [4].

Courts consider several factors in evaluating hardship, including the amount of time and money the client has invested in the lawyer, the foreseeability of the need for the lawyer's testimony, and the likely difficulty of obtaining substitute counsel. *See Int'l Res. Ventures v. Diamond Mining*, 934 S.W.2d 218 (Ark. 1996) (no substantial hardship in disqualifying plaintiff's lawyer when, according to plaintiff's press release, plaintiff had "famed Texas plaintiffs' lawyer" and three capable Arkansas lawyers already working on case); *People v. Pasillas-Sanchez*, 214 P.3d 520 (Colo. App. 2009) (no substantial hardship in disqualifying criminal defense lawyer who was only person other than defendant able to testify about material facts and defendant also represented by second lawyer; "it would undercut defendant's opportunity to freely choose whether to testify" if lawyer remained as trial counsel); *Cushing v. Greyhound Lines, Inc.*, 991 N.E.2d 28 (Ill. App. Ct. 2013) (substantial hardship to disqualify lawyer with "encyclopedic knowledge" of discovery occurring during "five years of aggressive litigation" involving national and international discovery and thousands of documents); *D.J. Inv. Grp., L.L.C. v. DAE/Westbrook, L.L.C.*, 147 P.3d 414 (Utah 2006) (substantial hardship exception applied; motion to disqualify filed two and a half years into litigation, after significant work done, and disqualification would require "exorbitant" expenditures of time and money); *see also Carta ex rel. Estate of Carta v. Lumbermens Mut. Cas. Co.*, 419 F. Supp. 2d 23 (D. Mass. 2006) (no substantial hardship in disqualifying lawyer from twelve-year-old case that involved "relatively straightforward" matter; successor would not need any specialized knowledge); *Forever Green Athletic Fields Inc. v. Lasiter Constr. Inc.*, 384 S.W.3d 540 (Ark. Ct. App. 2011) (disqualifying lawyer found to be material witness four days before trial "would have worked a great injustice on [the client] and forced a lengthy postponement of the trial").

## WHEN LAWYER-WITNESS IS ALSO LITIGANT

The rationales of the advocate-witness rule do not apply to the pro se lawyer-litigant. *See Duncan v. Poythress*, 777 F.2d 1508 (11th Cir. 1985); Conn. Informal Ethics Op. 05-03 (2005); N.C. Ethics Op. 2011-1 (2011). Accordingly, courts have generally allowed lawyers to represent themselves even when they were likely to be necessary witnesses. *See Waldrop v. Discover Bank*, No. 15-14689-JDL, 2016 WL 6090849, 2016 BL 346838 (Bankr. W.D. Okla. Oct. 18, 2016) (rule does not bar pro se lawyers from testifying); *Suchite v. Kleppin*, 784 F. Supp. 2d 1343 (S.D. Fla. 2011) (lawyer disqualified from representing co-defendants but not from representing self at trial); *Presnick v. Esposito*, 513 A.2d 165 (Conn. App. Ct. 1986) (lawyer-litigant may appear as both advocate and witness in action for collection of legal fees and in defense of counterclaim for malpractice in same action); *Farrington v. Law Firm of Sessions, Fishman*, 687 So. 2d 997 (La. 1997) (Rule 3.7 does not apply to lawyers representing themselves); *Horen v. Bd. of Educ.*, 882 N.E.2d 14 (Ohio Ct. App. 2007) (trial court erred as matter of law by disqualifying lawyer from serving as her own counsel); *Brooks v. S.C. Comm'n on Indigent Def.*, 797 S.E.2d 402 (S.C. Ct. App. 2017) (rule does not prohibit self-represented lawyer from acting as both advocate and fact witness); *Ayres v. Canales*, 790 S.W.2d 554 (Tex. 1990) (lawyer representing self may act as witness in fee-division dispute); *see also Cloud v. Barnes*, 116 So. 3d 67 (La. Ct. App. 2013) (Rule 3.7 inapplicable to motion for sanctions filed against lawyer). *But see McCulloch v. Velez*, 364 F.3d 1 (1st Cir. 2004) (disqualifying lawyer-plaintiff who was also represented by co-counsel; party has right to represent himself or to be represented by counsel, but "cannot have it both ways"; no right to hybrid representation in federal courts).

However, if a lawyer represents a corporation of which she is the sole shareholder and officer, Rule 3.7 will normally apply. *See Premium Prods., Inc. v. Pro Performance Sports, LLC*, 997 F. Supp. 2d 433 (E.D. Va. 2014) (disqualifying plaintiff corporation's sole owner, officer, director, patent attorney, and inventor from serving as counsel in patent infringement case in which he was necessary witness; if expense associated with disqualification constituted substantial hardship, "exception would soon swallow the rule"); *Harris & Hilton, P.A. v. Rassette*, 798 S.E.2d 154 (N.C. Ct. App. 2017) (rejecting argument that rule should not apply to lawyers representing own firm in fee collection cases); *Mt. Rushmore Broad., Inc. v. Statewide Collections*, 42 P.3d 478 (Wyo. 2002) (lawyer representing corporation of which he was sole shareholder, officer, and director prohibited from testifying on its behalf). *But see Nat'l Child Care, Inc. v. Dickinson*, 446 N.W.2d 810 (Iowa 1989) (lawyer representing corporation in which he was sole shareholder and chief executive officer not disqualified even though he would likely be witness at trial; policy reasons underlying rule not applicable to situation analogous to pro se representation).

## WHEN DUAL ROLE GIVES RISE TO CONFLICT OF INTEREST

Serving as both advocate and witness in the same trial may also give rise to a conflict of interest under Rule 1.7 or Rule 1.9. A conflict under either of those rules can result in the lawyer's disqualification (from the entire representation) even if Rule 3.7 does not prohibit the lawyer from serving as both advocate and witness. In some circumstances, obtaining the client's informed consent (confirmed in writing) will avert disqualification under those rules. *See* Rule 3.7, cmt. [6]. For further discussion, see the annotations to Rules 1.7 and 1.9.

## *Paragraph (b): Imputation*

### NO IMPUTED DISQUALIFICATION UNDER RULE

Unlike the provision in the predecessor Model Code, Rule 3.7 does not automatically extend the lawyer-witness prohibition to the partners and associates of a testifying lawyer. Rather, paragraph (b) specifically allows a lawyer to act as an advocate at trial even when it is likely that a colleague in the firm will be called as a witness, unless Rule 1.7 or Rule 1.9 would be violated. *See Emory Univ. v. Nova Biogenetics*, No. 06-CV-0141-TWT, 2006 WL 2708635, 2006 BL 99698 (N.D. Ga. Sept. 20, 2006) (lawyer who prosecuted patent could not be trial counsel in infringement suit, but other lawyers in firm could); *Brown v. Daniel*, 180 F.R.D. 298 (D.S.C. 1998) (in light of "drastic nature of disqualification," Rule 3.7(b) does not require disqualification of entire firm even though partner will be necessary witness); *Fognani v. Young*, 115 P.3d 1268 (Colo. 2005) (Rule 3.7 "does not mandate automatic disqualification of a disqualified attorney's law firm"); *In re Harris*, 934 P.2d 965 (Kan. 1997) (Rule 3.7 does not prevent deputy disciplinary administrator from prosecuting case in which another deputy disciplinary administrator is witness); *Cunningham v. Sams*, 588 S.E.2d 484 (N.C. Ct. App. 2003) (affirming disqualification of lawyer but reversing disqualification of firm); *State ex rel. Macy v. Owens*, 934 P.2d 343 (Okla. Crim. App. 1997) (district court judge could not disqualify entire district attorney's office because two assistant district attorneys likely to be necessary witnesses; office is required by law to prosecute all crimes within district, and Rule 3.7(b) specifically allows other lawyers in office to handle trial); *State v. Schmitt*, 102 P.3d 856 (Wash. Ct. App. 2004) (affirming disqualification of deputy prosecutor who was material witness, but reversing disqualification of entire prosecutor's office). *But see Norman v. Elkin*, No. 06-005-LPS, 2014 WL 556081, 2014 BL 34518 (D. Del. 2014) (even though not required by ethics rules, "equities" compelled disqualification of entire firm on retrial; "inappropriate" for jury to hear lawyer's testimony on credibility of client who implicated lawyer in fraud, and see lawyer's firm colleagues at counsel table); *United States v. Dyess*, 231 F. Supp. 2d 493 (S.D. W. Va. 2002) (disqualifying entire U.S. attorney's office; managing assistant U.S. attorney and other members of office all became potential witnesses in case involving allegations of theft, perjury, and witness tampering by government agents and witnesses); *cf.* N.Y. Rule 3.7(b)(1) (prohibiting lawyer from serving as advocate before tribunal if another member of firm is likely to be called to testify on significant issue other than on client's behalf and it appears that testimony may be prejudicial to client).

## Rule 3.8

### *Special Responsibilities of a Prosecutor*

The prosecutor in a criminal case shall:

(a) refrain from prosecuting a charge that the prosecutor knows is not supported by probable cause;

(b) make reasonable efforts to assure that the accused has been advised of the right to, and the procedure for obtaining, counsel and has been given reasonable opportunity to obtain counsel;

(c) not seek to obtain from an unrepresented accused a waiver of important pretrial rights, such as the right to a preliminary hearing;

(d) make timely disclosure to the defense of all evidence or information known to the prosecutor that tends to negate the guilt of the accused or mitigates the offense, and, in connection with sentencing, disclose to the defense and to the tribunal all unprivileged mitigating information known to the prosecutor, except when the prosecutor is relieved of this responsibility by a protective order of the tribunal;

(e) not subpoena a lawyer in a grand jury or other criminal proceeding to present evidence about a past or present client unless the prosecutor reasonably believes:

(1) the information sought is not protected from disclosure by any applicable privilege;

(2) the evidence sought is essential to the successful completion of an ongoing investigation or prosecution; and

(3) there is no other feasible alternative to obtain the information;

(f) except for statements that are necessary to inform the public of the nature and extent of the prosecutor's action and that serve a legitimate law enforcement purpose, refrain from making extrajudicial comments that have a substantial likelihood of heightening public condemnation of the accused and exercise reasonable care to prevent investigators, law enforcement personnel, employees or other persons assisting or associated with the prosecutor in a criminal case from making an extrajudicial statement that the prosecutor would be prohibited from making under Rule 3.6 or this Rule.

(g) When a prosecutor knows of new, credible and material evidence creating a reasonable likelihood that a convicted defendant did not commit an offense of which the defendant was convicted, the prosecutor shall:

(1) promptly disclose that evidence to an appropriate court or authority, and

(2) if the conviction was obtained in the prosecutor's jurisdiction,

(i) promptly disclose that evidence to the defendant unless a court authorizes delay, and

(ii) undertake further investigation, or make reasonable efforts to cause an investigation, to determine whether the defendant was convicted of an offense that the defendant did not commit.

(h) When a prosecutor knows of clear and convincing evidence establishing that a defendant in the prosecutor's jurisdiction was convicted of an offense that the defendant did not commit, the prosecutor shall seek to remedy the conviction.

## COMMENT

[1] A prosecutor has the responsibility of a minister of justice and not simply that of an advocate. This responsibility carries with it specific obligations to see that the defendant is accorded procedural justice, that guilt is decided upon the basis of sufficient evidence, and that special precautions are taken to prevent and to rectify the conviction of innocent persons. The extent of mandated remedial action is a matter of debate and varies in different jurisdictions. Many jurisdictions have adopted the ABA Standards for Criminal Justice Relating to the Prosecution Function, which are the product of prolonged and careful deliberation by lawyers experienced in both criminal prosecution and defense. Competent representation of the sovereignty may require a prosecutor to undertake some procedural and remedial measures as a matter of obligation. Applicable law may require other measures by the prosecutor and knowing disregard of those obligations or a systematic abuse of prosecutorial discretion could constitute a violation of Rule 8.4.

[2] In some jurisdictions, a defendant may waive a preliminary hearing and thereby lose a valuable opportunity to challenge probable cause. Accordingly, prosecutors should not seek to obtain waivers of preliminary hearings or other important pretrial rights from unrepresented accused persons. Paragraph (c) does not apply, however, to an accused appearing *pro se* with the approval of the tribunal. Nor does it forbid the lawful questioning of an uncharged suspect who has knowingly waived the rights to counsel and silence.

[3] The exception in paragraph (d) recognizes that a prosecutor may seek an appropriate protective order from the tribunal if disclosure of information to the defense could result in substantial harm to an individual or to the public interest.

[4] Paragraph (e) is intended to limit the issuance of lawyer subpoenas in grand jury and other criminal proceedings to those situations in which there is a genuine need to intrude into the client-lawyer relationship.

[5] Paragraph (f) supplements Rule 3.6, which prohibits extrajudicial statements that have a substantial likelihood of prejudicing an adjudicatory proceeding. In the context of a criminal prosecution, a prosecutor's extrajudicial statement can create the additional problem of increasing public condemnation of the accused. Although the announcement of an indictment, for example, will necessarily have severe consequences for the accused, a prosecutor can, and should, avoid comments which have no legitimate law enforcement purpose and have a substantial likelihood of increasing public opprobrium of the accused. Nothing in this Comment is intended to restrict the statements which a prosecutor may make which comply with Rule 3.6(b) or 3.6(c).

[6] Like other lawyers, prosecutors are subject to Rules 5.1 and 5.3, which relate to responsibilities regarding lawyers and nonlawyers who work for or are associated with the lawyer's office. Paragraph (f) reminds the prosecutor of the importance of these obligations in connection with the unique dangers of improper extrajudicial statements in a criminal case. In addition, paragraph (f) requires a prosecutor to exercise reasonable care to prevent persons assisting or associated with the prosecutor from making improper extrajudicial statements, even when such persons are not under the direct supervision of the prosecutor. Ordinarily, the reasonable care standard will be satisfied if the prosecutor issues the appropriate cautions to law enforcement personnel and other relevant individuals.

[7] When a prosecutor knows of new, credible and material evidence creating a reasonable likelihood that a person outside the prosecutor's jurisdiction was convicted of a crime that the person did not commit, paragraph (g) requires prompt disclosure to the court or other appropriate authority, such as the chief prosecutor of the jurisdiction where the conviction occurred. If the conviction was obtained in the prosecutor's jurisdiction, paragraph (g) requires the prosecutor to examine the evidence and undertake further investigation to determine whether the defendant is in fact innocent or make reasonable efforts to cause another appropriate authority to undertake the necessary investigation, and to promptly disclose the evidence to the court and, absent court-authorized delay, to the defendant. Consistent with the objectives of Rules 4.2 and 4.3, disclosure to a represented defendant must be made through the defendant's counsel, and, in the case of an unrepresented defendant, would ordinarily be accompanied by a request to a court for the appointment of counsel to assist the defendant in taking such legal measures as may be appropriate.

[8] Under paragraph (h), once the prosecutor knows of clear and convincing evidence that the defendant was convicted of an offense that the defendant did not commit, the prosecutor must seek to remedy the conviction. Necessary steps may include disclosure of the evidence to the defendant, requesting that the court appoint counsel for an unrepresented indigent defendant and, where appropriate, notifying the court that the prosecutor has knowledge that the defendant did not commit the offense of which the defendant was convicted.

[9] A prosecutor's independent judgment, made in good faith, that the new evidence is not of such nature as to trigger the obligations of sections (g) and (h), though subsequently determined to have been erroneous, does not constitute a violation of this Rule.

**Definitional Cross-References**

"Known" and "Knows" *See* Rule 1.0(f)
"Reasonable" *See* Rule 1.0(h)
"Reasonably believes" *See* Rule 1.0(i)
"Substantial" *See* Rule 1.0(l)
"Tribunal" *See* Rule 1.0(m)

**State Rules Comparison**

http://ambar.org/MRPCStateCharts

## ANNOTATION

### BACKGROUND OF RULE

Rule 3.8 imposes special obligations upon prosecutors in criminal cases. As a "minister of justice," a prosecutor has a duty "to see that the defendant is accorded procedural justice [and] that guilt is decided upon the basis of sufficient evidence." Cmt. [1]. The Supreme Court described this unique role in *Berger v. United States*, 295 U.S. 78 (1935):

> [The prosecutor] is the representative not of an ordinary party to a contro-
> versy, but of a sovereignty whose obligation to govern impartially is as com-
> pelling as its obligation to govern at all; and whose interest, therefore, in a
> criminal prosecution is not that it shall win a case, but that justice shall be
> done. As such, he is in a peculiar and very definite sense the servant of the
> law, the twofold aim of which is that guilt shall not escape or innocence suf-
> fer. He may prosecute with earnestness and vigor—indeed he should do so.
> But, while he may strike hard blows, he is not at liberty to strike foul ones. It
> is as much his duty to refrain from improper methods calculated to produce
> a wrongful conviction as it is to use every legitimate means to bring about a
> just one.

*Accord Pabst v. State*, 192 P.3d 630 (Kan. 2008) (although statute allows "prosecuting witnesses" to hire private lawyer to help in prosecution, prosecutor's duty "to assure justice is done" may require private lawyer's role to be "materially limited"); *Sedore v. Epstein*, 864 N.Y.S.2d 543 (App. Div. 2008) (prosecutor may not delegate prosecution to private lawyer retained by complaining witness; "conflict inherent in permitting the prosecutor to be paid by the complainant is readily apparent"); *see also* Susan W. Brenner & James Geoffrey Durham, *Towards Resolving Prosecutor Conflicts of Interest*, 6 Geo. J. Legal Ethics 415 (Winter 1993) (prosecutors charged with three inherently conflicting roles: politician, advocate, and "administrator of justice"); *cf.* Pa. Ethics Op. 2009-44 (2009) (part-time prosecutor in arson prosecution may also represent party in civil claim against accused arsonist if commonwealth consents). *See generally* John M. Burkoff, *Prosecutorial Ethics: The Duty Not "To Strike Foul Blows"*, 53 U. Pitt. L. Rev. 271 (Winter 1992); Bennett L. Gershman, *The Prosecutor's Duty to Truth*, 14 Geo. J. Legal Ethics 309 (Winter 2001); Bruce A. Green, *Prosecutors and Professional Regula-*

*tion*, 25 Geo. J. Legal Ethics 873 (Fall 2012); Catherine J. Lanctot, *The Duty of Zealous Advocacy and the Ethics of the Federal Government Lawyer: The Three Hardest Questions*, 64 S. Cal. L. Rev. 951 (May 1991); Kevin C. McMunigal, *Are Prosecutorial Ethics Standards Different?*, 68 Fordham L. Rev. 1453 (Apr. 2000); H. Richard Uviller, *The Neutral Prosecutor: The Obligation of Dispassion in a Passionate Pursuit*, 68 Fordham L. Rev. 1695 (Apr. 2000).

Other professional guidelines for prosecutors are codified in the National District Attorneys Association Prosecution Standards (3d ed. 2009), and the ABA Standards for Criminal Justice, Prosecution Function Standards (4th ed. 2015). *See generally* Bruce A. Green, *Developing Standards of Conduct for Prosecutors and Criminal Defense Lawyers*, 62 Hastings L.J. 1093 (May 2011); Charles E. MacLean & Stephen Wilks, *Keeping Arrows in the Quiver: Mapping the Contours of Prosecutorial Discretion*, 52 Washburn L.J. 59 (Fall 2012).

### • *Federal Prosecutors*

Federal prosecutors periodically argued, generally without success, that they were not subject to local ethics rules and so were immune from state bar disciplinary proceedings. *E.g., United States v. Colo. Supreme Court*, 189 F.3d 1281 (10th Cir. 1999); *United States v. Helmandollar*, 852 F.2d 498 (9th Cir. 1988); *Barrett v. United States*, 798 F.2d 565 (2d Cir. 1986). The issue was extensively litigated in *In re Doe*, 801 F. Supp. 478 (D.N.M. 1992), triggered by a state disciplinary proceeding against an assistant U.S. attorney, and the ensuing injunction suit brought in his behalf against New Mexico's chief disciplinary counsel, *United States v. Ferrara*, 54 F.3d 825 (D.C. Cir. 1995). After the federal courts dismissed the injunction suit, the authority-to-discipline issue was ultimately resolved in favor of the state disciplinary authority in *In re Howes*, 940 P.2d 159 (N.M. 1997) (imposing public censure on prosecutor). *See also United States ex rel. U.S. Att'ys ex rel. E., W. Dists. of Ky. v. Ky. Bar Ass'n*, 439 S.W.3d 136 (Ky. 2014) (rejecting argument that Ky. Ethics Op. E-435 (2012), prohibiting plea agreements containing ineffective assistance of counsel waivers, violated Supremacy Clause as applied to federal prosecutors). *But see United States v. Supreme Court of N.M.*, 839 F.3d 888 (10th Cir. 2016) (in grand jury investigations, federal law preempts New Mexico rule of professional conduct limiting power of prosecutors to issue subpoenas to other lawyers).

Passage of the McDade Amendment (28 U.S.C. § 530B) in 1998 subjected each federal prosecutor to the ethics rules of "the state where such attorney engages in that attorney's duties." The Department of Justice formally adopted that rule as part of its own regulations. 28 C.F.R. § 77.3. *See generally* Jennifer Blair, *The Regulation of Federal Prosecutorial Misconduct by State Bar Associations: 28 U.S.C. § 530B and the Reality of Inaction*, 49 UCLA L. Rev. 625 (Dec. 2001); Bruce A. Green & Fred C. Zacharias, *Regulating Federal Prosecutors' Ethics*, 55 Vand. L. Rev. 381 (Mar. 2002); Jesselyn Alicia Radack, *The Big Chill: Negative Effects of the McDade Amendment and the Conflict Between Federal Statutes*, 14 Geo. J. Legal Ethics 407 (Spring 2001); Bradley T. Tennis, *Uniform Ethical Regulation of Federal Prosecutors*, 120 Yale L.J. 144 (Oct. 2010); Note, *Federal Prosecutors, State Ethics Regulations, and the McDade Amendment*, 113 Harv. L. Rev. 2080 (June 2000).

• *Separation-of-Powers Challenges*

The argument that a prosecutor is a member of the executive branch and therefore cannot be subject to discipline by the judicial branch has been raised and rejected by state authorities. *See Massameno v. Statewide Grievance Comm.*, 663 A.2d 317 (Conn. 1995) (declaratory judgment that Connecticut judiciary may sanction conduct of prosecutor without violating doctrine of separation of powers; enumerated charges included violation of Rule 3.8(a), prosecution without probable cause); *Ramsey v. Bd. of Prof'l Responsibility*, 771 S.W.2d 116 (Tenn. 1989) (constitutional provision that prosecutors can be removed only by impeachment does not protect them against disciplinary proceedings). *See generally* Melissa K. Atwood, *Who Has the Last Word? An Examination of the Authority of State Bar Grievance Committees to Investigate and Discipline Prosecutors for Breaches of Ethics*, 22 J. Legal Prof. 201 (Spring 1998).

## CRIMINAL PROCEDURE AND DISCIPLINARY ENFORCEMENT

Prosecutorial misconduct is not in itself grounds for relief in criminal cases. Relief in the criminal case—such as suppression of evidence or reversal of a conviction—will not be granted unless the misconduct implicates a constitutional right and the defendant has been prejudiced. *E.g.*, *United States v. Isgro*, 974 F.2d 1091 (9th Cir. 1992) (reversing dismissal of indictment as sanction for prosecutor's failure to disclose exculpatory evidence; misconduct not to be a "windfall for the unprejudiced defendant"); *Lawson v. State*, 242 P.3d 993 (Wyo. 2010) (affirming conviction despite prosecution's failure to turn over evidence; "the aim of due process 'is not punishment of society for misdeeds of a prosecutor but avoidance of an unfair trial to the accused'" (quoting *Brady v. Maryland*, 373 U.S. 83 (1963))); *accord United States v. Jamil*, 707 F.2d 638 (2d Cir. 1983) (suppression of tape recording obtained in violation of ethics rules not required); *State v. Cornell*, 878 P.2d 1352 (Ariz. 1994) ("although the conduct was undeniably improper, we look first to determine whether counsel's actions were reasonably likely to have affected the jury's verdict, thereby denying the defendant a fair trial"); *Suarez v. State*, 481 So. 2d 1201 (Fla. 1985) (suppression would be "overkill"; appropriate remedy is disciplinary action); *State v. DeLeon*, 795 A.2d 776 (Md. Ct. Spec. App. 2002) (reversing dismissal of indictment for prosecutor's withholding of exculpatory lab tests). *But see State v. Sosinski*, 750 A.2d 779 (N.J. Super. Ct. App. Div. 2000) (statement obtained in "unconscionable" violation of Rule 3.8(b) would be suppressed for all purposes, even though it would have been constitutionally admissible as impeachment). *See generally* Frank O. Bowman, III, *A Bludgeon by Any Other Name: The Misuse of "Ethical Rules" Against Prosecutors to Control the Law of the State*, 9 Geo. J. Legal Ethics 665 (Spring 1996); H. Mitchell Caldwell, *The Prosecutor Prince: Misconduct, Accountability, and a Modest Proposal*, 63 Cath. U. L. Rev. 51 (Fall 2013); Bruce A. Green, *Prosecutorial Ethics in Retrospect*, 30 Geo. J. Legal Ethics 461 (Summer 2017); Bruce Green & Ellen Yaroshefsky, *Prosecutorial Accountability 2.0*, 92 Notre Dame L. Rev. 51 (Nov. 2016); Thomas P. Sullivan & Maurice Possley, *The Chronic Failure to Discipline Prosecutors for Misconduct: Proposals for Reform*, 105 J. Crim. L. & Criminology 881 (Fall 2015).

## Paragraph (a): Prosecutorial Discretion in Bringing Charges

Rule 3.8(a) prohibits a prosecutor from bringing a charge that the prosecutor has actual knowledge is unsupported by probable cause. *See, e.g., In re Livingston*, 744 S.E.2d 220 (Va. 2013) (prosecutor's "incompetent representation" demonstrated absence of "actual knowledge" that indictments lacked probable cause); *In re Lucareli*, 611 N.W.2d 754 (Wis. 2000) (endorsing "actual knowledge" test and affirming referee's finding of lack of "actual knowledge" that charge unsupported); S.C. Ethics Op. 14-02 (2014) (lawyer may not serve as contract prosecutor for municipality that prohibits prosecutors from exercising discretion to dismiss or negotiate charges); *see also Iowa Supreme Court Att'y Disciplinary Bd. v. Howe*, 706 N.W.2d 360 (Iowa 2005) (city prosecutor's agreements for some offenders to plead down to violation of traffic statute he knew to be obsolete violated analogous probable cause requirement in predecessor Model Code); Va. Ethics Op. 1879 (2015) (Rule 3.8 does not apply to lawyer presenting civil charges to administrative body); *cf.* N.D. Ethics Op. 95-2 (1995) (city lawyer directed by city council to dismiss criminal case voluntarily, to save city cost of paying for court-appointed counsel, must still exercise his own prosecutorial discretion in determining whether to proceed, but among factors he may consider are city's best interests, which could include time and expense of trial). *See generally* Carrie Leonetti, *When the Emperor Has No Clothes III: Personnel Policies and Conflicts of Interest in Prosecutors' Offices*, 22 Cornell J.L. & Pub. Pol'y 53 (Fall 2012); Daniel S. Medwed, *Emotionally Charged: The Prosecutorial Charging Decision and the Innocence Revolution*, 31 Cardozo L. Rev. 2187 (June 2010).

## Paragraphs (b) and (c): Right to Counsel; Seeking Waivers

Although paragraphs (b) and (c) describe the duties of a prosecutor toward "the accused," they may apply before any criminal charges are filed. *See United States v. Acosta*, 111 F. Supp. 2d 1082 (E.D. Wis. 2000) (rejecting argument that Rule 3.8(b) worded to secure only Sixth Amendment right to counsel, rather than broader, earlier-attaching Fifth Amendment right to counsel); *see also United States v. Hammad*, 858 F.2d 834 (2d Cir. 1988) (rejecting same argument regarding no-contact rule of DR 7-104(A) (1)); Ill. Ethics Op. 14-02 (2014) (prosecutor may offer plea agreement to pro se defendant before any court hearing if prosecutor advises defendant of right to counsel, ensures defendant understands prosecutor's role, and does not recommend or pressure defendant to accept agreement); Wis. Ethics Op. E-09-02 (2009) ("prosecutor's responsibilities under paragraph (c) may arise before the filing of formal charges"); *cf.* Va. Ethics Op. 1876 (2015) (prosecutor may not offer agreement entailing guilty plea to deportable offense to noncitizen defendant without requesting court colloquy or disclosing advisability of obtaining counsel to discuss potential deportation consequences).

## RELEASE-DISMISSAL AGREEMENTS

A prosecutor's agreement to dismiss criminal charges in exchange for the defendant's release of any civil claims arising out of the arrest is called a release-dismissal agreement. As a matter of federal common law, release-dismissal agreements are valid and enforceable if they are voluntary, if there is no evidence of prosecutorial misconduct, and if enforcement would not adversely affect the public interest. *Town of Newton v. Rumery*, 480 U.S. 386 (1987) (upholding waiver of civil rights claim in connection with release of criminal prosecution); *see also Price v. U.S. Dep't of Justice Att'y Office*, 865 F.3d 676 (D.C. Cir. 2017) (FOIA waiver as part of plea agreement held unenforceable because government failed to show it would serve any legitimate public interest). Authorities vary, however, regarding whether these agreements violate Rule 3.8. *Compare* Colo. Ethics Op. 62 (rev. 1988), Conn. Informal Ethics Op. 00-24 (2000), Or. Ethics Op. 2005-113 (2005), *and* Tex. Ethics Op. 571 (2006) (permissible in certain circumstances), *with* Ind. Ethics Op. 2005-2 (2005), N.J. Ethics Op. 661 (1992), *and* S.C. Ethics Op. 05-17 (2005) (never permissible). *See generally* Andrea Hyatt, *Release-Dismissal Agreement Validity—From Per Se Invalidity to Conditional Validity, and Now Turning Back to Per Se Invalidity*, 39 Vill. L. Rev. 1135 (1994) (collecting cases); Fred C. Zacharias, *Justice in Plea Bargaining*, 39 Wm. & Mary L. Rev. 1121 (Mar. 1998).

For discussion of whether plea agreements conditioned upon a defendant's agreement to waive claims of ineffective assistance of counsel and/or prosecutorial misconduct are permissible, see "Kansas Bar: Unethical to Negotiate IAC Waiver in Plea Deal," *ABA/BNA Lawyers' Manual on Professional Conduct*, 33 Law. Man. Prof. Conduct 201 (Current Reports, Apr. 19, 2017), and the annotation to Rule 8.4; also see Mass. Rule 3.8(h) (prohibiting prosecutors from seeking waiver of ineffective assistance of counsel or prosecutorial misconduct in plea agreements).

## Paragraph (d): Duty to Disclose Exculpatory Evidence

The U.S. Constitution requires prosecutors to provide the defense with any favorable evidence that is material to guilt, punishment, or impeachment. *Brady v. Maryland*, 373 U.S. 83 (1963) (prosecution did not disclose accomplice's confession to homicide for which defendant convicted). Favorable evidence is deemed material "if there is a reasonable probability that, had the evidence been disclosed to the defense, the result of the proceeding would have been different." *United States v. Bagley*, 473 U.S. 667 (1985). *See generally* Kirsten M. Schimpff, *Rule 3.8, The Jencks Act, and How the ABA Created a Conflict Between Ethics and the Law on Prosecutorial Disclosure*, 61 Am. U. L. Rev. 1729 (Aug. 2012); George A. Weiss, *Prosecutorial Accountability After* Connick v. Thompson, 60 Drake L. Rev. 199 (Fall 2011).

Rule 3.8's requirement to disclose all information that "tends to negate the guilt of the accused or mitigates the offense" is generally deemed to be broader than what is constitutionally required. ABA Formal Ethics Op. 09-454 (2009) (it is an "incorrect assumption that the rule requires no more from a prosecutor than compliance with the constitutional and other legal obligations"); *see Cone v. Bell*, 556 U.S. 449 (2009) (although *Brady* "only mandates the disclosure of material evidence," duty to disclose other evidence "may arise" under Rule 3.8(d)); *Kyles v. Whitley*, 514 U.S. 419 (1995) (*Brady* "requires less of the prosecution" than Rule 3.8(d) or the ABA Standards for Criminal Justice); *In re Kline*, 113 A.3d 202 (D.C. 2015) (D.C. rule "requires a prosecutor to disclose all potentially exculpatory information in his or her possession regardless of whether that information would meet the materiality requirements" of *Brady* and progeny); *In re Rain*, 79 N.Y.S.3d 387 (App. Div. 2018) (failure to disclose summary of exculpatory witness statement); *State ex rel. Okla. Bar Ass'n v. Miller*, 309 P.3d 108 (Okla. 2013) (prosecutor should have disclosed "all negating or mitigating evidence or information"); *In re Larsen*, 379 P.3d 1209 (Utah 2016) (Rule 3.8(d) differs from *Brady* and requires timely disclosure, not merely acknowledging exculpatory evidence after it surfaces during trial); N.Y. City Ethics Op. 2016-3 (2016) (duty to disclose exculpatory evidence is broader than *Brady* obligation); S.C. Ethics Op. 03-11 (2003) (rule requires prosecutor who discovers police officer failed to tell truth in internal police investigation to inform "each and every criminal defendant in cases in which that officer will be a witness during trial"); Tenn. Formal Ethics Op. 2017-F-163 (n.d.) (prosecutor's duty to disclose exculpatory evidence is broader than and in addition to those imposed by *Brady*); Va. Ethics Op. 1862 (2012) (ethical duty to timely disclose exculpatory evidence arises earlier than *Brady* requirement); *see also In re Hudson*, 105 N.E.3d 1089 (Ind. 2018) (failure to disclose victim's recantation violated Rule 3.8(d) regardless of whether disclosure requirements are broader than or coextensive with *Brady*); Ky. Ethics Op. E-440 (2016) (if prosecutor, but not defense counsel, is aware of defendant's diminished mental capacity, prosecutor should apprise defense counsel because of exculpatory potential); *cf. People v. Lincoln*, 161 P.3d 1274 (Colo. 2007) (prosecutor who formerly represented prosecution witnesses may "obtain consent from the prior client [for] disclosure of . . . exculpatory information[,] disqualify [himself] from prosecuting [or] disclose to the court that . . . he has exculpatory information, and reveal the information to the defense upon order of the court"). *But see In re Att'y C*, 47 P.3d 1167 (Colo. 2002) (importing materiality standard into Colorado's Rule 3.8(d); "we are disinclined to impose inconsistent obligations upon prosecutors"); *In re Seastrunk*, 236 So. 3d 509 (La. 2017) (Louisiana rule requiring timely disclosure of exculpatory evidence is coextensive with, not broader than, *Brady*); *Disciplinary Counsel v. Kellogg-Martin*, 923 N.E.2d 125 (Ohio 2010) (predecessor Model Code's analogous provision "imposes no requirement on a prosecutor to disclose information that he or she is not required to disclose by applicable law, such as *Brady v. Maryland*"); *State ex rel. Okla. Bar Ass'n v. Ward*, 353 P.3d 509 (Okla. 2015) (failure to disclose rap sheets or benefits to prosecution witnesses not shown to be material and therefore did not violate Rule 3.8(d)); *In re Riek*, 834 N.W.2d 384 (Wis. 2013) ("[p]rosecutors should not be subjected to disciplinary proceedings for complying with legal disclosure obligations").

A prosecutor's failure to disclose exculpatory evidence due to inadvertence, an erroneous belief that evidence was not exculpatory, or some other reason will not necessarily provide a shield from discipline. *See, e.g., In re Lee*, 799 S.E.2d 766 (Ga. 2017) (intent irrelevant in determining violation of *Brady* or Rule 3.8(d)); *In re Jordan*, 913 So. 2d 775 (La. 2005) (prosecutor claimed lone murder witness's statement was not exculpatory); *In re Feland*, 820 N.W.2d 672 (N.D. 2012) (prosecutor negligently failed to disclose exculpatory memo; intent is not necessary element of rule violation); *In re Russell*, 797 N.W.2d 77 (S.D. 2011) (elected prosecutor failed to disclose involvement of campaign contributor in prosecution concerning public golf course construction); *see also In re Howes*, 52 A.3d 1 (D.C. 2012) (prosecutor "compounded his misuse of witness voucher funds by failing to make mandatory disclosures of voucher distribution"); *Baker v. State*, 238 P.3d 10 (Okla. Crim. App. 2010) (if question whether *Brady* requires disclosure, then Rule 3.8(d) requires "the prosecutor [to] present the question to the trial judge"); ABA Formal Ethics Op. 467 (2014) (concerning best practices in prosecutor offices to support compliance with Rule 3.8(d)); *cf.* Rule 3.8, cmt. [9] (prosecutor's good-faith judgment that new evidence does not trigger post-conviction remedial obligations under Rule 3.8(g) or (h), "though subsequently determined to have been erroneous, does not constitute a violation of this Rule"). *See generally* R. Michael Cassidy, *Plea Bargaining, Discovery, and the Intractable Problem of Impeachment Disclosures,* 64 Vand. L. Rev. 1429 (Oct. 2011); Bruce A. Green, *Prosecutors' Ethical Duty of Disclosure in Memory of Fred Zacharias,* 48 San Diego L. Rev. 57 (Feb./ Mar. 2011); Steven Koppell, *An Argument Against Increasing Prosecutors' Disclosure Requirements Beyond Brady,* 27 Geo. J. Legal Ethics 643 (Summer 2014); Laurie L. Levenson, *The Politics of Ethics,* 69 Mercer L. Rev. 753 (Spring 2018); Jodi Nafzger, *Leveling Felony Charges at Prosecutors for Withholding Evidence,* 66 Drake L. Rev. 307 (Spring 2018); Christina Parajon, *Discovery Audits: Model Rule 3.8(d) and the Prosecutor's Duty to Disclose,* 119 Yale L.J. 1339 (Apr. 2010); Michael D. Ricciuti, Caroline E. Conti & Paolo G. Corso, *Criminal Discovery: The Clash Between Brady and Ethical Obligations,* 51 Suffolk U. L. Rev. 399 (2018); Ellen Yaroshefsky, *Prosecutorial Disclosure Obligations,* 62 Hastings L.J. 1321 (May 2011).

## *Paragraph (e): Lawyer Subpoenas*

Rule 3.8(e) limits a prosecutor's ability to subpoena other lawyers in grand jury and other criminal proceedings. The rule is rarely invoked in disciplinary matters but is sometimes invoked in the course of criminal proceedings. *See generally United States v. Supreme Court of N.M.,* 839 F.3d 888 (10th Cir. 2016) (federal law preempts New Mexico rule of professional conduct limiting power of federal prosecutors to issue subpoenas to other lawyers in grand jury investigations); *State v. Gonzalez,* 234 P.3d 1 (Kan. 2010) (reversing finding of contempt against public defender who refused to testify about former client; "crime-fraud" exception to lawyer-client privilege did not apply to information sought); *In re Grand Jury Investigation,* 902 N.E.2d 929 (Mass. 2009) ("Because the Commonwealth does not assert that Moe's communications [to his lawyer] come within the crime-fraud exception, they were privileged"; subpoena quashed); Bruce A. Green, *Prosecutorial Ethics in Retrospect,* 30 Geo. J. Legal Ethics 461 (Summer 2017).

A controversial 1990 amendment to the rule required judicial approval or an opportunity for hearing before a prosecutor could subpoena a defense lawyer about current or past clients. That requirement was eliminated by the ABA in 1995 on the theory that it belonged in a rule of criminal procedure rather than in an ethics code. ABA Report to the House of Delegates, No. 101 (Aug. 1995) (citing *Baylson v. Disciplinary Bd.,* 764 F. Supp. 328 (E.D. Pa. 1991)); *accord Stern v. U.S. Dist. Court,* 214 F.3d 4 (1st Cir. 2000) (judicial approval requirement in district court's Rule 3.8 added "novel procedural step" beyond court's rulemaking authority). *See generally* Max D. Stern & David A. Hoffman, *Privileged Informers: The Attorney Subpoena Problem and a Proposal for Reform,* 136 U. Pa. L. Rev. 1783 (June 1988); Fred C. Zacharias, *A Critical Look at Rules Governing Grand Jury Subpoenas of Attorneys,* 76 Minn. L. Rev. 917 (Apr. 1992).

## *Paragraph (f): Out-of-Court Statements*

Paragraph (f) prohibits a prosecutor from making extrajudicial comments that "have a substantial likelihood of heightening public condemnation of the accused," except for certain "legitimate" statements necessary to inform the public of the proceedings. *See, e.g., In re Gansler,* 889 A.2d 285 (D.C. 2005) (reciprocally disciplining prosecutor under Rule 3.8 for misconduct Maryland disciplined under Rule 3.6 in *Att'y Grievance Comm'n v. Gansler,* 835 A.2d 548 (Md. 2003)); *In re Brizzi,* 962 N.E.2d 1240 (Ind. 2012) (prosecutor made statements at press conference that evidence against murder defendant was "overwhelming" and failing to seek death penalty would be a "travesty"); *Lawyer Disciplinary Bd. v. Sims,* 574 S.E.2d 795 (W. Va. 2002) (disciplining prosecutor under both Rules 3.6 and 3.8); N.J. Ethics Op. 731 (2017) (prosecutors may not display seized contraband while making out-of-court announcements); *cf. State v. Polk,* 415 S.W.3d 692 (Mo. 2013) (prosecutor's use of social media during trial to "highlight" evidence against defendant and "dramatize" victim's circumstances risked tainting jury and heightening public condemnation of defendant and was unlikely necessary to inform public or serve other legitimate law enforcement purpose). *See generally* Jan L. Jacobowitz & John G. Browning, *Legal Ethics and Social Media: A Practitioner's Handbook* 127-38 (2017); Sebrina A. Mason, *Policing the Police: How Far Must a Prosecutor Go to Keep Officers Quiet?*, 26 S. Ill. U. L.J. 317 (Winter 2002).

The rule goes on to require the prosecutor to exercise "reasonable care" to prevent anyone "assisting or associated with" the prosecutor from making any statements the prosecutor could not make under Rule 3.8 or Rule 3.6, the trial publicity rule. (Rule 3.6 bars comments about pending litigation if they will have "a substantial likelihood of materially prejudicing an adjudicative proceeding.") *See Devine v. Robinson,* 131 F. Supp. 2d 963 (N.D. Ill. 2001) (dismissing prosecutors' First Amendment challenge to rules for lack of case or controversy; rules "fairly susceptible to an interpretation that would render them constitutional").

## *Paragraphs (g) and (h): Post-Conviction Exculpatory Evidence*

In 2008 paragraphs (g) and (h) were added to Rule 3.8. They create post-conviction duties for prosecutors to disclose "new, credible and material evidence" they come to know of that "creat[es] a reasonable likelihood that a convicted defendant did not commit an offense" (paragraph (g)), and to "seek to remedy [a] conviction" when they come to know of "clear and convincing evidence establishing that a defendant in the prosecutor's jurisdiction" did not commit the offense for which he or she was convicted (paragraph (h)). *See* ABA Report to the House of Delegates, No. 105B (Feb. 2008) ("The obligation to avoid and rectify convictions of innocent people, to which the proposed provisions give expression, is the most fundamental professional obligation of criminal prosecutors. The inclusion of these provisions in the rules of professional conduct . . . will express the vital importance that the profession places on this obligation."); N.Y. City Ethics Op. 2018-2 (2018); *cf. Comm'n for Lawyer Discipline v. Hanna,* 513 S.W.3d 175 (Tex. App. 2016) (Texas rule does not require post-conviction disclosure of exculpatory or mitigating evidence). *See generally* Wayne D. Garris, Jr., Current Development, *Model Rule of Professional Conduct 3.8: The ABA Takes a*

*Stand Against Wrongful Convictions*, 22 Geo. J. Legal Ethics 829 (Summer 2009) (new rule "will counter the institutional incentives for prosecutors to win by any means"); Bruce A. Green & Ellen Yaroshefsky, *Prosecutorial Discretion and Post-Conviction Evidence of Innocence*, 6 Ohio St. J. Crim. L. 467 (Spring 2009); "ABA Approves Conditional Admission Rule, Amends Rule Detailing Prosecutors' Duties," *ABA/BNA Lawyers' Manual on Professional Conduct*, 24 Law. Man. Prof. Conduct 92 (Current Reports, Feb. 20, 2008).

## Rule 3.9

*Advocate in Nonadjudicative Proceedings*

A lawyer representing a client before a legislative body or administrative agency in a nonadjudicative proceeding shall disclose that the appearance is in a representative capacity and shall conform to the provisions of Rules 3.3(a) through (c), 3.4(a) through (c), and 3.5.

## COMMENT

[1] In representation before bodies such as legislatures, municipal councils, and executive and administrative agencies acting in a rule-making or policy-making capacity, lawyers present facts, formulate issues and advance argument in the matters under consideration. The decision-making body, like a court, should be able to rely on the integrity of the submissions made to it. A lawyer appearing before such a body must deal with it honestly and in conformity with applicable rules of procedure. See Rules 3.3(a) through (c), 3.4(a) through (c) and 3.5.

[2] Lawyers have no exclusive right to appear before nonadjudicative bodies, as they do before a court. The requirements of this Rule therefore may subject lawyers to regulations inapplicable to advocates who are not lawyers. However, legislatures and administrative agencies have a right to expect lawyers to deal with them as they deal with courts.

[3] This Rule only applies when a lawyer represents a client in connection with an official hearing or meeting of a governmental agency or a legislative body to which the lawyer or the lawyer's client is presenting evidence or argument. It does not apply to representation of a client in a negotiation or other bilateral transaction with a governmental agency or in connection with an application for a license or other privilege or the client's compliance with generally applicable reporting requirements, such as the filing of income-tax returns. Nor does it apply to the representation of a client in connection with an investigation or examination of the client's affairs conducted by government investigators or examiners. Representation in such matters is governed by Rules 4.1 through 4.4.

### State Rules Comparison
http://ambar.org/MRPCStateCharts

## ANNOTATION

Rule 3.9 defines the general duties of a lawyer appearing before a legislative body or administrative agency in a nonadjudicative proceeding. Rule 3.9 requires the lawyer to disclose the fact that he or she appears in a representative capacity, and specifically incorporates some of the rules governing matters that *are* before a tribunal: Rule 3.3(a), (b), and (c) (Candor Toward the Tribunal); Rule 3.4(a), (b), and (c) (Fairness to Opposing Party and Counsel); and Rule 3.5 (Impartiality and Decorum of the Tribunal).

## WHEN DOES RULE APPLY?

Before 2002, Rule 3.9 referred to the representation of a client "before a legislative or administrative tribunal." In 2002, the rule was amended to refer to a "legislative body" or an "administrative agency" because Rule 1.0(m) defines "tribunal" as a body acting in an adjudicative capacity, so the change was necessary to emphasize that the rule applies only to nonadjudicative proceedings. American Bar Association, *A Legislative History: The Development of the ABA Model Rules of Professional Conduct, 1982–2013*, at 543 (2013); *cf.* N.Y. State Ethics Op. 838 (2010) (proposing several factors to consider when analyzing whether administrative matter is adjudicative or nonadjudicative).

Rule 3.9 expressly applies only to a lawyer's activities in an official proceeding—that is, "when a lawyer represents a client in connection with an official hearing or meeting of a governmental agency or a legislative body to which the lawyer or the lawyer's client is presenting evidence or argument." Cmt. [3]; *see* Ill. Ethics Op. 12-13 (2012) (city attorney's partner must comply with Rule 3.9 when appearing before city council or planning commission to oppose zoning change). The rule does *not* apply when a lawyer represents a client in matters involving negotiations "or other bilateral transaction[s] with a governmental agency," applications for licenses or other privileges, "the client's compliance with generally applicable reporting requirements, such as the filing of income-tax returns," or situations in which the client is under investigation by a governmental entity. Cmt. [3]; *see* ABA Formal Ethics Op. 93-375 (1993) (bank examination more akin to negotiation or bilateral transaction than rulemaking or policy-making proceeding, so Rule 3.9 inapplicable); N.Y. State Ethics Op. 1011 (2014) (activities in connection with visa application do not involve presenting evidence or argument and do not constitute adjudicative proceedings before tribunal). *See generally* George M. Cohen, *The Laws of Agency Lawyering*, 84 Fordham L. Rev. 1963 (Apr. 2016); Daniel Riesel & Victoria Shiah Treanor, *Ethical Considerations for the Clean Air Act Attorney*, 30 Prac. Real Est. Law. 5 (Sept. 2014); Harris Weinstein, *Attorney Liability in the Savings and Loan Crisis*, 1993 U. Ill. L. Rev. 53 (1993); Symposium, *In the Matter of Kaye, Scholer, Fierman, Hays & Handler: A Symposium on Government Regulation, Lawyers' Ethics, and the Rule of Law*, 66 S. Cal. L. Rev. 977 (Mar. 1993).

## • Disclosure of Representative Capacity

Rule 3.9 requires a lawyer to disclose that his or her appearance in a legislative or administrative proceeding is in a representative capacity. This requirement preserves the integrity of the forum by ensuring that all participants are aware that the lawyer is appearing as an advocate rather than as a concerned citizen. *See* Charles W. Wolfram, *Modern Legal Ethics* § 13.8.2, at 51 (1986); *see also Restatement (Third) of the*

*Law Governing Lawyers* § 104(1) (2000) (lawyer representing client before legislature or administrative agency must disclose fact that appearance is in representative capacity); Sean J. Griffith, *Ethical Rules and Collective Action: An Economic Analysis of Legal Ethics*, 63 U. Pitt. L. Rev. 347 (Winter 2002) (observing that Rule 3.9 is part of constellation of rules—with Rules 3.4(e), 3.7, and 6.4—intended to prevent "role misrepresentation": lawyers "misrepresent their role as advocates when they cast themselves instead as disinterested reporters of truth, and seek to exploit this misrepresentation by encouraging their audience to accept their legal conclusions as fact").

## RELATED OBLIGATIONS

Arguably, lawyers enjoy somewhat greater latitude in nonadjudicative administrative proceedings. For instance, Rule 3.9 does not incorporate Rules 3.1 and 3.2, which prohibit frivolous claims and other conduct designed to delay or harass. The justification for selective incorporation is that some of the rules have no bearing in nonadjudicative proceedings. *See* Richard S. Gruner, *General Counsel in an Area of Compliance Programs and Corporate Self-Policing*, 46 Emory L.J. 1113 (Summer 1997). *But see* Lars Noah, *Sham Petitioning as a Threat to the Integrity of the Regulatory Process*, 74 N.C. L. Rev. 1 (Nov. 1995) (arguing that rules governing behavior in front of regulatory agencies are inadequate and prone to abuse).

### • *Candor*

Questions concerning the degree of candor required of a lawyer turn on whether a "proceeding" is involved. When the matter is a "proceeding," Rule 3.9 applies and incorporates the provisions of Rule 3.3(a) through (c). But in all cases Rule 4.1 applies. *See* ABA Formal Ethics Op. 93-375 (1993) (lawyer representing bank in routine examination by banking agency not subject to Rule 3.9, but Rule 4.1's "obligation of truthfulness is unqualified, applies on all occasions, and contains no exceptions"); *cf.* Phila. Ethics Op. 2002-3 (2002) (lawyer who learns client misstated material fact to INS must reveal misstatement; even if Rules 3.3 and 3.9 do not apply, Rule 4.1 still requires disclosure).

### • *Ex Parte Communications*

A lawyer representing a client before a legal body or administrative agency in a nonadjudicative proceeding is prohibited by Rule 3.5(b) from ex parte communications with individual members of a legislative or administrative body unless authorized by law or court order.

# Transactions with Persons Other Than Clients

## Rule 4.1

### Truthfulness in Statements to Others

In the course of representing a client a lawyer shall not knowingly:

(a) make a false statement of material fact or law to a third person; or

(b) fail to disclose a material fact when disclosure is necessary to avoid assisting a criminal or fraudulent act by a client, unless disclosure is prohibited by Rule 1.6.

## COMMENT

### Misrepresentation

[1] A lawyer is required to be truthful when dealing with others on a client's behalf, but generally has no affirmative duty to inform an opposing party of relevant facts. A misrepresentation can occur if the lawyer incorporates or affirms a statement of another person that the lawyer knows is false. Misrepresentations can also occur by partially true but misleading statements or omissions that are the equivalent of affirmative false statements. For dishonest conduct that does not amount to a false statement or for misrepresentations by a lawyer other than in the course of representing a client, see Rule 8.4.

### Statements of Fact

[2] This Rule refers to statements of fact. Whether a particular statement should be regarded as one of fact can depend on the circumstances. Under generally accepted conventions in negotiation, certain types of statements ordinarily are not taken as statements of material fact. Estimates of price or value placed on the subject of a transaction and a party's intentions as to an acceptable settlement of a claim are ordinarily in this category, and so is the existence of an undisclosed principal except where non-disclosure of the principal would constitute fraud. Lawyers should be mindful of their obligations under applicable law to avoid criminal and tortious misrepresentation.

### Crime or Fraud by Client

[3] Under Rule 1.2(d), a lawyer is prohibited from counseling or assisting a client in conduct that the lawyer knows is criminal or fraudulent. Paragraph (b) states a specific application of the principle set forth in Rule 1.2(d) and addresses the situation where a client's crime or fraud takes the form of a lie or misrepresentation. Ordinarily, a lawyer can avoid assisting a client's crime or fraud by withdrawing from the

representation. Sometimes it may be necessary for the lawyer to give notice of the fact of withdrawal and to disaffirm an opinion, document, affirmation or the like. In extreme cases, substantive law may require a lawyer to disclose information relating to the representation to avoid being deemed to have assisted the client's crime or fraud. If the lawyer can avoid assisting a client's crime or fraud only by disclosing this information, then under paragraph (b) the lawyer is required to do so, unless the disclosure is prohibited by Rule 1.6.

**Definitional Cross-References**
"Fraudulent" *See* Rule 1.0(d)
"Knowingly" *See* Rule 1.0(f)

**State Rules Comparison**
http://ambar.org/MRPCStateCharts

## ANNOTATION

### "IN THE COURSE OF REPRESENTING A CLIENT"

As Rule 4.1 states, it applies to a lawyer's statements to others "[i]n the course of representing a client." *Compare In re Swanson*, 200 P.3d 1205 (Kan. 2009) (lawyer testifying falsely at own disciplinary proceeding violated Rule 8.4(c) but not Rule 4.1), *with In re Rausch*, 32 P.3d 1181 (Kan. 2001) (lawyer violated Rule 4.1(b) by failing to disclose sham investment program to investors; though lawyer argued he was not representing clients, court noted he did "act as an attorney" in various roles in investment program). *See generally* Peter J. Henning, *Lawyers, Truth and Honesty in Representing Clients*, 20 Notre Dame J.L. Ethics & Pub. Pol'y 209 (2006).

According to Comment [1], misrepresentations made "other than in the course of representing a client" are subject to Rule 8.4 rather than Rule 4.1.

Misrepresentations made to a tribunal are covered by the more rigorous Rule 3.3, which is not limited to materiality and supersedes the duty of confidentiality.

Rule 4.1(a) is not applicable to what a lawyer says to a client. *State ex rel. Okla. Bar Ass'n v. Bolusky*, 23 P.3d 268 (Okla. 2001) (declining to treat representative of corporate client as third person for purposes of Rule 4.1(a); rule involves "making a statement to a 'third person,' that is, someone other than the client"). *See generally* Raymond J. McKoski, *The Truth Be Told: The Need for a Model Rule Defining a Lawyer's Duty of Candor to a Client*, 99 Iowa L. Rev. Bull. 73 (2014). The analogous provision in the predecessor Model Code was not limited to third persons, however, so cases decided under the Model Code may involve statements made to clients as well.

The rule does, however, apply to false statements made to opposing parties, opposing counsel, and even co-counsel. *See, e.g., In re Malofiy*, 653 F. App'x 148 (3d Cir. 2016) (plaintiff's lawyer lied to unrepresented defendant); *Iowa Supreme Court Att'y Disciplinary Bd. v. Barnhill*, 885 N.W.2d 408 (Iowa 2016) (lying to opposing counsel); *Att'y Grievance Comm'n v. Zhang*, 100 A.3d 1112 (Md. 2014) (falsely telling co-counsel that client could not speak English fluently and had agreed to proposed settlement agreement).

## *Paragraph (a): False Statements*
### KNOWING MISREPRESENTATION

Rule 4.1(a) prohibits a lawyer from "knowingly" making false statements. According to Rule 1.0(f), this requires "actual knowledge of the fact in question," which "may be inferred from circumstances." *See Brown v. Genesee County*, 872 F.2d 169 (6th Cir. 1989) (defense counsel who only "believed it probable" that plaintiff and her lawyer were mistaken about damage computation in employment discrimination case was "under no legal or ethical duty" to correct them); *In re Tocco*, 984 P.2d 539 (Ariz. 1999) (violation of Rule 1.2, 3.3, or 4.1 requires knowledge; "mere showing that the attorney reasonably *should have known* her conduct was in violation of the rules, without more, is insufficient"); *In re Eliasen*, 913 P.2d 1163 (Idaho 1996) (collections lawyer who warned debtor his driver's license would be suspended if he did not pay violated Rule 4.1 by sending second letter with same warning after being informed by legal aid lawyer that DMV advised otherwise; "lawyer should have done more research before . . . reasserting his earlier misstatement of the law"); *In re McCray*, 755 N.W.2d 835 (N.D. 2008) (sending form letters purportedly written by clients disputing items on their credit reports; lawyer bought forms from another firm and knew recitations could not possibly be true for all 9,450 clients); *see also In re Chaplin*, 790 S.E.2d 386 (S.C. 2016) (lawyer who knew about IRS Form 8300 reporting requirement lied to federal agents by stating he did not know it applied to aggregate payments). *See generally* Bruce A. Green, *Criminal Defense Lawyering at the Edge: A Look Back*, 36 Hofstra L. Rev. 353 (Winter 2007) ("lawyer will sometimes be unsure what he does and does not 'know'").

### MATERIALITY

A statement is material for purposes of Rule 4.1(a) if it could or would influence the hearer. *In re Merkel*, 138 P.3d 847 (Or. 2006) (information is material if it "would or could have influenced the decision-making process significantly"); *see In re Malofiy*, 653 F. App'x 148 (3d Cir. 2016) (false statements to unrepresented defendant were material because they led to default judgment); *Att'y Grievance Comm'n v. Cocco*, 109 A.3d 1176 (Md. 2015) (after presenting third parties with invalid subpoena, lawyer told them they must comply with it); *In re Krigel*, 480 S.W.3d 294 (Mo. 2016) (in attempt to conceal adoption proceedings from birth father, lawyer for birth mother falsely told his lawyer that child would not be adopted without birth father's consent). Whether it actually did influence the hearer is beside the point. *See In re Winthrop*, 848 N.E.2d 961 (Ill. 2006) (lawyer falsely told social service agency's lawyer court order would not be required to freeze client's assets to protect them from client's malfeasing agent; not relevant that false statement had no effect upon agency lawyer's conduct); *In re Warner*, 851 So. 2d 1029 (La. 2003) (to avoid opening estate for client who just died, lawyer had client's daughter endorse settlement check in client's name; insurance adjuster's testimony that he would have made same settlement anyway not relevant to Rule 4.1(a) violation); *In re Smith*, 236 P.3d 137 (Or. 2010) (lawyer's false statements to clinic employees that he had court order or letter from attorney general authorizing his client to physically take over clinic were material even though employees called police anyway; reliance not part of materiality under Rule 4.1); *see also In re Pizur*, 84 N.E.3d 627 (Ind. 2017) (corporate counsel lied to reporter seeking information about dogs seized by the city); *cf. Office of Disciplinary Counsel v. DiAngelus*, 907 A.2d 452 (Pa. 2006) (materiality of defense counsel's false statement that arresting officer agreed to withdrawal of one charge was established by prosecutor's reliance upon it; client's actual innocence of that charge not relevant); *In re Carmick*, 48 P.3d 311 (Wash. 2002) (when lawyer's statement became material only because he was negotiating directly with obligee rather than her counsel, court would apply Rule 4.2 rather than Rule 4.1).

Note that DR 7-102(A)(5), the analogous provision of the predecessor Model Code, did not include a materiality requirement; many jurisdictions adopting Rule 4.1 retained this approach and omitted the materiality requirement. See http:// ambar.org/MRPCStateCharts for the variations.

## OMISSIONS THAT MISLEAD

Comment [1] explains that misrepresentations include "partially true but misleading statements or omissions that are the equivalent of affirmative false statements." This language was added in 2002 to replace the "vague" statement that "[m]isrepresentations can also occur by failure to act." American Bar Association, *A Legislative History: The Development of the ABA Model Rules of Professional Conduct, 1982–2013*, at 552 (2013). *See In re Summer*, 105 P.3d 848 (Or. 2005) ("misrepresentations by omission involve information that the lawyer had in mind and failed to disclose" though he knew it was material to case at hand). *But see* Neb. Ethics Op. 09-09 (n.d.) (lawyer for third-party defendant must comply with client's instructions not to volunteer that client is in hospice care).

A misrepresentation by omission under Rule 4.1(a) is different from a violation of Rule 4.1(b)'s affirmative obligation to disclose; Rule 4.1(b) comes into play only if nondisclosure would amount to assisting in a client's crime or fraud.

## DOCUMENTS

A document can be used in such a way that it becomes a false statement for purposes of Rule 4.1(a). *See, e.g., In re Apt*, 946 P.2d 1002 (Kan. 1997) (lawyer handling sale of deceased client's home used deed executed before client's death to complete sale, making it look as though sale effected before client died); *In re Wahlder*, 728 So. 2d 837 (La. 1999) (lawyer let client sign settlement documents on client's wife's behalf); *In re Aitken*, 787 N.W.2d 152 (Minn. 2010) (forging client's signature on plea petition was misleading statement that violated Rule 4.1); *In re Edison*, 724 N.W.2d 579 (N.D. 2006) (lawyer for defendant in auto accident case under no duty to disclose client's death before serving any pleadings, but serving answer and amended answer on her behalf violated Rule 4.1); *Disciplinary Counsel v. Land*, 6 N.E.3d 1183 (Ohio 2014) (submitting fraudulent documents to IRS); *Office of Disciplinary Counsel v. Price*, 732 A.2d 599 (Pa. 1999) (lawyer represented himself as doctor on medical assessment forms for public assistance, signing "Dr. Neil Price, J.D." in space designated for identification of medical provider); *In re Holland*, 713 A.2d 227 (R.I. 1998) (presenting purportedly valid foreclosure deed when foreclosure not yet complete); *Lawyer*

*Disciplinary Bd. v. Veneri*, 524 S.E.2d 900 (W. Va. 1999) (alteration of proposed order without notice to opposing counsel).

## SURREPTITIOUS RECORDING OF CONVERSATIONS

Lawyer participation in surreptitious recording of conversations is generally addressed under Rule 8.4, but Rule 4.1 will also be implicated if the lawyer lies about it. *See Miss. Bar v. Att'y ST*, 621 So. 2d 229 (Miss. 1993) (although lawyer may in certain circumstances surreptitiously record telephone conversations with nonclients, denying it to party on other end is false statement of material fact); *In re PRB Docket No. 2007-046*, 989 A.2d 523 (Vt. 2009) (when potential witness asked lawyers if they were recording their call with him, one lawyer said no and other did not correct her; violation of Rule 4.1 but not Rule 8.4(c)); *see also* ABA Formal Ethics Op. 01-422 (2001) (lawyer who is recording conversation without other party's knowledge may not say conversation is not being recorded).

## LITIGATION

Misrepresentations made in the course of litigation typically violate Rules 3.3, 3.4, and 8.4, but can also violate Rule 4.1. *See, e.g., Am. Airlines, Inc. v. Allied Pilots Ass'n*, 968 F.2d 523 (5th Cir. 1992) (submitting unsigned sworn statements made to look like they had actually been signed, in support of motion for temporary restraining order, violated Rules 3.3, 3.4, and 4.1; statements stricken); *In re Myers*, 981 P.2d 143 (Colo. 1999) (professing not to represent defendant in theft case, lawyer led complaining witness to believe that witness had criminal record of his own and that it would be used against him); *In re Crossen*, 880 N.E.2d 352 (Mass. 2008) (counsel orchestrated elaborate "job interview" ruse with judge's former law clerk in attempt to elicit, and then coerce, evidence with which to force judge's recusal and reversal of her prior rulings); *In re Gross*, 759 N.E.2d 288 (Mass. 2001) (lawyer for DUI defendant orchestrated impersonation scheme to confuse victim and cause misidentification at trial); *In re Breen*, 552 A.2d 105 (N.J. 1989) (lawyer called constable and court clerk during client's eviction and falsely claimed to have obtained federal stay of eviction); *Cavallaro v. Jamco Prop. Mgmt.*, 760 A.2d 353 (N.J. Super. Ct. App. Div. 2000) (violation of Rules 3.4(c) and 4.1 to send subpoena cover letter to doctors stating they could avoid appearing at deposition by forwarding copies of privileged treatment records); Ill. Ethics Op. 01-06 (2002) (lawyer served banks with citations to discover assets listing full judgment amount, rather than just unsatisfied portion); *see also Leysock v. Forest Labs., Inc.*, No. 12-11354-FDS, 2017 WL 1591833, 2017 BL 142553 (D. Mass. Apr. 28, 2017) (deceptively inducing doctors to disclose confidential patient information; analyzing circumstances under which deceptive evidence gathering is permissible under Rules 4.1 and 8.4(c)); *Meyer v. Kalanick*, 212 F. Supp. 3d 437 (S.D.N.Y. 2016) (hiring private investigators who used deception to conduct secret personal background investigations of opposing party and counsel); *cf. Cakebread v. Berkeley Millwork & Furniture Co.*, 218 F. Supp. 3d 1040 (N.D. Cal. 2016) (calling conduct "troubling," court found no basis in California ethics rules for sanctioning lawyer who misled third party in attempt to obtain unauthorized discovery (California subsequently adopted version of Model Rule 4.1)).

For discussion of the ethical propriety of lying in the course of a covert investigation, see the annotation to Rule 8.4.

## GAINING ACCESS TO RESTRICTED SOCIAL MEDIA SITES

Ethics opinions condemn covert attempts to gain access to restricted social media websites. *See* San Diego Cnty. Ethics Op. 2011-2 (2011) (lawyer may not send "friend" request to access private Facebook pages of employees of litigation adversary without disclosing his reason); Conn. Informal Ethics Op. 2011-04 (2011) (lawyer may not "friend" adverse party on social networking site); D.C. Ethics Op. 371 (2016) (pretexting in reviewing social media violates rule); Ky. Ethics Op. E-434 (2012) (lawyer may not make false statement to gain access to restricted social media webpage); N.H. Ethics Op. 2012-13/5 (2013) (by omitting identifying information from request to access witness's restricted social media information, lawyer makes false statement of material fact); N.Y. State Ethics Op. 843 (2010) (lawyer may access public pages of party's social networking website, but may not "friend" party or direct someone else to do so); N.Y. City Ethics Op. 2010-2 (2010) (may not use deception to "friend" someone on social media); Pa. Formal Ethics Op. 2014-300 (2014) (using intermediary to deceptively gain access to witness's social media profile constitutes false statement of material fact to witness); Phila. Ethics Op. 2009-2 (2009) (lawyer may not use third person to contact or "friend" nonparty witness to access her private Facebook or MySpace pages, even if no affirmative misrepresentations made); *see also* Tex. Ethics Op. 671 (2018) (lawyer may not anonymously contact alleged online tortfeasor to obtain jurisdictional and identifying information). *See generally* Steven C. Bennett, *Ethics of "Pretexting" in a Cyber World*, 41 McGeorge L. Rev. 271 (2010) (discussing application of Rules 4.1, 4.2, and 8.4 to "pretexting"); Allison Clemency, Comment, *"Friending," "Following," and "Digging Up" Evidentiary Dirt: The Ethical Implications of Investigating Information on Social Media Websites*, 43 Ariz. St. L.J. 1021 (Fall 2011). This issue is also discussed in the annotation to Rule 8.4.

## NEGOTIATION

A lawyer who makes a false statement in the course of negotiating may be subject to discipline under Rule 4.1(a). For cogent analysis see *Ausherman v. Bank of Am. Corp.*, 212 F. Supp. 2d 435 (D. Md. 2002), in which the court referred a lawyer to a disciplinary committee for untruthfulness in his letter to opposing counsel proposing settlement terms. *See also In re Filosa*, 976 F. Supp. 2d 460 (S.D.N.Y. 2013) (associate negotiating for plaintiff in employment discrimination suit used expert's damages report premised upon plaintiff's continued unemployment, even though associate knew plaintiff just accepted higher-paying position elsewhere); *In re Gilly*, 976 F. Supp. 2d 471 (S.D.N.Y. 2013) (lawyer instructed associate (see *Filosa, supra*) to serve and use expert's damages report in misleading manner); *In re Rosen*, 198 P.3d 116 (Colo. 2008) (as matter of first impression, lawyer's misrepresentations leading insurance company to believe his deceased client was still alive (client's "brain wasn't working") or, later, had not died until after settlement, violated Rule 4.1); *Ky. Bar Ass'n v. Geisler*, 938 S.W.2d 578 (Ky. 1997) (lawyer settled personal injury case without disclosing her client died; failure to disclose amounted to affirmative misrepresentation of material fact); *In re Lyons*, 780 N.W.2d 629 (Minn. 2010) (lawyer untruthful to opposing counsel about whether client died before or after settlement agreement reached); *State ex rel. Neb. State Bar Ass'n v. Addison*, 412 N.W.2d 855 (Neb. 1987) (personal injury plaintiff's lawyer negotiating release of hospital's lien on client's recovery had duty to tell hospital administrator defendant had additional umbrella policy); *Carpenito's Case*, 651 A.2d 1 (N.H. 1994) (after learning otherwise, lawyer in partnership dissolution failed to correct his earlier representation that certificate of deposit for escrow money had been opened); *In re Eadie*, 36 P.3d 468 (Or. 2001) (concealing intent to recover costs and failing to correct false impression that settlement agreement would resolve case violated analogous Model Code provision; trial court's denial of motion to set aside on basis of misrepresentation did not preclude discipline); ABA Formal Ethics Op. 95-397 (1995) (failure to inform court and opposing counsel of client's death before accepting settlement in personal injury case is tantamount to making false statement of material fact under Rule 4.1(a)); N.Y. Cnty. Ethics Op. 731 (2003) (if opposing side relying upon false information in accepting settlement proposal, *and* if lawyer or his client supplied the false information, lawyer must correct it). *But see* Pa. Ethics Op. 2001-26 (2001) (lawyer need not disclose client's one-year life expectancy when settling workers' compensation claim for equivalent of three years of benefits; unless lawyer determines nondisclosure would work a fraud, Rule 4.1(a) not implicated because no statement made and no question posed regarding life expectancy).

A lawyer's false statements in negotiation can also jeopardize the enforceability of any resulting agreement. *See Virzi v. Grand Trunk Warehouse & Cold Storage Co.*, 571 F. Supp. 507 (E.D. Mich. 1983) (looking to Model Code analogue to Rule 4.1 as well as to Model Rules 3.3 and 4.1, court vacated settlement that plaintiff's lawyer, knowing defendant believed plaintiff would make excellent trial witness, negotiated without disclosing client died). *See generally* Don Peters, *When Lawyers Move Their Lips: Attorney Truthfulness in Mediation and a Modest Proposal*, 2007 J. Disp. Resol. 119 (2007) (most "actual regulation" of lawyer honesty in negotiation occurs through challenges to negotiated agreement by party who discovers facts were not as represented; citing Carrie Menkel-Meadow, "Ethics, Morality, and Professional Responsibility in Negotiation," in *Dispute Resolution Ethics, A Comprehensive Guide* 139 (Phyllis Bernard & Bryant Garth eds., 2002)).

For scholarly analysis see Charles B. Craver, *Negotiation Ethics for Real World Interactions*, 25 Ohio St. J. on Disp. Resol. 299 (2010); Nathan M. Crystal, *The Lawyer's Duty to Disclose Material Facts in Contract or Settlement Negotiations*, 87 Ky. L.J. 1055 (1999); Monroe H. Freedman, *In Praise of Overzealous Representation—Lying to Judges, Deceiving Third Parties, and Other Ethical Conduct*, 34 Hofstra L. Rev. 771 (Spring 2006); James K. L. Lawrence, *Lying, Misrepresenting, Puffing and Bluffing: Legal, Ethical and Professional Standards for Negotiators and Mediation Advocates*, 29 Ohio St. J. on Disp. Resol. 35 (2014); E. Cliff Martin & T. Karena Dees, Current Development, *The Truth About Truthfulness: The Proposed Commentary to Rule 4.1 of the Model Rules of Professional Conduct*, 15 Geo. J. Legal Ethics 777 (Summer 2002); Peter Reilly, *Was Machiavelli Right? Lying in Negotiation and the Art of Defensive Self-Help*, 24 Ohio St. J. on Disp. Resol. 481 (2009); Douglas R. Richmond, *Lawyers' Professional Responsibilities and Liabilities in Negotiations*, 22 Geo. J. Legal Ethics 249 (Winter 2009); Hiroharu Saito, *Do Professional Ethics*

*Make Negotiators Unethical? An Empirical Study with Scenarios of Divorce Settlement*, 22 Harv. Negot. L. Rev. 325 (Spring 2017); Barry R. Temkin, *Misrepresentation by Omission in Settlement Negotiations: Should There Be a Silent Safe Harbor?*, 19 Geo. J. Legal Ethics 179 (Fall/Winter 2004); Daniel Walfish, *Making Lawyers Responsible for the Truth: The Influence of Marvin Frankel's Proposal for Reforming the Adversary System*, 35 Seton Hall L. Rev. 613 (2005) (analyzing impact of 1975 argument that ethics rules should forbid material omissions and should affirmatively compel certain disclosures); and Fred C. Zacharias & Bruce A. Green, *Reconceptualizing Advocacy Ethics*, 74 Geo. Wash. L. Rev. 1 (Nov. 2005).

### • *"Generally Accepted Conventions in Negotiation"*

Comment [2] recognizes that certain statements ordinarily are not taken as statements of material fact "[u]nder generally accepted conventions in negotiation," and goes on to note that these include estimates of price or value and a party's intentions regarding acceptable settlement. This "defines the conduct that is permissible in negotiation by reference to local norms of negotiation behavior," according to James E. Moliterno, *Modeling the American Lawyer Regulation System*, 13 Or. Rev. Int'l L. 47, 51 n.10 (2011) (noting culture-driven norms create opportunities for misunderstanding in cross-border negotiation). *See* Nelli Doroshkin, Current Development, *Candor and Integration: Codifying Collegial Truthfulness Requirements in Europe*, 25 Geo. J. Legal Ethics 503 (Summer 2012) (norms of lawyer-to-lawyer interactions, which are often more culture-specific than those governing lawyers' relations with clients and judges, become more important as cross-border transactions increase; author calls upon Council of Bars and Law Societies of Europe (CCBE) to adopt negotiation provision that, like Rule 4.1, leaves space for cultural variances).

The word "ordinarily" was added in 2002 to acknowledge that an estimate of price or value or a statement of intention regarding settlement could, under some circumstances, constitute a false statement of fact. American Bar Association, *A Legislative History: The Development of the ABA Model Rules of Professional Conduct, 1982–2013*, at 552 (2013); *see* ABA Formal Ethics Op. 06-439 (2006) (statements about party's negotiating goals or its willingness to compromise, as well as statements that can fairly be characterized as negotiation "puffing," ordinarily do not come within Rule 4.1(a)); Cal. Formal Ethics Op. 2015-194 (2015) (agreeing with ABA opinion prior to state's adoption of version of Model Rule 4.1).

### *Paragraph (b): Affirmative Duty to Speak Up to Avoid Assisting in Client's Crime or Fraud*

#### DUTY TO DISCLOSE MATERIAL FACTS

Under Rule 4.1(b), a lawyer must come forward with material facts if nondisclosure would amount to assisting in a client's crime or fraud. *See, e.g., In re McCarthy*, 173 A.3d 536 (Del. 2017) (failure to disclose existence of altered medical records and to correct client's testimony in medical malpractice case); *Att'y Grievance Comm'n v. Rohrback*, 591 A.2d 488 (Md. 1991) (lawyer assisted client's fraud by not disclosing client's true name to parole officer); *In re Cantrell*, 619 S.E.2d 434 (S.C. 2005) (Rule

4.1(b) violated when lawyer for client in workers' compensation case submitted loan application on his and client's behalf for loan to be repaid from proceeds of workers' compensation case, without disclosing client's bankruptcy filing). *See generally* Bruce A. Green, *Deceitful Silence*, 33 Litig. 24 (Winter 2007).

Comment [3] was expanded in 2002 to explain that the duty not to assist in a client's crime or fraud is a "specific application" of Rule 1.2(d) (lawyer may not assist client in conduct lawyer knows is criminal or fraudulent; remedial measures may include disclosure to extent permitted by Rule 1.6). American Bar Association, *A Legislative History: The Development of the ABA Model Rules of Professional Conduct, 1982–2013*, at 552 (2013). *See generally* Patrick McDermott, Current Development, *Lying by Omission? A Suggestion for the Model Rules*, 22 Geo. J. Legal Ethics 1015 (Summer 2009) (proposing deletion of Rule 4.1(b)'s limiting language; affirmative duty to disclose material facts should not be limited to situations "when disclosure is necessary to avoid assisting a criminal or fraudulent act by a client").

Rule 1.0(d) defines fraud as conduct that is fraudulent "under the substantive or procedural law of the applicable jurisdiction and has a purpose to deceive"; deceptive conduct that does not violate any law does not fit within the definition of the disciplinary offense. American Bar Association, *A Legislative History: The Development of the ABA Model Rules of Professional Conduct, 1982–2013*, at 29 (2013).

For discussion of other rules dealing with a lawyer's duty when confronted with a client's crime or fraud, see the annotations to Rule 1.2(d) (prohibition against counseling or assisting client in crime or fraud), Rule 1.6 (confidentiality and exceptions), Rule 1.16(b) (withdrawal when lawyer's services have been or will be used in client's fraud or crime), and Rule 3.3(b) (disclosure to tribunal when necessary to avoid assisting in client's crime or fraud).

## DISCLOSURE OF CONFIDENTIAL INFORMATION

Rule 4.1(b) requires disclosure of a material fact to avoid assisting in a client's crime or fraud "unless disclosure is prohibited by Rule 1.6." Rule 1.6 generally bars lawyers from disclosing any "information relating to the representation of a client," but an exception in Rule 1.6(b) permits disclosure when a client is using the lawyer's services to further certain crimes or frauds. Although the language used in Rule 4.1(b) is not perfectly congruent with that used in Rule 1.6(b)(2) and (3), Rule 4.1(b) requires the disclosure if the conditions of both rules are met. *See* Pa. Ethics Op. 2002-3 (2002) (Rule 4.1(b) requires lawyer representing family before INS to disclose family member's prior arrest; client's failure to disclose amounted to fraud in which he was using lawyer's services, thus triggering prevention/rectification exception to confidentiality rule); John A. Humbach, *Shifting Paradigms of Lawyer Honesty*, 76 Tenn. L. Rev. 993 (Summer 2009) ("Since Rule 4.1(b) requires its disclosures when Rule 1.6 permits them, a new and wide-ranging 'duty to warn' has emerged."); Peter R. Jarvis & Trisha M. Rich, *The Law of Unintended Consequences: Whether and When Mandatory Disclosure Under Model Rule 4.1(b) Trumps Discretionary Disclosure Under Model Rule 1.6(b)*, 44 Hofstra L. Rev. 421 (Winter 2015); *cf.* ABA Formal Ethics Op. 07-446 (2007) (fact that lawyer gives behind-the-scenes help to pro se litigant is not material; failure to disclose—or ensure that litigant discloses—does not implicate Rule 4.1(b)).

# TRANSACTIONS WITH PERSONS OTHER THAN CLIENTS

## Rule 4.2

### Communication with Person Represented by Counsel

In representing a client, a lawyer shall not communicate about the subject of the representation with a person the lawyer knows to be represented by another lawyer in the matter, unless the lawyer has the consent of the other lawyer or is authorized to do so by law or a court order.

## COMMENT

[1] This Rule contributes to the proper functioning of the legal system by protecting a person who has chosen to be represented by a lawyer in a matter against possible overreaching by other lawyers who are participating in the matter, interference by those lawyers with the client-lawyer relationship and the uncounselled disclosure of information relating to the representation.

[2] This Rule applies to communications with any person who is represented by counsel concerning the matter to which the communication relates.

[3] The Rule applies even though the represented person initiates or consents to the communication. A lawyer must immediately terminate communication with a person if, after commencing communication, the lawyer learns that the person is one with whom communication is not permitted by this Rule.

[4] This Rule does not prohibit communication with a represented person, or an employee or agent of such a person, concerning matters outside the representation. For example, the existence of a controversy between a government agency and a private party, or between two organizations, does not prohibit a lawyer for either from communicating with nonlawyer representatives of the other regarding a separate matter. Nor does this Rule preclude communication with a represented person who is seeking advice from a lawyer who is not otherwise representing a client in the matter. A lawyer may not make a communication prohibited by this Rule through the acts of another. See Rule 8.4(a). Parties to a matter may communicate directly with each other, and a lawyer is not prohibited from advising a client concerning a communication that the client is legally entitled to make. Also, a lawyer having independent justification or legal authorization for communicating with a represented person is permitted to do so.

[5] Communications authorized by law may include communications by a lawyer on behalf of a client who is exercising a constitutional or other legal right to communicate with the government. Communications authorized by law may also

include investigative activities of lawyers representing governmental entities, directly or through investigative agents, prior to the commencement of criminal or civil enforcement proceedings. When communicating with the accused in a criminal matter, a government lawyer must comply with this Rule in addition to honoring the constitutional rights of the accused. The fact that a communication does not violate a state or federal constitutional right is insufficient to establish that the communication is permissible under this Rule.

[6] A lawyer who is uncertain whether a communication with a represented person is permissible may seek a court order. A lawyer may also seek a court order in exceptional circumstances to authorize a communication that would otherwise be prohibited by this Rule, for example, where communication with a person represented by counsel is necessary to avoid reasonably certain injury.

[7] In the case of a represented organization, this Rule prohibits communications with a constituent of the organization who supervises, directs or regularly consults with the organization's lawyer concerning the matter or has authority to obligate the organization with respect to the matter or whose act or omission in connection with the matter may be imputed to the organization for purposes of civil or criminal liability. Consent of the organization's lawyer is not required for communication with a former constituent. If a constituent of the organization is represented in the matter by his or her own counsel, the consent by that counsel to a communication will be sufficient for purposes of this Rule. Compare Rule 3.4(f). In communicating with a current or former constituent of an organization, a lawyer must not use methods of obtaining evidence that violate the legal rights of the organization. See Rule 4.4.

[8] The prohibition on communications with a represented person only applies in circumstances where the lawyer knows that the person is in fact represented in the matter to be discussed. This means that the lawyer has actual knowledge of the fact of the representation; but such actual knowledge may be inferred from the circumstances. See Rule 1.0(f). Thus, the lawyer cannot evade the requirement of obtaining the consent of counsel by closing eyes to the obvious.

[9] In the event the person with whom the lawyer communicates is not known to be represented by counsel in the matter, the lawyer's communications are subject to Rule 4.3.

## Definitional Cross-References
"Knows" *See* Rule 1.0(f)

## State Rules Comparison
http://ambar.org/MRPCStateCharts

# ANNOTATION
## PURPOSE OF RULE

Rule 4.2 codifies what is often referred to as the no-contact or anticontact rule: If a person is represented in a matter, lawyers for others in the matter may not communicate about it with him directly but must go through his lawyer.

Comment [1], which was added in 2002, explains the rule's purposes: it "contributes to the proper functioning of the legal system" by preventing lawyers from overreaching, from interfering in other lawyers' relationships with their clients, and from eliciting protected information via "uncounselled disclosure." *See Polycast Tech. Corp. v. Uniroyal, Inc.*, 129 F.R.D. 621 (S.D.N.Y. 1990) (rule prevents lawyers from eliciting "unwise statements" from opponents, protects privileged information, and facilitates settlements by allowing lawyers to conduct negotiations); *Messing, Rudavsky & Weliky, P.C. v. President & Fellows of Harvard Coll.*, 764 N.E.2d 825 (Mass. 2002) (rule preserves counsel's "mediating role" and protects clients from other people's lawyers). *See generally* Jessica J. Berch & Michael A. Berch, *May I Have a Word with You: Oops, Have I Already Violated the No-Contact Rule?*, 6 Phoenix L. Rev. 433 (Spring 2013); George M. Cohen, *Beyond the No-Contact Rule: Ex Parte Contact by Lawyers with Nonclients*, 87 Tul. L. Rev. 1197 (June 2013) (rule protects the absent lawyer as much as it protects the person being contacted); Geoffrey C. Hazard, Jr. & Dana Remus Irwin, *Toward a Revised 4.2 No-Contact Rule*, 60 Hastings L.J. 797 (Mar. 2009) (suggesting changes to rule in order to implement its "proper purpose—protecting the client-lawyer relationship to the greatest extent consistent with legitimate implicated interests—those of the client, the adversary, the court, and the legal system as a whole").

### • No "Waiver"

Because the rule protects other interests in addition to the client's, a represented person cannot waive the rule's protection. *See United States v. Lopez*, 4 F.3d 1455 (9th Cir. 1993) (mistake to speak of waiving rights under anticontact rule; rule "is fundamentally concerned with the duties of attorneys, not with the rights of parties"); *Iowa Supreme Court Att'y Disciplinary Bd. v. Box*, 715 N.W.2d 758 (Iowa 2006) (testator did not waive her representation by presenting herself at another lawyer's office and, when he said he should not be talking to her, responding "testily" that she could speak to "whatever lawyer she chose"); *In re Charges of Unprof'l Conduct in Panel File No. 41755*, 912 N.W.2d 224 (Minn. 2018) (because right belongs to represented person's attorney, only attorney can waive right to be present); *In re Howes*, 940 P.2d 159 (N.M. 1997) (prosecutor violated Model Code analogue of Rule 4.2 by listening to criminal defendant discuss case on several occasions without defense counsel's knowledge, even though defendant initiated communications and prosecutor did not ask any questions); ABA Formal Ethics Op. 95-396 (1995) (irrelevant that client, not lawyer, initiates contact).

### Not Acting as Lawyer

If the lawyer is acting in a capacity other than that of lawyer, the anticontact rule is generally not applicable. *See HTC Corp. v. Tech. Props. Ltd.*, 715 F. Supp. 2d 968 (N.D. Cal. 2010) (alleged patent infringers seeking declaration of noninfringement could not prohibit defendant's CEO, a lawyer, from contacting them about settlement over their lawyer's objection; CEO acting strictly as business officer); *In re Rock Rubber & Supply of Conn., Inc.*, 345 B.R. 37 (Bankr. D. Conn. 2006) (Chapter 7 trustee who was also lawyer did not violate Rule 4.2 by sending letter to bank he knew to be represented demanding turnover of estate funds; lawyer acting as trustee); S.C. Ethics Op.

11-04 (2011) (federal investigator who happens to be lawyer not prohibited from contacting represented target of administrative investigation; communication not made in representing a client). *Contra* Va. Ethics Op. 1861 (2012) (rule prohibits lawyer serving as Chapter 7 bankruptcy trustee from communicating with represented debtor; opinion points out, however, that in Chapter 13 many such communications will come within rule's "authorized by law" exception).

## NOT REPRESENTING A CLIENT: SECOND OPINIONS

A sentence added to Comment [4] in 2002 makes an exception for communicating with a represented person seeking advice from "a lawyer who is not otherwise representing a client in the matter." Thus, a lawyer is free to talk to someone who already has counsel but wants a "second opinion from a lawyer who is not representing a party in the matter." American Bar Association, *A Legislative History: The Development of the ABA Model Rules of Professional Conduct, 1982–2013*, at 565 (2013). *See In re Charges of Unprof'l Conduct in Panel File No. 41755*, 912 N.W.2d 224 (Minn. 2018) (lawyer not authorized to provide "second opinion" to defendant in defamation action when lawyer represented co-defendant); Fla. Ethics Op. 02-05 (2003) (permitting second-opinion consultation); Ill. Ethics Op. 18-03 (2018) (same); La. Ethics Op. 07-RPCC-014 (2007) (same); N.Y. State Ethics Op. 1010 (2014) (lawyer may advertise willingness to provide second opinion to people "unhappy with [their] current attorney"; communication not made in course of representing a client); *see also* Phila. Ethics Op. 2004-1 (2004) (lawyer approached by prospective client who is dissatisfied with current counsel not only should not, but may not, notify current counsel without prospective client's permission); Or. Ethics Op. 2005-81 (rev. 2014) (same); *cf. United States v. Gonzalez-Lopez*, 403 F.3d 558 (8th Cir. 2005) (reversing criminal conviction on Sixth Amendment grounds; error to deny pro hac vice admission to defendant's new counsel as sanction for having talked to defendant without permission of defendant's then-lawyer).

## LAWYERS REPRESENTING THEMSELVES

The majority view is that Rule 4.2 applies to lawyers representing themselves. *See In re Lucas*, 789 N.W.2d 73 (N.D. 2010) (lawyer litigating against his condominium association violated rule by sending letters to association's board discussing litigation and suggesting settlement); *Medina Cnty. Bar Ass'n v. Cameron*, 958 N.E.2d 138 (Ohio 2011) (rule applies to lawyers acting pro se; collecting authorities); *In re Knappenberger*, 108 P.3d 1161 (Or. 2005) (lawyer violated rule by speaking to two of his employees about action they had just brought against him in federal court; "independent justification" defense rejected); *Vickery v. Comm'n for Lawyer Discipline*, 5 S.W.3d 241 (Tex. App. 1999) (lawyer representing himself in domestic relations proceeding cannot contact wife directly); *In re Haley*, 126 P.3d 1262 (Wash. 2006) (lawyer representing himself is representing a client within meaning of Rule 4.2); D.C. Ethics Op. 258 (1995) (pro se lawyers retain presumptively unfair advantage over opposing parties and therefore must comply with Rule 4.2); Haw. Ethics Op. 44 (2003) (rule applies to lawyer proceeding pro se); N.Y. City Ethics Op. 2011-1 (n.d.) (same). *Compare* N.Y. State Ethics Op. 879 (2011) (lawyer-litigant must comply with rule whether representing himself or being represented by counsel), *with* Pa. Formal Ethics Op. 2017-200 (2017) (rule applies when lawyer acting pro se, but not when represented by counsel). *But see Pinsky v. Statewide Grievance Comm.*, 578 A.2d 1075 (Conn. 1990) (lawyer acting on own behalf not "representing a client" and therefore did not violate rule by contacting represented opponent); *In re Benson*, 69 P.3d 544 (Kan. 2003) (lawyer suing law firm for refusing to represent him in various matters did not violate rule by sending letters directly to firm partners; letters not sent "[i]n representing a client"); Tex. Ethics Op. 653 (2016) (lawyer who is a party and not representing anyone else in a matter may communicate directly with adverse party; rejecting *Vickery, supra,* and adopting Restatement view); *Restatement (Third) of the Law Governing Lawyers* § 99(1)(b) (2000) (anticontact rule inapplicable to lawyer who is a party and does not represent anyone else in the matter). *See generally* Stephen J. Langs, Note, *Legal Ethics: The Question of Ex Parte Communications and Pro Se Lawyers Under Model Rule 4.2—Hey, Can We Talk?*, 19 W. New Eng. L. Rev. 421 (1997); Margaret Raymond, *Professional Responsibility for the Pro Se Attorney*, 1 St. Mary's J. Legal Mal. & Ethics 2 (2011).

## PARTICIPANTS MAY SPEAK TO EACH OTHER

Rule 4.2 does not restrict the participants from communicating with each other directly, whether or not they have their own lawyers. In addition, Comment [4] specifies that "a lawyer is not prohibited from advising a client concerning a communication that the client is legally entitled to make." *See* ABA Formal Ethics Op. 11-461 (2011) (lawyer may give client "substantial assistance" about issues and strategies for communicating with represented adversary; irrelevant whether idea originates with lawyer or with client); ABA Formal Ethics Op. 92-362 (1992) (lawyer who has serious doubts whether settlement offer he made to opponent's lawyer was communicated to offeree may not ask offeree, but may tell client that client is free to ask); *see also Miano v. AC & R Adver., Inc.*, 148 F.R.D. 68 (S.D.N.Y. 1993) (client, plaintiff in age discrimination action against corporation, surreptitiously recorded conversations with corporation's employees; after extended analysis, court refused to preclude use of tapes at trial, reasoning that lawyer had not "caused" taping in violation of Rule 4.2); Tex. Ethics Op. 613 (2011) (though insurance defense counsel may not tell plaintiff settlement money transferred to plaintiff's counsel's account, he need not discourage insurance company from notifying plaintiff directly). *But see* Ill. Ethics Op. 04-02 (2005) (general counsel involved in employment negotiations with lawyer representing potential new corporate hire may not contact candidate directly; nonlawyer managerial employee of corporation may, but general counsel may not suggest or assist in it); N.Y. City Ethics Op. 2002-3 (2002) (if client "conceives of the idea" of communicating with represented party, lawyer may offer advice).

The lawyer may not script the communication. *See Holdren v. Gen. Motors Corp.*, 13 F. Supp. 2d 1192 (D. Kan. 1998) (counsel for plaintiff in employment suit advised client about obtaining affidavits from other employees and, at client's request, showed client how to draft affidavit; saying counsel "stepped over [the] line," court issued protective order); *S.F. Unified Sch. Dist. ex rel. Contreras v. First Student, Inc.*, 153 Cal. Rptr. 3d 583 (Ct. App. 2013) (reversing lower court's finding that counsel indirectly communicated with defendant's employees by orchestrating clients' contacts with them; no evidence of coaching) (California rule expressly covers indirect communication); *In re Pyle*, 91 P.3d 1222 (Kan. 2004) (lawyer prepared affidavit for client's boyfriend, who was defendant in client's personal injury action, and "encouraged" her to deliver it to him knowing she would obtain boyfriend's signature without his counsel's consent); *Trumbull Cnty. Bar Ass'n v. Makridis*, 671 N.E.2d 31 (Ohio 1996) (personal injury plaintiff's lawyer suggested her client call defendant about client's anticipated trial testimony just before trial; during call, plaintiff handed telephone to lawyer, who continued conversation but then withdrew as plaintiff's counsel); *Bd. of Prof'l Responsibility v. Melchior*, 269 P.3d 1088 (Wyo. 2012) (divorce lawyer made revisions to agreement reached by client and her husband, and gave revisions to client without telling husband's lawyer, notwithstanding substantial risk client would deliver them to her husband); Va. Ethics Op. 1870 (2013) (government lawyer may ask social worker or investigator to contact and interview represented person and may advise "generally" on information needed); *cf.* Utah Ethics Op. 13-01 (2013) (defense lawyer in employment discrimination suit may not send litigation hold e-mail to group of employees that would include plaintiff, but may prepare form litigation hold e-mail for supervisor to send). *See generally* John K. Villa, *A Client's Direct Contact with a Represented Party: What, if Anything, Can You Advise Your Client to Say?*, 30 ACC Docket, no. 4, at 76 (May 2012).

## COMMUNICATING THROUGH SOMEONE ELSE

A lawyer's adventitious receipt of information from someone who has spoken with the represented person independently, not at the lawyer's behest, does not implicate Rule 4.2. *See, e.g.*, *Hayes v. Commonwealth*, 25 S.W.3d 463 (Ky. 2000) (detective who interviewed indicted defendant without prosecutor's knowledge was not prosecutor's agent; no breach of anticontact rule); *State v. P.Z.*, 703 A.2d 901 (N.J. 1997) (defendant made statements to social worker, who passed them on to prosecutor; Rule 4.2 not implicated); *cf.* Tex. Ethics Op. 600 (2010) (government regulatory lawyer not required to comply with request of counsel for person being investigated that all communications by enforcement personnel be carried out through him; lawyer has no direct supervision over enforcement personnel).

The lawyer may not, however, cause the contact. *See Bratcher v. Ky. Bar Ass'n*, 290 S.W.3d 648 (Ky. 2009) (plaintiff's lawyer in wrongful termination suit hired reference-check company to ascertain type of reference client's former employer would give); ABA Formal Ethics Op. 95-396 (1995) (lawyer accountable for ex parte contacts made by investigator she supervises if she either instructed him to make them or did not try to prevent him from making them, but if investigator makes them despite her instructions, she may use results; use not tantamount to ratification). *See generally* Douglas R. Richmond, *Deceptive Lawyering*, 74 U. Cin. L. Rev. 577 (Winter 2005).

## OBSERVATION VERSUS COMMUNICATION

Merely observing someone conduct business is not the same as "communicating" with him. *See Hill v. Shell Oil Co.*, 209 F. Supp. 2d 876 (N.D. Ill. 2002) (refusing to enjoin plaintiffs' counsel in putative civil rights class action against owners of gas stations from secretly videotaping station employees at work; employees' conversations with customers not audible on videotapes, so no communication for purposes of Rule 4.2); *Insituform of N. Am., Inc. v. Midwest Pipeliners, Inc.*, 139 F.R.D. 622 (S.D. Ohio 1991) (testimony obtained by lawyer—who had since withdrawn—in violation of rule would be excluded, but lawyer's own testimony about what he noticed when on defendant's property was admissible); *State ex rel. State Farm Fire & Cas. Co. v. Madden*, 451 S.E.2d 721 (W. Va. 1994) (private investigator's conversation with plaintiff violated Rule 4.2 but did not warrant exclusion of investigator's testimony that he saw allegedly disabled plaintiff apparently at work); Or. Ethics Op. 2005-164 (2005) (visiting public website of client's represented adversary does not involve communication; website considered public even if access fee or subscription fee charged); *see also Scranton Prods., Inc. v. Bobrick Washroom Equip., Inc.*, 190 F. Supp. 3d 419 (M.D. Pa. 2016) (lawyer who was present and listening when client phoned represented person did not violate Rule 4.2 where insufficient evidence that lawyer "directed or caused" communication, but "failure to disclose his presence and notetaking" violated Rule 8.4(c)); *cf. In re Peters*, Ill. Disciplinary Op. 04 CH 127, 2006 WL 6889164 (Ill. ARDC Sept. 22, 2006) (husband's lawyer did not "communicate" with represented wife by discussing settlement with him in court hallway such that wife could overhear). *Compare Gidatex, S.r.L. v. Campaniello Imps., Ltd.*, 82 F. Supp. 2d 119 (S.D.N.Y. 1999) (investigators posing as furniture customers "did nothing more than observe and record the manner in which Campaniello employees conducted routine business"), *with Midwest Motor Sports, Inc. v. Arctic Sales, Inc.*, 347 F.3d 693 (8th Cir. 2003) (excluding, as sanction for violating Rule 4.2, secret recordings of opposing party's salespeople, and testimony of agents posing as customers). *See generally* Phillip Barengolts, *Ethical Issues Arising from the Investigation of Activities of Intellectual Property Infringers Represented by Counsel*, 1 Nw. J. Tech. & Intell. Prop. 3 (Spring 2003); Erin Barrett, Note, *Who Is Patrolling the Border of Ethical Conduct? The Convergence of Federal Immigration Attorneys, Benefit Fraud, and Model Rule 4.2*, 55 Wm. & Mary L. Rev. 2255 (June 2014) (unannounced home visits to homes/workplaces of represented green-card applicants to check for marriage fraud probably violate Rule 4.2); Julian J. Moore, *Home Sweet Home: Examining the (Mis)Application of the Anti-Contact Rule to Housing Discrimination Testers*, 25 J. Legal Prof. 75 (2001).

### • *Viewing Social Media Sites*

Rule 4.2 prohibits lawyers from communicating ex parte with represented persons via social media, such as by making "friend" requests in order to view nonpublic portions of the person's social networking site. Merely viewing the public portion of a represented person's social media page does not implicate the rule. *See* D.C. Ethics Op. 371 (2016) (requesting access to information protected by privacy settings, such as making "friend" request to represented person, violates Rule 4.2); Me. Ethics Op. 217 (2017) (access and use of private portion of represented person's social media account is prohibited by Rule 4.2, even if action is fully automated through social media interface itself); Pa. Formal Ethics Op. 2014-300 (2014) ("friend" request violates rule, but lawyer may access public portion of represented party's social media site); W. Va. Ethics Op. 2015-02 (2015) (lawyer may not contact represented person through social media or send "friend" request to such person, but lawyer may access public portion of person's social media page); *see also* San Diego Cnty. Ethics Op. 2011-2 (2011) (lawyer may not make ex parte "friend" request of represented party; under former California Rule 2-100). *See generally* Yvette Ostolaza & Ricardo Pellafone, *Applying Model Rule 4.2 to Web 2.0: The Problem of Social Networking Sites*, 11 J. High Tech. L. 56 (2010).

Participation in covert investigations is discussed in the annotation to Rule 8.4.

## "Parties" versus "Persons"

Rule 4.2 originally prohibited direct contact with "parties" represented in a matter. "Parties" was replaced by "persons" in 1995 to clarify that the rule applies to anyone known to be represented regarding the subject of the intended communication, not just to those who have been named parties to a formally identified proceeding. *See* American Bar Association, *A Legislative History: The Development of the ABA Model Rules of Professional Conduct, 1982–2013*, at 559 (2013). (Rule 4.3 has always been phrased in terms of dealing with unrepresented persons, rather than parties.)

The amendment codified a conclusion most jurisdictions—and the ABA's own ethics committee—reached as a matter of interpretation. *See United States v. Jamil*, 546 F. Supp. 646 (E.D.N.Y. 1982) (person who retains counsel as protection against grand jury investigation is "represented party"; application of anticontact rule "depends on the existence of the attorney-client relationship, not upon the existence of a pending lawsuit"), *rev'd on other grounds*, 707 F.2d 638 (2d Cir. 1983); *Monceret v. Bd. of Prof'l Responsibility*, 29 S.W.3d 455 (Tenn. 2000) ("party" not limited to named plaintiff or defendant; may include witnesses); *In re Illuzzi*, 616 A.2d 233 (Vt. 1992) (anticontact provision in predecessor Model Code not limited to litigation but applies to all transactions for which lawyers hired); ABA Formal Ethics Op. 95-396 (1995) (rule's coverage should extend to any represented person "whose interests are potentially distinct from those of the client on whose behalf the communicating lawyer is acting").

## How Does the Lawyer "Know" Someone Is Represented?

Consent of a represented person's counsel is required only if the lawyer knows the person is represented. Knowledge, according to Rule 1.0(f), means actual knowledge and may be inferred from circumstances. Until 2002, the comment to Rule 4.2 went on to say that "such an inference may arise . . . where there is substantial reason to believe that the person . . . is represented." That sentence was deleted in 2002 because equating knowledge with "substantial reason to believe" was thought "inconsistent with the definition of 'knows' in Rule 1.0(f), which requires actual knowledge and involves no duty to inquire." American Bar Association, *A Legislative History: The Development of the ABA Model Rules of Professional Conduct, 1982–2013*, at 566 (2013). *See Jorgensen v. Taco Bell Corp.*, 58 Cal. Rptr. 2d 178 (Ct. App. 1996) (rejecting argument that because lawyer for potential plaintiff in suit against corporation knew corporation had in-house counsel, he should have known employee he interviewed was represented); *Allstate Ins. Co. v. Bowne*, 817 So. 2d 994 (Fla. Dist. Ct. App. 2002) (no disqualification of lawyer who took statement of defendant's employee; lawyer had good-faith belief she was employed by different entity); *Humco, Inc. v.*

*Noble*, 31 S.W.3d 916 (Ky. 2000) (fact that defendant's employee copied defendant's in-house counsel on letter to plaintiff's lawyer did not give plaintiff's lawyer actual knowledge that employee was represented in matter); *State ex rel. Okla. Bar Ass'n v. Harper*, 995 P.2d 1143 (Okla. 2000) (evidence did not support finding that insurer's lawyer knew insured was represented when he took her statement; records received from insurer indicated she was unrepresented at time of accident, and she said nothing about being represented when insurer's lawyer told her she could have lawyer present); Va. Ethics Op. 1863 (2012) (plaintiff's lawyer in personal injury case need not assume defense counsel jointly represents insurer as well, and may communicate with insurer unless he knows otherwise).

Although the black letter of the rule imposes no duty to inquire as to whether a person is represented, Comment [8] advises that a lawyer "cannot evade the requirement of obtaining the consent of counsel by closing eyes to the obvious." Accordingly, some authorities have concluded that there are some circumstance under which a lawyer should ask whether a person is represented. *See NorthPointe Holdings, Inc. v. Nationwide Emerging Managers, LLC*, No. 09C-11-141-JOH, 2011 WL 7657679, 2012 BL 24013 (Del. Super. Ct. Oct. 4, 2011, rev. Jan. 26, 2012) (when lawyer interviewing fired key player of corporate adversary was clearly seeking more than simple factual information, it was professional misconduct to interview him without first asking if he had a lawyer); *see also* ABA Formal Ethics Op. 472 (2015) (recommending lawyer inquire as to whether person is represented if circumstances suggest person is receiving limited-scope legal services; if person states he or she is or was represented in any part of a matter and does not indicate either that representation has ended or that issue to be discussed is outside scope of representation, lawyer must contact person's counsel); Ind. Ethics Op. 2008-2 (2008) (when circumstances suggest someone may be represented, lawyer has duty to investigate); Ky. Ethics Op. E-441 (2017) (if opposing pro se party has filed pleading indicating it was prepared with assistance of counsel, lawyer may contact party directly but should inquire about scope of representation; if it appears that party is or may be represented on matter at issue, lawyer should contact party's counsel to confirm scope of representation).

## HAS THE OTHER LAWYER BEEN FIRED?

A lawyer is not necessarily free to accept an individual's claim that he fired his lawyer and is now unrepresented. *See In re Capper*, 757 N.E.2d 138 (Ind. 2001) (must contact counsel even if individual claims to have discharged him); *Engstrom v. Goodman*, 271 P.3d 959 (Wash. Ct. App. 2012) (when defendant in personal injury suit e-mailed plaintiff's counsel to contact her directly because she was firing her lawyer, counsel should have forwarded e-mail to lawyer or submitted it to court rather than using it to prepare declaration in support of motion to strike); ABA Formal Ethics Op. 95-396 (1995) (lawyer should seek confirmation when confronted with claim that counsel discharged; if case involves appointed counsel, lawyer should not proceed ex parte "without reasonable assurance that the court has granted [counsel] leave to withdraw").

However, courts have acknowledged that "an uncritical application of [the anti-contact rule] would effectively defeat its goal of protecting the administration of justice." *United States v. Talao*, 222 F.3d 1133 (9th Cir. 2000) (no violation when book-keeper of company under criminal investigation initiated contact with prosecutor and answered questions, saying she did not want company's lawyer representing her because he would pressure her to testify falsely); *see In re Users Sys. Servs., Inc.,* 22 S.W.3d 331 (Tex. 1999) (defendant's letter to plaintiffs' counsel stating defendant "decided to terminate" his representation, was no longer represented by any lawyer in matter, and did not desire to be represented by counsel in connection with his discussions with plaintiffs' counsel, did not require confirmation; defendant may have had good reason not to alert his co-defendants, also represented by same lawyer, of his settlement overture); *see also People v. Stewart*, 656 N.Y.S.2d 210 (App. Div. 1997) (when defendant wants to "blow the whistle" on whoever is paying his defense lawyers and voluntarily reaches out to government, government may bring defendant to judge for appointment of independent counsel); *cf. People v. McLean*, 21 N.E.3d 218 (N.Y. 2014) (police did not violate suspect's right to counsel by questioning him after suspect's lawyer said he no longer represented suspect); N.Y. State Ethics Op. 959 (2013) (lawyer may contact adverse person whose lawyer has withdrawn or resigned from bar to ask whether he retained new counsel or will represent himself). *See generally* Brenna K. DeVaney, *The "No-Contact" Rule: Helping or Hurting Criminal Defendants in Plea Negotiations?*, 14 Geo. J. Legal Ethics 933 (Summer 2001).

### • *Lawyer May Not Contact Former Client Who Has New Counsel*

When a client fires his or her lawyer and hires a replacement, the discharged lawyer may no longer speak directly with the former client. *See* N.Y. City Ethics Op. 2011-1 (n.d.) (if former client has new counsel, lawyer may not communicate directly with him about anything on which lawyer has reason to believe new counsel represents him); R.I. Ethics Op. 2002-04 (2002) (if client fires lawyer and makes clear she does not want him to contact her, he may not communicate with her unless replacement counsel allows it); *see also* Ill. Ethics Op. 96-09 (1996) (discharged lawyer seeking fees and expenses from former client is representing his own interests and therefore must comply with Rule 4.2); *cf.* Mo. Informal Ethics Op. 2005-059 (n.d.) (lawyer may continue to have direct contact with client who is threatening to file bar complaint against him but has not retained other counsel; even after complaint filed, client not "represented" by disciplinary counsel).

### HAS THE OTHER LAWYER CONSENTED?

Consent to the communication by a represented person's lawyer may be implied from the circumstances. *See Restatement (Third) of the Law Governing Lawyers* § 99 cmt. j (2000) ("consent may be implied rather than express, such as where such direct contact occurs routinely as a matter of custom, unless the opposing lawyer affirmatively protests"); *see also* Cal. Formal Ethics Op. 2011-181 (n.d.) (listing factors relevant to determining whether lawyer has implied consent to communicate with represented party).

That a lawyer "cc"s a client in an e-mail to another lawyer does not necessarily constitute consent to the receiving lawyer to "reply-all" to the message. *See* N.C. Ethics Op. 2012-7 (2013) (other factors to be considered include how the matter is initiated, whether matter is transactional or adversarial, prior course of conduct and extent to which the communication might interfere with lawyer-client relationship); *see also* Alaska Ethics Op. 2018-1 (2018) (receiving lawyer has duty to ask sending lawyer for permission to include client in reply); Ky. Ethics Op. E-442 (2017) ("showing 'cc' to a client on an e-mail, without more, cannot reasonably be regarded as consent to communicate directly with the client"). *But see* N.Y. City Ethics Op. 2009-1 (2009) (in group e-mail communications involving multiple lawyers and their clients, important considerations include how group communication is initiated and whether communication occurs in adversarial setting; e-mail sent by lawyer to opposing counsel with copy to client would imply consent to "reply-all" limited to subject of e-mail "unless otherwise clearly indicated"); *cf.* N.Y. State Ethics Op. 1124 (2017) (lawyer may, but need not, comply with opposing counsel's direction to send copies of all written communication to opposing counsel's client).

## IS THERE A "MATTER" YET?

An important determinant of the applicability of the no-contact rule is whether events have ripened into a "matter." *See, e.g., SEC v. Lines*, 669 F. Supp. 2d 460 (S.D.N.Y. 2009) (SEC lawyer did not violate rule; contact with company president occurred early in course of investigation and there had been no "ripening adverse relationship"); *Johnson v. Cadillac Plastic Grp., Inc.*, 930 F. Supp. 1437 (D. Colo. 1996) (focus should be upon how much of adversarial relationship has developed); *Jorgensen v. Taco Bell Corp.*, 58 Cal. Rptr. 2d 178 (Ct. App. 1996) (lawyer for potential plaintiff in suit against corporation may interview corporate employee as part of pre-suit investigation because no "matter" exists yet).

## CLASS MEMBERS

The majority rule is that once a proceeding has been certified as a class action, Rule 4.2 is applicable to communication with members of the class. Prior to that time, Rule 4.3 applies. *See Jackson v. Bloomberg, L.P.*, No. 13-CV-2001 (JPO), 2015 WL 1822695, 2015 BL 114295 (S.D.N.Y. Apr. 22, 2015); *Bobryk v. Durand Glass Mfg. Co.*, Civ. No. 12–cv–5360 (NLH/JS), 2013 WL 5574504, 2013 BL 279736 (D.N.J. Oct. 9, 2013); *Restatement (Third) of the Law Governing Lawyers* § 99 cmt. 1 (2000). Communicating with putative class members before certification is granted is discussed in the annotation to Rule 4.3.

## JUST WHAT "MATTER" IS THE PERSON REPRESENTED IN?

Rule 4.2 does not prohibit a lawyer from communicating with a represented person about something other than the subject of the representation. *See United States v. Ford*, 176 F.3d 376 (6th Cir. 1999) (government could place informant in prison cell to investigate threats defendant allegedly made against government officials; threats not related to offense for which defendant imprisoned); *Grievance Comm. v. Simels*, 48 F.3d 640 (2d Cir. 1995) (lawyer for criminal defendant may interview potential witness against his client in one matter even though witness represented in another matter, in which witness is potential co-defendant with client; in neither case is individual a "party" in same "matter" within meaning of predecessor Model Code provision); *In re Haynes*, 577 B.R. 711 (E.D. Tenn. 2017) (bankruptcy trustee's communications with clients of law firm not prohibited by Rule 4.2 where "matter" to which communication relates is firm's practices of marketing, solicitation, and fee arrangements rather than clients' bankruptcy filings); *State Farm Mut. Auto. Ins. Co. v. Sanders*, 975 F. Supp. 2d 509 (E.D. Pa. 2013) (lawyers for auto insurer suing physician for insurance fraud were free to contact 130 of his patients, all of whom were personal injury plaintiffs being represented by same law firm; firm's fee agreements clearly limited its representation to the personal injury suits); *Miller v. Material Scis. Corp.*, 986 F. Supp. 1104 (N.D. Ill. 1997) (plaintiff's counsel in securities fraud action did not violate rule by discussing accounting irregularities at defendant corporation with its former plant controller, also named as defendant; former controller represented in SEC investigation but not in fraud action); *People v. Santiago*, 925 N.E.2d 1122 (Ill. 2010) (prosecutors questioning defendant charged with aggravated battery of her child were not required to contact lawyer appointed for her in civil dependency case in juvenile court arising out of same facts); *Iowa Supreme Court Att'y Disciplinary Bd. v. Box*, 715 N.W.2d 758 (Iowa 2006) (lawyer's letter saying individual "visited with [him] concerning her Last Will and Testament and her Revocable Trust, together with other personal matters[, and in] the event you would want to communicate with [her], you should contact [him] instead" was broad enough to include future sale of trust farm property to her nephew); *State ex rel. Okla. Bar Ass'n v. Harper*, 995 P.2d 1143 (Okla. 2000) (insurance defense lawyer's interview with insured driver about passenger's claim against her did not involve same matter as claims on which she was being represented, even though all claims arose out of same accident); ABA Formal Ethics Op. 95-396 (1995) (criminal defense lawyer cannot immunize client from all ex parte contacts by declaring lawyer represents client in all matters); D.C. Ethics Op. 263 (1996) (lawyer may not communicate with respondent about modification of civil protection order if counsel appointed to defend respondent on criminal contempt charges for violating order; modification proceeding and contempt are part of same "matter"); N.Y. State Ethics Op. 904 (2012) (lawyer for investor seeking restitution from investment manager represented by counsel in criminal investigation arising from same facts may contact investment manager without criminal defense counsel's consent); N.Y. State Ethics Op. 884 (2011) (criminal defense counsel may speak directly with complaining witness who is himself subject of separate criminal indictment on which he is represented); *see also United States v. Overseas Shipholding Grp., Inc.*, 625 F.3d 1 (1st Cir. 2010) (lawyer for whistleblower seeking award not required to contact client's appointed counsel from criminal proceeding; matters not the same); *Blanchard v. Edgemark Fin. Corp.*, 175 F.R.D. 293 (N.D. Ill. 1997) (defendants' counsel violated Rule 4.2 by negotiating with class representative through lawyer who was handling representative's related state court litigation but was not class counsel of record); Va. Ethics Op. 1820 (2006) (lawyers working in claims department of railroad prohibited from contacting any employee known to be represented in connection with his injuries, even if only to offer job retraining and disability support services).

## When Represented Person Is an Organization: Which Constituents Are "Represented"?

When an organization—a corporation, for example—is the represented person, certain officers and employees will be off-limits under Rule 4.2. Just who is off-limits has engendered a great deal of litigation. *See Wagner v. City of Holyoke*, 183 F. Supp. 2d 289 (D. Mass. 2001) ("that courts have to address Rule 4.2 so often, weighing the relative interests and needs of the parties case by case, is more a reflection of the rule's lack of clarity than any desire to insert themselves in what should be the self-executing application of the rules of professional conduct").

The issues are particularly well analyzed in *Snider v. Superior Court*, 7 Cal. Rptr. 3d 119 (Ct. App. 2003), and Wis. Ethics Op. E-07-01 (2007). *See generally* James L. Burt & Jeremy J. Cook, *Ethical Considerations Concerning Contacts by Counsel or Investigators with Present and Former Employees of an Opposing Party*, 38 St. Mary's L.J. 963 (2007); William Jacob, *Increased Access to Corporate Constituents Under New Model Rule 4.2*, 14 Prof. Law., no. 2, at 20 (Winter 2003); Lori W. Ketcham, *Skip Counsel Issues in NLRB Unfair Labor Practice Investigations*, 16 Prof. Law., no. 1, at 18 (2005).

### • Different Tests

Over the years, different tests emerged to determine whether an organization's officer or employee was deemed to be represented by the organization's counsel for purposes of Rule 4.2.

Many courts used a "managing/speaking" test, and prohibited direct contact with any individual who had managerial responsibility or who could speak for the company or whose acts or omissions could be imputed to the company. *See, e.g., Palmer v. Pioneer Inn Assocs., Ltd.*, 338 F.3d 981 (9th Cir. 2003) ("managing authority sufficient to give [him] the right to speak for, and bind," company); *NAACP v. Fla. Dep't of Corr.*, 122 F. Supp. 2d 1335 (M.D. Fla. 2000) (plaintiff's lawyer could interview rank-and-file prison employees; "unlikely" their statements could bind their employer or that their acts or omissions would be imputed to it); *S.F. Unified Sch. Dist. ex rel. Contreras v. First Student, Inc.*, 153 Cal. Rptr. 3d 583 (Ct. App. 2013) (because employee's act or omission within scope of employment could be imputed to employer under respondeat superior, no informal interviews allowed) (California's Rule 2-100(B)(2) applies if employee's acts or omissions may be imputed to employer); *Featherstone v. Schaerrer*, 34 P.3d 194 (Utah 2001) (secretary-treasurer of defendant corporation deemed represented; his statements could bind company); Alaska Ethics Op. 2011-2 (2011) (rule applies only if employee can speak for and bind corporation; construing "managerial responsibility" test adopted in state's version of comment).

Some courts looked to the phrase "any other person . . . whose statement may constitute an admission on the part of the organization" previously contained in Comment [4] (superseded in 2002 by Comment [7]) and invoked the evidentiary concept of an admission by a party opponent. (The phrase was deleted from the model version of the comment in 2002 but some jurisdictions continue to use the test.) *See, e.g., Weeks v. Indep. Sch. Dist. No. I-89*, 230 F.3d 1201 (10th Cir. 2000) (disqualifying lawyer for communicating ex parte with school employee whose statements about school procedures would be admissible under hearsay exception to federal rules of evidence); *Richards v. Holsum Bakery, Inc.*, No. CV09-00418-PHX-MHM, 2009 WL 3740725, 2009 BL 265670 (D. Ariz. Nov. 5, 2009) (because employee's statements "appear to meet the 801(d) standard [as admissions on organization's part], Ms. de Para is a 'party' under Rule 4.2"); *Calloway v. DST Sys., Inc.*, No. 98-1303-CV-W-6, 2000 WL 230244, 2000 BL 1285 (W.D. Mo. Feb. 28, 2000) (manager of company is "represented person" because his statements may be deemed admissions by company). The problematic meaning of "admission" in this context is discussed in *Palmer v. Pioneer Inn Assocs., Ltd.*, 338 F.3d 981 (9th Cir. 2003).

Some courts used the old "control group" or "Upjohn" test (see *Upjohn Co. v. United States*, 449 U.S. 383 (1981)) developed from federal privilege law. *See Weibrecht v. S. Ill. Transfer, Inc.*, 241 F.3d 875 (7th Cir. 2001).

Courts also looked to the constituent's relationship with the organization's lawyers. *See, e.g., Andrews v. Goodyear Tire & Rubber Co.*, 191 F.R.D. 59 (D.N.J. 2000) (manager of represented company not in litigation control group for purposes of anticontact rule); *Messing, Rudavsky & Weliky, P.C. v. President & Fellows of Harvard Coll.*, 764 N.E.2d 825 (Mass. 2002) (lawyer for plaintiff suing police department could contact certain lieutenants, patrol officers, and dispatcher employed by police department because they were witnesses rather than participants, were not involved in directing litigation, and were not authorized to make binding admissions on behalf of department).

New York courts developed an "alter ego" test that some other jurisdictions also took up. *See Niesig v. Team I*, 558 N.E.2d 1030 (N.Y. 1990) (only those corporate employees who could be considered company's alter egos and whose acts, omissions, or statements are binding on corporation are considered represented persons for purposes of anticontact rule); *see also Dent v. Kaufman*, 406 S.E.2d 68 (W. Va. 1991); *Strawser v. Exxon Co. U.S.A.*, 843 P.2d 613 (Wyo. 1992).

### • *2002 Amendment: New Test*

In 2002, the comment to Rule 4.2 was amended to provide clearer guidance. *See* American Bar Association, *A Legislative History: The Development of the ABA Model Rules of Professional Conduct, 1982–2013*, at 566 (2013) (noting criticism that managing/speaking test vague and overly broad).

Under the 2002 version of Comment [7], the permissibility of informal contacts no longer turns on the constituent's managerial responsibility or ability to make admissions on the organization's behalf. Instead it turns on whether the constituent "supervises, directs or regularly consults with the organization's lawyer concerning the matter or has authority to obligate the organization with respect to the matter." However, the amended comment retains the prohibition on communicating with a constituent whose act or omission in the matter may be imputed to the organization. *Goswami v. DePaul Univ.*, 8 F. Supp. 3d 1004 (N.D. Ill. 2014), thoroughly reviews the development of the various tests before rejecting an interpretation of the amended comment that would have barred contact with a constituent who either supervises or directs *anyone* in the organization or regularly consults with the organization's lawyers about the matter. *See Peterson v. Murphy*, No. 2:16-cv-00075-EJL-REB, 2018

WL 1526070, 2018 BL 107231 (D. Idaho Mar. 28, 2018) (lawyer for plaintiff in age discrimination suit violated rule by communicating with defendant's highest-ranking employee at facility who had signed plaintiff's performance evaluations and had authority to obligate defendant in matter, even if that authority was limited); *Sowell v. Dicara*, 127 A.3d 356 (Conn. App. Ct. 2015) (plaintiff's lawyer sent letter directly to members of defendant's board of directors; rule violation even though entity had been dissolved and was in process of winding up); Ill. Ethics Op. 09-01 (2009) (direct communication permitted if employee's acts or omissions not imputable to organization and employee does not supervise, direct, or regularly consult with organization's lawyer or have authority to obligate organization); Vt. Ethics Op. 2011-5 (n.d.) (defense lawyer in suit brought by condominium association's board of directors may contact individual condominium owners about litigation if they are not board members, do not supervise, direct, or regularly consult with association's lawyer, and have no authority to act on association's behalf regarding litigation); Wis. Ethics Op. E-07-01 (2007) (direct talks with corporate constituent permissible unless his job brings him into regular contact with corporate counsel, or his conduct imputable to organization; comprehensive review of authorities); *cf. Iowa Supreme Court Att'y Disciplinary Bd. v. Stowers*, 823 N.W.2d 1 (Iowa 2012) (charity's CFO was managerial level and therefore represented (using old managing/speaking test to interpret amended comment) but single member of charity's board of directors did not have power to bind it and therefore was not). *See generally* Bran C. Noonan, *The* Niesig *and NLRA Union: A Revised Standard for Identifying High-Level Employees for Ex Parte Interviews*, 54 N.Y.L. Sch. L. Rev. 261 (2010).

### • *Fact Witnesses*

Rule 4.2 does not preclude a lawyer from interviewing fact witnesses who are employed by a represented organization but who are not part of the group identified by Comment [7]. *See Perry v. City of Pontiac*, 254 F.R.D. 309 (E.D. Mich. 2008) (witnesses were rank-and-file police officers); *Cole v. Appalachian Power Co.*, 903 F. Supp. 975 (S.D. W. Va. 1995) (employees were "mere holders of factual information"); *see also Rivera v. Lutheran Med. Ctr.*, 866 N.Y.S.2d 520 (Sup. Ct. 2008) (to block employment discrimination plaintiff's informal access to witnesses who were or had been employed by defendant corporation, defense counsel offered to represent them in connection with case at defendant's expense; as sanction for solicitation, court disqualified defense counsel from representing witnesses but not defendants); *cf.* Rule 3.4, cmt. [4] (lawyer may advise client's employees to refrain from giving information to another party, "for the employees may identify their interests with those of the client").

### • *Former Employees of Corporation*

A 2002 amendment to Comment [7] unequivocally declares that the anticontact rule does not apply to former employees of a represented organization. American Bar Association, *A Legislative History: The Development of the ABA Model Rules of Professional Conduct, 1982–2013*, at 566 (2013); *see In re Digitek Prod. Liab. Litig.*, 648 F. Supp. 2d 795 (S.D. W. Va. 2009); *Bryant v. Yorktowne Cabinetry, Inc.*, 538 F. Supp. 2d 948 (W.D. Va. 2008); *Smith v. Kalamazoo Ophthalmology*, 322 F. Supp. 2d 883 (W.D. Mich. 2004); *Muriel*

*Siebert & Co. v. Intuit Inc.*, 868 N.E.2d 208 (N.Y. 2007) (permissible to interview terminated top executive even though he played key role in underlying events and litigation); Mich. Informal Ethics Op. RI-360 (2013) (permissible to contact unrepresented former supervisory employees); R.I. Ethics Op. 2012-02 (2012). *See generally* Susan J. Becker, *Discovery of Information and Documents from a Litigant's Former Employees: Synergy and Synthesis of Civil Rules, Ethical Standards, Privilege Doctrines, and Common Law Principles*, 81 Neb. L. Rev. 868 (2003).

### • *In-House or General Counsel of Corporation*

The fact that an organization has a general counsel does not itself prevent another lawyer from communicating directly with the organization's constituents. *See, e.g., SEC v. Lines*, 669 F. Supp. 2d 460 (S.D.N.Y. 2009) (neither organization nor president necessarily "represented" in particular matter simply because corporation has general counsel); *Terra Int'l, Inc. v. Miss. Chem. Corp.*, 913 F. Supp. 1306 (N.D. Iowa 1996) ("[A]n employer cannot unilaterally create or impose representation of employees by corporate counsel. . .. '[A]utomatic representation' [would] impede the course of investigation leading to or following the filing of a lawsuit."); *Humco, Inc. v. Noble*, 31 S.W.3d 916 (Ky. 2000) (knowledge that corporation has in-house counsel is not actual notice of representation); ABA Formal Ethics Op. 95-396 (1995) (general counsel cannot assert blanket representation of all employees); Alaska Ethics Op. 2006-1 (2006) (lawyer acting on own behalf in matter not in litigation may communicate directly with corporate management even though he knows corporation regularly represented by counsel, but once lawyer knows corporation asked counsel to deal with particular matter, Rule 4.2 applies); Ohio Sup. Ct. Ethics Op. 2005-3 (2005) (general counsel cannot assert blanket representation of all current and former employees; under predecessor Code); Wis. Ethics Op. E-07-01 (2007) (fact that organization has in-house counsel or regularly retains outside counsel does not make it "represented" in connection with any particular matter). *See generally* Joan Colson, Comment, *Rule of Ethics or Substantive Law: Who Controls an Individual's Right to Choose a Lawyer in Today's Corporate Environment*, 38 J. Marshall L. Rev. 1265 (Summer 2005).

A lawyer is generally free to communicate with a corporate opponent's in-house counsel about a case in which the corporation has hired outside counsel. ABA Formal Ethics Op. 06-443 (2006); *accord* D.C. Ethics Op. 331 (2005); Wis. Ethics Op. E-07-01 (2007); *see also* Phila. Ethics Op. 2000-11 (2000) (under certain circumstances, even though outside counsel has appeared for organization, in-house counsel may still represent organization for purposes of communications under Rule 4.2).

## "AUTHORIZED BY LAW" IN CIVIL CONTEXT

According to an ABA ethics opinion, the exception permitting communication authorized by law is satisfied by "a constitutional provision, statute or court rule, having the force and effect of law, that expressly allows a particular communication to occur in the absence of counsel." ABA Formal Ethics Op. 95-396 (1995). *See, e.g., Wilkerson v. Brown*, 995 P.2d 393 (Kan. Ct. App. 1999) (statutes allowing for service of demands and offers of judgment on opposing party trigger "authorized by law" exception to anticontact rule); *Lewis v. Bayer A.G.*, No. 2353 Aug. Term 2001, 2002 WL

1472339 (Pa. Com. Pl. June 12, 2002) (drug company's mailings to putative members of plaintiff class of patients with adverse drug reactions sent pursuant to FDA regulations and thus "authorized by law"); N.Y. State Ethics Op. 894 (2011) (statute authorizing landlord's lawyer to serve process on represented party challenging validity of original service also lets him ask for signed acknowledgment of service); Va. Ethics Op. 1861 (2012) (although anticontact rule generally binds lawyer serving as bankruptcy trustee, many direct contacts with debtor in Chapter 13 proceeding will come within "authorized by law" exception); *see also Parker v. Pepsi-Cola Gen. Bottlers, Inc.,* 249 F. Supp. 2d 1006 (N.D. Ill. 2003) (issuance of subpoena does not invoke "authorized by law" exception; lawyer who subpoenaed witness whom he knew to have counsel not authorized to conduct deposition in counsel's absence); Tex. Ethics Op. 613 (2011) (insurance defense counsel may not tell plaintiff settlement money transferred to plaintiff's counsel's account, notwithstanding that Texas Department of Insurance "strongly encourages" direct notice).

The only change to the blackletter rule, as opposed to the comment, made by the 2002 amendments was to expand "authorized by law" to "authorized . . . by law or a court order." Although "a communication with a represented person pursuant to a court order will ordinarily fall within the 'authorized by law' exception," the specific reference was added "to alert lawyers to the availability of judicial relief in the rare situations in which it is needed." American Bar Association, *A Legislative History: The Development of the ABA Model Rules of Professional Conduct, 1982–2013,* at 565 (2013).

The majority position is that a federal statute voiding any rule that interferes with a railway employee's ability to volunteer information about accidents does not supersede Rule 4.2 or trigger the "authorized by law" exception. *See Weibrecht v. S. Ill. Transfer, Inc.,* 241 F.3d 875 (7th Cir. 2001) (in maritime personal injury suit, section 60 of Federal Employer's Liability Act does not authorize plaintiff's lawyer to contact tugboat's pilot directly); *Hornick v. Am. Commercial Barge Line,* No. 5:07CV-140R, 2008 WL 2168893, 2008 BL 109046 (W.D. Ky. May 23, 2008) (collecting cases). *See generally* John E. Tyler, III, *FELA § 60 v. Ethical Rule 4.2: More Than Meets the Eye in a Conflict Between State's Rights and Federal Law,* 69 UMKC L. Rev. 791 (Summer 2001).

## COMMUNICATING WITH GOVERNMENT

Comment [5] was amended in 2002 to recognize "the possibility that a citizen's constitutional right to petition and the public policy of ensuring a citizen's right of access to government decisionmakers may create an exception to this Rule." American Bar Association, *A Legislative History: The Development of the ABA Model Rules of Professional Conduct, 1982–2013,* at 565 (2013). Before the amendment, ABA Formal Opinion 97-408 had already declared that Rule 4.2 permits a lawyer representing a private party in a controversy with the government to communicate about the matter with government officials having authority to recommend action in the matter, provided the sole purpose of the communication is to address a policy issue, including settlement, rather than the specific facts of the case. ABA Formal Ethics Op. 97-408 (1997). *See* D.C. Ethics Op. 340 (2007) (with disclosures, lawyer may discuss substantive legal issues with officer of government agency with which client in dispute, and with officers at other agencies notwithstanding they could affect government's position in matter); Ill. Ethics Op. 13-09 (2013) (lawyer whose client is appealing municipal tax assessment may communicate with municipal official who will decide appeal to talk about underlying policy issues, but not to talk about resolving appeal; rejecting in part reasoning of ABA Formal Opinion 97-408); Me. Ethics Op. 181 (2003) (lawyer representing municipal employee in grievance proceeding may not contact high-level town officials responsible for making litigation decisions unless town's lawyer consents; irrelevant that nonlawyers, who are permitted to represent employees in grievance proceedings, routinely do so); N.C. Ethics Op. 2005-5 (2006) (lawyer representing former county employee must comply with county attorney's request to direct communications about threatened litigation to him rather than to county manager or human resources director and may not, at public meeting of county board, approach board member to complain that county attorney trying to keep lawyer from communicating with board); *see also* Nev. Ethics Op. 54 (2018) (lawyer may make public records request to government entity with whom lawyer is involved in litigation, but any communication beyond records request would violate rule); Or. Ethics Op. 2005-144 (rev. 2007) (same). *Compare United States v. Sierra Pac. Indus.*, 759 F. Supp. 2d 1206 (E.D. Cal. 2010) (when lawyer for defendant in government's suit alleging corporate responsibility for forest fire attended Forest Service field trip open to public and questioned lower-level employees, without disclosing his role in the lawsuit, he was not exercising right of petition but was "attempting to gain information for use in the litigation" in violation of California's anticontact rule as well as Model Rule 4.2), *with United States v. County of Los Angeles*, No. CV 15-05903 DDP (JEMx), 2016 WL 4059712, 2016 BL 243919 (C.D. Cal. July 27, 2016) (lawyer suing over alleged ADA violations at county jail system did not violate California's no-contact rule by discussing matter with county health director at social gathering, after disclosing lawyer's involvement in case). *See generally* Matthew K. Corbin, Insights: "Restraints on Lawyers' Ex Parte Communications with Government Agencies," *ABA/BNA Lawyers' Manual on Professional Conduct*, 30 Law. Man. Prof. Conduct 392 (Current Reports, June 4, 2014); Julia E. Fish, Note, *A Practical Solution to the Government Contacts Problem: Opinion 340 Updates the D.C. Exception to the No-Contact Rule*, 21 Geo. J. Legal Ethics 739 (Summer 2008); Jana S. Pail, Note, *How Far Should the "No Contact" Rule Go to Protect Government Employees? Finding a Solution in the Land Use Regulation Context*, 20 J.L. & Com. 129 (Fall 2000).

## "AUTHORIZED BY LAW" IN CRIMINAL CONTEXT

### • *Prosecutors Communicating with Represented Suspects*

The majority of courts have long held that communication with represented criminal suspects as part of noncustodial investigations, before formal proceedings are initiated, does not violate the anticontact rule. *See, e.g., United States v. Elliott*, 684 F. App'x 685 (10th Cir. 2017) (prosecutor's use of undercover informant to elicit incriminating admissions prior to indictment fell within "authorized by law" exception notwithstanding rule amendment from "party" to "person"; construing Wyoming law); *United States v. Talao*, 222 F.3d 1133 (9th Cir. 2000) (preindictment noncustodial communication with defendant corporation's bookkeeper, who was represented by corporation's lawyer, did not violate Rule 4.2); *United States v. Balter*, 91 F.3d 427 (3d

Cir. 1996) (agreeing with all circuits—except Second Circuit—that Rule 4.2 does not apply to contacts made by prosecutors or their agents before indictment; prosecutor did not violate Rule 4.2 by having informant surreptitiously tape conversations with suspected instigator of murder-for-hire); *United States v. Sabean*, No. 2:15-cr-175-GZS, 2016 WL 5721135, 2016 BL 329356 (D. Me. Oct. 3, 2016) (preindictment, noncustodial interview by IRS agents of individual indicted more than twenty months later was "authorized by law"); *United States v. Isch*, No. CR-09-050-D, 2009 WL 2409548, 2009 BL 164641 (W.D. Okla. Aug. 3, 2009) (when suspect under investigation had retained counsel but not been indicted, government did not violate Rule 4.2 by causing suspect's supervisor to secretly record their conversations); *United States v. Joseph Binder Schweizer Emblem Co.*, 167 F. Supp. 2d 862 (E.D.N.C. 2001) (government agent could conduct preindictment interview with company manager, despite pending qui tam action against company, when government had not yet intervened); *In re John Doe, Inc.*, 194 F.R.D. 375 (D. Mass. 2000) (granting prosecutor's motion to interview three employees of corporation represented by counsel); *United States v. Marcus*, 849 F. Supp. 417 (D. Md. 1994) (neither Rule 4.2 nor its Model Code predecessor precludes preindictment undercover contacts between government and represented target in noncustodial setting; collecting cases). *Contra United States v. Tapp*, No. CR107-108, 2008 WL 2371422, 2008 BL 118738 (S.D. Ga. June 4, 2008) (endorsing reasoning in *United States v. Hammad*, 858 F.2d 834 (2d Cir. 1988), that "pre-indictment contact with represented persons should not be the Government's standard practice"); ABA Formal Ethics Op. 95-396 (1995) ("limiting the Rule to post-indictment communications could allow the government to manipulate grand jury proceedings to avoid its encumbrances"). *See generally* William Edmonson, Note, *A "New" No-Contact Rule: Proposing an Addition to the No-Contact Rule to Address Questioning of Suspects After Unreasonable Charging Delays*, 80 N.Y.U. L. Rev. 1773 (Dec. 2005); Caleb Mason, *The Police-Prosecutor Relationship and the No-Contact Rule: Conflicting Incentives After* Montejo v. Louisiana *and* Maryland v. Shatzer, 58 Clev. St. L. Rev. 747 (2010).

### • *Applicability of Rule 4.2 to Federal Prosecutors*

In 1988, a sharp debate arose over whether Rule 4.2 applies to federal prosecutors conducting criminal investigations. The U.S. Justice Department, in response to the decision in *United States v. Hammad*, 858 F.2d 834 (2d Cir. 1988), which suppressed evidence obtained by a prosecutor in violation of the anticontact provision of the predecessor Model Code, declared that federal prosecutors could not be sanctioned for contacts with a defendant "in the course of authorized law enforcement activity." *See* Richard Thornburgh, U.S. DOJ, Memorandum, *Communications with Persons Represented by Counsel* (June 6, 1989), reprinted in *In re Doe*, 801 F. Supp. 478 (D.N.M. 1992); *see also* "Analysis," *ABA/BNA Lawyers' Manual on Professional Conduct*, 5 Law. Man. Prof. Conduct 427 (Current Reports, Jan. 3, 1990).

In 1994, the Department of Justice promulgated regulations codifying much of the Thornburgh Memorandum. *See* 28 C.F.R. § 77 (1994). The regulations authorized certain federal prosecutors to make ex parte contacts—before charge, arrest, or indictment—with persons known to be represented in the matter being investigated. The Eighth Circuit invalidated the regulations as being "outside" any authority granted by Congress to the U.S. Attorney General and accordingly held that any ex parte contact made pursuant to the regulations but in violation of local ethics rules is not "authorized by law." *United States ex rel. O'Keefe v. McDonnell Douglas Corp.*, 132 F.3d 1252 (8th Cir. 1998); *see also In re Howes*, 940 P.2d 159 (N.M. 1997) (federal prosecutor's communication with represented party not authorized by law despite his compliance with office policy; U.S. Justice Department not authorized to issue policies or regulations absolving its lawyers from state-imposed ethics obligations). (The Justice Department's challenges to the state court's authority to discipline this prosecutor were resolved in favor of New Mexico in *In re Doe*, 801 F. Supp. 478 (D.N.M. 1992), and in *United States v. Ferrara*, 54 F.3d 825 (D.C. Cir. 1995).)

In 1998, Congress countered with the Citizens Protection Act, also known as the McDade Amendment, under which federal prosecutors are made subject to state ethics rules. 28 U.S.C. § 530B (1998). *See United States v. Singleton*, 165 F.3d 1297 (10th Cir. 1999) (Henry, J., concurring) (McDade "repeals" Thornburgh Memorandum); *United States v. Brown*, 356 F. Supp. 2d 470 (M.D. Pa. 2005) (rejecting argument that passage of McDade requires court to reexamine whether anticontact rule indeed applies to noncustodial preindictment communication). *See generally* Megan Browdie & Wei Xiang, Current Development, *Chevron Protects Citizens: Reviving the Citizens Protection Act*, 22 Geo. J. Legal Ethics 695 (Summer 2009) ("[Act] requires federal courts to fully defer to states' interpretations of their own ethics rules and to apply the states' remedies").

The history of the Citizens Protection Act is well explained in *United States v. Tapp*, No. CR107-108, 2008 WL 2371422, 2008 BL 118738, at *4–20 (S.D. Ga. June 4, 2008). *See generally* Bruce A. Green, *Prosecutors and Professional Regulation*, 25 Geo. J. Legal Ethics 873 (Fall 2012); Rima Sirota, *Reassessing the Citizens Protection Act: A Good Thing It Passed, and a Good Thing It Failed*, 43 Sw. L. Rev. 51 (2013) (praising act because it "succeeded in nullifying DOJ's ill-conceived claim of exclusive interpretive authority over the no-contact rule for its own lawyers" yet "failed to accomplish its proponents' ill-conceived goal of limiting federal involvement in pre-charge investigative communications with represented persons").

## CONSEQUENCES OF RULE VIOLATION

As a practical matter, violations of Rule 4.2 occurring in the course of a civil proceeding are generally addressed by the court hearing the proceeding; courts have ordered evidentiary remedies, return of documents, monetary sanctions, and even disqualification. *See, e.g., Hammond v. City of Junction City*, 126 F. App'x 886 (10th Cir. 2005) (affirming, as sanction for ex parte communications with city's director of human resources, order prohibiting counsel for putative plaintiff class in employment discrimination action from representing any class of individuals in any other action based upon class allegations in present case); *McClelland v. Blazin' Wings, Inc.*, 675 F. Supp. 2d 1074 (D. Colo. 2009) (in personal injury case arising out of bar fight, plaintiff barred from using interview with bartender that was surreptitiously obtained and recorded by investigator); *Parker v. Pepsi-Cola Gen. Bottlers, Inc.*, 249 F. Supp. 2d 1006 (N.D. Ill. 2003) (as sanction for deposing witness without his counsel, court barred employer from using deposition testimony or evidence gained from it, ordered transcripts destroyed, limited time allowed for future deposition of witness, and awarded fees arising from preparation of witness's sanctions motion); *Meachum v. Outdoor World Corp.*, 654 N.Y.S.2d 240 (Sup. Ct. 1996) (class certification denied as sanction for lawyer's contact with representatives of defendant corporation). *See generally* Fred C. Zacharias, *Evidence Laws and Ethics Rules*, 19 Prof. Law., no. 2, at 12 (2009).

In criminal cases, however, the approach is different. *See, e.g., United States v. Lopez*, 4 F.3d 1455 (9th Cir. 1993) (dismissal of indictment as sanction for prosecutor's violation of anticontact rule was abuse of discretion; "when there is no showing of substantial prejudice to the defendant, lesser sanctions, such as holding the prosecutor in contempt or referral to the state bar for disciplinary proceedings," can suffice); *United States v. McNaughton*, 848 F. Supp. 1195 (E.D. Pa. 1994) (suppression denied; ethics rules not enforced under constitutional exclusionary rule). *Compare United States v. Koerber*, 966 F. Supp. 2d 1207 (D. Utah 2013) (preindictment communication in violation of Rule 4.2 and McDade violated defendant's due process rights; exclusionary rule requires suppression), *with United States v. Sabean*, No. 2:15-cr-175-GZS, 2016 WL 5721135, 2016 BL 329356 (D. Me. Oct. 3, 2016) ("most courts have determined that suppression must be reserved for only the most egregious violations of the no-contact rule and have declined to order suppression"; collecting cases). *See generally* Neil Salon, Note, *Prosecutors and Model Rule 4.2: An Examination of Appropriate Remedies*, 12 Geo. J. Legal Ethics 393 (Winter 1999).

Notwithstanding remedies imposed by a tribunal in the course of a legal proceeding, the offending lawyer is still subject to discipline for violating Rule 4.2. *See, e.g., In re Hatcher*, 42 N.E.3d 80 (Ind. 2015); *Iowa Supreme Court Att'y Disciplinary Bd. v. Box*, 715 N.W.2d 758 (Iowa 2006); *Bratcher v. Ky. Bar Ass'n*, 290 S.W.3d 648 (Ky. 2009); *In re Williams-Bensaadat*, 181 So. 3d 684 (La. 2015); *see also In re Nguyen*, 215 So. 3d 668 (La. 2017) (out-of-state lawyer who violated Rule 4.2 and then failed to cooperate with disciplinary authorities barred from seeking temporary or limited admission for one year).

# TRANSACTIONS WITH PERSONS OTHER THAN CLIENTS

## Rule 4.3
### *Dealing with Unrepresented Person*

In dealing on behalf of a client with a person who is not represented by counsel, a lawyer shall not state or imply that the lawyer is disinterested. When the lawyer knows or reasonably should know that the unrepresented person misunderstands the lawyer's role in the matter, the lawyer shall make reasonable efforts to correct the misunderstanding. The lawyer shall not give legal advice to an unrepresented person, other than the advice to secure counsel, if the lawyer knows or reasonably should know that the interests of such a person are or have a reasonable possibility of being in conflict with the interests of the client.

## COMMENT

[1] An unrepresented person, particularly one not experienced in dealing with legal matters, might assume that a lawyer is disinterested in loyalties or is a disinterested authority on the law even when the lawyer represents a client. In order to avoid a misunderstanding, a lawyer will typically need to identify the lawyer's client and, where necessary, explain that the client has interests opposed to those of the unrepresented person. For misunderstandings that sometimes arise when a lawyer for an organization deals with an unrepresented constituent, see Rule 1.13(f).

[2] The Rule distinguishes between situations involving unrepresented persons whose interests may be adverse to those of the lawyer's client and those in which the person's interests are not in conflict with the client's. In the former situation, the possibility that the lawyer will compromise the unrepresented person's interests is so great that the Rule prohibits the giving of any advice, apart from the advice to obtain counsel. Whether a lawyer is giving impermissible advice may depend on the experience and sophistication of the unrepresented person, as well as the setting in which the behavior and comments occur. This Rule does not prohibit a lawyer from negotiating the terms of a transaction or settling a dispute with an unrepresented person. So long as the lawyer has explained that the lawyer represents an adverse party and is not representing the person, the lawyer may inform the person of the terms on which the lawyer's client will enter into an agreement or settle a matter, prepare documents that require the person's signature and explain the lawyer's own view of the meaning of the document or the lawyer's view of the underlying legal obligations.

**Definitional Cross-References**

"Knows" *See* Rule 1.0(f)

"Reasonable" *See* Rule 1.0(h)

"Reasonably should know" *See* Rule 1.0(j)

**State Rules Comparison**

http://ambar.org/MRPCStateCharts

## ANNOTATION

### CLARIFYING LAWYER'S ROLE

Under Rule 4.3, a lawyer acting on behalf of a client may not mislead an unrepresented person—or take advantage of an unrepresented person's misunderstanding—about the lawyer's role in the matter. *See Marino v. Usher*, 673 F. App'x 125 (3d Cir. 2016) (plaintiff's lawyer, who knew or reasonably should have known unrepresented defendant believed himself to be merely a witness in matter, violated rule by continuing to foster defendant's misunderstanding); *In re Katrina Canal Breaches Consol. Litig.*, No. 05-4182 "K" (2), 2008 WL 2066999 (E.D. La. May 14, 2008) (although investigators said they worked for private investigative agency and did not say they were working for lawyer, no Rule 4.3 violation because they did not deliberately foster "impression that [they] were on [the interviewees'] side"); *In re Air Crash Disaster*, 909 F. Supp. 1116 (N.D. Ill. 1995) (plaintiffs' lawyers sent questionnaires to unrepresented airline pilots employed by defendant, purporting to be part of "independent survey" of pilots whose names had been provided by Federal Aviation Administration; questionnaire results excluded as sanction for Rule 4.3 violation); *In re Hansen*, 868 N.W.2d 55 (Minn. 2015) (lawyer met with husband and wife about divorce but failed to clarify to wife that he only represented husband); D.C. Ethics Op. 321 (2003) (respondent's lawyer in domestic violence case may send investigator to interview unrepresented petitioner; lawyer must try to ensure petitioner understands roles and interests, but need not advise petitioner to obtain independent legal advice before signing any documents); Mont. Ethics Op. 011115 (2001) (lawyer representing client in civil matter that could also subject client to criminal charges may contact unrepresented putative victims, provided lawyer explains his role and interest); *see also Sisk v. Transylvania Cmty. Hosp., Inc.*, 695 S.E.2d 429 (N.C. 2010) (revoking pro hac vice admission; in suit against hospital, lawyers for plaintiff retained expert whom drug company retained in similar case; lawyers' failure to tell expert they were going to add drug company as defendant was "inconsistent with fair dealings as reflected in Rule 4.3"); *cf. Andrews v. Goodyear Tire & Rubber Co.*, 191 F.R.D. 59 (D.N.J. 2000) (plaintiffs' lawyer had no obligation to tell unrepresented employee of corporate defendant that corporation's lawyer was not representing him). *See generally* George M. Cohen, *Beyond the No-Contact Rule: Ex Parte Contact by Lawyers with Nonclients*, 87 Tul. L. Rev. 1197 (June 2013); Ben Kempinen, *Dealing Fairly with an Unrepresented Person*, 78 Wis. Law. 12 (Oct. 2005).

As to whether the lawyer should know the unrepresented person misunderstands the lawyer's role, compare *In re Millett*, 241 P.3d 35 (Kan. 2010) (lawyer for defendant charged with online sexual solicitation accompanied defendant's brother to police interview after advising brother he could safely testify that it was really he who had gone online, to play practical joke on defendant; lawyer "knew or should have known" brother thought he was protecting his interests), with *In re Jensen*, 191 P.3d 1118 (Kan. 2008) (although witness subpoenaed by other side in custody case clearly misunderstood father's lawyer's role, court rejected hearing panel's finding that lawyer "should have known" of witness's confusion; it was not readily apparent, and "other portions of the conversation might well have provided [the witness] with a clue as to Jensen's role").

To "avoid a misunderstanding," according to Comment [1], "a lawyer will typically need to identify the lawyer's client and, where necessary, explain that the client has interests opposed to those of the unrepresented person." *See, e.g., In re Greene*, 6 N.E.3d 947 (Ind. 2014) (letters sent by hospital to injured patients implied that its lawyer would advocate on behalf of patients in getting their insurance companies to pay their medical bills); *In re Klemp*, 418 P.3d 733 (Or. 2018) (lawyer who had client's incarcerated wife sign power of attorney failed to correct her mistaken impression that lawyer represented both spouses; telling her about bar's lawyer referral service and to contact another lawyer if she had questions insufficient). Some older authority, still frequently cited, also required in cases involving a corporate opponent that the lawyer advise an employee of the entity of his right to refuse to be interviewed without the company's lawyer (or other counsel) present. *See Monsanto Co. v. Aetna Cas. & Sur. Co.*, 593 A.2d 1013 (Del. Super. Ct. 1990); *see also McCallum v. C.S.X. Transp., Inc.*, 149 F.R.D. 104 (M.D.N.C. 1993) (applying *Monsanto* requirement to former employee interviews without drawing distinction); *In re Envtl. Ins. Declaratory Judgment Actions*, 600 A.2d 165 (N.J. Super. Ct. Law Div. 1991) (same). However, the courts in those cases had already found violations of Rule 4.3, and were setting ground rules in the course of granting remedial relief; the rule itself does not require any such advice. *See* Phila. Ethics Op. 2014-3 (2014) (lawyer must disclose her capacity, must not elicit privileged information, and must honor former employee's request that his personal lawyer or corporation's lawyer be present; no requirement that lawyer also advise of right to have counsel present); *see also* ABA Formal Ethics Op. 91-359 (1991) (Rule 4.3 requires lawyer to clearly explain his role, his client's identity, and fact that interviewee is adverse party).

## Social Networking Sites

A lawyer seeking access to the nonpublic portions of an unrepresented person's social networking site must do so in a way that does not involve deception or give the impression that the lawyer is disinterested. Authorities differ on the extent of disclosure required by Rule 4.3. *See* Colo. Ethics Op. 127 (2015) (must disclose lawyer's name, fact that lawyer is acting on behalf of a client, and general nature of matter; may also have to disclose other information, such as client's name or fact that client's interests are opposed to those of unrepresented person, if necessary to avoid misunderstanding); D.C. Ethics Op. 371 (2016) (lawyers should identify themselves, their client, and the matter and state that they are lawyers); Me. Ethics Op. 217 (2017) (whether and extent to which lawyer must disclose purpose for requesting access to unrepresented person's social media website depends on circumstances); Mass. Ethics Op. 2014-5 (2014) (lawyer seeking access to nonpublic portion of unrepresented potential adversary's social networking site must disclose her identity as party's lawyer); N.H. Ethics Op. 2012-13/5 (2013) (lawyer must identify self and role); Or. Ethics Op. 2013-189 (2013) (lawyer may ask represented person for access to non-public website information as long as no misrepresentation involved); Pa. Formal Ethics Op. 2014-300 (2014) (lawyer must disclose his or her identity and purpose; failure to disclose purpose would imply lawyer is disinterested); W. Va. Ethics Op. 2015-2 (2015) (same); *cf.* Phila. Ethics Op. 2009-02 (2009) (lawyer's use of third party to "friend" unrepresented witness to gain access to private website does not implicate Rule 4.3, but deception does implicate Rule 8.4). *Compare* N.Y. State Ethics Op. 843 (2010) (lawyer may access public Facebook and MySpace profiles but may not send "friend" request to unrepresented party), *with* N.Y. City Formal Ethics Op. 2010-2 (2010) (lawyer may "friend" unrepresented person without disclosing reason for request; no mention of Rule 4.3). *See generally* John G. Browning, *Digging for the Digital Dirt: Discovery and Use of Evidence from Social Media Sites*, 14 SMU Sci. & Tech. L. Rev. 465 (Summer 2011); Allison Clemency, Comment, *"Friending," "Following," and "Digging Up" Evidentiary Dirt: The Ethical Implications of Investigating Information on Social Media Websites*, 43 Ariz. St. L.J. 1021 (Fall 2011); Sandra Hornberger, *Social Networking Websites: Impact on Litigation and the Legal Profession in Ethics, Discovery, and Evidence*, 27 Touro L. Rev. 279 (2011); Ken Strutin, *Social Media and the Vanishing Points of Ethical and Constitutional Boundaries*, 31 Pace L. Rev. 228 (Winter 2011).

## "ON BEHALF OF A CLIENT"

Rule 4.3 does not apply unless the lawyer is "dealing on behalf of a client." *See, e.g., HTC Corp. v. Tech. Props. Ltd.*, 715 F. Supp. 2d 968 (N.D. Cal. 2010) (defendant corporation's CEO free to communicate directly with employees of plaintiff corporation about settlement; although a lawyer, he never represented defendant corporation in litigation); *Suck v. Sullivan*, No. 207488, 1999 WL 33437564 (Mich. Ct. App. Aug. 27, 1999) (lawyer representing himself in real estate transaction had no duty to advise unrepresented seller to seek independent counsel; lawyer not acting on behalf of client, and Rule 4.3 does not impose general duty to recommend unrepresented person consult lawyer); Conn. Informal Ethics Op. 2010-2 (2010) (hospital's risk manager who is not acting as its lawyer may negotiate with patients and third parties without mentioning he is a lawyer); *see also* Margaret Raymond, *Professional Responsibility for the Pro Se Attorney*, 1 St. Mary's J. Legal Mal. & Ethics 2 (2011) (rule "should plainly be applied to pro se lawyers" if it is to serve its purpose of protecting unrepresented persons).

## PRO SE LITIGANT GETTING LIMITED
## LEGAL HELP IS STILL "UNREPRESENTED"

A pro se litigant receiving limited or "unbundled" legal assistance remains unrepresented for purposes of Rule 4.3. *See McMillan v. Shadow Ridge at Oak Park Homeowner's Ass'n*, 81 Cal. Rptr. 3d 550 (Ct. App. 2008) (defense counsel entitled to speak directly with pro se plaintiff even though he knew lawyer was helping her in some aspects of case); Kan. Ethics Op. 09-01 (2009) (lawyer who receives from pro se litigant document bearing legend "Prepared with Assistance of Counsel" has no duty to refrain from communicating directly with that pro se litigant); Nev. Ethics Op. 34 (2009) (pro se litigant being assisted by disclosed ghost-lawyer is considered unrepresented for purposes of Rules 4.2 and 4.3); Utah Ethics Op. 08-01 (2008) (opposing lawyer may treat pro se litigant as unrepresented person even if he has reason to know litigant receiving undisclosed assistance from another lawyer); *see also* ABA Formal Ethics Op. 472 (2015) (lawyer may communicate directly with person receiving limited-scope representation on aspects of the matter for which there is no representation, or for which the representation is completed and not expected to resume); *cf.* Phila. Ethics Op. 2012-9 (2012) (lawyer for government agency in condemnation proceeding is free to communicate with condemnee purportedly represented by nonlawyer).

Limited representation of pro se litigants, including ghostwriting, is discussed in the annotation to Rule 1.2.

## GIVING "LEGAL ADVICE"

In 2002 Rule 4.3 was amended to prohibit a lawyer from giving "legal advice" other than the advice to secure counsel to an unrepresented person whose interests might conflict with those of the lawyer's client. With this amendment came the deletion of the comment's broader warning not to give advice to unrepresented persons (regardless of interests) other than the advice to secure counsel. American Bar Association, *A Legislative History: The Development of the ABA Model Rules of Professional Conduct, 1982–2013*, at 573–74 (2013).

Comment [2] explains that whether a lawyer is giving impermissible advice "may depend on the experience and sophistication of the unrepresented person, as well as the setting in which the behavior and comments occur." *See Hanlin-Cooney v. Frederick County*, No. WDQ-13-1731, 2014 WL 3421921, 2014 BL 191112 (D. Md. July 9, 2014) (lawyer handling two inmate-suicide cases against county met several times with correctional officer while preparing new suit, in which officer was to be a defendant; discussing officer's potential overtime claims against county and putting him in touch with wage-claim lawyers did not violate Rule 4.3); *Yates v. Belli Deli*, No. C 07-1405 WHA, 2007 WL 2318923 (N.D. Cal. Aug. 13, 2007) (plaintiffs' law firm suing hundreds of small mom-and-pop businesses under Americans with Disabilities Act offered quick, small settlements with "friendly advice" they not waste their money hiring lawyers); *Hopkins v. Troutner*, 4 P.3d 557 (Idaho 2000) (court relieved unrepresented plaintiff from agreement to settle case for $5,500; defendant's lawyer told him he thought case worth $3,000 to $4,000, but did not explain he was not disinterested and did not advise plaintiff to seek independent counsel); *First Nat'l Bank of St. Bernard v. Assavedo*, 764 So. 2d 162 (La. Ct. App. 2000) (woman served with citation and petition by bank suing her family on promissory note called bank's law firm and was told to have her son call bank; this was not "advice" under Rule 4.3); *Att'y Q v. Miss. State Bar*, 587 So. 2d 228 (Miss. 1991) (lawyer for owner of property damaged by automobile gave impermissible legal advice by saying "don't worry about it" when automobile owner asked him if she should contact her insurance company now that she had been served); *State ex rel. Okla. Bar Ass'n v. Berry*, 969 P.2d 975 (Okla. 1998) (creditor's lawyer told unrepresented bankruptcy petitioner she did not complete her petition properly and should convert from Chapter 7 to Chapter 13 proceeding); *Barrett v. Va. State Bar*, 611 S.E.2d 375 (Va. 2005) (when lawyer's wife left him, he e-mailed her he would assert "fault grounds, which means [she could] say good-bye to spousal support," and that she "could be socked with half [his debts]" and "might end up paying [him] spousal support"; court rejected board's finding that these and similar statements constituted legal advice within meaning of Rule 4.3) (Virginia's version of Rule 4.3 not limited to conduct on behalf of client); N.Y. State Ethics Op. 898 (2011) (lawyer sending notice to unrepresented debtor does not violate Rule 4.3 by including statutorily required language about statute of limitations); N.Y. City Ethics Op. 2009-2 (2009) (lawyer may provide unrepresented adverse person with "incontrovertible" information about, for example, client's negotiating position, "non-negotiable procedural requirements for doing business, or the existence of a legal right such as the right against self-incrimination"); Or. Ethics Op. 2005-16 (2005) (lawyer for automobile accident victim may not send letter to unrepresented driver recommending he instruct his insurer to accept policy-limits demand; lawyer representing criminal defendant may not advise unrepresented witness to assert Fifth Amendment when appearing before grand jury); *see also Banco Santos, S.A., v. Espirito Santo Bank*, No. 10-47543-BKC-LMI, 2014 WL 5655025, 2014 BL 310916 (S.D. Fla. Nov. 3, 2014) (no duty to advise unrepresented person to obtain counsel); N.Y. State Ethics Op. 768 (2003) (government agency's lawyer accompanying agency officers to meeting with unrepresented contractors may state government's legal position and may answer contractors' questions about agency filing requirements; ban on giving legal advice not implicated); Ben Kempinen, *The Ethics of Prosecutor Contact with the Unrepresented Defendant*, 19 Geo. J. Legal Ethics 1147 (Fall 2006). *See generally* Victoria J. Haneman, *The Ethical Exploitation of the Unrepresented Consumer*, 73 Mo. L. Rev. 707 (Summer 2008) ("ironic, but an unrepresented party will often rely on the perception of superior knowledge and expertise in the opposing attorney"; author proposes new rule, "Duty of Fairness Toward an Unrepresented Party Opponent," requiring "higher level of honest behavior"); Thomas M. Horan & Ericka Fredricks Johnson, *A Beginner's Guide to Effectively Addressing the Pro Se Opponent*, 32 Am. Bankr. Inst. J. 28 (Aug. 2013) (desire to be helpful when unrepresented opponent asks questions about legal process can result in rendering impermissible legal advice); Stephen Pepper, *Integrating Morality and Law in Legal Practice: A Reply to Professor Simon*, 23 Geo. J. Legal Ethics 1011 n.105 (Fall 2010) (declaration in Comment [2] that lawyer dealing with unrepresented person may explain lawyer's view of underlying legal obligation is "difficult to reconcile with the clear language of the rule, but does seem justifiable as a matter of practicality").

## • *Discouraging Unrepresented Person from Talking to Opposing Counsel*

Opinions vary about discouraging unrepresented people from talking to opposing counsel. *See* D.C. Ethics Op. 360 (2011) (if personal injury client's treating physician is legally permitted to communicate directly with opposing counsel, plaintiff's lawyer may not ask him not to, but may tell him he is not required to speak with opposing counsel at all); Md. Ethics Op. 2012-08 (n.d.) (lawyer may tell unrepresented potential witness he may, but need not, speak to other party, either with or without lawyer, but may not say client "prefers" witness not do so); N.Y. City Ethics Op. 2009-5 (n.d.) (lawyer in civil matter may advise unrepresented witness she has no obligation to provide information voluntarily to other side, and may ask her not to); Va. Ethics Op. 1795 (2004) (criminal defense lawyer may ask victim, who is defendant's mother, to speak to him before speaking to prosecutor, but may not tell her she does not have to speak to prosecutor or appear in court unless subpoenaed, or that prosecution will fail without her testimony).

This is also addressed by Rule 3.4(f), which specifically prohibits asking people not to give relevant information to other parties; see the annotation to Rule 3.4 for further discussion.

Whether offering to represent the witness constitutes solicitation is discussed in the annotation to Rule 7.3.

## SUBMITTING DOCUMENTS TO UNREPRESENTED PERSON

A lawyer must comply with Rule 4.3 when submitting documents to an unrepresented person. *See Marino v. Usher*, 673 F. App'x 125 (3d Cir. 2016) (plaintiff's lawyer persuaded unrepresented defendant to sign affidavit; e-mail stating "if you want to review [it] with a lawyer, that's fine too," was insufficient to satisfy rule); Ariz. Ethics Op. 05-07 (2005) (lawyer settling client's personal injury claim may not obtain release from client's wife unless both spouses have agreed to joint representation and waived potential conflict; if not, lawyer may not advise wife of her legal rights regardless of whether release would affect them); Md. Ethics Op. 2002-17 (2002) (landlord's lawyer may send unrepresented tenant notice of default along with draft complaint; lawyer merely informing tenant of client's intent to sue unless tenant alters behavior); N.C. Ethics Op. 2009-12 (2010) (lawyer may prepare affidavit and confession of judgment for unrepresented adverse party if he explains whom he represents and does not give legal advice, but may not prepare waiver of exemptions for him); N.C. Ethics Op. 2004-10 (2005) (because deed, unlike pleading, is not adversarial, buyer's lawyer in real estate closing may prepare deed for unrepresented seller as accommodation to her client; she must first explain deed will comply with contract specifications but will protect her client's interests); Ohio Sup. Ct. Ethics Op. 96-2 (1996) (lawyer hired by defendant's insurer may prepare application for appointment of guardian and approval of settlement for unrepresented minor plaintiff to sign if lawyer ensures parents, court, and guardian know he is hired by insurer and they may ask another lawyer to review the documents; "[p]reparation of these statutorily required documents does not constitute legal advice"; decided under predecessor Code); *see also* W. Va. Ethics Op. 2004-01 (2004) (lawyer retained by tortfeasor's insurance company to prepare petition on behalf of parents of injured minor to facilitate settlement must tell minor and parents in writing, in plain English, that she has been retained by tortfeasor's insurer and does not represent their interests, that their disclosures to her are not confidential, that she makes no representation as to fairness of settlement, and that they have right to obtain independent counsel; must also give them telephone number of state bar's referral service); *cf. Jones v. Allstate Ins. Co.*, 45 P.3d 1068 (Wash.

2002) (conduct of nonlawyer insurance claims adjuster fell below standard of care applicable to lawyers when she advised victim and spouse to sign release without properly advising them of its legal consequences or referring them to independent counsel as required by Rule 4.3).

## EMPLOYEES AND FORMER EMPLOYEES OF REPRESENTED ORGANIZATIONS

Certain otherwise unrepresented employees or constituents of an organization will be deemed to be represented by the organization's lawyer, depending upon their particular role in the organization or in the matter at issue. Communication with them is therefore governed by Rule 4.2 (communication with represented persons) rather than this rule. In general, Rule 4.2 applies if the employee meets some combination (depending upon the jurisdiction) of the following criteria: the employee has managerial responsibilities within the entity, the employee's actions or omissions could be imputed to the entity, the employee's statements could bind the entity, the employee's admissions would be admissible against the entity as an exception to the hearsay rule, and/or the employee is responsible for implementing the advice of the entity's lawyers. For discussion see the annotations to Rule 4.2 (Communication with Person Represented by Counsel) and Rule 1.13 (Organization as Client).

Employees who do not fit into one of these categories are, like former employees, not considered represented by the corporation's lawyer. (A 2002 amendment to Rule 4.2's comment clarified that "[c]onsent of the organization's lawyer is not required for communication with a former constituent"; Cmt. [7].) Communications with such individuals are therefore governed by Rule 4.3 rather than Rule 4.2. *See* N.M. Ethics Op. 2015-01 (n.d.) (lawyer who contacts unrepresented former managerial employee of opposing party must disclose his role in the matter, including identifying client and fact that former employer is adverse party); Ohio Sup. Ct. Ethics Op. 2016-5 (2016) (same).

## PUTATIVE CLASS MEMBERS

The majority view, shared by the *Restatement*, is that putative class members are unrepresented. *See, e.g., EEOC v. SVT, LLC*, 297 F.R.D. 336 (N.D. Ind. 2014) (until potential class members establish client-lawyer relationship with counsel, defendant's lawyers may contact them); *Hammond v. City of Junction City*, 167 F. Supp. 2d 1271 (D. Kan. 2001) (same); *In re McKesson HBOC, Inc. Sec. Litig.*, 126 F. Supp. 2d 1239 (N.D. Cal. 2000) (same); ABA Formal Ethics Op. 07-445 (2007) (contact permitted until class certified and opt-out period expires); Conn. Informal Ethics Op. 2011-09 (2011) (defense lawyer free to contact putative class members before certification); N.Y. City Ethics Op. 2004-1 (2004) (same); *Restatement (Third) of the Law Governing Lawyers* § 99 cmt. l (2000); *cf. Bobryk v. Durand Glass Mfg. Co.*, No. 12-cv-5360(NLH/JS), 2013 WL 5574504, 2013 BL 279736 (D.N.J. Oct. 9, 2013) (distinguishing between opt-out and opt-in class actions; precertification communication permitted in FLSA representative opt-in actions for unpaid wages or overtime); *Parks v. Eastwood Ins. Servs., Inc.*, 235 F. Supp. 2d 1082 (C.D. Cal. 2002) (same). *But see Dondore v. NGK Metals Corp.*, 152 F. Supp. 2d 662 (E.D. Pa. 2001) (corporation's lawyer must tell employee he may be part of plaintiff class and must identify plaintiffs' lawyers). *See generally* Debra Lyn Bassett, *Pre-Certification Communication Ethics in Class Actions*, 36 Ga. L. Rev. 353 (Winter 2002) (suggesting more nuanced approach); Craig M. Freeman, John Randall Whaley & Richard J. Arsenault, *Knowledge Is Power: A Practical Proposal to Protect Putative Class Members from Improper Pre-Certification Communication*, 2006 Fed. Cts. L. Rev. 2 (May 2006); Mindi Guttmann, Note, *Absent Class Members: Are They Really Absent? The Relationship Between Absent Class Members and Class Counsel with Regards to the Attorney-Client and Work-Product Privileges*, 7 Cardozo Pub. L. Pol'y & Ethics J. 493 (Spring 2009); Christopher Lage, *Avoiding and Dealing with Unethical Communications with Putative Class Members in Systemic Cases*, 27 A.B.A. J. Lab. & Emp. L. 43 (Fall 2011); Ellen J. Messing, James S. Weliky & Jessica A. Cunningham, *"Silence Like a Cancer Grows" or "You Talk Too Much?" Ethical and Strategic Issues in Communications by Plaintiff's Counsel with Putative Class Members*, 10 Emp. Rts. & Emp. Pol'y J. 649 (2006); Douglas R. Richmond, *Class Actions and Ex Parte Communications: Can We Talk?*, 68 Mo. L. Rev. 813 (Fall 2003); Hollis Saltzman, Meegan Hollywood & Noelle Feigenbaum, *Between a Rock and a Hard Place: Communicating with Absent Class Members*, 32 Antitrust 45 (Fall 2017).

# Transactions with Persons Other Than Clients

## Rule 4.4
### *Respect for Rights of Third Persons*

(a) In representing a client, a lawyer shall not use means that have no substantial purpose other than to embarrass, delay, or burden a third person, or use methods of obtaining evidence that violate the legal rights of such a person.

(b) A lawyer who receives a document or electronically stored information relating to the representation of the lawyer's client and knows or reasonably should know that the document or electronically stored information was inadvertently sent shall promptly notify the sender.

## COMMENT

[1] Responsibility to a client requires a lawyer to subordinate the interests of others to those of the client, but that responsibility does not imply that a lawyer may disregard the rights of third persons. It is impractical to catalogue all such rights, but they include legal restrictions on methods of obtaining evidence from third persons and unwarranted intrusions into privileged relationships, such as the client-lawyer relationship.

[2] Paragraph (b) recognizes that lawyers sometimes receive a document or electronically stored information that was mistakenly sent or produced by opposing parties or their lawyers. A document or electronically stored information is inadvertently sent when it is accidentally transmitted, such as when an email or letter is misaddressed or a document or electronically stored information is accidentally included with information that was intentionally transmitted. If a lawyer knows or reasonably should know that such a document or electronically stored information was sent inadvertently, then this Rule requires the lawyer to promptly notify the sender in order to permit that person to take protective measures. Whether the lawyer is required to take additional steps, such as returning the document or deleting electronically stored information, is a matter of law beyond the scope of these Rules, as is the question of whether the privileged status of a document or electronically stored information has been waived. Similarly, this Rule does not address the legal duties of a lawyer who receives a document or electronically stored information that the lawyer knows or reasonably should know may have been inappropriately obtained by the sending person. For purposes of this Rule, "document or electronically stored information" includes, in addition to paper documents, email and other forms of

electronically stored information, including embedded data (commonly referred to as "metadata"), that is subject to being read or put into readable form. Metadata in electronic documents creates an obligation under this Rule only if the receiving lawyer knows or reasonably should know that the metadata was inadvertently sent to the receiving lawyer.

[3] Some lawyers may choose to return a document or delete electronically stored information unread, for example, when the lawyer learns before receiving it that it was inadvertently sent. Where a lawyer is not required by applicable law to do so, the decision to voluntarily return such a document or delete electronically stored information is a matter of professional judgment ordinarily reserved to the lawyer. See Rules 1.2 and 1.4.

### Definitional Cross-References
"Knows" *See* Rule 1.0(f)
"Reasonably should know" *See* Rule 1.0(j)
"Substantial" *See* Rule 1.0(l)

### State Rules Comparison
http://ambar.org/MRPCStateCharts

## ANNOTATION

### SCOPE OF RULE 4.4

Rule 4.4, like the three other rules grouped under "Transactions with Persons Other Than Clients," tempers the zeal with which a lawyer is permitted to represent a client. (Canon 7 of the predecessor Model Code provided that "a lawyer should represent a client zealously within the bounds of the law," but the Model Rules relegate the obligation of zeal to the comment. *See* Rule 1.3, cmt. [1].)

Rule 4.4(a) prohibits conduct that has no substantial purpose other than to harass someone, and prohibits evidence-gathering tactics that violate someone else's rights.

Paragraph (b), added to the rule in 2002 (and amended in 2012 to specifically cover electronically transmitted information), declares that when a lawyer receives a document or electronically stored information and reasonably should know it was inadvertently transmitted, the lawyer must promptly notify the sender. Civil procedure rules and other law may well require more, however, as do the versions of Rule 4.4(b) adopted in several jurisdictions.

### Paragraph (a), Part I: No Substantial Purpose Other Than to Embarrass, Delay, or Burden Third Person

### "MIXED" PURPOSES

Rule 4.4(a) prohibits conduct that has no *substantial* purpose other than to embarrass, delay, or burden a third person. The wording replaces that of the predecessor Model Code provision, DR 7-102(A)(1), which forbade the lawyer from taking action that would serve *merely* to harass or maliciously injure another.

Most charges of violating Rule 4.4(a) therefore involve conduct that has both a "legitimate purpose and an illegitimate purpose." *In re Royer*, 78 P.3d 449 (Kan. 2003) (facilitating transfer of clients' unsafe building to homeless man so clients would not have to pay for its demolition); *see Idaho State Bar v. Warrick*, 44 P.3d 1141 (Idaho 2002) (county prosecutor who wrote "waste of sperm" and "scumbag" on jail's inmate control board next to name of criminal defendant had no substantial purpose other than to embarrass him; because Rule 4.4(a) focuses on purpose rather than effect, irrelevant whether inmate himself actually knew about it); *In re Campbell*, 199 P.3d 776 (Kan. 2009) (in effort to "shock" minors' parents into dealing with underage drinking, prosecutor showed them photos of their children drinking and engaging in sexual activity at party); *In re Comfort*, 159 P.3d 1011 (Kan. 2007) (lawyer wrote and publicized accusatory letter to another lawyer who made open-records request of his client; disseminating letter designed to embarrass is "means" explicitly contemplated by Rule 4.4); *In re Wallingford*, 799 S.W.2d 76 (Mo. 1990) (lawyer for father in child custody battle did not violate Rule 4.4 by advising client to pay child support to Missouri court administrator as tactic to force child's mother—who took child out of state without court permission—to appear in Missouri: "In confrontations of the kind shown by this record, . . . some pressure tactics are not necessarily inappropriate."); *In re Mertz*, 712 N.W.2d 849 (N.D. 2006) (lawyer defending daughter in vicious-dog-at-large infraction wrote letter to complainant calling him "animal hater or ignorant of animals, or both," and suggesting complainant had been "sneaking up" on daughter in the dark); *In re White*, 797 S.E.2d 411 (S.C. 2011) (lawyer wrote letter calling town officials "pagans" "pigheadedly" intent on crucifying client; court rejected lawyer's explanation that he was permissibly putting town on notice of client's intent to sue); *State ex rel. Scales v. Comm. on Legal Ethics*, 446 S.E.2d 729 (W. Va. 1994) (lawyer for woman in bitter divorce contacted husband's commanding officer to report husband's domestic violence in attempt to prevent further abuse, which constituted substantial purpose other than embarrassment and harassment); Tex. Ethics Op. 585 (2008) (if no substantial purpose other than to delay or burden opposing party, counseling client to preemptively hire all available local lawyers would violate rule even if party was not in fact delayed or burdened); *see also Kyko Global, Inc. v. Prithvi Info. Solutions, Ltd.*, No. C13-1034 MJP, 2014 WL 2694236, 2014 BL 168580 (W.D. Wash. June 13, 2014) (because hard drive may contain much that is not protected, plaintiffs' lawyers in civil fraud case had "legitimate purpose apart from the discovery of privileged documents" in buying one defendant's old computer at auction and having it examined; no violation of Rule 4.4(a)); *N.C. State Bar v. Sutton*, 791 S.E.2d 881 (N.C. 2016) (lawyer who posted video on internet accusing sheriff's office of engaging in criminal conduct admitted purpose was not to further representation but to be a "smart aleck"). *See generally* Carol Rice Andrews, *The First Amendment Problem with the Motive Restrictions in the Rules of Professional Conduct*, 24 J. Legal Prof. 13 (Spring 2000); Douglas R. Richmond, *Saber-Rattling and the Sound of Professional Responsibility*, 34 Am. J. Trial Advoc. 27 (Summer 2010) (neither dual purpose nor lawyer's naked assertion of permissible purpose is defense; court determines purpose objectively); Ellen Yankiver Suni, *Who Stole the Cookie from the Cookie Jar? The Law and Ethics of Shifting Blame in Criminal Cases*, 68 Fordham L. Rev. 1643 (Apr. 2000) ("[W]here the purpose is permitted, the Rule appears to tolerate a high level of negative effect. Thus, if [counsel] were acting with a permissible purpose and using otherwise legal means to defend, the fact that their examination of [the witness] was humiliating and degrading would not likely, by itself, lead to violation of Rule 4.4.").

Note that Rule 11(b)(1) of the Federal Rules of Civil Procedure uses still another standard, penalizing the presentation of documents for *any* "improper purpose, such as to harass, cause unnecessary delay, or needlessly increase the cost of litigation."

## LITIGATION BEHAVIOR

Rule 4.4 is not limited to litigation behavior. *See, e.g., In re Hanson*, 53 N.E.3d 412 (Ind. 2016) (sending threatening and obscene private social media message to client's ex-husband). However, most of the reported decisions arise in that context. Violations include frivolous court filings, abusive discovery tactics, and other harassing conduct—any of which may violate other ethics rules as well. *See Alexander v. Jesuits of Mo. Province*, 175 F.R.D. 556 (D. Kan. 1997) (lawyer's sole purpose in scheduling deposition of nonparty witness at 8:00 a.m. in city more than sixty miles from her home was harassment); *Thompson v. Comm. on Prof'l Conduct*, 252 S.W.3d 125 (Ark. 2007) (after being notified his lis pendens was improperly filed, lawyer took "nearly two months to make any attempt at correcting his mistake"); *People v. Beecher*, 224 P.3d 442 (Colo. O.P.D.J. 2009) (when all nonfinancial issues in divorce had been resolved, deposing client's husband and adult son about husband's alleged sexual abuse of son when son was minor violated rule); *In re Hurley*, 183 A.3d 703 (Del. 2018) (sending offensive letters to deputy attorneys general and making demeaning remarks to and about former client in letters to client and disciplinary authorities); *Fla. Bar v. Buckle*, 771 So. 2d 1131 (Fla. 2000) (criminal defense lawyer sent humiliating letter to crime victim to intimidate her into abandoning her complaint); *In re Anonymous*, 896 N.E.2d 916 (Ind. 2008) (before litigation commenced and without any authority, insurance company's lawyer served purported subpoenas on claimant); *In re Holste*, 358 P.3d 850 (Kan. 2015) (naming as defendant in breach of contract suit person who was not party to contract); *In re O'Dwyer*, 221 So. 3d 1 (La. 2017) (retaliatory attempts to sanction other lawyers and parties through frivolous motions and accusations); *In re Humphrey*, 15 So. 3d 960 (La. 2009) (lawyer said "f*** you" to opposing counsel and filed pleadings with unsubstantiated accusations of complicity in child molestation, perjury, and destruction of evidence); *Att'y Grievance Comm'n v. Powers*, 164 A.3d 138 (Md. 2017) (in attempt to collect fees, lawyer filed suit against former client and new lawyer in court that lacked jurisdiction); *Att'y Grievance Comm'n v. Cocco*, 109 A.3d 1176 (Md. 2015) (presenting invalid subpoena to third parties and threatening them with lawsuit if they did not comply); *Att'y Grievance Comm'n v. Mixter*, 109 A.3d 1 (Md. 2015) (routine discovery requests for irrelevant personal information about opposing parties); *In re Torgerson*, 870 N.W.2d 602 (Minn. 2015) (yelling at court staff); *In re Kurzman*, 871 N.W.2d 753 (Minn. 2015) (deposition questions included baseless allegations that deponent had been accused of sexual misconduct with minors); *In re Igbanugo*, 863 N.W.2d 751 (Minn. 2015) (stating in collection suit affidavit "I am deeply disturbed by [clients'] unholy efforts to steal my services"); *In re Kalil*, 773 A.2d 647 (N.H. 2001) (lawyer told pro se opponent he would "rip his face off" if he disobeyed court's order); *In re Dvorak*, 611 N.W.2d 147 (N.D. 2000) (in letter to witness's employer seeking access to documents witness may have stored on employer's computer, lawyer falsely claimed witness provided false information at deposition); *Sutch v. Roxborough Mem'l Hosp.*, 151 A.3d 241 (Pa. Super. Ct. 2016) (attempting to intimidate opponents' expert); *In re Whitlark*, 811 S.E.2d 794 (S.C. 2018) (failure to pay court reporter fees); *Flowers v. Bd. of Prof'l Responsibility*, 314 S.W.3d 882 (Tenn. 2010) (eighteen frivolous appeals in clients' immigration cases); *In re Cottingham*, 423 P.3d 818 (Wash. 2018) (frivolous litigation with intent to harass neighbors); *In re Eisenberg*, 778 N.W.2d 645 (Wis. 2010) (after successfully defending husband against estranged wife's domestic violence charges, lawyer "rushed" to file civil complaint against her just before pretrial conference in couple's divorce action, falsely announcing that jury in criminal case "stormed the judge's chambers and demanded to know why the woman was not being prosecuted for perjury"); Ill. Ethics Op. 01-06 (2002) (lawyer cannot tell business owner who defaulted that when lawyer "gets through" with him he would never be able to borrow again, and then tell banks not to renew his loans). *See generally* Douglas R. Richmond, *Saber-Rattling and the Sound of Professional Responsibility*, 34 Am. J. Trial Advoc. 27 (Summer 2010) (some degree of embarrassment, delay, and burden is inherent in litigation).

### • *Lawyer as Party Litigant*

Rule 4.4, like Rules 4.1, 4.2, and 4.3, is explicitly directed at a lawyer's conduct in representing a client. But like the other rules, it has also been applied to lawyers representing themselves; the rule's "intent and purpose" require that a lawyer who represents himself be deemed to be representing a client, according to *Att'y Grievance Comm'n v. Alison*, 565 A.2d 660 (Md. 1989). *See, e.g., In re Rozbicki*, No. CV116004519S, 2013 WL 1277298 (Conn. Super. Ct. Mar. 8, 2013) (as executor of former client's estate, lawyer filed own suit against beneficiaries to harass them for objecting to his fee claim in decedent's personal injury case); *In re Richardson*, 792 N.E.2d 871 (Ind. 2003) (misconduct in course of lawyer's own suit against estranged girlfriend); *In re Stratton*, 869 So. 2d 794 (La. 2004) (misconduct in course of lawyer's own suit against former secretary); *In re Yarborough*, 559 S.E.2d 836 (S.C. 2002) (threatening civil action against state witness in lawyer's own obstruction-of-justice case); *Barrett v. Va. State Bar ex rel. Second Dist. Comm.*, 634 S.E.2d 341 (Va. 2006) (applying Rule 4.4 to lawyer's harassment of witness in his own divorce case; lawyer was "functioning as an attorney"); *see also In re Johnson*, 743 N.W.2d 117 (N.D. 2007) (nineteen months after representation of client ended, lawyer threatened witness trying to collect witness fee lawyer had personally undertaken to pay him; court rejected lawyer's argument that he was no longer representing a client within meaning of Rule 4.4); *In re Isaacson*, 860 N.W.2d 490 (Wis. 2015) (lawyer serving as corporate officer engaged in pattern of bad faith litigation making false and defamatory statements about judges, other lawyers, appointed officers, and third parties).

## THREATENING TO PROSECUTE OR TO REPORT

The predecessor Model Code (DR 7-105(A)) barred a lawyer from presenting, participating in presenting, or threatening to present criminal charges "solely to obtain an advantage in a civil matter." This specific prohibition was deleted from the Model Rules. However, threatening either criminal or civil proceedings to gain leverage for a client in a civil matter violates Rule 4.4 if the threat is made with "no substantial purpose other than to embarrass, delay, or burden a third person" or is used as a method of "obtaining evidence that violate[s] the legal rights of such a person." *See In re Robertson*, 626 A.2d 397 (N.H. 1993) (plaintiff's civil rights lawyer persistently threatened city lawyers with criminal and disciplinary charges, and publicly maligned them in "aggressive" effort to settle case); *see also In re Barker*, 993 N.E.2d 1138 (Ind. 2013) (in dispute over mother's interference with father's visitation rights, father's lawyer claimed mother did not understand her legal obligations because she was "illegal alien"); *Att'y M. v. Miss. Bar*, 621 So. 2d 220 (Miss. 1992) (Rule 4.4 not violated when lawyer warned doctor that even though doctor "didn't do anything wrong," lawyer might be "forced" to join him as co-defendant in malpractice action if he was not willing to state plaintiff left his care in same condition as when she arrived at hospital; court noted threatened suit was "colorable"); *N.C. State Bar v. Livingston*, 809 S.E.2d 183 (N.C. 2017) (filing baseless complaint and threatening to file more); ABA Formal Ethics Op. 92-363 (1992) (may not use possibility of presenting criminal charges against client's opponent in civil case for leverage on client's behalf unless charges relate to civil matter and are well-founded); *cf.* Wash. Rule 4.4, cmt. [4] (added in 2013 to prohibit mentioning someone's immigration status as intimidation tactic in civil matter). *See generally* David P. Weber, *(Unfair) Advantage: Damocles' Sword and the Coercive Use of Immigration Status in a Civil Society*, 94 Marq. L. Rev. 613 (Winter 2010) (immigration status may be tangentially related to all sorts of cases; Rule 4.4(a) violation becomes harder to prove "as counsel who attempt to seek such information become more creative").

In the same vein, an ABA ethics opinion holds that threatening to file a disciplinary complaint—as opposed to a civil or criminal action—against opposing counsel to obtain an advantage in a civil case is "constrained" by the Model Rules even though not directly addressed. ABA Formal Ethics Op. 94-383 (1994). If opposing counsel's misconduct raises a substantial question of honesty, trustworthiness, or fitness as a lawyer, Rule 8.3(a) would already require the lawyer to report him; it would therefore be improper, the opinion reasons, to use the threat of reporting as a bargaining chip. *See In re Kenny*, 217 P.3d 36 (Kan. 2009) (threatening disciplinary complaint against client's former lawyer to coerce him into refunding client's money); *Ky. Bar Ass'n v. Blum*, 404 S.W.3d 841 (Ky. 2013) (focal point is purpose of threat, not whether opposing counsel actually behaved unethically); *In re Eicher*, 661 N.W.2d 354 (S.D. 2003) (repeatedly threatening to move for sanctions against opposing counsel and report him to disciplinary authorities); *Barrett v. Va. State Bar*, 611 S.E.2d 375 (Va. 2005) (lawyer's professed good-faith belief opposing counsel's behavior was unethical did not make lawyer's suggestion of disciplinary claim any less of a threat).

Threats of civil, criminal, or disciplinary proceedings can also implicate Rule 3.1 (Meritorious Claims and Contentions), Rule 4.1 (Truthfulness in Statements to Others), and Rule 8.4 (Misconduct). *See, e.g., In re King*, 232 P.3d 1095 (Wash. 2010). *See generally ABA/BNA Lawyers' Manual on Professional Conduct*, "Obligations to Third Persons: Threatening Prosecution," pp. 71:601 *et seq.*

## Paragraph (a), Part II: Methods of Obtaining Evidence That Violate Others' Rights

Rule 4.4(a) prohibits using evidence-gathering tactics that violate other people's rights. *See In re Neary*, 84 N.E.3d 1194 (Ind. 2018) (prosecutor eavesdropped on conversations between defendants and their lawyers); *In re Eisenstein*, 485 S.W.3d 759 (Mo. 2016) (using information divorce client obtained through unauthorized access to wife's e-mail account; material included list of direct examination questions sent by wife's attorney); Conn. Informal Ethics Op. 96-4 (1996) (even though lawyer did not participate in client's procurement of client's ex-wife's psychiatric records, statute prohibiting disclosure or transmission of psychiatric records meant that lawyer would be violating Rule 4.4 if he reviewed them); Pa. Ethics Op. 93-135 (1993) (lawyer seeking to impeach witness may not accept his expert's offer to examine witness's confidential psychiatric records, which happened to be maintained at expert's institution); Phila. Ethics Op. 2000-1 (2000) (at deposition, surreptitiously using software program that instantly analyzes speech patterns to assess speaker's truthfulness violates Rule 4.4). *See generally* Maura Irene Strassberg, *An Ethical Rabbit Hole: Model Rule 4.4, Intentional Interference with Former Employee Non-Disclosure Agreements and the Threat of Disqualification, Part II*, 90 Neb. L. Rev. 141 (2011).

Note that in 2002, Comment [1] was amended by adding "legal restrictions on . . . unwarranted intrusions into privileged relationships, such as the client-lawyer relationship" as an example of third-person rights.

### SURREPTITIOUS RECORDING OR TRACKING

A lawyer's surreptitious recording of conversations does not violate Rule 4.4 unless it is unlawful or is done to harass or burden a third person. ABA Formal Ethics Op. 01-422 (2001) (recording conversation without knowledge of other party to it violates Rule 4.4 only if prohibited by law or done with "no substantial purpose other than to embarrass or burden a third person"); *see also In re Nolan*, 796 S.E.2d 841 (S.C. 2017) (plaintiffs' lawyer violated rule by having investigators pose as defendant's customers, lie to its employees, prod them into making statements about product, and secretly record conversations).

Surreptitious use of e-mail tracking software may violate Rule 4.4(a). *See* Ill. Ethics Op. 18-01 (2018) (surreptitious use of tracking software violates Rules 4.4(a) and (b) and 8.4(c)); Pa. Formal Ethics Op. 2017-300 (2017) (use of e-mail tracker violates Rules 4.4(a) and 8.4(c)).

These issues are discussed in the annotation to Rule 8.4.

## Paragraph (b): Receipt of Documents Transmitted by Mistake

Rule 4.4(b) and accompanying Comments [2] and [3], which were added in 2002, provide that if a lawyer receives a document the lawyer knows or reasonably should know was sent inadvertently, he or she must promptly notify the sender.

Until the 2002 amendments the Model Rules had been silent on inadvertent delivery. An ABA ethics opinion had filled in by holding that a lawyer who receives documents that were clearly sent by mistake *and* look as though they were intended to be confidential not only must notify the sender (as Rule 4.4(b) would later require for any and all documents sent inadvertently), but also must refrain from examining them while awaiting the sender's instructions about what to do with them. ABA Formal Ethics Op. 92-368 (1992) (superseded). Two years later, ABA Formal Opinion 94-382 extended this holding to the lawyer who receives an adverse party's confidential-looking materials from an "unauthorized" source. ABA Formal Ethics Op. 94-382 (1994) (superseded).

Both ethics opinions were withdrawn after the adoption of Rule 4.4(b). *See* ABA Formal Ethics Op. 06-440 (2006) (withdrawing ABA Formal Opinion 94-382 "in its entirety"); ABA Formal Ethics Op. 05-437 (2005) (lawyer's only ethical obligation under Rule 4.4(b) is to promptly notify sender; ABA Formal Opinion 92-368 withdrawn).

There is considerable controversy about whether Rule 4.4(b) goes far enough. *See, e.g., Hill v. Hassan,* Civ. No. 09-1285, 2010 WL 419433, 2010 BL 19879 (W.D. Pa. Jan. 29, 2010) (Rule 4.4(b) "begs the question"; court therefore invoked its own inherent power to sanction lawyers for using anonymous-source documents whose provenance would have "raise[d] 'red flags' for any reasonable attorney"); Fla. Ethics Op. 07-1 (2007) ("to merely . . . point out that there are legal issues to be resolved does a disservice to the inquiring attorney"). *See generally* Peter J. Henning, *Lawyers, Truth & Honesty in Representing Clients,* 20 Notre Dame J.L. Ethics & Pub. Pol'y 209 (2006) (if documents reasonably believed to be confidential, receiving lawyer should be required to stop reading pending judicial review); Donald R. Lundberg, *Moral Dissonance in the Practice of Law: The Authentic Self,* 73 Or. St. B. Bull. (July 2013) (notwithstanding Rule 4.4's Comment [3] (receiving lawyer may return document to sender unread), it is "appropriate and probably mandatory" that lawyer and client discuss legal consequences, including disqualification, of reading inadvertently sent document); Andrew J. Perlman, *Untangling Ethics Theory from Attorney Conduct Rules: The Case of Inadvertent Disclosures,* 13 Geo. Mason L. Rev. 767 (Summer 2005) (upon notification by sending lawyer, receiving lawyer should be required to stop reading and follow sending lawyer's instructions); Paula Schaefer, *The Future of Inadvertent Disclosure: The Lingering Need to Revise Professional Conduct Rules,* 69 Md. L. Rev. 195 (2010) (receiving lawyer's duties should be triggered not when he "reasonably should know the document was inadvertently sent," but when he reasonably should know or is notified by sender that it is privileged; receiving lawyer should be required to follow sender's instructions).

Note that some jurisdictions have modified their versions of Rule 4.4(b) to require more than notification. *See, e.g., Stengart v. Loving Care Agency, Inc.,* 990 A.2d 650 (N.J. 2010) (under state's "stop, notify and return" version of Rule 4.4(b), defendants' counsel in employment discrimination suit should have set aside e-mail messages between plaintiff and her lawyer upon realizing they were lawyer-client communications; fact that trial court ultimately ruled they were not privileged was irrelevant); Ariz. Ethics Op. 07-03 (2007) (state's Rule 4.4(b) requires lawyer who receives document sent inadvertently to notify sender and preserve status quo so sender can take protective measures); Iowa Ethics Op. 15-02 (2015) (adopting requirement of stop, notify, and return if confidential material disclosed inadvertently, or under color of right). *See generally* James M. Altman, *Model Rule 4.4(b) Should Be Amended*, 21 Prof. Law., no. 1, at 16 n.7 (2011) (rule should offer greater protection to inadvertently disclosed confidential information).

## OBLIGATIONS UNDER OTHER LAW

Under Rule 4.4(b) the lawyer need not stop reading the document, return it, or comply with the sender's instructions. Comment [2] notes, however, that other laws—which would include rules of evidence and procedure as well as data privacy laws—may create additional obligations. *See* Cal. Formal Ethics Op. 2013-188 (n.d.) (receipt of another's potentially privileged documents from third party may implicate computer crime, receipt of stolen property, violation of Uniform Trade Secrets Act, or violation of protective order); N.Y. City Ethics Op. 2012-01 (2012) (withdrawing N.Y. City Ethics Op. 2003-04 "to the extent it imposes standards that go beyond" Rule 4.4(b); "Counsel would do well, however, to remember the New York State Bar Association comment [[2]] that 'a lawyer who reads or continues to read a document that contains privileged or confidential information may be subject to court-imposed sanctions, including disqualification and evidence-preclusion.'").

The analogous provision in the Federal Rules of Civil Procedure is Rule 26(b)(5)(B), called the claw-back rule. The rule imposes no duty upon the lawyer who receives inadvertently sent privileged material unless and until the lawyer is notified it was inadvertently sent. Once notified, though, the receiving lawyer must return, sequester, or destroy the document and any copies, must take reasonable steps to retrieve any information that was already disclosed, and may not use or disclose the information until the claim is resolved. *See Mt. Hawley Ins. Co. v. Felman Prod., Inc.,* 271 F.R.D. 125 (S.D. W. Va. 2010) (although defendants had no ethical obligation to tell plaintiffs they received inadvertently disclosed privileged document—West Virginia had not yet adopted Rule 4.4(b)—defendants violated Fed. R. Civ. P. 26(b)(5) by using document after plaintiffs notified them it was sent inadvertently); *Lund v. Myers,* 305 P.3d 374 (Ariz. 2013) (receiving lawyer who submits inadvertently sent documents to trial court for privilege ruling does not violate Arizona's Rule 4.4(b), requiring recipient to notify sender and preserve status quo, or its Civil Procedure Rule 26.1(f)(2), analogous to Fed. R. Civ. P. 26(b)(5)(B)); James M. Altman, *Model Rule 4.4(b) Should Be Amended*, 21 Prof. Law., no. 1, at 16 n.7 (2011) (finding similar claw-back protocols in rules in roughly half the states' civil procedure rules); *see also* Fed. R. Evid. 502(b) (inadvertent disclosure does not waive lawyer-client privilege or work-product protection if holder took reasonable steps to prevent it and promptly takes reasonable steps to respond to it).

Courts therefore must rule on claims of inadvertence not only for Rule 4.4(b) purposes, but also to determine if the sender took reasonable precautions to protect the material, and whether the sender waived its claims of confidentiality or privilege. This determination must take into account the sending lawyer's obligations of competence and confidentiality in addition to the obligations imposed upon the sender by other laws. The ethical obligations of competence and confidentiality, highlighted in the ABA's "technology" amendments to the Model Rules in 2012, include the duty to keep abreast of relevant technology (Rule 1.1, cmt. [8]) and the duty to protect against inadvertent disclosure of confidential information (Rule 1.6(c)). *See* American Bar Association, *A Legislative History: The Development of the ABA Model Rules of Professional Conduct, 1982–2013*, at 146 (2013) (duty to protect against inadvertent/unauthorized disclosure "needed to be specifically addressed . . . in light of the increase in electronic storage and dissemination of information"); *see also BNP Paribas Mortg. Corp. v. Bank of Am., N.A.*, Nos. 09 Civ. 9783, 9784 (RWS), 2013 WL 2322678, 2013 BL 290891 (S.D.N.Y. May 21, 2013) (given that 116 documents at issue represented less than .001 percent of 1.5 million documents reviewed, production was inadvertent rather than careless and therefore did not waive privilege); Michael H. Berger & Ann T. Lebeck, *Inadvertent Disclosure of Confidential or Privileged Information*, 40 Colo. Law. 65 (Jan. 2011) (comparing Rule 4.4, Fed. R. Civ. P. 26(b)(5), and Fed. R. Evid. 502).

## WHOSE INADVERTENCE?

Rule 4.4(b) applies to documents or data the receiving lawyer knows or reasonably should know were sent inadvertently. Comment [2] seems to assume the sender is an opposing party or counsel but the blackletter rule is not so limited, nor does the rule specify that the lawyer herself must be the one to whom the delivery was inadvertent. *See* Phila. Ethics Op. 2008-02 (2008) (if lawyer for defendant being sued by ex-wife determines client, who still has access to ex-wife's e-mail account, "came into possession" of her e-mail correspondence with her lawyer inadvertently, lawyer's ethical duty is limited to notification under Rule 4.4(b)).

## WHICH DOCUMENTS?

Unlike the duty articulated in the superseded ABA ethics opinions, the duty imposed by Rule 4.4 is not limited to documents that look confidential. Whether a document looks confidential is therefore relevant only insofar as it might bear upon whether the receiving lawyer reasonably should have known the document was not intended for him. *See, e.g., Castellano v. Winthrop*, 27 So. 3d 134 (Fla. Dist. Ct. App. 2010) (mother's law firm in paternity litigation spent over one hundred hours reviewing contents of defendant's USB flash drive "although it was apparent within moments of inspection that it belonged to the [opponent] and contained attorney/client communications"); *cf. Clark v. Superior Court*, 125 Cal. Rptr. 3d 361 (Ct. App. 2011) (affirming disqualification; lawyer for plaintiff suing former employer used documents plaintiff obtained while employed even though lawyer knew they were privileged) (California caselaw holds that if material clearly appears to be confidential and privileged and reasonably appears to have been provided inadvertently, receiving lawyer must stop reading and notify sender; Cal. Rule 4.4, adopted in 2018, has similar requirements).

## UNAUTHORIZED, AS OPPOSED TO INADVERTENT

Rule 4.4(b) addresses receipt of documents sent inadvertently; it does not address the receipt of documents sent intentionally but from an unauthorized source. *See* ABA Formal Ethics Op. 06-440 (2006) (lawyer's responsibility, if any, upon receiving material sent intentionally but from unauthorized source is "matter of law beyond the scope of Rule 4.4(b)"); *see also* ABA Formal Ethics Op. 11-460 (2011) (ethics rules do not impose notification obligations upon employer's lawyer who receives copies of employee's privileged communications retrieved from employer's computer system, but obligations may come from court exercising its supervisory authority, or from civil procedure rules; if no clear answer, notification decision should be left to fully informed client); N.C. Ethics Op. 2012-5 (2012) (same); *cf. Kyko Global, Inc. v. Prithvi Info. Solutions, Ltd.*, No. C13-1034 MJP, 2014 WL 2694236, 2014 BL 168580 (W.D. Wash. June 4, 2014) (plaintiffs' lawyers in civil fraud action had no Rule 4.4(b) duty to tell defendants they bought one defendant's old computer at public auction and had its contents analyzed).

Many jurisdictions reject this hands-off approach, either in their versions of Rule 4.4(b) (see *Fiber Materials, Inc. v. Subilia*, 974 A.2d 918 (Me. 2009)), or in their caselaw. *See Chamberlain Grp., Inc. v. Lear Corp.*, 270 F.R.D. 392 (N.D. Ill. 2010) ("Many courts, this Court included, fail to see why this same duty to disclose should cease where confidential documents are sent intentionally and without permission [citation omitted]. If anything, the duty to disclose should be stricter."); *Merits Incentives, LLC v. Eighth Judicial Dist. Court*, 262 P.3d 720 (Nev. 2011) (lower court correctly applied Rule 4.4(b) "by analogy" to lawyer's receipt of case documents from anonymous source; supreme court would henceforth require notification if documents received anonymously); *In re Wood*, 663 S.E.2d 496 (S.C. 2008) (lawyer who opened package addressed to client's spouse at marital home, where client still living, without first notifying spouse's counsel should have known it was "inadvertently" sent; no discussion of authorization); Iowa Ethics Op. 15-02 (2015) (in case of wrongfully obtained documents, lawyer must advise client of lawyer's duty to stop, notify and return; if client fails to permit lawyer to do so, lawyer should either return documents or file them with court under seal without explanation and withdraw); *see also* Cal. Formal Ethics Op. 2013-188 (n.d.) (under California caselaw, lawyer to whom anonymous sender e-mails copy of communication between opposing counsel and opposing counsel's client may not read it and must notify opposing counsel); N.Y. State Ethics Op. 945 (2012) (collecting cases requiring notification if client wrongly procures opposing party's documents; these cases "may be intended to impose obligations, pursuant to the courts' supervisory authority, that are independent of the ethics rules"). *See generally* Brian S. Faughnan & Douglas R. Richmond, "Model Rule 1.15: The Elegant Solution to the Problem of Purloined Documents," *ABA/BNA Lawyers' Manual on Professional Conduct*, 26 Law. Man. Prof. Conduct 623 (Current Reports, Oct. 13, 2010).

## METADATA

Documents created electronically are likely to contain more information than is visible in the final product. Such "metadata" may include information purged from prior drafts and information identifying recipients and authors. ABA Formal Opinion 06-442 (2006) declares that a lawyer is generally permitted to review and use metadata received from opposing counsel, an adverse party, or an adverse party's agent; however, the opinion's reception has been mixed. *See* Tomas J. Garcia & Shane T. Tela, Current Development, *Jurisdictional Discord in Applying Ethics Guidelines to Inadvertently Transmitted Metadata*, 23 Geo. J. Legal Ethics 585 (Summer 2010) (ABA opinion "falls short of promoting attorney-client confidence, diligent representation, and good faith between professional colleagues"; authors favor requiring sender to scrub, prohibiting recipient from mining, and requiring recipient to notify sender if metadata should happen to be discovered in regular course of review).

The ABA amended Rule 4.4(b) and its comment in 2012 to specifically address electronically stored information, including metadata. Amended Comment [3] declares that metadata creates no obligation under Rule 4.4 unless the receiving lawyer knows or reasonably should know it was inadvertently sent to him or her.

There is no consensus among jurisdictions. Some jurisdictions condemn searching for metadata as a violation of the ethics rules. *See* Ala. Ethics Op. 2007-02 (2007); Ariz. Ethics Op. 07-03 (2007); Me. Ethics Op. 196 (2008); N.H. Ethics Op. 2008-2009/4 (2009); N.Y. State Ethics Op. 782 (2004); N.Y. Cnty. Ethics Op. 738 (2008). But other jurisdictions conclude that the ethics rules permit or arguably even require the lawyer to look for metadata inadvertently included in documents received from opposing counsel. *See* D.C. Ethics Op. 341 (2007); Md. Ethics Op. 2007-09 (2006); Vt. Ethics Op. 2009-01 (2009).

Some jurisdictions require the lawyer to notify or even consult with the sender upon receiving a document that "inadvertently" includes confidential metadata. *See* Fla. Ethics Op. 06-2 (2006); Minn. Ethics Op. 22 (2010) (noting metadata could have been included intentionally "and for the mutual benefit of clients with adverse interests"); N.C. Ethics Op. 2009-1 (2010); Or. Ethics Op. 2011-186 (2011); Wash. Ethics Op. 2216 (2012); W. Va. Ethics Op. 2009-01 (2009); Wis. Formal Ethics Op. EF-12-01 (2012). Pennsylvania requires the lawyer to consult with the client about what to do. *See* Pa. Formal Ethics Op. 2009-100 (2009). *See generally* Steven C. Bennett & Jeremy Cloud, *Coping with Metadata: Ten Key Steps*, 61 Mercer L. Rev. 471 (Winter 2010); Tomas J. Garcia & Shane T. Tela, *Jurisdictional Discord in Applying Ethics Guidelines to Inadvertently Transmitted Metadata*, 23 Geo. J. Legal Ethics 585 (Summer 2010); David Hricik, *Mining for Embedded Data: Is It Ethical to Take Intentional Advantage of Other People's Failures?*, 8 N.C. J. L. & Tech. 231 (Spring 2007); Adam K. Israel, *To Scrub or Not to Scrub: The Ethical Implications of Metadata and Electronic Data Creation, Exchange, and Discovery*, 60 Ala. L. Rev. 469 (2009); Elizabeth W. King, *The Ethics of Mining for Metadata Outside of Formal Discovery*, 113 Penn St. L. Rev. 801 (Winter 2009); Bradley H. Leiber, *Applying Ethics Rules to Rapidly Changing Technology: The D.C. Bar's Approach to Metadata*, 21 Geo. J. Legal Ethics 893 (Summer 2008); Michael W. Loudenslager, *Why Shouldn't Attorneys Be Allowed to View Metadata? A Proposal for Allowing Attorneys to View Metadata as Long as Extraordinary Measures Are Not Taken to Do So and Opposing Counsel Is Contacted upon Discovery of Sensitive Information*, 15 J. Tech. L. & Pol'y 159 (Dec. 2010); Andrew M. Perlman, *The Legal Ethics of Metadata Mining*, 43 Akron L. Rev. 785 (2010); Ronald D. Rotunda, *Applying the Revised ABA Model Rules in the Age of the Internet: The Problem of Metadata*, 42 Hofstra L. Rev. 175 (Fall 2013); Hans P. Sinha, *The Ethics of Metadata: A Critical Analysis and a Practical Solution*, 63 Me. L. Rev. 175 (2010).

The ethical propriety of mining metadata is also discussed in the annotation to Rule 8.4.

## Rule 5.1

### *Responsibilities of Partners, Managers, and Supervisory Lawyers*

(a) A partner in a law firm, and a lawyer who individually or together with other lawyers possesses comparable managerial authority in a law firm, shall make reasonable efforts to ensure that the firm has in effect measures giving reasonable assurance that all lawyers in the firm conform to the Rules of Professional Conduct.

(b) A lawyer having direct supervisory authority over another lawyer shall make reasonable efforts to ensure that the other lawyer conforms to the Rules of Professional Conduct.

(c) A lawyer shall be responsible for another lawyer's violation of the Rules of Professional Conduct if:

(1) the lawyer orders or, with knowledge of the specific conduct, ratifies the conduct involved; or

(2) the lawyer is a partner or has comparable managerial authority in the law firm in which the other lawyer practices, or has direct supervisory authority over the other lawyer, and knows of the conduct at a time when its consequences can be avoided or mitigated but fails to take reasonable remedial action.

## COMMENT

[1] Paragraph (a) applies to lawyers who have managerial authority over the professional work of a firm. See Rule 1.0(c). This includes members of a partnership, the shareholders in a law firm organized as a professional corporation, and members of other associations authorized to practice law; lawyers having comparable managerial authority in a legal services organization or a law department of an enterprise or government agency; and lawyers who have intermediate managerial responsibilities in a firm. Paragraph (b) applies to lawyers who have supervisory authority over the work of other lawyers in a firm.

[2] Paragraph (a) requires lawyers with managerial authority within a firm to make reasonable efforts to establish internal policies and procedures designed to provide reasonable assurance that all lawyers in the firm will conform to the Rules of Professional Conduct. Such policies and procedures include those designed to detect and resolve conflicts of interest, identify dates by which actions must be taken in pending matters, account for client funds and property and ensure that inexperienced lawyers are properly supervised.

[3] Other measures that may be required to fulfill the responsibility prescribed in paragraph (a) can depend on the firm's structure and the nature of its practice. In a small firm of experienced lawyers, informal supervision and periodic review of compliance with the required systems ordinarily will suffice. In a large firm, or in practice situations in which difficult ethical problems frequently arise, more elaborate measures may be necessary. Some firms, for example, have a procedure whereby junior lawyers can make confidential referral of ethical problems directly to a designated senior partner or special committee. See Rule 5.2. Firms, whether large or small, may also rely on continuing legal education in professional ethics. In any event, the ethical atmosphere of a firm can influence the conduct of all its members, and the partners may not assume that all lawyers associated with the firm will inevitably conform to the Rules.

[4] Paragraph (c) expresses a general principle of personal responsibility for acts of another. See also Rule 8.4(a).

[5] Paragraph (c)(2) defines the duty of a partner or other lawyer having comparable managerial authority in a law firm, as well as a lawyer who has direct supervisory authority over performance of specific legal work by another lawyer. Whether a lawyer has supervisory authority in particular circumstances is a question of fact. Partners and lawyers with comparable authority have at least indirect responsibility for all work being done by the firm, while a partner or manager in charge of a particular matter ordinarily also has supervisory responsibility for the work of other firm lawyers engaged in the matter. Appropriate remedial action by a partner or managing lawyer would depend on the immediacy of that lawyer's involvement and the seriousness of the misconduct. A supervisor is required to intervene to prevent avoidable consequences of misconduct if the supervisor knows that the misconduct occurred. Thus, if a supervising lawyer knows that a subordinate misrepresented a matter to an opposing party in negotiation, the supervisor as well as the subordinate has a duty to correct the resulting misapprehension.

[6] Professional misconduct by a lawyer under supervision could reveal a violation of paragraph (b) on the part of the supervisory lawyer even though it does not entail a violation of paragraph (c) because there was no direction, ratification or knowledge of the violation.

[7] Apart from this Rule and Rule 8.4(a), a lawyer does not have disciplinary liability for the conduct of a partner, associate or subordinate. Whether a lawyer may be liable civilly or criminally for another lawyer's conduct is a question of law beyond the scope of these Rules.

[8] The duties imposed by this Rule on managing and supervising lawyers do not alter the personal duty of each lawyer in a firm to abide by the Rules of Professional Conduct. See Rule 5.2(a).

## Definitional Cross-References

"Firm" and "Law firm" *See* Rule 1.0(c)
"Knows" *See* Rule 1.0(f)
"Partner" *See* Rule 1.0(g)
"Reasonable" *See* Rule 1.0(h)

**State Rules Comparison**
http://ambar.org/MRPCStateCharts

## ANNOTATION

### GENERAL SUPERVISORY RESPONSIBILITY

Rule 5.1 imposes a duty upon partners, lawyers with comparable managerial authority, and lawyers who directly supervise other lawyers to oversee the conduct of lawyers within their firms or organizations. The rule establishes the principle of supervisory responsibility without introducing vicarious liability. American Bar Association, *A Legislative History: The Development of the ABA Model Rules of Professional Conduct, 1982–2013*, at 586 (2013); Rule 5.1, cmt. [7] ("Whether a lawyer may be liable civilly or criminally for another lawyer's conduct is a question of law beyond the scope of these Rules."); *see In re Phillips*, 244 P.3d 549 (Ariz. 2010) (rule does not provide for vicarious liability for subordinate's acts, but mandates independent duty of supervision); *In re Anonymous*, 552 S.E.2d 10 (S.C. 2001) (Rule 5.1 does not create vicarious liability); *Stewart v. Coffman*, 748 P.2d 579 (Utah Ct. App. 1988) (rejecting argument that Rule 5.1 creates vicarious liability for shareholder lawyers). *See generally* Rachel Reiland, *The Duty to Supervise and Vicarious Liability: Why Law Firms, Supervising Attorneys and Associates Might Want to Take a Closer Look at Model Rules 5.1, 5.2, and 5.3*, 14 Geo. J. Legal Ethics 1151 (Summer 2001); Douglas R. Richmond, *Law Firm Partners as Their Brothers' Keepers*, 96 Ky. L.J. 231 (2007–2008).

As originally enacted, Rule 5.1, like Rule 5.3, was directed only at partners and supervisors, but in 2002, both rules were amended to specifically include others with comparable managerial authority. The amendments were for clarification and were not intended to reflect a change in substance. American Bar Association, *A Legislative History: The Development of the ABA Model Rules of Professional Conduct, 1982–2013*, at 592 (2013) (changes meant to clarify that rules apply "to managing lawyers in corporate and government legal departments and legal services organizations, as well as to partners in private law firms"). *E.g., In re Dickens*, 174 A.3d 283 (D.C. 2017) (though not managing partner, lawyer had "managerial authority" based on role as founder, decision-maker, business-generator, and holder of controlling interest in firm); *In re Myers*, 584 S.E.2d 357 (S.C. 2003) ("RPC 5.1(a) applies to government agencies, as well as law firms."); *cf.* Wash. Ethics Op. 2219 (2012) (duties under Rule 5.1 not triggered for public utility's general counsel in connection with staff lawyer for whom he has no supervisory or management responsibility).

Some jurisdictions also extend responsibility for the ethical conduct of firm lawyers to the law firm itself. *See, e.g.,* N.J. Rule 5.1(a) ("Every law firm, government entity, and organization authorized . . . to practice law in this jurisdiction shall make reasonable efforts to ensure that member lawyers or lawyers otherwise participating in the organization's work undertake measures giving reasonable assurance that all lawyers conform to the Rules of Professional Conduct"); N.Y. Rule 5.1 (requiring law firm to "make reasonable efforts to ensure that all lawyers in the firm conform to [the ethics] rules" and to "ensure that the work of partners and associates is adequately supervised"). *See generally* Elizabeth Chambliss, *The Nirvana Fallacy in Law Firm Reg-*

*ulation Debates*, 33 Fordham Urb. L.J. 119 (Nov. 2005); Ted Schneyer, *On Further Reflection: How "Professional Self-Regulation" Should Promote Compliance with Broad Ethical Duties of Law Firm Management*, Ariz. L. Rev. 577 (Summer 2011).

## Paragraph (a): Duty of Partners/Managers to Ensure Compliance with Ethics Rules

Under paragraph (a), a lawyer who is a partner or who has "comparable managerial authority" in a firm must "make reasonable efforts" to establish measures ensuring that lawyers within the firm comply with the Rules of Professional Conduct. These measures include procedures for detecting and resolving conflicts of interest, ensuring compliance with deadlines, safeguarding client funds and property, and supervising inexperienced lawyers. Cmt. [2]. The adequacy of particular measures may depend upon the nature of the practice and the structure and size of the firm. For example, a small firm of experienced lawyers may require only "informal supervision and periodic review of compliance with the required systems," while at larger firms or in practice situations in which complex ethical issues often arise, "more elaborate measures may be necessary." Cmt. [3]. *E.g., Ky. Bar Ass'n v. Weinberg*, 198 S.W.3d 595 (Ky. 2006) (senior lawyers failed to supervise subordinate and to "maintain institutional controls, such as tickler systems, cover letters for transmitting copies of pleadings to clients, periodic review of files, or diary systems, in order to monitor and direct control over their files"); *Att'y Grievance Comm'n v. Kimmel*, 955 A.2d 269 (Md. 2008) ("partners and managing attorneys must adapt the level of supervision to a given attorney's experience and relative to the assigned tasks and the firm's nature and culture"; suspending two partners of Pennsylvania firm who hired inexperienced local lawyer to run high-volume Maryland office with little supervision or support; listing several indicators that should have alerted partners to need for heightened level of supervision); ABA Formal Ethics Op. 477R (2017) (managerial lawyers must establish policies and procedures, and periodically train employees in use of secure methods of electronic communication with clients, and periodically reassess and update policies); ABA Formal Ethics Op. 467 (2014) (providing guidance on specific measures prosecutors should take to comply with Rules 5.1 and 5.3; measures involve training, supervision, creating a culture of compliance, "up-the-ladder" reporting obligations and discipline); Colo. Ethics Op. 119 (2008) (supervising lawyer has duty to make reasonable efforts to ensure firm has "appropriate technology and systems in place so that subordinate lawyers and nonlawyer assistants can control transmission of metadata"); *see In re Roswold*, 249 P.3d 1199 (Kan. 2011) (lawyer serving as counsel of record in medical malpractice case allowed partner not admitted in jurisdiction to serve as lead counsel and perform all work; partner neglected matter and lied about it); *see also In re White-Steiner*, 198 P.3d 1195 (Ariz. 2009) (lawyer disciplined for maintaining client trust accounts improperly, even though lawyer relied upon husband/law partner to oversee accounts); Va. Ethics Op. 1872 (2013) (for virtual law office, "[a]dditional measures may be necessary to supervise staff who are not physically present where the lawyer works").

Notice of circumstances suggesting unethical behavior by firm lawyers will trigger the need for additional measures. *E.g., In re Dickens*, 174 A.3d 283 (D.C. 2017) (lax enforcement of firm policies led to lawyer's discipline for another partner's misappropriation of client funds; "once warning signs appeared, suggesting clear problems regarding ethical behavior, informal enforcement and occasional admonition no longer sufficed"); *In re Robinson*, 74 A.3d 688 (D.C. 2013) (trust account overdraft put law firm principal on notice that subordinate lawyer needed additional supervision in handling firm's accounting; failure to follow up led to second overdraft and misappropriation of clients' funds); *In re Fonte*, 905 N.Y.S.2d 173 (App. Div. 2010) (lawyer "ignored multiple warning signs and blatantly apparent indicators" of partner's misappropriation of escrow funds).

An example of how law firm policies can adversely affect the ability of individual lawyers to represent clients is seen in *Davis v. Ala. State Bar*, 676 So. 2d 306 (Ala. 1996). In *Davis*, both partners in a two-partner firm were suspended for imposing conditions upon associates that made it impossible to represent clients adequately. The conditions included huge caseloads, limits on the amount of time that could be spent with clients and on cases, a quota system requiring associates to open a specified number of files in a certain time period, and rules prohibiting associates from returning phone calls of existing clients so they would have more time to sign new clients. The court found that "the evidence presented amply showed that the two attorneys, in an effort to turn over a huge volume of cases, neglected their clients and imposed policies on associate attorneys that prevented the attorneys from providing quality and competent legal services." *Id.* at 308. *See also In re Cohen*, 847 A.2d 1162 (D.C. 2004) (firm failed to offer associates rudimentary ethics training or mechanism for review and guidance by supervisors); *Att'y Grievance Comm'n v. Ficker*, 924 A.2d 1105 (Md. 2007) (lawyer in high-volume practice failed to implement adequate system for assigning cases to associates, fostering "an environment where rules regarding diligent representation and communication with clients were almost inherently violated").

For analysis of issues relating to intra-firm ethics consultations, see ABA Formal Ethics Op. 08-453 (2008); Elizabeth Chambliss, *The Professionalization of Law Firm In-House Counsel*, 84 N.C. L. Rev. 1515 (June 2006); Elizabeth Chambliss & David B. Wilkins, *The Emerging Role of Ethics Advisors, General Counsel, and Other Compliance Specialists in Large Law Firms*, 44 Ariz. L. Rev. 559 (Fall/Winter 2002); and Alex B. Long, *Whistleblowing Attorneys and Ethical Infrastructures*, 68 Md. L. Rev. 786 (2009).

### *Paragraph (b): Duty of Supervisor*

Paragraph (b) requires a lawyer with direct supervisory responsibility over another lawyer to "make reasonable efforts" to ensure the other lawyer complies with the Rules of Professional Conduct. *See In re Moore*, 494 S.E.2d 804 (S.C. 1997) (lawyer who turned over all discovery matters to associate was responsible for ensuring associate appropriately responded to discovery requests); *see also In re Ritger*, 556 A.2d 1201 (N.J. 1989) ("when lawyers take on the significant burdens of overseeing the work of other lawyers, more is required than that the supervisor simply be 'available'"); Utah Ethics Op. 17-04 (2017) (local counsel must take reasonable steps to ensure pro hac vice lawyer follows ethics rules).

Adequate supervision is particularly important when dealing with inexperienced lawyers. *See, e.g., Fla. Bar v. Nowacki*, 697 So. 2d 828 (Fla. 1997) (lawyer undergoing cancer treatment delegated entire caseload to new associate; when client refused to let associate proceed and demanded refund, associate failed to comply and called police to settle matter); *In re Farmer*, 950 P.2d 713 (Kan. 1997) (lawyer hired inexperienced associates and failed to supervise and train them adequately); *Ky. Bar Ass'n v. Devers*, 936 S.W.2d 89 (Ky. 1996) (lawyer sent untrained and uninformed employee to represent clients at meeting of creditors in bankruptcy proceeding; employee gave inaccurate advice to clients); *In re Wilkinson*, 805 So. 2d 142 (La. 2002) (lawyer made no effort to oversee handling of client matter by newly admitted lawyer initially hired as law clerk); *Att'y Grievance Comm'n v. Ficker*, 706 A.2d 1045 (Md. 1998) (lawyer assigned difficult drunk-driving case to novice lawyer the day before trial and with minimum preparation); *In re Kaszynski*, 620 N.W.2d 708 (Minn. 2001) (lawyer failed to supervise and train inexperienced associate adequately and misinformed him about immigration law procedure); *In re Yacavino*, 494 A.2d 801 (N.J. 1985) ("attitude of leaving new lawyers to sink or swim will not be tolerated"; supervising lawyer has duty to ensure each lawyer in organization diligently represents clients in conformance with ethics rules).

Assigning excessive caseloads to subordinates may violate Rule 5.1(b). *See* ABA Formal Ethics Op. 06-441 (2006) (supervisory lawyer responsible for ensuring subordinate's caseload is not so excessive that subordinate cannot provide competent and diligent representation); S.C. Ethics Op. 04-12 (2004) (public defender's supervisor has duty to take steps to ensure subordinates do not carry excessive caseloads); Va. Ethics Op. 1798 (2004) (prosecutor who assigns to assistant caseload so large as to make competent and diligent representation impossible violates Rule 5.1); *see also* Or. Ethics Op. 2007-178 (2007) (supervisory lawyer in public defender office who knows subordinates have excessive caseloads must take remedial measures to alleviate excess under state's version of Model Rule 5.1(c)). See the annotation to Rule 5.2 for a discussion of the subordinate lawyer's obligations when assigned an excessive caseload.

When a supervisor knows a subordinate lawyer is impaired, reasonable measures to ensure compliance with the ethics rules may include confronting the lawyer, forcefully urging the lawyer to seek help, limiting the lawyer's workload, or preventing the lawyer from rendering legal services to firm clients. ABA Formal Ethics Op. 03-429 (2003); *accord* N.C. Ethics Op. 2013-8 (2014); Va. Ethics Op. 1886 (2016).

## SUPERVISION OF OUTSIDE LAWYERS

Rule 5.1 has been interpreted to apply to the supervision of lawyers not directly affiliated with the supervising lawyer's firm. ABA Formal Ethics Op. 08-451 n.2 (2008) ("A contrary interpretation would lead to the anomalous result that lawyers who outsource have a lower standard of care when supervising outsourced lawyers than they have with respect to lawyers within their own firm."); *accord* Colo. Ethics Op. 121 (2008); *see also In re Trahant*, 108 So. 3d 67 (La. 2012) (lawyer with voluminous caseload failed to supervise lawyer sharing office space whom he hired to perform title examinations and notarial services but who engaged in pattern of fraudulent real estate closings). For discussion of the means of ensuring the conduct of outsourced lawyers conforms to the lawyer's ethical duties, see ABA Formal Ethics Op. 08-451

(2008); L.A. Cnty. Ethics Op. 518 (2006); San Diego Cnty. Ethics Op. 2007-1 (2007); Colo. Ethics Op. 121 (2008); Fla. Ethics Op. 07-2 (2008); Iowa Ethics Op. 13-03 (2013); N.Y. City Ethics Op. 2006-3 (2006); Ohio Ethics Op. 2009-6 (2009); and Comm. on Prof'l Responsibility, Ass'n of the Bar of the City of N.Y., *Report on the Outsourcing of Legal Services Overseas* (2009). *See generally* Mary C. Daly & Carole Silver, *Flattening the World of Legal Services? The Ethical and Liability Minefields of Offshoring Legal and Law-Related Services*, 38 Geo. J. Int'l L. 401 (Spring 2007).

## *Paragraph (c): Responsibility for Another Lawyer's Ethical Violations*

Under paragraph (c), any lawyer may be held responsible in discipline for another lawyer's ethical violations if the lawyer orders or ratifies the specific conduct involved. *See, e.g., In re Gilly*, 976 F. Supp. 2d 471 (S.D.N.Y. 2013) (partner instructed associate to use misleading expert report in settlement negotiations and ratified his failure to timely produce documents requested during discovery); *In re Asher*, 772 A.2d 1161 (D.C. 2001) (lawyer lied to court about reason for former associate's failure to appear at trial and encouraged her to back up his story by dictating letter and having her mail it to court; when associate later informed lawyer about her intent to tell the truth, lawyer told her to "stick with the story and nobody will know"); *Fla. Bar v. Adams*, 198 So. 3d 593 (Fla. 2016) (lawyer directed or ratified conduct of subordinates in improperly causing DUI arrest of opposing counsel); *Ky. Bar Ass'n v. Chesley*, 393 S.W.3d 584 (Ky. 2013) (lawyer ratified and actively attempted to conceal misconduct of co-counsel in mass tort settlement); *In re Hartley*, 869 So. 2d 799 (La. 2004) (lawyer who directed another firm lawyer to notarize unwitnessed signatures violated Rules 5.1(c)(1) and 8.4(c); infractions "minor," no formal discipline); *Att'y Grievance Comm'n v. Johnson*, 976 A.2d 245 (Md. 2009) (lawyer-owner of title company who, along with lawyer-settlement agent, engaged in fraudulent lease/buy-back arrangement was responsible under Rule 5.1(c) for agent's misconduct, even if agent was independent contractor and even if lawyer-owner not acting as lawyer at the time).

In addition, if the lawyer is a partner, manager, or direct supervisor of the offending lawyer, he or she may be answerable in discipline for the misconduct merely by having knowledge of it "at a time when its consequences can be avoided or mitigated" and failing "to take reasonable remedial action." Rule 5.1(c)(2). *E.g., In re Conwell*, 69 P.3d 589 (Kan. 2003) (lawyer failed to take steps to protect funds in trust account after learning of complaints and judgment against law partner for mishandling funds); *Att'y Grievance Comm'n v. McDowell*, 93 A.3d 711 (Md. 2014) (no violation of Rule 5.1(c) when, after learning that lawyers robo-signed documents in 900 foreclosure actions, managing partner took timely reasonable remedial action); *In re Marshall*, 394 N.W.2d 790 (Minn. 1986) (failure to take reasonable remedial action to avoid or mitigate consequences of law partner's misconduct is grounds for discipline); *Whelan's Case*, 619 A.2d 571 (N.H. 1992) (with respondent's knowledge, law partner drafted codicil to client's will leaving substantial gift to respondent; both lawyers should have obtained client's informed waiver of conflict); *In re Kauffman*, 471 N.Y.S.2d 719 (App. Div. 1984) (lawyer lacking knowledge of letter sent by partner misrepresenting work completed is not responsible); *In re Myers*, 584 S.E.2d 357 (S.C.

2003) (solicitor told by deputy solicitor that law enforcement officers eavesdropped on defense counsel's privileged conversation with client violated Rule 5.1(b) and (c) by failing to ensure defense counsel was informed); *In re Mandelman*, 714 N.W.2d 512 (Wis. 2006) (lawyer who knew partner was neglecting client matters for which lawyer had direct responsibility violated Rule 5.1(c)(2) by failing to take remedial action); Ga. Ethics Op. 98-1 (1998) (lawyer serving as local counsel can be disciplined for discovery abuse by out-of-state lawyer if local counsel knows of it and ratifies it, or has supervisory authority over other lawyer); *see also In re Weston*, 442 N.E.2d 236 (Ill. 1982) (discipline for failure to correct problems caused by mentally ill associate once they became known); *In re Kline*, 311 P.3d 321 (Kan. 2013) (state attorney general who violated Rule 8.4 by directing staff lawyers to attach sealed documents to publicly filed brief, in violation of court order, also violated Rule 5.1(c)(2) by failing to mitigate or avoid consequences of staff's actions in carrying out directive); *cf. In re Anonymous*, 724 N.E.2d 1101 (Ind. 2000) (lawyer co-signed complaint with his partner but failed to ensure case prosecuted after partner left firm; violation of Rule 5.1(c)(2)).

## Rule 5.2

### Responsibilities of a Subordinate Lawyer

(a) A lawyer is bound by the Rules of Professional Conduct notwithstanding that the lawyer acted at the direction of another person.

(b) A subordinate lawyer does not violate the Rules of Professional Conduct if that lawyer acts in accordance with a supervisory lawyer's reasonable resolution of an arguable question of professional duty.

## COMMENT

[1] Although a lawyer is not relieved of responsibility for a violation by the fact that the lawyer acted at the direction of a supervisor, that fact may be relevant in determining whether a lawyer had the knowledge required to render conduct a violation of the Rules. For example, if a subordinate filed a frivolous pleading at the direction of a supervisor, the subordinate would not be guilty of a professional violation unless the subordinate knew of the document's frivolous character.

[2] When lawyers in a supervisor-subordinate relationship encounter a matter involving professional judgment as to ethical duty, the supervisor may assume responsibility for making the judgment. Otherwise a consistent course of action or position could not be taken. If the question can reasonably be answered only one way, the duty of both lawyers is clear and they are equally responsible for fulfilling it. However, if the question is reasonably arguable, someone has to decide upon the course of action. That authority ordinarily reposes in the supervisor, and a subordinate may be guided accordingly. For example, if a question arises whether the interests of two clients conflict under Rule 1.7, the supervisor's reasonable resolution of the question should protect the subordinate professionally if the resolution is subsequently challenged.

**Definitional Cross-References**

"Reasonable" *See* Rule 1.0(h)

**State Rules Comparison**

http://ambar.org/MRPCStateCharts

## ANNOTATION
### SUBORDINATE LAWYER'S
### INDEPENDENT DUTY TO ACT ETHICALLY

Rule 5.2 provides that a lawyer is not excused from the duty to act ethically simply because actions are taken at the direction of a supervisor. However, it also provides that a subordinate lawyer is not subject to discipline for acting in accordance with a supervisory lawyer's "reasonable" resolution of an "arguable question of professional duty." *See People v. Casey*, 948 P.2d 1014 (Colo. 1997) (lawyer's attempt to consult with senior partner did not absolve lawyer of responsibility for failing to tell court client using false identity, though consultation may serve as mitigating factor); *Kelley's Case*, 627 A.2d 597 (N.H. 1993) (rule is no defense to conflicts charge when conflict would be fundamental and clear to disinterested lawyer); *In re Howes*, 940 P.2d 159 (N.M. 1997) (assistant U.S. attorney's reliance upon advice of supervisory lawyers did not relieve him of responsibility for violating ethics rules; "ABA Comment to Model Rule 5.2 makes it clear that the rule, taken as a whole, is not meant to immunize attorneys from accountability for their misconduct"); *In re Bowden*, 613 S.E.2d 367 (S.C. 2005) (associate reprimanded for improprieties in safekeeping of funds and financial recordkeeping, even though these responsibilities handled by supervisor, who was not licensed in state and worked in out-of-state office); Pa. Ethics Op. 2001-23 (2001) (government lawyer may not comply with directive of non-lawyer agency executive to prosecute matter if lawyer believes no probable cause exists; lawyer should bring issue to supervising lawyer for resolution; if supervisor agrees with executive, lawyer may not abide by decision unless it is reasonable resolution of arguable ethics question); *see also In re Ockrassa*, 799 P.2d 1350 (Ariz. 1990) (lawyer disciplined for prosecuting defendant whom he defended in related matter; although lawyer's superiors did not believe this violated ethics rules, "[e]ven minimal research would have disclosed" violation of Rule 1.9); *McCurdy v. Kan. Dep't of Transp.*, 898 P.2d 650 (Kan. 1995) (reversing suspension of government lawyer who refused assignment because of conflict of interest and refused to tell her supervisor nature of conflict; Rule "5.2(b) does not require a subordinate to allow her supervisor to decide all questions involving her ethical duty"); Conn. Informal Ethics Op. 00-9 (2000) (government lawyer may not accept directions from supervisory paralegal if those directions conflict with lawyer's ethical duties); D.C. Ethics Op. 362 (2012) (lawyer who works for discovery service may rely upon management's explanation of service's compliance with prohibitions on unauthorized practice of law and on passive ownership of entities that practice law, but Rule 5.2's safe harbor unavailable if lawyer learns explanation inaccurate); Phila. Ethics Op. 2010-4 (2010) (Rule 5.2 applies to contract lawyers); S.C. Ethics Op. 10-08 (2010) (same); *cf. In re Lightfoot*, 217 F.3d 914 (7th Cir. 2000) ("Reliance on a supervisor's orders is a defense to a charge of misconduct only when reasonable . . . and it is not reasonable to believe that one is authorized to mislead a court."); *Daniels v. Alander*, 844 A.2d 182 (Conn. 2004) (associate sitting at counsel table violated Rule 3.3 by remaining silent while employer made false statements to court). The obligation to exercise independent professional judgment in representing a client is discussed in the annotation to Rule 2.1.

A lawyer's inexperience does not excuse compliance with instructions to engage in unethical conduct. *E.g., In re Alexander*, 300 P.3d 536 (Ariz. 2013) (inexperienced deputy county attorney who knew RICO suit against county board lacked merit could not avoid responsibility for maintaining it by blaming senior attorney); *Ky. Bar Ass'n v. Helmers*, 353 S.W.3d 599 (Ky. 2011) (permanent disbarment for lawyer who helped superiors defraud clients in multimillion-dollar class action even though lawyer was "inexperienced, impressionable, and may have been influenced, and perhaps even led astray, by those more seasoned lawyers"); *Disciplinary Counsel v. Smith*, 918 N.E.2d 992 (Ohio 2009) (inexperienced lawyer disciplined for charging, at direction of supervisor, fee that violated fee agreement and state insurance law; Rule 5.2(b)'s safe harbor provision did not absolve lawyer of duty to research fee issue even after raising it with supervisor, who said he would look into it); *In re Rivers*, 331 S.E.2d 332 (S.C. 1984) (inexperienced lawyer prepared questions for private investigator's interviews of prospective jurors in reliance upon senior partner's assurance that practice ethical if jurors not told name of case; lawyer held to same standard as experienced colleagues, but inexperience would be mitigating factor).

ABA Formal Opinion 06-441 considers the ethics dilemma faced by public defenders—as well as contract and court-appointed lawyers—when excessive caseloads make competent and diligent representation impossible. The opinion states that a supervisor's conscientious effort to resolve a public defender's workload issues will ordinarily constitute a "reasonable resolution of an arguable question of professional duty" within the meaning of Rule 5.2(b). ABA Formal Ethics Op. 06-441 (2006). If it does not, the opinion concludes that the lawyer must take the problem further; possible steps include appealing to the public defender's governing board or seeking court permission to withdraw from enough cases to bring the caseload to a manageable level. *Accord In re Edward S.*, 92 Cal. Rptr. 3d 725 (Ct. App. 2009) (ABA opinion "is fully consistent with the California Rules of Professional Conduct"; public defender's failure to move for substitution of counsel knowing he had insufficient time and resources to provide adequate defense "fell below an objective standard of reasonableness under prevailing professional norms" and resulted in ineffective assistance to defendant); *see* Mich. Informal Ethics Op. RI-252 (1996) (staff lawyer for legal aid agency must monitor workload and decline new clients if taking them would prevent lawyer from providing competent and diligent representation); N.Y. State Ethics Op. 751 (2002) (government agency lawyer may not accept more cases than she can reasonably handle, may not comply with agency official's directive to "just show up," and may defer to supervisor's decision only if reasonable resolution of doubtful ethical question); Or. Ethics Op. 2007-178 (2007) (lawyer representing indigent criminal defendants must take steps to ensure caseload not excessive; "ABA opinion offers useful guidance for Oregon lawyers").

For a discussion of the lawyer's duties of competence and diligence, see the annotations to Rule 1.1 (Competence) and Rule 1.3 (Diligence).

## SCHOLARLY ANALYSIS OF RULE 5.2

Some commentators have argued about whether Rule 5.2 is unduly protective of subordinate lawyers. *See* Robert R. Keatinge, *The Floggings Will Continue Until Morale*

*Improves: The Supervising Attorney and His or Her Firm*, 39 S. Tex. L. Rev. 279 (Mar. 1998) (effect of Rule 5.2 may be to reduce vigor of associates' examination of questionable ethics); Carol M. Rice, *The Superior Orders Defense in Legal Ethics: Sending the Wrong Message to Young Lawyers*, 32 Wake Forest L. Rev. 887 (Fall 1997) (criticizing Rule 5.2(b) for providing "Nuremberg defense" for subordinate lawyers); Douglas R. Richmond, *Subordinate Lawyers and Insubordinate Duties*, 105 W. Va. L. Rev. 449 (Winter 2003) (concluding that Rule 5.2 does not shield subordinate lawyers from discipline, but requires them to act ethically even when acting at superior's direction). *Compare* Andrew M. Perlman, *The Silliest Rule of Professional Conduct: Model Rule 5.2(b)*, 19 Prof. Law., no. 3, at 14 (2009), *with* Douglas R. Richmond, *Academic Silliness About Model Rule 5.2(b)*, 19 Prof. Law., no. 3, at 15 (2009). *See generally* Catherine Gage O'Grady, *Wrongful Obedience and the Professional Practice of Law*, 19 J.L. Bus. & Ethics 9 (Winter 2013); Andrew M. Perlman, *Unethical Obedience by Subordinate Attorneys: Lessons from Social Psychology*, 36 Hofstra L. Rev. 451 (Winter 2007); Douglas R. Richmond, *Professional Responsibilities of Law Firm Associates*, 45 Brandeis L.J. 199 (Winter 2007).

## Rule 5.3

*Responsibilities Regarding Nonlawyer Assistance*

With respect to a nonlawyer employed or retained by or associated with a lawyer:

(a) a partner, and a lawyer who individually or together with other lawyers possesses comparable managerial authority in a law firm shall make reasonable efforts to ensure that the firm has in effect measures giving reasonable assurance that the person's conduct is compatible with the professional obligations of the lawyer;

(b) a lawyer having direct supervisory authority over the nonlawyer shall make reasonable efforts to ensure that the person's conduct is compatible with the professional obligations of the lawyer; and

(c) a lawyer shall be responsible for conduct of such a person that would be a violation of the Rules of Professional Conduct if engaged in by a lawyer if:

(1) the lawyer orders or, with the knowledge of the specific conduct, ratifies the conduct involved; or

(2) the lawyer is a partner or has comparable managerial authority in the law firm in which the person is employed, or has direct supervisory authority over the person, and knows of the conduct at a time when its consequences can be avoided or mitigated but fails to take reasonable remedial action.

## COMMENT

[1] Paragraph (a) requires lawyers with managerial authority within a law firm to make reasonable efforts to ensure that the firm has in effect measures giving reasonable assurance that nonlawyers in the firm and nonlawyers outside the firm who work on firm matters act in a way compatible with the professional obligations of the lawyer. See Comment [6] to Rule 1.1 (retaining lawyers outside the firm) and Comment [1] to Rule 5.1 (responsibilities with respect to lawyers within a firm). Paragraph (b) applies to lawyers who have supervisory authority over such nonlawyers within or outside the firm. Paragraph (c) specifies the circumstances in which a lawyer is responsible for the conduct of such nonlawyers within or outside the firm that would be a violation of the Rules of Professional Conduct if engaged in by a lawyer.

## Nonlawyers Within the Firm

[2] Lawyers generally employ assistants in their practice, including secretaries, investigators, law student interns, and paraprofessionals. Such assistants, whether employees or independent contractors, act for the lawyer in rendition of the lawyer's professional services. A lawyer must give such assistants appropriate instruction and supervision concerning the ethical aspects of their employment, particularly regarding the obligation not to disclose information relating to representation of the client, and should be responsible for their work product. The measures employed in supervising nonlawyers should take account of the fact that they do not have legal training and are not subject to professional discipline.

## Nonlawyers Outside the Firm

[3] A lawyer may use nonlawyers outside the firm to assist the lawyer in rendering legal services to the client. Examples include the retention of an investigative or paraprofessional service, hiring a document management company to create and maintain a database for complex litigation, sending client documents to a third party for printing or scanning, and using an Internet-based service to store client information. When using such services outside the firm, a lawyer must make reasonable efforts to ensure that the services are provided in a manner that is compatible with the lawyer's professional obligations. The extent of this obligation will depend upon the circumstances, including the education, experience and reputation of the nonlawyer; the nature of the services involved; the terms of any arrangements concerning the protection of client information; and the legal and ethical environments of the jurisdictions in which the services will be performed, particularly with regard to confidentiality. See also Rules 1.1 (competence), 1.2 (allocation of authority), 1.4 (communication with client), 1.6 (confidentiality), 5.4(a) (professional independence of the lawyer), and 5.5(a) (unauthorized practice of law). When retaining or directing a nonlawyer outside the firm, a lawyer should communicate directions appropriate under the circumstances to give reasonable assurance that the nonlawyer's conduct is compatible with the professional obligations of the lawyer.

[4] Where the client directs the selection of a particular nonlawyer service provider outside the firm, the lawyer ordinarily should agree with the client concerning the allocation of responsibility for monitoring as between the client and the lawyer. See Rule 1.2. When making such an allocation in a matter pending before a tribunal, lawyers and parties may have additional obligations that are a matter of law beyond the scope of these Rules.

## Definitional Cross-References

"Firm" and "Law firm" *See* Rule 1.0(c)
"Knows" *See* Rule 1.0(f)
"Partner" *See* Rule 1.0(g)
"Reasonable" *See* Rule 1.0(h)

## State Rules Comparison

http://ambar.org/MRPCStateCharts

## ANNOTATION

### GENERAL DUTY REGARDING NONLAWYER ASSISTANCE

It is generally accepted that lawyers delegate certain duties to nonlawyers when providing legal services. *See* Cmt. [2]. However, a lawyer remains responsible for ensuring that nonlawyers perform their duties in a manner compatible with the lawyer's own ethical obligations. *See Mays v. Neal*, 938 S.W.2d 830 (Ark. 1997) (lawyer who delegates tasks to assistants retains "ultimate responsibility" for assistants' compliance with ethics rules); N.C. Ethics Op. 2005-2 (2005) (lawyer who hires nonlawyer to represent Social Security claimants must ensure nonlawyer's conduct is compatible with lawyer's professional obligations, notwithstanding law allowing nonlawyers to represent claimants); *see also* Ala. Ethics Op. 2008-01 (2008) (lawyer employing nonlawyer to communicate with clients in foreign language is responsible for accuracy of information relayed between employee and clients); Mich. Informal Ethics Op. RI-349 (2010) (lawyers may use nonlawyer assistants to communicate with clients and third parties if nonlawyers do not provide legal advice or use independent legal judgment and are properly trained and supervised); *cf.* Utah Ethics Op. 11-03 (2011) (violation of rule for lawyer to require or permit law clerk to use—or to fail to rectify use of—clerk's free law school electronic research account for firm research). *See generally* Douglas R. Richmond, *Watching Over, Watching Out: Lawyers' Responsibilities for Nonlawyer Assistants*, 61 U. Kan. L. Rev. 441 (Dec. 2012).

On the applicability of Rule 5.3 to lawyers when not acting as such, compare *In re Marriage of Redmond & Bezdek*, 131 P.3d 1167 (Colo. App. 2005) (Rule 5.3 applies only to lawyers engaged in practice of law and not to lawyer serving as special advocate in dissolution of marriage proceeding charged with investigating, reporting, and making recommendations about best interest of minor child), with *Att'y Grievance Comm'n v. Johnson*, 976 A.2d 245 (Md. 2009) (lawyer-owner of title company who engaged in fraudulent equity-stripping transaction was responsible for conduct of nonlawyer employee who distributed funds in transaction, regardless of whether lawyer acting as lawyer at the time). *See also In re Cater*, 887 A.2d 1 (D.C. 2005) (rule violated by inadequate supervision of secretary who embezzled over $47,000 from estates for which lawyer was court-appointed conservator).

### • *2002 and 2012 Amendments*

As originally enacted, Rule 5.3, like Rule 5.1, was directed only at partners and supervisors. In 2002, both rules were amended to include lawyers who possess managerial authority comparable to that of partners. The amendments were not intended to reflect a change in substance, but to clarify that rules apply "to managing lawyers in corporate and government legal departments and legal services organizations, as well as to partners in private law firms." American Bar Association, *A Legislative History: The Development of the ABA Model Rules of Professional Conduct, 1982–2013*, at 603–04 (2013).

In 2012, Rule 5.3 was further amended to clarify that it applies to the use of nonlawyers within and outside the firm. The word "assistants" in the title was replaced with the word "assistance"; the order of Comments [1] and [2] was reversed, with changes made to new Comment [1]; and Comments [3] and [4] were added. The word "monitoring" in Comment [4] introduces a new ethical concept to address situations in which the client directs the selection of an outside nonlawyer service provider and the lawyer cannot provide direct supervision. *See* American Bar Association, *A Legislative History: The Development of the ABA Model Rules of Professional Conduct, 1982–2013*, at 604–06 (2013).

## "RETAINED BY OR ASSOCIATED WITH"

Rule 5.3 concerns the conduct not only of nonlawyers whom the lawyer employs, but also of nonlawyers "retained by or associated with a lawyer." *See In re Flack*, 33 P.3d 1281 (Kan. 2001) (lawyer contracted with estate planning company to prepare documents and provide legal services to clients solicited by company; company's service representatives used lawyer's name, committed fraud, and engaged in unauthorized practice of law); *In re Emery*, 799 S.E.2d 295 (S.C. 2017) (lawyer used services of nonlawyer contractors who placed misleading content on lawyer's website and social media page and engaged in unauthorized practice of law); L.A. Cnty. Ethics Op. 522 (2009) (lawyer hired by debt-collection business must have "active role in supervision and direction" of business's employees, including "exercising due control over the preparation of legal pleadings and correspondence" and monitoring employees' compliance with laws governing debt collection); D.C. Ethics Op. 321 (2003) (investigator retained to interview unrepresented adverse party); Ill. Ethics Op. 03-07 (2004) (interpreter retained to communicate with hearing-impaired client); Md. Ethics Op. 2004-27 (2004) (marketing firm retained to contact recipients of mailing who did not respond to mailing); Mass. Ethics Op. 2005-04 (2005) (law firm's software provider); Mont. Ethics Op. 001027 (2000) (collection agency engaged to collect lawyer's unpaid fees); N.Y. State Ethics Op. 1116 (2017) (foreign migration agent who assists immigration lawyer in communicating with client and with gathering and translating documents); Phila. Ethics Op. 2012-1 (2012) (legal aid organization may use nonlawyer volunteers to reach out to community members in trouble and refer them to organization or other nonprofit, provided volunteers supervised by lawyers); Vt. Ethics Op. 2003-03 (2003) (computer consultant); *see also Fla. Bar v. Abrams*, 919 So. 2d 425 (Fla. 2006) (nonlawyer formed corporation to provide legal services and employed lawyer as "Managing Attorney"; lawyer failed to supervise nonlawyer, who mishandled client's immigration case); *In re Meltzer*, 741 N.Y.S.2d 240 (App. Div. 2002) (lawyer who formed corporation with nonlawyer and improperly permitted her to provide legal services was responsible in discipline for her neglect, incompetence, and misrepresentation); *N.C. State Bar v. Leonard*, 632 S.E.2d 183 (N.C. 2006) (lawyer worked on post-conviction cases with convicted felon whom he failed to supervise, and whose methods of acquiring clients or collecting fees he did not inquire into).

Rule 5.3 has also been applied to the supervision of individuals not normally thought of as being "retained by or associated with" the lawyer. In *Fla. Bar v. Flowers*, 672 So. 2d 526 (Fla. 1996), a lawyer was found to have violated Rule 5.3(c) by failing to supervise a nonlawyer "immigration consultant" with whom the lawyer shared office space. Because the office space was arranged to give persons meeting with the consultant the impression they were receiving legal assistance from the lawyer, the lawyer was answerable in discipline for the consultant's mishandling of an individual's immigration matter, notwithstanding that he had never met with, received fees from, or provided legal advice to the individual. *See also Sneed v. Bd. of Prof'l Responsibility*, 301 S.W.3d 603 (Tenn. 2010) (lawyer working out of nonlawyer's immigration business assisted in unauthorized practice of law and failed to provide proper supervision).

In *In re Cline*, 756 So. 2d 284 (La. 2000), a lawyer was found to have violated Rule 5.3(b) by failing to supervise a client adequately. The lawyer gave the client settlement checks erroneously made out to her former lawyer. The client had offered to take the checks to the former lawyer to obtain his endorsement. The Rule 5.3(b) violation lay in the lawyer's failure to take steps to ensure she would actually do so, such as by phoning the former lawyer to alert him that the client would soon be arriving.

### • *Outsourcing*

For discussion of how to ensure the conduct of outsourced service providers is compatible with the lawyer's ethical duties, see ABA Formal Ethics Op. 477R (2017); ABA Formal Ethics Op. 08-541 (2008); L.A. Cnty. Ethics Op. 518 (2006); San Diego Cnty. Ethics Op. 2007-1 (2007); Colo. Ethics Op. 121 (2008); Fla. Ethics Op. 07-2 (2008); N.Y. City Ethics Op. 2015-1 (2015); N.Y. City Ethics Op. 2006-3 (2006); N.C. Ethics Op. 2007-12 (2008); Ohio Ethics Op. 2009-6 (2009); Ohio State Bar Ethics Op. 2013-03 (2013); Va. Ethics Op. 1850 (2010); Comm. on Small Law Firms, N.Y. City Bar Ass'n, *The Cloud and the Small Law Firm: Business, Ethics and Privilege Considerations* (2012); and Comm. on Prof'l Responsibility, Ass'n of the Bar of the City of N.Y., *Report on the Outsourcing of Legal Services Overseas* (2009). *See generally* Laura D'Allaird, *"The Indian Lawyer": Legal Education in India and Protecting the Duty of Confidentiality While Outsourcing*, 18 Prof. Law., no. 3, at 1 (2007); Mary C. Daly & Carole Silver, *Flattening the World of Legal Services? The Ethical and Liability Minefields of Offshoring Legal and Law-Related Services*, 38 Geo. J. Int'l L. 401 (Spring 2007).

## SUPERVISION OF TRUST ACCOUNT MANAGEMENT

Lawyers are responsible under Rule 5.3 if nonlawyer assistants mishandle client funds; holding money in trust for clients is a nondelegable fiduciary responsibility that cannot be excused by someone else's ignorance, inattention, incompetence, or dishonesty. Although lawyers may employ nonlawyers to help discharge their fiduciary duties, lawyers must provide adequate training and supervision. "[T]here must be some system of timely review and internal control to provide reasonable assurance that the supervising lawyer will learn whether the employee is performing the delegated duties honestly and competently." *In re Cater*, 887 A.2d 1 (D.C. 2005) (inadequate supervision of secretary who embezzled over $47,000 from estates for which lawyer was court-appointed conservator). *See, e.g., In re Hawk*, No. 115-006, 2016 WL 7157977, 2016 BL 405332 (S.D. Ga. Dec. 6, 2016) (lawyer may be disciplined under rule even if unaware of assistant's misconduct "because violations of this rule rest on the lawyer's supervisory failures, not upon participation in or knowledge of the assistant's misconduct"; gross negligence in supervising paralegal who embezzled client funds and was subject of 253-count indictment that included charges of bank fraud and aggravated identity theft); *In re Struthers*, 877 P.2d 789 (Ariz. 1994) (lawyer failed to screen, instruct, or supervise nonlawyer employees, and signed pages of blank checks for employees to complete in his absence, thus allowing nonlawyers to decide whether and how much to pay clients from their trust accounts); *In re Bailey*, 821 A.2d 851 (Del. 2003) (managing partner of law firm has "enhanced duties" to ensure firm's compliance with recordkeeping obligations under ethics rules; list of ways to meet these duties at n.33); *Fla. Bar v. Hines*, 39 So. 3d 1196 (Fla. 2010) (lawyer allowed nonlawyer whom she did not employ, supervise, or control to have signatory authority over escrow account, resulting in misappropriation); *In re Grant*, 694 S.E.2d 647 (Ga. 2010) (failure to supervise paralegal who defrauded clients and stole money from trust account); *In re Krebes*, 36 N.E.3d 1047 (Ind. 2015) (failing to adequately supervise paralegal, to whom lawyer delegated authority to establish lawyer-client relationships, enabled paralegal to misappropriate over $100,000); *Curtis v. Ky. Bar Ass'n*, 959 S.W.2d 94 (Ky. 1998) (lawyer's office manager/spouse used trust account check to purchase dog, reimbursing account days later); *In re Joiner*, 209 So. 3d 718 (La. 2015) (failure to supervise assistant facilitated embezzlement of client funds); *Att'y Grievance Comm'n v. Shephard*, 119 A.3d 765 (Md. 2015) (not enough to instruct staff on proper procedures; lawyer had duty to supervise to ensure ethical duties concerning trust accounts were being met); *Att'y Grievance Comm'n v. Smith*, 116 A.3d 977 (Md. 2015) (despite knowledge that client trust account was being invaded, lawyer failed to take reasonable efforts to investigate; instead, he deposited personal funds on several occasions for over a year); *Att'y Grievance Comm'n v. Zuckerman*, 944 A.2d 525 (Md. 2008) (lawyer previously disciplined for failure to supervise assistant who embezzled more than $140,000 from trust account was suspended again when paralegal hired to replace her was similarly poorly supervised and stole more than $100,000); *In re Kaszynski*, 620 N.W.2d 708 (Minn. 2001) (lawyer who gave legal assistant unsupervised responsibility for client matters enabled assistant to forge trust account checks and client money orders); *In re Stransky*, 612 A.2d 373 (N.J. 1992) (lawyer improperly delegated signatory power over trust account and failed to supervise account from which secretary/bookkeeper would "borrow" client funds to pay office bills); *In re Galasso*, 978 N.E.2d 1254 (N.Y. 2012) (lawyer failed to supervise bookkeeper/brother adequately or heed warning signs of misappropriation); *Disciplinary Counsel v. Ball*, 618 N.E.2d 159 (Ohio 1993) (lawyer inadequately supervised bookkeeper who embezzled money from client trust accounts over ten-year period); *State ex rel. Okla. Bar Ass'n v. Mayes*, 977 P.2d 1073 (Okla. 1999) (lawyer's lax supervision allowed nonlawyer office manager to commingle and convert client funds); *In re McNelis*, 150 A.3d 185 (R.I. 2016) (lack of supervision enabled nonlawyer to overcharge client's credit cards and withdraw those funds from business account); *In re Ponder*, 654 S.E.2d 533 (S.C. 2007) (legal assistant who offered to manage trust account after lawyer developed serious health problems embezzled over $238,000; lawyer reviewed her reports but not cancelled checks); *In re PRB Docket No. 2016-042*, 154 A.3d 949 (Vt. 2016) (failure to supervise assistant created "fertile environment" for embezzlement); *In re Trejo*, 185 P.3d 1160 (Wash. 2008) (inadequate trust accounting procedures and inadequate supervision of nonlawyer assistant who misappropriated client funds).

## Paragraph (a): Duty of Partners/Managers to Ensure Conduct of Nonlawyers Is Compatible with Lawyers' Ethical Obligations

Partners, and lawyers with comparable managerial authority, have an obligation to "make reasonable efforts" to establish measures to ensure the conduct of non-lawyer assistants is compatible with the lawyers' ethical duties. Rule 5.3(a). Such measures include instructing nonlawyers about lawyers' ethical duties (especially confidentiality), supervising nonlawyers in ways that prevent them from engaging in the unauthorized practice of law, and, when appropriate, excluding nonlawyers from involvement in particular client matters. *See, e.g., In re Phillips*, 244 P.3d 549 (Ariz. 2010) (firm's policy of tying legal administrators' bonuses to client retention led to "high pressure tactics" and false statements to dissuade client from terminating representation; failure to implement policy to ensure prompt return of unearned fees caused client to wait more than five months for refund); *People v. Smith*, 74 P.3d 566 (Colo. O.P.D.J. 2003) (no violation of Rule 5.3(a) by lawyer who had in place procedures to reasonably ensure legal assistant would act in manner compatible with lawyer ethics rules, but assistant failed to follow them); *In re Saxton*, 791 S.E.2d 773 (Ga. 2016) (allowing unsupervised communications between clients and nonlawyer employees, one of whom advised client to file meritless bankruptcy petition pro se); *In re Mashek*, 758 S.E.2d 309 (Ga. 2014) (lawyer initiated system through which paralegals solicited clients based on tips from medical provider); *In re Farmer*, 950 P.2d 713 (Kan. 1997) (lawyer has duty to ensure nonlawyer assistants do not give legal advice to clients or other callers); *Att'y Grievance Comm'n v. McDowell*, 93 A.3d 711 (Md. 2014) (managing partner had no measures in place to reasonably ensure paralegals did not falsely notarize documents); *Disciplinary Counsel v. Blair*, 944 N.E.2d 1161 (Ohio 2011) (lawyer authorized nonlawyer staff to prepare and file court documents in guardianship matter with no oversight, resulting in filing of false guardian account and forged affidavit); *State ex rel. Okla. Bar Ass'n v. Patmon*, 939 P.2d 1155 (Okla. 1997) (lawyer regularly allowed secretary to sign lawyer's name on documents and file them with court without oversight); ABA Formal Ethics Op. 467 (2014) (providing guidance on specific measures prosecutors should take to comply with Rules 5.1 and 5.3; measures involve training, supervision, creating a culture of compliance, "up-the-ladder" reporting obligations, and discipline); Colo. Ethics Op. 119 (2008) (supervising lawyer has duty to make reasonable efforts to ensure firm has "appropriate technology and systems in place so that subordinate lawyers and nonlawyer assistants can control transmission of metadata"); N.Y. State Ethics Op. 762 (2003) (law firm with associates licensed only in foreign countries must ensure their compliance with ethics rules of their home jurisdictions does not compromise firm's compliance with New York Code).

On the adequacy of measures for dealing with nonlawyer assistants who previously worked for opposing counsel, see *Stewart v. Bee-Dee Neon & Signs, Inc.*, 751 So. 2d 196 (Fla. Dist. Ct. App. 2000) (nonlawyer employees who formerly worked for firm representing adverse party in litigation should be admonished not to discuss matter with anyone in new firm, and access to information about case should be restricted; court noted that former firm has duty under Rule 5.3 to instruct departing nonlawyer employees about ethical obligation not to disclose confidences of firm's clients); *In re Johnston*, 872 N.W.2d 300 (N.D. 2015) (failure to screen paralegal from matter on which he worked while employed by opposing firm violated Rule 5.3); Me. Ethics Op. 186 (2004) (adequate screening of nonlawyer employee to avoid conflicts of interest may fulfill lawyer's duty to make "reasonable efforts" to ensure nonlawyer's conduct is compatible with professional responsibilities of lawyer). For discussion about screening nonlawyer assistants formerly employed by a law firm representing an adverse party, see the annotation to Rule 1.10.

## Paragraph (b): Duties of Supervisory Lawyers

Paragraph (b) requires a lawyer with direct supervisory authority over a nonlawyer assistant to make reasonable efforts to ensure the assistant's conduct is compatible with the lawyer's ethical obligations. Compliance with paragraph (a), in other words, does not suffice if the lawyer also has direct supervisory authority over the nonlawyer whose conduct is in question. *Att'y Grievance Comm'n v. Glenn*, 671 A.2d 463 (Md. 1996) (existence of office procedures to ensure integrity of escrow account did not preclude finding that lawyer failed to supervise employees' management of account adequately); *see also In re Cater*, 887 A.2d 1 (D.C. 2005) (rule violation may result even if lawyer has reason to believe employee is honest and capable: "Internal controls and supervisory review are essential precisely because employee dishonesty and incompetence are not always identifiable in advance.").

Rule 5.3(b) requires the lawyer to provide both instruction and oversight. *In re Comish*, 889 So. 2d 236 (La. 2004) (proper supervision "includes adequate instruction when assigning projects, monitoring of the progress of the project, and review of the completed project"); *see, e.g., In re Anonymous*, 929 N.E.2d 778 (Ind. 2010) (impossible for lawyer employing incarcerated legal assistant to supervise inmate's work, prevent disclosure of client confidences, or ensure inmate's conduct compatible with lawyer's duties under rules); *In re Juhnke*, 41 P.3d 855 (Kan. 2002) (lawyer employed disbarred lawyer—who eventually converted client funds—as legal assistant, letting him meet with clients and write contracts, letters, and pleadings); *Ky. Bar Ass'n v. Mills*, 318 S.W.3d 89 (Ky. 2010) (lawyer involved in class-action litigation allowed nonlawyer employees to mislead clients about their rights under settlement agreement); *In re Wilkinson*, 805 So. 2d 142 (La. 2002) (lawyer told nonlawyer assistant, whose bar admission was pending, not to give legal advice, but had him meet privately with client and then made no attempt to learn what transpired at meeting); *Att'y Grievance Comm'n v. Mooney*, 753 A.2d 17 (Md. 2000) (member of lawyer's office staff incorrectly told client he did not need to attend own trial, resulting in issuance of bench warrant and two-day incarceration of client); *In re Bernstein*, 44 N.Y.S.3d 522 (App. Div. 2017) (lax supervision enabled paralegal to engage in unauthorized practice of law); *Cincinnati Bar Ass'n v. Britt*, 977 N.E.2d 620 (Ohio 2012) (failure to supervise nonlawyer assistant, who gave client flawed legal advice); *In re Vanderbeek*, 101 P.3d 88 (Wash. 2004) (failure to provide adequate supervision of bookkeeper/husband, who was overbilling clients).

Thus, a lawyer may not turn over the day-to-day operations of a law office—or any discrete part thereof—without continuously scrutinizing those operations. *See,*

*e.g., People v. Calvert*, 280 P.3d 1269 (Colo. O.P.D.J. 2011) (lawyer introduced paralegal as "my best attorney" and allowed her to provide legal services to clients without supervision); *In re Shamers*, 873 A.2d 1089 (Del. 2005) (failure to supervise firm
bookkeeping enabled nephew to embezzle funds); *In re Avant*, 603 S.E.2d 295 (Ga.
2004) (failure to supervise office assistant who conducted real estate closings and prepared settlement documents with inaccurate information); *In re Cartmel*, 676 N.E.2d
1047 (Ind. 1997) (lawyer failed to supervise paralegal who placed misleading advertisement in newspaper where it ran five times before being discovered; lawyer also
"abdicated many day-to-day functions of his legal office to legal assistants without
adequately supervising them"); *In re Mopsik*, 902 So. 2d 991 (La. 2005) (lawyer turned
over full responsibility for case to paralegal, who then represented client in court,
presented judge with pleading she prepared purporting to contain lawyer's signature, and failed to inform judge of preexisting restraining order against client); *Att'y
Grievance Comm'n v. Chapman*, 60 A.3d 25 (Md. 2013) (lawyer delegated all core case
responsibility to loan-modification consultant who obtained clients, staffed cases,
directed work, and "only tangentially" updated lawyer); *In re Kaszynski*, 620 N.W.2d
708 (Minn. 2001) (immigration lawyer gave legal assistant unsupervised responsibility for client files and allowed him to interview clients, complete government agency
forms, have ongoing communication with clients, and dispense legal advice); *State ex
rel. Okla. Bar Ass'n v. Martin*, 240 P.3d 690 (Okla. 2010) (lawyer's failure to supervise
nonlawyer employee who was allowed to operate "research center" in lawyer's office
made it possible for employee to defraud client); *In re Marshall*, 498 S.E.2d 869 (S.C.
1998) (lawyer delegated complete operation of office to office manager, who retained
clients and embezzled trust funds); *see also Fla. Bar v. Stein*, 916 So. 2d 774 (Fla. 2005)
(by permitting disbarred New York lawyer to sign her name on court documents as
attorney of record and failing to supervise him, lawyer became responsible for his
misconduct); *In re Foster*, 45 So. 3d 1026 (La. 2010) (all members of firm management
committee reprimanded for failing to supervise nonlawyer employee to whom firm
delegated responsibility for firm's website, which falsely implied former governor
was member of firm); *In re Guirard*, 11 So. 3d 1017 (La. 2009) (nonlawyers allowed
to advise clients on viability of claims and given leeway to negotiate claims without
lawyer supervision); *Att'y Grievance Comm'n v. Barton*, 110 A.3d 668 (Md. 2015) (lawyer encouraged office manager to engage in unauthorized practice of law, gave him
control of firm bank accounts, and failed to review bank statements even after manager was caught stealing client funds); *In re Evans*, 657 S.E.2d 752 (S.C. 2008) (lawyer
failed to properly supervise staff handling office accounting and document preparation, and allowed staff to sign her name as attorney on closing documents and then
sign as witness to her "signature").

However, the mere fact of employee misconduct, without more, does not necessarily denote a violation of Rule 5.3. *See, e.g., In re Phillips*, 244 P.3d 549 (Ariz. 2010)
(rule does not require lawyer to "guarantee" assistant will never engage in misconduct); *People v. Milner*, 35 P.3d 670 (Colo. O.P.D.J. 2001) (paralegal's single outburst
telling client to "stop calling and bit*hing," although "lacking in tact," could not
form basis for Rule 5.3(b) violation); *Statewide Grievance Comm. v. Pinciaro*, No. CV
970396643S, 1997 WL 155379 (Conn. Super. Ct. Mar. 21, 1997) (misconduct of nonlaw-

yer employee who took kickback from client when distributing settlement check did not, in itself, amount to ethical violation by lawyer who did not authorize, approve, or even suspect such conduct; no evidence presented about what lawyer should have done differently); *In re Eddings*, 795 S.E.2d 183 (Ga. 2016) (despite theft of $2.3 million from trust account by lawyer's financial manager/wife, no Rule 5.3 violation; lawyer was victim of "elaborate con" and took reasonable steps to address problems of which he was aware); *Att'y Grievance Comm'n v. Ficker*, 706 A.2d 1045 (Md. 1998) (nonlawyer assistant failed to timely convey client's message to lawyer that she would be out of town on scheduled trial date, resulting in bench warrant being issued against client; court "not prepared to conclude, on this record, that one missed communication, even though significant, constitutes a violation of . . . Rule 5.3").

## *Paragraph (c): Ordering, Ratifying, or Failing to Rectify Wrongful Conduct of Nonlawyers*

A lawyer who directs or ratifies a nonlawyer assistant's misconduct—that is, conduct that would violate the ethics rules if engaged in by the lawyer—is answerable in discipline for that misconduct. Under paragraph (c), if the lawyer is a partner or manager, or is the nonlawyer's supervisor, it is enough that the lawyer knew about the misconduct "at a time when its consequences [could have been] avoided or mitigated" and failed "to take reasonable remedial action." *Att'y Grievance Comm'n v. Smith*, 116 A.3d 977 (Md. 2015) (lawyer can't avoid responsibility under Rule 5.3(c)(2) "by remaining willfully ignorant . . . in the face of clear indications of [the employee's] misconduct"). *See, e.g., In re Lassen*, 672 A.2d 988 (Del. 1996) (lawyer directed accounting personnel to charge fictitious time to clients' accounts); *In re Moore*, 704 A.2d 1187 (D.C. 1997) (lawyer's blanket authorization of all banking transactions of spouse/ office manager resulted in commingling of client funds with third-party funds, misappropriation, and failure to pay third-party creditors of client on time); *Fla. Bar v. Adams*, 198 So. 3d 593 (Fla. 2016) (lawyer directed or ratified conduct of paralegal in orchestrating DUI arrest of opposing counsel); *In re Ehrlich*, 351 P.3d 1268 (Kan. 2015) (lawyer knew law clerk failed to obtain service on defendant at time when problem could have been remedied); *Att'y Grievance Comm'n v. Phillips*, 155 A.3d 476 (Md. 2017) (lawyer ratified son's unauthorized practice of law); *Att'y Grievance Comm'n v. Gracey*, 136 A.3d 798 (Md. 2016) (lawyer knew nonlawyer staff were improperly soliciting clients and allowed it to continue); *Att'y Grievance Comm'n v. McDowell*, 93 A.3d 711 (Md. 2014) (no Rule 5.3(c) violation when managing partner took reasonable remedial action upon learning that paralegals falsely notarized documents in 900 foreclosure cases); *In re Houge*, 764 N.W.2d 328 (Minn. 2009) (lawyer entered sham employment arrangement with client that appeared lawful but actually violated terms of client's court-ordered probation); *State ex rel. Okla. Bar Ass'n v. Taylor*, 4 P.3d 1242 (Okla. 2000) (lawyer ratified conduct of wife/office manager who improperly endorsed client's settlement checks); *see also Richards v. Jain*, 168 F. Supp. 2d 1195 (W.D. Wash. 2001) (disqualifying law firm for lawyers' failure to make reasonable efforts to ensure paralegal did not review privileged materials on computer disk provided by opposing party in discovery; "upon . . . learning that [disk] contained every e-mail from [plaintiff's] hard drive, [the firm's lawyers] had constructive knowledge that the [disk] contained privileged e-mail" and were required by Rule 5.3(c) to take steps to prevent further review, or remediate by removing paralegal from further contact with case).

For discussion of the prohibition against violating an ethics rule through the acts of another, see the annotation to Rule 8.4.

# LAW FIRMS AND ASSOCIATIONS

## Rule 5.4

### *Professional Independence of a Lawyer*

(a) A lawyer or law firm shall not share legal fees with a nonlawyer, except that:

(1) an agreement by a lawyer with the lawyer's firm, partner, or associate may provide for the payment of money, over a reasonable period of time after the lawyer's death, to the lawyer's estate or to one or more specified persons;

(2) a lawyer who purchases the practice of a deceased, disabled, or disappeared lawyer may, pursuant to the provisions of Rule 1.17, pay to the estate or other representative of that lawyer the agreed-upon purchase price;

(3) a lawyer or law firm may include nonlawyer employees in a compensation or retirement plan, even though the plan is based in whole or in part on a profit-sharing arrangement; and

(4) a lawyer may share court-awarded legal fees with a nonprofit organization that employed, retained or recommended employment of the lawyer in the matter.

(b) A lawyer shall not form a partnership with a nonlawyer if any of the activities of the partnership consist of the practice of law.

(c) A lawyer shall not permit a person who recommends, employs, or pays the lawyer to render legal services for another to direct or regulate the lawyer's professional judgment in rendering such legal services.

(d) A lawyer shall not practice with or in the form of a professional corporation or association authorized to practice law for a profit, if:

(1) a nonlawyer owns any interest therein, except that a fiduciary representative of the estate of a lawyer may hold the stock or interest of the lawyer for a reasonable time during administration;

(2) a nonlawyer is a corporate director or officer thereof or occupies the position of similar responsibility in any form of association other than a corporation; or

(3) a nonlawyer has the right to direct or control the professional judgment of a lawyer.

## COMMENT

[1] The provisions of this Rule express traditional limitations on sharing fees. These limitations are to protect the lawyer's professional independence of judgment. Where someone other than the client pays the lawyer's fee or salary, or recommends employment of the lawyer, that arrangement does not modify the lawyer's obligation to the client. As stated in paragraph (c), such arrangements should not interfere with the lawyer's professional judgment.

[2] This Rule also expresses traditional limitations on permitting a third party to direct or regulate the lawyer's professional judgment in rendering legal services to another. See also Rule 1.8(f) (lawyer may accept compensation from a third party as long as there is no interference with the lawyer's independent professional judgment and the client gives informed consent).

### Definitional Cross-References
"Firm" and "Law firm" *See* Rule 1.0(c)
"Partner" *See* Rule 1.0(g)

### State Rules Comparison
http://ambar.org/MRPCStateCharts

## ANNOTATION

### OVERVIEW

Rule 5.4 is intended to protect a lawyer's independent professional judgment by limiting the influence of nonlawyers on the lawyer-client relationship. *See* ABA Formal Ethics Op. 01-423 (2001) (rule's prohibitions are "directed mainly against entrepreneurial relationship with nonlawyers and primarily are for the purpose of protecting a lawyer's independence in exercising professional judgment on the client's behalf free from control by nonlawyers").

For a penetrating critique see Bruce A. Green, *Lawyers' Professional Independence: Overrated or Undervalued?*, 46 Akron L. Rev. 599 (2013) (questioning rhetoric of professional independence as invoked by opponents of multidisciplinary practice). *See generally* Charles S. Doskow, *Variations on Nonlawyer Ownership of Law Firms: The Full Monty, Accommodation or the (ABA) Stonewall*, 32 Miss. C. L. Rev. 267 (2013) (Rule 5.4(c) and (d) ignore fact that lawyers in military or employed full-time by corporations "have superiors with interests other than the practice of law, [who] in fact have the right and duty to direct the lawyer's activities").

The rule overlaps with Rules 1.8 and 2.1 and with the advertising rules' prohibitions on paying for recommendations and limitations on solicitation. The rule's subparagraphs also overlap with each other: Rule 5.4(a) concerns a nonlawyer's financial stake in a lawyer's work; Rules 5.4(b) and (d) are about affiliating with nonlawyers in partnerships (Rule 5.4(b)) or professional corporations (Rule 5.4(d)); and Rule 5.4(c) admonishes the lawyer to preserve his independence no matter who recommends, hires, or pays him.

### • Nonlawyer Ownership, Multidisciplinary Practice, and Litigation Funding

Rule 5.4 figures prominently in controversies over nonlawyer ownership, multidisciplinary practice, litigation funding, and online for-profit "matching" services. In each scenario the lawyer's relationship with the nonlawyer is said to pose a threat to the lawyer's independence and therefore a potential violation of Rule 5.4(a) and (c). Multidisciplinary practice and nonlawyer ownership present additional issues under Rule 5.4(b) and (d), which restrict forms of practice.

## Paragraph (a): Sharing Fees with Nonlawyers

### GENERAL PROHIBITION

Rule 5.4(a) prohibits a lawyer or law firm from paying a nonlawyer a portion of the legal fees generated by any particular matter unless one of the four narrow exceptions in Rule 5.4(a)(1–4) applies.

Nonlawyers have been permitted to enforce fee-sharing agreements that violate Rule 5.4; this is discussed in the annotation to the Preamble and Scope section.

### • Out-of-State Lawyers

Out-of-state lawyers have been treated as lawyers for purposes of Rule 5.4(a) in the context of trying to enforce a fee-sharing agreement. *See, e.g., Dietrich Corp. v. King Resources Co.*, 596 F.2d 422 (10th Cir. 1979) (out-of-state lawyer who consulted in securities litigation should be "treated as a lawyer whose services in the instant case did not constitute the unauthorized practice of law"); *Daynard v. Ness, Motley, Loadholt, Richardson & Poole, P.A.*, 188 F. Supp. 2d 115 (D. Mass. 2002) (law professor working in Massachusetts but licensed in New York not barred from trying to enforce oral fee-sharing agreement with Mississippi and South Carolina lawyers for advising them in multibillion-dollar tobacco litigation; policy concerns of Rule 5.4(a) not implicated); *Tomar, Seliger, Simonoff, Adourian & O'Brien, P.C. v. Snyder*, 601 A.2d 1056 (Del. Super. Ct. 1990) (lawyers licensed in other state not nonlawyers for purposes of Rule 5.4(a)); N.H. Ethics Op. 2016-17/1 (2017) (retiring lawyer who remains member of another state's bar is "lawyer" for purposes of Rule 5.4(b) and (d)). *Contra Peterson v. Anderson*, 745 P.2d 166 (Ariz. 1987) (lawyer licensed in another state is nonlawyer for purposes of fee-sharing rule). *See generally* Thomas D. Morgan, *The Rise of Institutional Law Practice*, 40 Hofstra L. Rev. 1005 (Summer 2012); Paul R. Tremblay, *Shadow Lawyering: Nonlawyer Practice Within Law Firms*, 85 Ind. L.J. 653 (Spring 2010).

The same issue comes up when applying Rule 5.4(d) to lawyers licensed in non-U.S. jurisdictions; see the discussion "Affiliating with Foreign Lawyers" at the end of this annotation.

### • Inactive, Suspended, or Disbarred Lawyers

Rule 5.4(a) prohibits sharing legal fees with a lawyer who is suspended, disbarred, or on inactive status. *See Att'y Grievance Comm'n v. Brennan*, 714 A.2d 157 (Md. 1998) (not a defense to limit suspended lawyer to paralegal role; rule prohibits sharing fee with paralegal); *Morris & Doherty, P.C. v. Lockwood*, 672 N.W.2d 884 (Mich. Ct.

App. 2003) (for purposes of fee-sharing rule, law professor on inactive status treated as nonlawyer); Pa. Ethics Op. 2007-02 (2007) (may not pay referral fee to lawyer who referred case while on inactive status); Tex. Ethics Op. 592 (2010) (may not share fees with suspended lawyer who refers client); *see also* Phila. Ethics Op. 2016-1 (2016) (once suspension is ordered but before it takes effect, lawyer is considered "formerly admitted" under rule of disciplinary enforcement and therefore may not enter into revised fee agreement with co-counsel).

However, the rule does not prohibit the inactive, suspended, or disbarred lawyer from receiving whatever portion of the fee was earned before the change in status. *See* Mo. Informal Ethics Op. 2015-05 (n.d.) (may divide fee with disbarred lawyer if disbarred lawyer's share is for work performed before disbarment); Pa. Formal Ethics Op. 2007-400 (n.d.) (may pay referral fee to inactive, suspended, or disbarred lawyer if referral was made before status change and client does not object); R.I. Ethics Op. 01-07 (2001) (may pay suspended lawyer on quantum meruit basis for services rendered before suspension).

### • *"Sharing" Fees with Client*

Rule 5.4(a) is not violated when a lawyer rebates some or all of a fee to the client himself. *See* D.C. Ethics Op. 351 (2009) (plaintiff's lawyer who settled case under fee-shifting statute may turn fee award over to client; characterizing this as fee-sharing misconstrues Rule 5.4(a)); Me. Ethics Op. 198 (2009) (although lawyer who takes over representation of Social Security claimant from nonlawyer advocate may not pay advocate out of lawyer's fees, lawyer may refund portion of his own fee for client to pay to nonlawyer advocate); N.Y. State Ethics Op. 1121 (2017) (when insurance carrier pays claimant corporation's attorney fees, to which corporation is statutorily entitled, to corporation's in-house counsel, in-house counsel may remit them to corporation without violating Rule 5.4(a)); N.Y. State Ethics Op. 1096 (2016) (may permit civil-rights client to keep court-awarded attorney fees; statutory fee award belongs to client as prevailing party, rather than to lawyer); N.Y. State Ethics Op. 819 (2007) (divorce lawyer who has been awarded fees to be paid by opponent may agree to accept smaller amount from client and then remit to client whatever portion thereof he eventually recovers from opponent); Va. Ethics Op. 1783 (2003) (lawyer who represents lender collecting on note obligating borrower to pay 25 percent of balance as attorneys' fees may rebate to lender any portion of it that exceeds actual cost of lawyer's services). *But see In re Van Cura*, 504 N.W.2d 610 (Wis. 1993) ("consulting agreement" by which client would finance product liability litigation conducted by law firm in return for half of legal fees violated Rule 5.4(a)).

### • *Consultants and Employees*

The prohibition against fee-sharing with nonlawyers extends to employees and consultants such as investigators, interpreters, jury psychologists, and others whose services the lawyer uses. *See, e.g., McIntosh v. Mills*, 17 Cal. Rptr. 3d 66 (Ct. App. 2004) (agreement to pay bank's former employee percentage of lawyer's fee for helping in suit against bank violated state's counterpart to Rule 5.4(a)); *People v. Easley*, 956 P.2d 1257 (Colo. 1998) (lawyer in sexual harassment case offered to share contingent fee with investigator and psychological counselor); *In re Guirard*, 11 So. 3d 1017 (La. 2009) (lawyer paid nonlawyer case-manager percentage of fees if nonlawyer settled case within specified time period, but nothing if case transferred to litigation); *Richland Cnty. Bar Ass'n v. Akers*, 835 N.E.2d 29 (Ohio 2005) (lawyer reviewed and approved documents prepared by secretary for clients he never spoke with, then told secretary how much to bill each client and to remit the rest to him after deducting $30/hour for her services); Me. Ethics Op. 198 (2009) (lawyer who takes over representation of Social Security claimant from nonlawyer advocate may not pay advocate as "costs" out of lawyer's fees, even though tribunal's rules specifically authorize nonlawyer advocates); Md. Ethics Op. 02-05 (2002) (may not be employed by or share profits of collection agency lawyer co-owns with nonlawyer; agency charges customers single fee and uses lawyer's firm for legal work); R.I. Ethics Op. 2016-05 (2016) (may not form partnership or corporation with owner or manager who is nonlawyer law school graduate; if lawyer pays nonlawyer to render nonlegal services to a client, fee must not be tied to lawyer's fee); *see also Son v. Margolius, Mallios, Davis, Rider & Tomar*, 709 A.2d 112 (Md. 1998) (retainer agreement's implicit requirement that law firm pay percentage of its fee to nonlawyer consultant serving as clients' translator and spokesperson violated public policy expressed in Rule 5.4(a)); *cf. State ex rel. Okla. Bar Ass'n v. Martin*, 240 P.3d 690 (Okla. 2010) (unsupervised nonlawyer employee engaged in unauthorized practice while running support-service business he set up under lawyer's name; no fee-sharing involved, however, because even though lawyer was to be paid percentage of business's income, nonlawyer's customers were never lawyer's clients).

Rule 5.4(a) also forbids tying an employment agency's payment to the fees generated by particular matters. *See In re Watley*, 802 So. 2d 593 (La. 2001) (may not split fees with agency providing secretarial and paralegal services); Ala. Ethics Op. 2007-03 (2007) (law firm hiring temporary lawyer should pay him directly and pay separate placement fee to staffing agency); Ariz. Ethics Op. 00-10 (2000) (may pay staffing agency based on number of hours temporary lawyer works, with agency in turn paying lawyer out of that amount; may not, however, base payment to agency on amounts actually received from client); N.C. Ethics Op. 2010-4 (2010) (permissible to participate in barter exchange program that charges transaction fee of 10 percent of value of services being purchased; surcharge is similar to credit-card bank's discount fee); *see also* ABA Formal Ethics Op. 88-356 (1988) (Rule 5.4(a) not implicated if law firm uses agency to locate, recruit, and screen temporary lawyer and bases agency's payment on lawyer's compensation).

### • *Paying to Recruit Clients*

A lawyer who shares legal fees in return for referrals violates Rule 5.4(a). *See, e.g., Fla. Bar v. Barrett*, 897 So. 2d 1269 (Fla. 2005) (paid bonus to employee, an ordained minister, for referring congregation members who had been in accidents); *In re Hear*, 755 N.E.2d 579 (Ind. 2001) (shared fees from debt-collection business with nonlawyer who recruited clients); *In re Flack*, 33 P.3d 1281 (Kan. 2001) (fee-sharing agreement with marketing company that solicited estate as lawyer's client violated Rule 5.4(a)); *Ky. Bar Ass'n v. Haas*, 985 S.W.2d 346 (Ky. 1999) (may not agree to give insurance company salesperson a portion of fees generated from personal injury claimants he refers); *In re Zak*, 73 N.E.3d 262 (Mass. 2017) (paid nonlawyer agents $1,000 to $1,500 for each mortgage-loan modification client they acquired); *In re McCray*, 755 N.W.2d 835 (N.D. 2008) (lawyer paid almost all his gross legal fees to company running credit-repair seminars at which it would recommend lawyer's services); *Disciplinary Counsel v. Stranke*, 852 N.E.2d 1202 (Ohio 2006) (lawyer shared fees with bankruptcy counseling firm that solicited and referred clients to him); *Cleveland Bar Ass'n v. Nosan*, 840 N.E.2d 1073 (Ohio 2006) (lawyer shared fees with debt-counseling company that advertised for clients and provided lawyer with office space and support staff); *In re Deddish*, 557 S.E.2d 655 (S.C. 2001) (lawyer did estate-planning work for, and split fees with, nonlawyer-owned limited-liability company); *Lawyer Disciplinary Bd. v. Duty*, 671 S.E.2d 763 (W. Va. 2008) (lawyer gave nonlawyer employee half of his eventual fee for securing her friend as his client in personal injury case); N.Y. State Ethics Op. 727 (2000) (may not accept referral of personal injury case from accounting firm in return for agreement to share contingent fee); *see also In re Holmes*, 304 B.R. 292 (Bankr. N.D. Miss. 2004) (paid nonlawyer employees incentive bonuses of $5 for each signed retainer agreement or durable power of attorney); Ill. Ethics Op. 06-02 (2006) (may not compensate marketing firm based upon fees received from clients it refers); Ill. Ethics Op. 01-05 (2002) (may not avoid Rule 5.4(a) by creating sham "mediation firm" in order to share legal fees with accounting firm in exchange for referrals); Md. Ethics Op. 2004-11 (2004) (may not agree for nonlawyer insurance brokers and financial planners to refer estate-planning customers to lawyer and pay his fee); Phila. Ethics Op. 04-3 (2004) (may not pay nonlawyer marketing director percentage of profits from cases he brings to firm). *See generally* John S. Dzienkowski & Robert J. Peroni, *Conflicts of Interest in Lawyer Referral Arrangements with Nonlawyer Professionals*, 21 Geo. J. Legal Ethics 197 (Spring 2008).

### • *Internet Matching Services and Discount Programs*

Online matching services typically involve some form of fee-sharing that implicates Rule 5.4. *See* Ohio Sup. Ct. Ethics Op. 2016-3 (2016) (may not accept referrals from service that determines legal services and fees for potential client, then charges lawyer for marketing based on fees generated); Pa. Formal Ethics Op. 2016-200 (2016) (may not accept referrals from Flat-Fee Limited-Scope [FFLS] program; matching service charges prospective client flat fee for desired legal service, remits fee to lawyer after services performed, and then charges lawyer a percentage as marketing fee); S.C. Ethics Op. 16-06 (2016) (same). *See generally* Nathan Crystal, *Legal Services Rendered by Nonlawyers: Neither "Thumbs Up Nor Down,"* 28 S.C. Law. 12 (Jan. 2017); Aviva Meridian Kaiser, *The "Uberization" of Legal Services: Consistent with Ethics Rules?*, 90 Wis. Law. 24 (Feb. 2017).

Group-discount coupons and "daily deal" programs present similar issues. *See* Md. Ethics Op. 2016-14 (n.d.) (may not participate in online fixed-fee legal services program that charges lawyer based on services for which lawyer is retained); Mich. Informal Ethics Op. RI-366 (2014) (group program by which potential client buys coupon from marketing company for specified legal services and company forwards payment to lawyer after deducting a percentage violates rule against splitting fees with nonlawyers); N.H. Ethics Op. 2013-14/8 (2014) (no per se prohibition against using group-coupon or daily-deal websites to offer discounted legal services but must ensure internet company's policies comply with ethics rules).

These arrangements are discussed in the annotation to Rule 7.2 in the context of the prohibition on paying for referrals.

### • Enforcing the Agreement

Enforceability of an agreement that violates Rule 5.4 is discussed in the annotation to the Preamble and Scope sections.

## EXCEPTIONS IN PARAGRAPHS (a)(1)–(a)(4)

### Paragraphs (a)(1) and (a)(2): Fee-Sharing with Estate or Representative of "Deceased, Disabled, or Disappeared" Lawyer

Rule 5.4(a)(1) permits a lawyer and a firm to agree that upon the lawyer's death, the firm will make payments to the lawyer's estate or other specified persons.

Rule 5.4(a)(2) clarifies that when a lawyer purchases the practice of a "deceased, disabled, or disappeared lawyer," payment to the estate or its nonlawyer representative does not implicate the fee-sharing rule. *See* American Bar Association, *A Legislative History: The Development of the ABA Model Rules of Professional Conduct, 1982–2013*, at 617 (2013); *see also* Ill. Ethics Op. 98-09 (1999) (lawyer who undertakes unfinished legal work of deceased lawyer may pay estate portion of fees allocable to work already performed); N.Y. State Ethics Op. 1128 (2017) (same); Pa. Ethics Op. 2015-039 (2015) (same); *cf.* Mo. Informal Ethics Op. 2017-05 (n.d.) (may not pay an attorney's lien if filing attorney has died and no estate has been opened).

### Paragraph (a)(3): Including Nonlawyer Employees in Compensation and Retirement Plans

Rule 5.4(a)(3) permits a lawyer or law firm to include nonlawyer employees in profit-sharing compensation and retirement plans. The rule has often been interpreted to prohibit nonlawyer participation in plans that tie the profits being shared to particular clients or particular matters. *See In re Bass*, 227 B.R. 103 (Bankr. E.D. Mich. 1998) (may not tie legal assistants' compensation to number of bankruptcy petitions firm filed); *In re Formal Advisory Op. 05-4*, 642 S.E.2d 686 (Ga. 2007) (may pay non-lawyer employees monthly bonuses based on percentage of office's gross revenue); *Doe v. Condon*, 532 S.E.2d 879 (S.C. 2000) (profit-sharing arrangement compensating paralegal based on volume and type of cases paralegal handles violates rule); Colo. Informal Ethics Op. 00/01-02 (2001) (may base nonlawyer employees' bonuses on firm's earnings in excess of preset levels of income or net profits, allocated according to each employee's regular compensation or length of service); Del. Ethics Op. 2009-1 (2009) (may not base bonuses to marketing professional on revenues from new clients, increase in total firm revenues, increase in revenues from existing clients, or percentage of revenues from new clients generated by marketer's efforts); Fla. Ethics Op. 02-1 (2002) (may pay bonus to nonlawyer employee based on "extraordinary efforts" on particular case or over specific time period, but bonus must not be tied to number of hours worked on that case or during that time period); N.Y. State Ethics Op. 733 (2000) (nonlawyer employee may receive compensation based on profit-sharing arrangement with law firm, but may not be paid percentage of profits or fees attributable to particular matters he refers); N.Y. City Ethics Op. 2015-1 (2015) (law firm using professional employer organization [PEO] for human resource management must structure PEO's compensation in compliance with Rule 5.4(a)); Phila. Ethics Op. 2014-8 (2015) (law firm's bonuses for high-level nonlawyer supervisors may be contingent on firm's general profitability but not on any specific fees); Phila. Ethics Op. 2004-3 (2004) (may compensate nonlawyer marketing director with percentage of firm's total profits, but not with percentage of profits from cases he refers); Tex. Ethics Op. 642 (rev. 2015) (may consider firm revenue, expenses, and profit in determining whether to pay bonuses to nonlawyer employees, but may not promise specified additional payment if firm meets particular revenue or profit goal); Utah Ethics Op. 02-07 (2002) (nonlawyer compensation plan may include legal fees if amounts not tied to specific cases). *But see In re Weigel*, 817 N.W.2d 835 (Wis. 2012) (bonus system that rewards paralegals with share of gross recoveries on cases they work on did not violate rule; no indication it impinged upon lawyers' professional independence); N.C. Ethics Op. 2005-6 (2005) (lawyer may base legal assistant's pay upon income generated from assistant's appearances before Social Security Administration, which permits nonlawyers to appear on behalf of others).

## *Paragraph (a)(4): Sharing Court-Awarded Fees with Nonprofit Organization*

Rule 5.4(a)(4), added in 2002, permits a lawyer to share court-awarded legal fees with a nonprofit organization that employs, retains, or recommends the lawyer.

The amendment codifies ABA Formal Opinion 93-374 (1993), which concluded that when a nonprofit organization is involved, there is less of a threat to the lawyer's independent judgment. *See Inmates of R.I. Training Sch. v. Martinez*, 465 F. Supp. 2d 131 (D.R.I. 2006) (policy behind federal civil rights laws authorizes exception to literal application of Rule 5.4(a), even without Rule 5.4(a)(4)); Ark. Ethics Op. 95-01 (1995) (collecting opinions, and citing estimate that 40 percent of bar association referral services charge on percentage basis); *see also Richards v. SSM Health Care, Inc.*, 724 N.E.2d 975 (Ill. App. Ct. 2000) (lawyer's agreement to pay percentage of fee in exchange for referrals from bar-sponsored lawyer referral service did not implicate Rule 5.4(a)); D.C. Ethics Op. 329 (2005) (permissible for nonprofit organization to pay lawyer $10,000 retainer to handle wage compensation claims for day laborers on contingent basis and then take first $10,000 of lawyer's fees to cover organization's expenses); D.C. Ethics Op. 307 (2001) (lawyer may participate in government-run program that negotiates contracts with lawyers to do legal work for federal agencies notwithstanding that lawyer is required to contribute 1 percent of legal fees to fund program; opinion notes nonprofit, public interest nature of plan); Ill. Ethics Op. 15-04 (2015) (law firm receiving referrals from nonprofit organization that does not qualify as not-for-profit lawyer referral service under Rule 7.2 may give its court-awarded fees to the organization but may not pay it a referral fee); Va. Ethics Op. 1751 (2001) (lawyer may pay local bar association reasonable percentage of fees earned from clients it refers); *cf.* D.C. Ethics Op. 369 (2015) (D.C. exception, which applies to settlement funds as well as court-awarded funds, is limited to litigated matters because D.C. cmt. [11] refers to funds "recovered from the opposing party" in a "case"); Phila. Ethics Op. 2017-1 (2017) (nonprofit legal services organization funded by bar foundation, directed and primarily staffed by lawyers, is considered a law firm for purposes of fee-sharing rule and may therefore receive percentage of any fee award or settlement in matters it refers to outside pro bono lawyers).

### *Paragraph (b): Partnership with Nonlawyer*

Paragraph (b) prohibits a lawyer from entering a partnership with a nonlawyer if any of the partnership's activities constitutes the practice of law. *See, e.g., Jacoby & Meyers, LLP v. Presiding Justices*, 852 F.3d 178 (2d Cir. 2017) (affirming dismissal of constitutional challenge to state's ban on nonlawyer investment in law firms); *Fla. Bar v. Glueck*, 985 So. 2d 1052 (Fla. 2008) (when lawyer shared immigration consulting business's office space, fees, and paralegal employee, law office and consulting business "blended together into one operation that was in essence a partnership"); *In re Whatley*, 621 S.E.2d 732 (Ga. 2005) (nonlawyer partner conducted all of bankruptcy firm's business, paying lawyer flat fee per case and later, per month, to close files and appear in court); N.Y. State Ethics Op. 801 (2006) (may not form partnership with out-of-state lawyer if other lawyer would be engaged in unauthorized practice in New York); Utah Ethics Op. 00-03 (2000) (may not enter partnership with nonlawyer to help clients challenge real estate tax assessments; representation of taxpayers in tax commission proceedings is "practice of law" under Rule 5.4(b)). *But see* Va. Ethics Op. 1843 (2008) (patent lawyers may form partnerships and share legal fees with nonlawyer patent agents if practice restricted to patent law; Rule 5.4(b) trumped by Supremacy Clause and by federal regulations governing patent practice).

The District of Columbia's pioneering version of Rule 5.4(b) specifically permits lawyers to enter partnerships with nonlawyers if (1) the sole purpose of the partnership is to provide legal services, (2) the nonlawyer partners agree to conform to the requirements of the lawyer ethics rules, and (3) lawyers with a financial stake or managerial authority in the partnership undertake responsibility for the nonlawyer partners as set out by Rule 5.1. *See* ABA Formal Ethics Op. 464 (2013) (lawyers do not violate fee-sharing prohibition if they work and divide fee with firms in D.C. or foreign countries where nonlawyer ownership permitted); ABA Formal Ethics Op. 91-360 (1991) (if lawyer licensed in D.C. as well as another jurisdiction, lawyer's primary place of practice determines whose Rule 5.4(b) applies); Fla. Ethics Op. 2017-1 (2017) (co-counsel may share fees with out-of-state firms that have nonlawyer owners); Mich. Informal Ethics Op. RI-225 (1995) (lawyer licensed in both Michigan and D.C. may obtain financial interest in D.C. firm owned in part by nonlawyer); N.Y. State Ethics Op. 1038 (2014) (New York lawyer with New York-based practice may not practice in law firm that is wholly owned subsidiary of Washington, D.C., firm that has nonlawyer partner); N.Y. State Ethics Op. 889 (2011) (New York lawyer also admitted in D.C. and principally practicing there would be governed by D.C.'s more liberal Rule 5.4); N.Y. City Ethics Op. 2015-8 (2015) (New York lawyer may share fees with out-of-state firm owned/managed in part by nonlawyers if arrangement permissible in other jurisdiction); Phila. Ethics Op. 2010-7 (2010) (Pennsylvania lawyer may enter fee-sharing agreement with D.C. firm owned in part by nonlawyer who will be sharing in profits pursuant to D.C. rule).

Washington State's Rules 5.9 and 5.10, adopted in 2015, recognize a new nonlawyer legal professional called a Limited License Legal Technician [LLLT]; the comment explains that the new provision "is designed as an exception to the general prohibition stated in Rule 5.4 that lawyers may not share fees or enter into business relationships with [nonlawyers]."

For a comprehensive analysis of multidisciplinary practice see Mary C. Daly, *Choosing Wise Men Wisely: The Risks and Rewards of Purchasing Legal Services from Lawyers in a Multidisciplinary Partnership*, 13 Geo. J. Legal Ethics 217 (Winter 2000). *See generally* Emil Sadykhov, Comment, *Nonlawyer Equity Ownership of Law Practices: A Free Market Approach to Increasing Access to Courts*, 55 Hous. L. Rev. 225 (Fall 2017); Gillian K. Hadfield, *The Cost of Law: Promoting Access to Justice Through the (Un)Corporate Practice of Law*, 38 Int'l Rev. L. & Econ. 43 (June 2014); Rees M. Hawkins, Note, *Not "If," But "When" and "How": A Look at Existing De Facto Multidisciplinary Practices and What They Can Teach Us About the Ongoing Debate*, 83 N.C. L. Rev. 481 (Jan. 2005); Paul R. Koppel, *Under Siege from Within and Without: Why Model Rule 5.4 Is Vital to the Continued Existence of the American Legal Profession*, 14 Geo. J. Legal Ethics 687 (Spring 2001); Charles W. Wolfram, *The ABA and MDPs: Context, History, and Process*, 84 Minn. L. Rev. 1625 (June 2000).

## Paragraph (c): Independent Professional Judgment: Interference by Third Parties

Rule 5.4(c) prohibits a lawyer from allowing "a person who recommends, employs, or pays the lawyer" to interfere with the lawyer's exercise of independent professional judgment on behalf of a client. *See* Ind. Ethics Op. 2004-1 (2004) (lawyer may not participate in bank's program to refer its estate planning customers to him exclusively, in exchange for which he would offer them discount); Ohio Sup. Ct. Ethics Op. 02-5 (2002) (improper for lawyer to donate legal services to be auctioned or raffled at fund-raiser for charitable organization; arrangement may limit exercise of professional judgment in deciding which clients to accept and what services to provide); Pa. Ethics Op. 99-10 (1999) (Rule 5.4(c) requires director of law school's legal clinic to protect interests of clinic client despite law school's admonition that clinic director reconsider commencement of high-profile environmental litigation); S.C. Ethics Op. 04-03 (2004) (arrangement under which nonprofit organization pays lawyer to draft estate-related documents for its prospective donors is permissible if fee not percentage of gift amount and lawyer protects independence of judgment); *cf. Bowers v. State Farm Auto. Ins. Co.*, 932 N.E.2d 607 (Ill. App. Ct. 2010) (Rule 5.4(c) and (d) did not implicitly overrule state law permitting insurance company to employ staff lawyers to represent its insureds); Phila. Ethics Op. 2014-8 (2015) (law firm may not designate high-level nonlawyer supervisory employees as "principals" or give them any managerial control, and must limit their voting authority to administrative matters).

## • *Litigation Funding*

Litigation-funding arrangements, whether tied to a particular case or to the firm's accounts receivable, may be permissible if they do not impinge on the lawyer's ability to exercise independent judgment. *See* N.Y. State Ethics Op. 1062 (2015) (lawyer may use crowdfunding to raise cash for new practice but donors must not receive any interest in or proceeds from the practice; as incentives lawyer may offer informational pamphlets and reports on firm's progress); Pa. Ethics Op. 2016-003 (2016) (may use crowdfunding websites to raise capital for law firm if no profit-sharing or partnership with nonlawyers, and may advise client to begin crowdfunding campaign for legal fees); Utah Ethics Op. 02-01 (2002) (lawyer may fund contingent-fee litigation with loan on which he is sole obligor but may not grant lender security interest in fee) (collecting opinions from other jurisdictions); W. Va. Ethics Op. 2016-01 (2016) (may obtain loan from third-party lender to advance costs and expenses in personal-injury case and with client's informed consent may deduct actual costs and interest from client's portion of settlement or judgment; may not use settlement or judgment to secure loan). *See generally* Thurbert Baker, *Paying to Play: Inside the Ethics and Implications of Third-Party Litigation Funding*, 23 Widener L.J. 229 (2013); Amber Hollister & Beverly Michaelis, *Tread Carefully: Crowdfunding Your Law Practice*, 75 Or. State B. Bull. 7 (May 2015) (crowdfunding not per se prohibited; permissibility depends on funding model used and specifics of implementation); Douglas R. Richmond, *Litigation Funding: Investing, Lending, or Loan Sharking?*, 2005 Prof. Law. Symp. 17 (2005); Victoria Shannon Sahani, *Reshaping Third-Party Funding*, 91 Tul. L. Rev. 4016 (Feb. 2017) (diagramming third-party funding and analyzing possible new ways to structure it).

New York courts have not only approved of litigation-funding arrangements but enforced them. *See Heer v. N. Moore St. Developers, LLC*, 36 N.Y.S.3d 93 (App. Div. 2016) (fee-sharing agreements with nonlawyers are illegal, but "litigation loans obtained by law firms and secured by their accounts receivable are permitted"), citing with approval *Hamilton Capital VII, LLC v. Khorrami, LLP*, 22 N.Y.S.3d 137 (Sup. Ct. 2015) (whether security interest is in contract rights or accounts receivable, "loan results in debt, not equity"; "[p]roviding law firms access to investment capital where the investors are effectively betting on the success of the firm promotes the sound public policy of making justice accessible to all, regardless of wealth").

Insofar as Rule 5.4(c) has been interpreted to prohibit financing by third-party litigation-funding companies, it has been widely criticized. *See* Marco de Morpurgo, *Comparative Legal and Economic Approach to Third-Party Litigation Funding*, 19 Cardozo J. Int'l & Comp. L. 343 (Spring 2011) (parties to third-party litigation-funding contract should be allowed to bargain over transfer of control over litigation, with claimholder paying less in exchange for giving up some control); Michele DeStefano, *Nonlawyers Influencing Lawyers: Too Many Cooks in the Kitchen or Stone Soup?*, 80 Fordham L. Rev. 2791 (May 2012) (after analyzing third-party litigation-funding industry author concludes that "granting nonlawyers more influence could stimulate much needed innovation in the provision and management of legal services"; requiring third-party funder to have absolutely no input in litigation decisions and case management is "unrealistic"); Anthony J. Sebok, *What Do We Talk About When*

*We Talk About Control?*, 82 Fordham L. Rev. 2939 (May 2014) (constraints on litigation investment and on fee-splitting with nonlawyers should not be construed to prevent laypersons from buying an interest in litigation; threat of interference with lawyers' professional independence overblown); Maya Steinitz, *Whose Claim Is This Anyway? Third-Party Litigation Funding*, 95 Minn. L. Rev. 1268 (Apr. 2011) (institutional litigation funders—including those wholly owned by law firms—seek to avoid prohibition on fee-sharing by contracting directly with clients rather than their lawyers; this may actually disserve interests Rule 5.4 seeks to protect).

## Paragraph (d): Professional Corporations and Associations
### NONLAWYER OWNERSHIP AND MANAGEMENT

Rule 5.4(d)—which prohibits a lawyer from practicing "with or in the form of" any for-profit professional corporation or association in which a nonlawyer has an ownership interest, a position of responsibility, or a right to direct the lawyer's professional judgment—restates the requirement of Rule 5.4(c) as well as Rule 2.1 that a lawyer exercise independent professional judgment on a client's behalf. *See, e.g., In re Whatley*, 621 S.E.2d 732 (Ga. 2005) (lawyer established bankruptcy law firm in which nonlawyer handled clients and paperwork, with lawyer making court appearances for flat monthly fee); *Att'y Grievance Comm'n v. Phillips*, 155 A.3d 476 (Md. 2017) (agreed to be part of law firm organized by son, who had graduated from law school but was not admitted, and "in effect" represented himself to opposing party as senior firm member); Ill. Ethics Op. 96-4 (1996) (lawyer may not enter arrangement with nonlawyer real estate broker who will form, own, and direct corporation that would contract with independent lawyers who would pay to use corporate name and hold themselves out as doing business in corporate name in return for corporation's provision of marketing and office space); N.Y. State Ethics Op. 911 (2012) (New York lawyers may not get around fee-sharing prohibition by establishing New York outpost of firm organized in United Kingdom, where alternative business structures permitted); N.D. Ethics Op. 00-09 (2000) (lawyer may not take salaried position with nonlawyer title company to review abstracts and prepare opinions, with title company billing set fee to buyers and sellers); Pa. Ethics Op. 98-90 (1998) (partnership between general-partner law firm and limited-partner real estate broker that provides real estate counseling and title insurance not allowed under Rule 5.4(d)(1); nonlawyer limited partner would be a beneficial owner).

Efforts to change ABA policy on nonlawyer ownership have long met with failure. For a scathing review of the ABA's failure to come to terms with nonlawyer ownership see Steven Gillers, *How to Make Rules for Lawyers: The Professional Responsibility of the Legal Profession*, 40 Pepp. L. Rev. 365 (2013). *See also* Barron Dickinson, *Nonlawyer Ownership of Law Firms in Florida: Issues with Corporate Governance*, 16 Fla. St. U. Bus. Rev. 99 (Spring 2017) (if nonlawyer investment is to be allowed, regulations must ensure clients' interests take precedence over fiduciary duty to shareholders); Roberta S. Karmel, *Will Law Firms Go Public?*, 35 U. Pa. J. Int'l L. 487 (Winter 2013); Joan C. Rogers, "Ethics 20/20 Ditches Idea of Recommending Option for Nonlawyer Owners in Law Firms," *ABA/BNA Lawyers' Manual on Professional Conduct*, 28 Law. Man. Prof. Conduct 250 (Current Reports, Apr. 25, 2012).

Like the Rule 5.4(a) ban on fee-sharing, the prohibition on nonlawyer ownership is widely condemned for impeding the development of multidisciplinary practices [MDPs], alternative legal practice structures [ALPSs], and alternative business structures [ABSs] in the United States. *See* Tyler Cobb, Note, *Have Your Cake and Eat It Too! Appropriately Harnessing the Advantages of Nonlawyer Ownership*, 54 Ariz. L. Rev. 765 (Fall 2012) (proposing more liberal rule based on rejected discussion draft issued by ABA Commission on Ethics 20/20); Jack A. Guttenberg, *Practicing Law in the Twenty-First Century in a Twentieth (Nineteenth) Century Straightjacket: Something Has to Give*, 2012 Mich. St. L. Rev. 415 (2012) ("nonlawyer ownership will bring needed capital and incentives to develop alternative and creative business models" meeting needs of middle- and lower-income clients). *See generally* Melissa Pender, Note, *Multijurisdictional Practice and Alternative Legal Practice Structures: Learning from EU Liberalization to Implement Appropriate Legal Regulatory Reforms in the United States*, 37 Fordham Int'l L.J. 1575 (July 2014) (Rule 5.4 should be amended to permit nonlawyer ownership if (1) firm practices law and nothing else, (2) percentage of nonlawyer ownership is 25 percent or less, and (3) all nonlawyer owners pass character and fitness test); Jayne R. Reardon, *Alternative Business Structures: Good for the Public, Good for the Lawyers*, 7 St. Mary's J. Legal Mal. & Ethics 30 (2017).

The United Kingdom has permitted nonlawyer ownership arrangements since passage of the 2007 Legal Services Act. *See* Judith A. McMorrow, *UK Alternative Business Structures for Legal Practice: Emerging Models and Lessons for the US*, 47 Geo. J. Int'l L. 665 (Winter 2016); Paul D. Paton, *Multidisciplinary Practice Redux: Globalization, Core Values, and Reviving the MDP Debate in America*, 78 Fordham L. Rev. 2193 (Apr. 2010). Nonlawyer ownership is also permitted in Australia, Germany, the Netherlands, New Zealand, and some Canadian provinces.

### • *Affiliating with Foreign Lawyers*

Most ethics opinions have concluded that lawyers licensed in non-U.S. jurisdictions "should be considered lawyers rather than nonlawyers for purposes of Rule 5.4." ABA Formal Ethics Op. 01-423 (2001) (lawyers may form partnerships and other entities to practice law in which foreign lawyers are partners or owners, if foreign lawyers are members of recognized legal profession in the foreign jurisdiction and arrangement complies with law of jurisdictions where firm practices). *E.g.*, Ala. Ethics Op. 02-02 (2002); Iowa Ethics Op. 97-25 (1997); N.Y. State Ethics Op.1072 (2015) (lawyer may form partnership with Japanese professional licensed to practice Japanese intellectual property law as a "benrishi," for which law school degree is not required, if lawyer ensures educational requirements for benrishi are equivalent to those for New York lawyers); Phila. Ethics Op. 92-19 (1992); Utah Ethics Op. 96-14 (1997); *see also* Ark. Ethics Op. 2004-03 (2004) ("Rule 5.4(d) permits only lawyers to be members of a firm, but does not require that they be admitted to practice in this state."); Wash. Ethics Op. 2201 (2009) (foreign legal consultant performing legal services pursuant to special admission rule is not "nonlawyer" for fee-sharing purposes); *cf.* N.Y. State Ethics Op. 1093 (2016) (New York lawyer living and practicing principally in U.K., in alternative business structure [ABS] with nonlawyer shareholders, may practice in separate New York firm); N.Y. State Ethics Op. 1041 (2014) (New York-licensed lawyer practicing principally in U.K. though not admitted there may establish or join U.K. alternative business structure [ABS] with nonlawyers/foreign lawyers as partners or supervisory personnel; she is deemed admitted to practice in U.K. for purposes of Rule 8.5(b)). *But see* Va. Ethics Op. 1743 (2000) (improper for Virginia lawyer to form partnership with foreign legal consultant not admitted in U.S.; lawyer licensed in another country is considered nonlawyer for purpose of state's unauthorized practice rules).

## Rule 5.5

### Unauthorized Practice of Law; Multijurisdictional Practice of Law

(a) A lawyer shall not practice law in a jurisdiction in violation of the regulation of the legal profession in that jurisdiction, or assist another in doing so.

(b) A lawyer who is not admitted to practice in this jurisdiction shall not:

(1) except as authorized by these Rules or other law, establish an office or other systematic and continuous presence in this jurisdiction for the practice of law; or

(2) hold out to the public or otherwise represent that the lawyer is admitted to practice law in this jurisdiction.

(c) A lawyer admitted in another United States jurisdiction, and not disbarred or suspended from practice in any jurisdiction, may provide legal services on a temporary basis in this jurisdiction that:

(1) are undertaken in association with a lawyer who is admitted to practice in this jurisdiction and who actively participates in the matter;

(2) are in or reasonably related to a pending or potential proceeding before a tribunal in this or another jurisdiction, if the lawyer, or a person the lawyer is assisting, is authorized by law or order to appear in such proceeding or reasonably expects to be so authorized;

(3) are in or reasonably related to a pending or potential arbitration, mediation, or other alternative dispute resolution proceeding in this or another jurisdiction, if the services arise out of or are reasonably related to the lawyer's practice in a jurisdiction in which the lawyer is admitted to practice and are not services for which the forum requires pro hac vice admission; or

(4) are not within paragraphs (c)(2) or (c)(3) and arise out of or are reasonably related to the lawyer's practice in a jurisdiction in which the lawyer is admitted to practice.

(d) A lawyer admitted in another United States jurisdiction or in a foreign jurisdiction, and not disbarred or suspended from practice in any jurisdiction or the equivalent thereof, or a person otherwise lawfully practicing as an in-house counsel under the laws of a foreign jurisdiction, may provide legal services through an office or other systematic and continuous presence in this jurisdiction that:

(1) are provided to the lawyer's employer or its organizational affiliates; are not services for which the forum requires pro hac vice admission; and, when performed by a foreign lawyer and requires advice on the law of this or another jurisdiction or of the United States, such advice shall be based upon the advice of a lawyer who is duly licensed and authorized by the jurisdiction to provide such advice; or

(2) are services that the lawyer is authorized by federal law or other law or rule to provide in this jurisdiction.

(e) For purposes of paragraph (d):

(1) the foreign lawyer must be a member in good standing of a recognized legal profession in a foreign jurisdiction, the members of which are admitted to practice as lawyers or counselors at law or the equivalent, and subject to effective regulation and discipline by a duly constituted professional body or a public authority; or

(2) the person otherwise lawfully practicing as an in-house counsel under the laws of a foreign jurisdiction must be authorized to practice under this Rule by, in the exercise of its discretion, [the highest court of this jurisdiction].

## COMMENT

[1] A lawyer may practice law only in a jurisdiction in which the lawyer is authorized to practice. A lawyer may be admitted to practice law in a jurisdiction on a regular basis or may be authorized by court rule or order or by law to practice for a limited purpose or on a restricted basis. Paragraph (a) applies to unauthorized practice of law by a lawyer, whether through the lawyer's direct action or by the lawyer assisting another person. For example, a lawyer may not assist a person in practicing law in violation of the rules governing professional conduct in that person's jurisdiction.

[2] The definition of the practice of law is established by law and varies from one jurisdiction to another. Whatever the definition, limiting the practice of law to members of the bar protects the public against rendition of legal services by unqualified persons. This Rule does not prohibit a lawyer from employing the services of paraprofessionals and delegating functions to them, so long as the lawyer supervises the delegated work and retains responsibility for their work. See Rule 5.3.

[3] A lawyer may provide professional advice and instruction to nonlawyers whose employment requires knowledge of the law; for example, claims adjusters, employees of financial or commercial institutions, social workers, accountants and persons employed in government agencies. Lawyers also may assist independent nonlawyers, such as paraprofessionals, who are authorized by the law of a jurisdic-

tion to provide particular law-related services. In addition, a lawyer may counsel nonlawyers who wish to proceed pro se.

[4] Other than as authorized by law or this Rule, a lawyer who is not admitted to practice generally in this jurisdiction violates paragraph (b)(1) if the lawyer establishes an office or other systematic and continuous presence in this jurisdiction for the practice of law. Presence may be systematic and continuous even if the lawyer is not physically present here. Such a lawyer must not hold out to the public or otherwise represent that the lawyer is admitted to practice law in this jurisdiction. See also Rule 7.1.

[5] There are occasions in which a lawyer admitted to practice in another United States jurisdiction, and not disbarred or suspended from practice in any jurisdiction, may provide legal services on a temporary basis in this jurisdiction under circumstances that do not create an unreasonable risk to the interests of their clients, the public or the courts. Paragraph (c) identifies four such circumstances. The fact that conduct is not so identified does not imply that the conduct is or is not authorized. With the exception of paragraphs (d)(1) and (d)(2), this Rule does not authorize a U.S. or foreign lawyer to establish an office or other systematic and continuous presence in this jurisdiction without being admitted to practice generally here.

[6] There is no single test to determine whether a lawyer's services are provided on a "temporary basis" in this jurisdiction, and may therefore be permissible under paragraph (c). Services may be "temporary" even though the lawyer provides services in this jurisdiction on a recurring basis, or for an extended period of time, as when the lawyer is representing a client in a single lengthy negotiation or litigation.

[7] Paragraphs (c) and (d) apply to lawyers who are admitted to practice law in any United States jurisdiction, which includes the District of Columbia and any state, territory or commonwealth of the United States. Paragraph (d) also applies to lawyers admitted in a foreign jurisdiction. The word "admitted" in paragraphs (c), (d) and (e) contemplates that the lawyer is authorized to practice in the jurisdiction in which the lawyer is admitted and excludes a lawyer who while technically admitted is not authorized to practice, because, for example, the lawyer is on inactive status.

[8] Paragraph (c)(1) recognizes that the interests of clients and the public are protected if a lawyer admitted only in another jurisdiction associates with a lawyer licensed to practice in this jurisdiction. For this paragraph to apply, however, the lawyer admitted to practice in this jurisdiction must actively participate in and share responsibility for the representation of the client.

[9] Lawyers not admitted to practice generally in a jurisdiction may be authorized by law or order of a tribunal or an administrative agency to appear before the tribunal or agency. This authority may be granted pursuant to formal rules governing admission pro hac vice or pursuant to informal practice of the tribunal or agency. Under paragraph (c)(2), a lawyer does not violate this Rule when the lawyer appears before a tribunal or agency pursuant to such authority. To the extent that a court rule or other law of this jurisdiction requires a lawyer who is not admitted to practice in this jurisdiction to obtain admission pro hac vice before appearing before a tribunal or administrative agency, this Rule requires the lawyer to obtain that authority.

[10] Paragraph (c)(2) also provides that a lawyer rendering services in this jurisdiction on a temporary basis does not violate this Rule when the lawyer engages

in conduct in anticipation of a proceeding or hearing in a jurisdiction in which the lawyer is authorized to practice law or in which the lawyer reasonably expects to be admitted pro hac vice. Examples of such conduct include meetings with the client, interviews of potential witnesses, and the review of documents. Similarly, a lawyer admitted only in another jurisdiction may engage in conduct temporarily in this jurisdiction in connection with pending litigation in another jurisdiction in which the lawyer is or reasonably expects to be authorized to appear, including taking depositions in this jurisdiction.

[11] When a lawyer has been or reasonably expects to be admitted to appear before a court or administrative agency, paragraph (c)(2) also permits conduct by lawyers who are associated with that lawyer in the matter, but who do not expect to appear before the court or administrative agency. For example, subordinate lawyers may conduct research, review documents, and attend meetings with witnesses in support of the lawyer responsible for the litigation.

[12] Paragraph (c)(3) permits a lawyer admitted to practice law in another jurisdiction to perform services on a temporary basis in this jurisdiction if those services are in or reasonably related to a pending or potential arbitration, mediation, or other alternative dispute resolution proceeding in this or another jurisdiction, if the services arise out of or are reasonably related to the lawyer's practice in a jurisdiction in which the lawyer is admitted to practice. The lawyer, however, must obtain admission pro hac vice in the case of a court-annexed arbitration or mediation or otherwise if court rules or law so require.

[13] Paragraph (c)(4) permits a lawyer admitted in another jurisdiction to provide certain legal services on a temporary basis in this jurisdiction that arise out of or are reasonably related to the lawyer's practice in a jurisdiction in which the lawyer is admitted but are not within paragraphs (c)(2) or (c)(3). These services include both legal services and services that nonlawyers may perform but that are considered the practice of law when performed by lawyers.

[14] Paragraphs (c)(3) and (c)(4) require that the services arise out of or be reasonably related to the lawyer's practice in a jurisdiction in which the lawyer is admitted. A variety of factors evidence such a relationship. The lawyer's client may have been previously represented by the lawyer, or may be resident in or have substantial contacts with the jurisdiction in which the lawyer is admitted. The matter, although involving other jurisdictions, may have a significant connection with that jurisdiction. In other cases, significant aspects of the lawyer's work might be conducted in that jurisdiction or a significant aspect of the matter may involve the law of that jurisdiction. The necessary relationship might arise when the client's activities or the legal issues involve multiple jurisdictions, such as when the officers of a multinational corporation survey potential business sites and seek the services of their lawyer in assessing the relative merits of each. In addition, the services may draw on the lawyer's recognized expertise developed through the regular practice of law on behalf of clients in matters involving a particular body of federal, nationally-uniform, foreign, or international law. Lawyers desiring to provide pro bono legal services on a temporary basis in a jurisdiction that has been affected by a major disaster, but in which they are not otherwise authorized to practice law, as well as lawyers from the

affected jurisdiction who seek to practice law temporarily in another jurisdiction, but in which they are not otherwise authorized to practice law, should consult the [*Model Court Rule on Provision of Legal Services Following Determination of Major Disaster*].

[15] Paragraph (d) identifies two circumstances in which a lawyer who is admitted to practice in another United States or a foreign jurisdiction, and is not disbarred or suspended from practice in any jurisdiction, or the equivalent thereof, may establish an office or other systematic and continuous presence in this jurisdiction for the practice of law. Pursuant to paragraph (c) of this Rule, a lawyer admitted in any U.S. jurisdiction may also provide legal services in this jurisdiction on a temporary basis. See also *Model Rule on Temporary Practice by Foreign Lawyers*. Except as provided in paragraphs (d)(1) and (d)(2), a lawyer who is admitted to practice law in another United States or foreign jurisdiction and who establishes an office or other systematic or continuous presence in this jurisdiction must become admitted to practice law generally in this jurisdiction.

[16] Paragraph (d)(1) applies to a U.S. or foreign lawyer who is employed by a client to provide legal services to the client or its organizational affiliates, i.e., entities that control, are controlled by, or are under common control with the employer. This paragraph does not authorize the provision of personal legal services to the employer's officers or employees. The paragraph applies to in-house corporate lawyers, government lawyers and others who are employed to render legal services to the employer. The lawyer's ability to represent the employer outside the jurisdiction in which the lawyer is licensed generally serves the interests of the employer and does not create an unreasonable risk to the client and others because the employer is well situated to assess the lawyer's qualifications and the quality of the lawyer's work. To further decrease any risk to the client, when advising on the domestic law of a United States jurisdiction or on the law of the United States, the foreign lawyer authorized to practice under paragraph (d)(1) of this Rule needs to base that advice on the advice of a lawyer licensed and authorized by the jurisdiction to provide it.

[17] If an employed lawyer establishes an office or other systematic presence in this jurisdiction for the purpose of rendering legal services to the employer, the lawyer may be subject to registration or other requirements, including assessments for client protection funds and mandatory continuing legal education. See *Model Rule for Registration of In-House Counsel*.

[18] Paragraph (d)(2) recognizes that a U.S. or foreign lawyer may provide legal services in a jurisdiction in which the lawyer is not licensed when authorized to do so by federal or other law, which includes statute, court rule, executive regulation or judicial precedent. See, e.g., *Model Rule on Practice Pending Admission*.

[19] A lawyer who practices law in this jurisdiction pursuant to paragraphs (c) or (d) or otherwise is subject to the disciplinary authority of this jurisdiction. See Rule 8.5(a).

[20] In some circumstances, a lawyer who practices law in this jurisdiction pursuant to paragraphs (c) or (d) may have to inform the client that the lawyer is not licensed to practice law in this jurisdiction. For example, that may be required when the representation occurs primarily in this jurisdiction and requires knowledge of the law of this jurisdiction. See Rule 1.4(b).

[21] Paragraphs (c) and (d) do not authorize communications advertising legal services in this jurisdiction by lawyers who are admitted to practice in other jurisdictions. Whether and how lawyers may communicate the availability of their services in this jurisdiction is governed by Rules 7.1 to 7.3.

**Definitional Cross-References**
"Reasonably" *See* Rule 1.0(h)
"Tribunal" *See* Rule 1.0(m)

**State Rules Comparison**
http://ambar.org/MRPCStateCharts

# ANNOTATION

Rule 5.5 has three basic components. First, paragraphs (a) and (b) set out the general prohibitions against out-of-state lawyers engaging or assisting in the unauthorized practice of law, representing to the public that they are licensed in the jurisdiction, or establishing an office in the state. Second, paragraph (c) relaxes these prohibitions somewhat by allowing lawyers admitted to practice in any U.S. jurisdiction (and, in some cases, in a foreign jurisdiction) to provide legal services in another jurisdiction on a limited or temporary basis. Finally, subject to several limitations, paragraphs (d) and (e) permit U.S. or foreign lawyers, primarily in-house counsel advising their employers or corporate affiliates, to maintain an office or otherwise establish a systematic and continuous presence in another jurisdiction.

## PARAGRAPHS *(a)* AND *(b)*: UNAUTHORIZED PRACTICE OF LAW
### Paragraph (a): Prohibition against Unauthorized Practice

Paragraph (a), as amended in 2002, prohibits a lawyer from practicing law in a jurisdiction in which the lawyer is not authorized or from assisting another in doing so. This combines the substance of what was formerly contained in paragraphs (a) and (b). American Bar Association, *A Legislative History: The Development of the ABA Model Rules of Professional Conduct, 1982–2013*, at 643–46 (2013); *see, e.g., In re Trester*, 172 P.3d 31 (Kan. 2007) (practicing law in California for nearly forty years without license violated rule); *State ex rel. Okla. Bar Ass'n v. Auer*, 376 P.3d 243 (Okla. 2016) (lawyer "repeatedly violated this rule by . . . drafting legal documents and . . . offering legal advice to clients" in another state); *see also In re Holmes*, 416 P.3d 143 (Kan. 2018) (practicing law while license suspended). The following sections provide the rationale behind the prohibition, illustrate issues in defining the practice of law, and cite examples of rule violations (or at least alleged violations).

### RATIONALE FOR PROSCRIPTION AGAINST UNAUTHORIZED PRACTICE OF LAW

Although several concerns drive the unauthorized-practice proscriptions, their primary purpose is to protect the public from the consequences of receiving legal services from unqualified persons. Cmt. [2]. The proscriptions are also aimed at facilitating the regulation of the legal profession and protecting the integrity of the judicial system. *See Fla. Bar v. Schramek*, 616 So. 2d 979 (Fla. 1993) (court's primary responsibility is to define and regulate practice of law to protect public from incompetent, unethical, or irresponsible representation and to ensure better access to courts); *In re Op. No. 26 of Comm. on Unauthorized Practice of Law*, 654 A.2d 1344 (N.J. 1995) (noting that ban against unauthorized practice of law protects against unskilled legal advice); *Renaissance Enters. Inc. v. Summit Teleservices Inc.*, 515 S.E.2d 257 (S.C. 1999) (stating that goal is to protect public from incompetent, unethical, or irresponsible representation).

## POWER TO REGULATE PRACTICE OF LAW

### • *State Jurisdiction*

The power to regulate the practice of law generally rests with the states. *United Mine Workers of Am. v. Ill. State Bar Ass'n*, 389 U.S. 217 (1967) (states have broad power to regulate practice of law). Normally, this "inherent" power is vested in the state judicial branch. *See, e.g., In re Flack*, 33 P.3d 1281 (Kan. 2001) (state supreme court has inherent power to define and regulate practice of law); *Hargis v. JLB Corp.*, 357 S.W.3d 574 (Mo. 2011) (noting that it is judiciary's responsibility to determine what constitutes practice of law); *State ex rel. Okla. Bar Ass'n v. Bourland*, 19 P.3d 289 (Okla. 2001) (observing that state supreme court exercises original jurisdiction in lawyer discipline cases); *Clinard v. Blackwood*, 46 S.W.3d 177 (Tenn. 2001) (stating "that the licensing and regulation of attorneys practicing law in courts of Tennessee is squarely within the inherent authority of the judicial branch of government"); *Shenandoah Sales & Serv., Inc. v. Assessor of Jefferson Cnty.*, 724 S.E.2d 733 (W. Va. 2012) (noting corporations must be represented by a lawyer and striking down as unconstitutional a statute that purported to permit nonlawyers to represent corporations). For more discussion of the inherent power of courts (typically state supreme courts) to regulate the practice of law, see generally *Restatement (Third) of the Law Governing Lawyers* § 1 cmt. c (2000); Deborah H. Rhode, *Policing the Professional Monopoly: A Constitutional and Empirical Analysis of Unauthorized Practice Prohibitions*, 34 Stan. L. Rev. 1 (Nov. 1981); Laurel A. Rigertas, *Lobbying and Litigating Against "Legal Bootleggers"—The Role of the Organized Bar in the Expansion of the Courts' Inherent Powers in the Early Twentieth Century*, 46 Cal. W. L. Rev. 65 (2009); Keith Swisher, *The Short History of Arizona Legal Ethics*, 45 Ariz. St. L.J. 813 (2013).

### • *Federal Jurisdiction and Preemption*

Federal courts have inherent power to regulate practice before them. *See, e.g., Chambers v. NASCO, Inc.*, 501 U.S. 32 (1991) (inherent power of federal court includes control over admission to its bar and discipline of lawyers who appear before it).

For those who limit their practice to federal law, federal law may preempt a state's power to regulate that practice. *See, e.g., Sperry v. Fla. ex rel. Fla. Bar*, 373 U.S. 379 (1963) (states may not prohibit nonlawyers registered to practice before U.S. Patent Office from engaging in activities authorized by federal patent law, even if those activities constitute practice of law under state law); *Surrick v. Killion*, 449 F.3d 520 (3d Cir. 2006) (suspension of lawyer by state supreme court cannot override federal district court's power to authorize lawyer to maintain law office in state dedicated exclusively to his practice in federal court); *Augustine v. Dep't of Veterans Affairs*, 429 F.3d 1334 (Fed. Cir. 2005) (federal law, not state law, controls whether lawyer not licensed in state may represent claimant and recover statutory fees in federal administrative proceeding); *NAAMJP v. Simandle*, No. CV 14-3678, 2015 WL 13273313, 2015 BL 282524 (D.N.J. Sept. 1, 2015) (noting that federal court may "adopt a rule that explicitly conditions membership in the court's bar on membership in New Jersey's state bar"); *Benninghoff v. Superior Court*, 38 Cal. Rptr. 3d 759 (Ct. App. 2006) (although state law barred former lawyer—who had resigned with disciplinary charges pending—from practicing law in California, state had no jurisdiction over his federal law practice); *State ex rel. York v. W. Va. Office of Disciplinary Counsel*, 744 S.E.2d 293 (W. Va. 2013) ("because [disciplinary counsel] will not seek to suspend or expel the petitioner from his federal practice, there is no conflict presently existing in the simultaneous federal and state disciplinary investigations"). For further discussion of out-of-state lawyers' permissible (and impermissible) federal practice, see "Paragraph (d): Provision of Legal Services on Regular Basis" below.

## WHAT IS THE "PRACTICE OF LAW"?

The definition of the practice of law varies from one jurisdiction to another, and states are often reluctant to adopt a comprehensive definition. *See In re Unauthorized Practice of Law Rules Proposed by S.C. Bar*, 422 S.E.2d 123 (S.C. 1992) (commending bar for its "Herculean" effort to define practice of law but concluding it was neither "practicable nor wise to attempt a comprehensive definition by way of a set of rules"); *see also In re Howard*, 721 N.E.2d 1126 (Ill. 1999) (noting that "[d]etermining what conduct constitutes 'practicing law' defies mechanistic formulation" and "encompasses not only court appearances, but also services rendered out of court and includes the giving of any advice or rendering of any service requiring the use of legal knowledge").

Nevertheless, each jurisdiction has identified—whether in decisional law, statutes, or court rules—certain activities that constitute the practice of law. *See Rattler v. United States*, No. 1:16-CV-00126-MR, 2018 WL 5839389, 2018 BL 411395 (W.D.N.C. Nov. 7, 2018) (jailhouse lawyer "attempting to represent the legal interests of anyone other than oneself, unless licensed to practice in the State of North Carolina or admitted elsewhere and specially admitted, constitutes the unauthorized practice of law, which is a criminal offense in the State of North Carolina"); *In re Henderson*, 426 B.R. 526 (Bankr. W.D. Pa. 2010) (preparation, filing, and prosecution of motion constitutes practice of law); *Att'y Grievance Comm'n v. James*, 735 A.2d 1027 (Md. 1999) (although difficult to craft "all encompassing definition" of practice of law, inquiry should focus on "whether the activity in question required legal knowledge and skill in order to apply legal principles and precedent"); *In re Charges of Unprof'l Conduct in Panel File No. 39302*, 884 N.W.2d 661 (Minn. 2016) (lawyer in Colorado engaged in unauthorized practice of law because he briefly represented his in-laws concerning "a Minnesota judgment and attempted to negotiate, via e-mail, the satisfaction of that judgment with a Minnesota lawyer"); *Lawyer Disciplinary Bd. v. McCloskey*, 793 S.E.2d 23 (W. Va. 2016) ("Court's long-standing 'Definition of the Practice of Law' expressly states that the practice of law includes 'undertak[ing], with or without compensation and whether or not in connection with another activity, to prepare for another legal instruments of any character' or 'represent[ing] the interest of another before any judicial tribunal or officer'"); *see also Benninghoff v. Superior Court*, 38 Cal. Rptr. 3d 759 (Ct. App. 2006) (representing parties in state administrative hearings constituted practice of law, even though laypeople permitted to do so); *LAS Collection Mgmt. v. Pagan*, 858 N.E.2d 273 (Mass. 2006) (property agent engaged in unauthorized practice of law because agent "filed a complaint for injunctive relief, signed the complaint as an agent of the property owner, managed the prosecution of the complaint, and cross-examined witnesses"); *Cincinnati Bar Ass'n v. Mullaney*, 894 N.E.2d 1210 (Ohio 2008) (advising debtors of their legal rights and terms and conditions of settlement constituted practice of law). *But see In re Chimko*, 831 N.E.2d 316 (Mass. 2005) (preparing reaffirmation agreement in out-of-state bankruptcy court "akin to the nonattorney's preparation of preprinted income tax returns" and did not constitute unauthorized practice of law); *In re Estate of Cooper*, 746 N.W.2d 653 (Neb. 2008) (in Nebraska probate proceeding, neither filing of statement of claim by nonlawyer manager of bank nor filing of demand for notice by Tennessee bank's Tennessee lawyer constituted unauthorized practice).

For a detailed discussion of the types of conduct found to constitute the unauthorized practice of law, see *ABA/BNA Lawyers' Manual on Professional Conduct*, "Qualifications: Unauthorized Practice of Law: Prohibitions on Practice of Nonlawyers," pp. 21:8001 *et seq.* For information regarding the ABA Task Force on the Model Definition of the Practice of Law and a state-by-state canvass of the definitions of the practice of law, see http://www.americanbar.org/groups/professional_responsibility/task_force_model_definition_practice_law.html.

### • *Limited Practice by Nonlawyers*

Federal law has long permitted nonlawyer participation in certain areas, such as patents, federal tax, and immigration law. Recently, a few states have allowed nonlawyers to undertake certain tasks that might otherwise have been considered the unauthorized practice of law. For example, Arizona authorizes "certified legal document preparers," and Utah and Washington now authorize "licensed paralegal practitioners" and "limited license legal technicians," respectively. Ariz. Code of Judicial Admin. § 7-208; Wash. Admission to Practice Rule 28, *available at* http://wsba.org/Licensing-and-Lawyer-Conduct/Limited-Licenses/Legal-Technicians. *See* American Bar Foundation & National Center for State Courts, *Preliminary Evaluation of the Washington State Limited License Legal Technician Program* (2017), *available at* http://www.americanbarfoundation.org/uploads/cms/documents/preliminary_evaluation_of_the_washington_state_limited_license_legal_technician_program_032117.pdf (recommending program be expanded in Washington and considered by other states to broaden access to justice). *See generally* Catherine J. Dupont, *Licensed Paralegal Practitioners*, 31 Utah B.J., no. 3, at 16 (May/June 2018); Lynn Crossett, *Regulation of the Paralegal Profession and Programs for Limited Practice by Non-Lawyers*, 2017 J. Prof. Law. 95, 121 (2017); Brooks Holland, *The Washington State Limited License Legal Technician Practice Rule: A National First in Access to Justice*, 82 Miss. L.J. Supra 75 (2013); Jack P. Sahl, *Cracks in the Profession's Monopoly Armor*, 82 Fordham L. Rev. 2635 (2014).

## PRACTICE BY LAWYERS WHO
## HAVE BEEN SUSPENDED OR DISBARRED

Lawyers who are suspended or disbarred may not practice law or hold themselves out as eligible to practice. *See In re Baars*, 683 N.E.2d 555 (Ind. 1997) (sentencing suspended lawyer to thirty days in jail and fining him $200 for engaging in practice of law); *In re Ellis*, 742 So. 2d 869 (La. 1999) (suspended lawyer improperly acted as notary in drafting two acts of sale and potentially misled public by failing to remove from office "attorney at law" designations, including office sign, law license, and other indicia of good standing); *Att'y Grievance Comm'n v. Hecht*, 184 A.3d 429 (Md. 2018) (suspended lawyer drafted discovery documents for client); *In re Giese*, 709 N.W.2d 717 (N.D. 2006) (suspended lawyer held himself out as being authorized to practice); *see also People v. Mason*, 212 P.3d 141 (Colo. O.P.D.J. 2009) (lawyer violated suspension order by providing legal advice to one client and preparing documents for another, even though he told them he was not a lawyer); *In re Contempt of Fox*, 796 N.E.2d 1186 (Ind. 2003) (ordering suspended lawyer to pay $500 and costs of proceedings for practicing law by, among other activities, appearing at sentencing hearing for criminal defendant); *In re Miller*, 238 P.3d 227 (Kan. 2010) (suspended sole practitioner cannot maintain financial control over professional corporation and "hire an independent contractor to do the legal work which the suspended attorney is precluded from doing").

### • *"Administrative" Suspensions*

Rule 5.5(a)'s prohibition against unauthorized practice applies to lawyers suspended for administrative reasons, such as failure to pay bar dues or comply with continuing legal education (CLE) requirements. *See In re Hall*, 377 P.3d 1149 (Kan. 2016) (lawyer on administrative suspension engaged in unauthorized practice by seeking and receiving pro hac vice admission before resuming practice in the state); *In re Holmberg*, 135 P.3d 1196 (Kan. 2006) (continuing to represent clients while on administrative suspension for failure to pay fees and fulfill CLE requirements); *Ky. Bar Ass'n v. Poteat*, 511 S.W.3d 909 (Ky. 2017) (lawyer continued to practice law although suspended for failure to comply with CLE requirements); *Hipwell v. Ky. Bar Ass'n*, 267 S.W.3d 682 (Ky. 2008) (continuing to work as in-house counsel for twenty-two years after being suspended for nonpayment of dues); *In re Oldenburg*, 19 So. 3d 455 (La. 2009) (practicing while ineligible due to failure to comply with administrative CLE requirements after check for payment of CLE seminar bounced); *In re Gomsrud*, 618 N.W.2d 803 (Minn. 2000) (suspending indefinitely a lawyer who "practiced law while suspended for failing to pay attorney registration fees and while on restricted status for failing to meet CLE requirements"); *see also People v. Harris*, 915 N.E.2d 103 (Ill. App. Ct. 2009) (lawyer convicted of impersonating a lawyer by giving legal advice on trademark matter knowing he was no longer authorized to practice law in Michigan or before patent office; lawyer had been suspended from Michigan bar for failing to pay registration fees and from patent office after failing to provide current address). *But see In re Sonnenreich*, 86 P.3d 712 (Utah 2004) (lawyer suspended for nonpayment of licensing fees may not be disciplined for unauthorized practice unless lawyer had actual notice of suspension).

**• *Law-Related Activities of Suspended or Disbarred Lawyers***

The extent to which suspended or disbarred lawyers may engage in law-related activities short of actual practice varies by jurisdiction. *See Wilson v. State Bar of Ga.*, 132 F.3d 1422 (11th Cir. 1998) (rules prohibiting practicing lawyers from allowing suspended or disbarred lawyers they employ to have contact with clients are not unconstitutionally vague); *In re Boyer*, 988 P.2d 625 (Colo. 1999) (suspended lawyer engaged in unauthorized practice by analyzing value of clients' personal injury claims, negotiating with insurer regarding claims, giving advice, and collecting attorneys' fees); *In re Anonymous*, 787 N.E.2d 883 (Ind. 2003) (Indiana prohibits suspended or disbarred lawyer from maintaining presence or occupying office where practice of law conducted "so the public is not misled into believing that the attorney is still authorized to practice law"); *In re Wiles*, 210 P.3d 613 (Kan. 2009) (disbarred or suspended lawyer may work for lawyer as law clerk, investigator, paralegal, or in any lay capacity but may do only preparatory work under lawyer's supervision and may not have client contact in person, by telephone, or in correspondence); *In re Rowe*, 604 N.E.2d 728 (N.Y. 1992) (publishing article on legal topic and identifying himself in it as "J.D." did not violate suspension directing lawyer not to practice law, give advice on law, or hold himself out as lawyer); *In re Chastain*, 587 S.E.2d 115 (S.C. 2003) (disbarring suspended lawyer who engaged in unauthorized practice by working as office manager for county lawyer); *see also Buckley v. Slocum Dickson Med. Grp., PLLC*, 111 F. Supp. 3d 218 (N.D.N.Y. 2015) (denying request for fees for paralegal work performed by disbarred attorney).

## LAWYERS ON INACTIVE OR RETIRED STATUS

Rule 5.5(a) also applies to lawyers on inactive or retired status. *See In re Cohen*, 612 S.E.2d 294 (Ga. 2005) (disbarring inactive lawyer in part because lawyer undertook representation of criminal defendant); *In re Rost*, 211 P.3d 145 (Kan. 2009) (retired lawyer violated Rule 5.5(a) by selling his practice and then setting up "consulting business" from same location, performing law-related services for same clients with same staff, corresponding with judge using stationery identifying himself as lawyer, and using lawyer registration number on court filings, even though he disclosed his retired status to clients); *In re Johnson*, 9 So. 3d 835 (La. 2009) (lawyer improperly represented client in divorce proceeding while on inactive status); *Disciplinary Counsel v. Cantrell*, 928 N.E.2d 1100 (Ohio 2010) (lawyer on inactive status improperly represented decedent's estate).

## ASSISTING IN UNAUTHORIZED PRACTICE OF LAW

Rule 5.5(a) prohibits a lawyer from helping someone else engage in the unauthorized practice of law. *See In re Crosley*, 99 N.E.3d 643 (Ind. 2018) (Indiana lawyer in "of counsel" relationship with Texas law firm reviewed and signed documents prepared by Texas lawyers for Indiana clients, with whom lawyer typically had no communication); *In re Flack*, 33 P.3d 1281 (Kan. 2001) (lawyer permitted marketing company's nonlawyer service representatives to use his name in soliciting estate planning clients, conducting interviews, explaining legal documents, and advising clients of legal rights); *In re LaMattina*, 858 N.Y.S.2d 222 (App. Div. 2008) (lawyer allowed his name to be used to form corporation run by nonlawyers who in turn represented lenders at real estate closings without lawyer's supervision); *Disciplinary Counsel v. Willard*, 913 N.E.2d 960 (Ohio 2009) (lawyer partnered with nonattorney organization to represent clients in mortgage foreclosure proceedings); ABA Formal Ethics Op. 14-469 (2014) (prosecutor who "supplies official letterhead to a debt collection company and allows the debt collection company to use it to send threatening letters to alleged debtors without any review by the prosecutor or staff lawyers to determine whether a crime was committed and prosecution is warranted, violates Rule 5.5(a) by aiding and abetting the unauthorized practice of law").

### • *Working with Suspended or Disbarred Lawyers*

Helping a suspended or disbarred lawyer engage in the practice of law is also a violation of Rule 5.5. *See, e.g., In re Zentz*, 891 A.2d 277 (D.C. 2006) (lawyer permitted disbarred lawyer to prepare and file documents in bankruptcy court and sign lawyer's name on them); *In re Gaff*, 524 S.E.2d 728 (Ga. 2000) (lawyer failed to supervise disbarred lawyer hired as paralegal who engaged in unauthorized practice and defrauded clients); *In re Discipio*, 645 N.E.2d 906 (Ill. 1994) (lawyer continued to accept referrals of workers' compensation cases from—and share work and divide fees with—disbarred lawyer); *In re Anonymous*, 787 N.E.2d 883 (Ind. 2003) ("it is impermissible for an Indiana attorney to employ a suspended or disbarred attorney to perform work of any kind in a law office"); *In re Juhnke*, 41 P.3d 855 (Kan. 2002) (lawyer employed disbarred lawyer as legal assistant and allowed him to write contracts and letters, meet with clients, prepare pleadings, provide legal advice, and bill at lawyer's own rate); *Ky. Bar Ass'n v. Unnamed Att'y*, 191 S.W.3d 640 (Ky. 2006) (lawyer employed suspended lawyer and permitted him to make presentation to clients and answer their legal questions; lawyer told clients that employee not practicing law for "health" and "other" reasons).

### • *Working with Out-of-State Lawyers*

Lawyers who work with out-of-state lawyers risk being deemed to have assisted them in the unauthorized practice of law. *See, e.g., In re Anonymous*, 932 N.E.2d 1247 (Ind. 2010) (local counsel signed appearance with out-of-state lawyer and allowed him to appear in court, sign answers to interrogatories, and take depositions in state court without ensuring he was admitted pro hac vice); *In re Roswold*, 249 P.3d 1199 (Kan. 2011) (local counsel failed to promptly seek pro hac vice admission of out-of-state counsel, which resulted in out-of-state counsel "participating in depositions, other pretrial matters with opposing counsel, and even mediation, without ever complying with" pro hac vice rules); *In re Lerner*, 197 P.3d 1067 (Nev. 2008) (lawyer allowed employee licensed only in Arizona to conduct initial consultations, decide whether to accept representation, negotiate claims, and serve as clients' sole contact with firm); *In re DuBre*, 656 S.E.2d 343 (S.C. 2007) (managing lawyer of out-of-state collection firm's South Carolina office signed firm's pleadings so they could be filed in state and took no other action in those cases, which were handled by out-of-state lawyers); *In re Knight*, 745 N.W.2d 77 (Wis. 2008) (lawyer allowed out-of-state lawyer to use her name and attorney number to represent clients in Wisconsin courts).

In 2012, the comment was amended to make explicit that, in situations such as outsourcing, "a lawyer may not assist a person in practicing law in violation of the rules governing professional conduct in that person's jurisdiction." Cmt. [1]. *See* American Bar Association, *A Legislative History: The Development of the ABA Model Rules of Professional Conduct, 1982–2013*, at 657–58 (2013). *See generally* ABA Formal Ethics Op. 08-451 (2008) (advising lawyers to be mindful of possibility of Rule 5.5(a) violation if outsourced lawyer's activities constitute unauthorized practice).

## • *Working with Nonlawyers*

Delegating tasks to nonlawyer employees or contractors does not amount to assisting in the unauthorized practice of law, provided the lawyer adequately supervises the nonlawyers. Failure to provide adequate supervision, however, may violate not only Rule 5.5 but also Rule 5.3. *See In re Guirard*, 11 So. 3d 1017 (La. 2009) (nonlawyers advised clients on viability of claims and on legal documents and negotiated claims without lawyer supervision); *Att'y Grievance Comm'n v. Phillips*, 155 A.3d 476 (Md. 2017) (lawyer helped nonlawyer son set up law firm and ratified son's act of sending cease and desist letter to client); *In re Hrones*, 933 N.E.2d 622 (Mass. 2010) (lawyer allowed unlicensed law school graduate to develop and handle employment discrimination practice with no supervision, sign lawyer's name on appearance forms and administrative complaints, and share fees); *Miss. Bar v. Thompson*, 5 So. 3d 330 (Miss. 2008) (lawyer who hired former prison inmate as paralegal violated rule "by giving him the position and resources necessary to practice law, and then failing to adequately supervise him"); *In re Op. No. 24 of Comm. on Unauthorized Practice of Law*, 607 A.2d 962 (N.J. 1992) (lawyer must maintain direct relationships with clients and must supervise and remain responsible for paralegals' work); *In re Pincelli*, 648 S.E.2d 578 (S.C. 2007) (lawyer allowed nonlawyer assistant to handle mortgage foreclosure aspect of practice with almost no supervision); Ill. Ethics Op. 06-02 (2006) (lawyer may not use marketing firm or nonlawyer employees to screen potential clients to determine whether they have valid claims); Vt. Ethics Op. 2001-05 (2001) (lawyer may not allow nonlawyer to sign lawyer's name, with nonlawyer's initials, on court documents); Va. Ethics Op. 1792 (2006) (lawyer may not train social workers to assist pro se litigants in filling out forms used in small-claims court if assistance goes beyond translation, transcription, or filing instructions); *cf. Doe v. Condon*, 532 S.E.2d 879 (S.C. 2000) (concluding in declaratory judgment action that law firm paralegal may not conduct informal seminars on wills and trusts in lawyer's absence); Ill. Ethics Op. 13-08 (2013) (out-of-state lawyer whose practice limited solely to federal law did not assist in unauthorized practice of law by employing assistant to collect information and meet with clients). *See generally* Paul R. Tremblay, *Shadow Lawyering: Nonlawyer Practice Within Law Firms*, 85 Ind. L.J. 653 (2010).

Rule 5.5(a) is similarly implicated when support services are outsourced. ABA Formal Ethics Op. 08-451 (2008) (noting that "if the activities of a lawyer, nonlawyer, or intermediary employed in an outsourcing capacity are held to be the unauthorized practice of law, and the outsourcing lawyer facilitated that violation of law by action or inaction, the outsourcing lawyer will have violated Rule 5.5(a)"); Fla. Ethics Op. 07-2 (2008) (lawyer may outsource to paralegals and foreign lawyers not admitted in Florida if work adequately supervised and does not amount to practice of law); N.Y. City Ethics Op. 2006-3 (2006) (lawyer outsourcing support services to nonlawyer located overseas must rigorously supervise work to avoid aiding in unauthorized practice); *see also* L.A. Cnty. Ethics Op. 518 (2006) (lawyer using services of out-of-state legal research and brief-writing firm does not assist in unauthorized practice as long as lawyer remains responsible for final product); San Diego Cnty. Ethics Op. 2007-1 (2007) (lawyers using outsourcing firm based in India did not assist in unauthorized practice of law when lawyers supervised and retained control of, and responsibility for, firm's work).

For further discussion of a lawyer's responsibility to supervise nonlawyers, see the annotation to Rule 5.3.

## Paragraph (b): Out-of-State Lawyers Generally May Not Maintain Continuous Presence or Hold Themselves Out as Licensed Lawyers in the State

### NO SYSTEMATIC OR CONTINUOUS PRESENCE

Rule 5.5(b)(1) states the general rule that unless "authorized by these Rules or other law," a lawyer may not "establish an office or other systematic and continuous presence" in a jurisdiction in which the lawyer is not admitted. *See, e.g.*, Me. Ethics Op. 198 (2005) (lawyer who maintains office and website holding himself out as able to provide legal services in Maine, although not licensed there, is engaged in unauthorized practice). *But cf.* Ill. Ethics Op. 14-04 (2014) (noting that "[s]olicitation of personal injury cases within Illinois by a lawyer not admitted to practice in Illinois is not, in and of itself, a form of unauthorized practice of law" but that such advertising must comply with the lawyer advertising rules).

Comment [4] notes that "systematic and continuous presence" in a state need not entail a lawyer's physical presence. *See, e.g.*, *Birbrower, Montalbano, Condon & Frank, P.C. v. Superior Court*, 949 P.2d 1 (Cal. 1998) (noting that one may impermissibly practice in California, though not physically present, through "telephone, fax, computer, or other modern technological means," but rejecting notion that lawyer's virtual presence in California automatically amounts to practicing law "in California"); *In re Towne*, 929 A.2d 774 (Del. 2007) ("physical presence is not required to establish that a person is providing or offering to provide legal services in this state"; disbarring Pennsylvania lawyer not licensed in Delaware who, though working from her Pennsylvania office, violated Rule 5.5(b)(1) by representing dozens of Delaware clients on continuing basis on matters involving Delaware law); Ill. Ethics Op. 12-09 (2012) ("A lawyer not admitted in Illinois may not primarily practice in this state, physically or through a virtual office, even if the co-owner of the law firm is a lawyer, licensed in Illinois, who has direct supervision of the nonadmitted lawyer on matters involving Illinois clients."). *See generally* Va. Ethics Op. 1872 (2013) (discussing ethical issues arising in virtual law practice); John D. D'Attomo, *The $1 Million Message—Lawyers Risk Fees and More When Representing Out-of-State Clients*, 39 Santa Clara L. Rev. 447 (1999) (discussing implications of *Birbrower* dicta regarding lawyer's "virtual contacts" and "continuing relationship" with client in foreign state).

Although not reflected in the Model Rules, a potentially growing state trend is to permit out-of-state lawyers to maintain an office in-state so long as they do not practice the host state's law. Ariz. Rule 5.5(b), (d) (prohibiting practice of Arizona law unless licensed in the state); N.H. Rule 5.5, cmt. [3] (new rule means that "a lawyer who is licensed in another jurisdiction but does not practice New Hampshire law need not obtain a New Hampshire license to practice law solely because the lawyer is present in New Hampshire"); *see also* Va. Ethics Op. 1856 (2011; supreme court approval 2016) (foreign lawyers in Virginia "may engage in their limited scope practice on a 'continuous and systematic' basis, and may engage in temporary and occasional practice" and "may advise clients and render legal opinions to clients located in other states or countries without violating Virginia's prohibition against the unauthorized practice of law"). These lawyers are still subject to the disciplinary authority of both their host state and their state of licensure; see also annotation to Rule 8.5.

## IMPROPER REPRESENTATION TO PUBLIC

Rule 5.5(b)(2) clearly articulates the established rule that lawyers may not represent to the public that they are licensed in a particular jurisdiction if that is not true. Cmts. [4], [21]; *see In re Gerber*, 868 N.W.2d 861 (N.D. 2015) (lawyer not licensed in state violated rule by identifying himself as "staff attorney" and "government relations attorney"); *see also In re Nadel*, 82 A.3d 716 (Del. 2013) ("[e]ven though [lawyer] did not represent that he was licensed in Delaware and did not actively solicit Delaware clients, he would often meet with many of these clients in Delaware, likely giving the impression that he was a Delaware lawyer"); *In re Geniuk*, 411 P.3d 320 (Kan. 2018) (suspended lawyer practiced law and held himself out as Kansas lawyer on website); *Att'y Grievance Comm'n v. Harris-Smith*, 737 A.2d 567 (Md. 1999) (lawyer admitted in federal but not state court in Maryland improperly used radio and newspaper advertisements to target prospective bankruptcy clients without noting her ineligibility to practice in Maryland state court); *N.C. State Bar v. Ely*, 810 S.E.2d 346 (N.C. Ct. App. 2018) (lawyer on administrative suspension offered legal services and listed "Esq." after name in e-mails); Or. Ethics Op. 2005-103 (2005; rev. 2015) (multistate firm may advertise to Oregon clients the availability of firm lawyers not admitted to Oregon bar if firm makes clear that non-Oregon lawyers would be available to render legal services only as allowed by Rule 5.5(c) and (d)). *Compare Sutton v. Hafner Valuation Grp., Inc.*, 982 N.Y.S.2d 185 (Sup. Ct. 2014) (certified real estate appraiser did not hold himself out as licensed lawyer by listing "Juris Doctor" on his résumé; fraud count against him properly dismissed), *with In re Strizic*, No. PDJ-2013-9014, 2013 WL 1963871 (Ariz. P.D.J. Apr. 10, 2013) (lawyer not licensed in jurisdiction violated rule "by operating as 'The Tax Edge' and using the designations 'J.D.' and 'LLM'").

For discussion of the rules governing lawyer advertising, see the annotations to Rules 7.1 through 7.3.

## *PARAGRAPHS (c), (d), AND (e): MULTIJURISDICTIONAL PRACTICE*
## MODERN FRAMEWORK FOR MULTIJURISDICTIONAL PRACTICE

In August 2002, the ABA House of Delegates added paragraphs (c) and (d) to Model Rule 5.5 as part of a package of proposals by the ABA Commission on Multijurisdictional Practice to enable licensed lawyers to engage in the practice of law on a limited basis in jurisdictions in which they are not admitted to practice. The package also included an amended version of Model Rule 8.5, amendments to Rules 6 and 22 of the ABA Model Rules for Lawyer Disciplinary Enforcement, a new ABA Model Rule on Pro Hac Vice Admission, a new ABA Model Rule on Admission by Motion, renewed support for the existing ABA Model Rule for Licensing Legal Consultants, a new ABA Model Rule on Temporary Practice by Foreign Lawyers, and other provisions intended to strengthen regulatory structures. American Bar Association, *A Legislative History: The Development of the ABA Model Rules of Professional Conduct, 1982–2013*, at 651–56 (2013); *see* ABA Report to the House of Delegates, No. 201A-J (Aug. 2002), *available at* http://ambar.org/CPRMJP; *see also Spencer v. Utah State Bar*, 293 P.3d 360 (Utah 2012) (upholding admission-on-motion rule against statutory and constitutional challenges and denying admission to applicant who had not practiced at least three of five preceding years in reciprocal jurisdiction). *See generally* Arthur F. Greenbaum, *Multijurisdictional Practice and the Influence of Model Rule of Professional Conduct 5.5—An Interim Assessment*, 43 Akron L. Rev. 729 (2010); Michael S. McGinniss, *Five Years Later: The Delaware Experience with Multi-Jurisdictional Practice*, 10 Del. L. Rev. 125 (2008).

### • *Recent Amendments: Multijurisdictional Practice in the Global Context*

In 2012 and 2013, as a result of the work of the ABA Commission on Ethics 20/20, Rule 5.5 was amended to address challenges presented in the international context. The changes included an amended paragraph (d), a new paragraph (e), and amendments to several comments. Notably, Rule 5.5 now permits foreign-licensed lawyers to serve as in-house counsel. Also amended was the ABA Model Rule on Admission by Motion, the ABA Model Rule for Registration of In-House Counsel, and the ABA Model Rule on Pro Hac Vice Admission. Additionally, a new ABA Model Rule on Practice Pending Admission was adopted. For details of these changes (as well as the accompanying amendments to Rules 1.0, 1.1, 1.4, 1.6, 1.7, 1.18, 4.4, 5.3, 5.5, 7.1, 7.2, 7.3, and 8.5), see https://www.americanbar.org/groups/professional_responsibility/committees_commissions/standingcommitteeonprofessionalism2/resources/ethics2020hompeage/; also see http://ambar.org/CPRMJP. *See generally* "ABA Approves Ethics 20/20 Proposals on Foreign Lawyers, Choice of Conflict Rules," *ABA/BNA Lawyers' Manual on Professional Conduct*, 29 Law. Man. Prof. Conduct 101 (Current Reports, Feb. 13, 2013); "Ethics 20/20 Rule Changes Approved by ABA Delegates with Little Opposition," *ABA/BNA Lawyers' Manual on Professional Conduct*, 28 Law. Man. Prof. Conduct 509 (Current Reports, Aug. 15, 2012); James E. Moliterno, *Ethics 20/20 Successfully Achieved Its Mission: It "Protected, Preserved, and Maintained,"* 47 Akron L. Rev. 149 (2014); Jack P. Sahl, *Real Metamorphosis or More of the Same: Navigating the Practice of Law in the Wake of Ethics 20/20—Globalization, New Technologies, and What It Means to Be a Lawyer in These Uncertain Times*, 47 Akron L. Rev. 1 (2014); Laurel S. Terry, *Globalization and the ABA Commission on Ethics 20/20: Reflections on Missed Opportunities and the Road Not Taken*, 43 Hofstra L. Rev. 95 (2014).

Finally, in 2016, paragraphs (d) and (e) were expanded to permit a broader array of foreign in-house counsel to "provide legal services through an office or other systematic and continuous presence" in the states. Prior to the amendment, a foreign in-house counsel was required to be a "member in good standing of a recognized legal profession in a foreign jurisdiction, the members of which are admitted to practice as lawyers or counselors at law or the equivalent, and are subject to effective regulation and discipline by a duly constituted professional body or a public authority." But this definition apparently "exclude[d] over 70% of foreign lawyers, particularly lawyers from civil law jurisdictions, who are either not required or not even legally allowed to be members of the bar when practicing as in-house counsel." ABA Report to the House of Delegates, No. 103 (Feb. 2016), *available at* https://www.americanbar.org/ content/dam/aba/administrative/professional_responsibility/2016_hod_midyear _rr_103_adopted.pdf. As an example, the drafters noted that a "lawyer admitted to the practice of law in France, upon going in-house, has to surrender her bar admission status, and consequently, does not fall under the current ABA definition of foreign lawyer." *Id.* The Rule and the Model Rule for Registration of In-House Counsel were thus amended to permit such a lawyer to establish a continuous presence if the highest state court agrees in its discretion to authorize the lawyer. In making this determination, the court may consider (among other criteria) the in-house lawyer's "legal education, references, and experience." Model Rule for Registration of In-House Counsel, *available at* https://www.americanbar.org/content/dam/aba/ administrative/professional_responsibility/mr_in_house_counsel_registration.pdf.

## BACKGROUND
### • *State of Law Leading to Amendments*

The case that brought the issue of multijurisdictional practice to national attention was *Birbrower, Montalbano, Condon & Frank, P.C. v. Superior Court*, 949 P.2d 1 (Cal. 1998). In *Birbrower*, the court concluded that a New York law firm had engaged in the unauthorized practice of law when it represented a California client in California in making preliminary arbitration arrangements and negotiating a settlement. As a result, the court denied the firm any recovery of legal fees for the work. This sparked a nationwide debate, ultimately resulting in the amendments to Model Rule 5.5 and accompanying changes recommended by the ABA Commission on Multijurisdictional Practice.

Although the seemingly harsh result in *Birbrower* took many in the legal profession by surprise, it was not the first such case. *See Ranta v. McCarney*, 391 N.W.2d 161 (N.D. 1986) (Minnesota lawyer could not recover fees for legal services rendered in North Dakota, where lawyer not licensed). Indeed, before the 2002 amendments, most courts considering the propriety of lawyers providing legal services in jurisdictions where they were not licensed had found such activities to be improper, resulting in adverse consequences that included disciplinary measures, injunctions, or denials of legal fees. *See Koscove v. Bolte*, 30 P.3d 784 (Colo. App. 2001) (lawyer licensed in Wisconsin who lived in Colorado and, before being admitted pro hac vice, investigated and pursued client's claim for royalty payments and assisted in contemplated lawsuit in Colorado, engaged in unauthorized practice of law); *Office of Disciplinary Counsel v. Fucetola*, 753 N.E.2d 180 (Ohio 2001) (issuing injunction against New Jersey lawyer who filed complaint in Ohio on behalf of longtime client and simultaneously filed motion for admission pro hac vice but appeared in court before court ruled on pro hac vice motion); *Cleveland Bar Ass'n v. Moore*, 722 N.E.2d 514 (Ohio 2000) (Pennsylvania lawyer who lived in Ohio and had office-sharing arrangement with several Ohio lawyers engaged in unauthorized practice in Ohio by negotiating on behalf of Ohio clients, communicating with their insurance companies, preparing settlement packages, making settlement demands, and agreeing to settlements, and Cleveland telephone directories listed lawyer as "attorney at law"); *see also Z.A. v. San Bruno Park Sch. Dist.*, 165 F.3d 1273 (9th Cir. 1999) (denying attorneys' fees for legal services rendered in state administrative proceeding because lawyer—though admitted in U.S. District Court for Northern District of California—was on inactive status with Pennsylvania bar and not admitted to practice in California). *Compare Torrey v. Leesburg Reg'l Med. Ctr.*, 769 So. 2d 1040 (Fla. 2000) (although Michigan lawyer not licensed in Florida engaged in unauthorized practice by preparing and filing wrongful death complaint in Florida, dismissal of complaint unnecessary because signature by out-of-state lawyer was amendable defect and other mechanisms for regulating unauthorized practice were available), *with Landrum v. Chippenham & Johnston-Willis Hosps., Inc.*, 717 S.E.2d 134 (Va. 2011) (excluding expert witness in part because notice not signed by local counsel), *and Wellmore Coal Corp. v. Harman Mining Corp.*, 568 S.E.2d 671 (Va. 2002) (dismissing appeal of $6 million trial court judgment because notice of appeal signed only by foreign counsel).

## *Paragraph (c): Provision of Legal Services on Temporary Basis*

Paragraph (c) permits a lawyer who is licensed in any U.S. jurisdiction "and not disbarred or suspended from practice in any jurisdiction" to provide legal services on a temporary basis in another jurisdiction, in four specifically enumerated circumstances discussed in turn below. As the comment concludes, allowing the temporary provision of legal services in these circumstances ordinarily does not pose an unreasonable risk to the interests of clients, the public, or the courts. Cmt. [5] (noting further that although rule identifies only four such circumstances, "[t]he fact that conduct is not so identified does not imply that the conduct is or is not authorized").

Comment [7] explains that for purposes of paragraph (c), the word "admitted" contemplates that the lawyer is authorized to practice law. It therefore excludes a lawyer who is technically admitted but not authorized to practice law "because, for example, the lawyer is on inactive status." *See In re Convisser*, 242 P.3d 299 (N.M. 2010) (inactive Virginia license did not authorize lawyer to provide legal services in New Mexico on temporary basis); *cf.* Ariz. Ethics Op. 10-04 (2010) (lawyer may share fees, in accordance with Rule 1.5, with out-of-state lawyer who referred matter to lawyer, if out-of-state lawyer eligible to provide temporary legal services under Rule 5.5 or if necessary is admitted pro hac vice).

## "TEMPORARY" BASIS

Rule 5.5(c) applies only if a lawyer's activities in another jurisdiction are performed on a temporary basis. The rule does not specify the number of visits a lawyer may make to another jurisdiction or offer any other bright-line test to determine when a lawyer's legal service in the jurisdiction is merely "temporary." Comment [6] does, however, note that services on a recurring basis or for an extended period of time, as in the case of a lengthy negotiation or litigation, can nonetheless be considered "temporary." ABA Report to the House of Delegates, No. 201B (Aug. 2002), *available at* http://ambar.org/CPRMJP ("application of the new standards leaves room for individual opinion and judicial interpretation"); *see Gould v. Fla. Bar*, 259 F. App'x 208 (11th Cir. 2007) (affirming district court's conclusion that New York-licensed lawyer's practice not "temporary" under Fla. Rule 4-5.5(c) because lawyer was Florida resident, who lived there more than twenty-nine years and had office in Miami); *In re Lerner*, 197 P.3d 1067 (Nev. 2008) (Arizona lawyer who regularly performed legal services in Nevada for Nevada clients not covered by safe-harbor provision of Rule 5.5 in part because work in Nevada not incidental to work in state of licensure); D.C. Unauthorized Practice of Law Op. 16-05 (2005) (contract lawyer who regularly undertakes short-term legal work in District of Columbia must be member of District of Columbia bar, even if individual assignments considered in isolation might constitute only incidental or occasional presence in jurisdiction). *See generally Restatement (Third) of the Law Governing Lawyers* § 3 cmt. e (2000) (discussing permissible multijurisdictional practice for litigation and transactional lawyers).

## TEMPORARILY PROVIDING LEGAL SERVICES IN WAKE OF MAJOR DISASTER

When the temporary provision of legal services in another jurisdiction is necessitated by a major disaster, a 2007 amendment to Comment [14] advises lawyers to consult the Model Court Rule on Provision of Legal Services Following Determination of Major Disaster. *Cf.* ABA Formal Ethics Op. 482 (2018) (warning that "[a]lthough displaced lawyers may be able to rely on Model Rule 5.5(c) allowing temporary multijurisdictional practice to provide legal services to their clients or displaced residents, they should not assume the Rule will apply in a particular jurisdiction"). That rule, also adopted in 2007, provides a framework under which courts can temporarily authorize lawyers from the affected jurisdiction to continue their practice somewhere else and can temporarily authorize out-of-state lawyers to provide pro bono legal services to victims of the disaster. *See generally* "ABA Delegates Approve Model Court Rule Easing Practice Restrictions During Disasters," *ABA/BNA Lawyers' Manual on Professional Conduct*, 23 Law. Man. Prof. Conduct 95 (Current Reports, Feb. 21, 2007); Dane S. Ciolino & Sandra S. Varnado, *Reconsidering Lawyers' Ethical Obligations in the Wake of a Disaster*, 19 Prof. Law., no. 4, at 8 (2009). For a chart showing which jurisdictions have adopted the rule, see https://www.americanbar.org/content/dam/aba/administrative/professional_responsibility/katrina_chart.pdf.

## *Paragraph (c)(1): Association with Local Lawyer*

Paragraph (c)(1) permits a lawyer admitted in one state to practice temporarily in another state without being admitted to that state's bar as long as the lawyer associates with local counsel who actively participates in the representation of the client and shares responsibility for the work. *See* Cmt. [8]; Nev. Ethics Op. 43 (2011);

*see also* ABA Report to the House of Delegates, No. 201B (Aug. 2002), *available at* http://ambar.org/CPRMJP (noting that, for provision to apply, local lawyer cannot serve "merely as a conduit" for out-of-state lawyer but must share actual responsibility for representation).

## Paragraph (c)(2): Legal Services Reasonably Related to Pending or Contemplated Proceedings

Paragraph (c)(2) permits a lawyer to provide legal services in a jurisdiction in which the lawyer is not admitted if the services are related to a pending or potential proceeding before a tribunal, provided the lawyer ("or a person the lawyer is assisting") is or reasonably expects to be admitted in the other jurisdiction. Permissible conduct under paragraph (c)(2) generally includes meeting with clients, interviewing witnesses, reviewing documents, and taking depositions. Cmt. [10]; *see Ky. Bar Ass'n v. Unnamed Att'y*, 476 S.W.3d 886 (Ky. 2015) (privately reprimanding Kentucky lawyer who filed objection to New York court's assumption of jurisdiction of Kentucky case, in part because lawyer had failed to file motion for pro hac vice admission in New York before filing objection); *Att'y Grievance Comm'n v. Hunt*, 135 A.3d 403 (Md. 2016) (imposing sixty-day suspension on D.C. lawyer who briefly represented client in Maryland criminal case in order to "deter Respondent and other non-Maryland attorneys from practicing law in Maryland courts without authorization, notwithstanding that such representation was on a limited, pro bono, basis"); *Carlson v. Workforce Safety & Ins.*, 765 N.W.2d 691 (N.D. 2009) (out-of-state lawyers' preparation of motion for reconsideration, filing of legal brief, and designation as counsel in administrative proceeding were not protected by safe-harbor provisions given that lawyers failed to timely seek pro hac vice admission as required); *see also Blume Const., Inc. v. State ex rel. Job Serv. N.D.*, 872 N.W.2d 312 (N.D. 2015) (voiding corporation's notice of appeal from administrative agency's tax determination because lawyer who filed notice was not licensed in the state and had not sought pro hac vice admission).

In some jurisdictions, out-of-state lawyers may be permitted to practice in the state while their admission-on-motion application is pending. *See* ABA Model Rule on Practice Pending Admission, *available at* https://www.americanbar.org/content/dam/aba/administrative/professional_responsibility/model_rule_practice_pending_admission.pdf. *Compare In re Jones*, No. 2018-0496, 2018 WL 5076017, 2018 BL 382036 (Ohio Oct. 17, 2018) (Kentucky lawyer permitted under Rule 5.5(c)(2) to practice Kentucky law from Ohio office while application for admission on motion to Ohio bar pending), *with In re Egan*, 90 N.E.3d 912 (Ohio 2017) (Kentucky lawyer who had practiced Kentucky law in Ohio for six years before applying for admission committed unauthorized practice of law). *See generally* Joan C. Rogers, "Although Many States Have Adopted MJP, Uncertainty Remains in Cross-Border Practice," *ABA/BNA Lawyers' Manual on Professional Conduct*, 31 Law. Man. Prof. Conduct 135 (Current Reports, Mar. 11, 2015).

## Paragraph (c)(3): Legal Services Reasonably Related to Pending or Potential Arbitration or Mediation Proceedings

Paragraph (c)(3) allows for the temporary cross-border provision of legal services that "are in or reasonably related to a pending or potential" alternative dispute resolution (ADR) proceeding, if the services arise out of or are reasonably related to the lawyer's practice in a jurisdiction in which the lawyer is admitted. *See* Phila. Ethics Op. 2003-13 (2003) (lawyer not admitted to practice in Pennsylvania but admitted elsewhere may represent longtime client in single ADR matter in Pennsylvania). *See generally* ABA Report to the House of Delegates, No. 201B (Aug. 2002), *available at* http://ambar.org/CPRMJP (recognizing that in ADR context there is strong justification for choosing lawyer who has ongoing relationship with client, even if not admitted to practice in state where proceeding takes place).

## Paragraph (c)(4): Reasonably Related to Lawyer's Practice—Transactional Matters

Paragraph (c)(4) permits the temporary cross-border provision of legal services that do not involve litigation or ADR proceedings if they "arise out of or are reasonably related to the lawyer's practice" where the lawyer is admitted. In this way, the Model Rules provide some latitude for transactional lawyers to provide legal services in jurisdictions in which they are not formally licensed. *See* ABA Report to the House of Delegates, No. 201B (Aug. 2002), *available at* http://ambar.org/CPRMJP (provision intended to cover services ancillary to matter in home state, to respect ongoing lawyer-client relationships by allowing client to retain same lawyer for multiple matters, and to allow for temporary cross-border services by recognized legal experts); *see also* Nev. Ethics Op. 43 (2011) (out-of-state transactional lawyer may practice in Nevada on temporary basis if work "incidental to" lawyer's work in state of licensure); *cf.* Tex. Ethics Op. 597 (2010) (under Texas rule similar to pre-2002 version of Model Rule 5.5, lawyer does not assist in unauthorized practice of law by permitting out-of-state partners to do legal work intermittently in firm's Texas office if partners do not establish continuous and systematic presence in state).

### "REASONABLY RELATED" SERVICES

Though Rule 5.5 does not explain how to determine when services "arise out of or are reasonably related to the lawyer's practice in a jurisdiction in which the lawyer is admitted"—the test used in paragraphs (c)(3) and (c)(4)—the comment mentions several potential factors, including the lawyer's previous representation of the client, the matter's connection to the lawyer's jurisdiction, and the involvement of that jurisdiction's law. Cmt. [14]; *see, e.g., In re Estate of Cooper*, 746 N.W.2d 653 (Neb. 2008) (under Rule 5.5(c)(4), Tennessee lawyer representing Tennessee bank did not engage in unauthorized practice by filing demand for notice in Nebraska probate proceeding). *But see In re Charges of Unprof'l Conduct in Panel File No. 39302*, 884 N.W.2d 661 (Minn. 2016) (Colorado lawyer's "representation of his in-laws did not 'arise out of' or 'reasonably relate' to his practice in Colorado simply because his in-laws contacted him in Colorado or [because he had previously] done collections work in Colorado"; "in-laws were not long-standing clients; nor was there any connection between the in-laws' case and the state or laws of Colorado").

## Paragraph (d): Provision of Legal Services on Regular Basis

Paragraph (d) specifies two situations in which a lawyer admitted in one jurisdiction "and not disbarred or suspended from practice in any jurisdiction" may provide legal services—on either a temporary or regular basis—in a jurisdiction where the lawyer is not admitted: when the lawyer provides the services to the lawyer's employer or its legal affiliate, and when the lawyer is authorized by federal or other law to provide legal services in the jurisdiction.

## Paragraph (d)(1): Providing Legal Services to Lawyer's Employer

Paragraph (d)(1) permits in-house counsel, government lawyers, and lawyers employed by other organizations to provide legal services to employers and their affiliates even if the work is performed in jurisdictions where the lawyers are not admitted. If the lawyer will be appearing before a tribunal, however, the lawyer must meet any pro hac vice requirements. *See Momot v. Silkworth Manor LLC*, No. 1 CA-CV 17-0274, 2018 WL 507345, 2018 BL 21316 (Ariz. Ct. App. Jan. 23, 2018) ("out-of-state attorney registered as in-house counsel must also secure pro hac vice status . . . before filing a brief or appearing in court on behalf of his corporate employer"). Furthermore, even if no court appearance will be involved, the lawyer may need to meet local requirements for registration, continuing legal education, or contributions to client protection funds. *See* Cmt. [17]. Finally, the rule does not extend to personal legal services provided to an entity's officers, employees, or customers. Cmt. [16]; *see* Ill. Ethics Op. 14-03 (2014) ("lawyer employed by a financial services company may not provide legal services to his employer's customers who are seeking social security appeals" in part "because . . . the lawyer may be at risk of assisting the employer, a non-legal entity, in the unauthorized practice of law").

Whether or not they have adopted a version of Model Rule 5.5(d), many states allow some form of expedited admission for in-house lawyers. For the text of the ABA Model Rule for Registration of In-House Counsel and links to state in-house counsel rules, see http://ambar.org/CPRMJP. *See generally* Carol A. Needham, *The Changing Landscape for In-House Counsel: Multijurisdictional Practice Considerations for Corporate Law Departments*, 43 Akron L. Rev. 985 (2010); Erica M. Spitzig, *License to Serve: Reevaluating Multijurisdictional Pro Bono Rules for In-House Counsel*, 21 Geo. J. Legal Ethics 1081 (2008).

### FOREIGN IN-HOUSE COUNSEL

In 2013, paragraph (d)(1) was amended to permit foreign-licensed lawyers to serve as in-house counsel. American Bar Association, *A Legislative History: The Development of the ABA Model Rules of Professional Conduct, 1982–2013*, at 659–61 (2013). At the same time, the Model Rule for Registration of In-House Counsel was amended to include foreign in-house counsel. *See* ABA Report to the House of Delegates, No. 107B (2013), *available at* https://www.americanbar.org/content/dam/aba/administrative/ethics_2020/20130201_revised_resolution_107b_resolution_only_redline.pdf.

Unlike domestic in-house counsel, however, when a foreign in-house counsel gives "advice on the law of this or another jurisdiction or of the United States, such advice shall be based upon the advice of a lawyer who is duly licensed and authorized by the jurisdiction to provide such advice." Rule 5.5(d)(1). *See generally* Carol A. Needham, *Globalization and Eligibility to Deliver Legal Advice: Inbound Legal Services Provided by Corporate Counsel Licensed Only in a Country Outside the United States*, 48 San Diego L. Rev. 379 (2011); "ABA Approves Ethics 20/20 Proposals on Foreign Lawyers, Choice of Conflict Rules," *ABA/BNA Lawyers' Manual on Professional Conduct*, 29 Law. Man. Prof. Conduct 101 (Current Reports, Feb. 13, 2013).

## Paragraph (d)(2): Providing Legal Services When Authorized by Federal or Other Law

Paragraph (d)(2) permits a lawyer to provide legal services in a jurisdiction in which the lawyer is not admitted, if authorized by federal or other law, court rules, executive regulations, or judicial precedents. Cmts. [15], [18]; *see, e.g., In re Desilets*, 291 F.3d 925 (6th Cir. 2002) (Texas lawyer with office in Michigan may practice before bankruptcy court in Western District of Michigan even though not admitted to Michigan state court, because lawyer admitted to practice before U.S. District Court for Western District of Michigan).

Although this rule recognizes that a lawyer may provide legal services when authorized by federal law, a lawyer's authority to practice before a federal tribunal or agency does not confer authority to provide general legal services in a state in which the lawyer is not admitted. *See Att'y Grievance Comm'n v. Harris-Smith*, 737 A.2d 567 (Md. 1999) (lawyer licensed in federal court in Maryland, but not in state court, engaged in unauthorized practice by holding herself out as Maryland lawyer and advising clients in Maryland office, even though practice limited to bankruptcy law); *see also* Alaska Ethics Op. 2010-1 (2010) (lawyer whose practice limited to immigration law may maintain Alaska office even though not licensed to practice law there, but must tell clients about jurisdictional restrictions and must avoid advising them on nonimmigration matters); D.C. Unauthorized Practice of Law Op. 17-06 (2006) (lawyers who are not active members of District of Columbia bar may engage in federal practice from District of Columbia office provided "entire practice" limited to federal matters and practice limitations made clear); Phila. Ethics Op. 2005-14 (2005) (out-of-state lawyer may open office in Pennsylvania for limited purpose of practicing immigration law before federal courts); *cf. Att'y Grievance Comm'n v. Ambe*, 38 A.3d 390 (Md. 2012) (to avoid false or misleading advertising, "Rule 7.1 requires out-of-state attorneys practicing federal law in Maryland to disclose that the attorney's practice is limited to federal matters and that the attorney is not authorized to practice law in Maryland"). For a discussion of federal preemption of state law, see "Power to Regulate Practice of Law" above.

## Paragraph (e): Qualifying Foreign Lawyers

In 2013, Rule 5.5(d)'s exceptions were extended to foreign-licensed lawyers, primarily in-house counsel, to permit them to "provide legal services through an office or other systematic and continuous presence" in the states. To qualify, paragraph (e)

(1) requires the foreign lawyer to be "a member in good standing of a recognized legal profession in a foreign jurisdiction, the members of which are admitted to practice as lawyers or counselors at law or the equivalent, and subject to effective regulation and discipline by a duly constituted professional body or a public authority." This is the same criterion long used in the ABA Model Rule for the Licensing and Practice of Foreign Legal Consultants, which is available at http://ambar.org/CPRMJP. In 2016, Rule 5.5 was further expanded to permit a broader array of foreign in-house lawyers in the states. Paragraph (e)(1) by its terms excludes many such in-house "lawyers, particularly lawyers from civil law jurisdictions, who are either not required or not even legally allowed to be members of the bar when practicing as in-house counsel." ABA Report to the House of Delegates, No. 103 (Feb. 2016), *available at* https://www.americanbar.org/content/dam/aba/administrative/professional_responsibility/2016_hod_midyear_rr_103_adopted.pdf. For example, a "lawyer admitted to the practice of law in France, upon going in-house, has to surrender her bar admission status, and consequently, does not fall under the current ABA definition of foreign lawyer." *Id.* Therefore, the rule, and the Model Rule for Registration of In-House Counsel, have been amended to permit such an in-house lawyer to establish a continuous presence if the highest state court agrees in its discretion to authorize the lawyer. Rule 5.5(e)(2). In making this determination, the court may consider (among other criteria) the in-house lawyer's "legal education, references, and experience." Model Rule for Registration of In-House Counsel, *available at* https://www.americanbar.org/content/dam/aba/administrative/professional_responsibility/mr_in_house_counsel_registration.pdf.

## HOST-STATE JURISDICTION AND RULE 8.5

Comment [19] notes that lawyers engaged in multijurisdictional practice under paragraph (c) or (d) are subject to discipline in the states in which they practice as well as in their states of licensure. Comment [20] further notes that lawyers may be required to inform clients that the lawyers are not licensed in a host jurisdiction, such as when the representation occurs primarily in the host jurisdiction and involves knowledge of the host jurisdiction's law. For further discussion, see the annotation to Rule 8.5.

## Rule 5.6

### *Restrictions on Right to Practice*

A lawyer shall not participate in offering or making:

(a) a partnership, shareholders, operating, employment, or other similar type of agreement that restricts the right of a lawyer to practice after termination of the relationship, except an agreement concerning benefits upon retirement; or

(b) an agreement in which a restriction on the lawyer's right to practice is part of the settlement of a client controversy.

## COMMENT

[1] An agreement restricting the right of lawyers to practice after leaving a firm not only limits their professional autonomy but also limits the freedom of clients to choose a lawyer. Paragraph (a) prohibits such agreements except for restrictions incident to provisions concerning retirement benefits for service with the firm.

[2] Paragraph (b) prohibits a lawyer from agreeing not to represent other persons in connection with settling a claim on behalf of a client.

[3] This Rule does not apply to prohibit restrictions that may be included in the terms of the sale of a law practice pursuant to Rule 1.17.

### State Rules Comparison

http://ambar.org/MRPCStateCharts

## ANNOTATION

### RATIONALE

Restrictive covenants involving lawyers are said to diminish the pool of legal talent available to the public. They are therefore regulated much more closely than similar agreements involving other professionals, to which courts will usually apply a common-law reasonableness test. Many critics disagree with this approach. *See* Thomas D. Morgan, *The Rise of Institutional Law Practice*, 40 Hofstra L. Rev. 1005 (Summer 2012) (reasonable restrictions would help firms establish compensation structures; firms pay $200,000 to $500,000 in recruiting costs per new associate but a substantial proportion leave before firms can recoup investment); Larry E. Ribstein, *Ethical Rules, Agency Costs, and Law Firm Structure*, 85 Va. L. Rev. 1707 (Nov. 1998) (restrictive covenants help younger lawyers by protecting firm's investment in client development; Rule 5.6(a) benefits the senior lawyers, who have the most to gain if they can sell their services elsewhere); Nathaniel Vargas Gallegos, *The Solo Lawyer Proportion: Explanations with the "Push & Pull" Factors Endemic in Legal Firm Organization*, 37 J. Legal Prof. 25 (Fall 2012) (ban on restrictive covenants leads to inefficient allocation of resources if firms try to appease lawyers who might take clients with them when they leave); *see also* Kevin D. Horvitz, Note, *An Unreasonable Ban on Reasonable Competition: The Legal Profession's Protectionist Stance Against Noncompete Agreements Binding In-House Counsel*, 65 Duke L.J. 1007 (Feb. 2016). *See generally* John Dwight Ingraham, *Covenants Not to Compete in the Professions*, 3 Fla. St. U. Bus. Rev. 11 (2002–2003); Asher L. Kitchings, Recent Development, *Non-Compete Agreements for Attorneys: Will We Continue to Be Treated Differently Than Other Professions?*, 38 Am. J. Trial Advoc. 433 (Fall 2014).

Close judicial scrutiny of restrictive covenants is also said to be necessary to protect lawyer independence, albeit by limiting the lawyer's freedom to contract it away. Again, many critics disagree. *See generally* Barbara C. Bentrup, Comment, *Friend or Foe: Reasonable Noncompete Restrictions Can Benefit Corporate In-House Counsel and Protect Corporate Employers*, 52 St. Louis U. L.J. 1037 (Spring 2008); Linda Sorenson Ewald, *Agreements Restricting the Practice of Law: A New Look at an Old Paradox*, 26 J. Legal Prof. 1 (2001–2002) (critical inquiry into whether rule actually serves policies invoked to support it); Robert W. Hillman, *Client Choice, Contractual Restraints, and the Market for Legal Services*, 36 Hofstra L. Rev. 65 (Fall 2007); Jessica Montello, *The Future of Non-Compete Agreements in In-House Practice*, 32 Ass'n Corp. Couns. Docket 72 (Nov. 2014).

## Paragraph (a): Restrictive Covenants in Employment Agreements

Rule 5.6(a) prohibits employment agreements designed to prevent lawyers from competing with their former firms after they change jobs. These include promises not to practice within a particular geographic or substantive area, promises not to represent any of the firm's clients, and restrictions on client contact or use of client information. *See, e.g., Dowd & Dowd v. Gleason*, 693 N.E.2d 358 (Ill. 1998) (lawyers cannot be allowed to agree to "onerous conditions that would unduly limit their mobility"; professional corporation's agreement prohibiting departing lawyers from soliciting or "endeavor[ing] to entice away" clients without corporation's written permission for two years after departure violated rule); *Pettingell v. Morrison, Mahoney & Miller*, 687 N.E.2d 1237 (Mass. 1997) (cannot require departing partners to forfeit annual partnership interest credits and right to portion of firm's cash profits if they compete); *Denburg v. Parker Chapin Flattau & Klimpl*, 624 N.E.2d 995 (N.Y. 1993) (cannot require departing partners who go into private practice to pay firm greater of 12.5 percent of firm's profits allocated to partner over previous two years, or 12.5 percent of next two years' billings to firm's former clients, notwithstanding firm's assertion that it was only trying to preserve enough income to pay for its new office space); *Gray v. Martin*, 663 P.2d 1285 (Or. Ct. App. 1983) (cannot condition withdrawing partner's right to payment upon his promise not to compete within geographical area); *Capozzi v. Latsha & Capozzi, P.C.*, 797 A.2d 314 (Pa. Super. Ct. 2002) (forfeiture clause providing that if co-founding partner left to compete his stock would be valued at amount of his initial capital contribution ($5,000) was not "reasonably necessary to protect the firm," which had grown considerably and was grossing $2.6 million); *Arena v. Schulman, LeRoy & Bennett*, 233 S.W.3d 809 (Tenn. Ct. App. 2006) (shareholder agreement cannot require lawyer to pay half of contingent fees earned on files he takes from firm if he practices in same or contiguous county); D.C. Ethics Op. 368 (2015) (employment agreement may not provide for substantial damages, actual or liquidated, if lawyer competes with firm after departure, nor may it interfere with lawyer's freedom of association by restricting his subsequent professional association or affiliation with firm's partners or employees); Ill. Ethics Op. 97-09 (1997) (cannot require withdrawing partners to forfeit 20 percent of amounts payable to them if they compete with firm); N.J. Ethics Op. 708 (2006) (employment agreement forbidding in-house lawyer from working for competitor after employment ends or recruiting corporation's legal staff to work for competitor is impermissible); N.C. Ethics Op. 2001-10 (2002) (condemning agreement that reduces deferred compensation of any shareholder-lawyer who leaves to engage in private practice within fifty-mile radius for two years); *cf. Heher v. Smith, Stratton, Wise, Heher & Brennan*, 785 A.2d 907 (N.J. 2001) (agreement's characterization of withdrawing partner's supplemental benefit as payment for his interest in partnership goodwill related only to tax treatment; court's invalidation of forfeiture provision did not entitle firm to prove loss in goodwill as offset against departing partner's benefits); Pa. Ethics Op. 2016-024 (2016) (may not require "of counsel" lawyer to agree that if any client follows him upon departure he will pay firm one-third of all fees firm had billed to that client in previous two years); Tex. Ethics Op. 656 (2016) (firm cannot require contract lawyer to agree not to represent firm clients after their affiliation ends; irrelevant that lawyer is independent contractor rather than employee for accounting and tax purposes). *See generally* Leslie D. Corwin, *Response to* Loyalty in the Firm, 55 Wash. & Lee L. Rev. 1055 (Fall 1998); Deborah A. DeMott, *The Faces of Loyalty: A Comment on Hillman*, Loyalty in the Firm, 55 Wash. & Lee L. Rev. 1041 (Fall 1998); Neil W. Hamilton, *Are We a Profession or Merely a Business? The Erosion of Rule 5.6 and the Bar Against Restrictions on the Right to Practice*, 22 Wm. Mitchell L. Rev. 1409 (1996); Robert W. Hillman, *Professional Partnerships, Competition, and the Evolution of Firm Culture: The Case of Law Firms*, 26 J. Corp. L. 1061 (Summer 2001); Robert W. Hillman, *Loyalty in the Firm: A Statement of General Principles on the Duties of Partners Withdrawing from Law Firms*, 55 Wash. & Lee L. Rev. 997 (Fall 1998); Kathleen Maher, *For Your Consideration: The Departed*, 18 Prof. Law., no. 1, at 12 (2007).

## "REASONABLE" DISINCENTIVES

A minority of jurisdictions will uphold reasonable financial disincentives notwithstanding their potential anticompetitive effect. *Haight, Brown & Bonesteel v. Superior Court*, 285 Cal. Rptr. 845 (Ct. App. 1991), equates law partnerships with other business partnerships: "Recognizing the sweeping changes in the practice of law, we can see no legal justification for treating partners in law firms differently [regarding noncompetition agreements] from partners in other businesses and professions." *Howard v. Babcock*, 863 P.2d 150 (Cal. 1993), likens a reasonable financial disincentive to "a tax on taking the former firm's clients—a tax that is not unreasonable, considering the financial burden the partner's competitive departure may impose on the former firm." *Accord Fearnow v. Ridenour, Swenson, Cleere & Evans*, 138 P.3d 723 (Ariz. 2006) (shareholder agreement requiring departing lawyer to relinquish his stock to professional corporation if he competes with it must be examined for reasonableness just like any other professional's employment agreement: "We are unable to conclude that the interests of a lawyer's clients are so superior to those of a doctor's patients (whose choice of a physician may literally be a life-or-death decision) as to require a unique rule applicable only to attorneys."); *Hoffman v. Levstik*, 860 N.E.2d 551 (Ill. App. Ct. 2006) (partnership agreement permitting firm to reduce payments of paid-in capital by greater of one-half the balance or $50,000 did not unduly limit withdrawing partner's mobility or hamper his clients in their choice of counsel); *Capozzi v. Latsha & Capozzi, P.C.*, 797 A.2d 314 (Pa. Super. Ct. 2002) (adopting *Howard's* "rule of reason" approach and enforcing oral agreement that any shareholder who leaves or competes will receive only the amount of capital he contributed for his stock). *See generally* Karen E. Komrada, Note, Fearnow v. Ridenour, Swenson, Cleere & Evans, P.C.: *Encouraging Firms to Punish Departing Attorneys?*, 48 Ariz. L. Rev. 677 (Fall 2006); Eli Wald, *Non-Compete Agreements in Colorado*, 40 Colo. Law. 63 (June 2011) ("first generation case law" viewed any financial penalties for competing as impermissible restrictions on practice, but minority view approves reasonable financial disincentives to compensate firm for its lost investment).

## PENALTIES FOR LEAVING VERSUS PENALTIES FOR COMPETING

Agreements that penalize lawyers for departing before retirement have been held not to violate Rule 5.6(a) if the penalty applies to any lawyer who leaves, whether or not the lawyer is leaving to compete with the firm. *See Pierce v. Morrison Mahoney LLP*, 897 N.E.2d 562 (Mass. 2008) (partnership provision denying payment of deferred income to all partners who leave voluntarily before turning sixty or completing twenty years of service—regardless of whether they continue to practice law—does not violate public policy embodied in Rule 5.6(a)), criticized in Lynne Bernabei & Alan R. Kabat, *Law Firms Penalizing Departing Partners?—That Goes Straight to the Penalty Box!*, 61 Prac. Law., no. 5, at 27 (Oct. 2015); *see also Hackett v. Milbank, Tweed, Hadley & McCloy*, 654 N.E.2d 95 (N.Y. 1995) (upholding partnership agreement reducing amount paid to withdrawing partner according to income derived from other sources; reduction applied to all departing partners whether or not they were going to compete); Miss. Ethics Op. 249 (2001) (buyout provision requiring any departing lawyer to pay specified amount to firm was not restriction on competition but was designed to protect firm's investment in lawyer); *cf.* D.C. Ethics Op. 325 (2004) (firm's merger agreement cannot condition receipt of enhanced amount of pre-merger income upon lawyer continuing to practice at firm for at least two years post-merger). *But see Weiss v. Carpenter, Bennett & Morrissey*, 672 A.2d 1132 (N.J. 1996) (cannot require partner to forfeit distribution of capital account if he withdraws for any reason other than death, disability, attainment of age sixty-five, or appointment to judiciary; "dominant purpose" was to dissuade partners from competing with firm after withdrawal).

## TAKING "FIRM" CLIENTS: FINANCIAL DISINCENTIVES

### • *Disguised Penalties*

Financial disincentives for taking "firm" clients violate Rule 5.6 if they are disguised attempts to penalize competition. *See, e.g., Moskowitz v. Jacobson Holman, PLLC,* No. 1:15-cv-336, 2016 WL 356035, 2016 BL 23398 (E.D. Va. Jan. 28, 2016) (cannot require departing shareholders to forfeit half their equity interest if they take clients with them) (applying D.C. law); *Minge v. Weeks,* 629 So. 2d 545 (La. Ct. App. 1993) (cannot require departing lawyer to pay firm 80 percent of all fees derived from representing firm clients who leave with him); *Eisenstein v. David G. Conlin, P.C.,* 827 N.E.2d 686 (Mass. 2005) (cannot require voluntarily withdrawing partners to remit 15 percent of all fees received at their new firms during next four years for work done for current or former clients of former firm); *Law Offices of Ronald J. Palagi, P.C., L.L.O. v. Howard,* 747 N.W.2d 1 (Neb. 2008) (agreeing with decisions from other jurisdictions; provision giving firm all fees on cases taken by departing lawyer provides "strong financial disincentive for that lawyer to perform services for that client" and therefore violates Rule 5.6(a)); *Cincinnati Bar Ass'n v. Hackett,* 950 N.E.2d 969 (Ohio 2011) (cannot require departing associates to pay firm 95 percent of fees generated in all cases involving former firm clients); Ariz. Ethics Op. 09-01 (2009) (cannot require departing associate to reimburse firm $3,500 for its marketing expenses for each client or prospective client she continues to represent); Fla. Ethics Op. 93-4 (1994) (cannot require departing lawyer to pay firm half of any fee received or firm's quantum meruit fee, whichever is greater, should he represent any firm clients), *petition for rescission of ethics opinion dismissed sub nom. Fla. Bar ex rel. Becker & Poliakoff, P.A.,* 771 So. 2d 1135 (Fla. 2000); Mich. Informal Ethics Op. RI-245 (1995) (recitation in agreement that one-third of all billed and collected amounts from departing clients was "fair and equitable compensation to the corporation for the loss of its good will associated with clients, and adequate and fair compensation for lost future profits of the corporation" did not suffice); N.C. Ethics Op. 2008-8 (2008) (cannot require departing associate to pay firm 70 percent of fees in all matters he takes with him); N.C. Ethics Op. 2007-6 (2007) (cannot reduce repurchase price of departing lawyer's shares by 125 percent of value of firm's prior year's work for clients who follow lawyer to his new firm).

### • *Impact of Partnership Law*

Questions of fee allocation when lawyers leave a dissolving law firm warrant consideration of statutory law as well as professional conduct rules. For example, partnership law provides that absent contrary agreement (called a *Jewel* waiver, after *Jewel v. Boxer,* 203 Cal. Rptr. 13 (Ct. App. 1984)), when a law firm dissolves its client matters constitute "unfinished business" and must be considered partnership assets. But not all client matters may fit within this rule. *See, e.g., Heller Ehrman LLP v. Davis Wright Tremaine LLP,* 411 P.3d 548 (Cal. 2018) ("Under California partnership law, a dissolved law firm does not have a property interest in legal matters handled on an hourly basis, or in the profits generated by former partners who continue to work on these hourly fee matters after they are transferred to the partners' new firms."). For discussion see Douglas R. Richmond, *Whither (Wither?) the Unfinished Business*

*Doctrine*, 20 Chap. L. Rev. 283 (Spring 2017). *See also* John W. Edson, *An Unworkable Result: Examining the Application of the Unfinished Business Doctrine to Law Firm Bankruptcies*, 32 Emory Bankr. Dev. J. 159, 189-90 (2015) ("[T]he unfinished business doctrine creates a disincentive for former partners to continue representing clients associated with their dissolved firm. This disincentive may in fact violate Rule 5.6(a) because it creates a barrier to an attorney's freedom to practice.").

• *Logical Basis*

Rule 5.6(a) does not, however, preclude enforcement of fee-allocation agreements logically related to the anticipated financial impact of the lawyer's departure. *See, e.g., Kelly v. Smith*, 611 N.E.2d 118 (Ind. 1993) (partnership agreement requiring withdrawing lawyer to give firm all fees earned from clients taken from firm except for percentage representing his stake in firm did not violate Rule 5.6); *Fox v. Heisler*, 874 So. 2d 932 (La. Ct. App. 2004) (approving oral agreement to split fees on case funded by former firm though handled exclusively by departing lawyer; but for firm's funding, lawyer "might have gone bankrupt and could no longer [have] represent[ed] Client"); *Warner v. Carimi Law Firm*, 678 So. 2d 561 (La. Ct. App. 1996) (requiring departing lawyer to reimburse firm for advanced costs simply keeps burden of financing case where it belongs); *McCroskey, Feldman, Cochrane & Brock, P.C. v. Waters*, 494 N.W.2d 826 (Mich. Ct. App. 1992) (contract requiring firm's former director to turn over 75 percent of fees from clients he referred to his former associates, and 25 percent of all other fees, was "reasonable attempt to relate [the departing lawyer's] fee entitlement to the amount of work done on a given file before it left the firm"); *Barna, Guzy & Steffen, Ltd. v. Beens*, 541 N.W.2d 354 (Minn. Ct. App. 1995) (permissible to require former partner to remit half of all contingent fees collected from clients who leave firm with him; he would have received less than that had he remained with firm); *Groen, Laveson, Goldberg & Rubenstone v. Kancher*, 827 A.2d 1163 (N.J. Super. Ct. App. Div. 2003) (enforcing fee-split; "partner or associate cannot be permitted to devote firm time and resources on a case with a potentially large contingency and then leave without owing the firm for its services"); *see also Gray v. Noteboom*, 159 S.W.3d 750 (Tex. App. 2005) (enforcing fee-split notwithstanding violation of Rule 5.6(a); "cost of preparing litigation is not only the efforts by the lawyer handling the case but also the efforts of the firm's legal staff[,] . . . investigative staff, clerical staff, and the time and expense of expert witnesses"), *discussed in* Jennifer Turner, Comment, Noteboom: *A Dramatic Deviation from Texas' Stand Against Non-Competition Clauses Among Lawyers*, 58 Baylor L. Rev. 1011 (Fall 2006). *See generally* Linda Sorenson Ewald, *Agreements Restricting the Practice of Law: A New Look at an Old Paradox*, 26 J. Legal Prof. 1 (2001–2002) (endorsing compensatory arrangements and differentiating them from practice-limiting arrangements).

## TAKING "FIRM" CLIENTS: OTHER RESTRICTIONS

Attempting to limit competition by forbidding client contact or use of "firm" information for a given period has been held to violate Rule 5.6. *See, e.g., In re Truman*, 7 N.E.3d 260 (Ind. 2014) (agreement gave employer sole right to notify clients if associate leaves, and forbad associate from contacting clients after leaving), *discussed*

*in* Donald R. Lundberg, *Breaking Up Is Hard to Do: Lawyers and Competition*, 58 Res
Gestae 28 (July/Aug. 2014); Ill. Ethics Op. 91-12 (1991) (agreement prevented lawyers from communicating with or representing former firm's clients for three years
after departure); Iowa Ethics Op. 89-48 (1990) (agreement prevented departing lawyer from practicing in same community or soliciting firm's clients for two years after
departure); Mich. Informal Ethics Op. RI-86 (1991) (agreement made client files exclusive property of firm and restricted departing lawyer from contacting firm's clients);
Pa. Ethics Op. 2012-006 (2012) (corporation may not require departing lawyer who
becomes affiliated with its vendors to obtain general counsel's consent before communicating with any of corporation's employees); Va. Ethics Op. 1403 (1991) (cannot
prohibit withdrawing lawyer from contacting firm clients until client has responded
to firm's letter asking client to choose counsel); Wash. Ethics Op. 2118 (2006) (cannot prohibit contract lawyers from communicating with firm clients without firm
approval "both during or after" contract's term; cannot prohibit solicitation of firm
clients or potential clients for two years after contract ends); *see also Jacob v. Norris,
McLaughlin & Marcus*, 607 A.2d 142 (N.J. 1992) (separation agreement denying termination compensation to members who, within one year of departure, represent firm's
clients or solicit firm's lawyers or staff was void as indirect restriction on practice;
"practice" includes not only lawyer-client interactions, but also lawyer-colleague
interactions); *Cohen v. Graham*, 722 P.2d 1388 (Wash. Ct. App. 1986) (lawyer could
agree not to solicit other lawyer's clients but could not agree to forbear representing
them if asked); *cf.* N.Y. State Ethics Op. 858 (2011) (in-house counsel for nonprofit corporation may require staff lawyers to sign confidentiality agreement giving special
protection to certain information, including employer's trade secrets, if agreement
makes plain that lawyer's right to practice after termination will not be restricted
thereby). *See generally* David L. Johnson, *The Parameters of "Solicitation" in an Era of
Non-Solicitation Covenants*, 28 A.B.A. J. Lab. & Emp. L. 99 (Fall 2012); Barry R. Temkin,
*The Ethical Issues of Lateral Moves: Whether, When and How to Notify Clients of a Lawyer's
Resignation*, 83 N.Y. St. B.J. 47 (Mar./Apr. 2011).

## RETIREMENT BENEFITS

A firm may condition receipt of retirement benefits upon a promise that the
retiree will not compete with the firm, but only if the payments are genuine "benefits upon retirement." *Compare Cummins v. Bickel & Brewer*, No. 00CV 3703, 2002 WL
187492 (N.D. Ill. Feb. 6, 2002) (provision calling for forfeiture of benefits if departing
partner "undertakes the representation of a Partnership Client within three (3) years
after . . . withdrawal" did not qualify as retirement provision and was therefore void),
*and Apfel v. Budd Larner Gross Rosenbaum Greenberg & Sade*, 734 A.2d 808 (N.J. Super.
Ct. App. Div. 1999) (invalidating ostensible retirement provision that defined retirement as ceasing to practice law in three states where firm had offices: "the benefits
depend not on age or years of service, but rather turn on competition or non-competition"), *with Donnelly v. Brown, Winick, Graves, Gross, Baskerville, Schoenebaum, &
Walker, P.L.C.*, 599 N.W.2d 677 (Iowa 1999) (although agreement conditioning benefits
upon lawyer's not practicing law in Iowa was covenant not to compete, it could still
be enforced as retirement plan; benefits payable only after attaining "ten years of

service and sixty years of age or twenty-five years of service"), *and Borteck v. Riker, Danzig, Scherer, Hyland & Perretti LLP*, 844 A.2d 521 (N.J. 2004) (provision for benefits upon early retirement—defined as permanent retirement but with exceptions for public service work and "of counsel" work for firm—after ten years with firm was valid, and was not applicable to lawyer who left after eleven years to work for another firm). For discussion of firms' attempts to use retirement penalties to discourage competition, see Robert W. Hillman, *Ties That Bind and Restraints on Lawyer Competition: Restrictive Covenants as Conditions to the Payments of Retirement Benefits*, 39 Ind. L. Rev. 1 (2005).

### • *What Qualifies as a Retirement Benefit?*

The phrase "benefits upon retirement" (not defined in the rules or comment) refers to amounts separately owed the departing lawyer out of the firm's retirement plan, over and above any other money due. It does not mean payment for the departing lawyer's interest in the firm's capital account or in its uncollected or undistributed earnings. Benefits that qualify under the exception "exhibit the objective indicia of retirement in terms of funding source, distribution period, and applicable eligibility criteria"; they are generally paid from future firm revenues, disbursed over an extended period, and conditioned upon age and length of service. *Schoonmaker v. Cummings & Lockwood of Conn., P.C.*, 747 A.2d 1017 (Conn. 2000) (benefits funded solely by firm's future earnings, to be paid if employee reaches sixty and worked for firm for twenty years); *see Neuman v. Akman*, 715 A.2d 127 (D.C. 1998) (payments qualified as retirement benefits because revenue to be distributed postdated lawyer's withdrawal and was payable only if lawyer turned sixty-five and fulfilled service requirement); *Miller v. Foulston, Siefkin, Powers & Eberhardt*, 790 P.2d 404 (Kan. 1990) (payments qualified as retirement benefits because conditioned upon age (sixty), length of service (thirty years), or permanent incapacity); *Bortek v. Riker, Danzig, Scherer, Hyland & Perretti*, 844 A.2d 521 (N.J. 2004) (early retirement plan included schedule of graduated, long-term payments keyed to age and years as partner); *see also Hoff v. Mayer, Brown & Platt*, 772 N.E.2d 263 (Ill. App. Ct. 2002) (affirming dismissal of suit for retirement benefits by former partner who resigned after thirty-six years to start another firm; the only benefits withheld were those derived from firm's future earnings). *See generally* ABA Formal Ethics Op. 06-444 (2006) (key features are age and length-of-service requirements; also whether benefits are calculated by a formula, increasing as years of service increase and payable over retired partner's lifetime, and whether they will decrease as payments from other retirement funds and defined-contribution retirement plans phase in); Robert W. Hillman, *Law Firm Management in an Era of Breakups and Lawyer Mobility: Limitations and Opportunities*, 43 Tex. Tech L. Rev. 449 (Winter 2011) (after age and length-of-service requirements, "additional criteria include (1) the existence of distinct withdrawal provisions governing non-retirement payouts, (2) the payment of benefits over an extended period of time, and (3) the payment or availability of ancillary benefits (primarily insurance and staff support). Some courts have suggested that payouts forfeitable under the retirement benefits exception must be sourced in future firm revenues rather than contributions previously made by the retired partner.").

## NONCOMPETITION AGREEMENTS INCIDENT TO SALE OF PRACTICE

With the adoption of Model Rule 1.17 (Sale of Law Practice) in 1990 came a corresponding amendment to Comment [3] of Rule 5.6, clarifying that Rule 5.6 does not apply to restrictions that may be included in the terms of the sale of a practice pursuant to Rule 1.17. *See* Wash. Ethics Op. 192 (1996) (seller and buyer of law practice may agree that they will not compete for clients).

### Paragraph (b): Restrictions That Are Part of Settlements

In settling their clients' cases, lawyers may not restrict their future work. In other words, a plaintiff's lawyer is not allowed to promise that he will not represent anyone else with similar claims against the defendant, and the defendant's lawyer is not allowed to ask for such a promise:

> First, permitting such agreements restricts the access of the public to lawyers who, by virtue of their background and experience, might be the very best available talent to represent these individuals. . . . Second, the use of such agreements may provide clients with rewards that bear less relationship to the merits of their claims than they do to the desire of the defendant to "buy off" plaintiff's counsel. Third, the offering of such restrictive agreements places the plaintiff's lawyer in a situation where there is conflict between the interests of present clients and those of future clients.

ABA Formal Ethics Op. 93-371 (1993). *Accord Fla. Bar v. St. Louis*, 967 So. 2d 108 (Fla. 2007) (Rule 5.6(b) passes rational-basis test and does not unconstitutionally infringe upon lawyer's property or liberty rights); *see In re Hager*, 812 A.2d 904 (D.C. 2002) (in settlement of mass products liability action, lawyer agreed not to sue defendant for same claims again); *Cardillo v. Bloomfield 206 Corp.*, 988 A.2d 136 (N.J. Super. Ct. App. Div. 2010) (plaintiffs' counsel's agreement to refrain from representing anyone adverse to defendants was "intertwined" with settlement of clients' case notwithstanding her consistent declarations during negotiations that it was separate); N.C. Ethics Op. 2003-9 (2003) (agreement not to represent potential clients with claims similar to settling client's claim "denies members of the public access to the very lawyer who may be best suited, by experience and background, to represent them"); Pa. Formal Ethics Op. 2016-300 (2016) (citing Rule 3.4 as well as Rule 5.6 and condemning agreements not to represent future claimants against settling defendant, not to use information acquired during the litigation in connection with a future matter, or not to advertise that lawyer "practices in a particular area or handles certain types of matters"; however, clause "that restricts the right to criticize the defendant in a non-litigation context—such as for publicity purposes—does not violate Rule 5.6(b)"); Tex. Ethics Op. 505 (1994) (lawyer may not agree to refrain from soliciting third parties to prosecute claims against defendant; restriction on otherwise permissible solicitation is restraint on practice of law); Va. Ethics Op. 1788 (2004) (settlement agreement calling for asbestosis plaintiffs' lawyers not to file future suits on behalf of asbestos manufacturer's employees violates Rule 5.6(b)); Wash. Ethics Op. 2125 (2006) (settlement provision preventing plaintiff's lawyer from filing additional unrelated suits against defendant on behalf of currently unidentified plaintiffs violates Rule 5.6(b)); *see also* ABA Formal Ethics Op. 94-381 (1994) (in-house counsel may not offer, and outside counsel may not accept, agreement by which outside counsel will never represent anyone against corporation, even on unrelated matters). *Compare DeSantis v. Snap-On Tools Co.*, No. 06-cv-2231, 2006 WL 3068584 (D.N.J. Oct. 27, 2006) (approving agreement reciting that plaintiffs' counsel has "no present intention" of representing anyone else with similar claims against defendant), *with La. Mun. Police Emps.' Ret. Sys. v. Black*, No. 9410-VCN, 2016 WL 790898, 2016 BL 57903 (Del. Ch. Feb. 19, 2016) (distinguishing no-present-intention language from plaintiffs' counsel's impermissible declaration it "would not be" suing).

The use of no-present-intention language as a work-around for Rule 5.6(b) is carefully analyzed in Lynn A. Baker, *Mass Torts and the Pursuit of Ethical Finality*, 85 Fordham L. Rev. 1943, 1957-62, 1966-68 (Apr. 2017). The author proposes an amended Rule 5.6(b) permitting a lawyer to promise "not to represent, or advertise for, new clients in matters arising out of the same transaction or event."

There is debate over whether Rule 5.6(b)'s restriction on lawyers' and litigants' freedom to contract is justified by the rule's purposes. *Compare* David A. Dana & Susan P. Koniak, *Secret Settlements and Practice Restrictions Aid Lawyer Cartels and Cause Other Harms*, 2003 U. Ill. L. Rev. 1217 (2003), *with* Stephen Gillers & Richard W. Painter, *Free the Lawyers: A Proposal to Permit No-Sue Promises in Settlement Agreements*, 18 Geo. J. Legal Ethics 291 (Spring 2005). *See generally* Yvette Golan, *Restrictive Settlement Agreements: A Critique of Model Rule 5.6(b)*, 33 Sw. U. L. Rev. 1 (2003).

## CONSULTING AGREEMENTS

Attempts to evade Rule 5.6 by agreeing the lawyers will become consultants for the other side have been condemned. *See Adams v. Bellsouth Telecomms., Inc.*, No. 96-2473-CIV, 2001 WL 34032759 (S.D. Fla. Jan. 29, 2001) (sanctioning both sides for agreeing plaintiffs' counsel would receive consulting fee from defendant, and condemning corporate co-option of plaintiffs' bar by "'consulting' agreements between plaintiffs' attorneys and former opposing parties"); *In re Brandt*, 10 P.3d 906 (Or. 2000) (settlement included plaintiff's lawyers' agreement to be retained by defendant; as matter of first impression, court found violation of disciplinary rule and suspended lawyers). For a thorough discussion of consultation agreements and nonbinding commitments as well as no-sue promises, see Ronnie Gomez, *Ethics Rules in Practice: An Analysis of Model Rule 5.6(b) and Its Impact on Finality in Mass Tort Settlements*, 32 Rev. Litig. 467 (Summer 2013).

## WITHDRAWAL AGREEMENTS

An agreement to withdraw from representing nonsettling clients violates Rule 5.6(b). *See* ABA Formal Ethics Op. 93-371 (1993) (settlement agreement requiring plaintiffs' lawyer to refuse to represent certain opt-out plaintiffs, even those who were already clients, would violate Rule 5.6(b)); Ala. Ethics Op. 92-01 (1992) (plaintiffs' lead counsel in consolidated multidistrict litigation may not agree, as part of settlement package, to withdraw from representing nonsettling clients); *see also* L.A. Cnty. Ethics Op. 468 (1992) (condemning agreement under which lawyers for settling defendants would agree not to represent nonsettling defendants, and settling defendants would agree to assert conflict-of-interest claim against them should they try).

Inclusion of a withdrawal promise in a major nonclass aggregate settlement, *In re Vioxx Prods. Liab. Litig.*, No. 05-md-1657 (E.D. La. Nov. 9, 2007), available at https://perma.cc/Y9B5-DXHM, brought renewed examination of Rule 5.6(b) in the context of mass actions. *See* Howard M. Erichson & Benjamin C. Zipursky, *Consent Versus Closure*, 96 Cornell L. Rev. 265 (Jan. 2011) ("Mandatory withdrawal compromises not only loyalty to clients but also the public policy of preventing malefactors from buying off lawyers qua private attorneys general."); Nancy J. Moore, *Ethical Issues in Mass Tort Plaintiffs' Representation: Beyond the Aggregate Settlement Rule*, 81 Fordham L. Rev. 3233 (May 2013) (Rule 5.6(b) makes it impossible for defendants to achieve finality); Richard Zitrin, *Regulating the Behavior of Lawyers in Mass Individual Representations: A Call for Reform*, 3 St. Mary's J. Legal Mal. & Ethics 86 (2013) (ethics rules should be amended to facilitate settlements of mass individual representations). *See generally* Lynn A. Baker, *Mass Torts and the Pursuit of Ethical Finality*, 85 Fordham L. Rev. 1943 (Apr. 2017); Rara Kang, Current Development, *Working with the Model Rules: Navigating Ethical Dilemmas in Aggregate Settlements of Non-Class Action Mass Toxic Tort Suits*, 27 Geo. J. Legal Ethics 585 (Summer 2014).

## ENFORCEABILITY VERSUS DISCIPLINE

Some jurisdictions distinguish between enforcing the agreement and disciplining the lawyers for making it. *See, e.g., Lee v. Fla. Dep't of Ins.*, 586 So. 2d 1185 (Fla. Dist. Ct. App. 1991) (enforcing provision in settlement agreement and disqualifying lawyer; any violation of Rule 5.6(b) was disciplinary issue); *Feldman v. Minars*, 658 N.Y.S.2d 614 (App. Div. 1997) (based upon settlement agreement in which plaintiffs' law firm promised not to "assist or cooperate" in any actions against settling defendants, court granted defendants' motion to disqualify firm in subsequent action; any violation of ethics rules was for disciplinary authorities to address); *Shebay v. Davis*, 717 S.W.2d 678 (Tex. App. 1986) (settlement agreement enforceable; state bar grievance committee should determine whether it violates ethics rules); *see also* N.Y. City Ethics Op. 1999-3 (1999) (restrictive settlement provisions violate ethics rule even if enforceable).

## REVEALING INFORMATION

A settlement agreement that restricts the right to *reveal*, as opposed to *use*, nonpublic information acquired in the representation does not necessarily violate the ethics rules. Because Rule 1.9(c), which governs confidentiality obligations to former clients, already forbids disclosure of information relating to the representation of a former client, the lawyer is agreeing to no more than what is required anyway: "[I]t does not necessarily limit the lawyer's future practice in the manner accomplished by a restriction on the use of information relating to the opposing party in the matter." ABA Formal Ethics Op. 00-417 (2000). *Accord* L.A. Cnty. Ethics Op. 512 (2004) (approving agreement prohibiting disclosure of fact and amount of settlement); Fla. Ethics Op. 04-2 (2005); N.C. Ethics Op. 2003-9 (2004); S.C. Ethics Op. 16-02 (2016); *cf.*

Ariz. Ethics Op. 95-04 (1995) (corporation's in-house lawyer may agree to nondisclosure of client confidences as condition of severance agreement). *But see Bassman v. Blackstone Assocs.*, 718 N.Y.S.2d 826 (App. Div. 2001) (rejecting distinction between use and revelation and disqualifying plaintiff's counsel based on his agreement, in settling earlier suit against defendant, not to disclose certain information; obligation "conflicts with [counsel's] ability to freely contemplate settlement strategies").

If the information has already become public, however, the restriction may violate Rule 5.6. *See* D.C. Ethics Op. 335 (2006) (settlement agreement providing lawyer will not further disclose public information about case in promotional materials or on law firm website diminishes opportunity for lawyer to represent future clients in similar matters); Md. Ethics Op. 2016-07 (n.d.) (lawyer settling case may neither propose nor agree not to discuss or disclose case's underlying facts that are already a matter of public record); N.Y. State Ethics Op. 730 (2000) (agreement not to reveal any information about corporate defendant's business or operations is overbroad because there is "almost certainly" information that is public, or that lawyer knew before he took case, or that lawyer could learn without relying upon client's confidences or secrets); N.D. Ethics Op. 1997-05 (1997) (may not agree to keep information confidential if it is otherwise available).

## USING INFORMATION

Unlike an agreement not to disclose, an agreement not to *use* information obtained in a representation is, as a practical matter, an impermissible restriction on future employment. According to ABA Formal Opinion 00-417 (2000), "the lawyer's inability to use certain information may materially limit his representation of [a] future client and, further, may adversely affect that representation." The opinion notes that Rule 1.9(c)(1) does not impose a blanket restriction on use of information relating to former clients. Rather, it prohibits using information to a former client's *disadvantage*, and then only if the information has not become generally known.

In *Hu-Friedy Mfg. Co. v. Gen. Elec. Co.*, No. 99C 0762, 1999 WL 528545 (N.D. Ill. July 19, 1999), the defendant moved to disqualify plaintiff's counsel based upon a protective order and joint defense and cooperation agreement counsel had entered into as part of settling another client's case against the same defendant. The court refused: "In effect, [defendant's] argument turns any protective order barring future use of confidential information that is independently relevant and discoverable in a subsequent action into a restriction on an attorney's right to practice law." Because any "reasonably competent" lawyer would routinely obtain the information in discovery, the court continued, counsel's previous exposure to it did not amount to an unfair head start. *See also Tradewinds Airlines, Inc. v. Soros*, No. 08 Civ. 5901 (JFK), 2009 WL 1321695 (S.D.N.Y. May 12, 2009) (protective order in earlier veil-piercing action specifying that litigation materials were to be used solely for prosecution and defense of that action did not preclude plaintiff's lawyer from later representing others against same defendant; defendant would have to produce same materials in discovery in subsequent case anyway); *State ex rel. Verizon W. Va., Inc. v. Matish*, 740 S.E.2d 84 (W. Va. 2013) (confidential settlement agreements and agreed protective orders must not be construed to restrict future representation "based solely upon the attorney's obligations to maintain the confidentiality of information subject to such protective order or confidential settlement agreement"); Ill. Ethics Op. 11-02 (2011) (lawyer's agreement not to divulge client's accountant's tax ideas may amount to impermissible restriction on his right to practice even though it is not part of employment or settlement agreement); Chicago Ethics Op. 12-10 (2013) (settlement agreement violates Rule 5.6(b) if it forecloses lawyer's use of information in future representations or disclosure of information that is already public); S.C. Ethics Op. 10-04 (2010) (lawyer for settling plaintiffs may not promise not to use defendant's name for commercially related publicity; right to advertise is constitutional right inherent in right to practice and cannot be restricted).

## OTHER KINDS OF RESTRICTIONS

Settlement agreements sometimes incorporate limitations other than a promise not to sue or a promise not to disclose/use information. If the limitation restricts or substantially impairs counsel's future employment, it violates Rule 5.6(b). *See In re World Trade Ctr. Disaster Site Litig.*, 83 F. Supp. 3d 519 (S.D.N.Y. 2015) (refusing to enforce provision of mass tort settlement agreement giving plaintiffs' counsel a percentage of contingent payments if, in each of next five years, fewer than designated number of new cases were filed; provision "incentivizes lawyers to refuse new clients who seek their expertise by providing that additional payments and proportionate attorneys' fees are contingent on an absence of future cases") (applying New York law); Colo. Ethics Op. 92 (1993) (lawyer for settling claimants may not agree to refrain from using certain expert witnesses or subpoenaing certain records or fact witnesses in future actions against defendant, or to limit forum or venue options in future cases brought on behalf of nonsettling claimants); Ind. Ethics Op. 2014-1 (2014) (nondisparagement clause violates Rule 5.6(b) if it would extend to lawyer's advocacy on behalf of future clients or would prevent lawyer from informing prospective clients about his relevant experience); N.M. Ethics Op. 1985-5 (1985) (even at client's request, lawyer may not agree to turn over work product to opposing counsel if this would restrict ability to represent future clients); N.D. Ethics Op. 1997-05 (1997) (same); Tenn. Formal Ethics Op. 2016-F-161 (2016) (same); *see also Blue Cross & Blue Shield of N.J. v. Philip Morris, Inc.*, 53 F. Supp. 2d 338 (E.D.N.Y. 1999) (plaintiffs' promise not to seek to disqualify defendant's counsel—who was also representing plaintiffs in unrelated matters—in exchange for counsel's promise not to appear in one of three coordinated actions plaintiffs were bringing comported with Rule 5.6(b); agreement concerned one defendant's right to be represented by its chosen counsel in one lawsuit and therefore did not implicate public's unfettered access to counsel); *Garfinkel v. Mager*, 57 So. 3d 221 (Fla. Dist. Ct. App. 2010) (settlement of lawyer's suit against former firm in which he promised not to assist or advise anyone else suing firm was "reasoned effort" to balance competing public interests and did not violate Rule 5.6).

Note also that Rule 3.4(f) prohibits a lawyer from asking anyone other than a client to refrain from voluntarily giving relevant information to third parties. Therefore, it can be argued that defense counsel may not ask plaintiff's counsel, in settlement negotiations, to promise not to disclose relevant information on behalf of another potential claimant. *See* David D. Dodge, *Settlement Agreement Terms May Cause Ethical Trouble*, 52 Ariz. Att'y 12 (Nov. 2015) ("And if the plaintiff's lawyer goes along with the scheme, isn't he assisting the defendant's lawyer in violating an ethical rule, . . . which is itself an ethical violation?") (citing Rule 8.4(a)). On the applicability of Rule 3.4(f) as well as Rule 5.6(b) to settlement agreements see generally Jon Bauer, *Buying Witness Silence: Evidence-Suppressing Settlements and Lawyers' Ethics*, 87 Or. L. Rev. 481 (2008).

## Rule 5.7

*Responsibilities Regarding*
*Law-Related Services*

(a) A lawyer shall be subject to the Rules of Professional Conduct with respect to the provision of law-related services, as defined in paragraph (b), if the law-related services are provided:

(1) by the lawyer in circumstances that are not distinct from the lawyer's provision of legal services to clients; or

(2) in other circumstances by an entity controlled by the lawyer individually or with others if the lawyer fails to take reasonable measures to assure that a person obtaining the law-related services knows that the services are not legal services and that the protections of the client-lawyer relationship do not exist.

(b) The term "law-related services" denotes services that might reasonably be performed in conjunction with and in substance are related to the provision of legal services, and that are not prohibited as unauthorized practice of law when provided by a nonlawyer.

## COMMENT

[1] When a lawyer performs law-related services or controls an organization that does so, there exists the potential for ethical problems. Principal among these is the possibility that the person for whom the law-related services are performed fails to understand that the services may not carry with them the protections normally afforded as part of the client-lawyer relationship. The recipient of the law-related services may expect, for example, that the protection of client confidences, prohibitions against representation of persons with conflicting interests, and obligations of a lawyer to maintain professional independence apply to the provision of law-related services when that may not be the case.

[2] Rule 5.7 applies to the provision of law-related services by a lawyer even when the lawyer does not provide any legal services to the person for whom the law-related services are performed and whether the law-related services are performed through a law firm or a separate entity. The Rule identifies the circumstances in which all of the Rules of Professional Conduct apply to the provision of law-related services. Even when those circumstances do not exist, however, the conduct of a lawyer involved in the provision of law-related services is subject to those Rules that apply generally to lawyer conduct, regardless of whether the conduct involves the provision of legal services. See, e.g., Rule 8.4.

[3] When law-related services are provided by a lawyer under circumstances that are not distinct from the lawyer's provision of legal services to clients, the lawyer in providing the law-related services must adhere to the requirements of the Rules of Professional Conduct as provided in paragraph (a)(1). Even when the law-related and legal services are provided in circumstances that are distinct from each other, for example through separate entities or different support staff within the law firm, the Rules of Professional Conduct apply to the lawyer as provided in paragraph (a)(2) unless the lawyer takes reasonable measures to assure that the recipient of the law-related services knows that the services are not legal services and that the protections of the client-lawyer relationship do not apply.

[4] Law-related services also may be provided through an entity that is distinct from that through which the lawyer provides legal services. If the lawyer individually or with others has control of such an entity's operations, the Rule requires the lawyer to take reasonable measures to assure that each person using the services of the entity knows that the services provided by the entity are not legal services and that the Rules of Professional Conduct that relate to the client-lawyer relationship do not apply. A lawyer's control of an entity extends to the ability to direct its operation. Whether a lawyer has such control will depend upon the circumstances of the particular case.

[5] When a client-lawyer relationship exists with a person who is referred by a lawyer to a separate law-related service entity controlled by the lawyer, individually or with others, the lawyer must comply with Rule 1.8(a).

[6] In taking the reasonable measures referred to in paragraph (a)(2) to assure that a person using law-related services understands the practical effect or significance of the inapplicability of the Rules of Professional Conduct, the lawyer should communicate to the person receiving the law-related services, in a manner sufficient to assure that the person understands the significance of the fact, that the relationship of the person to the business entity will not be a client-lawyer relationship. The communication should be made before entering into an agreement for provision of or providing law-related services, and preferably should be in writing.

[7] The burden is upon the lawyer to show that the lawyer has taken reasonable measures under the circumstances to communicate the desired understanding. For instance, a sophisticated user of law-related services, such as a publicly held corporation, may require a lesser explanation than someone unaccustomed to making distinctions between legal services and law-related services, such as an individual seeking tax advice from a lawyer-accountant or investigative services in connection with a lawsuit.

[8] Regardless of the sophistication of potential recipients of law-related services, a lawyer should take special care to keep separate the provision of law-related and legal services in order to minimize the risk that the recipient will assume that the law-related services are legal services. The risk of such confusion is especially acute when the lawyer renders both types of services with respect to the same matter. Under some circumstances the legal and law-related services may be so closely entwined that they cannot be distinguished from each other, and the requirement of disclosure and consultation imposed by paragraph (a)(2) of the Rule cannot be

met. In such a case a lawyer will be responsible for assuring that both the lawyer's conduct and, to the extent required by Rule 5.3, that of nonlawyer employees in the distinct entity that the lawyer controls complies in all respects with the Rules of Professional Conduct.

[9] A broad range of economic and other interests of clients may be served by lawyers' engaging in the delivery of law-related services. Examples of law-related services include providing title insurance, financial planning, accounting, trust services, real estate counseling, legislative lobbying, economic analysis, social work, psychological counseling, tax preparation, and patent, medical or environmental consulting.

[10] When a lawyer is obliged to accord the recipients of such services the protections of those Rules that apply to the client-lawyer relationship, the lawyer must take special care to heed the proscriptions of the Rules addressing conflict of interest (Rules 1.7 through 1.11, especially Rules 1.7(a)(2) and 1.8(a), (b) and (f)), and to scrupulously adhere to the requirements of Rule 1.6 relating to disclosure of confidential information. The promotion of the law-related services must also in all respects comply with Rules 7.1 through 7.3, dealing with advertising and solicitation. In that regard, lawyers should take special care to identify the obligations that may be imposed as a result of a jurisdiction's decisional law.

[11] When the full protections of all of the Rules of Professional Conduct do not apply to the provision of law-related services, principles of law external to the Rules, for example, the law of principal and agent, govern the legal duties owed to those receiving the services. Those other legal principles may establish a different degree of protection for the recipient with respect to confidentiality of information, conflicts of interest and permissible business relationships with clients. See also Rule 8.4 (Misconduct).

## Definitional Cross-References

"Knows" *See* Rule 1.0(f)
"Reasonable" *See* Rule 1.0(h)

## State Rules Comparison

http://ambar.org/MRPCStateCharts

# ANNOTATION

## GENERAL PROVISIONS

Rule 5.7 deals with the ethical obligations of lawyers providing "law-related," as opposed to "legal," services. The provision of law-related services by a lawyer can create confusion insofar as recipients of these services, who are business customers, might reasonably assume that the relationship between them and the lawyer is a lawyer-client relationship with its attendant ethical protections. *See* Cmt. [1]. The lawyer, on the other hand, might assume that because the services provided are not "legal services," she does not owe business customers the same ethical duties she would owe law clients. Rule 5.7 places the burden upon the lawyer to make clear to the business customer that the protections of a lawyer-client relationship do not apply to the provision of law-related services. If the burden is not met, the Rules of Professional Conduct will apply to the provision of these services just as if the lawyer were providing legal services.

## • *Legislative History*

Rule 5.7 in its current form (except for the 2002 amendments) was initially adopted in 1994. A prior version adopted in 1991 severely restricted the ability of lawyers to provide law-related services. That version proved controversial and was repealed the following year, without having been adopted by any state.

In 2002, paragraph (a)(2) of the rule was amended. Originally, this paragraph applied only to law-related services provided "by a separate entity controlled by the lawyer." The amended language, and that of contemporaneous changes to Comments [2] and [3], recognizes that the services may be provided distinctly from each other even if the law-related services are being provided by the firm itself, rather than via a separate entity.

The amended version of Rule 5.7 (or a variation thereof) has been adopted by a majority of jurisdictions. Some ethics authorities have cited Rule 5.7 as guidance in jurisdictions that have not adopted it. *See, e.g.,* Ill. Ethics Op. 98-03 (1999); Nev. Ethics Op. 52 (2014); N.J. Ethics Op. 730 (2015).

For a complete history of Rule 5.7, see American Bar Association, *A Legislative History: The Development of the ABA Model Rules of Professional Conduct, 1982–2013,* at 671 *et seq.* (2013).

## Paragraph (a): Separating Business from Law Practice and Clarifying Relationship to Business Customer

Rule 5.7 articulates two circumstances under which a lawyer's law-related business must be conducted in compliance with the full complement of ethics rules applicable to the lawyer's law practice: (1) when the lawyer operates the business in a manner indistinguishable from the lawyer's law practice, and (2) when the lawyer operates the business distinctly from the law practice, but does not take reasonable measures to assure that the business customer understands he or she is not entitled to the protections of a lawyer-client relationship.

## OPERATING BUSINESS AND LAW PRACTICE INDISTINGUISHABLY

A lawyer who operates her law-related business in a manner not readily distinguishable from her law practice must conduct the business in compliance with all the lawyer ethics rules. *See, e.g.,* Ariz. Ethics Op. 05-01 (2005) (lawyer subject to ethics rules when providing law-related services under circumstances indistinguishable from provision of legal services, even if lawyer provides no legal services to recipient of law-related services); Ind. Ethics Op. 2002-1 (2002) (lawyer must comply with lawyer ethics rules in operating his financial planning business if he cannot meet "substantial burden" of keeping business separate and distinct, and ensure customers understand they are not receiving legal services); N.Y. State Ethics Op. 1135 (2017) (lawyer-CPA who provides legal and accounting services as integrated operation must comply with lawyer advertising rules when marketing accounting services to persons with whom lawyer lacks preexisting relationship); N.D. Ethics Op. 01-03 (2001) (lawyer's tax preparation business subject to ethics rules if not distinct from his law practice).

## OPERATING BUSINESS SEPARATELY FROM LAW PRACTICE

If a lawyer operates her law-related business separately from her law practice—whether through her law practice or a separate entity—all the ethics rules still apply to her dealings with business customers if she "fails to take reasonable measures to assure that a person obtaining the law-related services knows that the services are not legal services and that the protections of the client-lawyer relationship do not exist." Rule 5.7(a)(2); cmts. [2], [3]. *See* N.Y. State Ethics Op. 938 (2012) (law firm owning business that provides nonlegal Social Security Disability Insurance claims services and employs only nonlawyers may pay for "leads" from marketing organization if business is run separately from firm and disclaims provision of legal services); *cf.* Tenn. Formal Ethics Op. 2017-F-164 (2017) (law firm using trade name SETCO Law and leasing office space from title company called SETCO Services must make clear to customers of title company that no lawyer-client relationship is created by their use of title services). *See generally* Hugh D. Spitzer, *Model Rule 5.7 and Lawyers in Government Jobs—How Can They Ever Be "Non-Lawyers"?*, 30 Geo. J. Legal Ethics 45 (Winter 2017) (advising lawyers employed in law-related government jobs to follow procedures contemplated by Rule 5.7 to ensure those the lawyer serves understand they are not receiving legal services and not entitled to protections of lawyer-client relationship).

The rule does not spell out the "reasonable measures" the lawyer is supposed to take. But Comment [6] says that the lawyer should inform a potential business client of "the practical effect or significance of the inapplicability of the Rules of Professional Conduct . . . in a manner sufficient to assure that the person understands the significance of [this] fact." This should be done, Comment [6] continues, "before entering into an agreement for provision of or providing law-related services, and preferably . . . in writing." *Cf.* Fla. Rule 5.7(d) (reasonable efforts to avoid misunderstanding "must include advising the recipient, preferably in writing, that the services are not legal services and that the protection of a client-lawyer relationship does not exist with respect to the provision of nonlegal services to the recipient"); Okla. Rule 5.7, cmt. [6] (specific measures include providing written notice of lawyer's interest in business with written acknowledgment of notice by business customer, keeping law office and business office physically separate, providing disclaimers in advertisements, and maintaining separate letterhead).

The necessary measures ultimately depend upon the circumstances, but the burden of proving their adequacy is on the lawyer. Cmt. [7]. Greater explanation is required for "someone unaccustomed to making distinctions between legal services and law-related services" than for a more "sophisticated user of law-related services." *Id. See In re Rost*, 211 P.3d 145 (Kan. 2009) (given unsophisticated nature of retired lawyer's clientele, merely changing name from "Attorney" to "Consulting" on office sign and telling clients he was retired does not meet notification burden when lawyer continues to do similar work using same office and staff); Ariz. Ethics

Op. 05-01 (2005) (written disclosure that protections of attorney-client relationship do not apply, while "prudent," may not always suffice); *see also* Vt. Ethics Op. 2011-1 (n.d.) (stating that lawyer's online data storage business does not provide legal services or afford protections of lawyer-client relationship is insufficient; lawyer should tailor information to individual client and explain that individuals wishing to use law-related service are not obligated to use lawyer's legal services).

In some circumstances, "the legal and law-related services may be so closely entwined that they cannot be distinguished from each other, and the requirement of disclosure and consultation imposed by paragraph (a)(2) of the Rule cannot be met." Cmt. [8]. In that case, the lawyer will be subject to the Rules of Professional Conduct in dealing with the business customer. *See* Me. Ethics Op. 182 (2003) (if lawyer-owned title company provides services to client of lawyer's law practice in same transaction, full disclosure that protections of lawyer-client relationship do not apply to title services would *not* suffice to preclude application of ethics rules to title services; legal services and title services are too "closely entwined"; however, full disclosure would be effective to preclude application of ethics rules to title company customer who is not also lawyer's client); N.Y. State Ethics Op. 1026 (2014) (lawyer-mediator subject to ethics rules in providing mediation services designed to result in a separate retainer for the drafting of documents necessary for parties to secure divorce; legal and nonlegal services are "intimately bound up with each other"); N.D. Ethics Op. 01-03 (2001) (disclaimer that lawyer's tax preparation business is unrelated to law practice will not avoid application of ethics rules if business customer is also client); Phila. Ethics Op. 2003-16 (2004) (if "legal and nonlegal services are truly indistinguishable, the Rules of Professional Conduct will apply to the provision of the nonlegal services, regardless of disclosures made by the attorney to the recipient of the services").

### • *Lawyer's Control over Separate Entity*

Paragraph (a)(2) applies when the law-related services are provided "by an entity controlled by the lawyer individually or with others." Whether a lawyer has control over the entity for purposes of this rule is a function of the lawyer's "ability to direct its operation," which will "depend upon the circumstances of the particular case." Cmt. [4]. *See, e.g.,* Pa. Ethics Op. 2002-07 (2002) (law firm with ownership interest in insurance agency to which partners refer some clients not subject to lawyer ethics rules with respect to provision of insurance services if firm's involvement in operation is almost nil and firm takes precautions to keep enterprises separate); *cf. In re Unnamed Att'y*, 645 A.2d 69 (N.H. 1994) (disciplinary authorities had authority under New Hampshire rule on random audits of lawyer trust accounts to audit financial records of title insurance company of which lawyer was majority shareholder; lawyer controlled company and shared office space and employees with it).

### *Paragraph (b): "Law-Related" Services*

Rule 5.7(b) defines "law-related services" as those "that might reasonably be performed in conjunction with and in substance are related to the provision of legal services, and that are not prohibited as unauthorized practice of law when provided by a nonlawyer." Specific examples are contained in Comment [9]: "providing title insurance, financial planning, accounting, trust services, real estate counseling, legislative lobbying, economic analysis, social work, psychological counseling, tax preparation, and patent, medical or environmental consulting." *See In re Rost*, 211 P.3d 145 (Kan. 2009) (accounting services and business advice provided by lawyer on retired status are law-related); *Bauer v. Pa. State Bd. of Auctioneer Exam'rs*, 153 A.3d 899 (Pa. Commw. Ct. 2017) (auctioning toy trains not law-related); Me. Ethics Op. 185 (2004) (file storage business is law-related service); Mich. Informal Ethics Op. RI-363 (2013) (law-related services do not include provision of basic administrative services normally associated with supporting law office); N.Y. State Ethics Op. 1026 (2014) (mediation is law-related service); N.C. Ethics Op. 2014-10 (2015) (for-profit adoption agency provides law-related services); Ohio State Bar Ethics Op. 2011-02 (2011) (business that provides human resource services is law-related); S.C. Ethics Op. 13-03 (n.d.) (title insurance agency is law-related service); Tenn. Formal Ethics Op. 2017-F-164 (2017) (real estate title company provides law-related service); Vt. Ethics Op. 2011-1 (n.d.) (online data storage service is law-related); *see also* Rule 1.8, cmt. [1] (identifying sale of title insurance or investment services as relating to practice of law and referencing Rule 5.7).

Sometimes the ancillary services are deemed to be legal services, rather than law-related services. This may be due to the fact that a lawyer is providing them, or because of the nature of the services themselves. In those situations, Rule 5.7 cannot be used to preclude the application of the Rules of Professional Conduct. *See* N.Y. State Ethics Op. 951 (2012) (statements disclaiming lawyer-client relationship ineffective if services rendered are actually legal services); Utah Ethics Op. 17-07 (2017) (lawyer serving as real estate agent under supervision of broker is providing law-related services, but would be practicing law if performing nonclerical activities such as drafting contracts or providing advice regarding contract or warranty interpretation or applicability of zoning or environmental laws); Iowa Rule 32:5.7, cmt. [12] (lawyers are bound by ethics rules when providing services treated as practice of law when performed by lawyers, notwithstanding that nonlawyers permitted to provide same services; these include "consummation of real estate transactions, preparation of tax returns, legislative lobbying, and estate planning"). *Compare* Me. Ethics Op. 200 (2010) (guardian ad litem under Maine law does not act as lawyer and therefore provides law-related services), *with* Mass. Ethics Op. 2009-01 (2009) (lawyer appointed as guardian ad litem to represent interests of ward is subject to ethics rules even though nonlawyers may serve as guardians ad litem).

## ETHICS RULES MAY STILL APPLY

Even if a law-related business is operated in a manner distinct from the lawyer's legal practice, or even if the lawyer does not have a law practice, the lawyer may still be subject to discipline under the lawyer ethics rules for conduct in connection with the law-related business.

### • *Business Customers Who Are Also Clients of Law Practice*

A lawyer's ethical obligations to a client (or a former client) are unaffected by entry into a business relationship with that client. Of particular importance are the duties concerning conflicts of interest, confidentiality, and adverse use of information relating to the legal representation. Cmt. [5] (lawyer who refers client to separate law-related business that lawyer controls must comply with Rule 1.8(a)); *see* Ariz. Ethics Op. 05-01 (2005) (lawyer referring current clients to lawyer's separate investment advisory business must meet "heavy burden" of complying with Rules 1.7 and 1.8; if business customer is former client, lawyer must comply with Rule 1.9's obligations regarding disclosure and adverse use of information relating to the former representation); Fla. Ethics Op. 02-8 (2004) (lawyer may refer client to lawyer's ancillary financial services business only if referral in client's best interests; "all activity related to the referral will be subject to the Rules Regulating the Florida Bar"); N.Y. State Ethics Op. 896 (2011) (law firm that performs lien searches for clients through wholly or partly owned business is subject to Rule 1.7(b) and must obtain client's informed consent even if business run separately); N.Y. State Ethics Op. 752 (2002) (lawyer may not serve as broker and lawyer in same transaction); N.C. Ethics Op. 2014-10 (2015) (lawyers who manage separate private adoption agency may refer clients to and accept referrals from agency, but must comply with Rules 1.7 and 1.8); N.C. Ethics Op. 2010-13 (2011) (lawyer providing financial services and products to law clients through separate business must comply with Rules 1.7 and 1.8); N.D. Ethics Op. 98-07 (1998) (lawyer who provides both legal and nonlegal services to same person "must take special care to heed" ethics rules relating to conflict of interest and confidentiality); Phila. Ethics Op. 2002-7 (2002) (lawyers providing ancillary mortgage and real estate brokerage services to clients of law firm must comply with conflict-of-interest rules); Utah Ethics Op. 17-07 (2017) (lawyer who refers client to separate real estate company that lawyer controls must comply with Rule 1.8(a)); Ronald D. Rotunda & John S. Dzienkowski, *Lawyer's Deskbook on Professional Responsibility* § 5.7-2(a) (2017–2018) (Rule 1.8(a) applies even if jurisdiction has not adopted Rule 5.7; "one can think of Rule 5.7 as an elaboration of the general principles found in Rule 1.8(a)"); *see also* Conn. Informal Ethics Op. 15-03 (2015) (lawyer serving as both lawyer and real estate agent for client in real estate transaction must comply with ethics rules relating to conflicts of interest, fees, and advertising). *See generally* Douglas R. Richmond, *Law Firm Ancillary Business . . . the Persistent Ethics and Liability Issues*, 23 Of Counsel, no. 12, at 12 (Dec. 2004); Robert Rubinson, *The Model Rules of Professional Conduct and Serving the Non-Legal Needs of Clients: Professional Regulation in a Time of Change*, 2008 J. Prof. Law. 119 (2008).

For discussion of a lawyer's ethical duties when engaging in a business transaction with a client, see the annotation to Rule 1.8.

## • *Nonclients*

Some ethics rules, notably Rule 8.4, apply to a lawyer's conduct outside the practice of law. Comment [2] to Rule 5.7 explains that "the conduct of a lawyer involved in the provision of law-related services is subject to those Rules that apply generally to lawyer conduct, regardless of whether the conduct involves the provision of legal services." *See* N.Y. State Ethics Op. 832 (2009) (Rule 8.4(c) prohibits deceptive advertising or solicitation of nonlegal services); Ohio Sup. Ct. Ethics Op. 2013-3 (2013) (use of judicial title by former judge engaged in law-related business violates

Rule 8.4(c) and (e) even though business distinct from law practice); *see also Att'y Grievance Comm'n v. Johnson*, 976 A.2d 245 (Md. 2009) (owner of title company and lawyer-settlement agent both engaged in fraudulent lease/buy-back arrangement); *Att'y Grievance Comm'n v. Bereano*, 744 A.2d 35 (Md. 2000) (mail fraud arising out of lobbying activities); *In re Pugh*, 710 N.W.2d 285 (Minn. 2006) (misappropriating over a million dollars from real estate closing company he owned); *Neb. ex rel. Counsel for Discipline v. Gilmour*, 674 N.W.2d 483 (Neb. 2004) (lawyer on inactive status working as bank officer personally accepted money from bank customer for whom "no additional bank services or any other services were provided"); *Disciplinary Counsel v. Carroll*, 831 N.E.2d 1000 (Ohio 2005) (submitting false timesheets while serving as executive director of state barber board); *In re Hurtgen*, 772 N.W.2d 923 (Wis. 2009) (revoking law license of director of investment bank convicted of aiding and abetting wire fraud). For further examples, see the annotation to Rule 8.4.

## Soliciting Business Customers

As to whether a lawyer who owns a separate law-related business may solicit legal business from business customers, see S.C. Ethics Op. 02-06 (n.d.) (lawyer who owns mortgage brokerage business may not solicit legal business from brokerage customers); Wis. Informal Ethics Op. IE-16-01 (2016) (lawyer who is part-owner of financial planning business may not offer to provide legal services to business customers). For a discussion of the ethical duties relating to the solicitation of clients, see the annotation to Rule 7.3.

## Rule 6.1

### Voluntary Pro Bono Publico Service

Every lawyer has a professional responsibility to provide legal services to those unable to pay. A lawyer should aspire to render at least (50) hours of pro bono publico legal services per year. In fulfilling this responsibility, the lawyer should:

(a) provide a substantial majority of the (50) hours of legal services without fee or expectation of fee to:

(1) persons of limited means; or

(2) charitable, religious, civic, community, governmental and educational organizations in matters that are designed primarily to address the needs of persons of limited means; and

(b) provide any additional services through:

(1) delivery of legal services at no fee or substantially reduced fee to individuals, groups or organizations seeking to secure or protect civil rights, civil liberties or public rights, or charitable, religious, civic, community, governmental and educational organizations in matters in furtherance of their organizational purposes, where the payment of standard legal fees would significantly deplete the organization's economic resources or would be otherwise inappropriate;

(2) delivery of legal services at a substantially reduced fee to persons of limited means; or

(3) participation in activities for improving the law, the legal system or the legal profession.

In addition, a lawyer should voluntarily contribute financial support to organizations that provide legal services to persons of limited means.

## COMMENT

[1] Every lawyer, regardless of professional prominence or professional work load, has a responsibility to provide legal services to those unable to pay, and personal involvement in the problems of the disadvantaged can be one of the most rewarding experiences in the life of a lawyer. The American Bar Association urges all lawyers to provide a minimum of 50 hours of pro bono services annually. States, however, may decide to choose a higher or lower number of hours of annual service (which may be expressed as a percentage of a lawyer's professional time) depending

upon local needs and local conditions. It is recognized that in some years a lawyer may render greater or fewer hours than the annual standard specified, but during the course of his or her legal career, each lawyer should render on average per year, the number of hours set forth in this Rule. Services can be performed in civil matters or in criminal or quasi-criminal matters for which there is no government obligation to provide funds for legal representation, such as post-conviction death penalty appeal cases.

[2] Paragraphs (a)(1) and (2) recognize the critical need for legal services that exists among persons of limited means by providing that a substantial majority of the legal services rendered annually to the disadvantaged be furnished without fee or expectation of fee. Legal services under these paragraphs consist of a full range of activities, including individual and class representation, the provision of legal advice, legislative lobbying, administrative rule making and the provision of free training or mentoring to those who represent persons of limited means. The variety of these activities should facilitate participation by government lawyers, even when restrictions exist on their engaging in the outside practice of law.

[3] Persons eligible for legal services under paragraphs (a)(1) and (2) are those who qualify for participation in programs funded by the Legal Services Corporation and those whose incomes and financial resources are slightly above the guidelines utilized by such programs but nevertheless, cannot afford counsel. Legal services can be rendered to individuals or to organizations such as homeless shelters, battered women's centers and food pantries that serve those of limited means. The term "governmental organizations" includes, but is not limited to, public protection programs and sections of governmental or public sector agencies.

[4] Because service must be provided without fee or expectation of fee, the intent of the lawyer to render free legal services is essential for the work performed to fall within the meaning of paragraphs (a)(1) and (2). Accordingly, services rendered cannot be considered pro bono if an anticipated fee is uncollected, but the award of statutory attorneys' fees in a case originally accepted as pro bono would not disqualify such services from inclusion under this section. Lawyers who do receive fees in such cases are encouraged to contribute an appropriate portion of such fees to organizations or projects that benefit persons of limited means.

[5] While it is possible for a lawyer to fulfill the annual responsibility to perform pro bono services exclusively through activities described in paragraphs (a)(1) and (2), to the extent that any hours of service remained unfulfilled, the remaining commitment can be met in a variety of ways as set forth in paragraph (b). Constitutional, statutory or regulatory restrictions may prohibit or impede government and public sector lawyers and judges from performing the pro bono services outlined in paragraphs (a)(1) and (2). Accordingly, where those restrictions apply, government and public sector lawyers and judges may fulfill their pro bono responsibility by performing services outlined in paragraph (b).

[6] Paragraph (b)(1) includes the provision of certain types of legal services to those whose incomes and financial resources place them above limited means. It also permits the pro bono lawyer to accept a substantially reduced fee for services. Examples of the types of issues that may be addressed under this paragraph include First

Amendment claims, Title VII claims and environmental protection claims. Additionally, a wide range of organizations may be represented, including social service, medical research, cultural and religious groups.

[7] Paragraph (b)(2) covers instances in which lawyers agree to and receive a modest fee for furnishing legal services to persons of limited means. Participation in judicare programs and acceptance of court appointments in which the fee is substantially below a lawyer's usual rate are encouraged under this section.

[8] Paragraph (b)(3) recognizes the value of lawyers engaging in activities that improve the law, the legal system or the legal profession. Serving on bar association committees, serving on boards of pro bono or legal services programs, taking part in Law Day activities, acting as a continuing legal education instructor, a mediator or an arbitrator and engaging in legislative lobbying to improve the law, the legal system or the profession are a few examples of the many activities that fall within this paragraph.

[9] Because the provision of pro bono services is a professional responsibility, it is the individual ethical commitment of each lawyer. Nevertheless, there may be times when it is not feasible for a lawyer to engage in pro bono services. At such times a lawyer may discharge the pro bono responsibility by providing financial support to organizations providing free legal services to persons of limited means. Such financial support should be reasonably equivalent to the value of the hours of service that would have otherwise been provided. In addition, at times it may be more feasible to satisfy the pro bono responsibility collectively, as by a firm's aggregate pro bono activities.

[10] Because the efforts of individual lawyers are not enough to meet the need for free legal services that exists among persons of limited means, the government and the profession have instituted additional programs to provide those services. Every lawyer should financially support such programs, in addition to either providing direct pro bono services or making financial contributions when pro bono service is not feasible.

[11] Law firms should act reasonably to enable and encourage all lawyers in the firm to provide the pro bono legal services called for by this Rule.

[12] The responsibility set forth in this Rule is not intended to be enforced through disciplinary process.

## Definitional Cross-References
"Substantial" *See* Rule 1.0(l)

## State Rules Comparison
http://ambar.org/MRPCStateCharts

# ANNOTATION
## NOT ENFORCEABLE THROUGH DISCIPLINE
Rule 6.1 declares that every lawyer has a professional responsibility to provide legal services to those unable to pay. However, the responsibility "is not intended to

be enforced through disciplinary process," according to Comment [12], and can be fulfilled in ways that do not involve providing any legal services to anyone.

In 1993, the ABA amended the rule to include a recommended "aspirational" minimum of fifty pro bono hours each year; individual jurisdictions are expected to make their own recommendations, according to Comment [1]. For detailed information about each state's version of Rule 6.1, including any recommended minimum hours and/or financial contributions, see https://www.americanbar.org/groups/ probono_public_service/policy/state_ethics_rules.html.

Over the years, there have been several unsuccessful efforts at the national and state levels to make pro bono service mandatory. *See* Leslie Boyle, Current Development, *Meeting the Demands of the Indigent Population: The Choice Between Mandatory and Voluntary Pro Bono Requirements*, 20 Geo. J. Legal Ethics 415 (Summer 2007); David J. Dreyer, *Culture, Structure, and Pro Bono Practice*, 33 J. Legal Prof. 185 (2009); Rima Sirota, *Making CLE Voluntary and Pro Bono Mandatory: A Law Faculty Test Case*, 78 La. L. Rev. 547 (Spring 2018).

Effective 2015, New York requires bar applicants to perform fifty hours of pro bono service. N.Y. Rules of Ct. App. for Admission of Attorneys and Counselors at Law § 520.16(a) (2014). The court rule defines pro bono far more expansively than does Rule 6.1, and recognizes legal work done for any nonprofit organization. *See* ABA Standing Comm. on Pro Bono & Pub. Serv., *New York's 50-Hour Preadmission Pro Bono Rule: Weighing the Potential Pros and Cons* (2013), *available at* https://www. americanbar.org/content/dam/aba/administrative/probono_public_service/ls _pb_preadmission_pro_bono_requirement_white_paper.authcheckdam.pdf. (rule's broad definition "could have the unintended effect of lessening the importance of traditional pro bono work, i.e., direct, uncompensated service to poor people and their communities"). *See generally* Justin Hansford, *Lippman's Law: Debating the Fifty-Hour Pro Bono Requirement for Bar Admission*, 41 Fordham Urb. L.J. 1141 (May 2014).

## • *2002 Amendments*

Amendments to Rule 6.1 in 2002 added a new Comment [11] calling on law firms to "act reasonably to enable and encourage" firm lawyers to do pro bono work. The comment addresses concerns about firm policies that might, for example, discourage lawyers from rendering pro bono services until they have achieved a certain number of billable hours. *See* Debra Lyn Bassett, *Redefining the "Public" Profession*, 36 Rutgers L.J. 721 (Spring 2005); Arthur T. Farrell, Current Development, *Public Interest Meets Public Ownership: Pro Bono and the Publicly Traded Law Firm*, 21 Geo. J. Legal Ethics 729 (Summer 2008); *see also* Barbara Graves-Poller, *Is Pro Bono Practice in Legal "Backwaters" Beyond the Scope of the Model Rules?*," 13 U. N.H. L. Rev. 1 (Spring 2015) (arguing that ethics rules provide inadequate guidance to private-sector lawyers offering pro bono legal services). The report on the Pro Bono Institute's 2017 Law Firm Pro Bono Challenge, available at http://www.probonoinst.org/wpps/wp-content/ uploads/2017-Challenge-Report.pdf, discusses variables such as billing parity for associates' pro bono time.

The 2002 amendments also added to the blackletter rule the declaration already contained in Comment [1] that it is every lawyer's responsibility "to provide legal services to those unable to pay." But no change was made to Rule 6.1(b)(3), which goes on to say that part of this responsibility may be fulfilled by "participation in activities for improving the law, the legal system or the legal profession" or, according to Comment [8], by serving on bar association committees, taking part in Law Day activities, or acting as a mediator, an arbitrator, or a continuing legal education instructor. Comments in some jurisdictions refine this even further. For example, Arizona's Comment [5] recognizes "activities in law-related education, both to the public and in training other lawyers; law enforcement personnel, or law-related personnel; speaking appearances where the topic is educational and is about the law or the legal system"). *See* Robert Granfield, *The Meaning of Pro Bono: Institutional Variations in Professional Obligations Among Lawyers,* 41 Law & Soc'y Rev. 113 (Mar. 2007); Leslie C. Levin, *Pro Bono Publico in a Parallel Universe: The Meaning of Pro Bono in Solo and Small Law Firms,* 37 Hofstra L. Rev. 699 (Spring 2009). *See generally* Scott L. Cummings, *The Politics of Pro Bono,* 52 U.C.L.A. L. Rev. 1 (Oct. 2004); Deborah L. Rhode, *Rethinking the Public in Lawyers' Public Service: Pro Bono, Strategic Philanthropy, and the Bottom Line,* 77 Fordham L. Rev. 1435 (Mar. 2009); Rebecca L. Sandefur, *Lawyers' Pro Bono Service and American-Style Civil Legal Assistance,* 41 Law & Soc'y Rev. 79 (Mar. 2007). For the Canadian perspective, see Lorne Sossin, *The Public Interest, Professionalism, and Pro Bono Public,* 46 Osgoode Hall L.J. 131 (Spring 2008) ("without elaborating on the meaning of publico, pro bono is adrift and rudderless").

The "substantial majority" of the hours devoted to fulfilling the responsibility should, however, be spent providing legal services at no fee or no expectation of fee to persons of limited means and organizations designed to address their needs, according to paragraph (a). *See* Ind. Rule 6.7(b)(1) (state's rule requiring lawyers to report pro bono work recognizes only legal services rendered free to persons of limited means; "activities for improving the law, the legal system or the legal profession" are, like services rendered at reduced fees to persons of limited means, considered pro bono services under Rule 6.1 but do not qualify as reportable).

Beginning in 2004, the ABA has published a number of empirical studies of pro bono participation by U.S. lawyers. *See* ABA Standing Comm. on Pro Bono & Pub. Serv., *Supporting Justice IV: A Report on the Pro Bono Work of America's Lawyers* (2018), *available at* https://www.americanbar.org/content/dam/aba/administrative/pro bono_public_service/ls_pb_supporting_justice_iv_final.authcheckdam.pdf. *See also* Scott L. Cummings & Rebecca L. Sandefur, *Beyond the Numbers: What We Know—and Should Know—About American Pro Bono,* 7 Harv. L. & Pol'y Rev. 83 (Winter 2013).

### • Government Lawyers

Comment [5] acknowledges that constitutional, statutory, and regulatory provisions may restrict judges, government lawyers, and lawyers in the public sector from engaging in private practice. The comment therefore permits them to fulfill their pro bono responsibilities "by performing services outlined in paragraph (b)." Presumably the reference is to paragraph (b)(3), as that is the only part of the rule that does not entail direct delivery of legal services.

Florida exempts government lawyers from Rule 6.1 altogether if the terms of their employment prohibit them from engaging in private practice. *Amendments to Rules Regulating Fla. Bar: Pro Bono Activities by Gov't Lawyers*, 841 So. 2d 443 (Fla. 2003).

Apart from the private practice issue, the government lawyer may not do pro bono work if it creates a conflict of interest. *See* N.D. Ethics Op. 09-02 (2009) (county court clerk may not represent child support defendants pro bono; official responsibilities would interfere with her independent professional judgment); Utah Ethics Op. 06-01 (2006) (assistant county attorney may do pro bono legal work for domestic violence victims seeking civil protective orders if his personal interest in his county employment does not materially limit the work, but may not participate in office's prosecution of perpetrator); *see also* N.C. Ethics Op. 2014-3 (2014) (encouraging government agencies and public sector offices to adopt pro bono policies specifying types of services to be performed, treatment of conflicts, use of employer's resources such as support staff and office equipment, and whether services may be provided during working hours). *See generally* John C. Cruden, *Promoting Pro Bono Service by Government Attorneys*, 53 Fed. Law. 30 (Nov./Dec. 2006) (restrictions on federally employed lawyers fall into four basic categories: conflicts of interest, acting in individual capacity, use of official time, and use of official resources); Peggy Love, *Ethics and Professional Conduct for Federal Government Attorneys*, 25 Nat. Resources & Env't 40 (Winter 2011) (to avoid criminal penalties under 18 U.S.C. § 205, federal employee may be able to give nonrepresentational assistance to people seeking government benefits; must also comply with Standards of Conduct at 5 C.F.R. Part 2635).

### • *Buyout Option*

Comment [9] provides that when it is "not feasible" to engage in pro bono services, lawyers may discharge their pro bono obligations by contributing money to organizations that give free legal representation to the poor. The District of Columbia, home to a large proportion of government lawyers, moves the buyout option into the black letter of the rule.

### REPORTING REQUIREMENT

Several jurisdictions require lawyers to report their voluntary pro bono activities. *See Att'y Grievance Comm'n v. Brady*, 30 A.3d 902 (Md. 2011) (noting respondent decertified by court of appeals for failure to file pro bono report). For a chart showing which jurisdictions require reporting, see https://www.americanbar.org/groups/probono_public_service/.

In *Schwarz v. Kogan*, 132 F.3d 1387 (11th Cir. 1998), a suit for declaratory and injunctive relief, the court rejected the argument that Florida's reporting requirement itself is designed to be unfairly coercive. *See generally* Leslie Boyle, Current Development, *Meeting the Demands of the Indigent Population: The Choice Between Mandatory and Voluntary Pro Bono Requirements*, 20 Geo. J. Legal Ethics 415 (Summer 2007) (mandatory reporting is most effective and efficient way to increase pro bono service hours); Kellie Isbell & Sarah Sawle, Current Development, *Pro Bono Publico: Voluntary Service and Mandatory Reporting*, 15 Geo. J. Legal Ethics 845 (Summer 2002); Donald R. Lundberg, *Pro Bono and Pro Bono Reporting*, 58 Res Gestae 10 (Oct. 2014) (confidentiality provision in state's rule would probably exempt pro bono reports from disclosure under public records law).

## PRO BONO AS A MITIGATOR, A SANCTION, OR A COMPONENT OF CLE

In addition to being a professional responsibility, the rendering of pro bono legal services has been invoked as a mitigator, a sanction, and a way to satisfy continuing legal education requirements.

### • *Mitigation*

Although pro bono work is not one of the mitigating factors listed in the ABA Standards for Imposing Lawyer Sanctions, it has been considered in mitigation of discipline in some jurisdictions, at least when "serious" misconduct is not involved. *See, e.g., People v. Maynard*, 219 P.3d 430 (Colo. O.P.D.J. 2008); *In re Parshall*, 878 A.2d 1253 (D.C. 2005); *Iowa Supreme Court Att'y Disciplinary Bd. v. Barnhill*, 847 N.W.2d 466 (Iowa 2014); *In re Princivil*, 991 N.Y.S.2d 338 (App. Div. 2014); *Cleveland Metro. Bar Ass'n v. Berk*, 969 N.E.2d 256 (Ohio 2012). *But see In re Vanderslice*, 116 A.3d 1244 (Del. 2015) (lawyer's considerable pro bono work did not mitigate misconduct or warrant reduced sanction "in light of his cumulative pattern of dishonesty"); *In re Doherty*, 650 A.2d 522 (Vt. 1994) (refusing to consider rendering legal services pro bono as mitigating factor because it is not one under ABA Standards).

### • *Sanction*

Lawyers have been ordered to render pro bono services as a sanction for misconduct. *See, e.g., In re Saxton*, 91 A.3d 348 (R.I. 2014) (requiring respondent, a Georgia lawyer who violated Rhode Island's solicitation rules, to provide legal services to twelve Georgia residents referred to him from county bar association and county legal aid; Rhode Island's disciplinary rules explicitly authorize pro bono and community service as sanctions); *Hughes v. Bd. of Prof'l Responsibility*, 259 S.W.3d 631 (Tenn. 2008); *Lawyer Disciplinary Bd. v. Nace*, 753 S.E.2d 618 (W. Va. 2013) (suspension plus fifty hours of pro bono service); *see also Reinhardt v. Gulf Ins. Co.*, 489 F.3d 405 (1st Cir. 2007) (pro bono service as sanction for violating Federal Rule of Civil Procedure 11); *Ricoh Co. v. Asustek Computer Inc.*, No. 06-C-0462-C, 2007 WL 5462420, 2007 BL 36486 (W.D. Wis. June 15, 2007) (court offered to rescind its order revoking pro hac vice admission as sanction for discovery misconduct if lawyer would agree to take prisoner case pro bono). *Contra Fla. Bar v. Herman*, 8 So. 3d 1100 (Fla. 2009) (state's rules do not allow for provision of pro bono legal services as disciplinary sanction); *cf. In re Knopp*, 384 P.3d 428 (Kan. 2016) (as condition of probation, lawyer prohibited from providing pro bono services without prior approval of practice supervisor after thorough discussion of means of handling client matter); *In re Braecklein*, No. 66015, 2014 WL 5454838, 2014 BL302428 (Nev. Oct. 24, 2014) (because performing pro bono services is ethical duty, "it is inappropriate to prohibit the performance of pro-bono services as a disciplinary condition").

• *CLE*

Some jurisdictions permit lawyers to earn part of their continuing legal education credits by taking pro bono cases. *See* https://www.americanbar.org/groups/probono_public_service/policy/cle_rules.html; *see also* American Bar Association, *Essential Qualities of the Professional Lawyer* 212 (2013) (pro bono work may help new lawyers satisfy their states' certification requirements).

## Rule 6.2

### *Accepting Appointments*

A lawyer shall not seek to avoid appointment by a tribunal to represent a person except for good cause, such as:

(a) representing the client is likely to result in violation of the Rules of Professional Conduct or other law;

(b) representing the client is likely to result in an unreasonable financial burden on the lawyer; or

(c) the client or the cause is so repugnant to the lawyer as to be likely to impair the client-lawyer relationship or the lawyer's ability to represent the client.

## COMMENT

[1] A lawyer ordinarily is not obliged to accept a client whose character or cause the lawyer regards as repugnant. The lawyer's freedom to select clients is, however, qualified. All lawyers have a responsibility to assist in providing pro bono publico service. See Rule 6.1. An individual lawyer fulfills this responsibility by accepting a fair share of unpopular matters or indigent or unpopular clients. A lawyer may also be subject to appointment by a court to serve unpopular clients or persons unable to afford legal services.

### *Appointed Counsel*

[2] For good cause a lawyer may seek to decline an appointment to represent a person who cannot afford to retain counsel or whose cause is unpopular. Good cause exists if the lawyer could not handle the matter competently, see Rule 1.1, or if undertaking the representation would result in an improper conflict of interest, for example, when the client or the cause is so repugnant to the lawyer as to be likely to impair the client-lawyer relationship or the lawyer's ability to represent the client. A lawyer may also seek to decline an appointment if acceptance would be unreasonably burdensome, for example, when it would impose a financial sacrifice so great as to be unjust.

[3] An appointed lawyer has the same obligations to the client as retained counsel, including the obligations of loyalty and confidentiality, and is subject to the same limitations on the client-lawyer relationship, such as the obligation to refrain from assisting the client in violation of the Rules.

**Definitional Cross-References**

"Tribunal" *See* Rule 1.0(m)

**State Rules Comparison**

http://ambar.org/MRPCStateCharts

# ANNOTATION

## OVERVIEW

Because of the logistics of court appointment, "seeking to avoid" court appointment within the meaning of Rule 6.2 usually means moving to withdraw upon learning of one's appointment. If the motion is made well into the representation, the analysis is likely to turn on Rule 1.16 rather than Rule 6.2.

### • *Court's Power to Appoint*

A court's power to appoint counsel is codified in many federal and state statutes, but it is fundamentally a matter of inherent judicial authority. *See United States v. Burk*, No. EP-14-CR-240-DCG, 2014 WL 2800759, 2014 BL 389629 (W.D. Tex. June 18, 2014) (court would exercise inherent authority to appoint counsel for insolvent corporate criminal co-defendant; court rule prohibited corporations from appearing pro se, but neither Sixth Amendment nor Criminal Justice Act supplied authority for court-appointed counsel); *see also Naranjo v. Thompson*, 809 F.3d 793 (5th Cir. 2015) (courts have inherent power to compel lawyers to accept uncompensated appointment in limited circumstances).

The power to appoint counsel is most frequently exercised in criminal trials. *See Montejo v. Louisiana*, 556 U.S. 778 (2009) (in half the states, criminal defense counsel is automatically appointed upon a finding of indigency). But appointment is designed to protect institutional interests that go beyond the rights of a particular criminal defendant; this is why even if a defendant asserts his right of self-representation under *Faretta v. California*, 422 U.S. 806 (1975), counsel can still be appointed for him over his objection. *See Martinez v. Court of Appeal of Cal.*, 528 U.S. 152 (2000) ("the government's interest in ensuring the integrity and efficiency of the trial at times outweighs the defendant's interest in acting as his own lawyer"); *see also United States v. Bertoli*, 994 F.2d 1002 (3d Cir. 1993) (notwithstanding law firm's discharge by nonindigent criminal defendant, court ordered it to remain as unpaid standby counsel "in order to further the efficient processing and disposition of [the court's] caseload").

The protection of systemic interests has occasionally warranted appointment of counsel in civil cases even in the absence of specific statutory authorization. *See Bothwell v. Republic Tobacco Co.*, 912 F. Supp. 1221 (D. Neb. 1995) (appointment necessary "to protect the integrity and proper functioning of the judicial branch"); *In re Amendments to Rules Regulating Fla. Bar*, 573 So. 2d 800 (Fla. 1990) (discussing rationales); *see also Evans v. Kuplinski*, 713 F. App'x 167 (4th Cir. 2017) (indigent plaintiff asserting §1983 claim entitled to appointed counsel if exceptional circumstances exist); *Naranjo v. Thompson*, 809 F.3d 793 (5th Cir. 2015) (same).

## • When Defendant Rejects Appointed Counsel

A criminal defendant who rejects competent, conflict-free appointed counsel may be said to have chosen to proceed pro se, according to *United States v. Garey*, 540 F.3d 1253 (11th Cir. 2008) (appointed counsel "caught between a rock and a hard place" by uncooperative and obstructionist client can ask court to find waiver of Sixth Amendment rights and either discharge lawyer as counsel or appoint lawyer as standby counsel). When this happens, the court may appoint standby counsel to protect the proceedings and at the same time protect the defendant's right to represent himself. *McKaskie v. Wiggins*, 465 U.S. 168 (1984) (standby counsel must not interfere with self-representing defendant's control or appearance of control over his defense); *see United States v. Morris*, No. 2:06CR218-MHT, 2009 WL 1109358, 2009 BL 86436 (M.D. Ala. Apr. 23, 2009) (defendant who refused to accept his court-appointed lawyer and refused to represent himself thereby waived his right to counsel; court discharged counsel but appointed him as standby counsel). *See generally* H. Patrick Furman, *Pro Se Defendants and the Appointment of Advisory Counsel*, 35 Colo. Law. 29 (Dec. 2006) (explaining roles of advisory counsel, standby counsel, and hybrid counsel).

According to ABA Formal Opinion 07-448 ("Appointed Counsel's Relationship to a Person Who Declines to Be Represented"), there can be no lawyer-client relationship if the would-be client does not accept the representation: "[T]he defendant's desire to proceed without a lawyer's assistance makes it impossible for the lawyer to provide, or to participate in, a true 'representation.' . . . Any legal obligation owed by the lawyer to the defendant, which may be analogous to those embodied in the ethics rules, arises from the authority of the appointing tribunal and includes whatever obligations the tribunal may identify. The lawyer's ethical duties are limited to complying with the rules defining a lawyer's obligations to persons other than a client." ABA Formal Ethics Op. 07-448 (2007).

In a rare decision construing this opinion, the court found that a criminal defendant who refused to meet with his appointed counsel and repeatedly "fired" her was not in a lawyer-client relationship with her. Therefore, counsel was "not ethically obligated to follow the Oregon Rules of Professional Conduct governing the attorney-client relationship"; however, she was still "obligated to defend Mr. Davis as previously ordered by the court." *United States v. Davis*, No. 3:12-cr-00109-SI, 2013 WL 796655, 2013 BL 55560 (D. Or. Mar. 4, 2013). *See United States v. Barton*, 712 F.3d 111 (2d Cir. 2013) (denial of motion to withdraw was abuse of discretion; district court may not "foist an unwilling attorney upon an unwilling defendant, who has actively refused the appointment of counsel and declined to demonstrate his financial eligibility under the [Criminal Justice Act]"); Iowa Ethics Op. 05-07 (2006) (in civil case, military lawyer appointed by military commission for defendant who expressly declines representation and asserts right to represent himself, though tribunal's rules do not permit self-representation, must "act in accordance with the rules of the tribunal and accept the representation" anyway).

According to the same ABA opinion, if a lawyer is appointed as standby counsel, then no lawyer-client relationship exists unless and until the defendant seeks counsel's help. ABA Formal Ethics Op. 07-448 (2007); *see* N.Y. State Ethics Op. 949 (2012) (if court appoints counsel to stand on sidelines, pro se is to be treated as prospective client under Rule 1.18; otherwise relationship should be treated as limited-scope representation under Rule 1.2(c)); *see also* N.H. Ethics Op. 2015-16/09 (2016) (standby counsel has lawyer-client relationship with client, but ethical duties differ; counsel should seek instructions from court); Anne Bowen Poulin, *Ethical Guidance for Standby Counsel in Criminal Cases: A Far Cry from Counsel?*, 50 Am. Crim. L. Rev. 211 (Winter 2013) (finding ABA position "problematic" and preferring *Restatement (Third) of the Law Governing Lawyers'* position that standby counsel "should be viewed as having at least some limited lawyer-client relationship from the moment of appointment").

## CHALLENGES TO APPOINTMENTS

### • *Due Process and Equal Protection*

Lawyers have successfully challenged many aspects of court appointments on due process and equal protection grounds. *See DeLisio v. Alaska Supreme Court*, 740 P.2d 437 (Alaska 1987) (requiring private lawyer to represent indigent criminal defendant without pay is a taking); *Arnold v. Kemp*, 813 S.W.2d 770 (Ark. 1991) (appointment system based upon lawyer's residence address violates equal protection); *Cunningham v. Superior Court*, 222 Cal. Rptr. 854 (Ct. App. 1986) (requiring lawyers as a class to underwrite protection of indigents' constitutional rights violates equal protection); *State ex rel. Stephan v. Smith*, 747 P.2d 816 (Kan. 1987) (lawyer's services are property; Fifth Amendment violated if appointment creates "genuine and substantial" interference with lawyer's private practice); *Lavalee v. Justices in Hampden Superior Court*, 812 N.E.2d 895 (Mass. 2004) (community at large, as beneficiary of police power underlying criminal justice system, must shoulder cost of indigent defense); *State ex rel. Mo. Pub. Defender Comm'n v. Pratte*, 298 S.W.3d 870 (Mo. 2009) (state's prerogative to dictate how lawyer discharges professional obligation is limited by prohibition on deprivation of property without due process); *State v. Lynch*, 796 P.2d 1150 (Okla. 1990) (appointment without adequate and speedy compensation and no opportunity to contest it violates due process clause of state constitution; appointment system based upon population of county in which lawyer practices violates equal protection); *Jewell v. Maynard*, 383 S.E.2d 536 (W. Va. 1989) (taking occurs if lawyer cannot make decent living due to appointments; no lawyer should be required to expend more than 10 percent of normal work year on appointed cases). *But see Scheehle v. Justices of Supreme Court*, 508 F.3d 887 (9th Cir. 2007) (after state supreme court, in *Scheehle v. Justices of Supreme Court*, 120 P.3d 1092 (Ariz. 2005), and in answer to certified question, upheld rule requiring superior courts to maintain lists of lawyers subject to appointment as arbitrators for up to two days per year with minimal compensation, federal court concluded appointment system not a regulatory taking requiring compensation under Fifth Amendment), *discussed in* Tracy Le, Case Note, Scheehle v. Justices of the Supreme Court: *The Arizona Supreme Court's Right to Compel Attorneys to Serve as Arbitrators*, 48 Ariz. L. Rev. 413 (Summer 2006); *State v. Sells*, No. 2005-CA-37, 2006 WL 2795340 (Ohio Ct. App. Sept. 29, 2006) (when lawyers voluntarily accepted appointment, $20,000 cap on compensation could not be deemed a "taking" even though they worked on case for almost 800 hours). *See generally* Jerry L. Anderson,

*The Constitutionality of Uncompensated Conscription*, 3 Geo. J. Legal Ethics 503 (Winter 1990) (twenty-one states have some authority limiting or rejecting uncompensated or undercompensated service).

### • Thirteenth Amendment

Challenges based upon the Thirteenth Amendment prohibition against involuntary servitude have not been successful. *See, e.g., Family Div. Trial Lawyers v. Moultrie,* 725 F.2d 695 (D.C. Cir. 1984) (no "involuntary servitude" involved); *Williamson v. Vardeman,* 674 F.2d 1211 (8th Cir. 1982) (Thirteenth Amendment does not forbid compulsion of traditional modes of public service); *In re Amendments to Rules,* 573 So. 2d 800 (Fla. 1990) (no Thirteenth Amendment problem if no deprivation of freedom).

### • Sixth Amendment

In criminal cases, lawyers have asserted the indigent defendant's Sixth Amendment right to effective assistance of counsel as a basis for challenging appointment systems and fee schedules, with mixed results. *See Zarabia v. Bradshaw,* 912 P.2d 5 (Ariz. 1996) (random appointment system that results in civil transactional lawyers being appointed to represent defendants charged with serious crimes is likely to violate defendants' rights); *Pub. Defender, Eleventh Judicial Circuit of Fla. v. State,* 115 So. 3d 261 (Fla. 2013) (statute providing that "[i]n no case shall the court approve a withdrawal by the public defender . . . based solely on the inadequacy of funding or excess workload" was facially constitutional but should not be applied to withdrawal motion alleging caseload or underfunding would result in ineffective representation of indigent defendants); *Maas v. Olive,* 992 So. 2d 196 (Fla. 2008) (statutory cap would be unconstitutional if applied to limit court's authority to protect defendant's right to counsel; therefore court must have authority to award fees in excess of statutory cap in extraordinary circumstances); *Sheppard & White, P.A. v. City of Jacksonville,* 827 So. 2d 925 (Fla. 2002) (evidence that court-appointed counsel in capital case could not cover his overhead if paid at statutory rate did not implicate defendant's right to effective assistance); *State v. Young,* 172 P.3d 138 (N.M. 2007) (compensation that would not cover appointed counsel's overhead violated defendant's Sixth Amendment rights; withdrawal not allowed, but prosecution stayed until state made adequate defense funds available); *see also State v. Lewis,* 33 So. 3d 1046 (La. Ct. App. 2010) (counsel must be appointed regardless of funding availability but court can, upon defense motion, halt prosecution until adequate funding provided); *N.Y. Cnty. Lawyers' Ass'n v. State,* 742 N.Y.S.2d 16 (App. Div. 2002) (lawyers' association had standing to argue statutory caps on fees for assigned counsel in criminal and family law cases created possibility of violating clients' rights; claim that lawyers felt pressured by judges to accept cases they could not handle adequately alleged injury-in-fact); *Flora v. Luzerne County,* 103 A.3d 125 (Pa. Commw. Ct. 2014) (rejecting claim based upon prospective constructive denial of right to counsel due to inadequate funding of public defender's office). *See generally* Christopher D. Aulepp, *Enslaving Paul by Freeing Peter: The Dilemma of Protecting Counsel's Constitutional Rights While Providing Indigent Defendants with Effective Assistance of Counsel,* 78 UMKC L. Rev. 291 (Fall 2009); Margaret A. Costello, *Fulfilling the Unfulfilled Promise of Gideon: Litigation as a*

*Viable Strategic Tool*, 99 Iowa L. Rev. 1951 (July 2014); Bruce A. Green, *Criminal Neglect: Indigent Defense from a Legal Ethics Perspective*, 52 Emory L.J. 1169 (2003).

## • *Separation of Powers*

On the separation-of-powers issue presented by inadequately funded indigent-defense systems, see *Lavalee v. Justices in Hampden Superior Court*, 812 N.E.2d 895 (Mass. 2004) (court could not authorize compensation beyond rates set by legislature nor could it order state to provide funding; instead, court would require dismissal without prejudice whenever court-appointed counsel does not file appearance within forty-five days of arraignment); *State ex rel. Mo. Pub. Defender Comm'n v. Pratte*, 298 S.W.3d 870 (Mo. 2009) (payment is "troubling question" that "lurks" behind application of only coercive remedy trial judges possess—the appointment power); *State v. Young*, 172 P.3d 138 (N.M. 2007) (as "guardians of the constitution," court would stay death penalty prosecutions until state made adequate funds available for court-appointed counsel); *Hurrell-Harring v. State*, 930 N.E.2d 217 (N.Y. 2010) (reinstating class action by indigent criminal defendants challenging indigent-defense system; fact that relief might require "re-ordering of legislative priorities" not grounds for dismissal); and *State v. Perala*, 130 P.3d 852 (Wash. Ct. App. 2006) ("courts *must* award an amount that will allow for the financial survival of [counsel's] practice, and the county is required to pay a reasonable amount for those services when they are not donated"). *See also* Adam M. Gershowitz, *The Invisible Pillar of Gideon*, 80 Ind. L.J. 571 (Summer 2005); Norman Lefstein, *In Search of Gideon's Promise: Lessons from England and the Need for Federal Help*, 55 Hastings L.J. 835, 929 n.66 (Mar. 2004). *See generally* Cara H. Drinan, *The Third Generation of Indigent Defense Litigation*, 33 N.Y.U. Rev. L. & Soc. Change 427 (2009); Martin Guggenheim, *The People's Right to a Well-Funded Indigent Defender System*, 36 N.Y.U. Rev. L. & Soc. Change 395 (2012) (arguing for reinvigorated separation-of-powers challenge based upon wrongful interference with judicial function).

## • *Non-Constitutional Objections*

Appointment of counsel can distort the relationship between bar and bench. In one case, the court denied an inmate's second request for appointment of counsel in his civil rights case and instead "invited" him to "shop his case to private lawyers"; the incentive for taking a civil rights case should come from the prospect of a fee award under 42 U.S.C. § 1988 and not from "professional compulsion," the court reasoned. *Williams v. Grant*, 639 F. Supp. 2d 1377 (S.D. Ga. 2009). "Consider a lawyer's reaction to [a judge's request]. Reminding himself that he has other cases before that judge, he might wonder what happens if he declines the request, especially if he has been asked and similarly declined in the past." *Id.* at 1381 & n.5; *see also Ashcroft v. Dep't of Corr.*, No. 05CV488, 2008 WL 4367540, 2008 BL 210400 (W.D.N.Y. Sept. 18, 2008) (granting second appointed counsel's motion to withdraw from representing abusive inmate plaintiff in civil rights action and noting "cost to the Court in expended good will with the bar"—even while appointing third lawyer); *Reese v. Owens-Corning Fiberglas*, 962 F. Supp. 1418 (D. Kan. 1997) (relieving counsel of appointment but suggesting he "seriously consider whether he should file civil cases in this court in the future"); Kenneth P. Troccoli, *Control Over the Defense: Represent-*

*ing Zacarias Moussaoui*, 33 Champion, Dec. 2009, at 30 n.153 ("most court-appointed lawyers rightly believe that it is imprudent to decline a request from the court to accept a case no matter how difficult the client or the case may be"); *cf* Tex. Ethics Op. 612 (2011) (lawyer may participate in bar association program excusing him from appointment to represent indigents in certain family court matters upon payment of annual fee that supplements county's payments to court-appointed lawyers).

## "GOOD CAUSE"

### *Paragraph (a): Violation of Ethics Rule or Other Law*

Lack of expertise or experience in a particular subject area is the basis upon which relief from appointment is most often sought.

A lawyer arguing that a particular appointment is beyond his abilities may be required to make a "showing of incompetence" before the court will grant a motion to withdraw. Even then, the court may decide the lawyer is capable of becoming competent, or may tell the lawyer to "affiliate" with other counsel. *Cunningham v. Sommerville*, 388 S.E.2d 301 (W. Va. 1989) (even if lawyer shows inability to become competent within reasonable time, court may choose to appoint more experienced lawyer as co-counsel); *see also Reese v. Owens-Corning Fiberglas*, 962 F. Supp. 1418 (D. Kan. 1997) (court first appointed mentor for sole practitioner objecting to appointment to represent indigent Title VII plaintiff but eventually removed him altogether in harshly worded opinion); *DeLisio v. Alaska Supreme Court*, 740 P.2d 437 (Alaska 1987) (although lawyer had not practiced criminal law in fifteen years, his assertion that he could not provide adequate representation was "disingenuous"); *Stern v. Cnty. Court*, 773 P.2d 1074 (Colo. 1989) (although lawyer had not voluntarily represented a criminal defendant in eleven years, court believed he could become competent); *In re Murray*, 47 A.3d 972 (Del. 2012) (lawyer who was not permitted to withdraw from appointments in three family court cases for which he believed he lacked necessary skills could have sought substitute counsel but persistently "attempted to throw the burden back on the Court").

Excessive workloads can make it impossible for criminal defense lawyers to represent their clients competently and diligently. *See State ex rel. Mo. Pub. Defender Comm'n v. Waters*, 370 S.W.3d 593 (Mo. 2012) (ethics rules "run parallel" to judge's duty to protect Sixth Amendment rights; trial court exceeded its authority by appointing public defender that had, pursuant to administrative rule, declared itself of limited availability due to excessive caseloads); *see also State v. Singleton*, 216 So. 3d 985 (La. Ct. App. 2016) (lawyer heading public defender's office had good cause to avoid appointment as pro bono counsel in personal capacity; appointment would violate terms of employment contract and, because office was facing increasing caseloads and shrinking budget, "would likely violate several ethics rules, and perhaps even his constitutional duties as counselor").

According to ABA Formal Opinion 06-441, which treats appointed counsel in pari materia with public defenders, a lawyer "must not accept new cases" if it would make it impossible to represent existing clients competently; the opinion suggests the lawyer ask her supervisor to transfer some of her cases to another lawyer and, if the supervisor's resolution of the problem is not "reasonable," the lawyer must take further action, such as going over the supervisor's head to a governing board (opinion footnotes "reporting up" obligation Rule 1.13 imposes on corporate lawyers encountering constituent wrongdoing), or moving to withdraw from cases until her workload is manageable. ABA Formal Ethics Op. 06-441 (2006). *See* Heather Baxter, *Too Many Clients, Too Little Time: How States Are Forcing Public Defenders to Violate Their Ethical Obligations*, 25 Fed. Sent'g Rep. 91 (Dec. 2012) (ABA solutions are "unrealistic and ineffective"; opinion "did nothing to help the ethical quagmires of public defenders"). *Compare* John P. Gross, *Case Refusal: A Right for the Public Defender but Not a Remedy for the Defendant*, 95 Wash. U. L. Rev. 253 (2017), *with* Stephen F. Hanlon, *Case Refusal: A Duty for a Public Defender and a Remedy for All of a Public Defender's Clients*, 51 Ind. L. Rev. 59 (2018). *See generally* Heidi Reamer Anderson, *Funding Gideon's Promise by Viewing Excessive Caseloads as Unethical Conflicts of Interest*, 39 Hastings Const. L.Q. 421 (Winter 2012); Bennett H. Brummer, *The Banality of Excessive Defender Workload: Managing the Systemic Obstruction of Justice*, 22 St. Thomas L. Rev. 104 (Fall 2009); Jessica Trieu, Current Development, *The Federal Budget Crisis and Its Unintended Ethical Consequences: How Will Judges, Prosecutors, and Public Defenders Meet Their Ethical Obligations?*, 27 Geo. J. Legal Ethics 917 (Summer 2014).

### *Paragraph (b): Unreasonable Financial Burden*

Rule 6.2(b) uses the same "unreasonable financial burden" test as Rule 1.16, the general rule on seeking to withdraw from a representation. *See Synergy Assocs., Inc. v. Sun Biotechnologies, Inc.*, 350 F.3d 681 (7th Cir. 2003) (trial judge allowed lawyer who was owed more than $93,000 in fees and costs to withdraw as retained counsel for defendant in commercial dispute, but appointed him three weeks later to represent same defendant on pro bono basis; appellate court reversed: "[a]ppointment under that circumstance would override the legitimate reasons for withdrawal as retained counsel in the first place"); *Hagopian v. Justice Admin. Comm'n*, 18 So. 3d 625 (Fla. Dist. Ct. App. 2009) (quashing order appointing counsel for indigent defendant in complex RICO case when "extraordinary time and effort" required—"together with the minimal and uncertain compensation offered"—threatened to ruin lawyer's solo practice); *State v. Perala*, 130 P.3d 852 (Wash. Ct. App. 2006) ("established tradition" notwithstanding, "present economic circumstances may make this obligation an unreasonable burden"); *Cunningham v. Sommerville*, 388 S.E.2d 301 (W. Va. 1989) (granting writ of prohibition against appointment of corporation's general counsel to represent indigent criminal defendant; corporate employer owned and had access to lawyer's office equipment and computer, corporate policy prohibited outside employment, and lawyer had no malpractice coverage for outside work); *cf. Cooper v. Reg'l Admin. Judge of Dist. Court for Region V*, 854 N.E.2d 966 (Mass. 2006) (lawyer's failure to seek relief under Rule 6.2's "good cause" exception required dismissal of her challenge to statutory compensation rate). *But see Hanson v. Morton*, 67 A.3d 437 (Del. 2013) (in-house counsel's lack of malpractice insurance not good cause to withdraw from court-appointed representation of indigent parent in child dependency and neglect proceeding; any malpractice claim "will be subject to dismissal based upon the qualified immunity under the Tort Claims Act").

## *Paragraph (c): Repugnance*

When it is not the money but the lawyer's aversion to the case or client that is the basis for withdrawal, the quantum of "repugnance" required to meet the good-cause test is higher for appointed counsel than for retained counsel.

Rule 1.16(b)(4) states the general rule: A lawyer may withdraw from a representation if "the client insists upon taking action that the lawyer considers repugnant or with which the lawyer has a fundamental disagreement." The more specific provision in Rule 6.2(c) for court appointments raises the threshold to "the client or the cause is so repugnant to the lawyer as to be likely to impair" the representation. Both formulations, however, take the lawyer's feelings more seriously than did the predecessor Model Code, which specified in EC 2-29 that repugnance does not constitute a compelling reason to seek to be excused from a court appointment. *See United States v. O'Connor*, 650 F.3d 839 (2d Cir. 2011) (defendant not deprived of fair trial by denial of appointed counsel's motion to withdraw based upon his revulsion when confronted on eve of trial with DNA evidence implicating his client in child sex abuse and prostitution; applying EC 2-29).

## WHEN MOTION NOT GRANTED

Rule 1.16(c) fits in with Rule 6.2 by providing that if a tribunal orders a lawyer to continue representing someone, the lawyer must obey "notwithstanding good cause for terminating the representation." *See Hawkins v. Comm'n for Lawyer Discipline*, 988 S.W.2d 927 (Tex. App. 1999) (Rule 1.16(c) specifically prohibits disobeying court order to continue representing someone and therefore takes precedence over Rule 3.4(c), which more generally provides that open disobedience of ruling whose validity is challenged does not constitute misconduct); *see also In re Kleinsmith*, 124 P.3d 579 (N.M. Ct. App. 2005) (affirming finding of criminal contempt and $500 fine against lawyer appointed to represent disabled child; although lawyer faxed letter to court explaining his vacation was scheduled the following day and he was booked solid until then, lawyer remained bound by order until otherwise notified, and could still have interviewed child by telephone).

## DISCIPLINARY CONSEQUENCES OF DISOBEYING

Although the obligation to accept the court's appointment is usually enforced by the judge making the appointment rather than through the disciplinary process, lawyers have been disciplined for refusing to proceed with a representation after losing the motion to withdraw. *See In re State Bar v. Gregan*, No. 06-0946, 2007 WL 5869712 (Ariz. Sup. Ct. Disciplinary Comm'n Nov. 20, 2007) (censure and probation following civil contempt for refusing to serve as appointed arbitrator in civil case); *Fla. Bar v. Rubin*, 549 So. 2d 1000 (Fla. 1989) (reprimand following thirty-day jail sentence for contempt); *Hawkins v. Comm'n for Lawyer Discipline*, 988 S.W.2d 927 (Tex. App. 1999) (suspension following refusal to comply with judge's order to continue with appointed representation; among terms of additional period of probated suspension was requirement that lawyer provide fifteen hours per month of pro bono services to indigents referred to him by county bar association). *But see* N.C. Ethics Op. RPC

199 (1995) (if lawyer unsuccessfully challenges appointment and still believes, "as a matter of professional responsibility," that he is not competent, it is "not unethical for [the lawyer] to refuse to serve and to accept the court's sanction").

## DISCIPLINARY CONSEQUENCES OF OBEYING

On the possible disciplinary consequences of *complying* with an order of appointment the lawyer believes will entail violation of the ethics rules, see *Burke v. Lewis*, 122 P.3d 533 (Utah 2005) ("Where an appointment raises ethical concerns, . . . we hold that good-faith compliance with an appointment order provides lawyers with a safe harbor in which they can be free from exposure to disciplinary action."); *In re S.C.*, 88 A.3d 1220 (Vt. 2014) (appointed counsel's concern that presenting unsupported argument at client's insistence instead of filing *Anders* brief would expose him to disciplinary charges "may be sufficiently assuaged by noting that even an arguably frivolous claim will not be deemed to violate Rule 3.1 where, as here, a court categorically refuses to grant motions to withdraw in deference to overriding state interests"); and Fla. Ethics Op. 81-9 (1982) ("it is the opinion of the Committee that a court-appointed attorney who, at the insistence of his client and in accordance with the procedure set forth by the United States Supreme Court [in *Anders v. California*, 386 U.S. 738 (1967),] commences a [meritless] appeal . . . may not thereafter be said to have acted unethically in commencing the appeal").

## Rule 6.3

### *Membership in Legal Services Organization*

A lawyer may serve as a director, officer or member of a legal services organization, apart from the law firm in which the lawyer practices, notwithstanding that the organization serves persons having interests adverse to a client of the lawyer. The lawyer shall not knowingly participate in a decision or action of the organization:

(a) if participating in the decision or action would be incompatible with the lawyer's obligations to a client under Rule 1.7; or

(b) where the decision or action could have a material adverse effect on the representation of a client of the organization whose interests are adverse to a client of the lawyer.

## COMMENT

[1] Lawyers should be encouraged to support and participate in legal service organizations. A lawyer who is an officer or a member of such an organization does not thereby have a client-lawyer relationship with persons served by the organization. However, there is potential conflict between the interests of such persons and the interests of the lawyer's clients. If the possibility of such conflict disqualified a lawyer from serving on the board of a legal services organization, the profession's involvement in such organizations would be severely curtailed.

[2] It may be necessary in appropriate cases to reassure a client of the organization that the representation will not be affected by conflicting loyalties of a member of the board. Established, written policies in this respect can enhance the credibility of such assurances.

### Definitional Cross-References

"Law firm" *See* Rule 1.0(c)
"Knowingly" *See* Rule 1.0(f)

### State Rules Comparison

http://ambar.org/MRPCStateCharts

## ANNOTATION

### WHAT IS A LEGAL SERVICES ORGANIZATION?

The Rules do not define a legal services organization but the following observations strongly suggest that the phrase refers to a pro bono organization that provides legal services to economically disadvantaged clients.

First, Rule 6.3 is part of the "public service" group of ethics rules (Rules 6.1 to 6.5).

Second, this interpretation is consistent with the use of the phrase elsewhere in the Rules and comment. *See* Rule 1.0, cmt. [4] ("legal aid and legal services organizations"); Rule 1.17, cmt. [3] (referring to lawyers "on the staff of a . . . legal services entity that provides legal services to the poor"); Rule 6.5, cmt. [1] ("[l]egal services organizations, courts and various nonprofit organizations"); *see also* Ky. Ethics Op. E-425 (2006) ("generally understood that [Rule 6.3] applies to public or charitable organizations serving the poor, such as Legal Aid and the Public Defender"); Ill. Rule 6.3 (adding "nonprofit" just before "legal services organization"); N.Y. Rule 6.3 (same); *cf. Restatement (Third) of the Law Governing Lawyers* § 135A cmt. e (2000) ("Service of a private-practice lawyer on the board of directors of a legal-services organization can usefully support the delivery of legal services to persons unable to pay for them.").

Third, the legislative history states that when the rule was first proposed in 1983 the term "was meant to include a legal aid society." American Bar Association, *A Legislative History: The Development of the ABA Model Rules of Professional Conduct, 1982-2013*, at 720 (2013). *See* Wis. Ethics Op. EM-16-01 (2016) (crime-prevention funding board that provides no legal services is not a board of a legal services organization; sole role is to distribute funds to nonprofit organizations and law enforcement agencies).

To encourage lawyers to serve as members, officers, and directors of legal services organizations, Rule 6.3 specifies that their service is not to be used as ammunition in seeking their disqualification from representing clients in the course of their practices. *See* Tom Lininger, *Deregulating Public Interest Law*, 88 Tul. L. Rev. 727 (Mar. 2014) (slight relaxation of conflict rules to help lawyers become involved with legal aid boards suggests that "the urgent need for legal aid in civil cases may provide a reason to dial down ethical regulations, if the bar can do so without impeding its most important mission of protecting clients").

Rule 6.3 codifies the holding of an ABA ethics opinion issued the year Congress created the Legal Services Corporation, which provides funding for most of the nation's legal services programs. ABA Formal Opinion 334 (1974) held that for conflicts purposes, only the organization's staff lawyers actually represent clients; board members do not. Legal services clients, the opinion noted, do not confer with or confide in board members. *See* N.Y. State Ethics Op. 794 (2006) (rule "distinguishes between lawyers who, on the one hand, administer the organization, make policy, or teach, and on the other hand, the lawyers who represent clients as part of the organization's rendition of legal services"); Utah Ethics Op. 06-05 (2006) (lawyers serving on organization's ad hoc legal advisory panel are not representing organization's clients; they are functional equivalent of directors, officers, or members); *see also* Mo. Formal Ethics Op. 121 (2006) (nonprofit public interest organization whose staff lawyers represent domestic violence victims is not engaging in unlicensed practice of law if organization has no role in lawyer-client relationship); *cf.* S.C. Ethics Op. 02-04 (n.d.) (nonlawyer board members' participation in "general organizational policies that identify the types of cases for which the organization is willing to provide representation" by its staff lawyers is not unlicensed practice of law).

## MATERIAL LIMITATIONS

Membership in a legal services organization will not create multiple-representation conflicts, but it may still create material-limitation conflicts. For example, a lawyer's interest in successful board service may conflict with representation of a particular client, or the lawyer's responsibilities to others who serve on the organization's board may be at odds with the lawyer's responsibilities to a client. *See* S.D. Ethics Op. 2012-05 (n.d.) (lawyer's service on board of nonprofit organization providing nonlawyer advocates for children in abuse and neglect cases may materially limit his representation of parents in abuse and neglect cases within meaning of Rule 1.7). *See generally* Donald R. Lundberg & Caitlin S. Schroeder, *Ethics Guideposts for Lawyers Serving on Organizational Boards*, 59 Res Gestae 19 (Mar. 2016) (conflict arises under Rule 1.7(a)(2) when client asks estate-planning lawyer for advice about reducing or eliminating bequest to organization on whose board lawyer serves).

Consistent with the social-policy goals of the public service rules, Rule 6.3 provides a relatively painless cure for these material-limitation conflicts: When a lawyer who also belongs to a legal services organization is representing a client and finds that participating in a particular organizational action or decision would be "incompatible" with the lawyer's obligations to that client under Rule 1.7, the lawyer simply is not allowed to participate in that action or decision. Similarly, if the organization is considering doing something that would be adverse to a legal services client whose opponent is being represented by the lawyer board member (in the course of his or her practice), the lawyer may not participate in the organization's decision. The cure for the conflict, in other words, is to remove the lawyer from the organization's decision-making process so the lawyer can continue to represent his or her client. *See* Utah Ethics Op. 06-05 (2006) (recommending that legal services organizations adopt written policies requiring advisory group members to identify—and disqualify themselves from participating in—group actions that could pose conflicts with their duties to their clients). *See generally* Esther F. Lardent, *Positional Conflicts in the Pro Bono Context: Ethical Considerations and Market Forces*, 67 Fordham L. Rev. 2279 (Apr. 1999); Norman W. Spaulding, *The Prophet and the Bureaucrat: Positional Conflicts in Service Pro Bono Publico*, 50 Stan. L. Rev. 1395 (Apr. 1998).

## ROLE OF BOARD MEMBER

Most opinions analyzing board membership in a legal services organization from a conflicts standpoint involve a legal services staff lawyer representing one party, and a private lawyer on the organization's board representing the opposing party. This is a multiple-representation conflict rather than a Rule 6.3 material-limitation conflict, but the analysis in both situations turns on the same questions: What is the board member's role in the organization? How involved is the board member in the organization's work?

ABA Formal Opinion 345 (1979), the "other half" of Opinion 334, *supra*, notes that the relationship between a staff lawyer and a director of a legal services organization differs from the relationship between two staff lawyers in the same legal services organization; the critical difference "is the absence of a general opportunity for shared knowledge by the board member of the affairs of the staff attorney's client." But even though a board member may have no contact with a particular case, the board member does have long-term authority over staff salaries and promotions, and this may create a "whole network of relationships between a director and the staff . . . that would give some pause to the director's client [opposing] the organization's [client]." *Id.* The opinion concludes that representation of opposing parties by a board member and a staff lawyer is permissible if (1) the board member does not participate in the particular case, (2) there is no infringement of the staff lawyer's representation of his or her client, and (3) the board member does not have access to any confidential information about the case by virtue of board membership. *See* Me. Ethics Op. 197 (2009) (family law practitioner serving as director of legal clinic for domestic violence victims may represent client whose adversary is clinic client; directors have no access to confidential information of clinic clients, and clinic staff not "affiliated" with lawyer; lawyer must, however, inform client of relationship with clinic and obtain informed consent if substantial risk clinic duties will materially and adversely affect representation); Or. Ethics Op. 2005-66 (2005) (in "not likely" event that Legal Aid Society board member's representation of client whose opponent is represented by Legal Aid Society staff lawyer would be materially limited by his responsibilities as board member, he may secure client's informed consent; in any event, he may not participate in board decisions that could materially adversely affect opponent's representation); Phila. Ethics Op. 89-29 (1989) (if client consents, staff lawyer with Community Legal Services may represent one parent in dependency proceeding even though court appoints Community Legal Services board member as counsel for other parent; given board's "minimal" involvement in personnel matters, staff member could reasonably conclude that representation would not be adversely affected); S.C. Ethics Op. 90-08 (1990) (private lawyer on board of legal services corporation may represent clients with interests adverse to those of staff lawyers' clients if he is not involved in decisions concerning specific cases, and has no access to confidential information about corporation's clients); *see also* Neb. Ethics Op. 11-04 (n.d.) (lawyers in legal services unit of state department of health and human services not disqualified from representing department in administrative hearing even though unit colleague sits on board of public advocacy organization that has retained one party's counsel) (interpreting Rule 1.11's nonimputation provision rather than Rule 6.3).

In *EEOC v. Luby's, Inc.*, 347 F. Supp. 2d 743 (D. Ariz. 2004), the court decided that a lawyer's past membership on the Arizona Center for Disability Law [ACDL] board of directors did not disqualify her from defending an employer in a discrimination suit brought by an employee represented by a staff lawyer for ACDL. As a board member, the lawyer did not have a lawyer-client relationship with the plaintiff, and she had not acquired any confidential information about the plaintiff during her board service. She received one e-mail message about the case but deleted it unread, and her resignation from the board ensured that she would not be receiving any further information. The court rejected ACDL's argument that her service on the board and the legal committee, which reviewed litigation proposals, gave her access to information about attorneys' fees it received in case settlements, which in turn might give her insight into ACDL's litigation strategies and likely settlement position:

> Rule 6.3 . . . reflects a strong policy of encouraging attorneys to serve on legal service organization boards provided that they exercise care not to acquire confidential information about the organization's clients. Disqualifying Fatica because she had general information about ACDL litigation strategies would nullify Rule 6.3 because directors virtually always acquire this kind of information from their organizations.

In *B.A. v. L.A.*, 761 N.Y.S.2d 805 (Fam. Ct. 2003), a husband sought to disqualify the wife's lawyer, who was president of the Legal Aid Society, on the ground that the law guardian appointed to represent the couple's children was a Legal Aid Society employee. The wife's lawyer, he argued, invoking DR 5-101 (New York's provision on conflicts arising from a lawyer's financial, business, property, or personal interests), "wields power and influence over the Legal Aid attorney's salary, tenure and working conditions." The court denied the motion to disqualify the wife's lawyer, but granted a subsequent motion made on the same grounds to disqualify the law guardian instead. The court ruled that the law guardian's professional judgment "reasonably may be influenced since her adversary is president of . . . the agency by which she is employed." The clients, the court noted, were children and so could not give the informed consent that might otherwise have remedied the problem. *See also Lovitch v. Lovitch*, 884 N.Y.S.2d 430 (App. Div. 2009) (rejecting claim that court-appointed lawyer from Children's Rights Society should have been disqualified from representing children in custody dispute because father's lawyer was board member and later president of society).

In 2002, a New Jersey ethics opinion declared that it is not invariably improper for a legal aid lawyer to represent a client in a matter adverse to a legal aid board member or to a client represented by the board member. N.J. Ethics Op. 693 (2002). The board member in question was also an executive of a nonprofit housing corporation that was the landlord for some of the legal aid program's tenant clients. Abandoning its earlier prohibition, the committee held that the material-limitation analysis of Rule 1.7 must be made on a case-by-case basis. The committee noted that requiring the board member to refrain from any direct involvement in or control over specific cases normally obviates any material-limitation conflict. But because roles of board members can vary from organization to organization, the committee could not adopt a general rule to that effect: "[I]t is possible to hypothesize situations in which an organization lawyer might feel 'materially limited' by this conflict or even by other connections or conduct of a board member." The opinion warns that "it is improper for legal representatives of public entities and officials, and those officials themselves, to serve as board members or staff of non-profit legal assistance organizations if those organizations periodically represent clients who have such public entities or officials as adversaries."

## Rule 6.4

### *Law Reform Activities Affecting Client Interests*

A lawyer may serve as a director, officer or member of an organization involved in reform of the law or its administration notwithstanding that the reform may affect the interests of a client of the lawyer. When the lawyer knows that the interests of a client may be materially benefitted by a decision in which the lawyer participates, the lawyer shall disclose that fact but need not identify the client.

## COMMENT

[1] Lawyers involved in organizations seeking law reform generally do not have a client-lawyer relationship with the organization. Otherwise, it might follow that a lawyer could not be involved in a bar association law reform program that might indirectly affect a client. See also Rule 1.2(b). For example, a lawyer specializing in antitrust litigation might be regarded as disqualified from participating in drafting revisions of rules governing that subject. In determining the nature and scope of participation in such activities, a lawyer should be mindful of obligations to clients under other Rules, particularly Rule 1.7. A lawyer is professionally obligated to protect the integrity of the program by making an appropriate disclosure within the organization when the lawyer knows a private client might be materially benefitted.

### Definitional Cross-Reference
"Knows" See Rule 1.0(f)

### State Rules Comparison
http://ambar.org/MRPCStateCharts

## ANNOTATION

### ORGANIZATIONS "INVOLVED IN REFORM OF THE LAW OR ITS ADMINISTRATION"

Rule 6.4 permits lawyers to serve in organizations involved in reforming the law or its administration, but it does not define what reforming the law or its administration means. Although the comment does not elaborate, it does offer two examples: involvement in a "bar association law reform program" and participation in "drafting revisions of rules" in a particular subject-area of law. The first seems to echo the language of Rule 6.1(b)(3), which encourages pro bono "participation in activities for improving the law, the legal system or the legal profession" such as "serving on bar association committees, . . . taking part in Law Day activities," or engaging in legislative lobbying to improve the law. *See* Elizabeth Chambliss & Bruce A. Green, *Some Realism About Bar Associations*, 57 De Paul L. Rev. 425 (Winter 2008) (scrutinizing history and nature of organized bar's participation in law reform efforts); William Jacob Downes, *Does the ABA Promote Democracy in America?*, 26 Geo. J. Legal Ethics 645 (Fall 2013) (criticizing application of Rule 6.4 to bar association involvement in political issues). As to the second, see N.Y. State Ethics Op. 1073 (2015) (some of the work done by a district attorney's conviction integrity committee could constitute "law reform activities"); Pa. Ethics Op. 93-176 (1994) (in light of policies advanced by Rule 6.4, "not ethically inappropriate" to form organization of adoption lawyers interested in "following and influencing adoption legislation affecting Pennsylvania residents"); *see also* Elizabeth Laposata, Richard Barnes & Stanton Glantz, *Tobacco Industry Influence on the American Law Institute's Restatements of Torts and Implications for Its Conflict of Interest Policies*, 98 Iowa L. Rev. 1 (Nov. 2012) (noting that American Law Institute requires its consultative group members and advisors to comply with Rule 6.4).

A lawyer's involvement in an organization that advocates for law reform and also provides legal services to the indigent is subject to both Rule 6.4 and Rule 6.3. *See* Utah Ethics Op. 06-05 (2006) (public interest organization that provides legal services to indigents and whose mission is to enforce and strengthen laws protecting rights of disadvantaged may constitute "organization involved in the reform of the law or its administration" under Rule 6.4 as well as legal services organization under Rule 6.3).

## SOCIAL POLICY GOALS OF RULE 6.4

While Rule 6.3 is designed to encourage lawyers to serve as directors, officers, or members of legal services organizations, Rule 6.4 is designed to encourage similar service in law reform organizations. Rule 6.4 permits a lawyer to serve in a law reform organization even if the reform may affect one of the lawyer's clients. The rule's only requirement is that if a lawyer knows that a client's interests may be materially *benefited* by an organizational decision in which the lawyer is participating, the lawyer must tell the organization. (A handful of jurisdictions require notice whenever a client's interests may be materially *affected*, rather than merely benefited, by the decision.) The rule does not prohibit the lawyer from participating in the decision, nor does it require the lawyer to identify the client.

Rule 6.4 does not itself require the lawyer to tell the client about the lawyer's role in the organization. *See* Ill. Ethics Op. 91-27 (1992) (assistant state's attorney may, in private capacity as president of genealogical organization, petition state legislature to change law on access to birth records even though county clerk, his client, opposes change; "Rule 6.4 specifically permits such activities regardless of the possible effect that the actions of the organization may have on the client.").

The comment does, however, warn that in determining whether to participate in a law reform organization the lawyer "should be mindful of obligations to clients under other Rules, particularly Rule 1.7." *See* N.Y. Cnty. Ethics Op. 744 (2011) (rule does not require lawyer to notify client before speaking publicly at law reform forum implicating client's interests nor does it prohibit participation over client's objections; conflict could, however, require lawyer to discontinue either the representation or the participation under Rule 1.7); R.I. Ethics Op. 2017-03 (2017) (lawyer whose firm represents board of elections may serve on board of organization involved in elections-law reform if organization's open-meetings and public-records complaints against board of elections are no longer pending; future claims, however, could implicate Rule 1.7). *See generally* John Levin, *Legal Activism and Client Relations*, 29 Chi. Bar Ass'n Rec. 42 (Sept. 2015) (lawyer must determine point at which level of involvement in organization presents risk of materially limiting client's representation within meaning of Rule 1.7).

On the positional conflicts that can arise out of involvement in a law reform organization, see generally Nathan M. Crystal, *Developing a Philosophy of Lawyering*, 14 Notre Dame J.L. Ethics & Pub. Pol'y 75 (2000); John S. Dzienkowski, *Positional Conflicts of Interest*, 71 Tex. L. Rev. 457, 531–36 (Feb. 1993); Esther S. Lardent, *Positional Conflicts in the Pro Bono Context: Ethical Considerations and Market Forces*, 67 Fordham L. Rev. 2279 (Apr. 1999); and Norman W. Spaulding, *The Prophet and the Bureaucrat: Positional Conflicts in Service Pro Bono Publico*, 50 Stan. L. Rev. 1395 (Apr. 1998).

## Rule 6.5

### *Nonprofit and Court-Annexed Limited Legal Services Programs*

(a) A lawyer who, under the auspices of a program sponsored by a nonprofit organization or court, provides short-term limited legal services to a client without expectation by either the lawyer or the client that the lawyer will provide continuing representation in the matter:

(1) is subject to Rules 1.7 and 1.9(a) only if the lawyer knows that the representation of the client involves a conflict of interest; and

(2) is subject to Rule 1.10 only if the lawyer knows that another lawyer associated with the lawyer in a law firm is disqualified by Rule 1.7 or 1.9(a) with respect to the matter.

(b) Except as provided in paragraph (a)(2), Rule 1.10 is inapplicable to a representation governed by this Rule.

## COMMENT

[1] Legal services organizations, courts and various nonprofit organizations have established programs through which lawyers provide short-term limited legal services—such as advice or the completion of legal forms—that will assist persons to address their legal problems without further representation by a lawyer. In these programs, such as legal-advice hotlines, advice-only clinics or pro se counseling programs, a client-lawyer relationship is established, but there is no expectation that the lawyer's representation of the client will continue beyond the limited consultation. Such programs are normally operated under circumstances in which it is not feasible for a lawyer to systematically screen for conflicts of interest as is generally required before undertaking a representation. See, e.g., Rules 1.7, 1.9 and 1.10.

[2] A lawyer who provides short-term limited legal services pursuant to this Rule must secure the client's informed consent to the limited scope of the representation. See Rule 1.2(c). If a short-term limited representation would not be reasonable under the circumstances, the lawyer may offer advice to the client but must also advise the client of the need for further assistance of counsel. Except as provided in this Rule, the Rules of Professional Conduct, including Rules 1.6 and 1.9(c), are applicable to the limited representation.

[3] Because a lawyer who is representing a client in the circumstances addressed by this Rule ordinarily is not able to check systematically for conflicts of interest,

paragraph (a) requires compliance with Rules 1.7 or 1.9(a) only if the lawyer knows that the representation presents a conflict of interest for the lawyer, and with Rule 1.10 only if the lawyer knows that another lawyer in the lawyer's firm is disqualified by Rules 1.7 or 1.9(a) in the matter.

[4] Because the limited nature of the services significantly reduces the risk of conflicts of interest with other matters being handled by the lawyer's firm, paragraph (b) provides that Rule 1.10 is inapplicable to a representation governed by this Rule except as provided by paragraph (a)(2). Paragraph (a)(2) requires the participating lawyer to comply with Rule 1.10 when the lawyer knows that the lawyer's firm is disqualified by Rules 1.7 or 1.9(a). By virtue of paragraph (b), however, a lawyer's participation in a short-term limited legal services program will not preclude the lawyer's firm from undertaking or continuing the representation of a client with interests adverse to a client being represented under the program's auspices. Nor will the personal disqualification of a lawyer participating in the program be imputed to other lawyers participating in the program.

[5] If, after commencing a short-term limited representation in accordance with this Rule, a lawyer undertakes to represent the client in the matter on an ongoing basis, Rules 1.7, 1.9(a) and 1.10 become applicable.

**Definitional Cross-References**
"Law firm" *See* Rule 1.0(c)
"Knows" *See* Rule 1.0(f)

**State Rules Comparison**
http://ambar.org/MRPCStateCharts

# ANNOTATION

## PURPOSE OF THE RULE

Rule 6.5 was adopted in 2002 in response to concerns that a strict application of the conflict-of-interest rules "may be deterring lawyers from serving as volunteers in programs [providing] short-term limited legal services under the auspices of a nonprofit organization or a court-annexed program." American Bar Association, *A Legislative History: The Development of the ABA Model Rules of Professional Conduct, 1982–2013*, at 728 (2013). The limited-legal-services paradigm "is the legal-advice hotline or pro se clinic, the purpose of which is to provide short-term limited legal assistance to persons of limited means who otherwise would go unrepresented." *Id. See* N.Y. City Ethics Op. 2017-4 (2017) ("Rule 6.5 reduces obstacles to participation in programs that provide short-term limited legal services, thereby increasing the availability of such services to people in need."); Wis. Informal Ethics Op. EI-11-01 (2011) (Rule 6.5 means lawyers "can participate in most walk-in, advice-only clinics without worrying about screening for conflicts").

Rule 6.5 and its comment do not actually use the word "volunteer," nor do they make any reference to a client's economic status, nor do they draw any distinctions based upon the participating lawyer's fee, if any. According to a white paper by the

ABA Standing Committee on the Delivery of Legal Services, reprinted in 45 Fam. L.Q. 64, at 88–89 (Spring 2011), the rule is not limited to "pro bono programs, nor to lawyers who volunteer their services." Some jurisdictions, however, add the phrase "pro bono" to their versions of the rule; New York's Rule 6.5, entitled "Participation in Limited Pro Bono Legal Services Programs," further specifies that the advice or representation must be provided free of charge.

Note that at the same time it adopted Rule 6.5, the ABA amended Rule 1.2(c) to allow lawyers to provide limited representation if "reasonable under the circumstances and the client gives informed consent." *Cf.* Pa. Ethics Op. 2006-04 (2006) (Rule 6.5 implicitly recognizes permissibility of legal services program that offers limited representation for clients in custody cases). Rule 6.5 itself does not require the client's informed consent, but its Comment [2] invokes the informed-consent requirement of Rule 1.2(c). *See* Ohio Sup. Ct. Ethics Op. 2017-07 (2017).

## CONFLICTS-CHECKING REQUIREMENT OBVIATED

Rule 6.5 applies only when it is expected the representation will not continue "beyond the limited consultation." Cmt. [1]. A lawyer who undertakes a Rule 6.5 representation "ordinarily is not able to check systematically for conflicts of interest," Comment [3] notes. "A strict duty to identify conflicts does not make sense in the context of the short-term limited representation provided through a hotline or pro se clinic." American Bar Association, *A Legislative History: The Development of the ABA Model Rules of Professional Conduct, 1982–2013*, at 729 (2013). *See* Boston Ethics Op. 2008-01 (n.d.) (Rule 6.5 covers initial consultation with volunteer lawyer in pro bono bankruptcy program, but if lawyer is preparing Chapter 7 petition he will have time to run conflicts check and therefore be in position to "know" of conflict). *Compare* La. Ethics Op. 005-RPPC-005 (2005) (Rule 6.5 authorizes volunteers to advise disaster victims through hotline or booth sponsored by nonprofit group without conducting conflicts check), *discussed in* Sandra S. Varnado & Dane S. Ciolino, *Reconsidering Lawyers' Ethical Obligations in the Wake of a Disaster*, 19 Prof. Law., no. 4, at 8 (2009), *with* N.C. Ethics Op. 2014-6 (2014) (lawyer providing free brief consultations to members of nonprofit professional association who might then retain him must conduct full conflicts check; Rule 6.5 not applicable).

Comment [1] to Rule 6.5 recognizes that even in programs like legal-advice hotlines, "a client-lawyer relationship is established." *See* N.J. Ethics Op. 712 (2008) (impossible to disclaim lawyer-client relationship when hotline lawyers provide short-term limited legal services to members of nonprofit trade association); N.Y. City Ethics Op. 2017-4 (2017) (legal services lawyer providing legal advice to Medicaid applicant's caseworker has lawyer-client relationship with applicant); Va. Ethics Op. 1869 (2013) (lawyers volunteering in Family Court Self-Help Center answering general questions, preparing support calculations, or handing out materials available on website are not providing legal services and therefore may use customer agreements disclaiming lawyer-client relationship altogether; if lawyer helps attendee complete legal documents or gives legal advice, however, relationship arises and Rule 6.5 will apply).

The duty of confidentiality is not affected; when the representation ends the lawyer must treat the former client's protected information just as she would that of any other former client. *See* Cmt. [2].

When there is an initial consultation but *no* resulting client-lawyer relationship, Rule 1.18 defines the duties owed to the former prospective client.

## IMPUTATION OF CONFLICTS RESULTING FROM LIMITED REPRESENTATION

If the limited representation qualifies for Rule 6.5 treatment, the lawyer's participation "will not preclude the lawyer's firm from undertaking or continuing the representation of a client with interests adverse to a client being represented under the program's auspices." Cmt. [4]. *See* N.Y. State Ethics Op. 1012 (2014) (in bar association pro bono program that requires clients to agree in writing that lawyers' services do not extend beyond the one interaction, conflicts resulting from lawyer's participation are not imputed to his firm members); Wis. Informal Ethics Op. EI-11-01 (2011) (lawyer presenting seminar on powers of attorney forms and supervising law students completing forms for attendees under auspices of law student organization has full lawyer-client relationship with attendees, but if law school sponsors seminar and there is no contemplation of further assistance, Rule 6.5 would apply and would obviate need to enter attendees' names into firm's conflicts-checking database).

## DISCLOSURE OF LAWYER'S PARTICIPATION

Rule 6.5 does not require the lawyer's participation to be disclosed to the court or to the other parties. *See* N.C. Ethics Op. 2008-3 (2009) (Rule 6.5 does not require participating lawyer to either disclose his assistance to court or ensure client does); Utah Ethics Op. 08-01 (2008) (reasoning that if rules' drafters wanted to prohibit undisclosed assistance to pro se litigants, "Rule 6.5 would have been a likely place" to do so); *see also* Pa.-Phila. Joint Formal Ethics Op. 2011-100 (2011) (requiring lawyer to disclose participation "misses the whole point" of limited representation).

However, if the representation extends beyond that contemplated by Rule 6.5, other ethics rules or court rules may require disclosure. See the annotations to Rules 1.2, 3.3, and 8.4.

# Information about Legal Services

## Rule 7.1

### Communications Concerning a Lawyer's Services

A lawyer shall not make a false or misleading communication about the lawyer or the lawyer's services. A communication is false or misleading if it contains a material misrepresentation of fact or law, or omits a fact necessary to make the statement considered as a whole not materially misleading.

## Comment

[1] This Rule governs all communications about a lawyer's services, including advertising. Whatever means are used to make known a lawyer's services, statements about them must be truthful.

[2] Misleading truthful statements are prohibited by this Rule. A truthful statement is misleading if it omits a fact necessary to make the lawyer's communication considered as a whole not materially misleading. A truthful statement is misleading if a substantial likelihood exists that it will lead a reasonable person to formulate a specific conclusion about the lawyer or the lawyer's services for which there is no reasonable factual foundation. A truthful statement is also misleading if presented in a way that creates a substantial likelihood that a reasonable person would believe the lawyer's communication requires that person to take further action when, in fact, no action is required.

[3] A communication that truthfully reports a lawyer's achievements on behalf of clients or former clients may be misleading if presented so as to lead a reasonable person to form an unjustified expectation that the same results could be obtained for other clients in similar matters without reference to the specific factual and legal circumstances of each client's case. Similarly, an unsubstantiated claim about a lawyer's or law firm's services or fees, or an unsubstantiated comparison of the lawyer's or law firm's services or fees with those of other lawyers or law firms, may be misleading if presented with such specificity as would lead a reasonable person to conclude that the comparison or claim can be substantiated. The inclusion of an appropriate disclaimer or qualifying language may preclude a finding that a statement is likely to create unjustified expectations or otherwise mislead the public.

[4] It is professional misconduct for a lawyer to engage in conduct involving dishonesty, fraud, deceit or misrepresentation. Rule 8.4(c). See also Rule 8.4(e) for the prohibition against stating or implying an ability to improperly influence a government agency or official or to achieve results by means that violate the Rules of Professional Conduct or other law.

[5] Firm names, letterhead and professional designations are communications concerning a lawyer's services. A firm may be designated by the names of all or some of its current members, by the names of deceased members where there has been a succession in the firm's identity or by a trade name if it is not false or misleading. A lawyer or law firm also may be designated by a distinctive website address, social media username or comparable professional designation that is not misleading. A law firm name or designation is misleading if it implies a connection with a government agency, with a deceased lawyer who was not a former member of the firm, with a lawyer not associated with the firm or a predecessor firm, with a nonlawyer or with a public or charitable legal services organization. If a firm uses a trade name that includes a geographical name such as "Springfield Legal Clinic," an express statement explaining that it is not a public legal aid organization may be required to avoid a misleading implication.

[6] A law firm with offices in more than one jurisdiction may use the same name or other professional designation in each jurisdiction.

[7] Lawyers may not imply or hold themselves out as practicing together in one firm when they are not a firm, as defined in Rule 1.0(c), because to do so would be false and misleading.

[8] It is misleading to use the name of a lawyer holding a public office in the name of a law firm, or in communications on the law firm's behalf, during any substantial period in which the lawyer is not actively and regularly practicing with the firm.

## State Rules Comparison
http://ambar.org/MRPCStateCharts

## 2018 Advertising Rule Changes
http://ambar.org/AdvRuleChanges2018

## ANNOTATION

Rule 7.1 prohibits lawyers from making false or misleading statements about the lawyer or the lawyer's services. The rule is most often implicated in the context of lawyer advertising, but it is not limited to that context. As Comment [1] explains "Whatever means are used to make known a lawyer's services, statements about them must be truthful."

Note that Rule 7.1 is one of several ethics rules prohibiting lawyers from making false or misleading statements. For a discussion of other ethics rules requiring truthfulness in a variety of contexts, see the annotations to Rule 3.3 (Candor Toward the Tribunal), Rule 3.9 (Advocate in Nonadjudicative Proceedings), Rule 4.1 (Truthfulness in Statements to Others), Rule 4.3 (Dealing with Unrepresented Person), Rule 8.1 (Bar Admission and Disciplinary Matters), Rule 8.2 (Judicial and Legal Officials), and Rule 8.4 (Misconduct). Also see the annotation to Rule 3.4 (Fairness to Opposing Party and Counsel).

## LEGISLATIVE HISTORY

### • *2002 and 2012 Amendments*

The provisions in Comment [3] explaining that certain communications about a lawyer's achievements for other clients and unsubstantiated comparisons "may be misleading" are variants of provisions that were formerly in the rule itself, which stated that such communications are, in fact, misleading. Those provisions were criticized as being overly broad. Accordingly, in 2002 the rule was amended to remove the provisions from the black letter and place these variants in Comment [3].

In 2012 Comment [3] was again amended to substitute "the public" for "a prospective client" in the last sentence to clarify the breadth of the rule's intended coverage. American Bar Association, *A Legislative History: The Development of the ABA Model Rules of Professional Conduct, 1982–2013*, at 741–43 (2013).

### • *2018 Amendments*

The rules governing advertising and other communications about a lawyer's services, Model Rules 7.1-7.5, were amended in 2018 to accommodate advances in technology, especially the use of the internet and social media; increasingly common multijurisdictional practice; and developments in First Amendment and antitrust law.

The black letter of Model Rule 7.1 remained unchanged, but the comment was revised. Comment [1] was amended to delete the language "permitted by Rule 7.2." Comment [2] was amended to clarify that information may be misleading, even if true, if potential users of legal services are thereby persuaded that they must take unnecessary action, and Comment [3] now includes language stating that unsubstantiated claims about a lawyer's services or fees may be misleading. Comment [4] adds a reference to Model Rule 8.4(c) and a reminder that conduct involving dishonesty, fraud, deceit, or misrepresentation is professional misconduct. Comments [5]-[8] now contain matter previously found in Model Rule 7.5, which, along with Model Rule 7.4, was deleted in 2018. *See* ABA Report to the House of Delegates, Revised Resolution 101 (Aug. 2018), *available at* http://ambar.org/AdvRuleChanges2018.

## FIRST AMENDMENT CONSIDERATIONS

It is well settled that the First Amendment protects commercial speech, which includes lawyer advertising and any communications about a lawyer's services. *See Bates v. State Bar*, 433 U.S. 350 (1977) (commercial speech "serves individual and societal interests in assuring informed and reliable decisionmaking"); *see also Zauderer v. Office of Disciplinary Counsel*, 471 U.S. 626 (1985) (lawyer may not be disciplined for soliciting legal business through print advertising containing truthful and nondeceptive information and advice regarding legal rights of potential client); *In re R.M.J.*, 455 U.S. 191 (1982) (even "relatively uninformative" ad is protected speech as long as not misleading).

First Amendment protection does not, however, extend to lawyers' commercial speech that is false or deceptive, or that concerns illegal activities. These communications may be banned outright. *Bates v. State Bar*, 433 U.S. 350 (1977) ("advertising concerning transactions that are themselves illegal obviously may be suppressed"); *Farrin v. Thigpen*, 173 F. Supp. 2d 427 (M.D.N.C. 2001) (television advertisement misleading on its face is not commercial speech protected by First Amendment); *Fla. Bar v. Pape*, 918 So. 2d 240 (Fla. 2005) ("[l]awyer advertising enjoys First Amendment protection only to the extent that it provides accurate factual information that can be objectively verified").

In the absence of deception or illegal activities, regulations concerning the content of advertisements are constitutionally permissible only if they are narrowly drawn to advance a substantial governmental interest. *See Cent. Hudson Gas & Elec. Corp. v. Pub. Serv. Comm'n of N.Y.*, 447 U.S. 557 (1980); *Alexander v. Cahill*, 598 F.3d 79 (2d Cir. 2010) (state's ban on "advertising techniques [that] are no more than potentially misleading" is unconstitutional because of broad, "categorical nature of [those] prohibitions"); *Rubenstein v. Fla. Bar*, 72 F. Supp. 3d 1298 (S.D. Fla. 2014) (state bar guidelines prohibiting lawyers from advertising past results were not narrowly tailored to achieve bar's stated objectives). *See generally* David L. Hudson, Jr., *Attorney Advertising in the Litigators and Modern-Day America: The Continued Importance of the Public's Need for Legal Information*, 48 U. Mem. L. Rev. 959 (Spring 2018); Rodney A. Smolla, *Regulating the Speech of Judges and Lawyers: The First Amendment and the Soul of the Profession*, 66 Fla. L. Rev. 961 (May 2014).

## FALSE OR MISLEADING STATEMENTS

A lawyer may not make statements about the lawyer or the lawyer's services that are false or misleading. This prohibition includes both explicit falsehoods and falsehoods implicit in other claims. *See, e.g., Feldman & Pinto, P.C. v. Seithel*, Civ. No. 11–5400, 2011 WL 6758460, 2011 BL 324804 (E.D. Pa. Dec. 22, 2011) (lawyer's letter soliciting clients of former firm after being fired contained exaggerations, omissions, and misrepresentations and was misleading); *Davis v. Westgate Planet Hollywood Las Vegas, LLC*, No. 2:08-cv-00722-RCJ-PAL, 2009 WL 5038508, 2009 BL 269303 (D. Nev. Dec. 15, 2009) (class counsel in opt-in wages cases included false information about geographic scope of case on firm website); *In re Lutheran Bhd. Variable Ins. Prods. Co. Sales Practices Litig.*, No. 99-MD-1309PAMJGL, 2002 WL 1205695 (D. Minn. May 31, 2002) (lawyer mailed postcards to potential members of certified plaintiff class falsely claiming court ruled on merits of case and misrepresenting scope of class); *In re Zang*, 741 P.2d 267 (Ariz. 1987) (television advertisements showing lawyers in courtroom arguing before jury false and misleading; no lawyer in firm ever tried personal injury case to its conclusion); *People v. Carpenter*, 893 P.2d 777 (Colo. 1995) (Yellow Pages advertisement implied referral service supplied many lawyers in thirteen fields, when no more than five lawyers available in four fields); *In re Smith*, 991 N.E.2d 106 (Ind. 2013) (lawyer-author's book biography stating he was "Certified Domestic Law Mediator" was false and misleading); *In re Weaver*, 281 P.3d 502 (Kan. 2012) (advertisement stating loan modification company consisting of two lawyers was "nationwide network of attorneys" was false and misleading); *Att'y Grievance Comm'n v. Narasimhan*, 92 A.3d 512 (Md. 2014) (lawyer misstated experience on résumé); *In re Zak*, 73 N.E.3d 262 (Mass. 2017) (false statements such as that lawyer was only lawyer who knew how to secure permanent loan modifications); *Richmond's Case*, 872 A.2d

1023 (N.H. 2005) (lawyer's website touted expertise in securities law but lawyer's only experience was drafting registration statements that had never been filed); *In re Shapiro*, 780 N.Y.S.2d 680 (App. Div. 2004) (ad falsely depicted lawyer as experienced trial lawyer—lawyer never tried case to conclusion); *N.C. State Bar v. Culbertson*, 627 S.E.2d 644 (N.C. 2006) (lawyer involved in cases disposed by federal courts misleadingly claimed he was "published in Federal Law Reports"); *In re Wells*, 709 S.E.2d 644 (S.C. 2011) (law firm website overstated lawyers' experience, reputation, and foreign language abilities, and falsely stated firm had offices in other states); *Neely v. Comm'n for Lawyer Discipline*, 196 S.W.3d 174 (Tex. App. 2006) (ad soliciting inquiries about pending class case failed to identify sponsor as private lawyer and so could lead readers to believe lawyer was court employee); ABA Formal Ethics Op. 465 (2013) (lawyer must ensure group coupon or deal-of-the-day advertisement for lawyer's services is accurate, complete, and not misleading); D.C. Ethics Op. 271 (1997) (lawyer may not claim admission to jurisdiction if on inactive status there); Ill. Ethics Op. 15-05 (2015) (lawyer may not link to outside websites if they contain false or misleading information about lawyer or lawyer's services); N.J. Advertising Ethics Op. 43 (2011) (pay-per-lead lawyer-client-matching advertising website was misleading); N.Y. State Ethics Op. 1021 (2014) (law firm domain name including word "expert" is misleading); N.C. Ethics Op. 2015-3 (2015) (lawyer's proposed solicitation offering tablet computer to new clients was misleading because it did not make clear that tablet would be loan, not gift); N.C. Ethics Op. 2010-10 (2011) (law firm's advertisement for "free" out-of-office initial consultations must disclose any charges for consultation expenses); Pa. Ethics Op. 2011-27 (2011) (Groupon advertisement for "simple will" at "87% discount" may be misleading); S.C. Ethics Op. 12-12 (2012) (lawyers affiliated solely to share expenses may not refer to themselves as partnership); Va. Ethics Op. 1750 (rev. 2018) (ads using actors who portray lawyers are misleading without clear disclosure that they are dramatizations by actors). *See generally* Jan L. Jacobowitz & John G. Browning, *Legal Ethics and Social Media: A Practitioner's Handbook* 185-206 (2017).

## TRUE, BUT MISLEADING, STATEMENTS

Rule 7.1 prohibits lawyers from making statements that are literally true, but misleading. Cmt. [2]. This may involve a lawyer omitting important information and/or providing information in a way that leads another to reach an unwarranted conclusion about the lawyer, the lawyer's services, or the results the lawyer could obtain for a client. *See In re Huelskamp*, 740 N.E.2d 846 (Ind. 2000) ("Choose a *Lawyer* with 20 years of United States Marine Corps Experience and a former Assistant Professor at Boston University" is misleading statement even though lawyer had such experience; "reasonable person might believe incorrectly that the respondent was a Marine Corps lawyer or a law professor at Boston University"); *Ky. Bar Ass'n v. Mandello*, 32 S.W.3d 763 (Ky. 2000) (lawyer's letter to potential medical malpractice plaintiff stating, "[I] feel that my background provides me with a strong basis of knowledge with which to protect your interests" is misleading; lawyer admitted for only two years and never handled medical malpractice action); *In re Zak*, 73 N.E.3d 262 (Mass. 2017) (misrepresenting and omitting "significant and relevant" information); *In re Defillo*,

762 S.E.2d 552 (S.C. 2014) (Florida lawyer targeting advertising to South Carolina residents failed to note she was not admitted to South Carolina bar, referred to her firm's "lawyers" and "attorneys" although she was sole practitioner, and claimed her firm was "unique" because she and her staff spoke English and Spanish); ABA Formal Ethics Op. 10-457 (2010) (legal information on lawyer website must be accurate, current, and not misleading); Va. Ethics Op. 1750 (rev. 2018) (compendium opinion addressing misleading communications in several contexts); *see also* Phila. Ethics Op. 2012-3 (2012) (suspended lawyer wishing to provide nonlawyer representation to Social Security disability claimants may not state he is a law school graduate).

### • *Omissions concerning Lawyer's Fees*

Lawyers advertising legal fees must disclose information about clients' responsibilities to pay costs. *See Zauderer v. Office of Disciplinary Counsel*, 471 U.S. 626 (1985) (advertisement that no fee will be charged is misleading unless it also states client remains liable for costs and expenses of litigation); *Lyon v. Ala. State Bar*, 451 So. 2d 1367 (Ala. 1984) (advertisement stating "above fees do not include court costs" sufficient to inform readers to inquire regarding amount of court costs); *Leoni v. State Bar*, 704 P.2d 183 (Cal. 1985) (misleading for lawyer to state in letter to prospective client that $60 cash needed to apply for debt relief and not mention that legal fees would cost client ten times that amount); *People v. Roehl*, 655 P.2d 1381 (Colo. 1983) (advertisement for routine legal services at fixed fee that did not disclose hidden costs is misleading); *Cincinnati Bar Ass'n v. Mezher & Espohl*, 982 N.E.2d 657 (Ohio 2012) (law firm's advertising "free consultation" was misleading by omitting that billing would begin once fee agreement signed); Ohio Sup. Ct. Ethics Op. 2017-1 (2017) (lawyer handling matters on contingent fee basis may not advertise "There is no charge unless we win your case" without clarifying that client will be responsible for costs and expenses even if no recovery, if that is the case); Phila. Ethics Op. 95-12 (1995) (ad stating "No recovery, no fee" is misleading if client must pay costs even if no recovery); Va. Ethics Op. 1750 (rev. 2018) (advertisements containing statements such as "no recovery, no fee" are misleading without explanation that clients may be liable for costs). Groupon or "daily deal" advertisements must offer genuine discounts from the lawyer's customary fees. *See, e.g.*, N.H. Ethics Op. 2013-14/8 (2014); N.Y. State Ethics Op. 897 (2011); N.C. Ethics Op. 2011-10 (2011).

### • *Creating Unjustified Expectations about Results Lawyer Can Achieve*

As Comment [3] notes, an otherwise true statement may be misleading if presented in a way that would lead a reasonable person to form an unjustified expectation that the lawyer can obtain the same results for that person as the lawyer obtained in previous matters, "without reference to the specific factual and legal circumstances of each client's case." (Before the 2002 amendments, this issue was addressed in paragraph (b) of the rule, which characterized a statement as false or misleading if it was "likely to create an unjustified expectation about results the lawyer can achieve.")

The underlying assumption is that each legal matter is unique, and prospective clients should not rely upon the lawyer's past performance as an indication of the outcome of the prospective client's matter. *See, e.g., Farrin v. Thigpen*, 173 F. Supp. 2d 427 (M.D.N.C. 2001) (dramatization in television advertisement misleading because it inaccurately portrayed insurance industry and implied insurance companies will settle with law firm because of firm's reputation); *In re Burton*, 442 B.R. 421 (Bankr. W.D.N.C. 2009) (bankruptcy lawyer's letters claiming ability to save prospective clients' homes "in the vast majority of cases" misleading); *In re Coale*, 775 N.E.2d 1079 (Ind. 2002) (out-of-state lawyers barred from practicing in state for violating state's advertising rules; lawyers sent materials to relatives of plane crash victims and victims themselves claiming lawyers "helped other victims through [their] tragedy" and "helped to lead to over $225,000,000 in compensation for the Plaintiffs"); *In re Wamsley*, 725 N.E.2d 75 (Ind. 2000) (advertisement stating lawyer could obtain best possible settlement in least amount of time likely to create unjustified expectation that lawyer could obtain such result in any case); *In re Lord*, 807 S.E.2d 696 (S.C. 2017) (use of telephone number (844) FIXTICKET by traffic lawyer found "likely to create unjustified expectations or an implication that he can achieve results by unethical means"); Conn. Informal Ethics Op. 88-3 (1988) (dummy newspaper article headlined "Biker Awarded $250,000 for Accident" is misleading, because article created only for advertisement and unjustifiably implied similar awards could be received in other cases); *see also* Mich. Informal Ethics Op. CI-830 (1982) (misleading to send client newspaper clippings of out-of-state verdicts without disclaimer that similar results in state may not be possible); *cf.* Or. Ethics Op. 2005-31 (rev. 2015) (lawyer who is part-time justice of peace or state legislator may not have firm employees refer to him as "Judge" or "Senator" because titles improperly imply influence with government agencies). *Compare* N.Y. State Ethics Op. 1005 (2014) (slogans "I know how to win for you" and "unsurpassed litigation skills" used in lawyer advertising are misleading), *with* R.I. Ethics Op. 2015-03 (2015) (use of word "win" with lawyer's name in marketing slogan does not reasonably risk creating unjustified expectations).

### • *Testimonials and Endorsements*

Until 2002, Rule 7.1 included a comment stating that paragraph (b) "would ordinarily preclude . . . advertisements containing client endorsements." This comment was deleted in 2002, and the rule no longer prohibits testimonials or endorsements. In general, the appropriateness of such communications depends upon whether they are false or misleading. *See, e.g.,* Conn. Informal Ethics Op. 01-07 (2001) (quotes from clients regarding lawyer's personal qualities—such as being knowledgeable, patient, accommodating, and courteous—do not violate Rule 7.1); Neb. Ethics Op. 12-04 (2012) (testimonials permissible if not false or misleading); N.Y. State Ethics Op. 661 (1994) (dramatizations of client testimonials not unethical per se but must avoid misleading imagery regarding client identity, must use reasonable disclaimers about results achieved, and clients must consent); N.C. Ethics Op. 2012-1 (2012) ("soft" client testimonials describing lawyer's services generally permissible and do not require disclaimer; "hard" testimonials referring to favorable results in particular matter permissible if accompanied by disclaimer); Pa. Formal Ethics Op. 2014-300 (2014) (lawyer may solicit and accept endorsement on social media but must monitor it for accuracy and correct or remove any false or misleading information);

S.C. Ethics Op. 09-10 (2009) (lawyer should communicate only those "endorsements [that] are presented in a way that is not misleading nor likely to create unjustified expectations"); Wash. Ethics Op. 2206 (2010) (lawyer may use client testimonials that mention dollar amounts of settlements or awards in advertising if not misleading); W. Va. Ethics Op. 2015-02 (2015) (lawyer must monitor endorsements on lawyer's social media websites and remove or correct any that are false or misleading); *see also Pub. Citizen v. La. Disciplinary Bd.*, 632 F.3d 212 (5th Cir. 2011) (rule regulating use of client testimonials unconstitutional); *Alexander v. Cahill*, 598 F.3d 79 (2d Cir. 2010) (categorical prohibition of testimonials from current clients unconstitutional); *In re Anonymous*, 6 N.E.3d 903 (Ind. 2014) (lawyer's affiliation with "Law Tigers" website maintained by for-profit lawyer marketing service and containing testimonials and accounts of prior results of other affiliate lawyers was misleading even though lawyer's own website contained disclaimers); Conn. Informal Ethics Op. 12-03 (2012) (client reviews displayed on lawyer's Martindale-Hubbell directory listing are not advertising and therefore not subject to Rule 7.1 unless lawyer drafts or edits reviews).

### • *Comparisons with Other Lawyers*

An unsubstantiated comparison of a lawyer's fees or services with those of other lawyers "may be misleading if presented with such specificity as would lead a reasonable person to conclude that the comparison . . . can be substantiated." Cmt. [3]. (Before the 2002 amendments, this issue was addressed in paragraph (c) of the rule, which characterized a statement as false or misleading if it "compares the lawyer's services with other lawyers' services, unless the comparison can be factually substantiated.") *See Mezrano v. Ala. State Bar*, 434 So. 2d 732 (Ala. 1983) (absent state rating system, lawyer should not claim superiority over other lawyers); *In re Anonymous*, 637 N.E.2d 131 (Ind. 1994) (inappropriate to state firm has "quickly become recognized as a premier personal injury law firm"); *Medina Cnty. Bar Ass'n v. Grieselhuber*, 678 N.E.2d 535 (Ohio 1997) (statement "We Do It Well" is unverifiable and misleading); *In re Lord*, 807 S.E.2d 696 (S.C. 2017) (lawyer's website claimed "unique insight into the South Carolina traffic laws that many other lawyers simply do not have"); Ala. Ethics Op. 89-18 (1989) (commercial suggesting viewers call lawyer referral service rather than "take a chance" on telephone book misleads viewers into believing participating lawyers' services are superior); Conn. Informal Ethics Op. 01-07 (2001) (quote from client in firm newsletter comparing firm lawyer with other lawyers violates rule unless it can be substantiated); D.C. Ethics Op. 172 (1986) (advertising "low-cost alternative" is misleading); Miss. Ethics Op. 256 (2008) (lawyer's advertisement that he will donate part of fees to children's charities impermissibly implies he is more charitable and more honest than other lawyers); Phila. Ethics Op. 95-12 (1995) (advertisement of "Big city experience, small town service" impermissibly implies lawyer's service better than other lawyers' services and uses subjective terms incapable of verification); *see also* Ill. Ethics Op. 92-8 (1993) (lawyer represented fees to particular client as "guaranteed reduced hourly rate," which was less than lawyer's customary fee; unless rate is less than fees charged in geographic area for similar services, representation of "reduced" fee may be misleading); *cf. Bates v. State Bar*, 433

U.S. 350 (1977) (offering legal services for uncontested divorce at "very reasonable prices" not inherently misleading if within low range of prices commonly charged in geographic area).

### • *Comparisons by Third Parties*

Comparisons or ratings of lawyers that are performed by sources other than the lawyers themselves, that can be substantiated, and that the lawyers have not purchased are generally held to be not misleading and may be used in lawyers' advertising. *E.g., Mason v. Fla. Bar*, 208 F.3d 952 (11th Cir. 2000) (stating "AV rating, the Highest Rating" by Martindale-Hubbell service not misleading even though rating system not generally known to public); *In re Op. 39 of Comm. on Att'y Adver.*, 961 A.2d 722 (N.J. 2008) (vacating opinion of court's lawyer advertising committee prohibiting use of titles "Best Lawyer" and "Super Lawyer" as bestowed by directory publisher); Alaska Ethics Op. 2009-2 (2009) (approving use of designation as "Best Lawyer" or "Super Lawyer" in marketing communication if accompanied by disclaimer showing date of designation and relevant practice area); *accord* Del. Ethics Op. 2008-2 (2008); Iowa Ethics Op. 07-09 (2007); Mich. Informal Ethics Op. RI-341 (2007); N.C. Ethics Op. 2007-14 (2008); Pa. Ethics Op. 2004-10 (2004); Va. Ethics Op. 1750 (rev. 2018).

## STATEMENTS FOUND NOT MISLEADING

The advertising that has been permitted under Rule 7.1 includes statements that convey verifiable factual information and those that are more generally descriptive but not inherently misleading. *See, e.g., Zauderer v. Office of Disciplinary Counsel*, 471 U.S. 626 (1985) (even though advertising might be embarrassing, offensive, or undignified, not misleading to target advertisement to persons with specific legal problems as long as statements not actually false or deceptive); *In re R.M.J.*, 455 U.S. 191 (1982) (permissible to list jurisdictions in which lawyer admitted to practice); *In re Anonymous*, 684 S.E.2d 560 (S.C. 2009) (not misleading for lawyer to advertise he would "work to protect" jobs of workers' compensation claimants because lawyer could invoke statutory prohibitions on retaliatory discharge); N.C. Ethics Op. 2015-9 (2015) (firm lawyer may be designated as "partner" even without holding equity if designation is made using legitimate criteria); Ohio Sup. Ct. Ethics Op. 92-12 (1992) (statement in farmers' trade magazine, by lawyer who is also farmer, that "[b]eing a farmer of over twenty years' experience, I understand [farmers'] problems," not inherently misleading); *see also Att'y Grievance Comm'n v. Ficker*, 572 A.2d 501 (Md. 1990) (use of word "palimony" in lawyer's newspaper advertisement not false or misleading despite term's imprecision; tasteless and crass not synonymous with false and misleading); Phila. Ethics Op. 2014-8 (2015) (law firm's use of titles such as "officer" or "director" for nonlawyer employees not misleading); Tex. Ethics Op. 550 (2004) (lawyer who earned J.D. degree may use title "Doctor" in professional communications).

## DISCLAIMERS

A comment added in 2002 and amended in 2012 states that the "inclusion of an appropriate disclaimer or qualifying language may preclude a finding that a statement is likely to create unjustified expectations or otherwise mislead the public."

Cmt. [3]. *See* American Bar Association, *A Legislative History: The Development of the ABA Model Rules of Professional Conduct, 1982–2013,* at 742 (2013) (noting that before 2002, many jurisdictions already had encouraged or required disclaimers in lawyer advertising); *see also* N.Y. State Ethics Op. 834 (2009) (lawyer must use disclaimer "Prior results do not guarantee a similar outcome" in any advertising containing client testimonials or endorsements); N.C. Ethics Op. 2009-6 (2009) (firm may have "case summary" section of website about past verdicts and settlements but must include explanations of cases' complexity, whether liability or damages were contested, and success in collecting judgments); Wash. Ethics Op. 201402 (2014) (lawyer must remove inaccurate client ratings or other information on social network profile and/or post appropriate disclaimer).

A number of authorities have addressed the adequacy of particular disclaimers. *See, e.g., Farrin v. Thigpen,* 173 F. Supp. 2d 427 (M.D.N.C. 2001) (it would "defeat the purpose" of advertising rules "if the advertiser could employ deceptive and misleading methods so long as the ad included a disclaimer of what was portrayed"; court noted that size, lightness, and brevity of disclaimer in television advertisement rendered disclaimer "entirely ineffective"); *In re Keller,* 792 N.E.2d 865 (Ind. 2003) (television ad claiming "insurance companies know the name Keller & Keller" suggests firm can create favorable outcome solely by its reputation, notwithstanding disclaimer that "no specific result implied"); *In re Foos,* 770 N.E.2d 335 (Ind. 2002) (explanatory disclaimer in small type insufficient to negate misleading information that precedes it in standard type); D.C. Ethics Op. 302 (2000) (when appearing on websites, disclaimers should be readily available to visitors and not be buried in links several clicks removed from main pages); N.C. Ethics Op. 2010-6 (2011) (lawyer who intends to associate with more experienced lawyer must include disclaimer to that effect in advertisements); Okla. Ethics Op. 320 (2004) (lawyer's ad may include amounts awarded in jury verdicts only if accompanied by disclaimer that is at least as prominent as notice of amounts); S.C. Ethics Op. 12-03 (2012) (buried, small-type disclaimers on website enabling viewers to pose questions calling for specific legal advice from lawyer "experts" were ineffective); Wash. Ethics Op. 2206 (2010) (disclaimers in advertisements must appear in same font size as advertising text and cannot be minimized or obscured).

## FIRM NAMES AND LETTERHEAD

Former Rule 7.5 (deleted 2018) addressed restrictions on what lawyers can say about themselves and their firms in their firm names and on their letterhead. Because these restrictions related to false and misleading statements, they are now addressed in Rule 7.1, Comments [5]-[8].

A law firm name or letterhead must not mislead the public about the nature of the services the firm provides, or the names, credentials, or affiliations of the lawyers in the firm. Traditionally, law firm names include the names of partners. *Cf.* N.Y. City Ethics Op. 1995-9 (1995) (ethics rules do not require firm name to consist exclusively of partners); Tex. Ethics Op. 640 (2014) (law firm name may include name of associate). But as Comment [5] explains, a lawyer or firm may use a trade name as long as it is not false or misleading. Examples of names that are inherently false or misleading are those that imply a connection with a government agency, with a nonlawyer, with a lawyer who has never been associated with the firm, or with a public or charitable legal services organization.

### • *Characterizing Nature of Law Firm or Services Provided*

A law firm's name or letterhead may not mislead the public about the nature of the law firm or the services it provides. *See, e.g., In re Shapiro*, 656 N.Y.S.2d 80 (App. Div. 1996) (lawyer's listing in legal directories as "Accident Legal Clinic of Shapiro and Shapiro" was misleading because it implied lawyer operated clinic separate from Shapiro and Shapiro, his law firm, and because lawyer's practice not limited to accident claims); *In re Shannon*, 638 P.2d 482 (Or. 1982) ("Shannon and Johnson's Hollywood Law Center" not misleading regarding services offered or identity of lawyers); La. Ethics Op. 07-RPCC-012 (2007) (firm may use trade name conveying areas of practice but may not "state or imply certification, specialization or expertise in contravention to the rules"); Neb. Ethics Op. 12-01 (2012) (firm may use distinct trade names for offices in different cities if names do not confuse or mislead public regarding nature of firm and lawyer relationships); N.Y. State Ethics Op. 1152 (2018) (use of first name without surname as name of firm would be misleading because of universal convention of using surnames in firm names, but lawyer may use first name alone as branding component); N.Y. State Ethics Op. 872 (2011) (lawyer may use nickname or English translation of first name on website, business cards, and informal communications if not misleading as to identity); N.C. Ethics Op. 2010-11 (2011) (lawyer may note membership in "Million Dollar Advocates Forum" on letterhead if disclaimer and qualifications for designation included); Pa. Ethics Op. 2007-25 (2007) (lawyer who is not certified as elder specialist may not put logo of National Academy of Elder Law Attorneys on stationery even if member of organization); Phila. Ethics Op. 98-17 (1998) (law firm may call itself "Medical Malpractice Trial Attorneys, Inc." only if it actually handles medical malpractice cases through trial); Tex. Ethics Op. 647 (2014) (nonprofit law firm may not use trade name containing name of lawyer's granddaughter who is not a lawyer and has never practiced with firm); *see also Alexander v. Cahill*, 598 F.3d 79 (2d Cir. 2010) (New York's Rule 7.1 prohibiting "nickname, moniker, motto or trade name that implies an ability to obtain results" unconstitutional because prohibited tags are only "potentially misleading [and] not inherently or actually misleading in all cases"); *Michel v. Bare*, 230 F. Supp. 2d 1147 (D. Nev. 2002) (enjoining rule forbidding private lawyers to use trade names other than "law offices of" or "and associates"; lawyer may do business under service marks "Your Legal Power" and "Su Poder Legal"); Tenn. Formal Ethics Op. 2017-F-164 (2017) (Tennessee law firm and Florida law firm forming partnership may use trade name that incorporates name of title company).

### • *Implying Partnership or Other Association*

Comment [7], formerly contained in Model Rule 7.5(d) (deleted 2018), explains that lawyers are prohibited from implying or holding themselves out as practicing together in a firm when that is not the case. *See, e.g., In re Schneider*, 710 N.E.2d 178 (Ind. 1999) (suspension of lawyer/CPA who used same letterhead for both practices, describing self as "Professional Services Group" and falsely listing two other lawyers and three other CPAs as additional members to suggest he was part of group); *Disciplinary Counsel v. McCord*, 905 N.E.2d 1182 (Ohio 2009) (sole practitioner used several firm names improperly implying partnership with lawyer with whom he merely shared offices); ABA Formal Ethics Op. 94-388 (1994) (law firms that form network with firms in other cities may not mislead clients into thinking each firm has access to each other's lawyers; separate network members may not share same firm name); D.C. Ethics Op. 255 (1995) (lawyer who subleases office space from and works for former firm on ad hoc contract basis should not be called "special counsel" because that term suggests continuous relationship); La. Ethics Op. 07-RPCC-013 (2007) (lawyers sharing office must have "separate letterhead, business cards, telephone listings, and building-directory listings"); Mich. Informal Ethics Op. RI-310 (1998) (firm names and letterhead must accurately reflect relationship between lawyer and firm; firm may not state or imply temporary lawyer is member of firm); N.Y. State Ethics Op. 732 (2001) (as long as lawyer practices with associates, the name "The [lawyer's surname] Group" is permissible; "Group" accurately describes nature of practice with associates); N.Y. City Ethics Op. 1995-8 (1995) (lawyers and firms sharing office space may not use trade name "Law Offices at X Square" but may hold themselves out as "association" or "affiliation" if they maintain continuing relationship akin to "of counsel" association); N.Y. Cnty. Ethics Op. 680 (1990) (lawyers in separate practices who share office space may not practice under single firm name); N.C. Ethics Op. 2004-09 (2004) (law firm that shares offices with financial services company may not use firm name similar to financial services company's name); Pa. Ethics Op. 04-06 (2004) (two law firms sharing suite of offices may not refer to themselves as "association of professional corporations"; designation misleadingly implies partnership); S.C. Ethics Op. 12-12 (2012) (sole practitioners who intend to share expenses for office space and professional liability policy but will otherwise maintain separate practices may not call themselves a law firm or partnership or refer to each other as partners); Utah Ethics Op. 00-07 (2000) (Utah lawyer who associates with lawyers or firms from foreign countries may not use joint letterhead or common name; misleading to imply they are all members of one firm, sharing responsibilities and liabilities); Utah Ethics Op. 95-04 (1995) (lawyer or law firm may not enter franchise agreement to market services under common trade name if not in fact combining as partnership or professional corporation); *cf.* Md. Ethics Op. 2001-11 (2001) (law firm may not list nonlegal investment and insurance brokerage on letterhead as "Client Services Affiliated Organization" if relationship limited to occasional cross-referrals). *Compare* Tex. Ethics Op. 638 (2013) (two Texas lawyers practicing in different law firms may not advertise for out-of-state business to be jointly handled using trade name that combines firm names), *with* Tex. Ethics Op. 640 (2014) (lawyer who is sole shareholder of firm, which employs one associate, may use assumed firm name that includes names of both lawyers).

A sole practitioner may not imply the firm includes other lawyers. *See Fla. Bar v. Elster*, 770 So. 2d 1184 (Fla. 2000) (sole practitioner passed out business cards for "Immigration Verification Associates"); *Disciplinary Counsel v. Furth*, 754 N.E.2d 219 (Ohio 2001) (sole practitioner used phrase "and Associates" in letterhead); *State ex rel. Okla. Bar Ass'n v. Leigh*, 914 P.2d 661 (Okla. 1996) (sole lawyer of legal corporation may not use title "Senior Attorney and Director of Services"); Minn. Ethics Op. 20 (2009) (firm may not use "Associates" in name unless three or more lawyers practice with it); S.C. Ethics Op. 05-19 (2005) (sole practitioner who employs only nonlawyer assistants may not use "Associates" in firm name); *cf.* D.C. Ethics Op. 332 (2005) (sole practitioner may use term "firm" in firm name; word does not imply practice with other lawyers).

### • *Implying Government or Pro Bono Connection*

Comment [5] explains that a law firm name that implies the firm has a connection to a government agency or public or charitable legal services organization is misleading. It also states that a law firm using a trade name that incorporates a geographical term may be required to include a disclaimer; for example, a firm using the name "Springfield Legal Clinic" may need to include a statement that it is not a public legal aid organization. *See* Cal. Formal Ethics Op. 04-167 (2004) (firm's name, "Workers Compensation Relief Center," improperly implies affiliation with governmental agency); Conn. Informal Ethics Op. 95-22 (1995) ("[X] County Legal Services" requires disclaimer of any connection with either government agency or public or charitable legal services organization); Md. Ethics Op. 2010-02 (2009) (firm's use of "generic name of a state administrative agency" improper); Md. Ethics Op. 04-10 (2004) ("Consumer Legal Services" is improper trade name because it implies firm is public or charitable legal services organization); S.C. Ethics Op. 98-35 (1998) ("[Community Name] Legal Clinic" permissible if accompanied by explanation that firm is not legal aid office); Utah Ethics Op. 01-07 (2001) ("Legal Center for the Wrongly Accused" does not imply connection with government or pro bono organization).

The Supreme Court has held that the phrase "legal clinic" is not inherently misleading. *Bates v. State Bar*, 433 U.S. 350 (1977); *see also Jacoby v. State Bar*, 562 P.2d 1326 (Cal. 1977) ("use of 'legal clinic' appears less misleading than the widespread custom of retaining in the title of a law firm the name of partners long since deceased"). *But see In re Vincenti*, 704 A.2d 927 (N.J. 1998) (lawyer may not use phrase "Legal Clinic" on letterhead without informing clients in writing that firm not affiliated with public or charitable organization).

### • *Clarifying Lawyers' Jurisdictional Limitations*

Comment [6] explains that a law firm with offices in more than one jurisdiction may use the same name for all its offices. Prior to 2018, this provision was contained in Model Rule 7.5(b) (deleted 2018), which also required the firm to specify on its letterhead "the jurisdictional limitations on those not licensed to practice in the jurisdiction where the office is located." *See Att'y Grievance Comm'n v. Ambe*, 38 A.3d 390 (Md. 2012) (New York lawyer practicing from office in Maryland failed to disclose limitations on practice on letterhead and business cards); *State ex rel. Okla. Bar Ass'n v. Burnett*, 91 P.3d 641 (Okla. 2004) (lawyer practicing from Texas office failed to indicate on letterhead that she was licensed only in Oklahoma); *In re Ness*, 651 N.W.2d 724 (Wis. 2002) (suspending Wisconsin lawyer who described his firm as "national" law firm and used letterhead, websites, and fax transmission cover sheets falsely suggesting he was also admitted in Minnesota and in federal courts); Ark. Ethics Op. 2004-03 (2004) (firm employing lawyer not licensed in firm's resident state may still list lawyer on letterhead if jurisdictional limitation noted); Conn. Informal Ethics Op. 83-3 (1983) (lawyers admitted in different states who form partnership may include both names in partnership's name, but letterhead and other listings must indicate jurisdictional limitations); Ill. Ethics Op. 14-04 (2014) (out-of-state personal injury lawyer's mail solicitations to Illinois residents must state in which jurisdictions lawyer licensed); Mich. Informal Ethics Op. RI-353 (2012) (law firm name may contain name of lawyer not admitted to practice in Michigan if precautions taken to avoid misleading public, such as noting lawyer's jurisdictional limitations on firm letterhead); N.Y. State Ethics Op. 704 (1998) (names of lawyers listed on letterhead of multijurisdictional firms must be accompanied by notation of any jurisdictional limitations on ability to practice); N.Y. Cnty. Ethics Op. 682 (1990) (lawyers licensed only in other states may be listed on firm letterhead and given business cards, as long as limitations on status disclosed); Ohio Ethics Op. 2008-1 (2008) (Ohio lawyer may be named as "Of Counsel" on out-of-state firm's letterhead but jurisdictional limitations must be indicated on letterhead); Phila. Ethics Op. 2005-14 (2005) (lawyer not licensed in Pennsylvania may practice federal immigration law in Pennsylvania but must indicate lack of Pennsylvania license in all professional communications); Utah Ethics Op. 00-02 (2000) (lawyer on inactive status in another jurisdiction may not list herself as "also admitted" or "licensed" there without further explanation); *see also In re Franco*, 66 P.3d 805 (Kan. 2003) (business card of lawyer admitted only in Missouri claimed lawyer "practicing in Missouri and Kansas"); *In re Jardine*, 764 S.E.2d 924 (S.C. 2014) (out-of-state lawyer's direct-mail solicitations to South Carolina residents contained misleading firm trade name, failed to note lawyer did not have South Carolina law license, and omitted name under which lawyer licensed).

As of 2018 the Model Rules and comment no longer contain a specific requirement that law firms disclose jurisdictional limitations of its lawyers. Nevertheless, Rule 7.1 would bar law firm communications that imply firm lawyers are licensed in jurisdictions where they are not.

## • *Listing Lawyers' Outside Credentials*

A lawyer may indicate that she is also qualified in another field, such as accounting, financial planning, or medicine. *See Ibanez v. Fla. Dep't of Bus. & Prof'l Regulation*, 512 U.S. 136 (1994) (cannot prohibit lawyer from including "Certified Public Accountant" and "Certified Financial Planner" on letterhead and other advertising); Ala. Ethics Op. 87-80 (1987) (lawyer who is also licensed engineer may include designation "P.E." after name on business cards and letterhead); Del. Ethics Op. 04-1 (2004) (lawyer who is also certified public accountant may include designation "C.P.A." in letterhead); Ohio Sup. Ct. Ethics Op. 2018-6 (2018) (lawyer who holds another degree or professional license may include that in communications about practice); Phila. Ethics Op. 86-171 (1986) (all professional licenses and academic degrees may be included on letterhead, business cards, and other advertising); S.C. Ethics Op. 15-03 (2015) ("CIPP/US" acronym standing for "Certified Information Privacy Professional/US" designation bestowed by recognized legitimate organization "truthfully reflects a recognized professional certification available to both lawyers and non-lawyer[s], is objectively verifiable, and is not misleading"); *see also State ex rel. Okla. Bar Ass'n v. Leigh*, 914 P.2d 661 (Okla. 1996) (lawyer who failed CPA exam may not indicate "CPA" on letterhead); Tenn. Formal Ethics Op. 98-F-142 (1998) (misleading to add "Approved Rule 31 Mediator" on letterhead; should specify "Tennessee Supreme Court Approved Mediator"). For discussion of communicating fields of legal specialization, see the annotation to Rule 7.2.

### • *Firm Members Holding Public Office*

Comment [8], formerly contained in Model Rule 7.5(c) (deleted 2018), states that a firm name is misleading if it includes the name of a lawyer who holds public office "during any substantial period in which the lawyer is not actively and regularly practicing with the firm." *See In re Riddle*, 700 N.E.2d 788 (Ind. 1998) (lawyer who became full-time county prosecutor should have removed name from sign and stationery of private law office); Mont. Ethics Op. 001029 (2000) (full-time public officeholder may not continue to practice in "off-hours" and must remove name from firm's name); N.H. Ethics Op. 1988-9/22 (1989) (letterhead may not include name of former member appointed to public office or designate him "on leave of absence"; notation could mislead clients to believe he wielded influence to firm's advantage); Pa. Ethics Op. 2007-21 (2007) (lawyer who bought practice of recently elected county prosecutor may not continue to use prosecutor's name in firm name); Utah Ethics Op. 18-01 (2018) (firm may continue to include name of partner elected part-time state legislator in firm name if partner actively and regularly practices in firm during legislature recesses).

### • *Former Judges*

Several ethics opinions have addressed the propriety of referring in a firm's name or letterhead to a lawyer's prior service as a judge. *See* ABA Formal Ethics Op. 95-391 (1995) (referring to prior service as judge "is misleading insofar as it is likely to create an unjustified expectation about the results a lawyer can achieve"); Ariz. Ethics Op. 87-1 (1987) (permissible to identify lawyer's prior service as judge on letterhead, though possible that potential clients "may unjustifiably assume" undue influence with current judges); Mich. Informal Ethics Op. RI-327 (2001) (former judge may not use firm name "Honorable XXX Doe and Associates" even if letterhead shows prior years of service as judge); Ohio Sup. Ct. Ethics Op. 2013-3 (2013) (former judge who has returned to practice of law may not use judicial title); Pa. Ethics Op. 99-156 (1999) (including statement on letterhead that member is former judge does not create unjustified expectations about results lawyer can achieve).

### • *Named Partners Who Leave, Die, or Retire*

In general, a law firm may use in its firm name the name of a deceased partner or a partner who has given up his partnership but not started another practice with another firm. However, there should be no implication the lawyer is still a partner with the firm. *See, e.g., Ashtabula Cnty. Bar Ass'n v. Brown*, 86 N.E.3d 269 (Ohio 2017) (lawyer may not use name of former partner, now a sitting supreme court justice, in firm name, even with justice's consent); Conn. Informal Ethics Op. 03-12 (2003) (firm may continue to use name of partner who left firm to relocate to another state, provided his name removed from list of active lawyers); Ill. Ethics Op. 03-02 (2004) (firm may continue to use name of retired partner if it is bona fide successor of original partnership and takes reasonable steps to show partner retired); N.Y. State Ethics Op. 622 (1991) (after named partner died, other partners formed two new firms; one, but not both, of the new firms may use deceased partner's name in firm name if substantial continuity with original firm's membership, clientele, and professional practice, new firm is legally or contractually entitled to use name, and name not misleading); Or. Ethics Op. 2005-169 (rev. 2015) (partner who retires from firm to become mediator and paid consultant to firm may still be listed on letterhead, which must note "available solely as mediator"); *see also In re Weigel*, 817 N.W.2d 835 (Wis. 2012) (lawyer's continued use of former partner's name in law firm name violated Rule 7.1).

If a lawyer begins practicing with another firm, the former firm should no longer use the lawyer's name in the firm name. Md. Ethics Op. 00-03 (1999) (professional corporation may not continue to include in its trade name the name of former member who is no longer shareholder but who continues practicing elsewhere); Neb. Ethics Op. 10-04 (2010) (firm may not continue to use name of retired partner once partner resumes practice in new firm); N.C. Ethics Op. 2006-20 (2007) (lawyer whose professional corporation bears his name may not sell corporation's right to use name if he withdraws and practices in another firm); Phila. Ethics Op. 2005-13 (2005) (former partner and current "of counsel" at one firm may not join new firm as partner or associate and still be listed by name in letterhead of former firm). *But see* D.C. Ethics Op. 338 (2007) (firm may continue to use name of former partner who retains "of counsel" relationship even though former partner has become partner in another firm).

## • *Lawyers Who Have Lost or Relinquished Their License*

Lawyers who lack an active law license should not be named in the firm letterhead as practicing lawyers. *In re Coleman*, 919 A.2d 1135 (D.C. 2007) (lawyer on inactive status in Pennsylvania continued to act as local counsel and was listed as "of counsel" to New Jersey firm); Ariz. Ethics Op. 2002-07 (2002) (name of lawyer who goes on disability inactive status should be removed from firm letterhead); Me. Ethics Op. 132 (1993) (names of suspended lawyers must be dropped from all communications, including letterhead, until they are authorized to resume practice); R.I. Ethics Op. 2001-07 (2001) (name of suspended lawyer must be removed from firm name). *But see* N.Y. City Ethics Op. 2005-6 (2005) (because New York rules allow inactive-status lawyers to continue practicing law as long as they do not charge fee, inactive lawyers may continue using professional letterhead). For a discussion of unauthorized practice by lawyers who have lost or relinquished their license, see the annotation to Rule 5.5.

## • *Nonlawyers*

Comment [5] explains that a law firm name that implies a connection with a nonlawyer is misleading. This provision, originally added in 2002 to the comment to Model Rule 7.5 (deleted 2018), reflects concern that law firms joining with nonlawyer professionals in multidisciplinary arrangements would create confusion if they added nonlawyer names to their firm name. American Bar Association, *A Legislative History: The Development of the ABA Model Rules of Professional Conduct, 1982–2013*, at 823 (2013).

Nonlawyers may be listed on firm letterhead, business cards, or other communications if it is clearly indicated they are not lawyers. *See, e.g., Att'y Grievance Comm'n v. Mitchell*, 872 A.2d 720 (Md. 2005) (lawyer who allowed his nonlawyer wife to pass out business cards implying she was member of firm violated both Rule 7.1 and Rule 7.5); Conn. Informal Ethics Op. 2012-05 (2012) (law firm may not identify nonlawyer employee as "principal" on letterhead); Fla. Ethics Op. 94-6 (1995) (law firm may list mediation department's nonlawyer mediators on firm letterhead if it makes clear their nonlawyer status); Mich. Informal Ethics Op. RI-323 (2001) (law firm may not list name of nonlawyer in letterhead with title "Estate Administrator" without clearly indicating administrator not a lawyer; adding "MBA" after administrator's name does not solve problem); Nassau Cnty. (N.Y.) Ethics Op. 91-32 (1991) (firm that includes nonlawyers on its letterhead must indicate their function and nonlawyer status); N.Y. Cnty. Ethics Op. 682 (1990) (firm may list name of recent law school graduate on its letterhead if it notes he is not yet admitted to bar); Phila. Ethics Op. 2012-1 (2012) (nonprofit legal services organization using nonlawyer "community advocates" to distribute flyers and refer community members to organization must disclose in flyer or handout that advocates not lawyers); Utah Ethics Op. 131 (1993) (firm may list nonlawyer employees on letterhead if designation clearly indicates they are nonlawyers); *see also* S.C. Ethics Op. 05-19 (2005) (lobbying firm created by lawyer may list nonlawyer employees in letterhead provided their nonlawyer status clearly articulated); *cf. People v. Ra'shadd*, 110 P.3d 388 (Colo. O.P.D.J. 2005) (lawyer placed newspaper ad touting firm's employment of law student "special advocate" after student quit firm).

## NONTRADITIONAL LAW OFFICE ARRANGEMENTS

Lawyers practicing through a "virtual" law office, or those using shared office space for client meetings, may generally list the address of a mailbox or shared office on their websites, letterhead, and other communications, but further clarification may be required. *See, e.g.,* N.Y. State Ethics Op. 964 (2013) (lawyer may use virtual law office mailbox address as sole office address on letterhead and business cards if not used as advertising and not misleading); N.Y. City Ethics Op. 2014-2 (2014) (letterhead containing only street address where lawyer rents shared business facilities not inherently misleading); N.C. Ethics Op. 2012-6 (2012) (lawyer using time-shared office space may list that address on letterhead and advertising if explanation such as "by appointment only" is included to make nature of address and lawyer's location clear; additionally, lawyer may use post office box on advertisements if that address is on file with state bar); Ohio Sup. Ct. Ethics Op. 2017-5 (2017) (lawyer practicing through virtual law office must make nature of virtual practice clear in all communications and must not imply existence of traditional physical office); Pa. Formal Ethics Op. 2010-200 (2010) (lawyer with virtual law practice need not list physical address on letterhead but must state city or town of office where lawyer principally performs legal services);

Va. Ethics Op. 1872 (2013) (lawyer may not hold out virtual or shared office space as "law office" unless lawyer provides legal services there); *see also Texans Against Censorship, Inc. v. State Bar*, 888 F. Supp. 1328 (E.D. Tex. 1995) (location of lawyer's branch offices, regardless of staffing or frequency of lawyer's presence, is information that cannot be prohibited in advertisements); *In re Charges of Unprof'l Conduct Against 95-30*, 550 N.W.2d 616 (Minn. 1996) (advertising and letterhead listing series of "offices near you," most of which were merely meeting spaces lawyer occasionally rented by hour, was "vague" but "not *materially* misleading" [emphasis in original]; court commended lawyer for revising letterhead "to remove any possible ambiguity").

## INTERNET ADDRESSES

A law firm's internet address need not be identical to the firm name. However, it is a professional designation subject to regulation under the Model Rules and must not be misleading. Cmt. [5]; *see, e.g.*, Ariz. Ethics Op. 2011-04 (2011) (firm may use ".org" as suffix but may not use domain name that falsely implies affiliation with governmental or nonprofit entity); Ky. Ethics Op. E-427 (2007) (firm may use domain name different from firm name as long as it is not false, deceptive, or misleading); Md. Ethics Op. 2004-15 (2004) ("www.marylandadoption.us" impermissibly implies affiliation with governmental organization); N.J. Advertising Ethics Op. 32 (2005) (internet address may be different from firm's name but must comply with advertising rules); N.C. Ethics Op. 2005-14 (2006) (firms may use addresses that fail to identify owners as law firms if addresses not otherwise misleading); Ohio Sup. Ct. Ethics Op. 2018-5 (2018) (firm internet domain name is subject to regulation under advertising rules); Ohio Sup. Ct. Ethics Op. 99-4 (1999) (domain name including "willwineverycaseforyou.com" is misleading); S.C. Ethics Op. 04-06 (2004) (firm may use descriptive internet address indicating field of practice, provided not false or misleading); Va. Ethics Op. 1873 (2014) (law firm need not immediately change web domain name and URL upon separation of named partner but must include information about change in firm name and membership when automatically redirecting internet traffic to new firm homepage); *see also* N.C. Ethics Op. 2005-08 (2005) (internet address that is more than minor variation on name of firm must be registered with state bar as trade name). *See generally* Louise L. Hill, *Change Is in the Air: Lawyer Advertising and the Internet*, 36 U. Rich. L. Rev. 21 (2002).

## "OF COUNSEL" DESIGNATION

Generally a lawyer may be called "of counsel" to a firm when the lawyer and firm enjoy "a close and continuing relationship"; daily contact is not required, but "frequent and continuing contact"—defined as more than "merely an availability for occasional consultations"—is required. Compensation arrangements are not relevant. ABA Formal Ethics Op. 90-357 (1990); *accord* Haw. Ethics Op. 43 (2003) ("of counsel" acceptable designation as long as relationship between lawyers is continuing, close, and regular); Iowa Ethics Op. 13-01 (2013) (Iowa lawyers and law firms may use variants of "of counsel" to characterize relationship); N.C. Ethics Op. 34 (1987) (lawyer who maintains office at firm, works there few days each month, and has frequent contact with firm's other lawyers and staff may be designated "of counsel").

A law firm's letterhead may include the names of lawyers who are of counsel to the firm, if their status is clearly indicated. *See, e.g.,* Ariz. Ethics Op. 12-01 (2012) (firm may include names of nonmember lawyers who are "of counsel" to firm on firm letterhead and advertisements if "of counsel" and any other relationship or practice limitations are clearly identified); Pa. Ethics Op. 97-81 (1997) (lawyer formerly employed by firm may use "of counsel" on letterhead, followed by name of law firm and list of lawyers in it, if lawyer has contractual responsibilities to firm and remains available for consultation).

In general, a firm's name may include the names of "of counsel" lawyers. *See, e.g.,* D.C. Ethics Op. 338 (2007) (firm may continue to use name of former partner who retains "of counsel" relationship even though former partner has become partner in another firm); Fla. Ethics Op. 00-01 (2000) (law firm may continue using name of former partner who becomes "of counsel" and works for firm exclusively); Md. Ethics Op. 2002-15 (2002) (firm may continue to use name of partner who becomes "of counsel"); N.Y. City Ethics Op. 1995-9 (1995) (ethics rules do not require firm name to consist exclusively of partners; firm name may include "of counsel" lawyer's name).

## LIMITED-LIABILITY STATUS

Several ethics opinions have addressed the indication of limited-liability status in firm names. *See, e.g.,* Kan. Ethics Op. 94-03 (1994) (although lawyers may practice as limited-liability company or limited-liability partnership, use of "limited-liability partnership" or "LLP" on letterhead may raise questions in clients' minds; lawyers should fully explain designation to their clients); Mich. Formal Ethics Op. R-17 (1994) (ethics rules do not require lawyers to include information about limited-liability status in firm name, other than "Professional Limited Liability Company," or abbreviation "P.L.L.C." or "P.L.C."); N.Y. City Ethics Op. 1995-7 (1995) (lawyers practicing as limited-liability company or limited-liability partnership must designate organizational form in firm name by specific words or abbreviations); Wash. Ethics Op. 2135 (2007) (firm operating as limited legal liability corporation need not include "PLLC" in name and letterhead, but "should consider" explaining corporate structure in marketing materials).

## IN-HOUSE LAWYERS—INSURANCE COMPANIES

A lawyer employed by an insurance company may not suggest that the lawyer practices as a separate independent entity. *Gafcon, Inc. v. Ponsor & Assocs.,* 120 Cal. Rptr. 2d 392 (Cal. 2002) (insurance company's in-house counsel must clearly indicate relationship to insurer on letterhead); *In re Foos,* 770 N.E.2d 335 (Ind. 2002) ("Conover & Foos, Litigation Section of the Warrior Insurance Group, Inc." misleadingly suggests independent entity, notwithstanding disclaimer in small print on bottom of letterhead); *In re Weiss, Healey & Rea,* 536 A.2d 266 (N.J. 1988) (use of "[X], [Y] & [Z]" as trade name by lawyer employees of insurer inaccurately indicated they practiced as partners); *In re Youngblood,* 895 S.W.2d 322 (Tenn. 1995) (deceptive for insurance company's in-house lawyer to hold self out as separate, independent firm); ABA Formal Ethics Op. 03-430 (2003) (in-house insurance lawyers permitted to refer to themselves as "firm," "law firm," or "association" of lawyers only if lawyers disclose their employment status to all clients); Ala. Ethics Op. 2007-01 (2007) (insurance company's in-house litigation lawyers may use trade name but must disclose their relationship to company on letterhead); Md. Ethics Op. 00-46 (2000) (in-house lawyer employed by insurance company must use employer's letterhead); Or. Ethics Op. 2005-153 (rev. 2015) (failure of in-house insurance lawyers to identify themselves as employees of insurance company would be misleading).

## Rule 7.2

### *Communications Concerning a Lawyer's Services: Specific Rules*

(a) A lawyer may communicate information regarding the lawyer's services through any media.

(b) A lawyer shall not compensate, give or promise anything of value to a person for recommending the lawyer's services except that a lawyer may:

(1) pay the reasonable costs of advertisements or communications permitted by this Rule;

(2) pay the usual charges of a legal service plan or a not-for-profit or qualified lawyer referral service;

(3) pay for a law practice in accordance with Rule 1.17;

(4) refer clients to another lawyer or a nonlawyer professional pursuant to an agreement not otherwise prohibited under these Rules that provides for the other person to refer clients or customers to the lawyer, if:

(i) the reciprocal referral agreement is not exclusive; and

(ii) the client is informed of the existence and nature of the agreement; and

(5) give nominal gifts as an expression of appreciation that are neither intended nor reasonably expected to be a form of compensation for recommending a lawyer's services.

(c) A lawyer shall not state or imply that a lawyer is certified as a specialist in a particular field of law, unless:

(1) the lawyer has been certified as a specialist by an organization that has been approved by an appropriate authority of the state or the District of Columbia or a U.S. Territory or that has been accredited by the American Bar Association; and

(2) the name of the certifying organization is clearly identified in the communication.

(d) Any communication made under this Rule must include the name and contact information of at least one lawyer or law firm responsible for its content.

## COMMENT

[1] This Rule permits public dissemination of information concerning a lawyer's or law firm's name, address, email address, website, and telephone number; the kinds of services the lawyer will undertake; the basis on which the lawyer's fees are determined, including prices for specific services and payment and credit arrangements; a lawyer's foreign language ability; names of references and, with their consent, names of clients regularly represented; and other information that might invite the attention of those seeking legal assistance.

### *Paying Others to Recommend a Lawyer*

[2] Except as permitted under paragraphs (b)(1)-(b)(5), lawyers are not permitted to pay others for recommending the lawyer's services. A communication contains a recommendation if it endorses or vouches for a lawyer's credentials, abilities, competence, character, or other professional qualities. Directory listings and group advertisements that list lawyers by practice area, without more, do not constitute impermissible "recommendations."

[3] Paragraph (b)(1) allows a lawyer to pay for advertising and communications permitted by this Rule, including the costs of print directory listings, on-line directory listings, newspaper ads, television and radio airtime, domain-name registrations, sponsorship fees, Internet-based advertisements, and group advertising. A lawyer may compensate employees, agents and vendors who are engaged to provide marketing or client development services, such as publicists, public-relations personnel, business-development staff, television and radio station employees or spokespersons and website designers.

[4] Paragraph (b)(5) permits lawyers to give nominal gifts as an expression of appreciation to a person for recommending the lawyer's services or referring a prospective client. The gift may not be more than a token item as might be given for holidays, or other ordinary social hospitality. A gift is prohibited if offered or given in consideration of any promise, agreement or understanding that such a gift would be forthcoming or that referrals would be made or encouraged in the future.

[5] A lawyer may pay others for generating client leads, such as Internet-based client leads, as long as the lead generator does not recommend the lawyer, any payment to the lead generator is consistent with Rules 1.5(e) (division of fees) and 5.4 (professional independence of the lawyer), and the lead generator's communications are consistent with Rule 7.1 (communications concerning a lawyer's services). To comply with Rule 7.1, a lawyer must not pay a lead generator that states, implies, or creates a reasonable impression that it is recommending the lawyer, is making the referral without payment from the lawyer, or has analyzed a person's legal problems when determining which lawyer should receive the referral. See Comment [2] (definition of "recommendation"). See also Rule 5.3 (duties of lawyers and law firms with respect to the conduct of nonlawyers); Rule 8.4(a) (duty to avoid violating the Rules through the acts of another).

[6] A lawyer may pay the usual charges of a legal service plan or a not-for-profit or qualified lawyer referral service. A legal service plan is a prepaid or group legal

service plan or a similar delivery system that assists people who seek to secure legal representation. A lawyer referral service, on the other hand, is any organization that holds itself out to the public as a lawyer referral service. Qualified referral services are consumer-oriented organizations that provide unbiased referrals to lawyers with appropriate experience in the subject matter of the representation and afford other client protections, such as complaint procedures or malpractice insurance require-ments. Consequently, this Rule only permits a lawyer to pay the usual charges of a not-for-profit or qualified lawyer referral service. A qualified lawyer referral service is one that is approved by an appropriate regulatory authority as affording adequate protections for the public. See, e.g., the American Bar Association's Model Supreme Court Rules Governing Lawyer Referral Services and Model Lawyer Referral and Information Service Quality Assurance Act.

[7] A lawyer who accepts assignments or referrals from a legal service plan or referrals from a lawyer referral service must act reasonably to assure that the activi-ties of the plan or service are compatible with the lawyer's professional obligations. Legal service plans and lawyer referral services may communicate with the public, but such communication must be in conformity with these Rules. Thus, advertising must not be false or misleading, as would be the case if the communications of a group advertising program or a group legal services plan would mislead the pub-lic to think that it was a lawyer referral service sponsored by a state agency or bar association.

[8] A lawyer also may agree to refer clients to another lawyer or a nonlawyer professional, in return for the undertaking of that person to refer clients or custom-ers to the lawyer. Such reciprocal referral arrangements must not interfere with the lawyer's professional judgment as to making referrals or as to providing substantive legal services. See Rules 2.1 and 5.4(c). Except as provided in Rule 1.5(e), a lawyer who receives referrals from a lawyer or nonlawyer professional must not pay any-thing solely for the referral, but the lawyer does not violate paragraph (b) of this Rule by agreeing to refer clients to the other lawyer or nonlawyer professional, so long as the reciprocal referral agreement is not exclusive and the client is informed of the referral agreement. Conflicts of interest created by such arrangements are governed by Rule 1.7. Reciprocal referral agreements should not be of indefinite duration and should be reviewed periodically to determine whether they comply with these Rules. This Rule does not restrict referrals or divisions of revenues or net income among lawyers within firms comprised of multiple entities.

### *Communications about Fields of Practice*

[9] Paragraph (c) of this Rule permits a lawyer to communicate that the lawyer does or does not practice in particular areas of law. A lawyer is generally permitted to state that the lawyer "concentrates in" or is a "specialist," practices a "specialty," or "specializes in" particular fields based on the lawyer's experience, specialized train-ing or education, but such communications are subject to the "false and misleading" standard applied in Rule 7.1 to communications concerning a lawyer's services.

[10] The Patent and Trademark Office has a long-established policy of designat-ing lawyers practicing before the Office. The designation of Admiralty practice also

has a long historical tradition associated with maritime commerce and the federal courts. A lawyer's communications about these practice areas are not prohibited by this Rule.

[11] This Rule permits a lawyer to state that the lawyer is certified as a specialist in a field of law if such certification is granted by an organization approved by an appropriate authority of a state, the District of Columbia or a U.S. Territory or accredited by the American Bar Association or another organization, such as a state supreme court or a state bar association, that has been approved by the authority of the state, the District of Columbia or a U.S. Territory to accredit organizations that certify lawyers as specialists. Certification signifies that an objective entity has recognized an advanced degree of knowledge and experience in the specialty area greater than is suggested by general licensure to practice law. Certifying organizations may be expected to apply standards of experience, knowledge and proficiency to ensure that a lawyer's recognition as a specialist is meaningful and reliable. To ensure that consumers can obtain access to useful information about an organization granting certification, the name of the certifying organization must be included in any communication regarding the certification.

## Required Contact Information

[12] This Rule requires that any communication about a lawyer or law firm's services include the name of, and contact information for, the lawyer or law firm. Contact information includes a website address, a telephone number, an email address or a physical office location.

### Definitional Cross-References
"Law firm" *See* Rule 1.0(c)

### State Rules Comparison
http://ambar.org/MRPCStateCharts

### 2018 Advertising Rule Changes
http://ambar.org/AdvRuleChanges2018

## ANNOTATION
### LEGISLATIVE HISTORY
• *2012 Amendments*

In 2012, the comment was amended to clarify that lawyers may use lead-generation services, including those based on the internet, consistent with the rules, and to eliminate the term "prospective client," to avoid confusion with the term as used in Rule 1.18. American Bar Association, *A Legislative History: The Development of the ABA Model Rules of Professional Conduct, 1982–2013*, at 767 (2013).

## • *2018 Amendments*

In 2018, Model Rule 7.2 was modified in several respects. The title of the rule was changed from "Advertising" to "Communications Concerning A Lawyer's Services: Specific Rules." Paragraph (a) was revised to replace the word "advertise" with "communicate information regarding the lawyer's services," and to replace the phrase "written, recorded or electronic communication" with "any media." Paragraph (b) added the words "compensate" and "promise" to the prohibition on giving anything of value for recommending the lawyer's services. A new paragraph (b)(5) was added to include "nominal gifts as an expression of appreciation" in the exceptions to the general prohibition. Paragraph (c), along with comments [9]-[11], was added to address what lawyers may say about their fields of practice, expertise, and certifications. These issues were previously covered by former Rule 7.4, which was deleted in 2018. Paragraph (d) (formerly paragraph (c)) was revised to replace the phrase "office address" with "contact information." *See* ABA Report to the House of Delegates, Revised Resolution 101 (Aug. 2018), *available at* http://ambar.org/ AdvRuleChanges2018.

## Paragraph (a): *Communications through Any Media*

Rule 7.2(a) makes clear that lawyers are free to advertise their services through any media. That broad statement eliminates ambiguity created by prior versions of the rule which, by listing specific acceptable types of media advertising, left it unclear whether other types of advertising were also permitted. *See* ABA Report to the House of Delegates, Revised Resolution 101 (Aug. 2018), *available at* http://ambar.org/ AdvRuleChanges2018. Many jurisdictions retain the prior wording, which provided that a lawyer may advertise legal services through "written, recorded or electronic communication, including public media."

### WRITTEN COMMUNICATIONS

*Bates v. State Bar*, 433 U.S. 350 (1977), established that lawyer advertising in print media is constitutionally protected if it is not false or misleading. As a result of *Bates*, all states now permit lawyer advertising in printed media such as newspapers, periodicals, and Yellow Pages.

### RECORDED COMMUNICATIONS

Although Rule 7.2(a) now explicitly permits lawyers to advertise through any media, the prior version of the rule was amended in 1989 to add "recorded" communications to the list of permitted advertising media. *See* American Bar Association, *A Legislative History: The Development of the ABA Model Rules of Professional Conduct, 1982–2013*, at 753–54 (2013); *see also* Ill. Ethics Op. 97-6 (1998) (lawyer may advertise using recorded telephone announcement featuring general legal information); Ind. Ethics Op. 1996-3 (1996) (lawyer may participate in arrangement whereby newspaper subscribers phone prerecorded informational tapes sponsored by law firm if recording identified as advertising); Iowa Ethics Op. 86-6 (1986) (lawyer may advertise with service in which potential clients call number and receive prerecorded message with name, number, and address of lawyer if disclaimer used); Md. Ethics Op. 88-61 (1988) (lawyer may use automated telephone system and follow-up letter to advertise legal services).

If the lawyer knows that the person receiving the recorded message does not want to be contacted, the call constitutes solicitation and is barred by Rule 7.3.

## ELECTRONIC COMMUNICATIONS

Even under prior formulations, the Model Rules and predecessor Model Code treated broadcast communications in the same manner as any other form of advertising. *See, e.g., Grievance Comm. for Hartford-New Britain Judicial Dist. v. Trantolo*, 470 A.2d 228 (Conn. 1984) ("DR 2-101 [of the Code of Professional Responsibility] does not contemplate a blanket prohibition on lawyer advertising through the electronic media"; restricting advertising to print media unconstitutionally denies information about legal services to those who are illiterate, handicapped, and financially disadvantaged).

Some jurisdictions have scrutinized broadcast advertising more closely on the theory that it is uniquely persuasive and therefore more likely to mislead people. *See, e.g., In re Zang*, 741 P.2d 267 (Ariz. 1987) (dramatic sales pitch more troublesome when little time given for viewer/listener reflection and deliberation); *Comm. on Prof'l Ethics & Conduct v. Humphrey*, 377 N.W.2d 643 (Iowa 1985) ("electronic advertising presents a very strong potential for abuse, justifying its regulation"); Mo. Informal Ethics Op. 960040 (1996) (lawyer may advertise on radio using dialogue format and voices of professional announcers if advertisement includes disclaimer that voices not actual clients). *See generally* Clive M. Doran, *Television Advertising by Attorneys: A Deception Exception?*, 29 New Eng. L. Rev. 425 (Winter 1995); J. Alick Henderson, *Attorney Advertising: Does Television Advertising Deserve Special Treatment?*, 28 J. Legal Prof. 153 (2004).

Advertisements over electronic media, including social media, text messaging, and lawyer blogs, must comply with ethics rules. *See, e.g.*, Ala. Ethics Op. RO-96-07 (1996); Ariz. Ethics Op. 97-04 (1997); Cal. Formal Ethics Op. 2001-155 (n.d.); Colo. Ethics Op. 122 (2008; rev. 2010); Haw. Ethics Op. 41 (2001; amended 2015); Ill. Ethics Op. 96-10 (1997); Iowa Ethics Op. 00-1 (2000); Md. Ethics Op. 97-26 (1997); Mich. Informal Ethics Op. RI-276 (1996); Mo. Informal Ethics Op. 970161 (1997); N.J. Advertising Ethics Op. 43 (2011); N.Y. State Ethics Op. 1039 (2014); N.Y. Cnty. Ethics Op. 721 (1997); N.C. Ethics Op. 2017-01 (2017); Ohio Sup. Ct. Ethics Op. 2013-2 (2013); Pa. Ethics Op. 96-17 (1996); S.C. Ethics Op. 97-08 (1997); Utah Ethics Op. 97-10 (1997); Vt. Ethics Op. 2012-1 (2012); W. Va. Ethics Op. 2015-02 (2015). *See generally* American Bar Association, *Essential Qualities of the Professional Lawyer* 189–205 (2013); Jan L. Jacobowitz & John G. Browning, *Legal Ethics and Social Media: A Practitioner's Handbook* 185-206 (2017); David Hricik, Prashant Patel & Natasha Chrispin, *An Article We Wrote to Ourselves in the Future: Early 21st Century Views on Ethics and the Internet*, 1 St. Mary's J. Legal Mal. & Ethics 114 (2011); Michael E. Lackey, Jr. & Joseph P. Minta, *Lawyers and Social Media: The Legal Ethics of Tweeting, Facebooking and Blogging*, 28 Touro L. Rev. 149 (2012); J.T. Westermaier, *Ethics and the Internet*, 17 Geo. J. Legal Ethics 267 (Winter 2004).

## Paragraph (b): Compensating, Giving, or Promising Something of Value for Recommending Lawyer

Unless the exceptions of paragraph (b) apply, a lawyer may not pay, promise to pay, or give anything of value to anyone else to recommend the lawyer's services. *See People v. Shipp*, 793 P.2d 574 (Colo. 1990) (suspending lawyer for paying his inmate client to refer other inmates to him); *In re Maniscalco*, 564 S.E.2d 186 (Ga. 2002) (payment to operator of lawyer referral business who used nonlawyer "runners" to obtain clients violates rule even if lawyer initially did not know about runners and believed operator was a lawyer and refused to pay percentage of fees after learning truth); *Office of Disciplinary Counsel v. Au*, 113 P.3d 203 (Haw. 2005) (lawyer paid nonlawyer runner 5 percent of fees earned on cases that runner referred); *In re Goff*, 837 So. 2d 1201 (La. 2003) (lawyer suspended for participating in scheme to employ nonlawyer "runners" to refer personal injury clients); *Son v. Margolius, Mallios, Davis, Rider & Tomar*, 709 A.2d 112 (Md. 1998) (sufficient evidence for trial whether fee paid to personal injury client's nonlawyer "consultant" who referred case to law firm was referral fee in violation of rule; summary judgment reversed); *Emil v. Miss. Bar*, 690 So. 2d 301 (Miss. 1997) (lawyer suspended for using paid investigator to find prospective personal injury clients); *In re McCray*, 755 N.W.2d 835 (N.D. 2008) (lawyer paid marketing firm to tout firm's services at credit repair seminars); *Cincinnati Bar Ass'n v. Haas*, 699 N.E.2d 919 (Ohio 1998) (lawyer suspended for paying insurance salesperson for referring personal injury clients); N.Y. State Ethics Op. 1162 (2019) (lawyer who forms tax credit business may not pay other lawyers for referrals); Or. Ethics Op. 2005-73 (2005) (lawyer may accept referrals from friends, acquaintances, and clients only if lawyer does not request referrals and does not compensate individuals for their referrals); Utah Ethics Op. 14-02 (2014) (arrangement in which telephone direct marketer is paid percentage of fees generated for referrals to lawyer is impermissible); Wash. Ethics Op. 2227 (2012) (lawyer may not pay percentage of fees resulting from referrals to national organization for Russian-speaking lawyers when organization not duly authorized lawyer referral service). *Compare* S.C. Ethics Op. 13-09 (2013) (lawyer may not pay real estate agency for "Preferred Closing Attorney" designation in agency materials and other opportunities to access agency clients), *with* S.C. Ethics Op. 13-03 (2013) (lawyer may rent office space from real estate agency as condition of "preferred attorney" status if rent amount commercially reasonable).

Paragraph (b) also prohibits indirect compensation for referrals. *See* Conn. Informal Ethics Op. 92-24 (1992) (doing legal work for existing client on pro bono or reduced-fee basis in exchange for referral of new client constitutes giving something "of value" in violation of Rule 7.2); Del. Ethics Op. 2009-1 (2009) (firm may not pay nonlawyer marketing employee bonus based upon increased revenues from new clients or revenues from clients received by efforts of marketing employee); Ind. Ethics Op. 2008-4 (2008) (lawyer who donates services at charity auction must ensure no ongoing professional relationship with sponsoring charity lest donation be deemed thing of value given in return for recommendation of employment); N.Y. State Ethics Op. 930 (2013) (lawyer's participation in exclusive arrangement with insurance agency in which agency would market summary plan description for price that would include lawyer's review for discounted fee for clients referred by agency may violate Rule 7.2 if lawyer charges higher fee to other clients); N.D. Ethics Op. 08-06 (2008) (firm may not pay agency to market firm's estate planning services to employees of particular corporation); Pa. Ethics Op. 05-81 (2005) (lawyer may not give nonlawyer employee paid day off for referring new client to firm); Pa. Ethics Op. 93-107 (1993) (lawyer may not reduce fees ordinarily charged to client after client refers other cases to lawyer); Phila. Ethics Op. 95-10 (1995) (lawyer may not give prepaid telephone cards to clients or members of public as incentive for recommending lawyer's services); Wash. Ethics Op. 2203 (2010) (lawyer may not pay state mortgage broker association members for future services to clients referred to lawyer); *cf.* Md. Ethics Op. 2016-13 (n.d.) (paying online legal referral service to augment visibility on website does not constitute prohibited payment for referral).

## PAYMENTS THAT ARE PERMITTED

### • *Reasonable Costs of Advertising*

Paragraph (b)(1) allows a lawyer to pay the "reasonable costs" of advertising; Comment [3] explains that lawyers "may compensate employees, agents and vendors who are engaged to provide marketing or client development services, such as publicists, public-relations personnel, business-development staff, television and radio station employees or spokespersons and website designers," but other payments remain forbidden. *See* Ohio Sup. Ct. Ethics Op. 2001-2 (2001) (when lawyer "pays an entity to perform only the ministerial function of placing the attorney's name, address, phone number, fields of practice, and biographical information into the view of the public that is considered payment for an advertisement, not payment for a referral").

Permissible advertising arrangements vary. For example, in *Ala. State Bar Ass'n v. R.W. Lynch Co.*, 655 So. 2d 982 (Ala. 1995), individual lawyers and firms paid for a television commercial that included a notice that the advertisement was paid for by the sponsoring lawyers and was not a lawyer referral service; viewers who responded gave their names and numbers to a receptionist who forwarded the information to the lawyers according to their geographical areas. The lawyers then responded by calling the viewers to discuss the need for legal services. This plan was held to be a permissible form of group advertising and not a referral service. *See also* Ariz. Ethics Op. 91-04 (1991) (lawyer may participate in networking group whose members communicate availability of services if membership fee not based upon business generated, referring prospective clients not sole purpose of group, and lawyer does not accept referrals from members in exchange for referring clients to other members); Conn. Informal Ethics Op. 04-06 (2004) (lawyer who participates with nonlawyers in joint marketing efforts may contribute only lawyer's actual share of marketing expenses); Md. Ethics Op. 88-78 (1988) (advertisements that route viewers' calls to participating lawyers are form of group advertising, rather than referral service; lawyers pay cost of advertising, not fee for referrals); Mo. Informal Ethics Op. 970238 (1997) (law firm may allow clients to distribute coupons to their customers in mailers, provided firm pays only for expense of producing coupons and not for their distribution, and provided firm has no agreement with clients that clients will receive anything of value from firm).

## • Usual Charges of Legal Service Plans and
### Not-for-Profit or Qualified Lawyer Referral Services

Paragraph (b)(2) permits lawyers to pay the "usual charges" of legal service plans and not-for-profit or qualified lawyer referral services. *See People v. Zimmerman*, 938 P.2d 131 (Colo. 1997) (lawyer violated rule by paying monthly installments to, and advertising with, for-profit referral agency not approved by state bar association); Ariz. Ethics Op. 10-01 (2010) (not-for-profit organization that refers cases to participating lawyers may receive percentage of "court-ordered" fees in referred cases as part of its usual charge for lawyers' participation); D.C. Ethics Op. 369 (2015) (permissible to pay qualified lawyer referral service percentage of fees earned if that is organization's "usual fee"); Ill. Ethics Op. 15-04 (2015) (referral fee taken out of fees paid by client, not awarded by court, may not be paid to nonprofit organization unless it qualifies as not-for-profit lawyer referral service); Mo. Informal Ethics Op. 960126 (1996) (impermissible to give organization 10 percent of fees from cases it refers to lawyer unless organization is qualified, registered referral service); Mont. Ethics Op. 960227 (1996) (impermissible to participate in chamber of commerce referral network that awards "points" for leads because leads are not usual charges under rule); Neb. Ethics Op. 14-01 (2014) (approving participation in nonprofit state bar association lawyer referral program, which requires payment of initial fee and percentage of fees generated by referrals to fund program's reasonable operating expenses); Or. Ethics Op. 2005-79 (2005) (approving accepting clients via church's prepaid legal services plan available to church members); R.I. Ethics Op. 95-5 (1995) (may not pay percentage of fees to nonprofit, charitable organization that refers clients because organization not registered with state bar); Wash. Ethics Op. 2146 (2007) (nonprofit organization's lawyer referral service complies with rules if participating lawyers pay annual dues, not discrete fees for referrals); *see also* N.Y. City Ethics Op. 2017-1 (2017) (qualified legal assistance organizations may share referral fees).

## • Online Referral Services

Whether a lawyer may participate in and pay the fees charged by online referral services depends on how the service works and the fees are arrived at. *Compare* Ariz. Ethics Op. 11-02 (2011) (lawyer may participate in internet advertising website whereby lawyer pays for exclusive rights to leads generated within geographic area), D.C. Ethics Op. 342 (2007) (lawyer may participate in internet referral service that charges participating lawyers only flat fees and not share of fees from referred clients), N.C. Ethics Op. 2013-10 (2013) (lawyer may participate in "Total Attorneys" advertising website whereby lawyer pays for exclusive geographic lead-generation privileges, if disclosures clear and lawyer does not share fees with service), Ohio Sup. Ct. Ethics Op. 2016-3 (2016) (lawyers must ensure communications made on their behalf by online referral service are not false or misleading and otherwise meet requirements of ethics rules), Or. Ethics Op. 2007-180 (2007) (lawyer may pay agency for online listing in its directory of lawyers if fee not based upon number of referrals, retained clients, or revenue generated by lawyer's listing), R.I. Ethics Op. 05-01 (2005) (lawyer may pay flat fee to be listed in online directory; membership fee represents reasonable cost of advertising and does not constitute fee-sharing), Utah Ethics Op.

15-05 (2015) (approving participation in online service permitting lawyers to bid for clients' business that does not "recommend" bidding lawyers but indicates lawyers are "interested in" or "available" for service), *and* Vt. Ethics Op. 2014-3 (n.d.) (lawyer may participate in smartphone application that provides vehicle accident victims with services including names of lawyers in area; app company charges lawyer flat annual fee for geographical listing and does not make recommendations), *with* Ind. Sup. Ct. Ethics Op. 1-18 (2018) ("marketing fee" charged by online legal referral service that is tied to fees charged by lawyer is not reasonable cost of advertising and is more similar to prohibited payment for referrals), Mich. Informal Ethics Op. RI-365 (2013) (lawyer may not participate in for-profit marketing website that charges lawyer per blind referral generated when viewer selects lawyer's area of concentration), N.J. Ethics Op. 732 (2014) (lawyer may not participate in online legal service plans not registered with courts' administrative office or that require lawyer to share fee with nonlawyer or pay for referral), N.Y. State Ethics Op. 1132 (2017) ("marketing fee" charged by online referral company constitutes improper payment for recommendation); Ohio Sup. Ct. Ethics Op. 2016-3 (2016) (online lawyer referral service's "marketing fee" based on fees generated is tantamount to payment for referral); Pa. Ethics Op. 96-112 (1996) (prohibiting participation in online real estate lead and referral program in which lawyer would pay fee in exchange for exclusive marketing rights within certain area of state, advertising, and leads from sponsoring broker), Utah Ethics Op. 17-05 (2017) (fee charged by online referral service that varies by type of legal service provided bears no relationship to cost of advertising and would amount to impermissible payment for referral), *and* W. Va. Ethics Op. 2018-01 (2018) (lawyer-client matching arrangement in which payments to matching company are calculated based on number of matters and amount of fees generated amounts to impermissible payment in exchange for referrals). *See generally* Colo. Ethics Op. 122 (2010) (discussing characteristics of permissible internet lawyer marketing and referral programs); N.J. Advertising Ethics Op. 43 (2011) (same); Alberto Bernabe, *Attorney-Client Matchmaking and For-Profit Referral Services: 21st Century Innovation Clashes with 20th Century Rules and the End of Avvo Legal Services*, 25 Prof. Law., no. 2, at 8 (2018).

### • Website "Daily Deals" and Group Coupons

Whether a lawyer's participation in an arrangement with a website company to market group coupons or "daily deals" for discounted legal services is permissible under Rule 7.2 hinges upon whether the portion of the coupon's purchase price retained by the third-party company is determined to constitute payment for the reasonable cost of advertising. *Compare* ABA Formal Ethics Op. 465 (2013) (fee percentages retained by group coupon or deal-of-the-day marketers are permissible costs of lawyer advertising as long as amounts reasonable), Md. Ethics Op. 2012-7 (2012) (lawyer may use website company to advertise internet "daily deal" coupon, whereby company receives client's coupon fee, retains portion, and forwards remainder to lawyer; retained sum is cost of advertising and not prohibited referral fee), Neb. Ethics Op. 12-03 (2012) (same), N.H. Ethics Op. 2013-14/8 (2014) (same); N.Y. State Ethics Op. 897 (2011) (same), N.C. Ethics Op. 2011-10 (2011) (same), *and* S.C. Ethics Op.

11-05 (2011) (same), *with* Ala. Ethics Op. 2012-01 (2012) (percentage of lawyer's fee retained by "daily deal" website company not reasonable cost of advertising), Ariz. Ethics Op. 13-01 (2013) (discouraging lawyers from using group coupons whereby potential client pays coupon price directly to marketer), Ind. Ethics Op. 2012-1 (2012) (percentage of lawyer's fee retained by website company bears no relation to reasonable cost of advertising), *and* Mich. Informal Ethics Op. RI-366 (2014) (group coupon arrangement in which percentage of legal services coupon purchase price is retained by marketing company constitutes impermissible fee-sharing with nonlawyer). *See generally* Aaron J. Russ, *Is Groupon for Lawyers Fraught with Ethical Danger? Why the Legal Community Should Embrace Innovative Internet-Marketing for Lawyers*, 2013 U. Ill. J.L. Tech. & Pol'y 393 (Fall 2013).

## • *Purchasing a Law Practice*

Paragraph (b)(3) specifically allows a lawyer to pay the purchase price of a law practice. For a discussion of the ethical obligations involved in the sale and purchase of a law practice, see the annotation to Rule 1.17.

## • *Referrals pursuant to Agreement*

Paragraph (b)(4), added in 2002, allows mutual referrals of clients between a lawyer and another lawyer or "nonlawyer professional" if otherwise permitted by the rules and (i) the agreement is not exclusive, and (ii) the client is informed of the existence and nature of the agreement. *E.g.*, Utah Ethics Op. 14-03 (2014) (exclusive referral arrangement between two lawyers is impermissible); Vt. Ethics Op. 2012-1 (2012) (lawyer may participate in marketing campaign with lender and real estate agent if arrangement not exclusive, lawyer discloses arrangement to clients, payments to nonlawyers are for costs of advertising and not referrals, and any referral arrangement is informal, not explicit, and disclosed to potential clients). The prohibition against exclusive referral arrangements is intended to ensure a lawyer is "free to exercise independent professional judgment when counseling clients to consult with other professionals." American Bar Association, *A Legislative History: The Development of the ABA Model Rules of Professional Conduct, 1982–2013*, at 764 (2013); *see also* Ill. Ethics Op. 10-02 (2009) (lawyer referral arrangement with real estate company that requires lawyer to solely use company's affiliated title insurer as condition of receiving referrals impermissible); N.C. Ethics Op. 2006-7 (2006) ("when advising a client to use the services of a third party, a lawyer must exercise independent professional judgment"); Va. Ethics Op. 1846 (2009) ("the rationale against permitting a lawyer to make such exclusive . . . referrals is that this activity may compromise the professional judgment of the lawyer"); *cf.* N.Y. City Ethics Op. 2014-1 (2014) (discussing factors for lawyer to consider before entering arrangement to review documents for nonlegal organization's customers).

Although Rule 7.2(b)(4) allows referrals from a lawyer or nonlawyer professional, a lawyer who receives such referrals "must not pay anything solely for the referral." Cmt. [8]. Business arrangements involving lawyers making such payments or receiving such referrals have been found impermissible. *See* ABA Formal Ethics Op. 94-388 (1995) (law firm may not lend money to another firm and receive referrals as purported return on investment, even if firms not associated, affiliated, or part of network); Ill. Ethics Op. 96-04 (1996) (real estate brokerage corporation may not market lawyers' services to public and charge lawyers marketing fee); Md. Ethics Op. 99-10 (1998) (impermissible for accounting firm to hire lawyer at modest weekly wage with "understanding" it will refer fee-paying clients to lawyer); Mo. Informal Ethics Op. 970237 (1997) (impermissible for accounting firm to refer customers to law firm as quid pro quo for law firm's agreement to hire accounting firm for its administrative work); Mont. Ethics Op. 960227 (1996) (lawyer may not participate in network that requires members to make certain number of referrals to other members; leads given by lawyer to network members would constitute something of value in exchange for referrals); N.Y. State Ethics Op. 1001 (2014) (law firm may sell advertising in its newsletter to other professionals if no improper fee-splitting or referral arrangements); Pa. Ethics Op. 2008-37 (2008) (lawyer may not pay referral fee to owner of financial services company for referring company customers to lawyer); Phila. Ethics Op. 93-15 (1993) (lawyer may pay referring out-of-state law firm per-case fee of $35 if reimbursement for actual costs incurred by referring firm, but not if referral fee); S.C. Ethics Op. 93-05 (1993) (lawyer may not participate in ancillary business with accountant whereby lawyer provides capital, management advice, and referrals in exchange for accounting business's cross-referrals to him).

### • *Nominal Gifts*

Paragraph (b)(5), added in 2018, explicitly permits a lawyer to give "nominal gifts as an expression of appreciation" that are not intended or expected to be compensation for recommending the lawyer's services—an exception to the general prohibition that many authorities had already condoned. *See* Ariz. Ethics Op. 2002-01 (2002) (lawyer may give de minimis gift after referral as professional courtesy if lawyer's independent judgment not affected); Conn. Informal Ethics Op. 18-05 (2018) (lawyer may give gift of nominal value to thank person for referral); N.Y. State Ethics Op. 1052 (2015) (clients who post internet review of lawyer's services may be given $50 credit toward legal services, but credit may not be contingent on rating's substance); Phila. Ethics Op. 93-26 (1994) (law firm that represents union workers may take union representatives to dinner or give gifts valued less than $100; nominal value of gifts supports firm's position that gifts not being given for referrals); S.C. Ethics Op. 15-02 (2015) (law firm may launch program to deliver weekly small gifts such as doughnuts, coupons, and firm-branded items of minimal value to vendors firm hopes will refer it business if deliveries are not contingent upon actual referrals).

See also the annotation to Rule 5.4 for discussion of sharing fees with nonlawyers.

## *Paragraph (c): Communicating Fields of Practice and Specialization*

Paragraph (c), which prohibits stating or implying that a lawyer is certified as a specialist in a particular field unless certification requirements have been met, was formerly contained in Model Rule 7.4(d) (deleted 2018) and was moved to Model Rule 7.2 in 2018.

## CONSTITUTIONAL FRAMEWORK

It is well-settled that lawyer advertising is a form of commercial speech that may be restricted only when "the particular content or method of the advertising suggests that it is inherently misleading or when experience has proved that in fact such advertising is subject to abuse." *In re R.M.J.*, 455 U.S. 191 (1982) (disciplining lawyer for describing practice as "real estate" and "personal injury" rather than using prescribed terms "property law" and "tort law" violated First Amendment; lawyer's choice of words not misleading); *see also Zauderer v. Office of Disciplinary Counsel*, 471 U.S. 626 (1985) (factual description of lawyer's experience litigating in particular products liability area was not inherently misleading, even though reader might infer some expertise).

## FIELDS OF PRACTICE

Comment [9] contains language formerly found in Model Rule 7.4(a) (deleted 2018) explicitly stating that a lawyer may communicate in what fields of law the lawyer does or does not practice and, in general, may also state that the lawyer "concentrates in," is a "specialist," or "specializes in" a particular field as long as the communication is not false or misleading. *See, e.g.*, S.C. Ethics Op. 15-03 (2015) ("CIPP/US" acronym standing for "Certified Information Privacy Professional/US" designation bestowed by recognized legitimate organization "truthfully reflects a recognized professional certification available to both lawyers and non-lawyer[s], is objectively verifiable, and is not misleading").

The Model Rules originally prohibited stating or implying the lawyer was a specialist, except in the areas of patent law and admiralty, or under the specialization provisions of the particular state. Rule 7.4 (1983) [superseded]. However, as a result of *Peel v. Att'y Registration & Disciplinary Comm'n of Ill.*, 496 U.S. 91 (1990) (discussed below), these restrictions were relaxed. American Bar Association, *A Legislative History: The Development of the ABA Model Rules of Professional Conduct, 1982–2013*, at 809 (2013).

Some jurisdictions continue to forbid claims of special expertise or specialization without accompanying certification. *See, e.g., Fla. Bar v. Doane*, 43 So. 3d 640 (Fla. 2010) (lawyer certified as civil trial specialist may not use trade name "Legal Experts" because it fails to indicate area of certification); *In re Anonymous*, 783 N.E.2d 1130 (Ind. 2003) (disciplining lawyer for advertising himself as "elder law" specialist when not so certified); Ariz. Ethics Op. 2000-01 (2000) (firm may not advertise it specializes in particular area of law unless a member is certified in area); Ill. Ethics Op. 96-8 (1997) (law firm may hold itself out as "concentrating" in intellectual property law, but may not state it "specializes" because no member is admitted to practice in Patent and Trademark Office); N.Y. State Ethics Op. 1100 (2016) (lawyer may not advertise accreditation as estate planner from private national association because program has not been approved by ABA as required by New York Rule 7.2(c)(1)); *see also* N.J. Advertising Ethics Op. 45 (2018) (terms "expertise," "specialist," and "specialization" not inherently misleading if true, but only lawyers certified by state supreme court or ABA-approved organization can call themselves "experts"). *But see* W. Va. Ethics Op. 2015-02 (2015) (West Virginia does not recognize or permit claims of specialization).

## DISCLAIMERS

In *Peel v. Att'y Registration & Disciplinary Comm'n of Ill.*, 496 U.S. 91 (1990), an Illinois lawyer identified himself on his letterhead as "Certified Trial Specialist by the National Board of Trial Advocacy." Illinois had no certification plan of its own and argued consumers would think the ad referred to some formal state certification process. The Court rejected the consumer-confusion argument, however, and ruled that states may not ban statements of specialty certification that are only "potentially"— rather than "inherently"—misleading. Therefore, claims of specialty certification cannot be categorically prohibited. The Court noted, however, that "a State might consider . . . requiring a disclaimer about the certifying organization or the standards of a specialty."

The ABA subsequently amended former Rule 7.4 (deleted 2018) to require a disclaimer if the certifying organization was unapproved. But in 2002 the ABA abandoned that disclaimer requirement, concluding it did not provide enough protection against "potentially misleading claims of certification by an unapproved organization." American Bar Association, *A Legislative History: The Development of the ABA Model Rules of Professional Conduct, 1982–2013*, at 815 (2013).

Rule 7.2(c), which replaces former Rule 7.4 (deleted 2018), now permits claims of certification only if the certifying organization has been approved by "an appropriate authority" of the jurisdiction or accredited by the ABA, and is clearly identified. For the ABA Standards for Specialty Certification Programs for Lawyers, see https://www.americanbar.org/groups/professional_responsibility/committees_ commissions/standing-committee-on-specialization/resources/resources_for_ programs/accreditation_standards/. Disclaimers are still required in some jurisdictions but must satisfy the constitutional standard for commercial speech restrictions. *See Hayes v. N.Y. Att'y Grievance Comm. of Eighth Judicial Dist.*, 672 F.3d 158 (2d Cir. 2012) (New York's required disclaimer that certification is not required to practice law in New York and does not necessarily indicate greater competence did not satisfy constitutional test for restrictions on commercial speech set forth in *Cent. Hudson Gas & Elec. Corp. v. Pub. Serv. Comm'n of N.Y.*, 447 U.S. 557 (1980)). *Compare* Colo. Rule 7.4(e) (requiring disclaimer that "Colorado does not certify attorneys as specialists in any field" to accompany any published claim of specialization), *and* Haw. Rule 7.4(d)(3) (requiring all certification claims to include disclaimer stating "The Supreme Court of Hawai'i grants Hawai'i certification only to lawyers in good standing who have successfully completed a specialty program accredited by the American Bar Association"), *with* Ill. Ethics Op. 03-03 (2004) (lawyer may note membership in "Capital Litigation Trial Bar" on letterhead without adding prescribed disclaimer that Illinois Supreme Court does not recognize certifications, because capital litigation trial bar was created by court itself).

## FALSE IMPRESSIONS

Any statement that creates a false impression about certification or expertise remains prohibited. *See, e.g., Fla. Bar v. Doane*, 43 So. 3d 640 (Fla. 2010) (lawyer used trade name containing phrase "Legal Experts" when he was not certified as specialist); *In re Wells*, 709 S.E.2d 644 (S.C. 2011) (lawyer's website referred to firm's "expertise" and said firm "specializes" in several areas of law); Ala. Ethics Op. 90-49(A)&(B) (1990) (Personal Injury Trial Lawyers Association marketing program created false impression that association was certifying organization and participating lawyers were specialists); Ark. Ethics Op. 04-02 (2004) (lawyer who has LL.M. degree in taxation may include this degree on business cards and stationery; mere listing of degree does not imply specialization); Del. Ethics Op. 04-1 (2004) (lawyer may advertise he is certified public accountant only in "language that does not imply a legal specialization"); Kan. Ethics Op. 92-03 (1992) (lawyers who participate in referral service that sets minimum experience standards may not use their participation as basis for advertising certification or specialization in any area of law); Mo. Informal Ethics Op. 20020080 (2002) (if phrase "trial lawyers" on firm letterhead implies certification or specialization, disclaimer must be included); N.Y. State Ethics Op. 972 (2013) (lawyer may not list practice areas under "Specialties" header on social networking site unless certified); Ohio State Bar Ethics Op. 2012-02 (2012) (lawyer may not describe self as "Advanced Collaborative Practitioner" because term falsely implies specialist certification, but may state fact of membership in collaborative divorce professional organization); Utah Ethics Op. 00-07 (2000) (designation "international lawyers" on firm's letterhead "could be interpreted as an indication of special competence and experience"; designation "appears to be misleading" by improperly suggesting all lawyers participating in proposed association are experts in international law); *cf. In re Hyderally*, 32 A.3d 1117 (N.J. 2011) (lawyer placed seal of state lawyer certification agency on website although he was not so certified). *But see In re Hughes & Coleman*, 60 S.W.3d 540 (Ky. 2001) (approving ads for self-styled "injury lawyers" because "[n]one of the ads use any form of the prohibited phrases such as 'certified', 'specialist', 'expert', or 'authority' at any time or in any manner").

## PATENT AND ADMIRALTY SPECIALISTS

Comment [10] includes language formerly contained in paragraphs (b) and (c) of Model Rule 7.4 (deleted 2018) that reflects the historical practice of designating lawyers admitted to practice in the Patent and Trademark Office and admiralty practitioners as recognized specialists. Versions of this language have been included in the rule from its first adoption.

## *Paragraph (d): Required Inclusion of Contact Information of Responsible Lawyer*

Paragraph (d) (formerly paragraph (c)) provides that any communication about a lawyer's or law firm's services must include the name and contact information of at least one lawyer or firm responsible for its content. Prior to 2018, the rule required an "office address" rather than "contact information." Comment [12] specifies that a website address, telephone number, e-mail address, or physical office location all satisfy the rule. *See* Md. Ethics Op. 2002-18 (2002) (if lawyer's internet domain name describes lawyer's practice, it resembles advertising and must also identify lawyer by name; if protocol restrictions preclude identification in domain name itself, lawyer's identity should be fully disclosed in all publications of domain name); N.Y. State Ethics Op. 1025 (2014) (nonresident lawyer who practices in New York need not have physical office and may provide internet address of virtual law office to comply with advertising rule); N.C. Ethics Op. 2012-6 (2012) (leased time-sharing office space address or post office box satisfy advertising contact information requirement if lawyer lives in same community as office space and includes explanation such as "by appointment only" and post office box is same address listed in state bar registration); Ohio Sup. Ct. Ethics Op. 2017-5 (2017) (lawyer's home address, shared office space location, or post office box may be used to satisfy "office address" requirement for written or electronic communications); S.C. Ethics Op. 17-01 (2017) (lawyer may use post office box instead of street address for advertising contact information if identical to address listed with state bar). *But see* Pa. Ethics Op. 2009-53 (2009) (lawyer practicing via "virtual office"—including answering service for incoming telephone calls and local mailbox service for incoming mail—must still display in advertisements geographic location where legal services principally performed).

## FILING AND RETENTION REQUIREMENTS

Before 2002, Rule 7.2(b) required a lawyer to retain copies or recordings of advertisements or communications for a specified period after dissemination, and to keep a record of when and where the advertisements were used. *See* American Bar Association, *A Legislative History: The Development of the ABA Model Rules of Professional Conduct, 1982–2013*, at 746–67 (2013). That requirement persists in several jurisdictions' versions of Rule 7.2, and several jurisdictions also require advertisements to be filed with regulatory agencies. *See, e.g.,* N.Y. State Ethics Op. 1009 (2014) (tweeted announcements of lawyer's availability for handling shareholder litigation must comply with filing, labeling, and retention requirements); N.Y. State Ethics Op. 1001 (2014) (educational component of articles in law firm newsletter does not negate its essential nature as advertising; consequently, newsletter must comply with advertising rules); S.C. Ethics Op. 09-10 (2009) (lawyer who "claims" listing in independent online directory and solicits comments for listing must file listing if it contains "anything beyond directory information").

## Rule 7.3

### Solicitation of Clients

(a) "Solicitation" or "solicit" denotes a communication initiated by or on behalf of a lawyer or law firm that is directed to a specific person the lawyer knows or reasonably should know needs legal services in a particular matter and that offers to provide, or reasonably can be understood as offering to provide, legal services for that matter.

(b) A lawyer shall not solicit professional employment by live person-to-person contact when a significant motive for the lawyer's doing so is the lawyer's or law firm's pecuniary gain, unless the contact is with a:

(1) lawyer;

(2) person who has a family, close personal, or prior business or professional relationship with the lawyer or law firm; or

(3) person who routinely uses for business purposes the type of legal services offered by the lawyer.

(c) A lawyer shall not solicit professional employment even when not otherwise prohibited by paragraph (b), if:

(1) the target of the solicitation has made known to the lawyer a desire not to be solicited by the lawyer; or

(2) the solicitation involves coercion, duress or harassment.

(d) This Rule does not prohibit communications authorized by law or ordered by a court or other tribunal.

(e) Notwithstanding the prohibitions in this Rule, a lawyer may participate with a prepaid or group legal service plan operated by an organization not owned or directed by the lawyer that uses live person-to-person contact to enroll members or sell subscriptions for the plan from persons who are not known to need legal services in a particular matter covered by the plan.

## COMMENT

[1] Paragraph (b) prohibits a lawyer from soliciting professional employment by live person-to-person contact when a significant motive for the lawyer's doing so is the lawyer's or the law firm's pecuniary gain. A lawyer's communication is not a solicitation if it is directed to the general public, such as through a billboard, an

Internet banner advertisement, a website or a television commercial, or if it is in response to a request for information or is automatically generated in response to electronic searches.

[2] "Live person-to-person contact" means in-person, face-to-face, live telephone and other real-time visual or auditory person-to-person communications where the person is subject to a direct personal encounter without time for reflection. Such person-to-person contact does not include chat rooms, text messages or other written communications that recipients may easily disregard. A potential for overreaching exists when a lawyer, seeking pecuniary gain, solicits a person known to be in need of legal services. This form of contact subjects a person to the private importuning of the trained advocate in a direct interpersonal encounter. The person, who may already feel overwhelmed by the circumstances giving rise to the need for legal services, may find it difficult to fully evaluate all available alternatives with reasoned judgment and appropriate self-interest in the face of the lawyer's presence and insistence upon an immediate response. The situation is fraught with the possibility of undue influence, intimidation, and overreaching.

[3] The potential for overreaching inherent in live person-to-person contact justifies its prohibition, since lawyers have alternative means of conveying necessary information. In particular, communications can be mailed or transmitted by email or other electronic means that do not violate other laws. These forms of communications make it possible for the public to be informed about the need for legal services, and about the qualifications of available lawyers and law firms, without subjecting the public to live person-to-person persuasion that may overwhelm a person's judgment.

[4] The contents of live person-to-person contact can be disputed and may not be subject to third party scrutiny. Consequently, they are much more likely to approach (and occasionally cross) the dividing line between accurate representations and those that are false and misleading.

[5] There is far less likelihood that a lawyer would engage in overreaching against a former client, or a person with whom the lawyer has a close personal, family, business or professional relationship, or in situations in which the lawyer is motivated by considerations other than the lawyer's pecuniary gain. Nor is there a serious potential for overreaching when the person contacted is a lawyer or is known to routinely use the type of legal services involved for business purposes. Examples include persons who routinely hire outside counsel to represent the entity; entrepreneurs who regularly engage business, employment law or intellectual property lawyers; small business proprietors who routinely hire lawyers for lease or contract issues; and other people who routinely retain lawyers for business transactions or formations. Paragraph (b) is not intended to prohibit a lawyer from participating in constitutionally protected activities of public or charitable legal-service organizations or bona fide political, social, civic, fraternal, employee or trade organizations whose purposes include providing or recommending legal services to their members or beneficiaries.

[6] A solicitation that contains false or misleading information within the meaning of Rule 7.1, that involves coercion, duress or harassment within the meaning of

Rule 7.3(c)(2), or that involves contact with someone who has made known to the lawyer a desire not to be solicited by the lawyer within the meaning of Rule 7.3(c)(1) is prohibited. Live, person-to-person contact of individuals who may be especially vulnerable to coercion or duress is ordinarily not appropriate, for example, the elderly, those whose first language is not English, or the disabled.

[7] This Rule does not prohibit a lawyer from contacting representatives of organizations or groups that may be interested in establishing a group or prepaid legal plan for their members, insureds, beneficiaries or other third parties for the purpose of informing such entities of the availability of and details concerning the plan or arrangement which the lawyer or lawyer's firm is willing to offer. This form of communication is not directed to people who are seeking legal services for themselves. Rather, it is usually addressed to an individual acting in a fiduciary capacity seeking a supplier of legal services for others who may, if they choose, become prospective clients of the lawyer. Under these circumstances, the activity which the lawyer undertakes in communicating with such representatives and the type of information transmitted to the individual are functionally similar to and serve the same purpose as advertising permitted under Rule 7.2.

[8] Communications authorized by law or ordered by a court or tribunal include a notice to potential members of a class in class action litigation.

[9] Paragraph (e) of this Rule permits a lawyer to participate with an organization which uses personal contact to enroll members for its group or prepaid legal service plan, provided that the personal contact is not undertaken by any lawyer who would be a provider of legal services through the plan. The organization must not be owned by or directed (whether as manager or otherwise) by any lawyer or law firm that participates in the plan. For example, paragraph (e) would not permit a lawyer to create an organization controlled directly or indirectly by the lawyer and use the organization for the person-to-person solicitation of legal employment of the lawyer through memberships in the plan or otherwise. The communication permitted by these organizations must not be directed to a person known to need legal services in a particular matter, but must be designed to inform potential plan members generally of another means of affordable legal services. Lawyers who participate in a legal service plan must reasonably assure that the plan sponsors are in compliance with Rules 7.1, 7.2 and 7.3(c).

## Definitional Cross-References
"Known" *See* Rule 1.0(f)

## State Rules Comparison
http://ambar.org/MRPCStateCharts

## 2018 Advertising Rule Changes
http://ambar.org/AdvRuleChanges2018

## ANNOTATION
### OVERVIEW

Rule 7.3 sets out the ethical requirements for lawyers when communicating directly with potential clients. As the comment explains, the underlying concern is to avoid exercising "undue influence, intimidation, and overreaching" when obtaining new clients. Cmt. [2].

The rule was amended in 2012 to clarify the definition of solicitation in light of lawyers' increasing use of different internet-based communication methods; at the same time, the term "prospective client" was eliminated, to avoid confusion with the term as used in Rule 1.18. (The rule had formerly been titled "Direct Contact with Prospective Clients.") American Bar Association, *A Legislative History: The Development of the ABA Model Rules of Professional Conduct, 1982–2013*, at 797 (2013).

### • *2018 Amendments*

Model Rule 7.3 was amended in 2018 to clarify and move the definition of "solicitation" from the comment to the blackletter rule. The restrictions on solicitation taking place through "in-person, live telephone or real-time electronic contact" were changed to cover solicitation occurring via "live person-to-person contact" and moved from paragraph (a), which now contains the definition of "solicitation," to paragraph (b). The categories of persons a lawyer is permitted to solicit, now found in Rule 7.3(b)(1), (2), and (3), were slightly expanded to include routine users of the sort of business legal services offered by the lawyer and persons with whom a lawyer or law firm has a prior business relationship. The requirement that targeted advertising be labeled "Advertising Material," found in former paragraph (c), was deleted. A new paragraph (d) was added to clarify that the rule does not prohibit communications authorized by law or an order of a tribunal. The comment was amended to define and explain "live person-to-person contact" and provide examples of persons who "routinely" use various sorts of business legal services. Former Comment [8] regarding labeling was deleted. New Comment [8], formerly contained in Rule 7.2, comment [4], cites notices to potential class members in class action litigation as examples of communications authorized by law or ordered by a court or tribunal.

### *Paragraph (a): Definition of "Solicitation"*

The definition of "solicitation" was moved in 2018 from the comment to the blackletter rule. New paragraph (a) states that solicitation is a "communication by or on behalf of a lawyer or law firm that is directed to a specific person the lawyer knows or reasonably should know needs legal services in a particular matter and that offers to provide, or reasonably can be understood as offering to provide, legal services for that matter."

### *Paragraph (b): Restriction of Live Person-to-Person Contact*
#### GENERAL RESTRICTION AGAINST "LIVE" SOLICITATION

Rule 7.3(b) restricts solicitation by "live person-to-person contact" for pecuniary gain, whether face-to-face, by live telephone, or by other real-time visual or auditory person-to-person communication, as Comment [2] explains. The rule recognizes that someone who needs a lawyer may feel overwhelmed by the "private importuning of the trained advocate in a direct interpersonal encounter." Cmt. [2]. "Unlike a public advertisement, which simply provides information and leaves the recipient free to act upon it or not, in-person solicitation may exert pressure and often demands an immediate response, without providing an opportunity for comparison or reflection. . . . [T]here is no opportunity for intervention or counter-education by agencies of the Bar, supervisory authorities, or persons close to the solicited individual." *Ohralik v. Ohio State Bar Ass'n*, 436 U.S. 447 (1978); *accord Fla. Bar v. Weinstein*, 624 So. 2d 261 (Fla. 1993) (lawyer visited brain-damaged patient in hospital to solicit representation); *In re Gibson*, 856 So. 2d 1173 (La. 2003) (lawyer visited prisoners in jail to solicit representation); *Att'y Grievance Comm'n v. Gregory*, 536 A.2d 646 (Md. 1988) (lawyer approached criminal defendants leaving courtroom and handed them solicitation form letters); *In re Crouppen*, 731 S.W.2d 247 (Mo. 1987) (at hospital bedside, lawyer solicited individual who had been injured at work and was about to undergo surgery; lawyer then sent card and balloons); *see also* Mo. Informal Ethics Op. 2018-13 (n.d.) (lawyer may not have nonlawyer hand out discount coupons for lawyer's services at live seminar given by lawyer); Ohio Sup. Ct. Ethics Op. 2015-2 (2015) (lawyer presenting educational seminar may have brochures regarding lawyer's legal services available for audience members to take but may not hand them to attendees); *cf. Rose v. Winters, Yonker & Rousselle, P.S.C.*, 391 S.W.3d 871 (Ky. Ct. App. 2012) (Kentucky solicitation rule provides for fee forfeiture upon disciplinary agency's finding of violation, which is precondition for private right of action for recovery); *Rivera v. Lutheran Med. Ctr.*, 866 N.Y.S.2d 520 (Sup. Ct. 2008) (disqualifying lawyers for defendant employer who solicited former employees identified as potential witnesses to gain tactical discovery advantage). *See generally* George M. Cohen, *Beyond the No-Contact Rule: Ex Parte Contact by Lawyers with Nonclients*, 87 Tul. L. Rev. 1197 (June 2013); Barry R. Temkin & Michael H. Stone, *Solicitation by Defense Counsel: Ethical Pitfalls When Corporate Defense Counsel Offers Representation to Witnesses*, 80 Def. Couns. J. 363 (Oct. 2013).

Solicitation by direct personal contact can be categorically prohibited without offending the First Amendment. *Shapero v. Ky. Bar Ass'n*, 486 U.S. 466 (1988) (state may ban all in-person solicitation by lawyers for profit regardless of its contents). The state's interest in preventing "those aspects of solicitation that involve fraud, undue influence, intimidation, overreaching, and other forms of vexatious conduct" overrides the lawyer's interest in communication. *Ohralik v. Ohio State Bar Ass'n*, 436 U.S. 447 (1978); *see also Zauderer v. Office of Disciplinary Counsel*, 471 U.S. 626 (1985) ("possibilities for overreaching, invasion of privacy, the exercise of undue influence[,] outright fraud" and other "unique features of in-person solicitation by lawyers . . . justify a prophylactic rule prohibiting lawyers from engaging in solicitation for pecuniary gain").

## • *Electronic Solicitation*

Rule 7.3(b), as amended in 2018, prohibits solicitation by "live person-to-person contact." Under the pre-2018 version of the Model Rules (and under rules still in effect in many jurisdictions), with respect to electronic communication, the key phrase was "real-time electronic contact." Rule 7.3(a) and (b) (superseded). Whether a solicitation constitutes "real-time electronic contact" is generally held to depend upon the ease with which the recipient can ignore the communication or delay responding. *See* Fla. Ethics Op. A-00-1 (2000) (lawyer may not solicit through real-time chat room); N.C. Ethics Op. 2017-01 (2017) (lawyer's advertising text messages are not real-time electronic contact); N.C. Ethics Op. 2011-8 (2011) (law firm may use live pop-up chat support service on website; viewer may ignore chat button or click to indicate lack of interest in chat); Ohio Sup. Ct. Ethics Op. 2013-2 (2013) (lawyer may solicit potential clients by text messages because standard text messaging is more similar to e-mail than to chat); Pa. Ethics Op. 2013-035 (2013) (lawyer may ask potential clients to "like" lawyer's Facebook page if they may easily ignore lawyer's request); Phila. Ethics Op. 2010-6 (2010) (rule does not apply to solicitations in chat rooms if done "in a way in which it would [not] be socially awkward or difficult for a recipient of a lawyer's overtures to not respond"); Utah Ethics Op. 2015-05 (2015) (paying internet forum service nominal fee to bid on potential client's request for legal services is not real-time electronic contact and does not violate rule on solicitation); W. Va. Ethics Op. 2015-02 (2015) (real-time electronic contact "arguably" includes live social media chat and comments to posts); *see also* N.Y. State Ethics Op. 1049 (2015) (tweeted invitation to contact lawyer, directed toward potential clients with particular issues, constitutes solicitation; however, lawyer's response to potential client's invitation for contact is not solicitation); *cf.* Md. Ethics Op. 2014-04 (n.d.) (responding to postings of potential clients on online referral website does not constitute solicitation). *See generally* Cheryl B. Preston, *Lawyers' Abuse of Technology*, 103 Cornell L. Rev. 879 (May 2018); Ronald D. Rotunda, *Applying the Revised ABA Model Rules in the Age of the Internet: The Problem of Metadata*, 42 Hofstra L. Rev. 175 (Fall 2013).

After the adoption of the 2018 amendments, the rule no longer prohibits real-time electronic solicitation, which includes texts and tweets. According to Revised Report 101 of the ABA Standing Committee on Ethics and Professional Responsibility (2018) (available at http://ambar.org/AdvRuleChanges2018), "[t]hese forms of communication are more like a written communication, which allows the reader to pause before responding and creates less pressure to immediately respond or respond at all, unlike a direct interpersonal encounter." Instead, Rule 7.3 prohibits "live person-to-person contact," which, as explained in Comment [2], includes "real-time visual or auditory person-to-person communications where the person is subject to a direct encounter without time for reflection," but "does not include chat rooms, text messages, or other written communications that recipients may easily disregard." Rule 7.3, cmt. [2].

## PUBLIC INTEREST EXCEPTION

In a companion case decided the same day as *Ohralik v. Ohio State Bar Ass'n*, 436 U.S. 447 (1978), the Supreme Court held it unconstitutional for a state to discipline a lawyer working for a nonprofit, public interest organization for her in-person and direct-mail solicitation. *In re Primus*, 436 U.S. 412 (1978) (lawyer personally spoke to women who had been sterilized as condition of continuation of Medicaid benefits, offering free legal representation by ACLU and later writing to one of the women she addressed). Noting the "political or ideological" character of the representation, the Court held that the presence of associational rights, as well as the unlikelihood of overreaching, distinguished *Primus* from *Ohralik*. *Accord Rivera v. Brickman Grp.*, Civ. No. 05-1518, 2006 WL 680926 (E.D. Pa. Mar. 10, 2006) (allowing class counsel to contact potential opt-in plaintiffs directly because "[p]laintiffs' counsel are employed by a non-profit legal services organization. If, like most non-profit organizations, plaintiffs' counsel's employer uses income to fund more projects rather than supplement the salaries of its employees, one can expect plaintiffs' counsel to receive no pecuniary gain whatsoever from their efforts in this litigation.").

Thus, lawyers affiliated with a group formed to further a group right or "ideological" interest may claim greater constitutional protection than is accorded under the commercial-speech analysis to lawyers soliciting primarily for personal gain. *See In re Teichner*, 387 N.E.2d 265 (Ill. 1979) (lawyer's in-person solicitation of accident victims not disciplinable because done at invitation of victims' pastor; behavior fell between "the two extremes of Primus, who had a strong ideological interest and no pecuniary interest, and Ohralik, who had a strong pecuniary interest and no ideological interest"); Ala. Ethics Op. 03-1 (2003) ("when attorneys provide, free of charge, their time, advice or other legal services for a charitable or eleemosynary purpose, the motive for offering those services is not one of 'pecuniary gain' within the meaning of [Rule 7.3(a)]"); *cf.* Tex. Ethics Op. 674 (2018) (law firm operating as qualified public charity nonprofit organization may not solicit potential clients who are not members of qualified nonprofit for limited-scope legal services at below-market rates). *See generally* Amy Busa & Carl G. Sussman, *Expanding the Market for Justice: Arguments for Extending In-Person Client Solicitation*, 34 Harv. C.R.-C.L. L. Rev. 487 (Summer 1999).

## SOLICITATION OF OTHER LAWYERS, FAMILY MEMBERS, AND FORMER CLIENTS

The restrictions on solicitation in paragraph (b) do not apply if the person contacted is a lawyer, has a family, close personal, or prior professional relationship with the lawyer making the contact, or routinely uses for business the type of legal services offered by the lawyer making the contact. *E.g.*, Ill. Ethics Op. 12-14 (2012) (former law firm associate may contact his former clients directly to inform them of his departure and/or solicit their business). There is less likelihood that a lawyer "would engage in overreaching against" such people. Cmt. [5]. *See, e.g., Goldthwaite v. Disciplinary Bd.*, 408 So. 2d 504 (Ala. 1982) (lawyer's close relationship with and previous representation of bank brought bank within "close friend, relative, [or] former client" exception of predecessor Model Code); *In re Appert*, 315 N.W.2d 204 (Minn. 1981) (lawyer's attempts to contact potential client referred to him by student researcher at law school with which lawyer had close relationship were not improper solicitation); *see also In re Blaylock*, 978 P.2d 381 (Or. 1999) (no violation; lawyer who was also practicing physician responded to telephone call from nurse co-worker that he interpreted to be invitation from family of hospitalized man to contact him).

Commentators have discussed the rule's application to the solicitation of a firm's clients by former associates and partners who know those clients' needs. *See generally*

Robert W. Hillman, *Law Firms and Their Partners: The Law and Ethics of Grabbing and Leaving*, 67 Tex. L. Rev. 1 (Nov. 1988); Vincent R. Johnson, *Solicitation of Law Firm Clients by Departing Partners and Associates*, 50 U. Pitt. L. Rev. 1 (Fall 1988).

## SOLICITATION OF CLIENTS OF ANCILLARY BUSINESSES

Rule 7.3 prohibits lawyers owning or working in businesses providing nonlegal services from soliciting customers of those businesses for legal services. *See, e.g.*, Conn. Informal Ethics Op. 18-03 (2018) (lawyer with real estate agent license may not solicit legal business from real estate customers); S.C. Ethics Op. 02-06 (n.d.) (lawyer who owns mortgage brokerage business may not solicit legal business from brokerage customers); Wis. Informal Ethics Op. IE-16-01 (2016) (lawyer who is part-owner of financial planning business may not offer to provide legal services to business customers); *cf.* N.Y. State Ethics Op. 1135 (2017) (lawyer-accountant may not make telephone cold-calls offering accounting services that are not distinct from legal services, even though accounting profession does not prohibit such solicitation).

## SOLICITATION BY THIRD PERSONS

Lawyers may not use other people to solicit for them, and Rule 7.3 is sometimes invoked along with either Rule 7.2(b) (prohibiting paid recommendations) or Rule 8.4(a) (prohibiting use of third persons to violate rules) to prohibit the practice. *See, e.g., In re O'Keefe*, 877 So. 2d 79 (La. 2004) (lawyer disbarred for paying "runners" to find and refer personal injury cases); *Miss. Bar v. Turnage*, 919 So. 2d 36 (Miss. 2005) (lawyer suspended for hiring former insurance salesperson to solicit clients for potential class suit against insurer); Md. Ethics Op. 98-30 (1998) (lawyer may not have bail bondsman distribute bondsman's business cards with lawyer's contact information printed on back); Phila. Ethics Op. 2010-12 (2010) (lawyer may not accept referrals from consulting firm that obtains names of injured victims from police reports, contacts them to see whether they need legal representation, and forwards signed fee agreements and other case materials to lawyer in exchange for flat fee); Wash. Ethics Op. 2203 (2010) (lawyer may not pay referral source for clients accepted); *see also Cincinnati Bar Ass'n v. Rinderknecht*, 679 N.E.2d 669 (Ohio 1997) (lawyer indefinitely suspended for setting up direct marketing service to solicit accident victims as clients for himself and chiropractor; decided under Model Code); *cf. Crook v. State*, No. 08-02-00382-CR, 2005 WL 1539187, 2005 BL 17672 (Tex. App. June 30, 2005) (lawyer convicted of felony barratry for hiring chiropractor's assistant to solicit auto accident victims; court invoked Rules 7.3 and 8.4 in analyzing offense).

## SOLICITATION OF EMPLOYMENT AND PECUNIARY GAIN

Paragraph (b) regulates only communications that "solicit" professional employment when a "significant motive" is the lawyer's "pecuniary gain." Authorities analyze whether these elements are present in various ways. *See Wells Fargo Bank, N.A. v. LaSalle Bank Nat'l Ass'n*, No. CIV-08-1125-C, 2010 WL 1558554, 2010 BL 86484 (W.D. Okla. Apr. 19, 2010) (primary motive of corporate defense lawyer who solicited former employees was desire to protect interests of corporate client and its former employees, not pecuniary gain); *In re Charges of Unprof'l Conduct Against 97-29*, 581

N.W.2d 347 (Minn. 1998) (though several reasons for lawyer's phone call, motive of pecuniary gain still found considering "totality of all the circumstances of the communication, including the background of the parties, the parties' previous relationship, [and] the attorney's conduct"); N.Y. State Ethics Op. 1110 (2016) (legal seminars or webinars that are designed to encourage viewers or audience members to hire lawyer constitute solicitation and, if live, real-time, or interactive, must be limited to lawyer's family, close friends, and current or former clients); N.Y. Cnty. Ethics Op. 747 (2014) (lawyer who represents corporation in lawsuit may interview corporate employees and offer to represent them at corporate expense in connection with lawsuit if lawyer determines joint representation permissible and employees would benefit from representation); Phila. Ethics Op. 2012-1 (2012) (nonprofit legal aid organization may recruit nonlawyer volunteers, supervised by organization's lawyers, to solicit potential clients for free legal services or refer them to other nonprofit organizations, but nonlawyer volunteers should not refer potential clients directly to private lawyers who have agreed to charge discounted fees); R.I. Ethics Op. 98-03 (1998) (may not solicit clients for free legal work if "significant motive for the solicitation is the personal gain of the inquiring attorney in qualifying for future employment and the eventual pecuniary benefit to be derived"); Tex. Ethics Op. 672 (2018) (plaintiff's employment lawyer's letter to employees of defendant corporation informing them of lawsuit's allegations regarding corporation's employment practices, opining that employees in same position as plaintiffs deserve compensation, and describing lawyer's services, may constitute solicitation); *see also* ABA Formal Ethics Op. 482 (2018) (must comply with advertising rules when soliciting disaster victims); San Diego Cnty. Ethics Op. 2000-1 (2000) (lawyer witnessing accident may give business card to person involved so that person may contact lawyer as witness; no solicitation involved). *See generally* Jan L. Jacobowitz & John G. Browning, *Legal Ethics and Social Media: A Practitioner's Handbook* 185-206 (2017); Isabella M. Leavitt, *Attorney Advertising in the Age of Reddit: Drafting Ethical Responses to Prospective Clients in Online Non-Legal Forums*, 29 Geo. J. Legal Ethics 1111 (Fall 2016); Alexander Schwab, *In Defense of Ambulance Chasing: A Critique of Model Rule of Professional Conduct 7.3*, 29 Yale L. & Pol'y Rev. 603 (Spring 2011).

### Paragraph (c): Unwanted, Coercive, or Harassing Solicitation

Notwithstanding any other provisions of the rule, paragraph (c) (formerly paragraph (b)) prohibits any solicitation of someone who has let the lawyer know he or she does not want to be solicited, and any solicitation that involves coercion, duress, or harassment.

## TARGETED-MAIL SOLICITATION

In 1988, the Supreme Court held that the First Amendment does not allow states to impose blanket bans on lawyers' targeted-mail solicitation of prospective clients. *Shapero v. Ky. Bar Ass'n*, 486 U.S. 466 (1988). *Shapero* distinguished targeted direct-mail solicitation from in-person solicitation, in which the risk of improper lawyer conduct through coercive tactics is much greater. The Court cited *Zauderer v. Office of Disciplinary Counsel*, 471 U.S. 626 (1985), which dealt with print advertising, for the proposition that written communication does not involve "the coercive force of the personal presence of a trained advocate" or the "pressure on the potential client for an immediate yes-or-no answer to the offer of representation." Any risk associated with a personalized letter, the Court concluded, can be minimized by requiring the lawyer to file the letter with a state agency having authority to supervise targeted mailings and penalize actual abuses. *See also Revo v. Disciplinary Bd. of Supreme Court for N.M.*, 106 F.3d 929 (10th Cir. 1997) (ban on direct mail to personal injury victims violates First Amendment).

In 1995, however, the Court upheld a Florida rule prohibiting lawyers from sending targeted direct mail to accident victims or their relatives for thirty days following an accident or disaster. *Fla. Bar v. Went For It, Inc.*, 515 U.S. 618 (1995). In *Went For It*, the Court focused not upon the lawyer's First Amendment rights, as it had in *Shapero*, but upon the public's negative perception of the profession. The Court said the state had a substantial interest in "protecting injured Floridians from invasive conduct by lawyers and in preventing the erosion of the confidence in the profession." A few jurisdictions subsequently added similar waiting periods to their own versions of Rule 7.3 (*e.g.*, Ga. Rule 7.3(a)(3); N.Y. Rule 7.3(e)), or imposed additional requirements such as verifying that a targeted defendant in a civil action has been served or including a notice in communications sent to accident victims (*e.g.*, Ohio Rule 7.3(d) and (e)). *See generally* David L. Hudson, Jr., *Attorney Advertising in the Litigators and Modern-Day America: The Continued Importance of the Public's Need for Legal Information*, 48 U. Mem. L. Rev. 959 (Spring 2018); Note, *Six Years After* The Florida Bar v. Went For It, Inc.: *The Continued Erosion of First Amendment Rights*, 14 Geo. J. Legal Ethics 197 (Fall 2000); *ABA/BNA Lawyers' Manual on Professional Conduct*, "Advertising and Solicitation: Direct Mail," pp. 81:601 *et seq.*

---

### *Former Paragraph (c): Labeling Requirement* [Deleted 2018]

Former paragraph (c) was deleted as part of the 2018 amendments. Before the amendment, it provided as follows:

> Every written, recorded or electronic communication from a lawyer soliciting professional employment from anyone known to be in need of legal services in a particular matter shall include the words "Advertising Material" on the outside envelope, if any, and at the beginning and ending of any recorded or electronic communication, unless the recipient of the communication is a person specified in paragraphs (a)(1) or (a)(2).

Many jurisdictions continue to have a rule requiring advertising materials to be labeled. The rationale for the labeling requirement was to ensure potential clients were not misled or intimidated. *See, e.g., Fla. Bar v. Herrick*, 571 So. 2d 1303 (Fla. 1990) (lawyer disciplined for mailing to prospective client unsolicited letter not marked as advertisement); *In re Benkie*, 892 N.E.2d 1237 (Ind. 2008) (lawyer's use of "Legal Advertising" instead of rule-prescribed label "Advertising Material" misleading because it "may create the impression that the Commission or some other body had reviewed [and approved] it"); *Iowa Supreme Court Bd. of Prof'l Ethics & Conduct v. Beckman*, 557 N.W.2d 94 (Iowa 1996) (lawyer mailed marketing letter without required "advertisement only" language); *Anderson v. Ky. Bar Ass'n*, 262 S.W.3d 636 (Ky. 2008) (lawyer's paralegal sent solicitation e-mail that was not labeled "THIS IS AN ADVERTISEMENT"); *In re MDK*, 534 N.W.2d 271 (Minn. 1995) (lawyer admonished for failure to include "advertisement" at beginning of solicitation letter); *In re Jardine*, 764 S.E.2d 924 (S.C. 2014) (out-of-state lawyer mailed solicitations to potential South Carolina clients without complying with labeling, disclaimer, and notice requirements); Ill. Ethics Op. 14-04 (2014) (out-of-state personal injury lawyer's mail solicitations to Illinois residents must comply with Illinois labeling requirements); Kan. Ethics Op. 08-03 (2008) (the legend "Advertising Material" must be printed at top and on envelope of direct-mail solicitations); N.Y. State Ethics Op. 1129 (2017) (law firm newsletter mailed to bank customers with aim of drumming up business constitutes solicitation and must comply with labeling requirements); Ohio Sup. Ct. Ethics Op. 2017-3 (2017) (e-mail solicitations must comply with labeling requirements, including placing "ADVERTISING MATERIAL" or "ADVERTISEMENT ONLY" statement in subject line and "Understanding Your Rights" statement, if applicable, in body of message and not in attachment or by hyperlink); Utah Ethics Op. 02-02 (2002) (newsletters, brochures, and e-mail messages used to attract new clients must be labeled "Advertising Material," but website and promotional items that display firm's logo, without more, need not); *cf.* Idaho Ethics Op. 134 (1992) (lawyer may properly use words "advertising materials" within complete sentence, as long as context does not defeat purpose of rule by causing less sophisticated readers to interpret letter as some form of official communication requiring response).

Former paragraph (c) applied only to communications with persons "known to be in need of legal services in a particular matter." *See In re Anonymous*, 687 S.E.2d 41 (S.C. 2009) (rule did not apply to "discount coupons" for lawyer's realty services left at Realtors' offices because they were "distributed randomly by real estate agents[,] . . . similar in fashion to the common practice of leaving business cards for distribution"); N.Y. State Ethics Op. 1010 (2014) (lawyer advertisements of availability for second opinions for litigants already represented were not solicitations); Ohio Ethics Op. 2007-5 (2007) (personally addressed letter was solicitation because "personalization implies a familiarity with the recipient and the recipient's . . . general legal needs or specific legal needs").

---

## Paragraph (d): Communications Authorized by Law or Ordered by a Court or Other Tribunal

The rule was amended in 2018 to add a new paragraph clarifying that communications authorized by law or ordered by a court or other tribunal do not violate the rule. Comment [8], formerly contained in Rule 7.2, comment [4], states that such communications include notices to potential class members in class action litigation.

Even before the 2018 amendments, some authorities held that Rule 7.3 regulated lawyer communications with potential class members not only before but also after filing and before certification of a class. *See Hamm v. TBC Corp.*, 597 F. Supp. 2d 1338 (S.D. Fla. 2009) (lawyers' telephone solicitation of opt-in plaintiffs to FLSA collective action before certification violated rule); ABA Formal Ethics Op. 07-445 (2007) ("majority" rule is that prior to certification potential class members are not clients of class counsel, so Rule 7.3 regulates, but does not prohibit, lawyer communication with potential class members). *See generally* Vance G. Camisa, *The Constitutional Right to Solicit Potential Class Members in a Class Action*, 25 Gonz. L. Rev. 95 (1989/1990). For discussion of communicating with putative class members, see the annotation to Rule 4.3.

### *Paragraph (e): Solicitation by Legal Service Programs*

Solicitation by legal service programs sponsored by organizations is constitutionally protected as the expression of an associational right. *See United Transp. Union v. Mich. State Bar*, 401 U.S. 576 (1971) (upholding right of union representatives to visit injured members and encourage them to retain union-selected private lawyers; courts cannot "deny associations of workers or others the means of enabling their members to meet the costs of legal representation").

Paragraph (e) goes beyond associational rights protection. It authorizes lawyers to participate in prepaid and group legal service plans generally, as long as the plan (1) is not owned or directed by the lawyers providing the services, and (2) does not engage in solicitations targeted to persons known to be in need of the particular legal services covered by the plan. *See* Cmt. [7] (noting that contact with representatives in their fiduciary capacities is functionally similar to advertising); *see also* Md. Ethics Op. 88-48 (1988) (lawyer may personally contact representatives of organizations in their fiduciary capacities to solicit business, but may not solicit individual members).

# INFORMATION ABOUT LEGAL SERVICES

## Rule 7.4
### *Communication of Fields of Practice and Specialization*

[Deleted 2018]

[Model Rule 7.4 was deleted in 2018. Issues relating to communication of fields of practice and specialization are covered in Model Rule 7.2, paragraph (c) and Comments [9]-[11]. For further information relating to the 2018 amendments to the advertising rules, see http://ambar.org/AdvRuleChanges2018.]

---

The following is the text of Model Rule 7.4 prior to its deletion in 2018.

### *Rule 7.4*
### *Communication of Fields of Practice and Specialization*

*(a) A lawyer may communicate the fact that the lawyer does or does not practice in particular fields of law.*

*(b) A lawyer admitted to engage in patent practice before the United States Patent and Trademark Office may use the designation "Patent Attorney" or a substantially similar designation.*

*(c) A lawyer engaged in Admiralty practice may use the designation "Admiralty," "Proctor in Admiralty" or a substantially similar designation.*

*(d) A lawyer shall not state or imply that a lawyer is certified as a specialist in a particular field of law, unless:*

*(1) the lawyer has been certified as a specialist by an organization that has been approved by an appropriate state authority or that has been accredited by the American Bar Association; and*

*(2) the name of the certifying organization is clearly identified in the communication.*

## COMMENT

*[1] Paragraph (a) of this Rule permits a lawyer to indicate areas of practice in communications about the lawyer's services. If a lawyer practices only in certain fields, or will not accept matters except in a specified field or fields, the lawyer is permitted to so indicate. A lawyer is generally permitted to state that the lawyer is a "specialist," practices a "specialty,"*

or "specializes in" particular fields, but such communications are subject to the "false and misleading" standard applied in Rule 7.1 to communications concerning a lawyer's services.

[2] Paragraph (b) recognizes the long-established policy of the Patent and Trademark Office for the designation of lawyers practicing before the Office. Paragraph (c) recognizes that designation of Admiralty practice has a long historical tradition associated with maritime commerce and the federal courts.

[3] Paragraph (d) permits a lawyer to state that the lawyer is certified as a specialist in a field of law if such certification is granted by an organization approved by an appropriate state authority or accredited by the American Bar Association or another organization, such as a state bar association, that has been approved by the state authority to accredit organizations that certify lawyers as specialists. Certification signifies that an objective entity has recognized an advanced degree of knowledge and experience in the specialty area greater than is suggested by general licensure to practice law. Certifying organizations may be expected to apply standards of experience, knowledge and proficiency to insure that a lawyer's recognition as a specialist is meaningful and reliable. In order to insure that consumers can obtain access to useful information about an organization granting certification, the name of the certifying organization must be included in any communication regarding the certification.

## Rule 7.5
### *Firm Names and Letterheads*

[Deleted 2018]

[Model Rule 7.5 was deleted in 2018. Issues relating to firm names and letterheads are covered in Model Rule 7.1, Comments [5]-[8]. For further information relating to the 2018 amendments to the advertising rules, see http://ambar.org/AdvRuleChanges 2018.]

---

The following is the text of Model Rule 7.5 prior to its deletion in 2018.

## *Rule 7.5*
### *Firm Names and Letterheads*

(a) *A lawyer shall not use a firm name, letterhead or other professional designation that violates Rule 7.1. A trade name may be used by a lawyer in private practice if it does not imply a connection with a government agency or with a public or charitable legal services organization and is not otherwise in violation of Rule 7.1.*

(b) *A law firm with offices in more than one jurisdiction may use the same name or other professional designation in each jurisdiction, but identification of the lawyers in an office of the firm shall indicate the jurisdictional limitations on those not licensed to practice in the jurisdiction where the office is located.*

(c) *The name of a lawyer holding a public office shall not be used in the name of a law firm, or in communications on its behalf, during any substantial period in which the lawyer is not actively and regularly practicing with the firm.*

(d) *Lawyers may state or imply that they practice in a partnership or other organization only when that is the fact.*

## COMMENT

[1] *A firm may be designated by the names of all or some of its members, by the names of deceased members where there has been a continuing succession in the firm's identity or by a trade name such as the "ABC Legal Clinic." A lawyer or law firm may also be designated by a distinctive website address or comparable professional designation. Although the United*

States Supreme Court has held that legislation may prohibit the use of trade names in professional practice, use of such names in law practice is acceptable so long as it is not misleading. If a private firm uses a trade name that includes a geographical name such as "Springfield Legal Clinic," an express disclaimer that it is a public legal aid agency may be required to avoid a misleading implication. It may be observed that any firm name including the name of a deceased partner is, strictly speaking, a trade name. The use of such names to designate law firms has proven a useful means of identification. However, it is misleading to use the name of a lawyer not associated with the firm or a predecessor of the firm, or the name of a nonlawyer.

[2] With regard to paragraph (d), lawyers sharing office facilities, but who are not in fact associated with each other in a law firm, may not denominate themselves as, for example, "Smith and Jones," for that title suggests that they are practicing law together in a firm.

## Rule 7.6

### *Political Contributions to Obtain Government Legal Engagements or Appointments by Judges*

A lawyer or law firm shall not accept a government legal engagement or an appointment by a judge if the lawyer or law firm makes a political contribution or solicits political contributions for the purpose of obtaining or being considered for that type of legal engagement or appointment.

## COMMENT

[1] Lawyers have a right to participate fully in the political process, which includes making and soliciting political contributions to candidates for judicial and other public office. Nevertheless, when lawyers make or solicit political contributions in order to obtain an engagement for legal work awarded by a government agency, or to obtain appointment by a judge, the public may legitimately question whether the lawyers engaged to perform the work are selected on the basis of competence and merit. In such a circumstance, the integrity of the profession is undermined.

[2] The term "political contribution" denotes any gift, subscription, loan, advance or deposit of anything of value made directly or indirectly to a candidate, incumbent, political party or campaign committee to influence or provide financial support for election to or retention in judicial or other government office. Political contributions in initiative and referendum elections are not included. For purposes of this Rule, the term "political contribution" does not include uncompensated services.

[3] Subject to the exceptions below, (i) the term "government legal engagement" denotes any engagement to provide legal services that a public official has the direct or indirect power to award; and (ii) the term "appointment by a judge" denotes an appointment to a position such as referee, commissioner, special master, receiver, guardian or other similar position that is made by a judge. Those terms do not, however, include (a) substantially uncompensated services; (b) engagements or appointments made on the basis of experience, expertise, professional qualifications and cost following a request for proposal or other process that is free from influence based upon political contributions; and (c) engagements or appointments made on a rotational basis from a list compiled without regard to political contributions.

[4] The term "lawyer or law firm" includes a political action committee or other entity owned or controlled by a lawyer or law firm.

[5] Political contributions are for the purpose of obtaining or being considered for a government legal engagement or appointment by a judge if, but for the desire

to be considered for the legal engagement or appointment, the lawyer or law firm would not have made or solicited the contributions. The purpose may be determined by an examination of the circumstances in which the contributions occur. For example, one or more contributions that in the aggregate are substantial in relation to other contributions by lawyers or law firms, made for the benefit of an official in a position to influence award of a government legal engagement, and followed by an award of the legal engagement to the contributing or soliciting lawyer or the lawyer's firm would support an inference that the purpose of the contributions was to obtain the engagement, absent other factors that weigh against existence of the proscribed purpose. Those factors may include among others that the contribution or solicitation was made to further a political, social, or economic interest or because of an existing personal, family, or professional relationship with a candidate.

[6] If a lawyer makes or solicits a political contribution under circumstances that constitute bribery or another crime, Rule 8.4(b) is implicated.

**Definitional Cross-References**

"Law firm" *See* Rule 1.0(c)

**State Rules Comparison**

http://ambar.org/MRPCStateCharts

# ANNOTATION

## INTRODUCTION

After several false starts, the ABA in 2000 adopted Rule 7.6, the "pay-to-play" rule for lawyers:

> The practice commonly known as pay-to-play addressed by the Rule is a system whereby lawyers and law firms are considered for or awarded government legal engagements or appointments by a judge only upon their making or soliciting contributions for the political campaigns of officials who are in a position to "steer" such business their way.

American Bar Association, *A Legislative History: The Development of the ABA Model Rules of Professional Conduct, 1982–2013*, at 827 (2013). The tortured history of the ABA's attempts to address pay-to-play is recounted in the report accompanying the rule, available at https://www.americanbar.org/content/dam/aba/directories/policy/2000_my_110.authcheckdam.pdf. *See generally* Brian C. Buescher, *ABA Model Rule 7.6: The ABA Pleases the SEC, but Does Not Solve Pay to Play*, 14 Geo. J. Legal Ethics 139 (Fall 2000); Jon B. Jordan, *The Regulation of "Pay-to-Play" and the Influence of Political Contributions in the Municipal Securities Industry*, 1999 Colum. Bus. L. Rev. 489 (1999).

Rule 7.6 prohibits a lawyer or law firm from accepting a government legal engagement or judicial appointment if the lawyer or firm makes political contributions "for the purpose of obtaining or being considered for that type of legal engagement or appointment." The comment broadly defines political contribution to include "any gift, subscription, loan, advance or deposit of anything of value made directly or indirectly to a candidate, incumbent, political party or campaign committee to influence or provide financial support for election to or retention in judicial or other government office." Cmt. [2]. The analogous rule in the ABA Model Code of Judicial Conduct (2010)—Rule 2.13(B), Administrative Appointments—does not apply unless the contribution was made to the judge's own election campaign; the judicial code provision is further limited to contributions in excess of a particular amount, made within a particular time period, and known to the judge.

Note that for purposes of Rule 7.6, the definition of law firm is also uniquely broad; it includes "a political action committee or other entity owned or controlled by a lawyer or law firm." Cmt. [4].

Rule 7.6, like its judicial code counterpart, specifically excludes donation of uncompensated services (as well as engagements based upon requests for proposals or made on a rotational basis). *See* Nancy M. Olson, *Judicial Elections and Courtroom Payola: A Look at the Ethical Rules Governing Lawyers' Campaign Contributions and the Common Practice of "Anything Goes,"* 8 Cardozo Pub. L. Pol'y & Ethics 341 (Spring 2010) (loophole allowing donation of uncompensated services to obtain appointments should be closed: "A judge is much more likely to remember favorably her campaign secretary than the name of a single donor on a list of many.").

Very few jurisdictions have adopted any version of Rule 7.6. *See* Lucian T. Pera, *Grading ABA Leadership on Legal Ethics Leadership: State Adoption of the Revised ABA Model Rules of Professional Conduct*, 30 Okla. City U. L. Rev. 637 (Fall 2005) (noting Rule 7.6's distinction as rule most decisively rejected by states, author gives it "Most Brilliant Mistake" award).

### • *"Government Legal Engagement"*

For purposes of Rule 7.6, a "government legal engagement" is any legal engagement "that a public official has the direct or indirect power to award." Cmt. [3]. Note that this is designed to include the selection of lead counsel in a securities fraud class action filed by a public institutional investment fund as lead plaintiff; it was in this context that the abuses targeted by Rule 7.6 were identified. Under the Private Securities Litigation Reform Act of 1995, 15 U.S.C. § 78u-4a(3)(B)(v), the lead plaintiff selects and retains class counsel, subject to the court's approval; the court is to use a "deferential standard." *In re Cendant Corp. Litig.*, 264 F.3d 201 (3d Cir. 2001), *on remand*, 243 F. Supp. 2d 166 (D.N.J. 2003); *see* Drew T. Johnson-Skinner, Note, *Paying-to-Play in Securities Class Actions: A Look at Lawyers' Campaign Contributions*, 84 N.Y.U. L. Rev. 1725 (Dec. 2009) (finding such contributions by law firms in forty-one of the seventy-four securities fraud class actions filed between 2002 and 2006 by institutional investors whose boards included an elected official or political appointee). *See generally* John H. Beisner, Matthew Shors & Jessica Davidson Miller, *Class Action "Cops": Public Servants or Private Entrepreneurs?*, 57 Stan. L. Rev. 1441 (Apr. 2005); Samantha M. Cohen, Note, *"Paying-to-Play" Is the New Rule of the Game: A Practical Implication of the Private Securities Litigation Reform Act of 1995*, 1999 U. Ill. L. Rev. 1331 (1999).

• *"Appointments by Judges"*

Positions to which judges appoint lawyers include "referee, commissioner, special master, receiver [and] guardian." Cmt. [3]. *See Kraham v. Lippman*, 478 F.3d 502 (2d Cir. 2007) (rejecting First Amendment challenge to state court rule barring party officials and their law firm associates from state court appointments as fiduciaries); *cf. Ross v. Thomas*, No. 09 Civ. 5631 (SAS), 2011 WL 2207550, 2011 BL 148328 (S.D.N.Y. June 6, 2011) (New York's rule—upheld in *Kraham*—was enacted to "curb some of the dysfunction inherent in a (state) judiciary that is elected rather than appointed" and therefore did not apply to federal judge's appointment of receiver or her retention as counsel).

The counterpart prohibition in the judicial code adds assigned counsel to this list. ABA Model Code of Judicial Conduct, Rule 2.13, cmt. [1] (2010); *see* Lisa L. Milord, *The Development of the ABA Judicial Code* 24 (ABA Ctr. for Prof'l Responsibility 1992) (list of appointive positions in commentary to predecessor judicial code provision was amended in 1990 to include assigned counsel).

## LAWYER'S PURPOSE

Unlike many state and federal laws on campaign finance and government contracting, and unlike its judicial code counterpart, Rule 7.6 does not bar employment for a fixed period of time after the contribution was made. Rather, using the present tense, it prohibits accepting certain employment if the lawyer or law firm "makes . . . or solicits political contributions" for the proscribed purpose. Comment [5] defines this to mean that but for the desire to be considered for that kind of job, the lawyer or law firm would not have made or solicited the contribution.

The recommendations of the ABA's Task Force on Lawyers' Political Contributions, the entity whose 1998 report underlies the rule adopted in 2000 (identical to the rule rejected in 1999), included a nonexhaustive list of factors a disciplinary authority should consider in assessing the purpose behind a particular contribution, including the amount of the contribution; whether it was made to further a political, social, or economic belief or interest; and whether there is a nonpolitical "request for proposal" process, a history of comparable contributions, and a preexisting personal, family, or nonclient professional relationship. ABA Task Force on Lawyers' Political Contributions, *Report with Recommendations, Part I* (Report 301A, July 1998), *available at* https://www.americanbar.org/content/dam/aba/directories/policy/1998_am_301a.pdf; *see* Joan C. Rogers, "Task Force Urges ABA to Ban Pay-to-Play," *ABA/ BNA Lawyers' Manual on Professional Conduct*, 14 Law. Man. Prof. Conduct 365 (Current Reports, Aug. 8, 1998). Most of these survive in Comment [5], which notes that it would "weigh against existence of the proscribed purpose" if a contribution or solicitation "was made to further a political, social, or economic interest or because of an existing personal, family, or professional relationship with a candidate." *See generally* Brian C. Buescher, *ABA Model Rule 7.6: The ABA Pleases the SEC, but Does Not Solve Pay to Play*, 14 Geo. J. Legal Ethics 139 (Fall 2000) ("it seems hard to imagine any potential pay-to-play scenario where an accused attorney could not make one or more of these defenses"); Nancy M. Olson, *Judicial Elections and Courtroom Payola: A Look at the Ethical Rules Governing Lawyers' Campaign Contributions and the Common Practice of "Anything Goes,"* 8 Cardozo Pub. L. Pol'y & Ethics J. 341 (Spring 2010) (proposing as additional criteria whether judge running unopposed and is "certain winner" or "certain loser," whether contributions made to both sides, and whether contribution made to winner after election).

As a practical matter, Rule 7.6 may be all but unenforceable. *See* John H. Beisner, Matthew Shors & Jessica Davidson Miller, *Class Action "Cops": Public Servants or Private Entrepreneurs?*, 57 Stan. L. Rev. 1441 (Apr. 2005) ("Rule 7.6 requires proof of illegal purpose and is therefore virtually unenforceable in all but the most extreme cases—cases that could also be prosecuted under existing state bribery laws."); John C. Coffee, Jr., *"When Smoke Gets in Your Eyes": Myth and Reality About the Synthesis of Private Counsel and Public Client*, 51 DePaul L. Rev. 241 (Winter 2001) ("[l]egal minds will have little difficulty finding [Rule 7.6] inapplicable to the facts of their case"); *cf. Dean v. Bondurant*, 193 S.W.3d 744 (Ky. 2006) (in all cases requiring recusal based upon judge's receipt of campaign contributions from parties or counsel, there has been a "substantial donation coupled with other activities that reasonably raise questions of impartiality"—as, for example, when lawyer and member of his immediate family both contribute maximum allowable amount to judge before whom lawyer has pending case); *In re Bolton*, 820 So. 2d 548 (La. 2002) (no improper motive established (under Rule 8.4) even though lawyer waited for judge in parking lot, asked judge's law clerk to leave them alone, "shifted position closer" before asking judge, "What if I wanted to give you $5,000?," asked judge to keep matter between them, and the next day paid co-counsel to prepare letter of apology for him to send judge). *See generally* Raymond J. McKoski, *Judicial Discipline and the Appearance of Impropriety: What the Public Sees Is What the Judge Gets*, 94 Minn. L. Rev. 1914, at 1972, "Favoritism in Appointments" (June 2010) (most recusals for appearance of impropriety in appointment context "contain conclusive proof of actual favoritism" anyway).

## UNSUCCESSFUL ATTEMPTS TO SECURE APPOINTMENT OR ENGAGEMENT

Rule 7.6 does not apply to the attempt to secure an appointment or an engagement. According to the rule's sponsors, it applies only "where the lawyer or law firm making [the] political contribution or solicitation . . . has been successful in obtaining the business." *See* https://www.americanbar.org/content/dam/aba/directories/policy/2000_my_110.authcheckdam.pdf.

But an unsuccessful attempt could implicate other laws and other rules, including Rule 3.5(a) (lawyer may not try to influence judge or other official by means prohibited by law), Rule 7.2(b) (lawyer may not give anything of value to someone in exchange for recommendation of employment), Rule 8.4(b) (prohibiting criminal acts reflecting adversely upon a lawyer's fitness), and Rule 8.4(d) (prohibiting conduct prejudicial to the administration of justice).

In addition, Rule 8.4(f) prohibits "assist[ing] a judge or judicial officer in conduct that is a violation of applicable rules of judicial conduct or other law." *See* ABA Model Code of Judicial Conduct, Rule 2.13 (2010) (judge must exercise appointment power impartially and may not appoint lawyer as assigned counsel, referee, commissioner, special master, receiver, or guardian if judge knows lawyer, lawyer's spouse, or lawyer's domestic partner contributed more than specified amount to judge's campaign within specified number of years); *cf. In re LeBlanc*, 972 So. 2d 315 (La. 2008) (Rule 8.4(f) violated; by complying with judge's request for contribution to judge's niece's political campaign, lawyer assisted judge in violating campaign laws and applicable rules of judicial conduct).

## DISCLOSURE

Rule 7.6 does not require lawyers to disclose political contributions or contributions to a judge's campaign. *See* Conn. Informal Ethics Op. 02-07 (2002) (nothing in ethics rules requires lawyer to disclose contribution to judicial candidate's campaign; "even if Connecticut were to adopt Model Rule 7.6, it does not require disclosure"); *cf. In re Cendant Corp. Litig.*, 264 F.3d 201 (3d Cir. 2001) (if publicly managed fund is presumptively most adequate plaintiff in class action, court should require fund's chosen counsel to disclose campaign contributions to any elected officials with direct authority over fund), *on remand*, 243 F. Supp. 2d 166 (D.N.J. 2003). For examination of the logistics of investigating/disclosing political contributions—albeit in the context of judicial disqualification rather than lawyer discipline—see Keith Swisher, *Legal Ethics and Campaign Contributions: The Professional Responsibility to Pay for Justice*, 24 Geo. J. Legal Ethics 225 (Spring 2011) (given that contributions are matter of public record in virtually every state, it is "positively odd no authority specifically tells lawyers to perform a public records search" for contributions to judge from opposing party or counsel).

# Maintaining the Integrity of the Profession

## Rule 8.1
### *Bar Admission and Disciplinary Matters*

An applicant for admission to the bar, or a lawyer in connection with a bar admission application or in connection with a disciplinary matter, shall not:

(a) knowingly make a false statement of material fact; or

(b) fail to disclose a fact necessary to correct a misapprehension known by the person to have arisen in the matter, or knowingly fail to respond to a lawful demand for information from an admissions or disciplinary authority, except that this Rule does not require disclosure of information otherwise protected by Rule 1.6.

## COMMENT

[1] The duty imposed by this Rule extends to persons seeking admission to the bar as well as to lawyers. Hence, if a person makes a material false statement in connection with an application for admission, it may be the basis for subsequent disciplinary action if the person is admitted, and in any event may be relevant in a subsequent admission application. The duty imposed by this Rule applies to a lawyer's own admission or discipline as well as that of others. Thus, it is a separate professional offense for a lawyer to knowingly make a misrepresentation or omission in connection with a disciplinary investigation of the lawyer's own conduct. Paragraph (b) of this Rule also requires correction of any prior misstatement in the matter that the applicant or lawyer may have made and affirmative clarification of any misunderstanding on the part of the admissions or disciplinary authority of which the person involved becomes aware.

[2] This Rule is subject to the provisions of the Fifth Amendment of the United States Constitution and corresponding provisions of state constitutions. A person relying on such a provision in response to a question, however, should do so openly and not use the right of nondisclosure as a justification for failure to comply with this Rule.

[3] A lawyer representing an applicant for admission to the bar, or representing a lawyer who is the subject of a disciplinary inquiry or proceeding, is governed by the Rules applicable to the client-lawyer relationship, including Rule 1.6 and, in some cases, Rule 3.3.

**Definitional Cross-References**

"Knowingly" and "Known" *See* Rule 1.0(f)

**State Rules Comparison**

http://ambar.org/MRPCStateCharts

## ANNOTATION

### DUTY OF CANDOR AND COOPERATION

Rule 8.1(a) imposes a duty of candor in connection with all communications with admission authorities and disciplinary authorities. Because the duty "extends to persons seeking admission to the bar as well as to lawyers," the rule also is a basis for disciplining a lawyer who has already been admitted by the time his or her lack of candor during the application process is discovered. Cmt. [1].

Rule 8.1(b) imposes a duty to cooperate with admission and disciplinary authorities. It requires a lawyer to reveal information in connection with an admission or a disciplinary matter not only when explicitly requested, but also whenever necessary to correct a misapprehension. *See Columbus Bar Ass'n v. Nyce*, 98 N.E.3d 226 (Ohio 2018) (providing false testimony in attempt to explain failure to cooperate with disciplinary authorities).

### STAND-ALONE OFFENSE

In the vast majority of cases Rule 8.1 is an "add-on" charge, added to whatever violations the disciplinary authority was investigating in the first place. However, a violation of Rule 8.1 can stand alone as an offense.

A lawyer who ignores or falsely responds to a disciplinary authority's request for information about how the lawyer handled a matter can be disciplined for violating Rule 8.1 even if the disciplinary authority does not bring, or dismisses, any other charges of misconduct. *See In re Clark*, 834 N.E.2d 653 (Ind. 2005) (repeated failure to provide timely response to discipline authorities merited discipline even though underlying charges not proved); *Ky. Bar Ass'n v. Miniard*, 289 S.W.3d 191 (Ky. 2009) (suspending lawyer under Rule 8.1(b), but finding him not guilty on all other charges); *Att'y Grievance Comm'n v. Butler*, 107 A.3d 1220 (Md. 2015) (lawyer reprimanded for two-month delay in responding to bar counsel's letters); *In re Brost*, 850 N.W.2d 699 (Minn. 2014) (failure to cooperate with disciplinary investigation itself may warrant indefinite suspension and, when accompanied by other misconduct, may increase sanction); *In re Bunstine*, 41 N.E.3d 384 (Ohio 2015) (lawyer who failed to respond to all requests for information suspended, even though underlying charges dismissed); *State ex rel. Okla. Bar Ass'n v. McCoy*, 240 P.3d 675 (Okla. 2010) (failure to timely respond to bar's request for information is itself grounds for discipline); *In re Atwater*, 684 S.E.2d 557 (S.C. 2009) (suspension for failing to respond to investigations of five successive grievances even though hearing panel dismissed two and found other three "not sanctionable"); *In re Joseph*, 60 V.I. 540 (V.I. 2014) (violating Rule 8.1(b) in six matters warranted discipline, although all underlying ethics charges rejected); *see also Disciplinary Counsel v. Wexler*, 13 N.E.3d 1168 (Ohio 2014) (although charges relating to alleged sexual relationship with client ultimately dismissed, lawyer reprimanded for making false and misleading statement to disciplinary authorities about hotel bill).

Responding falsely to disciplinary authorities may also violate other rules. *E.g., In re Parks*, 9 So. 3d 106 (La. 2009) (driving without valid insurance not the type of criminal conduct that violates 8.4(b), but lawyer suspended for failing to cooperate with disciplinary authorities under Louisiana's Rule 8.1(c) and for lying to them under Rule 8.4(a) and (c)); *In re Hicks*, 214 P.3d 897 (Wash. 2009) (lawyer violated Rule 8.4(c) and rule for enforcement of lawyer conduct requiring full and complete response to disciplinary board inquiries by sending letter in which he "fudged things" about his trust accounts and provided information "different than, you know, the facts"; no Rule 8.1 charge).

### *Paragraph (a): Knowingly Making a False Statement*

Rule 8.1(a) prohibits knowingly making a false statement of material fact. *In re Gill*, 181 So. 3d 669 (La. 2015) (lying to disciplinary authorities about circumstances of alcohol-related arrests); *Atty Grievance Comm'n v. Phillips*, 155 A.3d 476 (Md. 2017) (series of material falsehoods to bar counsel relating to involvement in son's unauthorized practice of law); *Cleveland Metro. Bar Ass'n v. Azman*, 66 N.E.3d 695 (Ohio 2016) (admitting accessing firm e-mail accounts after being fired but lying to bar authorities by denying deleting any e-mails). *Compare People v. Goodman*, 334 P.3d 241 (Colo. O.P.D.J. 2014) (lawyer who gave disciplinary authorities fabricated copies of documents and made false statements about them violated rule), *with People v. Greene*, 276 P.3d 94 (Colo. O.P.D.J. 2011) (no Rule 8.1(a) violation when lawyer believed statement to be true and prefaced comments by saying he "thought" statement was true; element of scienter lacking), *and In re Riebschlager*, 361 P.3d 499 (Kan. 2015) (no Rule 8.1(a) violation for lawyer who believed he need not disclose on pro hac vice application that he was subject to partially probated suspension in Texas, but conduct violated Rule 8.1(b)). Motive is irrelevant to the determination that a lawyer has violated Rule 8.1; it should come into play only as a mitigating or aggravating factor. *See, e.g., In re Bailey*, 976 A.2d 176 (D.C. 2009) (applicant had "indisputably known" of his Jamaican manslaughter conviction and whether he had to report it; evidence of "unreliability" of Jamaican proceedings not relevant to violation of Rule 8.1); *In re Bidjou*, 615 N.W.2d 275 (Minn. 2000) (though lawyer knowingly made false statement of material fact on bar application by claiming no involvement in any legal proceedings, lack of intent to deceive Board of Law Examiners accepted as mitigating factor); *see also* ABA Standards for Imposing Lawyer Sanctions, Standard 9.32(b) (2012) (listing "absence of a dishonest or selfish motive" as mitigating factor).

Note, however, that most cases involving Rule 8.1 evince a mental state beyond simple knowledge anyway. *See, e.g., In re Cueller*, 880 N.E.2d 1209 (Ind. 2008) (misstatements showed "an intent to mislead the Commission into believing [respondent's] trust fund problem was an isolated (and remedied) event rather than an on-going, systemic failure"); *Att'y Grievance Comm'n v. Fraidin*, 91 A.3d 1078 (Md. 2014) (statement that $15,000 wired into IOLTA account was for benefit of client and failure to reveal that funds came from personal liquidated retirement account were "knowing and intentional misrepresentations of fact . . . intended to mislead Bar Counsel"); *In re Ek*, 643 N.W.2d 611 (Minn. 2002) (noncooperation "appear[ed] to be knowing and willful"); *In re Giese*, 709 N.W.2d 717 (N.D. 2006) (suspended lawyer filed affidavit falsely claiming he complied with client-notification requirement); *see also In re Steele*, 45 N.E.3d 777 (Ind. 2015) (false statements to disciplinary authorities were "virtually pathological in frequency and scope"); *Ky. Bar Ass'n v. Chesley*, 393 S.W.3d 584 (Ky. 2013) (answers to interrogatories were "incomplete, misleading, and false"); *Att'y Grievance Comm'n v. Hunt*, 76 A.3d 1214 (Md. 2013) (applicant made "purposeful and artful" choice "to disclose only the criminal activity that he did not believe would impact negatively on his Bar Application, that is, the criminal matter that resulted in a nolle prosequi").

## MATERIALITY

A false statement of fact does not violate Rule 8.1(a) unless the fact is "material." *See, e.g., In re Davis*, 43 A.3d 856 (Del. 2012) (lying on reinstatement questionnaire about conduct during and after alcohol-related auto accident); *In re Starnes*, 829 A.2d 488 (D.C. 2003) (applicant misled admissions committee into believing his work had been supervised by licensed D.C. lawyer); *In re Chandler*, 641 N.E.2d 473 (Ill. 1994) (failures to provide correct Social Security number and to supplement bar application with information regarding false loan application were material, but failure to provide name as it appeared on birth certificate not material); *Ky. Bar Ass'n v. Marcum*, 336 S.W.3d 95 (Ky. 2011) (in letter to bar authorities investigating misuse of escrow account, lawyer falsely stated account contained no client funds); *In re Bidjou*, 615 N.W.2d 275 (Minn. 2000) (false statement on bar application was material even though court noted applicant "would have been permitted to sit for the bar examination had he disclosed the information"); *In re Chernyy*, 981 N.Y.S.2d 539 (App. Div. 2014) (application omitted guilty plea to DUI); *In re Melendez*, 957 N.Y.S.2d 740 (App. Div. 2012) (false statements on bar application that lawyer was not four months or more behind in child support payments and had not applied for bankruptcy discharge); *In re Defillo*, 762 S.E.2d 552 (S.C. 2014) (lawyer not licensed in state purporting to limit practice to immigration law made "false statements of material fact" concerning extent of practice and advertising within state); *Lawyer Disciplinary Bd. v. Haught*, 757 S.E.2d 609 (W. Va. 2014) (false statements about which party lawyer represented in real estate matter); *see also In re Pasyanos*, No. 02-O-11558, 2005 WL 103065 (Cal. Bar Ct. Review Dep't Jan. 13, 2005) (under California's analogous Rule 1-200(A), nondisclosure of misdemeanor charge arising out of long-standing domestic dispute was material even though applicant "could not reasonably have believed" it would affect her admission).

## DISCIPLINE AS A LAWYER FOR LACK OF CANDOR TO ADMISSIONS AUTHORITIES

Lack of candor about a material fact in the application process would normally result in denial of admission. But if the individual has already been admitted by the time the problem is discovered, he or she may still be disciplined under Rule 8.1. Discipline may include disbarment, license revocation, or suspension. *See In re Rodri-*

*guez*, 753 N.E.2d 1289 (Ind. 2001) (suspension; omission from 1992 bar application of attendance at two colleges, academic dismissal from both, and suspension from one); *Att'y Grievance Comm'n v. Van Dusen*, 116 A.3d 1013 (Md. 2015) (disbarring lawyer more than two years after admission for failure to report ongoing criminal conduct to admissions authorities); *Att'y Grievance Comm'n v. Kepple*, 68 A.3d 797 (Md. 2013) (lawyer who failed to disclose to admissions authorities that she lied to law school about her address to take advantage of in-state tuition was suspended more than thirteen years later, when disciplinary authorities became aware of misconduct); *Att'y Grievance Comm'n v. Gilbert*, 515 A.2d 454 (Md. 1986) (disbarment; bar application omitted mention of lawyer's involvement in litigation over insurance policies on wife, proceeds of which he was denied due to overwhelming evidence linking him to her murder); *In re Gouiran*, 613 A.2d 479 (N.J. 1992) (license revoked; bar application omitted mention of disciplinary proceedings in connection with real estate license in another state); *In re DeMaria*, 62 N.Y.S.3d 226 (App. Div. 2017) (bar admission revoked seven years after admission for lying on bar application and failing to disclose finding by Saskatchewan admission authorities that lawyer had engaged in "serious breach of integrity" warranting monetary and academic sanctions); *see also In re Pasyanos*, No. 02-O-11558, 2005 WL 103065 (Cal. Bar Ct. Review Dep't Jan. 13, 2005) (under California's analogous Rule 1-200(A), public reproval rather than license cancellation because nondisclosure of misdemeanor charge on application not motivated by intent to mislead). See the annotation to Rule 8.4 for further discussion of discipline for pre-admission conduct.

### • *Expunged Convictions; Sealed Records*

The duty of disclosure in bar applications can extend to information contained in sealed records. *See, e.g., In re Rodriguez*, 753 N.E.2d 1289 (Ind. 2001) (rejecting lawyer's argument that he was not required to disclose circumstances of academic suspension because underlying conduct had been basis for criminal charges, records of which were "expunged"); *Ky. Bar Ass'n v. Guidugli*, 967 S.W.2d 587 (Ky. 1998) (application omitted mention of lawyer's criminal conviction, the record of which was sealed but not expunged; lawyer's good-faith effort to determine whether he was required to disclose it was mitigating factor); *see also State v. Greene*, 573 N.E.2d 110 (Ohio 1991) (error to deny law student's petition to expunge his conviction out of concern that expunction would prevent bar admission authorities from learning of it; applicant would still be required to disclose it, and board would still have access to any sealed records); *cf. Att'y Grievance Comm'n v. Hunt*, 76 A.3d 1214 (Md. 2013) (bar applicant required to disclose criminal activities even if not charged and convicted). *See generally* Lydia Johnson, *The Illusion of a Second Chance: Expunctions Versus the Law School and State Bar Application Processes*, 9 Fla. A & M U. L. Rev. 183 (Fall 2013).

## Paragraph (b): Duty to Cooperate with Admission and Disciplinary Authorities

Rule 8.1(b) imposes what is usually described as a duty of cooperation. The duty is phrased in the negative: a lawyer or an applicant may not "knowingly fail to respond" to any lawful demand for information from admission and disciplinary authorities, and if a lawyer or an applicant knows that a misapprehension has arisen in connection with an application or a disciplinary matter, he or she must not "fail to disclose a fact necessary to correct" it.

## DUTY TO CORRECT MISAPPREHENSION

Rule 8.1(b) requires a lawyer or bar applicant to "disclose a fact necessary to correct a misapprehension known by the person to have arisen in the matter." *See In re Hartke,* 138 A.3d 478 (D.C. 2016) (failure to correct misrepresentations made to disciplinary authorities investigating lawyer for disrupting CLE seminar); *In re Riebschlager,* 361 P.3d 499 (Kan. 2015) (although lawyer seeking pro hac vice admission believed he need not disclose partially probated suspension in Texas, declining to do so constituted failure to correct misapprehension); *In re Kline,* 311 P.3d 321 (Kan. 2013) (Rule 8.1(b) requires lawyer to correct prior misstatement even when disciplinary authorities could learn of its falsity through third party); *In re Lafaye,* 731 S.E.2d 282 (S.C. 2012) (lawyer kept bar authorities from discovering misappropriation by failing to disclose existence of second trust account); *see also In re Usher,* 987 N.E.2d 1080 (Ind. 2013) (lawyer's "less than entirely forthcoming" response to grievance seemed to be "crafted to create misapprehensions rather than to dispel them"); *Att'y Grievance Comm'n v. Slate,* 180 A.3d 134 (Md. 2018) (disclosing to admission authorities he had been party to lawsuit, but omitting fact that court found he had engaged in bad-faith litigation); *Att'y Grievance Comm'n v. Tanko,* 45 A.3d 281 (Md. 2012) (failure to include client's name on list of pending clients did not violate rule when lawyer believed attorney-client relationship ended; lawyer did not "know" that "a misapprehension had arisen").

## DUTY TO RESPOND

### • *Lawful Demands for Information*

Rule 8.1(b) requires a lawyer to respond to any "lawful demand for information from an admissions or disciplinary authority." Letters from disciplinary counsel or admissions authorities seeking information constitute lawful demands; subpoenas are not required. *See Ky. Bar Ass'n v. Bierbauer,* 282 S.W.3d 318 (Ky. 2009) (bar complaint or charge constitutes "lawful demand for information" within meaning of Rule 8.1(b)); *In re Gray,* 234 So. 3d 65 (La. 2018) (failure to respond to disciplinary complaint); *Att'y Grievance Comm'n v. Kahl,* 84 A.3d 103 (Md. 2014) (rule requires lawyer "to respond to letters or telephone calls from a disciplinary authority without the use of a subpoena"); *Att'y Grievance Comm'n v. Lewis,* 85 A.3d 865 (Md. 2014) (Rule 8.1(b) violation each time lawyer failed to respond to bar counsel's letters and investigator's e-mail and phone messages); *Disciplinary Counsel v. Eichenberger,* 55 N.E.3d 1100 (Ohio 2016) (repeated refusals to provide copies of trust account records); *State ex rel. Okla. Bar Ass'n v. Simank,* 19 P.3d 860 (Okla. 2001) (failure to respond to letters from bar on ten occasions and five instances of failure to claim certified mail sent to lawyer's official bar address); *In re McCoy-Jacien,* 186 A.3d 626 (Vt. 2018) (failure to respond to numerous written and oral requests for information by disciplinary counsel or to subsequent petition of misconduct); *Lawyer Disciplinary Bd. v. Barber,* 566 S.E.2d 245 (W. Va. 2002) (violation of Rule 8.1(b) not contingent upon issuance of subpoena); *see also Att'y Grievance Comm'n v. Dyer*, 162 A.3d 970 (Md. 2017) (raising constitutional or jurisdictional objections is not adequate; lawyer must respond to substance of allegations); *Att'y Grievance Comm'n v. Khandpur*, 25 A.3d 165 (Md. 2011) (no requirement that bar counsel explain how requested records relate to investigation); *In re Bunstine*, 41 N.E.3d 384 (Ohio 2015) (failure to allege specific rule violation at earliest stages of investigation does not excuse lawyer's failure to respond to disciplinary authority's inquiries). *But see In re Taylor*, 60 V.I. 356 (V.I. 2014) (case investigator's demand that lawyer file motion to reopen long-closed divorce case not "lawful demand" under Rule 8.1(b)); *In re Merry*, 847 N.W.2d 174 (Wis. 2014) (dismissal warranted when information allegedly withheld "appear[ed] to be of dubious relevance").

### • *Response Must Be Timely*

The response to a demand for information must be timely. *See In re Stern*, 11 N.E.3d 917 (Ind. 2014) (despite being asked about his relationship with client, lawyer failed to disclose for more than two years that client was his "contract paralegal"); *Att'y Grievance Comm'n v. Queen*, 967 A.2d 198 (Md. 2009) (although immediate response not necessary, four-month delay before any acknowledgment of bar counsel's repeated inquiries violated Rule 8.1(b)); *In re McCray*, 825 N.W.2d 468 (N.D. 2012) (lawyer took over three years to respond to bar counsel's request for information); *see also Att'y Grievance Comm'n v. Moeller*, 46 A.3d 407 (Md. 2012) (rejecting lawyer's claim that health problems, about which he had never informed bar counsel, prevented timely response); *In re Taylor*, 60 V.I. 356 (V.I. 2014) (untimely answer to grievance does not, without more, violate Rule 8.1(b), but failure to file answer in subsequent disciplinary action before court does); *Lawyer Disciplinary Bd. v. Lusk*, 574 S.E.2d 788 (W. Va. 2002) (lawyer's failure to respond within reasonable time constituted admission under state's rules of disciplinary procedure, in addition to violation of Rule 8.1(b)).

A lawyer's eventual response does not cure the initial delay. *See Att'y Grievance Comm'n v. Weiers*, 102 A.3d 332 (Md. 2014) (after numerous delays, lawyer's eventual response to bar counsel's follow-up letters did not excuse conduct); *Att'y Grievance Comm'n v. Fezell*, 760 A.2d 1108 (Md. 2000) (lawyer's belated fifteen-minute telephone conversation with bar counsel did not excuse failure to respond to five previous letters); *In re Obert*, 282 P.3d 825 (Or. 2012) (rejecting argument that because rule does not contain timing requirement lawyer's eventual response to bar inquiries constituted compliance with rule; rule interpreted to include "reasonable deadlines"); *see also In re Krasnoff*, 78 N.E.3d 657 (Ind. 2017) (lawyer's failure to cooperate resulted in two show cause proceedings that were dismissed when lawyer belatedly complied; "prosecution of a Rule 8.1(b) violation is not rendered either *res judicata* or moot by the initiation and resolution of show cause proceedings").

### • *"Knowing" Failure to Respond*

The failure to respond to a lawful demand for information violates Rule 8.1(b) only if it is "knowing," which, according to Rule 1.0(f), may be inferred from circumstances. *See People v. Weisbard*, 59 P.3d 858 (Colo. O.P.D.J. 2002) (error to enter default finding that lawyer violated Rule 8.1(b); no evidence he ever actually received requests for information); *In re Godette*, 919 A.2d 1157 (D.C. 2007) (repeated failure to acknowledge bar counsel's mailings warranted inference that lawyer was deliberately evading personal service); *In re Doudin*, 249 P.3d 1190 (Kan. 2011) (retained counsel's failure to cooperate imputed to respondent unless he demonstrates he "could not reasonably know that retained counsel was obstructing the investigation"); *In re Anderson*, 759 N.W.2d 892 (Minn. 2009) ("failure to read the letters from the Director does not allow [respondent] to escape responsibility for failing to respond to requests made in those letters"); *In re Dyer*, 817 N.W.2d 351 (N.D. 2012) (lawyers' refusal to comply with request for information until court ruled on confidentiality objection violated rule; "plain language of Rule 1.6" permitted disclosure); *Hanzelik v. Bd. of Prof'l Responsibility*, 380 S.W.3d 669 (Tenn. 2012) (lawyer "repeatedly and consistently failed to respond" to requests for information; prolonged duration of investigation suggested lawyer's "sluggish compliance was indeed 'dilatory'"); *see also State ex rel. Okla. Bar Ass'n v. Krug*, 92 P.3d 67 (Okla. 2004) (reversing recommendation of discipline for lawyer who responded to disciplinary counsel by repeatedly requesting complainant's identity; her letters "were attempts to secure relevant information necessary to fully respond. . . . [S]he maintained communication with General Counsel and requested information to which she is entitled."). *Compare Att'y Grievance Comm'n v. Sapero*, 929 A.2d 483 (Md. 2007) (lawyer's failure to make timely and orderly reply was "knowing" within meaning of Rule 8.1(b), even if it resulted from disorganized recordkeeping), *with Dayton Bar Ass'n v. Hooks*, 12 N.E.3d 1212 (Ohio 2014) (Rule 8.1 charge dismissed; although lawyer failed to provide client file upon request, he made good-faith effort to find file, which had been misplaced).

### • *Duty to Supplement*

As part of the bar admission process itself, candidates are required to supplement their pending applications. Rule 8.1(b) separately imposes a similar duty. *See In re Small*, 760 A.2d 612 (D.C. 2000) (failure to update bar application after conviction for negligent homicide); *In re Conn*, 715 N.E.2d 379 (Ind. 1999) (failure to supplement pending application with information about FBI investigation for receipt of child pornography); *Ky. Bar Ass'n v. Claypoole*, 198 S.W.3d 589 (Ky. 2006) (failure to update pending application after arrest for drunk driving). The rule may also be implicated if a lawyer facing discipline fails to provide updated information to bar authorities. *See Att'y Grievance Comm'n v. Thomas*, 127 A.3d 562 (Md. 2015) (lawyer subject to conditional diversion agreement failed to inform bar counsel he was no longer attending substance abuse counseling and had resumed using alcohol or opiates).

## DUTY OF CANDOR IN CONNECTION WITH SOMEONE ELSE'S APPLICATION OR DISCIPLINARY PROCEEDINGS

Rule 8.1 requires a lawyer to be truthful and to respond to lawful demands for information "in connection with *a* bar admission application or in connection with *a* disciplinary matter" (emphasis added). The duty thus applies regardless of the lawyer's role in the admission or discipline process. *See Andrews v. Ky. Bar Ass'n*, 169 S.W.3d 862 (Ky. 2005) (lawyer sent letter to bar counsel containing false statements about someone else's pending disciplinary case and enclosing falsified supporting evidence); *Att'y Grievance Comm'n v. Oswinkle*, 772 A.2d 267 (Md. 2001) (reprimanding lawyer who failed to respond to bar counsel's inquiries about another lawyer); *In re Torgerson*, 870 N.W.2d 602 (Minn. 2015) (false statements in connection with ethics complaint lawyer had filed against assistant county attorney).

## FIFTH AMENDMENT

Comment [2] notes that a lawyer's obligations under Rule 8.1 are subject to the Fifth Amendment. *In re Gault*, 387 U.S. 1 (1967); *Spevack v. Klein*, 385 U.S. 511 (1967) (recognizing right to invoke Fifth Amendment in lawyer discipline proceedings); *In re Artis*, 883 A.2d 85 (D.C. 2005) (inasmuch as fraud can constitute a crime, lawyer had Fifth Amendment right to refuse to supply bar counsel with information about his role in alleged fraudulent conveyance); *Miss. State Bar v. Att'y L.*, 511 So. 2d 119 (Miss. 1987) (lawyer may raise Fifth Amendment only if answer could create actual risk of criminal prosecution); *In re Curtis*, 907 N.W.2d 91 (Wis. 2018) (lawyer properly asserted Fifth Amendment privilege to avoid answering questions about firm's payment of 401(k) funds); *see also* Colo. R. Civ. P. 251.18(d) (respondent in disciplinary proceeding cannot be required to testify if doing so would violate Fifth Amendment rights). *See generally* Geoffrey C. Hazard, Jr. & Cameron Beard, *A Lawyer's Privilege Against Self-Incrimination in Professional Disciplinary Proceedings*, 96 Yale L.J. 1060 (Apr. 1987).

### • *Lawyer Must Still Respond*

The availability of the Fifth Amendment does not relieve the lawyer of the duty to make some response to an inquiry from bar authorities. *See, e.g., People v. Smith*, 937 P.2d 724 (Colo. 1997) (requiring lawyer to appear for deposition in disciplinary case does not violate Fifth Amendment right against self-incrimination); *In re Barber*, 128 A.3d 637 (D.C. 2015) (no Fifth Amendment right to decline to take witness stand, but lawyer free to invoke Fifth Amendment with respect to specific questions if responding would provide evidence that could be used to convict him of crime); *In re Zisook*, 430 N.E.2d 1037 (Ill. 1981) (lawyer must appear in response to inquiry, bringing whatever documents requested, and must claim Fifth Amendment privilege with specificity for each area of inquiry).

### • *No Protection against Disciplinary Sanctions*

The privilege cannot be invoked as a protection against disciplinary sanctions themselves. *Spevack v. Klein*, 385 U.S. 511 (1967), does not confer "a constitutional privilege to withhold evidence which cannot lead to criminal prosecution and bears only upon [the] right to continue to practice law." *Zuckerman v. Greason*, 231 N.E.2d 718 (N.Y. 1967). *See In re Shannon*, 876 P.2d 548 (Ariz. 1994) ("[b]ecause the primary function of state bar disciplinary sanctions is remedial, the right against self-incrimination does not attach when disciplinary sanctions are the only penalties to which a respondent is exposed"); *In re Holliday*, 15 So. 3d 82 (La. 2009) (respondent's assertion of Fifth Amendment privilege when disciplinary counsel asked about arrests was "not reasonable" given that respondent already reached plea agreements on underlying DWI charges). *But see State ex rel. Okla. Bar Ass'n v. Wilcox*, 227 P.3d 642 (Okla. 2009) (court treated respondent's refusal to answer bar's questions based upon possible exposure to discipline, not criminal prosecution, as exercise of Fifth Amendment rights for which he could not be disciplined under Rule 8.1(b)).

### • *If Lawyer Faces Incarceration for Contempt of Prior Disciplinary Order*

A lawyer may, however, invoke the Fifth Amendment privilege when questioned about noncriminal conduct that could nonetheless subject the lawyer to incarceration for contempt of a prior disciplinary order. *See, e.g., People v. Razatos*, 699 P.2d 970 (Colo. 1985) (lawyer successfully invoked Fifth Amendment regarding production of written records that he argued would show noncompliance with earlier disciplinary order and thereby subject him to contempt finding); *In re Malvin*, 466 A.2d 1220 (D.C. 1983) (court refused to require lawyer to submit to audit as condition of temporary suspension because possibility of incarceration upon finding of contempt of suspension order triggered applicability of Fifth Amendment privilege).

### • *No Protection against Requests for Client Account Records*

A lawyer has no Fifth Amendment protection against compelled production of records of client fund accounts; they come within the "required-records" exception to the privilege. *In re Henderson*, 761 So. 2d 523 (La. 2000); *Agwara v. State Bar*, 406 P.3d 488 (Nev. 2017) ("the Fifth Amendment does not protect petitioner from disclosure of client accounting records"); *In re Reis*, 942 N.Y.S.2d 101 (App. Div. 2012) (lawyer cannot assert Fifth Amendment right against self-incrimination "merely to avoid production of records" lawyer is required by ethics rules to maintain); *see also In re Thomas*, 740 A.2d 538 (D.C. 1999) (in disciplinary proceeding for mishandling client funds, lawyer's Fifth Amendment rights not violated by his bank's compliance with subpoena for his account records; bank, not lawyer, was source of incriminating evidence); *cf. Att'y Grievance Comm'n v. Zdravkovich*, 852 A.2d 82 (Md. 2004) (failure to produce escrow account records violated Rule 8.1; Rule 1.6 does not protect information to which banks are required to give disciplinary authorities access); *In re Dyer*, 817 N.W.2d 351 (N.D. 2012) (same).

### • *Effect of Invoking Fifth Amendment*

Unlike in a criminal proceeding, a lawyer's assertion of the Fifth Amendment privilege in a disciplinary proceeding may result in an adverse inference being drawn in connection with the disciplinary charges. *See In re Saghir*, 632 F. Supp. 2d 328 (S.D.N.Y. 2009) (adverse inference may be drawn from assertion of privilege in disciplinary proceeding); *People v. McNamara*, 275 P.3d 792 (Colo. O.P.D.J. 2011) (adverse inference appropriate in some cases); *Fla. Bar v. Adams*, 198 So. 3d 593 (Fla. 2016) (refusal to testify on Fifth Amendment grounds by respondents and witness resulted in adverse inferences); *see also In re Burton*, 472 A.2d 831 (D.C. 1984) ("invocation of the fifth amendment does not allow a respondent to place the burden of proof on Bar Counsel to [disprove] affirmative defenses which Respondent does not raise"); *People v. Jobi*, 953 N.Y.S.2d 471 (Sup. Ct. 2012) (lawyer's statements made in disciplinary proceeding to avoid adverse inference had lawyer invoked Fifth Amendment could be used against him in criminal proceeding). *Compare In re Redding*, 501 S.E.2d 499 (Ga. 1998) (because lawyer's Fifth Amendment claim "may result in an adverse inference being drawn by the fact finder," lawyer's "outright admissions and her admissions by virtue of invoking the Fifth Amendment constitut[ed] admission of the essential allegations of the charges against her"), *and State ex rel. Okla. Bar Ass'n v. Gasaway*, 863 P.2d 1189 (Okla. 1993) (although lawyer's invocation of Fifth Amendment at disciplinary hearing prevented panel from deeming bar's complaint admitted, evidence of misappropriation independently warranted disbarment), *with In re Curtis*, 907 N.W.2d 91 (Wis. 2018) (adverse inference permitted, but more was needed to support finding of Rule 8.4(c) violation). Invoking the Fifth Amendment "should not serve as a separate ground for an interim suspension" in itself. *In re Kapchan*, 924 N.Y.S.2d 338 (App. Div. 2011). But the adverse inference drawn from it may be considered as evidence supporting an interim suspension. *In re Muraskin*, 731 N.Y.S.2d 458 (App. Div. 2001) (evidence supporting immediate interim suspension and appointment of receiver included adverse inference drawn from lawyer's invocation of Fifth Amendment at deposition by disciplinary counsel).

In the admissions (as opposed to discipline) context, the burden is on the applicant to affirmatively establish character and fitness; claiming Fifth Amendment protection may make it impossible to meet that burden. *See Petition of Bellino*, 478 N.W.2d 507 (Minn. 1991) (South Carolina lawyer's Fifth Amendment right not to answer questions about his alleged sexual assaults on clients while he was officer in Marine Corps did not relieve him of burden of establishing good character and fitness to practice law as prerequisite for admission to Minnesota bar).

# Maintaining the Integrity of the Profession

## Rule 8.2
### *Judicial and Legal Officials*

(a) A lawyer shall not make a statement that the lawyer knows to be false or with reckless disregard as to its truth or falsity concerning the qualifications or integrity of a judge, adjudicatory officer or public legal officer, or of a candidate for election or appointment to judicial or legal office.

(b) A lawyer who is a candidate for judicial office shall comply with the applicable provisions of the Code of Judicial Conduct.

## COMMENT

[1] Assessments by lawyers are relied on in evaluating the professional or personal fitness of persons being considered for election or appointment to judicial office and to public legal offices, such as attorney general, prosecuting attorney and public defender. Expressing honest and candid opinions on such matters contributes to improving the administration of justice. Conversely, false statements by a lawyer can unfairly undermine public confidence in the administration of justice.

[2] When a lawyer seeks judicial office, the lawyer should be bound by applicable limitations on political activity.

[3] To maintain the fair and independent administration of justice, lawyers are encouraged to continue traditional efforts to defend judges and courts unjustly criticized.

**Definitional Cross-References**

"Knows" *See* Rule 1.0(f)

**State Rules Comparison**

http://ambar.org/MRPCStateCharts

## ANNOTATION

### INTRODUCTION

Rule 8.2 prohibits lawyers from knowingly or recklessly making false statements about the integrity or qualifications of judges, "public legal officer[s]," and candidates (elective or appointive) for either position. The rule also imports unspecified parts of the Code of Judicial Conduct: a lawyer who is a candidate for judicial office is subject to discipline under Rule 8.2(b) for violating any "applicable" judicial ethics rules.

## Paragraph (a): False Criticism

### APPLICABILITY

Most of the caselaw and commentary construing Rule 8.2(a) involves criticism of judges, but the rule also applies to false statements about the integrity or qualifications of an "adjudicatory officer or public legal officer, or of a candidate for election or appointment to judicial or legal office." *See, e.g., Iowa Supreme Court Att'y Disciplinary Bd. v. Kennedy,* 837 N.W.2d 659 (Iowa 2013) (lawyer sent letter to attorney general accusing county attorney's office of misconduct); *In re Wells,* 36 So. 3d 198 (La. 2010) (lawyer filed affidavit falsely accusing district attorney, who filed felony charges against him, of conspiracy to commit murder); *State ex rel. Okla. Bar Ass'n v. Wilcox,* 227 P.3d 642 (Okla. 2009) (lawyer sent out mass mailing questioning judicial candidate's ethics and falsely claiming candidate's cancer was terminal); *Lawyer Disciplinary Bd. v. Hall,* 765 S.E.2d 187 (W. Va. 2014) ("administrative law judges are adjudicatory officers within the meaning of Rule 8.2(a)"); *cf. Att'y Grievance Comm'n v. Frost,* 85 A.3d 264 (Md. 2014) (state governor not "public legal officer" for purposes of rule).

Rule 8.2(a) applies to what lawyers say even when they are not representing clients. *See, e.g., Notopoulos v. Statewide Grievance Comm.,* 890 A.2d 509 (Conn. 2006) (lawyer acting pro se when he wrote letter accusing judge of "extorting" funds from lawyer's mother's estate to "line the pockets of his cronies" violated Rule 8.2); *In re Ireland,* 276 P.3d 762 (Kan. 2012) (lawyer falsely claimed she was "intimidated, threatened and sexually harassed" by judge assigned to attempt to mediate her divorce); *In re Howe,* 865 N.W.2d 844 (N.D. 2015) (suspended lawyer stated in notice posted on office door and in letters to clients that he was suspended and charged with crime as result of a "witch hunt" by drug task force, state's attorney, and district court judge); *In re Isaacson,* 860 N.W.2d 490 (Wis. 2015) (lawyer serving as managing member of corporate entity directed other counsel to file court documents on her behalf containing false and harassing statements impugning integrity of judges and others involved in litigation).

The rule would not, however, apply to false statements communicated solely to the target of the criticism—although such conduct may violate other rules. *See Iowa Supreme Court Att'y Disciplinary Bd. v. Doe,* 878 N.W.2d 189 (Iowa 2016) (no violation of Rule 8.2(a) when e-mail accusing judge of unethical conduct was sent to judge alone, but conduct violated Rule 3.5(b)); *Hancock v. Bd. of Prof'l Responsibility,* 447 S.W.3d 844 (Tenn. 2014) (lawyer's e-mail to judge impugning judge's integrity did not violate rule as it was not sent to third party, but conduct did violate Rule 3.5(a) and (c)).

### ARGUMENTS FOR AND AGAINST REGULATION;
### CONSTITUTIONALITY

The justifications advanced for regulating what lawyers say about judges are the need to maintain public confidence in the judiciary, and the proposition that lawyers give up certain rights when they become members of a regulated profession. On these rationales, the restrictions on lawyer speech embodied in Rule 8.2 have long withstood constitutional challenge. *See In re Snyder*, 472 U.S. 634 (1985) ("[t]he license granted by the court requires members of the bar to conduct themselves in a manner compatible with the role of courts in the administration of justice"); *In re Shearin*, 765 A.2d 930 (Del. 2000) ("there are ethical obligations imposed upon a Delaware lawyer, which qualify the lawyer's constitutional right to freedom of speech"), *cert. denied*, 534 U.S. 961 (2001); *Fla. Bar v. Ray*, 797 So. 2d 556 (Fla. 2001) (rules prohibiting lawyers from impugning integrity of judges are not designed to protect judges from criticism, but to preserve public confidence in fairness of justice system), *cert. denied*, 535 U.S. 930 (2002); *In re Wilkins*, 777 N.E.2d 714 (Ind. 2002) (state's interest in preserving public's confidence in judicial system and overall administration of justice far outweighs lawyer's need to express himself), *cert. denied*, 540 U.S. 813 (2003); *Ky. Bar Ass'n v. Blum*, 404 S.W.3d 841 (Ky. 2013) (regulating lawyer speech "is appropriate in order to maintain the public confidence and credibility of the judiciary and as a condition of '[t]he license granted by the court'" (citing *Snyder*)); *Att'y Grievance Comm'n v. Frost*, 85 A.3d 264 (Md. 2014) (purpose of rule is "to prevent damage to the integrity of the judicial system"; lawyer's knowingly false allegations of corruption by several judges and public legal officers "not entitled to protection under the First Amendment"); *Office of Disciplinary Counsel v. Gardner*, 793 N.E.2d 425 (Ohio 2003) (integral role lawyers play in judicial system requires them to refrain from speech or conduct that may obstruct fair administration of justice), *cert. denied*, 540 U.S. 1220 (2004); *Anthony v. Va. State Bar*, 621 S.E.2d 121 (Va. 2005) ("limitations on lawyers' rights of free speech are based upon a lawyer's obligation to abstain from public debate that will obstruct the administration of justice").

Countervailing considerations arise out of the public's right to know about its judiciary, and the special protection afforded political speech. *See, e.g., In re Green*, 11 P.3d 1078 (Colo. 2000) ("Restrictions on attorney speech burden not only the attorney's right to criticize judges, but also hinder the public's access to the class of people in the best position to comment on the functioning of the judicial system."); *State ex rel. Okla. Bar Ass'n v. Porter*, 766 P.2d 958 (Okla. 1988) (First Amendment right of members of public to receive information from lawyers about judiciary protects lawyer from discipline for public remarks criticizing judge for racism in conduct of trial; court noted, however, that "false speech" not involved, as lawyer had "rational basis" for concluding his remarks were factual). *See generally* Angela Butcher & Scott Macbeth, Current Development, *Lawyers' Comments About Judges: A Balancing of Interests to Ensure a Sound Judiciary*, 17 Geo. J. Legal Ethics 659 (Summer 2004); Douglas R. Richmond, *Appellate Ethics: Truth, Criticism, and Consequences*, 23 Rev. Litig. 301 (Spring 2004) (examining issues appellate lawyers face when criticizing judiciary).

Many commentators question the rationales for regulating judicial criticism. *See, e.g.,* Erwin Chemerinsky, *Silence Is Not Golden: Protecting Lawyer Speech Under the First Amendment*, 47 Emory L.J. 859 (Summer 1998) (requiring lawyers to relinquish First Amendment rights as condition of membership in bar should be seen as unconstitutional condition); Jeanne D. Dodd, Comment, *The First Amendment and Attorney Discipline for Criticism of the Judiciary: Let the Lawyer Beware*, 15 N. Ky. L. Rev. 129 (1988) (silencing all lawyer criticism is as likely to generate suspicion as to promote confidence in judicial system); Lawrence A. Dubin, *Fieger, Civility and the First Amendment: Should the Mouth That Roared Be Silenced?*, 82 U. Det. Mercy L. Rev. 377 (Spring 2005) ("civility" considerations should not be used as basis for limiting lawyers' freedom of speech); Margaret Tarkington, *The Truth Be Damned: The First Amendment, Attorney Speech, and Judicial Reputation*, 97 Geo. L.J. 1567 (Aug. 2009) (impugning judicial integrity is "core political speech"; for courts to punish speech to protect judicial reputation "damns self-governance, robust public debate, the unique sovereignty of the American people, and the ability of the people to check and define the abuse of judicial power and to call upon democratic correctives to fix such abuses"); W. Bradley Wendel, *Free Speech for Lawyers*, 28 Hastings Const. L.Q. 305 (Winter 2001) (courts should not be permitted to restrict criticism without having to establish that it does, in fact, decrease public confidence in judiciary, and that government's interest in maintaining public confidence is not outweighed by First Amendment values). *But see* Hal R. Lieberman, *Should Lawyers Be Free to Publicly Excoriate Judges?*, 25 Hofstra L. Rev. 785 (Spring 1997) (context crucial to validity of disciplinary response; author notes judges are generally prohibited by law and judicial ethics rules from publicly responding to attacks); Adam R. Long, Note, *Keeping Mud Off the Bench: The First Amendment and Regulation of Candidates' False or Misleading Statements in Judicial Elections*, 51 Duke L.J. 787 (Nov. 2001) (restrictions on knowingly false and misleading statements by judicial candidates "can be tailored narrowly to achieve the state's interest and fit within current First Amendment jurisprudence"). *See generally* Caprice L. Roberts, Note, Standing Committee on Discipline v. Yagman: *Missing the Point of Ethical Restrictions on Attorney Criticism of the Judiciary?*, 54 Wash. & Lee L. Rev. 817 (Spring 1997).

## "Knowledge or Reckless Disregard"

The U.S. Supreme Court has held that the First Amendment protects a lawyer from civil or criminal liability for derogatory statements about judges unless the lawyer speaks "with 'actual malice'—that is, with knowledge that [the statement] was false or with reckless disregard of whether it was false or not." *Garrison v. Louisiana*, 379 U.S. 64 (1964) (district attorney's accusations that state court judges were lazy and inefficient, and were hampering his efforts to enforce vice laws, were protected unless he knew they were false or recklessly disregarded whether they were false); *N.Y. Times v. Sullivan*, 376 U.S. 254 (1964).

Rule 8.2(a) adopts the same standard for professional responsibility purposes. *See, e.g., In re Green*, 11 P.3d 1078 (Colo. 2000) (discipline for criticizing judge is constitutionally permissible only if (1) disciplinary authority proves criticism was false statement of fact, or was statement of opinion that necessarily implied undisclosed assertion of fact; and (2) lawyer acted with actual malice—that is, with knowledge of or in reckless disregard of its falsity); *Pilli v. Va. State Bar*, 611 S.E.2d 389 (Va.) (bar must establish that lawyer made statement about judge's qualifications or integrity knowing it was false, or with reckless disregard of its truth or falsity), *cert. denied*, 546 U.S. 977 (2005); *see also Restatement (Third) of the Law Governing Lawyers* § 114 (2000) (discipline appropriate only for false statements made knowingly or recklessly).

## • *Knowingly Making False Statements*

False statements made with knowledge of their falsity clearly fall within the rule. *See In re Cooper*, 78 N.E.3d 1098 (Ind. 2017) (county prosecutor told local newspaper that he was "suspicious" of transfer of case to particular judge and attempted to support statement with "commentary that was false, misleading, and inflammatory"); *In re Clothier*, 344 P.3d 370 (Kan. 2015) (lawyer accused judge of colluding with opposing counsel, knowing accusation to be false); *In re Callaghan*, 796 S.E.2d 604 (W. Va. 2017) (judicial candidate violated rule by mailing campaign flyer depicting incumbent judge as "party[ing] at the White House," knowing judge had only attended federally required meeting and child-trafficking conference on White House compound).

## • *Test for "Reckless Disregard" Differs from That Used in Defamation Cases*

The interests protected by professional discipline are different from those protected by defamation law. *In re Terry*, 394 N.E.2d 94 (Ind. 1979) ("Defamation is a wrong directed against an individual and the remedy is a personal redress of this wrong," but professional discipline is imposed to redress the wrong "against society as a whole, the preservation of a fair, impartial judicial system, and the system of justice"), *cert. denied*, 444 U.S. 1077 (1980); *accord In re Cobb*, 838 N.E.2d 1197 (Mass. 2005); *In re Graham*, 453 N.W.2d 313 (Minn. 1990). Consequently, reckless disregard as to falsity does not mean quite the same thing in discipline as it does in public-official libel and slander cases.

### Objective Standard Used in Discipline Cases

In defamation cases, "reckless conduct is not measured by whether a reasonably prudent man would have published, or would have investigated before publishing." *St. Amant v. Thompson*, 390 U.S. 727 (1968). "The standard is a subjective one . . . . As a result, failure to investigate before publishing, even when a reasonably prudent person would have done so, is not sufficient to establish reckless disregard." *Harte-Hanks Commc'ns, Inc. v. Connaughton*, 491 U.S. 657 (1989). But in disciplinary cases, the lawyer's mental state—that is, whether the lawyer knew the statement was false or recklessly disregarded its falsity—is to be assessed objectively. *See In re Sandlin*, 12 F.3d 861 (9th Cir. 1993) (in view of compelling state interests served by Rule 8.2, appropriate test is "what the reasonable attorney, considered in light of all his professional functions, would do in the same or similar circumstances"); *Fla. Bar v. Ray*, 797 So. 2d 556 (Fla. 2001) (lawyer had no objectively reasonable factual basis for statements impugning judge's fairness, integrity, and veracity), *cert. denied*, 535 U.S. 930 (2002); *Idaho State Bar v. Topp*, 925 P.2d 1113 (Idaho 1996) (lawyer "objectively reckless" in telling media judge worried about political ramifications of his decision); *In re Dixon*, 994 N.E.2d 1129 (Ind. 2013) (adopting objective standard calling for assessment of whether lawyer lacked "any objectively reasonable basis for making the statement at issue, considering its nature and the context in which the statement was made"); *Iowa Supreme Court Att'y Disciplinary Bd. v. Weaver*, 750 N.W.2d 71 (Iowa 2008) (analyzing authorities and endorsing objective standard); *Ky. Bar Ass'n v. Blum*, 404 S.W.3d 841 (Ky. 2013) (adopting objective standard); *In re Cobb*, 838 N.E.2d 1197 (Mass. 2005) (system that permits lawyer without objective basis to challenge integrity of judge presiding over case elevates brazen and irresponsible conduct above competence and diligence); *In re Graham*, 453 N.W.2d 313 (Minn. 1990) (proper standard in lawyer discipline cases is objective inquiry into what reasonable lawyer, considered in light of all his or her professional functions, would do in same or similar circumstances); *Miss. Bar v. Lumumba*, 912 So. 2d 871 (Miss.) (lawyer had no "objectively reasonable factual basis" for making statements impugning judge's integrity and qualifications), *cert. denied*, 546 U.S. 825 (2005); *In re Westfall*, 808 S.W.2d 829 (Mo. 1991) (given interest in protecting public, administration of justice, and profession, purely subjective standard inappropriate); *In re Holtzman*, 577 N.E.2d 30 (N.Y. 1991) (applying objective standard of what reasonable lawyer would do in similar circumstances); *Disciplinary Counsel v. Frost*, 909 N.E.2d 1271 (Ohio 2009) ("no reasonable attorney would accept [respondent's] charges of bias and corruption as true"); *Pilli v. Va. State Bar*, 611 S.E.2d 389 (Va.) ("the very content of these accusations [that judge lied and skewed facts] refutes Pilli's argument" that his statements were objectively reasonable), *cert. denied*, 546 U.S. 977 (2005); *Lawyer Disciplinary Bd. v. Hall*, 765 S.E.2d 187 (W. Va. 2014) (state's interest in protecting public, administration of justice, and legal profession supports use of objectively reasonable standard; lawyer's accusations against administrative law judge made "without an objectively reasonable factual basis"); *cf. Att'y Grievance Comm'n v. Stanalonis*, 126 A.3d 6 (Md. 2015) (without deciding whether objective or subjective standard should apply, lawyer's statement in judicial campaign flyer did not violate Rule 8.2(a) when lawyer had "demonstrable basis for believing" it to be true).

Thus, a lawyer's subjective belief that the statements are true is no defense in the context of disciplinary proceedings. *In re Holtzman*, 577 N.E.2d 30 (N.Y. 1991) ("It is the reasonableness of the belief, not the state of mind of the attorney, that is determinative."). *See, e.g., Statewide Grievance Comm. v. Burton*, 10 A.3d 507 (Conn. 2011) (lawyer must have objective basis for accusations of judicial corruption, notwithstanding lawyer's claim that she believed allegations true); *In re Mire*, 197 So. 3d 656 (La. 2016) (notwithstanding "genuineness" of lawyer's belief, "objective facts in the record" support conclusion that lawyer acted knowingly or with reckless disregard for truth in alleging judges' "incompetence and/or corruption"); *In re Graham*, 453 N.W.2d 313 (Minn. 1990) ("fact that Graham's feelings were 'genuine' is insufficient to negate the referee's findings and conclusions that Graham acted with reckless disregard as to the truth or falsity of his statements"); *In re Madison*, 282 S.W.3d 350 (Mo. 2009) (lawyer baselessly accused one judge of being racist and part of "evil" network and accused another judge of "ruthless abuse of power"; his belief in the truth of his statements was no defense); *State ex rel. Counsel for Discipline v. Gast*, 896 N.W.2d 583 (Neb. 2017) (even if lawyer believed judge engaged in "cover up" of close personal friendship with opposing counsel, "[n]o reasonable attorney would make this accusation without first obtaining a significant factual basis to sustain it."; lawyer knew only that two were social acquaintances over thirty years ago); *Disciplinary Counsel v. Shimko*, 983 N.E.2d 1300 (Ohio 2012) (despite lawyer's "firmly held beliefs" that judge was biased and acted improperly, lawyer's statements "were proved . . . to be unreasonable and objectively false with a mens rea of recklessness"); *In re Riordan*,

824 N.W.2d 441 (Wis. 2012) (lawyer's subjective belief that his allegations of bias and abuse of power were compelled by his religious beliefs did "not relieve him of the obligation to demonstrate a factual basis for his comments to the court").

On the standard applicable to statements made in the course of judicial election campaigns, compare *In re Parish*, No. 12–O–15242, 2015 WL 514334 (Cal. Bar Ct. Review Dep't Feb. 5, 2015) (applying objective standard to find violation of Cal. Rule 1-700 by judicial candidate who falsely alleged incumbent judge was involved in bribery scheme), with *Att'y Grievance Comm'n v. Stanalonis*, 126 A.3d 6 (Md. 2015) (noting, but not deciding, that "even if a court would normally favor an objective test in assessing the 'reckless disregard' prong of MLRPC 8.2(a), there is a significant argument that a subjective test should be applied in an election context, in light of the 'core' First Amendment values at stake"), and *In re Charges of Unprof'l Conduct Involving File No. 17139*, 720 N.W.2d 807 n.6 (Minn. 2006) (noting court has "never held that an objective standard applies under Rule 8.2(a) to statements made during a political campaign," but declining to rule on the issue).

### • *Verifying the Accusation*

Failure to verify can serve as objective evidence of reckless disregard. *See In re McDonald*, 906 N.W.2d 238 (Minn. 2018) ("reasonable attorney would not have made serious allegations against a district judge without first verifying her client's account"); *In re Madison*, 282 S.W.3d 350 (Mo. 2009) ("Far from being 'careful' or 'well-researched,'" lawyer's allegations against judges were "completely without factual basis and were made in the heat of anger and pique"); *In re Holtzman*, 577 N.E.2d 30 (N.Y. 1991) (prosecutor released information to media before obtaining trial transcript to verify her allegations about judge's conduct toward rape victim); *Disciplinary Counsel v. Marshall*, 27 N.E.3d 481 (Ohio 2014) (unsubstantiated claims of racial and gender bias by judge who had ruled against lawyer on fee issue and jailed her for contempt; "no reasonable attorney would have made racial- or gender-bias allegations based on the limited information available"); *State ex rel. Okla. Bar Ass'n v. Wilcox*, 227 P.3d 642 (Okla. 2009) ("Respondent admits that he should have investigated the truth" before sending out mass mailing questioning judicial candidate's ethics and falsely claiming candidate's cancer was terminal); *Office of Disciplinary Counsel v. Price*, 732 A.2d 599 (Pa. 1999) (instead of conducting reasonably diligent inquiry, lawyer relied upon rumors, innuendo, and his own perceptions); *Lawyer Disciplinary Bd. v. Turgeon*, 557 S.E.2d 235 (W. Va. 2000) ("extreme nature of the allegations . . . should have alerted [respondent] to the need to investigate and not merely rely upon the word of his client"); *Bd. of Prof'l Responsibility v. Davidson*, 205 P.3d 1008 (Wyo. 2009) (in motion for reassignment of judge, lawyer baselessly accused judge of improper ex parte communication with opposing counsel: "[w]e cannot convince ourselves that any reasonable attorney would have filed this motion without any inquiry" into alleged improper contact); *see also Chief Disciplinary Counsel v. Rozbicki*, 167 A.3d 351 (Conn. 2017) (accusations of judicial impropriety against two judges repeated in motions, memoranda, and oral argument "for no apparent reason beyond the fact that those judges ruled in opposition to [lawyer]"); *Ky. Bar Ass'n v. Blum*, 404 S.W.3d 841 (Ky. 2013) (baselessly accusing hearing officers of corruption and bias, making no attempt to verify); *In re Wells*, 36 So. 3d 198 (La. 2010) (filing affidavit from incarcerated felon accusing district attorney of hiring him to commit murder, without first investigating allegations or possessing any credible information suggesting allegations were true).

## CRITICAL OPINIONS

Rule 8.2(a) applies to false statements about qualifications or integrity. It does not apply to a lawyer's opinions—unless the opinions are based, explicitly or implicitly, upon false assertions of fact. *See Pilli v. Va. State Bar*, 611 S.E.2d 389 (Va.) (lawyer accusing judge of lying and "skewing . . . the facts" was making statement of fact rather than opinion), *cert. denied*, 546 U.S. 977 (2005).

Accordingly, Rule 8.2(a) does not apply to opinions that are not susceptible of being objectively verified. *See Standing Comm. on Discipline v. Yagman*, 55 F.3d 1430 (9th Cir. 1995) ("statements of 'rhetorical hyperbole' aren't sanctionable, nor are statements that use language in a 'loose, figurative sense'"; construing local rule prohibiting conduct that "degrades or impugns the integrity of the Court"); *In re Oladiran*, No. MC–10–0025–PHX–DGC, 2010 WL 3775074, 2010 BL 223466 (D. Ariz. Sept. 21, 2010) (no violation for referring to judge as "dishonorable" and a "brainless coward"; statements are "rhetorical hyperbole," incapable of being objectively verified); *In re Green*, 11 P.3d 1078 (Colo. 2000) ("if an attorney criticizes a judge's ruling by saying it was 'incoherent,' he may not be sanctioned").

Similarly, opinions based upon disclosed facts are constitutionally protected. "Lawyers may freely voice criticisms supported by a reasonable factual basis even if they turn out to be mistaken." *Standing Comm. on Discipline v. Yagman*, 55 F.3d 1430 (9th Cir. 1995) (accusation of anti-Semitism protected as lawyer's opinion, for which lawyer gave adequate factual basis). *See Berry v. Schmitt*, 688 F.3d 290 (6th Cir. 2012) (unconstitutional to apply Rule 8.2(a) to letter stating that manner in which legislative ethics commission proceeding conducted "gave cause for some to speculate that the deck was stacked," when lawyer's opinions based upon stated facts); *see also United States v. Brown*, 72 F.3d 25 (5th Cir. 1995) (lawyer's motion for new trial claiming judge's gestures and expressions demonstrated bias did not warrant suspension under Rule 8.2(a), as claims made "in confines of the judicial process" to note how court's conduct may have appeared to jury; "attorneys should be free to challenge, in appropriate legal proceedings, a court's perceived partiality without the court misconstruing such a challenge as an assault on [its] integrity"); *In re Green*, 11 P.3d 1078 (Colo. 2000) ("statements that the judge was a 'racist and bigot' and having a 'bent of mind' [were] statements of opinion based upon fully disclosed and uncontested facts"; thus, discipline prohibited under First Amendment); *In re Dixon*, 994 N.E.2d 1129 (Ind. 2013) (interpreting rule's limits to be "least restrictive" when lawyer "engaged in good faith professional advocacy in a legal proceeding requiring critical assessment of a judge or a judge's decision"; thus, recusal motion's accusations of bias by judge, supported by "lengthy recitation of facts," did not violate rule); *Att'y Grievance Comm'n v. Dyer*, 162 A.3d 970 (Md. 2017) (letter to administrative law judge alleging bias by circuit court did not violate rule; criticism did not name specific judge and was based on statement of circumstances of underlying litigation).

Statements of opinion are not, however, protected if they imply the lawyer is privy to undisclosed facts. *See, e.g., Idaho State Bar v. Topp*, 925 P.2d 1113 (Idaho 1996) (statement implying judge worried about political ramifications of his ruling not constitutionally protected as opinion); *Iowa Supreme Court Att'y Disciplinary Bd. v. Weaver*, 750 N.W.2d 71 (Iowa 2008) (lawyer's statement to newspaper reporter that "I can't speculate about the reasons why [the judge] did this, . . . but he's not being honest about the reasons why he committed me to the Department of Corrections" was not opinion but was "a *specific* statement about *specific* wrongdoing, by the judge, capable of being proved true or false"; disclaimer about speculation "simply left the reader at liberty to assume that Weaver knew more than he was saying"); *In re Nathan*, 671 N.W.2d 578 (Minn. 2003) (lawyer called judge a "bad judge" who "substituted his personal view for the law" and "won election to the office of judge by appealing to racism"; "merely cloaking an assertion of fact as an opinion does not give that assertion constitutional protection"); *cf. Att'y Grievance Comm'n v. Dyer*, 162 A.3d 970 (Md. 2017) (rule not violated by statement in newspaper attributed to lawyer that "[u]nreported opinions are the way the appellate courts do their political dirty work . . . that tells you a lot"; no testimony presented as to whether she actually made statement); *In re Charges of Unprof'l Conduct Involving File No. 17139*, 720 N.W.2d 807 (Minn. 2006) (reversing denial of disciplinary authority's motion to compel; when respondent claims good-faith reliance on information from two credible sources, disciplinary authority is entitled to know their identities; any other result would make enforcement of Rule 8.2(a) "extremely difficult" whenever a respondent claimed a credible source).

### Paragraph (b): Application of Code of Judicial Conduct
#### VIOLATING JUDICIAL CODE IS GROUNDS FOR DISCIPLINE AS A LAWYER

Lawyers who are candidates for judicial office are subject to discipline under Rule 8.2(b) of the lawyer ethics rules for violating "applicable" judicial ethics rules. Comment [2] specifically invokes the judicial code's limitations on political activity, and Canon 4 of the ABA Model Code of Judicial Conduct (2010) ("[a] judge or candidate for judicial office shall not engage in political or campaign activity that is inconsistent with the independence, integrity, or impartiality of the judiciary") specifically regulates candidates as well as sitting judges. *See Fla. Bar v. Williams-Yulee*, 138 So. 3d 379 (Fla. 2014) (judicial candidate reprimanded under Rule 8.2(b) for violating judicial code prohibition against personally soliciting campaign contributions), *aff'd*, 575 U.S. __, 135 S. Ct. 1656 (2015) (Florida judicial code prohibition doesn't violate First Amendment); *see also Pa. Family Inst., Inc. v. Black*, 489 F.3d 156 n.3 (3d Cir. 2007) ("Although the Disciplinary Counsel only has formal responsibility for the enforcement of its own Rules of Professional Conduct, Rule 8.2(b) explicitly incorporates, and makes binding on candidate-lawyers, the entirety of the Code of Judicial Conduct.").

The judicial code as imported via Rule 8.2(b) restricts speech more severely than does Rule 8.2(a); Rule 4.1(A)(11) of the ABA Model Code of Judicial Conduct (2010) applies to *any* false or misleading statements (not merely to false statements about qualifications or integrity) made knowingly or with reckless disregard for the truth. A lawyer may therefore be disciplined as a judicial candidate under Rule 8.2(b) for a statement that does not violate Rule 8.2(a). *See In re Giardine*, 392 P.3d 89 (Kan. 2017) (lawyer running for district court judge made false public statements about nine-year-old misdemeanor marijuana charge, in violation of Rule 4.1(A)(4) of Kan. Code of Judicial Conduct); *N.C. State Bar v. Hunter*, 696 S.E.2d 201 (N.C. Ct. App. 2010) (judicial candidate referred to herself on campaign website as "Madame Justice," even though she never held judicial office, in violation of judicial code).

In *Republican Party of Minn. v. White*, 536 U.S. 756 (2002), the Supreme Court invalidated a judicial ethics rule prohibiting judges and judicial candidates from announcing their views on disputed legal and political issues. As applied to campaign speech, the Court held the "announce" rule to be an unconstitutional content-based restriction on political speech. *See* Nat Stern, *The Looming Collapse of Restrictions on Judicial Campaign Speech*, 38 Seton Hall L. Rev. 63 (2008) (*White* nullifies premise "that a state, having chosen to select judges through elections, can substantially modify the ordinary operation of principles governing political speech").

For further discussion of the ethical obligations of lawyers seeking judicial office, see American Bar Association, *Annotated Model Code of Judicial Conduct 477 et seq.* (3d ed. 2016).

# MAINTAINING THE INTEGRITY
## OF THE PROFESSION

### Rule 8.3
*Reporting Professional Misconduct*

(a) A lawyer who knows that another lawyer has committed a violation of the Rules of Professional Conduct that raises a substantial question as to that lawyer's honesty, trustworthiness or fitness as a lawyer in other respects, shall inform the appropriate professional authority.

(b) A lawyer who knows that a judge has committed a violation of applicable rules of judicial conduct that raises a substantial question as to the judge's fitness for office shall inform the appropriate authority.

(c) This Rule does not require disclosure of information otherwise protected by Rule 1.6 or information gained by a lawyer or judge while participating in an approved lawyers assistance program.

### COMMENT

[1] Self-regulation of the legal profession requires that members of the profession initiate disciplinary investigation when they know of a violation of the Rules of Professional Conduct. Lawyers have a similar obligation with respect to judicial misconduct. An apparently isolated violation may indicate a pattern of misconduct that only a disciplinary investigation can uncover. Reporting a violation is especially important where the victim is unlikely to discover the offense.

[2] A report about misconduct is not required where it would involve violation of Rule 1.6. However, a lawyer should encourage a client to consent to disclosure where prosecution would not substantially prejudice the client's interests.

[3] If a lawyer were obliged to report every violation of the Rules, the failure to report any violation would itself be a professional offense. Such a requirement existed in many jurisdictions but proved to be unenforceable. This Rule limits the reporting obligation to those offenses that a self-regulating profession must vigorously endeavor to prevent. A measure of judgment is, therefore, required in complying with the provisions of this Rule. The term "substantial" refers to the seriousness of the possible offense and not the quantum of evidence of which the lawyer is aware. A report should be made to the bar disciplinary agency unless some other agency, such as a peer review agency, is more appropriate in the circumstances. Similar considerations apply to the reporting of judicial misconduct.

[4] The duty to report professional misconduct does not apply to a lawyer

retained to represent a lawyer whose professional conduct is in question. Such a situation is governed by the Rules applicable to the client-lawyer relationship.

[5] Information about a lawyer's or judge's misconduct or fitness may be received by a lawyer in the course of that lawyer's participation in an approved lawyers or judges assistance program. In that circumstance, providing for an exception to the reporting requirements of paragraphs (a) and (b) of this Rule encourages lawyers and judges to seek treatment through such a program. Conversely, without such an exception, lawyers and judges may hesitate to seek assistance from these programs, which may then result in additional harm to their professional careers and additional injury to the welfare of clients and the public. These Rules do not otherwise address the confidentiality of information received by a lawyer or judge participating in an approved lawyers assistance program; such an obligation, however, may be imposed by the rules of the program or other law.

**Definitional Cross-References**

"Knows" *See* Rule 1.0(f)
"Substantial" *See* Rule 1.0(l)

**State Rules Comparison**

http://ambar.org/MRPCStateCharts

# ANNOTATION

## DUTY TO REPORT

If a lawyer knows that another lawyer or a judge has committed a violation of the Rules of Professional Conduct, and if the lawyer believes the violation raises a "substantial question" about honesty or fitness, Rule 8.3 requires the lawyer to report the misconduct. *E.g., Robison v. Orthotic & Prosthetic Lab, Inc.,* 27 N.E.3d 182 (Ill. App. Ct. 2015) (product liability defense counsel should have reported plaintiff's counsel's misrepresentations and failure to advise of plaintiff's death); *In re Lodes,* 985 N.Y.S.2d 108 (N.Y. 2014) (failure to report illegal kickback scheme). *See generally* Arthur F. Greenbaum, *The Attorney's Duty to Report Professional Misconduct: A Roadmap for Reform,* 16 Geo. J. Legal Ethics 259 (Winter 2003); Nikki Ott & Heather F. Newton, *A Current Look at Model Rule 8.3: How Is It Used and What Are Courts Doing About It?,* 16 Geo. J. Legal Ethics 747 (Summer 2003); Douglas R. Richmond, *The Duty to Report Professional Misconduct: A Practical Analysis of Lawyer Self-Regulation,* 12 Geo. J. Legal Ethics 175 (Winter 1999).

The duty to report misconduct under Rule 8.3 is nondiscretionary. It is therefore unethical merely to threaten to report. *See In re Kenny,* 217 P.3d 36 (Kan. 2009); *Tessier v. Rockefeller,* 33 A.3d 1118 (N.H. 2011); ABA Formal Ethics Op. 94-383 (1994); Fla. Ethics Op. 94-5 (1995); N.Y. City Ethics Op. 2015-5 (2015): Wis. Ethics Op. E-01-01 (2001); *see also* Iowa Ethics Op. 14-02 (2014) (lawyer who calls another lawyer unethical must report lawyer to state disciplinary board). It is also unethical to negotiate for relinquishment of a potential disciplinary complaint against oneself. *See In re Eicher,* 661 N.W.2d 354 (S.D. 2003) (duty to report "also embraces a responsibility not to frustrate the reporting by others or dissuad[e] others from cooperating in disciplinary investigations"); Utah Ethics Op. 16-02 (2016) (prohibiting conditioning settlement on forgoing reporting lawyer's misconduct). Also see the annotations to Rules 4.4 and 8.4.

### • Reporting "Another Lawyer" or Judge

Although Rule 8.3 does not require a lawyer to report his or her own misconduct, the lawyer must report the misconduct of others even if doing so would implicate the lawyer's own conduct as well. *See, e.g., In re Rivers*, 331 S.E.2d 332 (S.C. 1984) (inexperienced lawyer helped his partner use private investigator to contact potential jurors; lawyer disciplined for failing to report partner as well as for his own role); Conn. Informal Ethics Op. 89-21 (1989) (must report former partner who covered up failure to file suit by giving client money and claiming it was "settlement" proceeds; opinion notes that under imputed-responsibility principles of Rule 5.1, "by reporting his partner, he may also be reporting himself"); *see also In re Lodes*, 985 N.Y.S.2d 108 (App. Div. 2014) (county attorney did not report kickback demands of lawyer who was state senator).

A lawyer generally must report the misconduct of law firm colleagues and former law firm colleagues. *See, e.g., In re Rivers*, 761 S.E.2d 234 (S.C. 2014) (reporting partner's trust account misappropriations only after learning of disciplinary agency's investigation); ABA Formal Ethics Op. 03-429 (2003) (partner must report impaired associate's violation of ethics rules); Md. Ethics Op. 2003-11 (2003) (must report firm colleague's conversion of funds even if offender reached private settlement with victims, reported himself, and was denied further access to client funds); N.C. Ethics Op. 2013-8 (2014) (firm members must report impaired colleague who mishandles client funds and displays incompetence in litigation unless misconduct isolated and unlikely to recur because impairment has ended or come under control); S.C. Ethics Op. 05-21 (2005) (duty to report partner or former partner not affected by any professional or fiduciary relationship); Va. Ethics Op. 1886 (2017) (must report firm lawyer's misconduct involving dishonesty even if lawyer is in treatment for substance abuse problem that contributed to misconduct); *see also Skolnick v. Altheimer & Gray*, 730 N.E.2d 4 (Ill. 2000) (trial court abused discretion by refusing to modify protective order so associate could report misconduct by firm's former partner); *cf. Estate of Spencer v. Gavin*, 946 A.2d 1051 (N.J. Super. Ct. App. Div. 2008) (Rule 8.3 duty of lawyer to report officemate's embezzlement "strengthens" court's conclusion that "inaction [can expose] him to civil liability to those who were harmed" by failure to report); Va. Ethics Op. 1887 (2017) (no requirement to report lawyer's impairment if representation is competent, but must report if impairment results in incompetent representation). *See generally* Cynthia L. Gendry, *An Attorney's Duty to Report the Professional Misconduct of Co-Workers*, 18 S. Ill. U. L.J. 603 (Spring 1994); Kathryn W. Tate, *The Boundaries of Self-Policing: Must a Law Firm Prevent and Report a Firm Member's Securities Trading on the Basis of Client Confidences?*, 40 U. Kan. L. Rev. 807 (Summer 1992) (analyzing insider trading as ethics violation subject to mandatory reporting).

Misconduct by a suspended, out-of-state, or nonpracticing lawyer is treated as misconduct by "another lawyer" for reporting purposes. *See Att'y Grievance Comm'n v. Brennan*, 714 A.2d 157 (Md. 1998) (must report that suspended lawyer is misrepresenting his status); *In re Galmore*, 530 S.E.2d 378 (S.C. 2000) (must report suspended lawyer's offer to practice law); ABA Formal Ethics Op. 04-433 (2004) (must report misconduct of nonpracticing lawyer even if it involves activity completely removed from practice of law); Md. Ethics Op. 2005-2 (2005) (must report New York lawyers' unauthorized practice in Maryland); N.Y. State Ethics Op. 1091 (2016) (must report out-of-state lawyer's unauthorized practice in New York); Pa. Ethics Op. 2015-038 (2015) (must report suspended lawyer's misconduct).

Paragraph (b) requires that misconduct by a judge be reported to the appropriate authority. *Lisi v. Several Att'ys*, 596 A.2d 313 (R.I. 1991) (lawyers' loans to judge violated Rule 3.5; lawyers' failure to report judge violated Rule 8.3); *see also* Ohio Sup. Ct. Ethics Op. 2017-2 (2017) (judge must report misconduct of lawyer or another judge); *cf.* N.Y. State Ethics Op. 1099 (2016) (lawyer may report judge's noncriminal violation of Rules of Judicial Conduct if consistent with duty of confidentiality to lawyer's client; N.Y. Rule 8.3 does not address reporting judicial misconduct). *See generally* J. Nick Badgerow, *The Beam and the Mote: A Review of the Lawyer's Duty to Report*, 82 J. Kan. B. Ass'n 20 (Feb. 2013).

## "KNOWS"

Paragraphs (a) and (b) require reporting only when a lawyer "knows" of another lawyer's or judge's misconduct. "Knows" is defined as "actual knowledge of the fact in question," which "may be inferred from circumstances." Rule 1.0(f). *See, e.g., Skolnick v. Altheimer & Gray*, 730 N.E.2d 4 (Ill. 2000) (reasonable inference drawn from documents is sufficient to trigger reporting requirement); *In re Riehlmann*, 891 So. 2d 1239 (La. 2005) (duty triggered when lawyer's terminally ill friend, former prosecutor, confided he suppressed exculpatory evidence several years earlier); *Att'y U v. Miss. Bar*, 678 So. 2d 963 (Miss. 1996) (client's uncorroborated description of improper fee-splitting arrangement with another lawyer, who denied arrangement, did not trigger duty; "standard must be . . . objective[,] not tied to the subjective beliefs of the lawyer in question"); Ky. Ethics Op. E-430 (2010) ("While lawyers cannot turn a blind eye to obviously questionable conduct, as a general rule they do not have a duty to investigate."); N.Y. City Ethics Op. 1990-3 (1990) (absolute certainty not required, but mere suspicion not enough; collecting ethics opinions); Pa. Ethics Op. 97-40 (1997) (lawyer who believes opposing counsel's simultaneous representation of two clients creates conflict should report conflict to disciplinary authority only if lawyer has "reliable information" that dual representation will adversely affect relationship with one or both clients); R.I. Ethics Op. 95-40 (1995) ("the determination . . . is one which involves a credibility determination that is largely subjective and is therefore one to be made by the attorney witnessing such conduct"); *cf.* N.Y. State Ethics Op. 912 (2012) (lawyer may host or participate in blog publicizing another lawyer's unethical behavior but may also be required to report subject lawyer's conduct). *See generally* N.Y. State Ethics Op. 854 (2011) (analyzing nature of knowledge that would trigger duty to report); Vincent R. Johnson, *Legal Malpractice Litigation and the Duty to Report Misconduct*, 1 St. Mary's J. Legal Mal. & Ethics 40 (2011); Peter A. Joy, *The Relationship Between Civil Rule 11 and Lawyer Discipline: An Empirical Analysis Suggesting Institutional Choices in the Regulation of Lawyers*, 37 Loy. L.A. L. Rev. 765 (Winter 2004).

## "SUBSTANTIAL QUESTION" ABOUT HONESTY, TRUSTWORTHINESS, OR FITNESS

Rule 8.3 obliges lawyers to report only those violations of the ethics rules that raise "a substantial question" about honesty or fitness. "Substantial" is defined in the Model Rules as "of clear and weighty importance." Rule 1.0(l). *See* Colo. Ethics Op. 124 (2012) (substantial question regarding materially impaired lawyer's fitness as lawyer arises if he fails or refuses to cease representing clients); Conn. Informal Ethics Op. 01-04 (2001) (backdating motion and submitting false certificate of service raise substantial question about trustworthiness); Conn. Informal Ethics Op. 94-33 (1994) (ex parte contact with judge's clerk on housekeeping matter did not evince "requisite degree of odiousness" to warrant reporting); N.M. Ethics Op. 2005-2 (2005) (insurance company lawyer who believes claimants' lawyer's million-dollar fee in uncontested, simple matter was unreasonable must report to disciplinary authorities); Nassau Cnty. (N.Y.) Ethics Op. 09-01 (2009) (lawyer who sees other lawyer soliciting criminal defendants in holding cells, at arraignments, and at court hearings must report this "misconduct of a substantial degree"); N.D. Ethics Op. 01-05 (2001) (bank's lawyer-employee must report that depositor using client trust account to cover overdrafts); Tex. Ethics Op. 632 (2013) (lawyer's use of trade name in clear violation of advertising rule did not raise substantial question of honesty, trustworthiness, or fitness that triggers reporting requirement unless trade name "affirmatively false and misleading"); Utah Ethics Op. 98-12 (1998) (lawyer must report another lawyer's unlawful possession of controlled substance if it raises substantial question about other lawyer's honesty, trustworthiness, or fitness); *see also Bd. of Overseers of Bar v. Warren*, 34 A.3d 1103 (Me. 2011) (firm's executive committee members who did not report lawyer to bar disciplinary board upon initially learning lawyer took money from client's trust account did not violate reporting rule because they "did not subjectively believe" lawyer's acts called into question lawyer's honesty, trustworthiness, or fitness as a lawyer until discovering three months later that additional client accounts were involved, at which time committee fired lawyer and reported him); Kan. Ethics Op. 14-01 (2014) (lawyers need not report former partner's forgetfulness absent knowledge of resultant ethics violations). *See generally* Lizabeth L. Burrell, *Between Scylla and Charybdis: The Importance of Internal Calibration in Balancing Zeal for One's Client with Duties to the Legal System When Your Adversary Is Incompetent*, 23 U.S.F. Mar. L.J. 265 (2011); Ryan Williams, *Reputation and the Rules: An Argument for a Balancing Approach Under Rule 8.3 of the Model Rules of Professional Conduct*, 68 La. L. Rev. 931 (Spring 2008).

## WHEN TO REPORT

Rule 8.3 does not specify when the report must be made. *See In re Comfort*, 159 P.3d 1011 (Kan. 2007) (court "unwilling to use this case as a vehicle to impose a time limit for reporting lawyer misconduct to the Disciplinary Administrator"); *In re Riehlmann*, 891 So. 2d 1239 (La. 2005) (lawyer waited five years before reporting misconduct of dying friend, prosecutor who admitted withholding exculpatory evidence nine years earlier; discipline warranted even though lawyer acted in time to prevent execution); *In re Anderson*, 769 A.2d 1282 (Vt. 2000) (nine months was too long for former disciplinary board member to wait to report partner's mishandling of client trust account); N.Y. City Ethics Op. 1990-3 (1990) (although reporting must be "prompt," some delay may be warranted to protect client's interest; lawyer should balance severity of misconduct and likelihood of its repetition against possible prejudice to client); S.C. Ethics Op. 16-04 (2016) (lawyer may wait to report opposing counsel's misconduct until conclusion of matter if immediate reporting might damage client's interests); *cf. United States v. Cantor*, 897 F. Supp. 110 (S.D.N.Y. 1995) (reporting requirement "must be read to require reporting . . . within a reasonable time under the circumstances"). *See generally* Laurel Fedder, *Obstacles to Maintaining the Integrity of the Profession: Rule 8.3's Ambiguity and Disciplinary Board Complacency*, 23 Geo. J. Legal Ethics 71 (Summer 2010) (rule's "failure to specify when the report shall be made leaves open the possibility that delayed reporting, and the inexcusable third-party consequences it creates, fulfills the Rule's dictate"); Vincent R. Johnson, *Legal Malpractice Litigation and the Duty to Report Misconduct*, 1 St. Mary's J. Legal Mal. & Ethics 40 (2011).

## REPORT TO WHOM?

Paragraphs (a) and (b) do not specify what the "appropriate" authority to receive a report is, but Comment [1] mentions the need to "initiate [a] disciplinary investigation," and Comment [3] refers to making a report "to the bar disciplinary agency unless some other agency . . . is more appropriate in the circumstances." *See, e.g., In re Riehlmann*, 891 So. 2d 1239 (La. 2005) (giving criminal defendant's appellate counsel an affidavit reciting deceased prosecutor's admission that he suppressed evidence exculpating defendant did not satisfy reporting requirement); *Santander Sec. LLC v. Gamache*, Civ. No. 17-317, 2017 WL 1208066, 2017 BL 108486 (E.D. Pa. Apr. 3, 2017) (report must be made to lawyer disciplinary agency, not a court); Conn. Informal Ethics Op. 05-11 (2005) (initiating malpractice action against former counsel does not satisfy reporting requirement); N.Y. State Ethics Op. 1120 (2017) (discussing to whom government agency lawyer must report misconduct of another government lawyer); Ohio Ethics Op. 2007-1 (2007) (must make report to disciplinary counsel or certified grievance committee; duty not satisfied by reporting misconduct to tribunal); Phila. Ethics Op. 2008-12 (2009) (litigator must report opposing counsel's misconduct to disciplinary authority even if he already reported it to trial court); Utah Ethics Op. 98-12 (1998) (reporting requirement not satisfied by telling lawyers assistance program, in which participation is purely voluntary, about another lawyer's illegal drug use); W. Va. Ethics Op. 92-04 (1992) (lawyer who discovers alcoholic lawyer stole client funds cannot satisfy reporting requirement by contacting lawyer impairment committee, which is not charged with duty to protect public); *see also Schuff v. A.T. Klemens & Son*, 16 P.3d 1002 (Mont. 2000) (affirming denial of defense's pretrial motion to disqualify plaintiff's counsel but referring both counsel to disciplinary commission: "if [defense counsel] viewed [plaintiff's counsel's] conduct as being as serious as claimed, then, it is, likewise, appropriate that the Commission make inquiry into why such violations were not reported to the disciplinary authority with jurisdiction to address them"). Some jurisdictions have amended their versions of Rule 8.3 to identify the "appropriate" authority. *E.g.*, N.C. Ethics Op. 2013-8 (2014) (rule requires report to state bar or court having jurisdiction over matter, and report to state bar's lawyer assistance program does not satisfy duty).

Some courts invoke Rule 8.3 to find "standing" for a litigant to move for the disqualification of an opposing lawyer based upon a violation of the rules, even though the moving litigant suffered no harm from the violation; the Rule 8.3(a) obligation of the movant's lawyer to report the opposing lawyer's misconduct bestows standing for the motion. *See, e.g., Kevlik v. Goldstein*, 724 F.2d 844 (1st Cir. 1984) (invoking predecessor Model Code provision to find standing); *In re Universal Bldg. Prods.*, 486 B.R. 650 (Bankr. D. Del. 2010) (debtor and its lawyers had standing to object to requested appointment of creditor-committee lawyers based upon allegations of improper client solicitation); *Ex parte Wheeler*, 978 So. 2d 1 (Ala. 2007) (because Rule 8.3 "imposes a duty to report unethical behavior . . . defendants therefore have standing to seek the disqualification").

## NO DUTY TO DISCLOSE CONFIDENTIAL INFORMATION

Rule 8.3(c) makes the duty to report misconduct subordinate to the duty of confidentiality set forth in Rule 1.6. *See, e.g., In re Ethics Advisory Panel Op. No. 92-1*, 627 A.2d 317 (R.I. 1993) (if lawyer learns of another lawyer's misconduct while representing client, duty of confidentiality prohibits reporting it without client's consent, even if lawyer learned of it from other lawyer's admission rather than from client); ABA Formal Ethics Op. 08-453 (2008) ("information [a firm's inside] ethics counsel has about a constituent lawyer's misconduct will be information relating to the representation of the ethics counsel's client, the law firm, and therefore the mandatory reporting requirement of Rule 8.3(a) will be subject to the firm's consent"); ABA Formal Ethics Op. 07-449 (2007) (lawyer representing judge in one matter may not report judge's misconduct in separate matter without judge's consent); Ariz. Ethics Op. 94-09 (1994) (lawyer who has no doubt his client was charged excessive fee by another lawyer must report it, but only with client's consent); D.C. Ethics Op. 246 (1994) (lawyer representing plaintiff in legal malpractice action may not report misconduct alleged unless client consents; filing suit does not waive confidentiality of underlying information for reporting purposes); Mich. Informal Ethics Op. RI-314 (1999) (must respect client's decision not to report other lawyer's billing fraud); N.Y. City Ethics Op. 2017-2 (2017) (must report firm colleague's fraudulent billing unless client refuses consent); Or. Ethics Op. 2005-05 (2005) (must abide by client's direction not to report confidential information revealing misconduct of client's former lawyer and another lawyer); Pa. Ethics Op. 2009-10 (2009) (may not report judge's public finding of misconduct by adversary lawyer without client's consent); *cf.* Ohio Sup. Ct. Ethics Op. 2016-2 (2016) (must report unprivileged knowledge of another lawyer's misconduct and may report privileged knowledge if client gives informed consent). *But see In re Himmel*, 533 N.E.2d 790 (Ill. 1988) (suspending lawyer who abided by legal malpractice client's directive not to report her former counsel's conversion; applied version of reporting rule that exempted only "privileged" information); Ill. Ethics Op. 11-10 (2011) (lawyer-mediator who learns during confidential mediation that lawyer for party has violated Rule 8.4 must report misconduct). *See generally*

Rosemary J. Matthews, *Do I Have to Say More? When Mediation Confidentiality Clashes with the Duty to Report*, 34 Campbell L. Rev. 205 (Fall 2011); Joanne P. Pitulla, *Should Clients Be Able to Veto the Duty to Report?*, 7 Prof. Law., no. 4, at 2 (Aug. 1996); Peter K. Rofes, *Another Misunderstood Relation: Confidentiality and the Duty to Report*, 14 Geo. J. Legal Ethics 621 (Winter 2001); Ronald D. Rotunda, *The Lawyer's Duty to Report Another Lawyer's Unethical Violations in the Wake of* Himmel, 1988 U. Ill. L. Rev. 977 (1988).

## LAWYERS ASSISTANCE PROGRAMS

For reasons of social policy, Rule 8.3(c) exempts from the reporting requirement any information learned through participation in an approved lawyers assistance program. *See* N.C. Ethics Op. 2001-5 (2001) (extending exemption to disclosures made during program's support group meetings); *cf. In re Clegg*, 14 So. 3d 1141 (La. 2010) (approving admission of testimony of lawyer-witnesses regarding respondent lawyer's admission of cocaine use in connection with his agreement to enroll in lawyer assistance program because "Rule 8.3(c) . . . does not preclude voluntary disclosure of such information").

The exemption was broadened in 2002 to protect information learned by lawyers and judges who are "participating in"—as opposed to "serving as a member of"—these programs. American Bar Association, *A Legislative History: The Development of the ABA Model Rules of Professional Conduct, 1982–2013*, at 845–46 (2013).

# Maintaining the Integrity of the Profession

## Rule 8.4

### *Misconduct*

It is professional misconduct for a lawyer to:

(a) violate or attempt to violate the Rules of Professional Conduct, knowingly assist or induce another to do so, or do so through the acts of another;

(b) commit a criminal act that reflects adversely on the lawyer's honesty, trustworthiness or fitness as a lawyer in other respects;

(c) engage in conduct involving dishonesty, fraud, deceit or misrepresentation;

(d) engage in conduct that is prejudicial to the administration of justice;

(e) state or imply an ability to influence improperly a government agency or official or to achieve results by means that violate the Rules of Professional Conduct or other law;

(f) knowingly assist a judge or judicial officer in conduct that is a violation of applicable rules of judicial conduct or other law; or

(g) engage in conduct that the lawyer knows or reasonably should know is harassment or discrimination on the basis of race, sex, religion, national origin, ethnicity, disability, age, sexual orientation, gender identity, marital status or socioeconomic status in conduct related to the practice of law. This paragraph does not limit the ability of a lawyer to accept, decline or withdraw from a representation in accordance with Rule 1.16. This paragraph does not preclude legitimate advice or advocacy consistent with these Rules.

## COMMENT

[1] Lawyers are subject to discipline when they violate or attempt to violate the Rules of Professional Conduct, knowingly assist or induce another to do so or do so through the acts of another, as when they request or instruct an agent to do so on the lawyer's behalf. Paragraph (a), however, does not prohibit a lawyer from advising a client concerning action the client is legally entitled to take.

[2] Many kinds of illegal conduct reflect adversely on fitness to practice law, such as offenses involving fraud and the offense of willful failure to file an income tax return. However, some kinds of offenses carry no such implication. Traditionally,

the distinction was drawn in terms of offenses involving "moral turpitude." That concept can be construed to include offenses concerning some matters of personal morality, such as adultery and comparable offenses, that have no specific connection to fitness for the practice of law. Although a lawyer is personally answerable to the entire criminal law, a lawyer should be professionally answerable only for offenses that indicate lack of those characteristics relevant to law practice. Offenses involving violence, dishonesty, breach of trust, or serious interference with the administration of justice are in that category. A pattern of repeated offenses, even ones of minor significance when considered separately, can indicate indifference to legal obligation.

[3] Discrimination and harassment by lawyers in violation of paragraph (g) undermine confidence in the legal profession and the legal system. Such discrimination includes harmful verbal or physical conduct that manifests bias or prejudice towards others. Harassment includes sexual harassment and derogatory or demeaning verbal or physical conduct. Sexual harassment includes unwelcome sexual advances, requests for sexual favors, and other unwelcome verbal or physical conduct of a sexual nature. The substantive law of antidiscrimination and anti-harassment statutes and case law may guide application of paragraph (g).

[4] Conduct related to the practice of law includes representing clients; interacting with witnesses, coworkers, court personnel, lawyers and others while engaged in the practice of law; operating or managing a law firm or law practice; and participating in bar association, business or social activities in connection with the practice of law. Lawyers may engage in conduct undertaken to promote diversity and inclusion without violating this Rule by, for example, implementing initiatives aimed at recruiting, hiring, retaining and advancing diverse employees or sponsoring diverse law student organizations.

[5] A trial judge's finding that peremptory challenges were exercised on a discriminatory basis does not alone establish a violation of paragraph (g). A lawyer does not violate paragraph (g) by limiting the scope or subject matter of the lawyer's practice or by limiting the lawyer's practice to members of underserved populations in accordance with these Rules and other law. A lawyer may charge and collect reasonable fees and expenses for a representation. Rule 1.5(a). Lawyers also should be mindful of their professional obligations under Rule 6.1 to provide legal services to those who are unable to pay, and their obligation under Rule 6.2 not to avoid appointments from a tribunal except for good cause. See Rule 6.2(a), (b) and (c). A lawyer's representation of a client does not constitute an endorsement by the lawyer of the client's views or activities. See Rule 1.2(b).

[6] A lawyer may refuse to comply with an obligation imposed by law upon a good faith belief that no valid obligation exists. The provisions of Rule 1.2(d) concerning a good faith challenge to the validity, scope, meaning or application of the law apply to challenges of legal regulation of the practice of law.

[7] Lawyers holding public office assume legal responsibilities going beyond those of other citizens. A lawyer's abuse of public office can suggest an inability to fulfill the professional role of lawyers. The same is true of abuse of positions of private trust such as trustee, executor, administrator, guardian, agent and officer, director or manager of a corporation or other organization.

**Definitional Cross-References**

"Fraud" *See* Rule 1.0(d)
"Knowingly" *See* Rule 1.0(f)
"Reasonably should know" *See* Rule 1.0(j)

**State Rules Comparison**

http://ambar.org/MRPCStateCharts

## ANNOTATION

### MISCONDUCT IN GENERAL

Rule 8.4 contains a list of loosely related categories of prohibited behavior under the general heading of "misconduct." It is derived primarily from the Model Code's misconduct rule in DR 1-102(A), adding paragraph (e) (similar to the Model Code's DR 9-101(C)), and introducing provisions that prohibit a lawyer from attempting to violate the ethics rules (paragraph (a)), assisting a judge in violating rules of judicial conduct (paragraph (f)), and engaging in harassment or improper discrimination (paragraph (g)).

#### • *"Personal" Conduct*

Rule 8.4 reaches conduct outside the practice of law. *See, e.g., People v. Parsley*, 109 P.3d 1060 (Colo. O.P.D.J. 2005) (fraudulently obtaining loan from mortgage company); *In re Richmond*, 996 So. 2d 282 (La. 2008) (member of state legislature lied about domicile when attempting to run in city council election); *Att'y Grievance Comm'n v. Young*, 124 A.3d 210 (Md. 2015) (working as home improvement contractor without valid license); *In re Grella*, 777 N.E.2d 167 (Mass. 2002) (assaulting estranged wife); *In re Trudeau*, 705 N.W.2d 409 (Minn. 2005) (lying to police while intoxicated, interfering with 911 call, and unauthorized computer access by installing spyware); *State ex rel. Counsel for Discipline v. Council*, 853 N.W.2d 844 (Neb. 2014) (state senator used campaign contributions to support gambling habit); *Lorain County Bar Ass'n v. Lewis*, 99 N.E.3d 404 (Ohio 2018) (lawyer involved in alcohol-related traffic accident falsely told police that an unknown African-American man had been driving the car when it crashed); *In re Carpenter*, 95 P.3d 203 (Or. 2004) (posting message on internet site in name of local high school teacher, implying teacher engaged in sexual relations with students); *In re Taylor*, 768 A.2d 1273 (Vt. 2000) (lawyer on inactive status suspended for failing to pay child support); *In re Whitney*, 120 P.3d 550 (Wash. 2005) (testifying falsely while acting as guardian ad litem); *Lawyer Disciplinary Bd. v. Plants*, 801 S.E.2d 225 (W. Va. 2017) (violating domestic violence protective order); ABA Formal Ethics Op. 336 (1974) (lawyer must comply with applicable rules whether or not acting in professional capacity); *cf. In re Fahy*, 5 Cal. State Bar Ct. Rptr. 141 (Cal. Bar Ct. 2009) (disbarment for lawyer who while serving as juror changed his vote to break deadlock so he could get back to his law practice, and then lied to judge about his motive; under California Business and Professions Code). Other examples are provided throughout this annotation.

### • Pre-admission Conduct

Lawyers have been disciplined under Rule 8.4 for misconduct that occurred before bar admission. *See, e.g., Att'y Grievance Comm'n v. Hunt*, 76 A.3d 1214 (Md. 2013) (criminal conduct involving unauthorized disclosure of taxpayer information while serving as IRS revenue officer before bar admission and failure to inform admissions authorities); *In re Mikus*, 131 P.3d 653 (N.M. 2006) (suspension based on pre-admission assault resulting in felony conviction, and failure to supplement bar application after indictment); *In re Wong*, 710 N.Y.S.2d 57 (App. Div. 2000) (pre-admission criminal sexual misconduct with minor); *Office of Disciplinary Counsel v. Clark*, 531 N.E.2d 671 (Ohio 1988) (felony convictions for pre-admission drug smuggling, tax evasion); *State ex rel. Okla. Bar Ass'n v. Flanery*, 863 P.2d 1146 (Okla. 1993) (embezzling $71,000 from relatives who hired lawyer as manager/bookkeeper before bar admission); *In re Brown*, 605 S.E.2d 509 (S.C. 2004) (pre-admission misconduct included conducting real estate closings, signing supervisor's name to closing documents, and having other employees sign as witness or notary on documents executed outside their presence). Also see the discussion of the duty of candor in the admissions process in the annotation to Rule 8.1.

## Paragraph (a): Violating, Attempting to Violate, or Assisting in Violation of Ethics Rules

### VIOLATING OR ATTEMPTING TO VIOLATE ETHICS RULES

Paragraph (a) characterizes the violation of any of the ethics rules as an act of misconduct. Thus, in a disciplinary proceeding, a finding that a lawyer violated any ethics rule may be accompanied by a finding that the lawyer thereby violated Rule 8.4(a). *E.g., In re Winterburg*, 41 P.3d 842 (Kan. 2002); *In re Shaw*, 141 So. 3d 795 (La. 2014); *Att'y Grievance Comm'n v. Powers*, 164 A.3d 138 (Md. 2017); *O'Meara's Case*, 54 A.3d 762 (N.H. 2012); *In re McAuley*, 759 S.E.2d 743 (S.C. 2014); *Kuchinsky v. Va. State Bar ex rel. Third Dist. Comm.*, 756 S.E.2d 475 (Va. 2014). *But see Iowa Supreme Court Att'y Disciplinary Bd. v. Templeton*, 784 N.W.2d 761 (Iowa 2010) (purpose of rule is to give notice to lawyers that they are subject to discipline for violating ethics rules, "not to create a separate violation"; court would neither discipline lawyer for violating rule nor consider it a separate violation when determining sanction, and advised disciplinary board not to allege Rule 8.4(a) violation in future complaints); Utah Rule 8.4, cmt. [1a] ("A violation of paragraph (a) based solely on the lawyer's violation of another Rule of Professional Conduct shall not be charged as a separate violation.").

Additionally, in a departure from the predecessor Model Code, Rule 8.4(a) states that it is misconduct even to *attempt* to violate an ethics rule. *See People v. Katz*, 58 P.3d 1176 (Colo. O.P.D.J. 2002) (attempted conversion of funds; "The fortuitous discovery and frustration of [respondent's] intended misappropriation of those funds does not lessen the seriousness of his actions."); *In re Bash*, 880 N.E.2d 1182 (Ind. 2008) (attempt to have sexual relationship with client); *In re Cushing*, 646 N.E.2d 662 (Ind. 1995) (attempt to file motion in state where lawyer not licensed); *In re Swarts*, 30 P.3d 1011 (Kan. 2001) (attempt to falsify evidence); *Geauga City Bar Ass'n v. Bond*, 52 N.E.3d 1181 (Ohio 2016) (attempting to violate Rule 1.8(e) by loaning money to person lawyer believed to be a client; no lawyer-client relationship found because putative client was perpetrating fraud); *In re Fink*, 22 A.3d 461 (Vt. 2011) (contracting to charge unreasonable fee, though lawyer did not try to collect it); *Lawyer Disciplinary Bd. v. Stanton*, 760 S.E.2d 453 (W. Va. 2014) (lawyer attempted to have sexual relationship with incarcerated client).

## ASSISTING IN VIOLATION, OR VIOLATING RULES THROUGH ACTS OF ANOTHER

Paragraph (a) prohibits a lawyer from knowingly assisting or inducing another to violate the ethics rules, or from violating the rules through the acts of another. *See People v. Cozier*, 74 P.3d 531 (Colo. O.P.D.J. 2003) (lawyer asked notary public to notarize signature neither had witnessed); *State v. Grossberg*, 705 A.2d 608 (Del. Super. Ct. 1997) (criminal defense lawyer appeared on television news program with client and guided client in making statements lawyer could not make without violating pretrial publicity rule); *In re Asher*, 772 A.2d 1161 (D.C. 2001) (inducing another lawyer to lie to court); *In re Usher*, 987 N.E.2d 1080 (Ind. 2013) (having paralegal disseminate e-mail containing false information about young attorney who rejected lawyer's romantic advances); *In re Pyle*, 156 P.3d 1231 (Kan. 2007) (plaintiff's lawyer tried to circumvent Rule 4.2 by drafting affidavit and encouraging client to give it directly to defendant); *Bratcher v. Ky. Bar Ass'n*, 290 S.W.3d 648 (Ky. 2009) (plaintiff's lawyer in wrongful discharge suit violated Rule 4.2 by hiring company to contact defendant and pose as prospective employer doing reference check on plaintiff); *In re McCool*, 172 So. 3d 1058 (La. 2015) (engaging in social media campaign that urged others to contact judges in attempt to influence outcome of pending litigation); *In re Abrams*, 767 N.E.2d 15 (Mass. 2002) (lawyer acting through business associate offered to pay client $20,000 to withdraw bar discipline complaint); *Grievance Adm'r v. Rostash*, 577 N.W.2d 452 (Mich. 1998) (knowingly aiding prosecutor in impermissible representation of private clients); *In re Isaacson*, 860 N.W.2d 490 (Wis. 2015) (lawyer serving as officer of corporate entity directed other counsel to file documents with court containing false and offensive statements); Phila. Ethics Op. 2009-02 (2009) (lawyer may not use third party to gain access to adverse witness's social networking pages by concealing "highly material fact" that any information obtained would be used to impeach her testimony); Va. Ethics Op. 1794 (2004) (lawyer may not direct client to pose as prospective client and consult with other lawyers to disqualify them from representing adverse party; violation of Virginia Rule 3.4(j)); *cf. In re Ositis*, 40 P.3d 500 (Or. 2002) (knowing private investigator was planning to pose as journalist to interview client's neighbor and potential adversary, lawyer suggested line of inquiry for him to use; lawyer made misrepresentations "through the acts of another"; under predecessor Code).

## *Paragraph (b): Criminal Conduct*

### SCOPE OF RULE

Paragraph (b) subjects a lawyer to discipline for certain types of criminal conduct. Unlike the predecessor Model Code, which prohibited illegal conduct involving "moral turpitude" (DR 1-102(A)(3)), Rule 8.4(b) prohibits criminal conduct only if it reflects adversely on the lawyer's honesty, trustworthiness, or fitness as a lawyer. As Comment [2] explains, "[o]ffenses involving violence, dishonesty, breach of trust, or serious interference with the administration of justice are in that category. A pattern of repeated offenses, even ones of minor significance when considered separately, can indicate indifference to legal obligation." *See Iowa Supreme Court Att'y Disciplinary Bd. v. Templeton*, 784 N.W.2d 761 (Iowa 2010) ("mere commission of a criminal act does not necessarily reflect adversely on the fitness of an attorney to practice law"); *In re White*, 815 P.2d 1257 (Or. 1991) (case-by-case determination required; "Pertinent considerations include the lawyer's mental state; the extent to which the act demonstrates disrespect for the law or law enforcement; the presence or absence of a victim; the extent of actual or potential injury to a victim; and the presence or absence of a pattern of criminal conduct."); *see also In re Mitrano*, 952 A.2d 901 (D.C. 2008) (to determine whether conduct is criminal under Rule 8.4(b), court may look to law of any jurisdiction that could have prosecuted lawyer). *Compare Iowa Supreme Court Att'y Disciplinary Bd. v. Keele*, 795 N.W.2d 507 (Iowa 2011) (felony conviction for possessing firearm while being unlawful user of or addicted to controlled substance did not violate Rule 8.4(b); lawyer legally took possession of firearm for benefit of client before lawyer's struggles with addiction began and stored it unloaded in empty closet; collecting cases in which illegal firearm possession or use did violate rule), *In re Parks*, 9 So. 3d 106 (La. 2009) (driving without auto insurance not type of crime covered by Rule 8.4(b)), *and State ex rel. Okla. Bar Ass'n v. Whitworth*, 183 P.3d 984 (Okla. 2008) (driving with suspended license does not itself violate Rule 8.4(b)), *with In re Tidwell*, 831 A.2d 953 (D.C. 2003) (leaving scene of fatal auto accident and failing to report it violates rule), *In re D'Emic*, 972 N.Y.S.2d 299 (App. Div. 2013) (misdemeanor conviction for sharing fees with disbarred lawyer violated rule), *In re Souls*, 669 A.2d 532 (R.I. 1996) (leaving scene of fatal accident with pedestrian without conducting diligent search for victim violates rule), *and Tate v. State Bar*, 920 S.W.2d 727 (Tex. App. 1996) (lawyer disbarred based upon felony conviction for failing to stop and render assistance in auto accident in which he injured two children and killed another child).

### • *Crimes Committed in Nonlawyer Capacity*

The rule reaches criminal conduct whether or not the lawyer was acting as a lawyer at the time. *See In re Cross*, 155 A.3d 835 (D.C. 2017) (video voyeurism; secretly taping man undressing in gym locker room); *In re Wright*, 76 P.3d 1018 (Kan. 2003) (lawyer holding power of attorney for great aunt living in nursing facility and who served as secretary/treasurer of Topeka Lawyers' Club took money from accounts for personal use); *In re Brown*, 674 So. 2d 243 (La. 1996) (negligent homicide conviction for shooting roommate during argument); *Att'y Grievance Comm'n v. Thompson*, 786 A.2d 763 (Md. 2001) (conviction for stalking thirteen-year-old boy violated rule; rejecting arguments that practice was limited to estates and trusts and other areas not involving minors, and that stalking had not been in course of representing client); *In re Trudeau*, 705 N.W.2d 409 (Minn. 2005) (misdemeanor convictions for interference with 911 call and unauthorized computer access); *In re Capone*, 689 A.2d 128

(N.J. 1997) (false statement on loan application); *In re Bonilla*, 60 N.Y.S.3d 405 (App. Div. 2017) (lawyer accused of sexual harassment while serving as town clerk unlawfully pressured employee to provide him with compromising photographs of complainant).

### • *Conviction Not Necessary*

It is not necessary for a lawyer to be convicted of, or even charged with, a crime to violate Rule 8.4(b). *See, e.g., In re Ivy*, 374 P.3d 374 (Alaska 2016) (lawyer's false testimony violated rule, though never charged with perjury; rule does not require conviction, but only that it "would be criminal" under state law); *People v. Odom*, 941 P.2d 919 (Colo. 1997) (lawyer disciplined for committing crime for which he never was charged); *In re Meaden*, 902 A.2d 802 (D.C. 2006) (attempted theft violated rule even though charges dismissed and records expunged; also disciplined in New Jersey and Minnesota); *In re Riddle*, 700 N.E.2d 788 (Ind. 1998) (prosecutor used deputy to work in prosecutor's private law office; rule violated even though no criminal charges filed); *Iowa Supreme Court Att'y Disciplinary Bd. v. Stowers*, 823 N.W.2d 1 (Iowa 2012) ("absence of criminal charges, or even acquittal of criminal charges, is not a defense to this rule"); *In re Frahm*, 241 P.3d 1010 (Kan. 2010) (fact that convictions for reckless driving and leaving scene of accident set aside irrelevant to discipline; "it is the conduct that warrants discipline, not the technicality of the conviction"); *In re King*, 33 So. 3d 873 (La. 2010) (that felony conviction was set aside and expunged at conclusion of probationary period did not preclude use for disciplinary purposes); *Att'y Grievance Comm'n v. Smith*, 950 A.2d 101 (Md. 2008) (lawyer who left voicemail message for trial witness and falsely represented himself as police officer violated rule even though convictions reversed); *State ex rel. Counsel for Discipline v. Janousek*, 674 N.W.2d 464 (Neb. 2004) (lawyer may be disciplined for conduct that "might be found to have been illegal" even if "no criminal prosecution has been instituted or conviction had"); *In re Treinen*, 131 P.3d 1282 (N.M. 2006) ("a criminal conviction is not a prerequisite to disciplining an attorney for criminal conduct"); *In re Hassenstab*, 934 P.2d 1110 (Or. 1997) (lawyer violated three criminal sex offense statutes; irrelevant that criminal proceedings resulted only in plea of no contest to one count of prostitution); *see also In re Varner*, 780 So. 2d 1 (Fla. 2001) (disciplining lawyer for violating insurance fraud statute and noting "[i]t is not necessary for the attorney to have been convicted or even charged with the violation of the criminal statute in question"); *Iowa Supreme Court Att'y Disciplinary Bd. v. Taylor*, 887 N.W.2d 369 (Iowa 2016) (failure to file tax returns, but never charged; "It is the commission of a criminal act . . . not the act of getting caught" that constitutes rule violation); *N.C. State Bar v. Simmons*, 757 S.E.2d 357 (N.C. Ct. App. 2014) (lawyer disbarred for embezzlement although not convicted of crime); *State ex rel. Okla. Bar Ass'n v. Dobbs*, 94 P.3d 31 (Okla. 2004) ("witness immunity doctrine does not preclude imposition of professional discipline for a lawyer's perjury"); *In re McEnaney*, 718 A.2d 920 (R.I. 1998) (entering nolo contendere plea amounted to admission of "sufficient facts to be found guilty of the crimes charged").

## OFFENSES COVERED
### • *Drug and Alcohol Offenses*

Crimes involving alcohol and drugs are generally deemed to fall within Rule 8.4(b). *In re Quinn*, 696 N.E.2d 863 (Ind. 1998) ("Criminal offenses such as driving while intoxicated, public intoxication, and gambling, while not directly linked to the practice of law, may nonetheless reflect adversely on one's fitness as an attorney because such conduct tends to indicate a general indifference to legal standards of conduct . . . . That perception is magnified where there is a pattern of such offenses."); *In re Musto*, 704 A.2d 6 (N.J. 1997) (lawyers who violate controlled-substance laws "demonstrate a disrespect for the law, denigrate the entire profession, and destroy public confidence in the practicing bar"); *see People v. Miller*, 409 P.3d 667 (Colo. O.P.D.J. 2017) (lawyer's first DUI, causing no harm to himself or others, violated rule; conduct carried risk of serious harm due to high blood alcohol content); *Iowa Supreme Court Att'y Disciplinary Bd. v. Khowassah*, 890 N.W.2d 647 (Iowa 2017) (public intoxication and OWI); *In re Frahm*, 241 P.3d 1010 (Kan. 2010) (DUI and leaving scene of accident involving personal injury and property damage); *Ky. Bar Ass'n v. Dunn*, 965 S.W.2d 158 (Ky. 1998) (plea of guilty to DUI established violation of rule notwithstanding lawyer's argument that his actions were product of addiction); *In re Pastorek*, 239 So. 3d 798 (La. 2018) (lawyer/physician convicted of conspiracy to improperly dispense controlled substances); *In re Mecca*, 214 So. 3d 827 (La. 2017) (accepting marijuana in exchange for legal services); *In re McEnaney*, 718 A.2d 920 (R.I. 1998) (possession of crack cocaine and marijuana); *In re Inglimo*, 740 N.W.2d 125 (Wis. 2007) (supplying clients with marijuana and using it with them).

### *"Legal" Marijuana*

Some state bar ethics opinions have concluded that using or distributing marijuana in conformance with state law would not violate Rule 8.4(b) even if the conduct would violate federal law. *See* Colo. Ethics Op. 124 (2012) (lawyer's medical use of marijuana in compliance with state law "does not, in and of itself, violate [Rule 8.4(b)]" even if it violates federal law; must be "additional evidence" conduct adversely implicates lawyer's fitness); Conn. Informal Ethics Op. 14-08 (2014) (lawyer who is "qualified patient" under state medical marijuana law does not violate Rule 8.4 by using or possessing marijuana); Pa. Ethics Op. 2016-017 (2016) (lawyer may participate as principal or backer in medical marijuana organization authorized under state law even if it violates federal law); Wash. Ethics Op. 201501 (2015) (lawyer may use, consume, or sell marijuana in accordance with state law to the same extent as nonlawyers; opinion relies on federal policy of not enforcing drug laws against persons complying with state marijuana laws). *But see* N.D. Ethics Op. 14-02 (2014) (moving to another state to participate in its medical marijuana treatment program would constitute "pattern of repeated offenses" indicating indifference to legal obligations in violation of Rule 8.4(b)). On the ethical implication of advising clients on operating marijuana businesses under state law, see the annotation to Rule 1.2.

• *Crimes Involving Dishonesty or Fraud*

Crimes involving dishonesty or fraud are covered by Rule 8.4(b). *See People v. Sugar*, 360 P.3d 1041 (Colo. O.P.D.J. 2015) (conspiracy to defraud government by helping more than 150 clients avoid tax obligations); *In re Brown*, 766 N.E.2d 363 (Ind. 2002) (forgery of client's signature on check and theft of client's portion of settlement); *Iowa Supreme Court Att'y Disciplinary Bd. v. Stowe*, 830 N.W.2d 737 (Iowa 2013) (stealing client funds to support drug habit); *In re Najim*, 405 P.3d 1223 (Kan. 2017) (structuring transaction to evade reporting of receipt of more than $10,000 as required by federal law); *In re Ellis*, 204 P.3d 1161 (Kan. 2009) (in-house counsel repeatedly took food from cafeteria without paying); *Ky. Bar Ass'n v. Thornsbury*, 511 S.W.3d 379 (Ky. 2017) (judge conspired to frame secretary's husband for crimes he did not commit after secretary broke off affair); *Ky. Bar Ass'n v. Maze*, 397 S.W.3d 891 (Ky. 2013) (county attorney convicted of vote buying and perjury); *In re Alfortish*, 145 So. 3d 1024 (La. 2014) (conspiracy to commit mail, wire, health care, and identification document fraud in attempt to be reelected president of Louisiana Horsemen's Benevolent and Protective Association); *Att'y Grievance Comm'n v. Bellamy*, 162 A.3d 848 (Md. 2017) (failing to remit funds to client after receiving judgment from opposing party); *Att'y Grievance Comm'n v. Nusbaum*, 84 A.3d 98 (Md. 2014) (conspiring to rig bids at tax lien auctions in violation of Sherman Antitrust Act); *In re Bonner*, 896 N.W.2d 98 (Minn. 2017) (felony theft by swindle); *Disciplinary Counsel v. Doumbas*, 76 N.E.3d 1185 (Ohio 2017) (attempting to bribe sexual assault victims to induce them to support leniency at client's sentencing hearing); *Ohio State Bar Ass'n v. McCafferty*, 17 N.E.3d 521 (Ohio 2014) (judge convicted of making false statements to FBI agents); *In re Leisure*, 113 P.3d 412 (Or. 2005) (lawyer wrote over 200 NSF checks and repeatedly misrepresented to creditors when she would provide full payment); *In re Kenyon*, 559 S.E.2d 590 (S.C. 2002) (racketeering convictions premised on money laundering, wire fraud, and murder); *In re Mross*, 657 N.W.2d 342 (Wis. 2003) (unlawfully delivering cigarettes to inmates of county jail); *Bd. of Prof'l Responsibility v. Krone*, 418 P.3d 253 (Wyo. 2018) (stealing nearly $10,000 from county bar association while serving as its treasurer).

• *Sex Offenses*

Crimes of a sexual nature violate Rule 8.4(b). *See People v. Bauder*, 941 P.2d 282 (Colo. 1997) (lawyer solicited prostitution during telephone call to client's wife by offering to pay wife and client's girlfriend for sexual rendezvous); *In re Cross*, 155 A.3d 835 (D.C. 2017) (voyeurism; taping man undressing in gym locker room); *In re Hall*, 761 S.E.2d 51 (Ga. 2014) (sexual battery against client); *In re Holloway*, 469 S.E.2d 167 (Ga. 1996) (felonious invasion of privacy arising from surreptitious videotaping of secretary in bathroom); *In re Conn*, 715 N.E.2d 379 (Ind. 1999) (child pornography); *In re Haecker*, 664 N.E.2d 1176 (Ind. 1996) (voyeurism; videotaping neighbors through holes drilled in their bathroom and bedroom walls); *Roberts v. Ky. Bar Ass'n*, 245 S.W.3d 207 (Ky. 2008) (indecent exposure); *Ky. Bar Ass'n v. Martin*, 205 S.W.3d 210 (Ky. 2006) (sexual assaults against employee and client); *In re Boudreau*, 815 So. 2d 76 (La. 2002) (smuggling and possessing child pornography); *State ex rel. Counsel for Discipline v. Cording*, 825 N.W.2d 792 (Neb. 2013) (public indecency); *In re Legato*, 161

A.3d 111 (N.J. 2017) (sex offenses in which intended victims were children); *Ohio State Bar Ass'n v. Jacob*, 80 N.E.3d 440 (Ohio 2017) (soliciting prostitution); *State ex rel. Okla. Bar Ass'n v. Hixson*, 397 P.3d 483 (Okla. 2017) (pressuring client to trade sex for money and legal services); *State ex rel. Okla. Bar Ass'n v. Wilburn*, 142 P.3d 420 (Okla. 2006) (misdemeanors involving inappropriate sexual contact with female courthouse security guards); *In re Hassenstab*, 934 P.2d 1110 (Or. 1997) (nonconsensual sexual contact with clients); *In re Parrott*, 804 S.E.2d 852 (S.C. 2017) (using cell phone to take photo up woman's skirt in grocery store); *see also State ex rel. Okla. Bar Ass'n v. Olmstead*, 285 P.3d 1110 (Okla. 2012) (judge downloaded obscene materials on state-issued computer). Also see the following section on violent crimes.

## • *Violent Crimes*

Violent crimes are clearly among those covered by Rule 8.4(b). *See People v. Bertagnolli*, 922 P.2d 935 (Colo. 1996) (criminal sexual assault); *Fla. Bar v. Bartholf*, 775 So. 2d 957 (Fla. 2000) (lawyer assaulted individual with golf cart); *In re Davidson*, 761 N.E.2d 854 (Ind. 2002) (assaulting police officers trying to arrest lawyer for public intoxication); *Iowa Supreme Court Att'y Disciplinary Bd. v. Blessum*, 861 N.W.2d 575 (Iowa 2015) (assaulting client); *In re Estiverne*, 741 So. 2d 649 (La. 1999) (threatening another lawyer with handgun during deposition); *In re Pastor*, 60 N.Y.S.3d 685 (App. Div. 2017) (killing girlfriend's dog); *In re Day*, 173 P.3d 915 (Wash. 2008) (sexual assault of eleven-year-old former client); *In re Perez-Pena*, 168 P.3d 408 (Wash. 2007) (assaulting client during dispute); *see also In re Harkins*, 899 A.2d 755 (D.C. 2006) ("sexually abusive contact, because of its inherently violent nature, calls into question one's fitness as a lawyer and thus falls within the ambit of Rule 8.4(b)"); *In re Keaton*, 29 N.E.3d 103 (Ind. 2015) (stalking, harassing, and intimidation of daughter's roommate); *Lawyer Disciplinary Bd. v. Robinson*, 736 S.E.2d 18 (W. Va. 2012) (beating client with baseball bat); *In re Hubatch*, 839 N.W.2d 579 (Wis. 2013) (robbing credit union with toy gun).

This includes acts of domestic violence. *See People v. Scott*, 121 P.3d 366 (Colo. O.P.D.J. 2005) (assault, false imprisonment, and harassment of ex-wife); *In re Knight*, 42 N.E.3d 80 (Ind. 2015) (domestic battery); *Iowa Supreme Court Att'y Disciplinary Bd. v. Deremiah*, 875 N.W.2d 728 (Iowa 2016) (criminal trespass and domestic assault); *In re Grella*, 777 N.E.2d 167 (Mass. 2002) (assaulting estranged wife); *In re Toronto*, 696 A.2d 8 (N.J. 1997) (conviction for assault of wife); *In re Falco*, 52 N.Y.S.3d 469 (App. Div. 2017) (assaulting pregnant wife; also disciplined in Colorado); *Ohio State Bar Ass'n v. Mason*, 94 N.E.3d 556 (Ohio 2017) (judge brutally assaulted wife); *State ex rel. Okla. Bar Ass'n v. Zannotti*, 330 P.3d 11 (Okla. 2014) (lawyer assaulted former client he had been dating). *But see In re Michaels*, 67 A.3d 1023 (Del. 2013) (lawyer's misdemeanor conviction for grabbing minor daughter by ponytail and refusing to let her go to prevent child from running away from home bore "no relationship to [his] fitness to practice law"); *In re Stoneburner*, 882 N.W.2d 200 (Minn. 2016) (throwing something at wife during heated argument did not violate rule; conduct did not result in harm to victim or any client, was not related to practice of law, and lawyer had no previous record of criminal conduct).

• *Tax Law Violations*

As Comment [2] indicates, tax law violations may violate Rule 8.4(b). *See In re Moore,* 691 A.2d 1151 (D.C. 1997) (willful failure to file federal income tax returns); *Iowa Supreme Court Bd. of Prof'l Ethics & Conduct v. Morris,* 604 N.W.2d 653 (Iowa 2000) (failure to pay employee withholding taxes and file required forms); *In re Cook,* 33 So. 3d 155 (La. 2010) (failure to file income tax returns); *Att'y Grievance Comm'n v. Gore,* 845 A.2d 1204 (Md. 2004) (failure to file sales tax returns and pay sales tax on behalf of restaurant lawyer owned); *In re Peterson,* 718 N.W.2d 849 (Minn. 2006) (tax evasion in connection with purchase of motor vehicle); *In re Lewis,* 70 A.3d 601 (N.J. 2013) (filing false tax return); *In re Cohen,* 71 N.Y.S.3d 46 (App. Div. 2018) (obstructing and impeding IRS and failing to file tax returns); *In re Chung,* 656 N.Y.S.2d 250 (App. Div. 1997) (failure to file required IRS Form 8300 after receiving cash in excess of $10,000); *Bd. of Prof'l Responsibility v. Barnes,* 297 P.3d 77 (Wyo. 2013) (falsification of motorcycle sales documents to pay lower sales taxes); *see also In re Cramer,* 225 P.3d 881 (Wash. 2010) (after lawyer's business license revoked for nonpayment of taxes, lawyer removed revocation notice from office door and continued to practice under different firm name); *cf. In re Waite,* 782 N.W.2d 820 (Minn. 2010) (failure to file federal and state income tax returns "for as many as 12 years" violated Rule 8.4(d) but not 8.4(b)).

## THREATENING PROSECUTION

DR 7-105(A) of the Model Code specifically prohibited a lawyer from using or threatening a criminal prosecution to gain an advantage in a civil matter. Although this provision has no counterpart in the Model Rules, threatening criminal prosecution—or disciplinary action against opposing counsel—will, under some circumstances, violate Rule 8.4(b). ABA Formal Ethics Op. 94-383 (1994) (threatening disciplinary complaint against opposing counsel to gain advantage in civil case may violate Rule 8.4(b) if conduct extortionate under criminal law of jurisdiction); ABA Formal Ethics Op. 92-363 (1992) ("The Model Rules do not prohibit a lawyer from using the possibility of presenting criminal charges against the opposing party in a civil matter, to gain relief for a client, provided that the criminal matter is related to the client's civil claim, the lawyer has a well-founded belief that both the civil claim and the criminal charges are warranted by the law and the facts, and the lawyer does not attempt to exert or suggest improper influence over the criminal process."; threat might, however, contravene Rule 8.4 if it violates criminal law); *accord* Alaska Ethics Op. 97-2 (1997); Md. Ethics Op. 03-16 (2003); *cf. State ex rel. Okla. Bar Ass'n v. Worsham,* 957 P.2d 549 (Okla. 1998) (statement that client intended to file criminal charges if defendant in civil action did not respond to settlement offer accurately reflected client's intent and therefore did not violate Rule 8.4(b)); *Comm. on Legal Ethics v. Printz,* 416 S.E.2d 720 (W. Va. 1992) (lawyer who threatened client's employee with criminal prosecution if employee did not make restitution of funds embezzled from client did not violate DR 7-105(A), which "has proven to be unworkable"; court emphasized DR 7-105(A) was "deliberately omitted [from the Rules of Professional Conduct] as redundant or overbroad or both"). This type of conduct may violate Rule 8.4(d); see the discussion below.

Note that several jurisdictions have retained a specific provision similar to DR 7-105(A). *See generally ABA/BNA Lawyers' Manual on Professional Conduct*, "Obligations to Third Persons: Threatening Prosecution," pp. 71:601 *et seq.*

## Paragraph (c): Dishonesty, Fraud, Deceit, or Misrepresentation

Paragraph (c)'s prohibition of "conduct involving dishonesty, fraud, deceit or misrepresentation" is broad and, like the other provisions of Rule 8.4, encompasses conduct outside the practice of law. *See, e.g.*, D.C. Ethics Op. 336 (2006) (lawyer acting as guardian—but not as lawyer—for incapacitated individual must "at all times" comply with Rule 8.4(c); thus, lawyer must discontinue using individual's name upon learning claimed identity is false).

The concepts of dishonesty, fraud, deceit, and misrepresentation, though closely related, are not the same. Fraud is defined by Model Rule 1.0(d) as "conduct that is fraudulent under the substantive or procedural law of the applicable jurisdiction and has a purpose to deceive." Neither damages nor detrimental reliance is a necessary element of the ethics violation, as opposed to the tort. Rule 1.0, cmt. [5].

The Model Rules do not define dishonesty, deceit, or misrepresentation. One court explained the difference by concluding that fraud and deceit require an intent to deceive, but misrepresentation does not, and that dishonesty involves "conduct indicating a disposition to 'lie, cheat or defraud.'" *In re Obert*, 89 P.3d 1173 (Or. 2004); *see In re Scanio*, 919 A.2d 1137 (D.C. 2007) ("dishonesty" includes "conduct evincing a lack of honesty, probity or integrity in principle; a lack of fairness and straightforwardness," but need not involve conduct legally characterized as fraud, deceit, or misrepresentation). *See generally Fla. Bar v. Ross*, 732 So. 2d 1037 (Fla. 1998) ("dishonesty" not unconstitutionally vague; "a person of common intelligence could be expected to understand the conduct proscribed by the rule").

A lawyer's intent or purpose to deceive is generally irrelevant to Rule 8.4(c). *See In re Lawrence*, 884 So. 2d 561 (La. 2004) (lawyer who submitted false timesheets to firm violated rule regardless of intent or motive); *State ex rel. Special Counsel v. Shapiro*, 665 N.W.2d 615 (Neb. 2003) (misrepresentation does not require proof of intent to deceive or defraud); *Disciplinary Counsel v. McCord*, 905 N.E.2d 1182 (Ohio 2009) (use of misleading firm name violated rules even if lawyer did not intend to deceive public); *In re Dann*, 960 P.2d 416 (Wash. 1998) (in determining whether lawyer violated Rule 8.4(c), "the question is whether the attorney lied"; motive irrelevant); *cf. Att'y Grievance Comm'n v. Dore*, 73 A.3d 161 (Md. 2013) ("dishonesty and misrepresentation under Rule 8.4(c) have no requirement of intent to deceive"; intent to deceive relevant only when fraud or deceit alleged). *But see State ex rel. Okla. Bar Ass'n v. Wilcox*, 318 P.3d 1114 (Okla. 2014) (Rule 8.4(c) violation requires "intent or purpose to deceive"; no violation for "negligent misrepresentation or failure to apprise another of relevant information").

Courts do, however, seem to look for some culpable mental state. "[T]he better view is to require some level of scienter that is greater than negligence to find a violation of [Rule 8.4(c),]" according to *Iowa Supreme Court Att'y Disciplinary Bd. v. Netti*, 797 N.W.2d 591 (Iowa 2011). *See In re Skagen*, 149 P.3d 1171 (Or. 2006) ("Although proving that a lawyer acted dishonestly does not require evidence that the lawyer *intended* to deceive, it does require a mental state of knowledge—that is, that the accused lawyer *knew* that his conduct was culpable in some respect."; reckless preparation of client bills did not violate ethics rule); *see also In re Surrick*, 338 F.3d 224 (3d Cir. 2003) (well settled that misrepresentation includes "statements made with reckless disregard for the truth"); *Romero-Barcelo v. Acevedo-Vila*, 275 F. Supp. 2d 177 (D.P.R. 2003) (Rule 8.4(c) encompasses misrepresentations made with reckless ignorance of their truth or falsity; collecting cases); *In re Clark*, 87 P.3d 827 (Ariz. 2004) ("lawyer cannot violate ER 8.4(c) by acting negligently; a violation of ER 8.4(c) must rest upon behavior that is knowing or intentional and purposely deceives or involves dishonesty or fraud"); *People v. Head*, 332 P.3d 117 (Colo. O.P.D.J. 2013) (must show "lawyer acted knowingly or with a reckless state of mind"); *Ansell v. Statewide Grievance Comm.*, 865 A.2d 1215 (Conn. App. Ct. 2005) (reckless misrepresentations to judge violated rule even though judge not ultimately misled; neither scienter nor injury required); *Fla. Bar v. Riggs*, 944 So. 2d 167 (Fla. 2006) (intent requirement of Rule 8.4(c) satisfied when lawyer "knowingly" assigned trust account responsibilities to paralegal, whom he failed to supervise); *In re Kline*, 311 P.3d 321 (Kan. 2013) (rule covers intentional dishonesty as opposed to mere mistake; showing of "malevolent" intent not required); *Att'y Grievance Comm'n v. Mahone*, 150 A.3d 870 (Md. 2016) (no violation of rule when misconduct is result of negligent rather than intentional conduct). *See generally* Nancy J. Moore, *Mens Rea Standards in Lawyer Disciplinary Codes*, 23 Geo. J. Legal Ethics 1 (Winter 2010).

## DISHONESTY TOWARD CLIENTS

### • *Lying*

A lawyer may not mislead or lie to a client. *See, e.g., People v. Maynard*, 275 P.3d 780 (Colo. 2010) (lawyer attempted to secretly negotiate with opposing parties for additional attorneys' fees); *People v. Parwatikar*, No. 04PDJ064, 2004 WL 1859850 (Colo. O.P.D.J. July 22, 2004) (general counsel for nurse staffing firm started competing business without employer's knowledge and used employer's trade secrets to operate business); *In re Hager*, 812 A.2d 904 (D.C. 2002) (lawyer settling potential class action failed to tell clients he and co-counsel were receiving $225,000 from opposing party); *Fla. Bar v. Russo*, 117 So. 3d 756 (Fla. 2013) (continuing to represent clients and deposit their money in trust account without disclosing account was seriously underfunded); *Fla. Bar v. Herman*, 8 So. 3d 1100 (Fla. 2009) (lawyer secretly set up own business in direct competition with corporate client); *In re Meyers*, 808 S.E.2d 650 (Ga. 2017) (outside counsel performed work for inside counsel's private clients and billed corporate client for the work); *In re Trester*, 172 P.3d 31 (Kan. 2007) (practicing law in state where not licensed); *Cunningham v. Ky. Bar Ass'n*, 266 S.W.3d 808 (Ky. 2008) (lawyers misled clients about how they disposed of millions of dollars from class action settlement); *In re Brown*, 813 So. 2d 325 (La. 2002) (lawyer deceived clients into believing paralegal was lawyer working with him); *In re Zak*, 73 N.E.3d 262 (Mass. 2017) (lawyer made false and misleading advertisements about himself, his law firm, and his loan modification services); *In re Frost*, 793 A.2d 699 (N.J. 2002) (lawyer entered "patently unfair" loan agreement with client, misrepresented extent of his interests in certain assets, and never intended to provide security for loan); *see also Liebling v. Miss. Bar*, 929 So. 2d 911 (Miss. 2006) (lawyer guaranteed client's father he would obtain client's early release from prison by specific date).

### • Stealing

Knowing misappropriation of client funds violates Rule 8.4(c). *See In re Blumenstyk*, 704 A.2d 1 (N.J. 1997) (although lawyer borrowed client funds only temporarily and made restitution, his intent and motives irrelevant to violation of Rules 1.15 and 8.4(c)); *In re Munzer*, 697 N.Y.S.2d 49 (App. Div. 1999) (lawyer's unauthorized personal use of funds entrusted to him as escrow agent violated New York Code analogue of Rules 1.15 and 8.4(c), notwithstanding that he returned money and never intended to deprive client of it permanently, and notwithstanding his personal relationship with client and his certainty deal would close and client would have been willing to lend him the money); *In re White*, 559 S.E.2d 583 (S.C. 2002) (lawyer hired to collect debt owed to client kept funds for himself); *see also People v. Clough*, 74 P.3d 552 (Colo. O.P.D.J. 2003) (failure to return unearned fees to former client); *Iowa Supreme Court Att'y Disciplinary Bd. v. Green*, 888 N.W.2d 398 (Iowa 2016) (lawyer entered into business transactions with clients, lying about the work he was undertaking and misappropriating funds); *In re Bergman*, 382 P.3d 455 (Kan. 2016) (lawyer billed corporate client for legal work benefiting client's top executive with whom she was having secret affair).

## MISLEADING, DEFRAUDING, OR LYING TO TRIBUNALS

Although Rule 3.3 expressly requires candor toward tribunals, Rule 8.4(c) is also implicated when a lawyer misleads or lies to a tribunal. *See In re Alcorn*, 41 P.3d 600 (Ariz. 2002) (defense lawyers secretly settled with plaintiff and agreed to engage in sham trial to create record for use against other defendant); *Ligon v. Stilley*, 371 S.W.3d 615 (Ark. 2010) (lawyer applying for pro hac vice admission misled court about disciplinary history); *People v. Casey*, 948 P.2d 1014 (Colo. 1997) (failing to inform court that client was using someone else's identity); *In re Lemmons*, 522 S.E.2d 650 (Ga. 1999) (lawyer falsely represented to IRS, courts, and others that he was certified public accountant); *In re Fieger*, 887 N.E.2d 87 (Ind. 2008) (failing to disclose disciplinary actions pending in other states in pro hac vice application); *Att'y Grievance Comm'n v. Goodman*, 850 A.2d 1157 (Md. 2004) (prosecuting case using another lawyer's name); *In re Balliro*, 899 N.E.2d 794 (Mass. 2009) (lawyer who was assaulted by her boyfriend testified falsely about source of her injuries at boyfriend's trial); *O'Meara's Case*, 834 A.2d 235 (N.H. 2003) (in his own divorce, lawyer filed pleading containing "gross embellishments on the truth"); *In re Forrest*, 730 A.2d 340 (N.J. 1999) (failing to disclose client's death, misrepresenting to arbitrator the reasons for client's absence, encouraging client's wife not to tell arbitrator, and misleading opposing counsel throughout discovery and negotiation processes); *Disciplinary Counsel v. Cicero*, 34 N.E.3d 60 (Ohio 2014) (lawyer who received speeding ticket obtained blank, signed judgment entry from court, used it to reduce charge, and falsely told court and prosecutor's office that prosecutor had approved reduction); *Disciplinary Counsel v. Rohrer*, 919 N.E.2d 180 (Ohio 2009) (leaking information to local newspaper in violation of court order, then lying to court about it); *In re Diggs*, 544 S.E.2d 628 (S.C. 2001) (submitting false report of attendance at CLE seminar); *In re Conteh*, 284 P.3d 724 (Wash. 2012) (lawyer lied about his employment history on asylum application); *Lawyer Disciplinary Bd. v. Cooke*, 799 S.E.2d 117 (W. Va. 2017) (overbilling for court-appointed work); *Bd. of Prof'l Responsibility v. Custis*, 348 P.3d 823 (Wyo. 2015) (filing brief misrepresenting testimony of witness); ABA Formal Ethics Op. 97-407 (1997) (lawyer who served as expert witness subject to discipline under Rule 8.4 for testifying falsely); *see also People v. Roose*, 69 P.3d 43 (Colo. 2003) (filing notice of appeal containing omissions and misstatements of fact); *Att'y Grievance Comm'n v. Brown*, 725 A.2d 1069 (Md. 1999) (paying court filing fee with check drawn on insufficient funds); *cf. Iowa Supreme Court Att'y Disciplinary Bd. v. Barnhill*, 885 N.W.2d 408 (Iowa 2016) (when court finds violation of specific rule involving deceit, such as Rule 3.3, it will not also find same conduct violates Rule 8.4(c)).

### • *Plagiarizing*

Plagiarizing another's work may violate Rule 8.4(c). *See Venesevich v. Leonard*, No. 1:07-CV-2118, 2008 WL 5340162 n.2, 2008 BL 280879 n.2 (M.D. Pa. Dec. 19, 2008) ("[p]lagiarism constitutes misrepresentation and is therefore a violation of Rule 8.4(c)"; significant portion of lawyer's brief plagiarized from court opinions without attribution); *In re Burghoff*, 374 B.R. 681 (Bankr. N.D. Iowa 2007) (lawyer plagiarized material in two briefs; in one brief, plagiarized material consisted of string cites); *In re Ayeni*, 822 A.2d 420 (D.C. 2003) (appointed counsel filed brief in criminal appeal that was virtually identical to brief filed earlier by co-defendant; he then submitted voucher for payment claiming he spent more than nineteen hours researching and writing it); *Iowa Supreme Court Att'y Disciplinary Bd. v. Cannon*, 789 N.W.2d 756 (Iowa 2010) (lawyer's brief included seventeen pages of material copied from published article without attribution); *Iowa Supreme Court Bd. of Prof'l Ethics & Conduct v. Lane*, 642 N.W.2d 296 (Iowa 2002) (lawyer submitted brief plagiarized from legal treatise, then applied to court for $16,000 in fees for eighty hours spent working on it); *In re Steinberg*, 620 N.Y.S.2d 345 (App. Div. 1994) (in application for appointment to criminal defense panel, lawyer submitted writing samples of other lawyers claiming they were his own); *see also Lohan v. Perez*, 924 F. Supp. 2d 447 (E.D.N.Y. 2013) (lawyer sanctioned for filing plagiarized memorandum; court noted conduct "would likely be found to violate [Rule 8.4(c)]"); *United States v. Sypher*, No. 3:09-CR-0085, 2011 WL 579156 n.4, 2011 BL 33239 n.4 (W.D. Ky. Feb. 9, 2011) (reminding lawyer whose statement of law contained material cut and pasted from Wikipedia without attribution that doing so amounts to plagiarism and may violate Rule 8.4); *In re Lamberis*, 443 N.E.2d 549 (Ill. 1982) (lawyer enrolled in LL.M. program submitted thesis containing material plagiarized from two published works); *cf. Newegg, Inc. v. Ezra Sutton, P.A.*, No. 2:15-cv-01395, 120 U.S.P.Q.2d 1111 (C.D. Cal. Sept. 13, 2016) (copying substantial portions of other party's brief without permission constituted copyright infringement). *But see* N.Y. City Ethics Op. 2018-3 (2018) (copying without attribution in brief not per se deceptive under Rule 8.4(c); opinion explains that academic writing and litigation have different purposes and norms and analyzes differences in various contexts); N.C. Ethics Op. 2008-14 (2009) (lawyer does not violate ethics rules by filing brief or using contract or other documents incorporating, without attribution or permission, material written by other lawyers). *See generally* Douglas E. Abrams, *Plagiarism in Lawyers' Advocacy: Imposing Discipline for Conduct Prejudicial to the Administration of Justice*, 47 Wake Forest L. Rev. 921 (Winter 2012) (arguing that lawyer plagiarism also violates Rule 8.4(d) by creating "risk of inadvertent plagiarism by the court" and distorting "the meaning and import of the adversarial argument that underlies reasoned decisionmaking"); Peter A. Joy & Kevin C. McMunigal, *The Problems of Plagiarism as an Ethics Offense*, 26 Crim. Just. 56 (Summer 2011) (arguing against labeling lawyer copying as plagiarism and treating it as per se ethics violation).

## • *Ghostwriting and Undisclosed Assistance to Pro Se Litigants*

Jurisdictions vary on whether, and the extent to which, a lawyer may provide legal services (generally in the form of drafting documents) to a pro se litigant without disclosing the lawyer's role to the court, adverse party, or opposing counsel. The resolution of this issue turns on an analysis of court rules (particularly Fed. R. Civ. P. 11), as well as several ethics rules, including—but not limited to—Rule 1.2(c) (limited-scope representation), Rule 3.3 (candor toward tribunals), Rule 4.1 (truthfulness in statements to others), and Rule 8.4(c) (misrepresentation). A major sticking point is whether the lack of disclosure misleads the court, adverse party, or opposing counsel.

Most ethics opinions conclude that ghostwriting pleadings for pro se litigants does not itself violate Rule 8.4(c), although disclosure of the lawyer's participation may be required by other rules, law, or circumstances. *E.g.*, ABA Formal Ethics Op. 07-446 (2007) (failure to disclose assistance to pro se litigant does not mislead court and thus does not violate Rule 8.4(c)); Ariz. Ethics Op. 05-06 (2005) (submitting ghostwritten documents without informing court "not inherently misleading," but disclosure may be required by law); Mich. Informal Ethics Op. RI-347 (2010) (disclosure of lawyer's role in assisting pro se litigant not required unless client makes "affirmative representation" no assistance has been provided); Miss. Ethics Op. 261 (2018) (undisclosed limited representation such as drafting document for pro se litigant is not deception under Rule 8.4(c)); N.Y. Cnty. Ethics Op. 742 (2010) (must disclose assistance to pro se litigant if required by court rule or order or if failure to do so would constitute misrepresentation; otherwise, notation "Prepared with the assistance of counsel admitted in New York" will normally suffice); Va. Ethics Op. 1874 (2014) (absent court rule or law to contrary, rule does not require lawyer to notify court of assistance to pro se litigant); *accord* Pa.-Phila. Joint Formal Ethics Op. 2011-100 (2011); *see also* N.J. Ethics Op. 713 (2008) (disclosure not required by Rule 8.4(c) and (d) and Rule 3.3 unless undisclosed assistance is tactic to take advantage of leeway accorded pro se litigants, or lawyer effectively controls wording of pleadings and conduct of litigation); Tenn. Formal Ethics Op. 2007-F-153 (2007) (lawyer may prepare pleadings for pro se litigant to protect claim from being barred by statute of limitation or other rule but may not create false impression that litigant is without substantial legal assistance); *cf. Persels & Assocs., LLC v. Capital One Bank*, 481 S.W.3d 501 (Ky. 2017) ("attorneys providing limited-representation of any kind may not deceptively engage in a more complete role"). *But see Iowa Supreme Court Att'y Disciplinary Bd. v. Rauch*, 746 N.W.2d 262 (Iowa 2008) (suspended lawyer who ghostwrote and filed pleadings without telling court violated Iowa Code analogue of Rule 8.4(c)); Nev. Ethics Op. 34 (rev. 2009) (lawyer providing "substantial" legal assistance to pro se litigant must disclose involvement to court or, if matter not in litigation, to other lawyer). *See generally* Michael W. Loudenslager, *Giving Up the Ghost: A Proposal for Dealing with Attorney "Ghostwriting" of Pro Se Litigants' Court Documents Through Explicit Rules Requiring Disclosure and Allowing Limited Appearances for Such Attorneys*, 92 Marq. L. Rev. 103 (Fall 2008) (concluding that Rule 8.4(c) and other ethics rules require disclosure, and urging jurisdictions to adopt more explicit rules).

Federal courts are split on this issue. *Compare In re Mungo*, 305 B.R. 762 (Bankr. D.S.C. 2003) (ghostwriting pleading for litigant filing pro se violates rule), *with In re Liu*, 664 F.3d 367 (2d Cir. 2011) (ghostwriting did not constitute misconduct given "lack of any rule or precedent governing attorney ghostwriting, and the various authorities that permit that practice"). *See generally* "Federal Courts Play Catch Up on Ghostwriting as States Cheer 'Unbundled' Legal Services," *ABA/BNA Lawyers' Manual on Professional Conduct*, 28 Law. Man. Prof. Conduct 42 (Current Reports, Jan. 18, 2012); Salman Bhojani, Comment, *Attorney Ghostwriting for Pro Se Litigants—A Practical and Bright-Line Solution to Resolve the Split of Authority Among Federal Circuits and State Bar Associations*, 65 SMU L. Rev. 653 (Summer 2012); Jessie M. Brown, *Ghostwriting and the Erie Doctrine: Why Federalism Calls for Respecting States' Ethical Treatment of Ghostwriting*, 2013 J. Prof. Law. 217 (2013).

## DECEIVING OTHERS: NONCLIENTS

### • *Adverse Parties and Opposing Counsel*

Deceiving an adverse party or opposing counsel can violate Rule 8.4(c). *See In re Piepes*, 692 N.Y.S.2d 716 (App. Div. 1999) (sending letter to woman involved in altercation with client falsely stating that client's father offered to amend will to bequeath her $25,000 in exchange for signed admission of fault in incident); *In re Gallagher*, 26 P.3d 131 (Or. 2001) (lawyer who knew opposing counsel made mistake regarding amounts of settlement checks had duty to clarify matter before disbursing proceeds); *In re Kronenberg*, 117 P.3d 1134 (Wash. 2005) (lawyer who bribed witness in attempt to get him to leave town and not testify against client deceived prosecutors about witness's whereabouts and lawyer's role); S.C. Ethics Op. 05-03 (2005) (reportable violation of Rule 8.4 if lawyer sent client's ex-husband letter falsely stating that divorce decree required him to submit to drug test and that refusal could be used as proof of positive result); *see also In re Pautler*, 47 P.3d 1175 (Colo. 2002) (prosecutor misled unrepresented murder suspect into believing prosecutor was public defender); *In re Holyoak*, 372 P.3d 1205 (Kan. 2016) (attempting to extort money from oil company by falsely claiming lawyer represented fifty other landowners with claims against it); *In re Eisenstein*, 485 S.W.3d 759 (Mo. 2016) (lawyer whose divorce client sent him information obtained through unauthorized access to wife's e-mail account used the information and failed to disclose it to opposing counsel); *In re Wisehart*, 721 N.Y.S.2d 356 (App. Div. 2001) (lawyer condoned photocopying and use of privileged documents taken from adverse party at discovery conference by client who was also his paralegal, failed to advise court and opponent immediately of theft of documents, used documents to extract settlement from adversary, and disregarded court's order to make no use of documents in litigation and secure all copies); *Cincinnati Bar Ass'n v. Statzer*, 800 N.E.2d 1117 (Ohio 2003) (lawyer deposing former legal assistant placed nine audiotapes in front of her, implying lawyer had recorded conversations with her); *In re Alia*, 709 N.W.2d 399 (Wis. 2006) (lawyer induced expert witness to authenticate report that lawyer secretly altered, and then falsely accused opposing counsel of fabricating evidence and being untruthful with court); Colo. Ethics Op. 108 (2000) (if lawyer receives from adverse party privileged or confidential documents that lawyer knows were sent inadvertently, lawyer would violate Rule 8.4(c) by examining them). See the annotations to Rule 3.4 and Rule 4.1.

### • *Members of Law Firm*

Stealing from one's own law firm violates Rule 8.4(c). *See In re Thompson*, 991 P.2d 820 (Colo. 1999) (associate accepted fees from clients and placed them in locked drawer for own use); *In re Vanderslice*, 55 A.3d 322 (Del. 2012) (misappropriation of law firm funds); *In re Wallace*, 232 So. 3d 1216 (La. 2017) (submitting hundreds of inflated billable hour statements to firm); *In re Renshaw*, 298 P.3d 1216 (Or. 2013) (miscoding over $150,000 in personal expenses as business expenses to obtain funds from law firm); *In re Moses*, 785 S.E.2d 364 (S.C. 2016) (stealing more than $70,000 from firm by asking clients to pay lawyer directly); *In re Siderits*, 824 N.W.2d 812 (Wis. 2013) (padding billing records to qualify for firm's year-end bonus); *see also Fla. Bar v. Winters*, 104 So. 3d 299 (Fla. 2012) (departing associates secretly took client files for their own use, violating criminal theft statute, to set up new practice); *Fla. Bar v. Kossow*, 912 So. 2d 544 (Fla. 2005) (associate used firm's resources to represent private clients and tried to conceal it from firm); *Att'y Grievance Comm'n v. Penn*, 65 A.3d 125 (Md. 2013) (title insurer's claims counsel secretly formed law firm and used his authority to farm out litigation work to firm); *Att'y Grievance Comm'n v. Keiner*, 27 A.3d 153 (Md. 2011) (lawyer planning to leave firm secretly altered or deleted client files and solicited hundreds of firm clients, using firm resources); *In re Placide*, 414 P.3d 1124 (Wash. 2018) (while working for two different firms, lawyer repeatedly lied about extent of her off-the-books practice; rejecting lawyer's argument that she did "not owe a duty of honesty of some sort").

Other forms of dishonesty to a lawyer's own firm, colleagues, supervisors, or employees can also violate the rule. *In re Sullivan*, 727 A.2d 832 (Del. 1999) (lawyer falsely told supervisor he filed complaint for client and that client failed to follow instructions); *In re Slaughter*, 929 A.2d 433 (D.C. 2007) (forging fee agreement and other documents, causing firm to expend over one million dollars in billable hours and costs for "client" it did not represent); *Fla. Bar v. Nowacki*, 697 So. 2d 828 (Fla. 1997) (lawyer failed to pay former associate and blocked her phone calls so she could not contact him about salary dispute); *In re Schwartz*, 599 S.E.2d 184 (Ga. 2004) (accessing, listening to, and randomly deleting messages from former law firm's voicemail system); *Att'y Grievance Comm'n v. Floyd*, 929 A.2d 61 (Md. 2007) (lawyer who obtained job with federal agency failed to disclose that former employer and primary reference was her husband, and used his letter offering to pay her $55,000 per year to win higher starting salary); *In re Bonner*, 896 N.W.2d 98 (Minn. 2017) (failing to deposit withheld employee contributions into retirement accounts and using funds to pay firm expenses); *In re Rennie*, 696 N.Y.S.2d 444 (App. Div. 1999) (failing to tell new employer about pending civil litigation against lawyer); *Cleveland Metro. Bar Ass'n v. Azman*, 66 N.E.3d 695 (Ohio 2016) (terminated lawyer accessed firm e-mail accounts without authorization and deleted messages); *In re Walton*, 287 P.3d 1098 (Or. 2012) (unauthorized use of former employer's Westlaw password); *In re Strouse*, 34 A.3d 329 (Vt. 2011) (lawyer concealed from her law firm her renewed romantic relationship with husband of firm's divorce client); *In re Beatse*, 722 N.W.2d 385 (Wis. 2006) (assistant district attorney viewed pornographic images on office computer and falsely blamed his son); *see also In re Hawn*, 917 A.2d 693 (D.C. 2007) (falsifying résumé and altering law school transcripts to obtain employment).

### • *Other Nonclients*

Rule 8.4(c) also extends to dishonesty in dealings with the world at large. *See People v. Rishel*, 50 P.3d 938 (Colo. O.P.D.J. 2002) (misappropriating funds received from third parties for purchase of baseball tickets); *In re Scanio*, 919 A.2d 1137 (D.C. 2007) (attempting to deceive insurer in claim for lost income); *In re Mitchell*, 822 A.2d 1106 (D.C. 2003) (lying to client's creditor about status of personal injury suit and allocation of proceeds); *Fla. Bar v. Schultz*, 712 So. 2d 386 (Fla. 1998) (giving postdated check to travel agent and stopping payment the same day); *Iowa Supreme Court Bd. of Prof'l Ethics & Conduct v. Visser*, 629 N.W.2d 376 (Iowa 2001) (defense lawyer's letter to newspaper containing "partially true" statement about judge's ruling on plaintiff's claims violated rule even though lawyer attached copy of court order to letter); *In re Royer*, 78 P.3d 449 (Kan. 2003) (lawyer for client facing condemnation proceedings sold client's dilapidated building to homeless man for one dollar to avoid incurring costs of demolition); *In re Albin*, 982 P.2d 385 (Kan. 1999) (lawyer wrote on envelope containing highly personal letters to inmate, "legal mail—re representation on car accident"); *Bonar v. Ky. Bar Ass'n*, 405 S.W.3d 465 (Ky. 2013) (misrepresentations in capacity as president of state bar association); *In re McCool*, 172 So. 3d 1058 (La. 2015) (disseminating false and misleading statements about judges through social media and in court motions); *In re Hutton*, 25 So. 3d 767 (La. 2009) (defrauding ex-sister-in-law of life insurance proceeds to which she was entitled); *Att'y Grievance Comm'n v. Young*, 124 A.3d 210 (Md. 2015) (falsely telling state authorities that he had license to work as home improvement contractor); *Att'y Grievance Comm'n v. Coppock*, 69 A.3d 1092 (Md. 2013) (lying to lender); *Att'y Grievance Comm'n v. Ellison*, 867 A.2d 259 (Md. 2005) (lying to client's physical therapist to avoid paying off lien from settlement proceeds); *In re Rios*, 965 N.Y.S.2d 418 (App. Div. 2013) (concealing investigative information from outside counsel hired to try client's personal injury case); *Disciplinary Counsel v. McCord*, 905 N.E.2d 1182 (Ohio 2009) (lawyer induced expert witness to attend deposition with promise of compensation but stopped payment on check day after deposition; also used firm name that included name of deceased lawyer with whom he had never practiced and phrase "and associates" when he had none); *In re Herman*, 348 P.3d 1125 (Or. 2015) ("Although no rule explicitly requires lawyers to be candid and fair with their business associates or employers, such an obligation is implicit in the prohibitions set out in [Rule 8.4(c)]"; lawyer diverted corporate assets from business associates); *In re Kluge*, 27 P.3d 102 (Or. 2001) (lawyer falsely claimed to be notary and administered oath at deposition, and told professional liability fund he was exempt from coverage requirement because he did not engage in private practice); *Lawyer Disciplinary Bd. v. Markins*, 663 S.E.2d 614 (W. Va. 2008) (secretly accessing e-mail accounts of wife and other lawyers at her firm for over two years); ABA Formal Ethics Op. 469 (2014) (prosecutors may not allow debt collection firms to use official letterhead of prosecutor's office for purposes of collection demand letters when no lawyer from prosecutor's office reviews letter and case file); *see also People v. Furtado*, No. 15PDJ056, 2015 WL 7574128, 2015 BL 388728 (Colo. O.P.D.J. Nov. 2, 2015) (opening trust accounts to pay bills of client medical marijuana dispensaries without disclosing purpose of accounts to bank, whose policies prohibited marijuana-related businesses to open accounts); *In re Usher*, 987 N.E.2d 1080 (Ind. 2013) (lawyer had paralegal disseminate e-mail containing false information about young attorney who rejected lawyer's romantic advances). *But see Att'y Grievance Comm'n v. Hall*, 969 A.2d 953 (Md. 2009) (lawyer having affair with client did not violate Rule 8.4(c) by lying to her about his affairs with other clients).

## CRIMINAL CONDUCT

A lawyer's criminal conduct involving dishonesty violates Rule 8.4(c) in addition to Rule 8.4(b). *See In re McIntosh*, 991 P.2d 403 (Kan. 1999) (bankruptcy fraud); *In re Scott*, 805 So. 2d 137 (La. 2002) (fraudulent bidding scheme); *In re Trudeau*, 705 N.W.2d 409 (Minn. 2005) (unauthorized computer access by installing and using e-mail spyware program); *In re Ellner*, 686 N.Y.S.2d 806 (App. Div. 1999) (attempted tax evasion); *Dayton Bar Ass'n v. Seall*, 690 N.E.2d 1271 (Ohio 1998) (conspiracy to commit tax fraud); *In re Kenyon*, 559 S.E.2d 590 (S.C. 2002) (racketeering convictions premised on money laundering, wire fraud, and murder).

## FALSIFICATION OF DOCUMENTS

Falsification of documents is prohibited under Rule 8.4(c). *See In re Sealed Appellant*, 194 F.3d 666 (5th Cir. 1999) (backdating endorsement on stock certificate); *In re Brown*, 766 N.E.2d 363 (Ind. 2002) (forging client's signature on check and stealing client's portion of settlement); *In re Wahlder*, 728 So. 2d 837 (La. 1999) (letting client sign wife's name to documents settling client's personal injury case, and directing law office employee to notarize signature); *In re Brost*, 763 N.W.2d 637 (Minn. 2009) (using expired notary stamp of deceased notary, altering expiration date, forging notary's signature, and submitting fraudulent document to bank); *Disciplinary Counsel v. Roberts*, 881 N.E.2d 1236 (Ohio 2008) (signing clients' names to release and notarizing signatures); *In re Poole*, 125 P.3d 954 (Wash. 2006) (creating backdated invoice and giving it to opposing counsel).

## SURREPTITIOUSLY OBTAINING INFORMATION
### • Covert Investigations

How does a lawyer's involvement in covert investigations square with Rule 8.4(c)'s prohibition of conduct involving deception? This issue was brought to the forefront in *In re Gatti*, 8 P.3d 966 (Or. 2000), in which the Oregon Supreme Court held that a lawyer violated Oregon's analogue of Model Rule 8.4(c) by engaging in subterfuge when investigating the grounds for a lawsuit. In response, the U.S. Department of Justice sought an injunction barring the Oregon bar from disciplining prosecutors involved in undercover investigations. *See* "DOJ Sues Oregon Bar Over Dishonesty Rule, Asserts Need for 'Prosecutorial Exception,'" *ABA/BNA Lawyers' Manual on Professional Conduct*, 17 Law. Man. Prof. Conduct 407 (Current Reports, July 4, 2001). Ultimately, Oregon's ethics rule was amended to permit lawyers "to advise clients or others about or to supervise lawful covert activity in the investigation of violations of civil or criminal law or constitutional rights" if the lawyer's conduct otherwise complies with the ethics rules. *See* "Oregon Amends Disciplinary Rule to Clarify That Lawyers May Supervise Covert Activity," *ABA/BNA Lawyers' Manual on Professional Conduct*, 18 Law. Man. Prof. Conduct 94 (Current Reports, Feb. 13, 2002); *see also* Or. Ethics Op. 2005-173 (2005) (lawyer may supervise and give advice about, but not participate in, covert investigation if lawyer believes unlawful activity may be occurring).

Most jurisdictions have reached similar conclusions with or without amending their rules. *See United States v. Parker*, 165 F. Supp. 2d 431 (W.D.N.Y. 2001) (ethics rule prohibiting dishonesty "does not apply to prosecuting attorneys who provide supervision and advice to undercover investigations"); *Gidatex v. Campaniello Imps., Ltd.*, 82 F. Supp. 2d 119 (S.D.N.Y. 1999) (ethics rule prohibiting dishonesty does not apply to private counsel in trademark infringement case using undercover investigators posing as interior decorators to elicit statements from salesclerks; no indication investigators caused clerks to say anything they would not otherwise have said); *Apple Corps Ltd. v. Int'l Collectors Soc'y*, 15 F. Supp. 2d 456 (D.N.J. 1998) (lawyers' use of undercover investigators posing as customers to detect violations of consent decree by opposing party did not violate Rule 8.4(c)); D.C. Ethics Op. 323 (2004) ("Lawyers employed by government agencies who act in a non-representational official capacity in a manner they reasonably believe to be authorized by law do not violate Rule 8.4 if, in the course of their employment, they make misrepresentations that are reasonably intended to further the conduct of their official duties."); Utah Ethics Op. 02-05 (2002) (government lawyer's authorized participation in lawful government covert investigation does not violate Rule 8.4(c)); Va. Ethics Op. 1738 (2000) (lawyer engaged in criminal investigation or housing discrimination investigation may make "otherwise lawful" misrepresentations necessary to conduct investigation without violating Rule 8.4); *see also* N.Y. Cnty. Ethics Op. 737 (2007) (under very limited circumstances, non-government lawyers may supervise investigators who use "dissemblance" regarding their identity and purpose in order to gather evidence); N.C. Ethics Op. 2014-9 (2015) (describing circumstances under which lawyer, "in pursuit of a legitimate public interest," may supervise private investigator using deceptive tactics); Va. Ethics Op. 1845 (2009) (bar counsel may direct investigators who use covert methods to gather evidence of unauthorized practice of law when no other reasonable alternatives available); *cf. Scott v. Frankel*, 562 F. App'x 950 (11th Cir. 2014) (rejecting argument that provision of Florida's Rule 8.4(c) stating "it shall not be professional misconduct for a lawyer for a criminal law enforcement agency or regulatory agency to advise others about or to supervise another in an undercover investigation" violated Fourteenth Amendment). *See generally* David B. Isbell & Lucantonio N. Salvi, *Investigators and*

*Discrimination Testers: An Analysis of the Provisions Prohibiting Misrepresentation Under the Model Rules of Professional Conduct*, 8 Geo. J. Legal Ethics 791 (Summer 1995); Tory L. Lucas, *To Catch a Criminal, To Cleanse a Profession: Exposing Deceptive Practices by Attorneys to the Sunlight of Public Debate and Creating an Express Investigation Deception Exception to the ABA Model Rules of Professional Conduct*, 89 Neb. L. Rev. 219 (2010); Douglas R. Richmond, *Deceptive Lawyering*, 74 U. Cin. L. Rev. 577 (Winter 2005) (concluding that state ethics rules adequately regulate lawyers' surreptitious recording of conversations, but not their participation in covert investigations); Barry R. Temkin, *Deception in Undercover Investigations: Conduct-Based vs. Status-Based Ethical Analysis*, 32 Seattle U. L. Rev. 123 (Fall 2008) (arguing that Model Rules should be amended to permit limited deception in investigations regardless of lawyer's status or subject area of law if evidence not otherwise available, lawyer's involvement indirect, and no ethics rules or laws broken).

For analysis of the circumstances under which deceptive evidence gathering is permitted under Rule 8.4(c) (and 4.1(a)), see *Leysock v. Forest Labs., Inc.*, No. 12-11354-FDS, 2017 WL 1591833, 2017 BL 142553 (D. Mass. Apr. 28, 2017) (depends on nature and degree of deception, nature of targeted information and targeted persons, and necessity of deception; rule violated where lawyers engaged in elaborate scheme of deceit under guise of legitimate medical research study inducing doctors to disclose confidential patient information without legal justification).

### • *Secretly Recording Conversations with Third Parties*

Surreptitious recording of conversations with third parties is generally permissible under Rule 8.4(c) if it does not violate applicable law and is not "accompanied by other circumstances that make it unethical." ABA Formal Ethics Op. 01-422 (2001) (unless illegal, recording of conversation with third party without party's knowledge or consent does not necessarily violate ethics rules; lawyer may not, however, falsely state that conversation not being recorded); *accord* Alaska Ethics Op. 2003-1 (2003); Ohio Sup. Ct. Ethics Op. 2012-1 (2012); *see Midwest Motor Sports v. Arctic Cat Sales, Inc.*, 347 F.3d 693 (8th Cir. 2003) (lawyer violated Rule 8.4(a) and (c) by hiring investigator to talk to and secretly record adverse party's employees under false pretenses; "unethical contact with [adverse party's employees] combined with the nonconsensual recording presents the type of situation where even [ABA Formal Opinion 01-422] would authorize sanctions"); *Iowa Supreme Court Bd. of Prof'l Ethics & Conduct v. Plumb*, 546 N.W.2d 215 (Iowa 1996) (no violation of ethics rule to record conversation secretly unless lawyer intended to deceive or mislead person being recorded: "It is not the use of recording devices, but the employment of artifice or pretense, that truly poses a threat to the trust which is the bedrock of our professional relationships."); *In re Curry*, 880 N.E.2d 388 (Mass. 2008), and *In re Crossen*, 880 N.E.2d 352 (Mass. 2008) (lawyers disbarred for attempting to obtain judge's recusal by engaging in and secretly recording sham interview with judge's former law clerk and trying to coerce clerk into making damaging statements about judge); *Miss. Bar v. Att'y ST*, 621 So. 2d 229 (Miss. 1993) (lawyer who secretly recorded conversations with city judge and police chief to protect client's interests did not thereby violate ethics rule, but "stepped over the line" and violated Rule 4.1 by denying it when asked); *In re PRB Docket No. 2007-046*, 989 A.2d 523 (Vt. 2009) (lawyers who mis-led potential witness about whether telephone conversation being recorded violated Rule 4.1 but not Rule 8.4(c)); Me. Ethics Op. 168 (1999) (no per se prohibition against secretly recording conversations; depends upon circumstances); N.M. Ethics Op. 2005-3 (2005) (although lawyer may not secretly record conversation with witness if it would involve "deceiving the witness either by commission or omission," such as if witness indicates he believes conversation to be off record or that he would not participate if recording made, "there may be instances where clandestine recording might be permissible"); Or. Ethics Op. 2005-156 (2005) (lawyer may secretly record telephone, but not in-person, conversation if permitted by law and if lawyer does not mislead person into believing no recording being made); Va. Ethics Op. 1814 (2011) (criminal defense lawyer may secretly record conversation with unrepresent-ed witness if witness informed of lawyer's identity); *see also* Wis. Ethics Op. E-94-5 (1994) (routine secret recording would "almost certainly" violate ethics rules; secretly recording conversations with clients would violate Rule 1.4; secretly recording tele-phone conversations with judges and their staffs is "generally impermissible"). *See generally* Kathleen Maher, *Tale of the Tape: Lawyers Recording Conversations*, 15 Prof. Law., no. 3, at 10 (2004); Alison A. Vana, Note, *Attorney Private Eyes: Ethical Implica-tions of a Private Attorney's Decision to Surreptitiously Record Conversations*, 2003 U. Ill. L. Rev. 1605 (2003).

Some authorities start from the position that surreptitious recording is imper-missible, but then carve out exceptions. *See, e.g., In re Att'y General's Petition*, 417 S.E.2d 526 (S.C. 1992) (lawyer may not record conversation without prior knowledge and consent of all participants absent prior consent of law enforcement agency per-forming criminal investigation); Colo. Ethics Op. 112 (2003) (lawyer may not secretly record conversations except to gather evidence in criminal trial, or if recording unre-lated to practice of law); N.Y. City Ethics Op. 2003-2 (2003) (secret recordings not permitted as routine practice, but may be permissible "if the lawyer has a reasonable basis for believing that disclosure of the taping would significantly impair pursuit of a generally accepted societal good"); *see also* Mo. Formal Ethics Op. 123 (2006) (may not secretly record conversation with client); *cf.* S.C. Ethics Op. 08-13 (2008) (party in divorce action who happens to be lawyer may secretly tape record phone conversa-tion with spouse if lawful, and if she is acting solely as private citizen).

### • *Tracking Software*

The undisclosed use of tracking software may violate Rule 8.4(c). *See* Alaska Eth-ics Op. 2016-1 (2016) (lawyer may not use "web bug" or other tracking device in doc-uments sent to opposing counsel); N.Y. State Ethics Op. 749 (2001) (same); Pa. Formal Ethics Op. 2017-300 (2017) (same); *see also* Ill. Ethics Op. 18-01 (2018) (lawyers may not use tracking software, also known as "web bugs," "web beacons," or "spymail," without informed consent of each recipient of such software).

### • *Mining of Metadata*

There is no clear consensus on the ethical propriety of examining metadata embedded in documents received by an opposing party or counsel to glean information the sender may not have intended to disclose. The issue implicates Rule 8.4(c) and (d) (as well as Rule 4.4).

Some authorities have concluded that examining metadata does not necessarily violate Rule 8.4. *See* ABA Formal Ethics Op. 06-442 (2006) (reviewing embedded information in electronic documents sent by adverse party or agent or counsel would not violate Rule 8.4(c) or (d)); Colo. Ethics Op. 119 (2008) (as nothing "inherently deceitful or surreptitious about searching for metadata," lawyer may search for and review metadata embedded in electronic document sent by opposing counsel or other third party; lawyer who finds confidential information in metadata should assume it was sent inadvertently and act in accordance with Rule 4.4(b)); D.C. Ethics Op. 341 (2007) (lawyer free to review metadata in documents provided by adversary unless lawyer knows it was inadvertently provided, as may be the case when lawyer notices metadata contains protected information); Tex. Ethics Op. 665 (2016) (ethics rules do not prohibit lawyer from searching for metadata); Vt. Ethics Op. 2009-1 (2009) (nothing in Rule 8.4 prohibits receiving lawyer from searching metadata); *see also* Or. Ethics Op. 2011-187 (rev. 2015) (using special software to search for metadata may violate rule); Wash. Ethics Op. 2216 (2012) (lawyer may view metadata if easily accessible, but using sophisticated software to read "scrubbed" document would violate Rules 4.4(a) and 8.4(d)). *See generally* Michael W. Loudenslager, *Why Shouldn't Attorneys Be Allowed to View Metadata? A Proposal for Allowing Attorneys to View Metadata as Long as Extraordinary Measures Are Not Taken to Do So and Opposing Counsel Is Contacted Upon Discovery of Sensitive Information*, 15 J. Tech. L. & Pol'y 159 (Dec. 2010); Andrew M. Perlman, *The Legal Ethics of Metadata Mining*, 43 Akron L. Rev. 785 (2010).

Others conclude that such conduct would amount to misconduct under Rule 8.4. *See* Ala. Ethics Op. 2007-02 (2007) (mining metadata for confidential information violates Rule 8.4; production of metadata in discovery is matter for courts); Me. Ethics Op. 196 (2008) (trying to unearth confidential information embedded in document from counsel for another party would violate Maine's version of Rule 8.4(c) and (d)); N.Y. State Ethics Op. 749 (2001) (use of computer technology to surreptitiously mine metadata would violate rule); *see also* Ariz. Ethics Op. 07-03 (2007) (lawyers should "refrain from conduct that amounts to an unjustified intrusion into the client-lawyer relationship that exists between the opposing party and his or her counsel. ER 8.4(a)–(d)"); N.C. Ethics Op. 2009-1 (2010) (violation of Rule 8.4(d) to search for or use confidential information in metadata of communication from another party or lawyer without authorization by law or court, or consent of other party).

For discussion of a lawyer's duty upon receipt of information—including metadata—sent inadvertently or without authorization, see the annotation to Rule 4.4.

## • *Deceit When Using Social Media*

A lawyer may not use deception to seek access to nonpublic portions of social media websites. Some authorities have concluded that a lawyer must disclose his or her identity and may not avoid this obligation by engaging a third party to make a "friend" request. *See Disciplinary Counsel v. Brockler*, 48 N.E.3d 557 (Ohio 2016) (assistant prosecutor violated rule by using fictitious social media identity to chat with alibi witnesses; refusing to carve out exception for "prosecutorial investigation deception"); Conn. Informal Ethics Op. 2011-4 (2011) (lawyer may not engage private investigator to "friend" adverse parties in litigation to obtain information to use against them); D.C. Ethics Op. 371 (2016) (rule prohibits pretexting when requesting access to private portions of social media); Mass. Ethics Op. 2014-5 (2014) (lawyer may access nonpublic information on potential adverse party's social networking site only if lawyer able to send message disclosing role; insufficient that lawyer's identity contained in "profile"); N.Y. City Ethics Op. 2012-2 (2012) (may not use deception to research jurors on social media sites); N.Y. City Ethics Op. 2010-2 (2010) (lawyer may not "friend" unrepresented person under false pretenses, such as by using false profile); *see also* Or. Ethics Op. 2013-189 (2013) (lawyer may not use deception to access nonpublic information in social media account unless exception for covert investigations under Oregon's Rule 8.4(b) applies); Tex. Ethics Op. 671 (2018) (lawyer may not anonymously contact alleged anonymous online defamer in order to obtain jurisdictional information).

Some authorities also conclude that the lawyer must disclose the purpose of the request. *See* San Diego Cnty. Ethics Op. 2011-2 (2011) (lawyer should not make friend requests of witnesses or parties without disclosing his purpose); Colo. Ethics Op. 127 (2015) (lawyer sending friend request to unrepresented person must disclose his identity, role, and general nature of matter); N.H. Ethics Op. 2012-13/5 (2013) (lawyer seeking permission to access witness's restricted social media account must identify himself and his role); Pa. Formal Ethics Op. 2014-300 (2014) (lawyer seeking access to unrepresented person's social networking site must use real name and state purpose of request); Phila. Ethics Op. 2009-02 (2009) (lawyer may not use third party to gain access to adverse witness's social networking pages concealing "highly material fact" that he was looking for impeachment material); W. Va. Ethics Op. 2015-02 (2015) (lawyer contacting unrepresented person through social media must state name and purpose for contact); *see also* N.Y. Cnty. Ethics Op. 750 (2017) (lawyer may not send friend request on Snapchat to adverse party or witness because there is no means to disclose lawyer's role in pending adversarial proceeding prior to recipient acting on request). *See generally* Commercial & Fed. Litig. Section, N.Y. State Bar Ass'n, *Social Media Ethics Guidelines* (2014), *available at* http://www.nysba.org/workarea/DownloadAsset.aspx?id=47547; Shane Witnov, *Investigating Facebook: The Ethics of Using Social Networking Websites in Legal Investigations*, 28 Santa Clara Computer & High Tech. L.J. 31 (Nov. 2011).

For further discussion of accessing social media websites, see the annotations to Rules 3.5, 4.1, and 4.3.

## *Paragraph (d): Conduct Prejudicial to the Administration of Justice*

### RULE USUALLY APPLIED TO CONDUCT CONNECTED WITH PROCEEDINGS OF TRIBUNAL

Paragraph (d), identical to DR 1-102(A)(5) of the Model Code, prohibits a lawyer from engaging in "conduct that is prejudicial to the administration of justice." The rule is most often applied to conduct connected with proceedings before a tribunal. *See, e.g., In re Friedman*, 23 P.3d 620 (Alaska 2001) ("[t]he cases suggest that DR

1-102(A)(5) contemplates conduct which impedes or subverts the process of resolving disputes; it is conduct which frustrates the fair balance of interests or 'justice' essential to litigation or other proceedings"; thus, although lawyer's mishandling of client funds in trust account violated other ethics rules, it did not violate this rule); *People v. Jaramillo*, 35 P.3d 723 (Colo. O.P.D.J. 2001) (violation of Rule 8.4(d) "requires proof of some nexus between the conduct charged and an adverse effect upon the administration of justice"); *In re Carter*, 11 A.3d 1219 (D.C. 2011) (to violate rule, conduct must be improper, bear directly on judicial process, and "taint the judicial process in more than a *de minimis* way"; lawyer's failure to pay arbitration awards did "not bear directly upon the judicial process" and therefore did not violate rule); *In re Winkler*, 834 N.E.2d 85 (Ind. 2005) (suspending two prosecutors who stole notes from defense lawyer's legal pad after he left room to consult with client during deposition: "Not only did they potentially jeopardize a criminal prosecution, they also damaged the public's perception of the criminal justice system, attempted to evade the authority of the judge, and ignored the protections created by our rules of procedure."); *Iowa Supreme Court Att'y Disciplinary Bd. v. Kingery*, 871 N.W.2d 109 (Iowa 2015) ("dispositive inquiry" is whether lawyer's conduct hampered "efficient and proper operation of the courts or of ancillary systems upon which the courts rely"; neglect of criminal matters causing numerous delays violated rule); *In re Pyle*, 156 P.3d 1231 (Kan. 2007) (rule can be violated "even if a legal proceeding has ended and even if the lawyer stops somewhere short of spreading outright lies"; disciplined lawyer sent letters to people complaining disciplinary process "stacked against him"); *In re Bilbe*, 841 So. 2d 729 (La. 2003) (failure to pay court reporter does not violate rule); *Att'y Grievance Comm'n v. Elmendorf*, 946 A.2d 542 (Md. 2008) (lawyer violated rule by suggesting to acquaintance seeking no-fault divorce that she could avoid one-year separation requirement by lying to court about it); *Miss. Bar v. Rogers*, 731 So. 2d 1158 (Miss. 1999) (conduct must be "connected to judicial proceedings"; conversion of fees in connection with title work and loan closings did not violate rule); *In re Smith*, 848 P.2d 612 (Or. 1993) (lawyer must have engaged in improper conduct "in the course of some judicial proceeding or a matter directly related thereto," and conduct "must have caused or had the potential to cause . . . more than minimal harm"); *see also In re Schaeffer*, 45 A.3d 149 (Del. 2012) (lawyer involved in dispute with another lawyer called 911 and falsely reported "hostage situation"; false reporting to police is prejudicial to administration of justice because "filing of charges with the police is often a starting place for charges in the criminal justice system"); *cf. In re Discipline of Att'y*, 815 N.E.2d 1072 (Mass. 2004) (conduct that does not violate any other ethics rule cannot violate this rule "unless it is so 'egregious' and 'flagrantly violative of accepted professional norms' as to 'undermine the legitimacy of the judicial process'").

### • Broader Interpretation

The rule has also been applied to conduct not connected with proceedings before a tribunal. *See Fla. Bar v. Frederick*, 756 So. 2d 79 (Fla. 2000) (rule not limited to conduct affecting particular proceeding, but encompasses "conduct that prejudices our system of justice as a whole"; lawyer required clients to agree not to complain to disciplinary authorities about him as condition of releasing funds); *In re Mears*, 723 N.E.2d 873

(Ind. 2000) (lawyer serving as county judge used members of county staff to perform personal tasks); *Att'y Grievance Comm'n v. Penn*, 65 A.3d 125 (Md. 2013) (Rule 8.4(d) violated when lawyer engages in "conduct which erodes public confidence in the legal profession"; title insurer's claims counsel secretly formed law firm and referred work to own firm); *Att'y Grievance Comm'n v. Goodman*, 43 A.3d 988 (Md. 2012) ("commingling of personal and client funds, including the failure to maintain a separate trust account, is prejudicial to the administration of justice"); *In re Waite*, 782 N.W.2d 820 (Minn. 2010) ("We have never . . . limited the scope of conduct sanctionable under Rule 8.4(d)" to conduct before tribunals; failure to file tax returns); *In re Bruner*, 469 S.E.2d 55 (S.C. 1996) (real estate lawyer falsely certified to client's title insurer that all title insurance requirements met); *see also Lawyer Disciplinary Bd. v. Kupec*, 505 S.E.2d 619 (W. Va. 1998) (misuse of client trust account funds; citing cases in which lawyers found to have violated rule in matters "only tangentially related to litigation").

## Criminal Conduct

In some cases, the rule has been applied to a lawyer's criminal conduct. *See, e.g., In re Vanderslice*, 55 A.3d 322 (Del. 2012) (theft of $1,780 from law firm violated rule); *Att'y Grievance Comm'n v. Reno*, 83 A.3d 781 (Md. 2014) (lawyer gave boyfriend gun knowing his gun application had been denied by state police); *Att'y Grievance Comm'n v. Childress*, 770 A.2d 685 (Md. 2001) (rule encompasses criminal conduct by lawyer; lawyer used internet to solicit sex with underage girls); *In re Gherity*, 673 N.W.2d 474 (Minn. 2004) (convictions for assault and disorderly conduct violated Rule 8.4(b) and (d)). *But see Iowa Supreme Court Att'y Disciplinary Bd. v. Templeton*, 784 N.W.2d 761 (Iowa 2010) ("mere act of committing a crime does not constitute a violation of this rule"; no violation for criminal conduct related to peering into windows of house owned by several women); *State ex rel. Okla. Bar Ass'n v. Giger*, 37 P.3d 856 (Okla. 2001) (lawyer's six arrests for drug-related vehicular crimes not prejudicial to administration of justice; though potentially dangerous to lawyer and others, conduct did not interfere with any judicial proceeding or harm legal system as a whole).

### • *Intent Not an Element*

A lawyer need not have intended to prejudice the administration of justice to violate the rule. *See In re Alexander*, 300 P.3d 536 (Ariz. 2013) (Rule 8.4(d) requires no mental state other than negligence; lawyer's motives "immaterial"); *In re Kennedy*, 864 N.W.2d 342 (Minn. 2015) (whether lawyer intended to prejudice administration of justice not relevant to whether he violated Rule 8.4(d)).

## MISCONDUCT WHEN NOT REPRESENTING CLIENTS

A lawyer is subject to discipline under Rule 8.4(d) for conduct that does not involve the representation of a client. *See, e.g., Neal v. Clinton*, No. CIV 2000-5677, 2001 WL 34355768 (Ark. Cir. Ct. Jan. 19, 2001) ("evasive and misleading answers" in deposition amounted to conduct prejudicial to administration of justice), *discussed in* "Clinton Accepts Five-Year Suspension to End Disbarment Case, Criminal Probe," *ABA/BNA Lawyers' Manual on Professional Conduct*, 17 Law. Man. Prof. Conduct 73 (Current Reports, Jan. 31, 2001); *People v. Coulter*, 950 P.2d 176 (Colo. 1998) (lawyer acting as guardian ad litem appeared in court while intoxicated); *In re Mason*, 736 A.2d 1019 (D.C. 1999) (lawyer lied under oath to Federal Home Loan Bank Board in course of agency investigation); *In re Davidson*, 761 N.E.2d 854 (Ind. 2002) (lawyer facing prosecution on misdemeanor offenses failed to appear in court on three occasions); *Iowa Supreme Court Att'y Disciplinary Bd. v. Rhinehart*, 827 N.W.2d 169 (Iowa 2013) (although lawyer's fraudulent conduct in own divorce proceedings did not affect property distribution or support award, it necessitated additional court proceedings); *In re Mintz*, 317 P.3d 756 (Kan. 2014) (lawyer lied to police after finding girlfriend's body); *Att'y Grievance Comm'n v. Gore*, 845 A.2d 1204 (Md. 2004) ("well settled that willful failure to pay taxes constitutes conduct prejudicial to the administration of justice"); *In re Ring*, 692 N.E.2d 35 (Mass. 1998) (lawyer transferred $406,000 in marital assets to overseas account one day after being served with divorce papers); *In re Stoneburner*, 882 N.W.2d 200 (Minn. 2016) (forcibly hindering wife's attempt to report domestic violence to 911 operator); *In re Waite*, 782 N.W.2d 820 (Minn. 2010) (failure to file federal and state income tax returns); *In re Stanbury*, 561 N.W.2d 507 (Minn. 1997) (lawyer stopped payment on personal check tendered for court filing fee and refused to satisfy law library's judgment against him); *In re Isaacson*, 860 N.W.2d 490 (Wis. 2015) (lawyer serving as corporate officer engaged in pattern of bad-faith litigation involving making false and defamatory statements about judges, other lawyers, appointed officers, and third parties).

## RULE HAS WITHSTOOD SCRUTINY

The proscription against "conduct that is prejudicial to the administration of justice" found in Model Rule 8.4(d) and its Model Code counterpart, DR 1-102(A)(5), has long withstood constitutional challenges for vagueness and overbreadth. *See Howell v. State Bar*, 843 F.2d 205 (5th Cir. 1988) (denying vagueness challenge, in part because lawyers are professionals and "have the benefit of guidance provided by case law, court rules and the lore of the profession"); *In re Keiler*, 380 A.2d 119 (D.C. 1977) (rule written by and for lawyers; "The language of a rule setting guidelines for members of the bar need not meet the precise standards of clarity that might be required of rules of conduct for laymen."); *State v. Nelson*, 504 P.2d 211 (Kan. 1972) (rule not unconstitutionally vague; "It cannot be seriously contended that 'prejudicial' does not sufficiently define the degree of conduct which is expected of an attorney."); *In re Crossen*, 880 N.E.2d 352 (Mass. 2008) (provision not unconstitutionally vague; lawyer should have known that using threats to coerce law clerk into making damaging statements about judge was prejudicial to administration of justice); *In re Stanbury*, 561 N.W.2d 507 (Minn. 1997) (Rule 8.4(d) not impermissibly broad); *Comm. on Legal Ethics v. Douglas*, 370 S.E.2d 325 (W. Va. 1988) (general consensus that rule not unconstitutionally vague "because the standard is considered in light of the traditions of the legal profession and its established practices").

## ABUSIVE OR DISRUPTIVE BEHAVIOR

Conduct that is abusive or disruptive or that impedes the proper functioning of the legal system can violate Rule 8.4(d). *See Chief Disciplinary Counsel v. Rozbicki*, 167 A.3d 351 (Conn. 2017) (motions, memoranda, and oral argument tainted by repetitive and baseless attacks on integrity of two judges); *In re White*, 11 A.3d 1226 (D.C. 2011) (former government lawyer's representation of age discrimination plaintiff in federal court in violation of Rule 1.11 delayed and disrupted proceedings, resulted in court striking deposition, and threatened to give plaintiff unfair advantage in litigation); *Fla. Bar v. Ratiner*, 238 So. 3d 117 (Fla. 2018) (disrupting proceedings by kicking table where opposing counsel was sitting); *In re McClellan*, 754 N.E.2d 500 (Ind. 2001) (disparaging remarks in petition for rehearing, including statement that court's decision "reads (sic) like a bad lawyer joke," was "conduct that demeaned the judiciary and the legal profession"); *In re Clothier*, 344 P.3d 370 (Kan. 2015) (during show-cause hearing lawyer falsely accused judge of colluding with opposing counsel); *In re Small*, 294 P.3d 1165 (Kan. 2013) (use of threats and intimidation tactics toward opposing counsel, judge, and disciplinary authorities and "two hour battering of [former client] on cross-examination"); *In re Gilman*, 126 P.3d 1115 (Kan. 2006) (lawyer appeared in court after consuming several whiskeys, requiring judge to call recess to address lawyer's condition); *Att'y Grievance Comm'n v. Mixter*, 109 A.3d 1 (Md. 2015) (repeated misrepresentations to tribunals in order to browbeat opponents into complying with unnecessary discovery requests, abusive behavior toward colleagues, and regular attempts to obtain medical records irrelevant to various cases "purely to harass members of the public"); *Att'y Grievance Comm'n v. Mahone*, 76 A.3d 1198 (Md. 2013) (disrupting proceedings inside and outside courtroom); *In re Torgerson*, 870 N.W.2d 602 (Minn. 2015) (yelling at court staff); *Miss. Bar v. Lumumba*, 912 So. 2d 871 (Miss. 2005) (lawyer told judge he would "pay for justice" if necessary and that judge's "henchmen" were going to throw him out of courtroom, and told newspaper reporter that judge "had the judicial temperament of a barbarian"); *N.C. State Bar v. Foster*, 808 S.E.2d 920 (N.C. Ct. App. 2017) (lawyer used offensive and vulgar language when addressing magistrate); *Disciplinary Counsel v. LoDico*, 833 N.E.2d 1235 (Ohio 2005) (defense lawyer engaged in pattern of disruptive behavior during murder trial by speaking loudly at sidebars so jurors could hear his statements suggesting witnesses were lying, by throwing money and credit cards on bench in anticipation of sanctions, by telling judge "[go] ahead and fine me," and by making inappropriate "dramatic" facial expressions in front of jury as witnesses testified); *In re Jeffrey*, 898 P.2d 752 (Or. 1995) (on day set for trial, lawyer threatened to create reversible error by refusing to represent client responsibly); *Bd. of Prof'l Responsibility v. Slavin*, 145 S.W.3d 538 (Tenn. 2004) (lawyer made numerous disparaging remarks in court documents about administrative law judges, referring to one as "[p]etty, barbarous and cruel," and used peer review process to harass and attempt to intimidate judges; lawyer's speech not protected by First Amendment if "highly likely to obstruct or prejudice the administration of justice"); *see also In re McCool*, 172 So. 3d 1058 (La. 2015) (lawyer engaged in social media blitz in order to influence judges in pending litigation).

### • *Abusive Behavior toward Clients*

    Abusive behavior toward clients can also violate Rule 8.4(d). *See Fla. Bar v. Knowles*, 99 So. 3d 918 (Fla. 2012) (disparaging client's integrity in motions to withdraw); *In re Freeman*, 835 N.E.2d 494 (Ind. 2005) (lawyer responded to incarcerated client's request for file and refund of fees by sending letter threatening to "make trouble" for client if he ever sent another letter); *Att'y Grievance Comm'n v. Basinger,* 109 A.3d 1165 (Md. 2015) (lawyer sent insulting letters containing profane language to sister-in-law who was either client or former client); *State ex rel. Okla. Bar Ass'n v. Moody,* 394 P.3d 223 (Okla. 2017) (leaving threatening phone messages for client in attempt to get client to pay fee); *see also State ex rel. Counsel for Discipline v. Sipple,* 660 N.W.2d 502 (Neb. 2003) (lawyer attempted to coerce client to accept settlement offer and engaged in "campaign to intimidate" client by contacting judge and challenging client's truthfulness, and by telling opposing counsel he did not want client to receive larger settlement than was being offered).

### • Behavior toward Opposing Parties, Their Counsel, or Witnesses

Rule 8.4(d) encompasses abusive or uncivil behavior toward opposing counsel, as well as parties and witnesses. *See In re Fletcher,* 424 F.3d 783 (8th Cir. 2005) (pattern of unprofessional conduct "in an attempt to harass, humiliate and intimidate deponents and their counsel" by, for example, "selectively quoting deposition testimony in a way that grossly mischaracterized deponents' statements"); *People v. Maynard,* 275 P.3d 780 (Colo. O.P.D.J. 2010) (threatening to sue subpoenaed witnesses in attempt to keep them from testifying); *In re Abbott,* 925 A.2d 482 (Del. 2007) (briefs included personal attacks against opposing counsel and implied court was biased against client); *Fla. Bar v. Adams,* 198 So. 3d 593 (Fla. 2016) (lawyers improperly effectuated DUI arrest of opposing counsel and tried to cover up scheme); *In re Moore,* 665 N.E.2d 40 (Ind. 1996) (hitting opposing counsel hard enough to send him across table); *In re Greenburg,* 9 So. 3d 802 (La. 2009) (two lawyers exchanged vulgarities in open court, then fell to floor when one lawyer grabbed other); *In re Eisenstein,* 485 S.W.3d 759 (Mo. 2016) (sending threatening e-mail to opposing counsel); *State ex rel. Counsel for Discipline v. Island,* 894 N.W.2d 804 (Neb. 2017) (issuing press release suggesting prosecutor was attempting to force client/witness to perjure herself); *In re Moran,* 840 N.Y.S.2d 847 (App. Div. 2007) (posting on website information about confidential investigation into conduct of rival law firm); *In re Golden,* 496 S.E.2d 619 (S.C. 1998) (insulting and degrading comments to adverse party during deposition); *see also In re Hammer,* 784 S.E.2d 678 (S.C. 2016) (lawyer backing out of parking space hit car of process server and left scene to avoid personal service in family court matter). *But see In re Hurley,* 183 A.3d 703 (Del. 2018) (violation of Rule 4.4(a) but not Rule 8.4(d) by sending offensive letters to deputy attorneys general; no evidence conduct "affected performance of opposing counsel or had some other distinct impact on the judicial process").

### • Failure to Comply with Court Rules and Orders

Failure to comply with court rules and orders can violate Rule 8.4(d). *See People v. Roose,* 69 P.3d 43 (Colo. 2003) (leaving courtroom midtrial in defiance of judge's order); *In re Kline,* 311 P.3d 321 (Kan. 2013) (attorney general directed staff to attach sealed documents to brief in violation of court order); *In re Johnson,* 877 N.E.2d 249 (Mass. 2007) (posting on website information court had impounded in child molestation case; lawyer not free to ignore court orders and challenge them for first time in disciplinary proceeding); *In re Estrada*, 143 P.3d 731 (N.M. 2006) (failure to respond properly to discovery requests); *Disciplinary Counsel v. Rohrer*, 919 N.E.2d 180 (Ohio 2009) (leaking information to local newspaper in violation of court order); *In re Nelson*, 750 S.E.2d 85 (S.C. 2013) (assistant prosecutor exchanged more than thirty phone calls and text messages with cousin serving as juror in criminal trial handled by other prosecutors); *Cody v. Bd. of Prof'l Responsibility*, 471 S.W.3d 420 (Tenn. 2015) (continuing to represent clients after being disqualified and disciplined for conduct); *Gilbert v. Utah State Bar*, 379 P.3d 1247 (Utah 2016) (lawyer claiming to have good-faith belief court order was invalid simply ignored it "without taking any action to appeal, stay, or otherwise object to the order"); *In re McGrath*, 280 P.3d 1091 (Wash. 2012) (lawyer falsely certified that he made reasonable inquiry into accuracy of discovery responses); *see also Daniels v. Statewide Grievance Comm.*, 804 A.2d 1027 (Conn. App. Ct. 2002) (failure to pay judgment on time); *Fla. Bar v. Walton*, 952 So. 2d 510 (Fla. 2006) (failure to record satisfaction of judgment despite statutory duty); *In re Hemphill*, 971 N.E.2d 665 (Ind. 2012) (lawyer concerned about safety of client/father's children picked them up from school and did not inform mother of their whereabouts; lawyer "took matters into her own hands and acted precipitously in disregard for the laws and agencies designed to deal with allegations of child abuse"); *In re Guirard*, 11 So. 3d 1017 (La. 2009) (permitting nonlawyer assistants to engage in unauthorized practice of law); *In re Westby*, 639 N.W.2d 358 (Minn. 2002) (practicing law while suspended). *But see In re Lawrence*, 256 P.3d 1070 (Or. 2011) (release of partial transcript of juvenile hearing to press did not violate rule when press had already reported on hearing; no showing that conduct harmed or had potential to harm proceeding or substantive rights of client, other defendants, victims, or state); *Utah State Bar v. Jardine*, 289 P.3d 516 (Utah 2012) (single instance of failing to appear at hearing, causing no harm to client, did not violate rule).

The willful failure to pay court-ordered child or spousal support can also violate Rule 8.4(d). *See, e.g., People v. Verce*, 286 P.3d 1107 (Colo. O.P.D.J. 2012); *In re Vanderbilt*, 253 P.3d 774 (Kan. 2011); *In re Giberson*, 581 N.W.2d 351 (Minn. 1998); *see also Disciplinary Counsel v. McCord*, 905 N.E.2d 1182 (Ohio 2009) (lawyer challenging child support determination "needlessly prolonged" litigation, during which time he failed to make payments, engaged in "dilatory" tactics, and was held in contempt at least twice); *In re Taylor*, 768 A.2d 1273 (Vt. 2000) (lawyer on inactive status suspended for failure to pay child support).

### • *Failure to Cooperate with Disciplinary Investigation*

The failure to cooperate with bar counsel can also violate Rule 8.4(d) as well as the more specific Rule 8.1. *See People v. Nelson*, 35 P.3d 641 (Colo. O.P.D.J. 2001); *In re Cater*, 887 A.2d 1 (D.C. 2005); *In re Stanbury*, 614 N.W.2d 209 (Minn. 2000); *In re Skagen*, 149 P.3d 1171 (Or. 2006); *In re Poole*, 193 P.3d 1064 (Wash. 2008); *see also Fla. Bar v. Walton*, 952 So. 2d 510 (Fla. 2006) (telling disciplinary authorities that complainant was a "liar" and had "some mental disorder"). *Compare Att'y Grievance Comm. v. Phillips*, 155 A.3d 476 (Md. 2017) (refusing to speak with bar counsel and filing frivolous motion to quash subpoena obstructed investigation "in a manner prejudicial to the administration of justice"), *with Att'y Grievance Comm'n v. Butler*, 107 A.3d 1220 (Md.

2015) (choosing to ignore bar counsel "impeded the investigative process but did not prejudice the administration of justice"; violation of Rule 8.1(b) but not Rule 8.4(d)).

• *Abuse of Process/Frivolous Claims*

A lawyer's abuse of legal process can violate Rule 8.4(d). *See In re Alexander*, 300 P.3d 536 (Ariz. 2013) (deputy county attorney maintained baseless RICO suit against judges); *In re Olsen*, 326 P.3d 1004 (Colo. 2014) (advancing "frivolous arguments" and making "repetitive and often unsupported motions"); *Henry v. Statewide Grievance Comm.*, 957 A.2d 547 (Conn. App. Ct. 2008) (inducing court to issue bench warrant for physician by falsely stating physician failed to appear for deposition); *In re Spikes*, 881 A.2d 1118 (D.C. 2005) (baseless defamation suit based upon complaints made to bar counsel); *Fla. Bar v. Committe*, 916 So. 2d 741 (Fla. 2005) (lawyer who was defendant in collection case filed two frivolous lawsuits to harass lawyer for creditor); *Iowa Supreme Court Att'y Disciplinary Bd. v. Barnhill*, 885 N.W.2d 408 (Iowa 2016) (frivolous claims and discovery violations); *In re Raspanti*, 8 So. 3d 526 (La. 2009) (filing defamation action based upon disciplinary complaint filed against him); *Att'y Grievance Comm'n v. Powers*, 164 A.3d 138 (Md. 2017) (in attempt to collect fees, lawyer filed federal suit against former client and new lawyer in state where neither defendant had any contacts); *Att'y Grievance Comm'n v. Cocco*, 109 A.3d 1176 (Md. 2015) (presenting invalid subpoena to third parties and threatening them with lawsuit if they did not comply); *In re Lupo*, 851 N.E.2d 404 (Mass. 2006) (frivolous suit against lawyer who filed grievance against him); *In re Hess*, 406 S.W.3d 37 (Mo. 2013) (frivolous claims and liens against former clients; fact that lawyer acting as litigant and had his own lawyer was no defense to discipline); *see also In re Brunton*, 144 P.3d 606 (Kan. 2006) (failing to amend client's bankruptcy plan knowing it purported to discharge nondischargeable debt); *Columbus Bar Ass'n v. Finneran*, 687 N.E.2d 405 (Ohio 1997) (lawyer routinely failed to respond to discovery requests, and voluntarily dismissed cases and refiled them later in hope of obtaining better settlement offers).

## SEXUAL MISCONDUCT

Inappropriate conduct of a sexual nature may violate Rule 8.4(d). *In re Manson*, 676 N.E.2d 347 (Ind. 1997) (lawyer, lieutenant in Judge Advocate General Corps in Naval Reserve, engaged in sexual activity with client in Naval Legal Services courtroom); *Att'y Grievance Comm'n v. Marcalus*, 112 A.3d 375 (Md. 2015) (sexting with unrepresented opposing party in custody modification proceeding); *In re Bulmer*, 899 N.W.2d 183 (Minn. 2017) (having sexual relations with client and witness in separate matters); *In re Weinstock*, 669 N.Y.S.2d 368 (App. Div. 1998) (lawyer assigned to represent indigent clients in family court had sexual encounters with client); *Disciplinary Counsel v. Krieger*, 843 N.E.2d 765 (Ohio 2006) (public defender engaged in sexual relationship with client and concealed it from authorities); *In re Munden*, 559 S.E.2d 589 (S.C. 2002) (adulterous relationship with client's spouse); *see also In re Dean*, 129 P.3d 943 (Ariz. 2006) (prosecutor had romantic relationship with superior court judge before whom she appeared 485 times); *People v. Biddle*, 180 P.3d 461 (Colo. O.P.D.J. 2007) (lawyer serving as magistrate and then as judge had affair with deputy district attorney who practiced in his courtroom); *In re Pattison*, 121 P.3d 423 (Kan. 2005) (lawyer serving as guardian ad litem for four children failed to withdraw after he became "infatuated" with children's mother); *Att'y Grievance Comm'n v. Hall*, 969 A.2d 953 (Md. 2009) (sexual relationship with client despite "knowledge of her fragile emotional state"); *Lawyer Disciplinary Bd. v. Chittum*, 689 S.E.2d 811 (W. Va. 2010) (flirtatious telephone and letter-writing relationship with incarcerated client in attempt to establish sexual relationship violated Rule 8.4(a) and (d)). *But see Iowa Supreme Court Att'y Disciplinary Bd. v. Monroe*, 784 N.W.2d 784 (Iowa 2010) (sexual relationship between lawyer and client does not automatically prejudice administration of justice; Rule 8.4(d) violation requires "proof the relationship actually hampered the proper functioning of the court system"). Sexual harassment is discussed under Rule 8.4(g) below.

## ABUSE OF PUBLIC OFFICE OR PRIVATE POSITION OF TRUST

Rule 8.4(d) can be violated by abuse of public office or of "positions of private trust such as trustee, executor, administrator, guardian, agent and officer, director or manager of a corporation or other organization." Rule 8.4, cmt. [7]. *See In re Alexander*, 300 P.3d 536 (Ariz. 2013) (deputy county attorney maintained baseless RICO suit against judges); *In re Favata*, 119 A.3d 1283 (Del. 2015) (prosecutor expressed personal opinion about defendant's guilt and vouched for credibility of witness); *In re Howes*, 52 A.3d 1 (D.C. 2012) (prosecutor issued witness vouchers to ineligible people and concealed improper payments from court and defendants); *In re Christoff*, 690 N.E.2d 1135 (Ind. 1997) (county prosecutor and deputy prosecutor renewed long-dormant criminal investigation and filed disciplinary complaint against lawyer seeking election as prosecutor); *In re Holste*, 358 P.3d 850 (Kan. 2015) (county attorney with part-time practice threatened to file felony charges against opposing party in civil matter if he did not withdraw motion to set aside default judgment); *In re Campbell*, 199 P.3d 776 (Kan. 2009) (county prosecutor allowed parents of minors who attended party to view photos taken at party of minors consuming alcohol and of minor sexual abuse victim engaged in intercourse with minor perpetrator); *In re Swarts*, 30 P.3d 1011 (Kan. 2001) (county attorney made arrangements for parents to bring their children to courthouse after business hours for public paddlings); *In re King*, 33 So. 3d 873 (La. 2010) (lawyer serving as district judge personally solicited campaign contributions and required court staff to campaign for him, then lied about it under oath); *In re Schwehm*, 860 So. 2d 1108 (La. 2003) (malfeasance by elected justice of the peace); *Att'y Grievance Comm'n v. Hodes*, 105 A.3d 533 (Md. 2014) (abusing position as trustee of client trust and using trust funds to pay personal debts); *Att'y Grievance Comm'n v. McDonald*, 85 A.3d 117 (Md. 2014) (deputy assistant state's attorney fixed tickets for and interfered with embezzlement investigation of employee with whom he was infatuated); *In re Finneran*, 919 N.E.2d 698 (Mass. 2010) (former speaker of Massachusetts House of Representatives gave false testimony in federal voting rights lawsuit about his role in redistricting plan); *In re Blakely*, 772 N.W.2d 516 (Minn. 2009) (judge negotiated and received substantial fee reduction from personal lawyer while appointing her to provide mediation services in matters pending before him); *Disciplinary Counsel v. Phillabaum*, 44 N.E.3d 271 (Ohio 2015) (assistant prosecutor signed indictment knowing it contained false statement); *Disciplinary Counsel v.*

*Gaul*, 936 N.E.2d 28 (Ohio 2010) (judge made comments on and off record indicating bias against defendant); *In re Harding*, 104 P.3d 1220 (Utah 2004) (district court judge pleaded guilty to drug charges after having "publicly maintain[ed] his innocence and malign[ed] his accusers for over a year"); *Lawyer Disciplinary Bd. v. Sims*, 574 S.E.2d 795 (W. Va. 2002) (county prosecutor repeatedly used prehearing publicity to prejudice proceedings); *Bd. of Prof'l Responsibility v. Murray*, 143 P.3d 353 (Wyo. 2006) (after deadlocked jury discharged, prosecutor made derogatory remark about jury member who held out for acquittal); *see also In re Gelof*, 142 A.3d 506 (Del. 2016) (deputy attorney general convinced security officer to pull gun on colleague in courthouse witness room as practical joke); *In re Flatt-Moore*, 959 N.E.2d 241 (Ind. 2012) (surrendering prosecutorial discretion in plea negotiations entirely to pecuniary demands of crime victim); *In re Kline*, 311 P.3d 321 (Kan. 2013) (attorney general failed to inform grand jury of relevant statute and of "the only federal court decision interpreting" statute, which "specifically rejected his assessment of that statute"); *In re Cofield*, 937 So. 2d 330 (La. 2006) (lawyer acting as trustee for mentally disabled client loaned money to himself from trust and took advantage of client's diminished capacity in attempt to thwart family's effort to remove him as trustee); *Lawyer Disciplinary Bd. v. Stanton*, 760 S.E.2d 453 (W. Va. 2014) (improper use of status as lawyer to further romantic relationship with vulnerable incarcerated client). *Compare In re Karavidas*, 999 N.E.2d 296 (Ill. 2013) (lawyer's breach of fiduciary duty while serving as executor of father's estate did not violate rule "because he was not acting as an attorney and he was not involved in the judicial process at the time of the breach"), *with Att'y Grievance Comm'n v. Storch*, 124 A.3d 204 (Md. 2015) (lawyer serving as personal representative of estate violated rule by failing to timely file interim accounts, appear for hearings, or comply with court order removing him from position).

## CONDUCT INVOLVING DISHONESTY: DECEPTION, FRAUD, OR THEFT

Conduct that is deceitful can violate Rule 8.4(d). *See In re Mason*, 736 A.2d 1019 (D.C. 1999) (lying under oath to Federal Home Loan Bank Board in course of agency investigation); *Fla. Bar v. Gardiner*, 183 So. 3d 240 (Fla. 2014) (judge in capital murder case failed to disclose her "significant personal and emotional relationship" with lead prosecutor); *In re Petition for Review of Hearing Comm. of Prof'l Conduct Bd.*, 102 P.3d 1119 (Idaho 2004) (prosecutor obtained grand jury transcript without court order and gave copy to third party engaged in civil litigation against defendant; actual prejudice in particular case not necessary for ethics rule violation); *In re Gamble*, 338 P.3d 576 (Kan. 2014) (lawyer representing biological father in adoption matter sent message containing false statements and legal advice to child's unrepresented teenage mother in attempt to coerce her to revoke her consent to adoption); *In re Hunsaker*, 217 P.3d 962 (Kan. 2009) (providing financial assistance to son who was evading criminal prosecution); *Att'y Grievance Comm'n v. Sheinbein*, 812 A.2d 981 (Md. 2002) (lawyer helped fugitive son flee country); *In re Czarnik*, 759 N.W.2d 217 (Minn. 2009) (lying in deposition violates rule, even if not material; duty to answer truthfully does not depend on materiality); *Cleveland Metro. Bar Ass'n v. Azman*, 66 N.E.3d 695 (Ohio 2016) (discharged lawyer accessed firm e-mails and deleted messages after former employer threatened legal action against him); *Dayton Bar Ass'n v. Parisi*, 965 N.E.2d 268 (Ohio 2012) (while guardianship petition was pending for client lawyer claimed was incompetent, lawyer had client sign document designating lawyer attorney-in-fact, and used it to pay her own fees without court approval); *In re Conteh*, 284 P.3d 724 (Wash. 2012) (lawyer lied about his employment history on asylum application); *see also In re Hopkins*, 687 A.2d 938 (D.C. 1996) (lawyer failed to take appropriate remedial action once she learned client took funds belonging to another beneficiary of probate estate); N.J. Ethics Op. 698 (2005) (lawyers may not imply in letters to prospective clients that prosecutors, police officers, and IRS regularly behave unethically). *But see Att'y Grievance Comm'n v. Kalil*, 936 A.2d 854 (Md. 2007) (rule not violated by lawyer who placed three calls to Merit Systems Protection Board falsely stating he was acting on behalf of D.C. bar counsel; calls were "minimally intrusive" and did not disrupt board's work).

### • *Lying to or Misleading Courts*

Lying to or misleading a court can violate Rule 8.4(d). *See In re Alcorn*, 41 P.3d 600 (Ariz. 2002) (lawyers for one defendant secretly colluded with plaintiff in conducting sham trial to create record to use against other defendant); *In re Forrester*, 916 So. 2d 647 (Fla. 2005) (falsely stating in pleading that individual was "convicted felon"); *In re Warrum*, 724 N.E.2d 1097 (Ind. 2000) (lawyer seeking increased child support failed to inform court of out-of-state decree governing post-dissolution matters); *In re Small*, 294 P.3d 1165 (Kan. 2013) (practice of signing signature page, giving it to employee to notarize, and attaching affidavit later); *Ky. Bar Ass'n v. Jacob*, 950 S.W.2d 832 (Ky. 1997) (lying on interrogatory about insurance coverage of car driven by daughter); *Att'y Grievance Comm'n v. Geesing*, 80 A.3d 718 (Md. 2014) (lawyer instructed nonlawyer staff to "robo-sign" his name to affidavits submitted in mortgage foreclosures and to falsely notarize them); *Att'y Grievance Comm'n v. Paul*, 31 A.3d 512 (Md. 2011) (lawyer cut and pasted opposing counsel's signature onto stipulation filed with court); *Cleveland Metro. Bar Ass'n v. Donchatz*, 80 N.E.3d 444 (Ohio 2017) (filing motion containing false statements and submitting "stipulated entry and consent judgment" to which other parties had not agreed); *State ex rel. Okla. Bar Ass'n v. Gassaway*, 196 P.3d 495 (Okla. 2008) (obtaining court orders by misleading judges); *In re Howard*, 127 A.3d 914 (R.I. 2015), and *In re Thurston*, 127 A.3d 917 (R.I. 2015) (pattern of filing documents with bankruptcy court without obtaining debtors' signatures and containing inaccurate disclosures of compensation).

### • *Representation without Authorization*

A lawyer who purports to represent a party without authorization violates Rule 8.4(d). *See In re Jarvis*, 349 P.3d 445 (Kan. 2015) (lawyer took legal action on behalf of client with diminished capacity without obtaining authorization from client's guardian and conservator); *In re Schaefer*, 25 P.3d 191 (Nev. 2001) (without any authorization, lawyer filed frivolous lawsuit purporting to represent trust as plaintiff); *In re Baker*, 797 N.Y.S.2d 200 (App. Div. 2005) (at request of longtime friend, lawyer agreed to represent person seeking divorce and let friend act as person's agent; after divorce judgment entered, lawyer learned that client—with whom he never met—was inmate at correctional facility and had no knowledge of proceedings); *Disciplinary Counsel v. Mamich*, 928 N.E.2d 691 (Ohio 2010) (lawyer represented client's daughter in debt collection case without her knowledge or consent); *see also In re Eugster*, 209 P.3d 435 (Wash. 2009) (after client fired him, lawyer petitioned court to have guardian appointed for client, and represented to court that he was still her lawyer). The unauthorized practice of law can itself violate the rule. *See In re Thomas*, 962 N.E.2d 454 (Ill. 2012) (suspended lawyer's unauthorized practice of law violated rule by jeopardizing interests of clients, and, in bankruptcy case, jeopardizing interests of creditors); *In re Hall*, 377 P.3d 1149 (Kan. 2016) (suspended lawyer improperly obtained pro hac vice admission and represented two criminal defendants). For further discussion on the unauthorized practice of law, see the annotation to Rule 5.5.

## LACK OF COMPETENCE OR DILIGENCE

Negligent or incompetent representation can violate Rule 8.4(d). *See Walker v. Supreme Court Comm. on Prof'l Conduct*, 246 S.W.3d 418 (Ark. 2007) (suspended lawyer agreed to represent personal injury client and then failed to file suit before statute of limitations had run); *People v. Crist*, 948 P.2d 1020 (Colo. 1997) (lawyer abandoned law practice and left state, leaving some sixty pending cases); *In re Cutright*, 910 N.E.2d 581 (Ill. 2009) (lawyer's neglect of estate while representing executor violated rule; two heirs died before receiving their share of any distribution and others had to wait seventeen years before receiving theirs); *In re McCord*, 722 N.E.2d 820 (Ind. 2000) ("extraordinarily deficient" handling of client's claim); *Iowa Supreme Court Att'y Disciplinary Bd. v. Curtis*, 749 N.W.2d 694 (Iowa 2008) (failing to meet deadlines in post-conviction relief action and handling estate matter incompetently); *In re Swisher*, 41 P.3d 847 (Kan. 2002) (failure to obtain service in personal injury case or to prosecute workers' compensation case); *Att'y Grievance Comm'n v. Smith*, 109 A.3d 1184 (Md. 2015) (gross negligence in child sexual abuse case by prosecutor who failed to provide victim and her foster mother with crucial information relating to prosecution); *Att'y Grievance Comm'n v. Walker-Turner*, 51 A.3d 553 (Md. 2012) (failure to appear at trial); *In re Cohen & Slamowitz, LLP*, 981 N.Y.S.2d 100 (App. Div. 2014) ("pattern and practice" of pursuing debt collection actions without reasonable investigation to verify identity of alleged debtors and their property and validity of alleged debts); *State ex rel. Okla. Bar Ass'n v. Benefield*, 125 P.3d 1191 (Okla. 2005) (criminal defense lawyer neglected client matters and failed to appear for court hearings, leading judges to appoint public defenders for clients); *In re Atwater*, 725 S.E.2d 686 (S.C. 2012) (nearly decade-long neglect of client matter); *cf. In re LaJeunesse*, 416 P.3d 1122 (Utah 2018) (ALJ did not violate Rule 8.4(d) by adopting good-faith but mistaken interpretation of law). See the annotations to Rule 1.1 (Competence) and Rule 1.3 (Diligence).

## UNETHICAL SETTLEMENT INDUCEMENTS

Attempting to settle a matter through unethical or illegal means can violate Rule 8.4(d). *See Iowa Supreme Court Att'y Disciplinary Bd. v. Buchanan*, 757 N.W.2d 251 (Iowa 2008) (settlement proposal included offer to destroy evidence of purported forgery and agreement not to cooperate with criminal investigation); *In re Kennedy*, 864 N.W.2d 342 (Minn. 2015) (lawyer sent letters to criminal defense counsel implying that client would not testify in criminal matter if client was paid $300,000 to settle civil claim); *State v. Koenig*, 769 N.W.2d 378 (Neb. 2009) (lawyer representing client charged with violating vehicle registration law sent letter to chief deputy county attorney alleging that newly elected county attorney was in violation of same law, but lawyer would keep quiet if client's case dismissed); *In re Geoghan*, 686 N.Y.S.2d 839 (App. Div. 1999) (lawyer offered to have client testify falsely in criminal matter in exchange for defendant's settlement of civil matter); *Disciplinary Counsel v. Doumbas*, 76 N.E.3d 1185 (Ohio 2017) (trying to bribe sexual assault victims by offering substantial payments as "civil settlements" to induce them to support leniency at client's sentencing hearing); *cf. In re Coleman*, 295 S.W.3d 857 (Mo. 2009) (lawyer "wasted judicial resources" by filing motion to enforce prohibited agreement purporting to give him sole right to settle client's case).

An agreement prohibiting a client from complaining to disciplinary authorities or requiring a client to withdraw a disciplinary complaint violates Rule 8.4(d). *See In re Martin*, 67 A.3d 1032 (D.C. 2013) (well settled that entering into settlement agreement with client requiring client to either refrain from filing or withdraw bar complaint violates rule; collecting cases); *Fla. Bar v. Frederick*, 756 So. 2d 79 (Fla. 2000) (as condition of releasing funds to clients, lawyer required them to agree not to complain to disciplinary authorities about him and to withdraw complaints already filed); *In re Johnson*, 877 N.E.2d 249 (Mass. 2007) (lawyer posted on her website confidential information about former clients, saying she might remove information if clients withdrew their bar complaint); *In re Abrams*, 767 N.E.2d 15 (Mass. 2002) (lawyer acting through business associate offered to pay client $20,000 to withdraw bar complaint); *Lawyer Disciplinary Bd. v. Artimez*, 540 S.E.2d 156 (W. Va. 2000) (lawyer who had sexual relationship with client's wife agreed to pay client in exchange for client's agreement not to complain to disciplinary authorities about it); Mo. Formal Ethics Op. 122 (2006) (may not enter settlement agreement that requires party to withdraw, refrain from filing, or decline to cooperate with disciplinary complaint); N.J. Ethics Op. 721 (2011) (asking client to withdraw or refrain from filing ethics complaint as condition of settling dispute with lawyer violates Rule 8.4(d)).

### • *Threatening Prosecution*

Threatening to press criminal charges or to file a disciplinary grievance to gain advantage in a civil matter may violate Rule 8.4(d). *See Ligon v. Stilley*, 371 S.W.3d 615 (Ark. 2010) (lawyer threatened judge with criminal prosecution and disciplinary proceedings and threatened to file and then filed grievances with bar authorities against opposing counsel in attempt to gain advantage in civil matter); *In re Campanella*, 56 N.E.3d 631 (Ind. 2016) (threatening to file bar grievance if settlement demand was not met); *In re Pyle*, 91 P.3d 1222 (Kan. 2004) (threatening to report opposing counsel to disciplinary authorities unless case settled within twenty days); *In re Ulanowski*, 800 N.W.2d 785 (Minn. 2011) (threatening prosecution to coerce payment in civil matter violates Rule 8.4(d)); *see also In re Young*, 621 S.E.2d 359 (S.C. 2005) (violation of state ethics rule prohibiting lawyers from threatening criminal prosecution to gain advantage in civil matter also constituted conduct prejudicial to administration of justice). This type of conduct may also violate Rule 8.4(b); see the discussion above.

### • *Plea Agreements*

State ethics opinions have advised that prosecutors and criminal defense counsel can run afoul of Rule 8.4(d) by participating in plea deals requiring defendants to waive important rights. *See* Ind. Ethics Op. 2005-2 (2005) (prosecutor and defense lawyer would violate Rule 8.4(d) by entering release-dismissal agreement requiring defendant to waive civil claims against public entity); Kan. Ethics Op. 17-02 (2017) (violation of Rule 8.4(d) for prosecutor or defense counsel to seek waiver of prosecutorial misconduct or ineffective assistance claims by defendant); Nev. Ethics Op. 48 (2011) (defense counsel may not include waiver of ineffective assistance of counsel claims in plea agreement); N.Y. State Ethics Op. 1098 (2016) (prosecutors may not routinely offer plea agreements requiring defendants to waive ineffective assistance claims); S.C. Ethics Op. 05-17 (2005) (solicitor engaged in plea negotiations may not offer or accept release-dismissal agreement that provides for dismissal of criminal charges in exchange for defendant releasing all government employees and entities from all claims arising out of incident); *see also* Fla. Ethics Op. 12-1 (2012) (prosecutor who offers plea agreement conditioned upon defendant's waiver of claims of ineffective assistance of counsel and prosecutorial misconduct violates Rule 8.4(a) and (d)); Mo. Formal Ethics Op. 126 (2009) (conduct prejudicial to administration of justice for prosecutor to negotiate plea agreement in which defendant waives post-conviction claims of ineffective assistance of counsel or prosecutorial misconduct); Ohio Sup. Ct. Ethics Op. 2001-6 (2001) (same); *cf.* Ky. Ethics Op. E-435 (2012) (prosecutor may not propose plea agreement requiring defendant to waive claim of ineffective assistance of counsel; Rule 8.4(a) violation); Nev. Ethics Op. 48 (2011) (same); Va. Ethics Op. 1957 (2011) (same). *But see* Or. Ethics Op. 2005-113 (2005) (prosecutor may offer plea bargain requiring defendant to waive civil remedies against arresting officers and their government employers or requiring simultaneous resolution of civil forfeiture proceeding prosecutor is bringing against defendant). Note that participation in these types of plea agreements may violate Rule 3.8 for prosecutors and Rule 1.7(a) and/ or 1.8(h) for defense lawyers. Release-dismissal agreements are also discussed in the annotation to Rule 3.8.

## CONDUCT DESIGNED TO FORCE DISQUALIFICATION OR RECUSAL

Trying to force a judge's recusal or a lawyer's disqualification can also violate Rule 8.4(d). *See In re Mole*, 822 F.3d 798 (5th Cir. 2016) (lawyer hired friend of judge as co-counsel in attempt to force judge's recusal); *Grievance Adm'r v. Fried*, 570 N.W.2d 262 (Mich. 1997) (lawyers participated as co-counsel in suits for sole purpose of obtaining recusals of judges with whom they had familial relationships); *Bd. of Prof'l Responsibility v. Davidson*, 205 P.3d 1008 (Wyo. 2009) (in effort to force recusal, lawyer recklessly accused judge of engaging in improper ex parte communication with opposing counsel); N.J. Ethics Op. 703 (2006) (violation of Rule 8.4(d) for lawyer to advise clients to contact other lawyers on pretext of seeking representation in order to disqualify those lawyers from representing adverse party); Utah Ethics Op. 01-03 (2001) (lawyer may not bring lawyer from judge's former firm into case in attempt to force judge's recusal); *see also In re Curry*, 880 N.E.2d 388 (Mass. 2008), and *In re Crossen*, 880 N.E.2d 352 (Mass. 2008) (lawyers attempted to obtain judge's recusal by arranging and secretly recording sham interview with judge's former law clerk and trying to coerce clerk into making damaging statements about judge).

## Paragraph (e): Suggesting Ability to Influence Government Agencies or Officials Improperly

### GENERAL PROHIBITION

Pursuant to paragraph (e), a lawyer may not "state or imply an ability to influence improperly a government agency or official or to achieve results by means that violate the Rules of Professional Conduct or other law." *See In re Reines*, 771 F.3d 1326 (Fed. Cir. 2014) (forwarding to clients and potential clients e-mail from judge praising his legal skills; message and lawyer's accompanying comments implied "special relationship" with judge); *In re Gorecki*, 802 N.E.2d 1194 (Ill. 2003) (former assistant state's attorney left message on answering machine of acquaintance suggesting acquaintance's boyfriend could get job by bribing local politician); *In re Johnson*, 74 N.E.3d 550 (Ind. 2017) (public defender's threats against ex-girlfriend suggested he could influence her probation officer and judge in criminal case against her); *In re Smith*, 991 N.E.2d 106 (Ind. 2013) (writing book with information about former client, dropping names of government officials to imply lawyer had ability to influence them improperly); *In re Holste*, 358 P.3d 850 (Kan. 2015) (county attorney with part-time private practice threatened to bring criminal charges against opposing party in civil litigation in order to benefit client in that matter); *In re Swarts*, 30 P.3d 1011 (Kan. 2001) (county attorney implied he could influence special prosecutor); *In re Dickson*, 968 So. 2d 136 (La. 2007) (criminal defense lawyer asked client for money to pay off judge and district attorney); *In re Andrade*, 736 N.W.2d 603 (Minn. 2007) (lawyer attempted to swindle money from client by saying it was needed to bribe police official); *State v. Koenig*, 769 N.W.2d 378 (Neb. 2009) (lawyer representing client charged with violating vehicle registration law sent letter to chief deputy county attorney alleging newly elected county attorney was in violation of same law but lawyer would keep quiet if client's case dismissed); *Cuyahoga City Bar Ass'n v. Wise*, 842 N.E.2d 35 (Ohio 2006) (lawyer representing parents in child custody dispute with child's aunt threatened to bring kidnapping charges against aunt, mentioning county prosecutor was his "friend"); *State ex rel. Okla. Bar Ass'n v. Moon*, 295 P.3d 1 (Okla. 2012) (lawyer arrested on drunk-driving charges "invoked the names of respected members of the legal community in an attempt to avoid prosecution and gain favorable treatment"); *In re Pstrak*, 575 S.E.2d 559 (S.C. 2003) (lawyer representing clients charged with traffic offenses falsely told court clerks he was town prosecutor and knew specific government officials, and suggested one client would make contribution to charity as "good-faith gesture"); *In re Bennett*, 376 N.W.2d 861 (Wis. 1985) (allowing client to believe bankruptcy-related matter would be resolved in some "extra-legal" way); Ohio Sup. Ct. Ethics Op. 2014-1 (2014) (lawyer who discloses involvement in presiding judge's election campaign to opposing counsel must not do so in way that "[conveys] an impression that the lawyer is in particular good favor with the judge"); *see also In re Mole*, 822 F.3d 798 (5th Cir. 2016) (attempting to effectuate judge's recusal by hiring judge's friend as co-counsel violates Rules 8.4(d) and (e)); *In re Pavilack*, 488 S.E.2d 309

(S.C. 1997) (lawyer used commercials in which police officer requests lawyer to come to accident scene to determine who was at fault and lawyer directs police officer to interview accident victims; decided under Rule 7.1(b)).

## APPLICATION TO JUDGES

The proscription against implying an ability to use influence improperly extends to lawyers who serve or have served as judges. *See In re Chiles*, 495 S.E.2d 202 (S.C. 1998) (while municipal judge, lawyer arranged dismissal of charges against friend for driving under influence and driving with suspended license); ABA Formal Ethics Op. 95-391 (1995) (former judge's use of title "Judge" in practice of law may constitute professional misconduct under Rule 8.4(e); ex-judge free to describe judicial experience, but descriptions should not imply special influence); Ohio Sup. Ct. Ethics Op. 2013-3 (2013) (violation of Rule 8.4(e) for former judge to use judicial title while engaged in practice of law or provision of law-related services, or for "acting" or "private" judges to use title outside judicial duties); Or. Ethics Op. 2005-31 (rev. 2015) (lawyer who serves as part-time justice of peace or state legislator may not permit employees of his private law office to answer phones with "Judge ___'s office" or "Senator ___'s office"); Joanne Pelton Pitulla, *Trading on Titles*, 6 Prof. Law., no. 4, at 14 (Aug. 1995); *see also* ABA Model Code of Judicial Conduct (2010) (Rule 1.3 prohibits judges from using or allowing others to use judicial office for personal gain, and Rule 2.4(c) prohibits judges from conveying, or allowing others to convey, impression that "any person or organization is in a position to influence the judge").

## *Paragraph (f): Assisting Judicial Misconduct*

Paragraph (f) prohibits a lawyer from knowingly assisting a judicial officer in conduct that violates the applicable rules of judicial conduct. *See In re Wilder*, 764 N.E.2d 617 (Ind. 2002) (lawyer obtained ex parte injunction without following proper procedures, for which judge issuing order was suspended for violating Code of Judicial Conduct); *In re White*, 996 So. 2d 266 (La. 2008) (lawyer convicted of misprision of felony for failure to report judge's conspiracy to deprive litigant of right to trial before impartial tribunal); *In re LeBlanc*, 972 So. 2d 315 (La. 2007) (lawyer acceded to judge's improper request for contribution to political campaign of judge's niece); *Lisi v. Several Att'ys*, 596 A.2d 313 (R.I. 1991) (lawyers made loans to judge before whom some regularly appeared); *see also In re Dean*, 129 P.3d 943 (Ariz. 2006) (prosecutor had romantic relationship with judge hearing felony cases in which prosecutor involved, and misrepresented relationship to state bar authorities); ABA Formal Ethics Op. 07-449 (2007) (lawyer with pending cases before judge whom lawyer is representing in another matter must withdraw from one or both matters if judge refuses to recuse himself); Mich. Formal Ethics Op. R-20 (2008) (same); Ohio Sup. Ct. Ethics Op. 2014-1 (2014) (violation of Rule 8.4(f) to participate in case before judge with whom lawyer has substantial political relationship if judge violates Judicial Code by failing to disqualify self or to disclose relationship); *cf.* Pa. Formal Ethics Op. 2014-300 (2014) (lawyer may connect with judge on social media site provided no attempt to influence outcome of a case or otherwise cause judge to violate Judicial Code).

## *Paragraph (g): Harassment and Discrimination*

Paragraph (g) was adopted in 2016, along with amended Comments [3], [4], and [5]. *See* http://ambar.org/antibiasrule. This provision prohibits lawyers from engaging in harassment or discrimination based on "race, sex, religion, national origin, ethnicity, disability, age, sexual orientation, gender identity, marital status or socioeconomic status" when the conduct is "related to the practice of law." The rule explicitly states that it does not "limit the ability of a lawyer to accept, decline or withdraw from a representation in accordance with Rule 1.16," and "does not preclude legitimate advice or advocacy consistent with these Rules."

Prior to 2016, discrimination was addressed in former Comment [3] to Rule 8.4 (adopted in 1998), which stated: "A lawyer who, in the course of representing a client, knowingly manifests by words or conduct, bias or prejudice based upon race, sex, religion, national origin, disability, age, sexual orientation or socioeconomic status, violates paragraph (d) when such actions are prejudicial to the administration of justice." *See* American Bar Association, *A Legislative History: The Development of the ABA Model Rules of Professional Conduct, 1982–2013*, at 859–860 (2013).

The new provision, whose prohibitions are contained in the black letter, has generated a fair amount of scholarship. *See, e.g.,* Rebecca Aviel, *Rule 8.4(g) and The First Amendment: Distinguishing Between Discrimination and Free Speech*, 31 Geo. J. Legal Ethics 31 (Winter 2018); Andrew F. Halaby & Brianna L. Long, *New Model Rule of Professional Conduct 8.4(g): Legislative History, Enforceability Questions, and a Call for Scholarship*, 41 J. Legal Prof. 201 (Spring 2017). *Compare* Stephen Gillers, *A Rule to Forbid Bias and Harassment in Law Practice: A Guide for State Courts Considering Model Rule 8.4(g)*, 30 Geo. J. Legal Ethics 195 (Spring 2017), *with* Josh Blackman, *Reply: A Pause for State Courts Considering Model Rule 8.4(g)*, 30 Geo. J. Legal Ethics 241 (Spring 2017).

Over half of all jurisdictions have a specific rule addressing bias and/or harassment—all of which differ in some way from the Model Rule and from each other. Several jurisdictions—including many that have adopted a specific rule—retain former Comment [3]. For charts comparing state rules, see http://ambar.org/MRPC StateCharts.

Whether or not a state has adopted an analogue to Model Rule 8.4(g), lawyers have been subject to discipline or sanctions for improper bias or harassment. *See In re Barker*, 993 N.E.2d 1138 (Ind. 2013) (lawyer's letter to opposing counsel accusing opposing party of being "illegal alien" violated Indiana Rule 8.4(g)); *In re Dempsey*, 986 N.E.2d 816 (Ind. 2013) (anti-Semitic statements and accusations of mental impairment); *In re McCarthy*, 938 N.E.2d 698 (Ind. 2010) (e-mail containing racist insult); *In re Kelley*, 925 N.E.2d 1279 (Ind. 2010) (ridiculing man with feminine-sounding voice by asking if he was "gay" or "sweet"); *In re Campiti*, 937 N.E.2d 340 (Ind. 2009) (disparaging references to opposing party's status as noncitizen receiving free legal services); *Iowa Supreme Court Att'y Disciplinary Bd. v. Moothart*, 860 N.W.2d 598 (Iowa 2015) (sexually harassing clients and employee); *In re Igbanugo*, 863 N.W.2d 751 (Minn. 2015) (sending threatening letters to former client, referring to client's religion and stating client must "answer to God" for nonpayment of fees and report to disciplinary authorities); *In re Charges of Unprof'l Conduct Contained in Panel Case No. 15976*, 653 N.W.2d 452 (Minn. 2002) (lawyer for plaintiff in personal injury case brought motion for new trial, objecting to presence of paralyzed court clerk in court-room; lawyer intended to argue that client, who was less disabled than clerk, was unable to work); *In re Charges of Unprof'l Conduct Contained in Panel File 98-26*, 597 N.W.2d 563 (Minn. 1999) (prosecutor brought motion in limine to prohibit public defender from "hav[ing] a person of color as co-counsel for the sole purpose of play-ing upon the emotions of the jury"); *In re Robinson*, No. 2018-112, 2019 WL 850501 (Vt. Feb. 22, 2019) (lawyer sexually harassed employee and pressured her to sign agree-ment not to file harassment claims); *In re McGrath*, 280 P.3d 1091 (Wash. 2012) (lawyer sent two ex parte communications to judge disparaging opposing party on basis of national origin and immigration status); *In re Baratki*, 902 N.W.2d 250 (Wis. 2017) (sexually harassing client, through text messages and physical contact); *In re Isaacson*, 860 N.W.2d 490 (Wis. 2015) (lawyer serving as officer of corporate entities involved in litigation executed documents containing religious slurs directed at judges, other counsel, and others, then directed other counsel to file them with federal courts in three states); *In re Kratz*, 851 N.W.2d 219 (Wis. 2014) (prosecutor sent sexually harass-ing text messages to domestic abuse victim and made sexually harassing comments to witness in another case; Rule 8.4(i) violation); *see also United States v. Kouri-Perez*, 8 F. Supp. 2d 133 (D.P.R. 1998) (in motion, lawyer accused prosecutor of hiding her true identity as granddaughter of former Dominican Republic dictator Rafael Trujil-lo; filing motion with "false statements and unnecessary and offensive references to ancestry" violates Rule 8.4(d)); *In re Williams*, 414 N.W.2d 394 (Minn. 1987) (lawyer unsuccessfully argued he should not be disciplined for making anti-Semitic remark to opposing counsel at deposition because he had right to represent his clients vig-orously, aggressively, and zealously); *In re Teague*, 15 N.Y.S.3d 312 (App. Div. 2015) (derogatory racial, ethnic, homophobic, and sexist remarks to other attorneys; under New York Rule 8.4(h)); *In re Monaghan*, 743 N.Y.S.2d 519 (App. Div. 2002) (lawyer repeatedly harangued opposing counsel at deposition for mispronouncing words; court found conduct to be racially motivated). For practical guidance on addressing the issue of sex-based harassment, see ABA Commission on Women in the Profes-sion, *Zero Tolerance: Best Practices for Combating Sex-Based Harassment in the Legal Pro-fession* (2018).

# MAINTAINING THE INTEGRITY OF THE PROFESSION

## Rule 8.5
### *Disciplinary Authority; Choice of Law*

(a) Disciplinary Authority. A lawyer admitted to practice in this jurisdiction is subject to the disciplinary authority of this jurisdiction, regardless of where the lawyer's conduct occurs. A lawyer not admitted in this jurisdiction is also subject to the disciplinary authority of this jurisdiction if the lawyer provides or offers to provide any legal services in this jurisdiction. A lawyer may be subject to the disciplinary authority of both this jurisdiction and another jurisdiction for the same conduct.

(b) Choice of Law. In any exercise of the disciplinary authority of this jurisdiction, the rules of professional conduct to be applied shall be as follows:

(1) for conduct in connection with a matter pending before a tribunal, the rules of the jurisdiction in which the tribunal sits, unless the rules of the tribunal provide otherwise; and

(2) for any other conduct, the rules of the jurisdiction in which the lawyer's conduct occurred, or, if the predominant effect of the conduct is in a different jurisdiction, the rules of that jurisdiction shall be applied to the conduct. A lawyer shall not be subject to discipline if the lawyer's conduct conforms to the rules of a jurisdiction in which the lawyer reasonably believes the predominant effect of the lawyer's conduct will occur.

## COMMENT
### *Disciplinary Authority*

[1] It is longstanding law that the conduct of a lawyer admitted to practice in this jurisdiction is subject to the disciplinary authority of this jurisdiction. Extension of the disciplinary authority of this jurisdiction to other lawyers who provide or offer to provide legal services in this jurisdiction is for the protection of the citizens of this jurisdiction. Reciprocal enforcement of a jurisdiction's disciplinary findings and sanctions will further advance the purposes of this Rule. See, Rules 6 and 22, ABA *Model Rules for Lawyer Disciplinary Enforcement*. A lawyer who is subject to the disciplinary authority of this jurisdiction under Rule 8.5(a) appoints an official to be designated by this court to receive service of process in this jurisdiction. The fact that the

lawyer is subject to the disciplinary authority of this jurisdiction may be a factor in determining whether personal jurisdiction may be asserted over the lawyer for civil matters.

## Choice of Law

[2] A lawyer may be potentially subject to more than one set of rules of professional conduct which impose different obligations. The lawyer may be licensed to practice in more than one jurisdiction with differing rules, or may be admitted to practice before a particular court with rules that differ from those of the jurisdiction or jurisdictions in which the lawyer is licensed to practice. Additionally, the lawyer's conduct may involve significant contacts with more than one jurisdiction.

[3] Paragraph (b) seeks to resolve such potential conflicts. Its premise is that minimizing conflicts between rules, as well as uncertainty about which rules are applicable, is in the best interest of both clients and the profession (as well as the bodies having authority to regulate the profession). Accordingly, it takes the approach of (i) providing that any particular conduct of a lawyer shall be subject to only one set of rules of professional conduct, (ii) making the determination of which set of rules applies to particular conduct as straightforward as possible, consistent with recognition of appropriate regulatory interests of relevant jurisdictions, and (iii) providing protection from discipline for lawyers who act reasonably in the face of uncertainty.

[4] Paragraph (b)(1) provides that as to a lawyer's conduct relating to a proceeding pending before a tribunal, the lawyer shall be subject only to the rules of professional conduct of that tribunal. As to all other conduct, including conduct in anticipation of a proceeding not yet pending before a tribunal, paragraph (b)(2) provides that a lawyer shall be subject to the rules of the jurisdiction in which the lawyer's conduct occurred, or, if the predominant effect of the conduct is in another jurisdiction, the rules of that jurisdiction shall be applied to the conduct. In the case of conduct in anticipation of a proceeding that is likely to be before a tribunal, the predominant effect of such conduct could be where the conduct occurred, where the tribunal sits or in another jurisdiction.

[5] When a lawyer's conduct involves significant contacts with more than one jurisdiction, it may not be clear whether the predominant effect of the lawyer's conduct will occur in a jurisdiction other than the one in which the conduct occurred. So long as the lawyer's conduct conforms to the rules of a jurisdiction in which the lawyer reasonably believes the predominant effect will occur, the lawyer shall not be subject to discipline under this Rule. With respect to conflicts of interest, in determining a lawyer's reasonable belief under paragraph (b)(2), a written agreement between the lawyer and client that reasonably specifies a particular jurisdiction as within the scope of that paragraph may be considered if the agreement was obtained with the client's informed consent confirmed in the agreement.

[6] If two admitting jurisdictions were to proceed against a lawyer for the same conduct, they should, applying this rule, identify the same governing ethics rules. They should take all appropriate steps to see that they do apply the same rule to the same conduct, and in all events should avoid proceeding against a lawyer on the basis of two inconsistent rules.

[7] The choice of law provision applies to lawyers engaged in transnational practice, unless international law, treaties or other agreements between competent regulatory authorities in the affected jurisdictions provide otherwise.

**Definitional Cross-References**
"Reasonably believes" *See* Rule 1.0(i)
"Tribunal" *See* Rule 1.0(m)

**State Rules Comparison**
http://ambar.org/MRPCStateCharts

# ANNOTATION

## LEGISLATIVE HISTORY

As first adopted in 1983, Rule 8.5 simply stated that "[a] lawyer admitted to practice in this jurisdiction is subject to the disciplinary authority of this jurisdiction although engaged in practice elsewhere."

### • *1993 Amendments*

In 1993, the rule was amended to clarify that a lawyer admitted in more than one jurisdiction is subject to the disciplinary authority of each licensing jurisdiction for the same conduct. Choice-of-law provisions were also added. *See* American Bar Association, *A Legislative History: The Development of the ABA Model Rules of Professional Conduct, 1982–2013*, at 867–69 (2013). Few jurisdictions adopted the 1993 amendments to Rule 8.5, however.

### • *2002 Amendments*

In 2002, Rule 8.5 was again amended, following the ABA Commission on Multijurisdictional Practice's proposals. *See* ABA Comm'n on Multijurisdictional Practice, Report to the House of Delegates No. 201A-J (Aug. 2002), *available at* http://ambar.org/CPRMJP. These amendments clarify jurisdictional and choice-of-law provisions in light of concurrent amendments to Rule 5.5, which made it easier for lawyers to provide certain legal services in jurisdictions in which they are not licensed. *See generally* American Bar Association, *A Legislative History: The Development of the ABA Model Rules of Professional Conduct, 1982–2013*, at 651–56, 873–76 (2013); Keith Swisher, *Disciplinary Authority and Choice of Law in Online Advertising: Disclaimers or Double Deontology*, 21 Prof. Law., no. 1, at 8 (2011); Charles W. Wolfram, *Expanding State Jurisdiction to Regulate Out-of-State Lawyers*, 30 Hofstra L. Rev. 1015 (2002). Jurisdictions have widely adopted these amendments. *See* annotation to Rule 5.5.

### • *2013 Amendments*

In 2013, as a result of the ABA Commission on Ethics 20/20's proposals, the comment to Rule 8.5 was amended to address conflicts of interest in multijurisdictional practice. The amendment provides that "in determining a lawyer's reasonable belief under paragraph (b)(2) [as to where the "predominant effect" of the lawyer's conduct will occur], a written agreement between the lawyer and client that reasonably specifies a particular jurisdiction as within the scope of that paragraph may be considered if the agreement was obtained with the client's informed consent confirmed in the agreement." Cmt. [5]. This essentially permits a lawyer and client to enter a choice-of-law agreement regarding the applicable conflict-of-interest rules, although the agreement is not binding on a court or disciplinary authority. The change "was intended to provide more predictability to clients and their lawyers by permitting them to specify a particular jurisdiction as within the scope of Rule 8.5(b)(2)." American Bar Association, *A Legislative History: The Development of the ABA Model Rules of Professional Conduct, 1982–2013*, at 877 (2013). *See generally* Francesca Giannoni-Crystal & Nathan M. Crystal, *Choice of Law in Lawyers' Engagement Agreements*, 121 Penn St. L. Rev. 683 (2017). The drafters implicitly recognized that this new comment allows lawyers to "contract around" the ethical rules and thus explicitly limited the comment's reach to agreements concerning conflict-of-interest rules. *See* ABA Comm'n on Ethics 20/20, Report to the House of Delegates (2012), *available at* http://www.americanbar.org/content/dam/aba/administrative/ethics_2020/20121112_ethics_20_20_choice_of_rule_resolution_and_report_final.pdf. Beyond conflicts, however, "such agreements . . . should not be used to specify the rules of a jurisdiction on other issues, such as the duty of confidentiality," because that would "authorize parties to contract around rules intended to protect adverse parties or tribunals." *Id.*

## Paragraph (a): Disciplinary Authority

Under Rule 8.5(a), a lawyer is subject to the disciplinary authority of every jurisdiction in which the lawyer is licensed, regardless of where the misconduct occurs. The rule also subjects the lawyer to the disciplinary authority of a jurisdiction in which she is not licensed if she provides or offers to provide legal services in that jurisdiction. Accordingly, the same misconduct can serve as the basis for disciplinary proceedings by two or more disciplinary authorities. *See generally* Alan M. Colvin, *Reciprocal Discipline: Double Jeopardy or a State's Right to Protect Its Citizens?*, 25 J. Legal Prof. 143 (2001); Margaret Raymond, *Inside, Outside: Cross-Border Enforcement of Attorney Advertising Restrictions*, 43 Akron L. Rev. 801 (2010).

Note that a jurisdiction's disciplinary authority can be distinct from a court's inherent authority to sanction those who appear before it. *See Sisk v. Transylvania Cmty. Hosp., Inc.*, 695 S.E.2d 429 (N.C. 2010) (lawyer discipline can be enforced through disciplinary proceedings and through court's inherent authority; Rule 8.5's choice-of-law provision applicable to former, but not to latter).

## DISCIPLINE FOR MISCONDUCT
## OUTSIDE LICENSING JURISDICTION

Any jurisdiction in which a lawyer is licensed can discipline the lawyer for misconduct, no matter where the misconduct occurred and no matter what any other jurisdiction has or has not done about it. *See People v. Rozan*, 277 P.3d 942 (Colo. O.P.D.J. 2011) (fact that lawyer practiced from office in Texas "does not divest the Colorado Supreme Court . . . of jurisdiction over this matter"); *Haymond v. Statewide Grievance Comm.*, 723 A.2d 821 (Conn. 1997) (disciplining Connecticut-licensed lawyer for advertising violations in Massachusetts); *In re Vega*, 241 So. 3d 993 (La. 2018) ("respondent is subject to the disciplinary authority of this court" even though "misconduct occurred in Texas"); *Att'y Grievance Comm'n v. Gore*, 845 A.2d 1204 (Md. 2004) (Maryland lawyer subject to discipline under Rule 8.5(a) for ethics rules violations committed in District of Columbia); *In re Overboe*, 745 N.W.2d 852 (Minn. 2008) (disciplining Minnesota lawyer for trust account violations in connection with law practice in North Dakota); *State ex rel. Counsel for Discipline v. Carter*, 808 N.W.2d 342 (Neb. 2011) (disbarring Nebraska lawyer in part for misappropriating client funds involving Iowa trust account); *State ex rel. Counsel for Discipline v. Horneber*, 708 N.W.2d 620 (Neb. 2006) (upholding court's authority to discipline Nebraska lawyer for drafting quitclaim deed in attempt to help client frustrate divorce decree, notwithstanding that property involved was in Iowa); *Rose v. Office of Prof'l Conduct*, 424 P.3d 134 (Utah 2018) (citing Rule 8.5(a) and rejecting lawyer's "challenge to the court's disciplinary authority that the Supremacy Clause divests our jurisdiction over discipline cases when the actions giving rise to the discipline occur in federal or tribal court"); *see also State ex rel. Counsel for Discipline v. Rokahr*, 675 N.W.2d 117 (Neb. 2004) (disciplining Nebraska lawyer for conduct that occurred in South Dakota for which South Dakota Disciplinary Board had already issued sanctions does not offend principles of Full Faith and Credit Clause). *But cf. Robertsson v. Misetic*, 116 N.E.3d 205 (Ill. App. Ct. 2018) (rejecting civil plaintiff's "argument that Illinois has personal jurisdiction over Misetic because Misetic was subject to the Illinois Rules of Professional Conduct" through Rule 8.5). *See generally* Alexandra Grossman, Current Developments, *Reciprocal Discipline: An Interest-Based Approach*, 29 Geo. J. Legal Ethics 1047 (2016) (noting that a "majority of states provide in their disciplinary rules for identical or substantially similar discipline to be imposed on attorneys originally disciplined in another forum").

A state generally may discipline a lawyer for misconduct in connection with the lawyer's federal court practice. *See Canatella v. California*, 404 F.3d 1106 (9th Cir. 2005) (California court can discipline California lawyer even though he practices exclusively in federal court and before federal agencies: "Barring the States from disciplining their bar members based on misconduct occurring in federal court would lead to the unacceptable consequence that an attorney could engage in misconduct at will in one federal district without jeopardizing the state-issued license that facilitates the attorney's ability to practice in other federal and state venues."); *Haagensen v. Supreme Court of Pa.*, 651 F. Supp. 2d 422 (W.D. Pa. 2009) (Pennsylvania court did not act without jurisdiction in disciplining lawyer for conduct in federal court; collecting cases); *Gillette v. Edison*, 593 F. Supp. 2d 1063 (D.N.D. 2009) (refusing to enjoin state disciplinary proceedings based upon misconduct occurring in Indian tribal court); *In re Chang*, 83 A.3d 763 (D.C. 2014) (imposing reciprocal suspension for misconduct in multiple bankruptcy cases); *In re Howes*, 940 P.2d 159 (N.M. 1997) (disciplining New Mexico lawyer for actions undertaken as assistant U.S. attorney prosecuting criminal case in District of Columbia); *In re Villanueva*, 42 N.Y.S.3d 5 (App. Div. 2016) (imposing reciprocal discipline for misconduct in federal criminal cases); *In re Vialet*, 987 N.Y.S.2d 65 (App. Div. 2014) (imposing reciprocal discipline after Second Circuit disciplined lawyer for misconduct in immigration proceedings); *Flowers v. Bd. of*

*Prof'l Responsibility*, 314 S.W.3d 882 (Tenn. 2010) (disciplining lawyer for misconduct in handling immigration cases); *In re Joseph*, 60 V.I. 540, 2014 WL 547513 (V.I. 2014) (noting that "this Court and the District Court, as well as the Third Circuit, each possess the authority to regulate our respective bars") (quotation marks omitted).

A lawyer remains subject to discipline even if suspended or on inactive status. *See In re Morrissey*, 305 F.3d 211 (4th Cir. 2002) (disbarring lawyer for conduct occurring while suspended; collecting cases); *In re Davis*, 43 A.3d 856 (Del. 2012) (disbarring lawyer in part for engaging in unauthorized practice of law during his one-year suspension in state); *In re Cohen*, 612 S.E.2d 294 (Ga. 2005) (disbarring lawyer for misconduct in connection with representation of client while on inactive status); *In re Arnold*, 56 P.3d 259 (Kan. 2002) (disciplining Kansas lawyer on inactive status for intemperate judicial criticism in course of federal litigation); *Barrett v. Va. State Bar*, 675 S.E.2d 827 (Va. 2009) ("lawyer whose license is suspended is still an active member of the bar and, although not in good standing, is subject to the Rules"); *see also In re Davy*, 25 A.3d 70 (D.C. 2011) (imposing reciprocal discipline several years after lawyer disciplined in Maryland; lawyer's voluntary resignation from District of Columbia bar before imposition of discipline in Maryland did not exempt her from reciprocal discipline).

## DISCIPLINE FOR OUT-OF-STATE LAWYER FOR IN-STATE MISCONDUCT

Under Rule 8.5(a), a lawyer who "provides or offers to provide" legal services in a jurisdiction is subject to the disciplinary authority of that jurisdiction, even if the lawyer is not licensed there. *See In re Edelstein*, 99 A.3d 227 (Del. 2014) (Pennsylvania lawyer who had represented dozens of Delaware auto accident clients in "getting information from the insurance company, getting information from the doctor and then sending out a letter trying to resolve these matters preliminarily" committed unauthorized practice of law); *In re Coale*, 775 N.E.2d 1079 (Ind. 2002) (barring out-of-state lawyers from "acts constituting the practice of law in [the] state (including pro hac vice admission)" until further order); *Iowa Supreme Court Att'y Disciplinary Bd. v. Carpenter*, 781 N.W.2d 263 (Iowa 2010) (enjoining out-of-state lawyer with federal practice in Iowa from practicing law in Iowa in part based on ethics rule violations involving clients in seventeen federal immigration matters); *Ky. Bar Ass'n v. Yocum*, 294 S.W.3d 437 (Ky. 2009) (Indiana lawyer who provided legal services in Kentucky was thereby subject to Kentucky disciplinary authority and his misconduct warranted prohibition "from requesting permission to practice law in [Kentucky], pro hac vice or otherwise, for 120 days"); *Att'y Grievance Comm'n v. Ndi*, 184 A.3d 25 (Md. 2018) (citing Rule 8.5(a) and noting that when out-of-state attorney chose to conduct practice in Maryland, he "subjected that practice to the consumer protection rules that govern legal practice in Maryland"); *Lawyer Disciplinary Bd. v. Lakin*, 617 S.E.2d 484 (W. Va. 2005) (prohibiting Illinois lawyer regularly admitted to practice in West Virginia on pro hac vice basis from practicing in West Virginia for twelve months as sanction for improper solicitation in West Virginia); Alaska Ethics Op. 2010-1 (2010) (lawyer who maintains Alaska office solely to practice immigration law is subject to Alaska disciplinary authority even though not licensed there); N.D. Ethics Op. 98-02 (1998) (California lawyer representing plaintiff in North Dakota arbitration against North Dakota corporation is subject to North Dakota's disciplinary authority).

## DISCIPLINARY AUTHORITY OF
## FEDERAL COURTS AND GOVERNMENT ENTITIES

Federal courts have their own independent power to regulate the conduct of lawyers practicing before them and can impose their own discipline—including suspension and disbarment from federal practice. *Chambers v. NASCO, Inc.*, 501 U.S. 32 (1991) (federal court has inherent power "to control admission to its bar and to discipline attorneys who appear before it"); *Theard v. United States*, 354 U.S. 278 (1957) ("The two judicial systems of courts, the state judicatures and the federal judiciary, have autonomous control over the conduct of their officers."); *In re Landerman*, 7 F. Supp. 2d 1202 (D. Utah 1998).

Many federal administrative agencies—including the Internal Revenue Service, the Securities and Exchange Commission, the Patent and Trademark Office, and the Board of Immigration Appeals—have authority to prescribe and enforce their own ethics rules for lawyers practicing before them. This authority supplements traditional state regulatory authority. *See Gadda v. Ashcroft*, 377 F.3d 934 (9th Cir. 2004) (federal law does not preempt California's authority to suspend or disbar California lawyers for misconduct in federal immigration proceedings; on the contrary, California disbarment warrants reciprocal disbarment by Board of Immigration Appeals and by Ninth Circuit Court of Appeals); *State ex rel. York v. Office of Disciplinary Counsel*, 744 S.E.2d 293 (W. Va. 2013) (refusing to enjoin state disciplinary authorities from investigating patent lawyer who practiced in state because "federal law does not preempt this state's disciplinary proceedings").

## *Paragraph (b): Choice of Law*

Rule 8.5(b) seeks to specify one set of ethics rules when a disciplinary proceeding involves a lawyer who practices in more than one jurisdiction. Rule 8.5(b)(1) provides that when a lawyer's misconduct relates to a matter pending before a tribunal, the rules of the jurisdiction in which the tribunal sits will apply, unless the rules of the tribunal provide otherwise. For all other conduct, Rule 8.5(b)(2) provides that the applicable rules are those of the jurisdiction in which the conduct either "occurred" or had its "predominant effect."

## *Paragraph (b)(1): Conduct Connected*
## *with Matter Pending before Tribunal*

When the misconduct takes place before a tribunal, the disciplinary authority is to apply the ethics rules of the jurisdiction in which the tribunal sits, unless the tribunal's own rules specify otherwise. *See, e.g., Alzheimer's Inst. of Am., Inc. v. Avid Radiopharmaceuticals*, Civ. No. 10-6908, 2011 WL 6088625, 2011 BL 307203 (E.D. Pa. Dec. 7, 2011) ("Because Bryan Cave's motion to withdraw pertains to a proceeding pending in this court and the Pennsylvania Rules of Professional Conduct govern this tribunal, Pennsylvania's Rules of Professional Conduct apply in this case."); *In re*

*Ponds*, 876 A.2d 636 (D.C. 2005) (censuring District of Columbia lawyer for violating Maryland ethics rules by disclosing confidential information in motion to withdraw in Maryland case); *In re Lyons*, 780 N.W.2d 629 (Minn. 2010) (applying Montana ethics rules to misconduct in connection with federal court litigation in Montana, and Minnesota rules to misconduct during disciplinary proceedings); *In re Marks*, 665 N.W.2d 836 (Wis. 2003) (Rule 8.5(b)(1) authorized discipline of lawyer licensed in both Michigan and Wisconsin for litigating frivolous lawsuit in Michigan court, in violation of Michigan Rules of Professional Conduct); Mass. Ethics Op. 12-02 (2012) (under Rule 8.5(b)(1) and (2), "[w]hen a suit to recover damages for personal injuries incurred on tribal lands in State X is contemplated, the ethics rules governing a contingent fee agreement between a Massachusetts attorney and her Massachusetts client are those of State X or the tribal court in State X and not the Massachusetts Rules of Professional Conduct"). *See generally* Andrea Lynn Evenson, *Disciplining Out-of-State Conduct and Lawyers Licensed in Other States*, 15 Prof. Law., no. 1, at 12 (Spring 2004).

## Paragraph (b)(2): Place Where Conduct Occurred / Predominant-Effect Test

If the misconduct did not occur before a tribunal, the ethics rules to be applied will depend on where the misconduct occurred and where its predominant effect was felt. *See In re Overboe*, 745 N.W.2d 852 (Minn. 2008) (in disciplining lawyer licensed in both Minnesota and North Dakota, applicable rules for allegations of trust account violations were those of North Dakota, where lawyer practiced and had bank accounts, but Minnesota rules applied to allegations of failure to cooperate with disciplinary authorities); *see also Daynard v. Ness, Motley, Loadholt, Richardson & Poole, P.A.*, 178 F. Supp. 2d 9 (D. Mass. 2001) (applying Rule 8.5 in determining that oral fee-splitting agreement made in Illinois between law professor licensed in New York and lawyers from both South Carolina and Mississippi was enforceable; although Illinois requires written client consent to fee division, no party was licensed in Illinois and Illinois had no interest in case); *In re Vega*, 241 So. 3d 993 n.2 (La. 2018) (because Louisiana lawyer's "misconduct occurred in Texas," Texas ethics rules applied); *In re Schiller*, 808 S.E.2d 378 n.1 (S.C. 2017) (North Carolina ethics rules applied to South Carolina lawyer's conduct while representing North Carolina citizen involved in car accident in North Carolina); N.Y. State Ethics Op. 1093 (2016) ("New York lawyer who is also admitted in a foreign jurisdiction and is practicing with non-lawyer partners in that jurisdiction may also practice in a separate New York law firm without violating the New York Rules of Professional Conduct as long as the lawyer (i) principally practices in the foreign jurisdiction or (ii) the predominant effect of the lawyer's practice with the foreign firm is in the foreign jurisdiction"); N.Y. State Ethics Op. 1058 (2015) (New York lawyer who exclusively practices immigration law in Illinois will be governed by rules of Illinois, not New York, but both jurisdictions maintain disciplinary authority over the lawyer); N.Y. State Ethics Op. 1027 (2014) (in determining "predominant effect," factors to consider include where: clients live and work, payments will be deposited, contract will be performed, and new business will operate). *See generally* Clara C. Ward, *The Law of Choice: Implementation of ABA Model Rule 8.5*, 30 J. Legal Prof. 173 (2005–2006).

Paragraph (b)(2) also provides that a lawyer is not subject to discipline if the lawyer's conduct conforms to the rules of a jurisdiction in which the lawyer "reasonably believes the predominant effect of the lawyer's conduct will occur." Comment [5] explains that this protects a lawyer from being subject to discipline when the lawyer's conduct involves significant contacts with more than one jurisdiction, and it is unclear where the predominant effect of the conduct will occur. *Cf.* ABA Formal Ethics Op. 464 (2013) (lawyer may divide fees with lawyers practicing in jurisdictions allowing nonlawyers to share fees).

To increase certainty about which conflict-of-interest rules will apply in a multi-jurisdictional matter, the comment was amended in 2013 to permit lawyers to enter an agreement with their clients to specify the jurisdiction in which the "predominant effect" will occur. Cmt. [5]. The agreement, however, is not binding on a court or disciplinary authority. American Bar Association, *A Legislative History: The Development of the ABA Model Rules of Professional Conduct, 1982–2013*, at 877 (2013); *see* Francesca Giannoni-Crystal & Nathan M. Crystal, *Choice of Law in Lawyers' Engagement Agreements*, 121 Penn St. L. Rev. 683, 741 (2017). *See generally* Mark J. Fucile, *Important Choices: Choice of Law Under Model Rule 8.5(b)*, 19 Prof. Law., no. 2, at 20 (2009); J. Mark Little, *The Choice of Rules Clause: A Solution to the Choice of Law Problem in Ethics Proceedings*, 88 Tex. L. Rev. 855 (2010); Nancy J. Moore, *Choice of Law for Professional Responsibility Issues in Aggregate Litigation*, 14 Roger Williams U. L. Rev. 73 (2009); Laurel S. Terry, *Transnational Legal Practice (United States)*, 47 Int'l Law. 499 (2013).

# ABA Commission on Multijurisdictional Practice

## Chair

WAYNE J. POSITAN
Roseland, New Jersey

## Members

| | | |
|---|---|---|
| ALAN T. DIMOND<br>Miami, Florida | W. ANTHONY JENKINS<br>Detroit, Michigan | HON. RANDALL T. SHEPARD<br>Indianapolis, Indiana |
| PETER D. EHRENHAFT<br>Washington, D.C. | CHARLES E. MCCALLUM<br>Grand Rapids, Michigan | MARNA S. TUCKER<br>Washington, D.C. |
| JOANNE M. GARVEY<br>San Francisco, California | CHERYL I. NIRO<br>Chicago, Illinois | DIANE C. YU<br>New York, New York |
| STEPHEN GILLERS<br>New York, New York | HON. LARRY RAMIREZ<br>Las Cruces, New Mexico | |

## Reporter

BRUCE A. GREEN
New York, New York

## Liaisons

ANTHONY E. DAVIS
Denver, Colorado
*Association of Professional
Responsibility Lawyers*

ERICA MOESER
Madison, Wisconsin
*National Conference
of Bar Examiners*

BURNELE V. POWELL
Kansas City, Missouri
*Coordinating Council of the Center
for Professional Responsibility*

THOMAS A. DECKER
Philadelphia, Pennsylvania
*Standing Committee on
Professional Discipline*

M. PETER MOSER
Baltimore, Maryland
*Standing Committee on Ethics and
Professional Responsibility*

WILLIAM P. SMITH, III
Atlanta, Georgia
*National Organization
of Bar Counsel*

SUSAN HACKETT
Washington, D.C.
*American Corporate
Counsel Association*

LUCIAN T. PERA
Memphis, Tennessee
*Commission on Evaluation of the
Rules of Professional Conduct*

JAMES E. TOWERY
San Jose, California
*Standing Committee on
Client Protection*

JOHN L. MCDONNELL, JR.
Oakland, California
*Board of Governors*

## American Bar Association
## Center for Professional Responsibility

JEANNE P. GRAY
*Director*

JOHN A. HOLTAWAY
*Commission Counsel*

CHARLOTTE K. STRETCH
*Special Counsel*

# AMERICAN BAR ASSOCIATION
## COMMISSION ON MULTIJURISDICTIONAL PRACTICE

In response to professional concerns about the regulation of multijurisdictional law practice, ABA President Martha Barnett appointed the Commission on Multijurisdictional Practice in July 2000 to undertake the following responsibilities:

(1) Research, study and report on the application of current ethics and bar admission rules to the multijurisdictional practice of law, (2) analyze the impact of those rules on the practice of in-house counsel, transactional lawyers, litigators and arbitrators and on lawyers and law firms maintaining offices and practicing in multiple state and federal jurisdictions, (3) make policy recommendations to govern the multijurisdictional practice of law that serve the public interest and take any other actions as may be necessary to carry out its jurisdictional mandate, and (4) review international issues related to multijurisdictional practice in the United States.

In November 2001, the Commission issued an Interim Report describing its preliminary recommendations. In June 2002, the Commission filed its Final Report with the ABA House of Delegates. When the Commission brought the Final Report before the House of Delegates, on August 12, 2002, it accepted friendly amendments to Recommendation 3 (Disciplinary Authority), Recommendation 6 (Pro Hac Vice Admission), and Recommendation 7 (Admission by Motion). Recommendation 2 (Rule 5.5: Unauthorized Practice of Law; Multijurisdictional Practice of Law) and Recommendation 3 (Rule 8.5: Disciplinary Authority; Choice of Law) were accepted as filed. The ABA House of Delegates then adopted all nine recommendations contained in the Final Report, as revised.

Information about the work of the Commission on Multijurisdictional Practice and the text of its Report can be found at http://ambar.org/CPRMJP.

# ABA STANDING COMMITTEE
## ON ETHICS AND PROFESSIONAL RESPONSIBILITY

## COMPOSITION AND JURISDICTION

The Standing Committee on Ethics and Professional Responsibility, which consists of ten members, may:

by the concurrence of a majority of its members, express its opinion on proper professional or judicial conduct, either on its own initiative or when requested to do so by a member of the bar or the judiciary;

periodically publish its issued opinions to the profession in summary or complete form and, on request, provide copies of opinions to members of the bar, the judiciary and the public;

provide under its supervision informal responses to ethics inquiries the answers to which are substantially governed by applicable ethical codes and existing written opinions;

on request, advise or otherwise assist professional organizations and courts in their activities relating to the development, modification and interpretation of statements of the ethical standards of the profession such as the Model Rules of Professional Conduct, the predecessor Model Code of Professional Responsibility, and the Code of Judicial Conduct;

recommend amendments to or clarifications of the Model Rules of Professional Conduct or the Code of Judicial Conduct; and

adopt rules relating to the procedures to be used in issuing opinions, effective when approved by the Board of Governors.

[The above Composition and Jurisdiction statement is found at Section 31.7 of the Bylaws of the American Bar Association.]

# CORRELATION TABLES

## TABLES A AND B:
### RELATED SECTIONS IN THE ABA MODEL CODE OF PROFESSIONAL RESPONSIBILITY

## TABLE A*

| ABA<br>MODEL RULES | ABA<br>MODEL CODE |
|---|---|
| *Competence* | |
| Rule 1.1 | EC 1-1, EC 1-2, EC 6-1, EC 6-2, EC 6-3, EC 6-4, EC 6-5, DR 6-101(A) |
| | |
| *Scope of Representation and Allocation of Authority between Client and Lawyer* | |
| Rule 1.2(a) | EC 5-12, EC 7-7, EC 7-8, DR 7-101(A)(1) |
| Rule 1.2(b) | EC 7-17 |
| Rule 1.2(c) | EC 7-8, EC 7-9, DR 7-101(B)(1) |
| Rule 1.2(d) | EC 7-1, EC 7-2, EC 7-5, EC 7-22, DR 7-102(A)(6), (7) & (8), DR 7-106 |
| | |
| *Diligence* | |
| Rule 1.3 | EC 2-31, EC 6-4, EC 7-1, EC 7-38, DR 6-101(A)(3), DR 7-101(A)(1) & (3) |
| | |
| *Communication* | |
| Rule 1.4(a) | EC 7-8, EC 9-2, DR 2-110(C)(1)(c), DR 6-101(A)(3), DR 9-102(B)(1) |
| Rule 1.4(b) | EC 7-8 |
| | |
| *Fees* | |
| Rule 1.5(a) | EC 2-16, EC 2-17, EC 2-18, DR 2-106(A) & (B) |
| Rule 1.5(b) | EC 2-19 |
| Rule 1.5(c) | EC 2-20, EC 5-7 |
| Rule 1.5(d) | EC 2-20, DR 2-106(C) |
| Rule 1.5(e) | EC 2-22, DR 2-107(A) |
| | |
| *Confidentiality of Information* | |
| Rule 1.6(a) | EC 4-1, EC 4-2, EC 4-3, EC 4-4, DR 4-101(A), (B) & (C) |
| Rule 1.6(b)(1) | EC 4-2, DR 4-101(C)(3), DR 7-102(B) |
| Rule 1.6(b)(2) | DR 4-101(C)(3) |
| Rule 1.6(b)(3) | None |
| Rule 1.6(b)(4) | None |
| Rule 1.6(b)(5) | DR 4-101(C)(4) |
| Rule 1.6(b)(6) | DR 4-101(C)(2) |
| Rule 1.6(b)(7) | None |
| Rule 1.6(c) | None |

\* Table A provides cross-references to related provisions, but only in the sense that the provisions consider substantially similar subject matter or reflect similar concerns. A cross-reference does not indicate that a provision of the ABA Model Code of Professional Responsibility has been incorporated by the provision of a Model Rule. The Canons of the Code are not cross-referenced.

| ABA MODEL RULES | ABA MODEL CODE |
|---|---|

*Conflict of Interest: Current Clients*

| Rule 1.7(a) | EC 2-21, EC 5-1, EC 5-2, EC 5-3, EC 5-9, EC 5-11, EC 5-13, EC 5-14, EC 5-15, EC 5-17, EC 5-21, EC 5-22, EC 5-23, DR 5-101(A) & (B), DR 5-102, DR 5-104(A), DR 5-105(A) & (B), DR 5-107(A) & (B) |
|---|---|
| Rule 1.7(b) | EC 2-21, EC 5-15, EC 5-16, EC 5-17, EC 5-19, EC 5-23, DR 5-101(A) & (B), DR 5-102, DR 5-104(A), DR 5-105(C), DR 5-107(A) |

*Conflict of Interest: Current Clients: Specific Rules*

| Rule 1.8(a) | EC 5-3, EC 5-5, DR 5-104(A) |
|---|---|
| Rule 1.8(b) | EC 4-5, DR 4-101(B) |
| Rule 1.8(c) | EC 5-1, EC 5-2, EC 5-5, EC 5-6 |
| Rule 1.8(d) | EC 5-1, EC 5-3, EC 5-4, DR 5-104(B) |
| Rule 1.8(e) | EC 5-1, EC 5-3, EC 5-7, EC 5-8, DR 5-103(B) |
| Rule 1.8(f) | EC 2-21, EC 5-1, EC 5-22, EC 5-23, DR 5-107(A) & (B) |
| Rule 1.8(g) | EC 5-1, DR 5-106(A) |
| Rule 1.8(h) | EC 6-6, DR 6-102(A) |
| Rule 1.8(i) | EC 5-1, EC 5-7, DR 5-101(A), DR 5-103(A) |
| Rule 1.8(j) | None |
| Rule 1.8(k) | None |

*Duties to Former Clients*

| Rule 1.9(a) | DR 5-105(C) |
|---|---|
| Rule 1.9(b) | EC 4-5, EC 4-6 |
| Rule 1.9(c) | None |

*Imputation of Conflicts of Interest: General Rule*

| Rule 1.10(a) | EC 4-5, DR 5-105(D) |
|---|---|
| Rule 1.10(b) | EC 4-5, DR 5-105(D) |
| Rule 1.10(c) | DR 5-105(A) |
| Rule 1.10(d) | None |

*Special Conflicts of Interest for Former and Current Government Officers and Employees*

| Rule 1.11(a) | EC 9-3, DR 9-101(B) |
|---|---|
| Rule 1.11(b) | None |
| Rule 1.11(c) | None |
| Rule 1.11(d) | EC 8-8 |
| Rule 1.11(e) | None |

*Former Judge, Arbitrator, Mediator or Other Third-Party Neutral*

| Rule 1.12(a) & (b) | EC 5-20, EC 9-3, DR 9-101(A) & (B) |
|---|---|
| Rule 1.12(c) | DR 5-105(D) |
| Rule 1.12(d) | None |

| ABA<br>MODEL RULES | ABA<br>MODEL CODE |
|---|---|

### *Organization as Client*

| | |
|---|---|
| Rule 1.13(a) | EC 5-18, EC 5-24 |
| Rule 1.13(b) | EC 5-18, EC 5-24, DR 5-107(B) |
| Rule 1.13(c) | EC 5-18, EC 5-24, DR 5-105(D), DR 5-107(B) |
| Rule 1.13(d) | None |
| Rule 1.13(e) | None |
| Rule 1.13(f) | EC 5-16 |
| Rule 1.13(g) | EC 4-4, EC 5-16, DR 5-105(B) & (C) |

### *Client with Diminished Capacity*

| | |
|---|---|
| Rule 1.14(a) | EC 7-11, EC 7-12 |
| Rule 1.14(b) | EC 7-12 |
| Rule 1.14(c) | None |

### *Safekeeping Property*

| | |
|---|---|
| Rule 1.15 | EC 5-7, EC 9-5, EC 9-7, DR 5-103(A)(1), DR 9-102 |

### *Declining or Terminating Representation*

| | |
|---|---|
| Rule 1.16(a)(1) | EC 2-30, EC 2-31, EC 2-32, DR 2-103(E), DR 2-104(A), DR 2-109(A), DR 2-110(B)(1) & (2) |
| Rule 1.16(a)(2) | EC 1-6, EC 2-30, EC 2-31, EC 2-32, DR 2-110(B)(3), DR 2-110(C)(4) |
| Rule 1.16(a)(3) | EC 2-31, EC 2-32, DR 2-110(B)(4) |
| Rule 1.16(b)(1) | EC 2-32, DR 2-110(A)(2), DR 2-110(C)(5) |
| Rule 1.16(b)(2) | EC 2-31, EC 2-32, DR 2-110(C)(1)(b) & (c), DR 2-110(C)(2) |
| Rule 1.16(b)(3) | EC 2-31, EC 2-32, DR 2-110(C)(2) |
| Rule 1.16(b)(4) | EC 2-30, EC 2-31, EC 2-32, DR 2-110(C)(1)(d) |
| Rule 1.16(b)(5) | EC 2-31, EC 2-32, DR 2-110(C)(1)(f)(i)(j) |
| Rule 1.16(b)(6) | EC 2-32, DR 2-110(C)(1)(d) & (e) |
| Rule 1.16(b)(7) | EC 2-32, DR 2-110(C)(6) |
| Rule 1.16(c) | EC 2-32, DR 2-110(A)(1) |
| Rule 1.16(d) | EC 2-32, DR 2-110(A)(2) & (3) |

### *Sale of Law Practice*

| | |
|---|---|
| Rule 1.17 | None |

### *Duties to Prospective Client*

| | |
|---|---|
| Rule 1.18 | EC 4-1 |

### *Advisor*

| | |
|---|---|
| Rule 2.1 | EC 5-11, EC 7-3, EC 7-8, DR 5-107(B) |

### *Evaluation for Use by Third Persons*

| | |
|---|---|
| Rule 2.3 | None |

| ABA MODEL RULES | ABA MODEL CODE |
|---|---|

*Lawyer Serving as Third-Party Neutral*

Rule 2.4          EC 5-20

*Meritorious Claims and Contentions*

Rule 3.1          EC 7-1, EC 7-4, EC 7-5, EC 7-14, EC 7-25, DR 5-102(A)(5), DR 2-109(A)(B)(1), DR 7-102(A)(1) & (2)

*Expediting Litigation*

Rule 3.2          EC 7-20, DR 1-102(A)(5), DR 7-101(A)(1) & (2)

*Candor Toward the Tribunal*

Rule 3.3(a)(1)    EC 7-4, EC 7-26, EC 7-32, EC 8-5, DR 1-102(A)(4) & (5), DR 7-102(A)(4) & (5)

Rule 3.3(a)(2)    EC 7-23, DR 1-102(A)(5), DR 7-106(B)(1)

Rule 3.3(a)(3)    EC 7-5, EC 7-6, EC 7-26, EC 8-5, DR 1-102(A)(4) & (5), DR 7-102(A)(4), (6) & (7), DR 7-102(B)(1) & (2)

Rule 3.3(b)       EC 7-5, EC 7-26, EC 7-27, EC 7-32, EC 8-5, DR 1-102(A)(4) & (5), DR 7-102(A)(4), (6) & (7), DR 7-102(B)(1) & (2), DR 7-108(G), DR 7-109(A) & (B)

Rule 3.3(c)       EC 8-5, DR 7-102(B)

Rule 3.3(d)       EC 7-24, EC 7-27

*Fairness to Opposing Party and Counsel*

Rule 3.4(a)       EC 7-6, EC 7-27, DR 1-102(A)(4) & (5), DR 7-106(C)(7), DR 7-109(A) & (B)

Rule 3.4(b)       EC 7-6, EC 7-28, DR 1-102(A)(4), (5) & (6), DR 7-102(A)(6), DR 7-109(C)

Rule 3.4(c)       EC 7-22, EC 7-25, EC 7-38, DR 1-102(A)(5), DR 7-106(A), DR 7-106(C)(5) & (7)

Rule 3.4(d)       DR 1-102(A)(5), DR 7-106(A), DR 7-106(C)(7)

Rule 3.4(e)       EC 7-24, EC 7-25, DR 1-102(A)(5), DR 7-106(C)(1), (2), (3) & (4)

Rule 3.4(f)       EC 7-27, DR 1-102(A)(5), DR 7-104(A)(2), DR 7-109(B)

*Impartiality and Decorum of the Tribunal*

Rule 3.5(a)       EC 7-20, EC 7-29, EC 7-31, EC 7-32, EC 7-34, DR 7-106, DR 7-108, DR 7-109, DR 7-110, DR 8-101(A)

Rule 3.5(b)       EC 7-35, DR 7-108, DR 7-110(A) & (B)

Rule 3.5(c)       EC 7-29, EC 7-30, EC 7-31, EC 7-32, DR 7-108

Rule 3.5(d)       EC 7-20, EC 7-25, EC 7-36, EC 7-37, DR 7-101(A)(1), DR 7-106(C)(6)

*Trial Publicity*

Rule 3.6          EC 7-25, EC 7-33, DR 7-107

| ABA MODEL RULES | ABA MODEL CODE |
|---|---|

*Lawyer as Witness*

| Rule 3.7(a) | EC 5-9, EC 5-10, DR 5-101(B)(1) & (2), DR 5-102 |
| Rule 3.7(b) | EC 5-9, DR 5-101(B), DR 5-102 |

*Special Responsibilities of a Prosecutor*

| Rule 3.8(a) | EC 7-11, EC 7-13, EC 7-14, DR 7-103(A) |
| Rule 3.8(b) | EC 7-11, EC 7-13 |
| Rule 3.8(c) | EC 7-11, EC 7-13, EC 7-18 |
| Rule 3.8(d) | EC 7-11, EC 7-13, DR 7-103(B) |
| Rule 3.8(e) | None |
| Rule 3.8(f) | EC 7-14 |
| Rule 3.8(g) | None |
| Rule 3.8(h) | None |

*Advocate in Nonadjudicative Proceedings*

| Rule 3.9 | EC 7-11, EC 7-15, EC 7-16, EC 8-4, EC 8-5, DR 7-106(B)(2), DR 9-101(C) |

*Truthfulness in Statements to Others*

| Rule 4.1 | EC 7-5, DR 7-102(A)(3), (4), (5) & (7), DR 7-102(B) |

*Communication with Person Represented by Counsel*

| Rule 4.2 | EC 2-30, EC 7-18, DR 7-104(A)(1) |

*Dealing with Unrepresented Person*

| Rule 4.3 | EC 2-3, EC 7-18, DR 7-104(A)(2) |

*Respect for Rights of Third Persons*

| Rule 4.4(a) | EC 7-10, EC 7-14, EC 7-21, EC 7-25, EC 7-29, EC 7-30, EC 7-37, DR 2-110(B)(1), DR 7-101(A)(1), DR 7-102(A)(1), DR 7-106(C)(2), DR 7-107(D), (E) & (F), DR 7-108(D), (E), & (F) |
| Rule 4.4(b) | None |

*Responsibilities of Partners, Managers, and Supervisory Lawyers*

| Rule 5.1(a) & (b) | EC 4-5, DR 4-101(D), DR 7-107(J) |
| Rule 5.1(c) | DR 1-102(A)(2), DR 1-103(A), DR 7-108(E) |

*Responsibilities of a Subordinate Lawyer*

| Rule 5.2 | None |

*Responsibilities Regarding Nonlawyer Assistance*

| Rule 5.3(a) | EC 3-6, EC 4-2, EC 4-5, EC 7-28, DR 4-101(D), DR 7-107(J) |
| Rule 5.3(b) | DR 1-102(A)(2), DR 7-107(J), DR 7-108(B), DR 7-108(E) |
| Rule 5.3(c) | None |

# TABLE A
*(continued)*

| ABA MODEL RULES | ABA MODEL CODE |
|---|---|

## Professional Independence of a Lawyer

Rule 5.4(a)    EC 2-33, EC 3-8, EC 5-24, DR 2-103(D)(1), DR 2-103(D)(2), DR 2-103(D)(4)(a), (d), (e) & (f), DR 3-102(A), DR 5-107(C)(3)

Rule 5.4(b)    EC 2-33, EC 3-8, DR 3-103(A)

Rule 5.4(c)    EC 2-33, EC 5-22, EC 5-23, DR 2-103(C), DR 5-107(B)

Rule 5.4(d)    EC 2-33, EC 3-8, DR 5-107(C)

## Unauthorized Practice of Law; Multijurisdictional Practice of Law

Rule 5.5(a)    DR 3-101(A) & (B)

Rule 5.5(b)    None

Rule 5.5(c)    None

Rule 5.5(d)    None

Rule 5.5(e)    None

## Restrictions on Right to Practice

Rule 5.6    DR 2-108

## Responsibilities Regarding Law-Related Services

Rule 5.7    None

## Voluntary Pro Bono Publico Service

Rule 6.1    EC 1-2, EC 1-4, EC 2-1, EC 2-2, EC 2-16, EC 2-24, EC 2-25, EC 6-2, EC 8-1, EC 8-2, EC 8-3, EC 8-7, EC 8-9

## Accepting Appointments

Rule 6.2 (a)    EC 2-1, EC 2-25, EC 2-27, EC 2-28, EC 2-29, EC 8-3

Rule 6.2(b)    EC 2-16, EC 2-25, EC 2-29, EC 2-30

Rule 6.2(c)    EC 2-25, EC 2-27, EC 2-29, EC 2-30

## Membership in Legal Services Organization

Rule 6.3    EC 2-33, DR 5-101(A)

## Law Reform Activities Affecting Client Interests

Rule 6.4    EC 2-33, DR 5-101(A), DR 8-101

## Nonprofit and Court-Annexed Limited Legal Services Programs

Rule 6.5    None

## Communications Concerning a Lawyer's Services

Rule 7.1    EC 2-8, EC 2-9, EC 2-10, DR 2-101(A), (B), (C), (E), (F) & (G), DR 2-102(E)

## Advertising

Rule 7.2(a)    EC 2-1, EC 2-2, EC 2-6, EC 2-7, EC 2-8, EC 2-15, DR 2-101(B) & (H), DR 2-102(A) & (B), DR 2-103(B), DR 2-104(A)(4) & (5)

# TABLE A

*(continued)*

| ABA MODEL RULES | ABA MODEL CODE |
|---|---|
| Rule 7.2(b) | EC 2-8, EC 2-15, DR 2-101(I), DR 2-103(B), (C) & (D) |
| Rule 7.2(c) | EC 2-8, EC 2-14, DR 2-105(A)(2) & (3). |
| Rule 7.2(d) | None |

### Solicitation of Clients

| | |
|---|---|
| Rule 7.3 | EC 2-3, EC 2-4, EC 5-6, DR 2-103(A), DR 2-103(C)(1), DR 2-103(D)(4)(b) & (c), DR 2-104(A)(1), (2), (3), & (5) |

### Communication of Fields of Practice and Specialization

| | |
|---|---|
| Rule 7.2(c) | EC 2-1, EC 2-7, EC 2-8, EC 2-14, DR 2-101(B)(2), DR 2-102(A)(3), DR 2-102(E), DR 2-105(A) |

### Firm Names and Letterheads

| | |
|---|---|
| Rule 7.1 (Comment) | EC 2-11, EC 2-12, EC 2-13, DR 2-102(A)(4), DR 2-102(B), (C), (D) & (E), DR 2-105 |

### Political Contributions to Obtain Government Legal Engagements or Appointments by Judges

| | |
|---|---|
| Rule 7.6 | None |

### Bar Admission and Disciplinary Matters

| | |
|---|---|
| Rule 8.1(a) | EC 1-1, EC 1-2, EC 1-3, DR 1-101(A) & (B) |
| Rule 8.1(b) | DR 1-102(A)(5), DR 1-103(B) |

### Judicial and Legal Officials

| | |
|---|---|
| Rule 8.2(a) | EC 8-6, DR 8-102 |
| Rule 8.2(b) | DR 8-103 |

### Reporting Professional Misconduct

| | |
|---|---|
| Rule 8.3 | EC 1-3, DR 1-103(A) |

### Misconduct

| | |
|---|---|
| Rule 8.4(a) | EC 1-5, EC 1-6, EC 9-6, DR 1-102(A)(1) & (2), DR 2-103(E), DR 7-102(A) & (B) |
| Rule 8.4(b) | EC 1-5, DR 1-102(A)(3) & (6), DR 7-102(A)(8), DR 8-101(A)(3) |
| Rule 8.4(c) | EC 1-5, EC 9-4, DR 1-102(A)(4), DR 8-101(A)(3) |
| Rule 8.4(d) | EC 3-9, EC 8-3, DR 1-102(A)(5), DR 3-101(B) |
| Rule 8.4(e) | EC 1-5, EC 9-2, EC 9-4, EC 9-6, DR 9-101(C) |
| Rule 8.4(f) | EC 1-5, EC 7-34, EC 9-1, DR 1-102(A)(3), (4), (5) & (6), DR 7-110(A), DR 8-101(A)(2) |
| Rule 8.4(g) | None |

### Disciplinary Authority; Choice of Law

| | |
|---|---|
| Rule 8.5 | None |

# TABLE B**

| ABA MODEL CODE | ABA MODEL RULES |
|---|---|

### Canon 1: Integrity of Profession

| | |
|---|---|
| EC 1-1 | Rule 1.1, 8.1(a) |
| EC 1-2 | Rules 1.1, 6.1, 8.1(a) |
| EC 1-3 | Rules 8.1(a), 8.3 |
| EC 1-4 | Rule 6.1 |
| EC 1-5 | Rule 8.4(a), (b), (c), (e) & (f) |
| EC 1-6 | Rules 1.16(a)(2), 8.4(a) |
| DR 1-101 | Rule 8.1(a) |
| DR 1-102(A)(1) | Rule 8.4(a) |
| DR 1-102(A)(2) | Rules 5.1(c), 5.3(b), 8.4(a) |
| DR 1-102(A)(3) | Rules 8.4(b) & (f) |
| DR 1-102(A)(4) | Rules 3.3(a)(1), (3) & (b), 3.4(a) & (b), 8.4(c) & (f) |
| DR 1-102(A)(5) | Rules 3.1, 3.2, 3.3(a) & (b), 3.4, 8.4(d) & (f) |
| DR 1-102(A)(6) | Rules 3.4(b), 8.4(b) & (f) |
| DR 1-103(A) | Rules 5.1(c), 8.3 |
| DR 1-103(B) | Rules 8.1(b) |

### Canon 2: Making Counsel Available

| | |
|---|---|
| EC 2-1 | Rules 6.1, 6.2(a), 7.2(a) & (c) |
| EC 2-2 | Rules 6.1, 7.2(a) |
| EC 2-3 | Rules 4.3, 7.3 |
| EC 2-4 | Rule 7.3 |
| EC 2-5 | None |
| EC 2-6 | Rule 7.2(a) |
| EC 2-7 | Rules 7.2(a) & (c) |
| EC 2-8 | Rules 7.1, 7.2(a), (b) & (c) |
| EC 2-9 | Rule 7.1 |
| EC 2-10 | Rule 7.1 |
| EC 2-11 | Rule 7.1 (Comment) |
| EC 2-12 | Rule 7.1 (Comment) |
| EC 2-13 | Rule 7.1 (Comment) |
| EC 2-14 | Rule 7.2(c) |
| EC 2-15 | Rule 7.2(a) & (b) |
| EC 2-16 | Rules 1.5(a), 6.1, 6.2(b) |
| EC 2-17 | Rule 1.5(a) |
| EC 2-18 | Rule 1.5(a) |
| EC 2-19 | Rule 1.5(b) |
| EC 2-20 | Rule 1.5(c) & (d) |
| EC 2-21 | Rules 1.7(a), 1.8(f) |

** Table B provides cross-references to related provisions, but only in the sense that the provisions consider substantially similar subject matter or reflect similar concerns. A cross-reference does not indicate that a provision of the ABA Model Code of Professional Responsibility has been incorporated by the provision of a Model Rule. The Canons of the Code are not cross-referenced.

| ABA MODEL CODE | ABA MODEL RULES |
|---|---|
| EC 2-22 | Rule 1.5(c) |
| EC 2-23 | None |
| EC 2-24 | Rule 6.1 |
| EC 2-25 | Rules 6.1, 6.2 |
| EC 2-26 | None |
| EC 2-27 | Rule 6.2(a) & (c) |
| EC 2-28 | Rule 6.2(a) |
| EC 2-29 | Rule 6.2 |
| EC 2-30 | Rules 1.16(a)(1) & (2), 1.16(b)(4), 4.2, 6.2(b) & (c) |
| EC 2-31 | Rules 1.3, 1.16(a) & (b) |
| EC 2-32 | Rule 1.16 |
| EC 2-33 | Rules 5.4, 6.3, 6.4 |
| DR 2-101(A) | Rule 7.1 |
| DR 2-101(B) | Rules 7.1, 7.2(a) |
| DR 2-101(C) | Rule 7.1 |
| DR 2-101(D) | None |
| DR 2-101(E) | Rule 7.1 |
| DR 2-101(F) | Rule 7.1 |
| DR 2-101(G) | Rule 7.1 |
| DR 2-101(H) | Rule 7.2 |
| DR 2-101(I) | Rule 7.2(b) |
| DR 2-102(A) | Rule 7.2(a) & (c) |
| DR 2-102(B) | Rules 7.1 (Comment), 7.2(a) |
| DR 2-102(C) | Rule 7.1 (Comment) |
| DR 2-102(D) | Rule 7.1 (Comment) |
| DR 2-102(E) | Rules 7.1, 7.2(c) |
| DR 2-103(A) | Rule 7.3 |
| DR 2-103(B) | Rule 7.2(a) & (b) |
| DR 2-103(C) | Rules 5.4(a), 7.2(b), 7.3 |
| DR 2-103(D) | Rules 1.16(a)(1), 5.4(a), 7.2(b), 7.3 |
| DR 2-103(E) | Rules 1.16(a), 7.2(a), 7.3 |
| DR 2-104 | Rules 1.16(a), 7.3 |
| DR 2-105 | Rule 7.2(c) |
| DR 2-106(A) | Rule 1.5(a) |
| DR 2-106(B) | Rule 1.5(a) |
| DR 2-106(C) | Rule 1.5(d) |
| DR 2-107(A) | Rule 1.5(e) |
| DR 2-107(B) | Rule 5.4(a)(1) |
| DR 2-108(A) | Rule 5.6 |
| DR 2-108(B) | Rule 5.6 |
| DR 2-109(A) | Rules 1.16(a)(1), 3.1 |
| DR 2-110(A) | Rule 1.16(b)(1), (c) & (d) |
| DR 2-110(B) | Rules 1.16(a), 3.1, 4.4(a) |
| DR 2-110(C) | Rules 1.4(a)(5), 1.16(a) & (b) |

# TABLE B

*(continued)*

<table>
<tr><td>**ABA**<br>**MODEL CODE**</td><td>**ABA**<br>**MODEL RULES**</td></tr>
</table>

*Canon 3: Unauthorized Practice*

| | |
|---|---|
| EC 3-1 | None |
| EC 3-2 | None |
| EC 3-3 | Rule 8.4(e) |
| EC 3-4 | None |
| EC 3-5 | None |
| EC 3-6 | Rule 5.3(a) |
| EC 3-7 | None |
| EC 3-8 | Rule 5.4(a), (b) & (d) |
| EC 3-9 | Rule 8.4(d) |
| DR 3-101(A) | Rule 5.5(a) |
| DR 3-101(B) | Rules 5.5(a), 8.4(d) |
| DR 3-102 | Rule 5.4(a) |
| DR 3-103 | Rule 5.4(b) |

*Canon 4: Confidences and Secrets*

| | |
|---|---|
| EC 4-1 | Rules 1.6(a), 1.18 |
| EC 4-2 | Rules 1.6(a) & (b)(1), 5.3(a) |
| EC 4-3 | Rule 1.6(a) |
| EC 4-4 | Rules 1.6(a), 1.13(g) |
| EC 4-5 | Rules 1.8(b), 1.9(b), 1.10(a) & (b), 5.1(a) & (c), 5.3(a) |
| EC 4-6 | Rule 1.9(b) |
| DR 4-101(A) | Rule 1.6(a) |
| DR 4-101(B) | Rules 1.6(a), 1.8(b), 1.9(b) |
| DR 4-101(C) | Rules 1.6(a) & (b) |
| DR 4-101(D) | Rules 5.1(a) & (b), 5.3(a) & (b) |

*Canon 5: Independent Judgment*

| | |
|---|---|
| EC 5-1 | Rules 1.7(a), 1.8(c), (d), (e), (f), (g) & (i) |
| EC 5-2 | Rules 1.7(a), 1.8(c) |
| EC 5-3 | Rules 1.7, 1.8(a), (d) & (e) |
| EC 5-4 | Rule 1.8(d) |
| EC 5-5 | Rule 1.8(a) & (c) |
| EC 5-6 | Rules 1.8(c), 7.3 |
| EC 5-7 | Rules 1.5(c), 1.8(e) & (i), 1.15 |
| EC 5-8 | Rule 1.8(e) |
| EC 5-9 | Rules 1.7(a), 3.7 |
| EC 5-10 | Rule 3.7(a) |
| EC 5-11 | Rules 1.7(a), 2.1 |
| EC 5-12 | Rule 1.2(a) |
| EC 5-13 | Rule 1.7(a) |
| EC 5-14 | Rule 1.7(a) |
| EC 5-15 | Rule 1.7 |
| EC 5-16 | Rules 1.7(b), 1.13(f) & (g) |

| ABA MODEL CODE | ABA MODEL RULES |
|---|---|
| EC 5-17 | Rule 1.7 |
| EC 5-18 | Rule 1.13(a), (b) & (c) |
| EC 5-19 | Rule 1.7(b) |
| EC 5-20 | Rules 1.12(a) & (b), 2.4 |
| EC 5-21 | Rule 1.7 |
| EC 5-22 | Rule 1.7 |
| EC 5-23 | Rules 1.7(a), 1.8(f), 5.4(c) |
| EC 5-24 | Rules 1.13(a), (b) & (c), 5.4(a) |
| DR 5-101(A) | Rule 1.7, 1.8(i), 6.3, 6.4 |
| DR 5-101(B) | Rules 1.7, 3.7 |
| DR 5-102(A) | Rules 1.7, 3.7 |
| DR 5-102(B) | Rules 1.7(b), 3.7 |
| DR 5-103(A) | Rules 1.8(i), 1.15 |
| DR 5-103(B) | Rule 1.8(e) |
| DR 5-104(A) | Rules 1.7, 1.8(a) |
| DR 5-104(B) | Rule 1.8(d) |
| DR 5-105(A) | Rules 1.7, 1.10(c) |
| DR 5-105(B) | Rules 1.7, 1.13(g) |
| DR 5-105(C) | Rules 1.7(b), 1.13(g), 1.9(a) |
| DR 5-105(D) | Rules 1.10(a), 1.12(c), 1.13(c) |
| DR 5-106 | Rule 1.8(g) |
| DR 5-107(A) | Rules 1.7(b), 1.8(f) |
| DR 5-107(B) | Rules 1.7(a), 1.8(f), 1.13(b) & (c), 2.1, 5.4(c) |
| DR 5-107(C) | Rule 5.4(a) & (d) |

*Canon 6: Competence*

| | |
|---|---|
| EC 6-1 | Rule 1.1 |
| EC 6-2 | Rules 1.1, 5.1(a) & (b), 6.1 |
| EC 6-3 | Rule 1.1 |
| EC 6-4 | Rules 1.1, 1.3 |
| EC 6-5 | Rule 1.1 |
| EC 6-6 | Rule 1.8(h) |
| DR 6-101 | Rules 1.1, 1.3, 1.4(a) |
| DR 6-102 | Rule 1.8(h) |

*Canon 7: Zeal Within the Law*

| | |
|---|---|
| EC 7-1 | Rules 1.2(d), 1.3, 3.1 |
| EC 7-2 | Rules 1.2(d) |
| EC 7-3 | Rule 2.1 |
| EC 7-4 | Rules 3.1, 3.3(a)(1) |
| EC 7-5 | Rules 1.2(d), 3.1, 3.3(a)(3) & (b), 4.1 |
| EC 7-6 | Rule 3.4(a) & (b) |
| EC 7-7 | Rule 1.2(a) |
| EC 7-8 | Rules 1.2(a) & (c), 1.4, 2.1 |
| EC 7-9 | Rule 1.2(c) |

# TABLE B

*(continued)*

| ABA MODEL CODE | ABA MODEL RULES |
|---|---|
| EC 7-10 | Rule 4.4(a) |
| EC 7-11 | Rules 1.14(a), 3.8(a), (b), (c) & (d), 3.9 |
| EC 7-12 | Rule 1.14 |
| EC 7-13 | Rule 3.8 |
| EC 7-14 | Rules 3.1, 3.8(a) & (f), 4.4(a) |
| EC 7-15 | Rule 3.9 |
| EC 7-16 | Rule 3.9 |
| EC 7-17 | Rule 1.2(b) |
| EC 7-18 | Rule 3.8(c), 4.2, 4.3 |
| EC 7-19 | None |
| EC 7-20 | Rules 3.2, 3.5(a) & (d) |
| EC 7-21 | Rule 4.4(a) |
| EC 7-22 | Rules 1.2(d), 3.4(c) |
| EC 7-23 | Rule 3.3(a)(2) |
| EC 7-24 | Rules 3.3(d), 3.4(e) |
| EC 7-25 | Rules 3.1, 3.4(c) & (e), 3.5(d), 3.6, 4.4(a) |
| EC 7-26 | Rule 3.3(a)(3) & (b) |
| EC 7-27 | Rules 3.3(b) & (d), 3.4(a) & (f) |
| EC 7-28 | Rules 3.4(b), 5.3(a) |
| EC 7-29 | Rules 3.5(a) & (c), 4.4(a) |
| EC 7-30 | Rules 3.5(c), 4.4(a) |
| EC 7-31 | Rule 3.5(a) & (c) |
| EC 7-32 | Rules 3.3(a)(1) & (b), 3.5(a) & (c) |
| EC 7-33 | Rule 3.6 |
| EC 7-34 | Rules 3.5(a), 8.4(f) |
| EC 7-35 | Rule 3.5(b) |
| EC 7-36 | Rule 3.5(d) |
| EC 7-37 | Rules 3.5(d), 4.4(a) |
| EC 7-38 | Rules 1.3, 3.4(c) |
| EC 7-39 | None |
| DR 7-101(A) | Rules 1.2(a), 1.3, 3.2, 3.5(d), 4.4(a) |
| DR 7-101(B) | Rules 1.2(b), 1.16(b) |
| DR 7-102(A)(1) | Rules 3.1, 4.4(a) |
| DR 7-102(A)(2) | Rule 3.1 |
| DR 7-102(A)(3) | Rules 3.3(a)(1), (a)(3) & (b), 4.1 |
| DR 7-102(A)(4) | Rules 3.3(a) & (b), 4.1 |
| DR 7-102(A)(5) | Rules 3.3(a)(1), 4.1 |
| DR 7-102(A)(6) | Rules 1.2(d), 3.3(b), 3.4(b) |
| DR 7-102(A)(7) | Rules 1.2(d), 3.3(a)(3) & (b), 4.1 |
| DR 7-102(A)(8) | Rules 1.2(d), 8.4(a) & (b) |
| DR 7-102(B) | Rules 1.6(b)(1), 3.3(b) & (c), 4.1 |
| DR 7-103(A) | Rule 3.8(a) |
| DR 7-103(B) | Rule 3.8(d) |
| DR 7-104 | Rules 3.4(f), 4.2, 4.3 |
| DR 7-105 | None |

# TABLE B

*(continued)*

| ABA MODEL CODE | ABA MODEL RULES |
|---|---|
| DR 7 106(A) | Rules 1.2(d), 3.4(c) & (d), 3.5(a) |
| DR 7-106(B) | Rules 3.3(a)(2), 3.9 |
| DR 7-106(C) | Rules 3.4(a), (c), (d) & (e), 3.5(d), 4.4(a) |
| DR 7-107(A)-(I) | Rule 3.6 |
| DR 7-107(D)-(F) | Rule 4.4(a) |
| DR 7-107(J) | Rules 5.1(a) & (b), 5.3(a) & (b) |
| DR 7-108(A) | Rules 3.5(a), (b) & (c) |
| DR 7-108(B) | Rules 3.5(a), (b) & (c), 5.3(b) |
| DR 7-108(C) | Rules 3.5(a), (b) & (c) |
| DR 7-108(D) | Rules 3.5(c)(3), 4.4(a) |
| DR 7-108(E) | Rules 3.5(a), (b) & (c), 4.4(a), 5.1(c), 5.3(b) |
| DR 7-108(F) | Rules 3.5(a), (b) & (c), 4.4(a) |
| DR 7-108(G) | Rules 3.3(b), 3.5(c) |
| DR 7-109(A) | Rules 3.3(a)(1), (a)(3) & (b), 3.4(a) |
| DR 7-109(B) | Rules 3.3(b), 3.4(a) & (f) |
| DR 7-109(C) | Rule 3.4(b) |
| DR 7-110(A) | Rules 3.5(a), 8.4(f) |
| DR 7-110(B) | Rule 3.5(a) & (b) |

*Canon 8: Improving Legal System*

| | |
|---|---|
| EC 8-1 | Rule 6.1 |
| EC 8-2 | Rule 6.1 |
| EC 8-3 | Rules 6.1, 6.2(a), 8.4(d) |
| EC 8-4 | Rule 3.9 |
| EC 8-5 | Rules 3.3(a)(1), (a)(3) & (b), 3.9 |
| EC 8-6 | Rule 8.2(a) |
| EC 8-7 | Rule 6.1 |
| EC 8-8 | Rule 1.11(d) |
| EC 8-9 | Rule 6.1 |
| DR 8-101 | Rules 3.5, 8.4(b), (c) & (f) |
| DR 8-102 | Rule 8.2(a) |
| DR 8-103 | Rule 8.2(b) |

*Canon 9: Appearance of Impropriety*

| | |
|---|---|
| EC 9-1 | Rule 8.4(f) |
| EC 9-2 | Rules 1.4(a), 8.4(e) |
| EC 9-3 | Rules 1.11(a), 1.12(a) & (b) |
| EC 9-4 | Rule 8.4(c) & (e) |
| EC 9-5 | Rule 1.15 |
| EC 9-6 | Preamble, Rule 8.4(e) |
| EC 9-7 | Rule 1.15 |
| DR 9-101(A) | Rule 1.12(a) & (b) |
| DR 9-101(B) | Rules 1.11(a), 1.12(a) & (b) |
| DR 9-101(C) | Rules 1.4(a)(5), 3.9, 8.4(e) |
| DR 9-102 | Rules 1.4(a), 1.15 |

# Amendments to the Model Rules of Professional Conduct (by Rule)

# Amendments to the Model Rules of Professional Conduct (by Rule)

*(continued)*

**Rule 1.16**
Amended 2002 per
  Midyear Meeting Report 401.

**Rule 1.17**
Added 1990 per
  Midyear Meeting Report 8A.
Amended 2002 per
  Midyear Meeting Report 401.
Amended 2012 per
  Annual Meeting Report 105F.

**Rule 1.18**
Added 2002 per
  Midyear Meeting Report 401.
Amended 2012 per
  Annual Meeting Report 105B.

**Rule 2.1**
Amended 2002 per
  Midyear Meeting Report 401.

**Rule 2.2**
Deleted 2002 per
  Midyear Meeting Report 401.

**Rule 2.3**
Amended 2002 per
  Midyear Meeting Report 401.

**Rule 2.4**
Added 2002 per
  Midyear Meeting Report 401.

**Rule 3.1**
Amended 2002 per
  Midyear Meeting Report 401.

**Rule 3.2**
Amended 2002 per
  Midyear Meeting Report 401.

**Rule 3.3**
Amended 2002 per
  Midyear Meeting Report 401.

**Rule 3.4**
Amended 2002 per
  Midyear Meeting Report 401.

**Rule 3.5**
Amended 2002 per
  Midyear Meeting Report 401.

**Rule 3.6**
Amended 1994 per
  Annual Meeting Report 100.

Amended 2002 per
  Midyear Meeting Report 401.

**Rule 3.7**
Amended 2002 per
  Midyear Meeting Report 401.

**Rule 3.8**
Amended 1990 per
  Midyear Meeting Report 118.
Amended 1994 per
  Annual Meeting Report 100.
Amended 1995 per
  Annual Meeting Report 101.
Amended 2002 per
  Midyear Meeting Report 401.
Amended 2008 per
  Midyear Meeting Report 105B.

**Rule 3.9**
Amended 2002 per
  Midyear Meeting Report 401.

**Rule 4.1**
Amended 2002 per
  Midyear Meeting Report 401.

**Rule 4.2**
Amended 1995 per
  Annual Meeting Report 100.
Amended 2002 per
  Midyear Meeting Report 401.

**Rule 4.3**
Amended 2002 per
  Midyear Meeting Report 401.

**Rule 4.4**
Amended 2002 per
  Midyear Meeting Report 401.
Amended 2012 per
  Annual Meeting Report 105A.

**Rule 5.1**
Amended 2002 per
  Midyear Meeting Report 401.

**Rule 5.3**
Amended 2002 per
  Midyear Meeting Report 401.
Amended 2012 per
  Annual Meeting Report 105C.

**Rule 5.4**
Amended 1990 per
  Midyear Meeting Report 8A.

Amended 2002 per
Midyear Meeting Report 401.

## RULE 5.5
Amended 2002 per
Annual Meeting Report 201B.
Amended 2007 per
Midyear Meeting Report 104.
Amended 2012 per Annual
Meeting Reports 105B and C.
Amended 2013 per
Midyear Meeting Report 107A.
Amended 2016 per
Midyear Meeting Report 103.

## RULE 5.6
Amended 1990 per
Midyear Meeting Report 8A.
Amended 2002 per
Midyear Meeting Report 401.

## RULE 5.7
Added 1994 per
Midyear Meeting Report 113.
Amended 2002 per
Midyear Meeting Report 401.

## RULE 6.1
Amended 1993 per
Midyear Meeting Report 8A.
Amended 2002 per
Midyear Meeting Report 401.

## RULE 6.3
Amended 1987 per
Midyear Meeting Report 121.

## RULE 6.5
Added 2002 per
Midyear Meeting Report 401.

## RULE 7.1
Amended 2002 per
Midyear Meeting Report 401.
Amended 2012 per
Annual Meeting Report 105B.
Amended 2018 per
Annual Meeting Report 101.

## RULE 7.2
Amended 1989 per
Midyear Meeting Report 120B.
Amended 1990 per
Midyear Meeting Report 8A.
Amended 2002 per
Midyear Meeting Report 401.

Amended 2002 per
Annual Meeting Report 114.
Amended 2012 per
Annual Meeting Report 105B.
Amended 2018 per
Annual Meeting Report 101.

## RULE 7.3
Amended 1989 per Midyear
Meeting Reports 115 and 120B.
Amended 2002 per
Midyear Meeting Report 401.
Amended 2012 per
Annual Meeting Report 105B.
Amended 2018 per
Annual Meeting Report 101.

## RULE 7.4
Deleted 2018 per
Annual Meeting Report 101.

## RULE 7.5
Deleted 2018 per
Annual Meeting Report 101.

## RULE 7.6
Added 2000 per
Midyear Meeting Report 110.

## RULE 8.1
Amended 2002 per
Midyear Meeting Report 401.

## RULE 8.3
Amended 1991 per
Midyear Meeting Report 108C.
Amended 2002 per
Midyear Meeting Report 401.

## RULE 8.4
Amended 1998 per
Annual Meeting Report 117.
Amended 2002 per
Midyear Meeting Report 401.
Amended 2016 per
Annual Meeting Report 109.

## RULE 8.5
Amended 1993 per
Annual Meeting Report 114.
Amended 2002 per
Annual Meeting Report 201C.
Amended 2013 per
Midyear Meeting Report 107D.

# AMENDMENTS TO THE MODEL RULES OF PROFESSIONAL CONDUCT (BY DATE)

**1987 MIDYEAR MEETING**
Rules 1.7, 1.8, 1.9, 1.11, 1.12 and 6.3

**1989 MIDYEAR MEETING**
Rules 1.9, 1.10, 7.2, 7.3 and 7.4

**1990 MIDYEAR MEETING**
Rules 1.17, 3.8, 5.4, 5.6 and 7.2

**1991 MIDYEAR MEETING**
Rule 8.3

**1992 ANNUAL MEETING**
Rule 7.4

**1993 MIDYEAR MEETING**
Rule 6.1

**1993 ANNUAL MEETING**
Rule 8.5

**1994 MIDYEAR MEETING**
Rule 5.7

**1994 ANNUAL MEETING**
Rules 3.6, 3.8 and 7.4

**1995 ANNUAL MEETING**
Rules 3.8 and 4.2

**1997 MIDYEAR MEETING**
Rule 1.14

**1998 ANNUAL MEETING**
Rule 8.4

**2000 MIDYEAR MEETING**
Rule 7.6

**2002 MIDYEAR MEETING**
Preamble, Scope, Rules 1.0, 1.1, 1.2,
1.3, 1.4, 1.5, 1.6, 1.7, 1.8, 1.9, 1.10,
1.11, 1.12, 1.13, 1.14, 1.15, 1.16, 1.17,
1.18, 2.1, 2.2, 2.3, 2.4, 3.1, 3.2, 3.3, 3.4,
3.5, 3.6, 3.7, 3.8, 3.9, 4.1, 4.2, 4.3, 4.4,
5.1, 5.3. 5.4, 5.6, 5.7, 6.1, 6.5, 7.1, 7.2,
7.3, 7.4, 7.5, 8.1, 8.3 and 8.4

**2002 ANNUAL MEETING**
Rules 5.5, 7.2, 7.5 and 8.5

**2003 ANNUAL MEETING**
Rules 1.6 and 1.13

**2007 MIDYEAR MEETING**
Rule 5.5

**2008 MIDYEAR MEETING**
Rule 3.8

**2009 MIDYEAR MEETING**
Rules 1.0 and 1.10

**2009 ANNUAL MEETING**
Rule 1.10

**2012 ANNUAL MEETING**
Rules 1.0, 1.1, 1.4, 1.6, 1.17, 1.18, 4.4,
5.3, 5.5, 7.1, 7.2 and 7.3

**2013 MIDYEAR MEETING**
Rules 5.5 and 8.5.

**2016 MIDYEAR MEETING**
Rule 5.5

**2016 ANNUAL MEETING**
Rule 8.4

**2018 ANNUAL MEETING**
Rules 7.1, 7.2, 7.3, 7.4 and 7.5

776

# TABLE OF CASES

*Alphabetization is letter-by-letter (e.g., "Newman" precedes "New York.")*

McCulloch v. Velez, 364 F.3d 1 (1st Cir. 2004), 425

McCullum; Commonwealth v., 602 A.2d 313 (Pa. 1992), 412

McCurdy v. Kansas Dep't of Transp., 898 P.2d 650 (Kan. 1995), 506

McDaniel; Kentucky Bar Ass'n v., 170 S.W.3d 400 (Ky. 2005), 358

McDaniels; Commonwealth v., 785 A.2d 120 (Pa. Super. Ct. 2001), 21

McDonald, In re, 906 N.W.2d 238 (Minn. 2018), 691

McDonald; Attorney Grievance Comm'n v., 85 A.3d 117 (Md. 2014), 735

McDowell; Attorney Grievance Comm'n v., 93 A.3d 711 (Md. 2014), 503, 515, 518

McDowell; State v., 669 N.W.2d 204 (Wis. Ct. App. 2003), 376

McEnaney, In re, 718 A.2d 920 (R.I. 1998), 709, 710

McGee; State ex rel. Okla. Bar Ass'n v., 48 P.3d 787 (Okla. 2002), 131

McGrath, In re Disciplinary Proceeding against, 280 P.3d 1091 (Wash. 2012), 396, 733, 744

McGraw, In re, 414 P.3d 841 (Or. 2018), 347

McGraw; Lawyer Disciplinary Bd. v., 461 S.E.2d 850 (W. Va. 1995), 112, 115

McGregor; United States v., 838 F. Supp. 2d 1256 (M.D. Ala. 2012), 411

McIntosh, In re, 991 P.2d 403 (Kan. 1999), 722

McIntosh v. Mills, 17 Cal. Rptr. 3d 66 (Ct. App. 2004), 524

McKaskie v. Wiggins, 465 U.S. 168 (1984), 593

McKechnie, In re, 708 N.W.2d 310 (N.D. 2006), 81

McKenzie Constr. v. St. Croix Storage Corp., 961 F. Supp. 857 (D.V.I. 1997), 342

McKesson HBOC, Inc. Sec. Litig., In re, 126 F. Supp. 2d 1239 (N.D. Cal. 2000), 482

McKittrick; Iowa Supreme Court Bd. of Prof'l Ethics & Conduct v., 683 N.W.2d 554 (Iowa 2004), 79

McLain v. Allstate Prop. & Cas. Ins. Co., Civ. No. 3:16CV843-TSL-RHW, 2017 WL 1513090, 2017 BL 136582 (S.D. Miss. Apr. 25, 2017), 187

McLaren; State v. See Humphrey ex rel. State v. McLaren

McLaughlin v. State, 173 P.3d 1014 (Alaska Ct. App. 2007), 39

McLean; People v., 21 N.E.3d 218 (N.Y. 2014), 462

McMillan v. Shadow Ridge at Oak Park Homeowner's Ass'n, 81 Cal. Rptr. 3d 550 (Ct. App. 2008), 478

McMillen v. State, No. A08-1917, 2010 WL 10367, 2010 BL 1648 (Minn. Ct. App. Jan. 5, 2010), 217

McNair v. Rainsford, 499 S.E.2d 488 (S.C. Ct. App. 1998), 8

McNamara; People v., 275 P.3d 792 (Colo. O.P.D.J. 2011), 682

McNaughton; United States v., 848 F. Supp. 1195 (E.D. Pa. 1994), 473

McNaul; SEC v., 277 F.R.D. 439 (D. Kan. 2011), 294

McNelis, In re, 150 A.3d 185 (R.I. 2016), 514

McVeigh; United States v., 964 F. Supp. 313 (D. Colo. 1997), 411

MDK, In re, 534 N.W.2d 271 (Minn. 1995), 661

Meachum v. Outdoor World Corp., 654 N.Y.S.2d 240 (Sup. Ct. 1996), 473

Meaden, In re, 902 A.2d 802 (D.C. 2006), 709

Mears, In re, 723 N.E.2d 873 (Ind. 2000), 728

Mecca, In re, 214 So. 3d 827 (La. 2017), 710

Mecham; State v., 9 P.3d 777 (Utah Ct. App. 2000), 40

Medina v. California, 505 U.S. 437 (1992), 262

Medina v. Draslow, 53 N.Y.S.3d 116 (App. Div. 2017), 97

Medina Cnty. Bar Ass'n v. Cameron, 958 N.E.2d 138 (Ohio 2011), 456

Medina Cnty. Bar Ass'n v. Grieselhuber, 678 N.E.2d 535 (Ohio 1997), 622

Megale; United States v., 235 F.R.D. 151 (D. Conn. 2006), 412

Mehaffy, Rider, Windholz & Wilson v. Central Bank Denver N.A., 892 P.2d 230 (Colo. 1995) (en banc), 331

Meier v. Meier, 835 So. 2d 379 (Fla. Dist. Ct. App. 2003), 388

Melchior; Board of Prof'l Responsibility v., 269 P.3d 1088 (Wyo. 2012), 458

Melendez, In re, 957 N.Y.S.2d 740 (App. Div. 2012), 676

Melton; United States v., 948 F. Supp. 2d 998 (N.D. Iowa 2013), 420

Opinion No. 39 of Comm. on Att'y Adver., In re, 961 A.2d 722 (N.J. 2008), 623

Opinion No. 583 of Advisory Comm. on Prof'l Ethics, In re, 526 A.2d 692 (N.J. 1987), 399

Oram v. 6 B's, Inc., No. 332925, 2018 WL 442213, 2018 BL 14335 (Mich. Ct. App. Jan. 16, 2018), 237

Orren, In re, 590 N.W.2d 127 (Minn. 1999), 67

Orsini, In re, 661 N.Y.S.2d 321 (App. Div. 1997), 270

Orsini v. Larry Moyer Trucking, Inc., 833 S.W.2d 366 (Ark. 1992), 10

Ortlieb; United States v., 274 F.3d 871 (5th Cir. 2001), 402

Osbon, Ex parte, 888 So. 2d 1236 (Ala. 2004), 149

Osicka, In re, 765 N.W.2d 775 (Wis. 2009), 352

Ositis, In re, 40 P.3d 500 (Or. 2002), 707

Oswinkle; Attorney Grievance Comm'n v., 772 A.2d 267 (Md. 2001), 681

Overboe, In re, 745 N.W.2d 852 (Minn. 2008), 749, 752

Overseas Shipholding Grp., Inc.; United States v., 625 F.3d 1 (1st Cir. 2010), 464

Owens, In re, 806 A.2d 1230 (D.C. 2002), 366

Owens v. McDermott, Will & Emery, 736 N.E.2d 145 (Ill. App. Ct. 2000), 8

**P**

Pabst v. State, 192 P.3d 630 (Kan. 2008), 430

Paige; Statewide Grievance Comm. v., No. CV030198335S, 2004 WL 1833462 (Conn. Super. Ct. July 14, 2004), 131

Pallon v. Roggio, Nos. 04-3625 (JAP), 06-1068 (FLW), 2006 WL 2466854, 2006 BL 91075 (D.N.J. Aug. 24, 2006), 192

Palmer v. Pioneer Inn Assocs., Ltd., 338 F.3d 981 (9th Cir. 2003), 465, 466

Panel Case No. 17289, In re, 669 N.W.2d 898 (Minn. 2003), 12

Panel File No. 99-5, In re, 607 N.W.2d 429 (Minn. 2000), 36

Pape; Florida Bar v., 918 So. 2d 240 (Fla. 2005), 618

Pappas v. Waggoner's Heating & Air, Inc., 108 P.3d 9 (Okla. Civ. App. 2004), 223, 228

Papyrus Tech. Corp. v. N.Y. Stock Exch., 325 F. Supp. 2d 270 (S.D.N.Y. 2004), 202

Parallel Networks, LLC v. Abercrombie & Fitch Co., No. 6:10-CV-111, 2016 WL 3883392, 2016 BL 109705 (E.D. Tex. Apr. 1, 2016), 228

Parish, In re, No. 12–O–15242, 2015 WL 514334 (Cal. Bar Ct. Review Dep't Feb. 5, 2015), 691

Park Apartments at Fayetteville, LP v. Plants, 545 S.W.3d 755 (Ark. 2018), 191

Parker v. Pepsi-Cola Gen. Bottlers, Inc., 249 F. Supp. 2d 1006 (N.D. Ill. 2003), 469, 472

Parker; United States v., 165 F. Supp. 2d 431 (W.D.N.Y. 2001), 723

Park-N-Shop, Ltd. v. City of Highwood, 864 F. Supp. 82 (N.D. Ill. 1994), 210

Parks, In re, 9 So. 3d 106 (La. 2009), 675, 708

Parks v. Eastwood Ins. Servs., Inc., 235 F. Supp. 2d 1082 (C.D. Cal. 2002), 482

Parnoff; Disciplinary Counsel v., 152 A.3d 1222 (Conn. 2016), 269

Parrinello, In re, 67 N.Y.S.3d 355 (App. Div. 2017), 118

Parrish v. Mississippi Bar, 691 So. 2d 904 (Miss. 1996), 51

Parrott, In re, 804 S.E.2d 852 (S.C. 2017), 712

Parshall, In re, 878 A.2d 1253 (D.C. 2005), 589

Parsley; People v., 109 P.3d 1060 (Colo. O.P.D.J. 2005), 705

Partee v. Compton, 653 N.E.2d 454 (Ill. App. Ct. 1995), 96

Partington, In re, Civ. No. 11-00753 SOM, 2017 WL 4560070, 2017 BL 366267 (D. Haw. Oct. 12, 2017), 348

Parwatikar; People v., No. 04PDJ064, 2004 WL 1859850 (Colo. O.P.D.J. July 22, 2004), 715

Paschal, In re, 772 S.E.2d 271 (S.C. 2015), 178

Pasillas-Sanchez; People v., 214 P.3d 520 (Colo. App. 2009), 423, 424

Pastor, In re, 60 N.Y.S.3d 685 (App. Div. 2017), 712

Pastorek, In re, 239 So. 3d 798 (La. 2018), 710

Pasyanos, In re, No. 02-O-11558, 2005 WL 103065 (Cal. Bar Ct. Review Dep't Jan. 13, 2005), 676, 677

Pate v. Robinson, 383 U.S. 375 (1966), 262

Patmon; State ex rel. Okla. Bar Ass'n v., 939 P.2d 1155 (Okla. 1997), 515

*Pfizer, Inc. v. Farr*, No. M2011-0139-COA-R10-CV, 2012 WL 2370619, 2012 BL 159661 (Tenn. Ct. App. June 22, 2012), 159

*Philbrick v. University of Conn.*, 51 F. Supp. 2d 164 (D. Conn. 1999), 24

*Philin Corp. v. Westhood, Inc.*, No. CV-04-1228-HU, 2005 WL 582695 (D. Or. Mar. 11, 2005), 237

*Philip Morris Inc.; United States v.*, 312 F. Supp. 2d 27 (D.D.C. 2004), 212

*Phillabaum; Disciplinary Counsel v.*, 44 N.E.3d 271 (Ohio 2015), 735

*Phillips, In re*, 766 A.2d 47 (D.C. 2001), 23

*Phillips, In re*, 107 P.3d 615 (Or. 2005), 171

*Phillips, In re*, 244 P.3d 549 (Ariz. 2010), 499, 515, 517

*Phillips; Attorney Grievance Comm'n v.*, 155 A.3d 476 (Md. 2017), 348, 518, 532, 547, 675, 733

*Phillips v. Washington Legal Found.*, 524 U.S. 156 (1998), 272

*Piaskoski & Assocs. v. Ricciardi*, 686 N.W.2d 675 (Wis. Ct. App. 2004), 100

*Piazza; Iowa Supreme Court Att'y Disciplinary Bd. v.*, 756 N.W.2d 690 (Iowa 2008), 92

*Pickett v. Sheridan Health Care Ctr.*, 664 F.3d 632 (7th Cir. 2011), 89

*Piepes, In re*, 692 N.Y.S.2d 716 (App. Div. 1999), 719

*Pierce, In re*, 706 N.W.2d 749 (Minn. 2005), 359

*Pierce v. Cook*, 992 So. 2d 612 (Miss. 2008), 9

*Pierce v. Morrison Mahoney LLP*, 897 N.E.2d 562 (Mass. 2008), 562

*Pilli v. Virginia State Bar*, 611 S.E.2d 389 (Va.), *cert. denied*, 546 U.S. 977 (2005), 688, 690, 692

*Pincelli, In re*, 648 S.E.2d 578 (S.C. 2007), 547

*Pinciaro; Statewide Grievance Comm. v.*, No. CV 970396643S, 1997 WL 155379 (Conn. Super. Ct. Mar. 21, 1997) (unpublished), 517

*Pinck, In re*, 94 A.3d 905 (N.J. 2014), 305

*Pinno; Attorney Grievance Comm'n v.*, 85 A.3d 159 (Md. 2014), 293

*Pinsky v. Statewide Grievance Comm.*, 578 A.2d 1075 (Conn. 1990), 457

*Pizur, In re*, 84 N.E.3d 627 (Ind. 2017), 446

*Placide, In re*, 414 P.3d 1124 (Wash. 2018), 81, 720

*Plants; Lawyer Disciplinary Bd. v.*, 801 S.E.2d 225 (W. Va. 2017), 705

*Plotts v. Chester Cycles LLC*, No. CV-14-00428-PHX-GMS, 2016 WL 614023, 2016 BL 43138 (D. Ariz. Feb. 16, 2016), 190

*Plumb; Iowa Supreme Court Bd. of Prof'l Ethics & Conduct v.*, 546 N.W.2d 215 (Iowa 1996), 724

*Polk, In re*, 174 So. 3d 1131 (La. 2015), 284

*Polk; State v.*, 415 S.W.3d 692 (Mo. 2013), 437

*Poll; People v.*, 65 P.3d 483 (Colo. O.P.D.J. 2003), 370

*Polycast Tech. Corp. v. Uniroyal, Inc.*, 129 F.R.D. 621 (S.D.N.Y. 1990), 455

*Poly Software Intern., Inc. v. Su*, 880 F. Supp. 1487 (D. Utah 1995), 341

*Ponder, In re*, 654 S.E.2d 533 (S.C. 2007), 514

*Ponds, In re*, 876 A.2d 636 (D.C. 2005), 752

*Pony v. County of L.A.*, 433 F.3d 1138 (9th Cir. 2006), 89

*Poole, In re*, 125 P.3d 954 (Wash. 2006) (en banc), 381, 722

*Poole, In re*, 193 P.3d 1064 (Wash. 2008), 733

*Poole v. Prince*, 61 So. 3d 258 (Ala. 2010), 14

*Poole v. United States*, 832 F.2d 561 (11th Cir. 1987), 39

*Porter, In re*, 930 So. 2d 875 (La. 2006), 369

*Porter; State ex rel. Okla. Bar Ass'n v.*, 766 P.2d 958 (Okla. 1988), 687

*Portland Gen. Elec. Co. v. Duncan, Weinberg, Miller & Pembroke, P.C.*, 986 P.2d 35 (Or. Ct. App. 1999), 12

*Poseidon Pools of Am., Inc., In re*, 180 B.R. 718 (Bankr. E.D.N.Y. 1995), 83

*Post v. Bregman*, 707 A.2d 806 (Md. 1998), 14

*Poteat; Kentucky Bar Ass'n v.*, 511 S.W.3d 909 (Ky. 2017), 544

*Pound v. Cameron*, 36 Cal. Rptr. 3d 922 (Ct. App. 2005), 201

*Powell, In re*, 953 N.E.2d 1060 (Ind. 2011), 93

*Powell; Attorney Disciplinary Bd. v.*, 830 N.W.2d 355 (Iowa 2013), 269

*Powell; Attorney Grievance Comm'n v.*, 192 A.3d 633 (Md. 2018), 267, 268

*Powell Mountain Energy, LLC v. Manalapan Land Co.*, Civ. No. 09-305-JBC, 2011 WL 3880512, 2011 BL 223860 (E.D. Ky. Aug. 31, 2011), 65

*Theard v. United* States, 354 U.S. 278 (1957), 751

*Theodore; People v.*, 926 P.2d 1237 (Colo. 1996), 45

*Thomas, In re*, 740 A.2d 538 (D.C. 1999), 61, 682

*Thomas, In re*, 962 N.E.2d 454 (Ill. 2012), 738

*Thomas, In re*, 193 P.3d 907 (Kan. 2008), 359

*Thomas; Attorney Grievance Comm'n v.*, 127 A.3d 562 (Md. 2015), 54, 680

*Thomas; State ex rel. Okla. Bar Ass'n v.*, 886 P.2d 477 (Okla. 1994), 357

*Thomas v. Tenneco Packaging Co.*, 293 F.3d 1306 (11th Cir. 2002), 402

*Thomas, State ex rel. v. Schneider*, 130 P.3d 991 (Ariz. Ct. App. 2006), 247

*Thomas B. Olson & Assoc. v. Leffert Jay & Polglaze P.A.*, 756 N.W.2d 907 (Minn. Ct. App. 2008), 280

*Thompson, In re*, 991 P.2d 820 (Colo. 1999), 720

*Thompson; Attorney Grievance Comm'n v.*, 786 A.2d 763 (Md. 2001), 708

*Thompson v. Hiter*, 826 N.E.2d 503 (Ill. App. Ct. 2005), 102

*Thompson; Mississippi Bar v.*, 5 So. 3d 330 (Miss. 2008), 547

*Thompson v. Supreme Court Comm. on Prof'l Conduct*, 252 S.W.3d 125 (Ark. 2007), 488

*Thompson, State ex rel. v. Dueker*, 346 S.W.3d 390 (Mo. Ct. App. 2011), 314

*Thorn; Lawyer Disciplinary Bd. v.*, 783 S.E.2d 321 (W. Va. 2016), 55

*Thornsbury; Kentucky Bar Ass'n v.*, 511 S.W.3d 379 (Ky. 2017), 711

*Thornton, In re Marriage of*, 486 N.E.2d 1288 (Ill. App. Ct. 1985), 228

*Threadgill v. Board of Prof'l Responsibility*, 299 S.W.3d 792 (Tenn. 2009), 60

*Thul v. Onewest Bank*, No. 12 C 6380, 2013 WL 212926 (N.D. Ill. Jan. 18, 2013), 373

*Thurston, In re*, 127 A.3d 917 (R.I. 2015), 737

*Thyden, In re*, 877 A.2d 129 (D.C. 2005), 62

*Ticktin; Florida Bar v.*, 14 So. 3d 928 (Fla. 2009), 169

*Tidball, In re*, 503 N.W.2d 850 (S.D. 1993), 268

*Tidwell, In re*, 831 A.2d 953 (D.C. 2003), 708

*Tiller v. Semonis*, 635 N.E.2d 572 (Ill. App. Ct. 1994), 52, 55

*Tillman, In re*, 462 S.E.2d 283 (S.C. 1995), 297

*Tilton v. Trezza*, 819 N.Y.S.2d 213 (Sup. Ct. 2006), 10

*Timbers; Statewide Grievance Comm. v.*, 796 A.2d 565 (Conn. App. Ct. 2002), 96

*Tina X v. John X*, 32 N.Y.S.3d 332 (App. Div. 2016), 215

*Toaston, In re*, 225 So. 3d 1066 (La. 2017), 357

*Tocco, In re*, 984 P.2d 539 (Ariz. 1999), 47, 445

*Tofflemire; Iowa Supreme Court Bd. of Prof'l Ethics & Conduct v.*, 689 N.W.2d 83 (Iowa 2004), 79

*Toigo, In re*, 385 P.3d 585 (Nev. 2016), 131

*Toledo Bar Ass'n v. Rust*, 921 N.E.2d 1056 (Ohio 2010), 349

*Toledo Bar Ass'n v. Wroblewski*, 512 N.E.2d 978 (Ohio 1987), 25

*Toler, Ex parte*, 710 So. 2d 415 (Ala. 1998), 10

*Tomar, Seliger, Simonoff, Adourian & O'Brien, P.C. v. Snyder*, 601 A.2d 1056 (Del. Super. Ct. 1990), 523

*Topp; Idaho State Bar v.*, 925 P.2d 1113 (Idaho 1996), 689, 693

*Torgerson, In re*, 870 N.W.2d 602 (Minn. 2015), 488, 681, 731

*Tornow, In re*, 835 N.W.2d 912 (S.D. 2013), 381

*Toronto, In re*, 696 A.2d 8 (N.J. 1997), 712

*Torre, In re*, 127 A.3d 690 (N.J. 2015), 169

*Torrey v. Leesburg Reg'l Med. Ctr.*, 769 So. 2d 1040 (Fla. 2000), 552

*Toups, In re*, 773 So. 2d 709 (La. 2000), 153

*Town of. See name of town*

*Towne, In re*, 929 A.2d 774 (Del. 2007), 548

*Tracy v. Dennie*, 411 S.W.3d 702 (Ark. 2012), 421

*Tradewinds Airlines, Inc. v. Soros*, No. 08 Civ. 5901 (JFK), 2009 WL 1321695 (S.D.N.Y. May 12, 2009), 570

*Trahant, In re*, 108 So. 3d 67 (La. 2012), 502

*Trainor v. Kentucky Bar Ass'n*, 311 S.W.3d 719 (Ky. 2010), 349

*Treinen, In re*, 131 P.3d 1282 (N.M. 2006), 709

*Trejo, In re*, 185 P.3d 1160 (Wash. 2008), 268, 271, 514

*Trester, In re*, 172 P.3d 31 (Kan. 2007), 540, 715

# INDEX

## A

Abandonment of case or client, 55

Abuse of process, 734. *See also* Frivolous litigation

Abuse of public office or position of trust, 735–736

Academic degrees, 628, 649

"Accommodation" clients as former clients, 186

Accountants
  designation in advertising and on letterhead, 628
  referral fees for, 646

Accounting of client's funds. *See* Funds of client

Acquiring interest in litigation
  business transactions between client and lawyer, 168, 177–178
  champerty and maintenance, 167, 177
  conflicts of interest, 166–167
  contingent fee as, 165
  liens for fees and expenses, 162, 167, 178
  securities in lieu of cash fee as, 170

Adjudicative officers. *See* Judges

Administration of justice, conduct prejudicial to, 703
  by lawyer, 727–729

Administrative proceedings
  appearance before, 439–441
  disciplinary authority of, 751
  ex parte communications in, 397, 398–399, 441

Administrators
  fees, 76
  misconduct by, 735–736

Admiralty attorneys, 649, 664

Admission to the bar, 369, 372, 673–683

Adoptions
  conflicts of interest, 153
  reform of law on, 607

Advanced fees. *See* Fee advances

Advancing funds to client. *See* Financial assistance to client; Loans

Adverse persons. *See* Communication with adverse persons; Conflicts of interest; Former clients

Advertising, 615–666. *See also* Letterhead; Name of firm; Solicitation
  comparisons or ratings, 615, 622–623
  costs of, 642
  disclaimers, 623–624, 661
  electronic media, 310, 311–312, 636, 640, 654, 661
  e-mail, 656
  endorsements, 621–622
  fees, statements about, 620
  fields of practice, 646–649, 663–664
  filing and retention requirements, 650
  First Amendment considerations, 617–618, 647
  former judges who have returned to practice, 629
  group, 625–627, 642
  group coupons, 644–645
  identification of, as "advertising material," 654, 660–661
  internet, 310, 311–312, 617. *See also* Social networking
  labeling, 661
  lawyers not admitted to practice in jurisdiction, 540
  marketing and referral arrangements, 276–277
  media permitted, 639–640, 654
  misrepresentation, 618–623
  multijurisdictional practice, 627–628
  name and address of responsible lawyer in, 649–650
  prepaid legal service plans, 643, 662
  prior results in, 620–621, 623
  qualifications in field other than law, 628–629
  recommendations and referrals, payment prohibited for, 622, 636–637, 641–646

notice of departing firm, 66–67

organization as client, 58, 232, 465–468

participants in matter communicating with each other, 457–458

plea bargains, 57, 64

promptness, 52–53, 62–63

prospective clients, 307–309

responding to requests for information, 58–59, 67

settlement offers, 57, 61

status of matter, 61, 67

through others, 65–66

withholding information from client, 58–59, 65

Communication with corporate employees

advice to unrepresented, 476

alter ego test, 466

confidentiality, 123, 231

control group test, 466

former employees of opponent, 467–468, 482

identity of client, clarifying, 236, 247–248, 476–477

informing fully, 58

interviews, 476

managing/speaking test, 465–466

of opponent, 465–468

"Upjohn" test, 466

Communication with judges

abuse by judge, 393

administrative law judges, 397, 398–399

ex parte, prohibited, 393, 395–399

in ex parte proceedings, 364, 397–398

hearing officers, 399

initiated by judge, 397–398

written submissions, 398

Communication with jurors

after trial, 393, 400–401

pretrial publicity causing prejudice, 407

during proceeding, 393, 399

respecting juror's desire not to communicate, 401

social networking, 448

Communication with prospective clients, 307–309

Communication with witnesses

advising to give false testimony, 384–385

bribing, 385

discouraging voluntary disclosure by, 390–391

employees as fact witnesses, 467

interviewing, 476

obstructing other party's access to, 382–383

questioning, 390–391

Competence, 19–30. *See also* Ineffective assistance of counsel

of appointed counsel, 29, 597

diligence related to, 50

misconduct for lack of, 738

Competency of clients. *See* Criminal representation; Diminished capacity, clients with

Computers. *See* Electronic media

Conduct prejudicial to administration of justice

intent, 729

by lawyer, 703, 727–729, 741–742

Confidentiality, 103–137. *See also* Disclosure of confidential information; Encryption

account records of client, 682

actions to preserve, 108, 130–137

alternative dispute resolution, 339–340

assistance programs for lawyers and judges, 696

attorney-client privilege, distinguished from, 104, 109–111

corporate client, 118–119, 123, 242

crime-fraud exception, 122–123

in disciplinary proceedings, 680

domestic relations proceedings, 406

duty of candor conflicting with, 366

duty to raise issue, 131

evaluation, information used in preparing, 328, 330–331

evaluation for use by third persons, 330–331

exceptions, 119–130

former clients, 108, 118–119, 181, 184–191, 192–193

informed consent to disclose
information, 117–118

lawyer as witness, 418

perjury, 374–376

related civil proceeding, 98–99

subpoenas, grand jury, 427, 428

third-party payment of fees, 176

trial publicity, 405, 406, 412

uncharged suspects, 428, 470–471

withdrawal, 287–288, 292

Criticism of judges. *See* Judges, criticism of

Custody of children, 60

# D

"Daily deal" payments, 276

Death penalty cases. *See* Capital cases

"Death row syndrome," 263

Deceased lawyers. *See also* Sale of law practice

name, in firm's name, 629–630

payments to estate of, 527

solo practitioners, 50

Deceit by lawyer. *See* Fraud/fraudulent conduct; Misrepresentation

Decision-making authority of client

appeals, 39

clients with diminished capacity, 32, 40–41, 254

disagreement between lawyer and client, 31–32

jury trials, 31, 39

for objectives of representation, 31, 34–35

pleas, 31, 39

for self-representation, 39

settlements, 31, 36–37

testifying, 31, 39

Declining representation. *See* Court-appointed lawyers; Termination of lawyer-client relationship

Defense lawyers. *See* Criminal representation

Degrees, academic, 628, 649

Delay, 355–359

appeals, 358–359

communicating with client, 61

court orders, obeying, 357

discipline for, 356

discovery, 357–358

disposition, 358

hearings, appearance at scheduled, 357

impeding administration of justice, 355

for lawyer's convenience, 355

pleadings and motions, 356–357

unreasonable, 52–53

Delegation of work to others, 27, 56. *See also* Supervisory duties

Departing lawyer

confidential information, 191

financial disincentives, 563–564

imputed disqualification, 203

joining new firm, 182–183, 199, 202–203

notice to clients, 66–67

reasonable disincentives, 561–562

restrictions on practice of law, 559, 560–561

retirement benefits, 565–566

solicitation of clients, 661

Depositions

conduct during, 402

false evidence in, 361–362, 363, 365

lawyer as witness conducting, 423

out-of-state lawyer taking, 546

Derivative actions, 235

Destruction of evidence. *See* Evidence

Diligence, 49–56

in investigation, 330

misconduct for lack of, 738

Diminished capacity, clients with, 251–264. *See also* Guardians

assessment of degrees of competence, 251, 258–259

client with poor judgment, 258–259

communication with, 58

confidentiality of mental disability proceedings, 406

decisions of, abiding by, 32, 40–41, 252

discharge of lawyer by, 282

disclosure of disability of, 253, 261–264

emergency legal assistance to, 253, 263–264

implied authorization to disclose confidential information, 117

incompetence to stand trial, 262–263

lawyer-client relationship, 251–252

legal representative already in place, 257

minor clients. *See* Minor clients

protective action, 257–260

suicidal client, 261–262

withdrawal from representing, 260

Directories, legal, 643

Disability discrimination. *See* Discrimination or bias on part of lawyer

Disabled clients. *See* Diminished capacity, clients with

Disabled lawyers

lawyer assistance program, information learned in, 696, 702

payments to representative of, 527

solo practitioner, diligence and, 50

withdrawal from representation by, 285–286

Disaster response, temporary provision of legal services, 538, 553

Disbarment. *See* Disciplined lawyers

Discharge of lawyer, 281–298

appointed by court, 461

client's right, 32, 282, 286–287

clients with diminished capacity, 282

communication with client after, 462

with contingency agreement, 95, 96–97

mitigating effect of discharge, 283

organizational representation, 234, 243, 247

protection of client after, 292–296

return of unearned advanced or retainer fees, 93

upon sale of law practice, 301

withdrawal upon, 287

Disciplinary proceedings

candor and cooperation, 369, 372, 674, 676–678, 680–681, 733–734

disclosure of client confidences, 103, 106, 118

duty to respond, 678–680

Fifth Amendment protection, 673, 681–683

good-faith challenge, 704

jurisdictional authority, 745, 748–751

pro bono work as mitigating factor, 589–590

prosecutors, 432

representation, 673

responding to, 674–675

stand-alone offense, 674–675

Discipline

abusive litigation tactics, 380

"administrative" suspensions, 544

advocate-witness role and, 417

authority for, 745–746

conflicts of law in, 752–753

conversion and misappropriation of client funds, 268

court appointment, refusal or withdrawal, 599–600

delay as grounds for, 356

disruptive behavior during litigation, 402

frivolous litigation, 347–348, 352–353

inexperience as mitigating factor, 507

judicial candidates, 693–694

misconduct outside licensing jurisdiction, 748–750

out-of-state lawyers, 750–751

prosecutors, 432

threat of disciplinary action, 489–490, 739

unauthorized communication with represented persons, 472–473

unreasonable fees as grounds for, 84–85

Disciplined lawyers

fee-splitting with, 523–524

on letterhead, 630

as paralegals, 545

reporting misconduct of, 697–698

sale of practice of law by, 306

unauthorized practice of law, 544–545, 546

Disclaimers, 623–624, 648, 661

Disclosure. *See also* Disclosure of confidential information

adverse legal authority, 362, 372–373

to bar, 677

Impropriety, appearance of, 159

Imputed disqualification. *See also* Screening
  co-counsel, 201
  confidences presumed shared, 217
  conflicts of interest, 142, 168
  consent, 203
  contract lawyers, 200
  of counsel relationship, 199–200, 425–426
  departing lawyers, 203
  "double imputation," 201
  of firm, 195–203
  former clients, 183, 191
  former government lawyers, 196, 203, 205–220
  of former judge's or arbitrator's firm, 229
  government lawyers, 216–218
  joint defense agreements, 201
  lawyer as witness, 417–418, 425–426
  legal services organizations, 201, 612
  nonlawyer employees, 201–202
  principles of, 196–198
  prosecutors' offices, 210
  prospective clients, 309, 316
  public defenders, 211
  sharing office space, 200–201
  substantial relationship test, 188
  temporary lawyers, 200
  waiver, 203

Inactive lawyers
  fee-sharing agreements, 523–524
  firm letterhead including, 630
  unauthorized practice of law, 545

Inadvertent disclosures of confidential client information, 109, 115, 137, 485–486, 491–496

Incompetency. *See* Diminished capacity, clients with

Independence from client's views or activities, 32

Independent professional judgment
  conflicts of interest, 178, 318–322
  detached advice, 141–142
  generally, 521–534
  insurance defense, 318–319
  legal service plans, 530–532

obligations to others, 319–320
  payment by third person, impaired by, 142, 165, 174, 530–532
  personal interests of lawyer and, 320–321
  sexual relations with clients, 321–322

Indigent persons
  court costs and expenses, 161, 165, 173
  pro bono representation, 583–584. *See also* Pro bono publico service
  withdrawal of appointed lawyer, 292

Ineffective assistance of counsel, 29, 98, 262

Inexperienced lawyers, 27–29

Informed consent. *See also* Confirmed in writing
  aggregate settlements, 166, 176
  business transactions with lawyer, 161, 169
  communication of need for, 59–60
  confirmed in writing, 16, 17–18, 143–144, 159, 161, 174, 183
  conflicts of interest, 140, 143, 158–160, 162
  definition of, 15, 17–18
  disclosure of information, 103, 104, 113, 117–118
  evaluation for use by third persons, client's, 327, 328
  former client, 183, 190–191
  inferring, 18
  information used to client's disadvantage, 161, 171
  lawyer as witness, 416
  limited scope of representation, 31, 44–45
  payment by third party, 165
  prospective clients, 301, 308, 315
  retaining or contracting with other lawyers, 20

In-house counsel, 242–243. *See also* Organizational representation
  confidentiality of communications with, 62
  as constituent representative, 468
  ethical consultations on professional responsibility issue, 62
  foreign in-house counsel, 550–551
  former, suits against former employers, 125–126

Prosecutors

communication with represented suspects by, 470–471

constitutional rights of accused, 433–434

discretion in bringing charges, 433

ethical guidelines, 431

exculpatory evidence, duty to disclose, 427, 434–436

extrajudicial statements, 427, 429, 437

federal, 471–472

imputed disqualification, 210

judicial remedies for ethical violations, 431

misconduct as grounds for relief, 432

National District Attorneys Association Prosecution Standards, 431

release-dismissal agreements, 433–434

responsibilities, 427–438

subpoena of lawyer by, 427, 428

testimony by, 417–418, 425–426

Pro se representation. *See also* Lawyer as party litigant

after discharge of appointed counsel, 282

in alternative dispute resolution, 343

assisting pro se litigant, 537, 547

ghostwriting and undisclosed assistance, 41–43, 377, 718–719

by lawyers representing themselves, 456–457

plea agreement, 433–434

"unrepresented" status, 478–479

Prospective clients, 307–316

confidentiality, 118–119, 310–312

conflicts of interest, 154, 159–160, 186–188, 308, 312, 315

consultation, 310

duty of loyalty, 314

good faith, 312

reasonable expectation of relationship, 310–312

restricting future representation, 571

solicitation of. *See* Solicitation

subsequent adverse representation in substantially related matter, 314–315

Protective action

diminished capacity, clients with, 257–260

upon termination of representation, 292–296

Protective orders, 427

Public defenders. *See also* Court-appointed lawyers

competence, 29

heavy caseloads, 30, 502, 507

imputed disqualification, 211

Publicity. *See* Advertising; Solicitation; Trial publicity

Publicly available information, disclosure of, 111–112, 192

Public officials. *See also* Government lawyers

firm's use of name, 629

improper influence or conduct, 703, 735–736, 741–742

misconduct, 703, 735–736

negotiating for private employment, 218, 227

Puffing, 450

# R

Racial discrimination. *See* Discrimination or bias on part of lawyer

Radio, 636

Rating services, 623

Real estate transactions

disclosure, 114

multiple representation, 150

opinion letters, 333

Reasonable belief/reasonably believes

definition of, 15

perjury, 363, 374

Reasonableness

defined, 15

fees, 73, 74, 76–90

limited scope of representation, 43–44

when review available, 84

Reasonably should know

adverse interests, 234, 247, 329

definition of, 16

misunderstanding of lawyer's role, 476

trial publicity, 407

Recorded communications, in advertising, 654

Recorded conversations, 447, 491, 724–725

Rectification and mitigation, 283, 507, 589–590

Recusal, 396, 671, 740–741

Referral fees
  in business transactions, 171
  as fee-sharing, 525–526
  indirect compensation, 641–642
  payment for referral prohibited, 643–644
  usual charges of, 643

Referrals. *See also* Lawyer referral services
  fees. *See* Referral fees
  group coupons, 276–277, 644–645
  online referral services, 643–644
  to other lawyer, 19, 645–646
  to other professionals, 171
  reciprocal agreements, 626, 645–646
  from relatives, 657–658
  website "daily deals," 644–645

Reform of law, 607–609

Relatives
  of client with diminished capacity, 287
  conflicts of interest, 141–142, 156–157
  gifts from, 161, 172
  referrals from, 657–658

Releases, 740. *See also* Waiver

Religious discrimination. *See* Discrimination or bias on part of lawyer

Reporting misconduct, 695–702
  authority to whom to report, 700–701
  of corporate or organizational client, 246
  duty of confidentiality vs., 682, 701–702
  of judge, 697–698
  knowledge required, 698
  of lawyer, 682, 695–702
  lawyer assistance program, information learned in, 696, 702
  of partner, 697
  of self, 697–698
  "substantial question" standard, 695, 699
  timing, 699–700

Reporting of abuse
  child abuse reporting statutes, 119, 129–130
  child sexual abuse, 256

Research
  competence in, 22, 25–26
  fees, 86–87

Restrictive covenants in employment contracts, 559–572
  enforceability vs. discipline, 569
  financial disincentives, 563–564
  impermissible restrictions on practice, 561
  penalties for competing, 562
  retirement benefits, 565–566
  sale of practice and, 567
  taking clients from firm, 563–565

Restrictive covenants in settlement agreements, 567–572

Retainers
  as client funds, 274
  fee advances, compared to, 91–93, 274–275
  forms of, 92, 274–275
  refundable/nonrefundable, 90, 91–93, 274
  settlement authority in, 37
  unearned, return of, 93

Retaining liens, 271

Retired lawyers
  benefits for, 565–566
  on letterhead, 629–630
  sale of practice upon retirement, 300
  unauthorized practice of law, 545

Retirement plans, inclusion of nonlawyers, 527–528

Rule 11 frivolous litigation, 352–353

Rule-making entities, lawyer appearing before, 365

## S

Safekeeping of client's property, 265–280. *See also* Property of client

Sale of law practice, 299–306
  covenants not to compete, 567
  payment to estate, 527
  referral in, 645

Sarbanes-Oxley Act
  confidential information and, 126, 129
  reporting SEC violations, 242, 245, 332